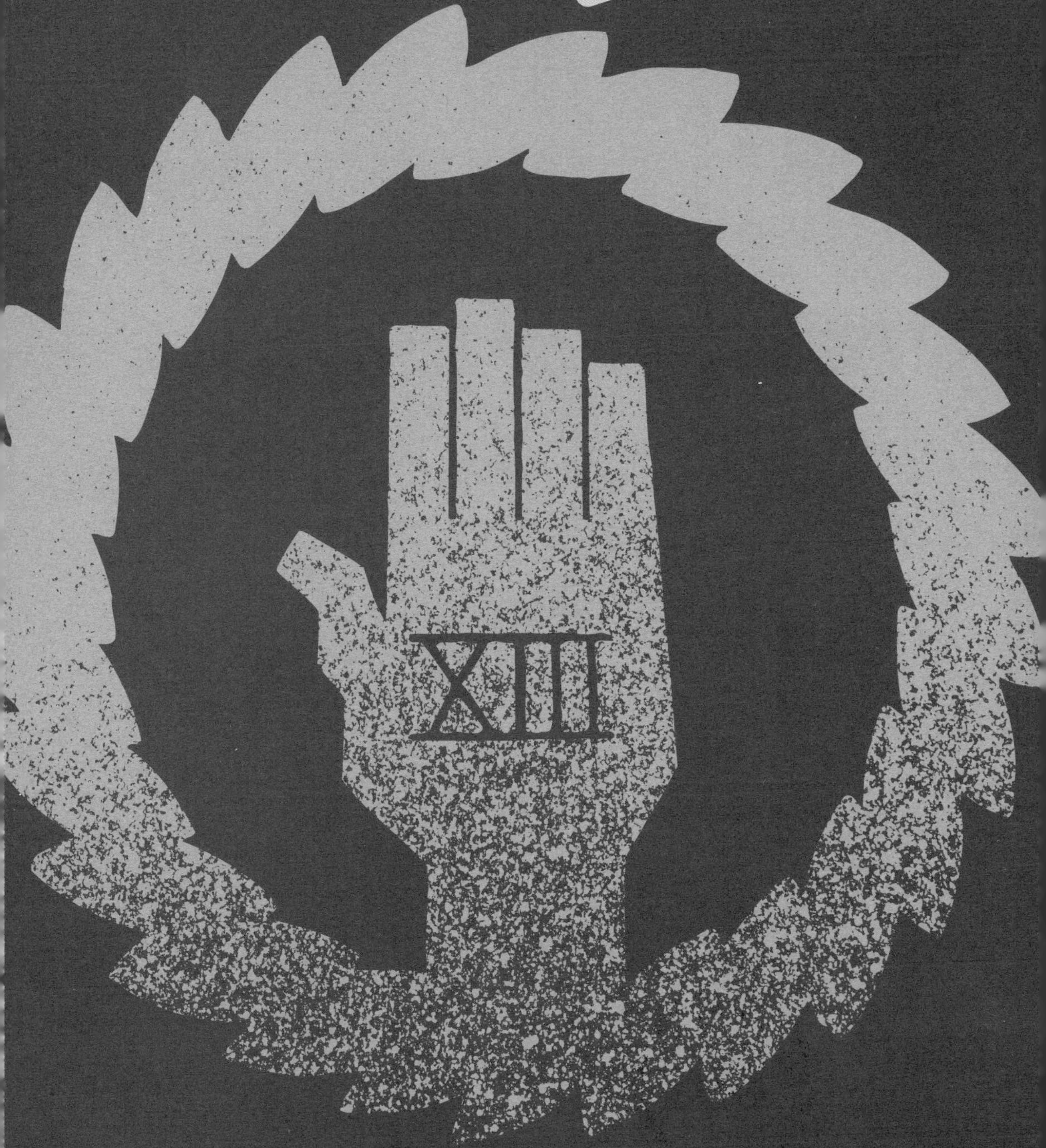
XIII

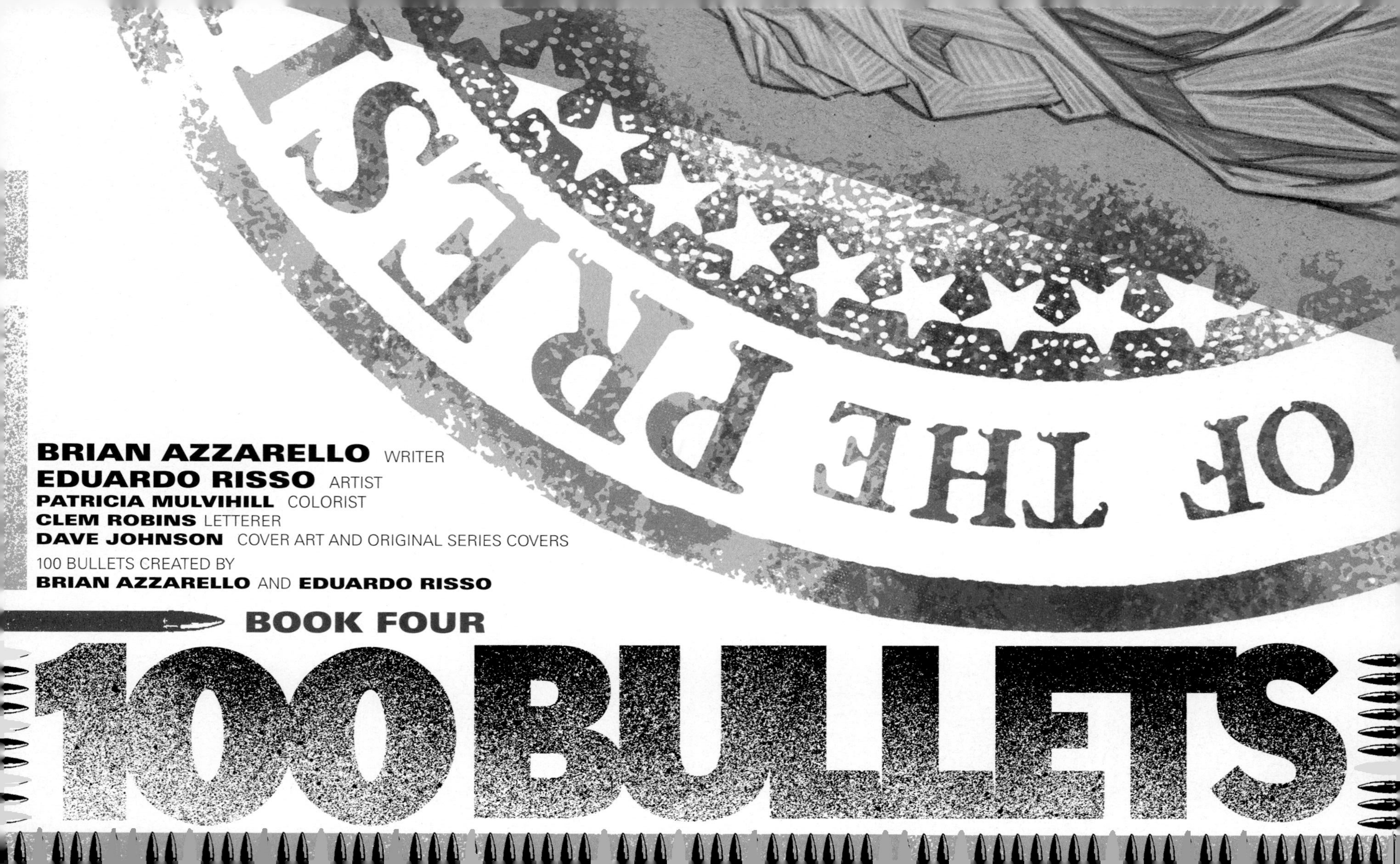
OF THE PRES

BRIAN AZZARELLO WRITER
EDUARDO RISSO ARTIST
PATRICIA MULVIHILL COLORIST
CLEM ROBINS LETTERER
DAVE JOHNSON COVER ART AND ORIGINAL SERIES COVERS
100 BULLETS CREATED BY
BRIAN AZZARELLO AND **EDUARDO RISSO**

BOOK FOUR

100 BULLETS

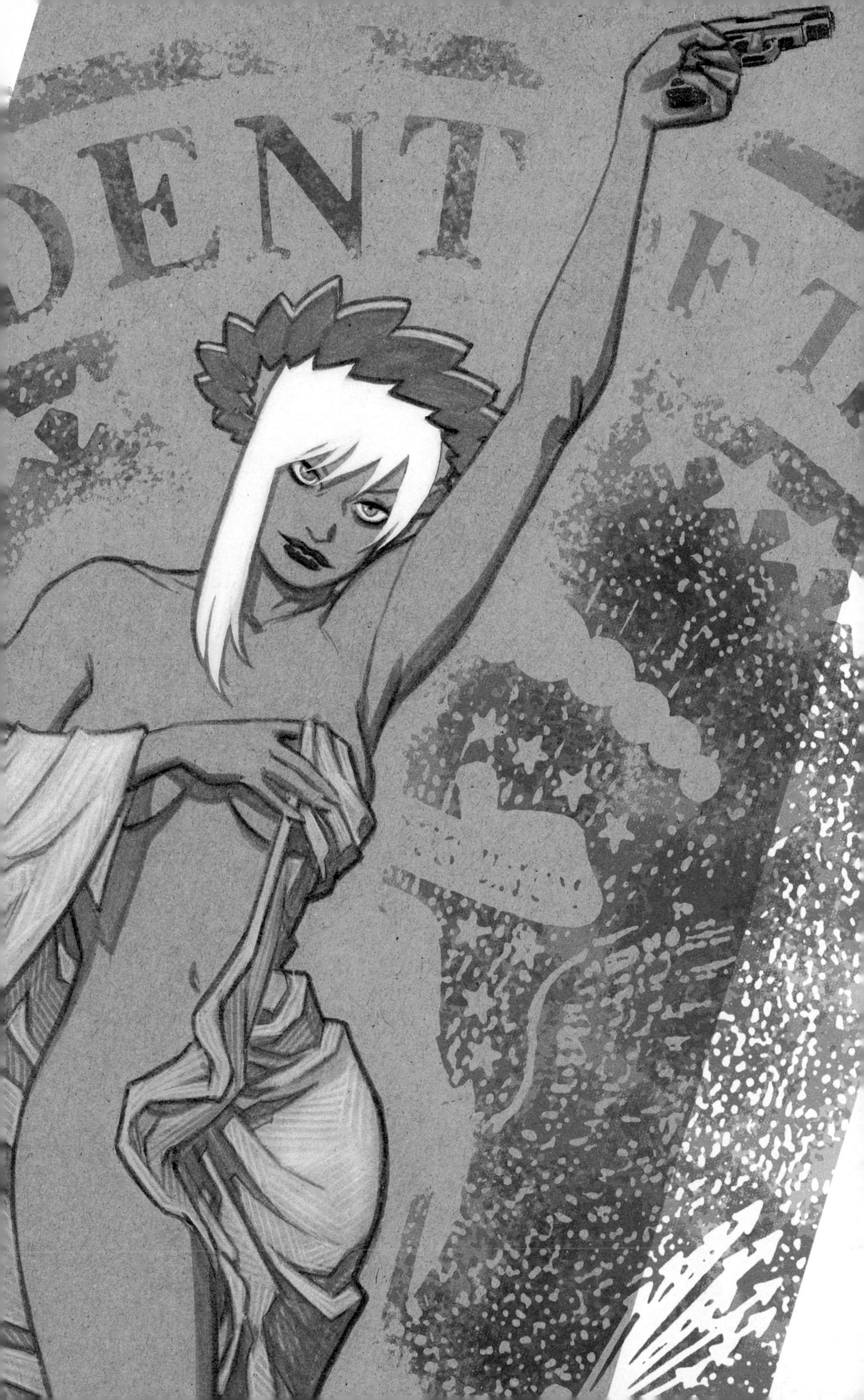
DENT
F T

Will Dennis Editor – Original Series
Casey Seijas Assistant Editor – Original Series
Jeb Woodard Group Editor – Collected Editions
Scott Nybakken Editor – Collected Edition
Louis Prandi Publication Design
Steve Cook Design Director - Books

Bob Harras Senior VP – Editor-in-Chief, DC Comics
Mark Doyle Executive Editor, Vertigo & Black Label

Dan DiDio Publisher
Jim Lee Publisher & Chief Creative Officer
Amit Desai Executive VP – Business & Marketing Strategy,
Direct to Consumer & Global Franchise Management
Bobbie Chase VP & Executive Editor, Young Reader & Talent Development
Mark Chiarello Senior VP – Art, Design & Collected Editions
John Cunningham Senior VP – Sales & Trade Marketing
Briar Darden VP – Business Affairs
Anne DePies Senior VP – Business Strategy, Finance & Administration
Don Falletti VP – Manufacturing Operations
Lawrence Ganem VP – Editorial Administration & Talent Relations
Alison Gill Senior VP – Manufacturing & Operations
Jason Greenberg VP – Business Strategy & Finance
Hank Kanalz Senior VP – Editorial Strategy & Administration
Jay Kogan Senior VP – Legal Affairs
Nick J. Napolitano VP – Manufacturing Administration
Lisette Osterloh VP – Digital Marketing & Events
Eddie Scannell VP – Consumer Marketing
Courtney Simmons Senior VP – Publicity & Communications
Jim (Ski) Sokolowski VP – Comic Book Specialty Sales & Trade Marketing
Nancy Spears VP – Mass, Book, Digital Sales & Trade Marketing
Michele R. Wells VP – Content Strategy

Special thanks to Eduardo A. Santillan Marcus
for his translating assistance.

PEFC Certified
This product is from sustainably managed forests and controlled sources
PEFC
PEFC/29-31-337   www.pefc.org

Library of Congress Cataloging-in-Publication Data

Azzarello, Brian.
  100 Bullets Book four / Brian Azzarello, Eduardo Risso.
     pages cm
  ISBN 978-1-4012-5794-1
  1. Graphic novels. I. Risso, Eduardo, illustrator. II. Title. III. Title: One hundred bullets.
  PN6728.A14A996 2013
  741.5'973—dc23
                                      2012048309

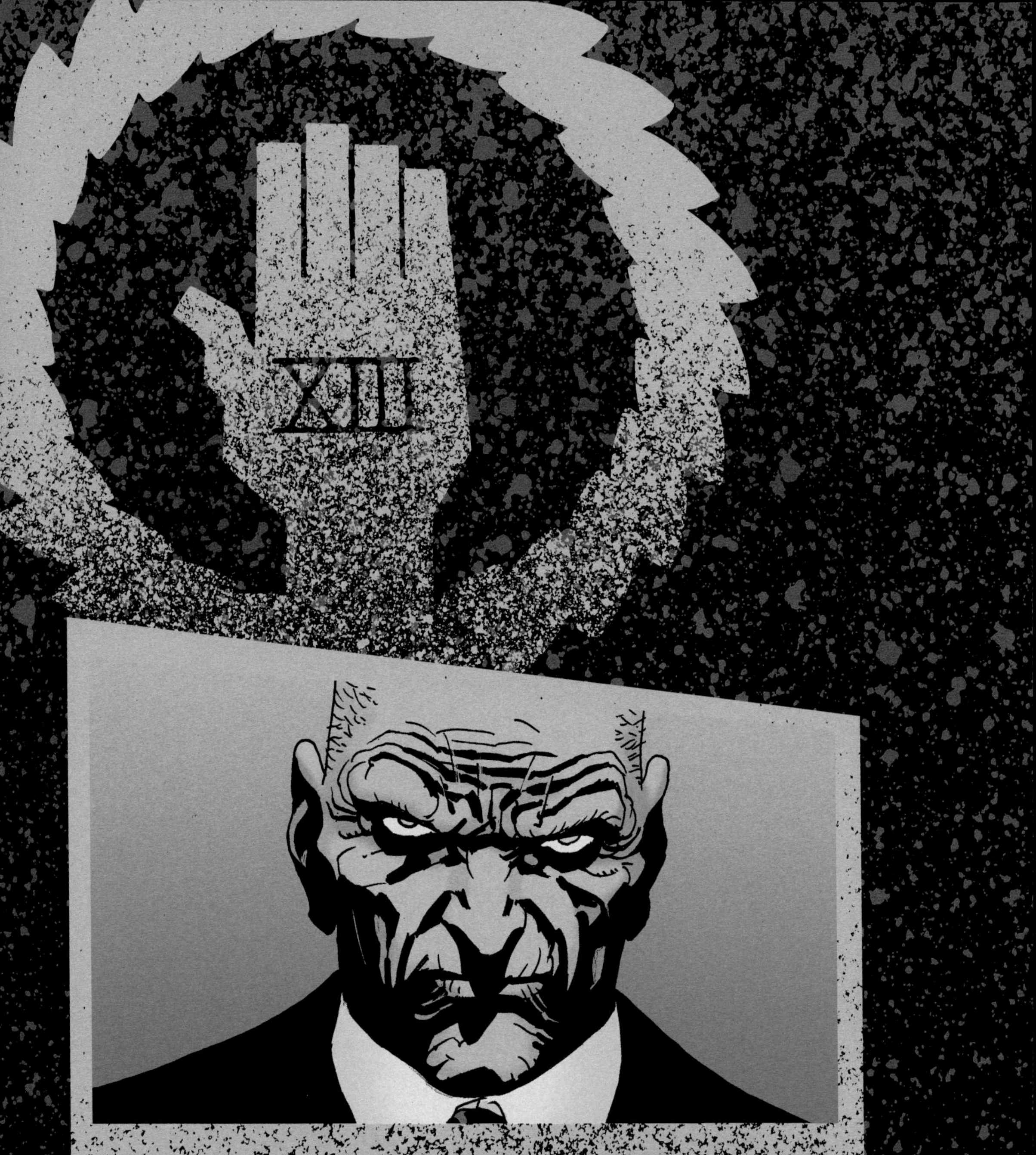
XIII

Table of Contents

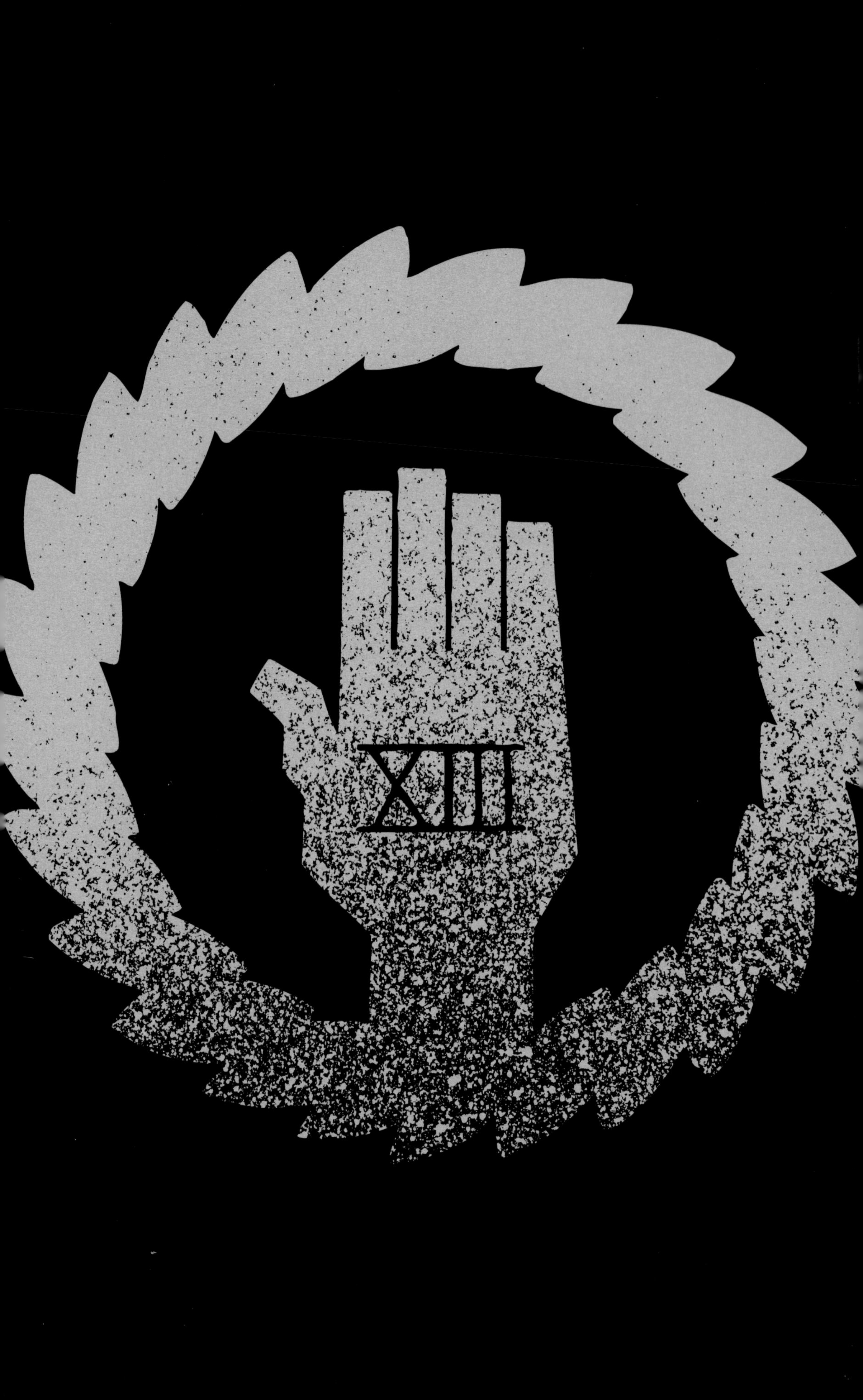
XIII

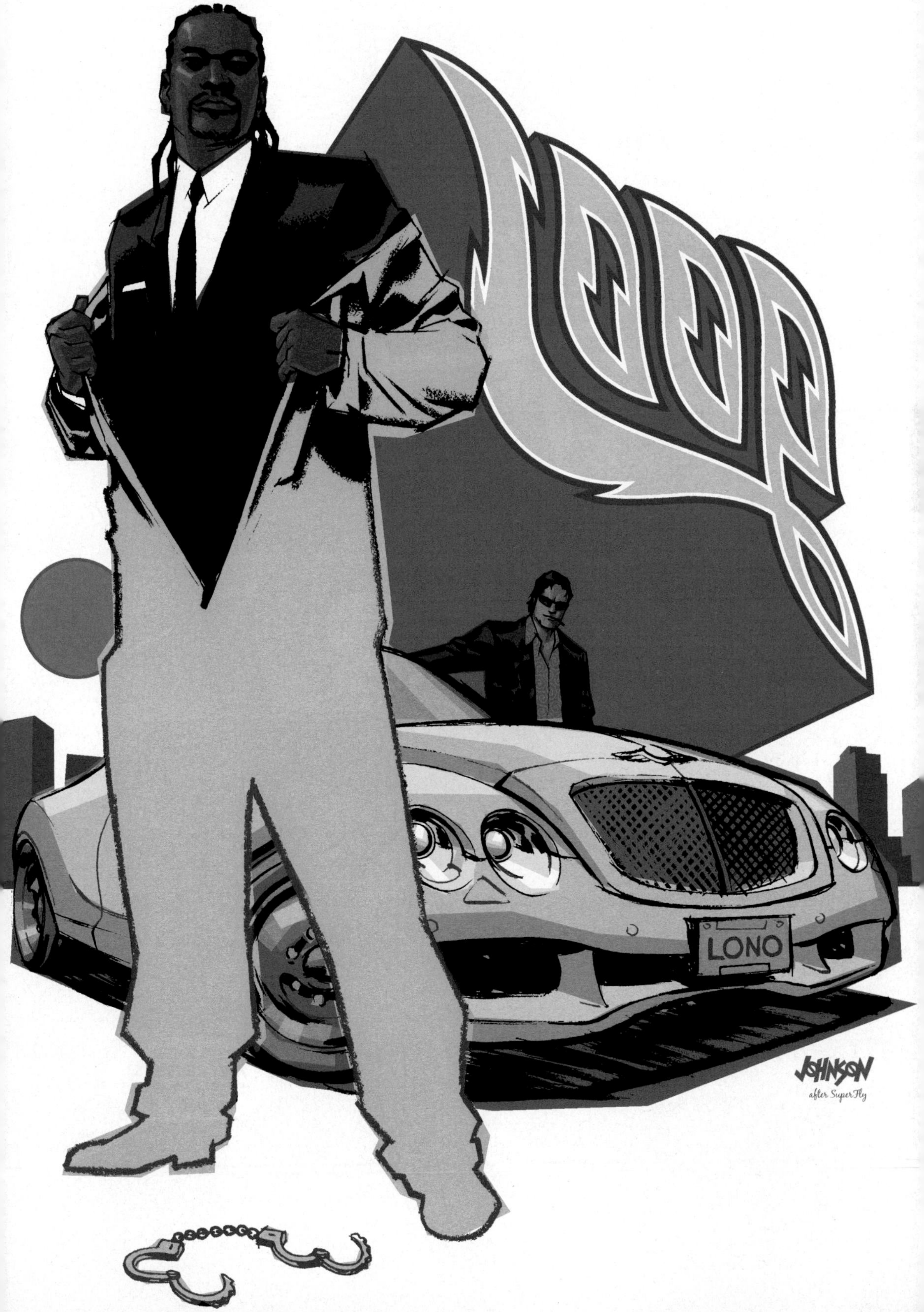
LONO
JOHNSON
after SuperFly

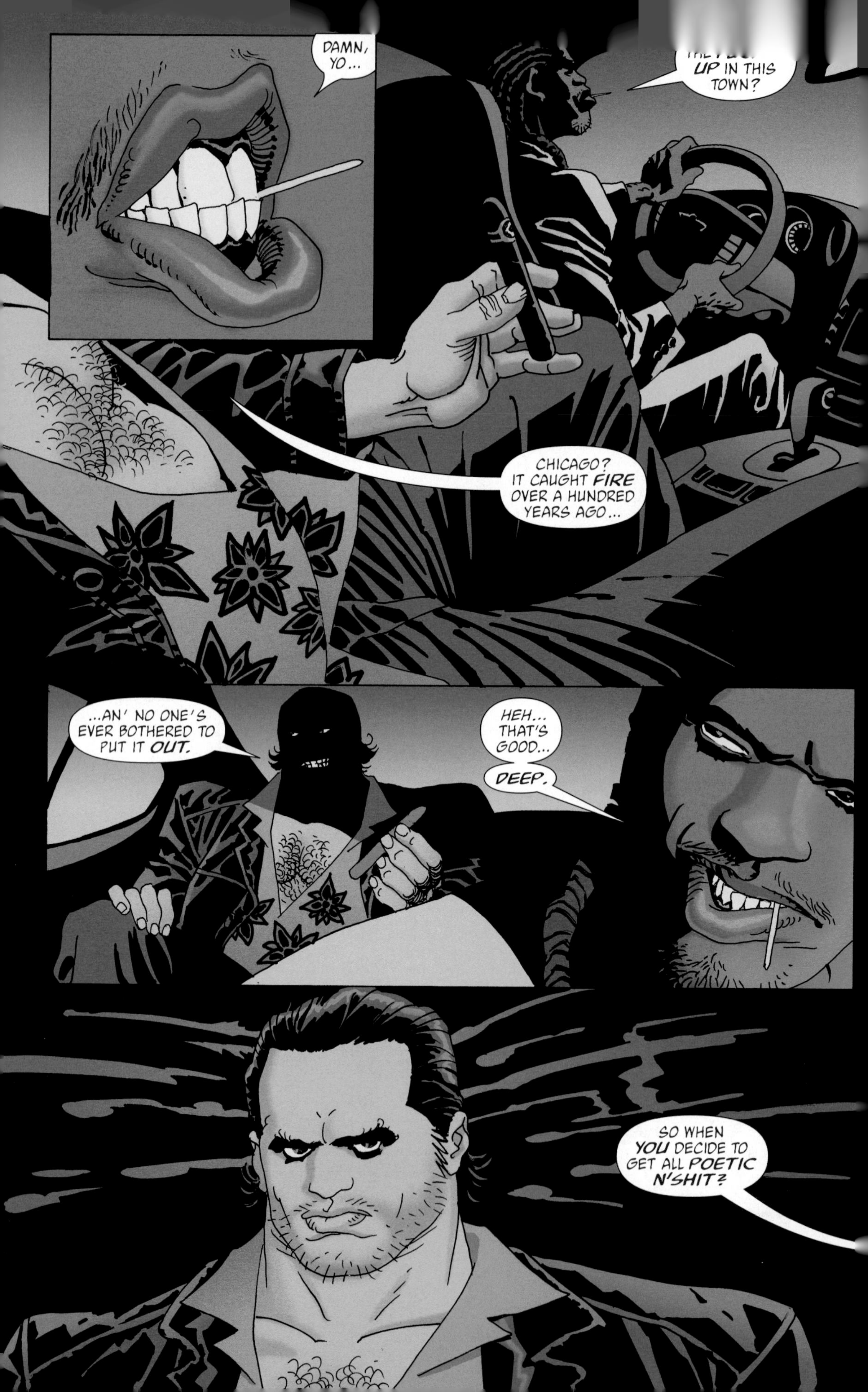
DAMN, YO...
UP IN THIS TOWN?
CHICAGO? IT CAUGHT FIRE OVER A HUNDRED YEARS AGO...
...AN' NO ONE'S EVER BOTHERED TO PUT IT OUT.
HEH... THAT'S GOOD...
DEEP.
SO WHEN YOU DECIDE TO GET ALL POETIC N'SHIT?

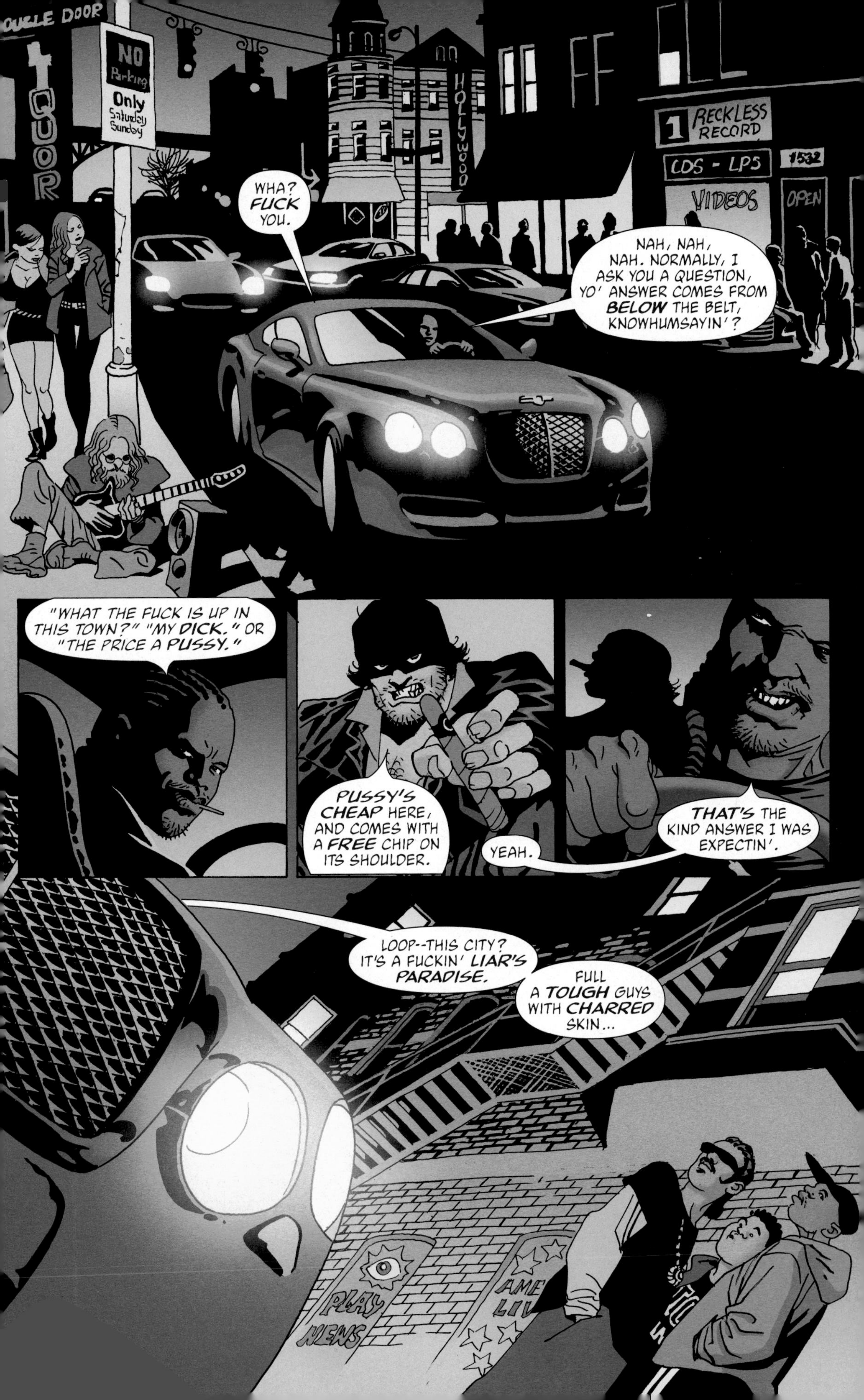

OUBLE DOOR
QUOR
NO Parking Only Saturday Sunday
HOLLYWOOD
RECKLESS RECORD
CDS - LPS
1532
VIDEOS
OPEN
WHA? FUCK YOU.
NAH, NAH, NAH. NORMALLY, I ASK YOU A QUESTION, YO' ANSWER COMES FROM BELOW THE BELT, KNOWHUMSAYIN'?
"WHAT THE FUCK IS UP IN THIS TOWN?" "MY DICK." OR "THE PRICE A PUSSY."
PUSSY'S CHEAP HERE, AND COMES WITH A FREE CHIP ON ITS SHOULDER.
YEAH.
THAT'S THE KIND ANSWER I WAS EXPECTIN'.
LOOP--THIS CITY? IT'S A FUCKIN' LIAR'S PARADISE.
FULL A TOUGH GUYS WITH CHARRED SKIN...
PLAY
NEWS

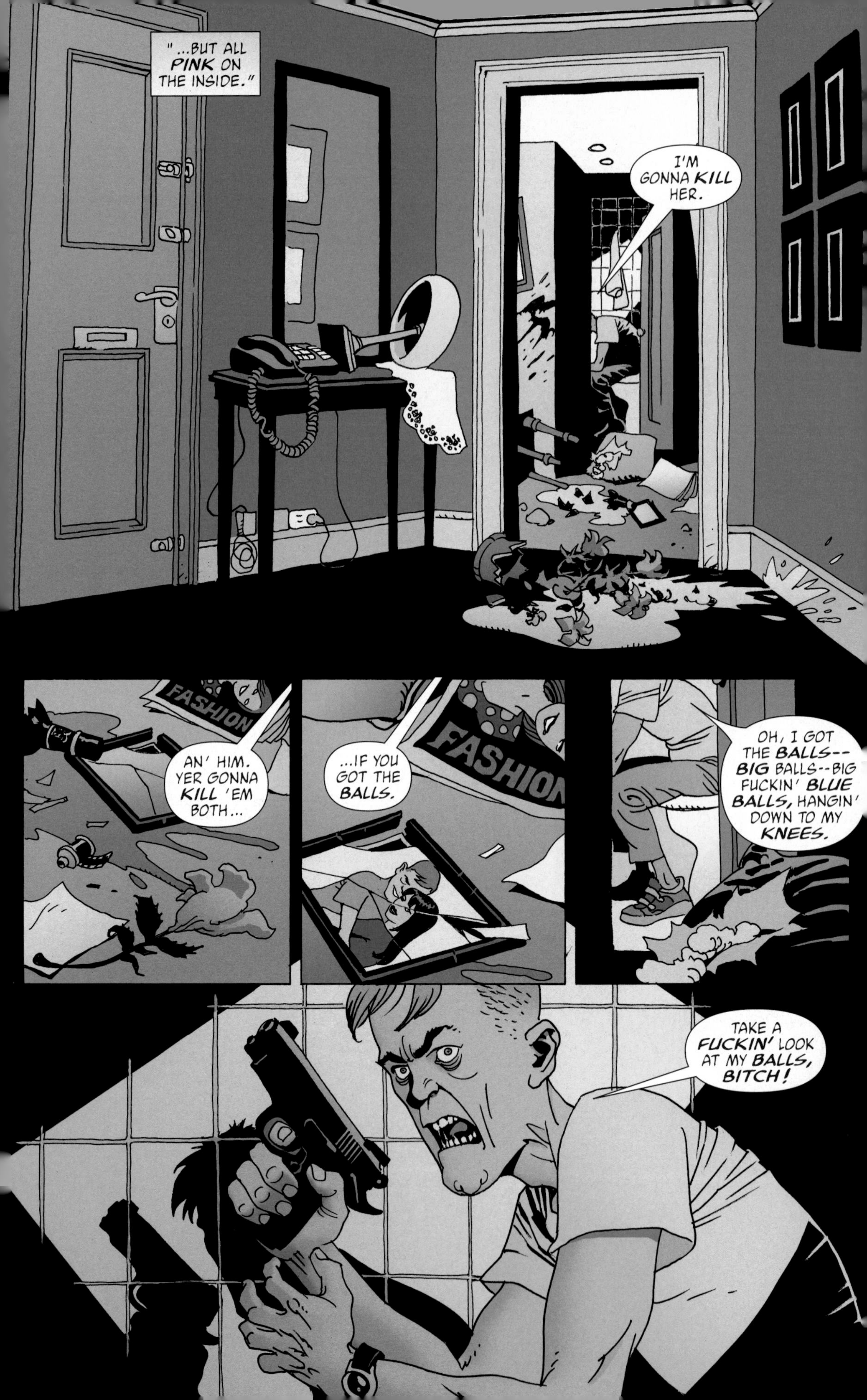
"...BUT ALL PINK ON THE INSIDE."
I'M GONNA KILL HER.
AN' HIM. YER GONNA KILL 'EM BOTH...
...IF YOU GOT THE BALLS.
FASHION
OH, I GOT THE BALLS--BIG BALLS--BIG FUCKIN' BLUE BALLS, HANGIN' DOWN TO MY KNEES.
TAKE A FUCKIN' LOOK AT MY BALLS, BITCH!

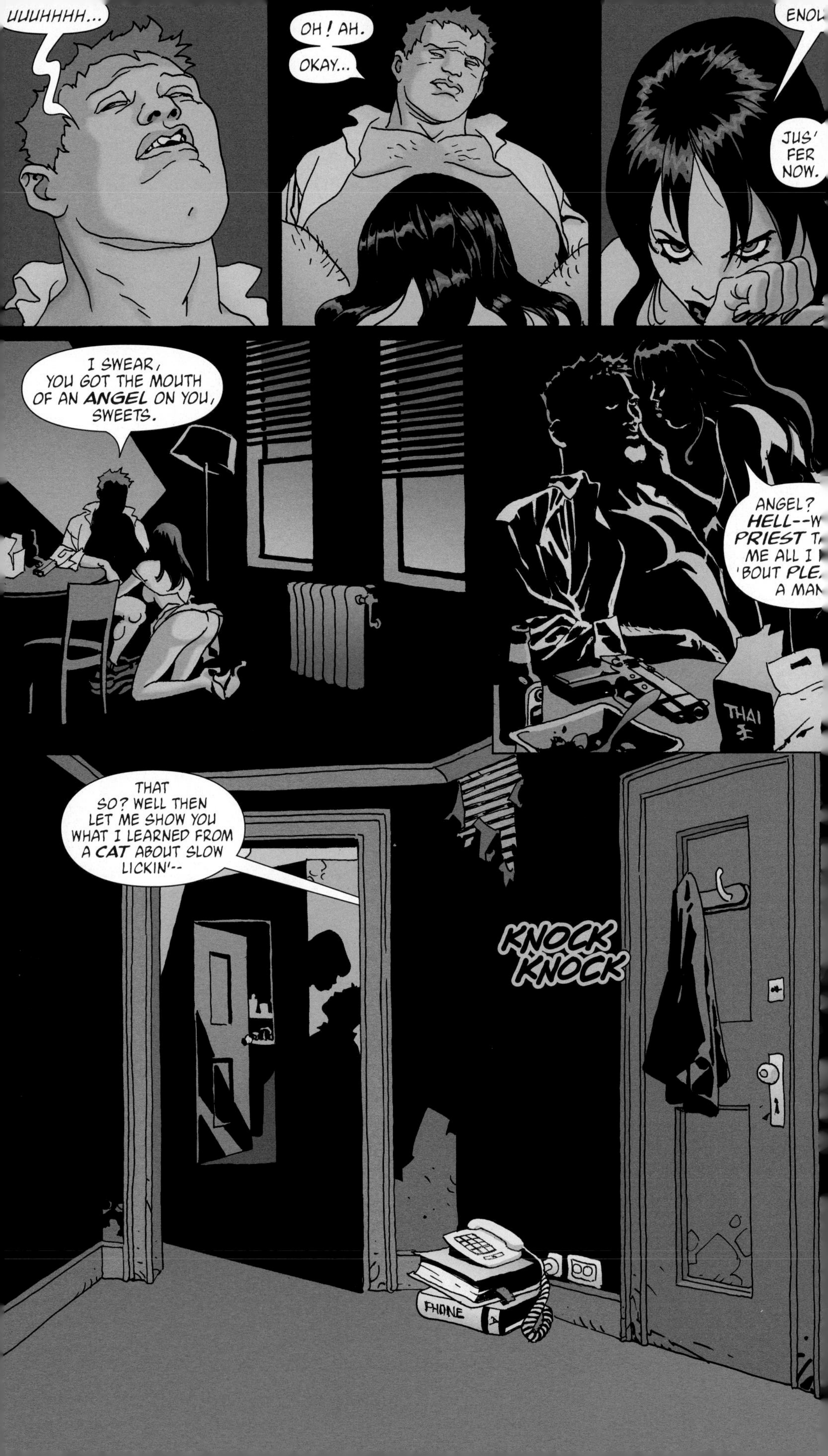

UUUHHHH...
OH! AH.
OKAY...
JUS' FER NOW.
I SWEAR, YOU GOT THE MOUTH OF AN ANGEL ON YOU, SWEETS.
ANGEL? HELL--
THAI
THAT SO? WELL THEN LET ME SHOW YOU WHAT I LEARNED FROM A CAT ABOUT SLOW LICKIN'--
KNOCK KNOCK
PHONE

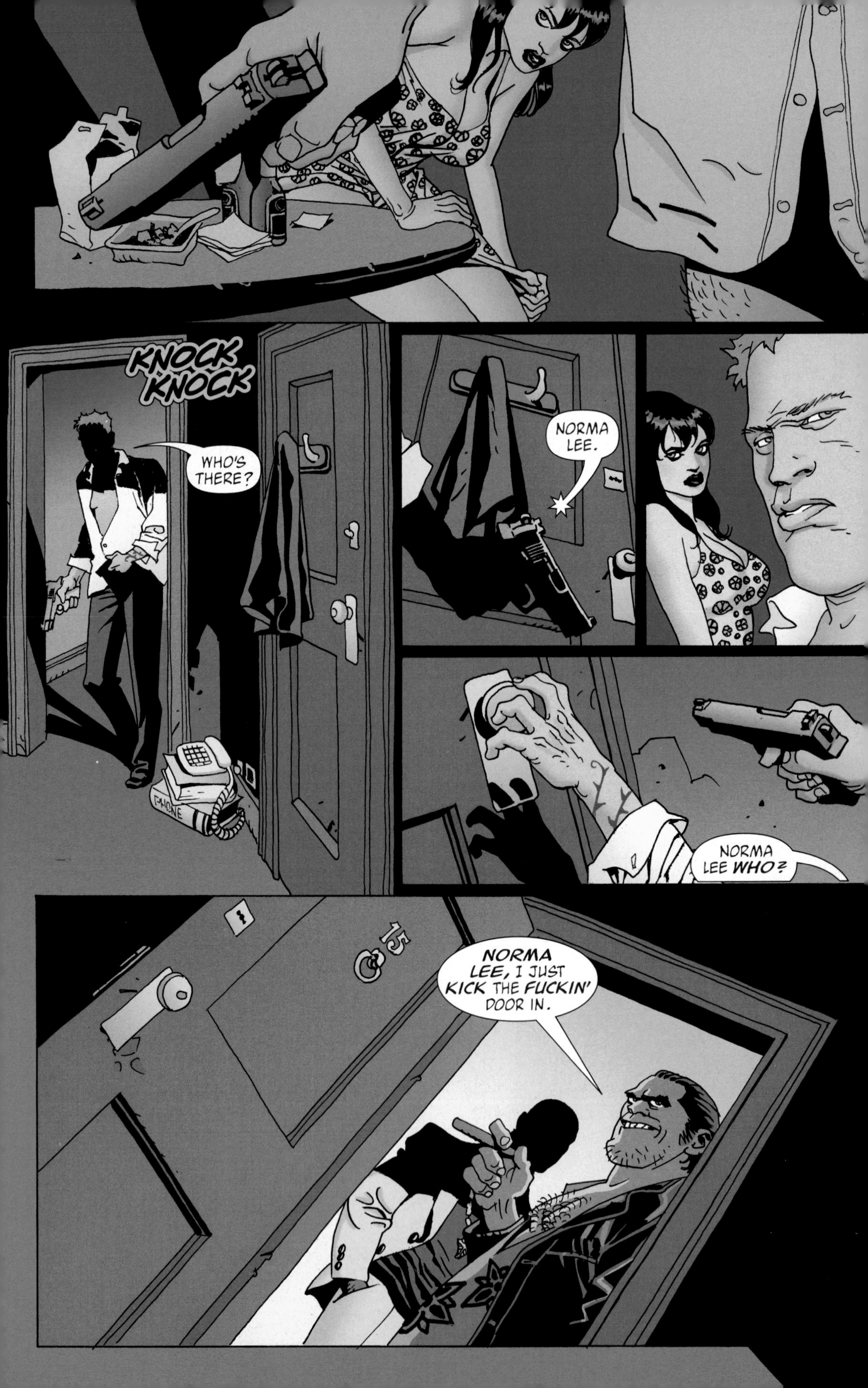
KNOCK KNOCK
WHO'S THERE?
NORMA LEE.
NORMA LEE WHO?
NORMA LEE, I JUST KICK THE FUCKIN' DOOR IN.
15

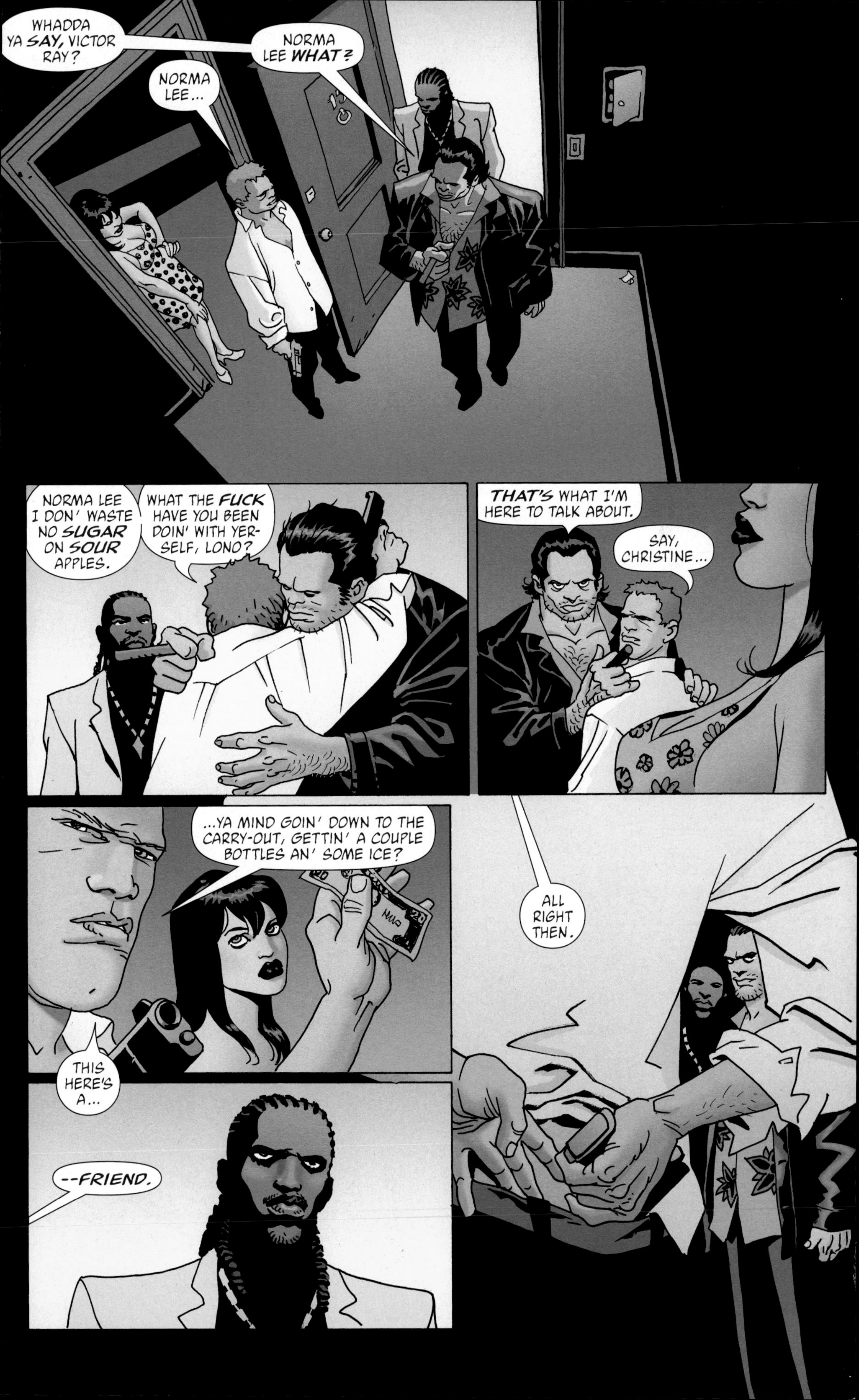
WHADDA YA SAY, VICTOR RAY?
NORMA LEE...
NORMA LEE WHAT?
NORMA LEE I DON' WASTE NO SUGAR ON SOUR APPLES.
WHAT THE FUCK HAVE YOU BEEN DOIN' WITH YER-SELF, LONO?
THAT'S WHAT I'M HERE TO TALK ABOUT.
SAY, CHRISTINE...
...YA MIND GOIN' DOWN TO THE CARRY-OUT, GETTIN' A COUPLE BOTTLES AN' SOME ICE?
ALL RIGHT THEN.
THIS HERE'S A...
--FRIEND.

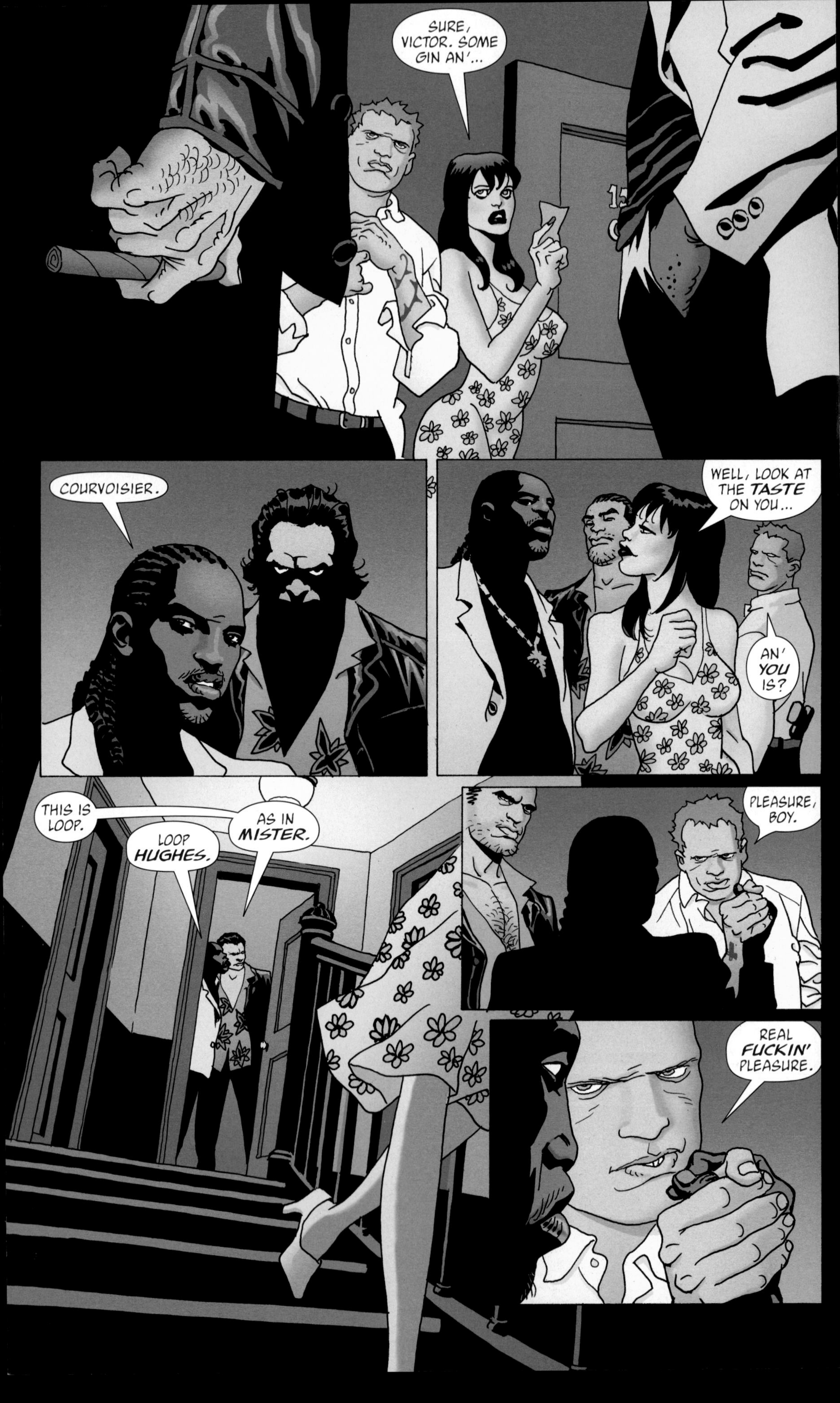
SURE, VICTOR. SOME GIN AN'...
COURVOISIER.
WELL, LOOK AT THE TASTE ON YOU...
AN' YOU IS?
THIS IS LOOP.
LOOP HUGHES.
AS IN MISTER.
PLEASURE, BOY.
REAL FUCKIN' PLEASURE.

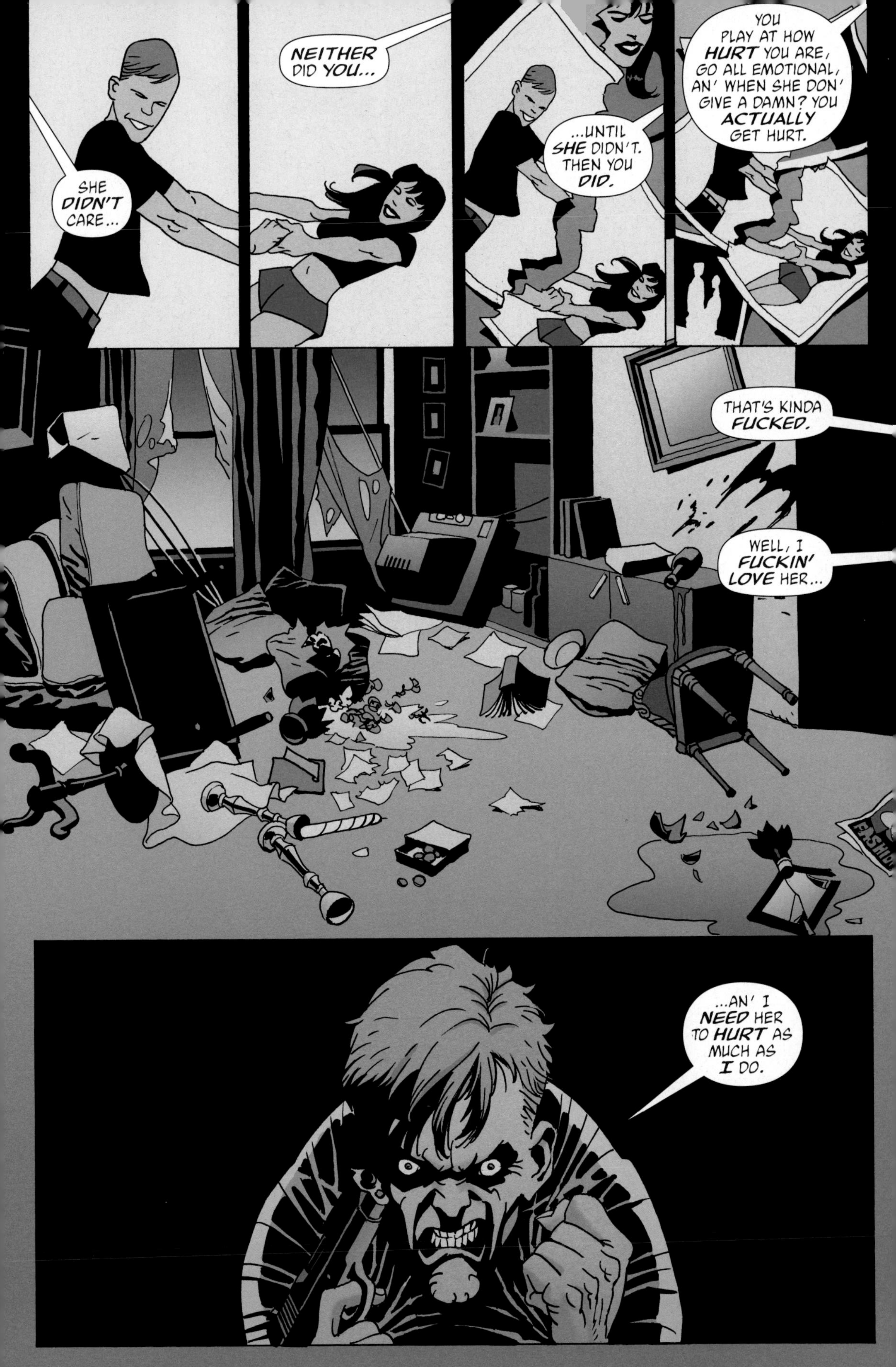
SHE DIDN'T CARE...
NEITHER DID YOU...
...UNTIL SHE DIDN'T. THEN YOU DID.
YOU PLAY AT HOW HURT YOU ARE, GO ALL EMOTIONAL, AN' WHEN SHE DON' GIVE A DAMN? YOU ACTUALLY GET HURT.
THAT'S KINDA FUCKED.
WELL, I FUCKIN' LOVE HER...
FASHION
...AN' I NEED HER TO HURT AS MUCH AS I DO.

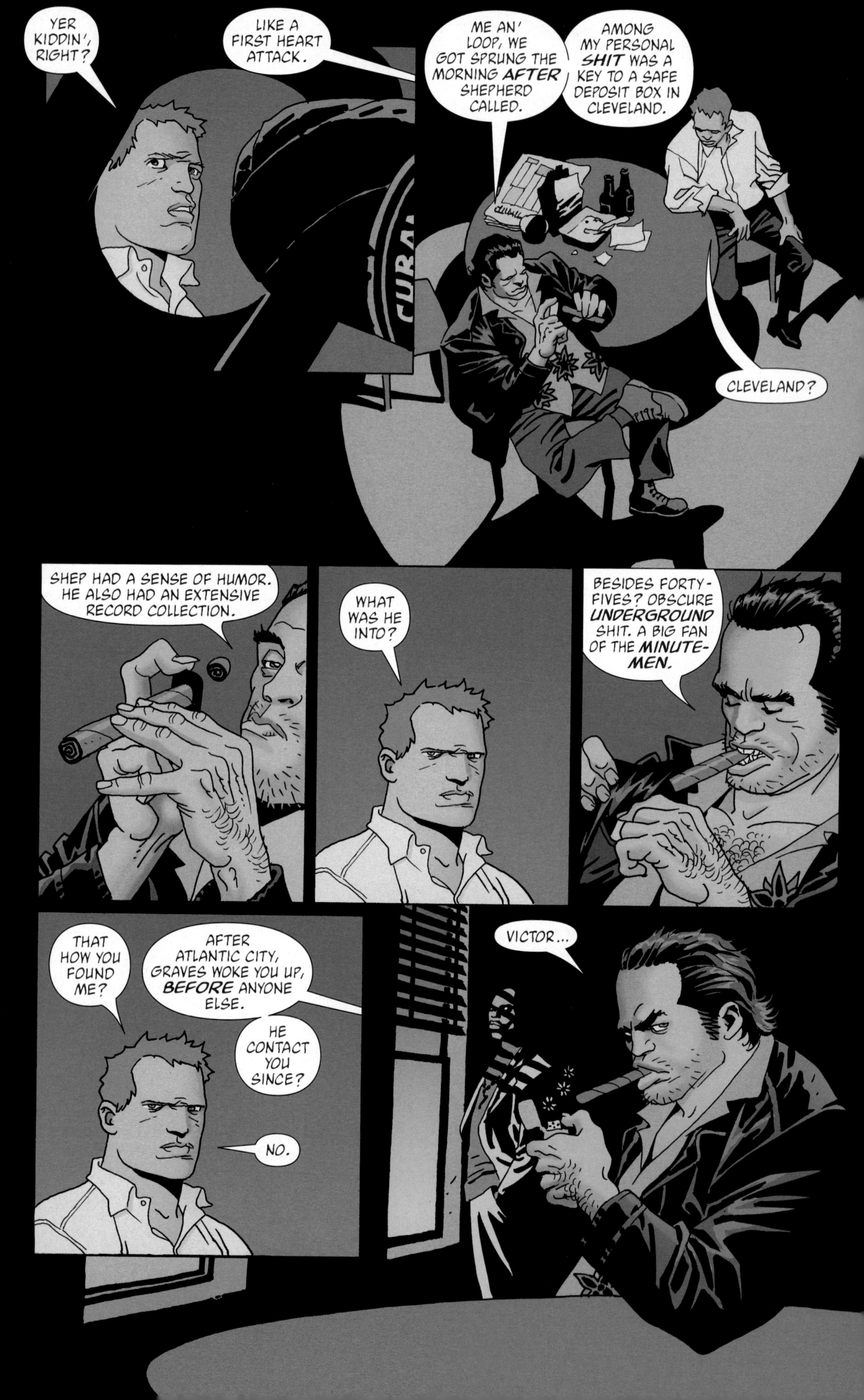
YER KIDDIN', RIGHT?
LIKE A FIRST HEART ATTACK.
ME AN' LOOP, WE GOT SPRUNG THE MORNING AFTER SHEPHERD CALLED.
AMONG MY PERSONAL SHIT WAS A KEY TO A SAFE DEPOSIT BOX IN CLEVELAND.
CLEVELAND?
SHEP HAD A SENSE OF HUMOR. HE ALSO HAD AN EXTENSIVE RECORD COLLECTION.
WHAT WAS HE INTO?
BESIDES FORTY-FIVES? OBSCURE UNDERGROUND SHIT. A BIG FAN OF THE MINUTE-MEN.
THAT HOW YOU FOUND ME?
AFTER ATLANTIC CITY, GRAVES WOKE YOU UP, BEFORE ANYONE ELSE.
HE CONTACT YOU SINCE?
NO.
VICTOR...

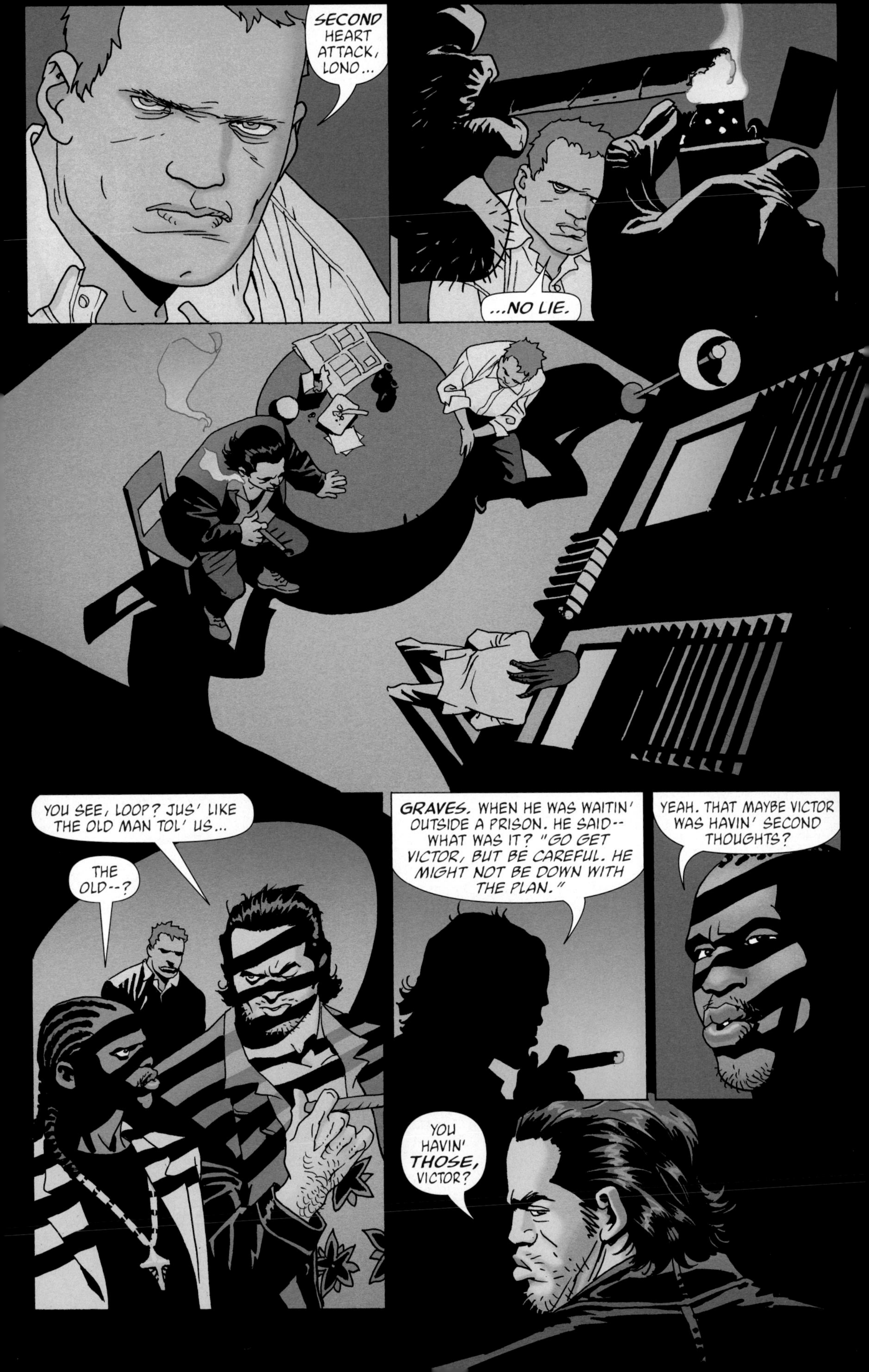
SECOND HEART ATTACK, LONO...
...NO LIE.
YOU SEE, LOOP? JUS' LIKE THE OLD MAN TOL' US...
THE OLD--?
GRAVES. WHEN HE WAS WAITIN' OUTSIDE A PRISON. HE SAID-- WHAT WAS IT? "GO GET VICTOR, BUT BE CAREFUL. HE MIGHT NOT BE DOWN WITH THE PLAN."
YEAH. THAT MAYBE VICTOR WAS HAVIN' SECOND THOUGHTS?
YOU HAVIN' THOSE, VICTOR?

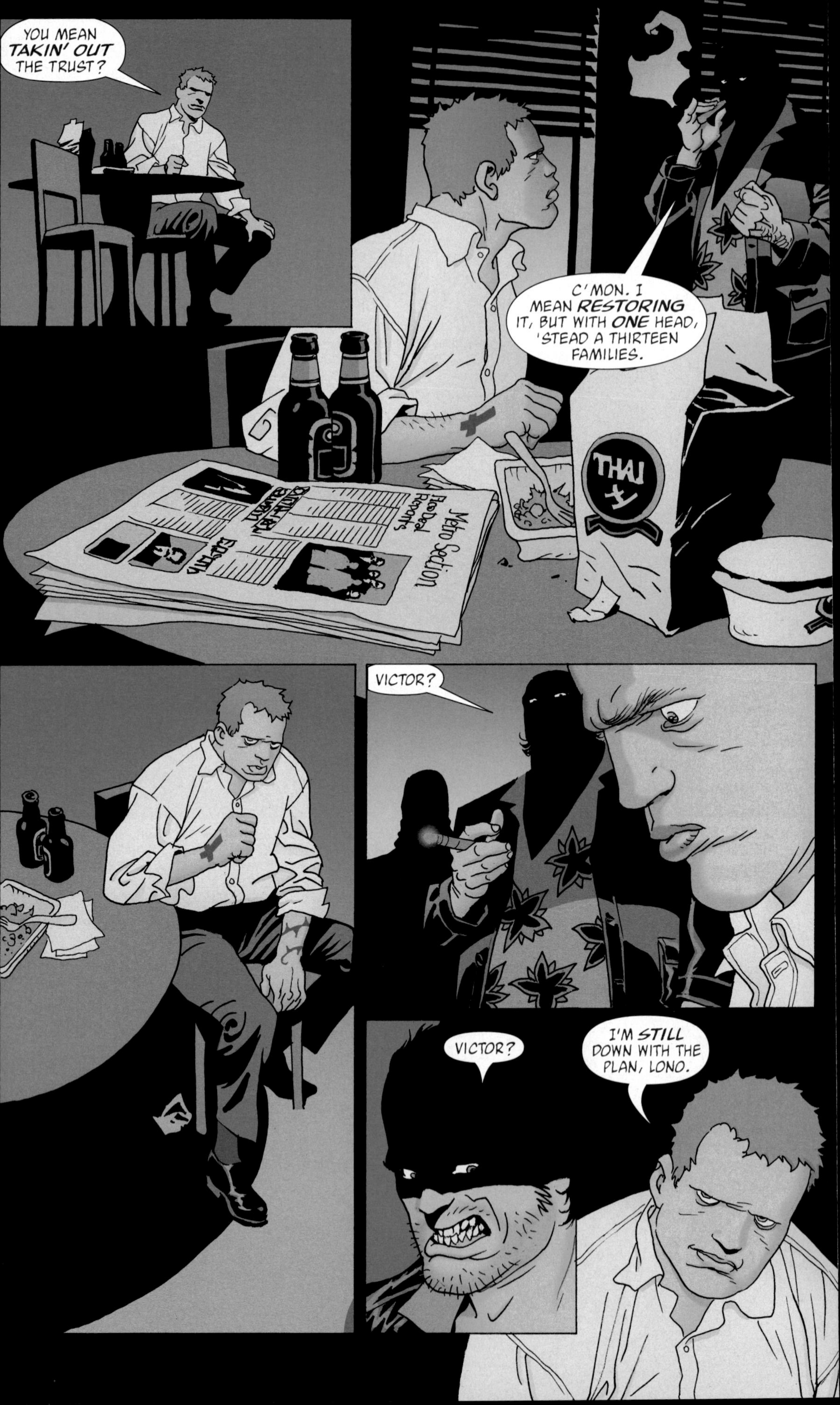
YOU MEAN TAKIN' OUT THE TRUST?
C'MON. I MEAN RESTORING IT, BUT WITH ONE HEAD, 'STEAD A THIRTEEN FAMILIES.
THAI
Metro Section
VICTOR?
VICTOR?
I'M STILL DOWN WITH THE PLAN, LONO.

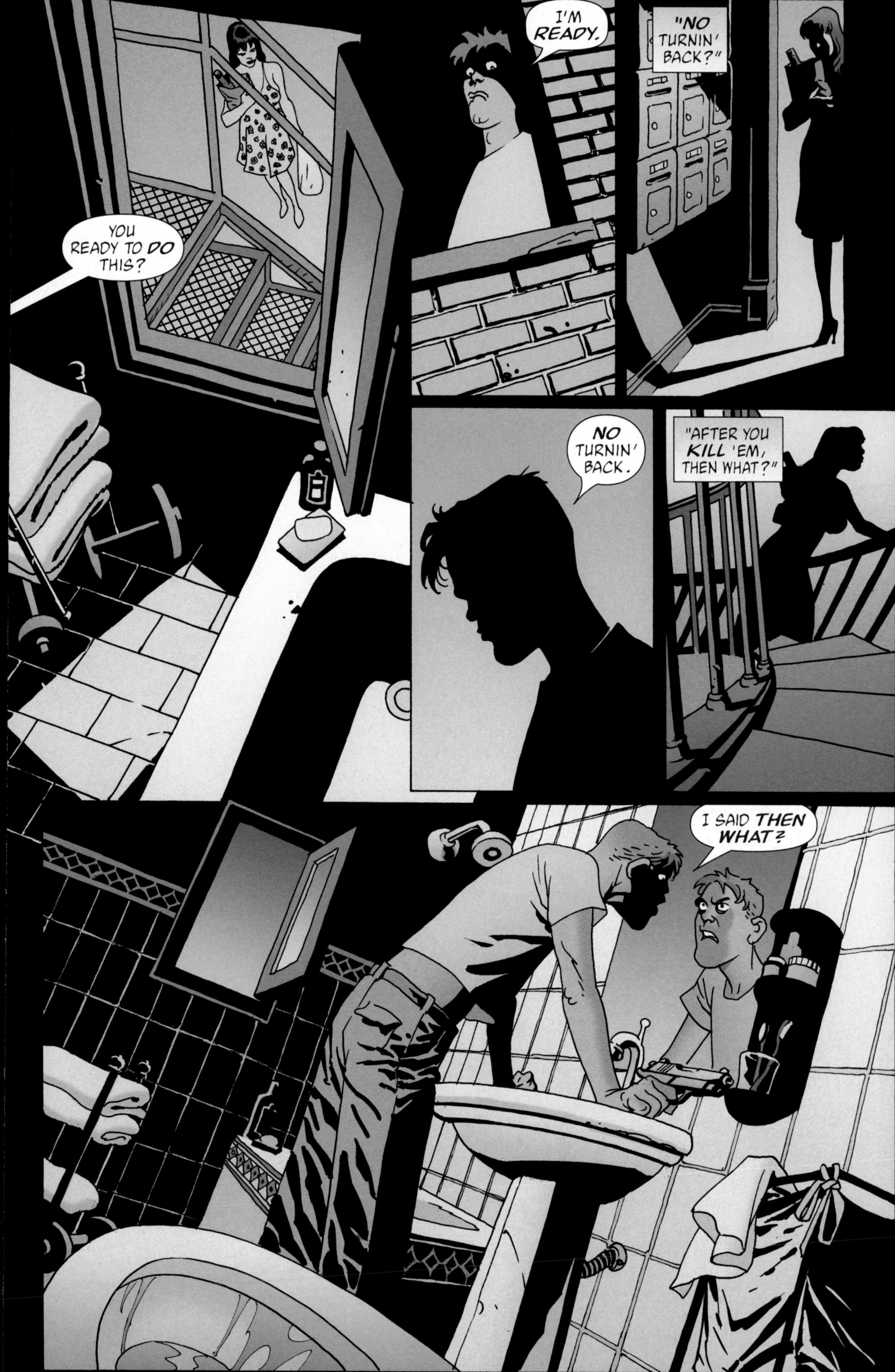
YOU READY TO DO THIS?
I'M READY.
"NO TURNIN' BACK?"
NO TURNIN' BACK.
"AFTER YOU KILL 'EM, THEN WHAT?"
I SAID THEN WHAT?

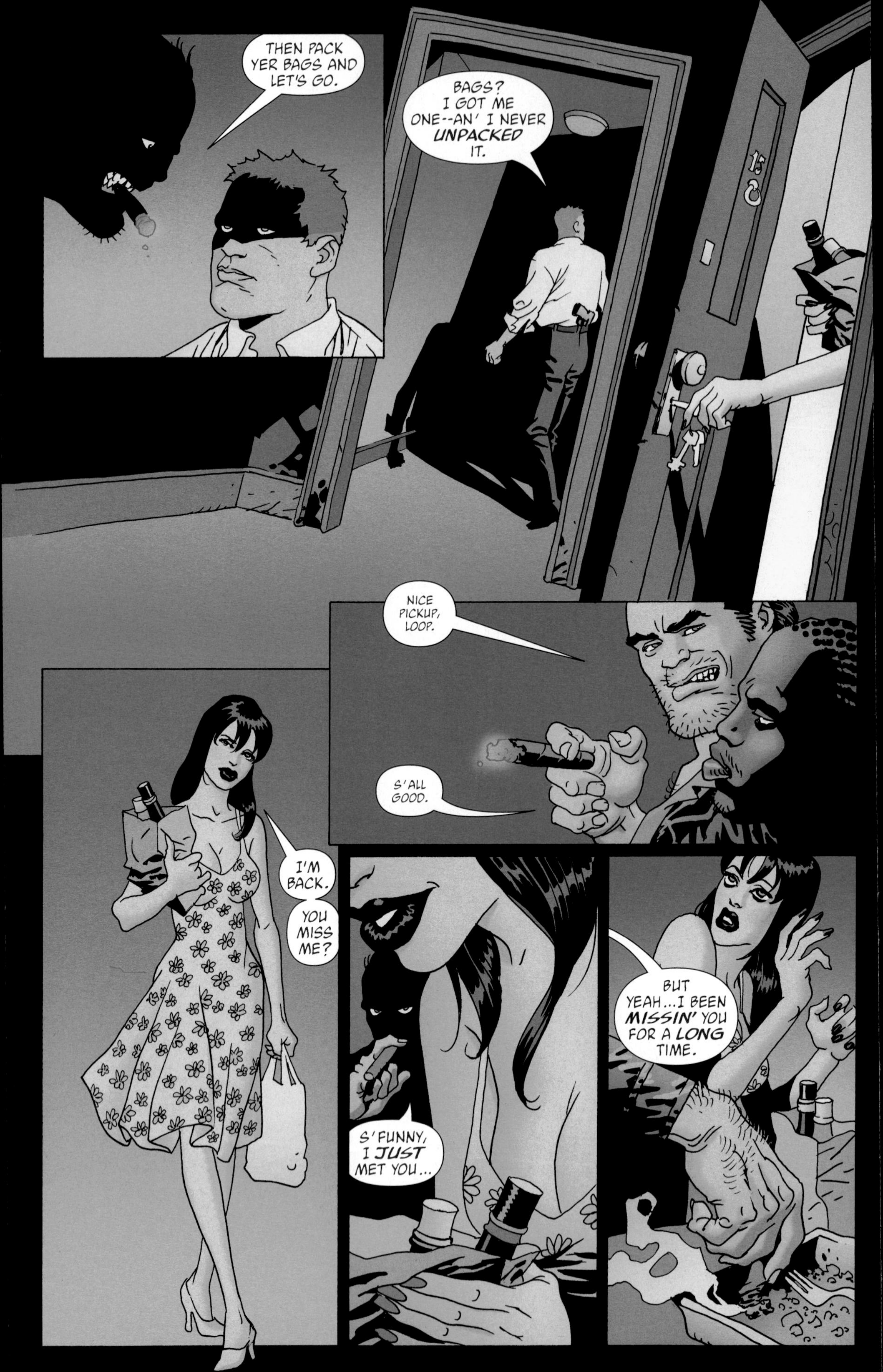
THEN PACK YER BAGS AND LET'S GO.
BAGS? I GOT ME ONE--AN' I NEVER UNPACKED IT.
NICE PICKUP, LOOP.
S'ALL GOOD.
I'M BACK.
YOU MISS ME?
S'FUNNY, I JUST MET YOU...
BUT YEAH...I BEEN MISSIN' YOU FOR A LONG TIME.

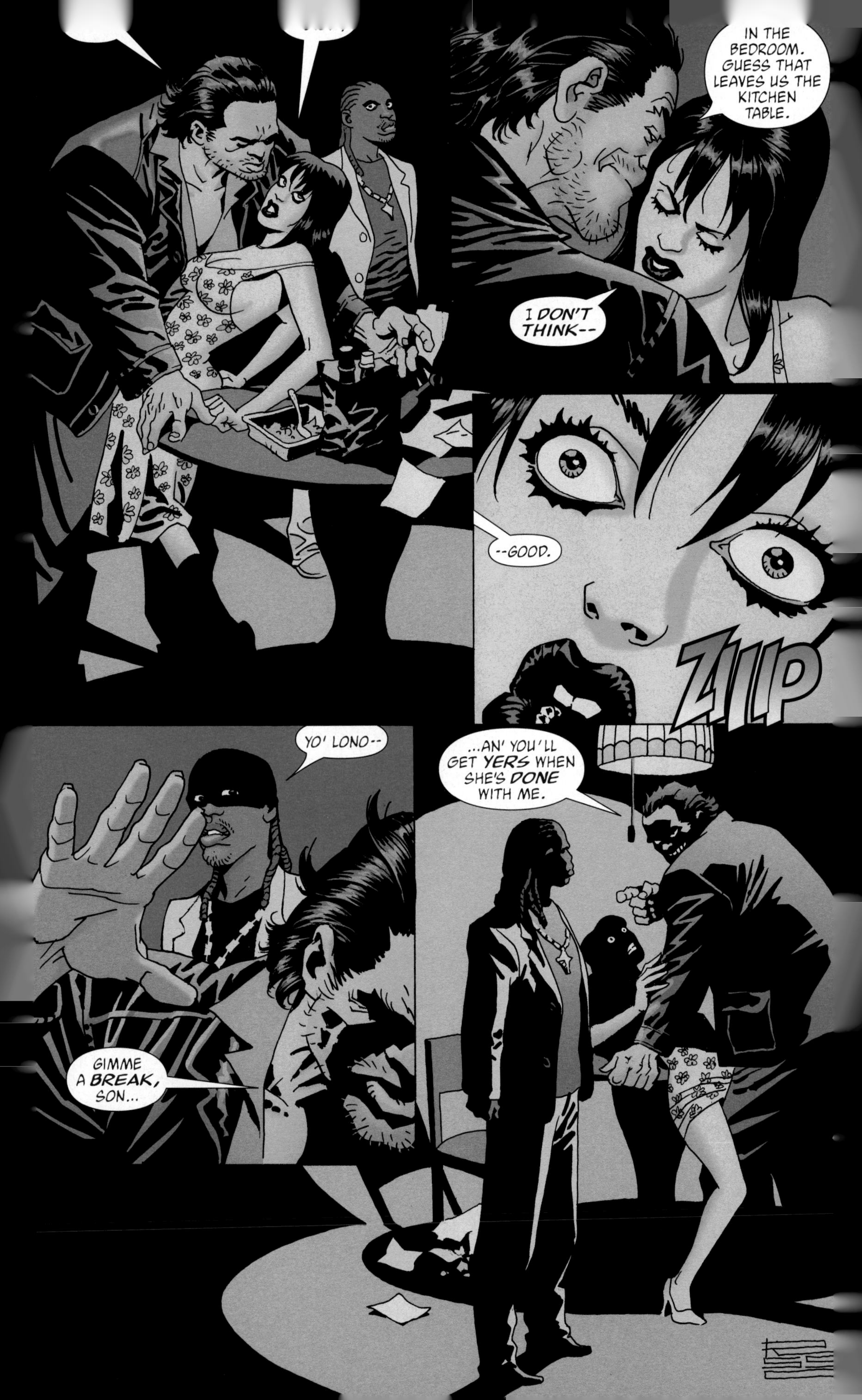
IN THE BEDROOM. GUESS THAT LEAVES US THE KITCHEN TABLE.
I DON'T THINK--
--GOOD.
ZIIP
YO' LONO--
GIMME A BREAK, SON...
...AN' YOU'LL GET YERS WHEN SHE'S DONE WITH ME.

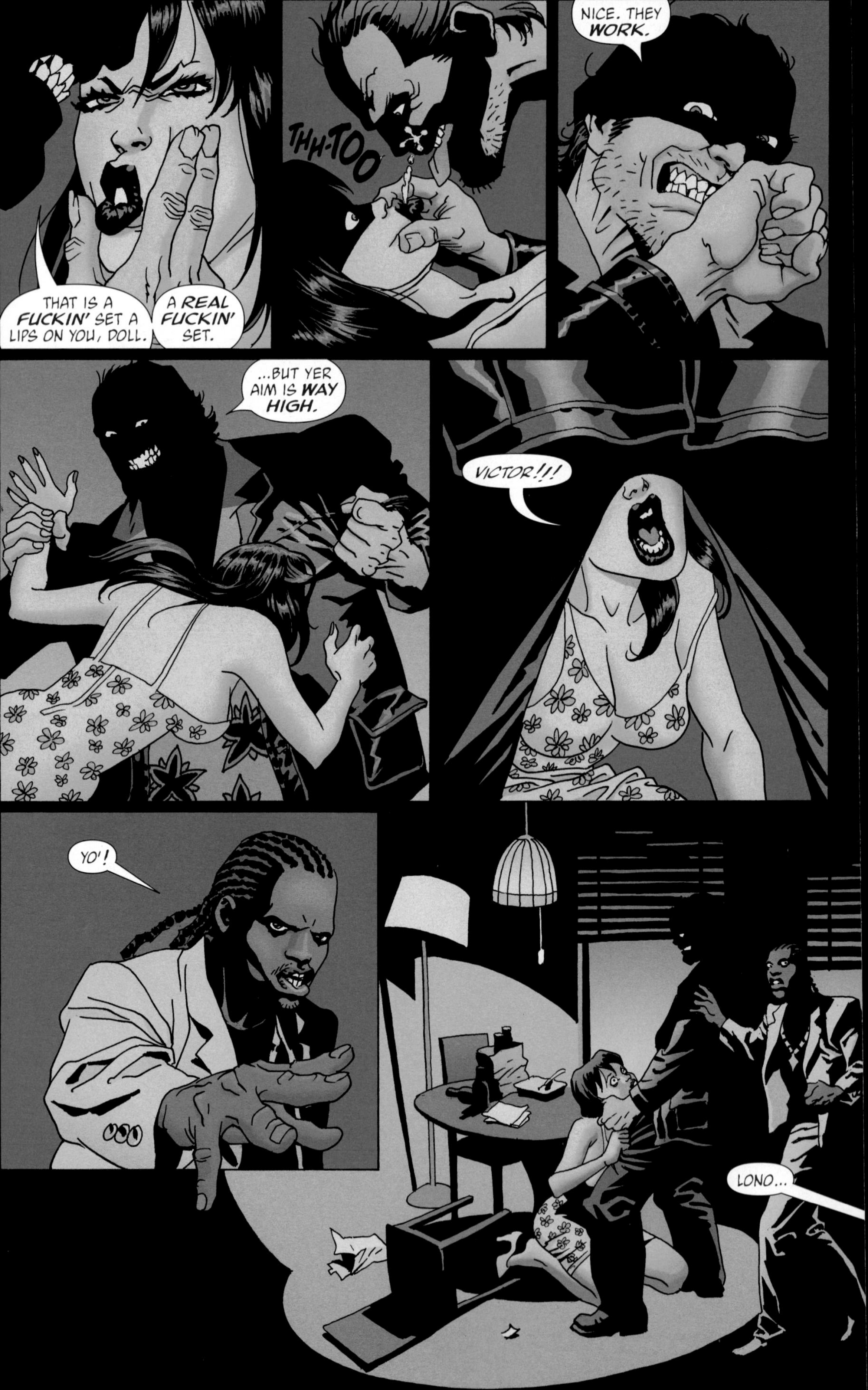
THAT IS A FUCKIN' SET A LIPS ON YOU, DOLL.
A REAL FUCKIN' SET.
THH-TOO
NICE. THEY WORK.
...BUT YER AIM IS WAY HIGH.
VICTOR!!!
YO'!
LONO...

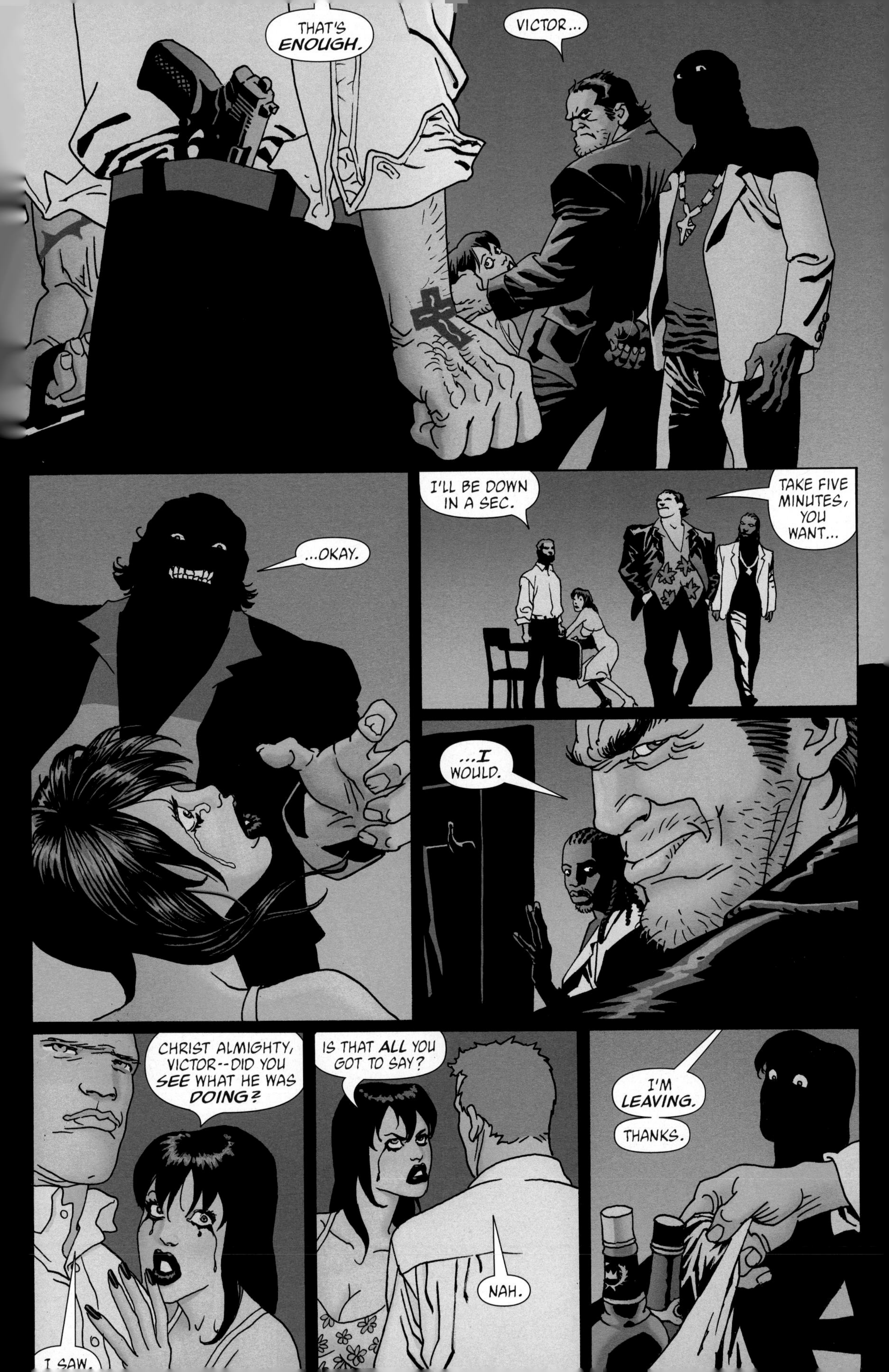
THAT'S ENOUGH.
VICTOR...
...OKAY.
I'LL BE DOWN IN A SEC.
TAKE FIVE MINUTES, YOU WANT...
...I WOULD.
CHRIST ALMIGHTY, VICTOR--DID YOU SEE WHAT HE WAS DOING?
I SAW.
IS THAT ALL YOU GOT TO SAY?
NAH.
I'M LEAVING.
THANKS.

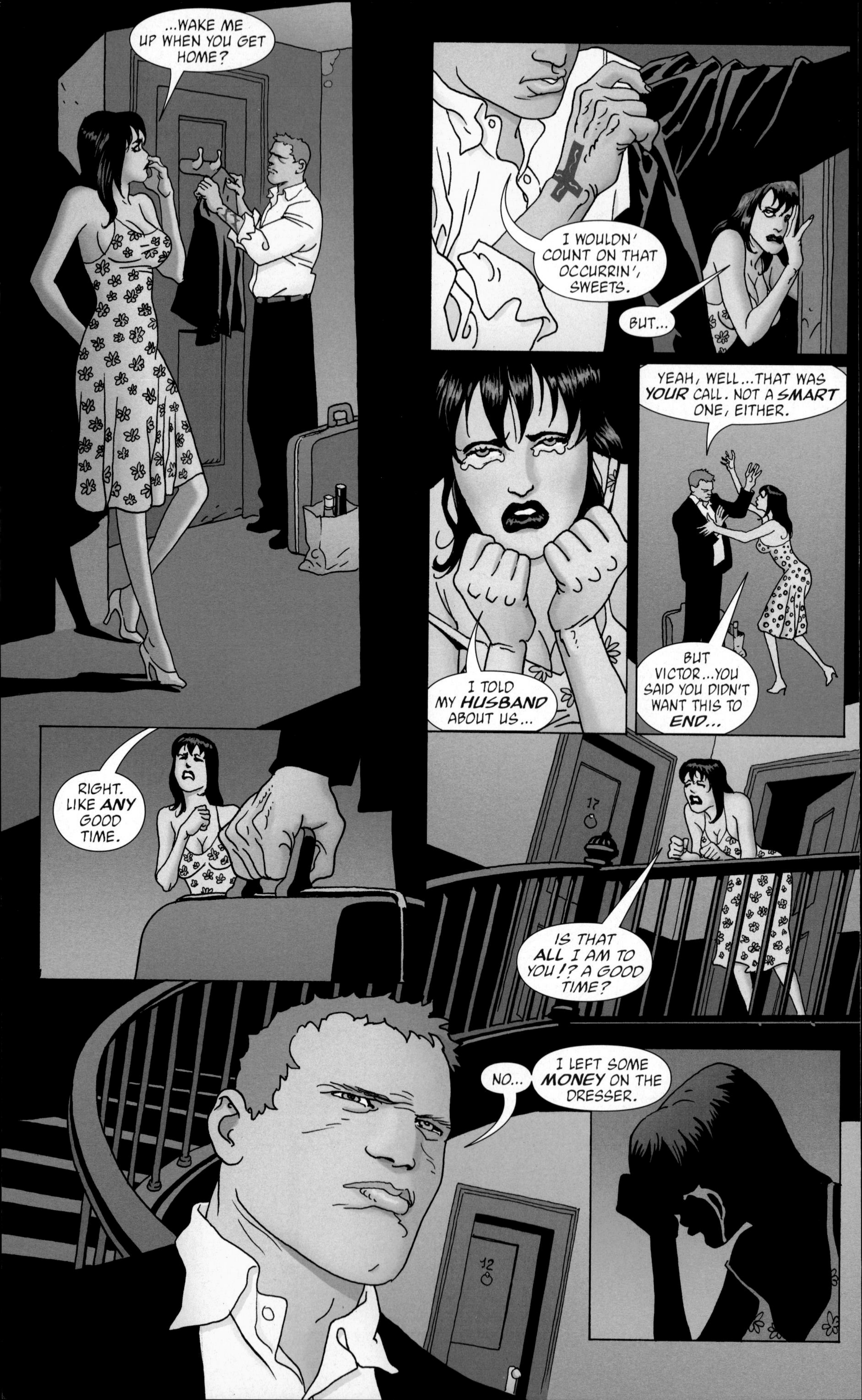
...WAKE ME UP WHEN YOU GET HOME?
I WOULDN' COUNT ON THAT OCCURRIN', SWEETS.
BUT...
I TOLD MY **HUSBAND** ABOUT US...
YEAH, WELL...THAT WAS **YOUR** CALL. NOT A **SMART** ONE, EITHER.
BUT VICTOR...YOU SAID YOU DIDN'T WANT THIS TO **END...**
RIGHT. LIKE **ANY** GOOD TIME.
IS THAT **ALL** I AM TO YOU!? A GOOD TIME?
NO...
I LEFT SOME **MONEY** ON THE DRESSER.

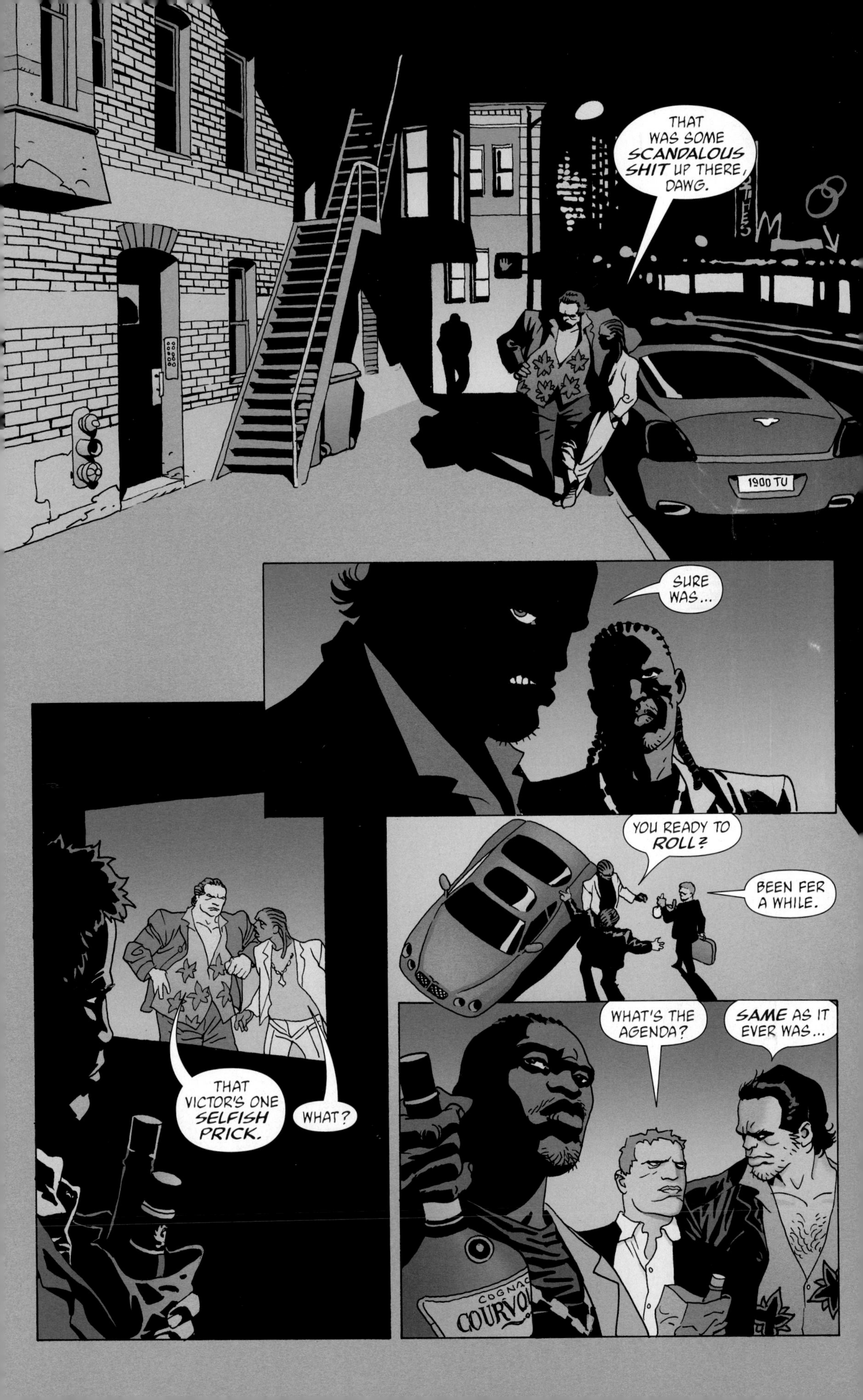
THAT WAS SOME SCANDALOUS SHIT UP THERE, DAWG.
1900 TU
SURE WAS...
THAT VICTOR'S ONE SELFISH PRICK.
WHAT?
YOU READY TO ROLL?
BEEN FER A WHILE.
WHAT'S THE AGENDA?
SAME AS IT EVER WAS...
COGNAC
COURVO

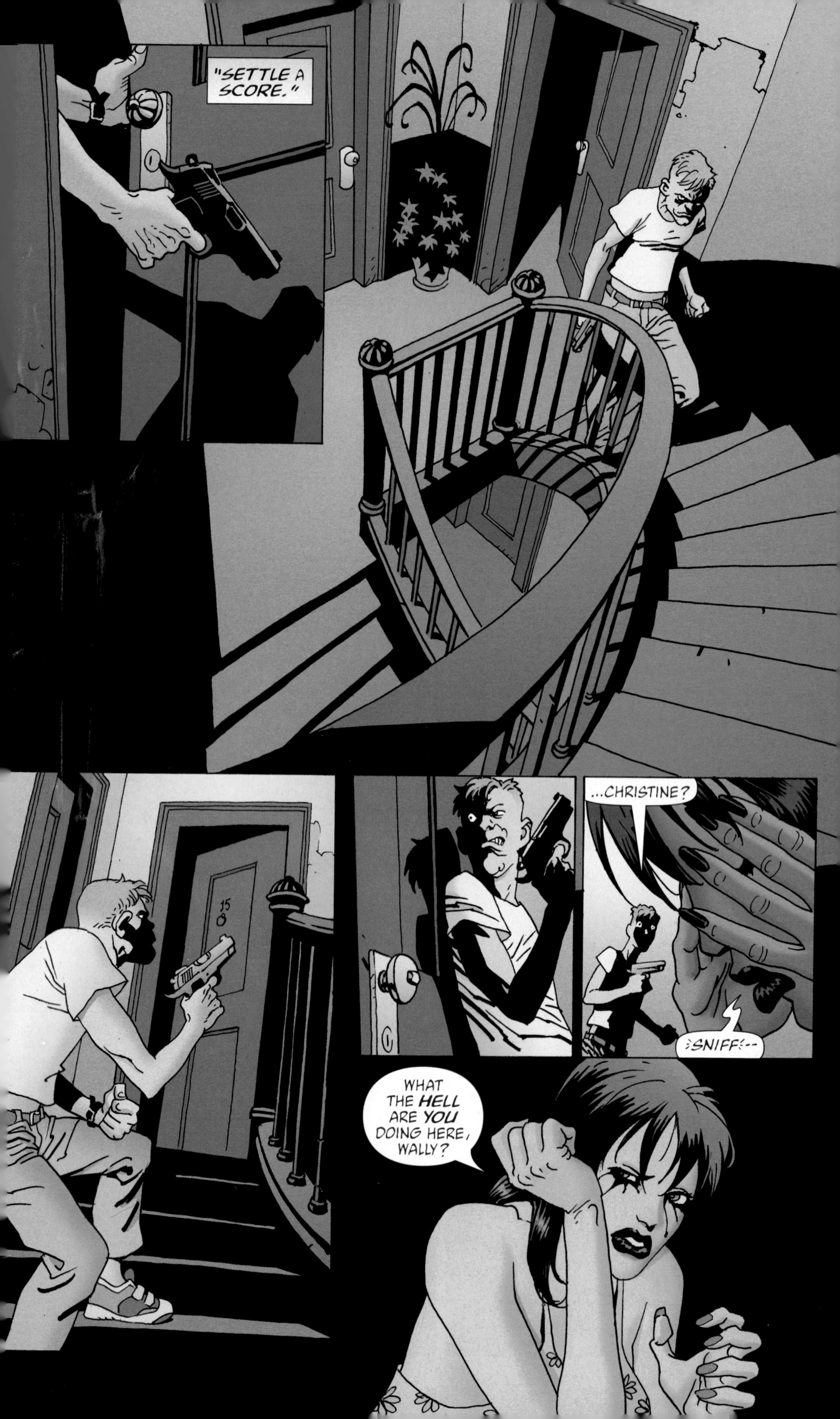
"SETTLE A SCORE."
...CHRISTINE?
SNIFF--
WHAT THE HELL ARE YOU DOING HERE, WALLY?

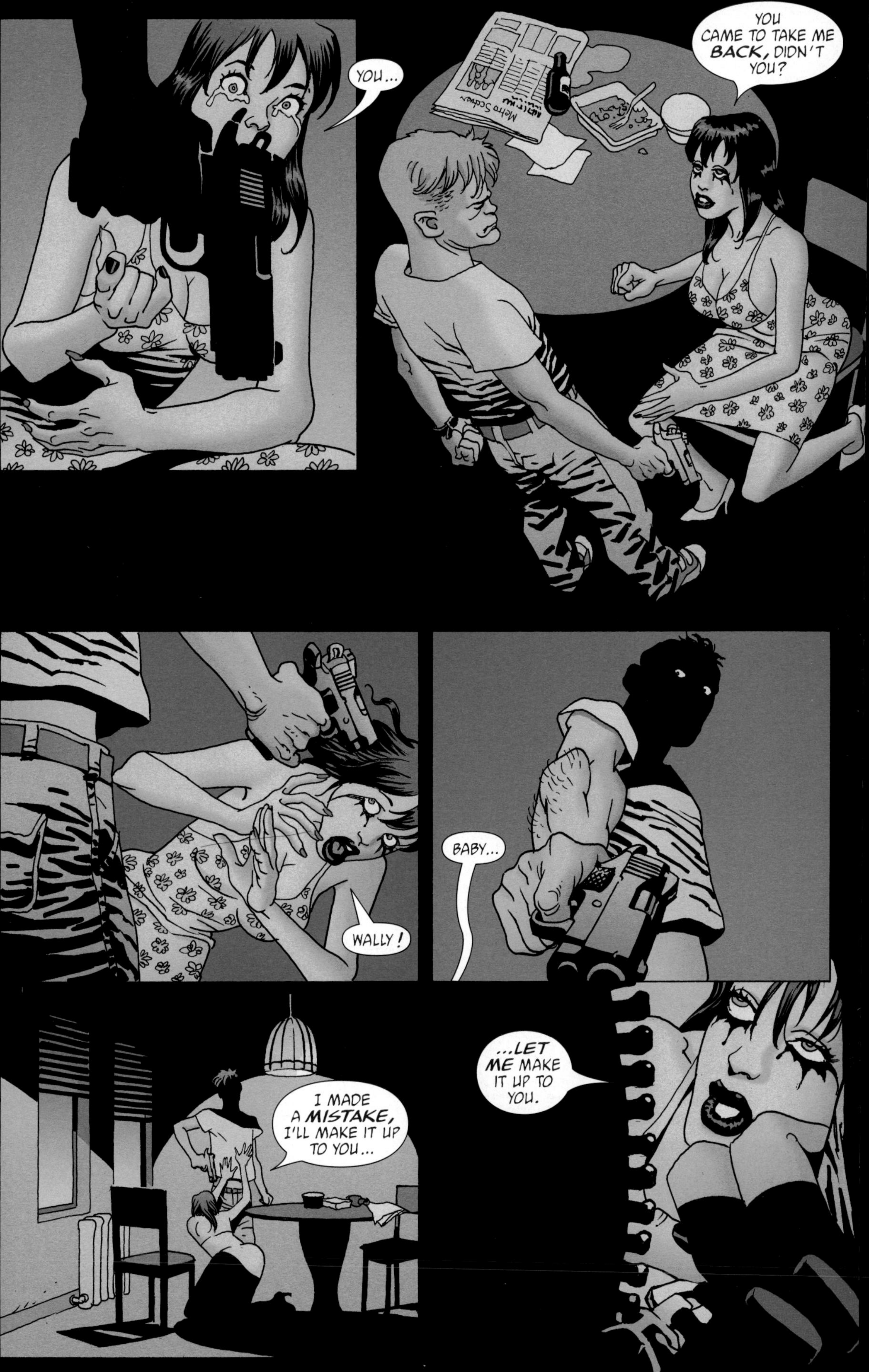
YOU...
YOU CAME TO TAKE ME BACK, DIDN'T YOU?
WALLY!
BABY...
I MADE A MISTAKE, I'LL MAKE IT UP TO YOU...
...LET ME MAKE IT UP TO YOU.

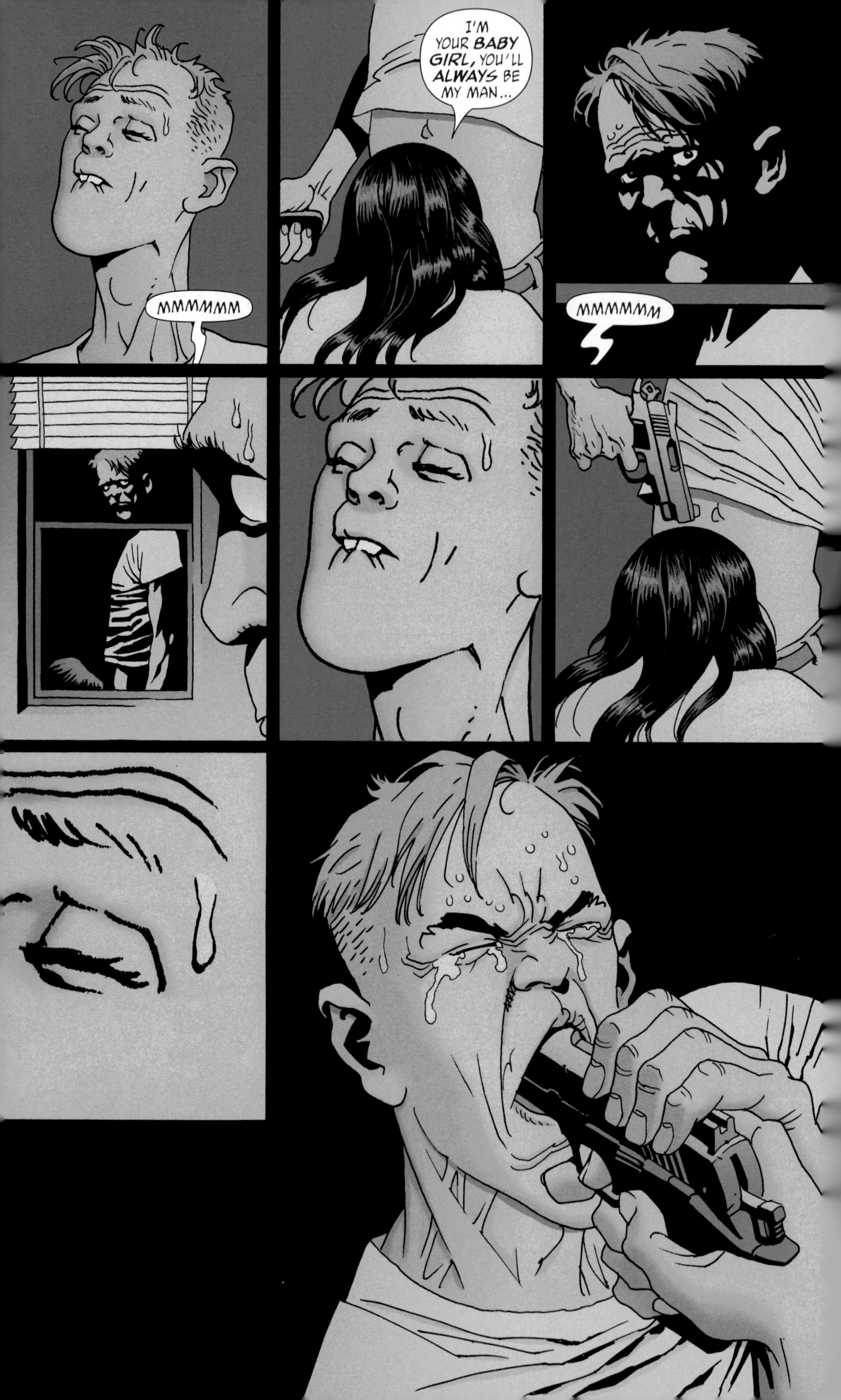
MMMMMM
I'M YOUR BABY GIRL, YOU'LL ALWAYS BE MY MAN...
MMMMMM

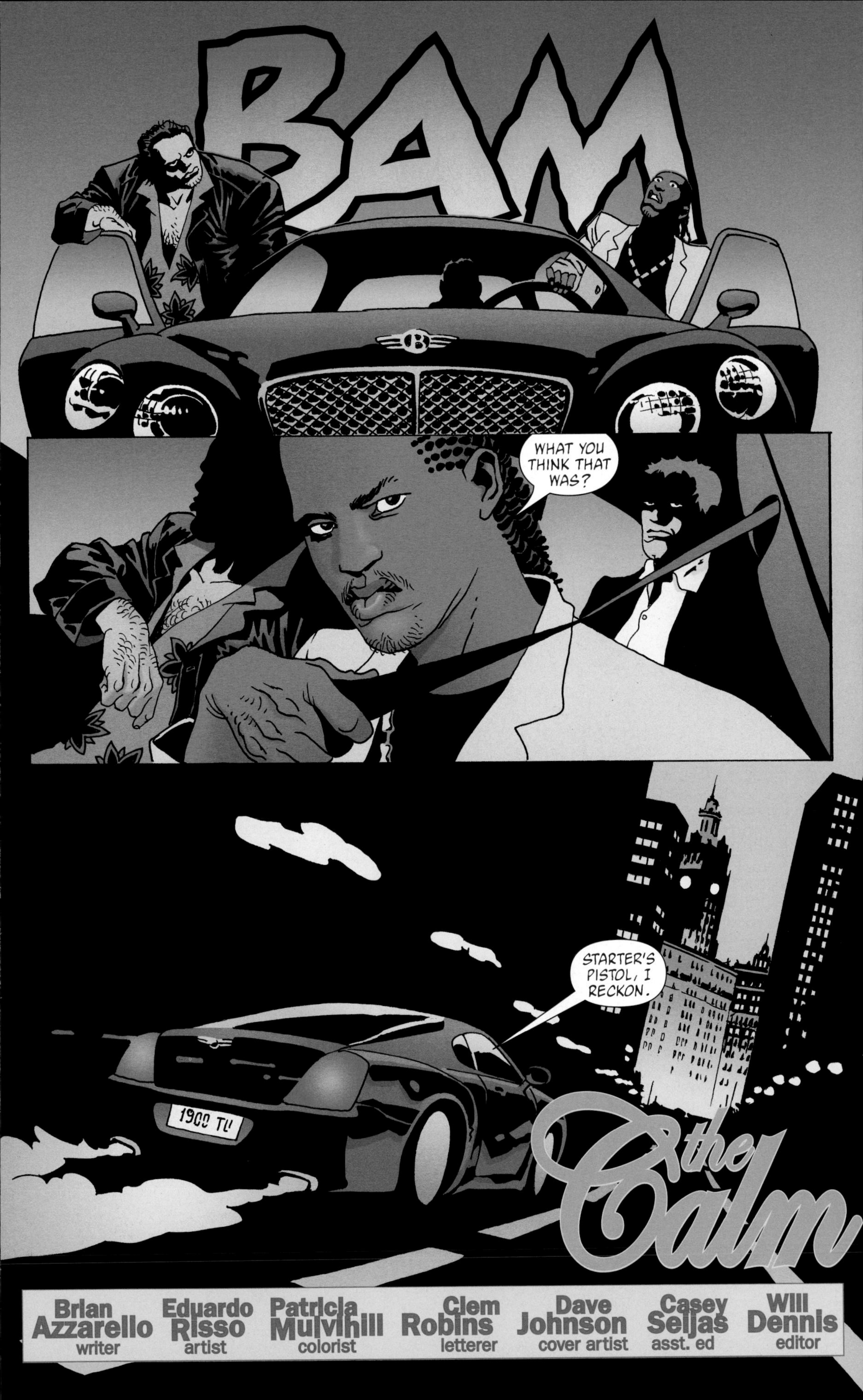
BAM
WHAT YOU THINK THAT WAS?
STARTER'S PISTOL, I RECKON.
1900 TU
the Calm
Brian Azzarello writer
Eduardo Risso artist
Patricia Mulvihill colorist
Clem Robins letterer
Dave Johnson cover artist
Casey Seijas asst. ed
Will Dennis editor

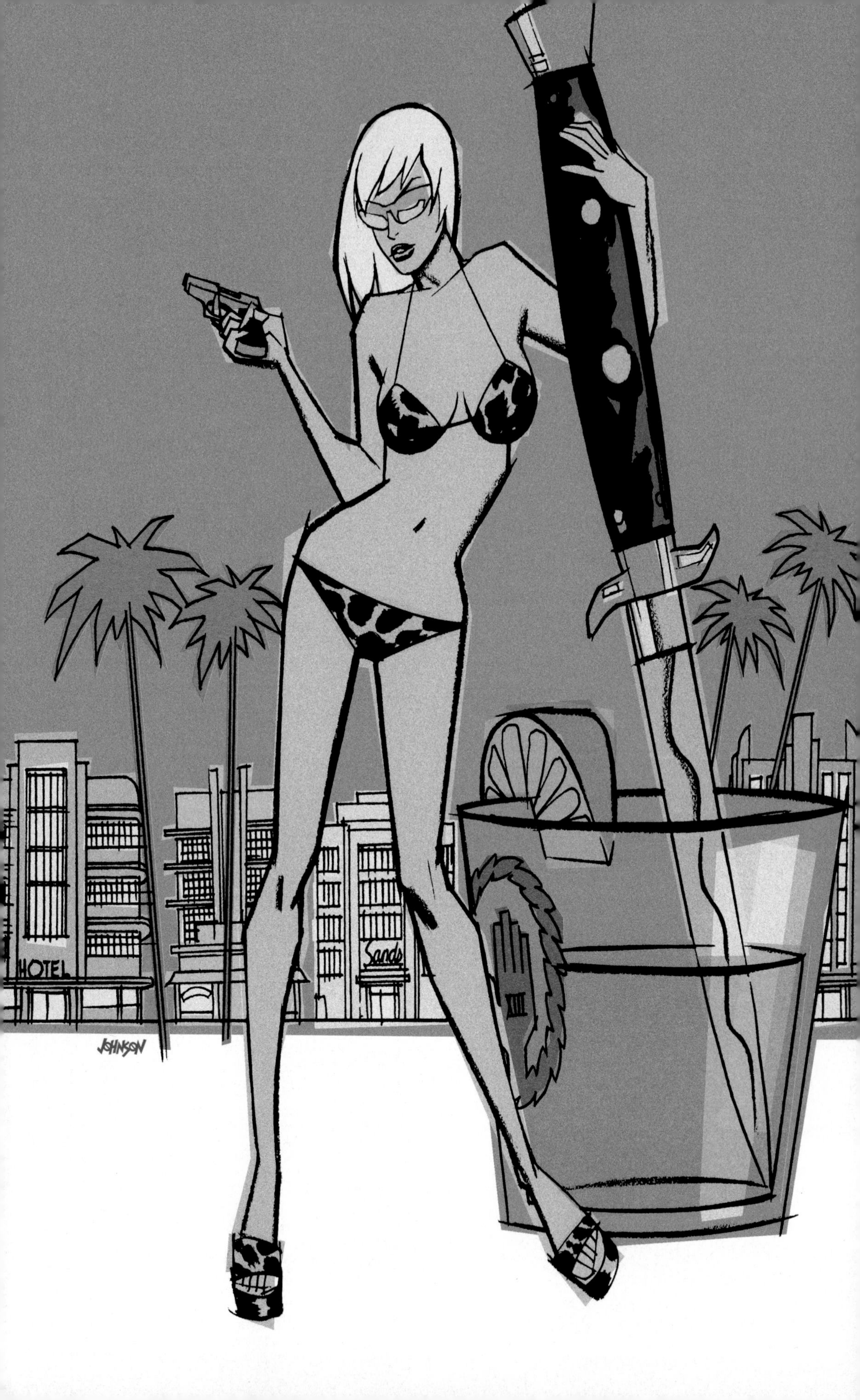
HOTEL
Sands
JOHNSON

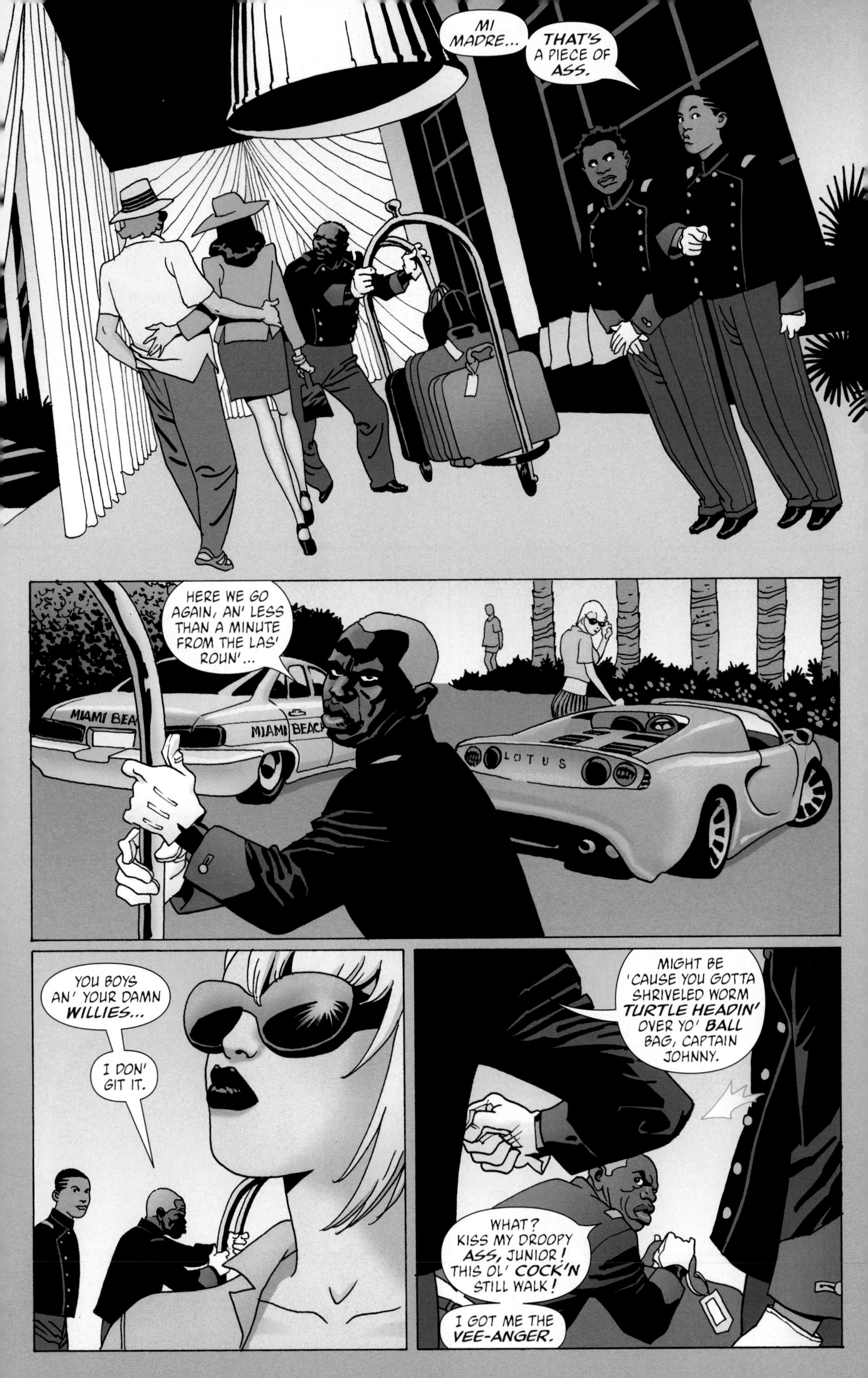
MI MADRE...
THAT'S A PIECE OF ASS.
HERE WE GO AGAIN, AN' LESS THAN A MINUTE FROM THE LAS' ROUN'...
MIAMI BEACH
MIAMI BEACH
LOTUS
YOU BOYS AN' YOUR DAMN WILLIES...
I DON' GIT IT.
MIGHT BE 'CAUSE YOU GOTTA SHRIVELED WORM TURTLE HEADIN' OVER YO' BALL BAG, CAPTAIN JOHNNY.
WHAT? KISS MY DROOPY ASS, JUNIOR! THIS OL' COCK'N STILL WALK!
I GOT ME THE VEE-ANGER.

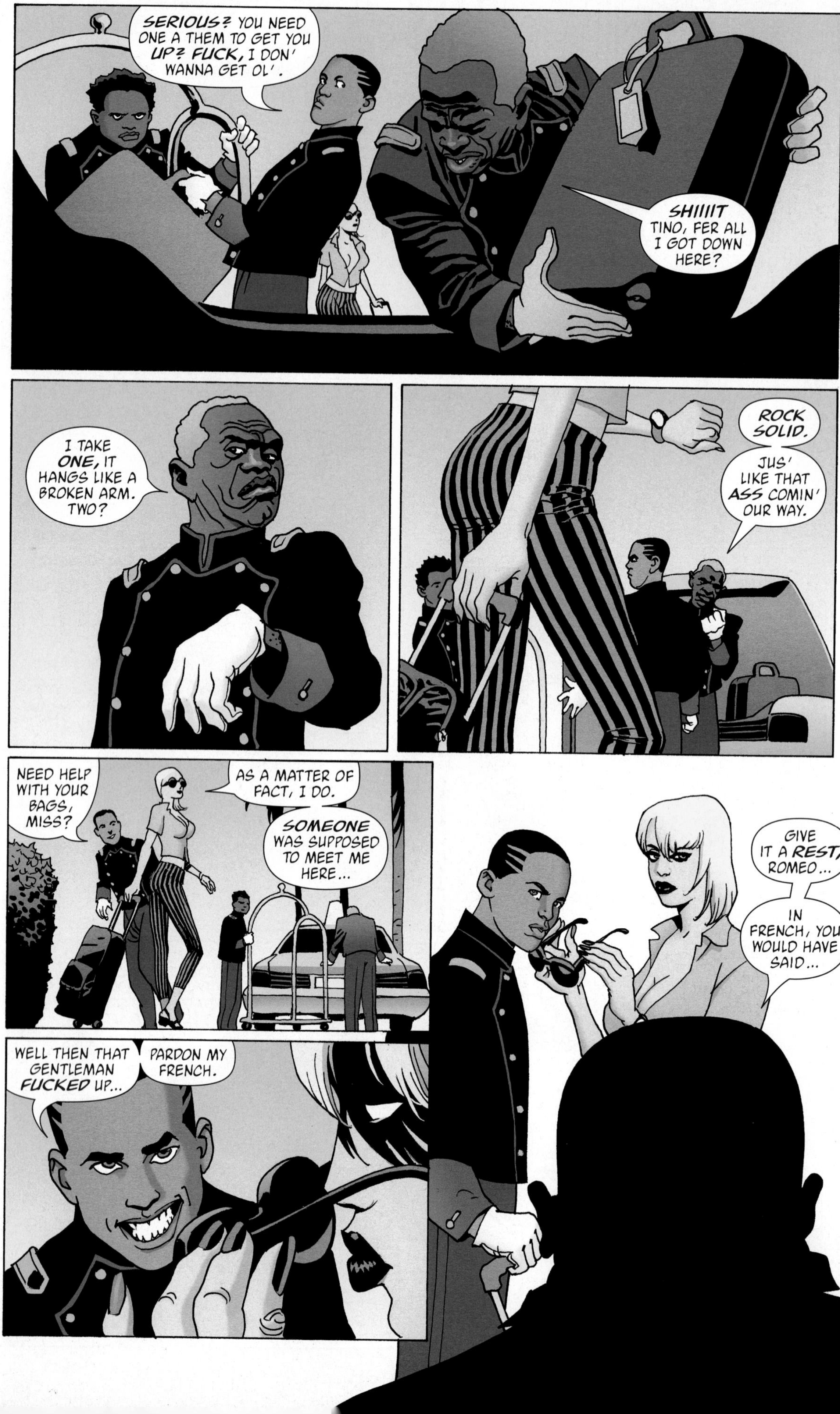
SERIOUS? YOU NEED ONE A THEM TO GET YOU UP? FUCK, I DON' WANNA GET OL'.
SHIIIIT TINO, FER ALL I GOT DOWN HERE?
I TAKE ONE, IT HANGS LIKE A BROKEN ARM. TWO?
ROCK SOLID.
JUS' LIKE THAT ASS COMIN' OUR WAY.
NEED HELP WITH YOUR BAGS, MISS?
AS A MATTER OF FACT, I DO.
SOMEONE WAS SUPPOSED TO MEET ME HERE...
WELL THEN THAT GENTLEMAN FUCKED UP...
PARDON MY FRENCH.
GIVE IT A REST, ROMEO...
IN FRENCH, YOU WOULD HAVE SAID...

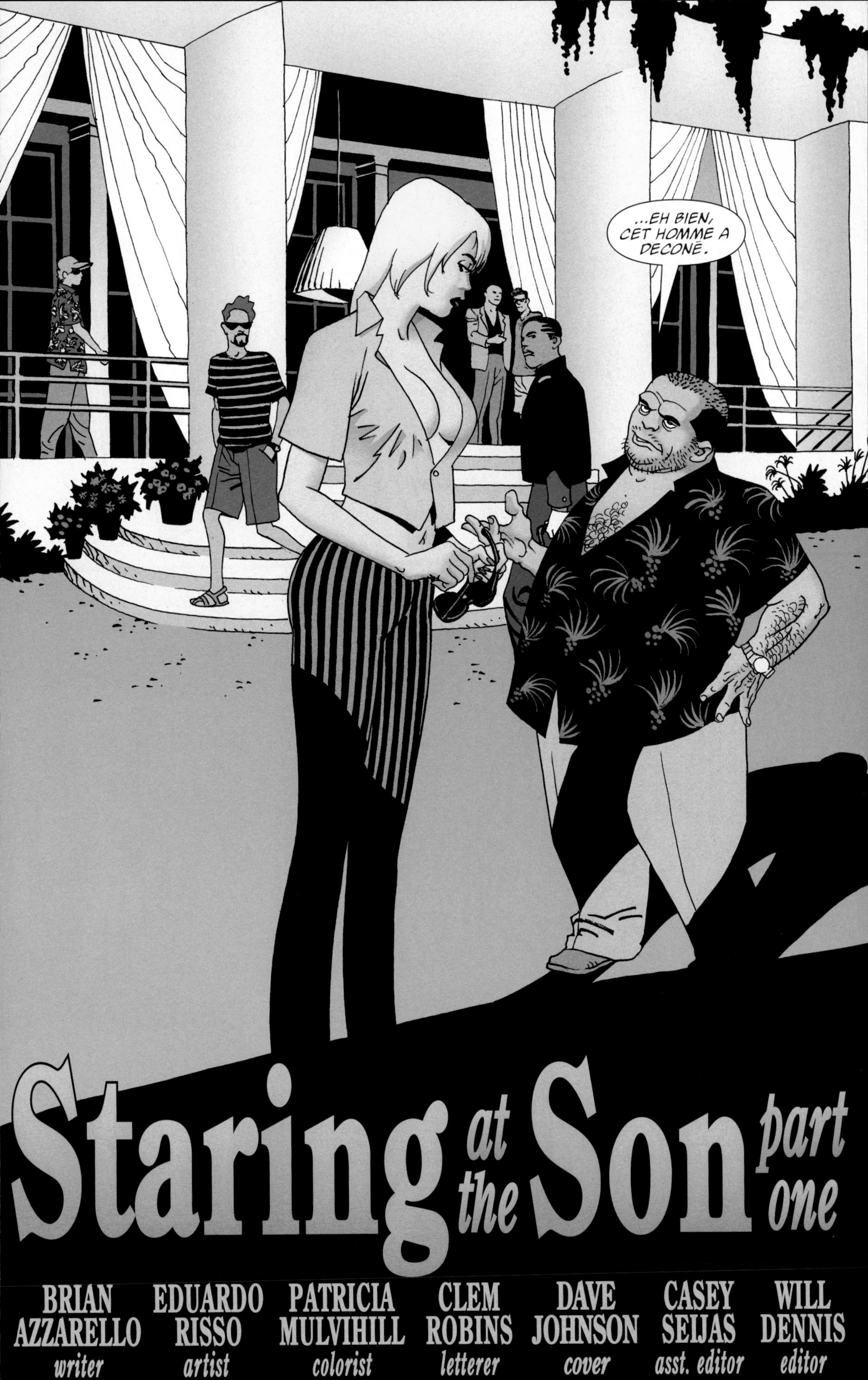
...EH BIEN, CET HOMME A DECONÉ.
Staring at the Son part one
BRIAN AZZARELLO writer
EDUARDO RISSO artist
PATRICIA MULVIHILL colorist
CLEM ROBINS letterer
DAVE JOHNSON cover
CASEY SEIJAS asst. editor
WILL DENNIS editor

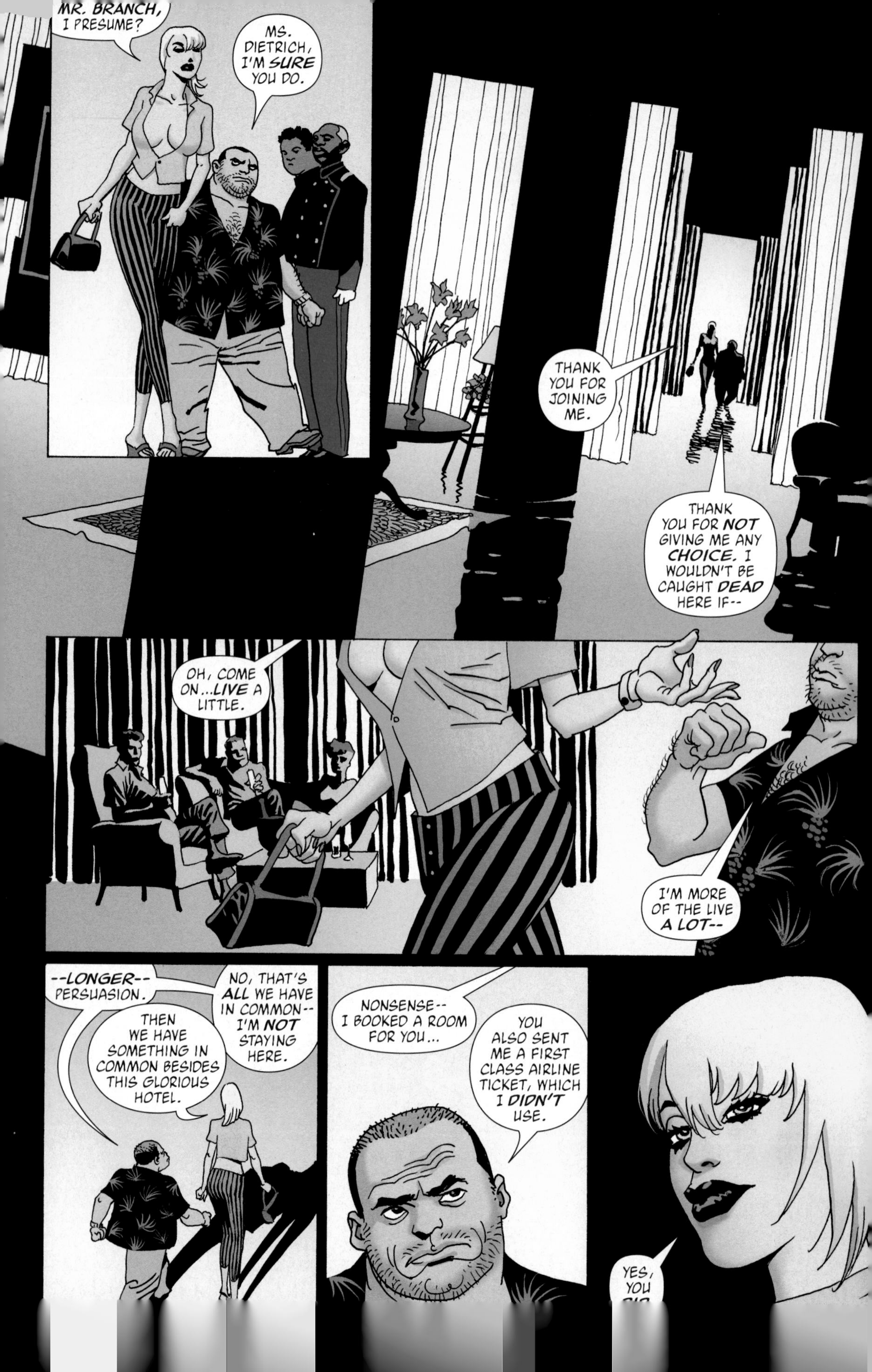

MR. BRANCH, I PRESUME?
MS. DIETRICH, I'M SURE YOU DO.
THANK YOU FOR JOINING ME.
THANK YOU FOR NOT GIVING ME ANY CHOICE. I WOULDN'T BE CAUGHT DEAD HERE IF--
OH, COME ON...LIVE A LITTLE.
I'M MORE OF THE LIVE A LOT--
--LONGER-- PERSUASION.
THEN WE HAVE SOMETHING IN COMMON BESIDES THIS GLORIOUS HOTEL.
NO, THAT'S ALL WE HAVE IN COMMON-- I'M NOT STAYING HERE.
NONSENSE-- I BOOKED A ROOM FOR YOU...
YOU ALSO SENT ME A FIRST CLASS AIRLINE TICKET, WHICH I DIDN'T USE.
YES, YOU

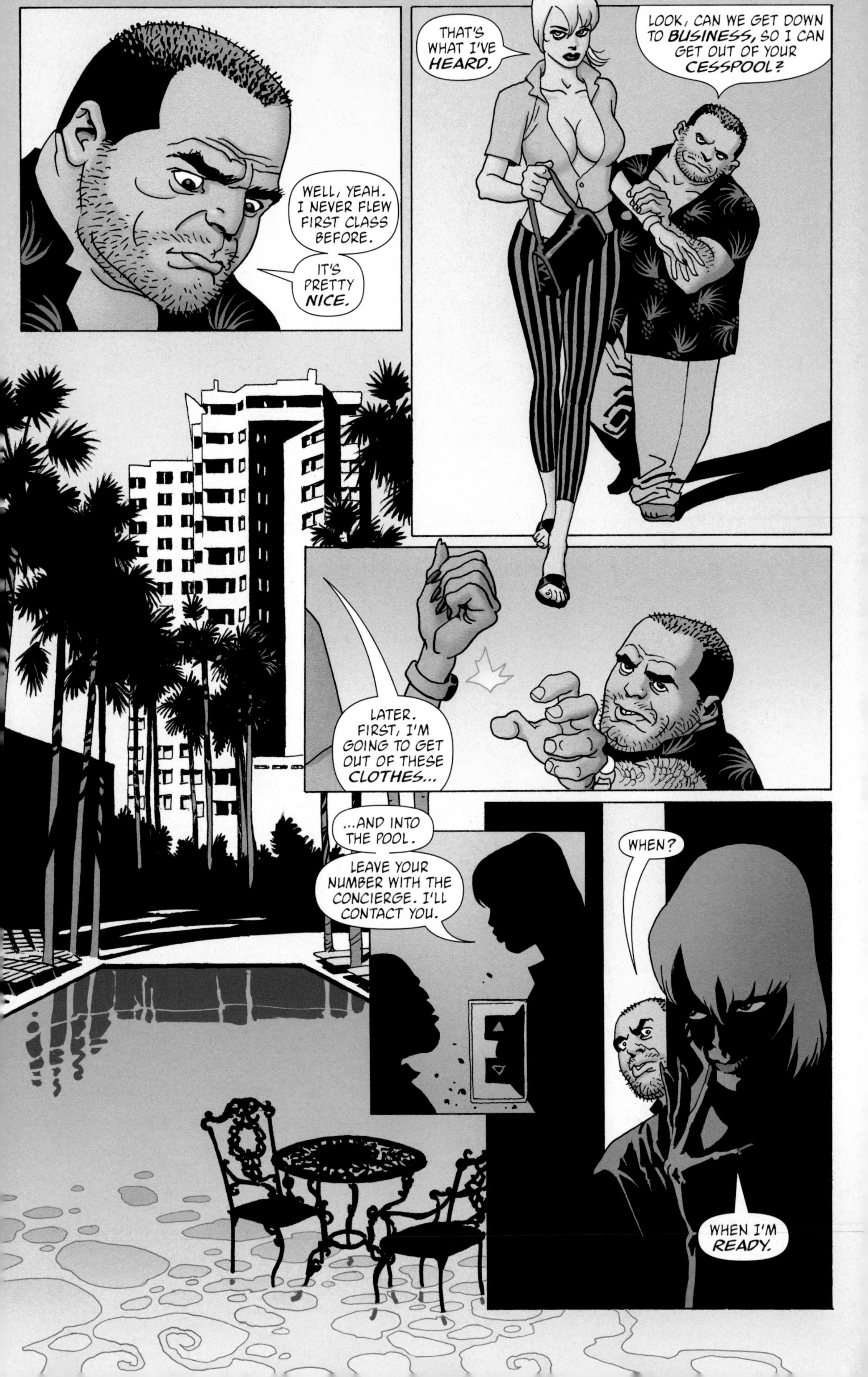
WELL, YEAH. I NEVER FLEW FIRST CLASS BEFORE.
IT'S PRETTY NICE.
THAT'S WHAT I'VE HEARD.
LOOK, CAN WE GET DOWN TO BUSINESS, SO I CAN GET OUT OF YOUR CESSPOOL?
LATER. FIRST, I'M GOING TO GET OUT OF THESE CLOTHES...
...AND INTO THE POOL.
LEAVE YOUR NUMBER WITH THE CONCIERGE. I'LL CONTACT YOU.
WHEN?
WHEN I'M READY.

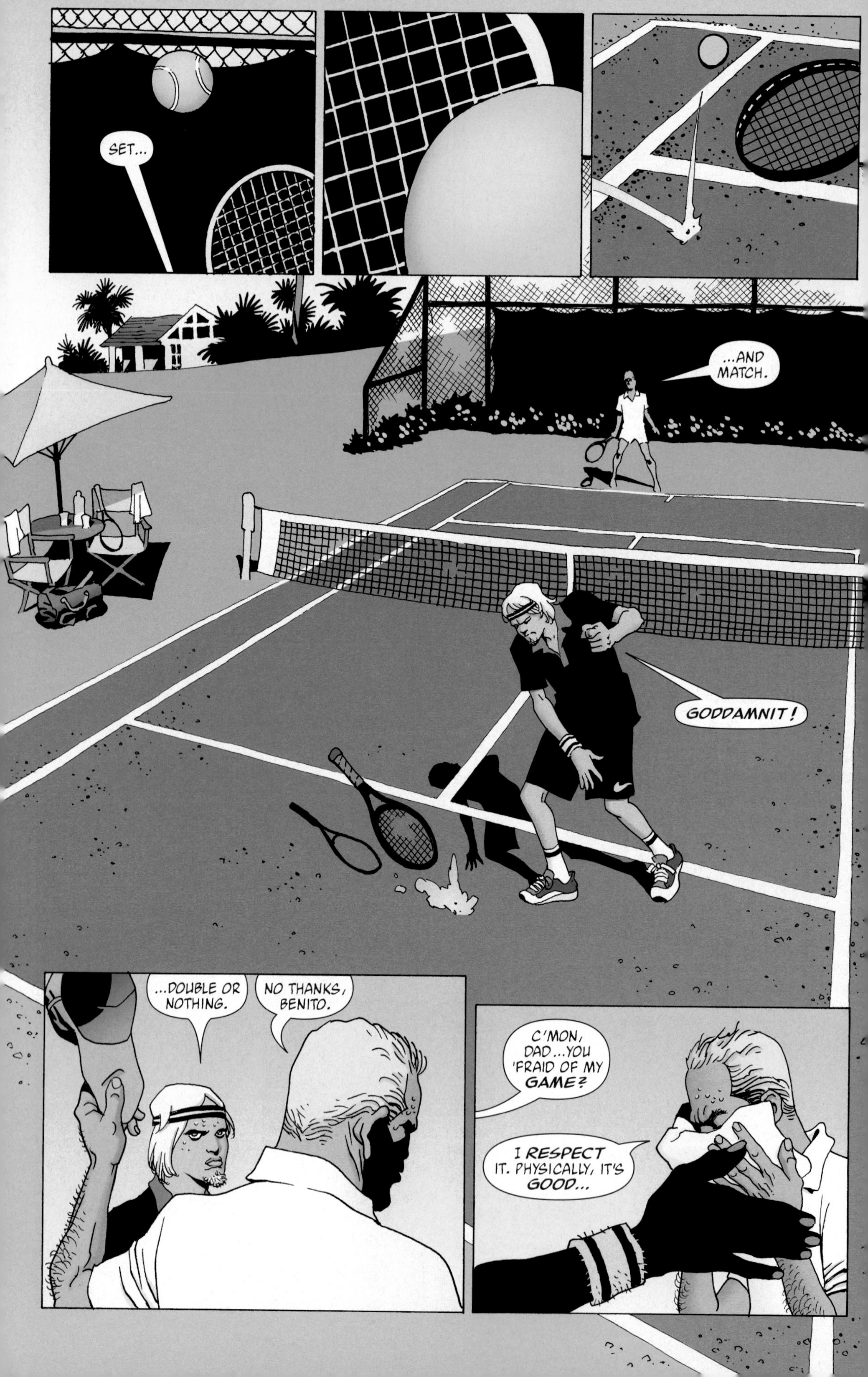
SET...
...AND MATCH.
GODDAMNIT!
...DOUBLE OR NOTHING.
NO THANKS, BENITO.
C'MON, DAD...YOU 'FRAID OF MY GAME?
I RESPECT IT. PHYSICALLY, IT'S GOOD...

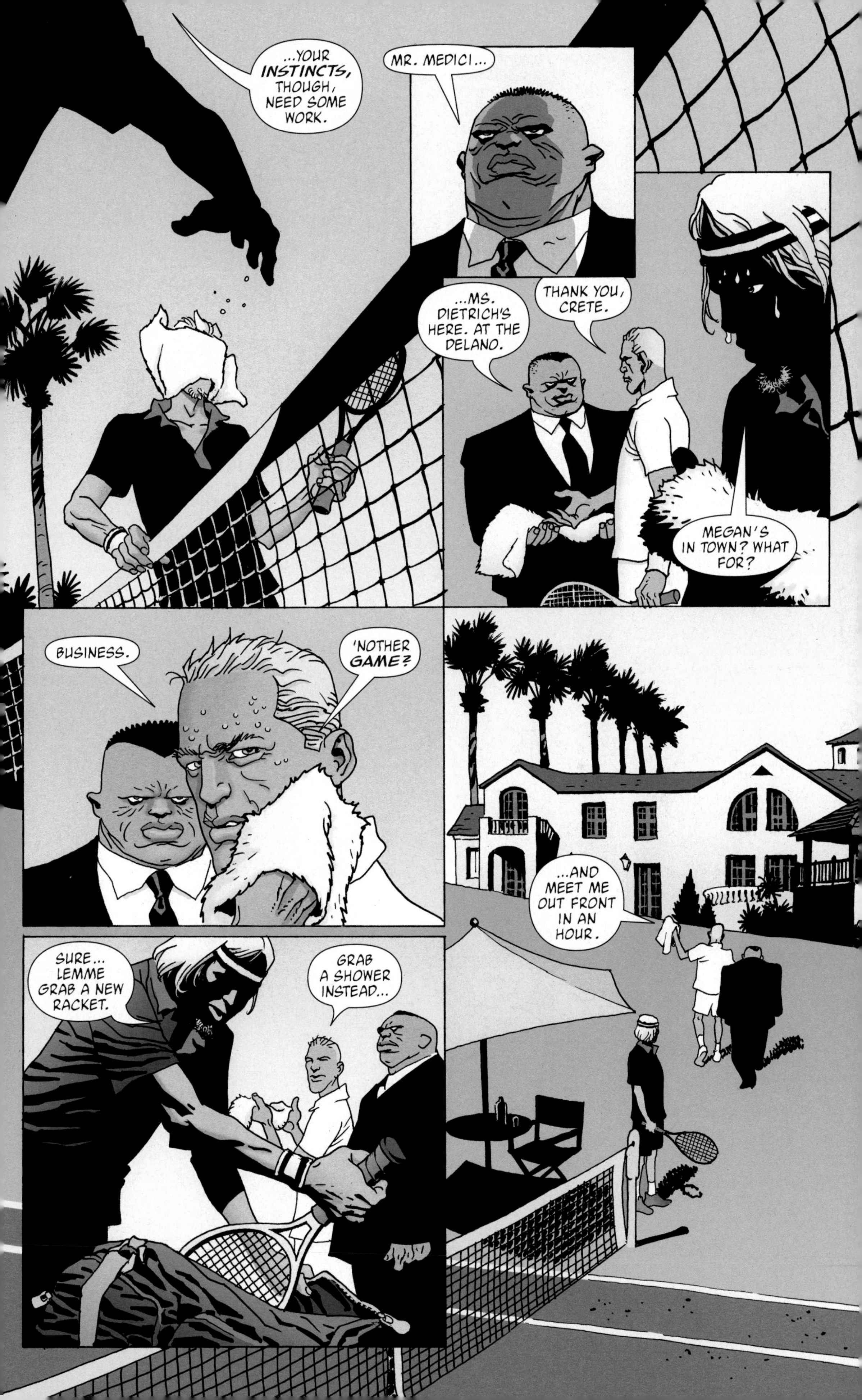
...YOUR INSTINCTS, THOUGH, NEED SOME WORK.
MR. MEDICI...
...MS. DIETRICH'S HERE. AT THE DELANO.
THANK YOU, CRETE.
MEGAN'S IN TOWN? WHAT FOR?
BUSINESS.
'NOTHER GAME?
SURE... LEMME GRAB A NEW RACKET.
GRAB A SHOWER INSTEAD...
...AND MEET ME OUT FRONT IN AN HOUR.

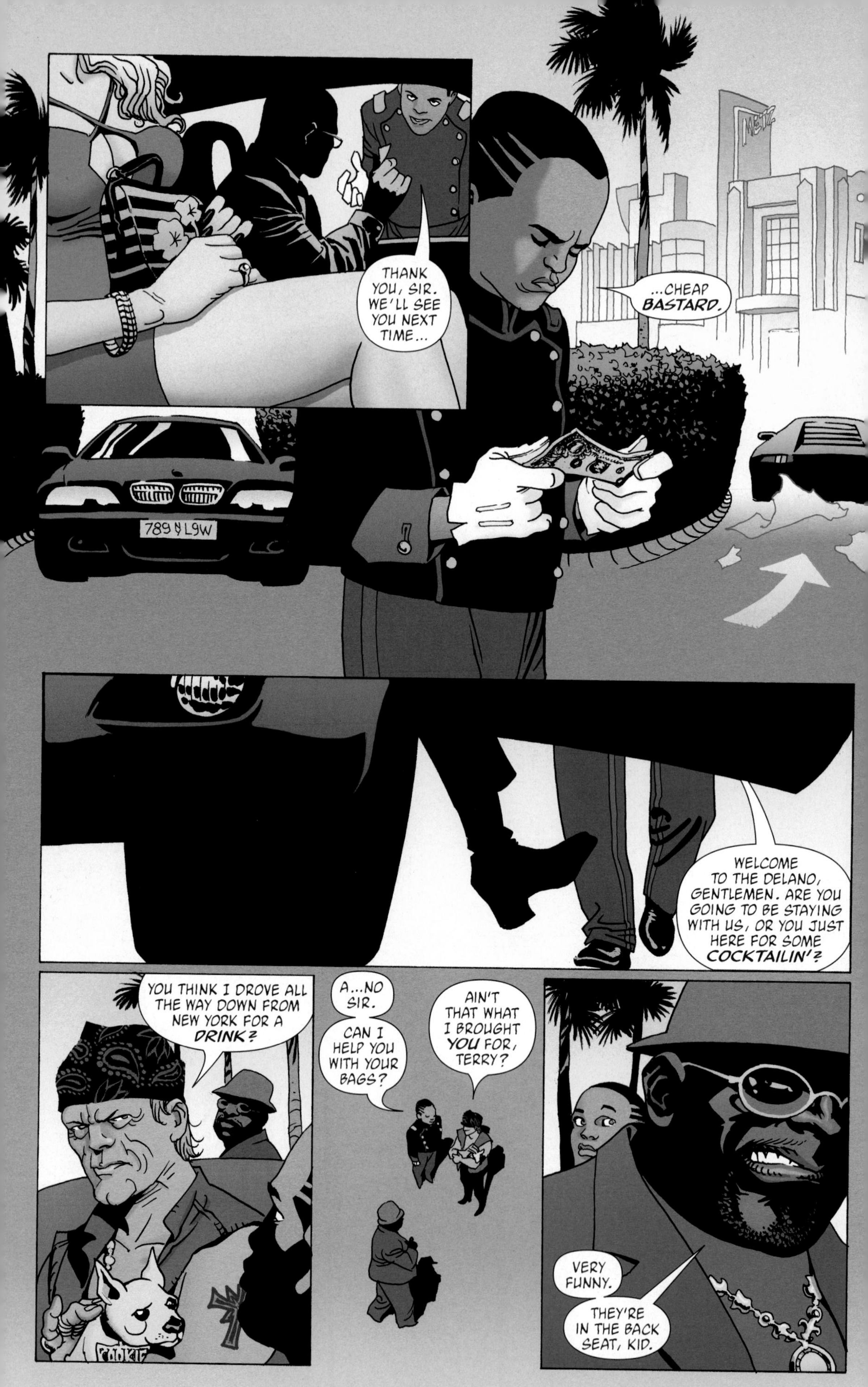

THANK YOU, SIR. WE'LL SEE YOU NEXT TIME...
...CHEAP BASTARD.
789 L9W
WELCOME TO THE DELANO, GENTLEMEN. ARE YOU GOING TO BE STAYING WITH US, OR YOU JUST HERE FOR SOME COCKTAILIN'?
YOU THINK I DROVE ALL THE WAY DOWN FROM NEW YORK FOR A DRINK?
A...NO SIR.
CAN I HELP YOU WITH YOUR BAGS?
AIN'T THAT WHAT I BROUGHT YOU FOR, TERRY?
VERY FUNNY.
THEY'RE IN THE BACK SEAT, KID.

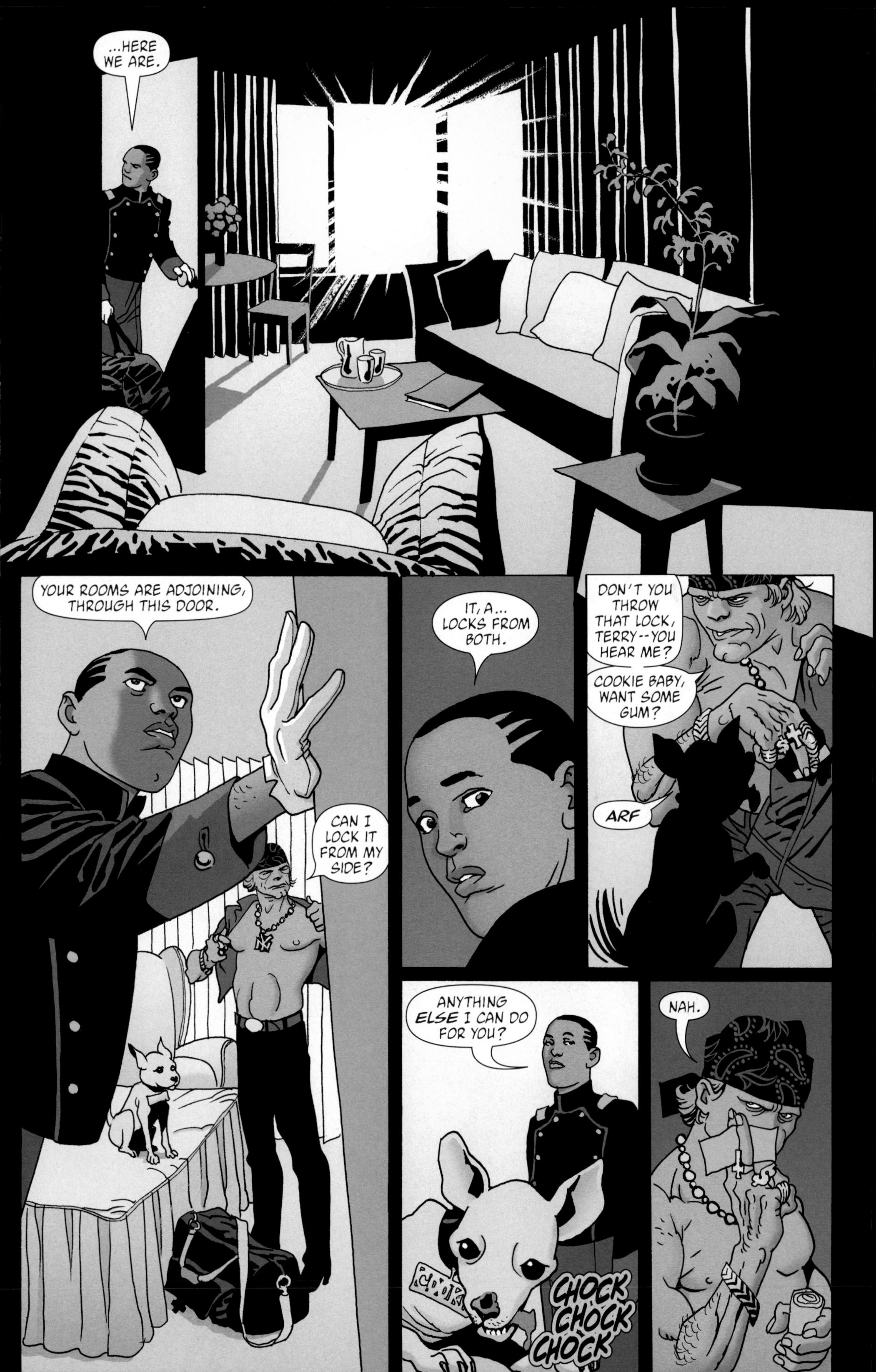
...HERE WE ARE.
YOUR ROOMS ARE ADJOINING, THROUGH THIS DOOR.
CAN I LOCK IT FROM MY SIDE?
IT, A... LOCKS FROM BOTH.
DON'T YOU THROW THAT LOCK, TERRY--YOU HEAR ME?
COOKIE BABY, WANT SOME GUM?
ARF
ANYTHING ELSE I CAN DO FOR YOU?
CHOCK CHOCK CHOCK
NAH.

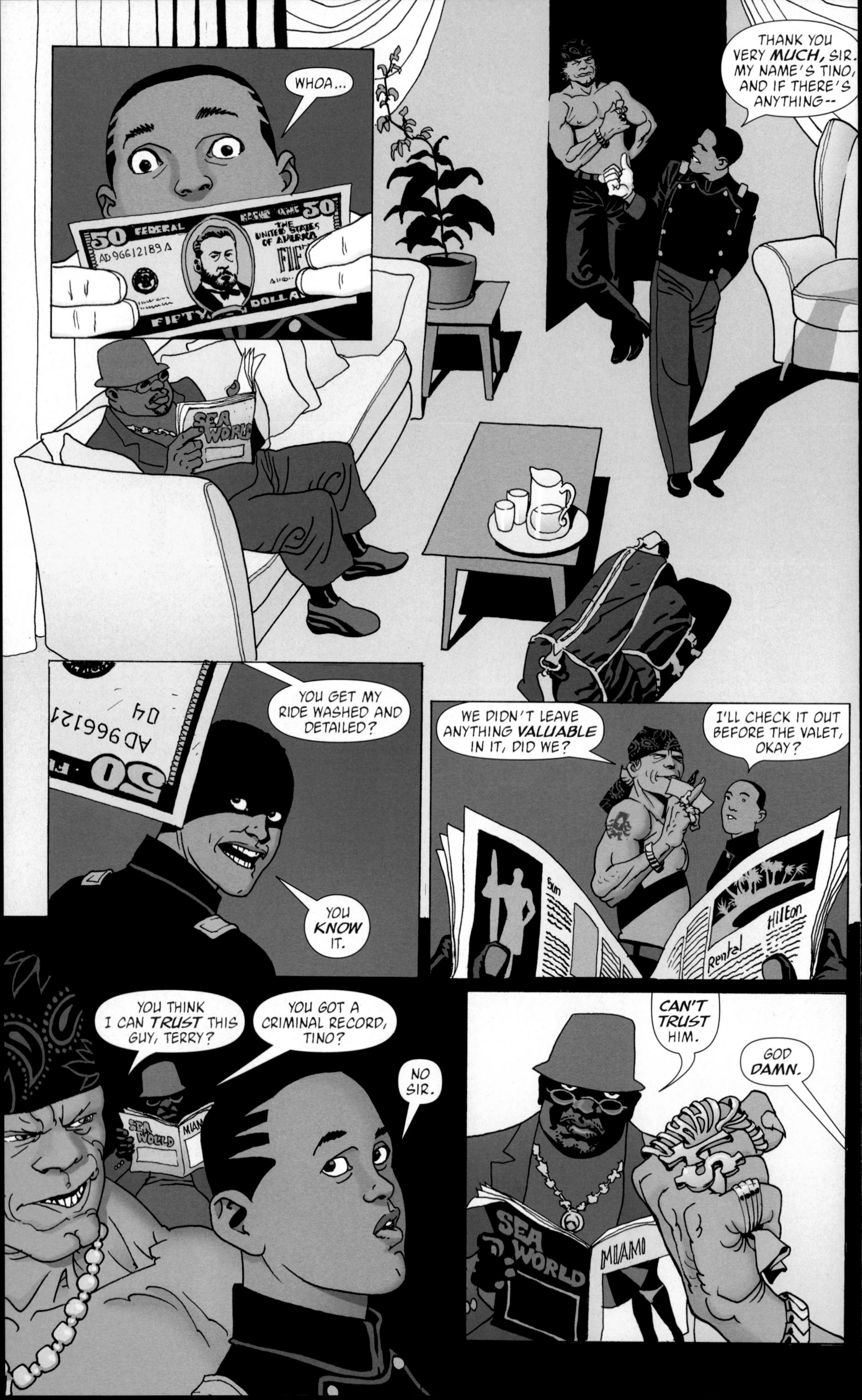
WHOA...
THANK YOU VERY MUCH, SIR. MY NAME'S TINO, AND IF THERE'S ANYTHING--
YOU GET MY RIDE WASHED AND DETAILED?
YOU KNOW IT.
WE DIDN'T LEAVE ANYTHING VALUABLE IN IT, DID WE?
I'LL CHECK IT OUT BEFORE THE VALET, OKAY?
YOU THINK I CAN TRUST THIS GUY, TERRY?
YOU GOT A CRIMINAL RECORD, TINO?
NO SIR.
CAN'T TRUST HIM.
GOD DAMN.

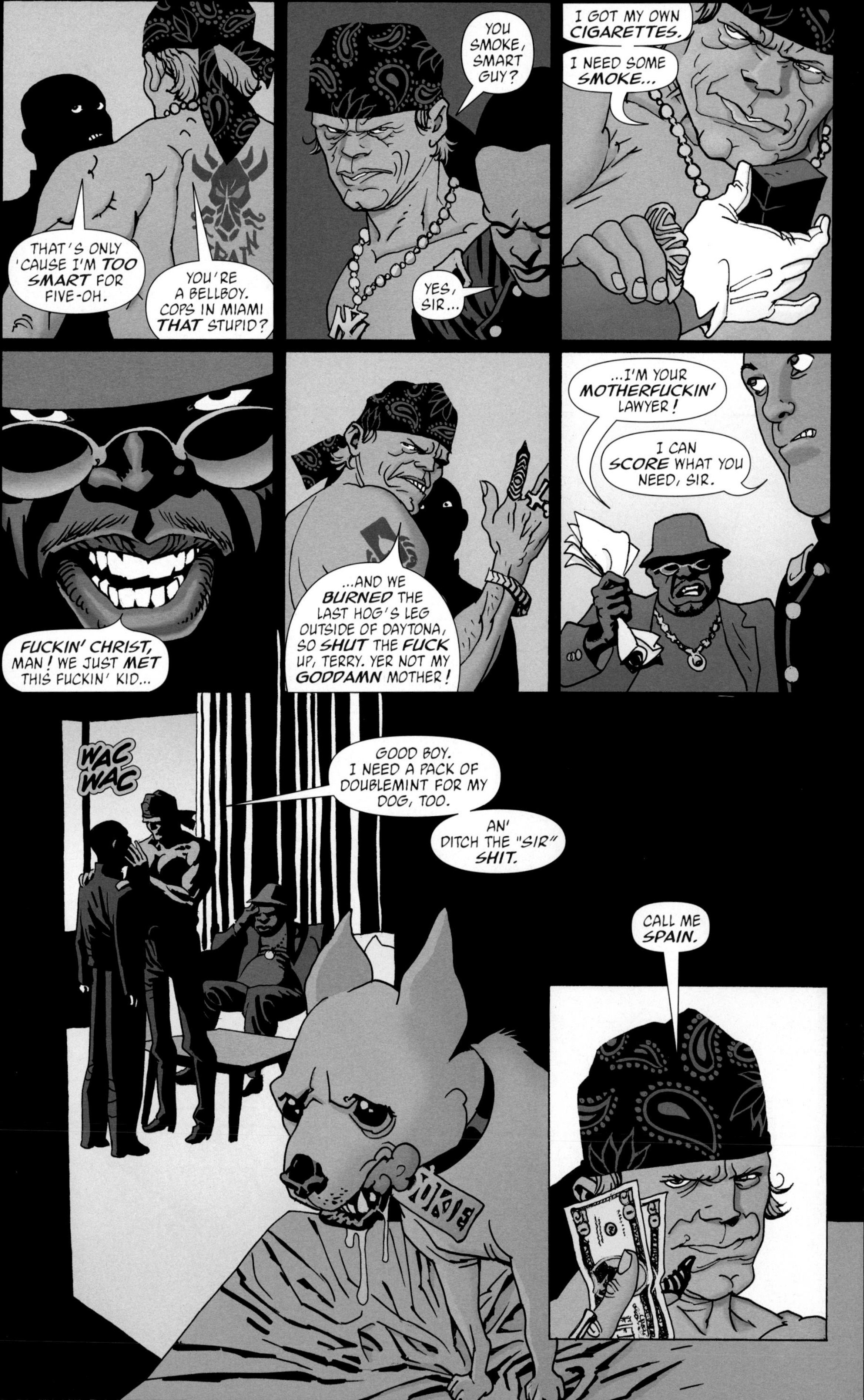
THAT'S ONLY 'CAUSE I'M TOO SMART FOR FIVE-OH.
YOU'RE A BELLBOY. COPS IN MIAMI THAT STUPID?
YOU SMOKE, SMART GUY?
YES, SIR...
I GOT MY OWN CIGARETTES.
I NEED SOME SMOKE...
FUCKIN' CHRIST, MAN! WE JUST MET THIS FUCKIN' KID...
...AND WE BURNED THE LAST HOG'S LEG OUTSIDE OF DAYTONA, SO SHUT THE FUCK UP, TERRY. YER NOT MY GODDAMN MOTHER!
...I'M YOUR MOTHERFUCKIN' LAWYER!
I CAN SCORE WHAT YOU NEED, SIR.
WAC WAC
GOOD BOY. I NEED A PACK OF DOUBLEMINT FOR MY DOG, TOO.
AN' DITCH THE "SIR" SHIT.
CALL ME SPAIN.

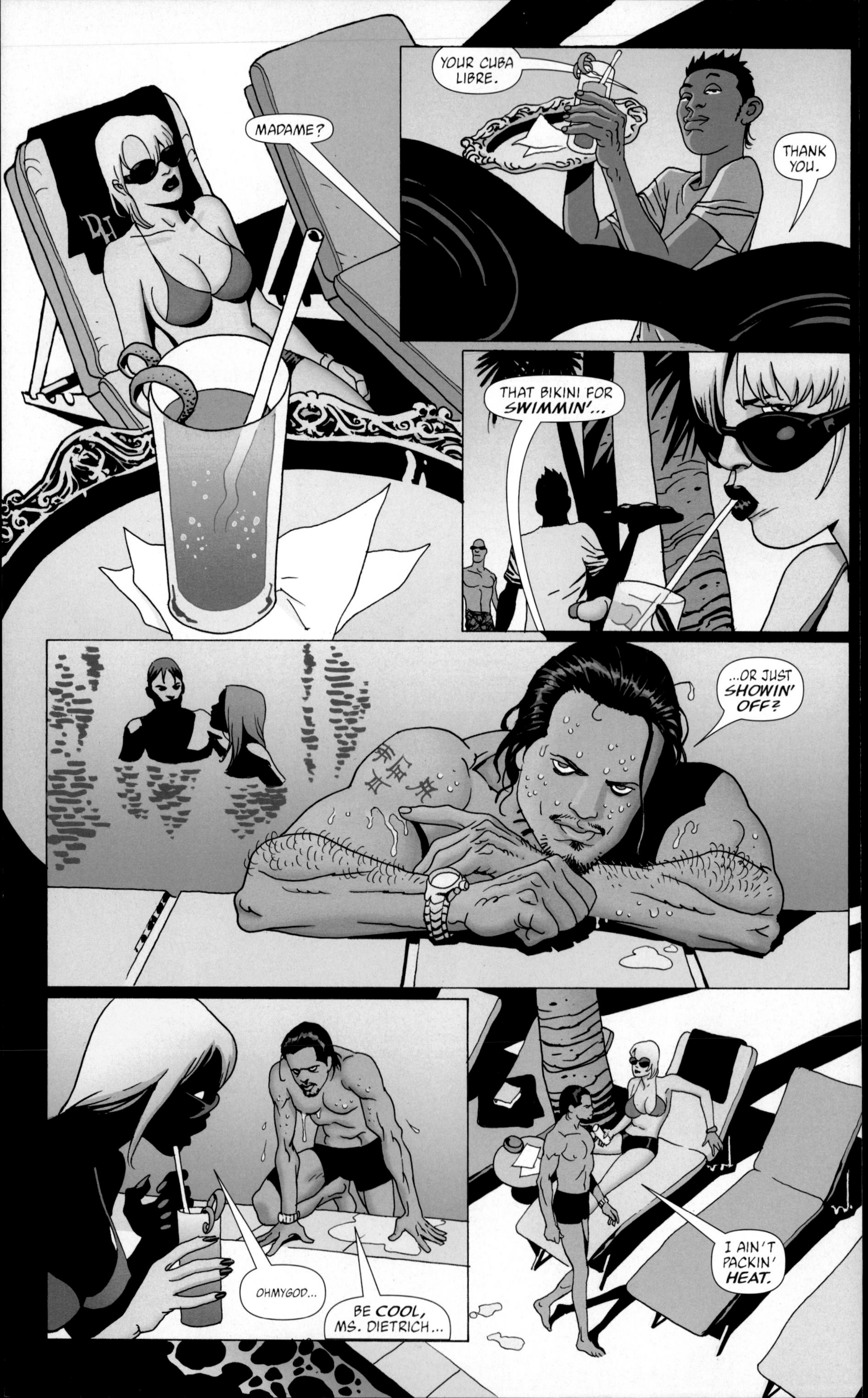
MADAME?
YOUR CUBA LIBRE.
THANK YOU.
THAT BIKINI FOR SWIMMIN'...
...OR JUST SHOWIN' OFF?
OHMYGOD...
BE COOL, MS. DIETRICH...
I AIN'T PACKIN' HEAT.

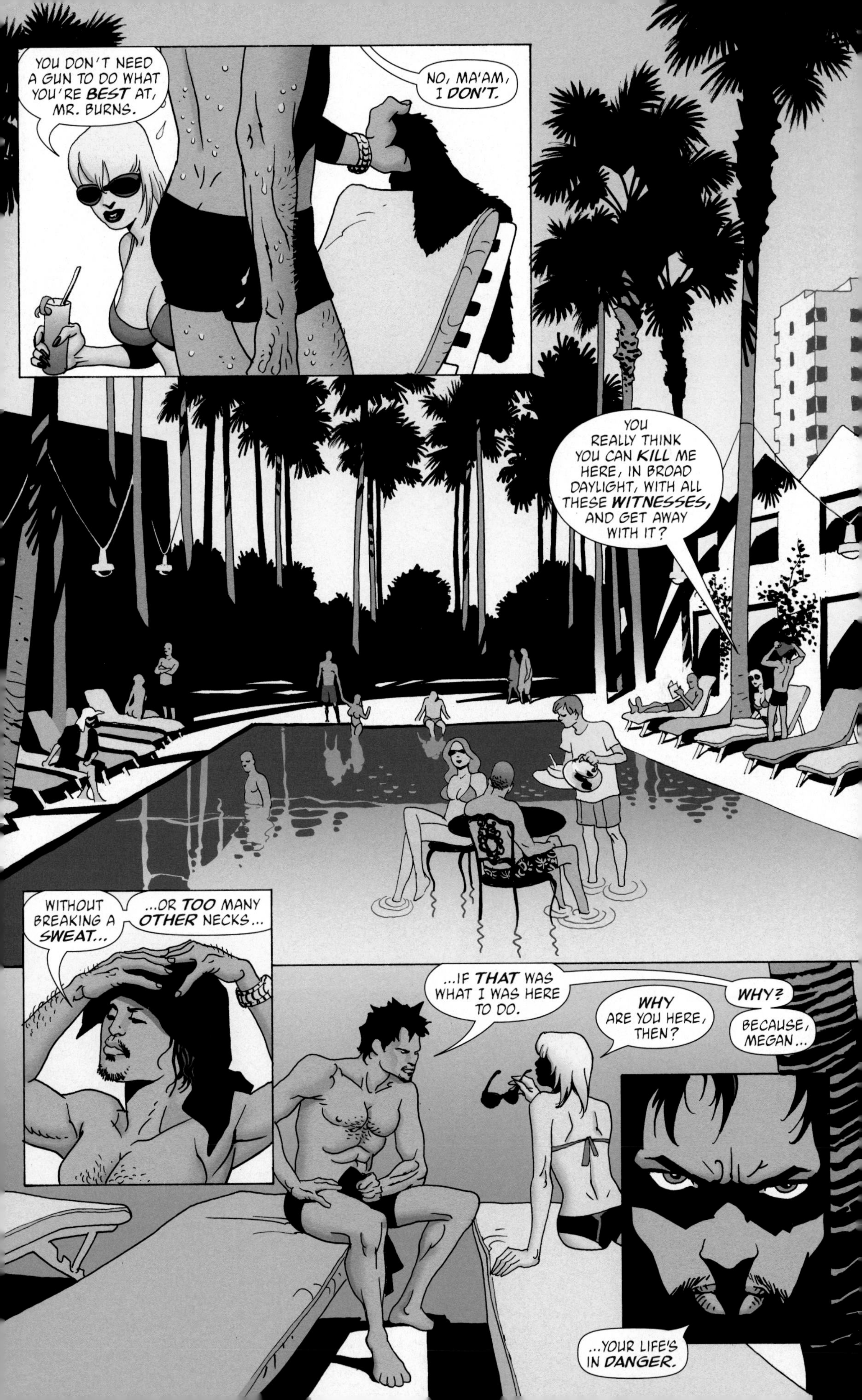
YOU DON'T NEED A GUN TO DO WHAT YOU'RE BEST AT, MR. BURNS.
NO, MA'AM, I DON'T.
YOU REALLY THINK YOU CAN KILL ME HERE, IN BROAD DAYLIGHT, WITH ALL THESE WITNESSES, AND GET AWAY WITH IT?
WITHOUT BREAKING A SWEAT...
...OR TOO MANY OTHER NECKS...
...IF THAT WAS WHAT I WAS HERE TO DO.
WHY ARE YOU HERE, THEN?
WHY?
BECAUSE, MEGAN...
...YOUR LIFE'S IN DANGER.

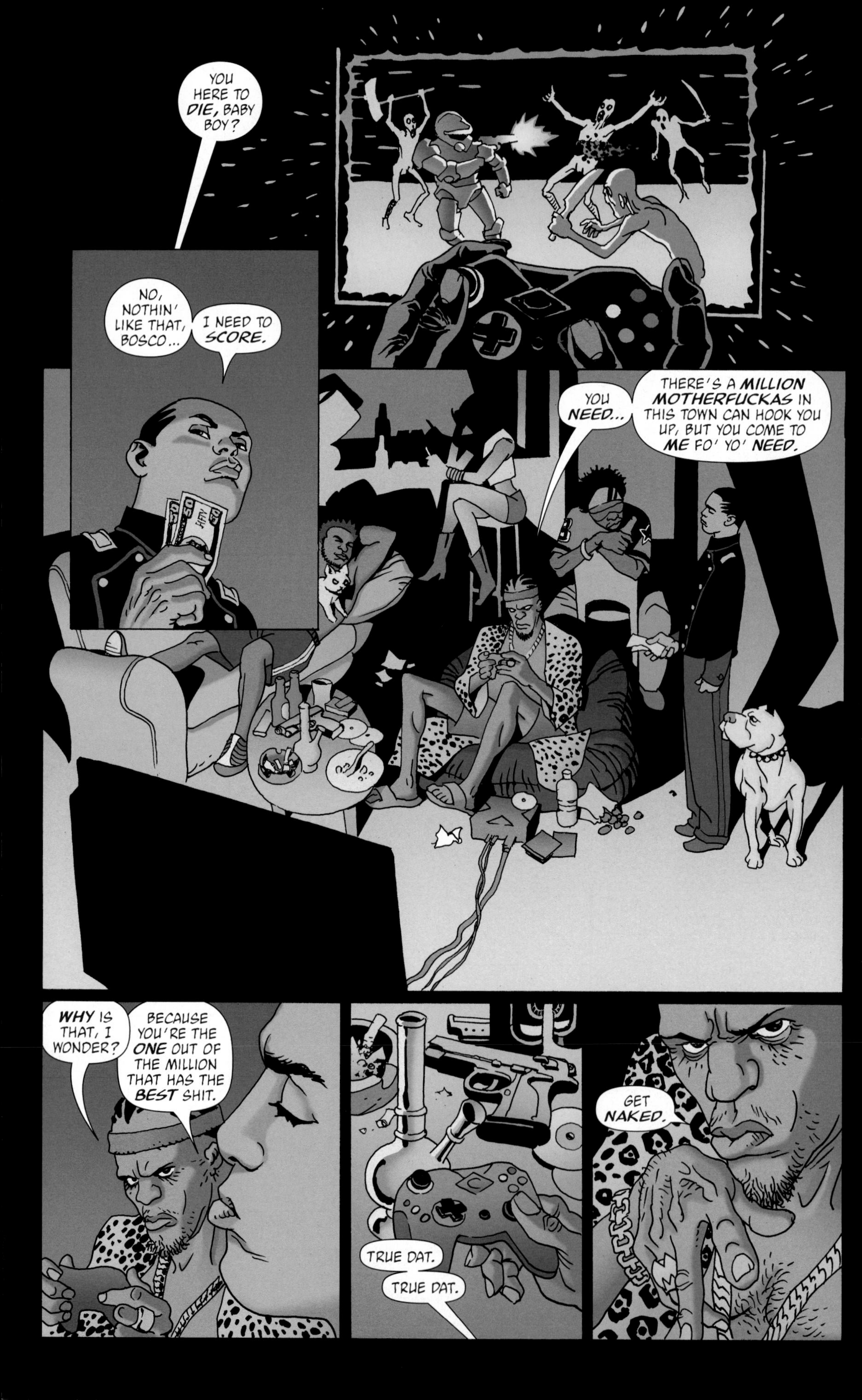

YOU HERE TO DIE, BABY BOY?
NO, NOTHIN' LIKE THAT, BOSCO...
I NEED TO SCORE.
YOU NEED...
THERE'S A MILLION MOTHERFUCKAS IN THIS TOWN CAN HOOK YOU UP, BUT YOU COME TO ME FO' YO' NEED.
WHY IS THAT, I WONDER?
BECAUSE YOU'RE THE ONE OUT OF THE MILLION THAT HAS THE BEST SHIT.
TRUE DAT.
TRUE DAT.
GET NAKED.

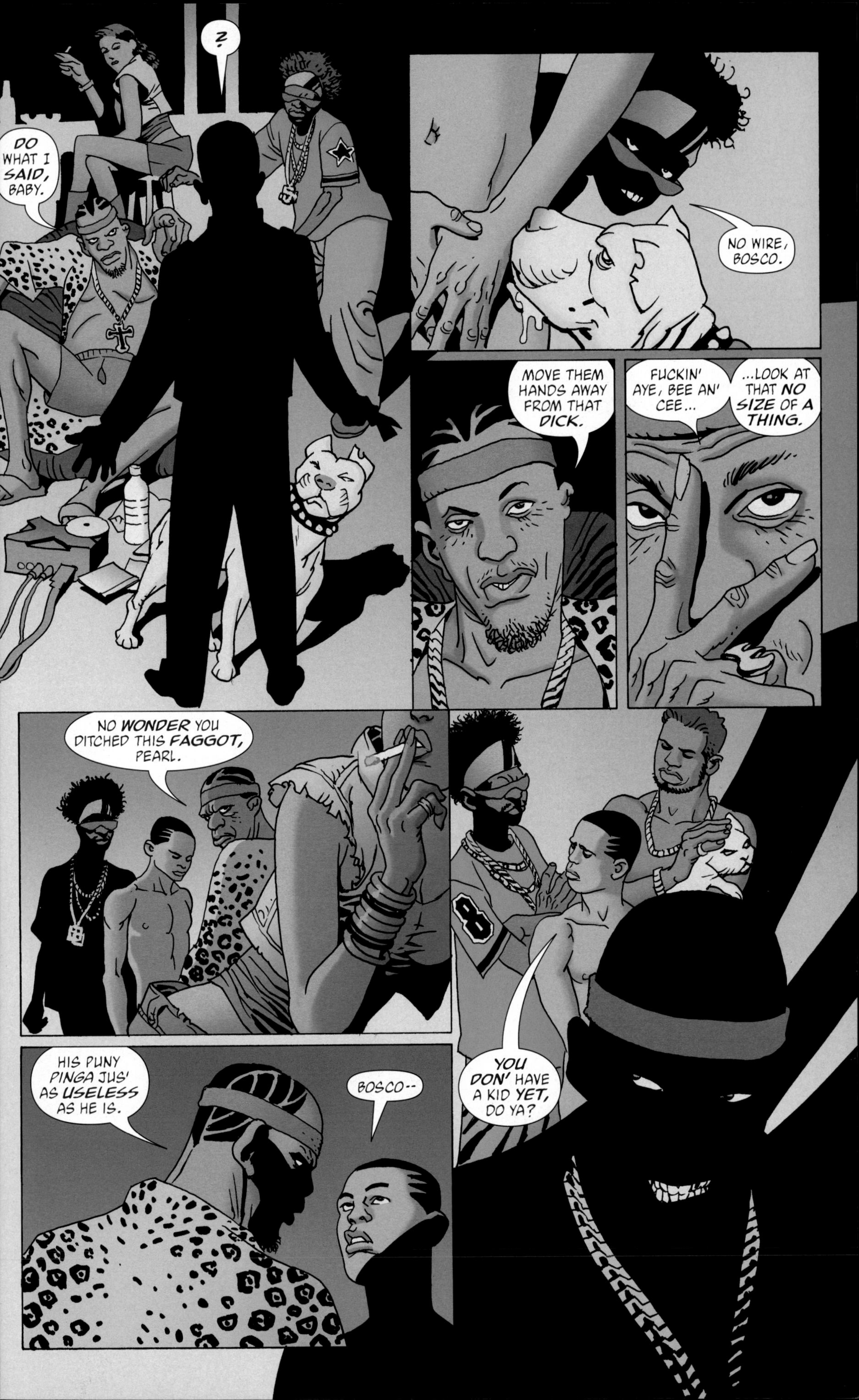
?
DO WHAT I SAID, BABY.
NO WIRE, BOSCO.
MOVE THEM HANDS AWAY FROM THAT DICK.
FUCKIN' AYE, BEE AN' CEE...
...LOOK AT THAT NO SIZE OF A THING.
NO WONDER YOU DITCHED THIS FAGGOT, PEARL.
HIS PUNY PINGA JUS' AS USELESS AS HE IS.
BOSCO--
YOU DON' HAVE A KID YET, DO YA?

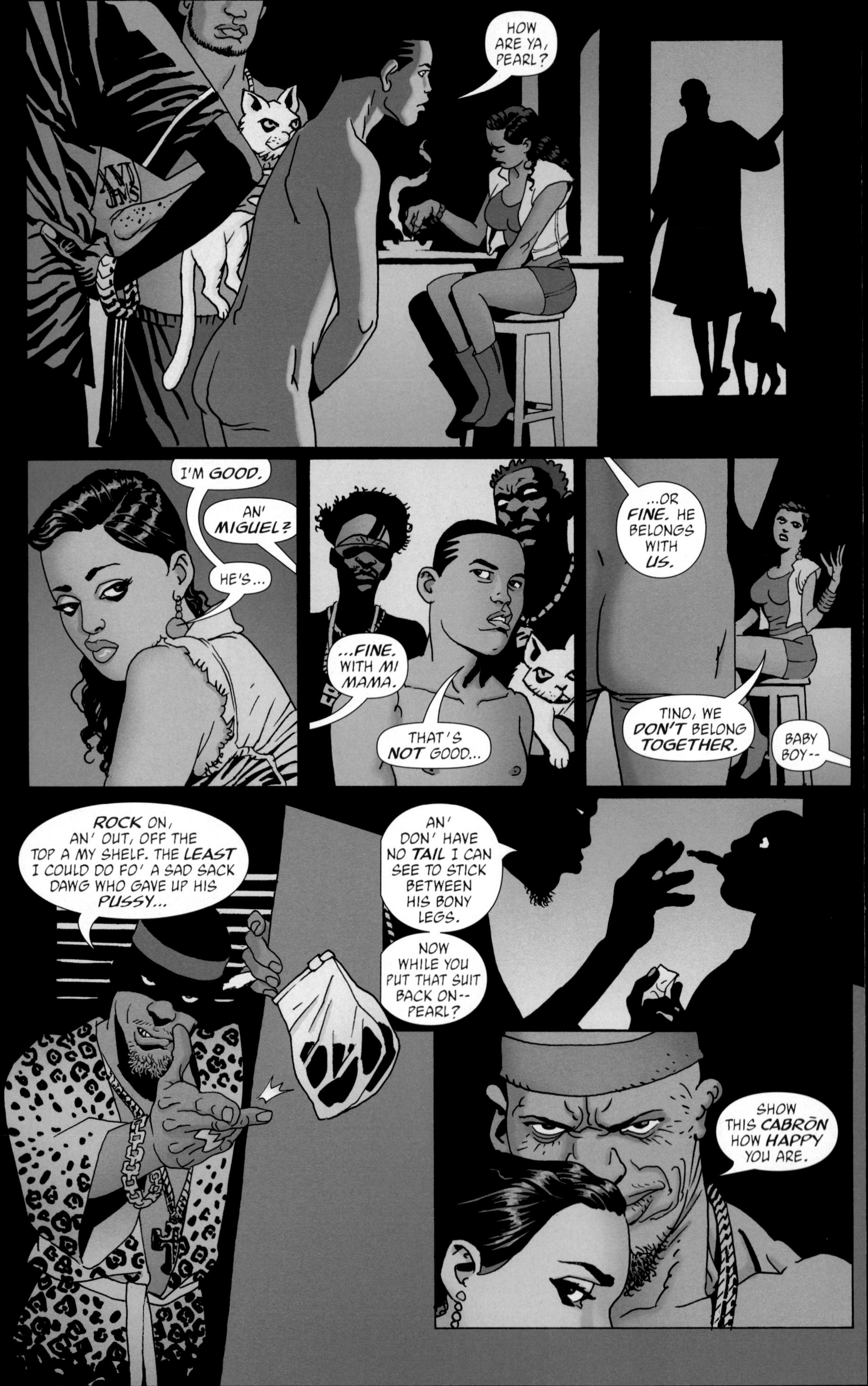
HOW ARE YA, PEARL?
I'M GOOD.
AN' MIGUEL?
HE'S...
...FINE. WITH MI MAMA.
THAT'S NOT GOOD...
...OR FINE. HE BELONGS WITH US.
TINO, WE DON'T BELONG TOGETHER.
BABY BOY--
ROCK ON, AN' OUT, OFF THE TOP A MY SHELF. THE LEAST I COULD DO FO' A SAD SACK DAWG WHO GAVE UP HIS PUSSY...
AN' DON' HAVE NO TAIL I CAN SEE TO STICK BETWEEN HIS BONY LEGS.
NOW WHILE YOU PUT THAT SUIT BACK ON-- PEARL?
SHOW THIS CABRŌN HOW HAPPY YOU ARE.

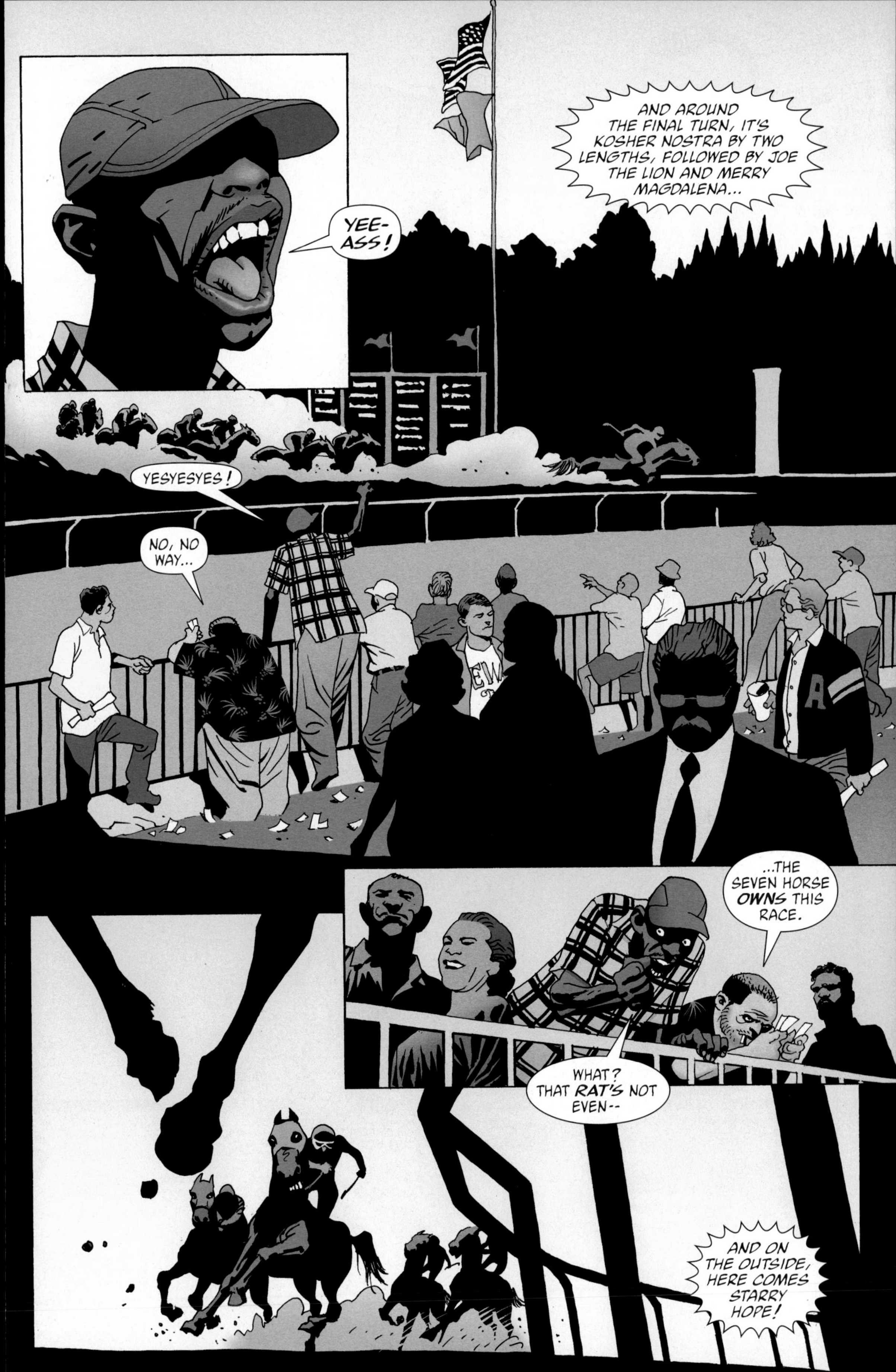
AND AROUND THE FINAL TURN, IT'S KOSHER NOSTRA BY TWO LENGTHS, FOLLOWED BY JOE THE LION AND MERRY MAGDALENA...
YEE-ASS!
YESYESYES!
NO, NO WAY...
...THE SEVEN HORSE OWNS THIS RACE.
WHAT? THAT RAT'S NOT EVEN--
AND ON THE OUTSIDE, HERE COMES STARRY HOPE!

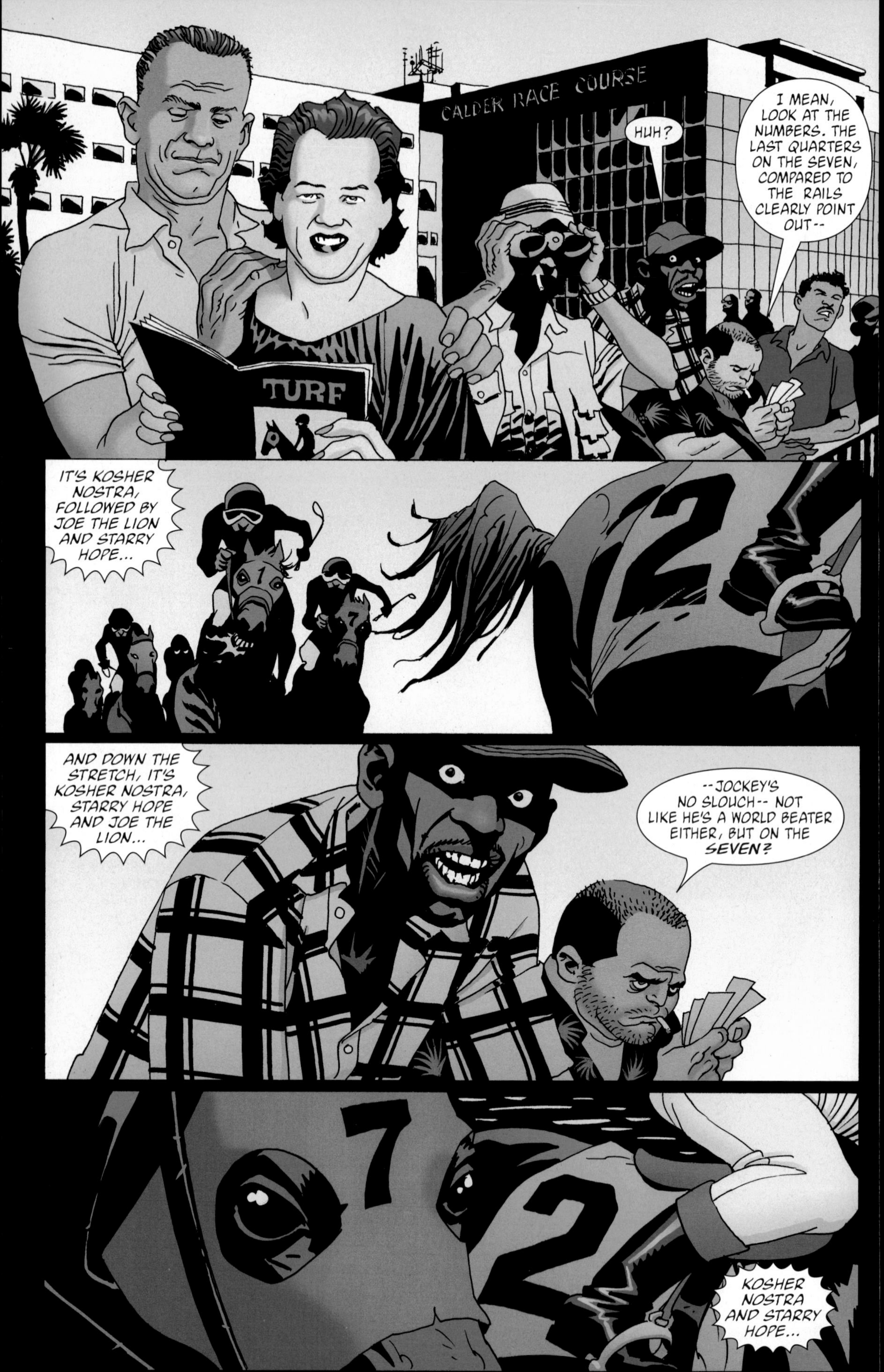
CALDER RACE COURSE
HUH?
I MEAN, LOOK AT THE NUMBERS. THE LAST QUARTERS ON THE SEVEN, COMPARED TO THE RAILS CLEARLY POINT OUT--
TURF
IT'S KOSHER NOSTRA, FOLLOWED BY JOE THE LION AND STARRY HOPE...
AND DOWN THE STRETCH, IT'S KOSHER NOSTRA, STARRY HOPE AND JOE THE LION...
--JOCKEY'S NO SLOUCH-- NOT LIKE HE'S A WORLD BEATER EITHER, BUT ON THE SEVEN?
KOSHER NOSTRA AND STARRY HOPE...

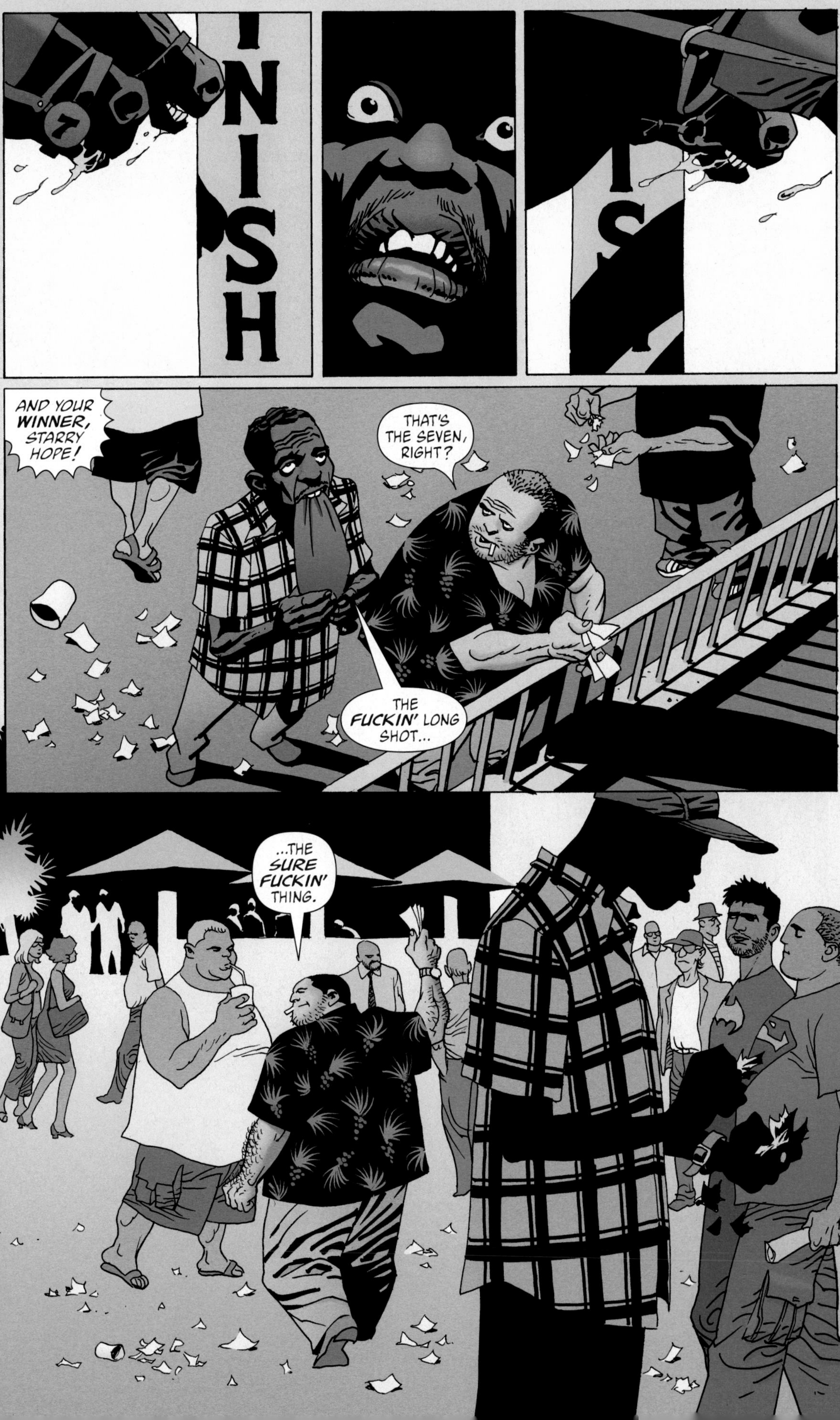
NISH
S
AND YOUR WINNER, STARRY HOPE!
THAT'S THE SEVEN, RIGHT?
THE FUCKIN' LONG SHOT...
...THE SURE FUCKIN' THING.

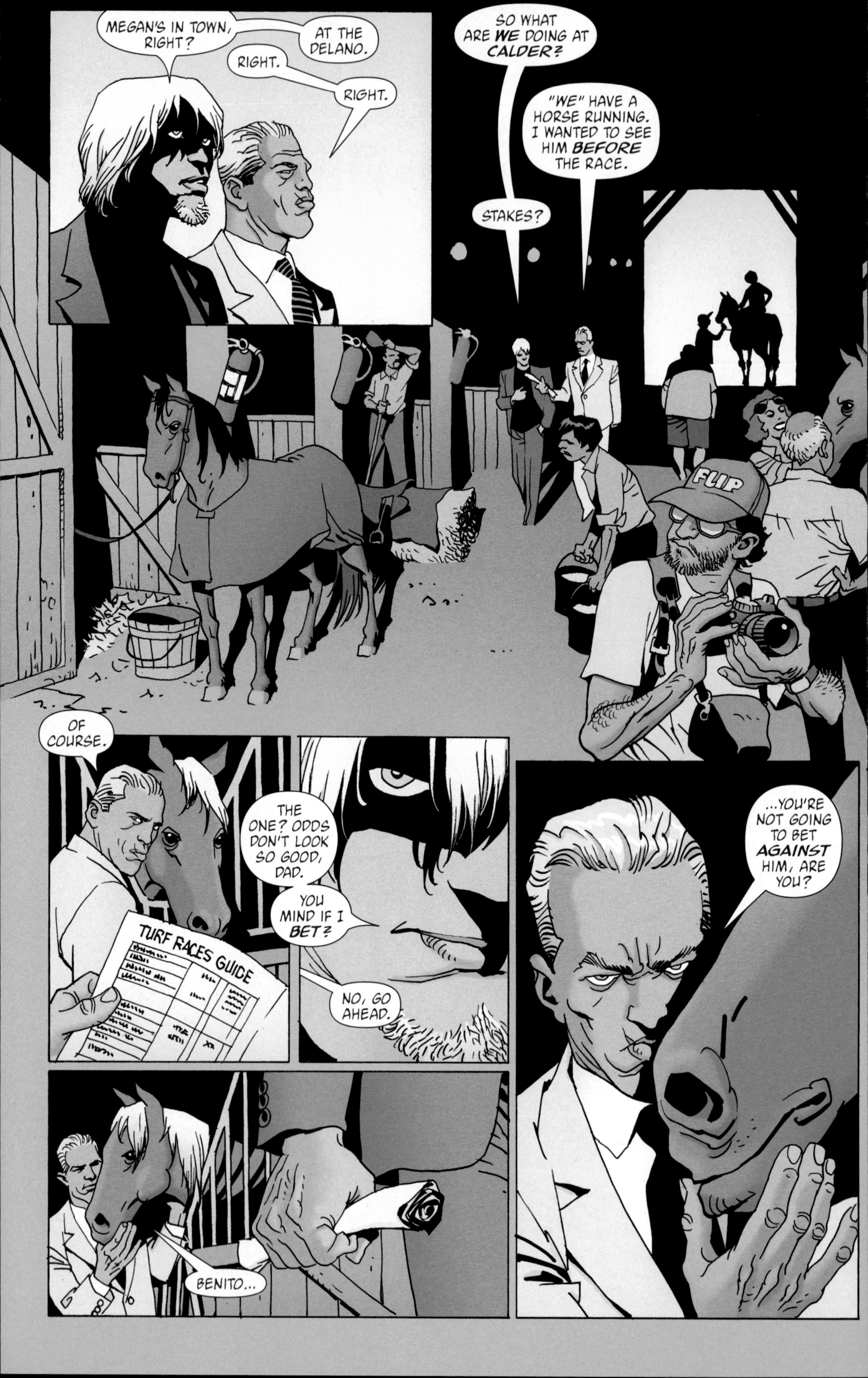
MEGAN'S IN TOWN, RIGHT?
AT THE DELANO.
RIGHT.
RIGHT.
SO WHAT ARE WE DOING AT CALDER?
"WE" HAVE A HORSE RUNNING. I WANTED TO SEE HIM BEFORE THE RACE.
STAKES?
OF COURSE.
TURF RACES GUIDE
THE ONE? ODDS DON'T LOOK SO GOOD, DAD.
YOU MIND IF I BET?
NO, GO AHEAD.
...YOU'RE NOT GOING TO BET AGAINST HIM, ARE YOU?
BENITO...

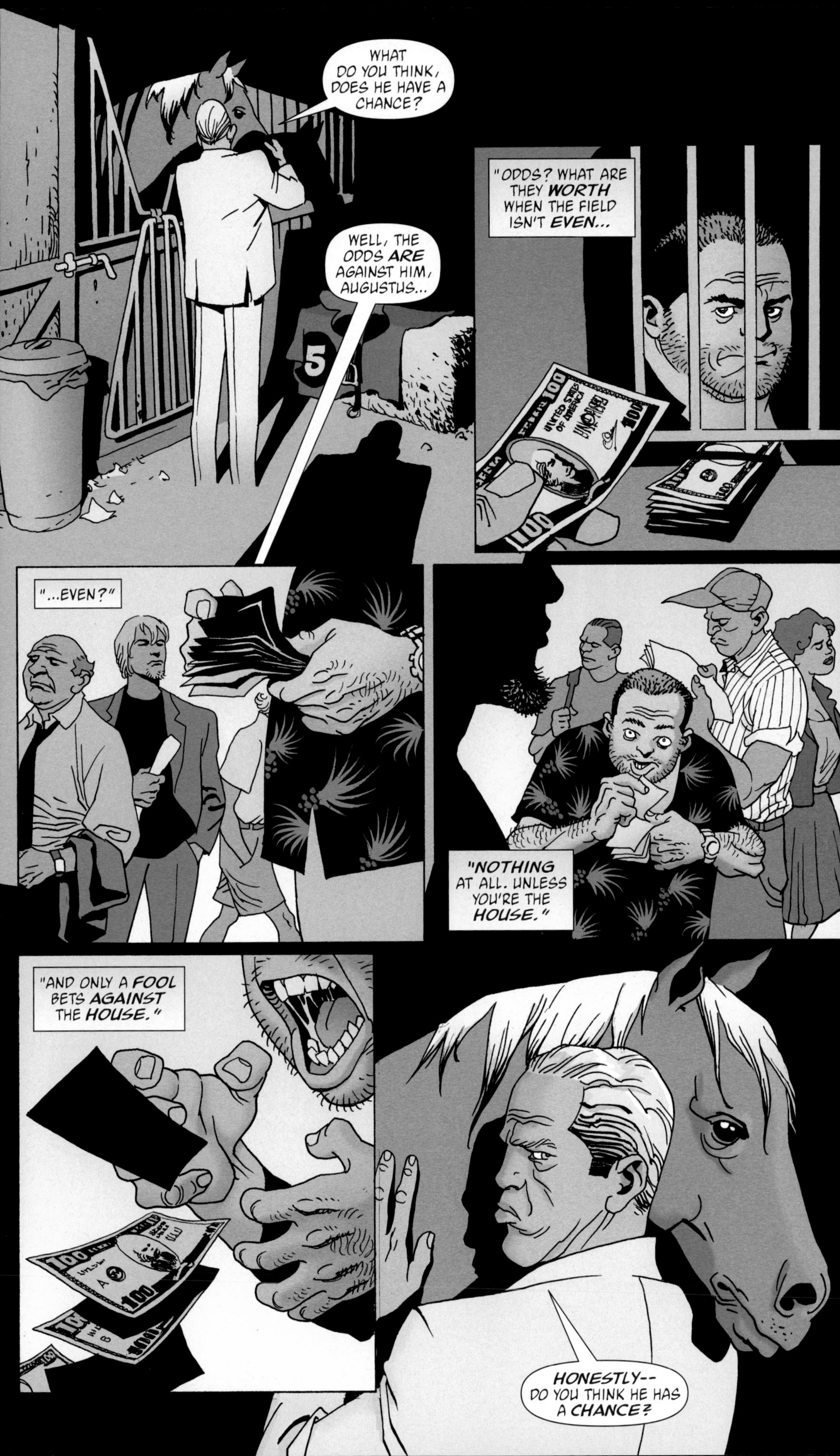
WHAT DO YOU THINK, DOES HE HAVE A CHANCE?
WELL, THE ODDS ARE AGAINST HIM, AUGUSTUS...
"ODDS? WHAT ARE THEY WORTH WHEN THE FIELD ISN'T EVEN...
"...EVEN?"
"NOTHING AT ALL. UNLESS YOU'RE THE HOUSE."
"AND ONLY A FOOL BETS AGAINST THE HOUSE."
HONESTLY-- DO YOU THINK HE HAS A CHANCE?

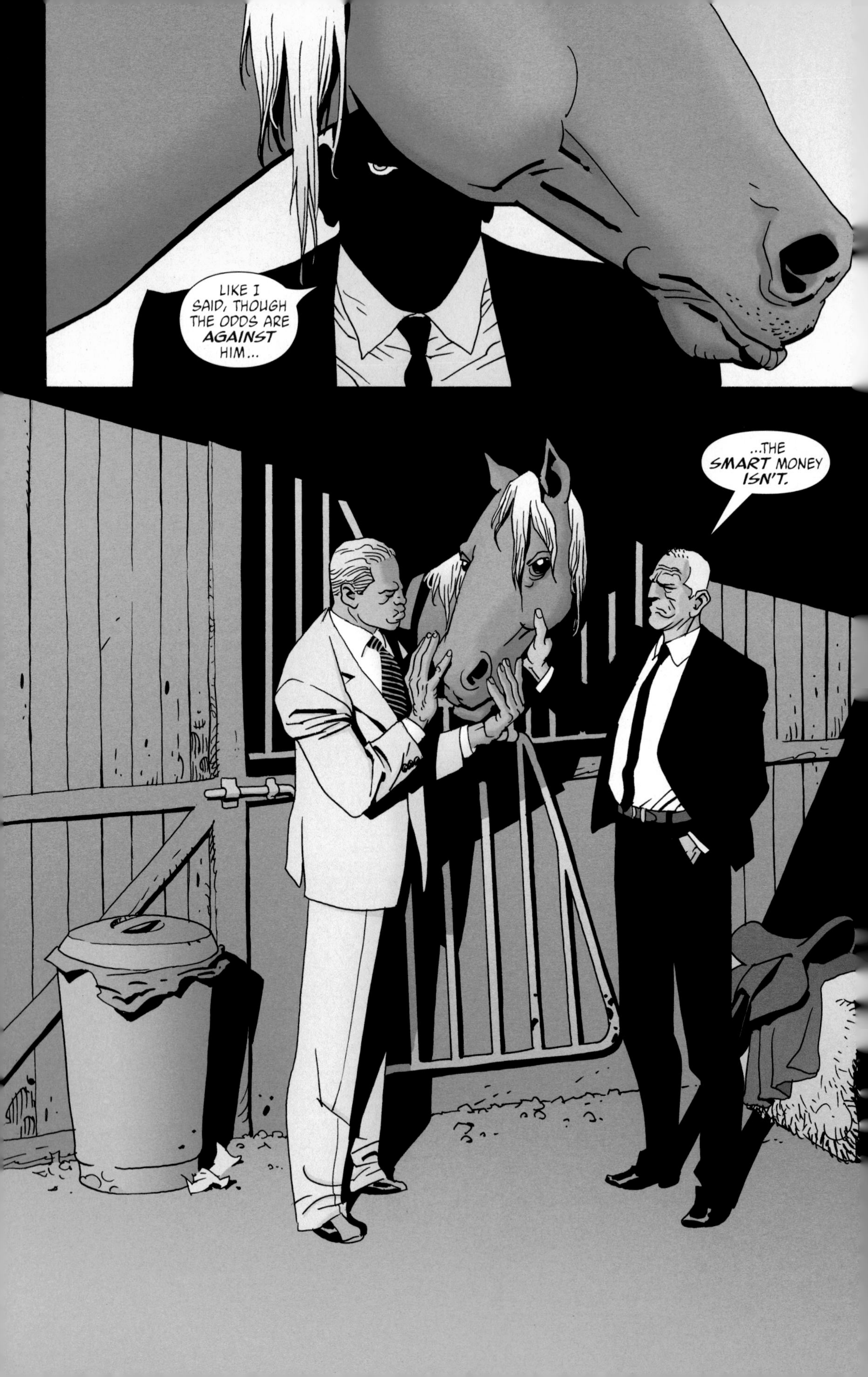
LIKE I SAID, THOUGH THE ODDS ARE AGAINST HIM...
...THE SMART MONEY ISN'T.

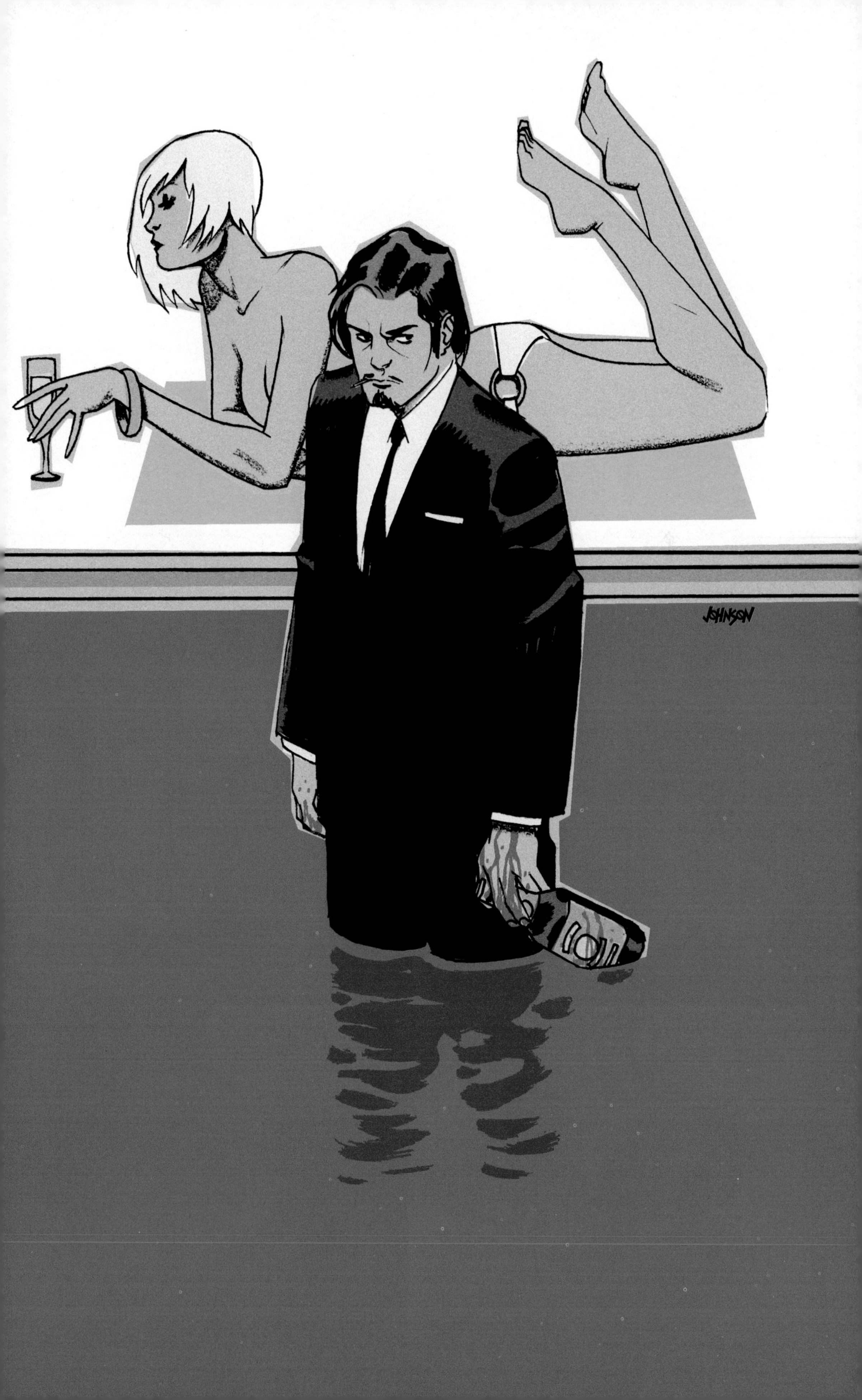
JOHNSON

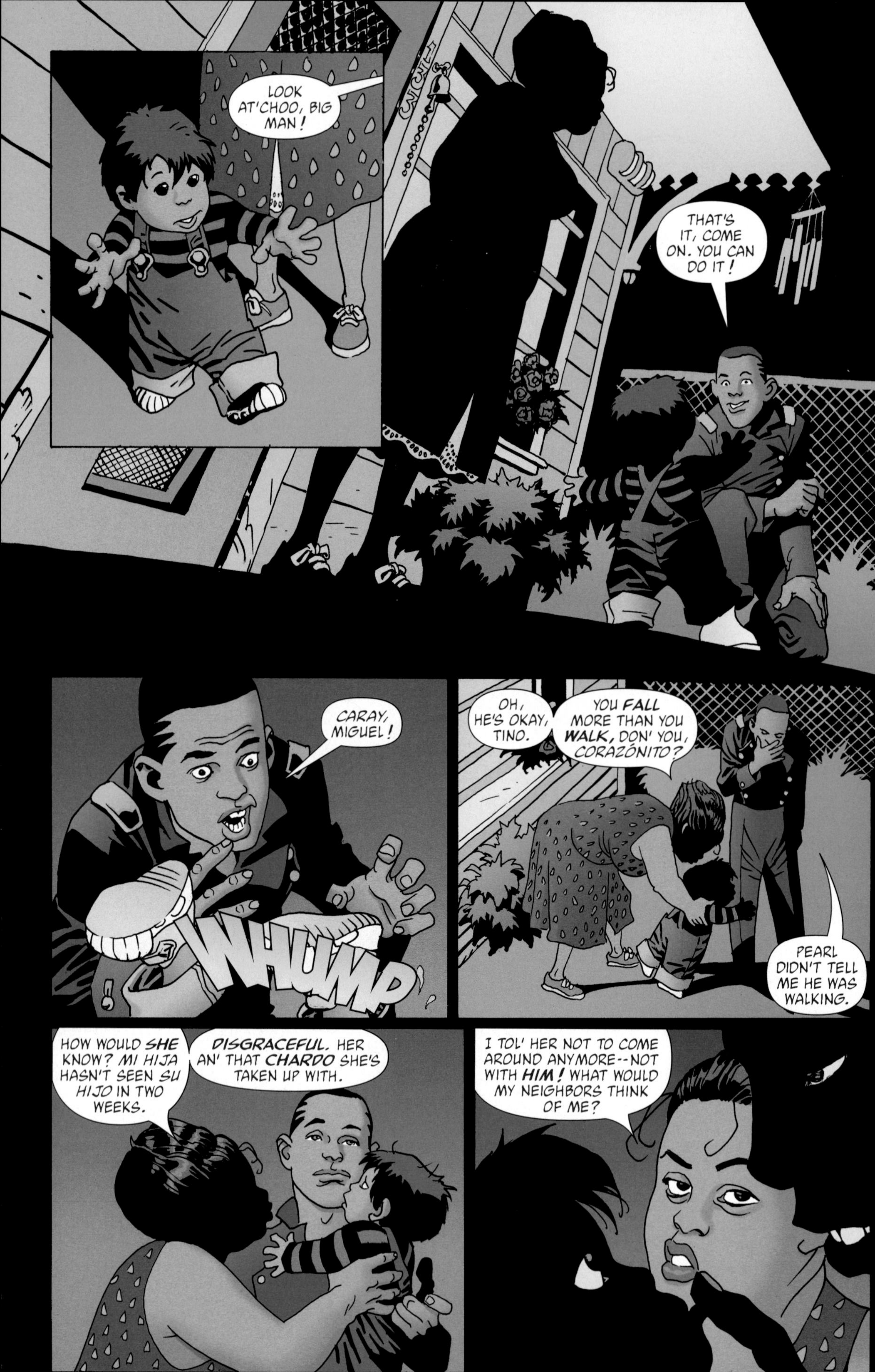
LOOK AT'CHOO, BIG MAN!
THAT'S IT, COME ON. YOU CAN DO IT!
CARAY, MIGUEL!
WHUMP
OH, HE'S OKAY, TINO.
YOU FALL MORE THAN YOU WALK, DON' YOU, CORAZÓNITO?
PEARL DIDN'T TELL ME HE WAS WALKING.
HOW WOULD SHE KNOW? MI HIJA HASN'T SEEN SU HIJO IN TWO WEEKS.
DISGRACEFUL. HER AN' THAT CHARDO SHE'S TAKEN UP WITH.
I TOL' HER NOT TO COME AROUND ANYMORE--NOT WITH HIM! WHAT WOULD MY NEIGHBORS THINK OF ME?

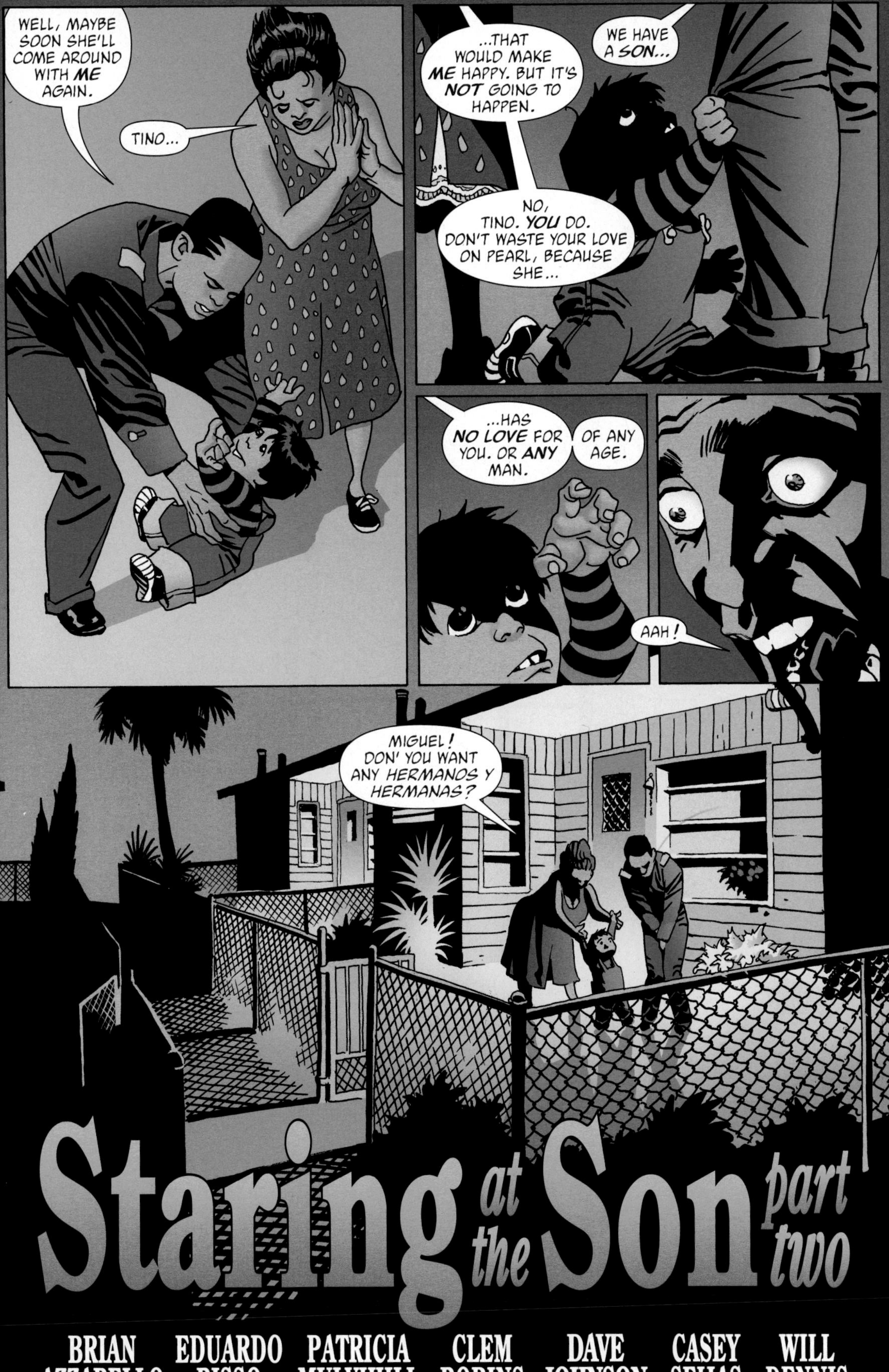
WELL, MAYBE SOON SHE'LL COME AROUND WITH ME AGAIN.
TINO...
WE HAVE A SON...
...THAT WOULD MAKE ME HAPPY. BUT IT'S NOT GOING TO HAPPEN.
NO, TINO. YOU DO. DON'T WASTE YOUR LOVE ON PEARL, BECAUSE SHE...
...HAS NO LOVE FOR YOU. OR ANY MAN.
OF ANY AGE.
AAH!
MIGUEL! DON' YOU WANT ANY HERMANOS Y HERMANAS?
Staring at the Son part two

BRIAN AZZARELLO · EDUARDO RISSO · PATRICIA MULVIHILL · CLEM ROBINS · DAVE JOHNSON · CASEY SEIJAS · WILL DENNIS

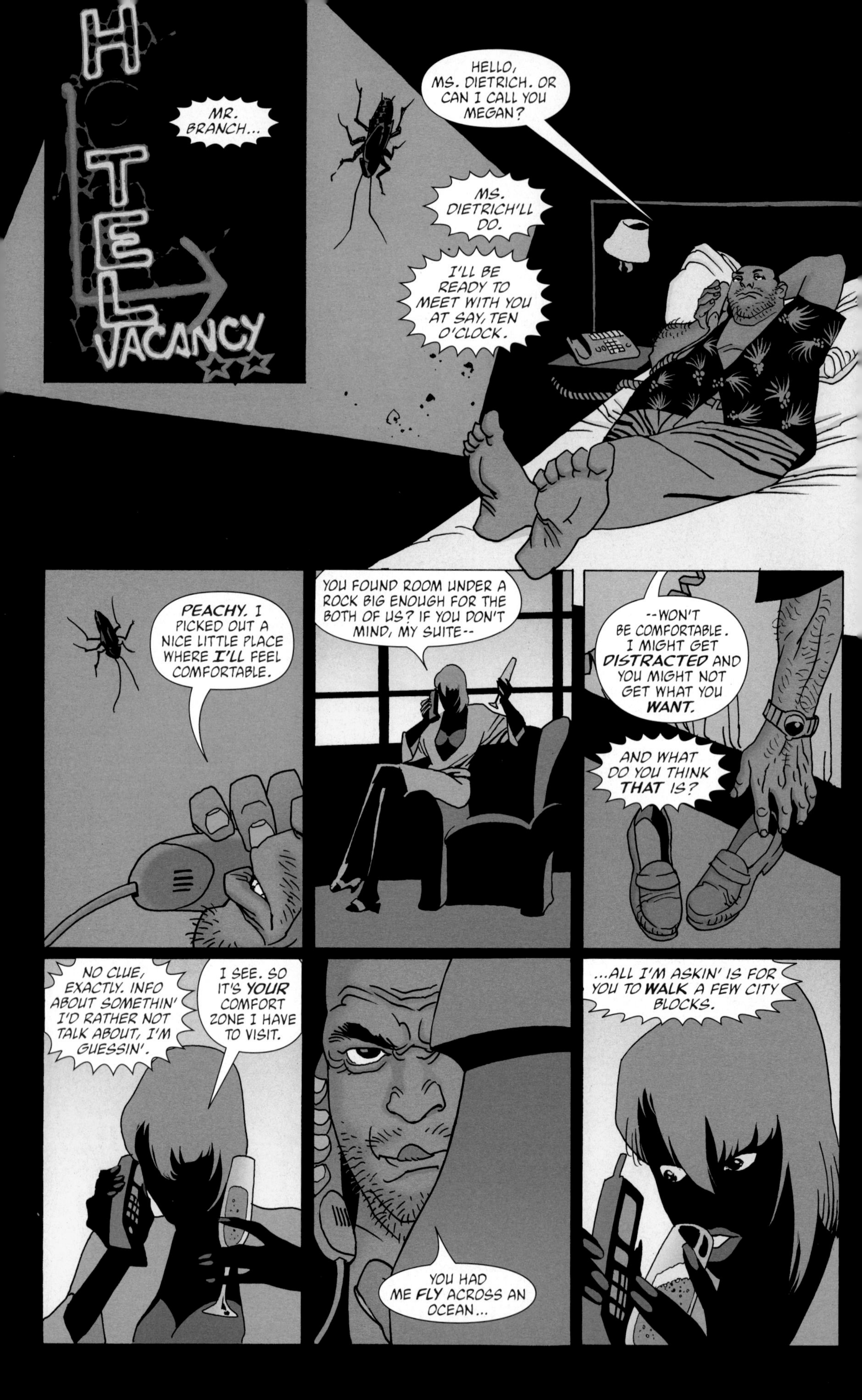
HOTEL
VACANCY
MR. BRANCH...
HELLO, MS. DIETRICH. OR CAN I CALL YOU MEGAN?
MS. DIETRICH'LL DO.
I'LL BE READY TO MEET WITH YOU AT SAY, TEN O'CLOCK.
PEACHY. I PICKED OUT A NICE LITTLE PLACE WHERE I'LL FEEL COMFORTABLE.
YOU FOUND ROOM UNDER A ROCK BIG ENOUGH FOR THE BOTH OF US? IF YOU DON'T MIND, MY SUITE--
--WON'T BE COMFORTABLE. I MIGHT GET DISTRACTED AND YOU MIGHT NOT GET WHAT YOU WANT.
AND WHAT DO YOU THINK THAT IS?
NO CLUE, EXACTLY. INFO ABOUT SOMETHIN' I'D RATHER NOT TALK ABOUT, I'M GUESSIN'.
I SEE. SO IT'S YOUR COMFORT ZONE I HAVE TO VISIT.
YOU HAD ME FLY ACROSS AN OCEAN...
...ALL I'M ASKIN' IS FOR YOU TO WALK A FEW CITY BLOCKS.

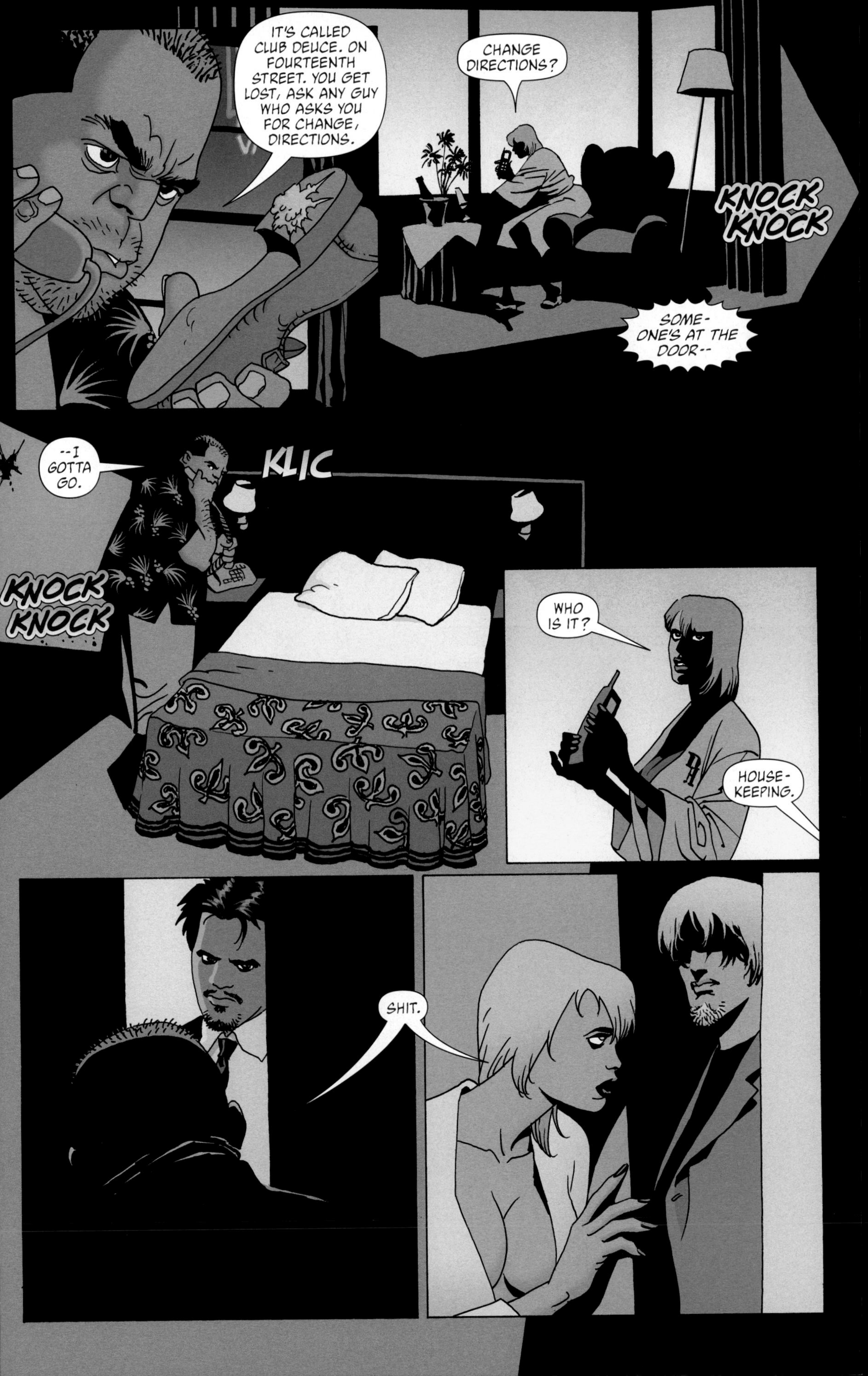
IT'S CALLED CLUB DEUCE. ON FOURTEENTH STREET. YOU GET LOST, ASK ANY GUY WHO ASKS YOU FOR CHANGE, DIRECTIONS.
CHANGE DIRECTIONS?
KNOCK KNOCK
SOME-ONE'S AT THE DOOR--
--I GOTTA GO.
KLIC
KNOCK KNOCK
WHO IS IT?
HOUSE-KEEPING.
SHIT.

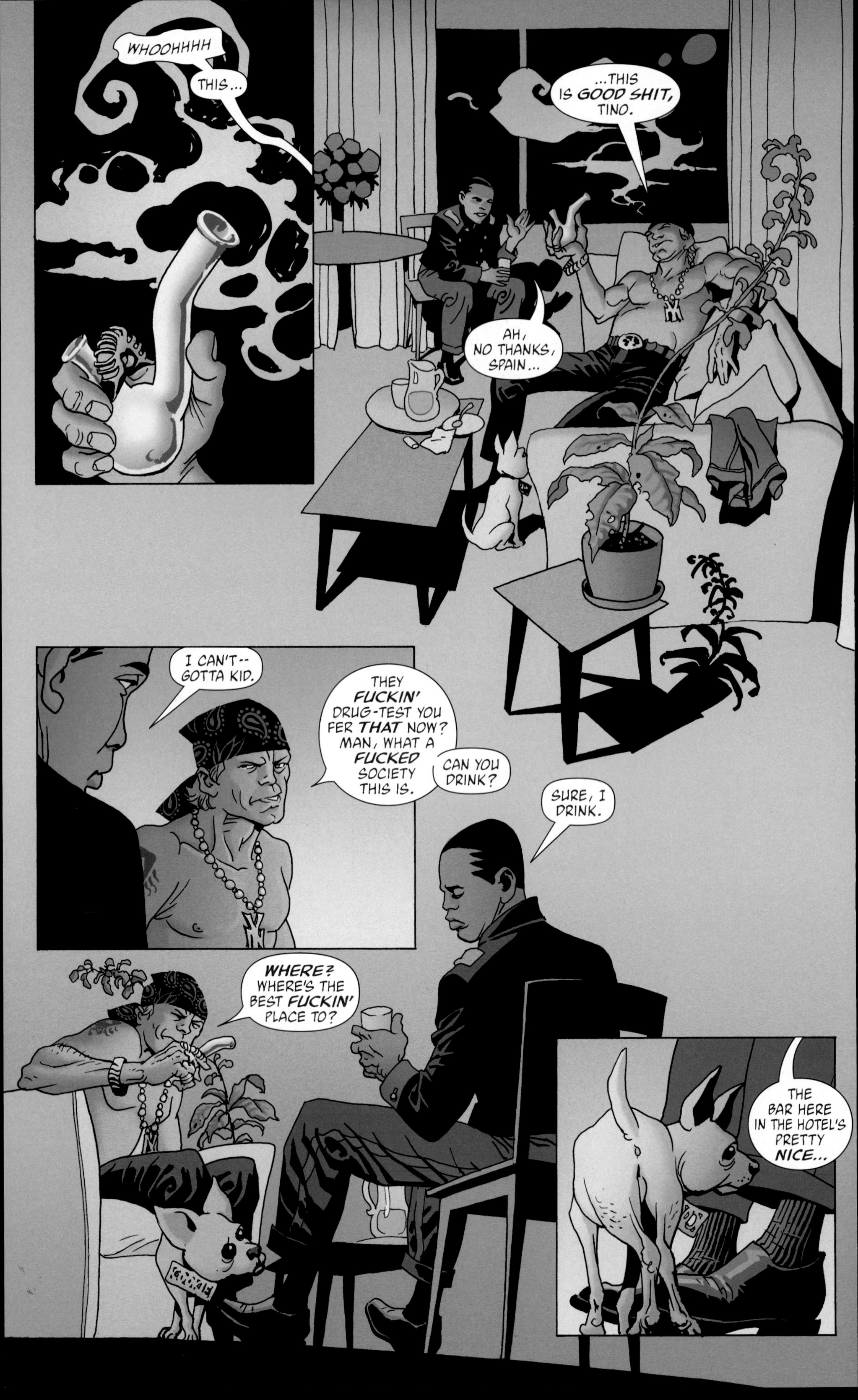
WHOOHHHH
THIS...
...THIS IS GOOD SHIT, TINO.
AH, NO THANKS, SPAIN...
I CAN'T-- GOTTA KID.
THEY FUCKIN' DRUG-TEST YOU FER THAT NOW? MAN, WHAT A FUCKED SOCIETY THIS IS.
CAN YOU DRINK?
SURE, I DRINK.
WHERE? WHERE'S THE BEST FUCKIN' PLACE TO?
THE BAR HERE IN THE HOTEL'S PRETTY NICE...

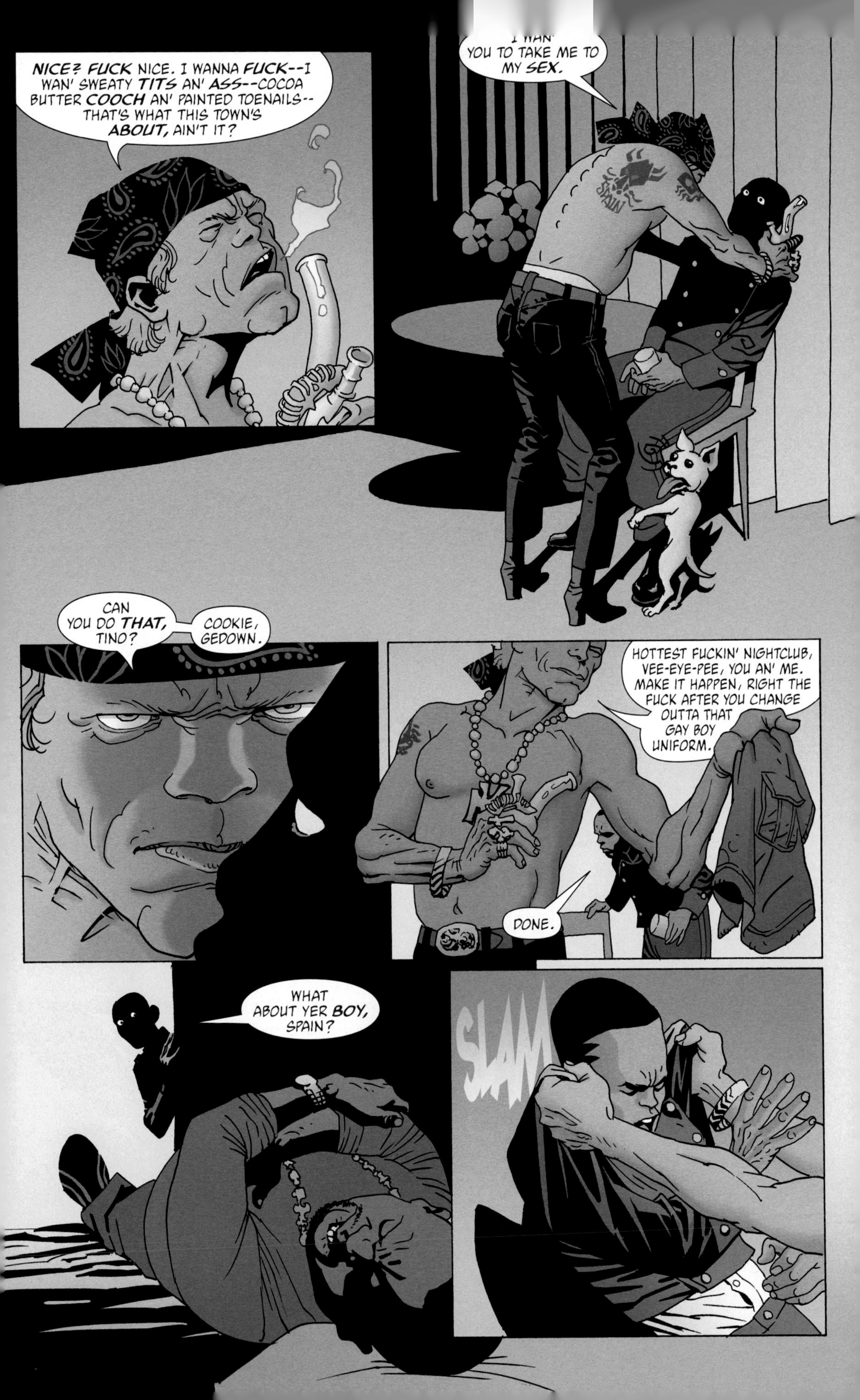
NICE? FUCK NICE. I WANNA FUCK--I WAN' SWEATY TITS AN' ASS--COCOA BUTTER COOCH AN' PAINTED TOENAILS-- THAT'S WHAT THIS TOWN'S ABOUT, AIN'T IT?
I WAN' YOU TO TAKE ME TO MY SEX.
SPAIN
CAN YOU DO THAT, TINO?
COOKIE, GEDOWN.
HOTTEST FUCKIN' NIGHTCLUB, VEE-EYE-PEE, YOU AN' ME. MAKE IT HAPPEN, RIGHT THE FUCK AFTER YOU CHANGE OUTTA THAT GAY BOY UNIFORM.
DONE.
WHAT ABOUT YER BOY, SPAIN?
SLAM

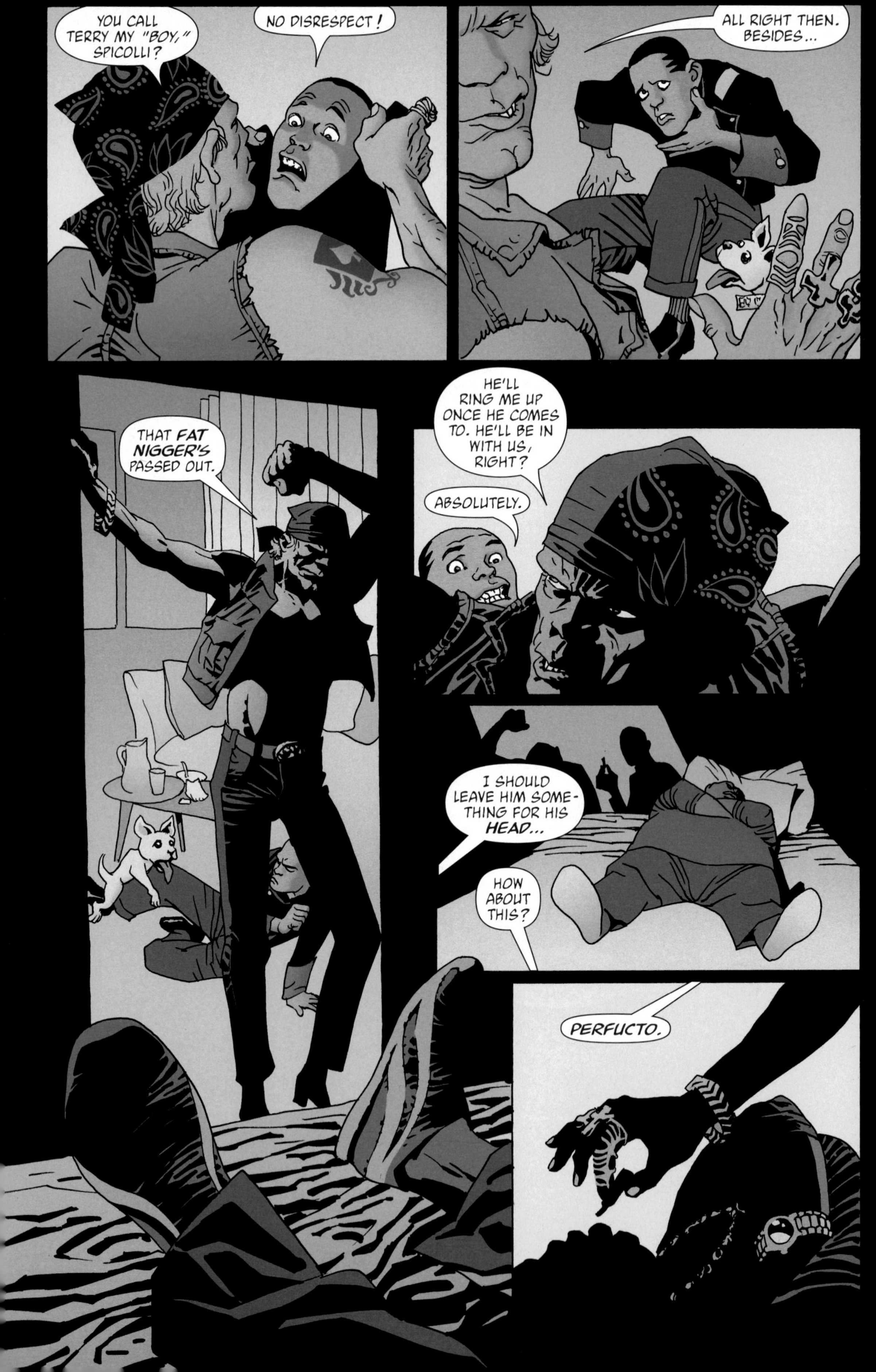
YOU CALL TERRY MY "BOY," SPICOLLI?
NO DISRESPECT!
ALL RIGHT THEN. BESIDES...
THAT FAT NIGGER'S PASSED OUT.
HE'LL RING ME UP ONCE HE COMES TO. HE'LL BE IN WITH US, RIGHT?
ABSOLUTELY.
I SHOULD LEAVE HIM SOME-THING FOR HIS HEAD...
HOW ABOUT THIS?
PERFUCTO.

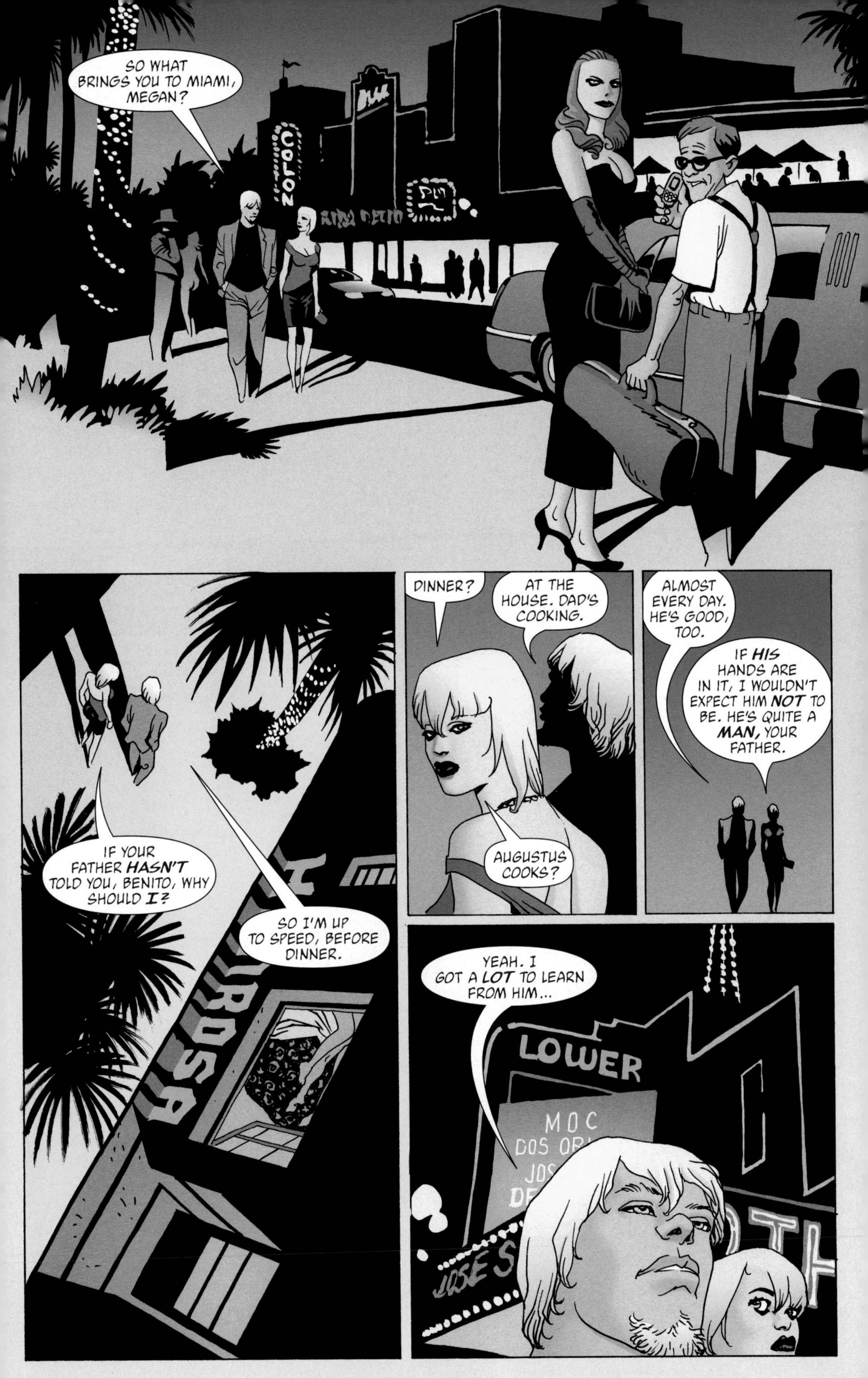
SO WHAT BRINGS YOU TO MIAMI, MEGAN?
COLON
IF YOUR FATHER HASN'T TOLD YOU, BENITO, WHY SHOULD I?
SO I'M UP TO SPEED, BEFORE DINNER.
DINNER?
AT THE HOUSE. DAD'S COOKING.
AUGUSTUS COOKS?
ALMOST EVERY DAY. HE'S GOOD, TOO.
IF HIS HANDS ARE IN IT, I WOULDN'T EXPECT HIM NOT TO BE. HE'S QUITE A MAN, YOUR FATHER.
YEAH. I GOT A LOT TO LEARN FROM HIM...
LOWER

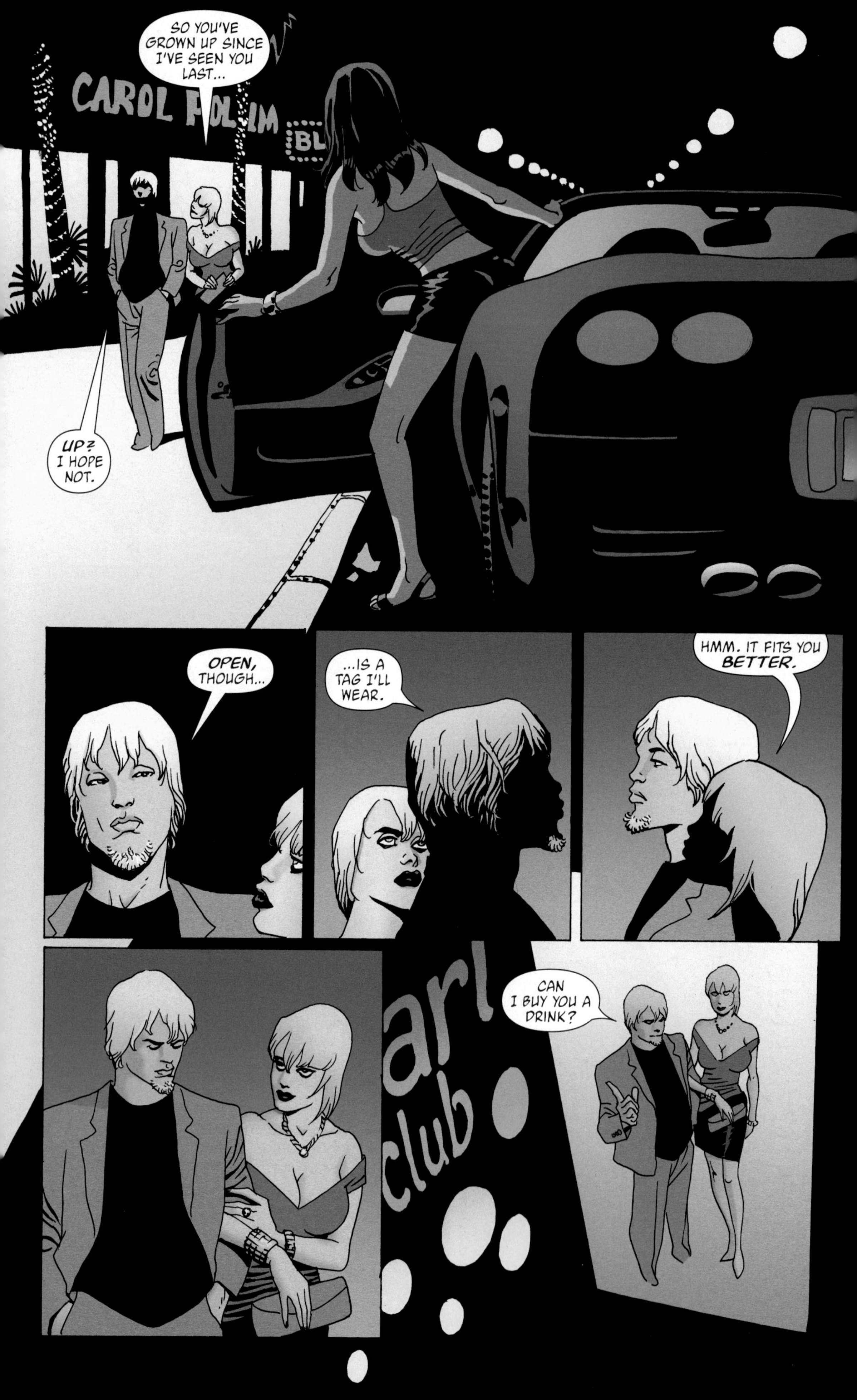
SO YOU'VE GROWN UP SINCE I'VE SEEN YOU LAST...
UP? I HOPE NOT.
OPEN, THOUGH...
...IS A TAG I'LL WEAR.
HMM. IT FITS YOU BETTER.
CAN I BUY YOU A DRINK?

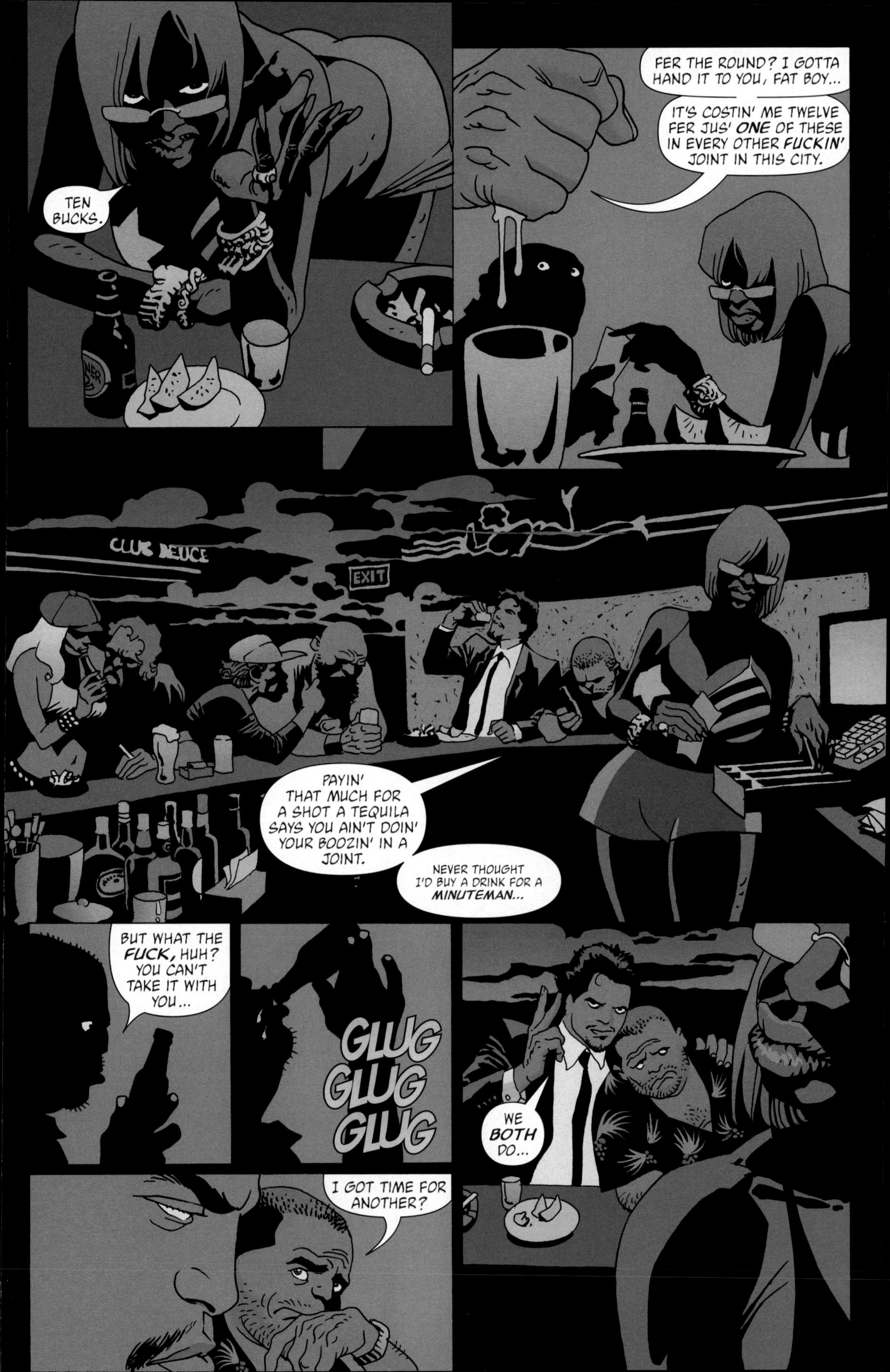
TEN BUCKS.
FER THE ROUND? I GOTTA HAND IT TO YOU, FAT BOY...
IT'S COSTIN' ME TWELVE FER JUS' ONE OF THESE IN EVERY OTHER FUCKIN' JOINT IN THIS CITY.
CLUB DEUCE
EXIT
PAYIN' THAT MUCH FOR A SHOT A TEQUILA SAYS YOU AIN'T DOIN' YOUR BOOZIN' IN A JOINT.
NEVER THOUGHT I'D BUY A DRINK FOR A MINUTEMAN...
BUT WHAT THE FUCK, HUH? YOU CAN'T TAKE IT WITH YOU...
GLUG GLUG GLUG
WE BOTH DO...
I GOT TIME FOR ANOTHER?

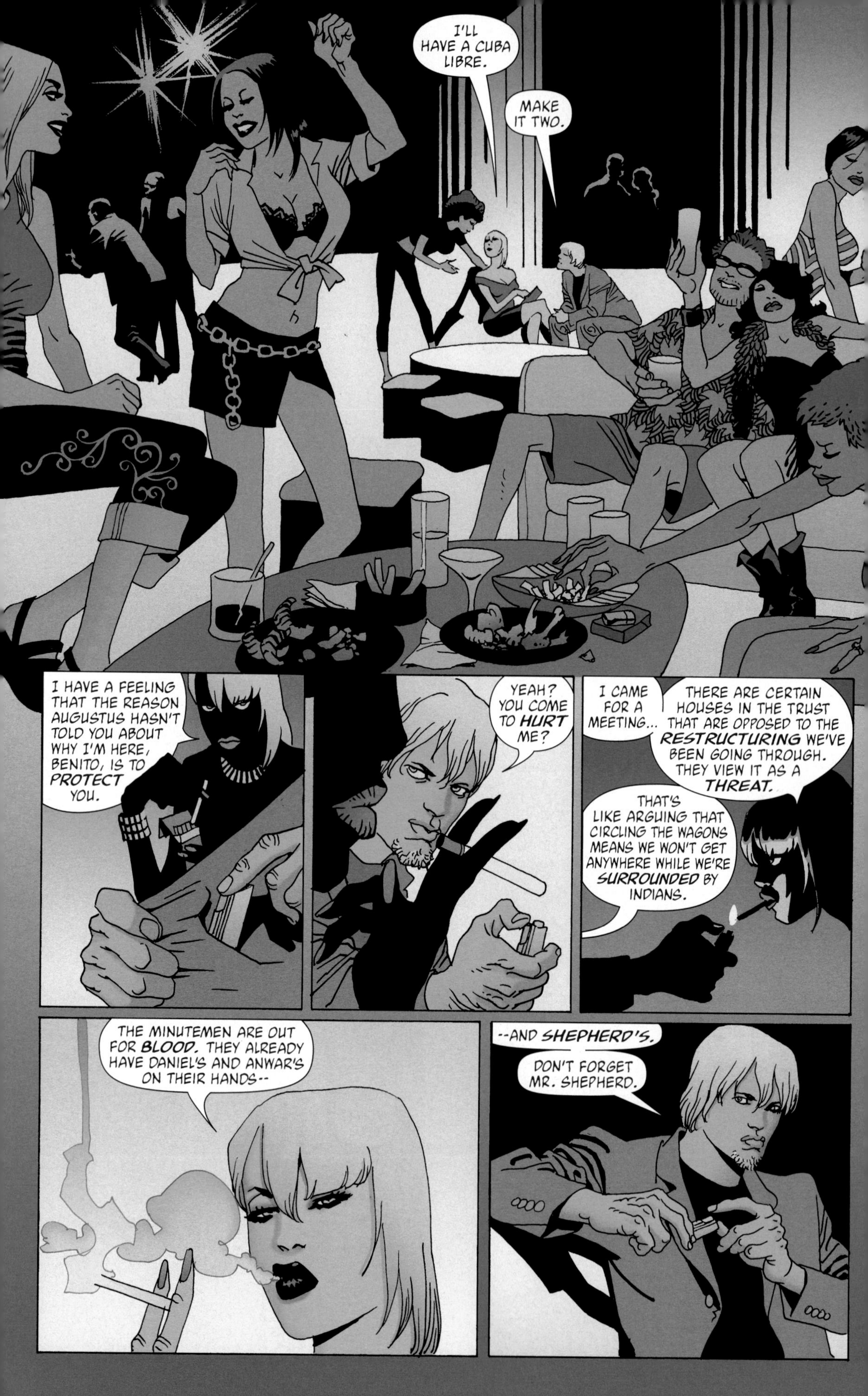
I'LL HAVE A CUBA LIBRE.
MAKE IT TWO.
I HAVE A FEELING THAT THE REASON AUGUSTUS HASN'T TOLD YOU ABOUT WHY I'M HERE, BENITO, IS TO *PROTECT* YOU.
YEAH? YOU COME TO *HURT* ME?
I CAME FOR A MEETING...
THERE ARE CERTAIN HOUSES IN THE TRUST THAT ARE OPPOSED TO THE *RESTRUCTURING* WE'VE BEEN GOING THROUGH. THEY VIEW IT AS A *THREAT.*
THAT'S LIKE ARGUING THAT CIRCLING THE WAGONS MEANS WE WON'T GET ANYWHERE WHILE WE'RE *SURROUNDED* BY INDIANS.
THE MINUTEMEN ARE OUT FOR *BLOOD.* THEY ALREADY HAVE DANIEL'S AND ANWAR'S ON THEIR HANDS--
--AND *SHEPHERD'S.*
DON'T FORGET MR. SHEPHERD.

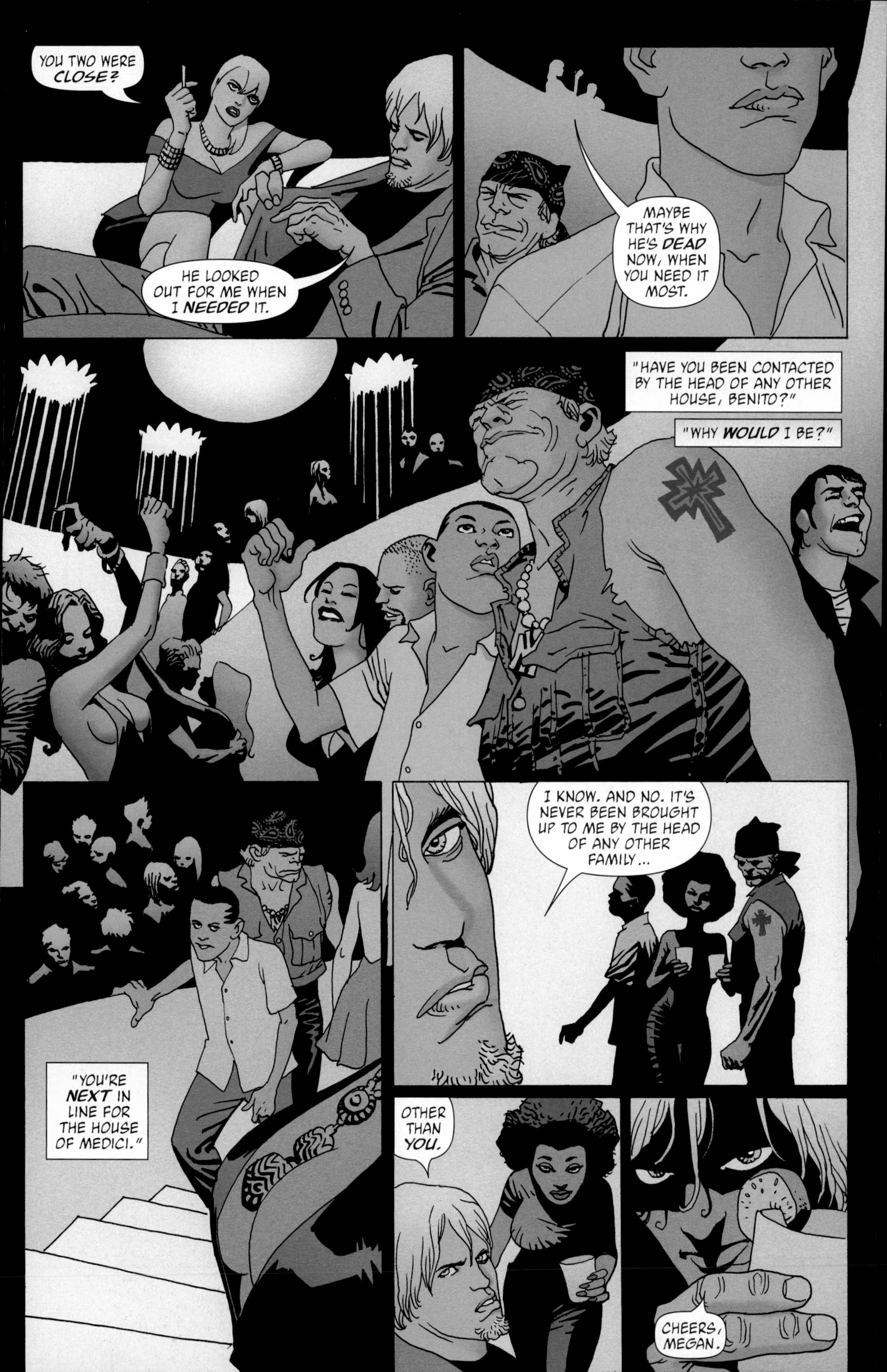

YOU TWO WERE CLOSE?
HE LOOKED OUT FOR ME WHEN I NEEDED IT.
MAYBE THAT'S WHY HE'S DEAD NOW, WHEN YOU NEED IT MOST.
"HAVE YOU BEEN CONTACTED BY THE HEAD OF ANY OTHER HOUSE, BENITO?"
"WHY WOULD I BE?"
"YOU'RE NEXT IN LINE FOR THE HOUSE OF MEDICI."
I KNOW. AND NO. IT'S NEVER BEEN BROUGHT UP TO ME BY THE HEAD OF ANY OTHER FAMILY...
OTHER THAN YOU.
CHEERS, MEGAN.

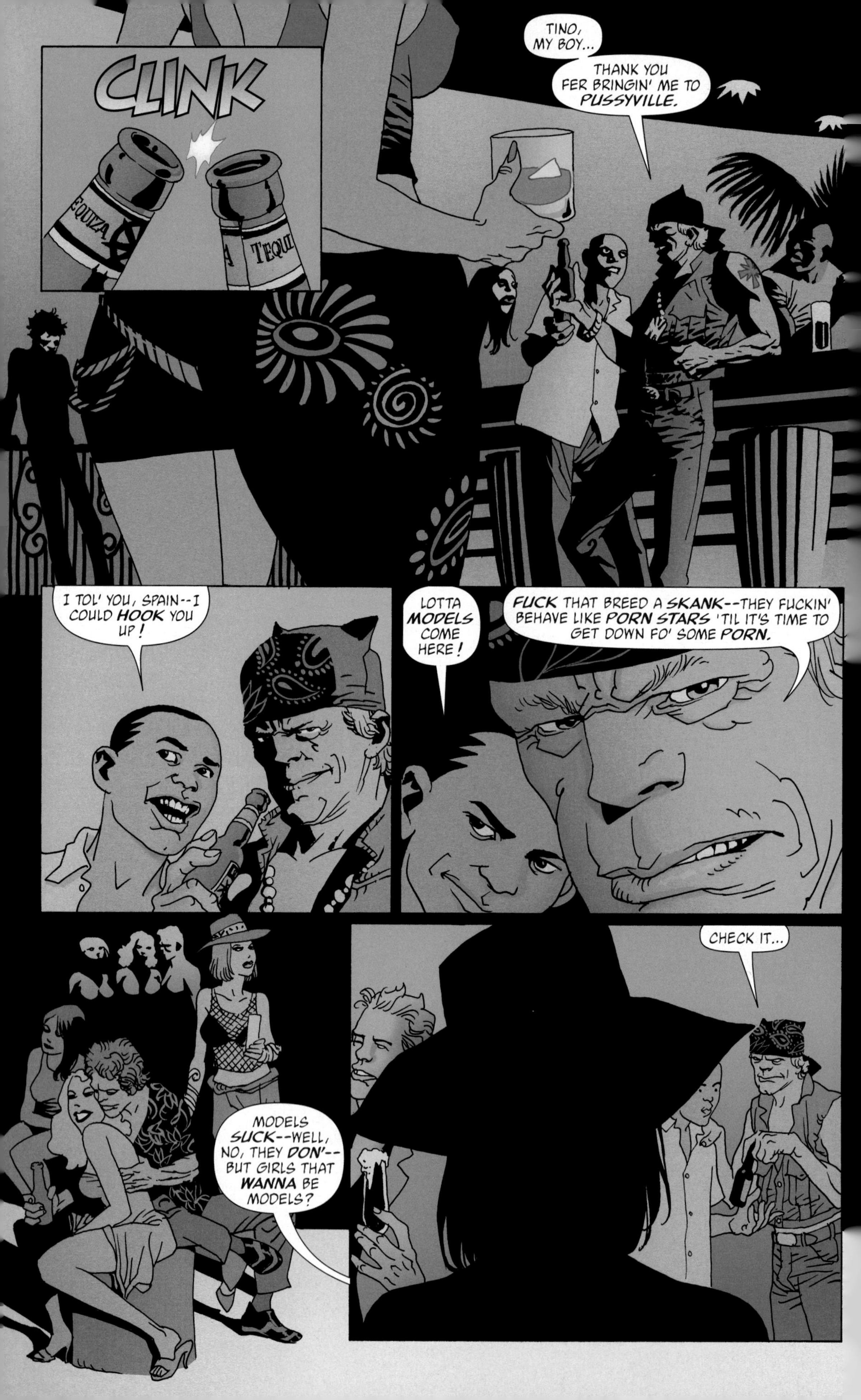
CLINK
TEQUIZA
TEQUI
TINO, MY BOY...
THANK YOU FER BRINGIN' ME TO PUSSYVILLE.
I TOL' YOU, SPAIN--I COULD HOOK YOU UP!
LOTTA MODELS COME HERE!
FUCK THAT BREED A SKANK--THEY FUCKIN' BEHAVE LIKE PORN STARS 'TIL IT'S TIME TO GET DOWN FO' SOME PORN.
MODELS SUCK--WELL, NO, THEY DON'--BUT GIRLS THAT WANNA BE MODELS?
CHECK IT...

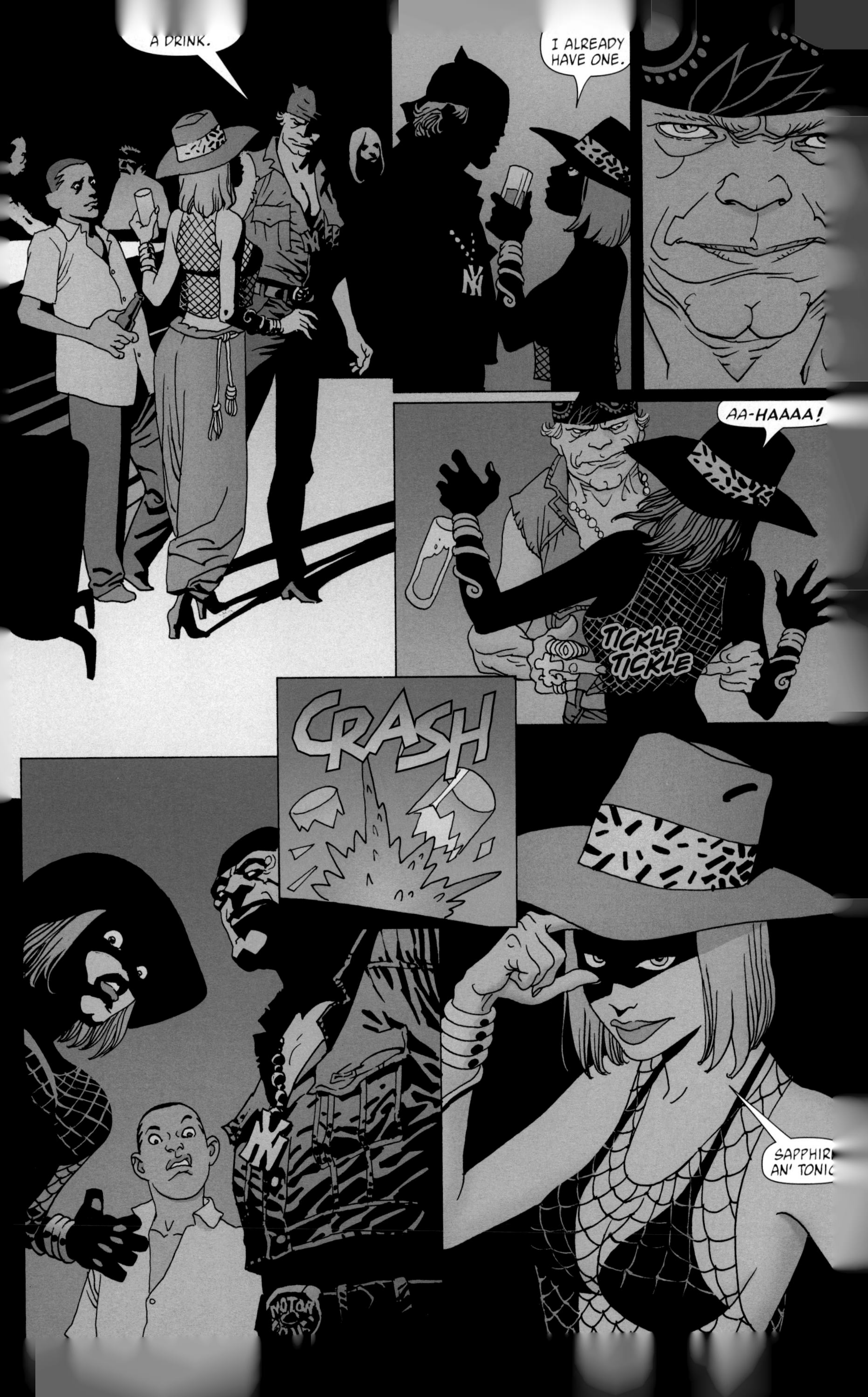
A DRINK.
I ALREADY HAVE ONE.
AA-HAAAA!
TICKLE TICKLE
CRASH
SAPPHIRE AN' TONIC

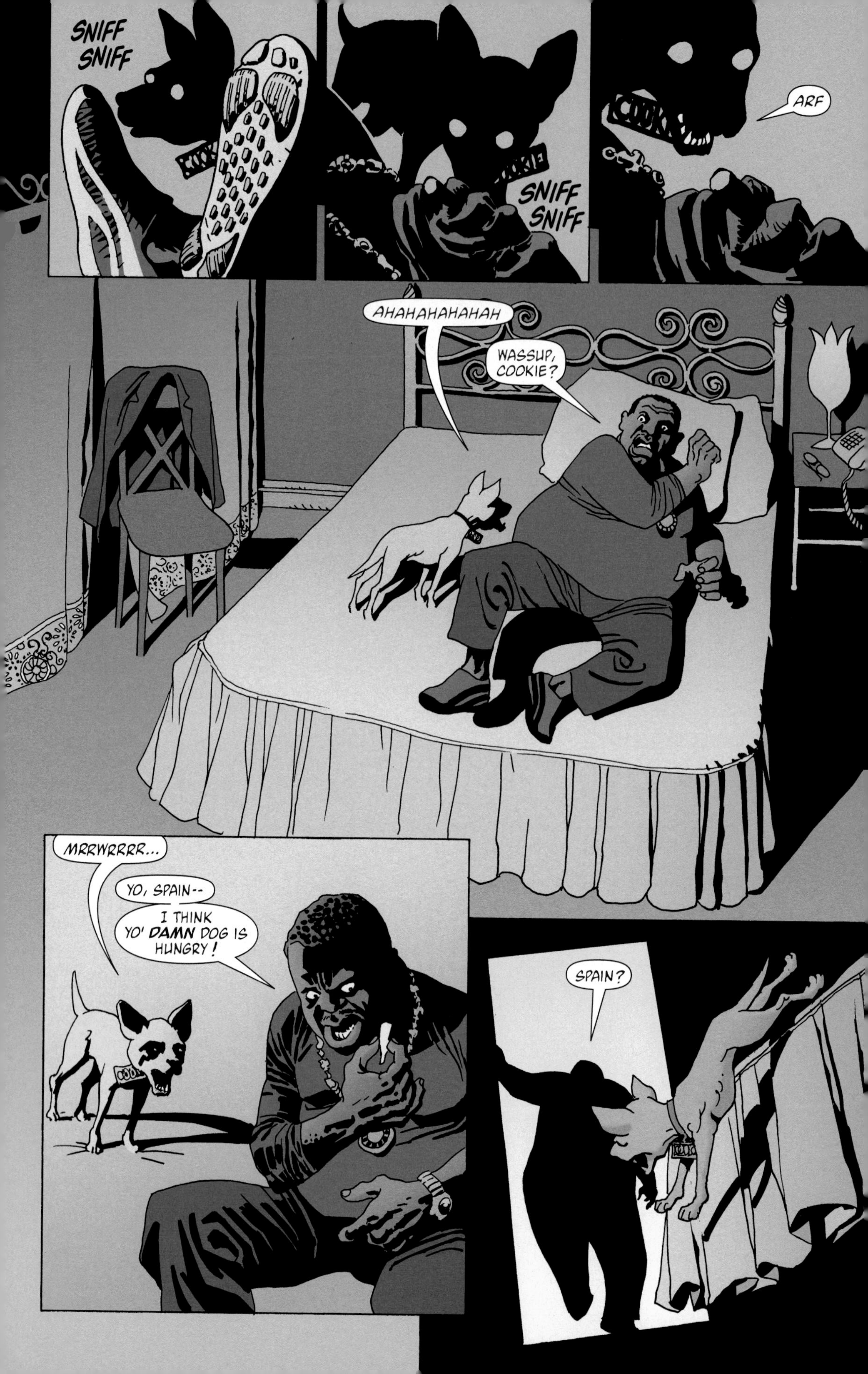
SNIFF
SNIFF
SNIFF
SNIFF
ARF
AHAHAHAHAHAH
WASSUP, COOKIE?
MRRWRRRR...
YO, SPAIN--
I THINK YO' DAMN DOG IS HUNGRY!
SPAIN?

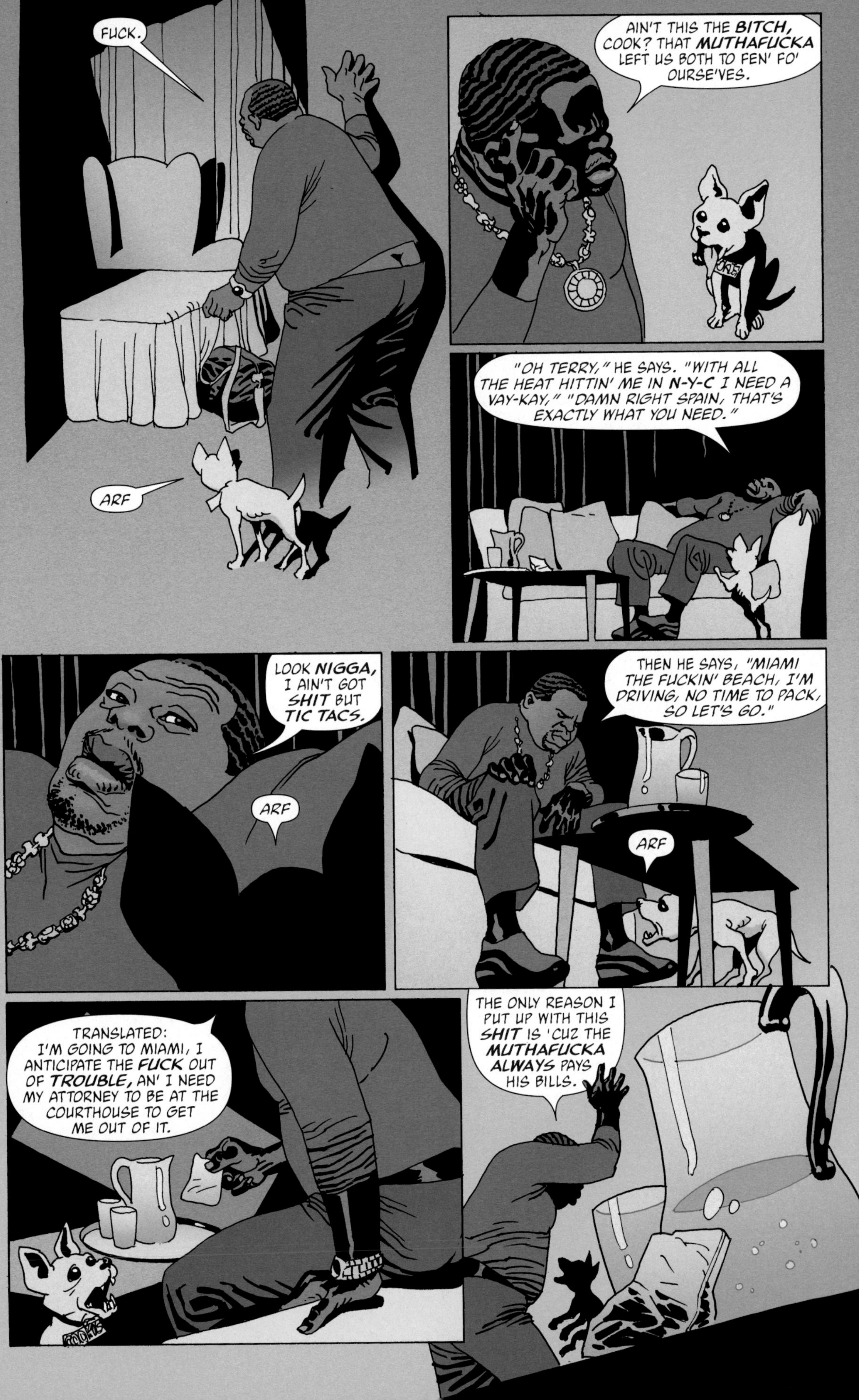
FUCK.
ARF
AIN'T THIS THE BITCH, COOK? THAT MUTHAFUCKA LEFT US BOTH TO FEN' FO' OURSE'VES.
"OH TERRY," HE SAYS. "WITH ALL THE HEAT HITTIN' ME IN N-Y-C I NEED A VAY-KAY," "DAMN RIGHT SPAIN, THAT'S EXACTLY WHAT YOU NEED."
LOOK NIGGA, I AIN'T GOT SHIT BUT TIC TACS.
ARF
THEN HE SAYS, "MIAMI THE FUCKIN' BEACH, I'M DRIVING, NO TIME TO PACK, SO LET'S GO."
ARF
TRANSLATED: I'M GOING TO MIAMI, I ANTICIPATE THE FUCK OUT OF TROUBLE, AN' I NEED MY ATTORNEY TO BE AT THE COURTHOUSE TO GET ME OUT OF IT.
THE ONLY REASON I PUT UP WITH THIS SHIT IS 'CUZ THE MUTHAFUCKA ALWAYS PAYS HIS BILLS.

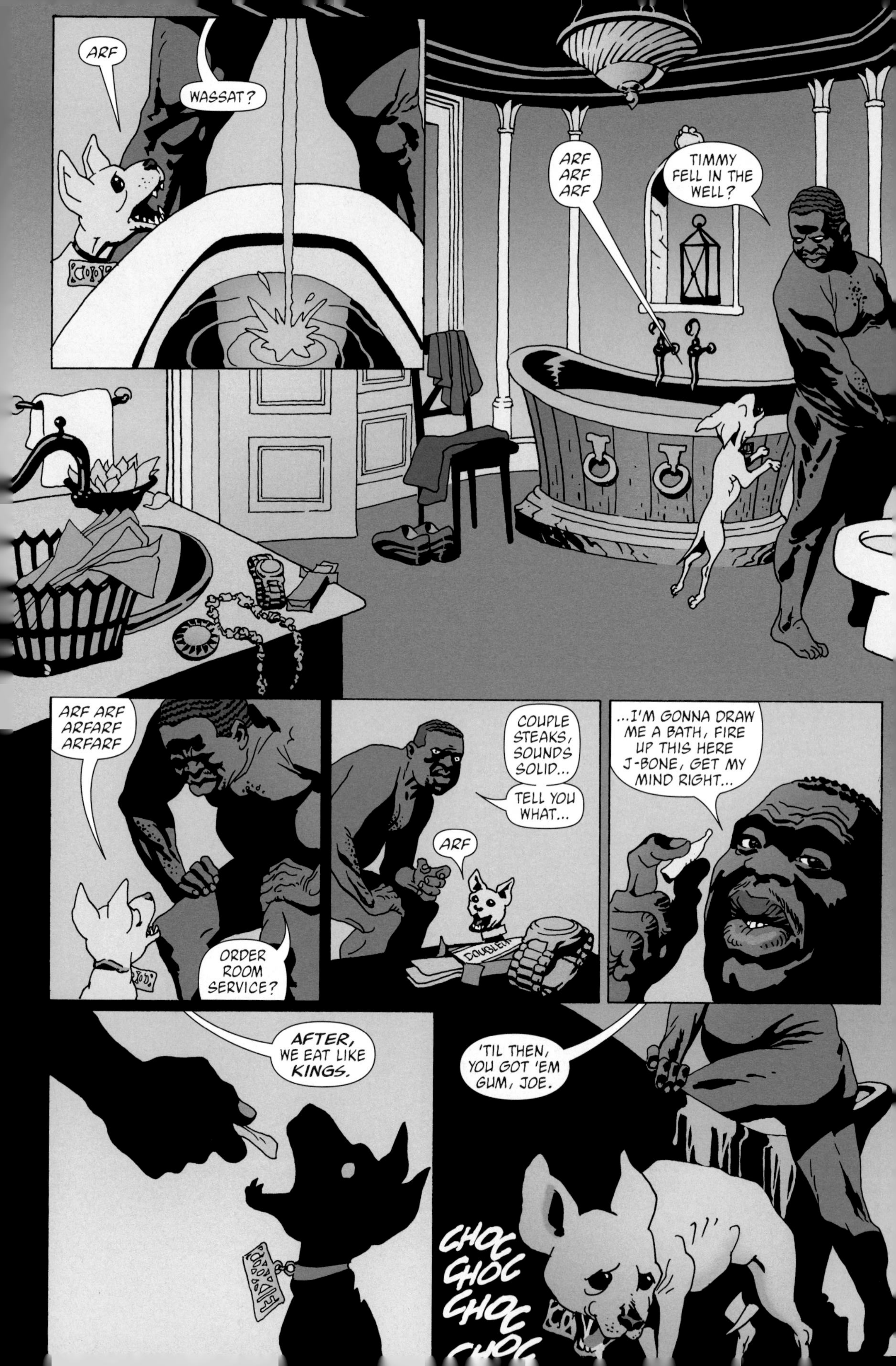
ARF
WASSAT?
ARF ARF ARF
TIMMY FELL IN THE WELL?
ARF ARF ARFARF ARFARF
ORDER ROOM SERVICE?
COUPLE STEAKS, SOUNDS SOLID...
TELL YOU WHAT...
ARF
...I'M GONNA DRAW ME A BATH, FIRE UP THIS HERE J-BONE, GET MY MIND RIGHT...
AFTER, WE EAT LIKE KINGS.
'TIL THEN, YOU GOT 'EM GUM, JOE.
CHOC CHOC CHOC CHOC

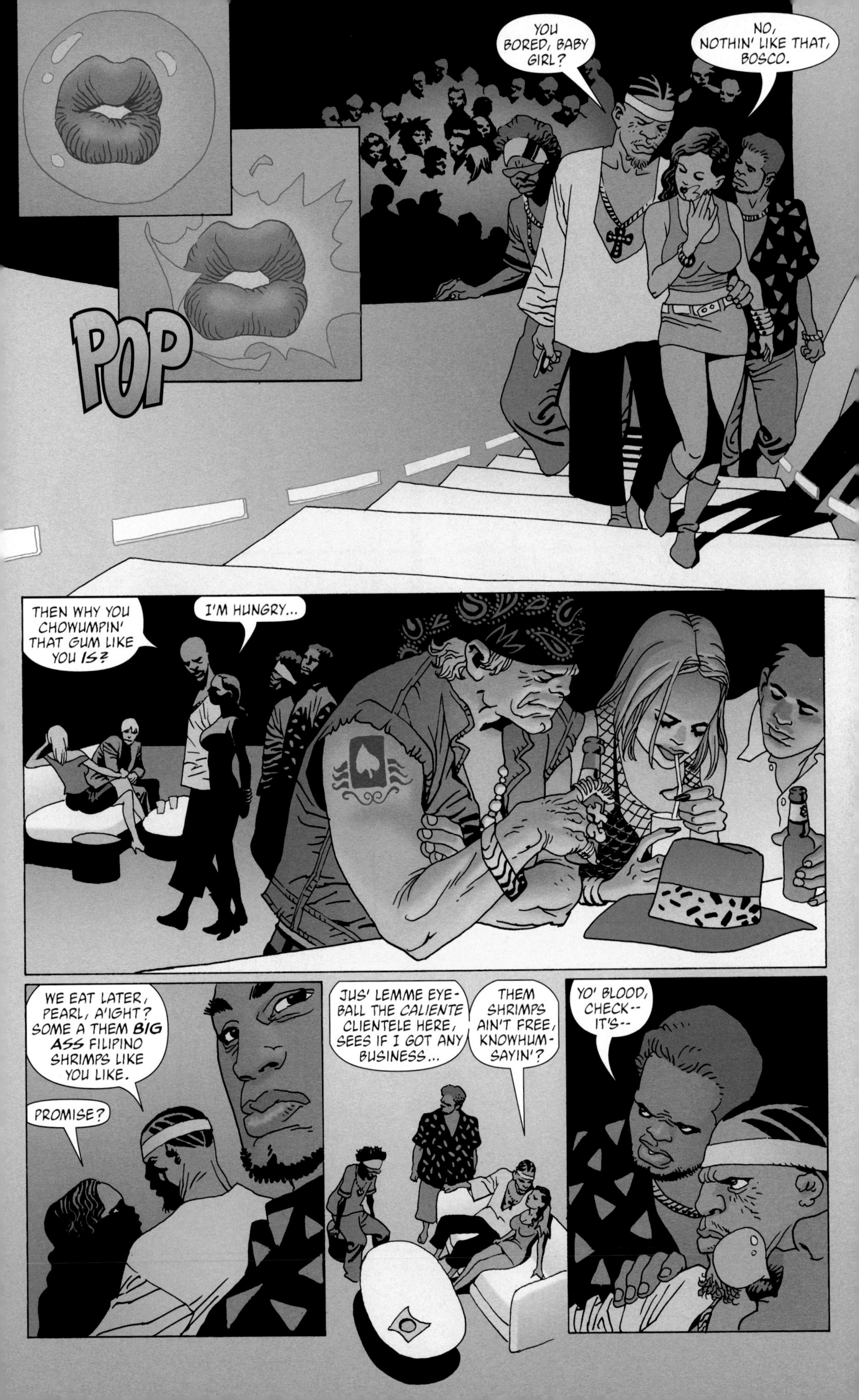
POP
YOU BORED, BABY GIRL?
NO, NOTHIN' LIKE THAT, BOSCO.
THEN WHY YOU CHOWUMPIN' THAT GUM LIKE YOU *IS*?
I'M HUNGRY...
WE EAT LATER, PEARL, A'IGHT? SOME A THEM **BIG ASS** FILIPINO SHRIMPS LIKE YOU LIKE.
PROMISE?
JUS' LEMME EYE-BALL THE *CALIENTE* CLIENTELE HERE, SEES IF I GOT ANY BUSINESS...
THEM SHRIMPS AIN'T FREE, KNOWHUM-SAYIN'?
YO' BLOOD, CHECK-- IT'S--

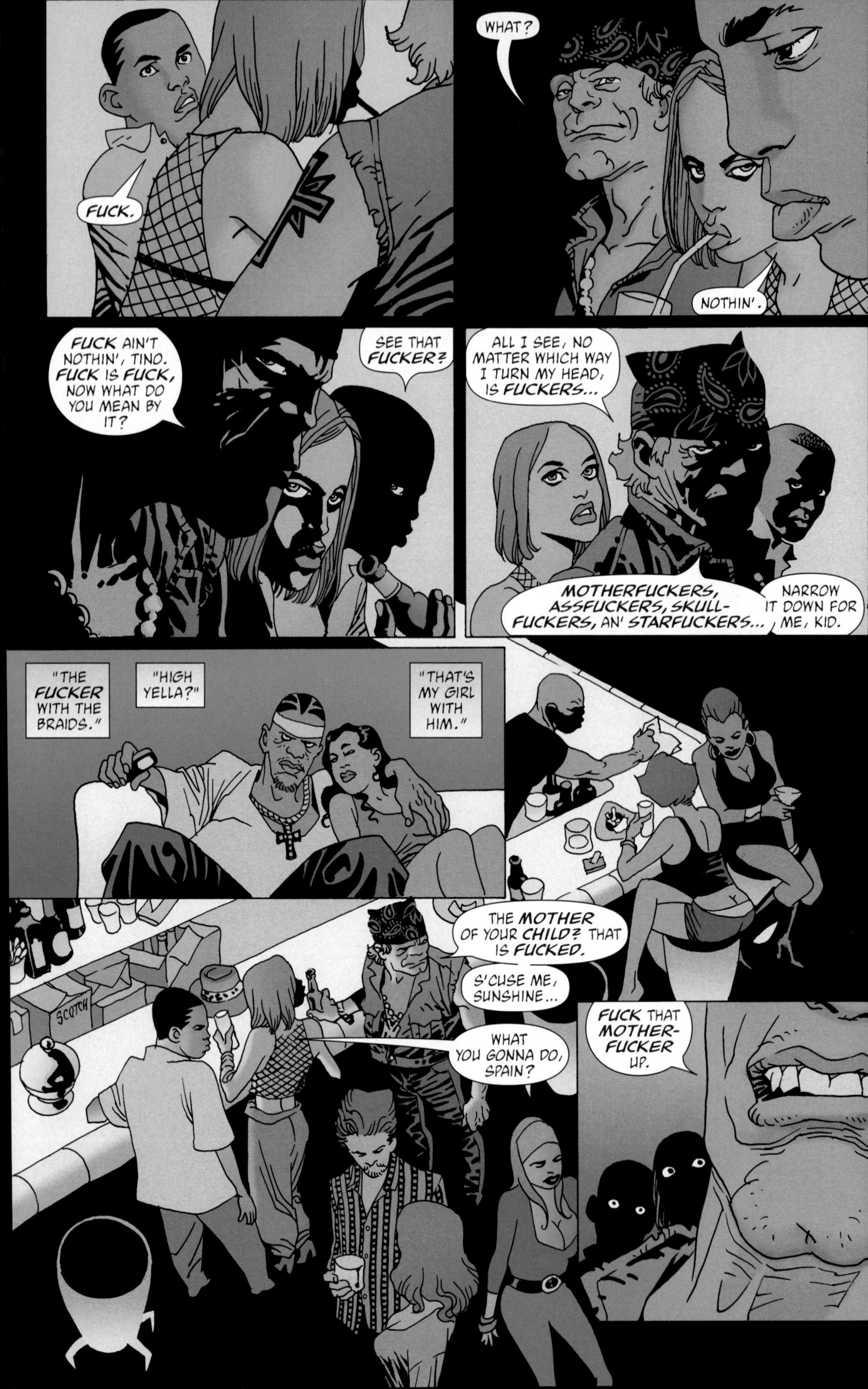
FUCK.
WHAT?
NOTHIN'.
FUCK AIN'T NOTHIN', TINO. FUCK IS FUCK, NOW WHAT DO YOU MEAN BY IT?
SEE THAT FUCKER?
ALL I SEE, NO MATTER WHICH WAY I TURN MY HEAD, IS FUCKERS...
MOTHERFUCKERS, ASSFUCKERS, SKULL-FUCKERS, AN' STARFUCKERS...
NARROW IT DOWN FOR ME, KID.
"THE FUCKER WITH THE BRAIDS."
"HIGH YELLA?"
"THAT'S MY GIRL WITH HIM."
THE MOTHER OF YOUR CHILD? THAT IS FUCKED.
S'CUSE ME, SUNSHINE...
WHAT YOU GONNA DO, SPAIN?
FUCK THAT MOTHER-FUCKER UP.
SCOTCH

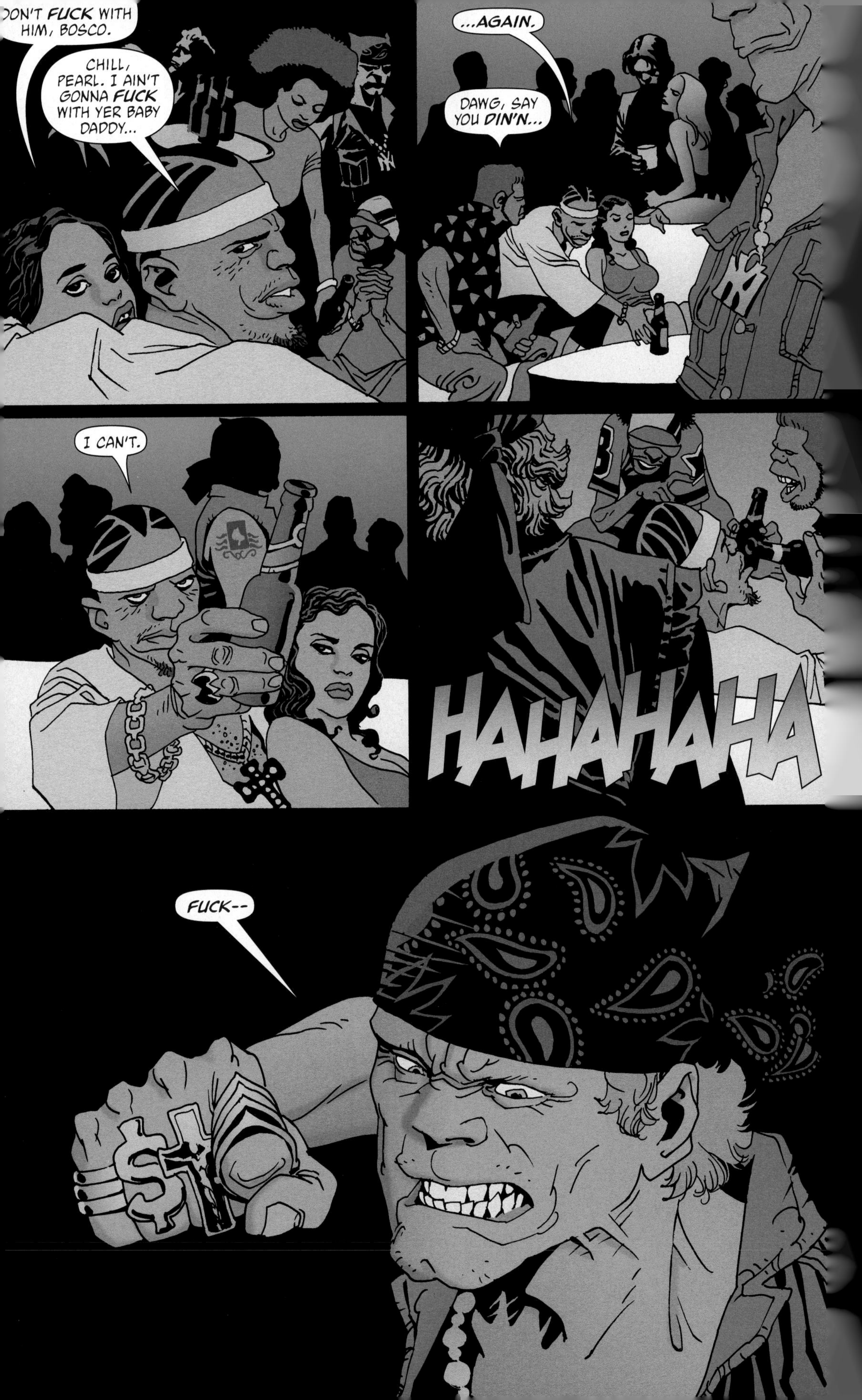
DON'T FUCK WITH HIM, BOSCO.
CHILL, PEARL. I AIN'T GONNA FUCK WITH YER BABY DADDY...
...AGAIN.
DAWG, SAY YOU DIN'N...
I CAN'T.
HAHAHAHA
FUCK--

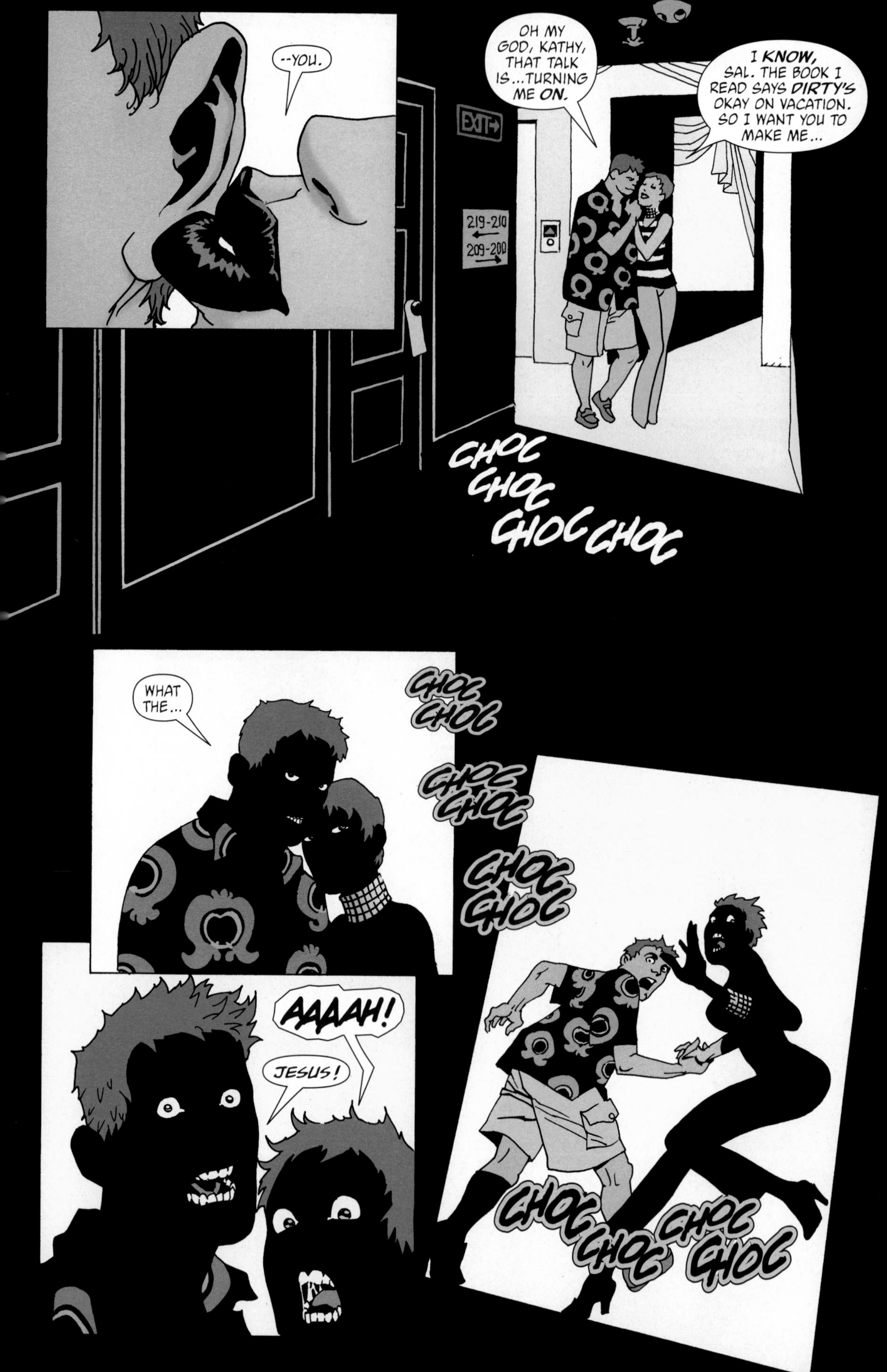
--YOU.
EXIT
219-210
209-200
OH MY GOD, KATHY, THAT TALK IS...TURNING ME ON.
I KNOW, SAL. THE BOOK I READ SAYS DIRTY'S OKAY ON VACATION. SO I WANT YOU TO MAKE ME...
CHOC CHOC CHOC CHOC
WHAT THE...
CHOC CHOC
CHOC CHOC
CHOC CHOC
AAAAH!
JESUS!
CHOC CHOC CHOC CHOC

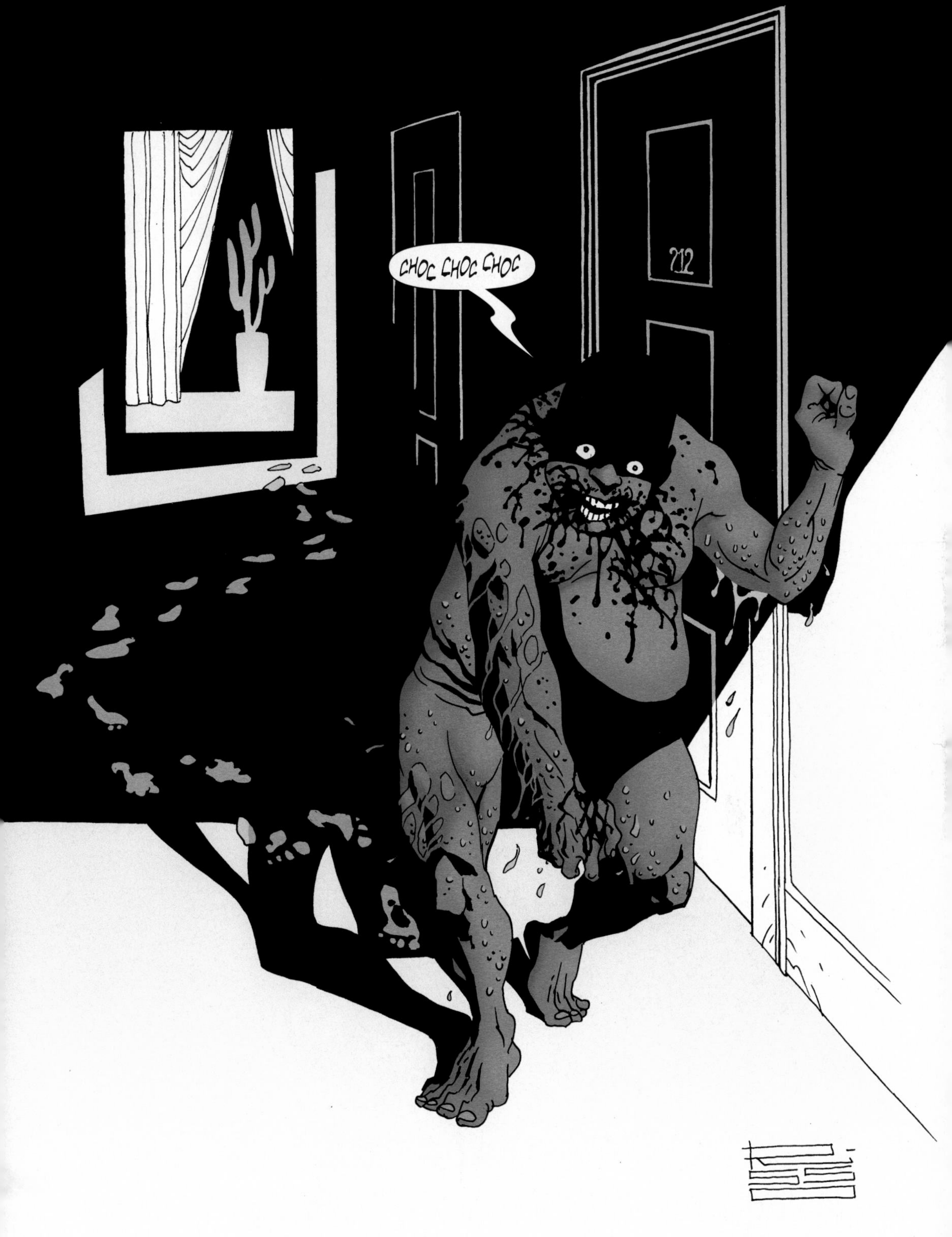
CHOC CHOC CHOC
212

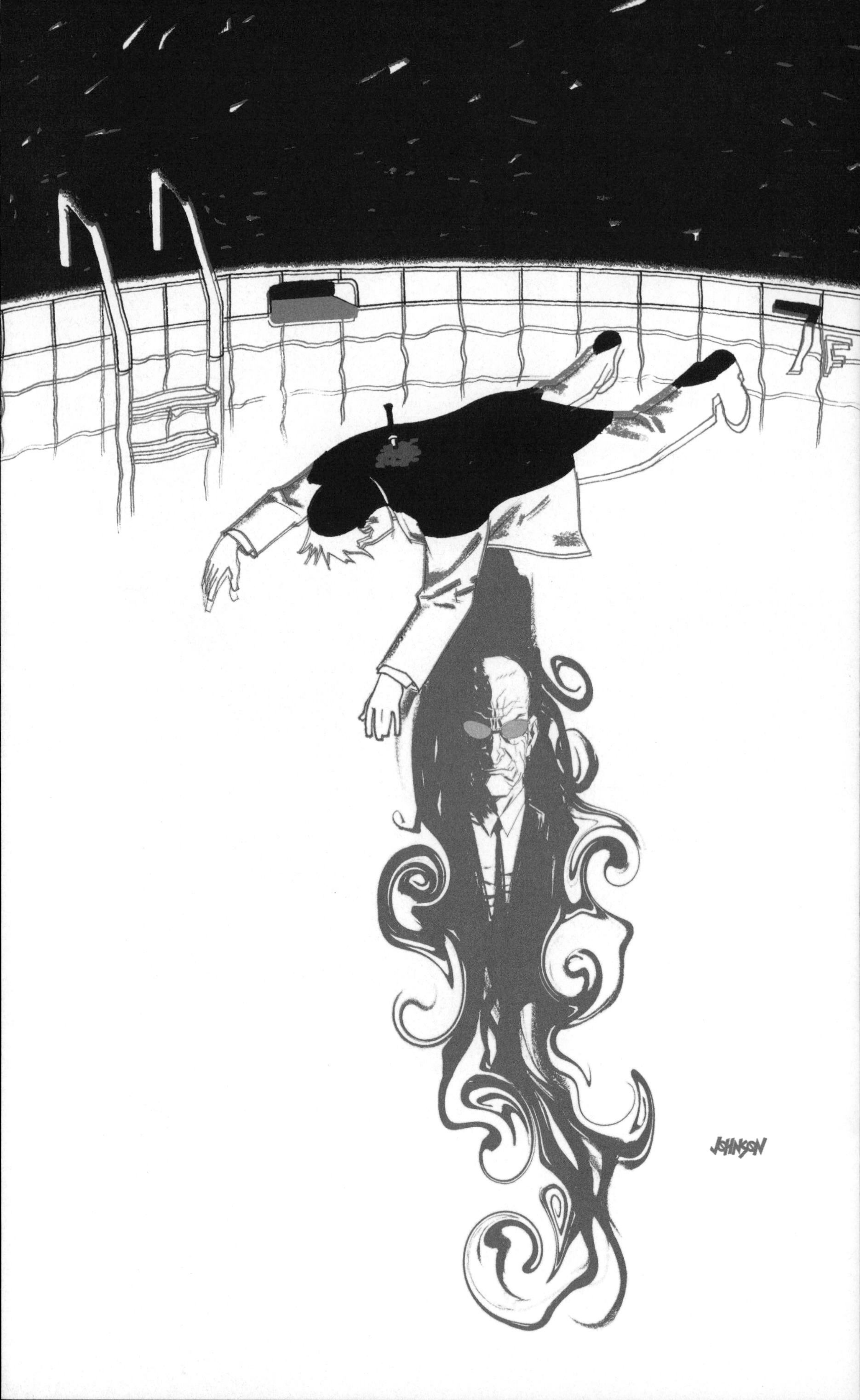
JOHNSON

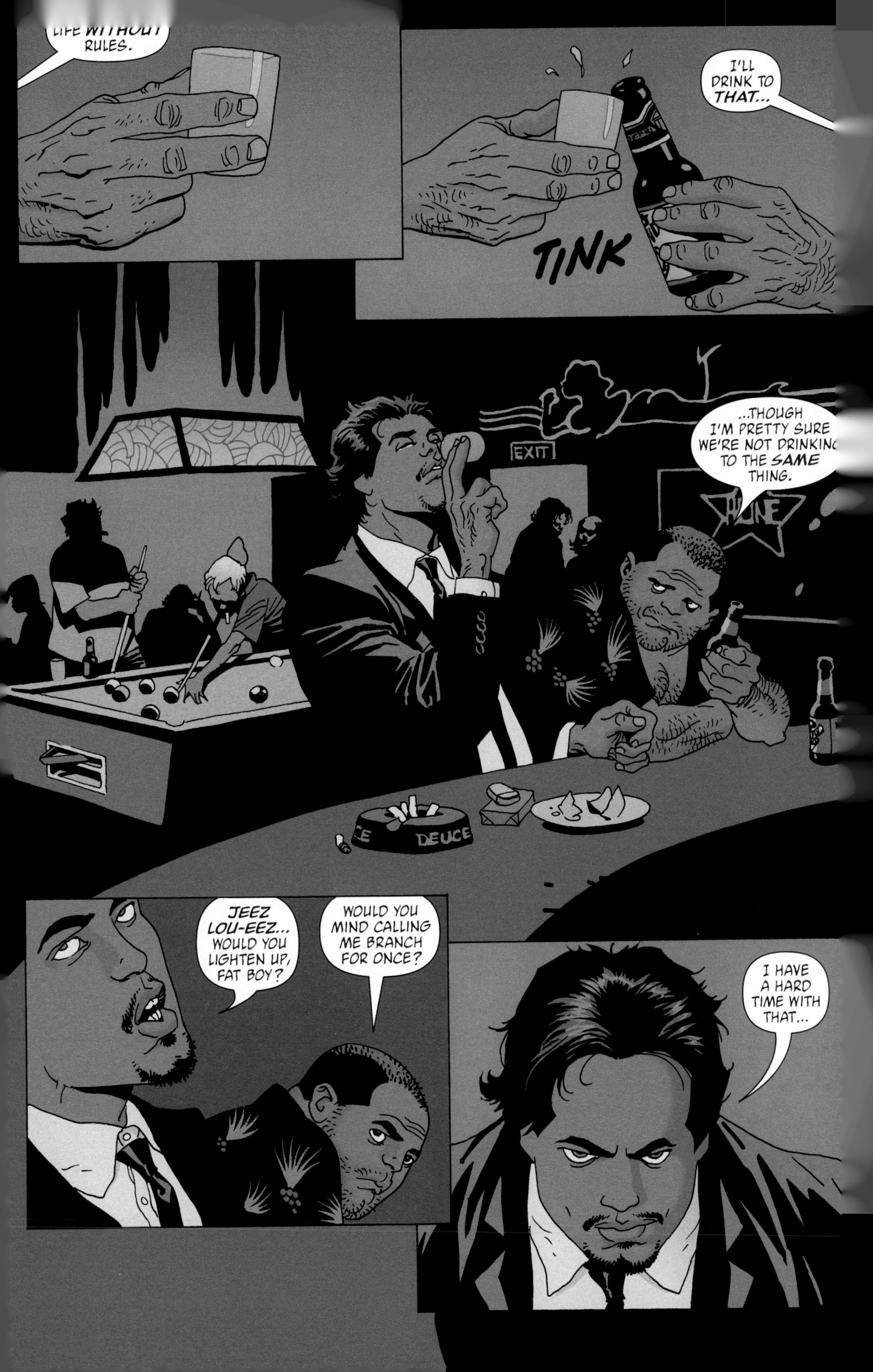
LIFE WITHOUT RULES.
I'LL DRINK TO THAT...
TINK
...THOUGH I'M PRETTY SURE WE'RE NOT DRINKING TO THE SAME THING.
EXIT
DEUCE
JEEZ LOU-EEZ... WOULD YOU LIGHTEN UP, FAT BOY?
WOULD YOU MIND CALLING ME BRANCH FOR ONCE?
I HAVE A HARD TIME WITH THAT...

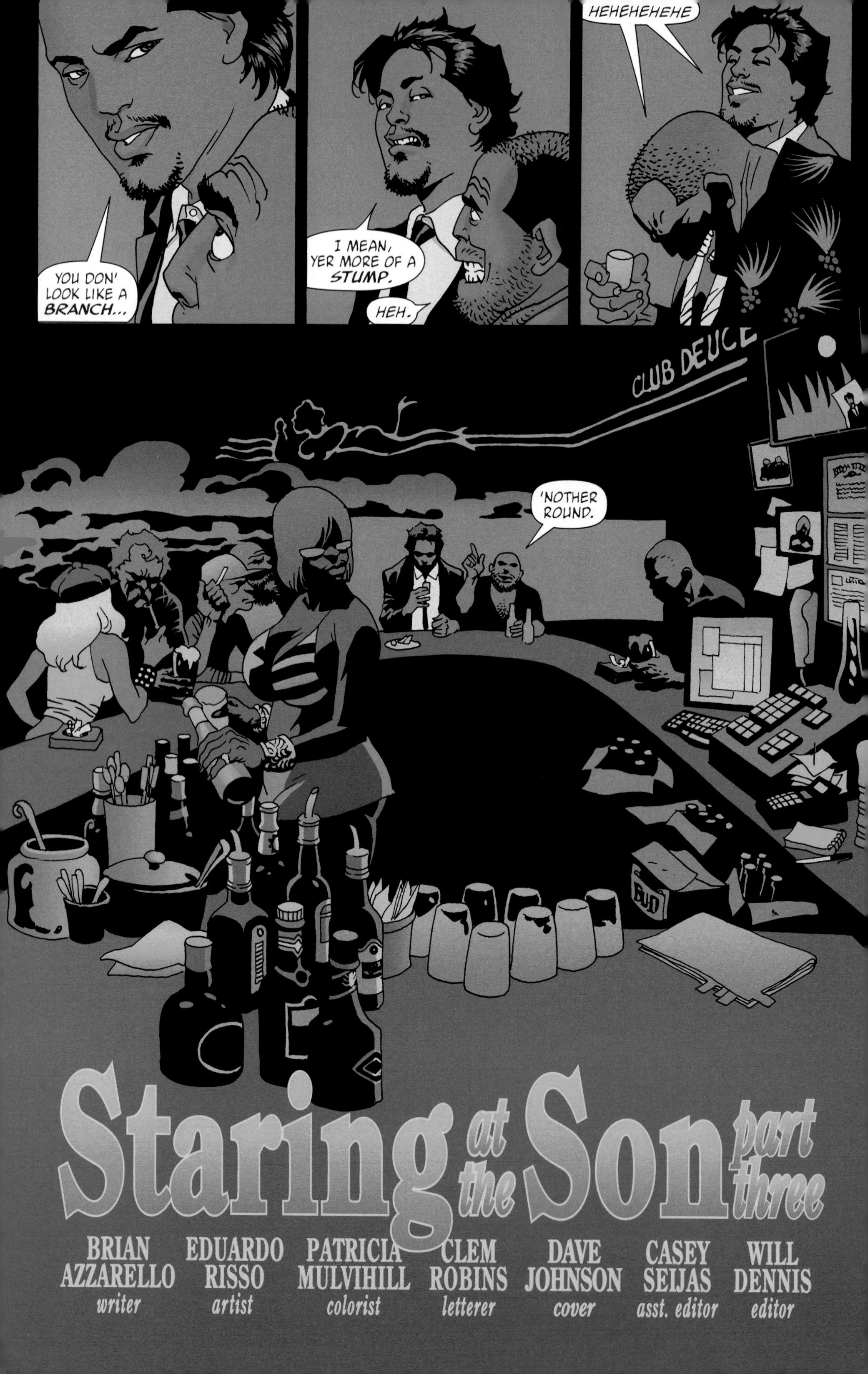
YOU DON' LOOK LIKE A BRANCH...
I MEAN, YER MORE OF A STUMP.
HEH.
HEHEHEHEHE
CLUB DEUCE
'NOTHER ROUND.
BUD
Staring at the Son part three
BRIAN AZZARELLO writer
EDUARDO RISSO artist
PATRICIA MULVIHILL colorist
CLEM ROBINS letterer
DAVE JOHNSON cover
CASEY SEIJAS asst. editor
WILL DENNIS editor

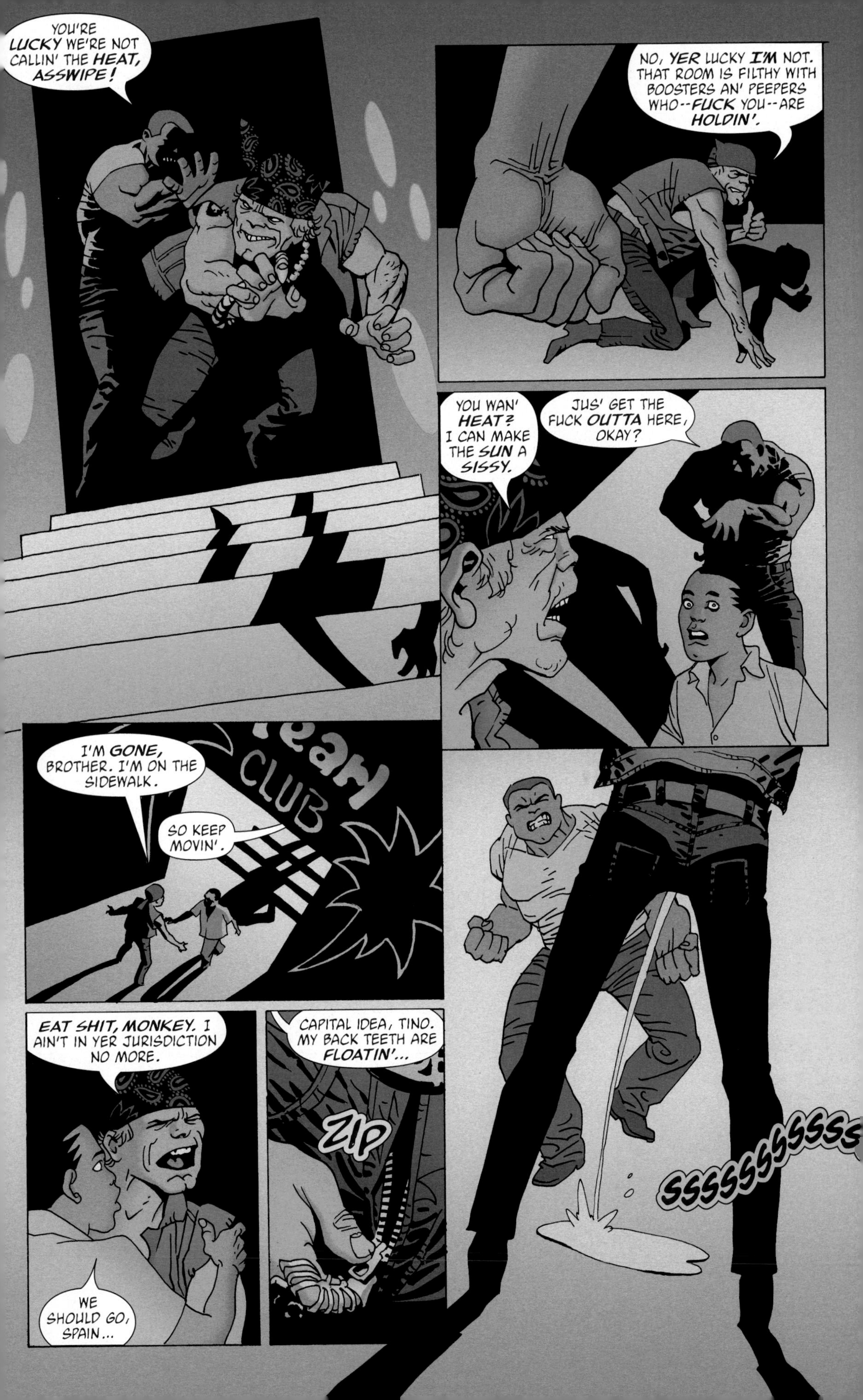
YOU'RE LUCKY WE'RE NOT CALLIN' THE HEAT, ASSWIPE!
NO, YER LUCKY I'M NOT. THAT ROOM IS FILTHY WITH BOOSTERS AN' PEEPERS WHO--FUCK YOU--ARE HOLDIN'.
YOU WAN' HEAT? I CAN MAKE THE SUN A SISSY.
JUS' GET THE FUCK OUTTA HERE, OKAY?
I'M GONE, BROTHER. I'M ON THE SIDEWALK.
SO KEEP MOVIN'.
CLUB
EAT SHIT, MONKEY. I AIN'T IN YER JURISDICTION NO MORE.
WE SHOULD GO, SPAIN...
CAPITAL IDEA, TINO. MY BACK TEETH ARE FLOATIN'...
ZIP
SSSSSSSSSSSSSSSS

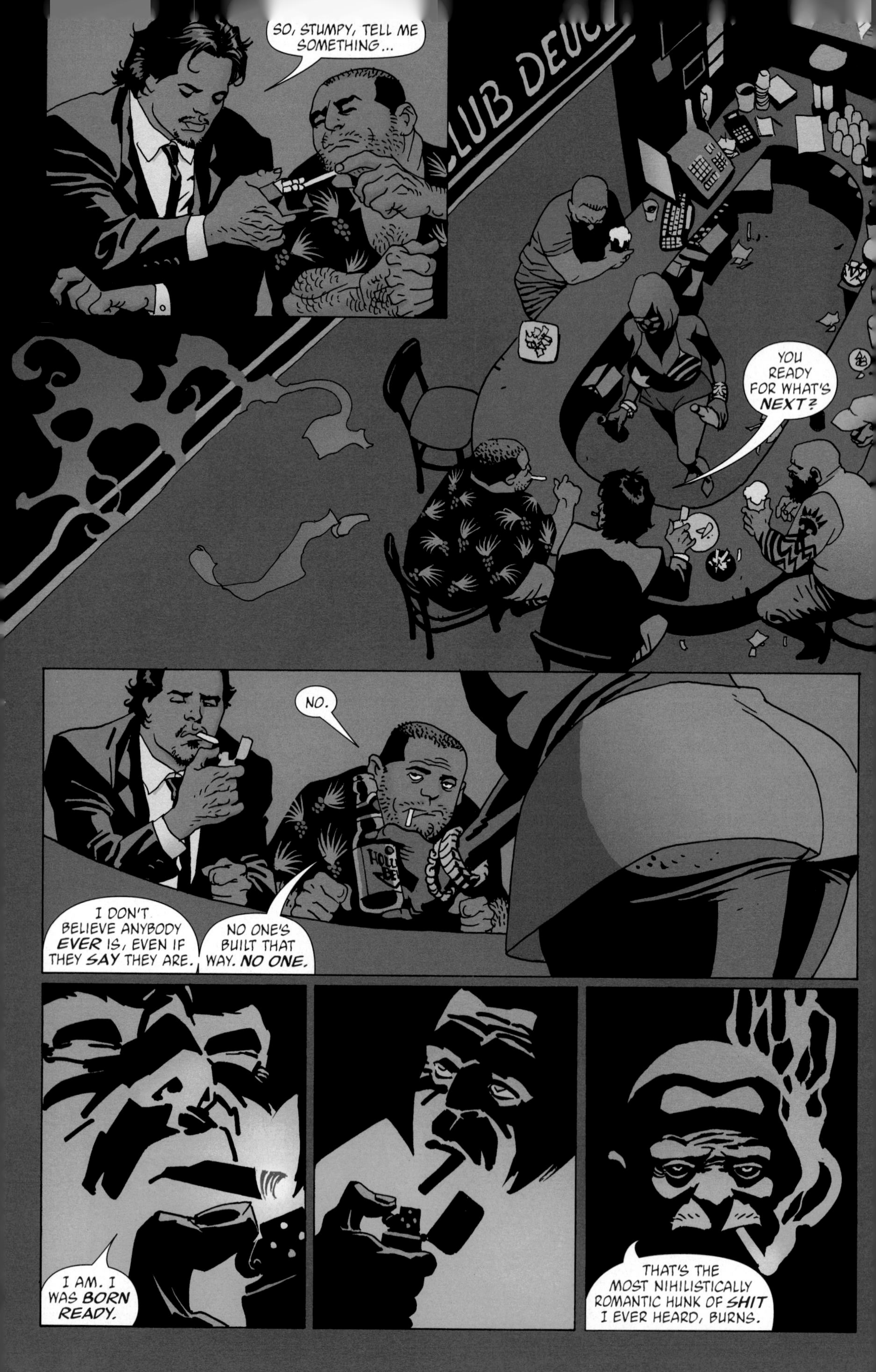
SO, STUMPY, TELL ME SOMETHING...
CLUB DEUCE
YOU READY FOR WHAT'S NEXT?
NO.
I DON'T. BELIEVE ANYBODY EVER IS, EVEN IF THEY SAY THEY ARE.
NO ONE'S BUILT THAT WAY. NO ONE.
I AM. I WAS BORN READY.
THAT'S THE MOST NIHILISTICALLY ROMANTIC HUNK OF SHIT I EVER HEARD, BURNS.

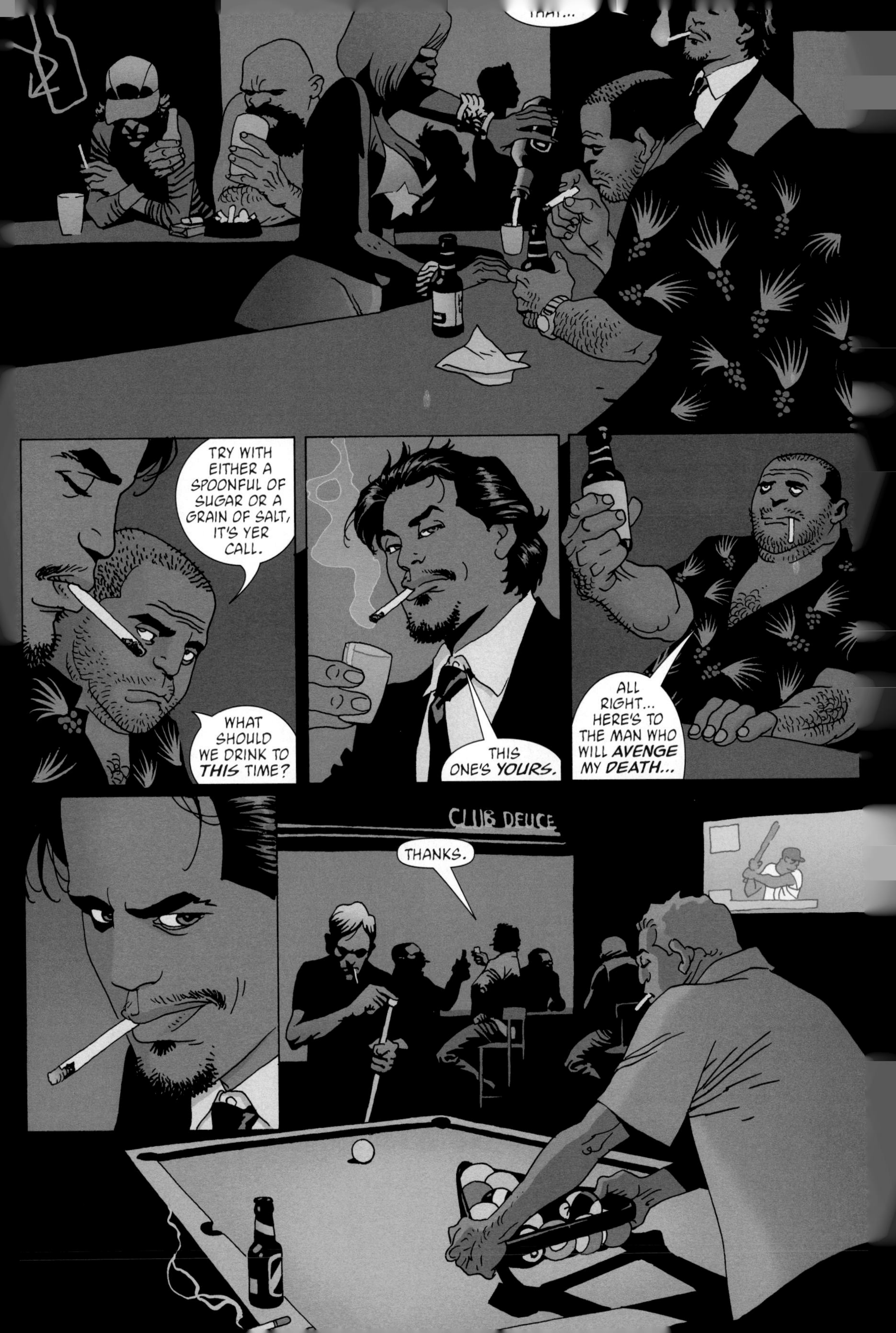
TRY WITH EITHER A SPOONFUL OF SUGAR OR A GRAIN OF SALT, IT'S YER CALL.
WHAT SHOULD WE DRINK TO *THIS* TIME?
THIS ONE'S *YOURS.*
ALL RIGHT... HERE'S TO THE MAN WHO WILL *AVENGE* MY *DEATH...*
CLUB DEUCE
THANKS.

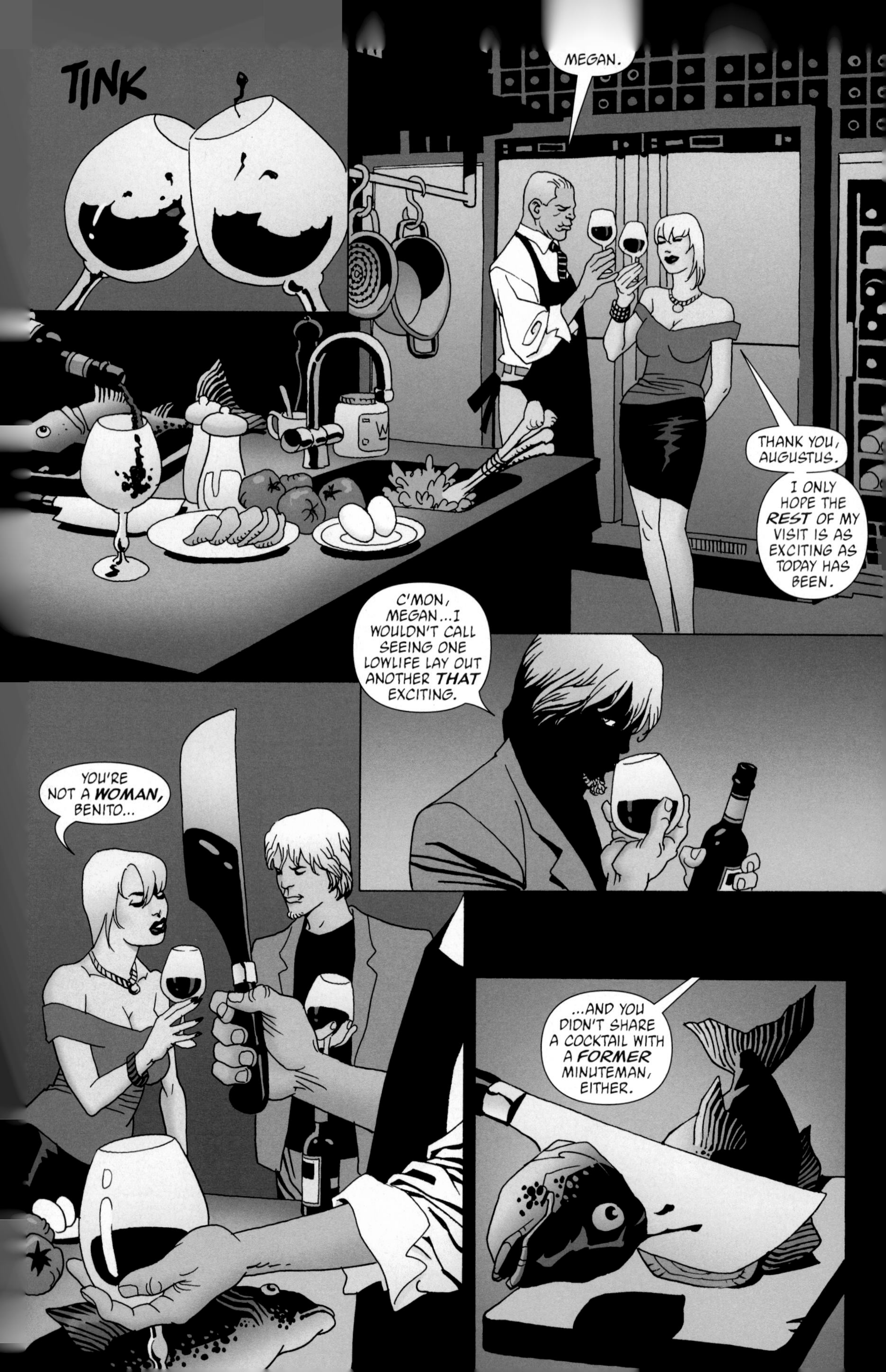
TINK
MEGAN.
THANK YOU, AUGUSTUS.
I ONLY HOPE THE REST OF MY VISIT IS AS EXCITING AS TODAY HAS BEEN.
C'MON, MEGAN...I WOULDN'T CALL SEEING ONE LOWLIFE LAY OUT ANOTHER THAT EXCITING.
YOU'RE NOT A WOMAN, BENITO...
...AND YOU DIDN'T SHARE A COCKTAIL WITH A FORMER MINUTEMAN, EITHER.

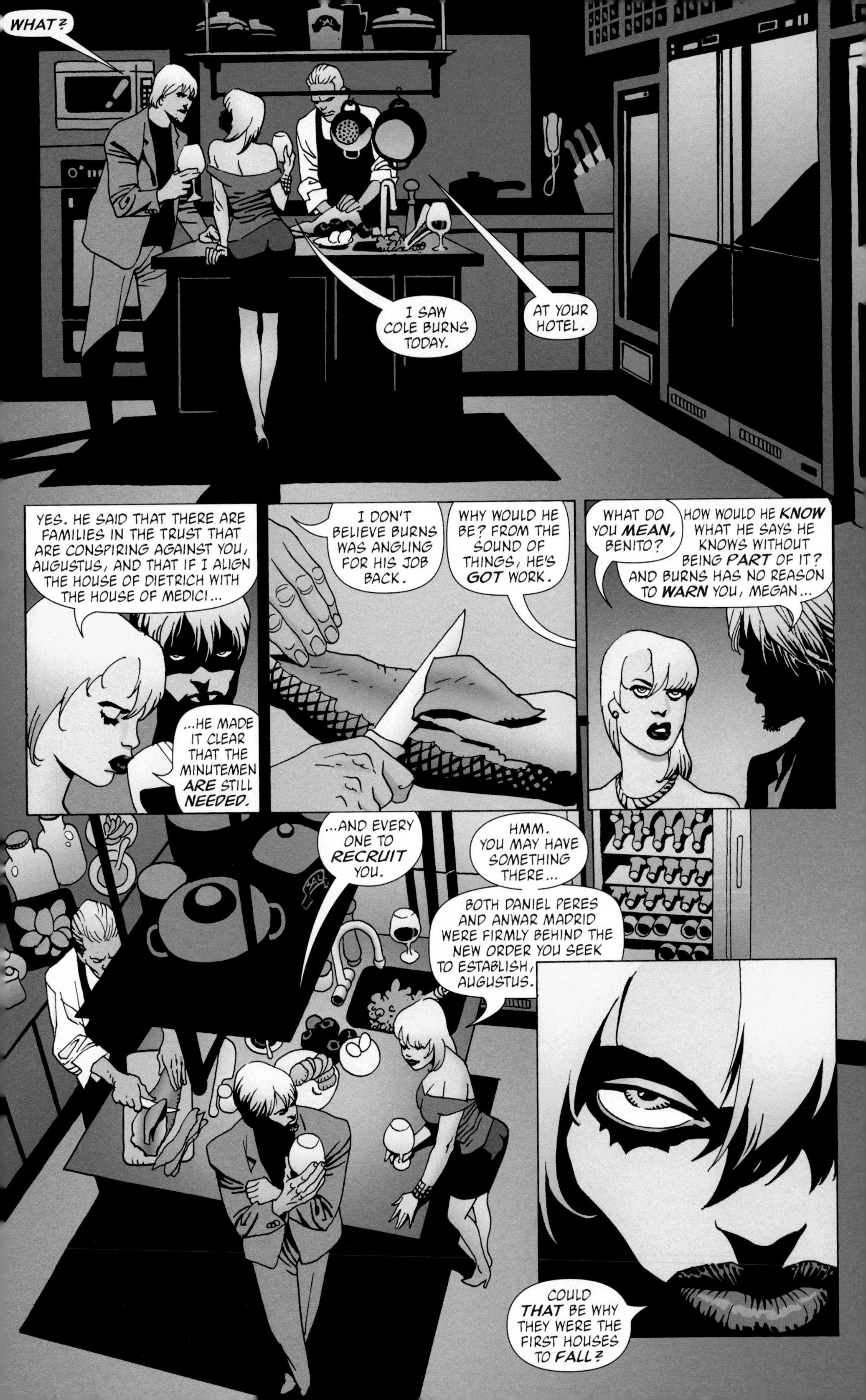
WHAT?
I SAW COLE BURNS TODAY.
AT YOUR HOTEL.
YES. HE SAID THAT THERE ARE FAMILIES IN THE TRUST THAT ARE CONSPIRING AGAINST YOU, AUGUSTUS, AND THAT IF I ALIGN THE HOUSE OF DIETRICH WITH THE HOUSE OF MEDICI...
...HE MADE IT CLEAR THAT THE MINUTEMEN ARE STILL NEEDED.
I DON'T BELIEVE BURNS WAS ANGLING FOR HIS JOB BACK.
WHY WOULD HE BE? FROM THE SOUND OF THINGS, HE'S GOT WORK.
WHAT DO YOU MEAN, BENITO?
HOW WOULD HE KNOW WHAT HE SAYS HE KNOWS WITHOUT BEING PART OF IT? AND BURNS HAS NO REASON TO WARN YOU, MEGAN...
...AND EVERY ONE TO RECRUIT YOU.
HMM. YOU MAY HAVE SOMETHING THERE...
BOTH DANIEL PERES AND ANWAR MADRID WERE FIRMLY BEHIND THE NEW ORDER YOU SEEK TO ESTABLISH, AUGUSTUS.
COULD THAT BE WHY THEY WERE THE FIRST HOUSES TO FALL?

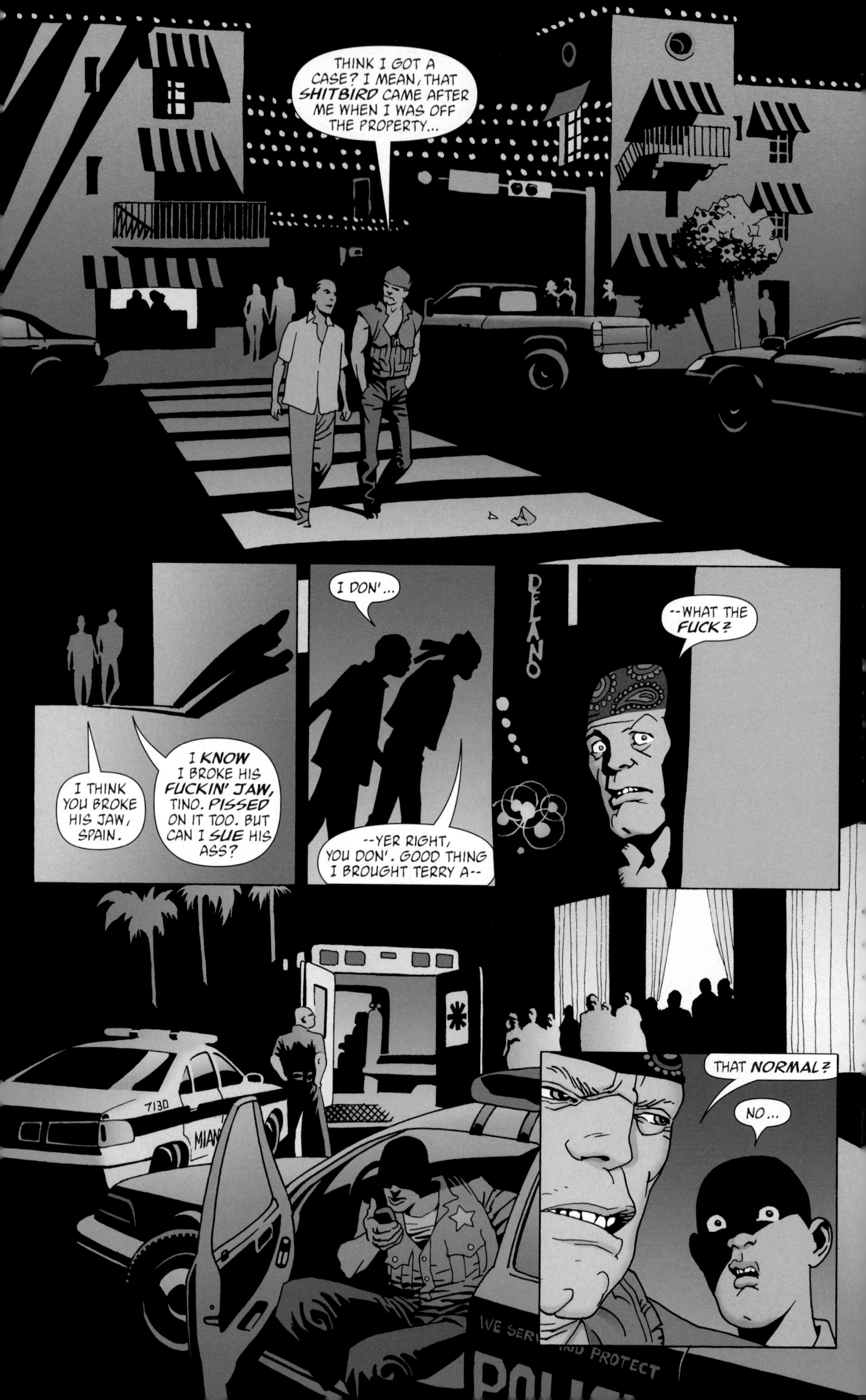
THINK I GOT A CASE? I MEAN, THAT SHITBIRD CAME AFTER ME WHEN I WAS OFF THE PROPERTY...
I THINK YOU BROKE HIS JAW, SPAIN.
I KNOW I BROKE HIS FUCKIN' JAW, TINO. PISSED ON IT TOO. BUT CAN I SUE HIS ASS?
I DON'...
--YER RIGHT, YOU DON'. GOOD THING I BROUGHT TERRY A--
DELANO
--WHAT THE FUCK?
7130
MIAM
THAT NORMAL?
NO...
WE SERV ND PROTECT
POLI

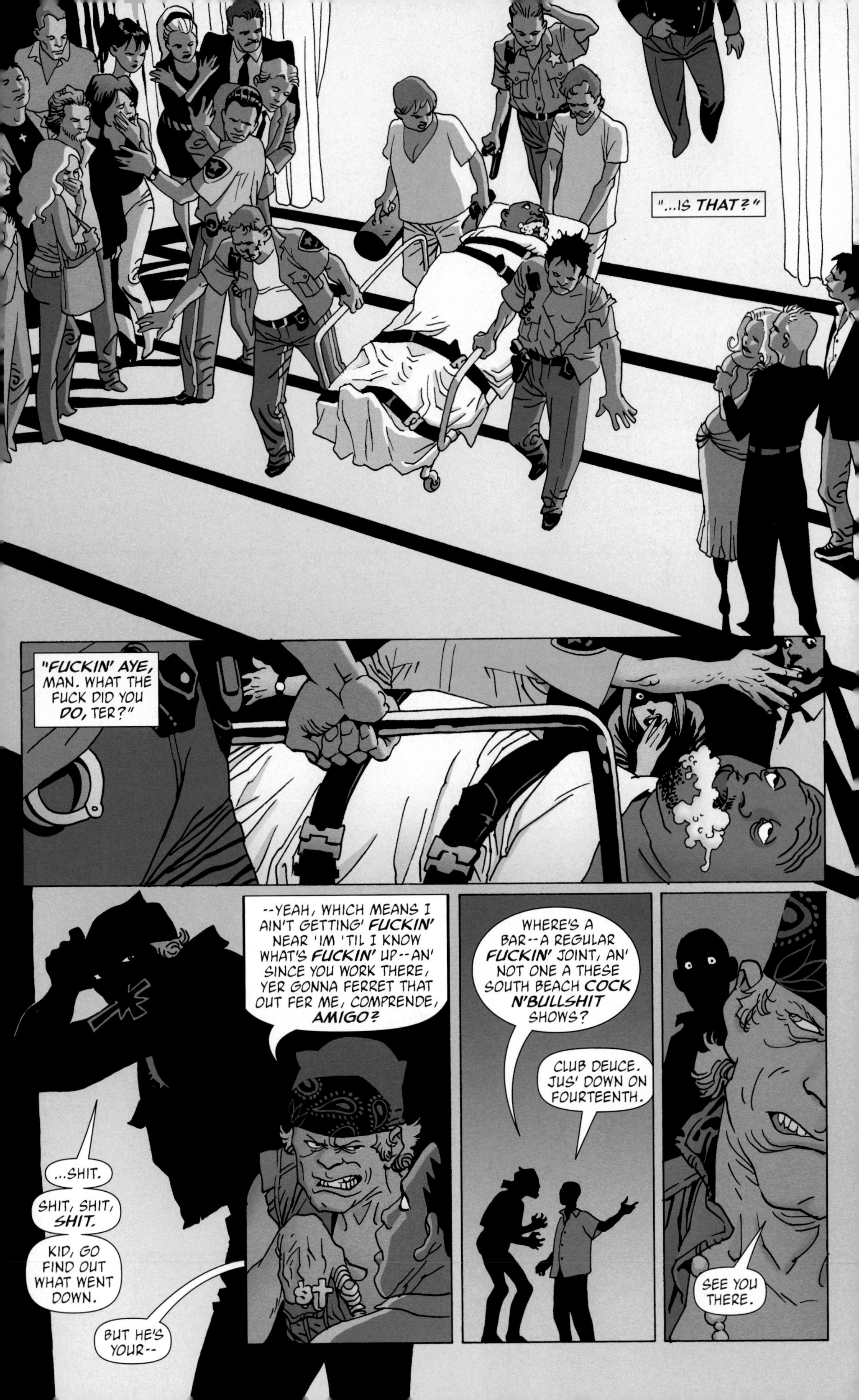
"...IS *THAT?*"
"FUCKIN' AYE, MAN. WHAT THE FUCK DID YOU *DO,* TER?"
...SHIT.
SHIT, SHIT, *SHIT.*
KID, GO FIND OUT WHAT WENT DOWN.
BUT HE'S YOUR--
--YEAH, WHICH MEANS I AIN'T GETTING' *FUCKIN'* NEAR 'IM 'TIL I KNOW WHAT'S *FUCKIN'* UP--AN' SINCE YOU WORK THERE, YER GONNA FERRET THAT OUT FER ME, COMPRENDE, *AMIGO?*
WHERE'S A BAR--A REGULAR *FUCKIN'* JOINT, AN' NOT ONE A THESE SOUTH BEACH *COCK N'BULLSHIT* SHOWS?
CLUB DEUCE. JUS' DOWN ON FOURTEENTH.
SEE YOU THERE.

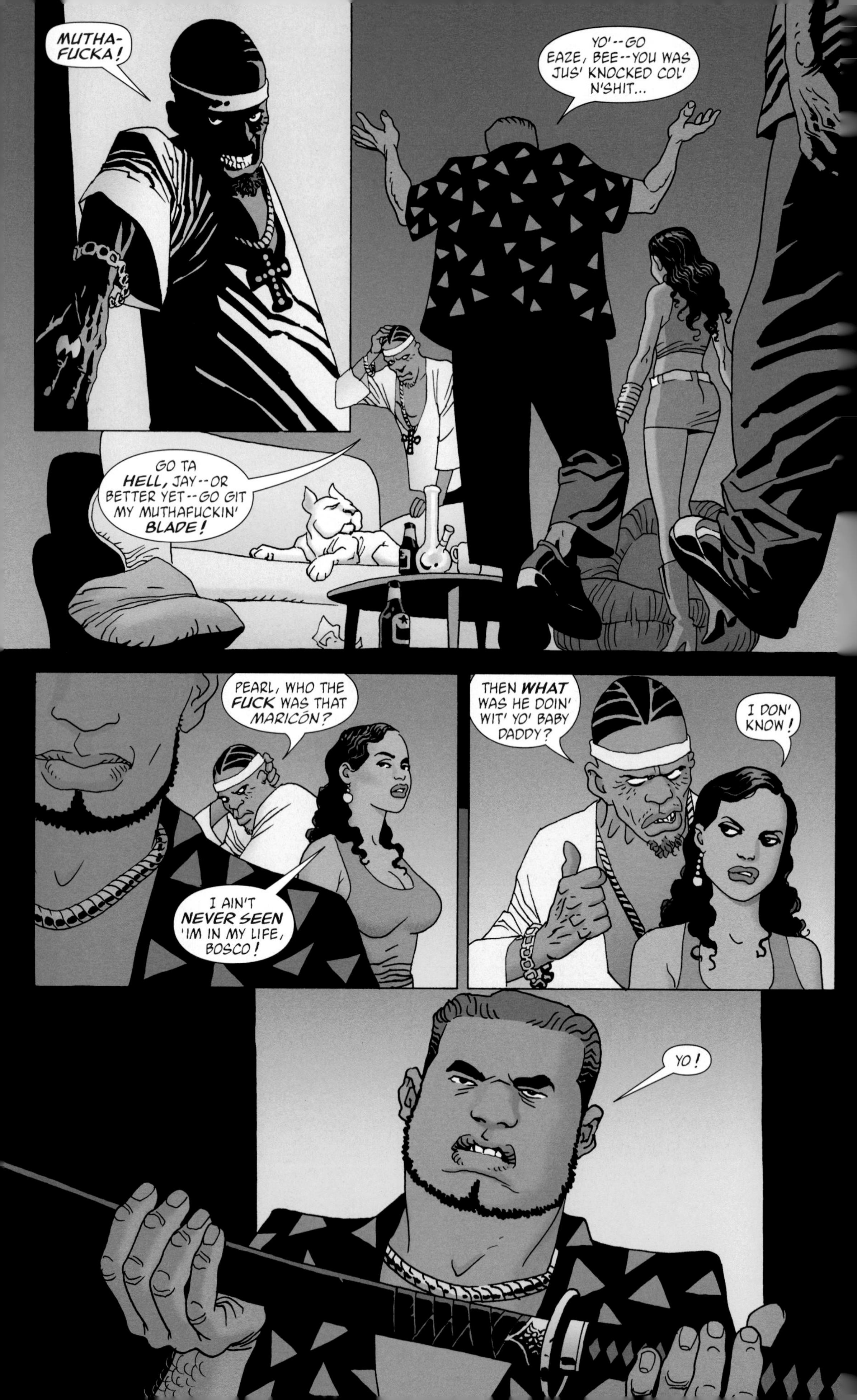
MUTHA-FUCKA!
YO'--GO EAZE, BEE--YOU WAS JUS' KNOCKED COL' N'SHIT...
GO TA HELL, JAY--OR BETTER YET--GO GIT MY MUTHAFUCKIN' BLADE!
PEARL, WHO THE FUCK WAS THAT MARICÓN?
I AIN'T NEVER SEEN 'IM IN MY LIFE, BOSCO!
THEN WHAT WAS HE DOIN' WIT' YO' BABY DADDY?
I DON' KNOW!
YO!

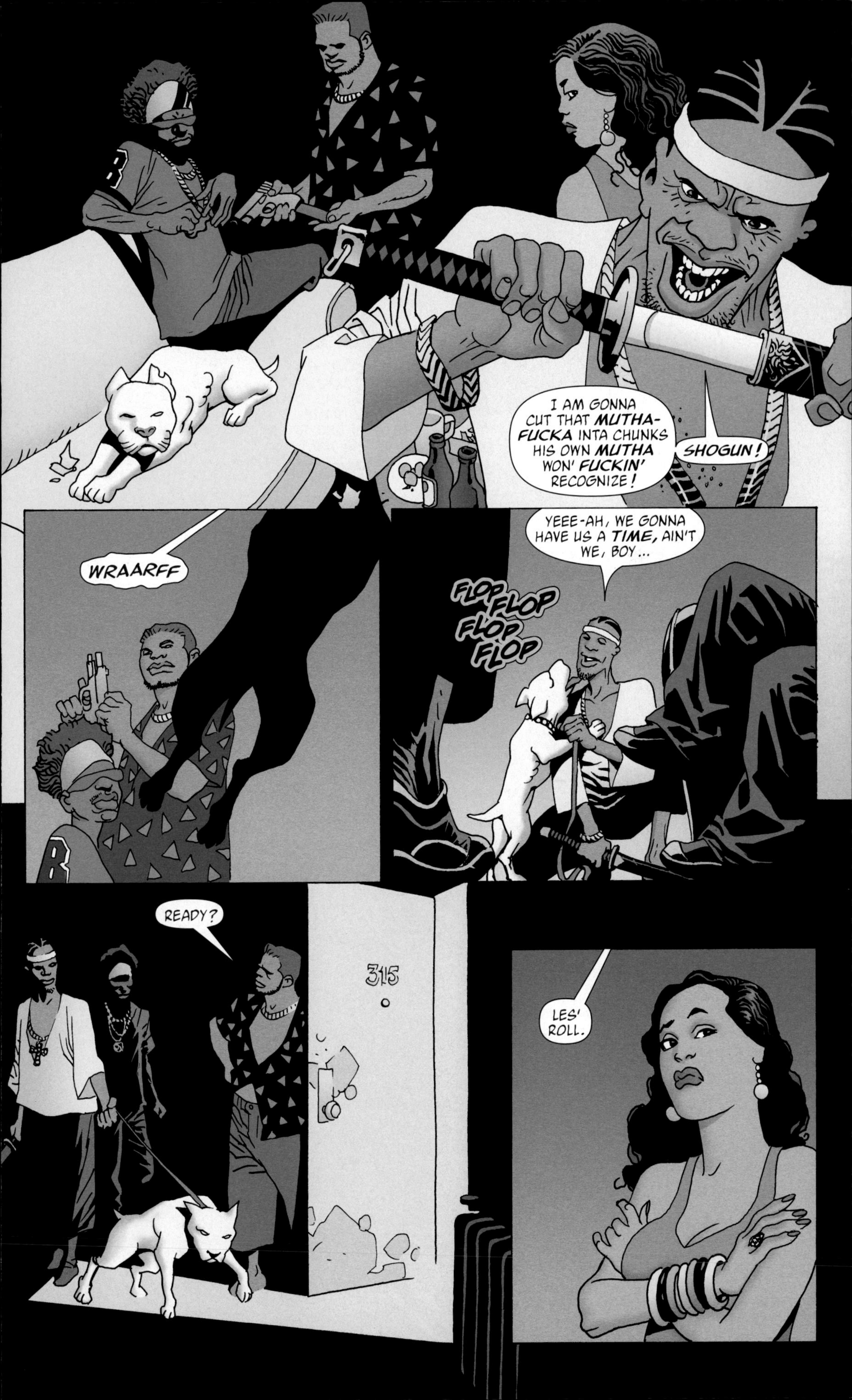
I AM GONNA CUT THAT MUTHA-FUCKA INTA CHUNKS HIS OWN MUTHA WON' FUCKIN' RECOGNIZE!
SHOGUN!
WRAARFF
YEEE-AH, WE GONNA HAVE US A TIME, AIN'T WE, BOY...
FLOP FLOP FLOP FLOP
READY?
315
LES' ROLL.

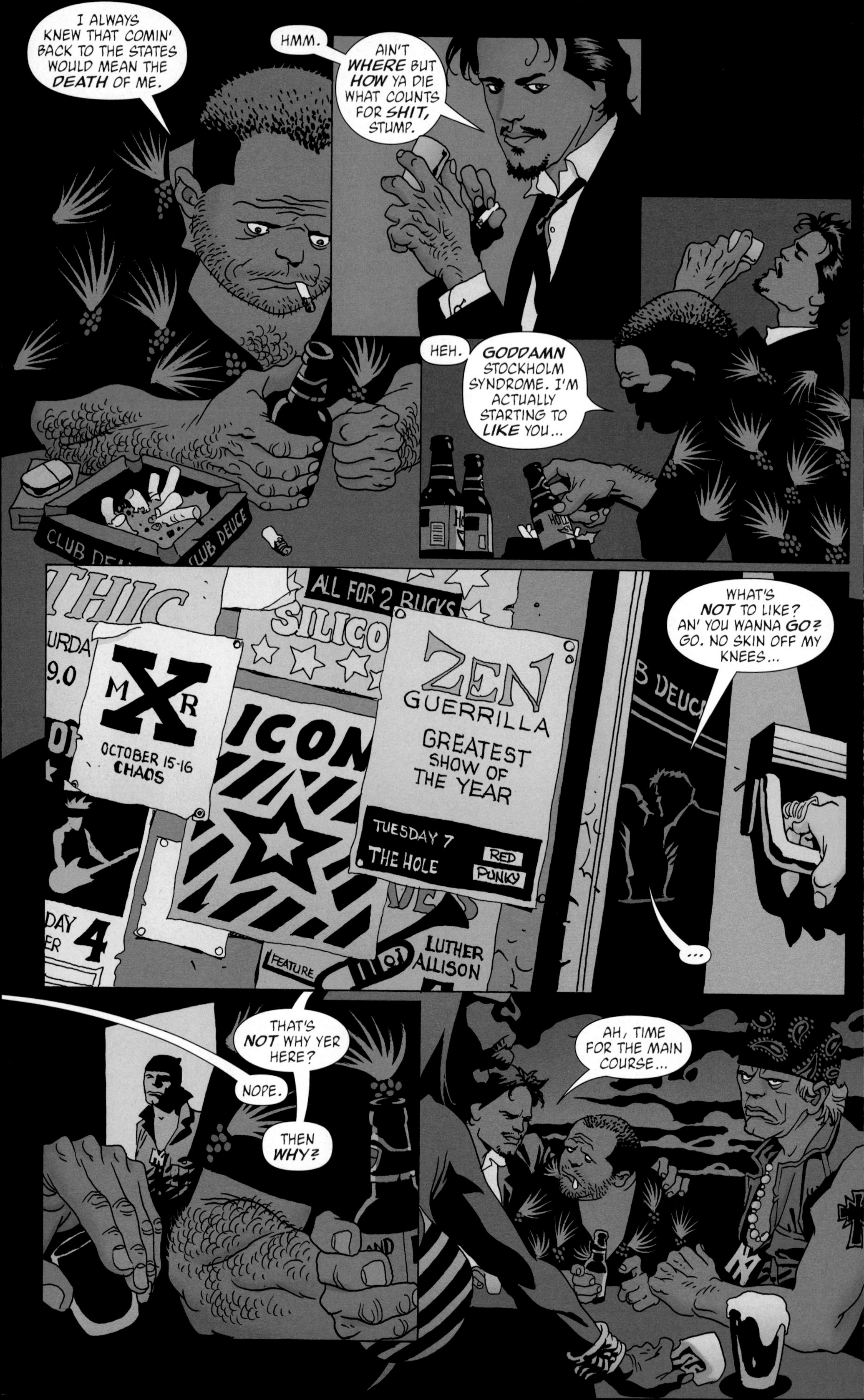
I ALWAYS KNEW THAT COMIN' BACK TO THE STATES WOULD MEAN THE DEATH OF ME.
HMM.
AIN'T WHERE BUT HOW YA DIE WHAT COUNTS FOR SHIT, STUMP.
CLUB DEUCE
CLUB DEUCE
HEH.
GODDAMN STOCKHOLM SYNDROME. I'M ACTUALLY STARTING TO LIKE YOU...
ALL FOR 2 BUCKS
SILICO
OCTOBER 15-16
CHAOS
ICON
ZEN
GUERRILLA
GREATEST SHOW OF THE YEAR
TUESDAY 7
THE HOLE
RED
PUNKY
LUTHER ALLISON
FEATURE
WHAT'S NOT TO LIKE? AN' YOU WANNA GO? GO. NO SKIN OFF MY KNEES...
...
THAT'S NOT WHY YER HERE?
NOPE.
THEN WHY?
AH, TIME FOR THE MAIN COURSE...

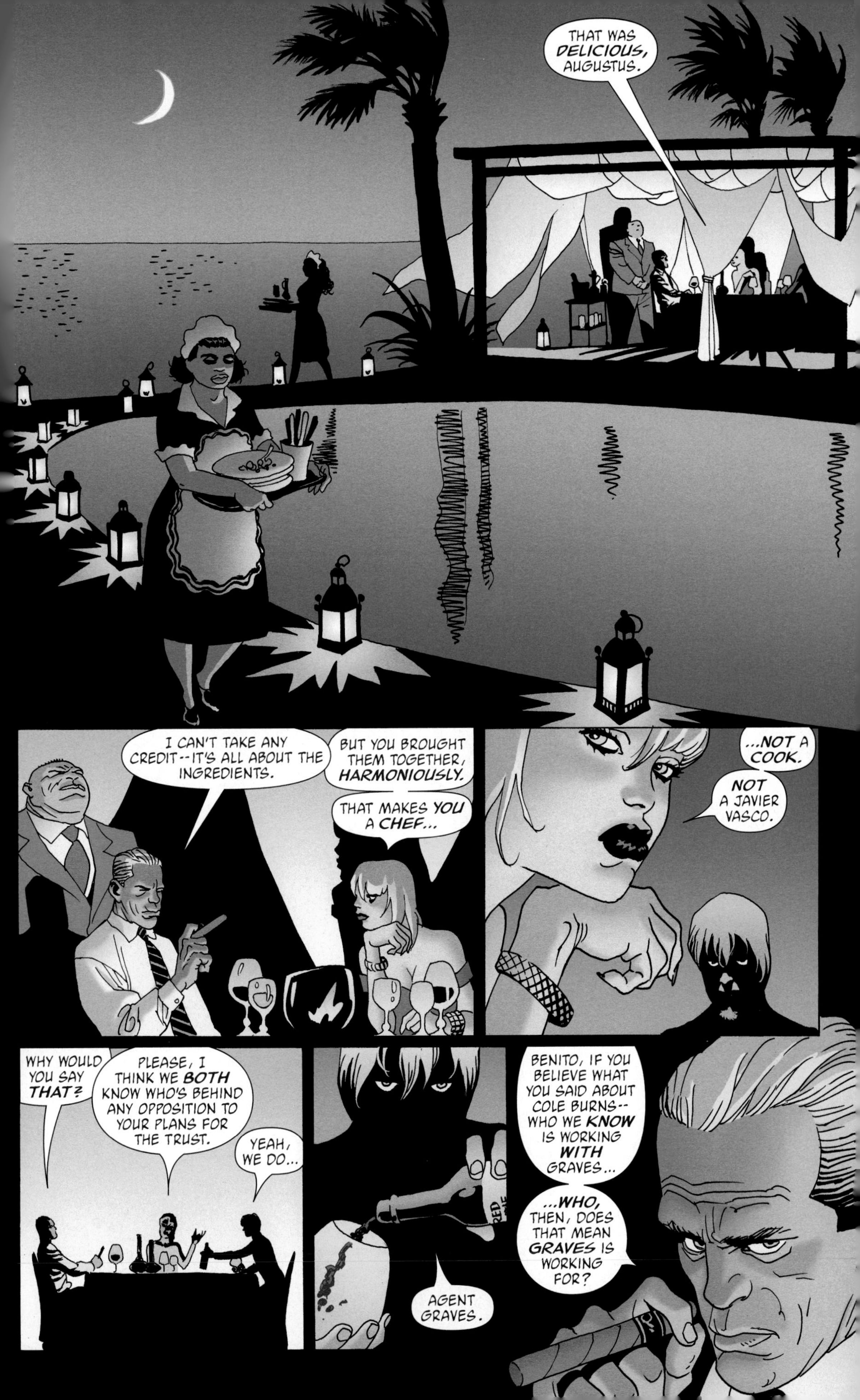
THAT WAS DELICIOUS, AUGUSTUS.
I CAN'T TAKE ANY CREDIT--IT'S ALL ABOUT THE INGREDIENTS.
BUT YOU BROUGHT THEM TOGETHER, HARMONIOUSLY.
THAT MAKES YOU A CHEF...
...NOT A COOK.
NOT A JAVIER VASCO.
WHY WOULD YOU SAY THAT?
PLEASE, I THINK WE BOTH KNOW WHO'S BEHIND ANY OPPOSITION TO YOUR PLANS FOR THE TRUST.
YEAH, WE DO...
AGENT GRAVES.
BENITO, IF YOU BELIEVE WHAT YOU SAID ABOUT COLE BURNS--WHO WE KNOW IS WORKING WITH GRAVES...
...WHO, THEN, DOES THAT MEAN GRAVES IS WORKING FOR?

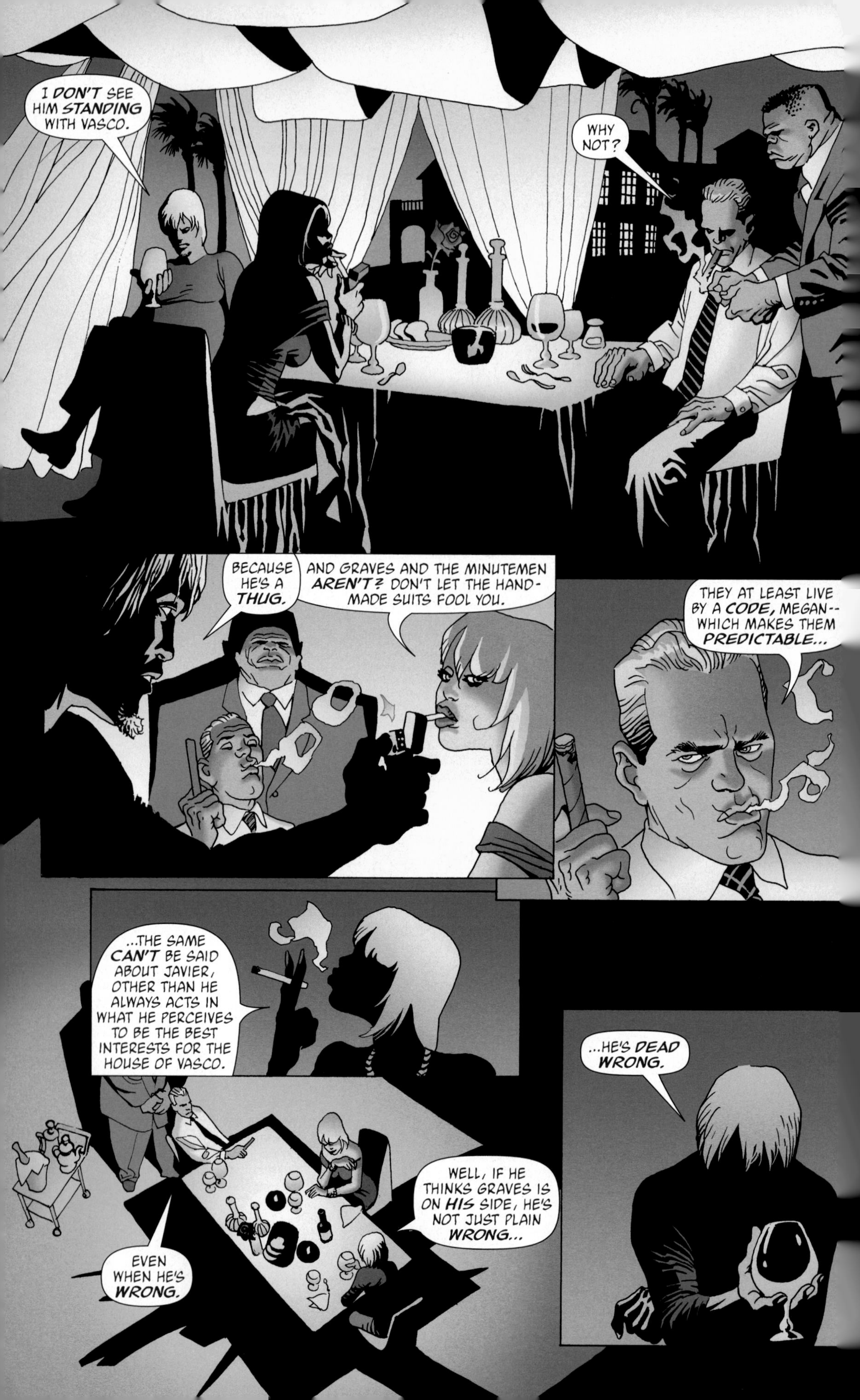
I DON'T SEE HIM STANDING WITH VASCO.
WHY NOT?
BECAUSE HE'S A THUG.
AND GRAVES AND THE MINUTEMEN AREN'T? DON'T LET THE HAND-MADE SUITS FOOL YOU.
THEY AT LEAST LIVE BY A CODE, MEGAN-- WHICH MAKES THEM PREDICTABLE...
...THE SAME CAN'T BE SAID ABOUT JAVIER, OTHER THAN HE ALWAYS ACTS IN WHAT HE PERCEIVES TO BE THE BEST INTERESTS FOR THE HOUSE OF VASCO.
EVEN WHEN HE'S WRONG.
WELL, IF HE THINKS GRAVES IS ON HIS SIDE, HE'S NOT JUST PLAIN WRONG...
...HE'S DEAD WRONG.

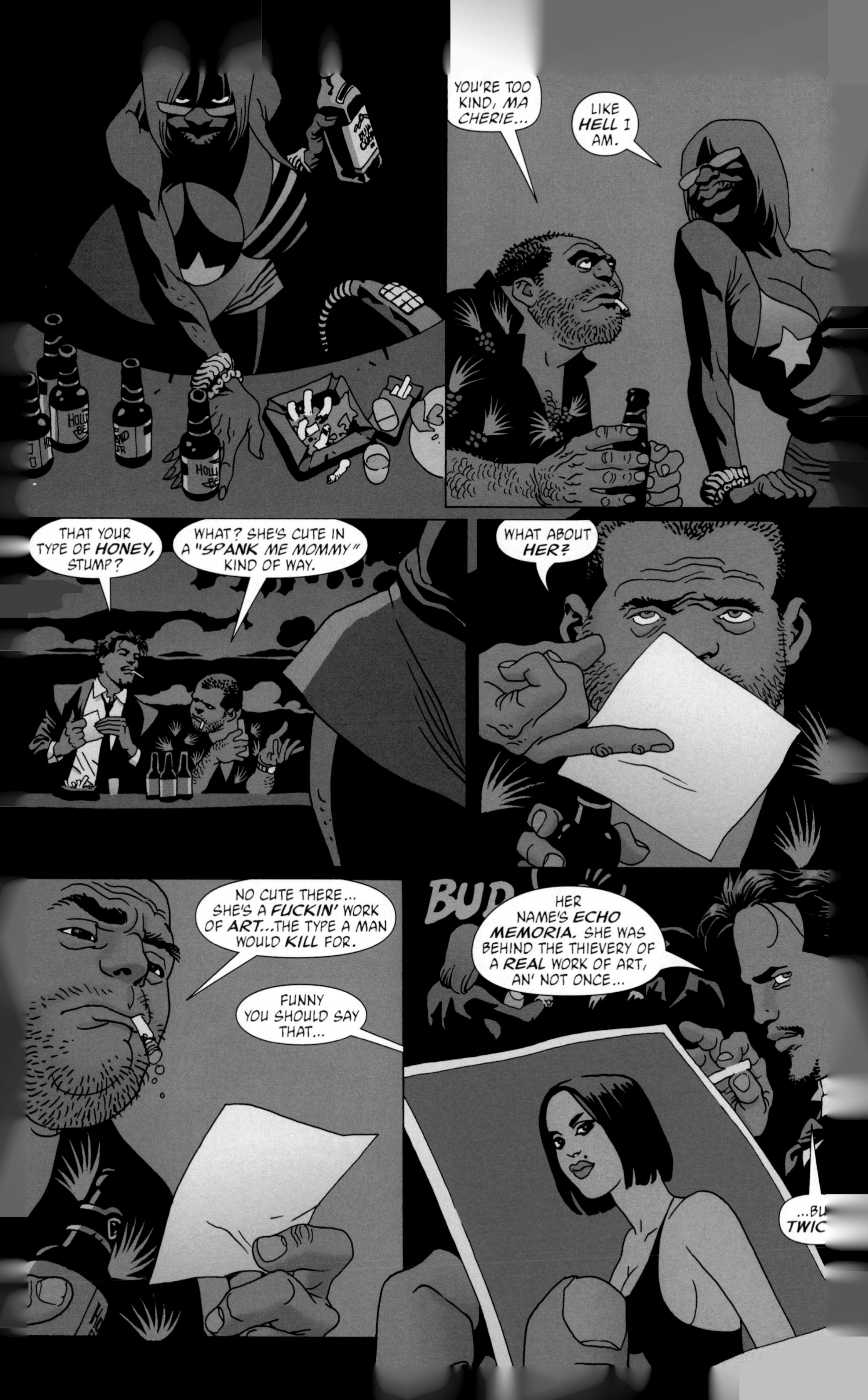
YOU'RE TOO KIND, MA CHERIE...
LIKE HELL I AM.
THAT YOUR TYPE OF HONEY, STUMP?
WHAT? SHE'S CUTE IN A "SPANK ME MOMMY" KIND OF WAY.
WHAT ABOUT HER?
NO CUTE THERE... SHE'S A FUCKIN' WORK OF ART...THE TYPE A MAN WOULD KILL FOR.
FUNNY YOU SHOULD SAY THAT...
BUD
HER NAME'S ECHO MEMORIA. SHE WAS BEHIND THE THIEVERY OF A REAL WORK OF ART, AN' NOT ONCE...
...BU
TWIC

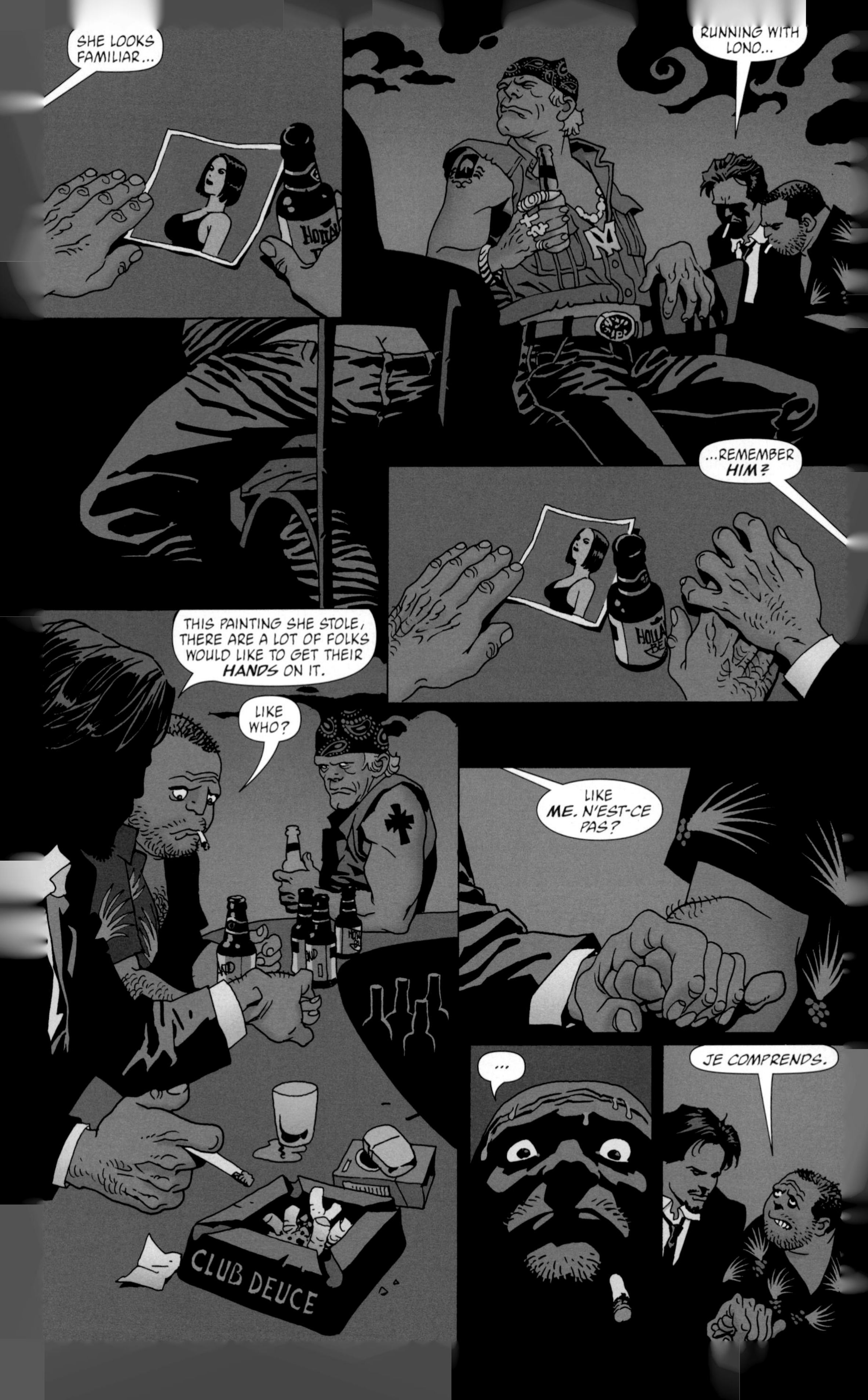

SHE LOOKS FAMILIAR...
RUNNING WITH LONO...
...REMEMBER HIM?
THIS PAINTING SHE STOLE, THERE ARE A LOT OF FOLKS WOULD LIKE TO GET THEIR HANDS ON IT.
LIKE WHO?
LIKE ME. N'EST-CE PAS?
...
JE COMPRENDS.
CLUB DEUCE

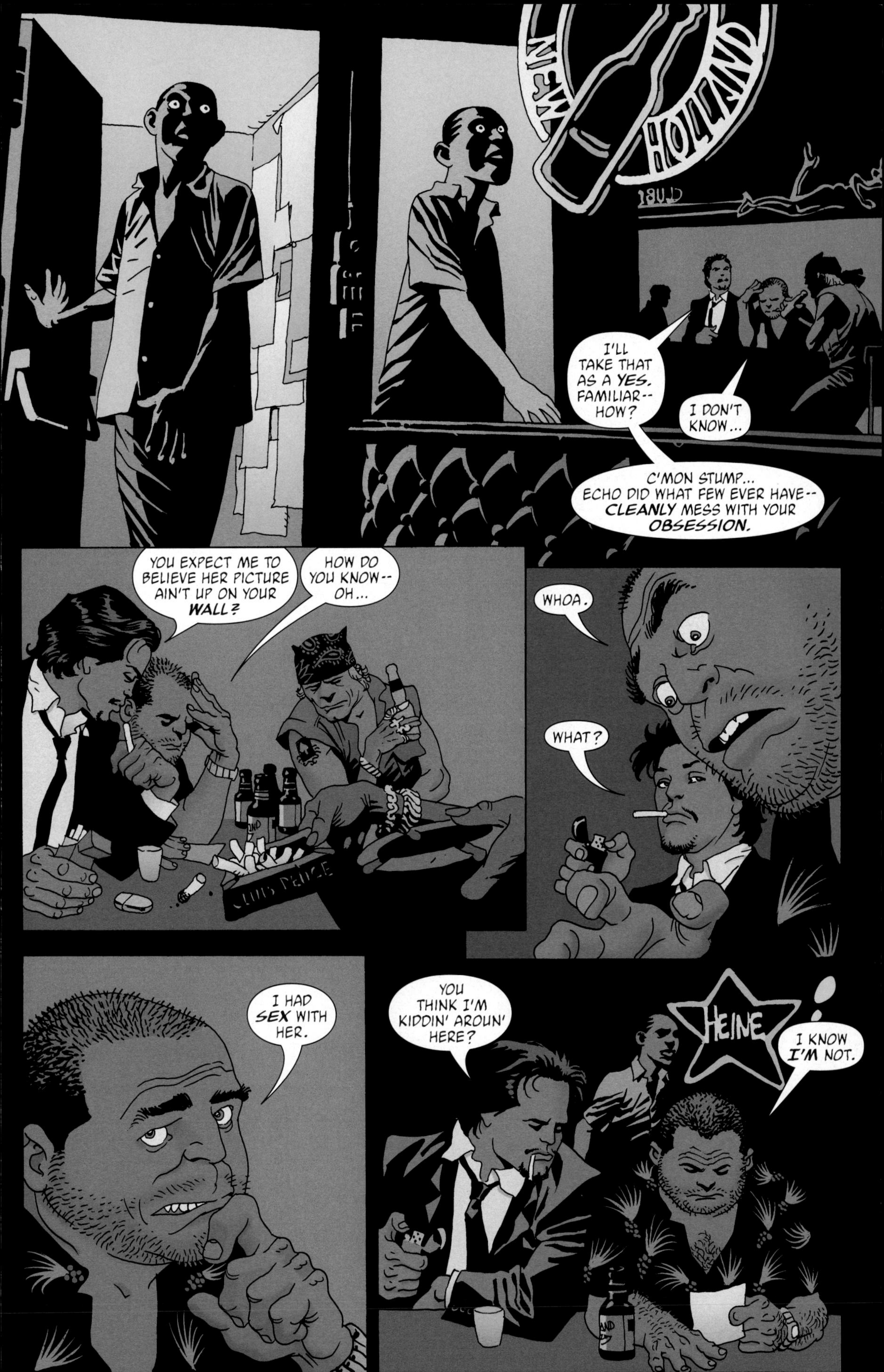
NEW HOLLAND
CLUB
I'LL TAKE THAT AS A YES. FAMILIAR--HOW?
I DON'T KNOW...
C'MON STUMP... ECHO DID WHAT FEW EVER HAVE-- CLEANLY MESS WITH YOUR OBSESSION.
YOU EXPECT ME TO BELIEVE HER PICTURE AIN'T UP ON YOUR WALL?
HOW DO YOU KNOW-- OH...
WHOA.
WHAT?
I HAD SEX WITH HER.
YOU THINK I'M KIDDIN' AROUN' HERE?
HEINE
I KNOW I'M NOT.

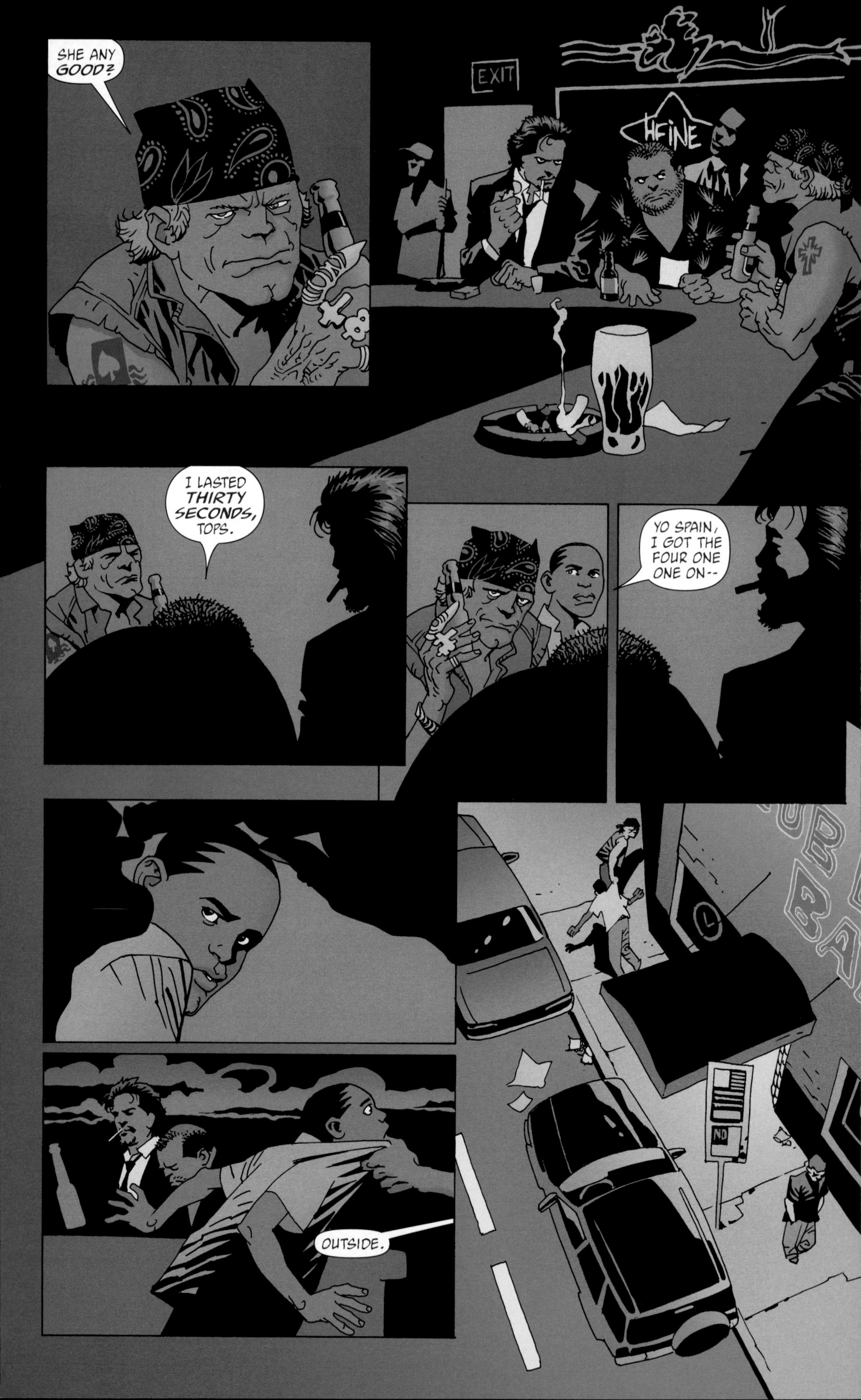
SHE ANY GOOD?
I LASTED THIRTY SECONDS, TOPS.
YO SPAIN, I GOT THE FOUR ONE ONE ON--
OUTSIDE.

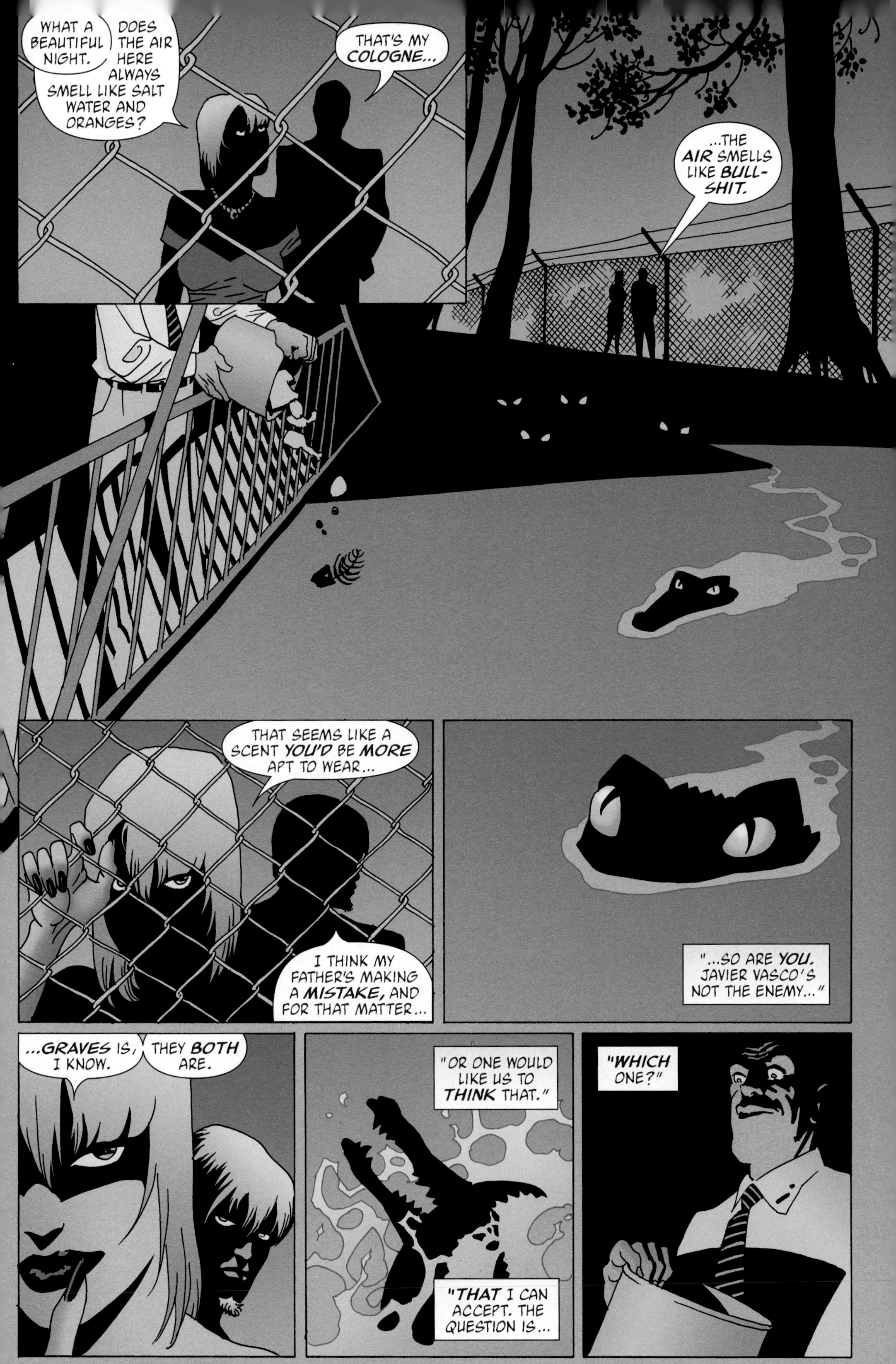
WHAT A BEAUTIFUL NIGHT.
DOES THE AIR HERE ALWAYS SMELL LIKE SALT WATER AND ORANGES?
THAT'S MY COLOGNE...
...THE AIR SMELLS LIKE BULL-SHIT.
THAT SEEMS LIKE A SCENT YOU'D BE MORE APT TO WEAR...
I THINK MY FATHER'S MAKING A MISTAKE, AND FOR THAT MATTER...
"...SO ARE YOU. JAVIER VASCO'S NOT THE ENEMY..."
...GRAVES IS, I KNOW.
THEY BOTH ARE.
"OR ONE WOULD LIKE US TO THINK THAT."
"THAT I CAN ACCEPT. THE QUESTION IS...
"WHICH ONE?"

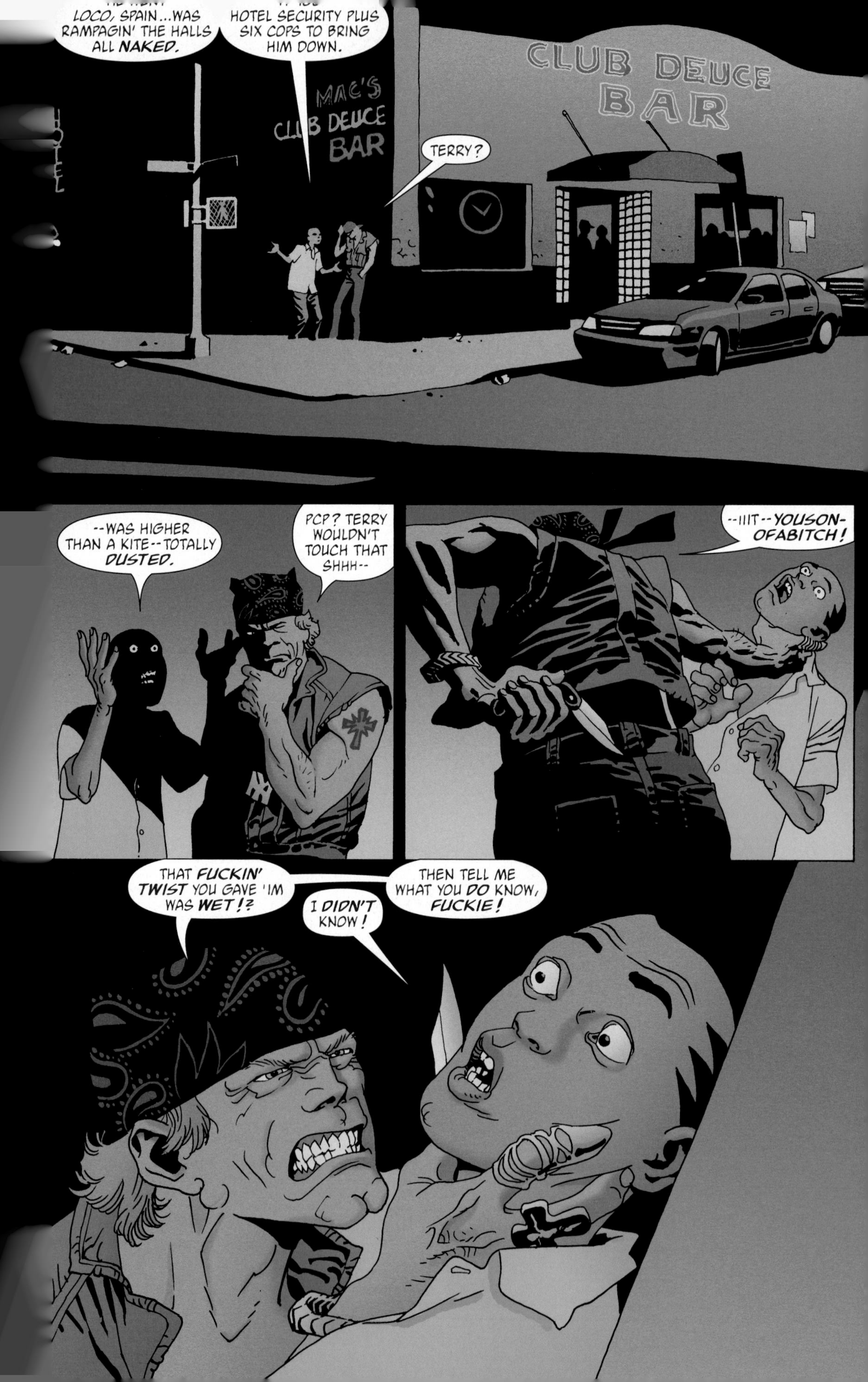
LOCO, SPAIN...WAS RAMPAGIN' THE HALLS ALL NAKED.
HOTEL SECURITY PLUS SIX COPS TO BRING HIM DOWN.
MAC'S CLUB DEUCE BAR
HOTEL
CLUB DEUCE BAR
TERRY?
--WAS HIGHER THAN A KITE--TOTALLY DUSTED.
PCP? TERRY WOULDN'T TOUCH THAT SHHH--
--IIIT--YOUSON-OFABITCH!
THAT FUCKIN' TWIST YOU GAVE 'IM WAS WET!?
I DIDN'T KNOW!
THEN TELL ME WHAT YOU DO KNOW, FUCKIE!

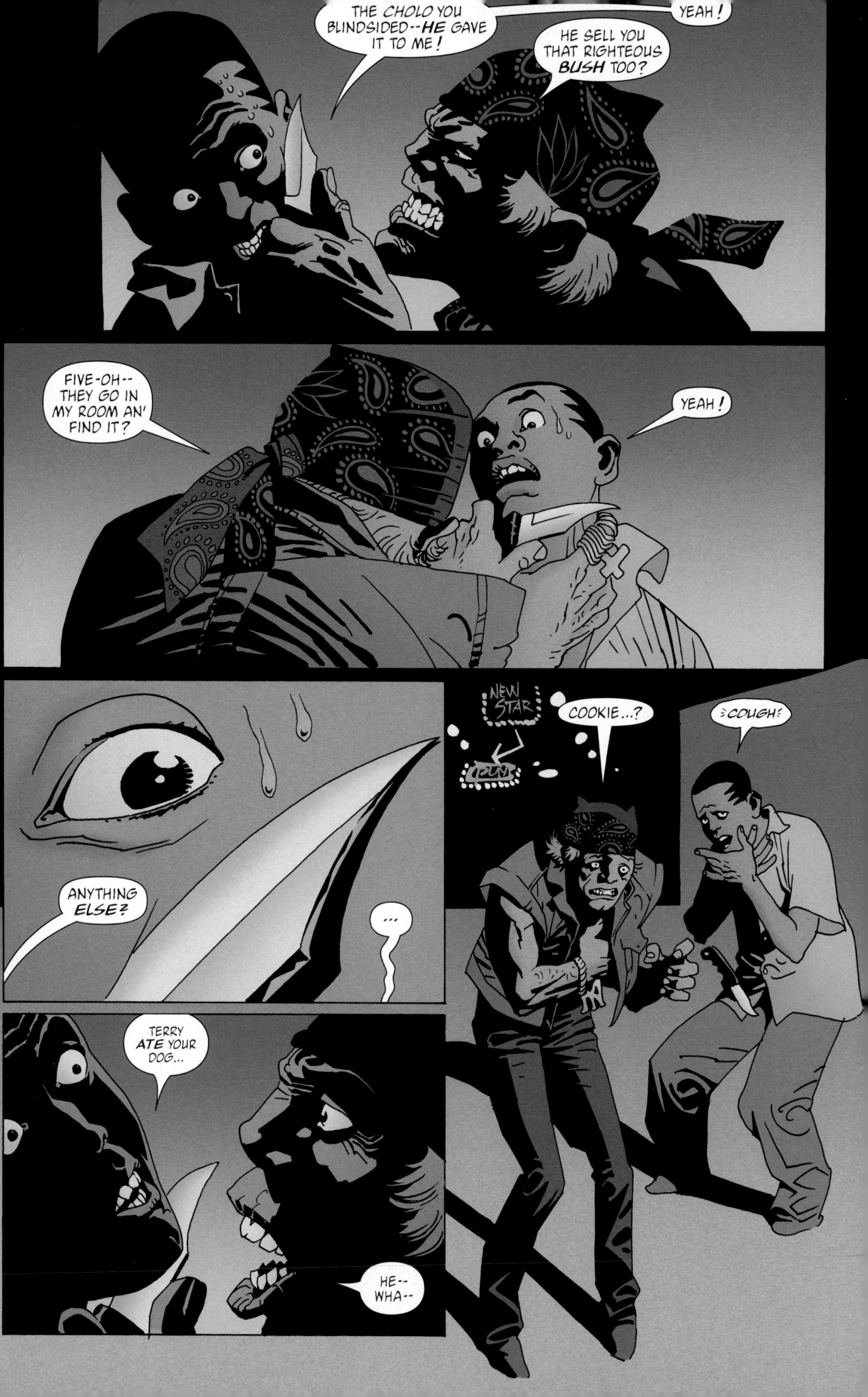
THE CHOLO YOU BLINDSIDED--HE GAVE IT TO ME!
YEAH!
HE SELL YOU THAT RIGHTEOUS BUSH TOO?
FIVE-OH--THEY GO IN MY ROOM AN' FIND IT?
YEAH!
ANYTHING ELSE?
...
TERRY ATE YOUR DOG...
HE--WHA--
NEW STAR
PUN
COOKIE...?
COUGH

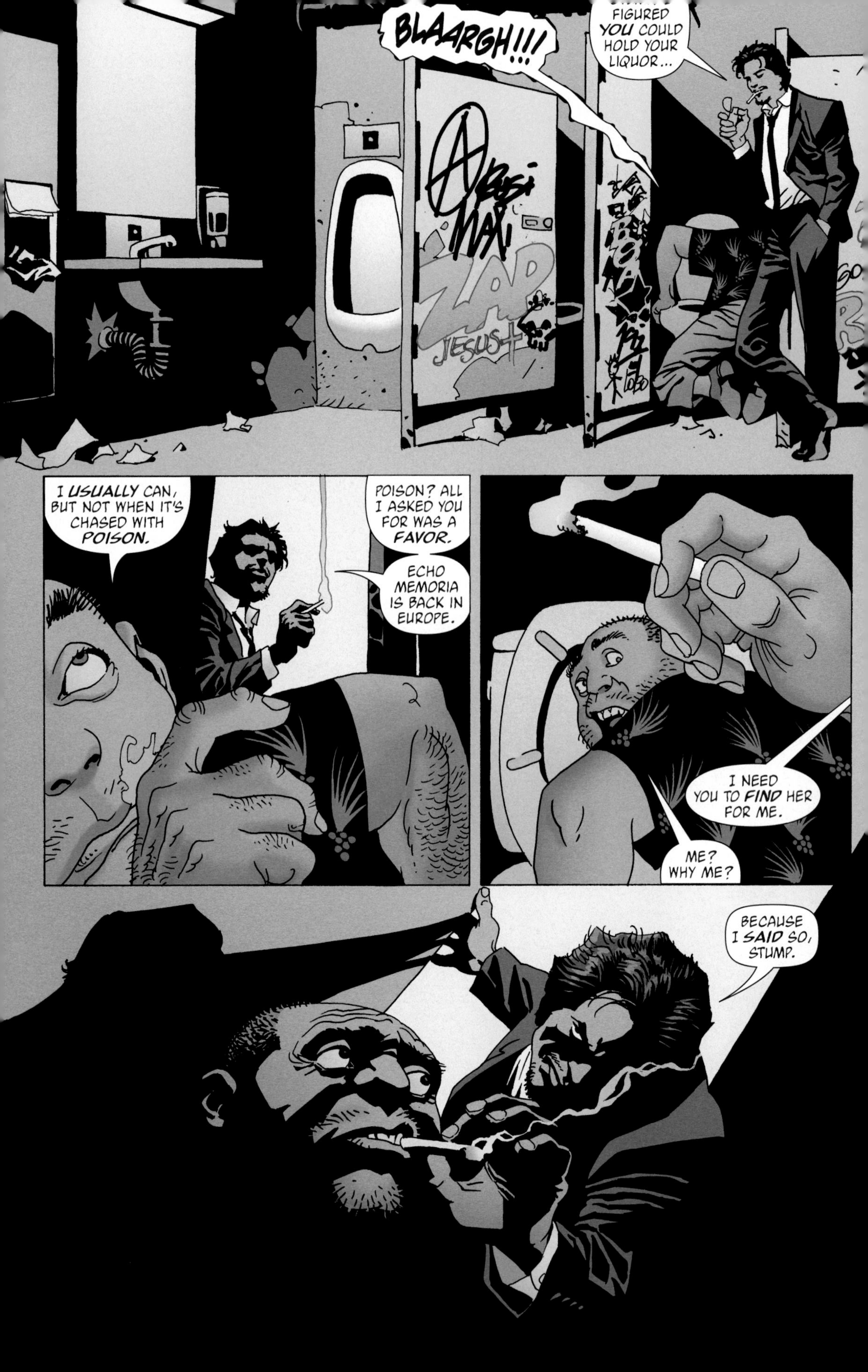

BLAARGH!!!
FIGURED YOU COULD HOLD YOUR LIQUOR...
I USUALLY CAN, BUT NOT WHEN IT'S CHASED WITH POISON.
POISON? ALL I ASKED YOU FOR WAS A FAVOR.
ECHO MEMORIA IS BACK IN EUROPE.
I NEED YOU TO FIND HER FOR ME.
ME? WHY ME?
BECAUSE I SAID SO, STUMP.

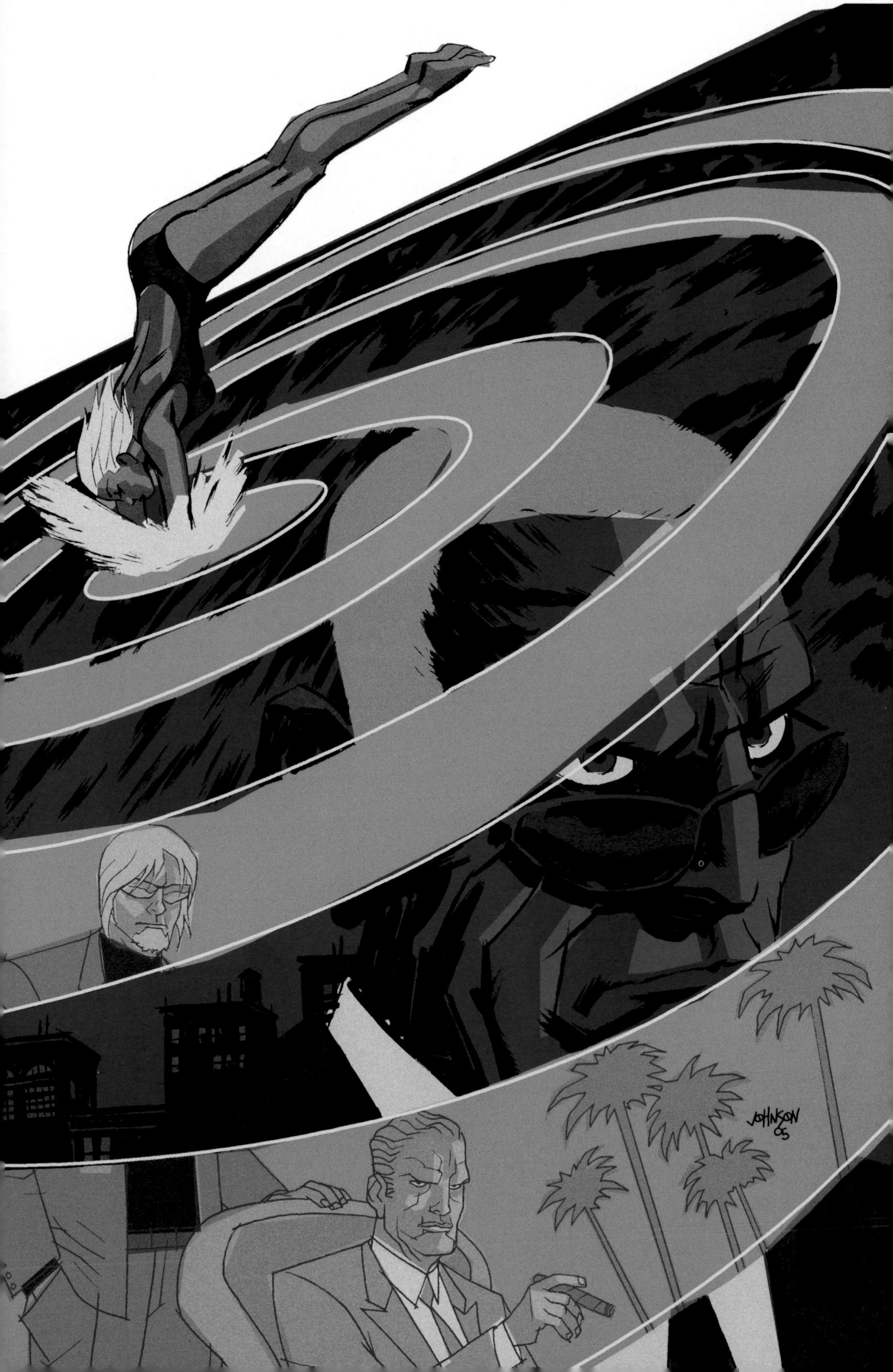
JOHNSON 05

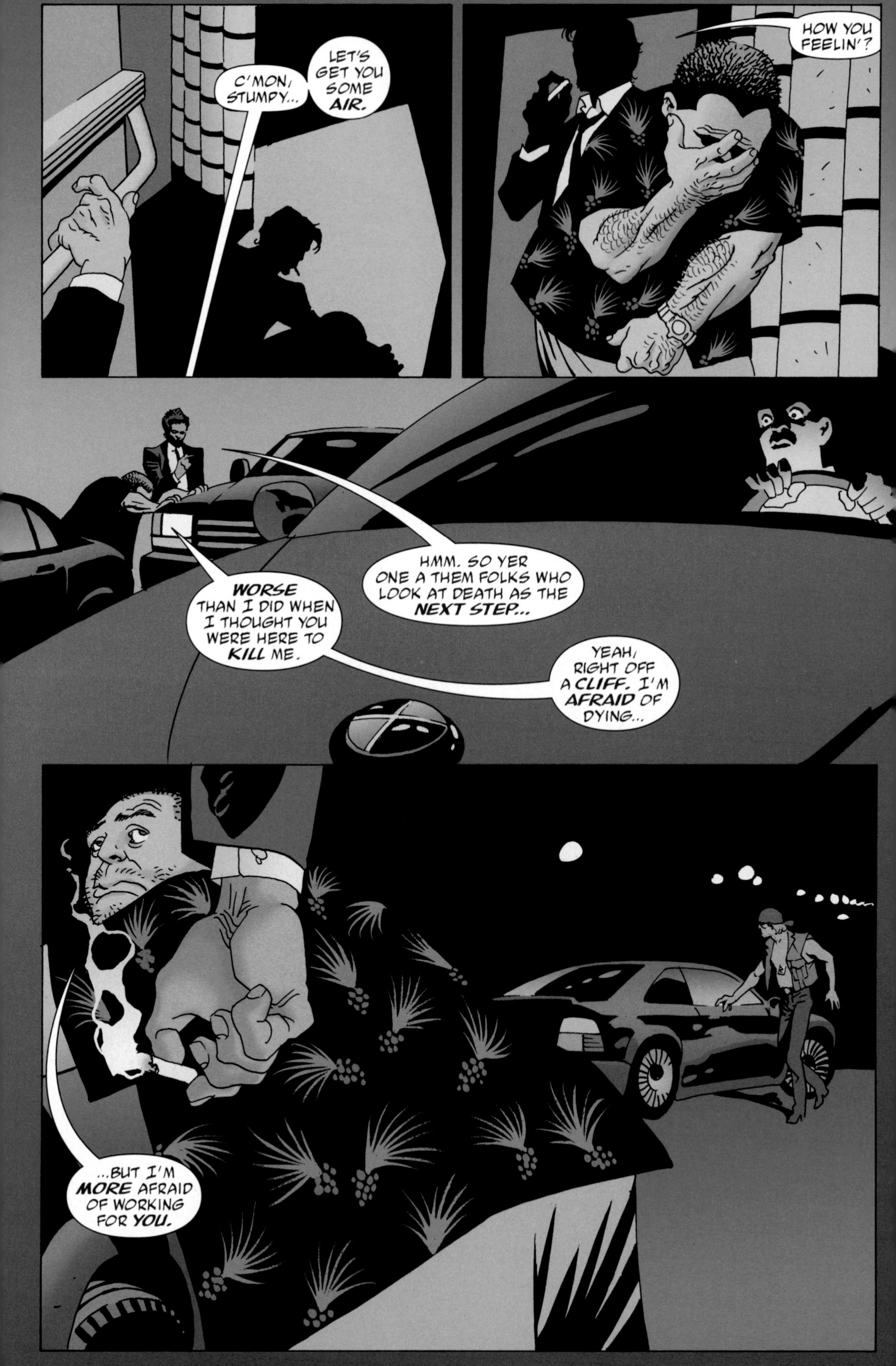
C'MON, STUMPY...
LET'S GET YOU SOME AIR.
HOW YOU FEELIN'?
WORSE THAN I DID WHEN I THOUGHT YOU WERE HERE TO KILL ME.
HMM. SO YER ONE A THEM FOLKS WHO LOOK AT DEATH AS THE NEXT STEP...
YEAH, RIGHT OFF A CLIFF. I'M AFRAID OF DYING...
...BUT I'M MORE AFRAID OF WORKING FOR YOU.

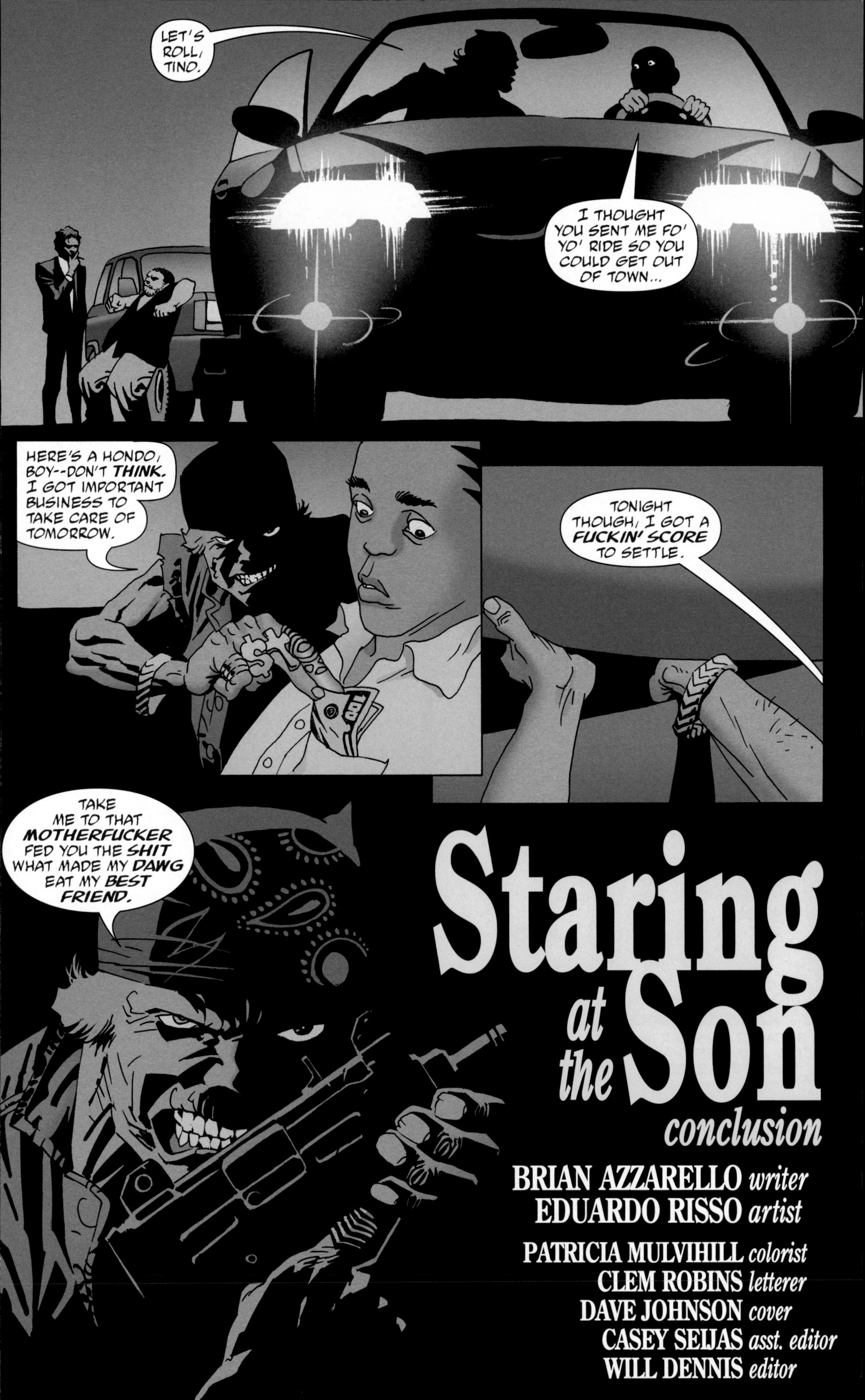
LET'S ROLL, TINO.
I THOUGHT YOU SENT ME FO' YO' RIDE SO YOU COULD GET OUT OF TOWN...
HERE'S A HONDO, BOY--DON'T THINK. I GOT IMPORTANT BUSINESS TO TAKE CARE OF TOMORROW.
TONIGHT THOUGH, I GOT A FUCKIN' SCORE TO SETTLE.
TAKE ME TO THAT MOTHERFUCKER FED YOU THE SHIT WHAT MADE MY DAWG EAT MY BEST FRIEND.
Staring at the Son
conclusion
BRIAN AZZARELLO writer
EDUARDO RISSO artist
PATRICIA MULVIHILL colorist
CLEM ROBINS letterer
DAVE JOHNSON cover
CASEY SEIJAS asst. editor
WILL DENNIS editor

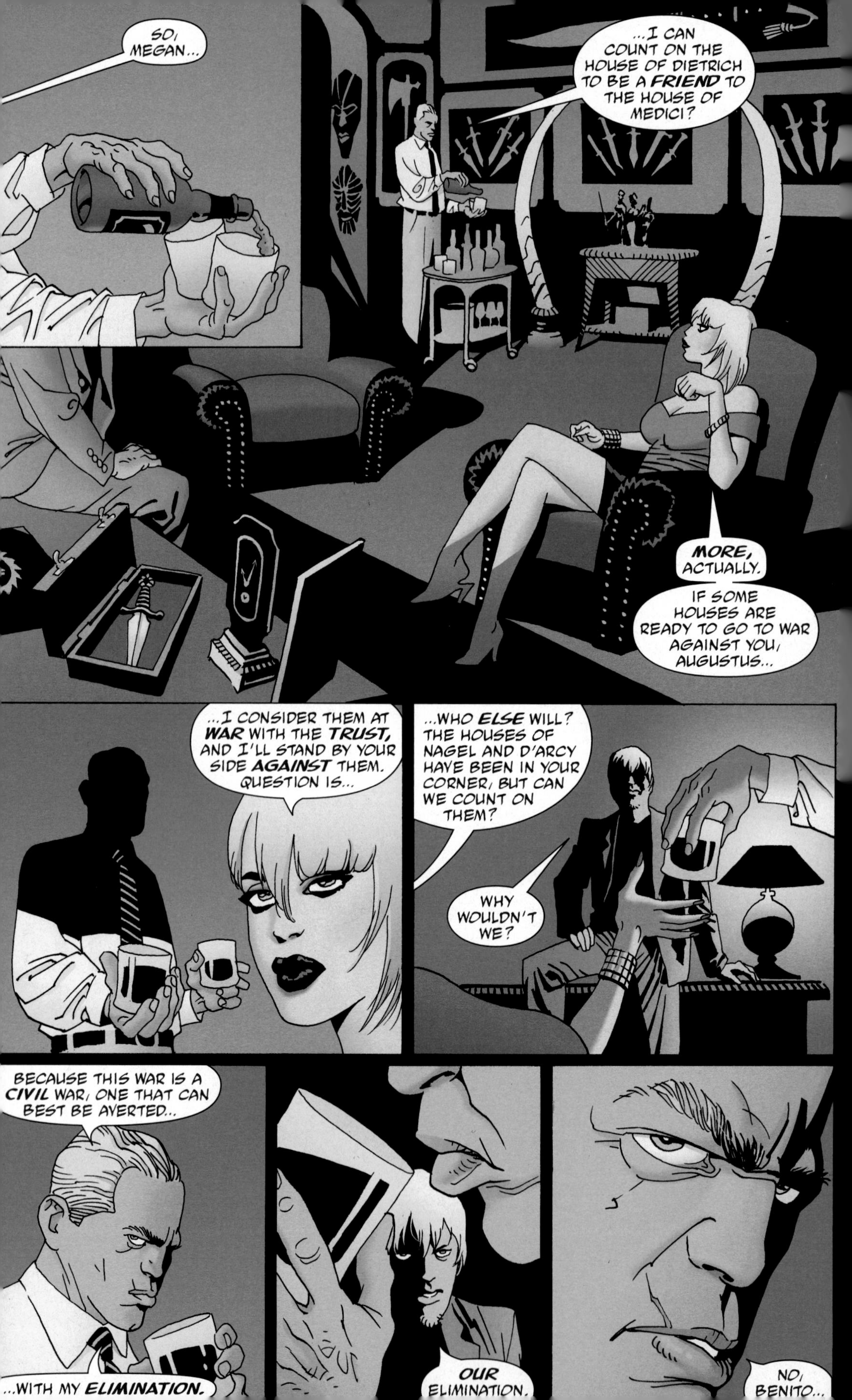
SO, MEGAN...
...I CAN COUNT ON THE HOUSE OF DIETRICH TO BE A **FRIEND** TO THE HOUSE OF MEDICI?
MORE, ACTUALLY.
IF SOME HOUSES ARE READY TO GO TO WAR AGAINST YOU, AUGUSTUS...
...I CONSIDER THEM AT **WAR** WITH THE **TRUST,** AND I'LL STAND BY YOUR SIDE **AGAINST** THEM. QUESTION IS...
...WHO **ELSE** WILL? THE HOUSES OF NAGEL AND D'ARCY HAVE BEEN IN YOUR CORNER, BUT CAN WE COUNT ON THEM?
WHY WOULDN'T WE?
BECAUSE THIS WAR IS A **CIVIL** WAR, ONE THAT CAN BEST BE AVERTED...
...WITH MY **ELIMINATION.**
OUR ELIMINATION.
NO, BENITO...

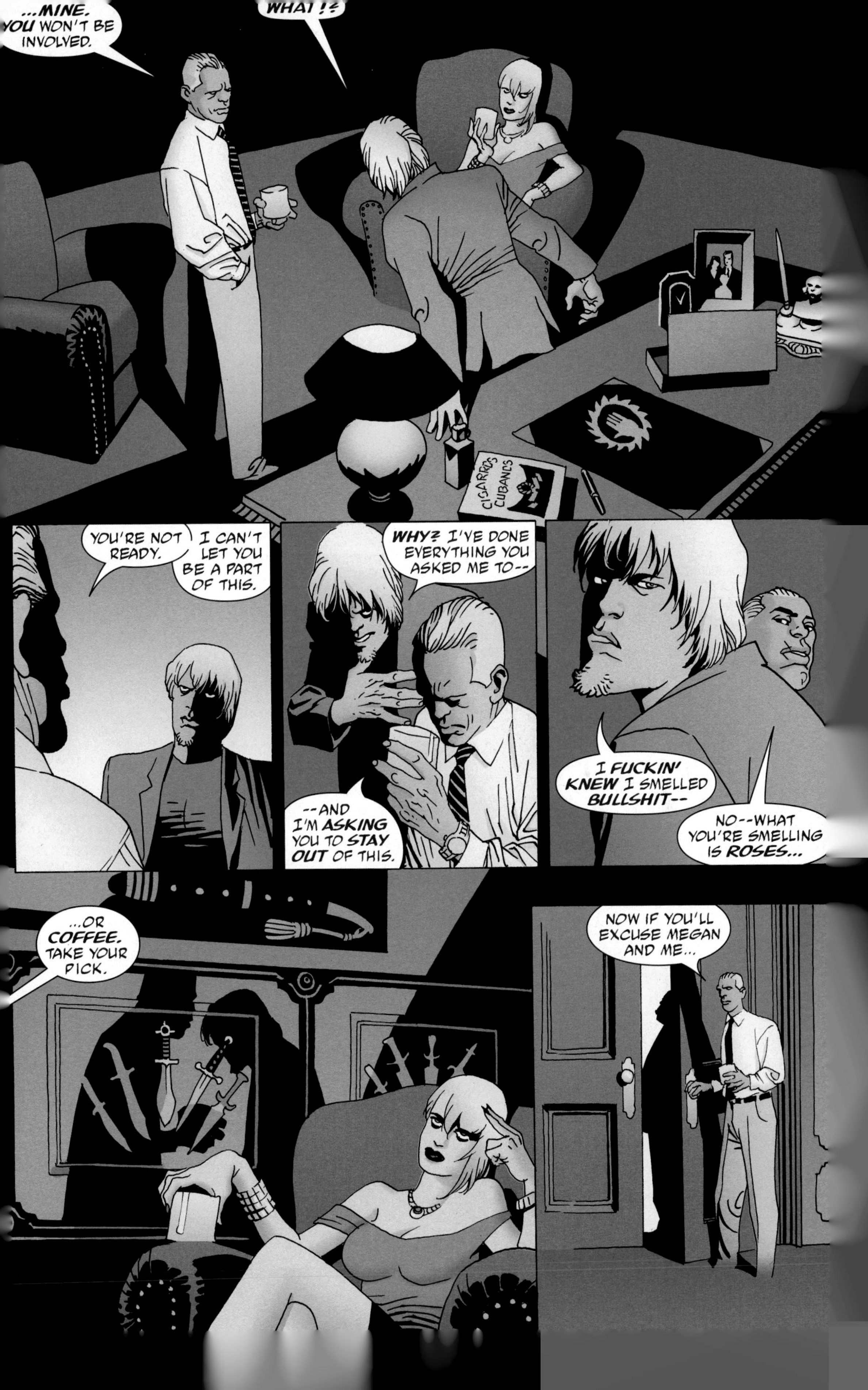
...MINE. YOU WON'T BE INVOLVED.
WHAT!?
YOU'RE NOT READY.
I CAN'T LET YOU BE A PART OF THIS.
WHY? I'VE DONE EVERYTHING YOU ASKED ME TO--
--AND I'M ASKING YOU TO STAY OUT OF THIS.
I FUCKIN' KNEW I SMELLED BULLSHIT--
NO--WHAT YOU'RE SMELLING IS ROSES...
...OR COFFEE. TAKE YOUR PICK.
NOW IF YOU'LL EXCUSE MEGAN AND ME...
CIGARROS CUBANOS

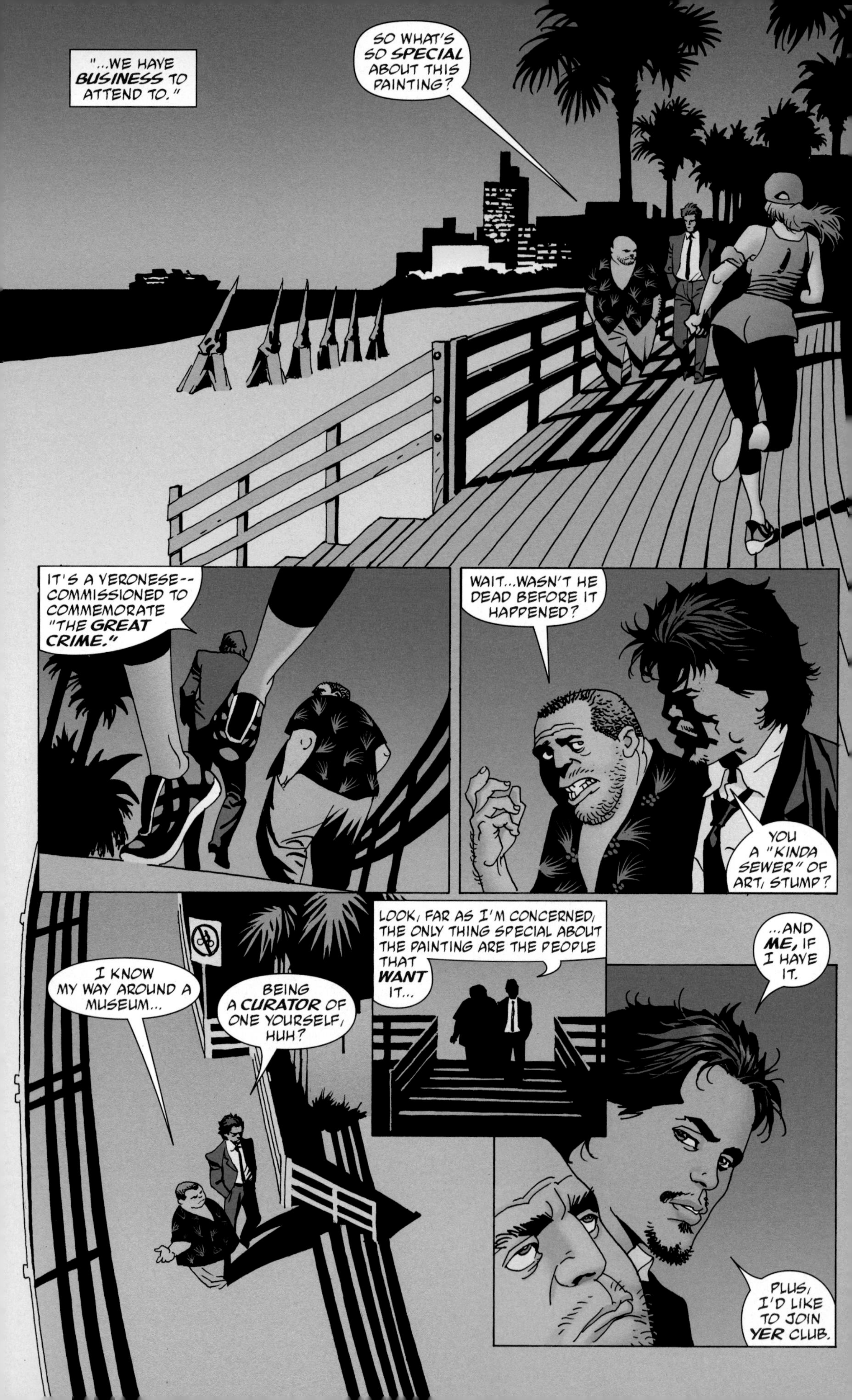
"...WE HAVE BUSINESS TO ATTEND TO."
SO WHAT'S SO SPECIAL ABOUT THIS PAINTING?
IT'S A VERONESE-- COMMISSIONED TO COMMEMORATE "THE GREAT CRIME."
WAIT...WASN'T HE DEAD BEFORE IT HAPPENED?
YOU A "KINDA SEWER" OF ART, STUMP?
I KNOW MY WAY AROUND A MUSEUM...
BEING A CURATOR OF ONE YOURSELF, HUH?
LOOK, FAR AS I'M CONCERNED, THE ONLY THING SPECIAL ABOUT THE PAINTING ARE THE PEOPLE THAT WANT IT...
...AND ME, IF I HAVE IT.
PLUS, I'D LIKE TO JOIN YER CLUB.

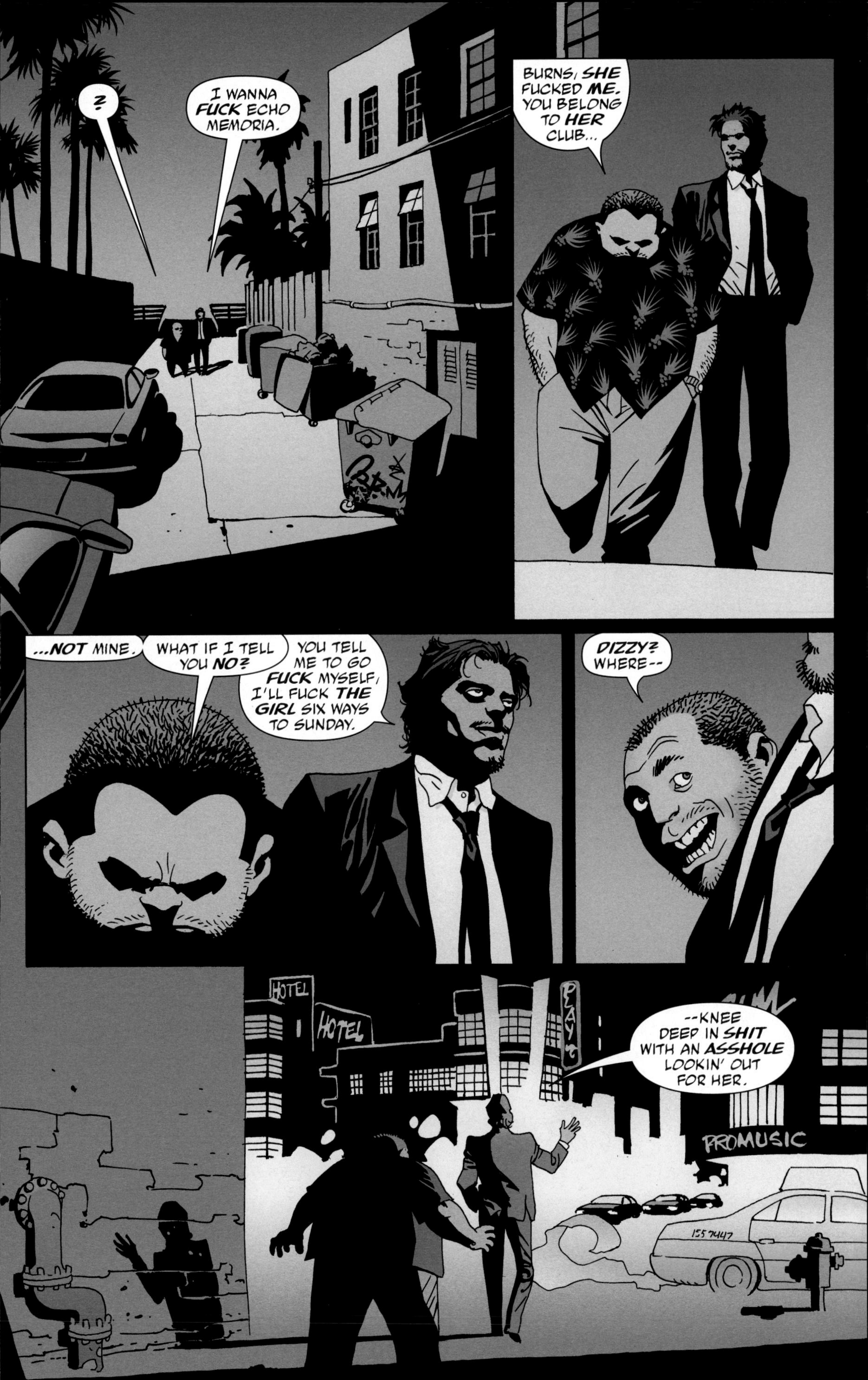
?
I WANNA FUCK ECHO MEMORIA.
BURNS, SHE FUCKED ME. YOU BELONG TO HER CLUB...
...NOT MINE.
WHAT IF I TELL YOU NO?
YOU TELL ME TO GO FUCK MYSELF, I'LL FUCK THE GIRL SIX WAYS TO SUNDAY.
DIZZY? WHERE--
--KNEE DEEP IN SHIT WITH AN ASSHOLE LOOKIN' OUT FOR HER.
HOTEL
HOTEL
PLAY
PROMUSIC
155 7447

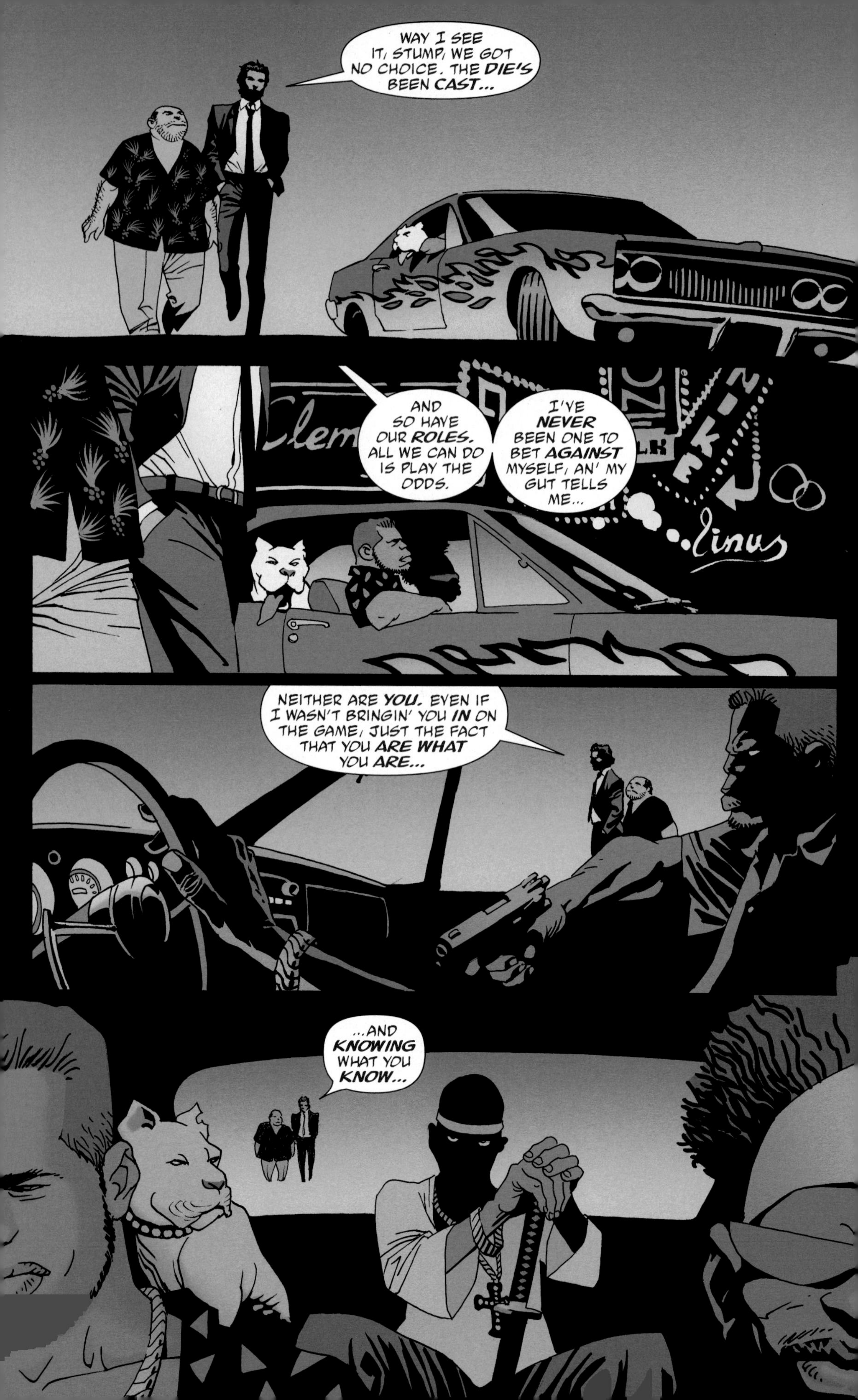
WAY I SEE IT, STUMP, WE GOT NO CHOICE. THE DIE'S BEEN CAST...
AND SO HAVE OUR ROLES. ALL WE CAN DO IS PLAY THE ODDS.
I'VE NEVER BEEN ONE TO BET AGAINST MYSELF, AN' MY GUT TELLS ME...
linus
NEITHER ARE YOU. EVEN IF I WASN'T BRINGIN' YOU IN ON THE GAME, JUST THE FACT THAT YOU ARE WHAT YOU ARE...
...AND KNOWING WHAT YOU KNOW...

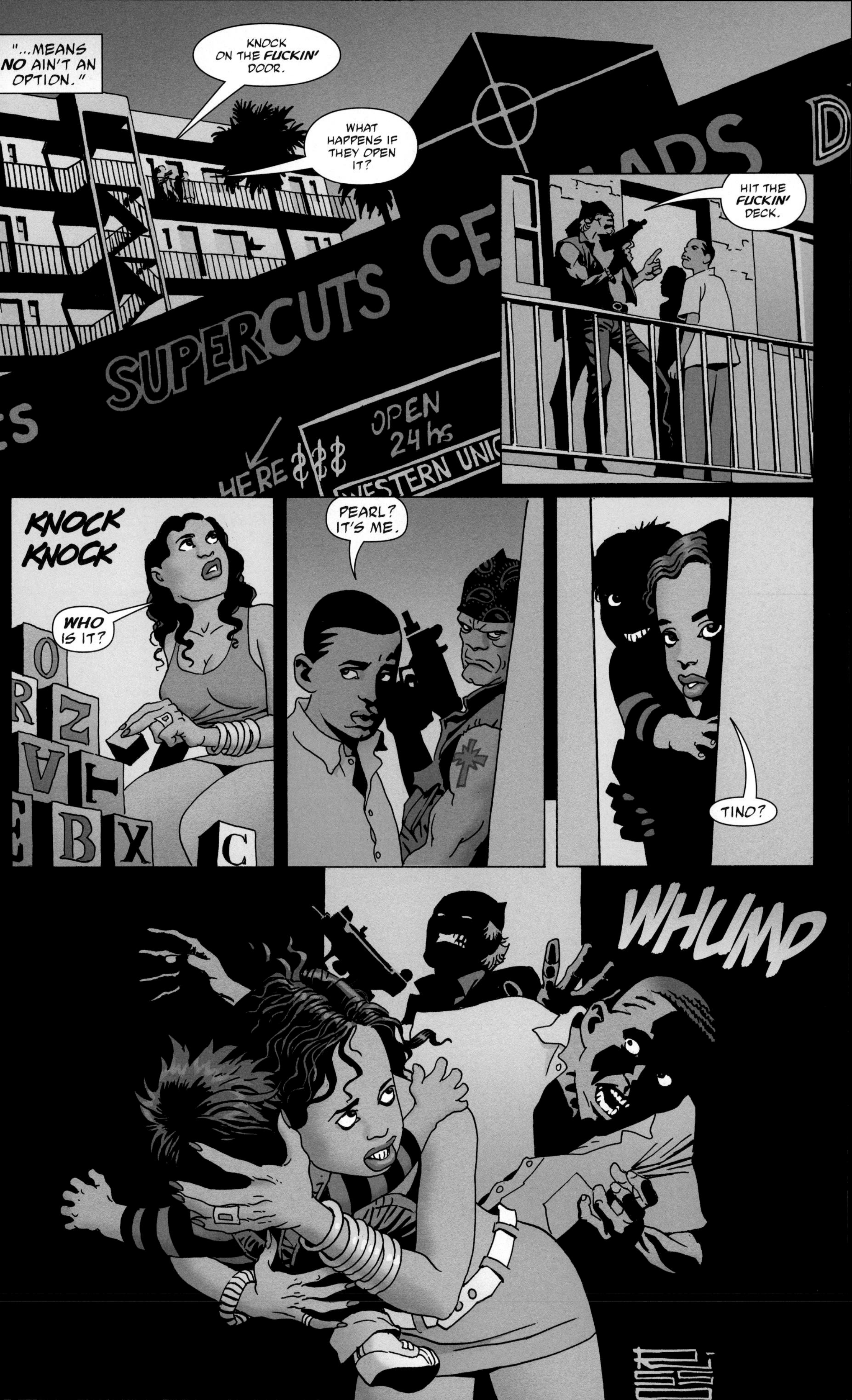
"...MEANS NO AIN'T AN OPTION."
KNOCK ON THE FUCKIN' DOOR.
WHAT HAPPENS IF THEY OPEN IT?
SUPERCUTS CE
HERE $$$
OPEN 24 hs
WESTERN UNI
HIT THE FUCKIN' DECK.
KNOCK KNOCK
WHO IS IT?
PEARL? IT'S ME.
TINO?
WHUMP

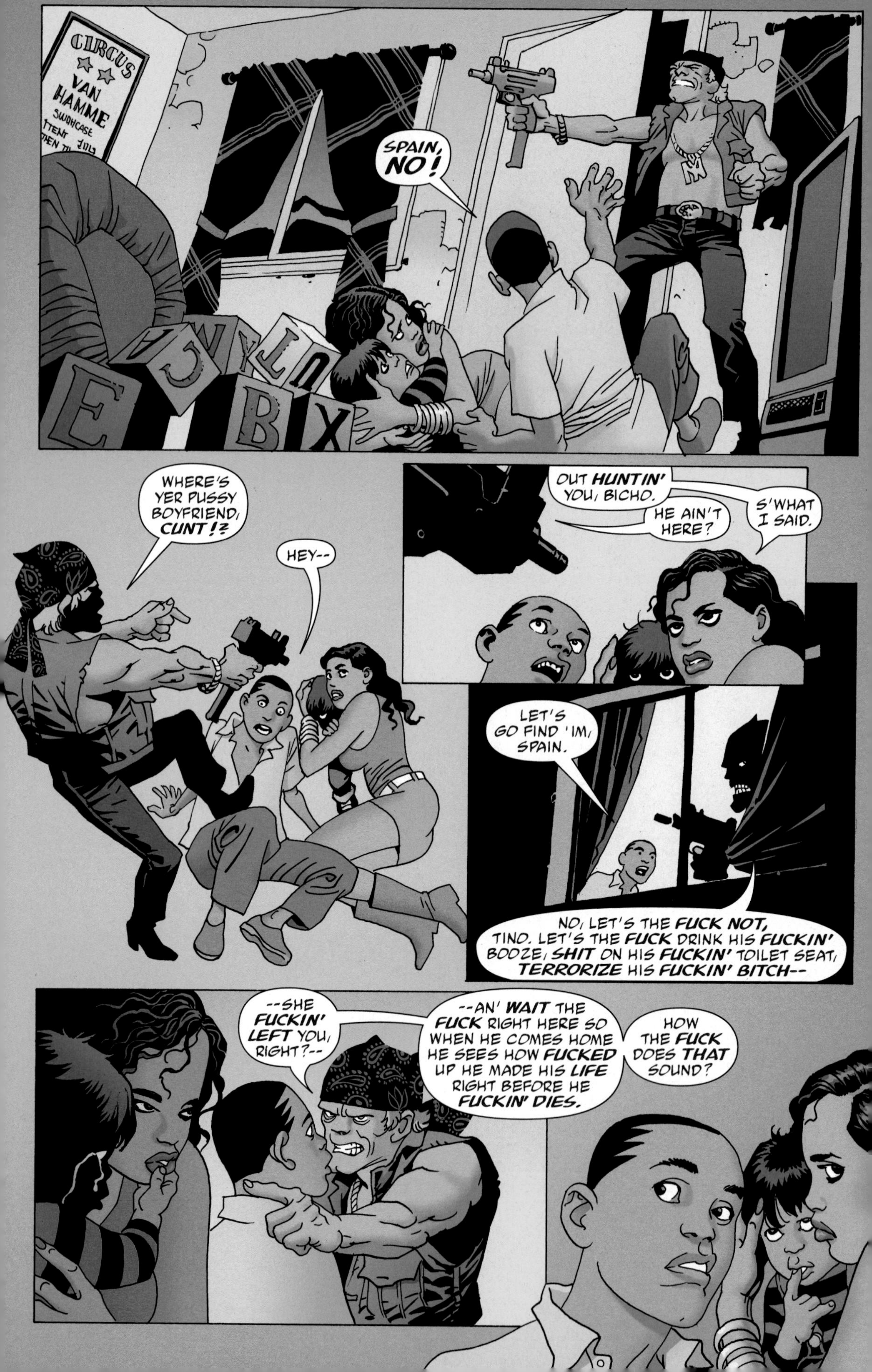

CIRCUS
VAN HAMME
SPAIN, NO!
WHERE'S YER PUSSY BOYFRIEND, CUNT!?
HEY--
OUT HUNTIN' YOU, BICHO.
HE AIN'T HERE?
S'WHAT I SAID.
LET'S GO FIND 'IM, SPAIN.
NO, LET'S THE FUCK NOT, TINO. LET'S THE FUCK DRINK HIS FUCKIN' BOOZE, SHIT ON HIS FUCKIN' TOILET SEAT, TERRORIZE HIS FUCKIN' BITCH--
--SHE FUCKIN' LEFT YOU, RIGHT?--
--AN' WAIT THE FUCK RIGHT HERE SO WHEN HE COMES HOME HE SEES HOW FUCKED UP HE MADE HIS LIFE RIGHT BEFORE HE FUCKIN' DIES.
HOW THE FUCK DOES THAT SOUND?

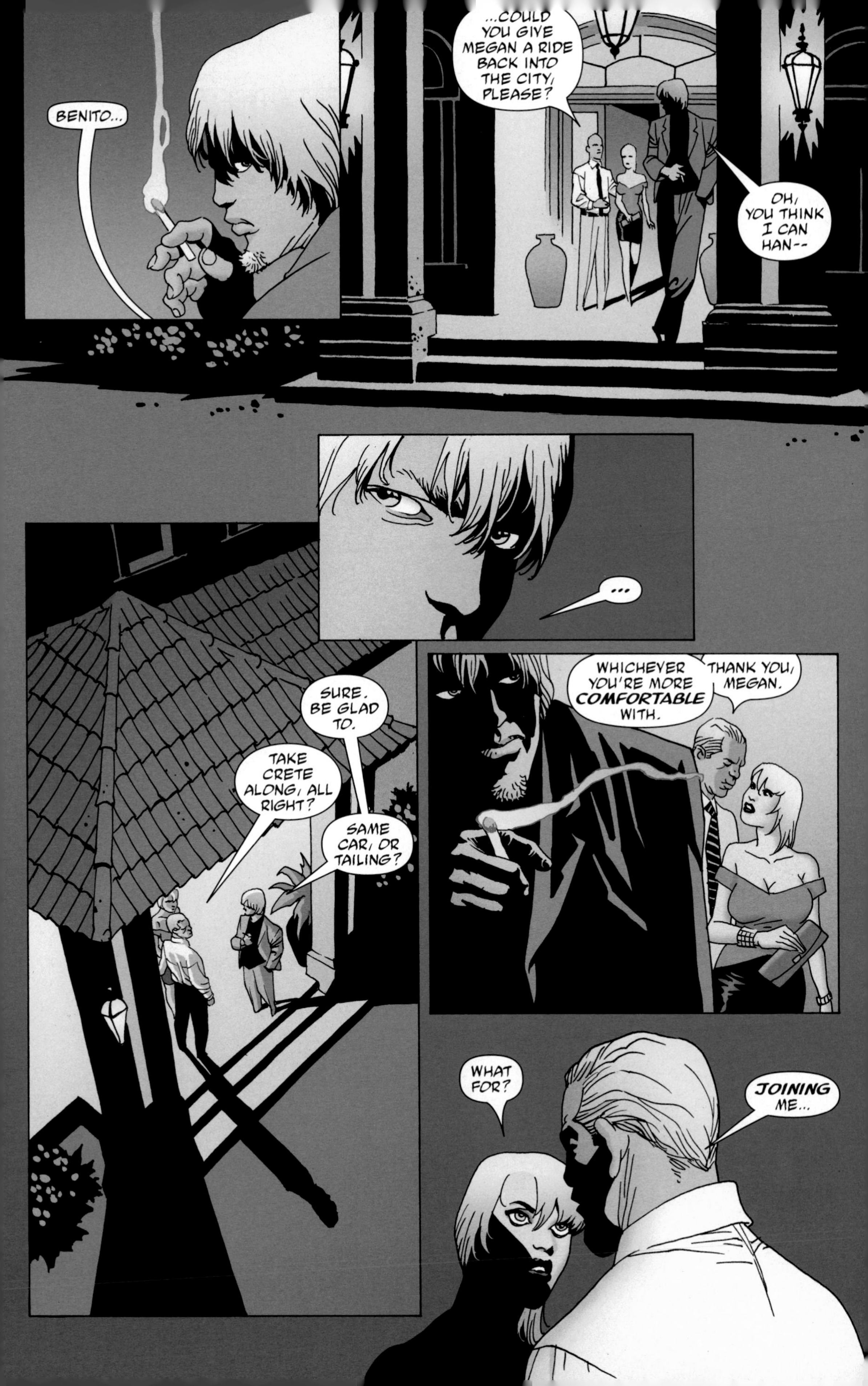
BENITO...
...COULD YOU GIVE MEGAN A RIDE BACK INTO THE CITY, PLEASE?
OH, YOU THINK I CAN HAN--
...
SURE. BE GLAD TO.
TAKE CRETE ALONG, ALL RIGHT?
SAME CAR, OR TAILING?
WHICHEVER YOU'RE MORE COMFORTABLE WITH.
THANK YOU, MEGAN.
WHAT FOR?
JOINING ME...

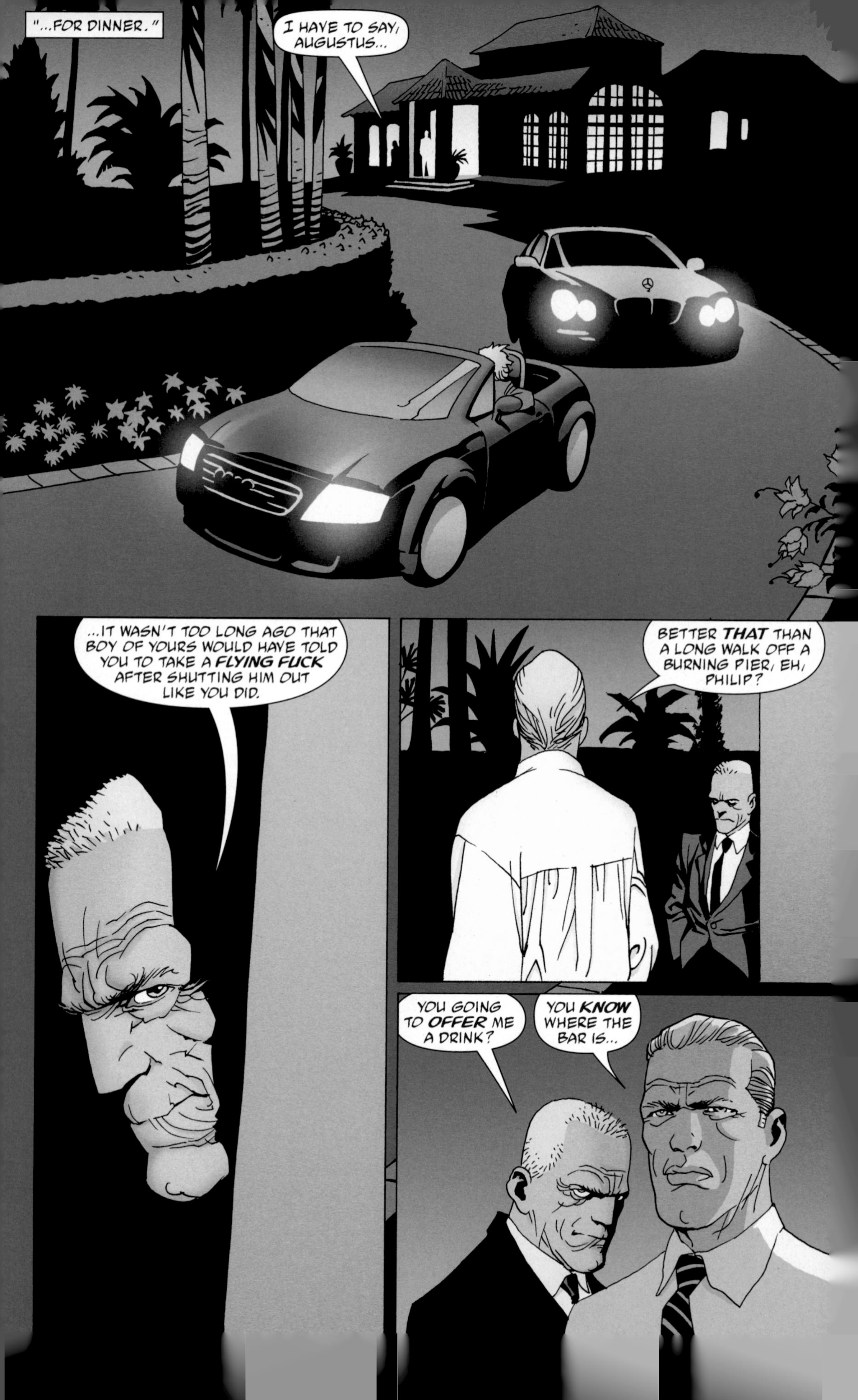
"...FOR DINNER."
I HAVE TO SAY, AUGUSTUS...
...IT WASN'T TOO LONG AGO THAT BOY OF YOURS WOULD HAVE TOLD YOU TO TAKE A FLYING FUCK AFTER SHUTTING HIM OUT LIKE YOU DID.
BETTER THAT THAN A LONG WALK OFF A BURNING PIER, EH, PHILIP?
YOU GOING TO OFFER ME A DRINK?
YOU KNOW WHERE THE BAR IS...

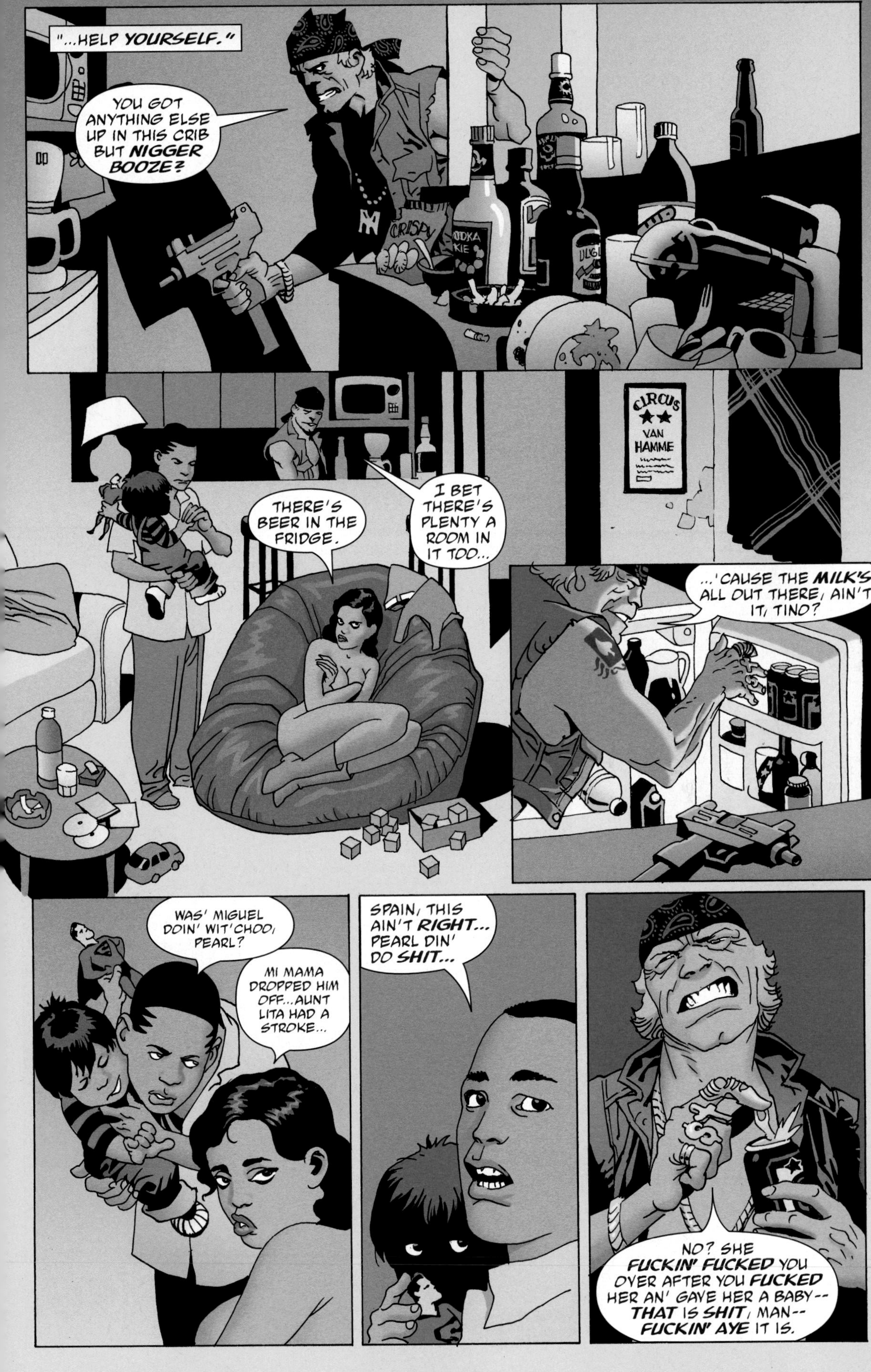
"...HELP YOURSELF."
YOU GOT ANYTHING ELSE UP IN THIS CRIB BUT NIGGER BOOZE?
THERE'S BEER IN THE FRIDGE.
I BET THERE'S PLENTY A ROOM IN IT TOO...
...'CAUSE THE MILK'S ALL OUT THERE, AIN'T IT, TINO?
WAS' MIGUEL DOIN' WIT'CHOO, PEARL?
MI MAMA DROPPED HIM OFF...AUNT LITA HAD A STROKE...
SPAIN, THIS AIN'T RIGHT... PEARL DIN' DO SHIT...
NO? SHE FUCKIN' FUCKED YOU OVER AFTER YOU FUCKED HER AN' GAVE HER A BABY-- THAT IS SHIT, MAN-- FUCKIN' AYE IT IS.

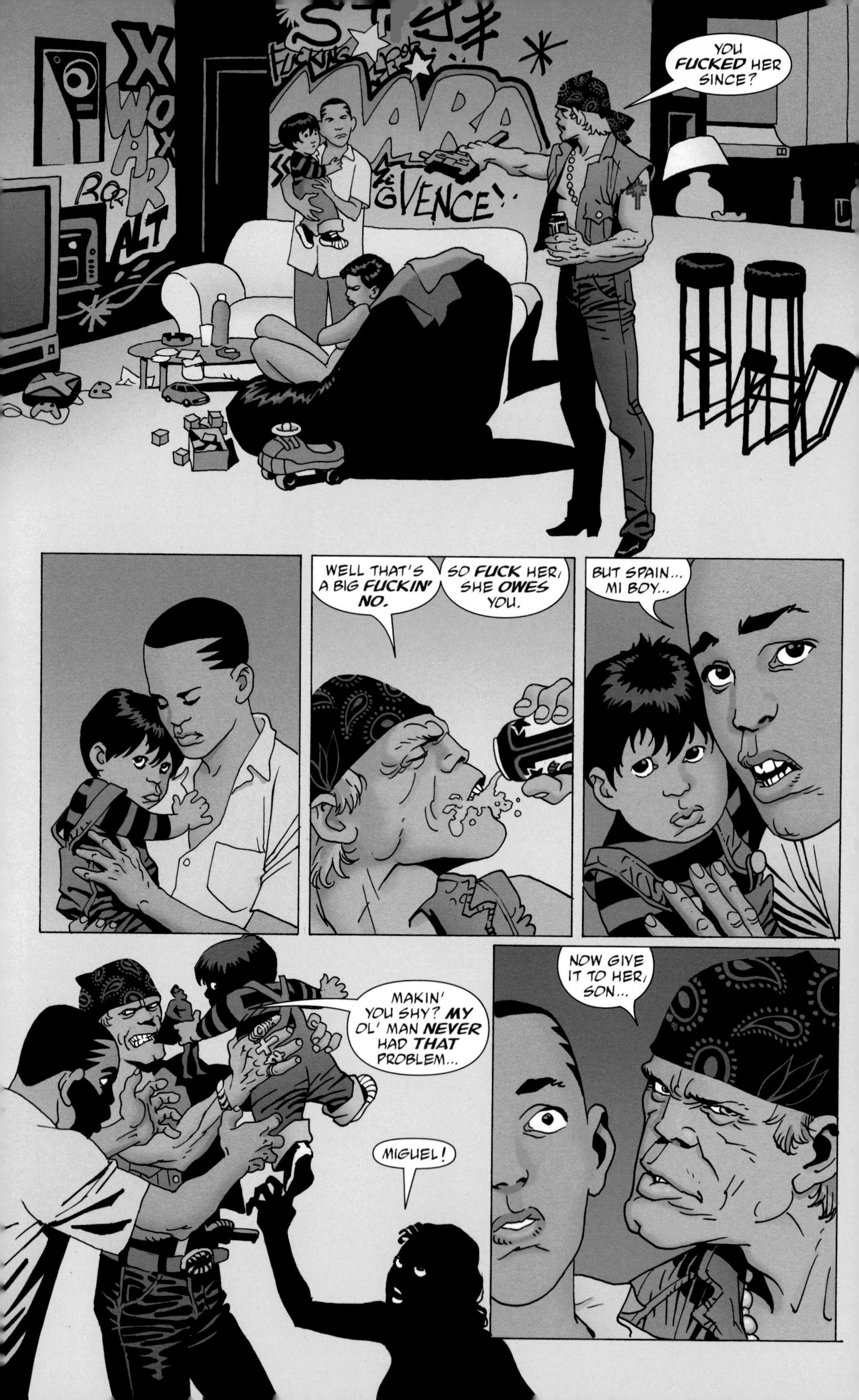
YOU FUCKED HER SINCE?
WELL THAT'S A BIG FUCKIN' NO.
SO FUCK HER, SHE OWES YOU.
BUT SPAIN... MI BOY...
MAKIN' YOU SHY? MY OL' MAN NEVER HAD THAT PROBLEM...
MIGUEL!
NOW GIVE IT TO HER, SON...

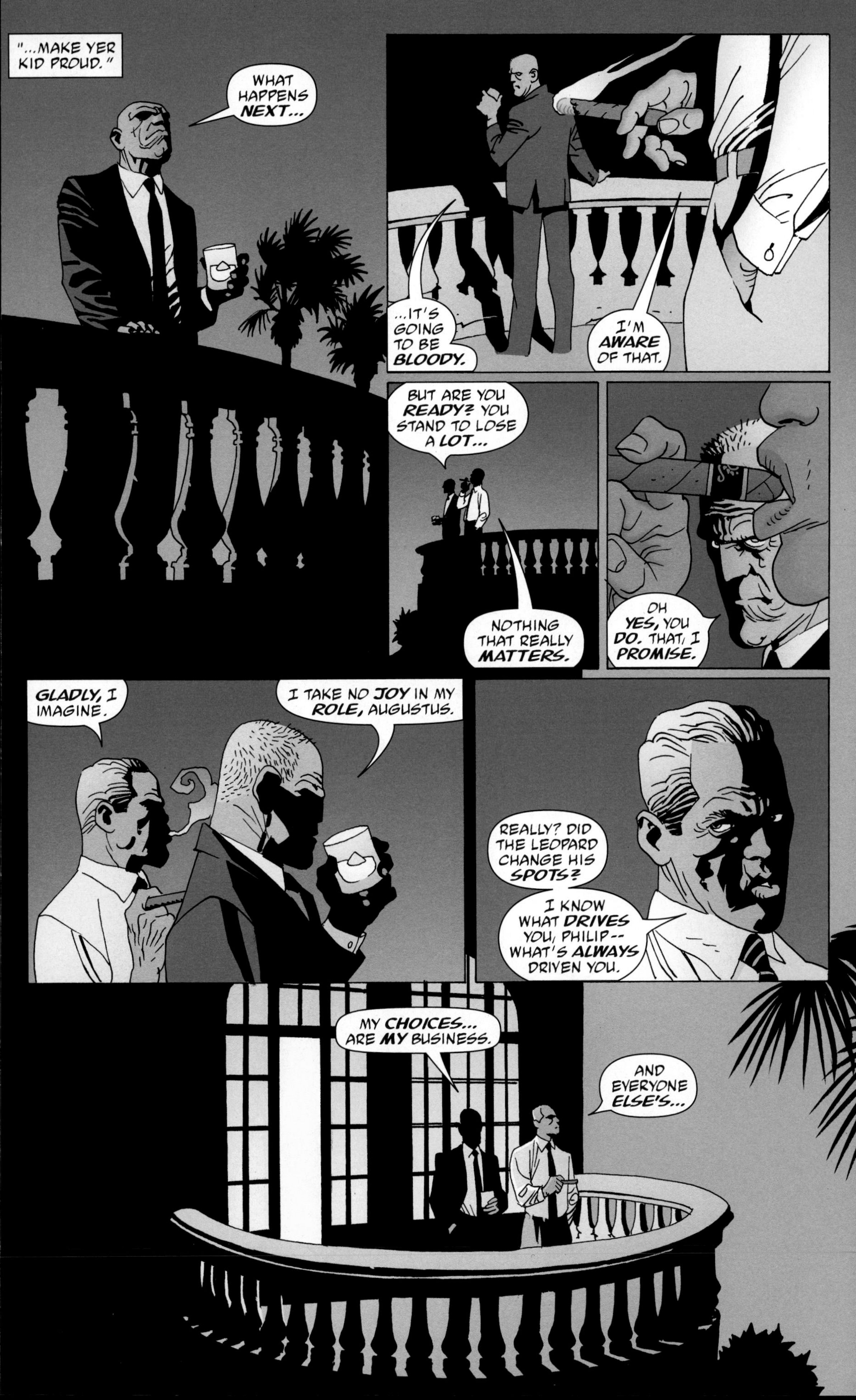
"...MAKE YER KID PROUD."
WHAT HAPPENS NEXT...
...IT'S GOING TO BE BLOODY.
I'M AWARE OF THAT.
BUT ARE YOU READY? YOU STAND TO LOSE A LOT...
NOTHING THAT REALLY MATTERS.
OH YES, YOU DO. THAT, I PROMISE.
GLADLY, I IMAGINE.
I TAKE NO JOY IN MY ROLE, AUGUSTUS.
REALLY? DID THE LEOPARD CHANGE HIS SPOTS?
I KNOW WHAT DRIVES YOU, PHILIP-- WHAT'S ALWAYS DRIVEN YOU.
MY CHOICES... ARE MY BUSINESS.
AND EVERYONE ELSE'S...

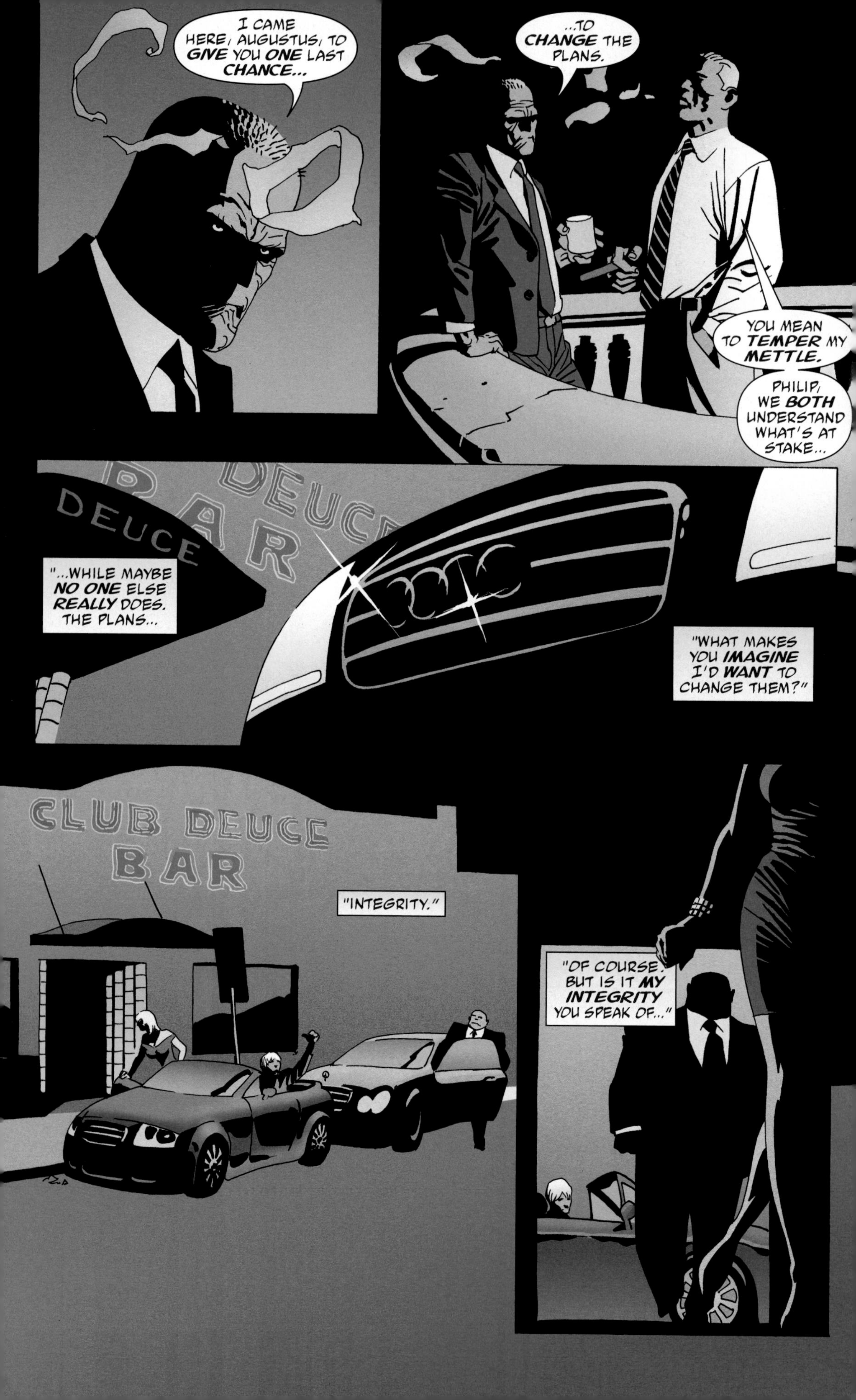

I CAME HERE, AUGUSTUS, TO GIVE YOU ONE LAST CHANCE...
...TO CHANGE THE PLANS.
YOU MEAN TO TEMPER MY METTLE.
PHILIP, WE BOTH UNDERSTAND WHAT'S AT STAKE...
DEUCE
DEUCE
BAR
"...WHILE MAYBE NO ONE ELSE REALLY DOES. THE PLANS...
"WHAT MAKES YOU IMAGINE I'D WANT TO CHANGE THEM?"
CLUB DEUCE
BAR
"INTEGRITY."
"OF COURSE. BUT IS IT MY INTEGRITY YOU SPEAK OF..."

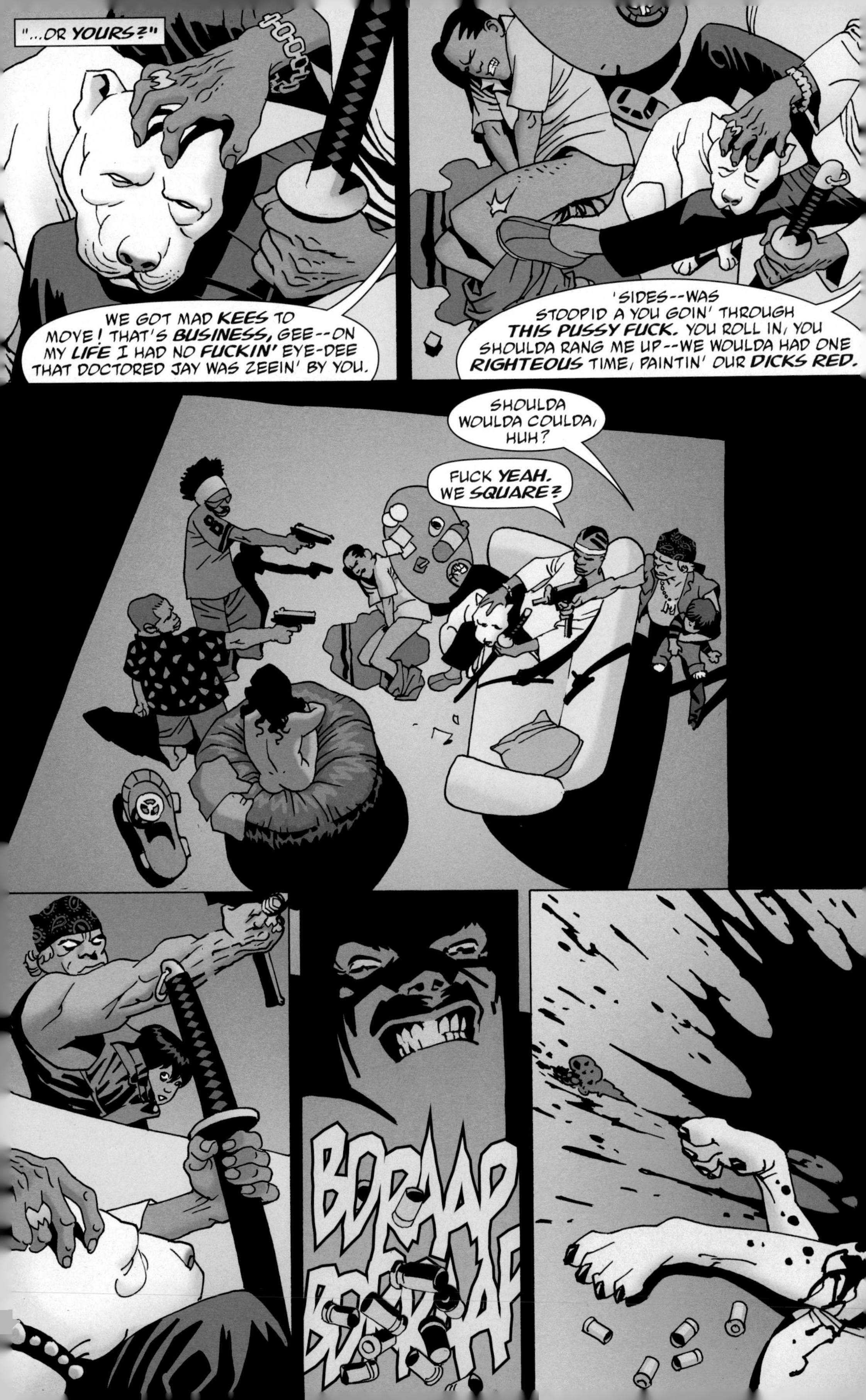
"...OR YOURS?"
WE GOT MAD KEES TO MOVE! THAT'S BUSINESS, GEE--ON MY LIFE I HAD NO FUCKIN' EYE-DEE THAT DOCTORED JAY WAS ZEEIN' BY YOU.
'SIDES--WAS STOOPID A YOU GOIN' THROUGH THIS PUSSY FUCK. YOU ROLL IN, YOU SHOULDA RANG ME UP--WE WOULDA HAD ONE RIGHTEOUS TIME, PAINTIN' OUR DICKS RED.
SHOULDA WOULDA COULDA, HUH?
FUCK YEAH. WE SQUARE?
BDRAAP

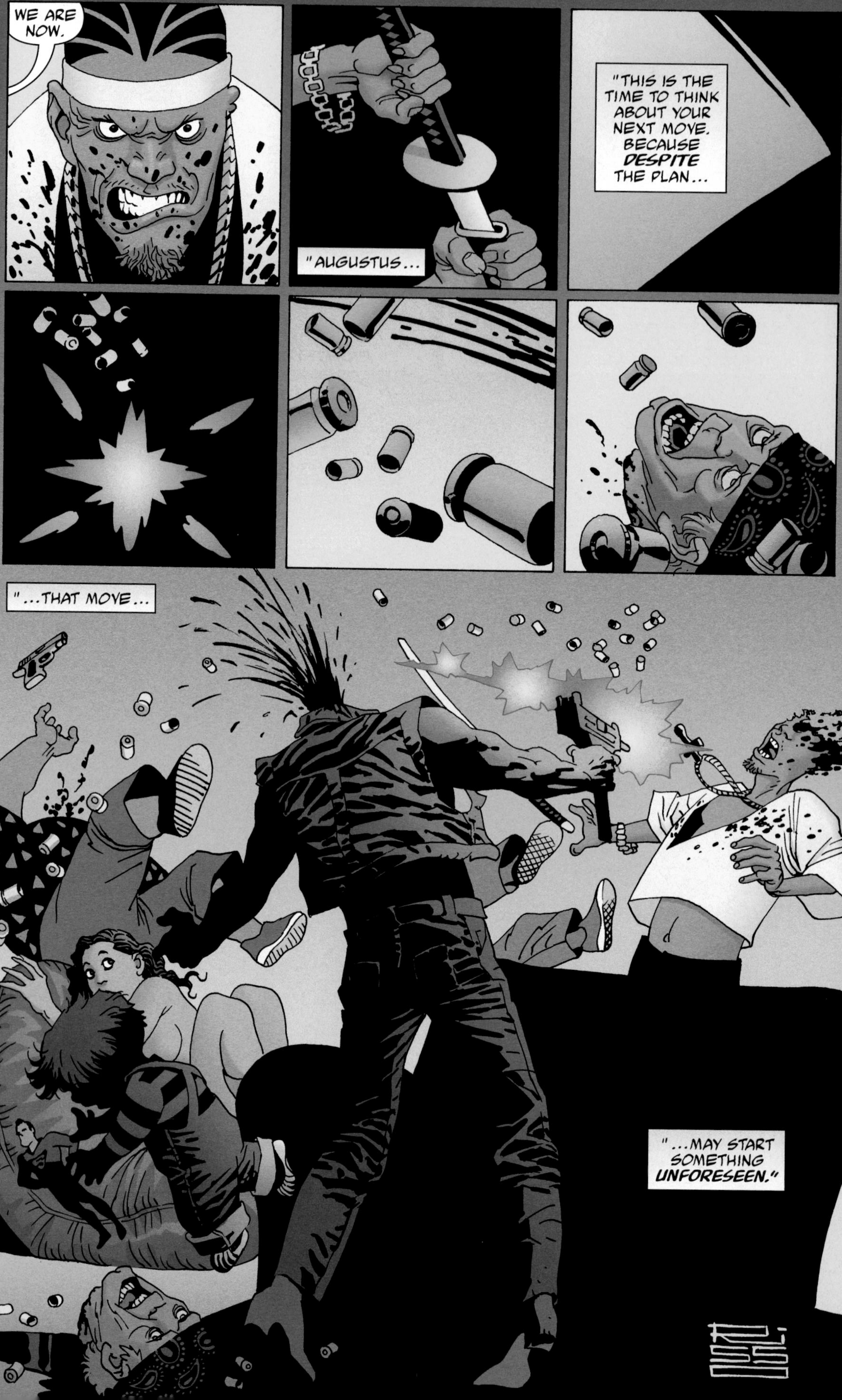
WE ARE NOW.
"AUGUSTUS...
"THIS IS THE TIME TO THINK ABOUT YOUR NEXT MOVE. BECAUSE DESPITE THE PLAN...
"...THAT MOVE...
"...MAY START SOMETHING UNFORESEEN."

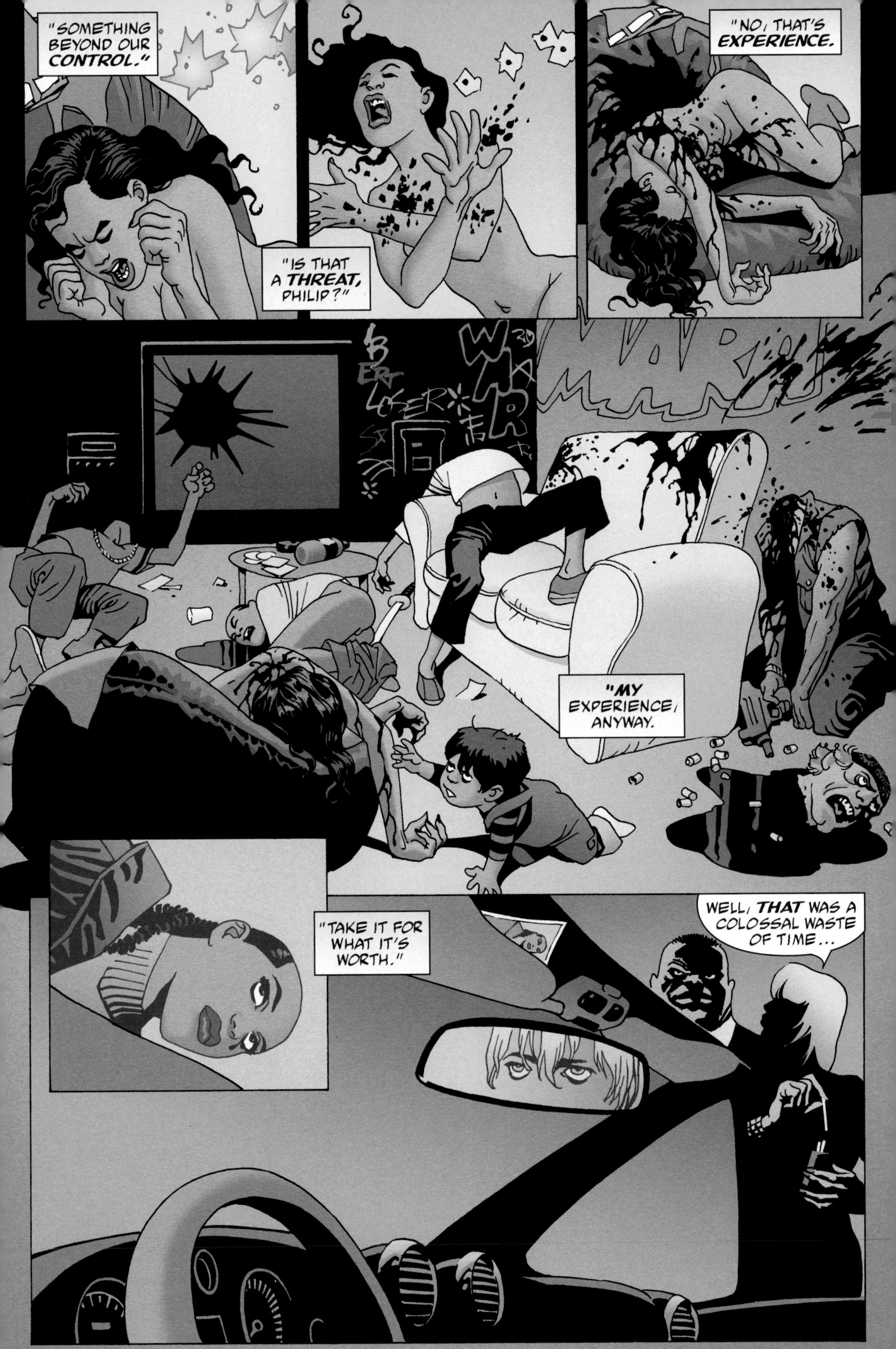
"SOMETHING BEYOND OUR CONTROL."
"IS THAT A THREAT, PHILIP?"
"NO, THAT'S EXPERIENCE.
"MY EXPERIENCE, ANYWAY.
"TAKE IT FOR WHAT IT'S WORTH."
WELL, THAT WAS A COLOSSAL WASTE OF TIME...

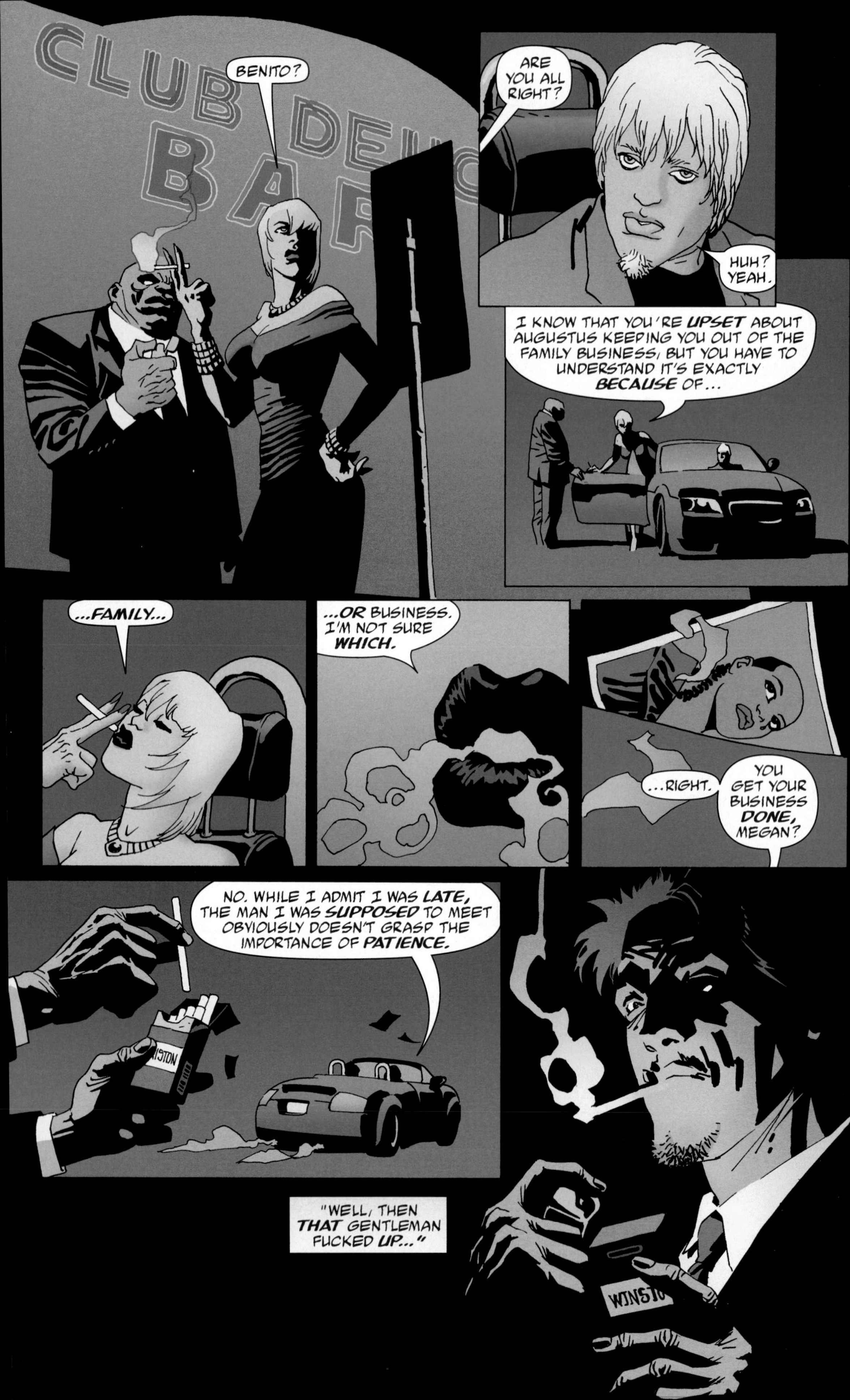
CLUB DELUXE BAR
BENITO?
ARE YOU ALL RIGHT?
HUH? YEAH.
I KNOW THAT YOU'RE UPSET ABOUT AUGUSTUS KEEPING YOU OUT OF THE FAMILY BUSINESS, BUT YOU HAVE TO UNDERSTAND IT'S EXACTLY BECAUSE OF...
...FAMILY...
...OR BUSINESS. I'M NOT SURE WHICH.
...RIGHT.
YOU GET YOUR BUSINESS DONE, MEGAN?
NO. WHILE I ADMIT I WAS LATE, THE MAN I WAS SUPPOSED TO MEET OBVIOUSLY DOESN'T GRASP THE IMPORTANCE OF PATIENCE.
"WELL, THEN THAT GENTLEMAN FUCKED UP..."

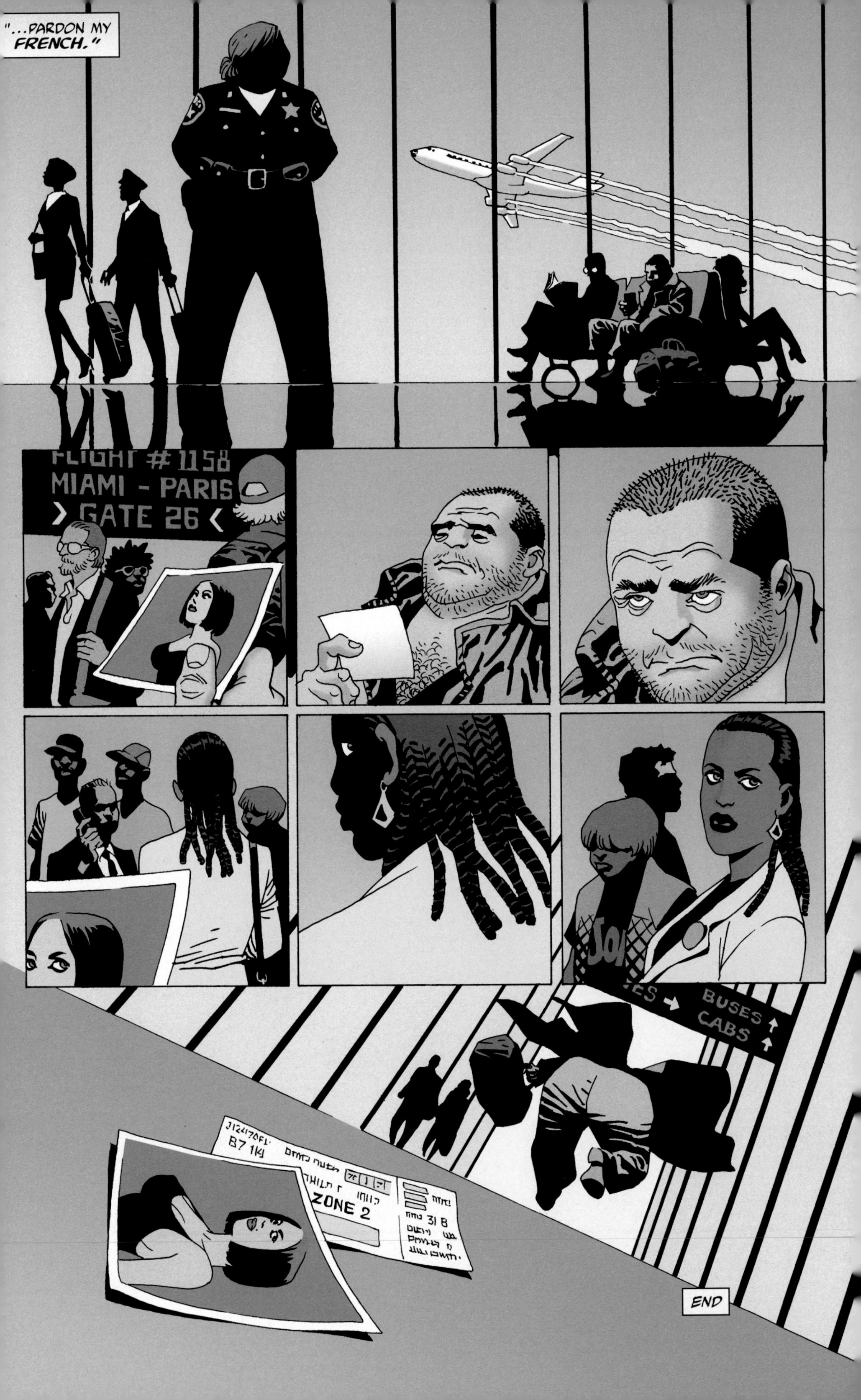
"...PARDON MY FRENCH."
FLIGHT # 1158
MIAMI - PARIS
GATE 26
BUSES
CABS
ZONE 2
END

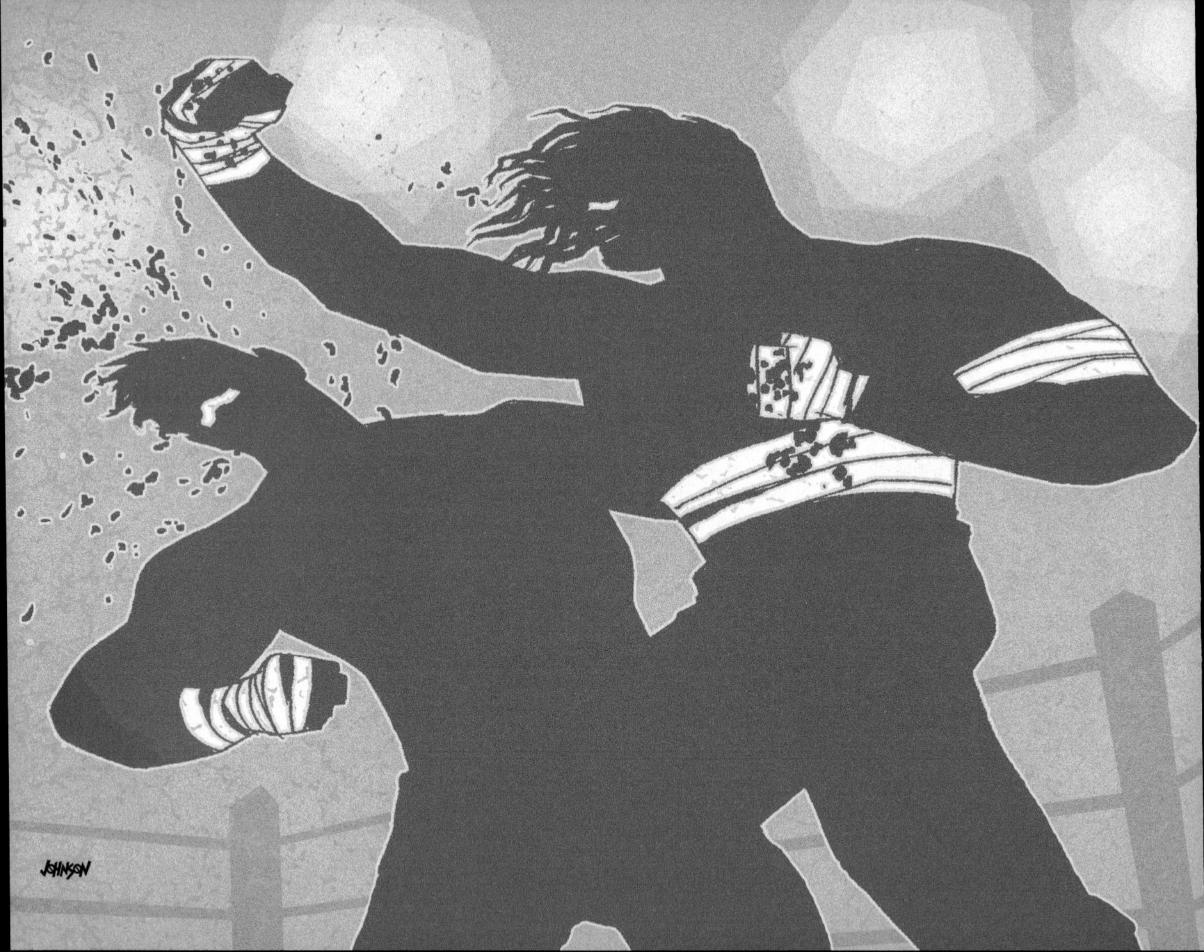
JOHNSON

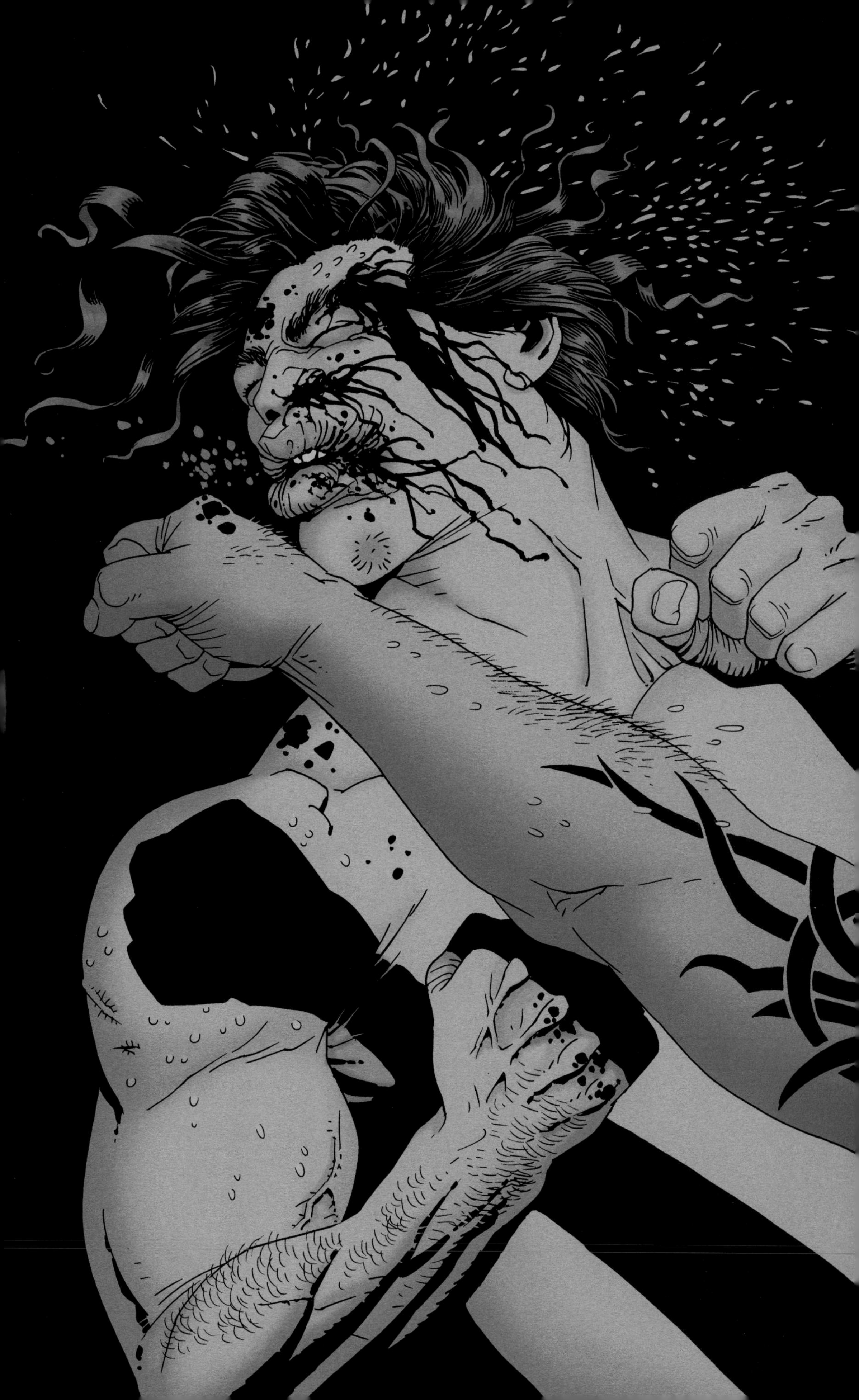

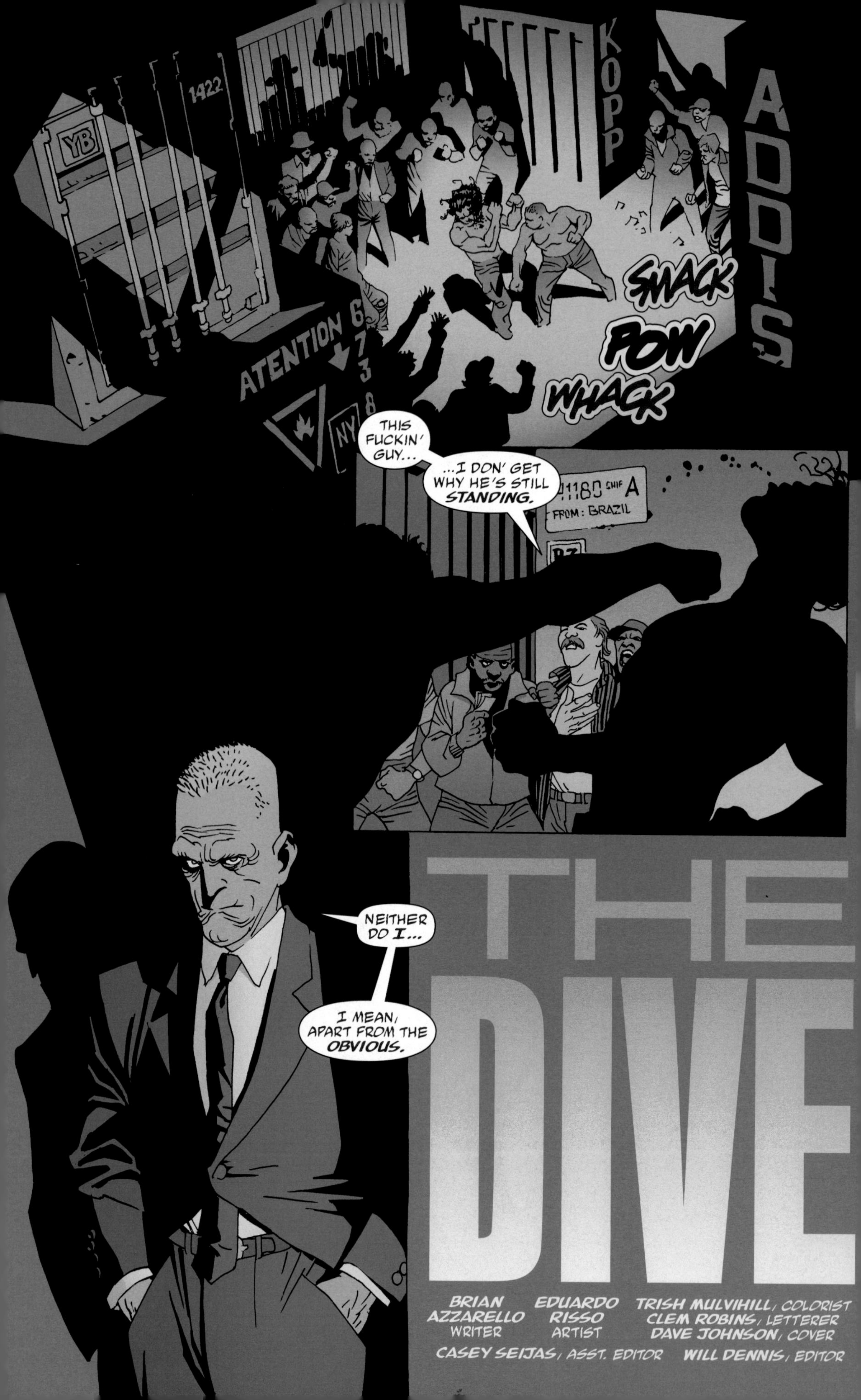
1422
YB
KOPP
ADDIS
SMACK
POW
WHACK
ATENTION
THIS FUCKIN' GUY...
...I DON' GET WHY HE'S STILL STANDING.
FROM: BRAZIL
NEITHER DO I...
I MEAN, APART FROM THE OBVIOUS.
THE DIVE
BRIAN AZZARELLO WRITER
EDUARDO RISSO ARTIST
TRISH MULVIHILL, COLORIST
CLEM ROBINS, LETTERER
DAVE JOHNSON, COVER
CASEY SEIJAS, ASST. EDITOR
WILL DENNIS, EDITOR

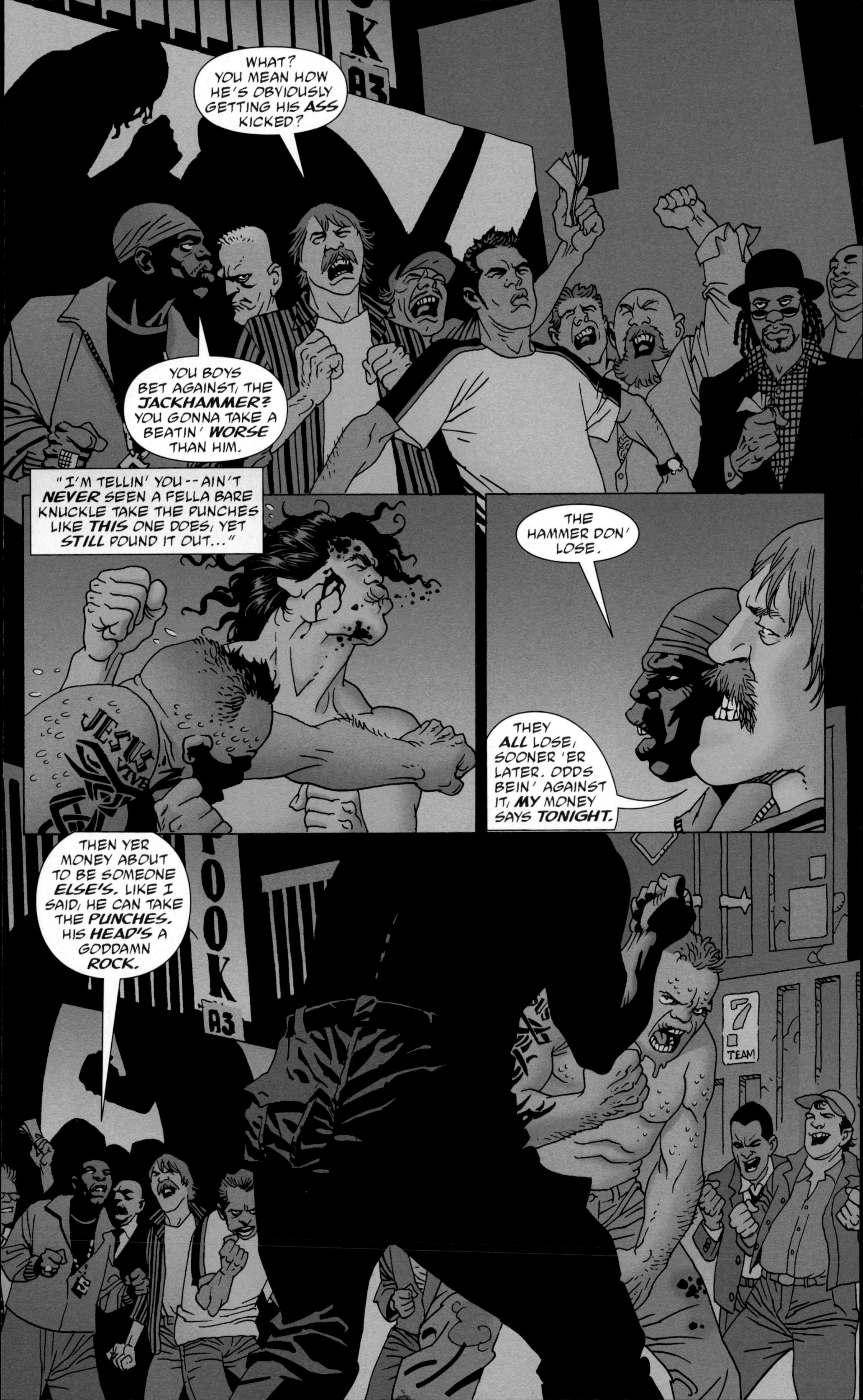
WHAT? YOU MEAN HOW HE'S OBVIOUSLY GETTING HIS ASS KICKED?
YOU BOYS BET AGAINST, THE JACKHAMMER? YOU GONNA TAKE A BEATIN' WORSE THAN HIM.
"I'M TELLIN' YOU--AIN'T NEVER SEEN A FELLA BARE KNUCKLE TAKE THE PUNCHES LIKE THIS ONE DOES, YET STILL POUND IT OUT..."
THE HAMMER DON' LOSE.
THEY ALL LOSE, SOONER 'ER LATER. ODDS BEIN' AGAINST IT, MY MONEY SAYS TONIGHT.
THEN YER MONEY ABOUT TO BE SOMEONE ELSE'S. LIKE I SAID, HE CAN TAKE THE PUNCHES. HIS HEAD'S A GODDAMN ROCK.
TEAM

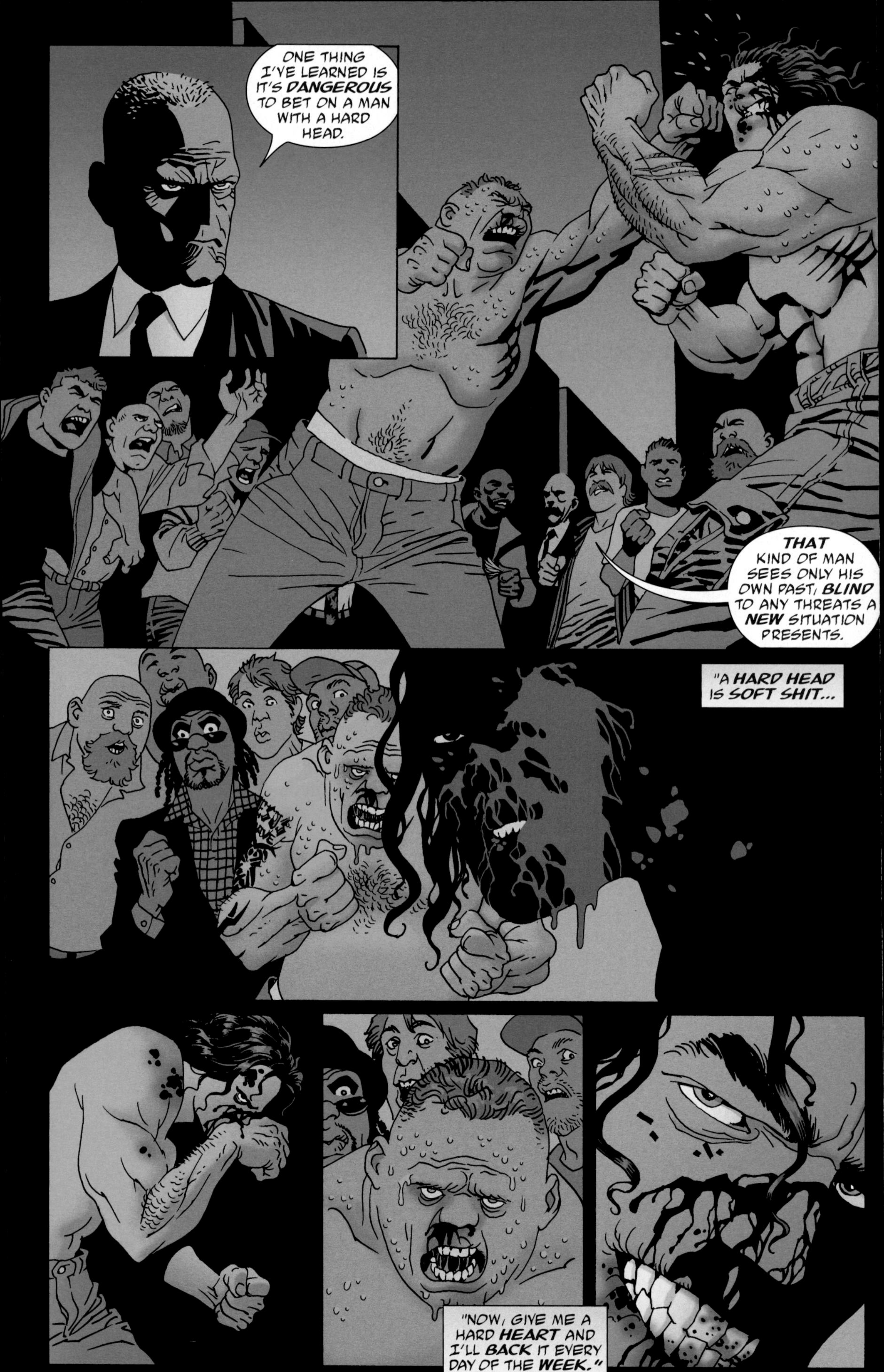
ONE THING I'VE LEARNED IS IT'S DANGEROUS TO BET ON A MAN WITH A HARD HEAD.
THAT KIND OF MAN SEES ONLY HIS OWN PAST, BLIND TO ANY THREATS A NEW SITUATION PRESENTS.
"A HARD HEAD IS SOFT SHIT...
"NOW, GIVE ME A HARD HEART AND I'LL BACK IT EVERY DAY OF THE WEEK."

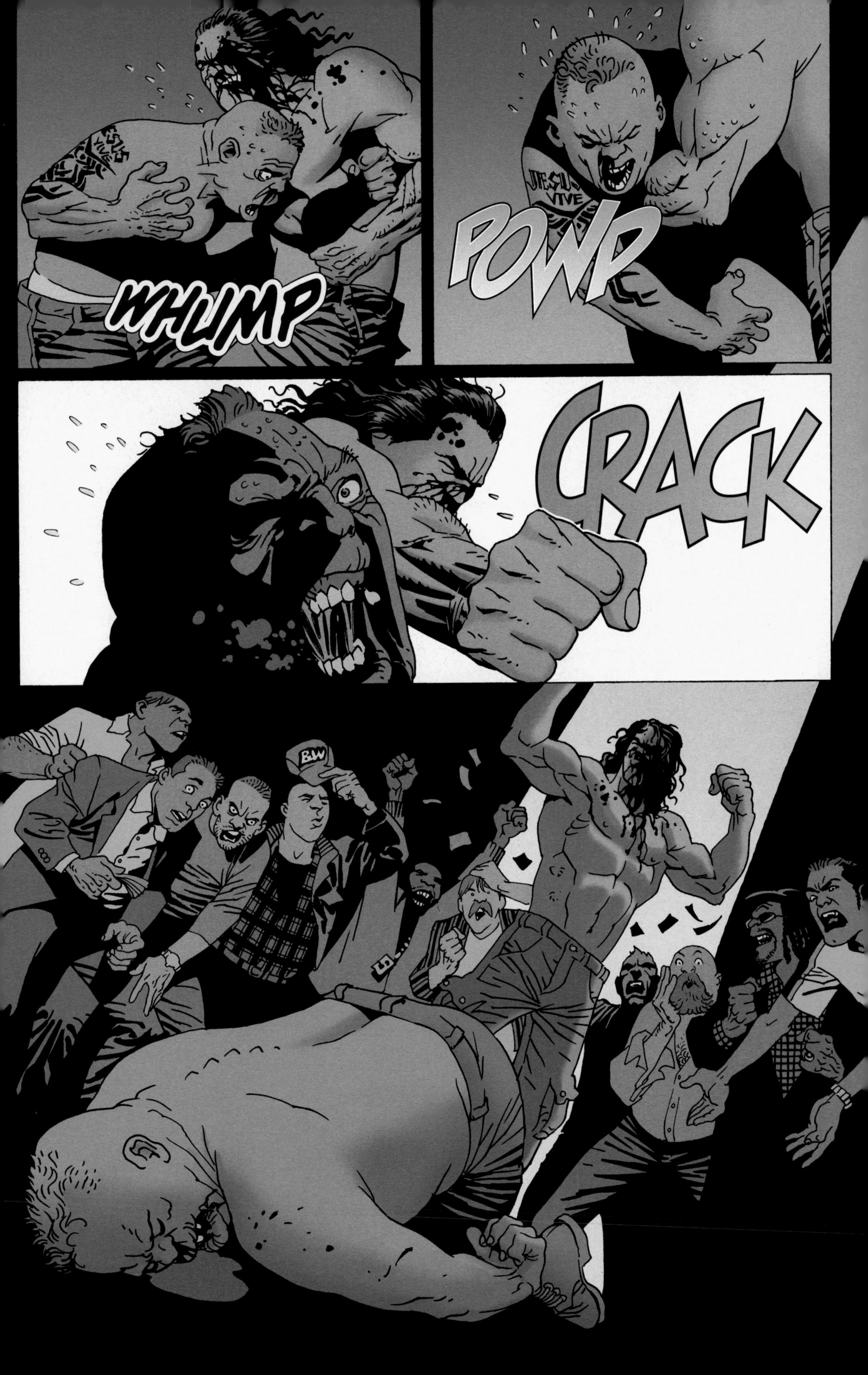
WHLIMP
JESUS VIVE
POWP
CRACK
BW

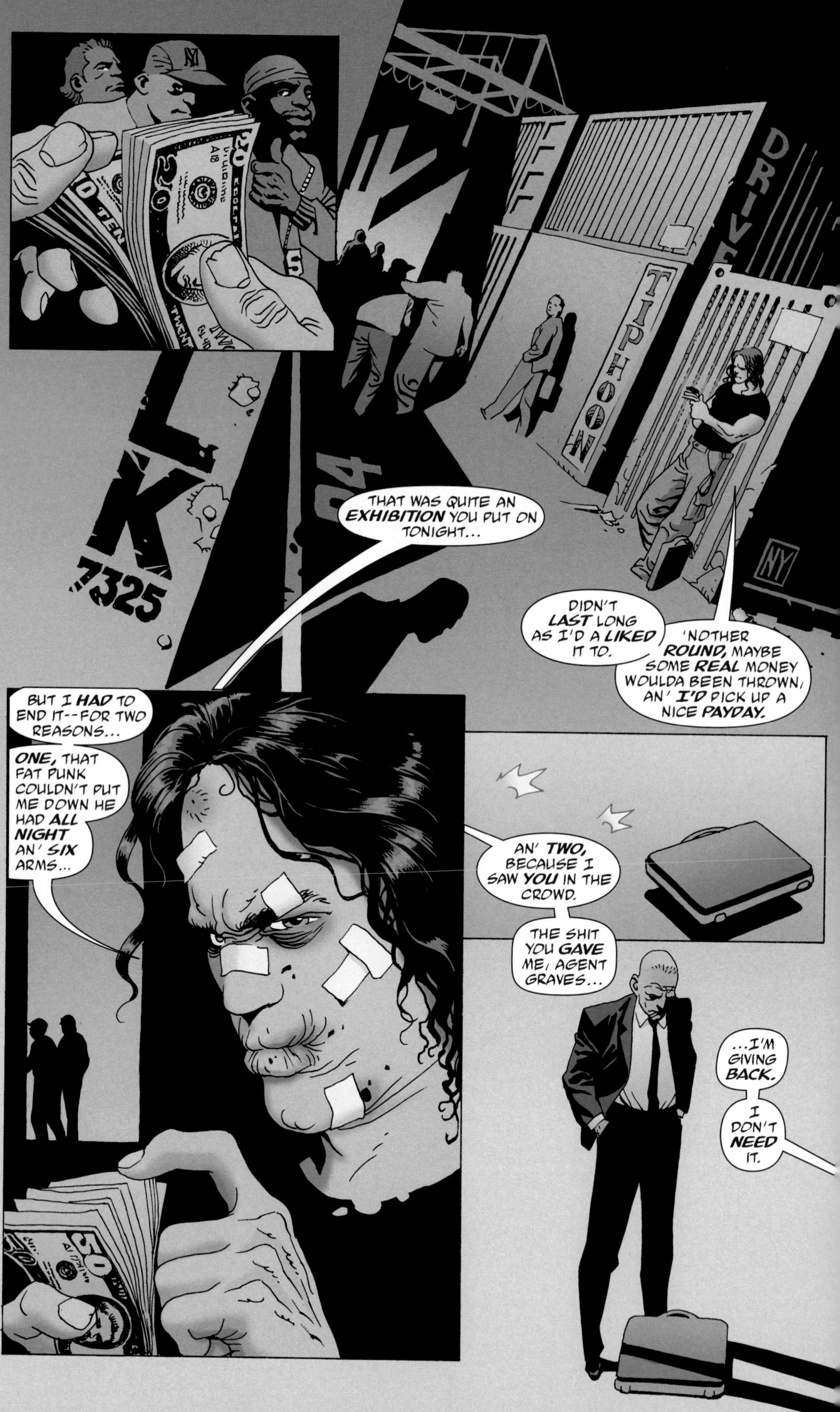
THAT WAS QUITE AN EXHIBITION YOU PUT ON TONIGHT...
DIDN'T LAST LONG AS I'D A LIKED IT TO.
'NOTHER ROUND, MAYBE SOME REAL MONEY WOULDA BEEN THROWN, AN' I'D PICK UP A NICE PAYDAY.
BUT I HAD TO END IT--FOR TWO REASONS...
ONE, THAT FAT PUNK COULDN'T PUT ME DOWN HE HAD ALL NIGHT AN' SIX ARMS...
AN' TWO, BECAUSE I SAW YOU IN THE CROWD.
THE SHIT YOU GAVE ME, AGENT GRAVES...
...I'M GIVING BACK.
I DON'T NEED IT.

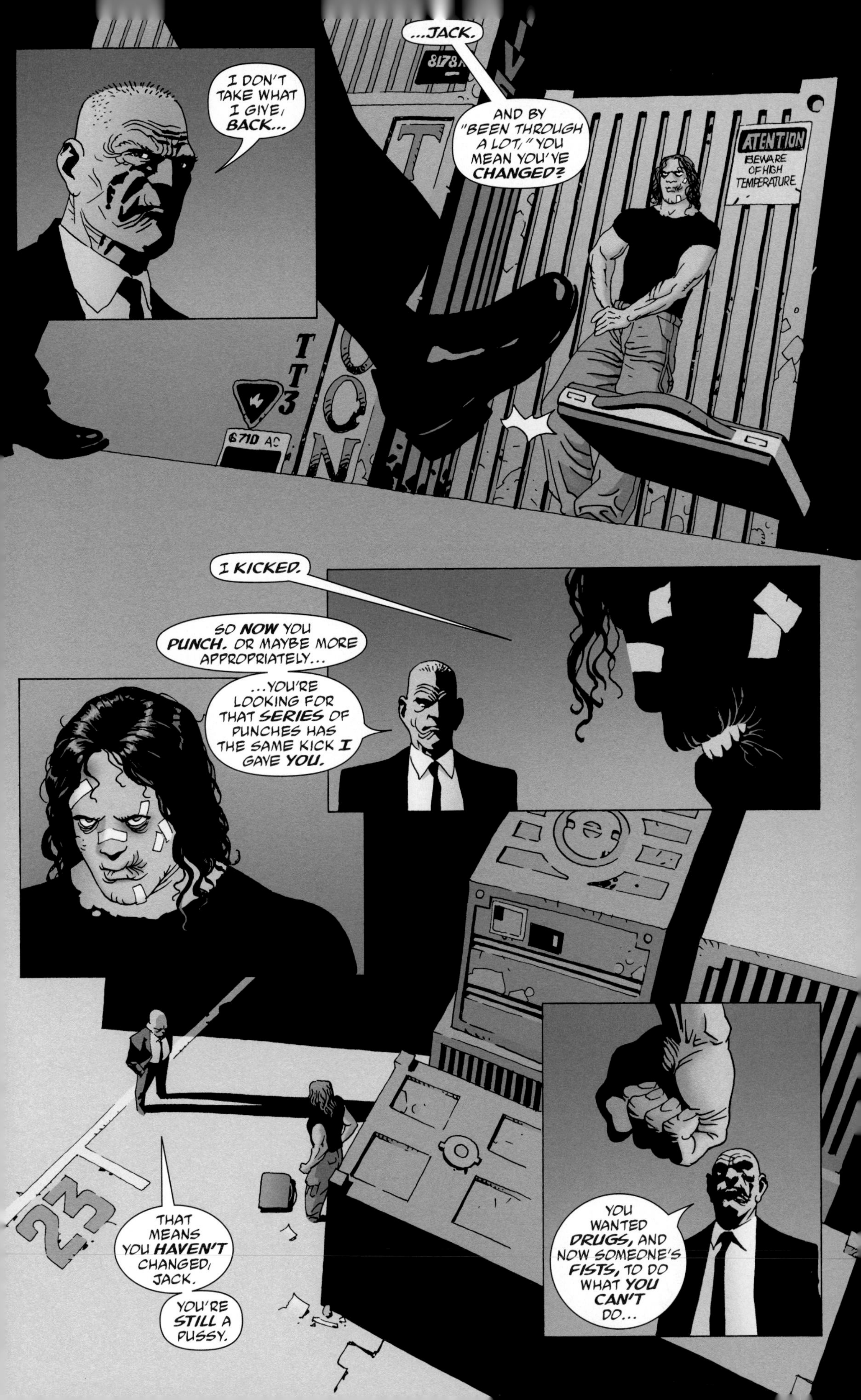
I DON'T TAKE WHAT I GIVE, BACK...
...JACK.
AND BY "BEEN THROUGH A LOT," YOU MEAN YOU'VE CHANGED?
ATENTION
BEWARE OF HIGH TEMPERATURE
TT3
6710 AC
I KICKED.
SO NOW YOU PUNCH. OR MAYBE MORE APPROPRIATELY...
...YOU'RE LOOKING FOR THAT SERIES OF PUNCHES HAS THE SAME KICK I GAVE YOU.
THAT MEANS YOU HAVEN'T CHANGED, JACK.
YOU'RE STILL A PUSSY.
YOU WANTED DRUGS, AND NOW SOMEONE'S FISTS, TO DO WHAT YOU CAN'T DO...

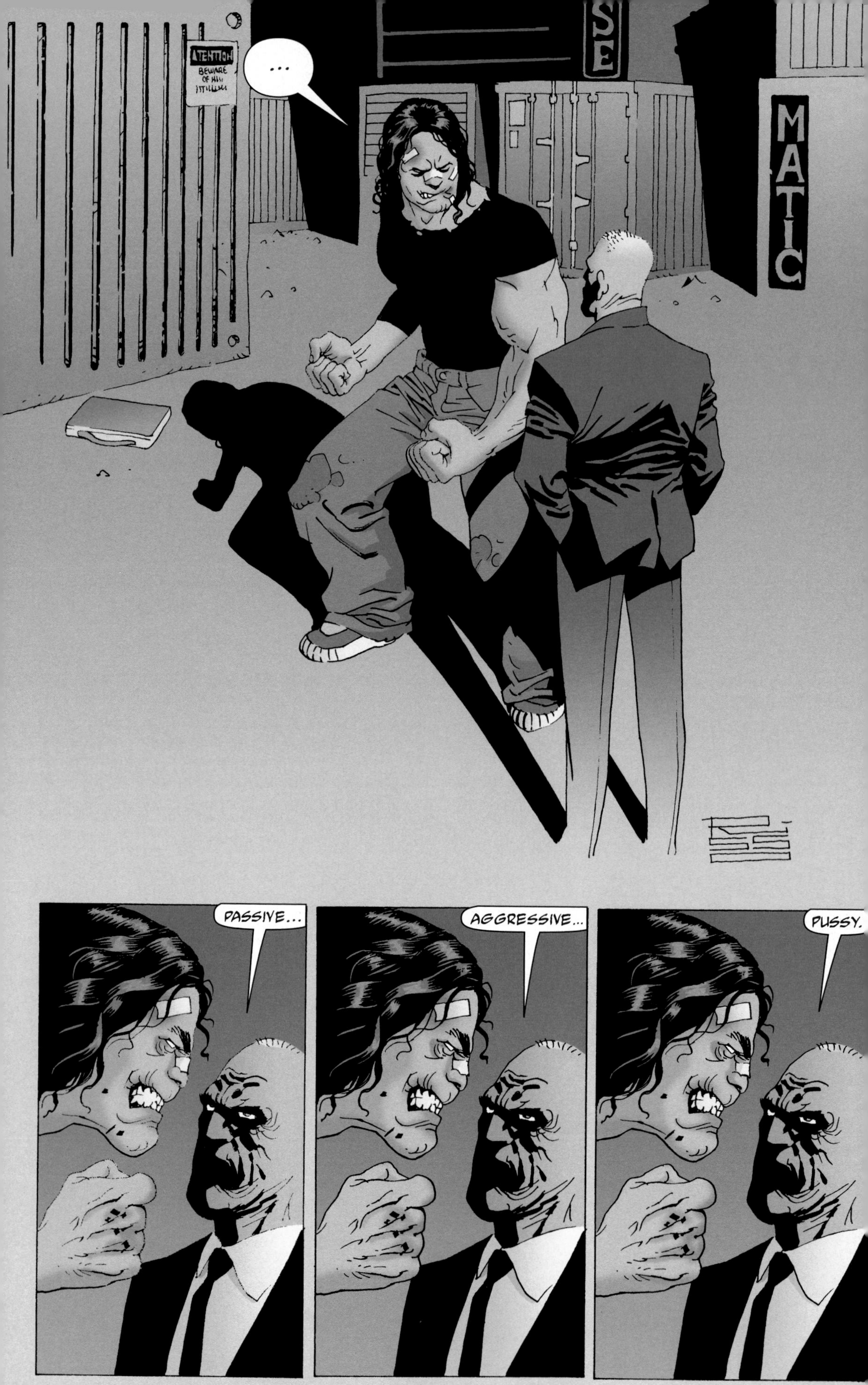

BEWARE
...
SE
MATIC
PASSIVE...
AGGRESSIVE...
PUSSY.

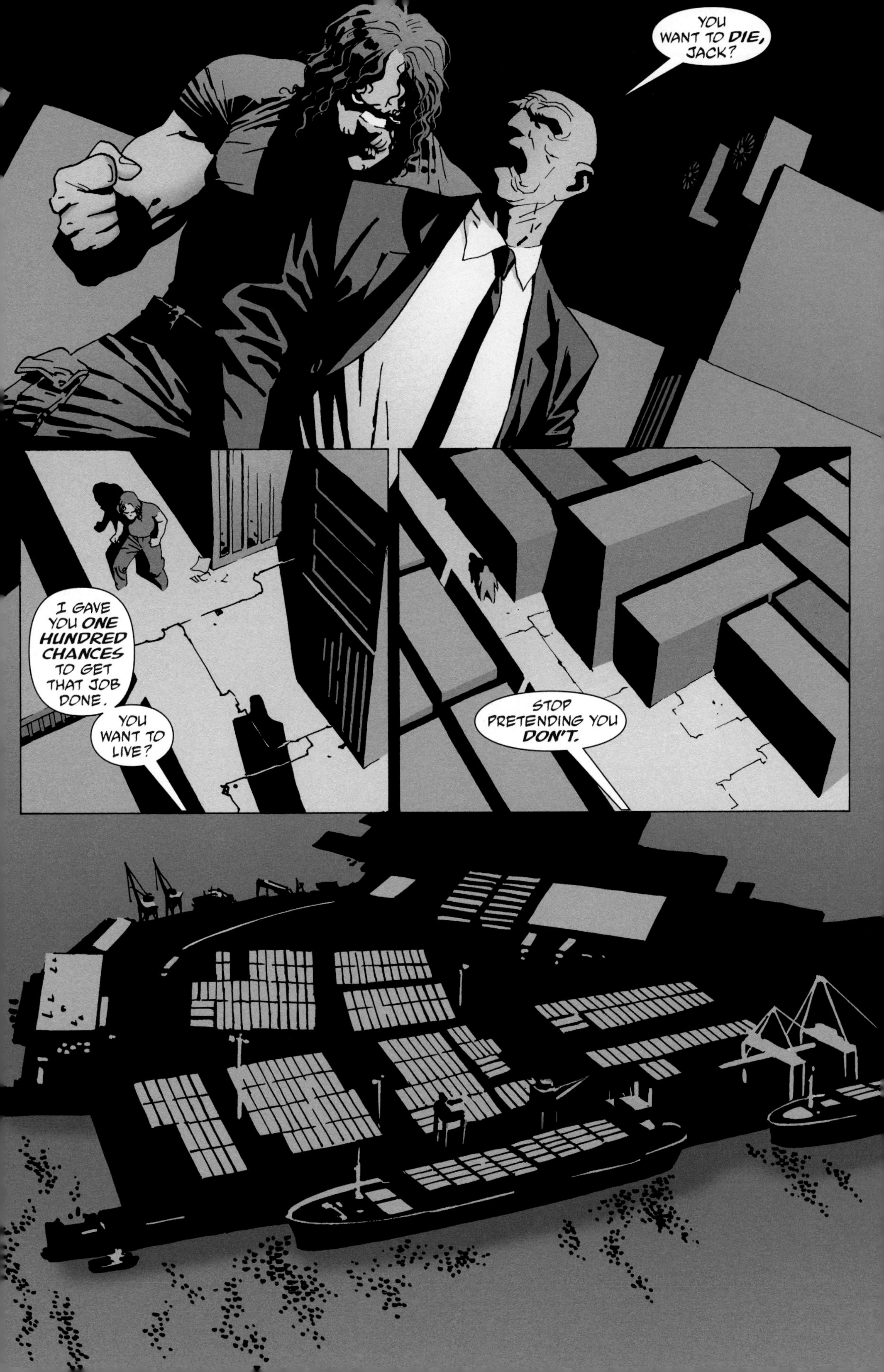
YOU WANT TO DIE, JACK?
I GAVE YOU ONE HUNDRED CHANCES TO GET THAT JOB DONE.
YOU WANT TO LIVE?
STOP PRETENDING YOU DON'T.

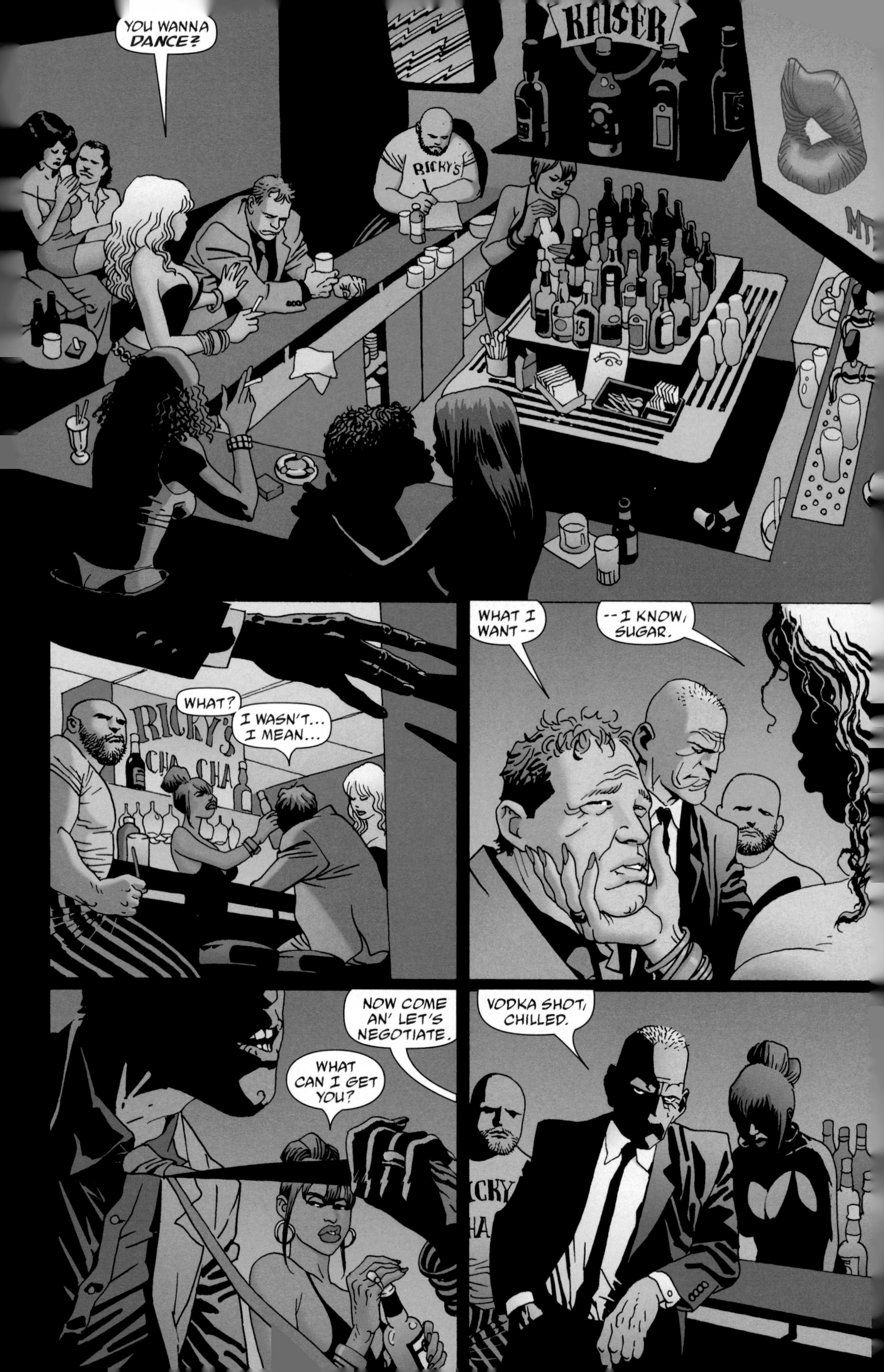
YOU WANNA DANCE?
KAISER
RICKY'S
WHAT?
I WASN'T... I MEAN...
RICKY'S CHA CHA
WHAT I WANT--
--I KNOW, SUGAR.
NOW COME AN' LET'S NEGOTIATE.
WHAT CAN I GET YOU?
VODKA SHOT, CHILLED.

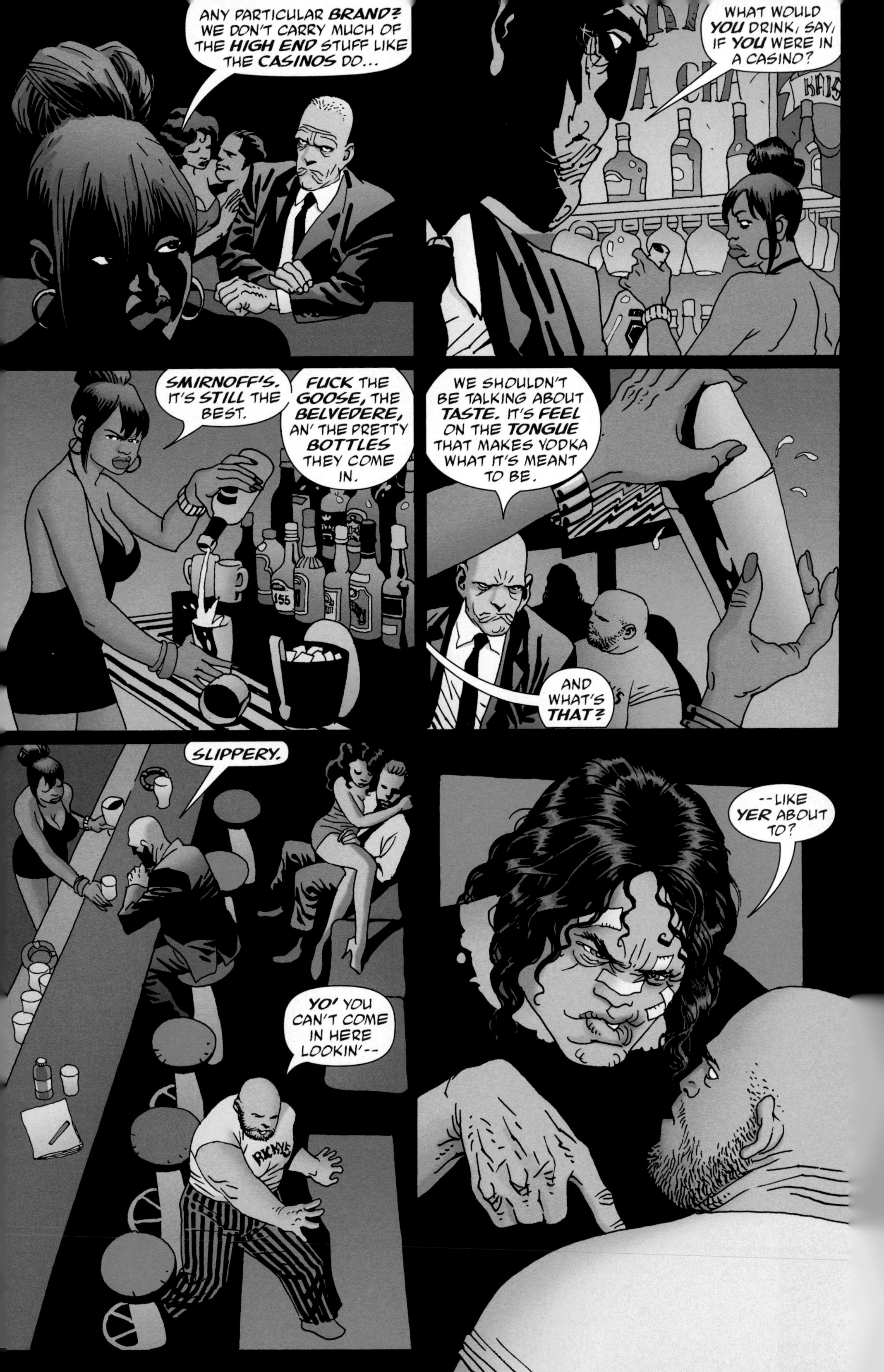
ANY PARTICULAR BRAND? WE DON'T CARRY MUCH OF THE HIGH END STUFF LIKE THE CASINOS DO...
WHAT WOULD YOU DRINK, SAY, IF YOU WERE IN A CASINO?
SMIRNOFF'S. IT'S STILL THE BEST.
FUCK THE GOOSE, THE BELVEDERE, AN' THE PRETTY BOTTLES THEY COME IN.
WE SHOULDN'T BE TALKING ABOUT TASTE. IT'S FEEL ON THE TONGUE THAT MAKES VODKA WHAT IT'S MEANT TO BE.
AND WHAT'S THAT?
SLIPPERY.
YO' YOU CAN'T COME IN HERE LOOKIN'--
--LIKE YER ABOUT TO?

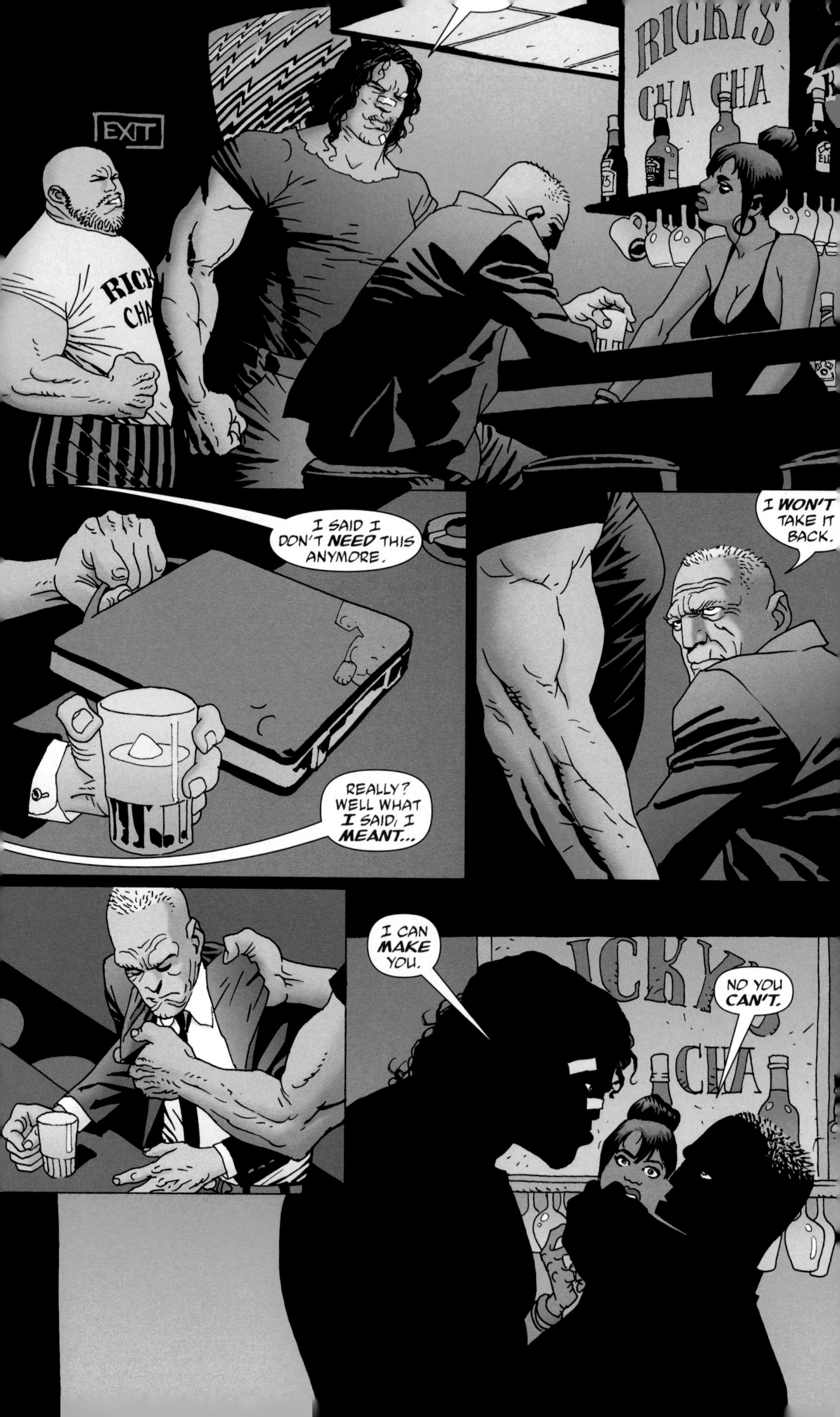
EXIT
RICKYS' CHA CHA
I SAID I DON'T **NEED** THIS ANYMORE.
REALLY? WELL WHAT **I** SAID, I **MEANT...**
I **WON'T** TAKE IT BACK.
I CAN **MAKE** YOU.
NO YOU **CAN'T.**

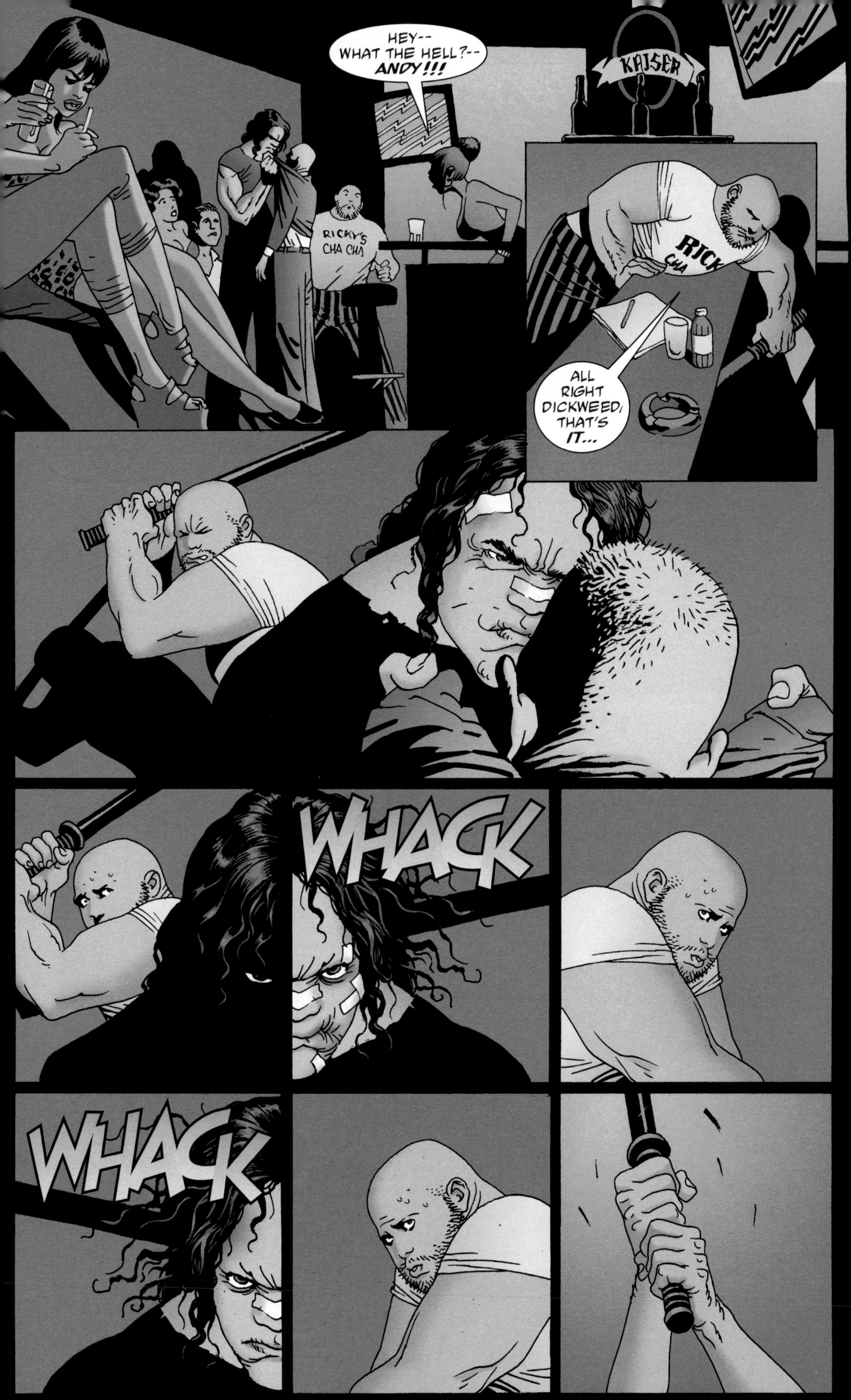
HEY--
WHAT THE HELL?--
ANDY!!!
KAISER
RICKY'S
CHA CHA
RICK
CHA
ALL RIGHT DICKWEED, THAT'S IT...
WHACK
WHACK

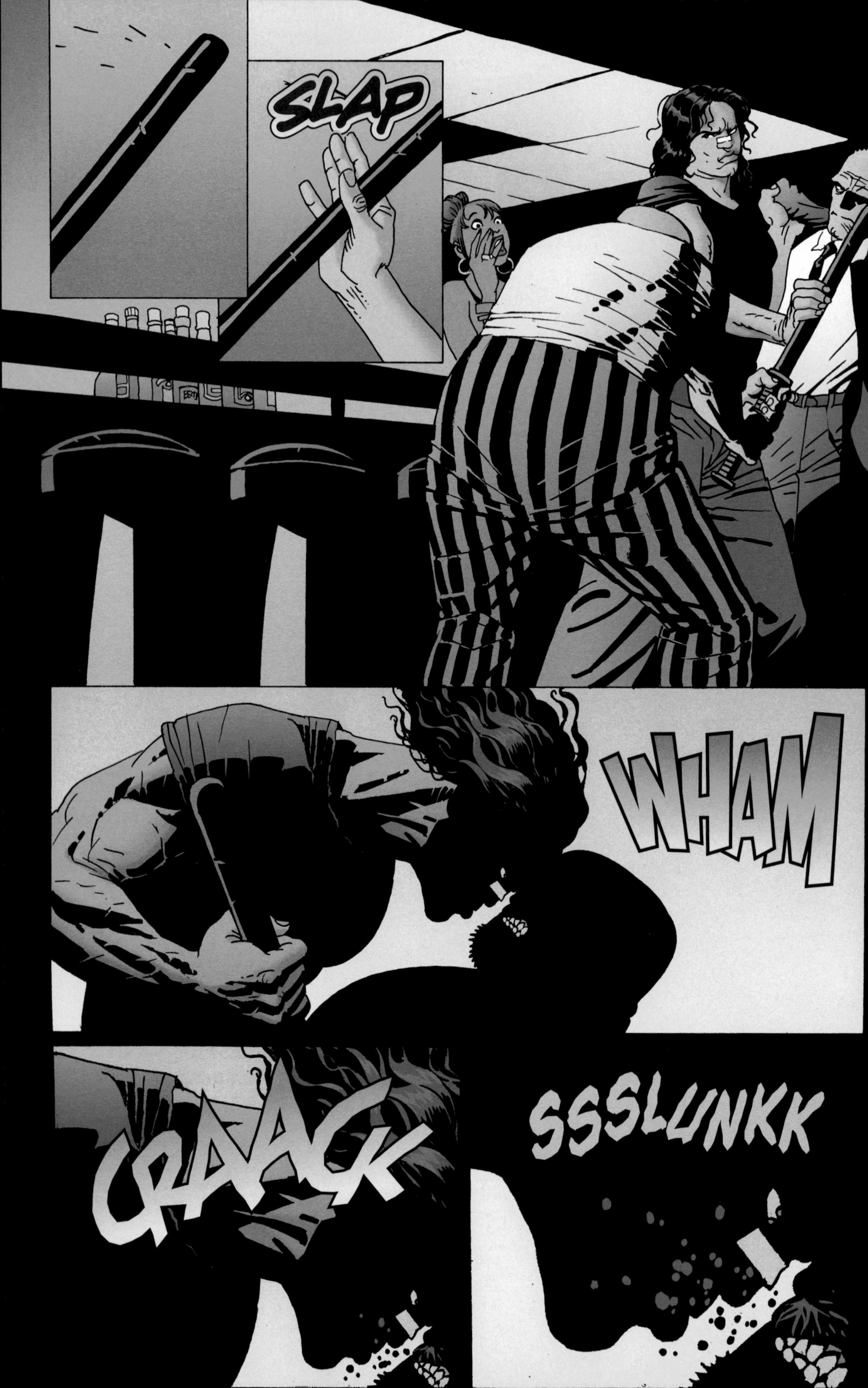
SLAP
WHAM
CRAACK
SSSLUNKK

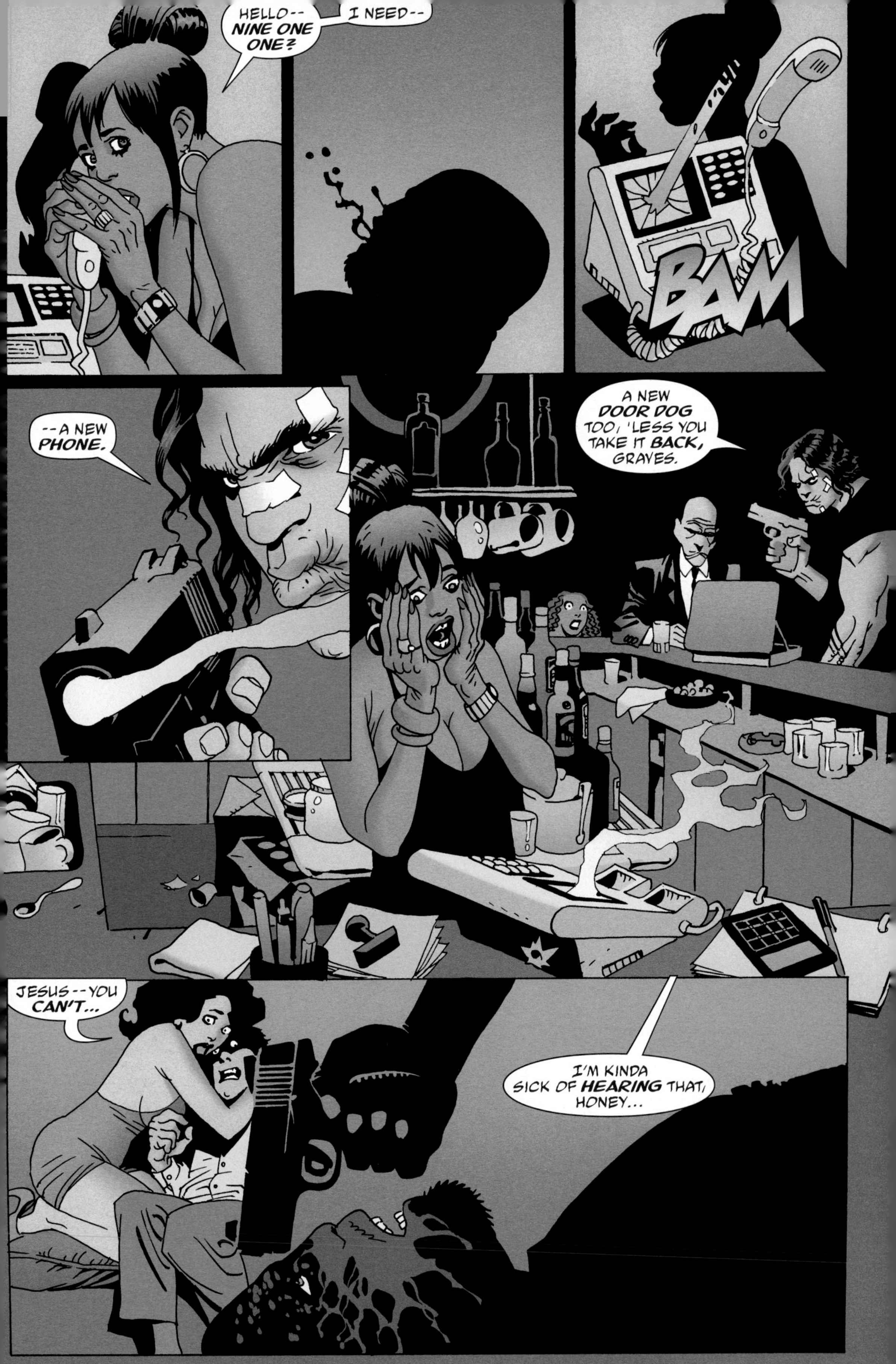
HELLO-- NINE ONE ONE?
I NEED--
BAM
--A NEW PHONE.
A NEW DOOR DOG TOO, 'LESS YOU TAKE IT BACK, GRAVES.
JESUS--YOU CAN'T...
I'M KINDA SICK OF HEARING THAT, HONEY...

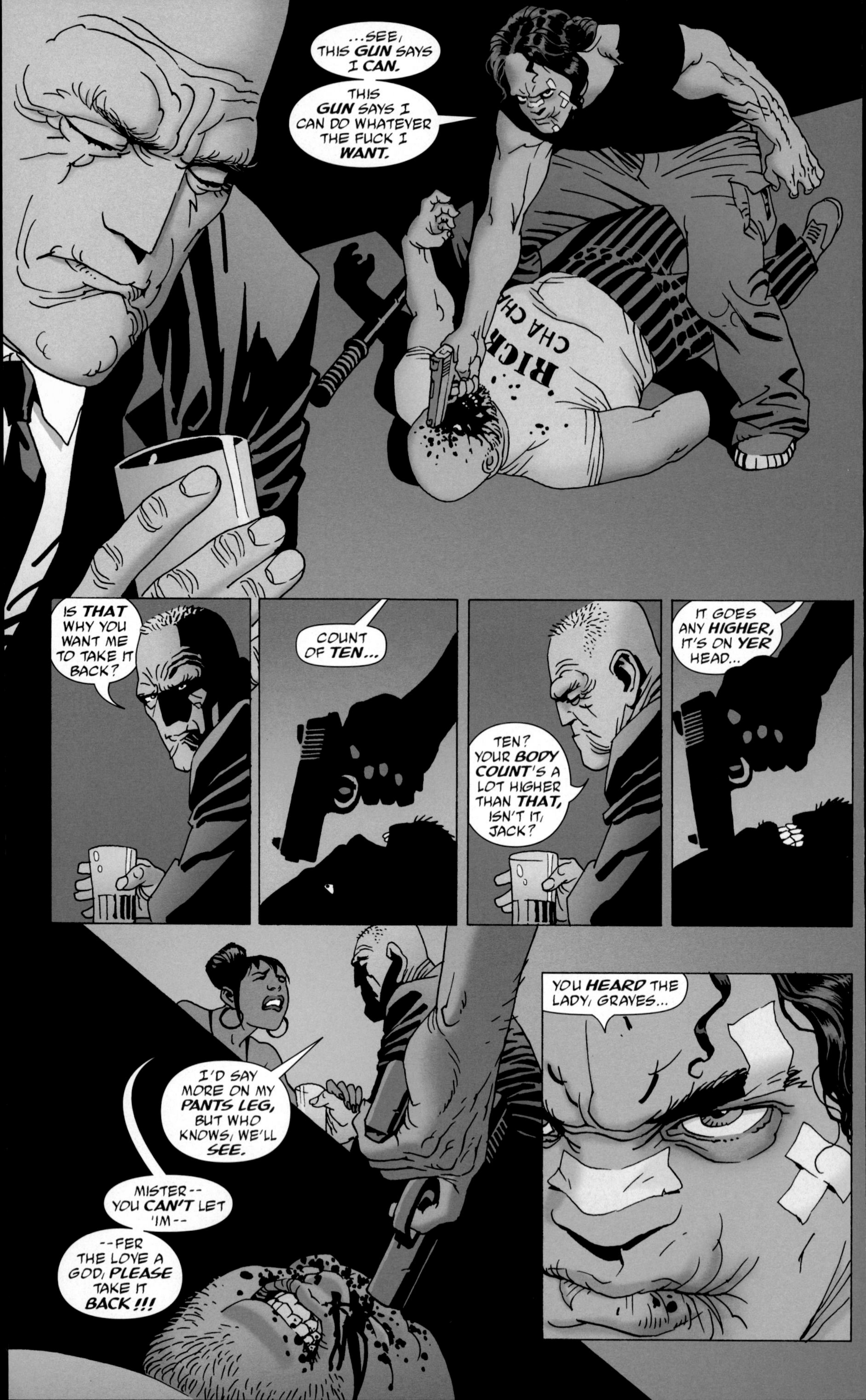
...SEE, THIS GUN SAYS I CAN.
THIS GUN SAYS I CAN DO WHATEVER THE FUCK I WANT.
RICK
CHA CHA
IS THAT WHY YOU WANT ME TO TAKE IT BACK?
COUNT OF TEN...
TEN? YOUR BODY COUNT'S A LOT HIGHER THAN THAT, ISN'T IT, JACK?
IT GOES ANY HIGHER, IT'S ON YER HEAD...
I'D SAY MORE ON MY PANTS LEG, BUT WHO KNOWS, WE'LL SEE.
MISTER-- YOU CAN'T LET 'IM--
--FER THE LOVE A GOD, PLEASE TAKE IT BACK!!!
YOU HEARD THE LADY, GRAVES...

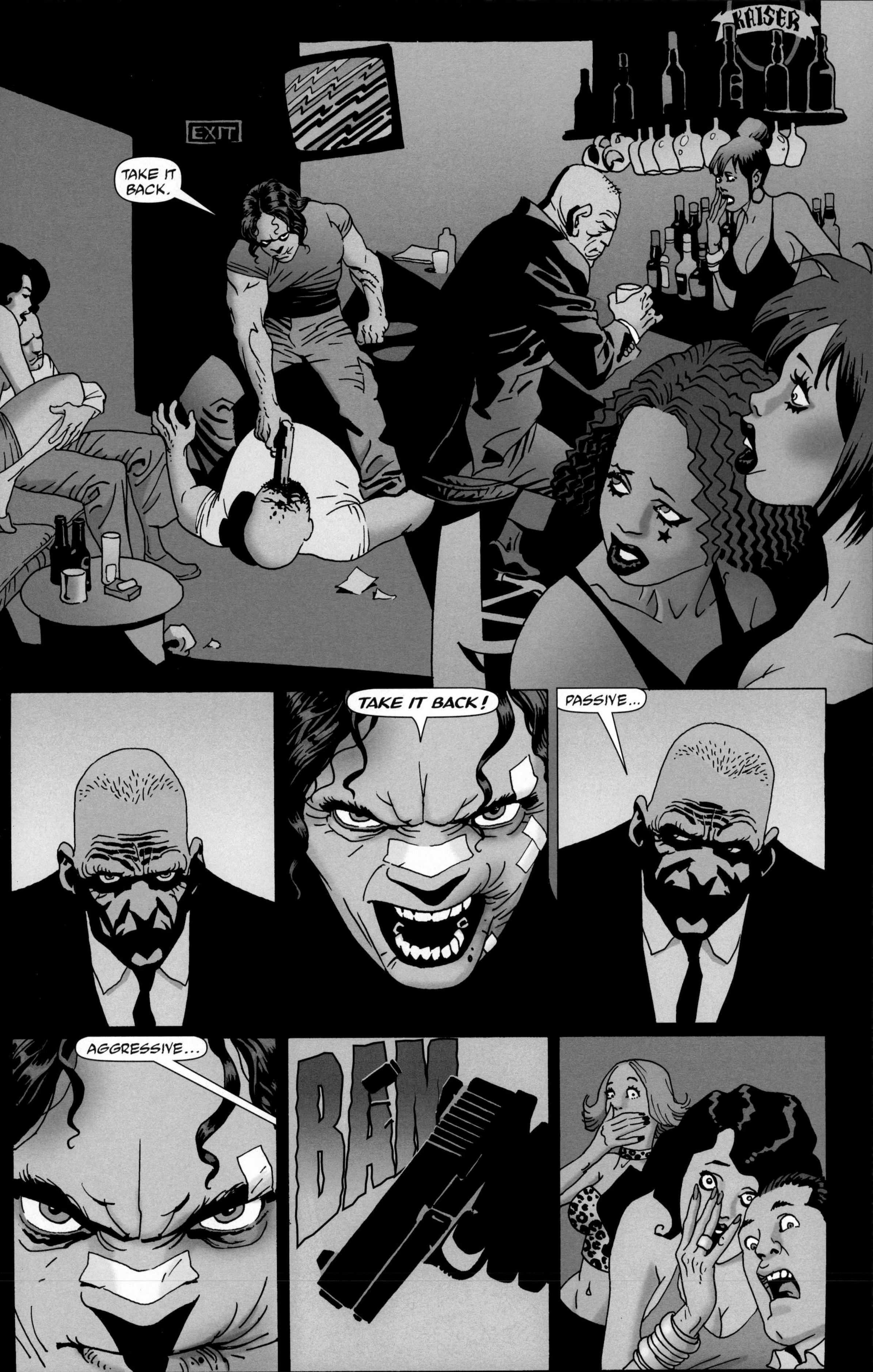
KAISER
EXIT
TAKE IT BACK.
TAKE IT BACK!
PASSIVE...
AGGRESSIVE...
BAM

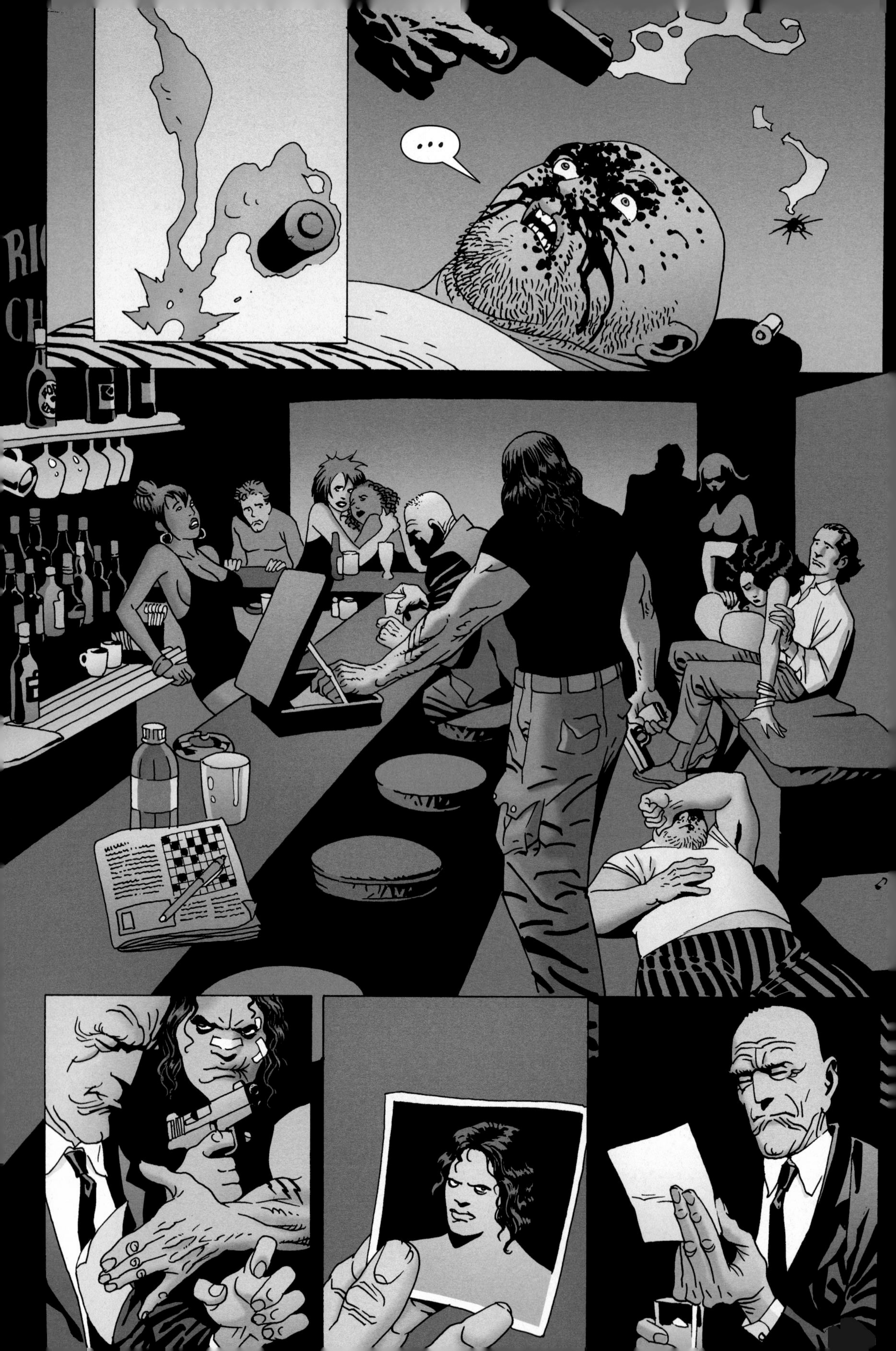
...

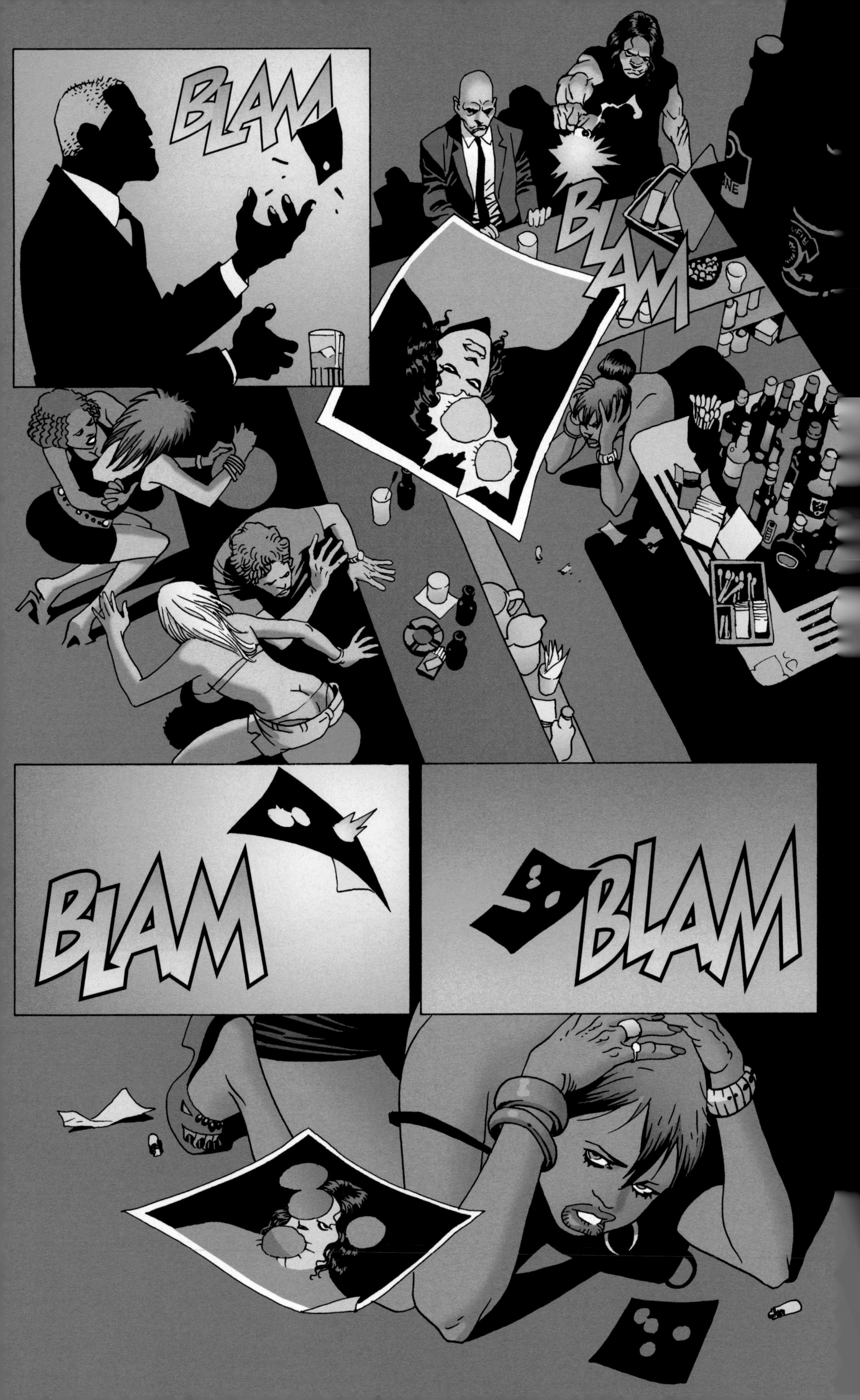
BLAM
BLAM
BLAM
BLAM

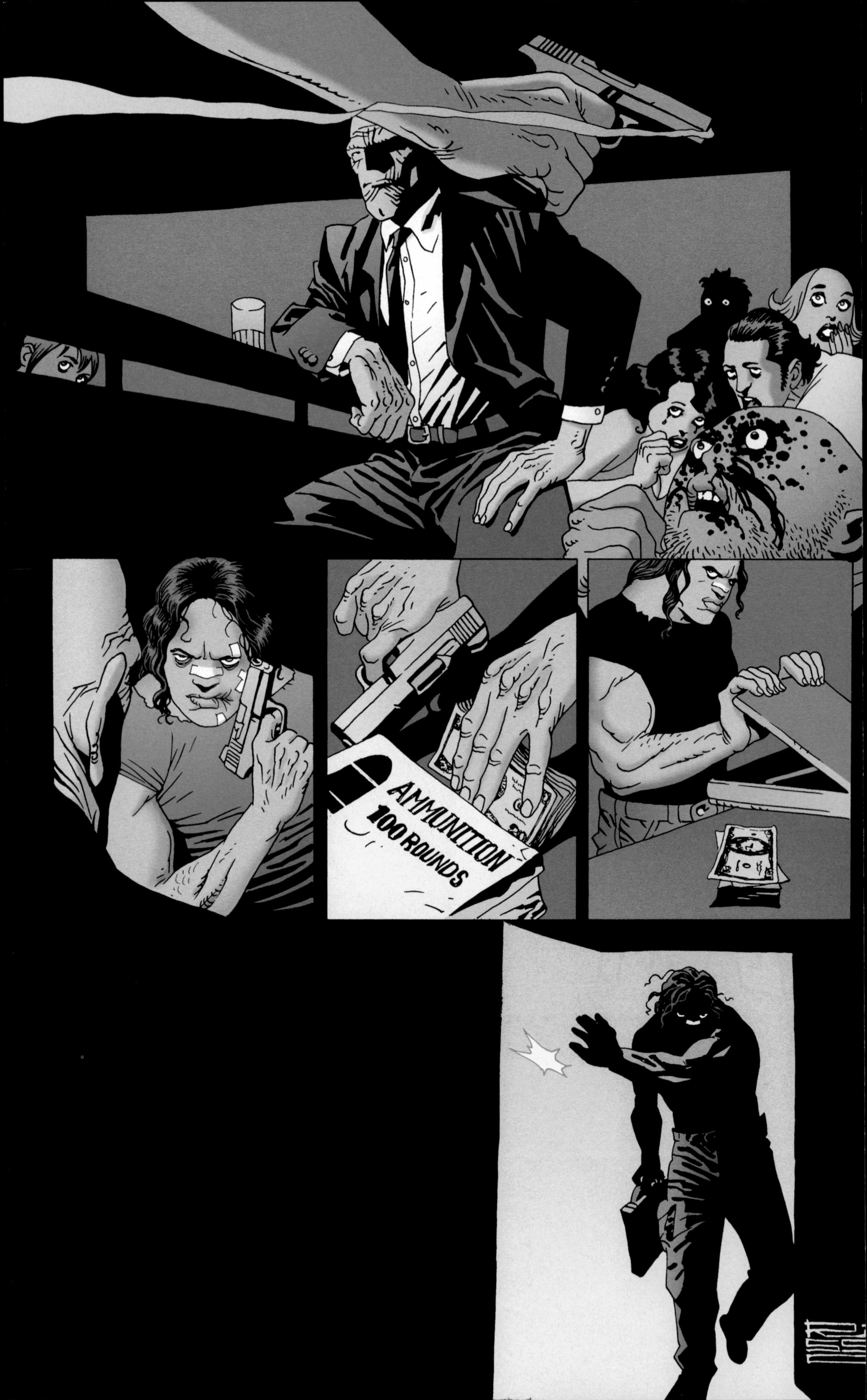
AMMUNITION
100 ROUNDS

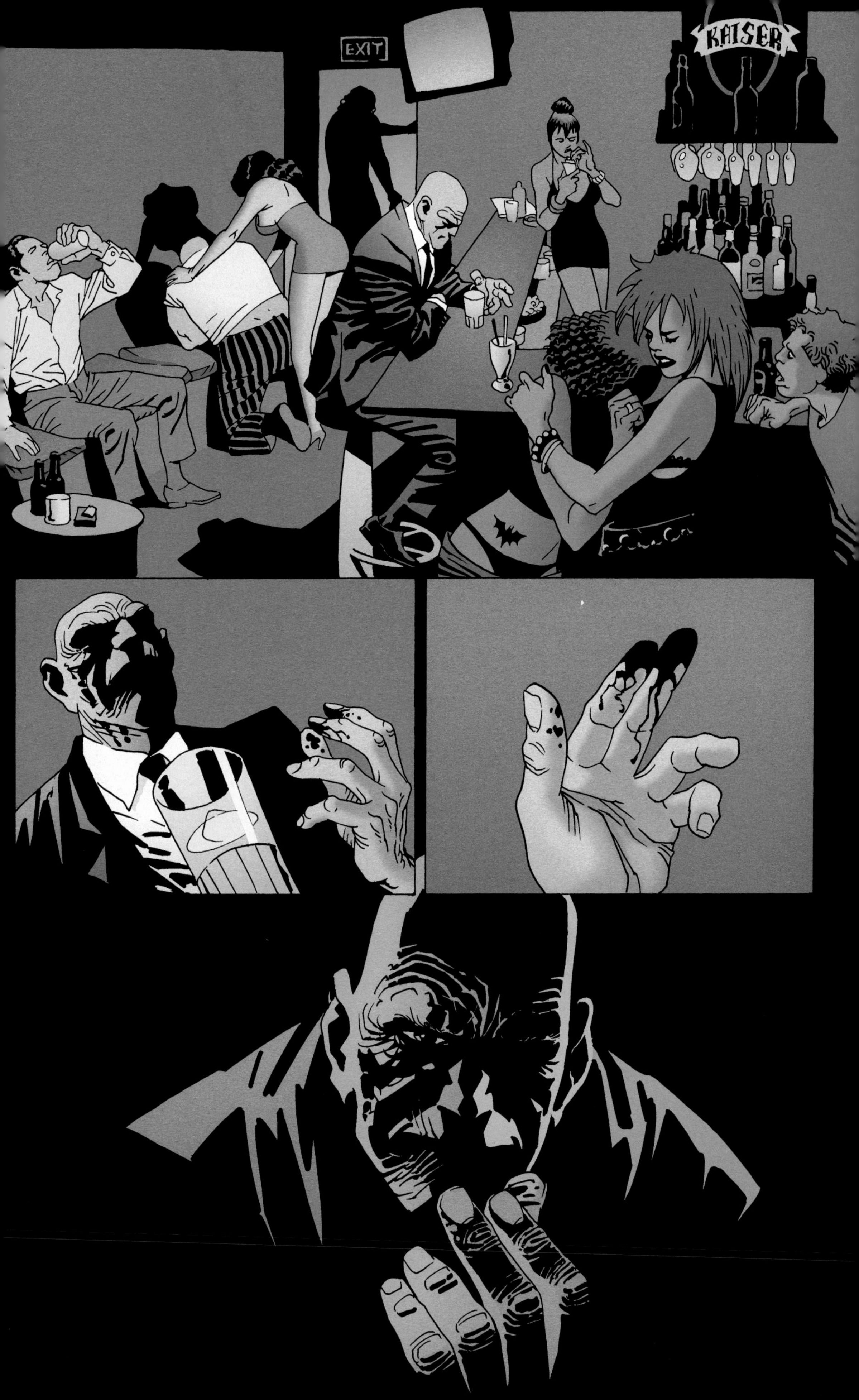
EXIT
KAISER

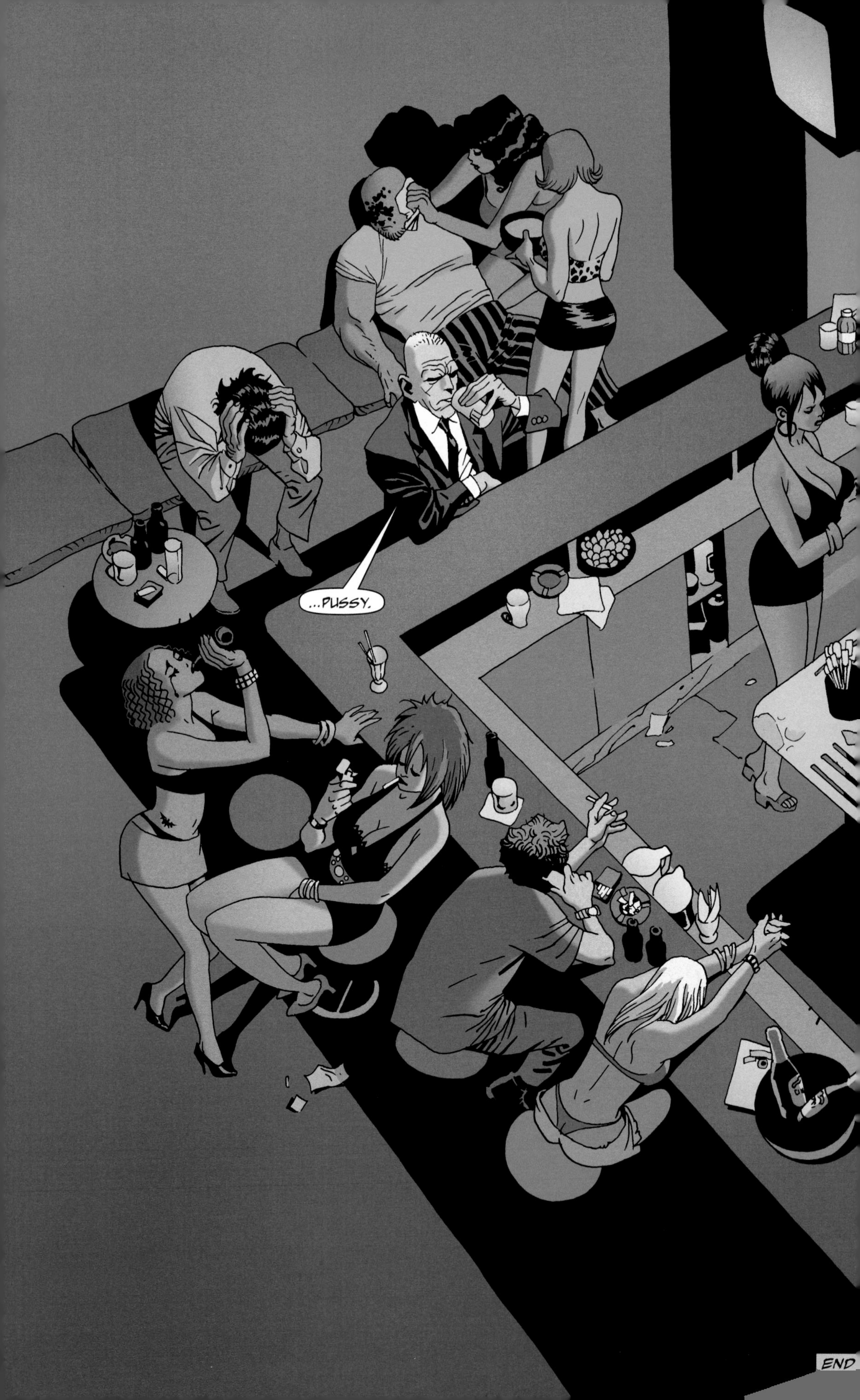
...PUSSY.
END

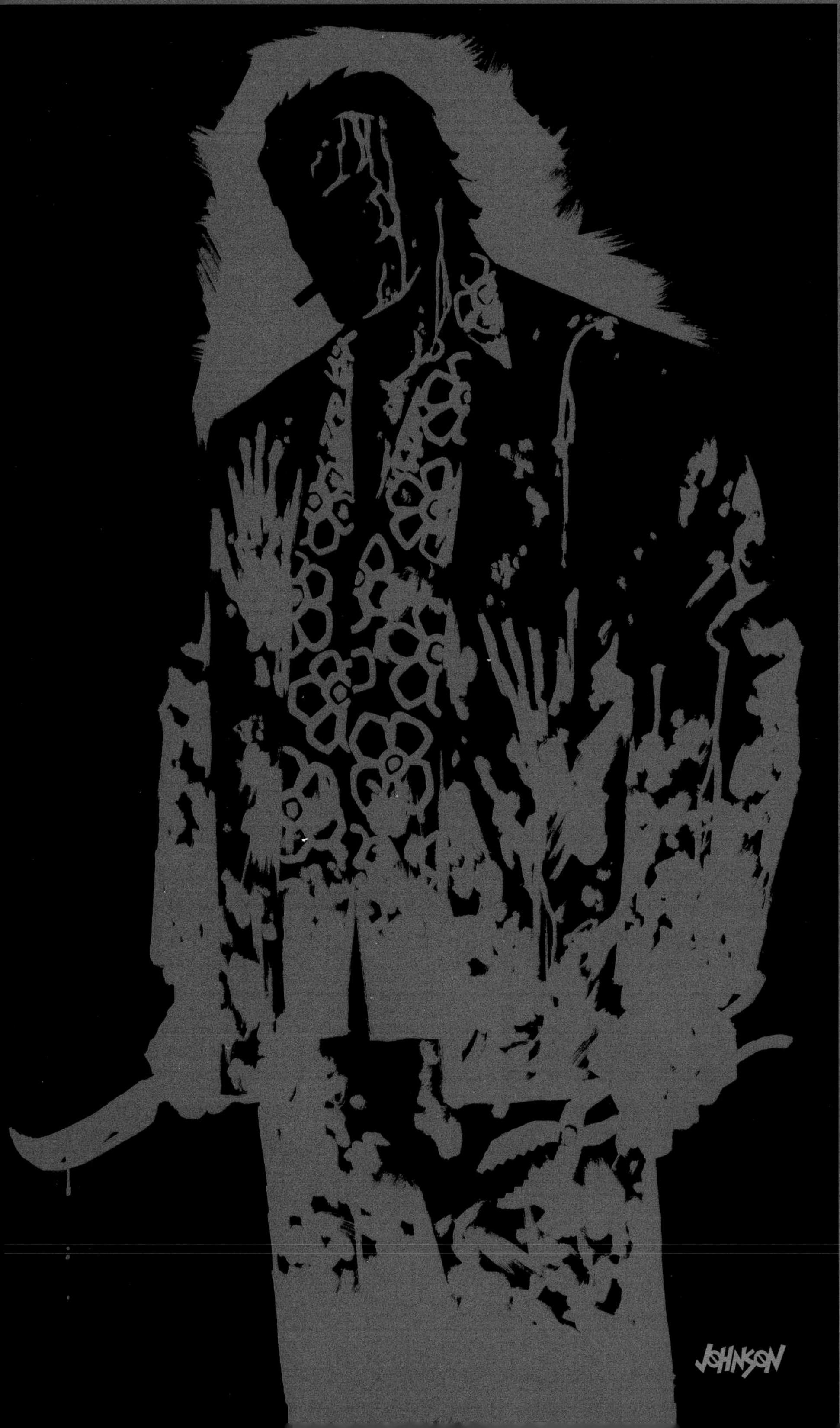
JOHNSON

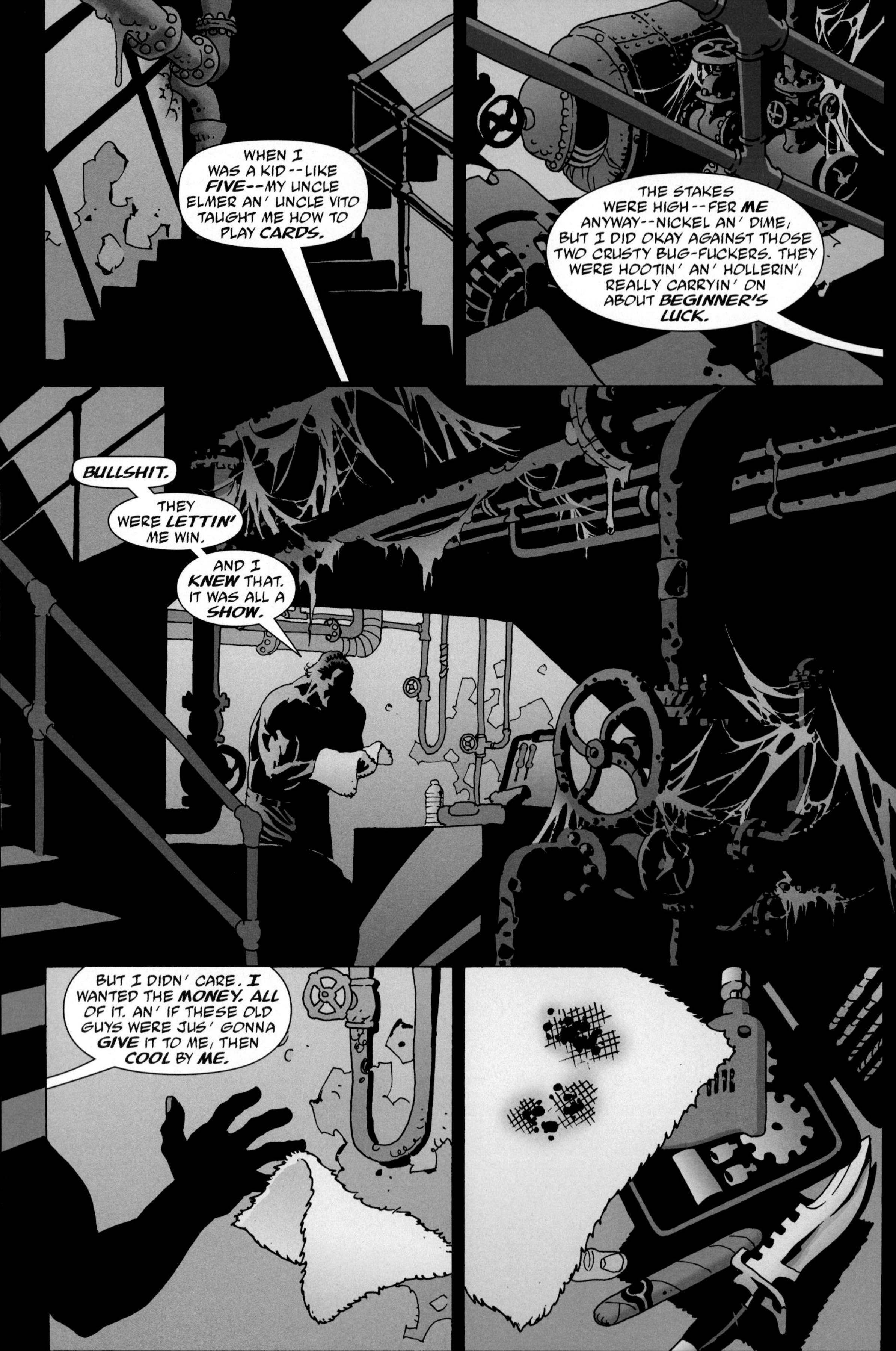
WHEN I WAS A KID--LIKE FIVE--MY UNCLE ELMER AN' UNCLE VITO TAUGHT ME HOW TO PLAY CARDS.
THE STAKES WERE HIGH--FER ME ANYWAY--NICKEL AN' DIME, BUT I DID OKAY AGAINST THOSE TWO CRUSTY BUG-FUCKERS. THEY WERE HOOTIN' AN' HOLLERIN', REALLY CARRYIN' ON ABOUT BEGINNER'S LUCK.
BULLSHIT.
THEY WERE LETTIN' ME WIN.
AND I KNEW THAT. IT WAS ALL A SHOW.
BUT I DIDN' CARE. I WANTED THE MONEY. ALL OF IT. AN' IF THESE OLD GUYS WERE JUS' GONNA GIVE IT TO ME, THEN COOL BY ME.

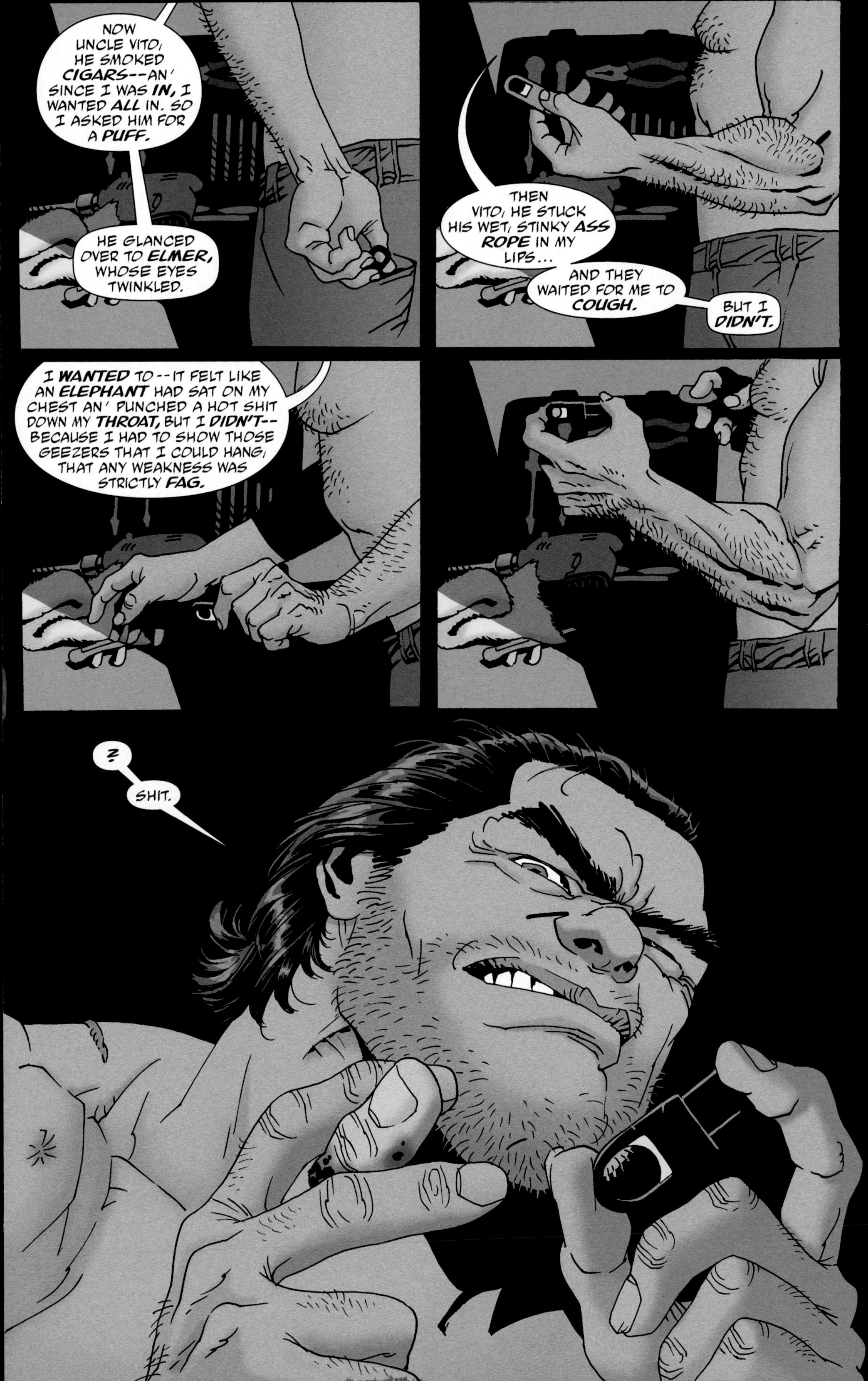
NOW UNCLE VITO, HE SMOKED CIGARS--AN' SINCE I WAS IN, I WANTED ALL IN. SO I ASKED HIM FOR A PUFF.
HE GLANCED OVER TO ELMER, WHOSE EYES TWINKLED.
THEN VITO, HE STUCK HIS WET, STINKY ASS ROPE IN MY LIPS...
AND THEY WAITED FOR ME TO COUGH.
BUT I DIDN'T.
I WANTED TO--IT FELT LIKE AN ELEPHANT HAD SAT ON MY CHEST AN' PUNCHED A HOT SHIT DOWN MY THROAT, BUT I DIDN'T--BECAUSE I HAD TO SHOW THOSE GEEZERS THAT I COULD HANG, THAT ANY WEAKNESS WAS STRICTLY FAG.
?
SHIT.

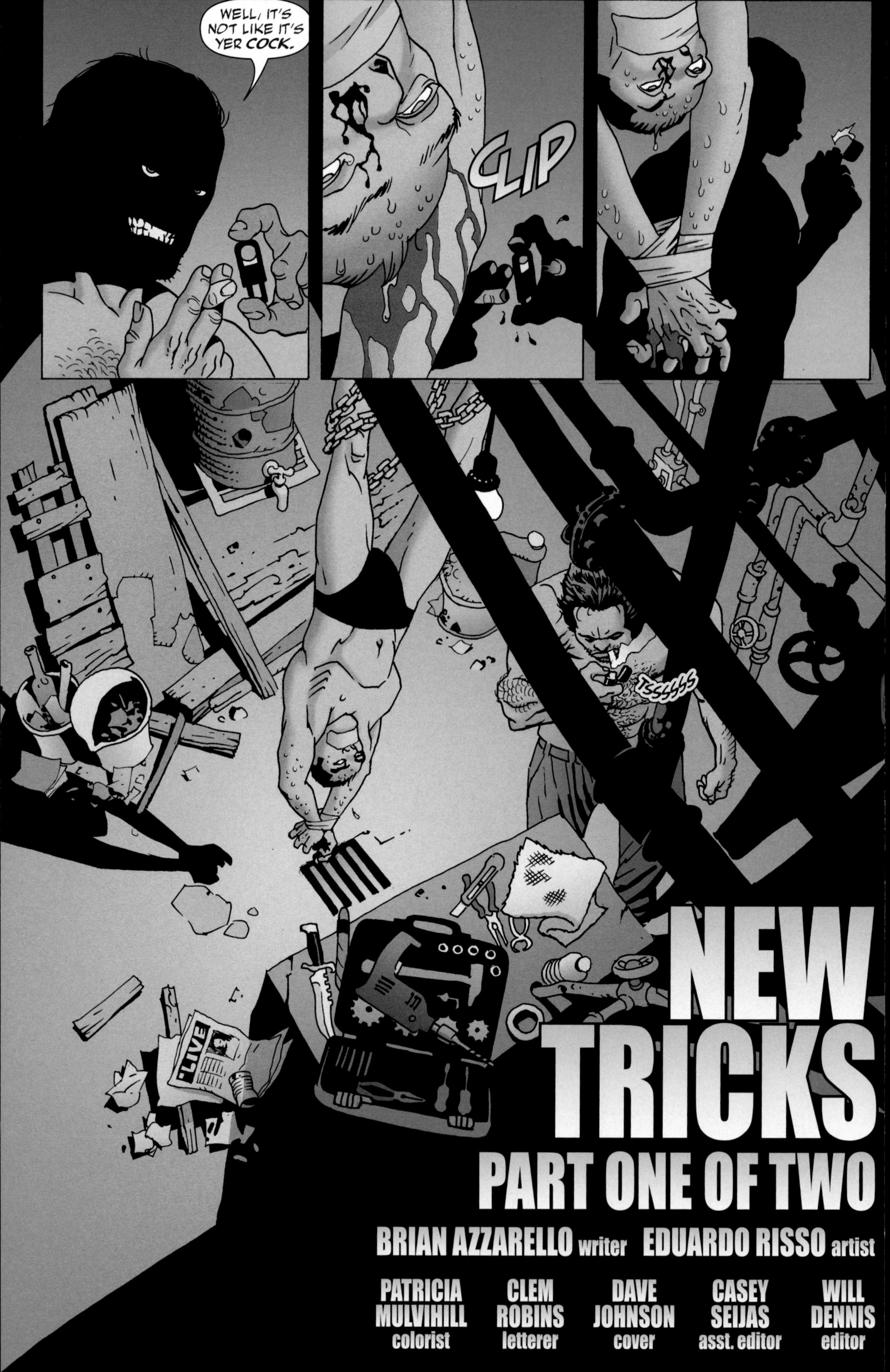
WELL, IT'S NOT LIKE IT'S YER COCK.
CLIP
TSSSSSS
LIVE

NEW TRICKS

PART ONE OF TWO

BRIAN AZZARELLO writer **EDUARDO RISSO** artist

PATRICIA MULVIHILL colorist **CLEM ROBINS** letterer **DAVE JOHNSON** cover **CASEY SEIJAS** asst. editor **WILL DENNIS** editor

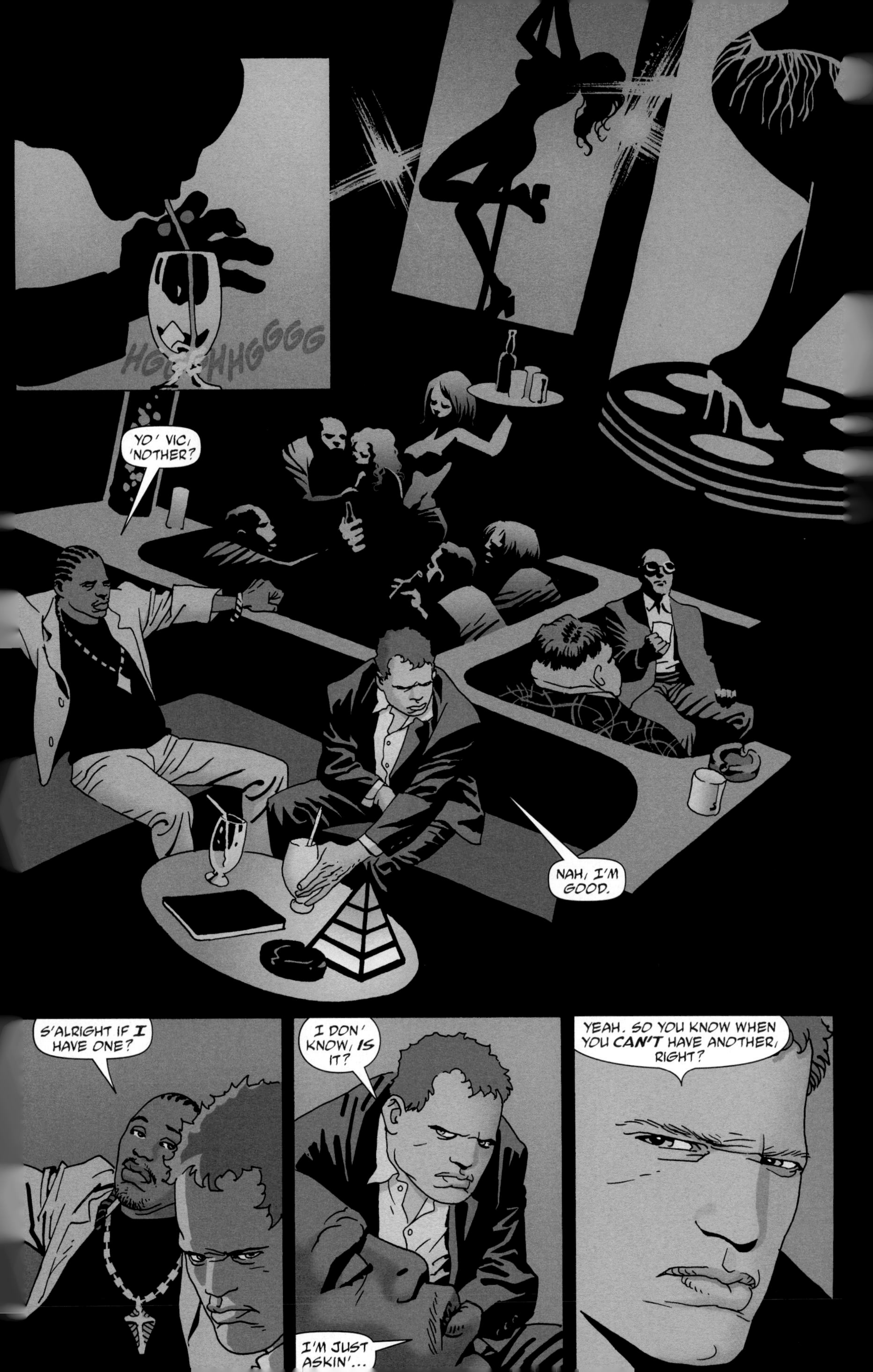
HGGGHHGGGG
YO' VIC, 'NOTHER?
NAH, I'M GOOD.
S'ALRIGHT IF I HAVE ONE?
I DON' KNOW, IS IT?
I'M JUST ASKIN'...
YEAH. SO YOU KNOW WHEN YOU CAN'T HAVE ANOTHER, RIGHT?

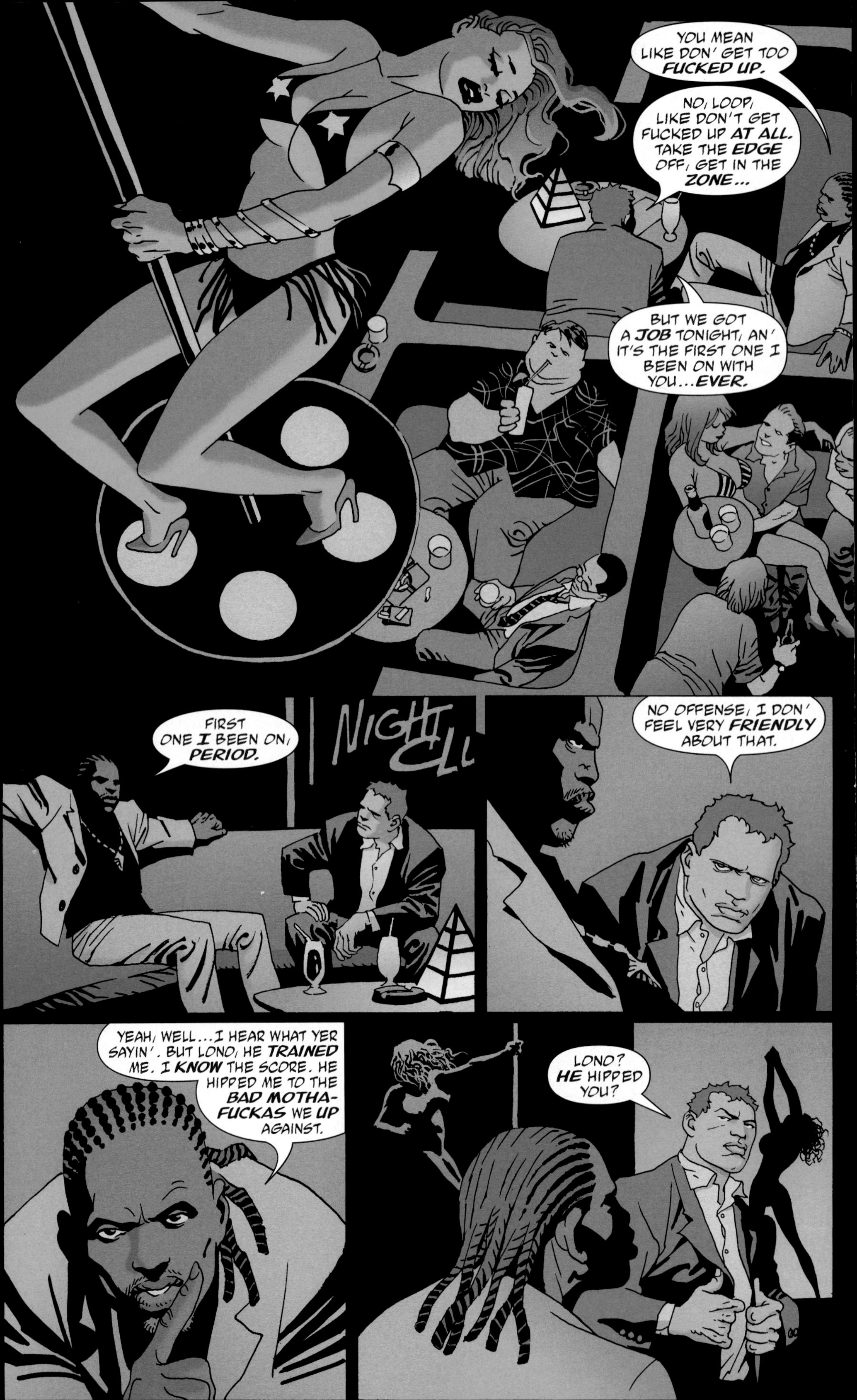
YOU MEAN LIKE DON' GET TOO FUCKED UP.
NO, LOOP, LIKE DON'T GET FUCKED UP AT ALL. TAKE THE EDGE OFF, GET IN THE ZONE...
BUT WE GOT A JOB TONIGHT, AN' IT'S THE FIRST ONE I BEEN ON WITH YOU... EVER.
FIRST ONE I BEEN ON, PERIOD.
NIGHT CLU
NO OFFENSE, I DON' FEEL VERY FRIENDLY ABOUT THAT.
YEAH, WELL... I HEAR WHAT YER SAYIN'. BUT LONO, HE TRAINED ME. I KNOW THE SCORE. HE HIPPED ME TO THE BAD MOTHA-FUCKAS WE UP AGAINST.
LONO? HE HIPPED YOU?

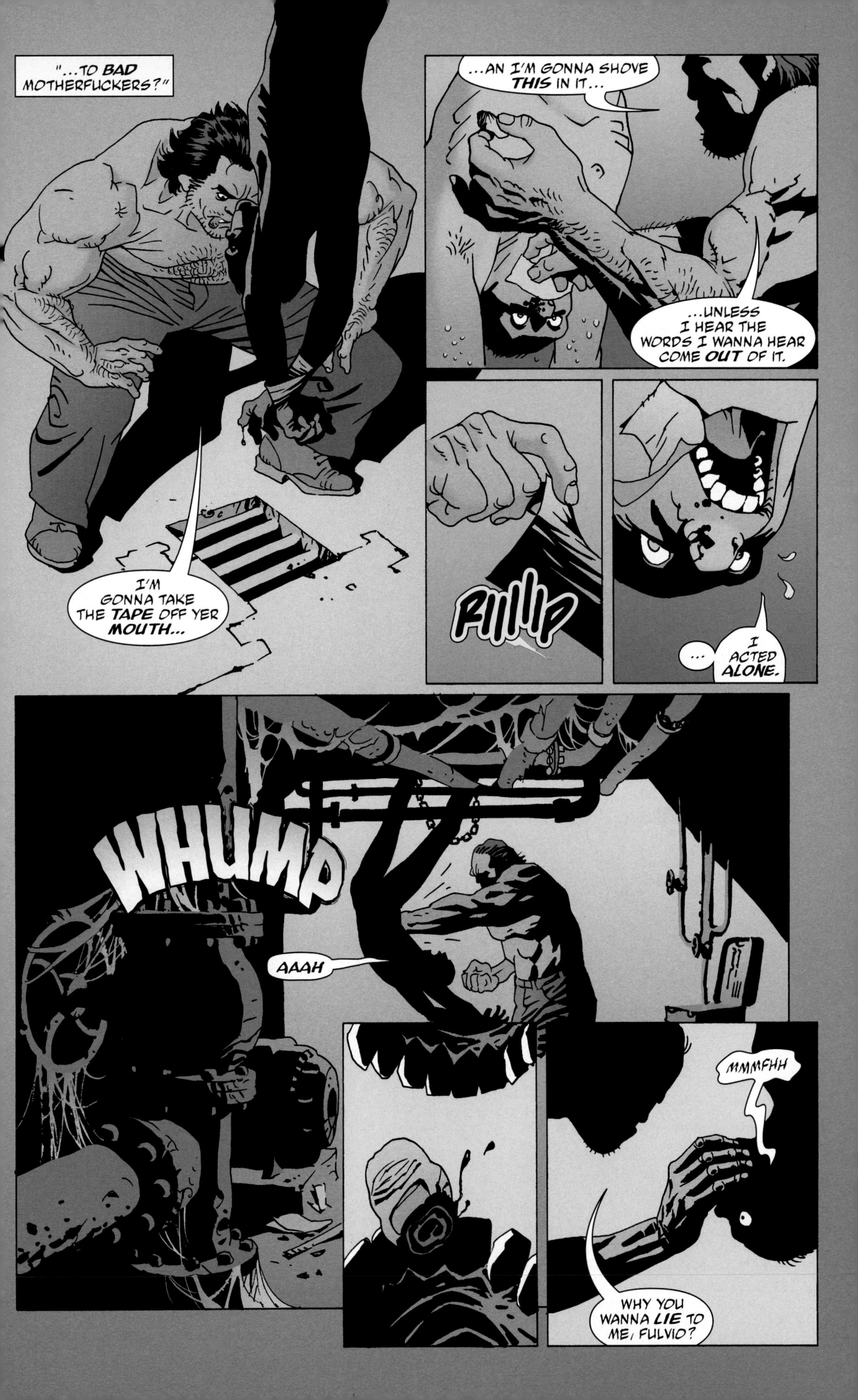
"...TO BAD MOTHERFUCKERS?"
I'M GONNA TAKE THE TAPE OFF YER MOUTH...
...AN I'M GONNA SHOVE THIS IN IT...
...UNLESS I HEAR THE WORDS I WANNA HEAR COME OUT OF IT.
RIIIIP
...
I ACTED ALONE.
WHUMP
AAAH
MMMFHH
WHY YOU WANNA LIE TO ME, FULVIO?

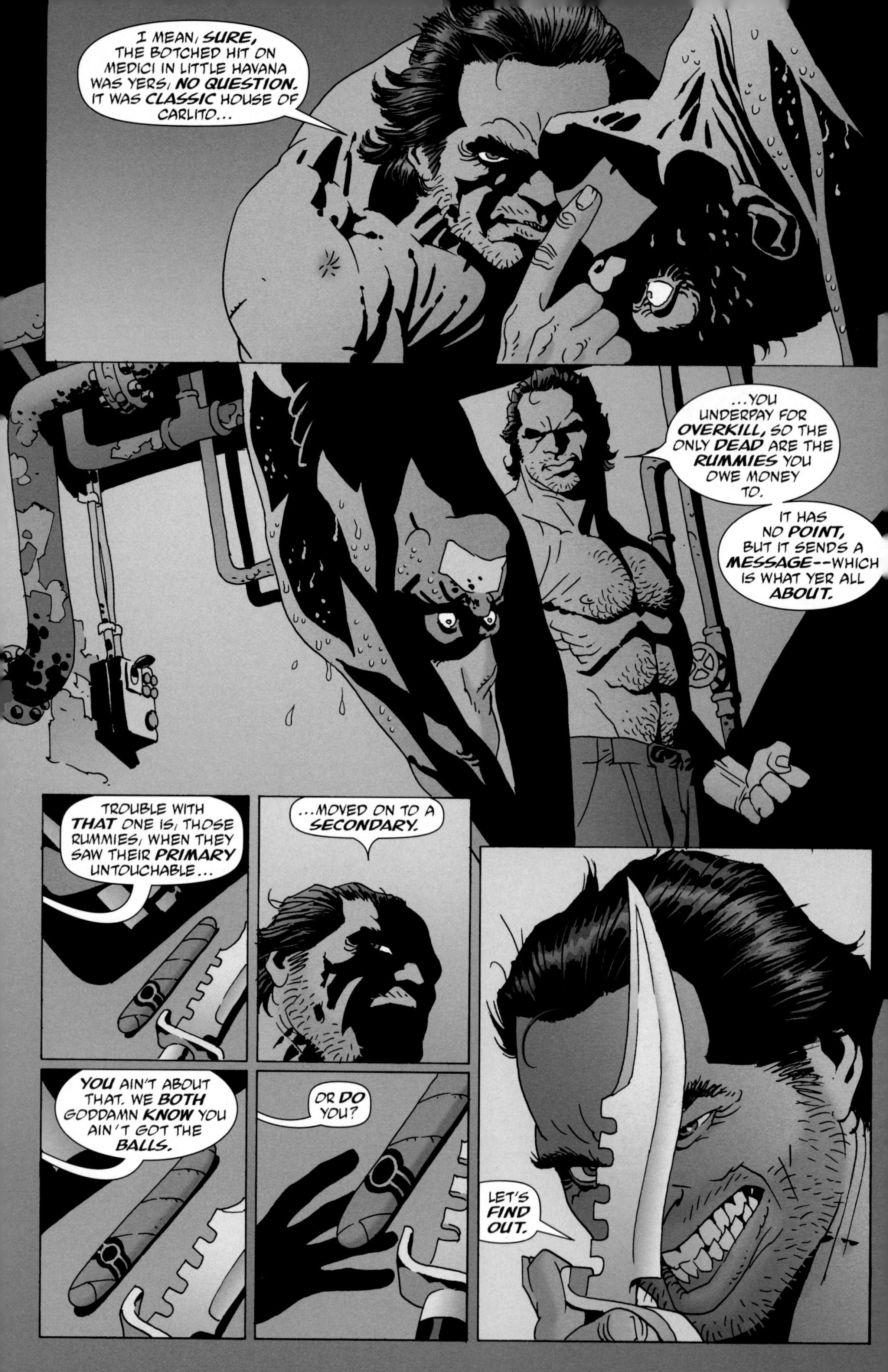
I MEAN, SURE, THE BOTCHED HIT ON MEDICI IN LITTLE HAVANA WAS YERS, NO QUESTION. IT WAS CLASSIC HOUSE OF CARLITO...
...YOU UNDERPAY FOR OVERKILL, SO THE ONLY DEAD ARE THE RUMMIES YOU OWE MONEY TO.
IT HAS NO POINT, BUT IT SENDS A MESSAGE--WHICH IS WHAT YER ALL ABOUT.
TROUBLE WITH THAT ONE IS, THOSE RUMMIES, WHEN THEY SAW THEIR PRIMARY UNTOUCHABLE...
...MOVED ON TO A SECONDARY.
YOU AIN'T ABOUT THAT. WE BOTH GODDAMN KNOW YOU AIN'T GOT THE BALLS.
OR DO YOU?
LET'S FIND OUT.

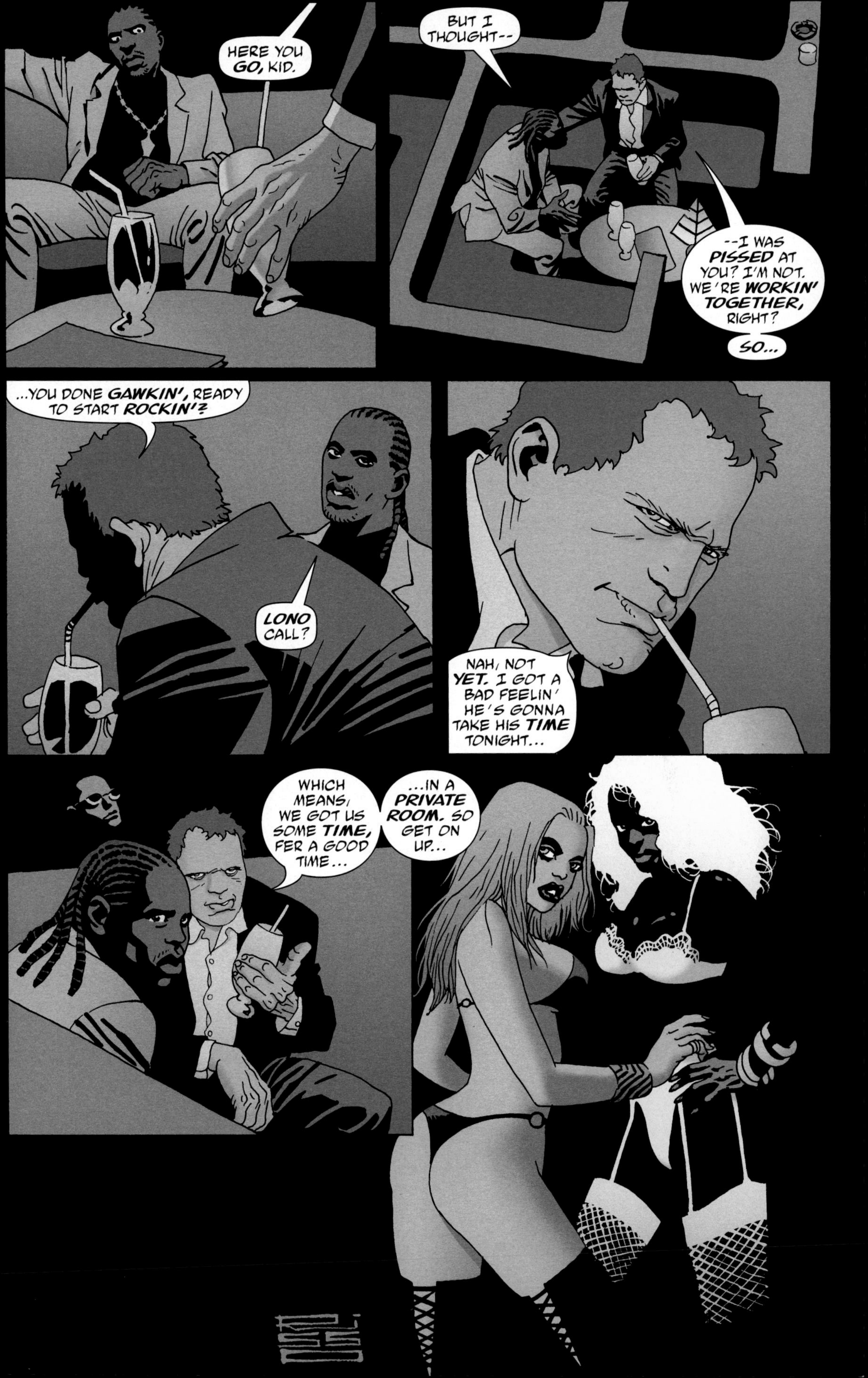
HERE YOU GO, KID.
BUT I THOUGHT--
--I WAS PISSED AT YOU? I'M NOT. WE'RE WORKIN' TOGETHER, RIGHT?
SO...
...YOU DONE GAWKIN', READY TO START ROCKIN'?
LONO CALL?
NAH, NOT YET. I GOT A BAD FEELIN' HE'S GONNA TAKE HIS TIME TONIGHT...
WHICH MEANS, WE GOT US SOME TIME, FER A GOOD TIME...
...IN A PRIVATE ROOM. SO GET ON UP...

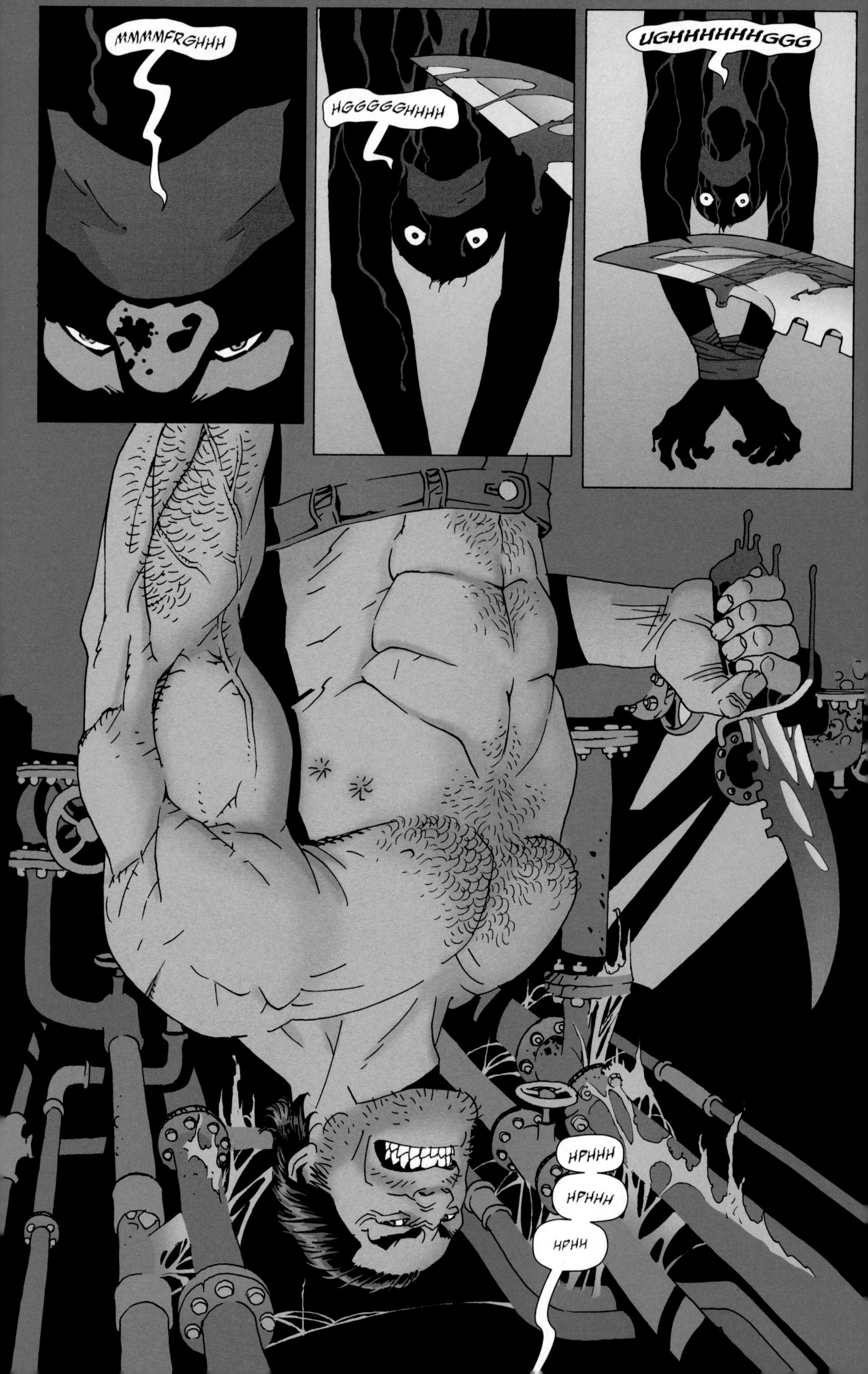
MMMMFRGHHH
HGGGGGHHHH
UGHHHHHHGGG
HPHHH
HPHHH
HPHH

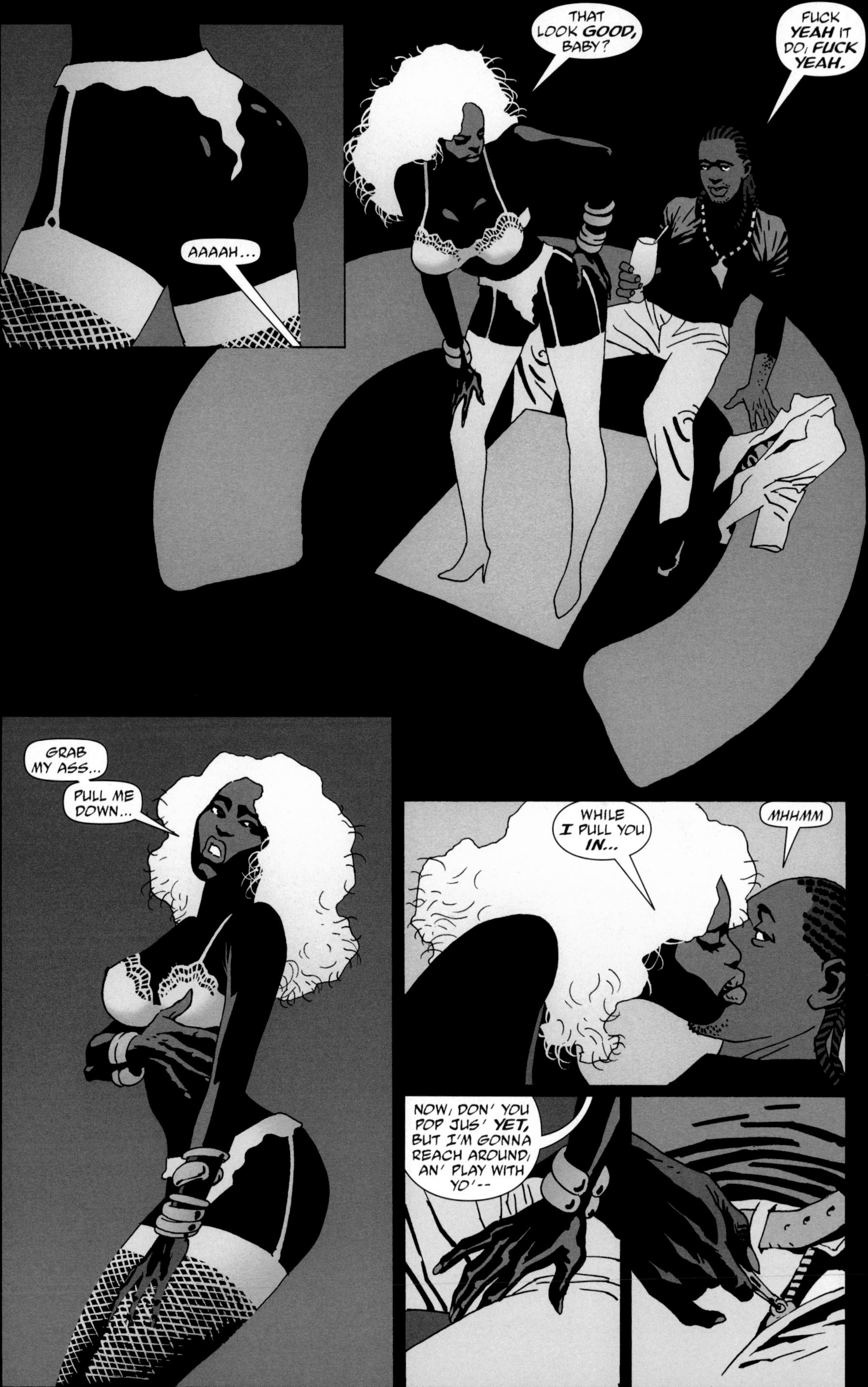
AAAAH...
THAT LOOK GOOD, BABY?
FUCK YEAH IT DO, FUCK YEAH.
GRAB MY ASS...
PULL ME DOWN...
WHILE I PULL YOU IN...
MHHMM
NOW, DON' YOU POP JUS' YET, BUT I'M GONNA REACH AROUND, AN' PLAY WITH YO'--

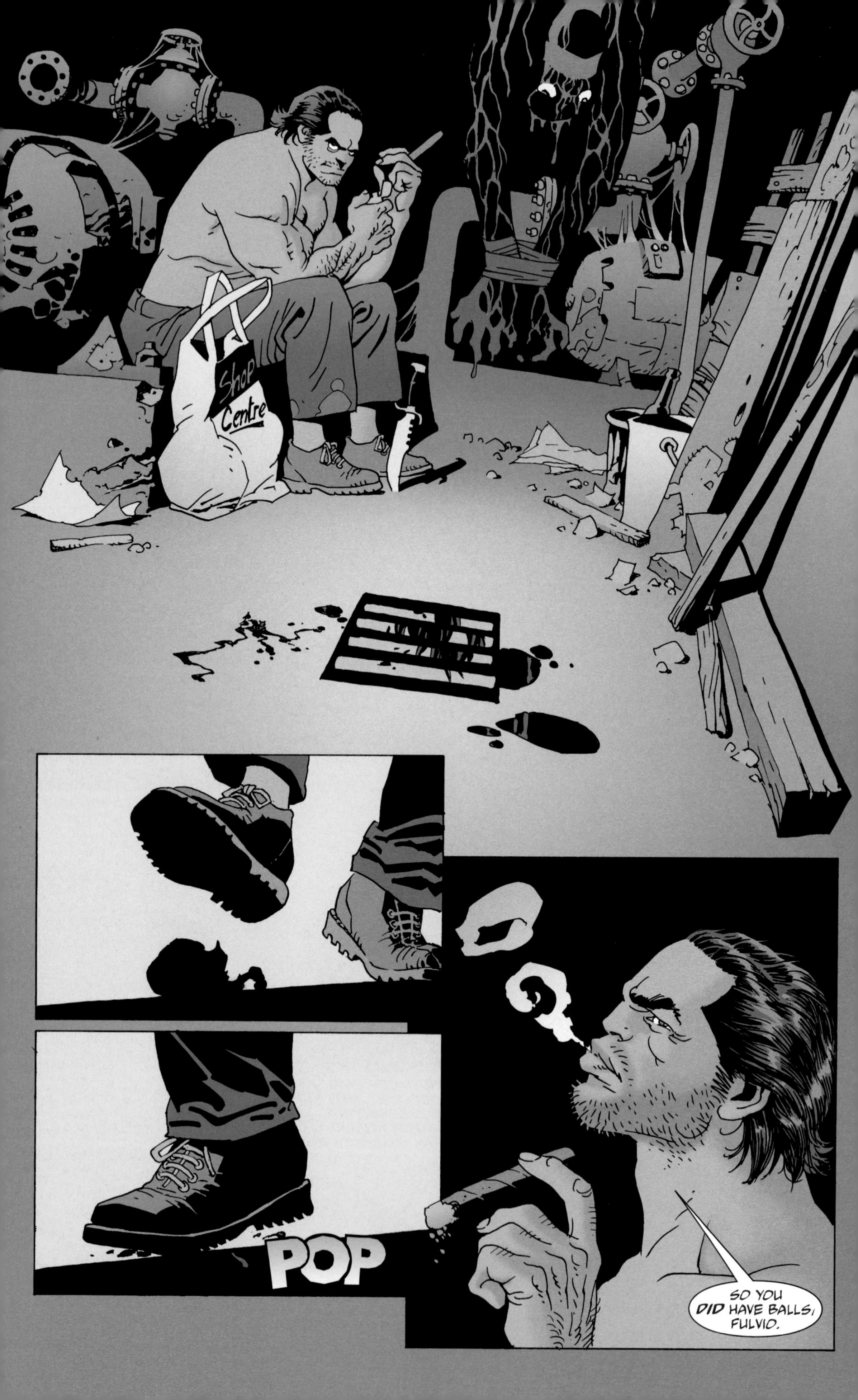
Shop Centre
POP
SO YOU DID HAVE BALLS, FULVIO.

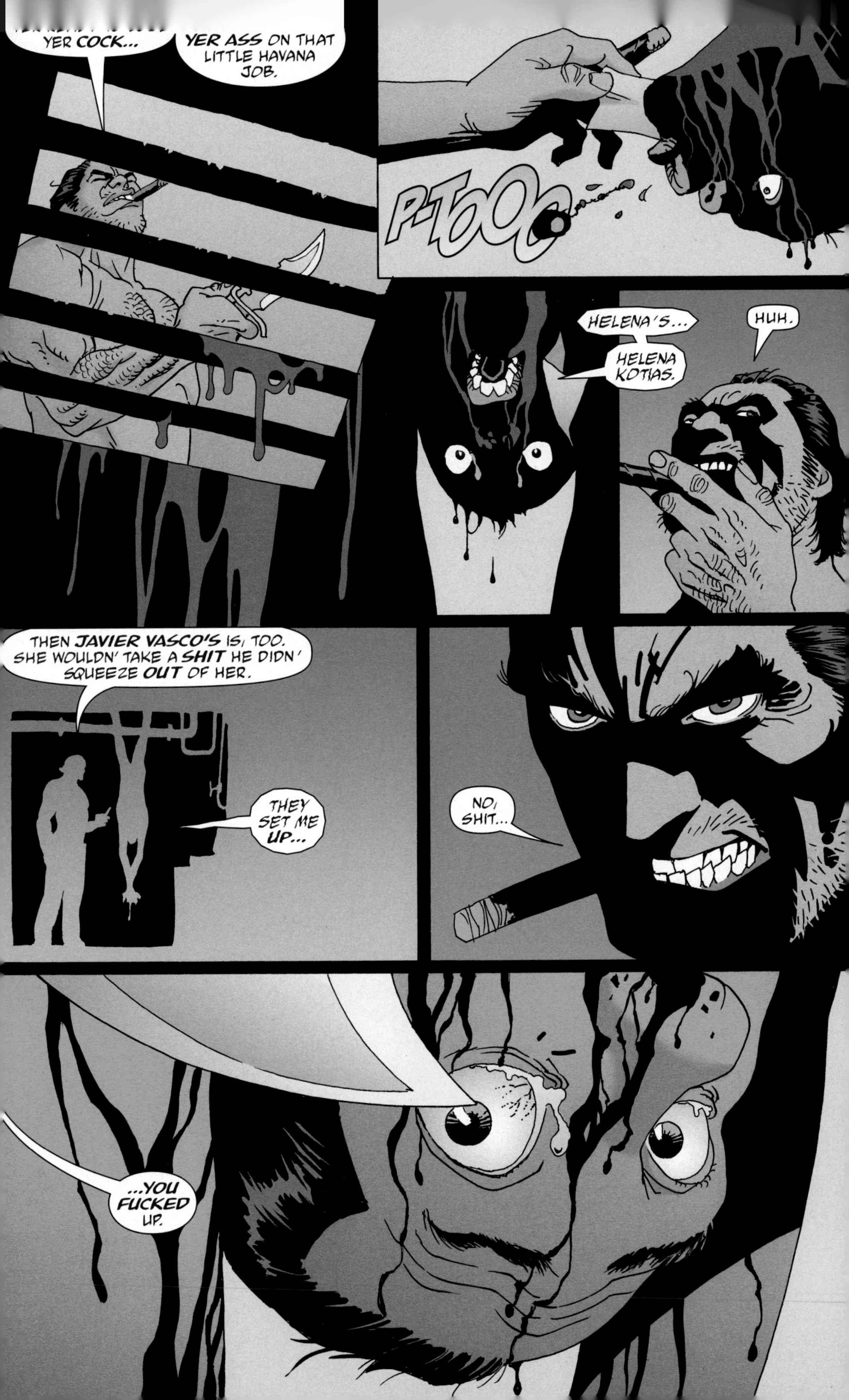
YER COCK...
YER ASS ON THAT LITTLE HAVANA JOB.
P-TOOO
HELENA'S...
HELENA KOTIAS.
HUH.
THEN JAVIER VASCO'S IS, TOO. SHE WOULDN' TAKE A SHIT HE DIDN' SQUEEZE OUT OF HER.
THEY SET ME UP...
NO, SHIT...
...YOU FUCKED UP.

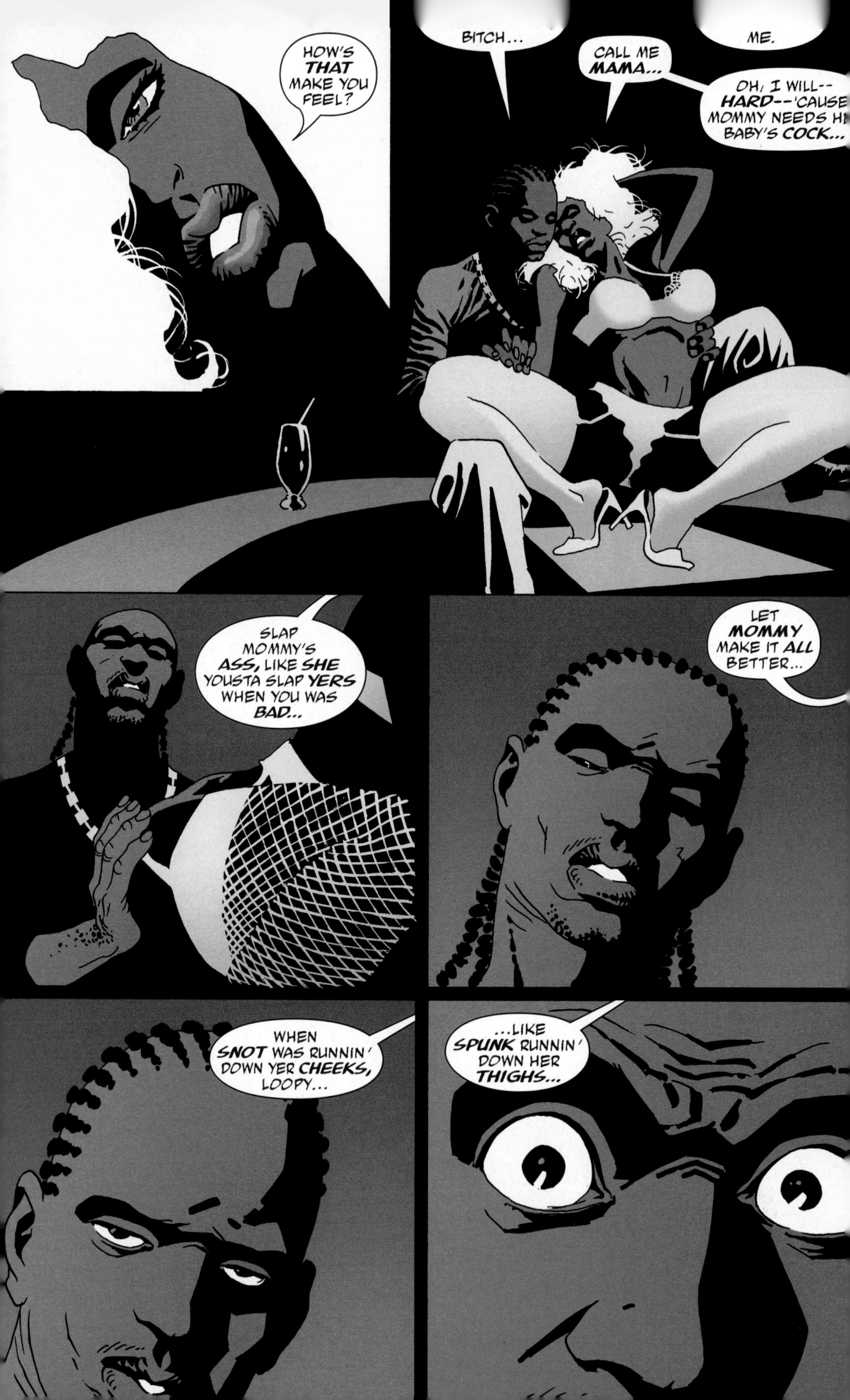
HOW'S **THAT** MAKE YOU FEEL?
BITCH...
ME.
CALL ME **MAMA...**
OH, I WILL-- **HARD--**'CAUSE MOMMY NEEDS H
BABY'S **COCK...**
SLAP MOMMY'S **ASS,** LIKE **SHE** YOUSTA SLAP **YERS** WHEN YOU WAS **BAD...**
LET **MOMMY** MAKE IT **ALL** BETTER...
WHEN **SNOT** WAS RUNNIN' DOWN YER **CHEEKS,** LOOPY...
...LIKE **SPUNK** RUNNIN' DOWN HER **THIGHS...**

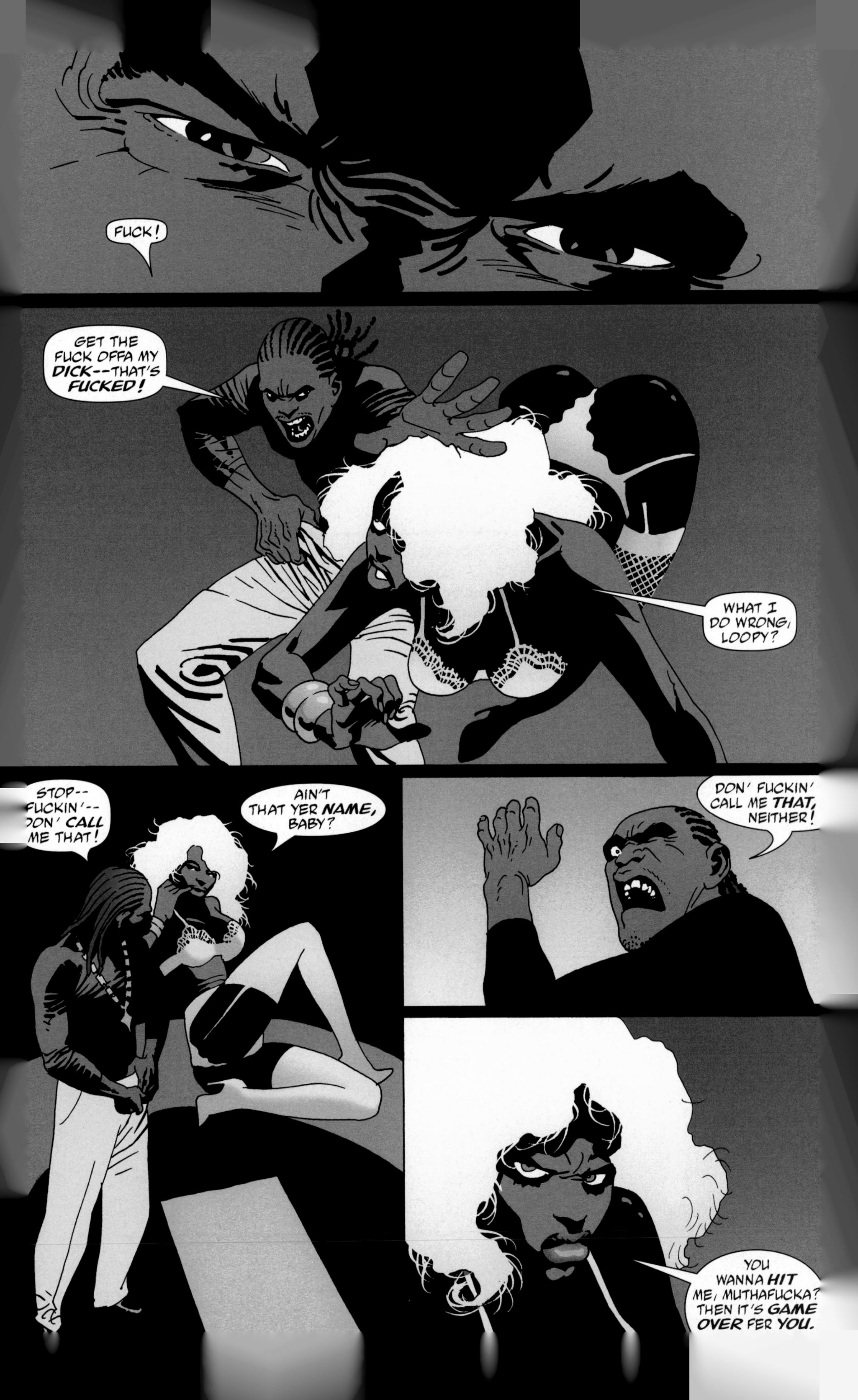
FUCK!
GET THE FUCK OFFA MY **DICK**--THAT'S **FUCKED!**
WHAT I DO WRONG, LOOPY?
STOP--FUCKIN'--DON' **CALL** ME THAT!
AIN'T THAT YER **NAME,** BABY?
DON' FUCKIN' CALL ME **THAT,** NEITHER!
YOU WANNA **HIT** ME, MUTHAFUCKA? THEN IT'S **GAME OVER** FER **YOU.**

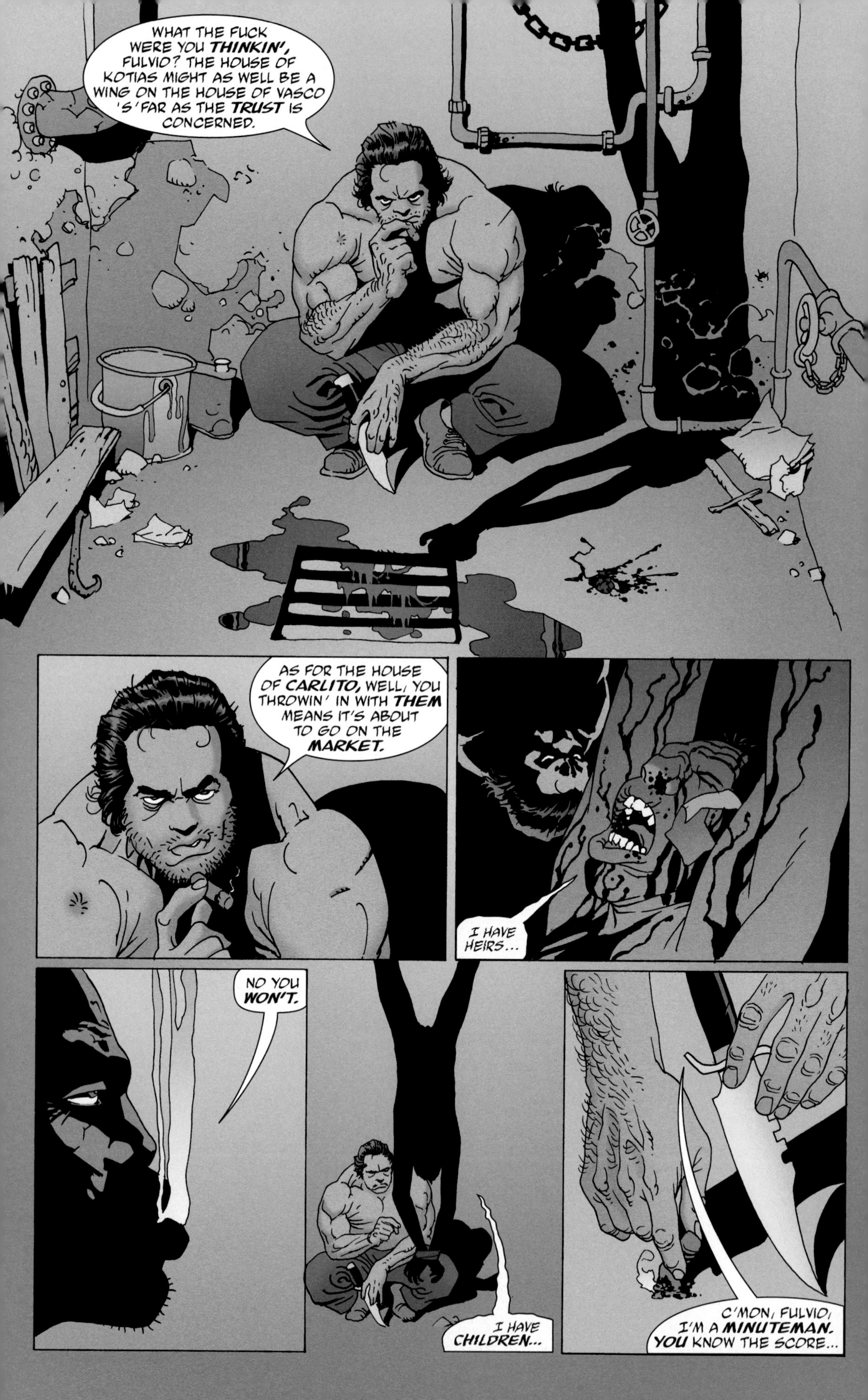

WHAT THE FUCK WERE YOU THINKIN', FULVIO? THE HOUSE OF KOTIAS MIGHT AS WELL BE A WING ON THE HOUSE OF VASCO 'S'FAR AS THE TRUST IS CONCERNED.
AS FOR THE HOUSE OF CARLITO, WELL, YOU THROWIN' IN WITH THEM MEANS IT'S ABOUT TO GO ON THE MARKET.
I HAVE HEIRS...
NO YOU WON'T.
I HAVE CHILDREN...
C'MON, FULVIO, I'M A MINUTEMAN. YOU KNOW THE SCORE...

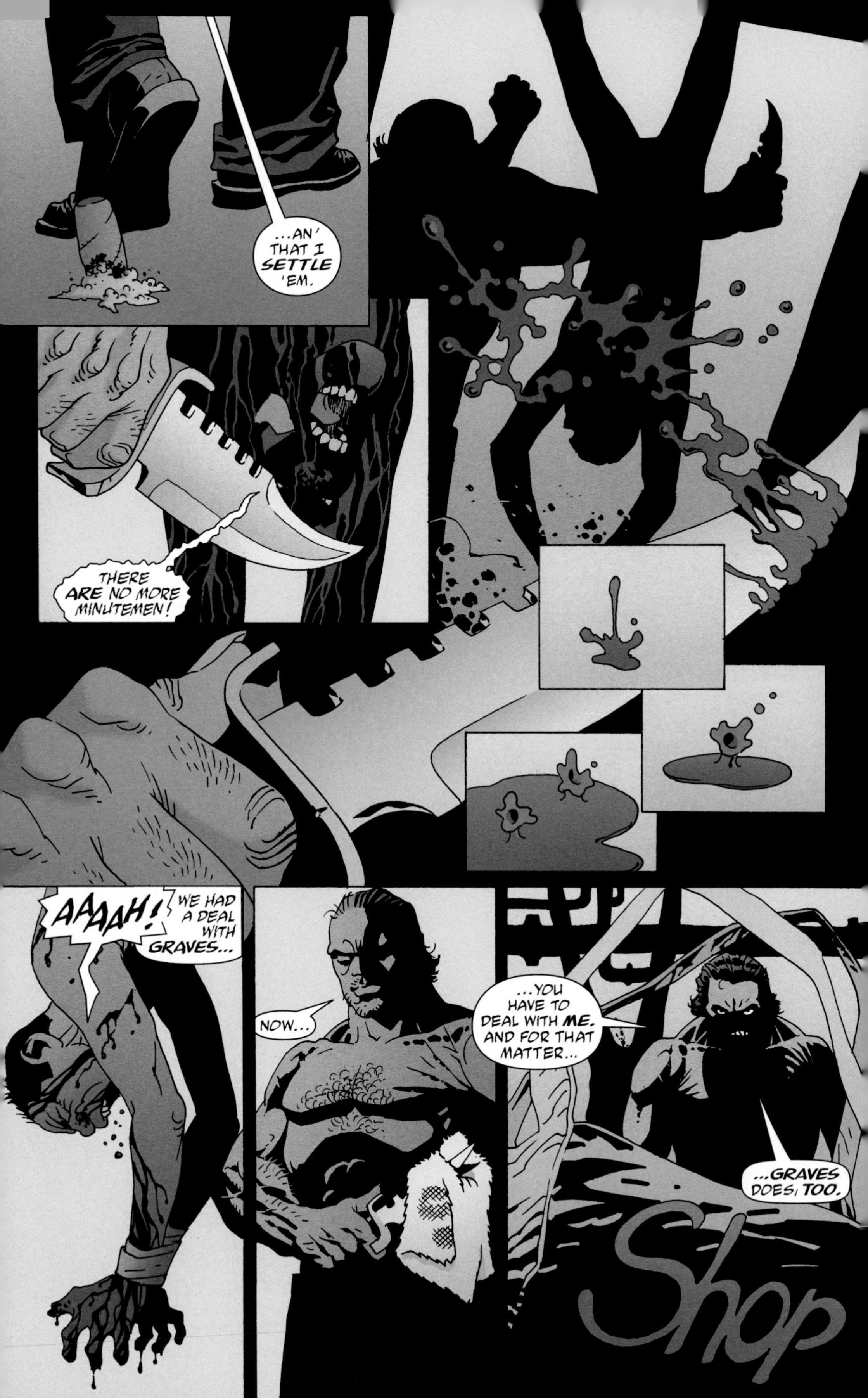
...AN' THAT I SETTLE 'EM.
THERE ARE NO MORE MINUTEMEN!
AAAAH!
WE HAD A DEAL WITH GRAVES...
NOW...
...YOU HAVE TO DEAL WITH ME. AND FOR THAT MATTER...
...GRAVES DOES, TOO.
Shop

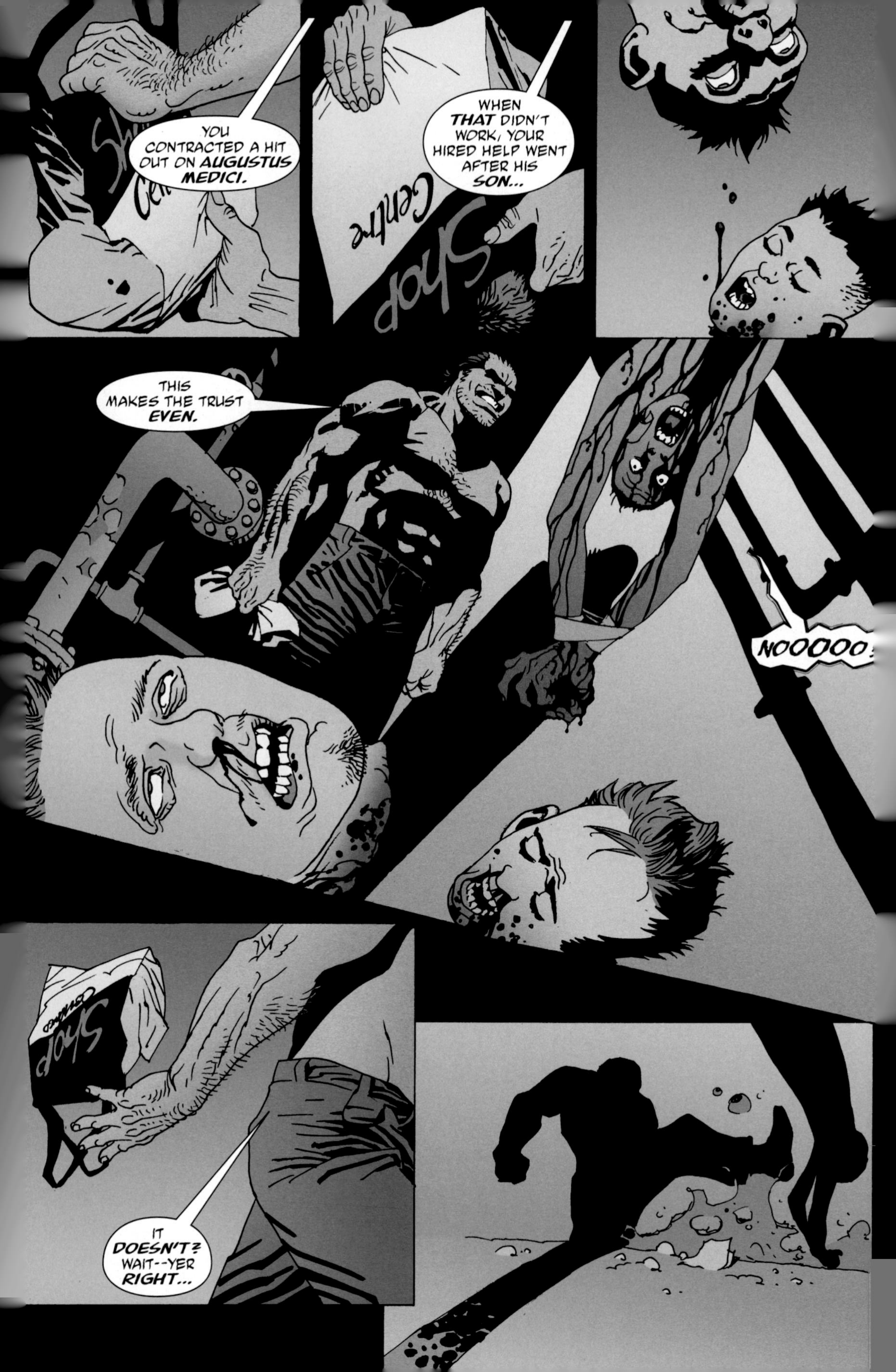
YOU CONTRACTED A HIT OUT ON AUGUSTUS MEDICI.
WHEN THAT DIDN'T WORK, YOUR HIRED HELP WENT AFTER HIS SON...
THIS MAKES THE TRUST EVEN.
NOOOOO
IT DOESN'T? WAIT--YER RIGHT...

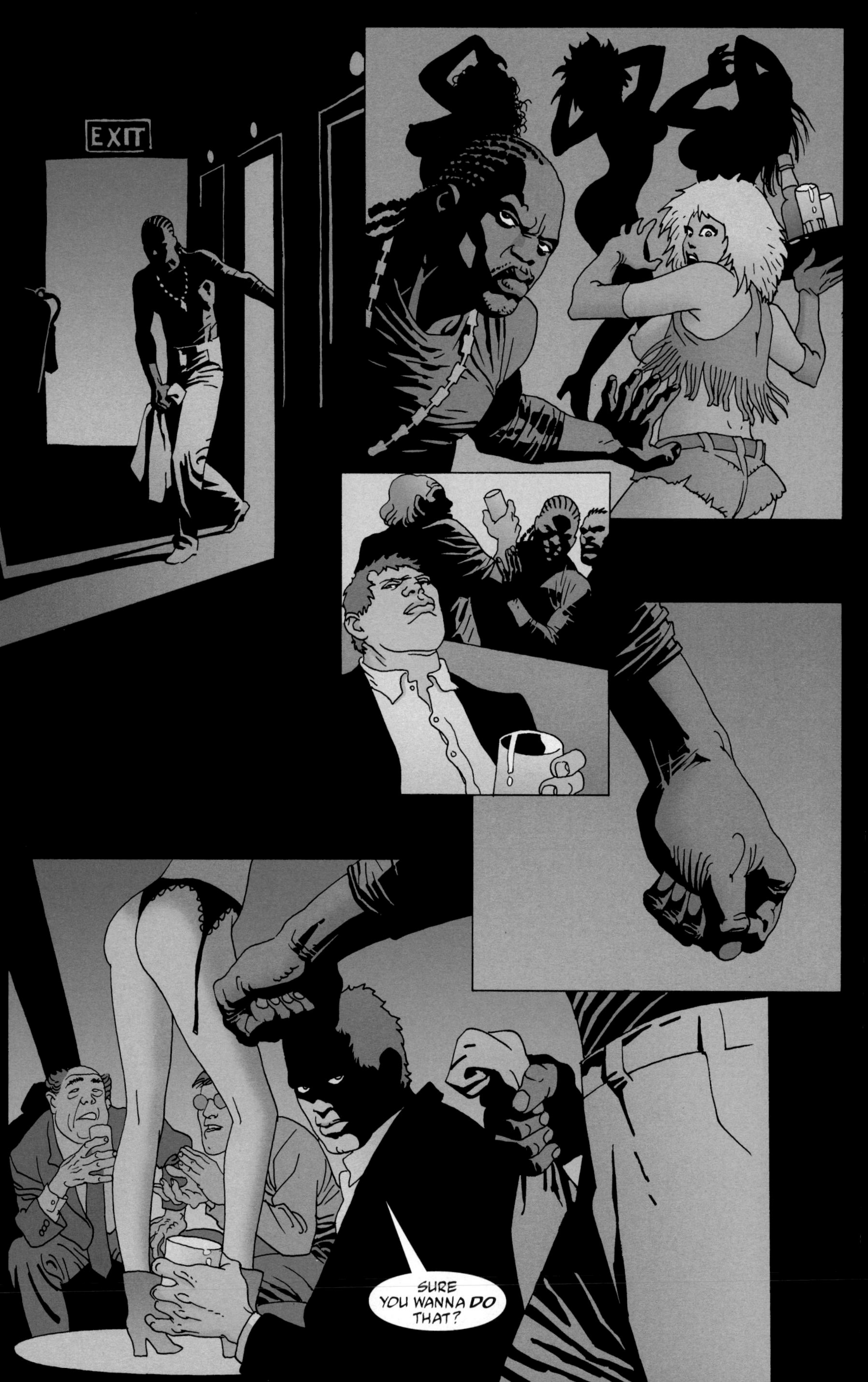
EXIT
SURE YOU WANNA DO THAT?

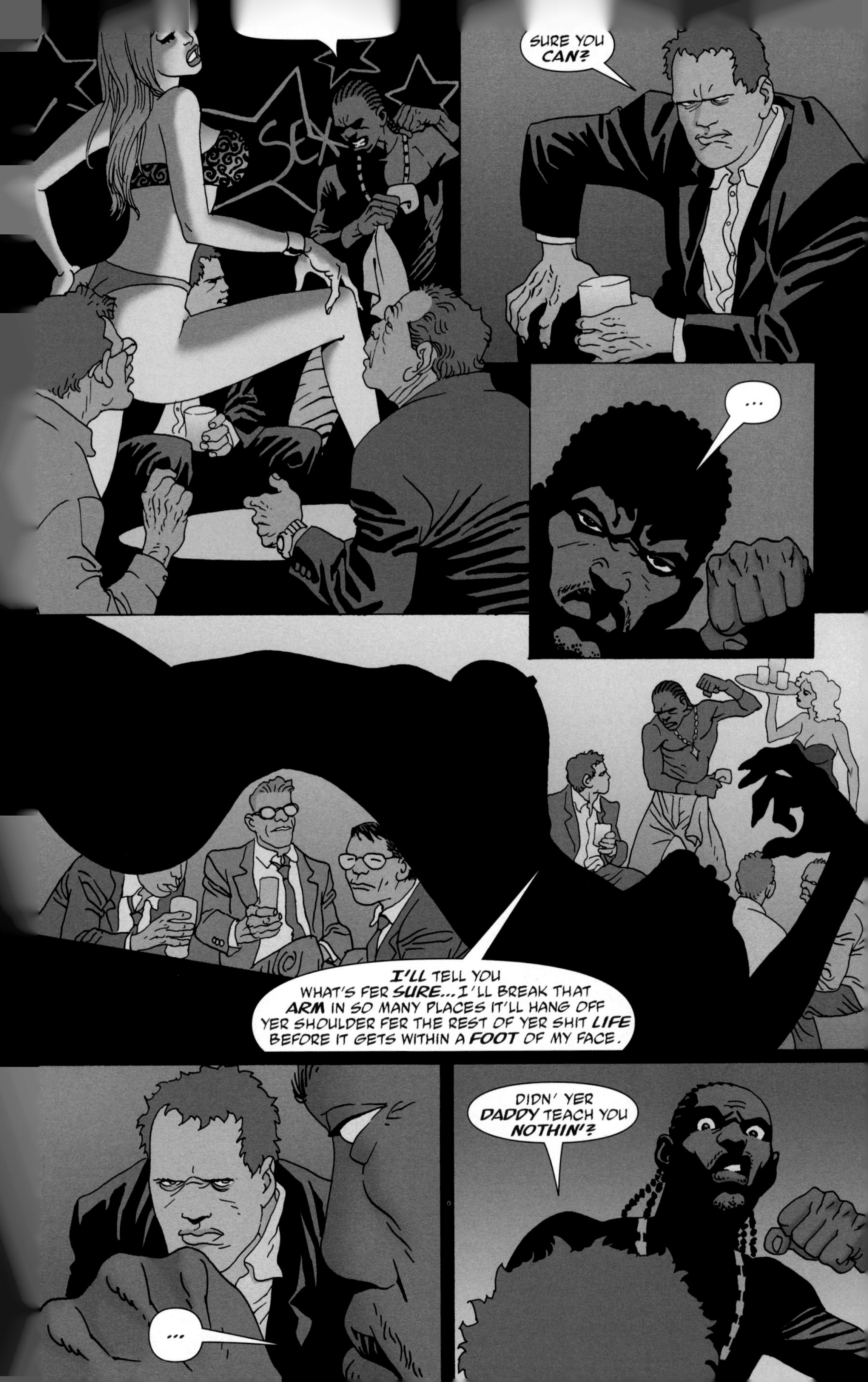
SURE YOU CAN?
...
I'LL TELL YOU WHAT'S FER SURE... I'LL BREAK THAT ARM IN SO MANY PLACES IT'LL HANG OFF YER SHOULDER FER THE REST OF YER SHIT LIFE BEFORE IT GETS WITHIN A FOOT OF MY FACE.
...
DIDN' YER DADDY TEACH YOU NOTHIN'?

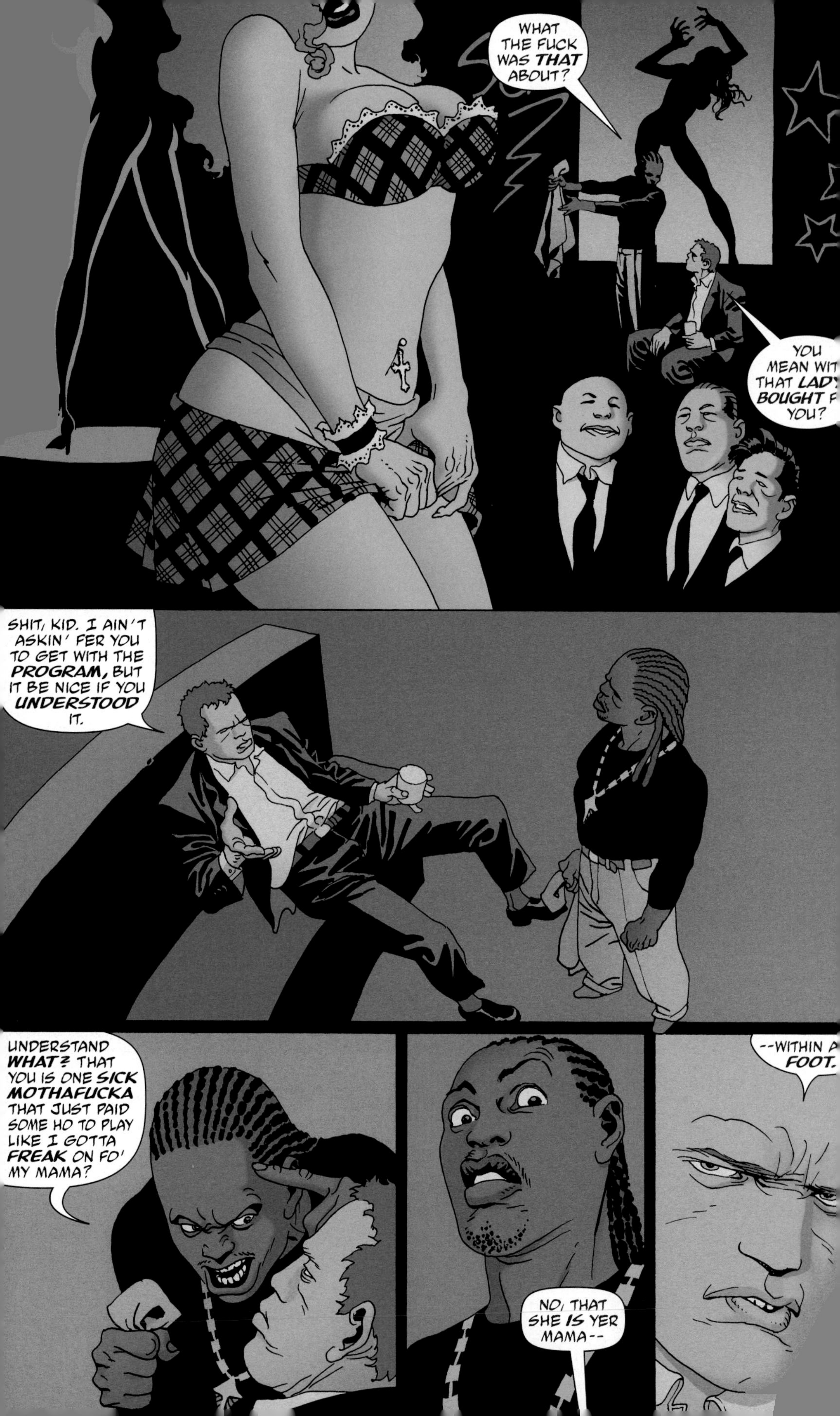
WHAT THE FUCK WAS THAT ABOUT?
YOU MEAN WIT THAT LAD BOUGHT YOU?
SHIT, KID. I AIN'T ASKIN' FER YOU TO GET WITH THE PROGRAM, BUT IT BE NICE IF YOU UNDERSTOOD IT.
UNDERSTAND WHAT? THAT YOU IS ONE SICK MOTHAFUCKA THAT JUST PAID SOME HO TO PLAY LIKE I GOTTA FREAK ON FO' MY MAMA?
NO, THAT SHE IS YER MAMA--
--WITHIN A FOOT.

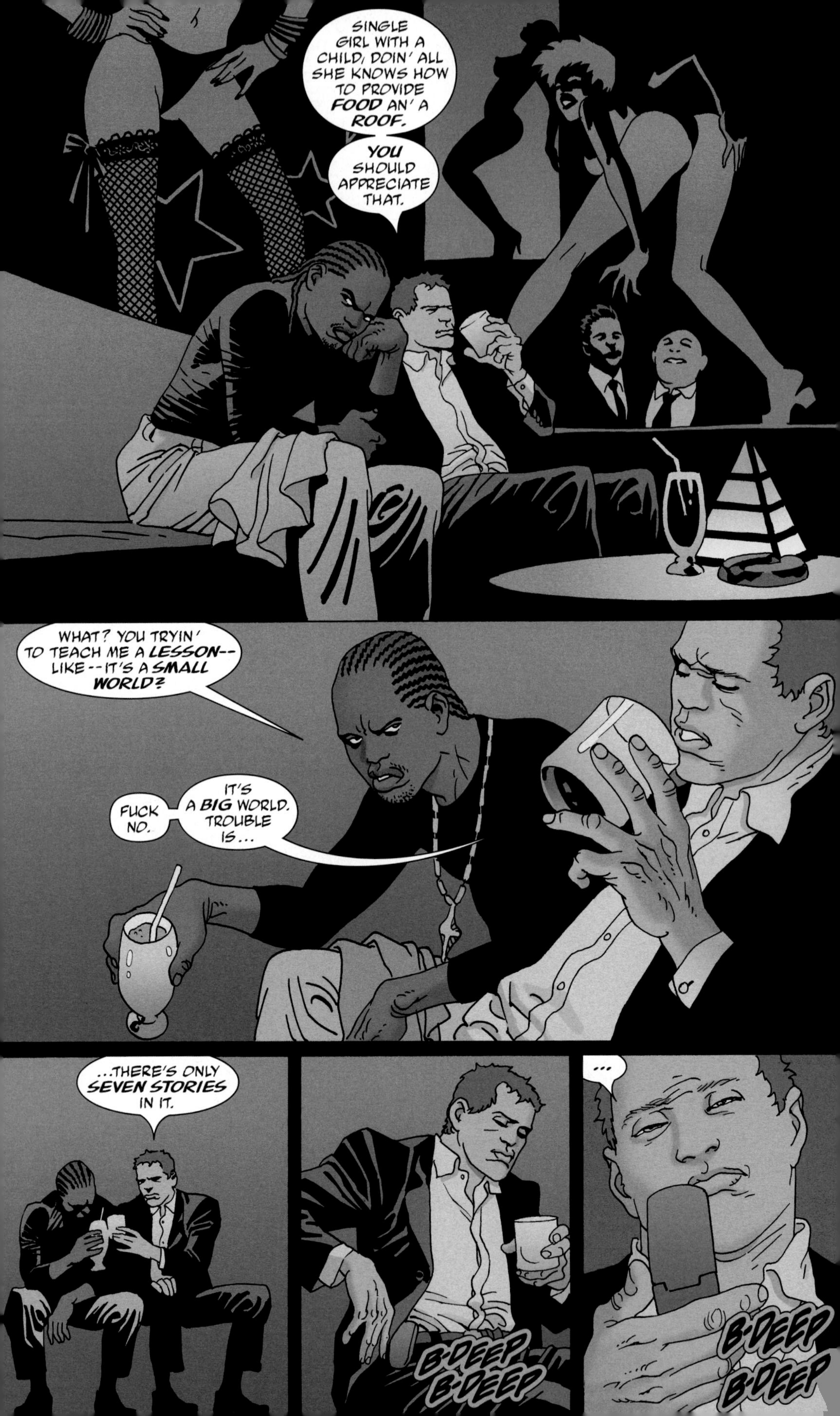

SINGLE GIRL WITH A CHILD, DOIN' ALL SHE KNOWS HOW TO PROVIDE FOOD AN' A ROOF.
YOU SHOULD APPRECIATE THAT.
WHAT? YOU TRYIN' TO TEACH ME A LESSON-- LIKE--IT'S A SMALL WORLD?
FUCK NO.
IT'S A BIG WORLD. TROUBLE IS...
...THERE'S ONLY SEVEN STORIES IN IT.
B-DEEP B-DEEP
...
B-DEEP B-DEEP

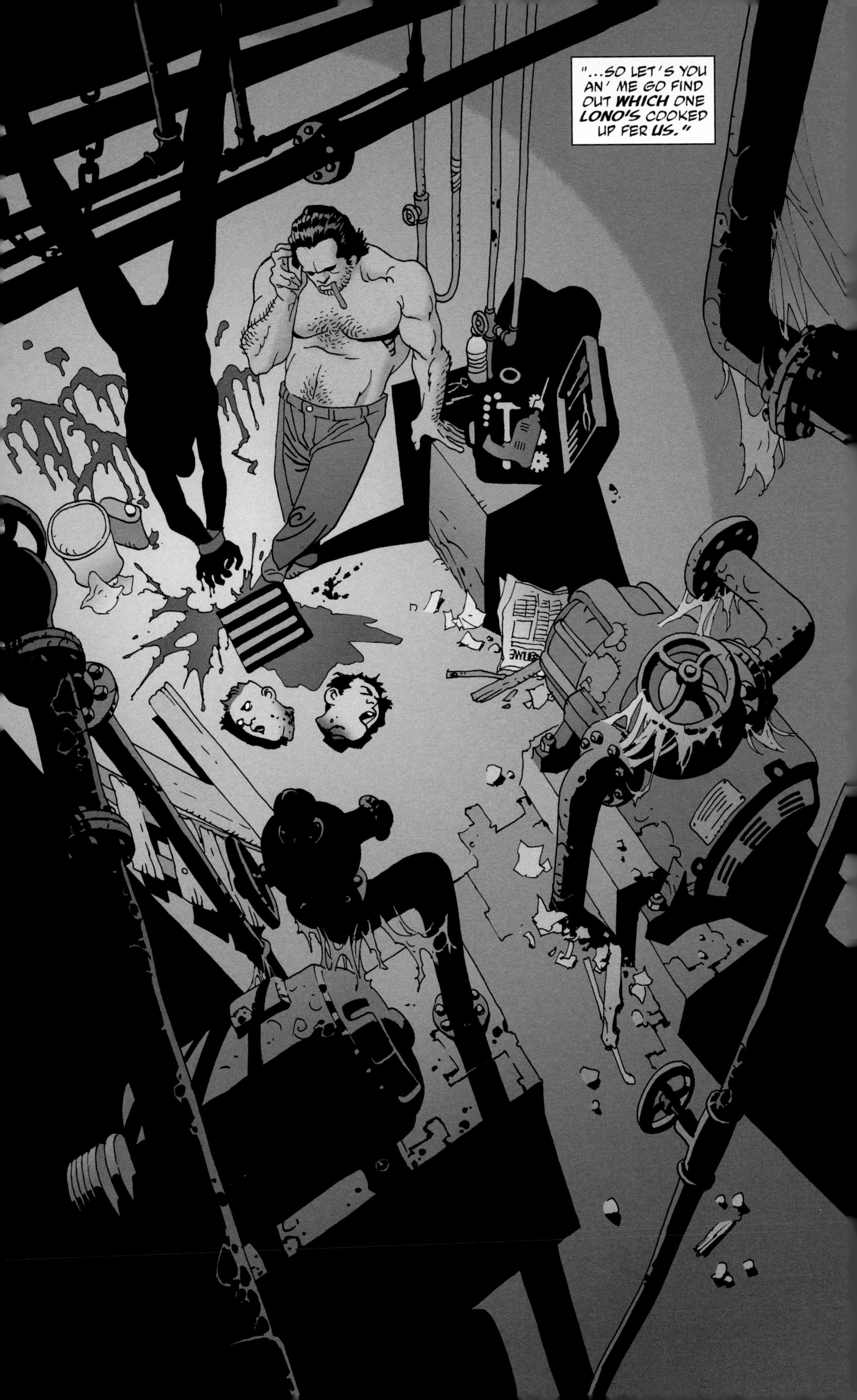
"...SO LET'S YOU AN' ME GO FIND OUT WHICH ONE LONO'S COOKED UP FER US."

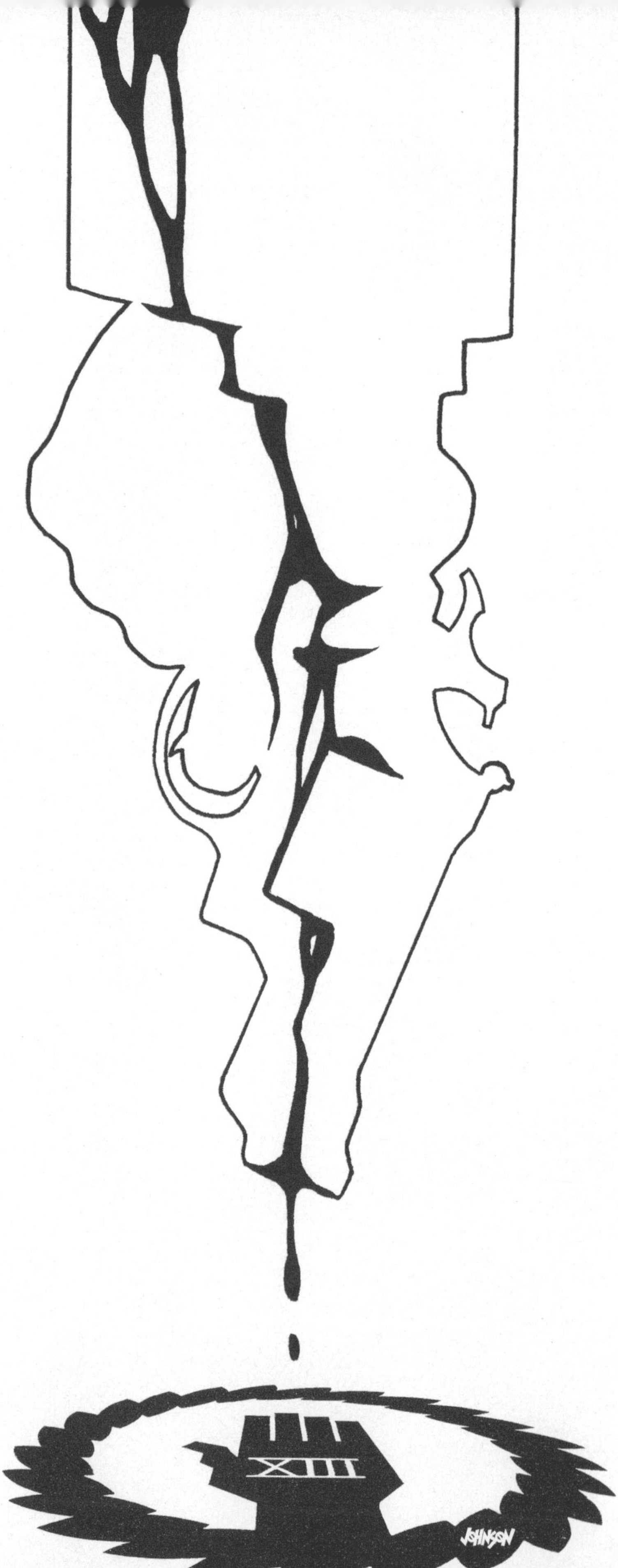
XIII
JOHNSON

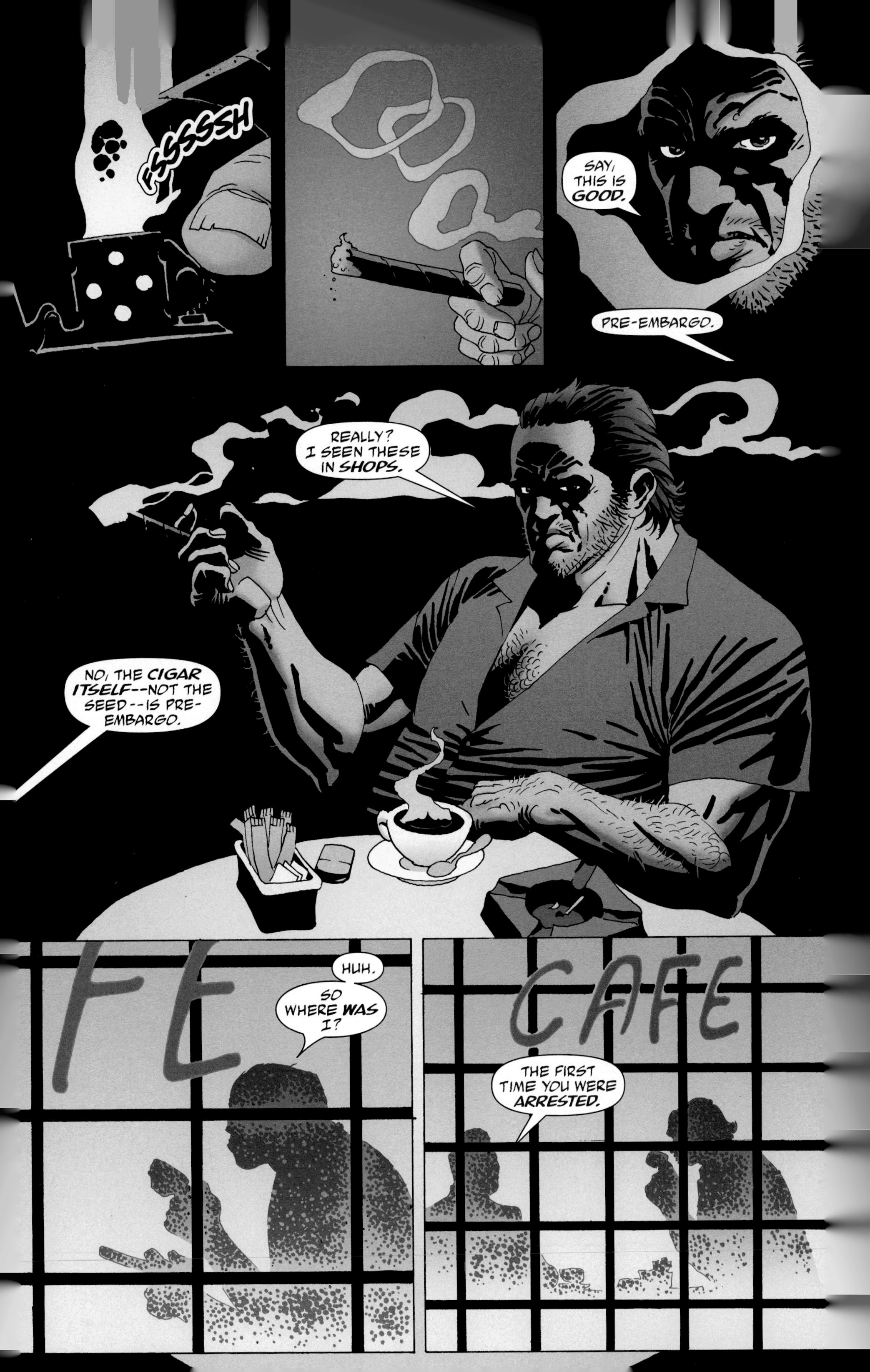
FSSSSSH
SAY, THIS IS GOOD.
PRE-EMBARGO.
REALLY? I SEEN THESE IN SHOPS.
NO, THE CIGAR ITSELF--NOT THE SEED--IS PRE-EMBARGO.
FE
HUH.
SO WHERE WAS I?
CAFE
THE FIRST TIME YOU WERE ARRESTED.

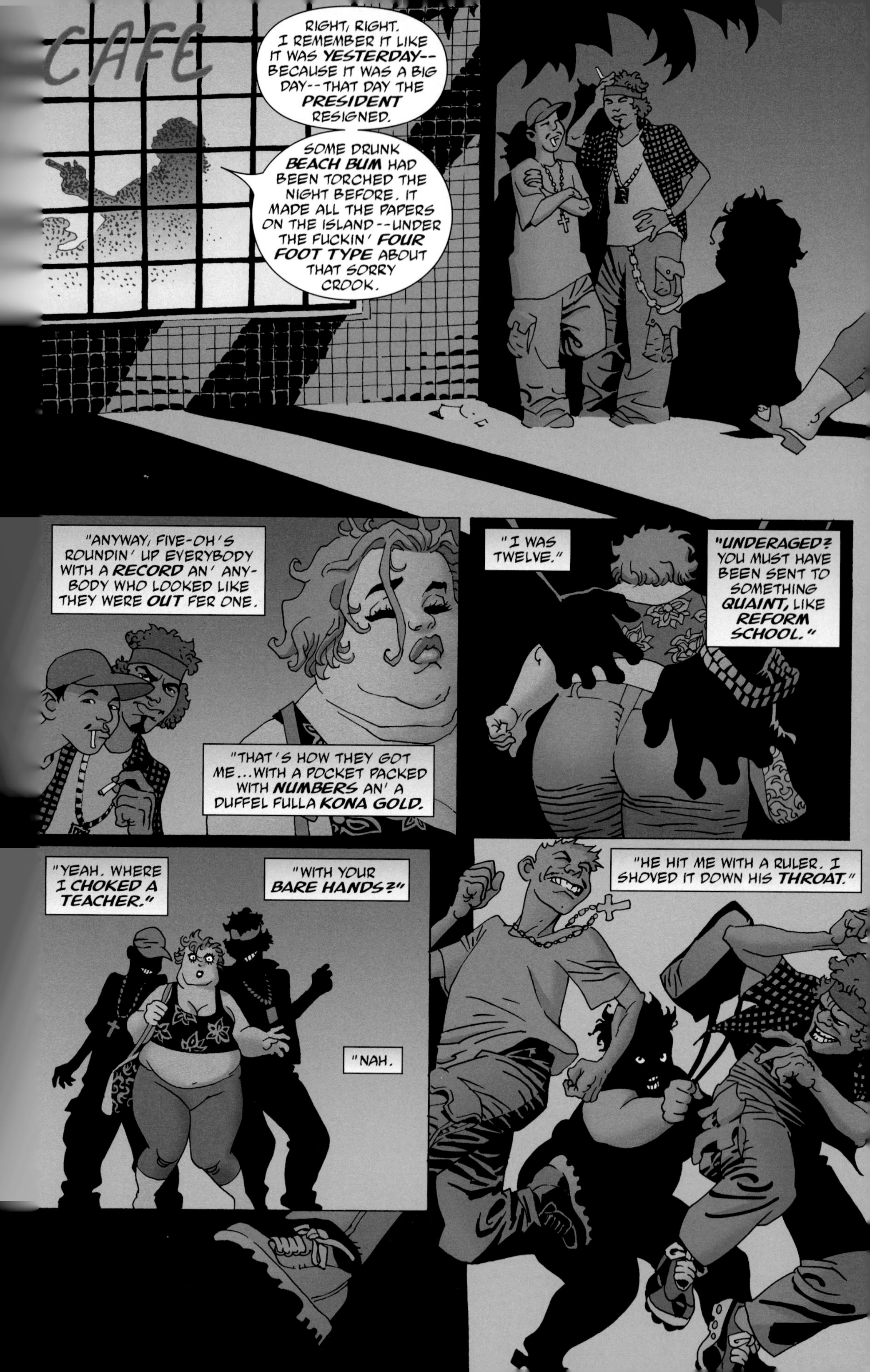
CAFE
RIGHT, RIGHT. I REMEMBER IT LIKE IT WAS YESTERDAY-- BECAUSE IT WAS A BIG DAY--THAT DAY THE PRESIDENT RESIGNED.
SOME DRUNK BEACH BUM HAD BEEN TORCHED THE NIGHT BEFORE. IT MADE ALL THE PAPERS ON THE ISLAND--UNDER THE FUCKIN' FOUR FOOT TYPE ABOUT THAT SORRY CROOK.
"ANYWAY, FIVE-OH'S ROUNDIN' UP EVERYBODY WITH A RECORD AN' ANY-BODY WHO LOOKED LIKE THEY WERE OUT FER ONE.
"THAT'S HOW THEY GOT ME...WITH A POCKET PACKED WITH NUMBERS AN' A DUFFEL FULLA KONA GOLD.
"I WAS TWELVE."
"UNDERAGED? YOU MUST HAVE BEEN SENT TO SOMETHING QUAINT, LIKE REFORM SCHOOL."
"YEAH. WHERE I CHOKED A TEACHER."
"WITH YOUR BARE HANDS?"
"NAH.
"HE HIT ME WITH A RULER. I SHOVED IT DOWN HIS THROAT."

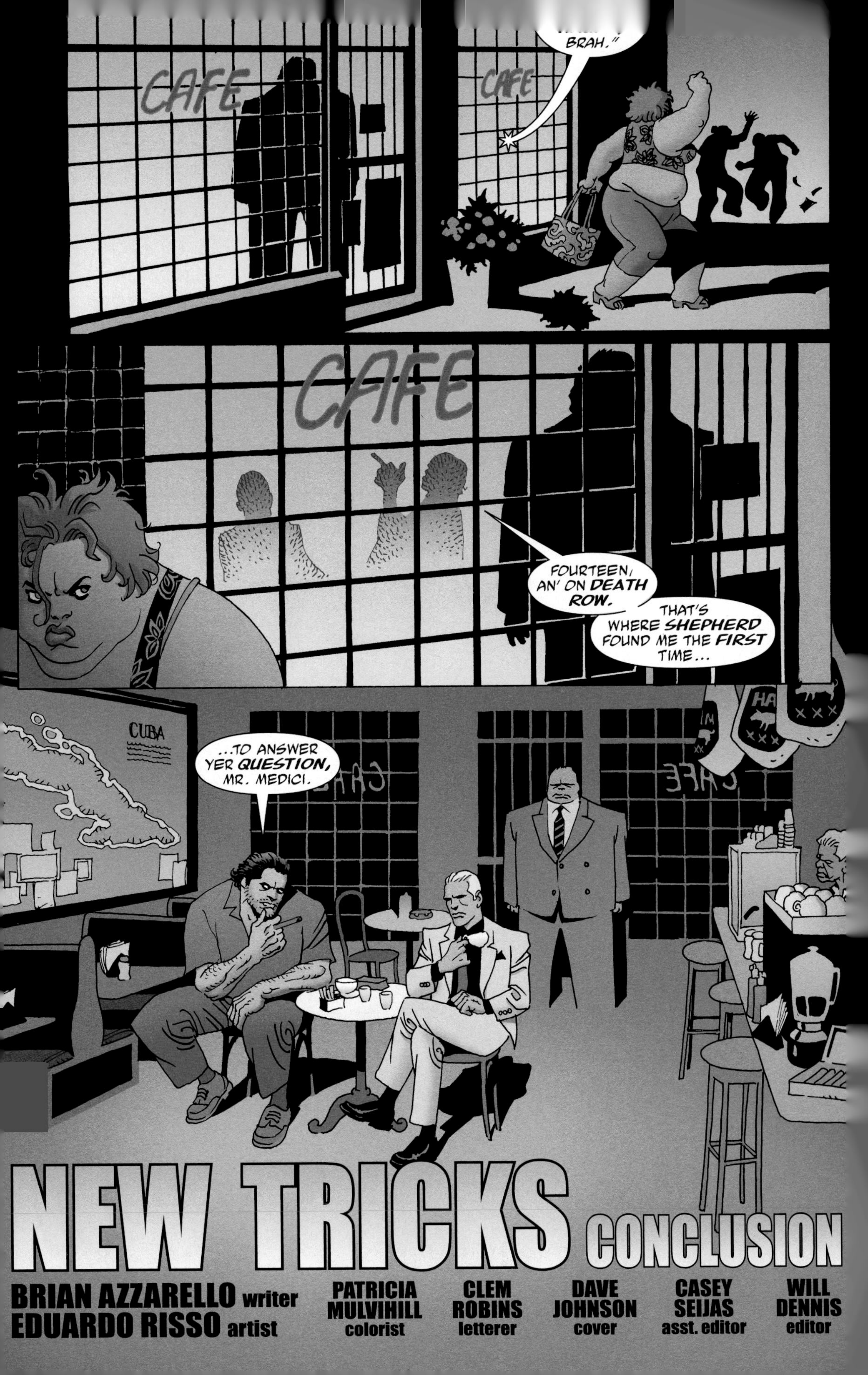
BRAH."
CAFE
CAFE
CAFE
FOURTEEN, AN' ON DEATH ROW.
THAT'S WHERE SHEPHERD FOUND ME THE FIRST TIME...
CUBA
...TO ANSWER YER QUESTION, MR. MEDICI.

NEW TRICKS CONCLUSION

BRIAN AZZARELLO writer
EDUARDO RISSO artist
PATRICIA MULVIHILL colorist
CLEM ROBINS letterer
DAVE JOHNSON cover
CASEY SEIJAS asst. editor
WILL DENNIS editor

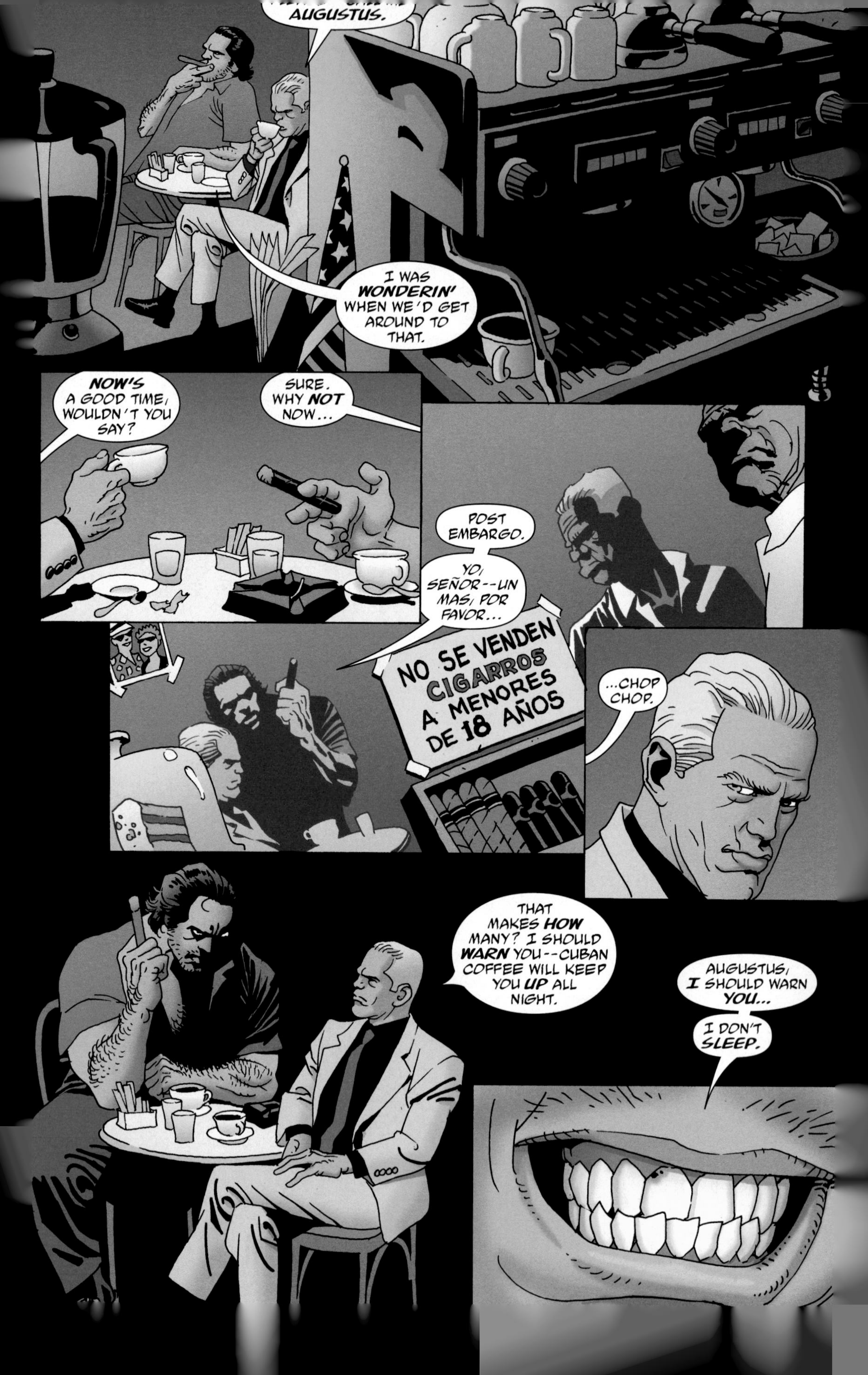
AUGUSTUS.
I WAS WONDERIN' WHEN WE'D GET AROUND TO THAT.
NOW'S A GOOD TIME, WOULDN'T YOU SAY?
SURE. WHY NOT NOW...
POST EMBARGO.
YO, SEÑOR--UN MAS, POR FAVOR...
NO SE VENDEN CIGARROS A MENORES DE 18 AÑOS
...CHOP CHOP.
THAT MAKES HOW MANY? I SHOULD WARN YOU--CUBAN COFFEE WILL KEEP YOU UP ALL NIGHT.
AUGUSTUS, I SHOULD WARN YOU...
I DON'T SLEEP.

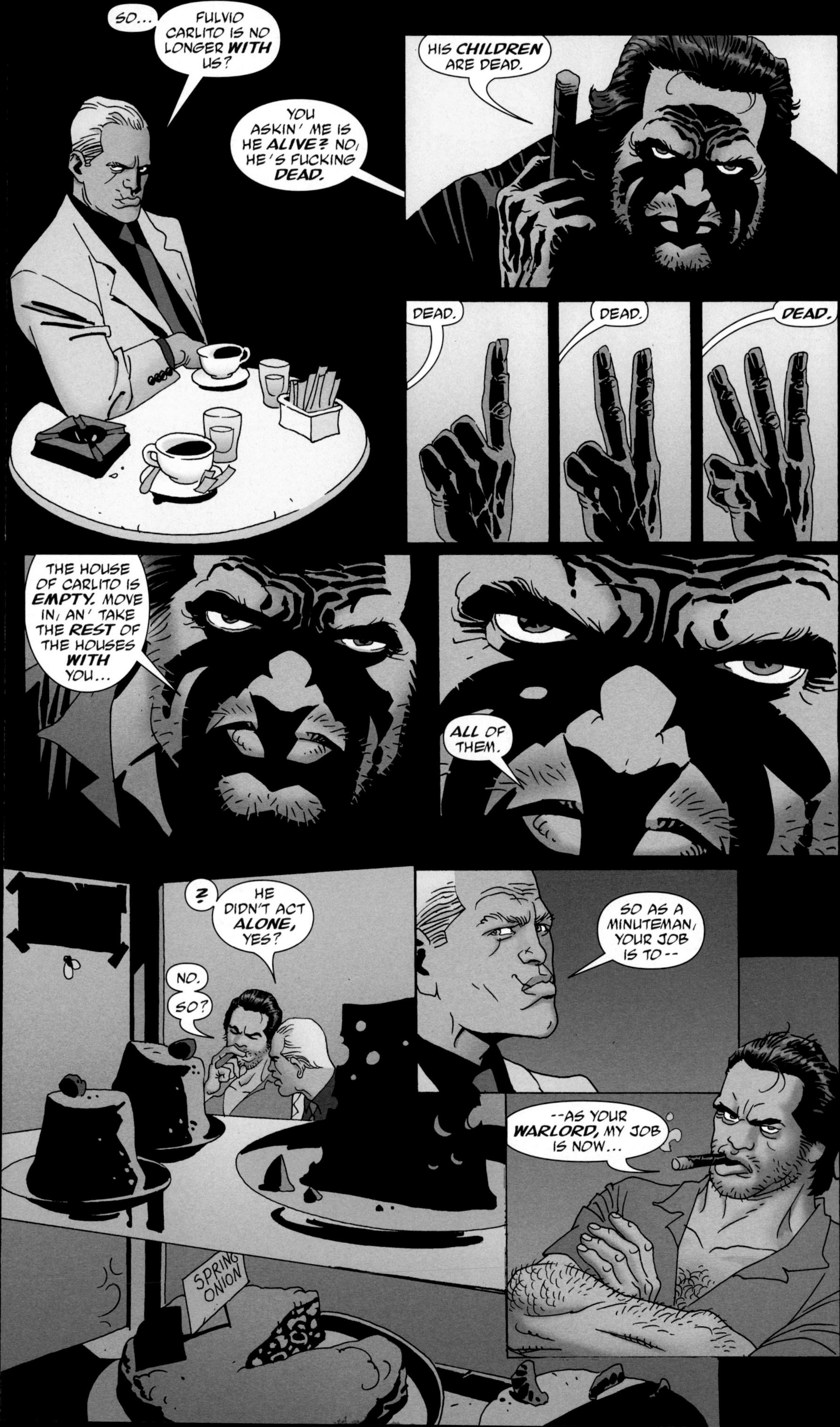

SO... FULVIO CARLITO IS NO LONGER WITH US?
YOU ASKIN' ME IS HE ALIVE? NO, HE'S FUCKING DEAD.
HIS CHILDREN ARE DEAD.
DEAD.
DEAD.
DEAD.
THE HOUSE OF CARLITO IS EMPTY. MOVE IN, AN' TAKE THE REST OF THE HOUSES WITH YOU...
ALL OF THEM.
?
HE DIDN'T ACT ALONE, YES?
NO.
SO?
SO AS A MINUTEMAN, YOUR JOB IS TO--
--AS YOUR WARLORD, MY JOB IS NOW...
SPRING ONION

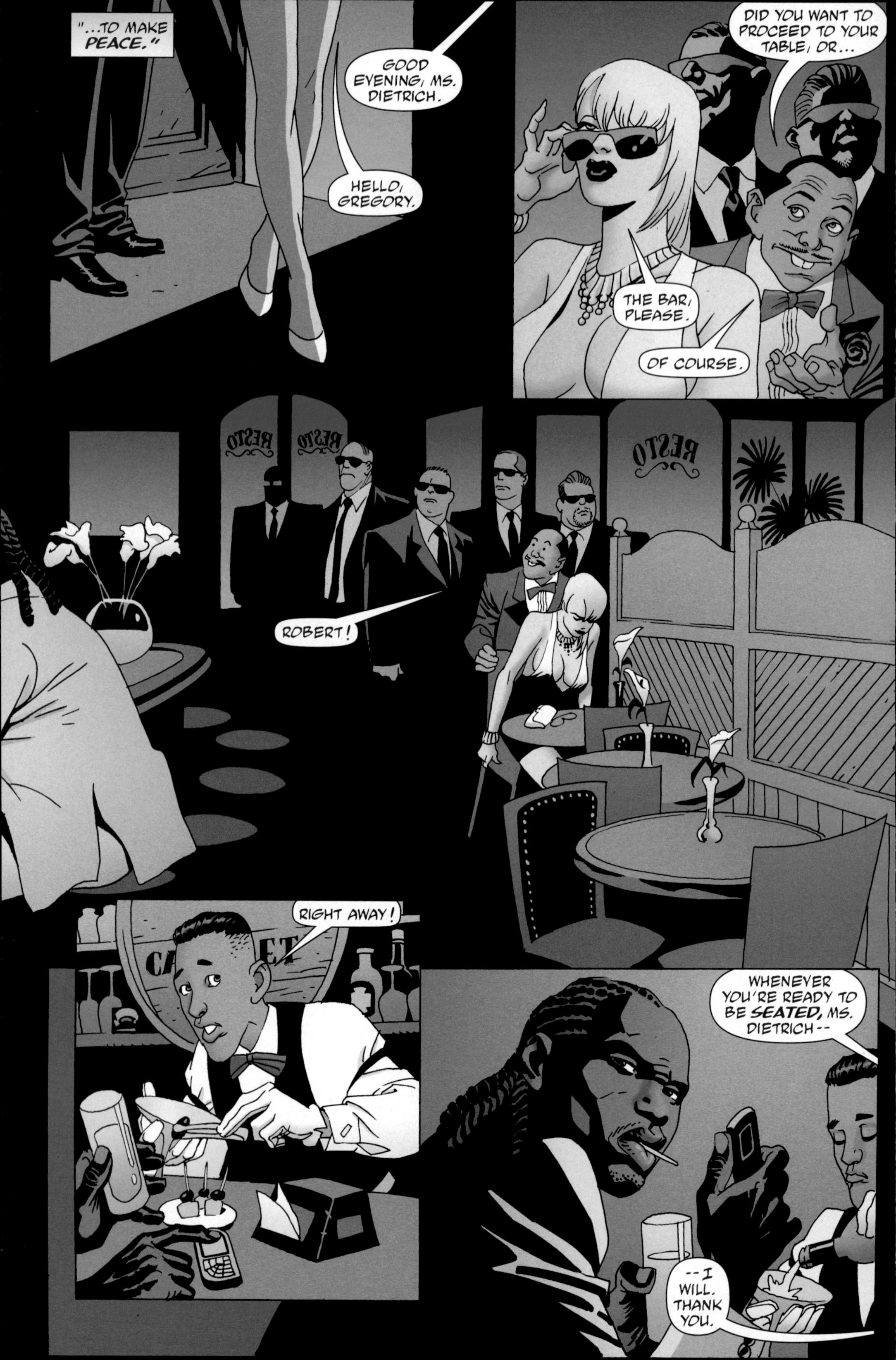
"...TO MAKE PEACE."
GOOD EVENING, MS. DIETRICH.
HELLO, GREGORY.
DID YOU WANT TO PROCEED TO YOUR TABLE, OR...
THE BAR, PLEASE.
OF COURSE.
ROBERT!
RIGHT AWAY!
WHENEVER YOU'RE READY TO BE SEATED, MS. DIETRICH--
--I WILL. THANK YOU.

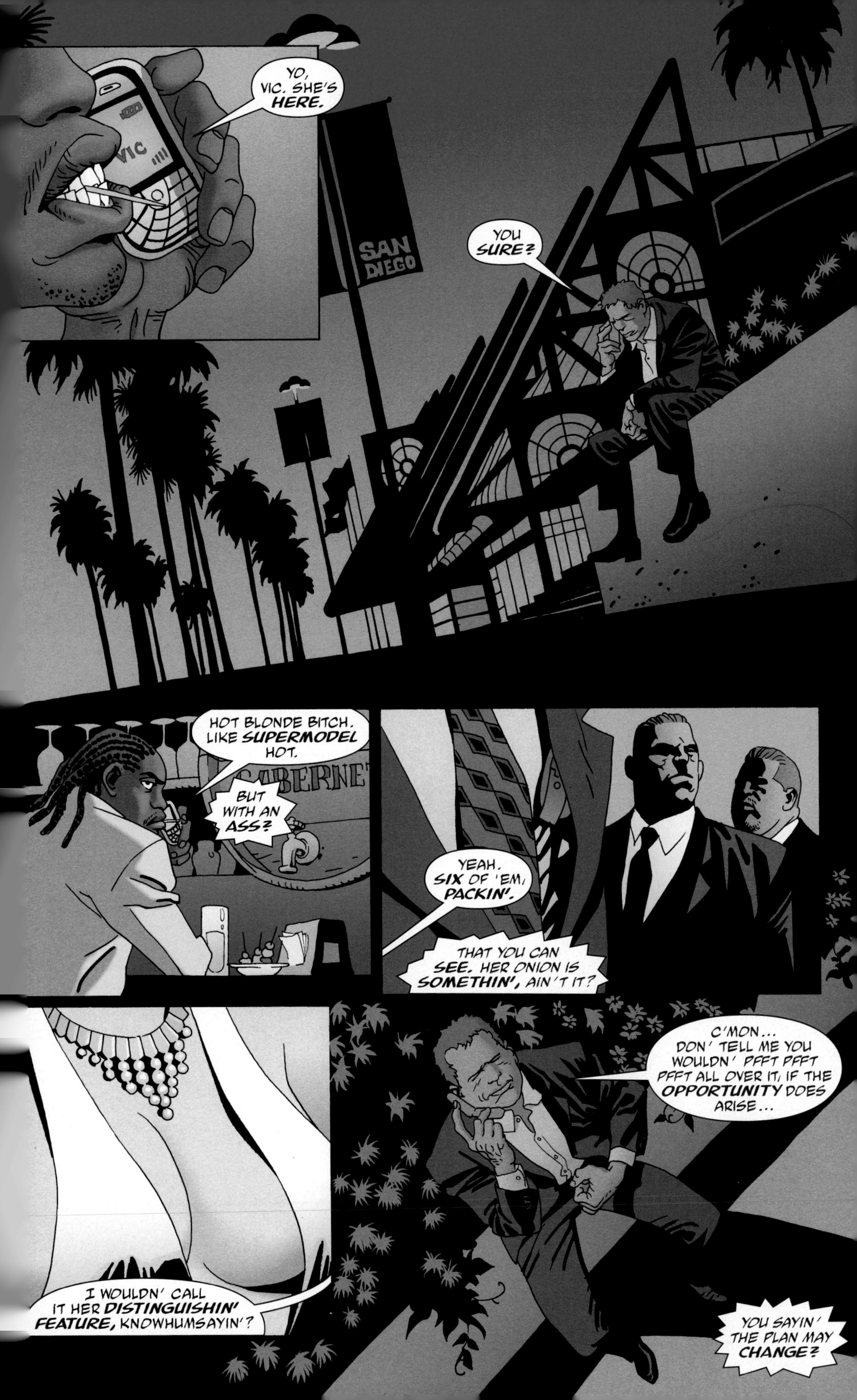
YO, VIC. SHE'S HERE.
VIC
SAN DIEGO
YOU SURE?
HOT BLONDE BITCH. LIKE SUPERMODEL HOT.
BUT WITH AN ASS?
YEAH. SIX OF 'EM, PACKIN'.
THAT YOU CAN SEE. HER ONION IS SOMETHIN', AIN'T IT?
I WOULDN' CALL IT HER DISTINGUISHIN' FEATURE, KNOWHUMSAYIN'?
C'MON... DON' TELL ME YOU WOULDN' PFFT PFFT PFFT ALL OVER IT, IF THE OPPORTUNITY DOES ARISE...
YOU SAYIN' THE PLAN MAY CHANGE?

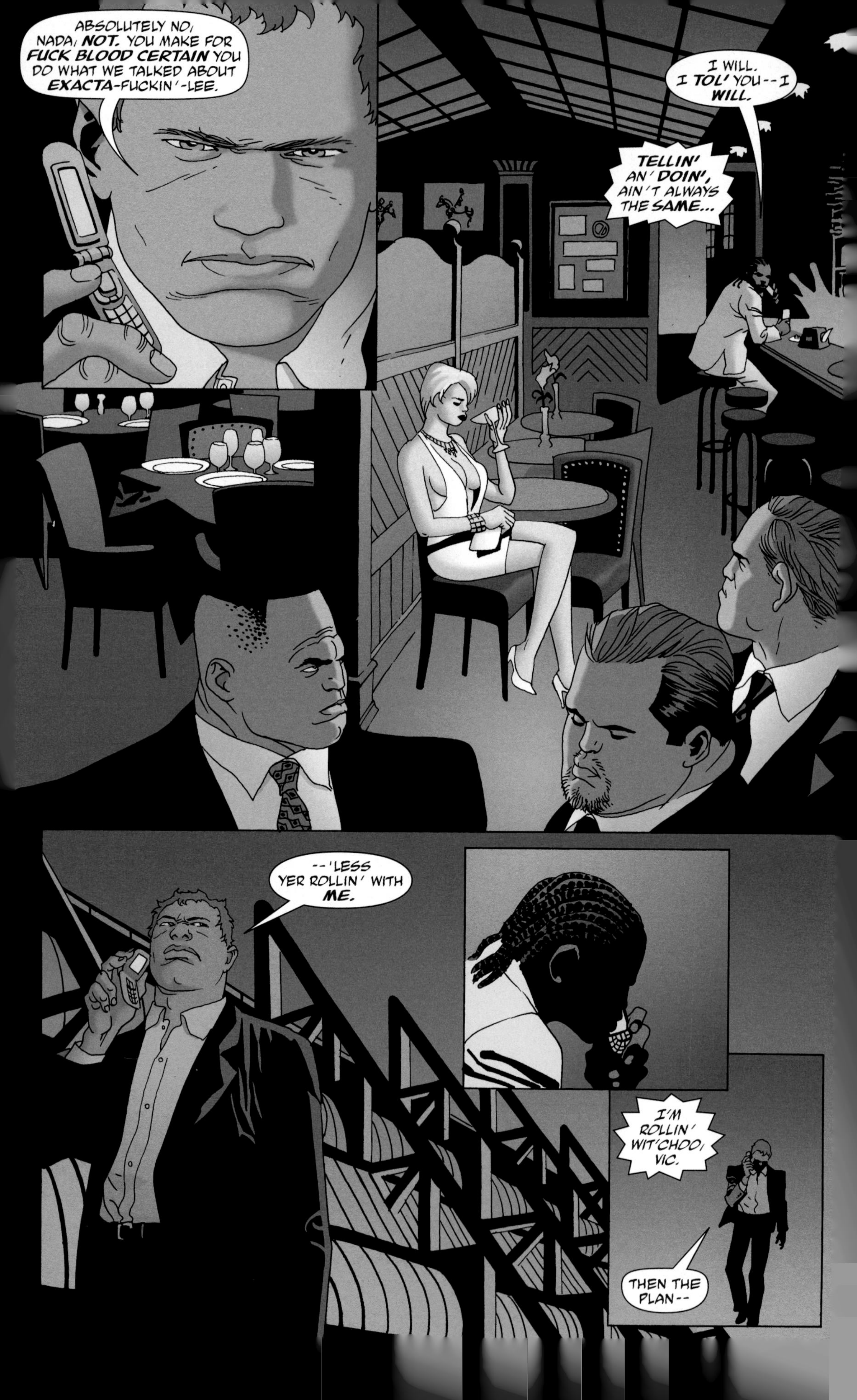
ABSOLUTELY NO, NADA, **NOT.** YOU MAKE FOR **FUCK BLOOD CERTAIN** YOU DO WHAT WE TALKED ABOUT **EXACTA**-FUCKIN'-LEE.
I WILL. I **TOL'** YOU-- I **WILL.**
TELLIN' AN' **DOIN',** AIN'T ALWAYS THE **SAME...**
--'LESS YER ROLLIN' WITH **ME.**
I'M ROLLIN' WIT'CHOO, VIC.
THEN THE PLAN--

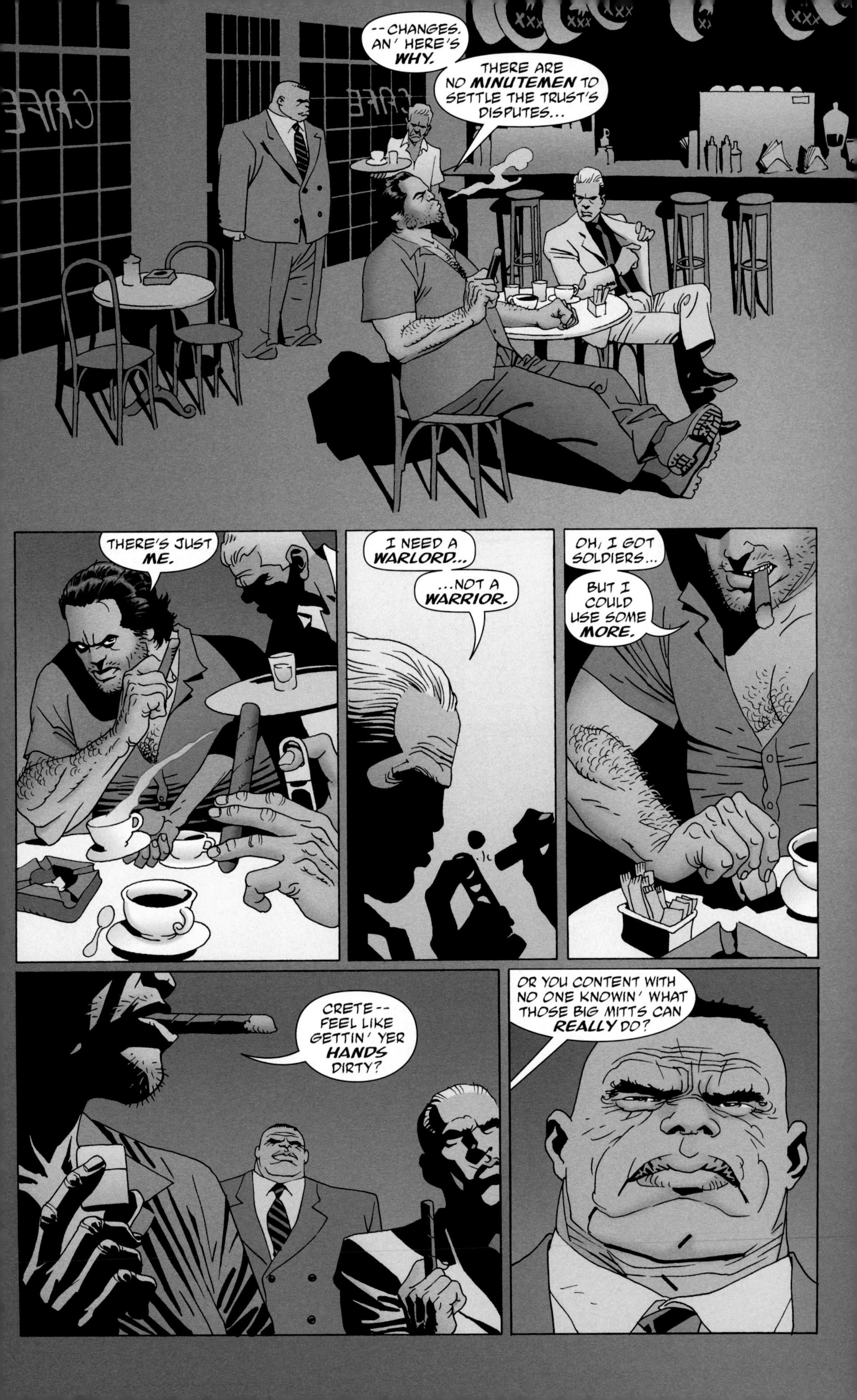

--CHANGES. AN' HERE'S **WHY.**
THERE ARE NO **MINUTEMEN** TO SETTLE THE TRUST'S DISPUTES...
THERE'S JUST **ME.**
I NEED A **WARLORD...**
...NOT A **WARRIOR.**
OH, I GOT SOLDIERS...
BUT I COULD USE SOME **MORE.**
CRETE-- FEEL LIKE GETTIN' YER **HANDS** DIRTY?
OR YOU CONTENT WITH NO ONE KNOWIN' WHAT THOSE BIG MITTS CAN **REALLY** DO?

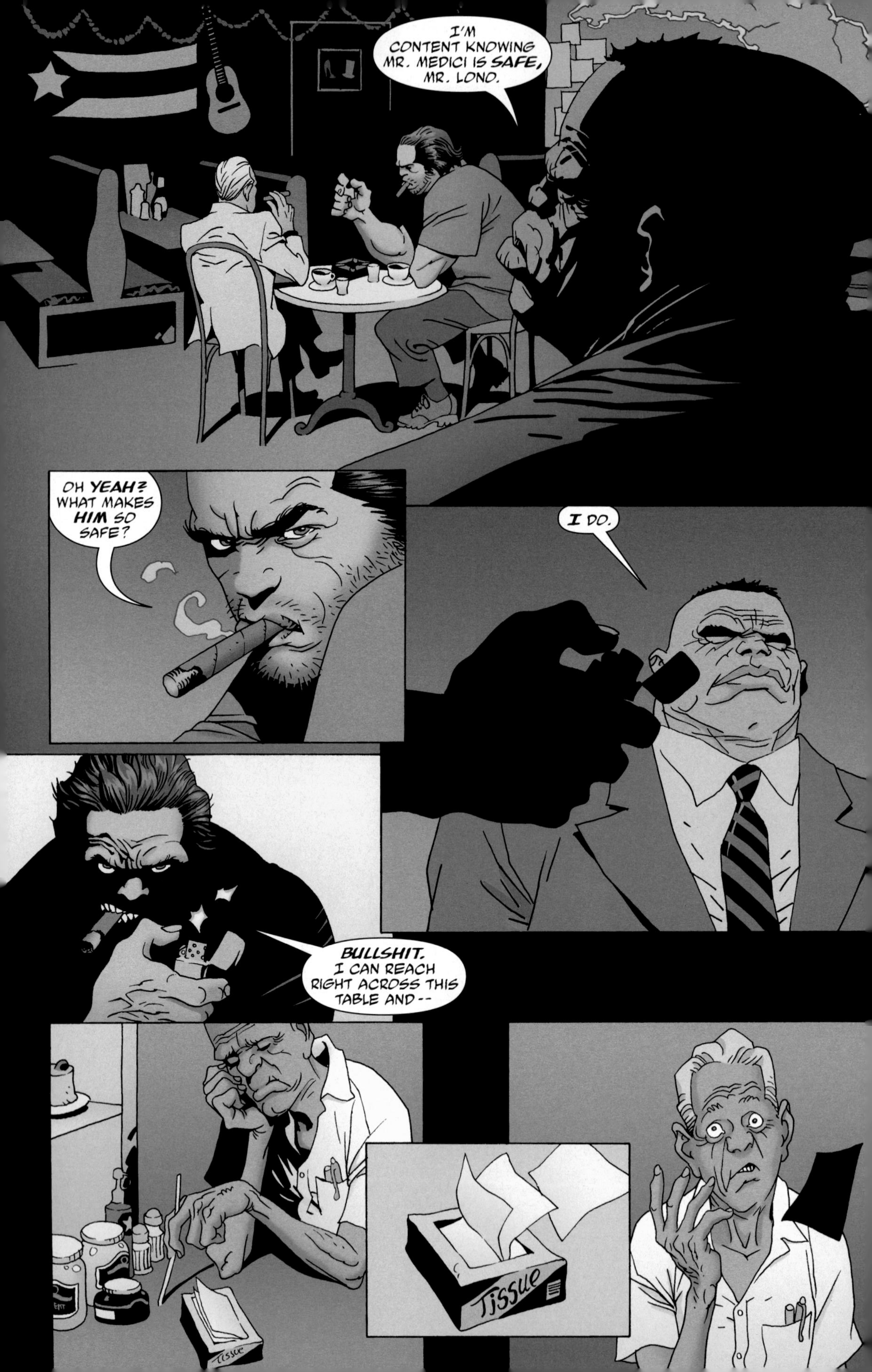
I'M CONTENT KNOWING MR. MEDICI IS **SAFE,** MR. LONO.
OH **YEAH?** WHAT MAKES **HIM** SO SAFE?
I DO.
BULLSHIT. I CAN REACH RIGHT ACROSS THIS TABLE AND --
TISSUE
TISSUE

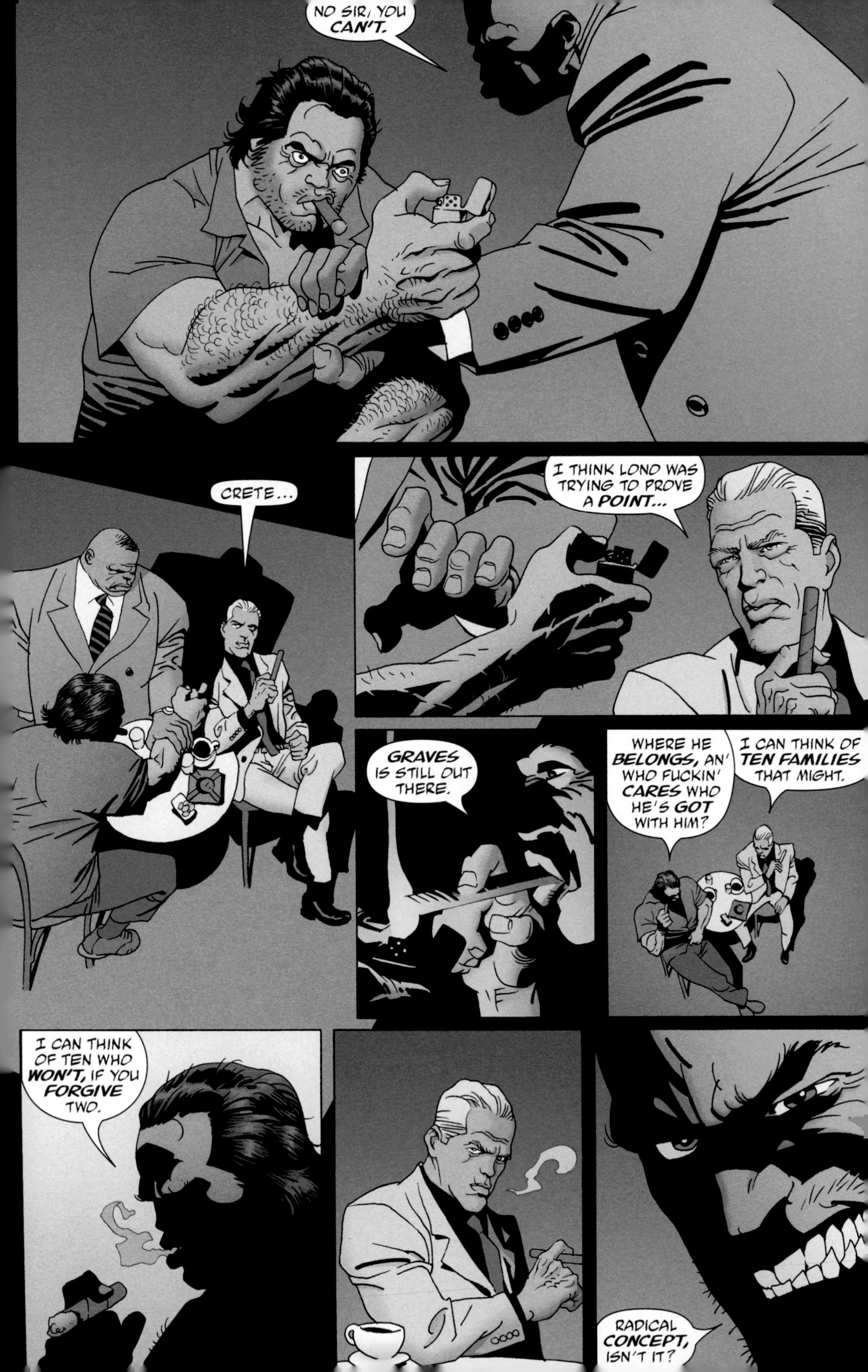
NO SIR, YOU CAN'T.
CRETE...
I THINK LONO WAS TRYING TO PROVE A POINT...
GRAVES IS STILL OUT THERE.
WHERE HE BELONGS, AN' WHO FUCKIN' CARES WHO HE'S GOT WITH HIM?
I CAN THINK OF TEN FAMILIES THAT MIGHT.
I CAN THINK OF TEN WHO WON'T, IF YOU FORGIVE TWO.
RADICAL CONCEPT, ISN'T IT?

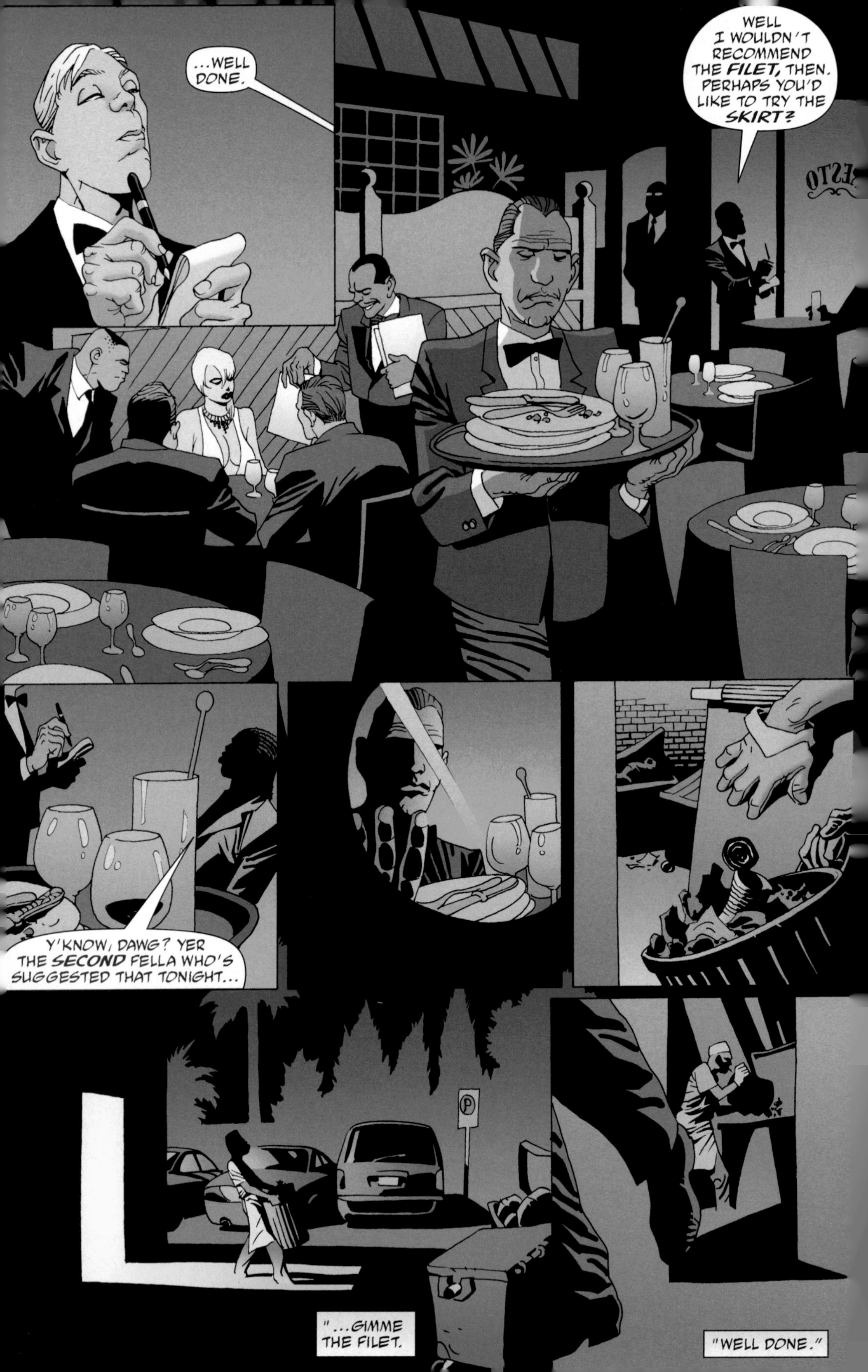

...WELL DONE.
WELL I WOULDN'T RECOMMEND THE FILET, THEN. PERHAPS YOU'D LIKE TO TRY THE SKIRT?
Y'KNOW, DAWG? YER THE SECOND FELLA WHO'S SUGGESTED THAT TONIGHT...
"...GIMME THE FILET.
"WELL DONE."

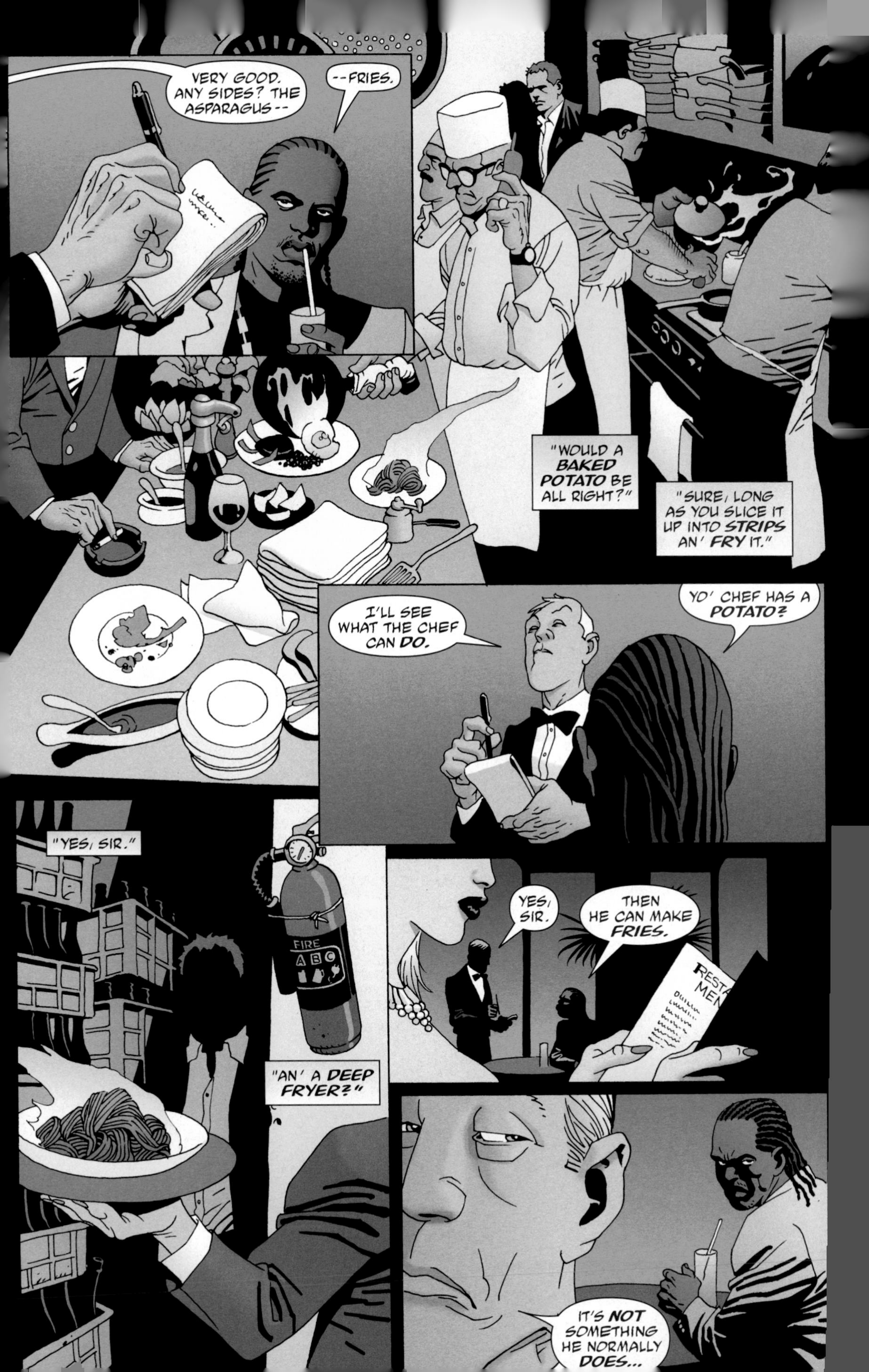
VERY GOOD. ANY SIDES? THE ASPARAGUS--
--FRIES.
"WOULD A BAKED POTATO BE ALL RIGHT?"
"SURE, LONG AS YOU SLICE IT UP INTO STRIPS AN' FRY IT."
I'LL SEE WHAT THE CHEF CAN DO.
YO' CHEF HAS A POTATO?
"YES, SIR."
"AN' A DEEP FRYER?"
FIRE
A B C
YES, SIR.
THEN HE CAN MAKE FRIES.
IT'S NOT SOMETHING HE NORMALLY DOES...

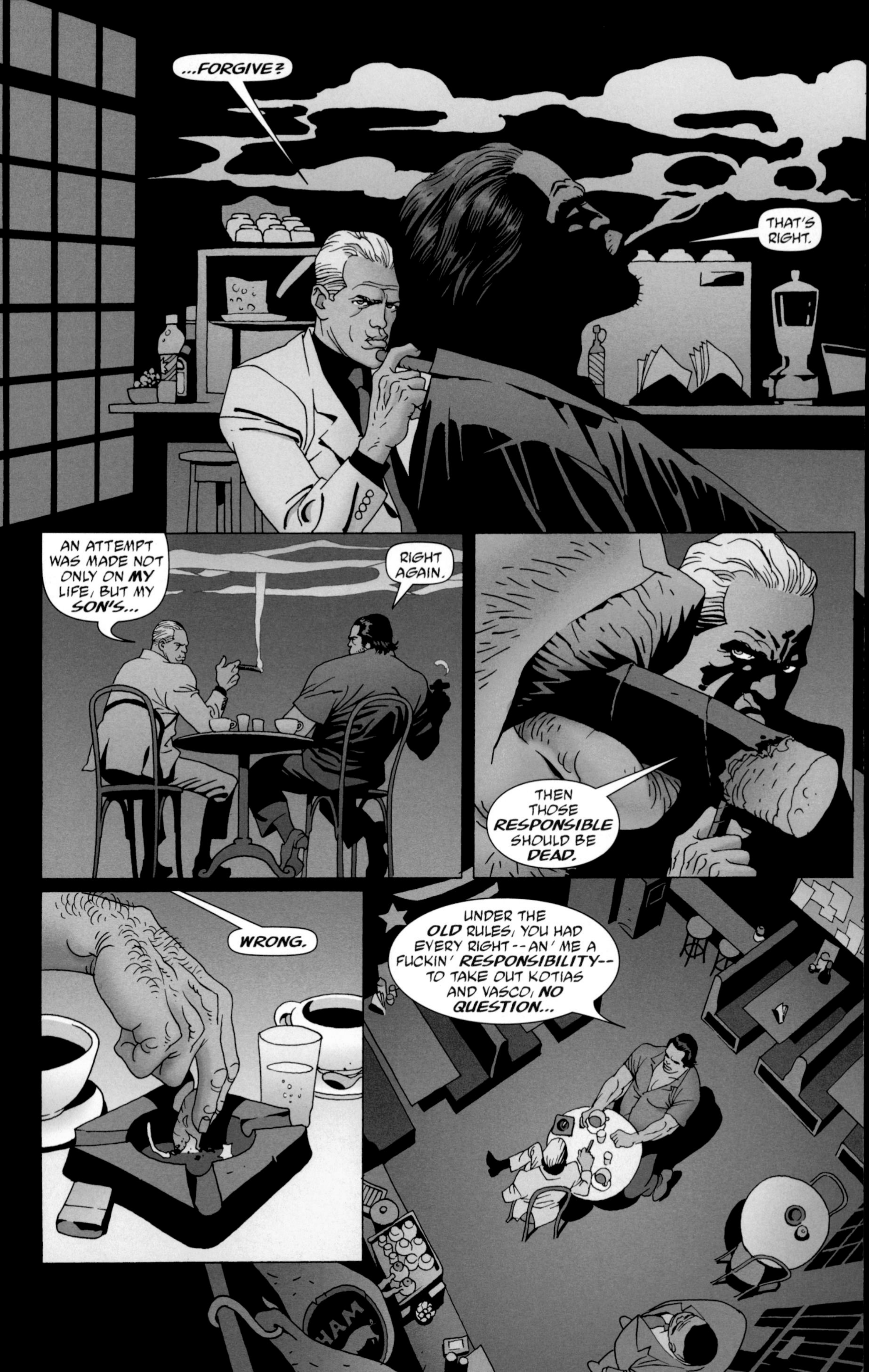
...FORGIVE?
THAT'S RIGHT.
AN ATTEMPT WAS MADE NOT ONLY ON MY LIFE, BUT MY SON'S...
RIGHT AGAIN.
THEN THOSE RESPONSIBLE SHOULD BE DEAD.
WRONG.
UNDER THE OLD RULES, YOU HAD EVERY RIGHT--AN' ME A FUCKIN' RESPONSIBILITY--TO TAKE OUT KOTIAS AND VASCO, NO QUESTION...

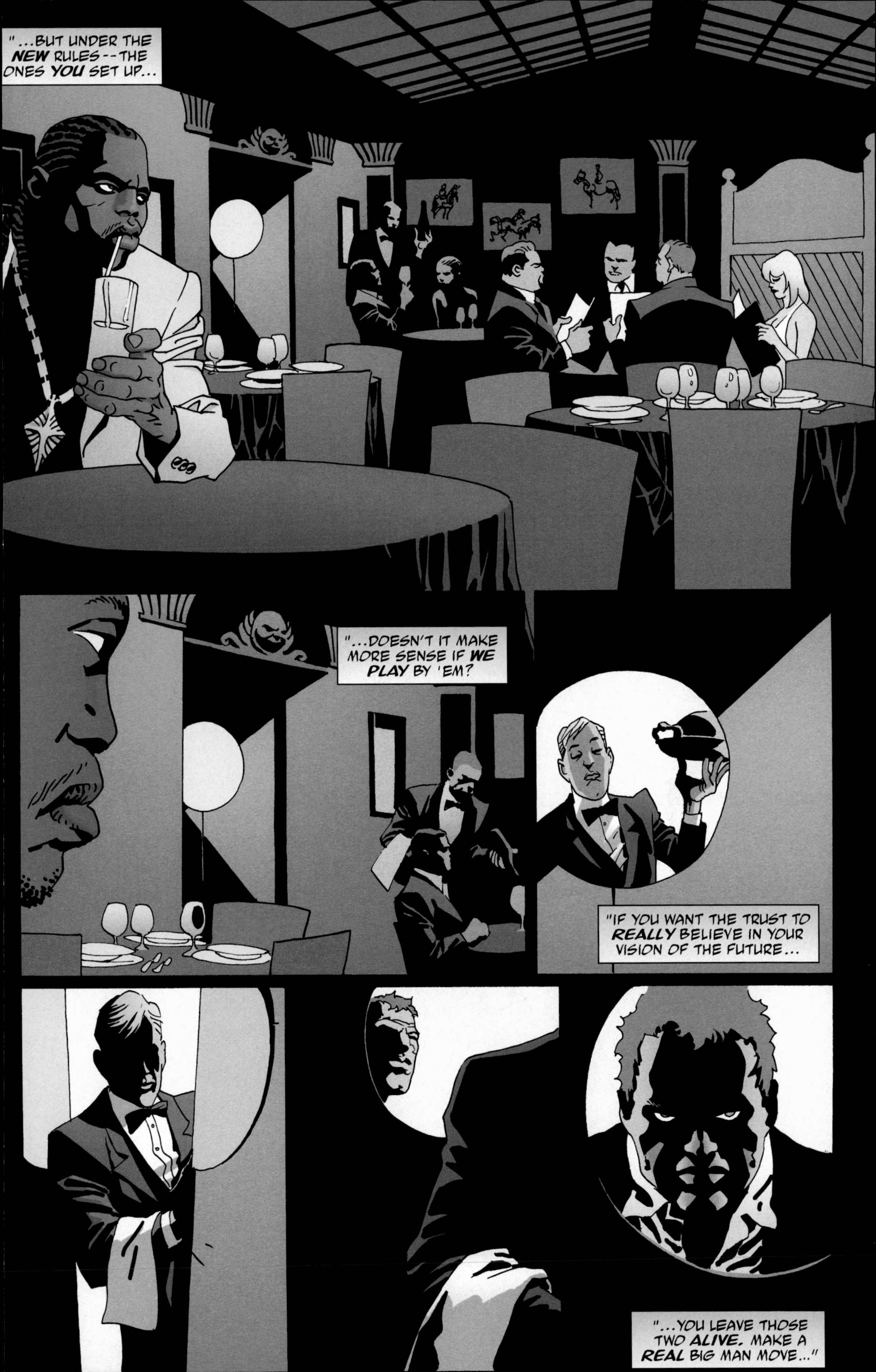
"...BUT UNDER THE NEW RULES--THE ONES YOU SET UP...
"...DOESN'T IT MAKE MORE SENSE IF WE PLAY BY 'EM?
"IF YOU WANT THE TRUST TO REALLY BELIEVE IN YOUR VISION OF THE FUTURE...
"...YOU LEAVE THOSE TWO ALIVE. MAKE A REAL BIG MAN MOVE..."

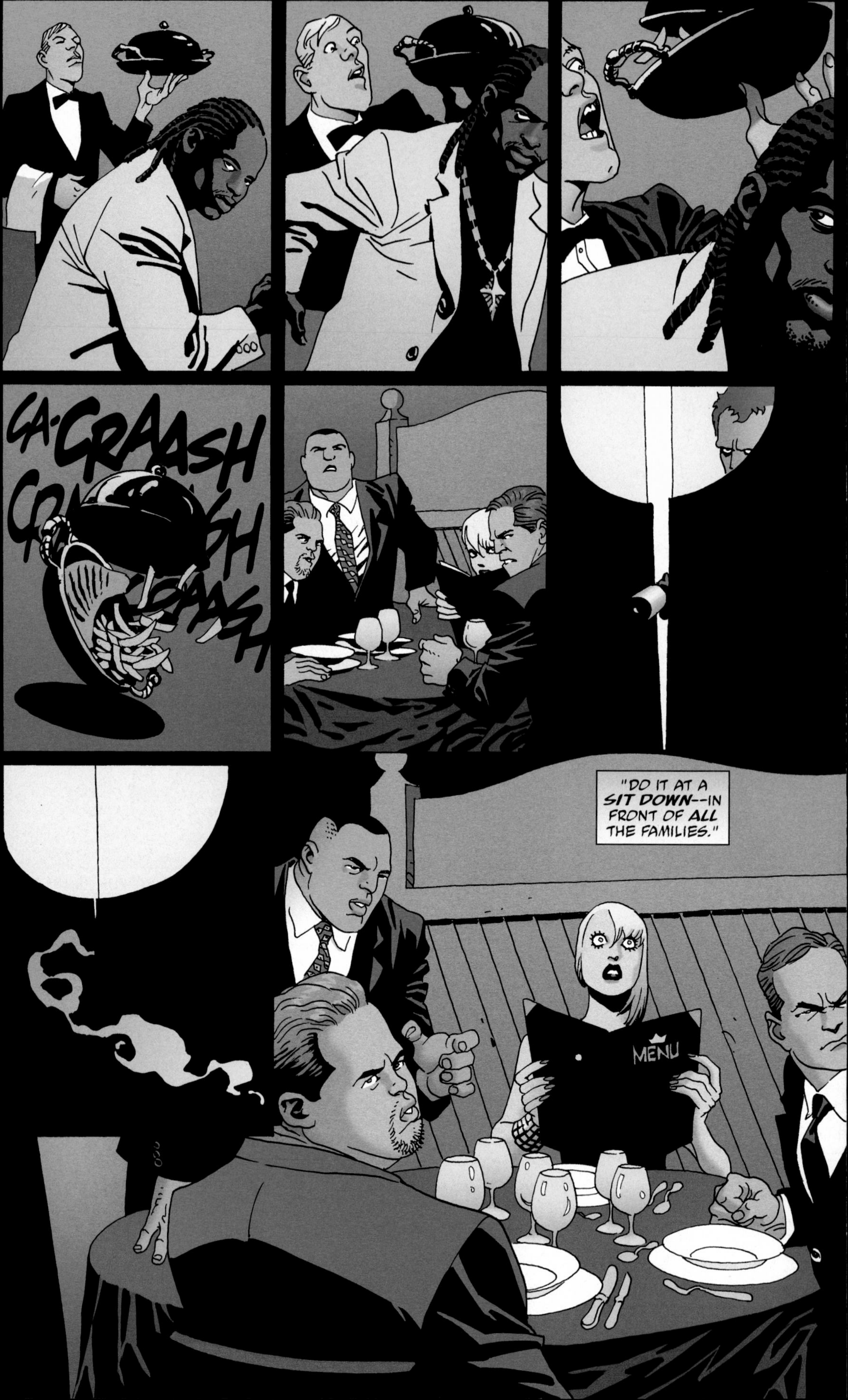
CA-CRAASH
CRAASH
CRAASH
"DO IT AT A SIT DOWN--IN FRONT OF ALL THE FAMILIES."
MENU

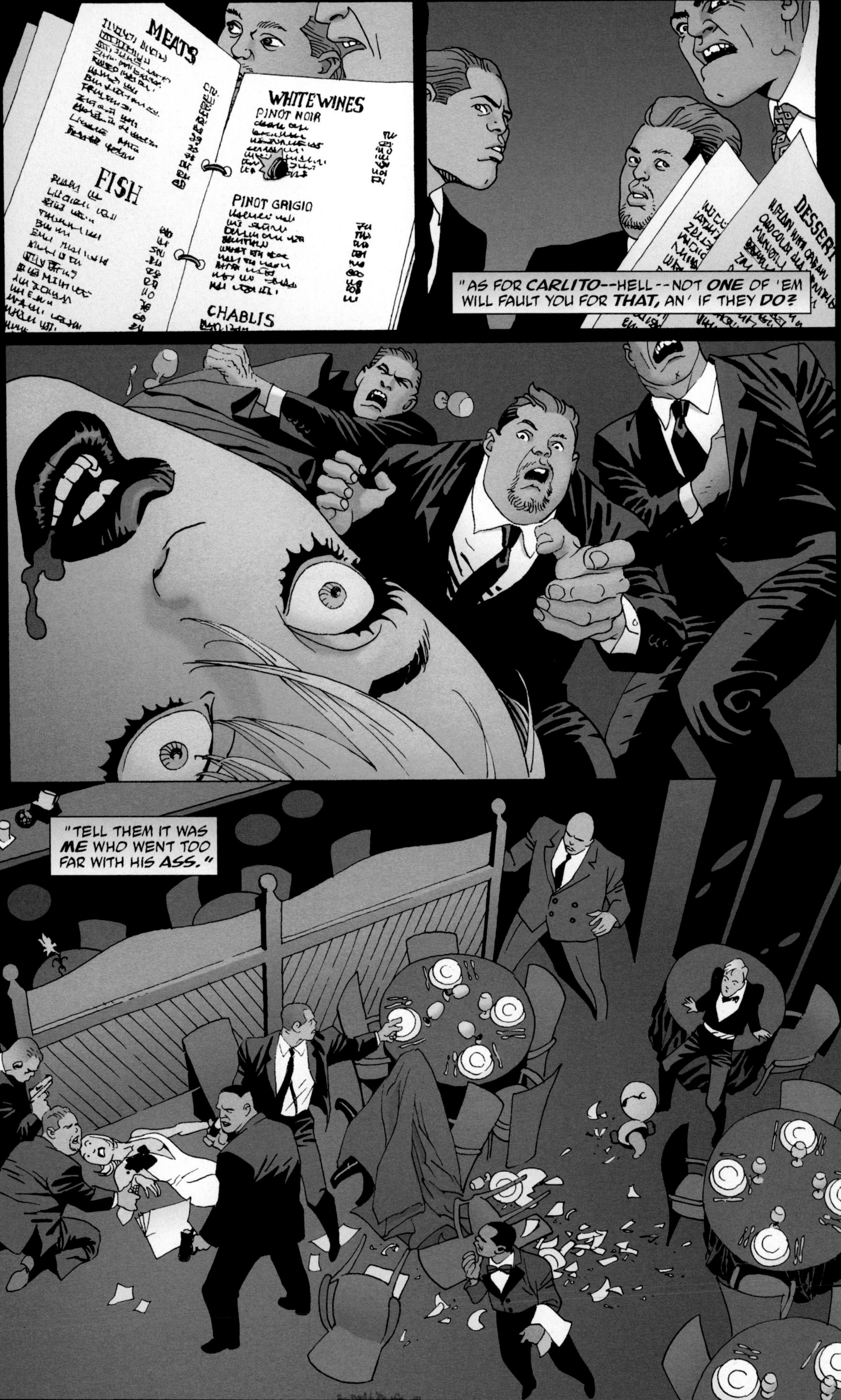
MEATS
WHITE WINES
PINOT NOIR
FISH
PINOT GRIGIO
CHABLIS
DESSERT
"AS FOR CARLITO--HELL--NOT ONE OF 'EM WILL FAULT YOU FOR THAT, AN' IF THEY DO?
"TELL THEM IT WAS ME WHO WENT TOO FAR WITH HIS ASS."

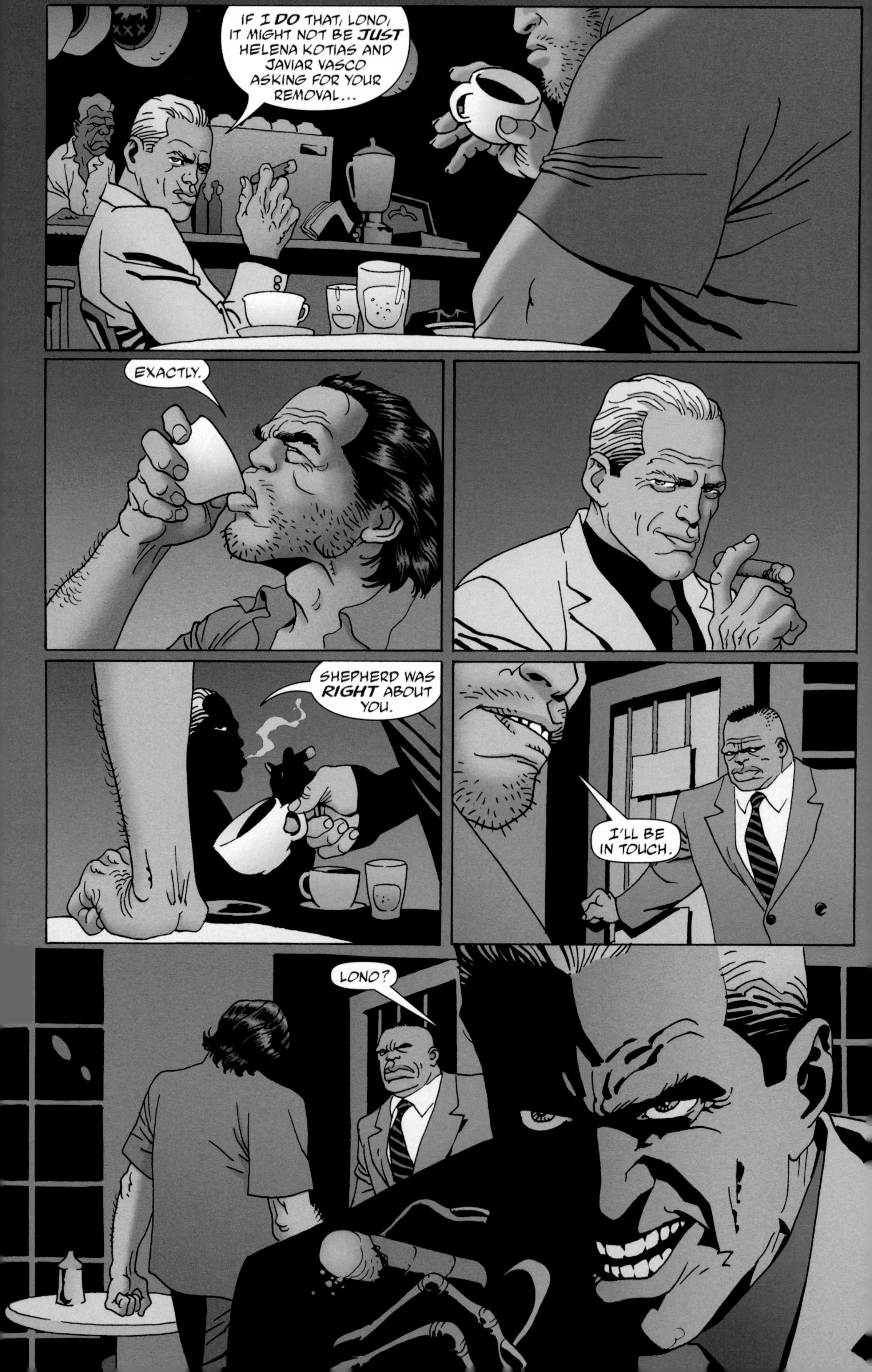
IF I DO THAT, LONO, IT MIGHT NOT BE JUST HELENA KOTIAS AND JAVIAR VASCO ASKING FOR YOUR REMOVAL...
EXACTLY.
SHEPHERD WAS RIGHT ABOUT YOU.
I'LL BE IN TOUCH.
LONO?

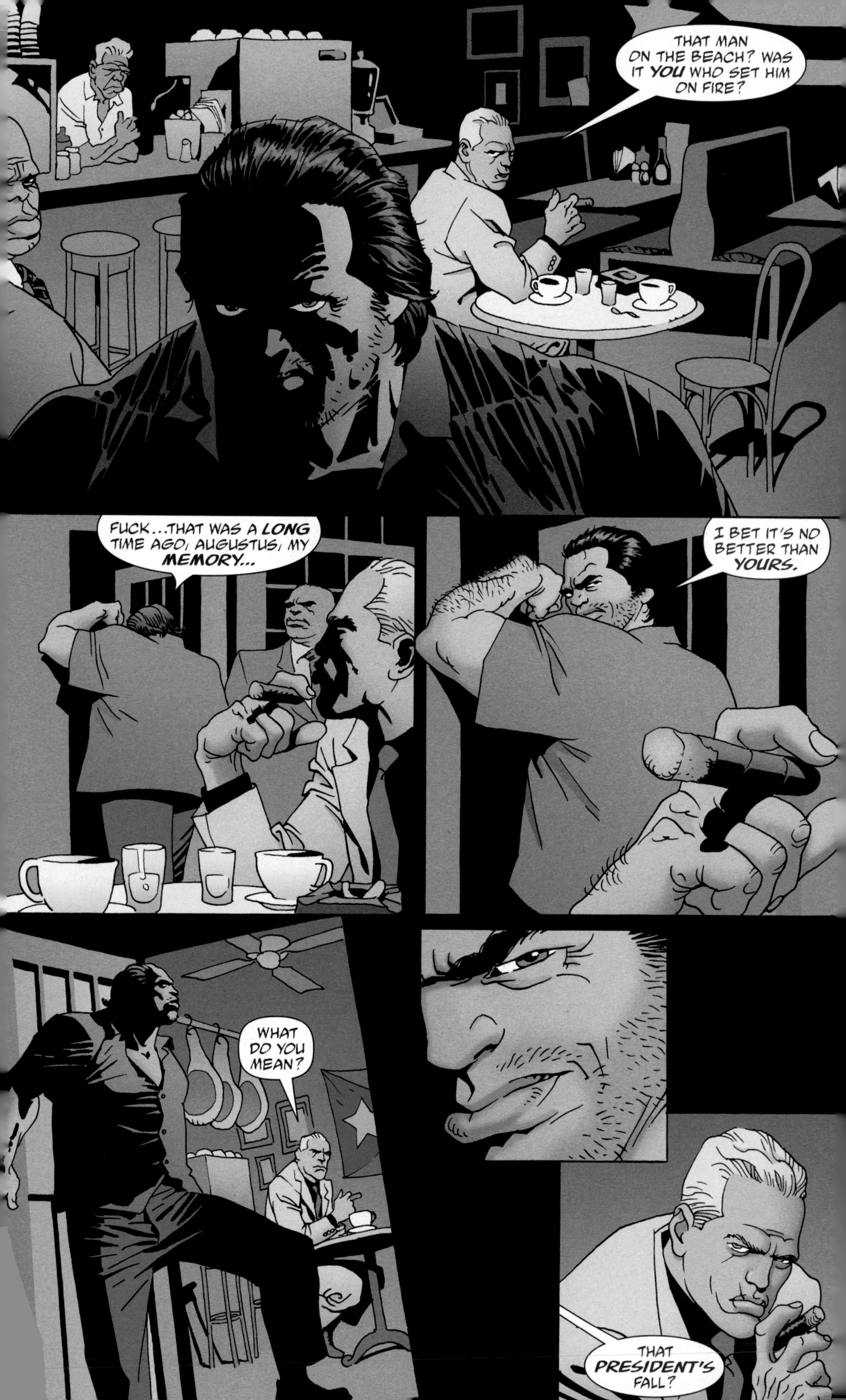
THAT MAN ON THE BEACH? WAS IT YOU WHO SET HIM ON FIRE?
FUCK...THAT WAS A LONG TIME AGO, AUGUSTUS, MY MEMORY...
I BET IT'S NO BETTER THAN YOURS.
WHAT DO YOU MEAN?
THAT PRESIDENT'S FALL?

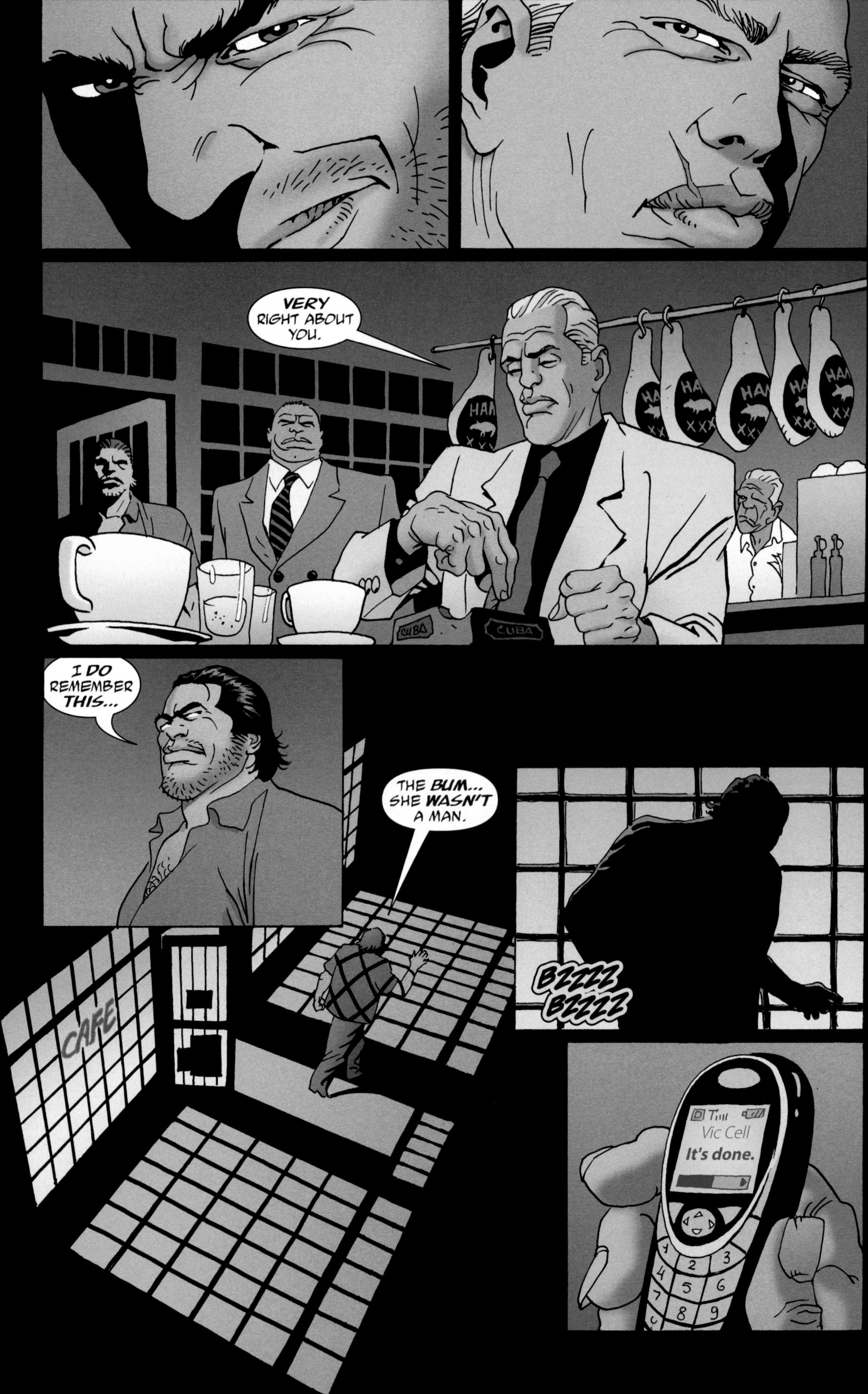
VERY RIGHT ABOUT YOU.
CUBA
CUBA
HAM
I DO REMEMBER THIS...
THE BUM... SHE WASN'T A MAN.
CAFE
BZZZZ BZZZZ
Vic Cell
It's done.

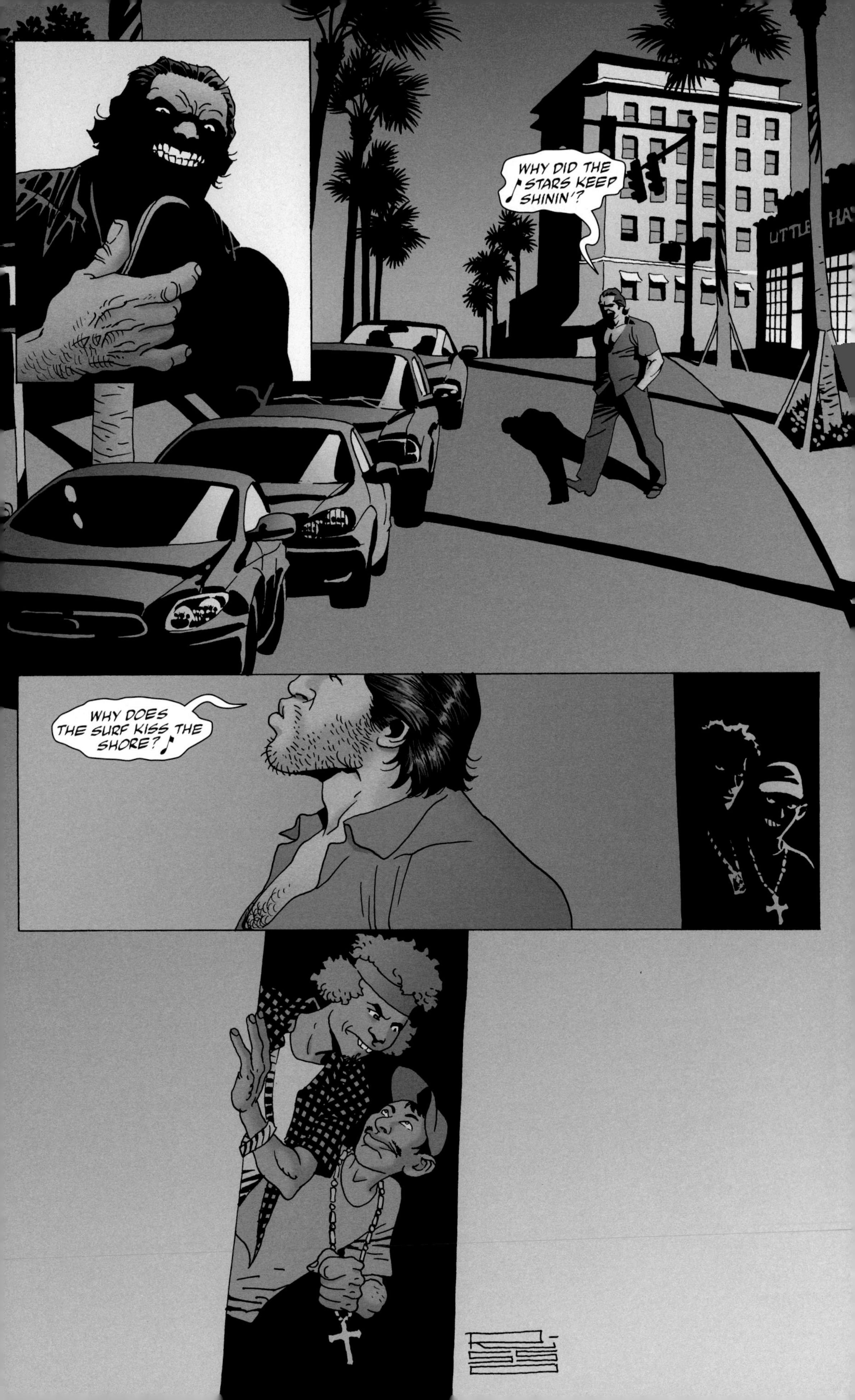

WHY DID THE ♪ STARS KEEP SHININ'?
LITTLE HA
WHY DOES THE SURF KISS THE SHORE? ♪

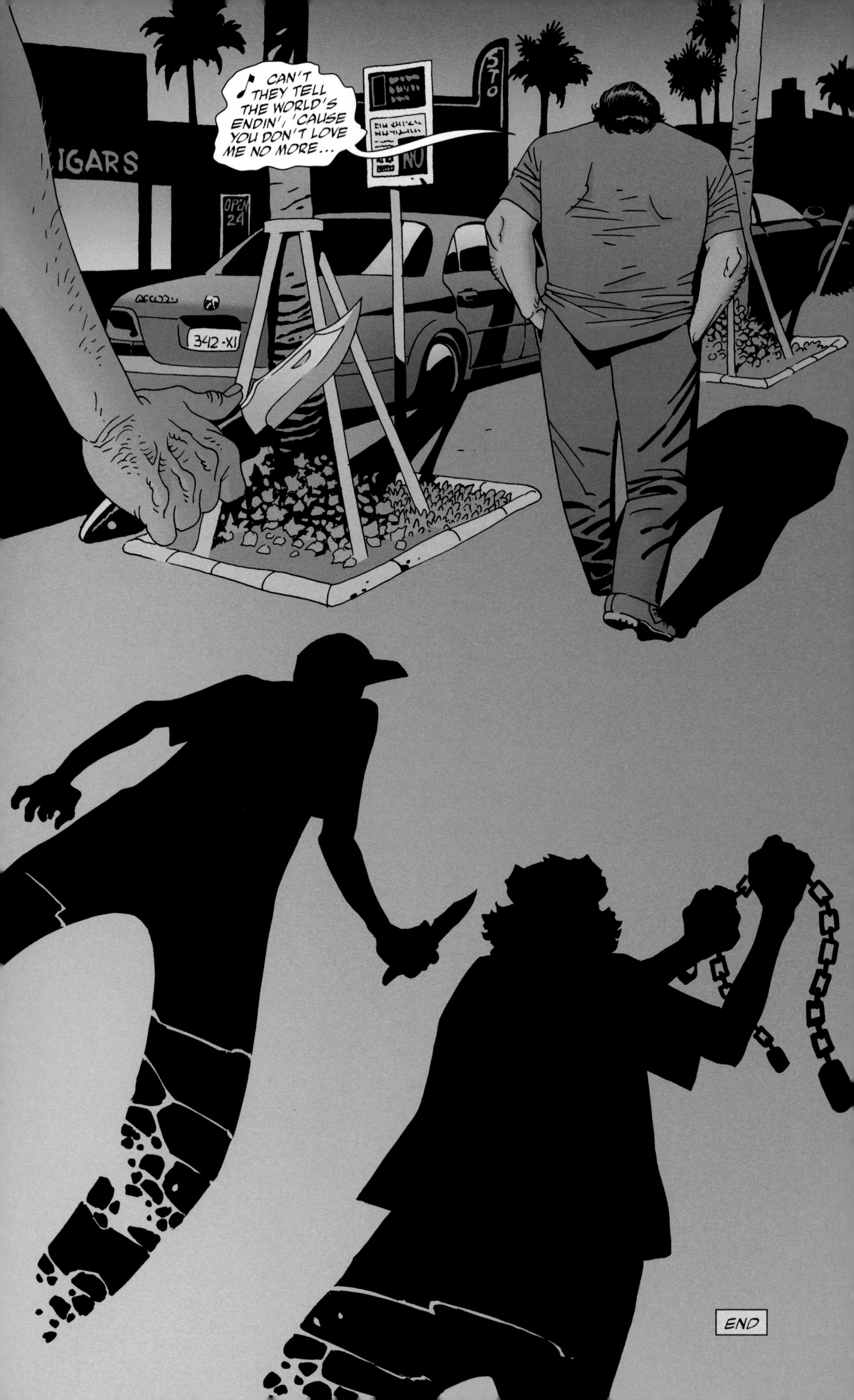
♪ CAN'T THEY TELL THE WORLD'S ENDIN', 'CAUSE YOU DON'T LOVE ME NO MORE...
IGARS
OPEN 24
342-XI
END

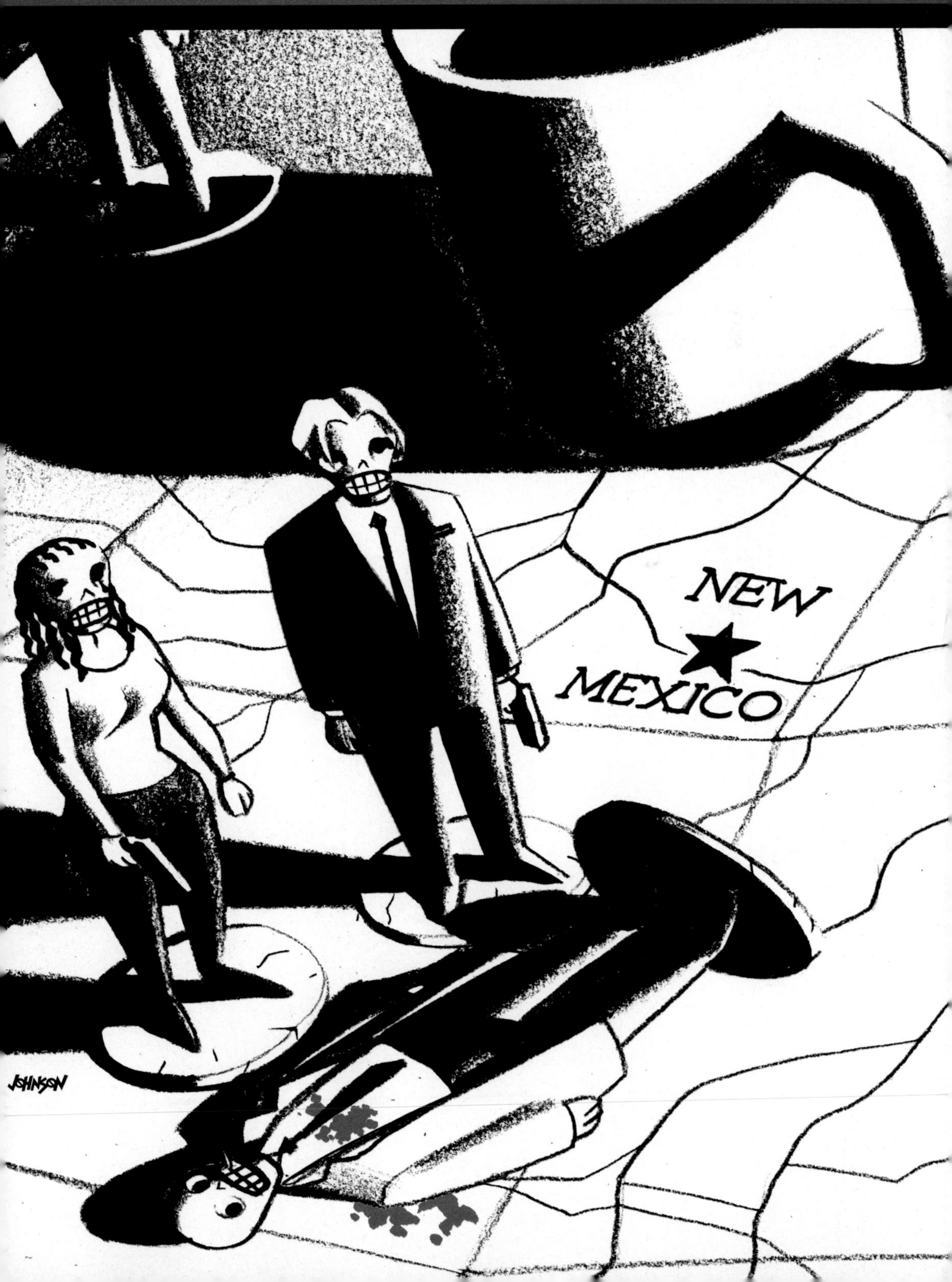
NEW
MEXICO
JOHNSON

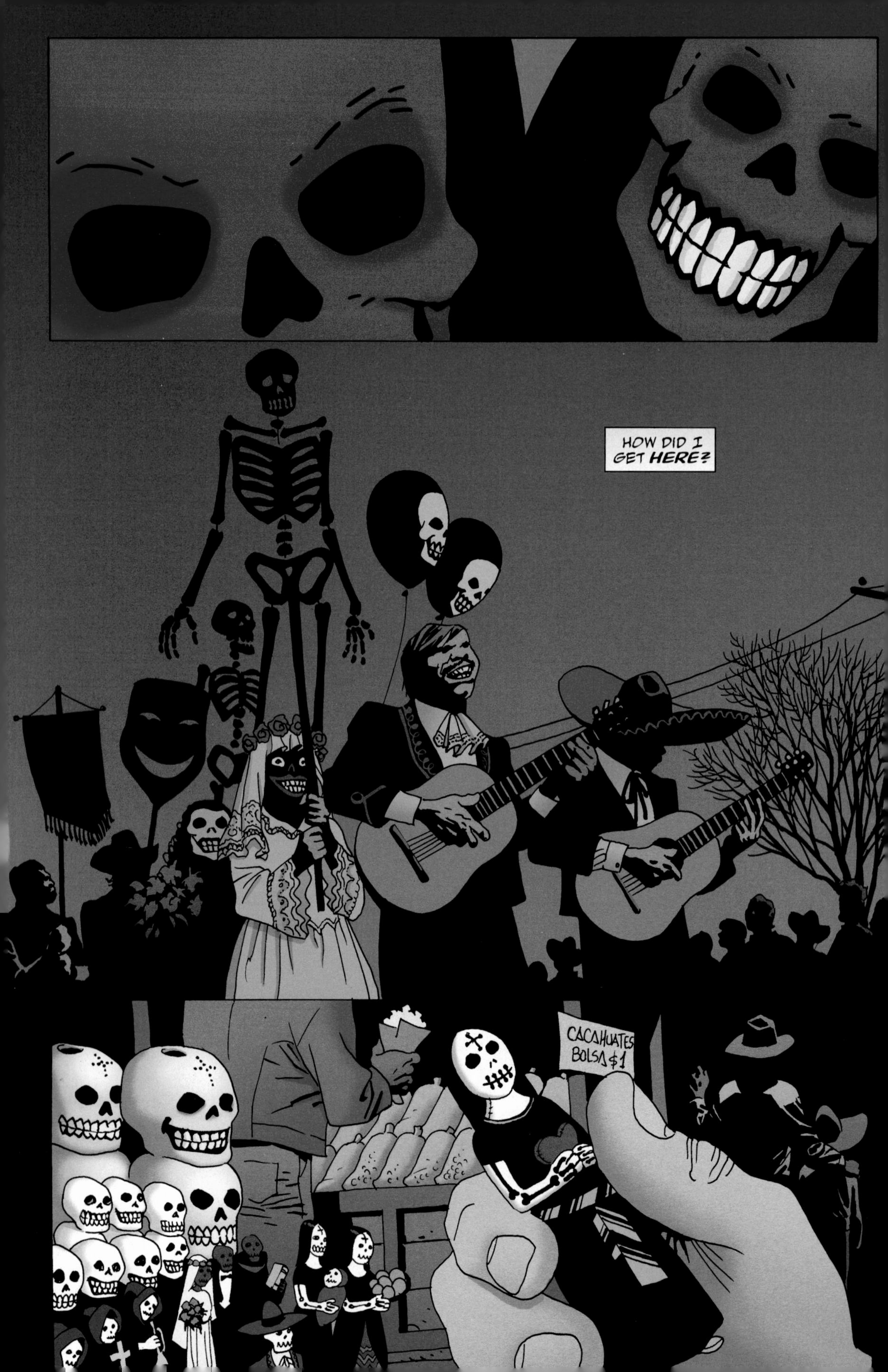
HOW DID I GET HERE?
CACAHUATES
BOLSA $1

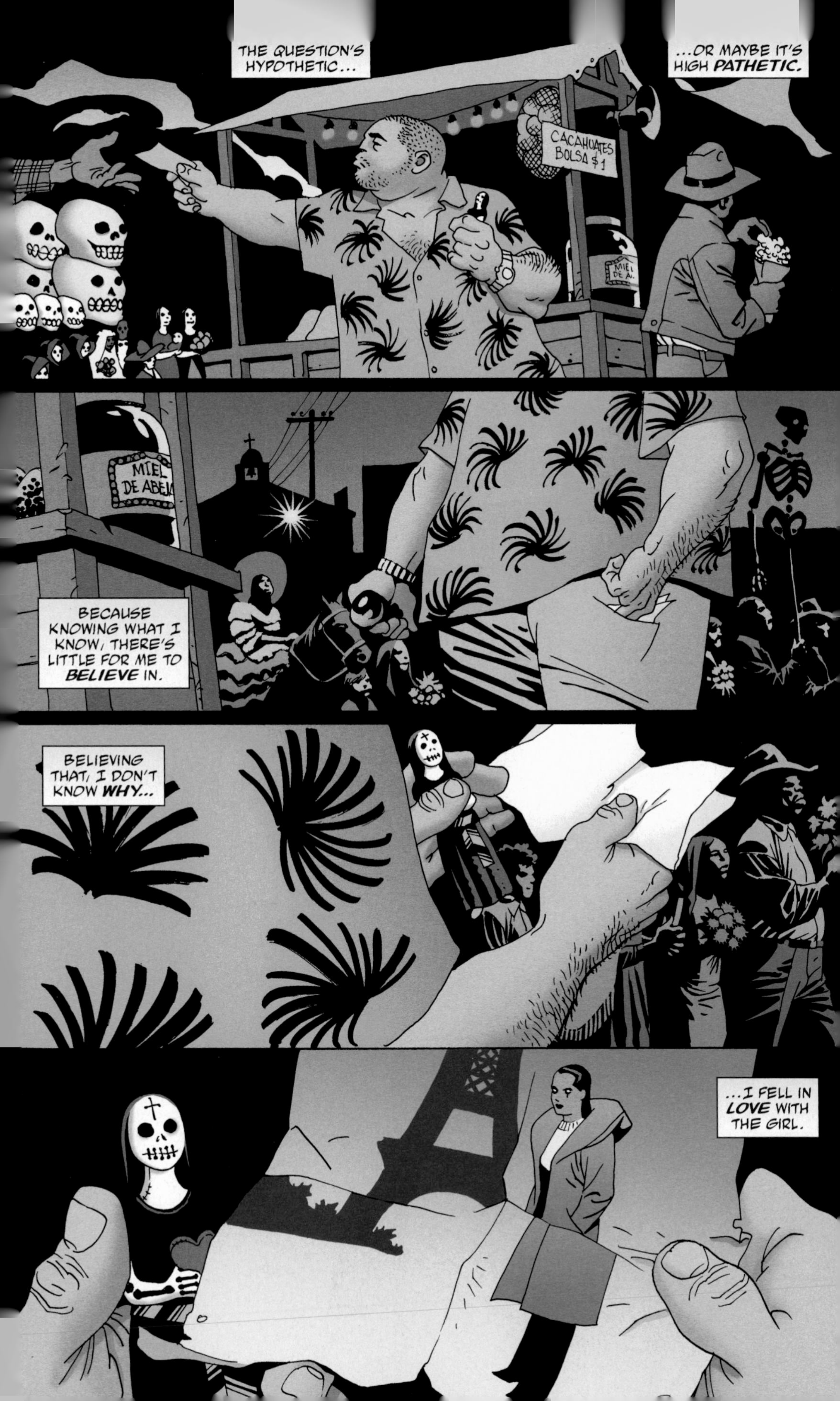
THE QUESTION'S HYPOTHETIC...
...OR MAYBE IT'S HIGH PATHETIC.
CACAHUATES BOLSA $1
BECAUSE KNOWING WHAT I KNOW, THERE'S LITTLE FOR ME TO BELIEVE IN.
MIEL DE ABEJA
BELIEVING THAT, I DON'T KNOW WHY...
...I FELL IN LOVE WITH THE GIRL.

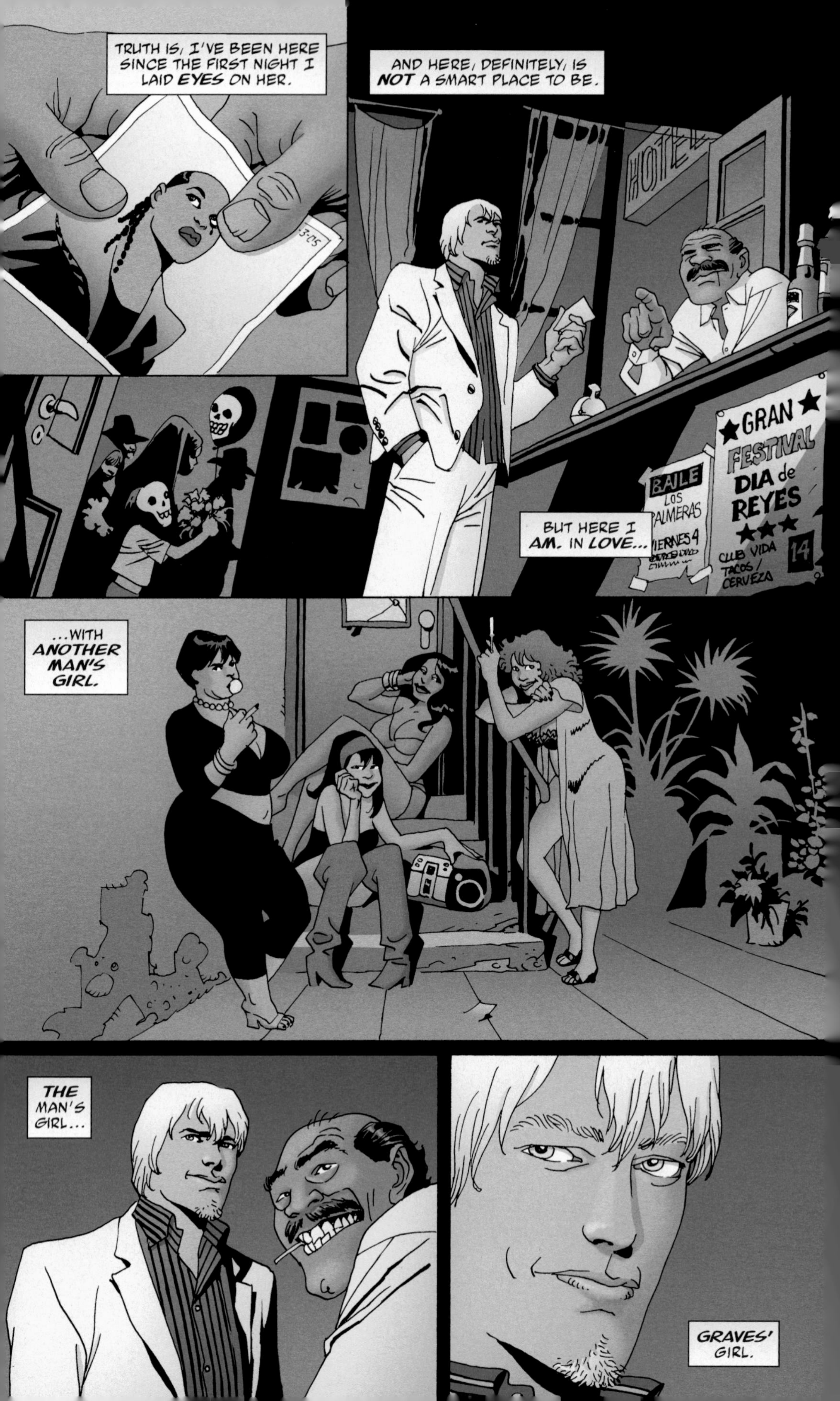
TRUTH IS, I'VE BEEN HERE SINCE THE FIRST NIGHT I LAID EYES ON HER.
AND HERE, DEFINITELY, IS NOT A SMART PLACE TO BE.
HOTEL
BAILE
LOS PALMERAS
VIERNES 4
GRAN FESTIVAL DIA de REYES
CLUB VIDA
TACOS / CERVEZA
14
BUT HERE I AM. IN LOVE...
...WITH ANOTHER MAN'S GIRL.
THE MAN'S GIRL...
GRAVES' GIRL.

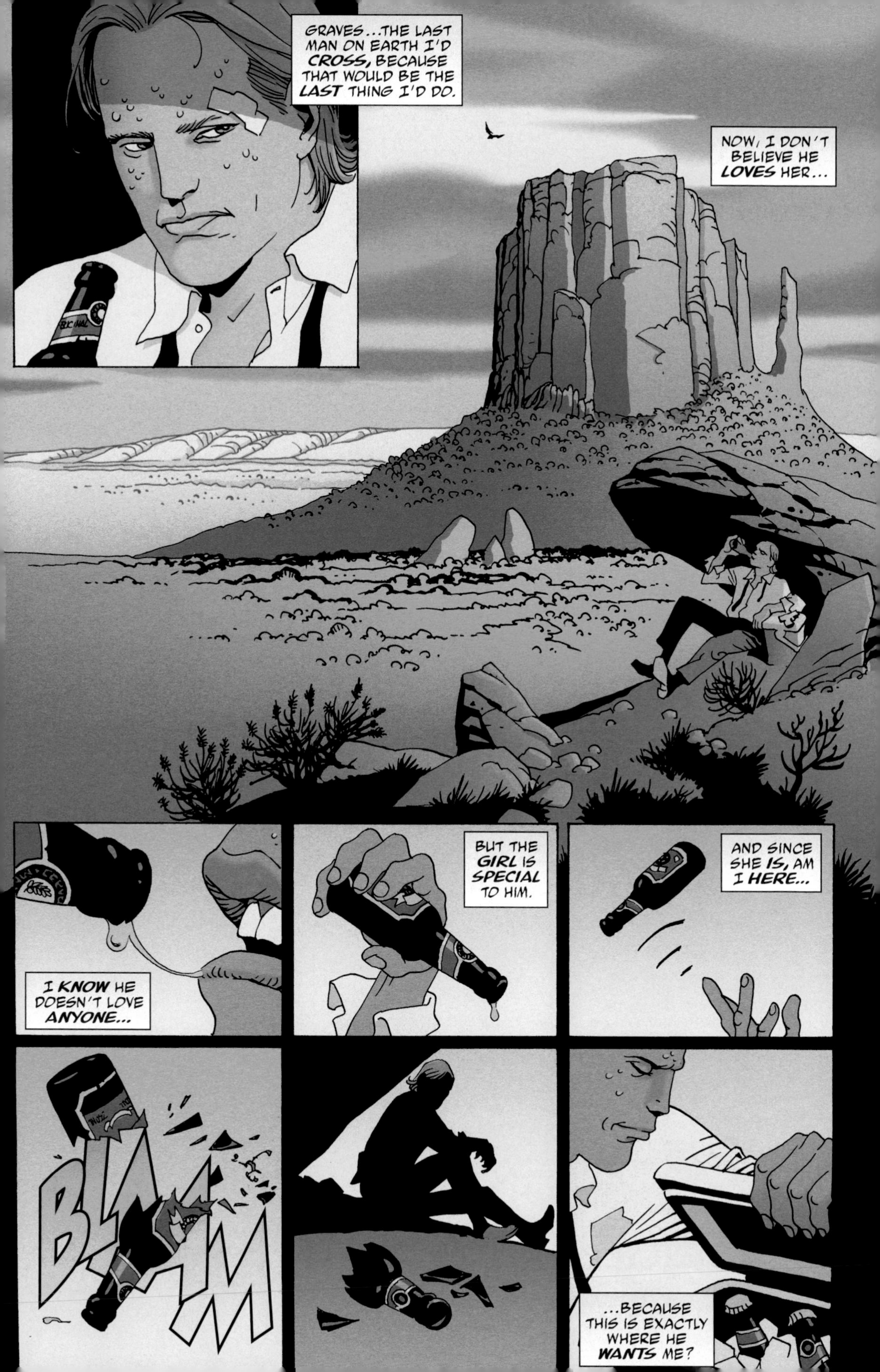
GRAVES...THE LAST MAN ON EARTH I'D CROSS, BECAUSE THAT WOULD BE THE LAST THING I'D DO.
NOW, I DON'T BELIEVE HE LOVES HER...
I KNOW HE DOESN'T LOVE ANYONE...
BUT THE GIRL IS SPECIAL TO HIM.
AND SINCE SHE IS, AM I HERE...
BLAMM
...BECAUSE THIS IS EXACTLY WHERE HE WANTS ME?

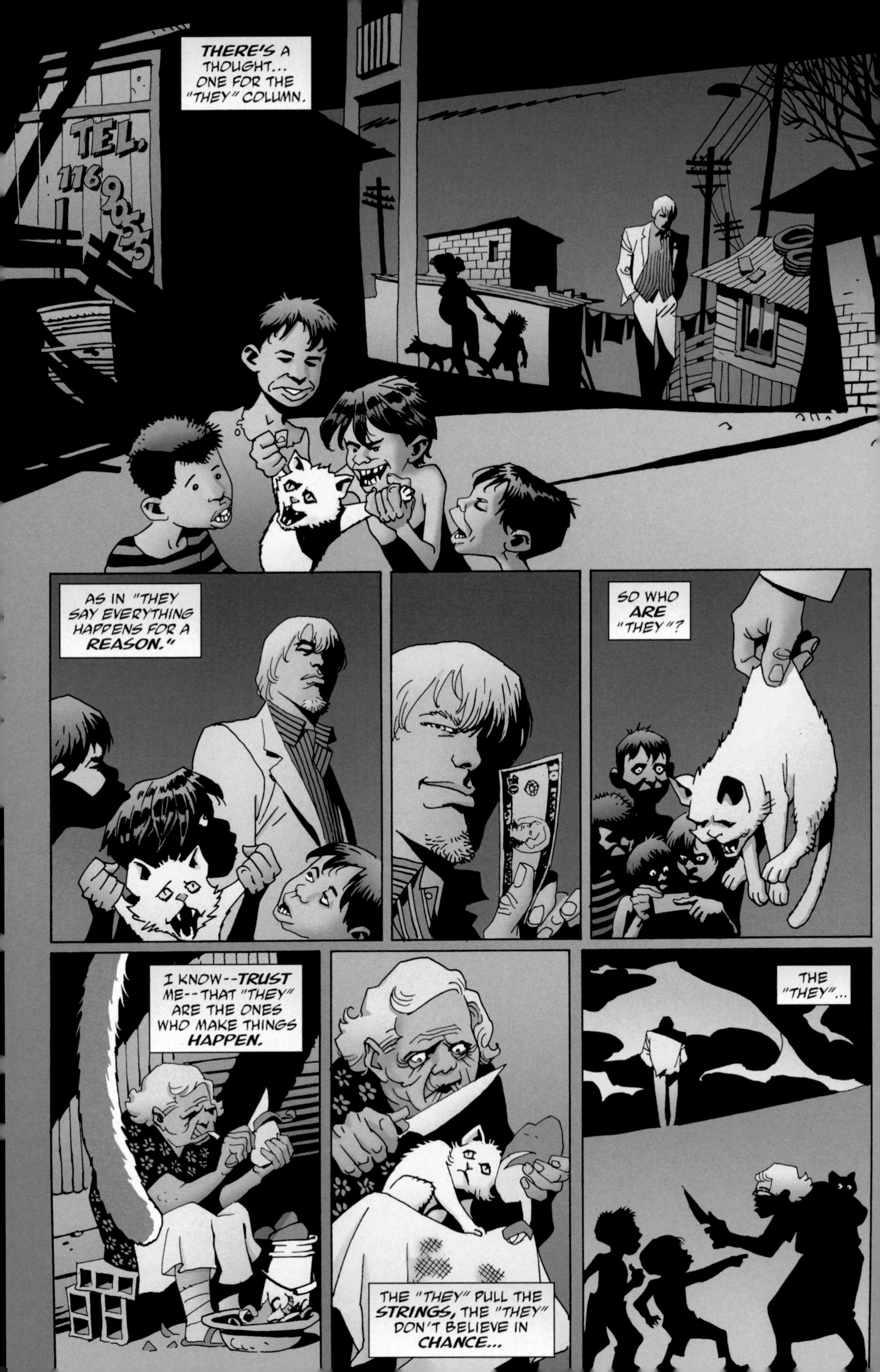
THERE'S A THOUGHT... ONE FOR THE "THEY" COLUMN.
TEL. 116 9055
AS IN "THEY SAY EVERYTHING HAPPENS FOR A REASON."
SO WHO ARE "THEY"?
I KNOW--TRUST ME--THAT "THEY" ARE THE ONES WHO MAKE THINGS HAPPEN.
THE "THEY" PULL THE STRINGS, THE "THEY" DON'T BELIEVE IN CHANCE...
THE "THEY"...

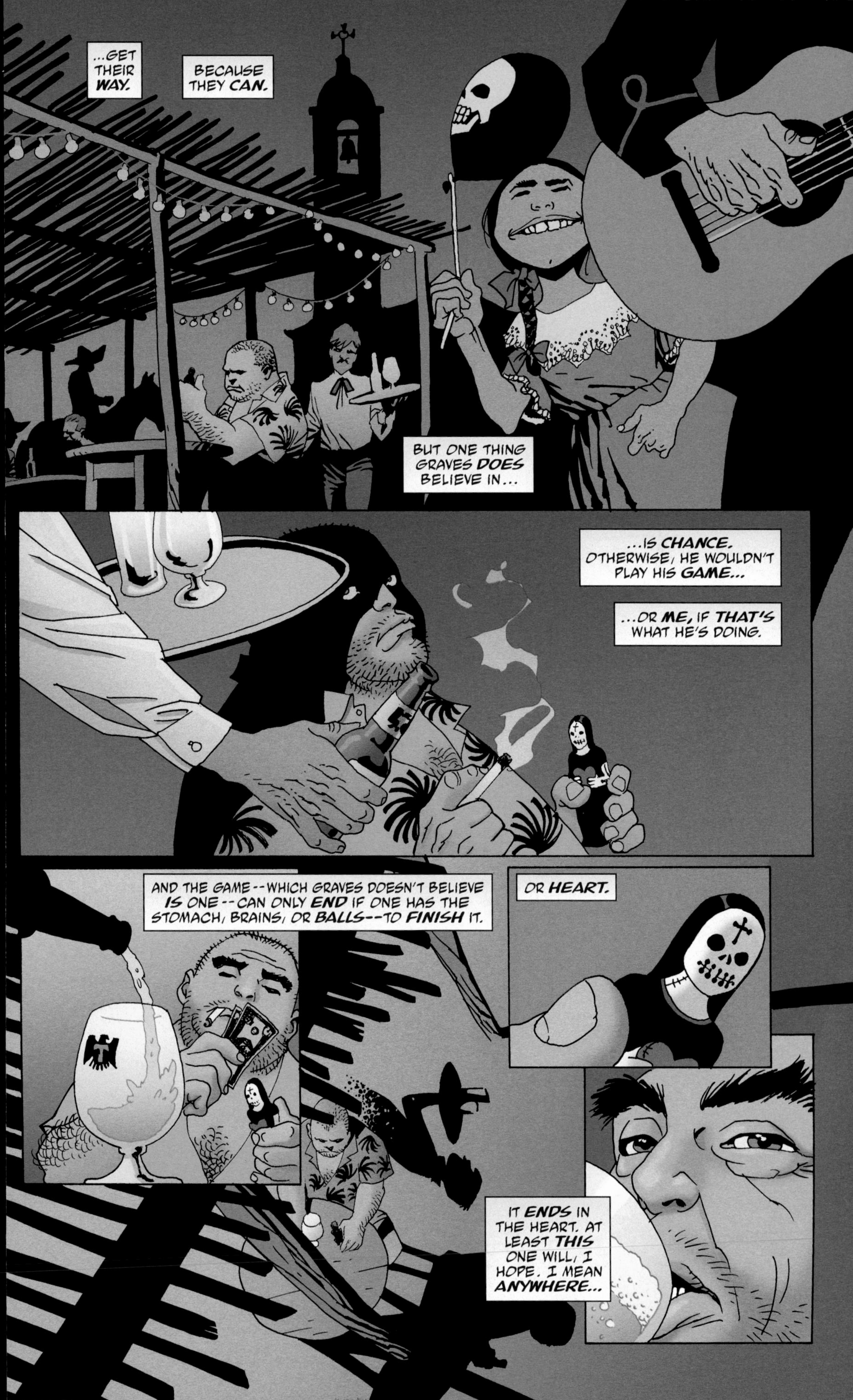
...GET THEIR WAY.
BECAUSE THEY CAN.
BUT ONE THING GRAVES DOES BELIEVE IN...
...IS CHANCE. OTHERWISE, HE WOULDN'T PLAY HIS GAME...
...OR ME, IF THAT'S WHAT HE'S DOING.
AND THE GAME--WHICH GRAVES DOESN'T BELIEVE IS ONE--CAN ONLY END IF ONE HAS THE STOMACH, BRAINS, OR BALLS--TO FINISH IT.
OR HEART.
IT ENDS IN THE HEART. AT LEAST THIS ONE WILL, I HOPE. I MEAN ANYWHERE...

ONE FOR ME...

...BUT THE FACE.

AND ONE...

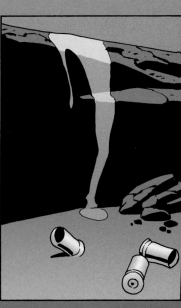

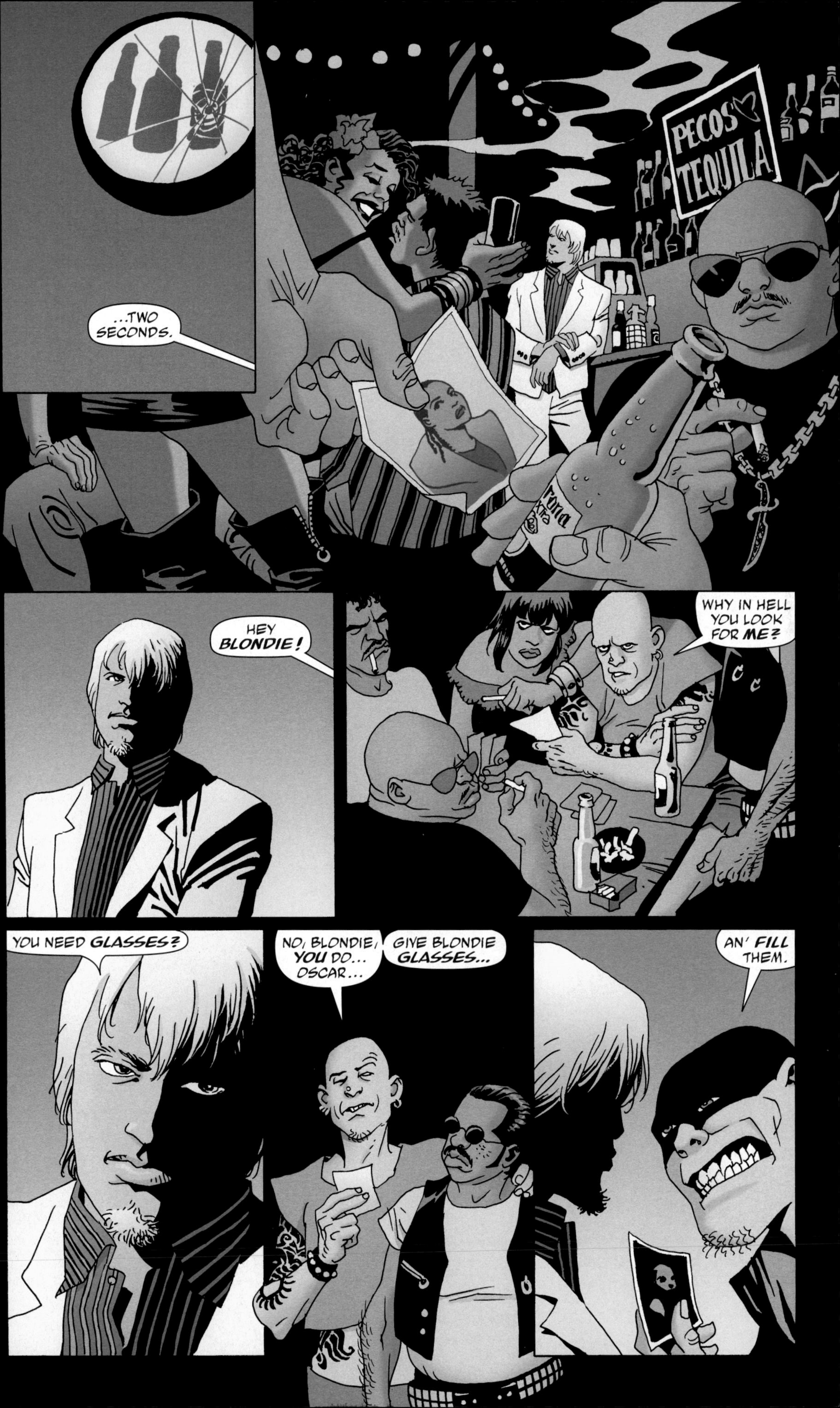

...TWO SECONDS.
PECOS TEQUILA
HEY BLONDIE!
WHY IN HELL YOU LOOK FOR ME?
YOU NEED GLASSES?
NO, BLONDIE, YOU DO... OSCAR...
GIVE BLONDIE GLASSES...
AN' FILL THEM.

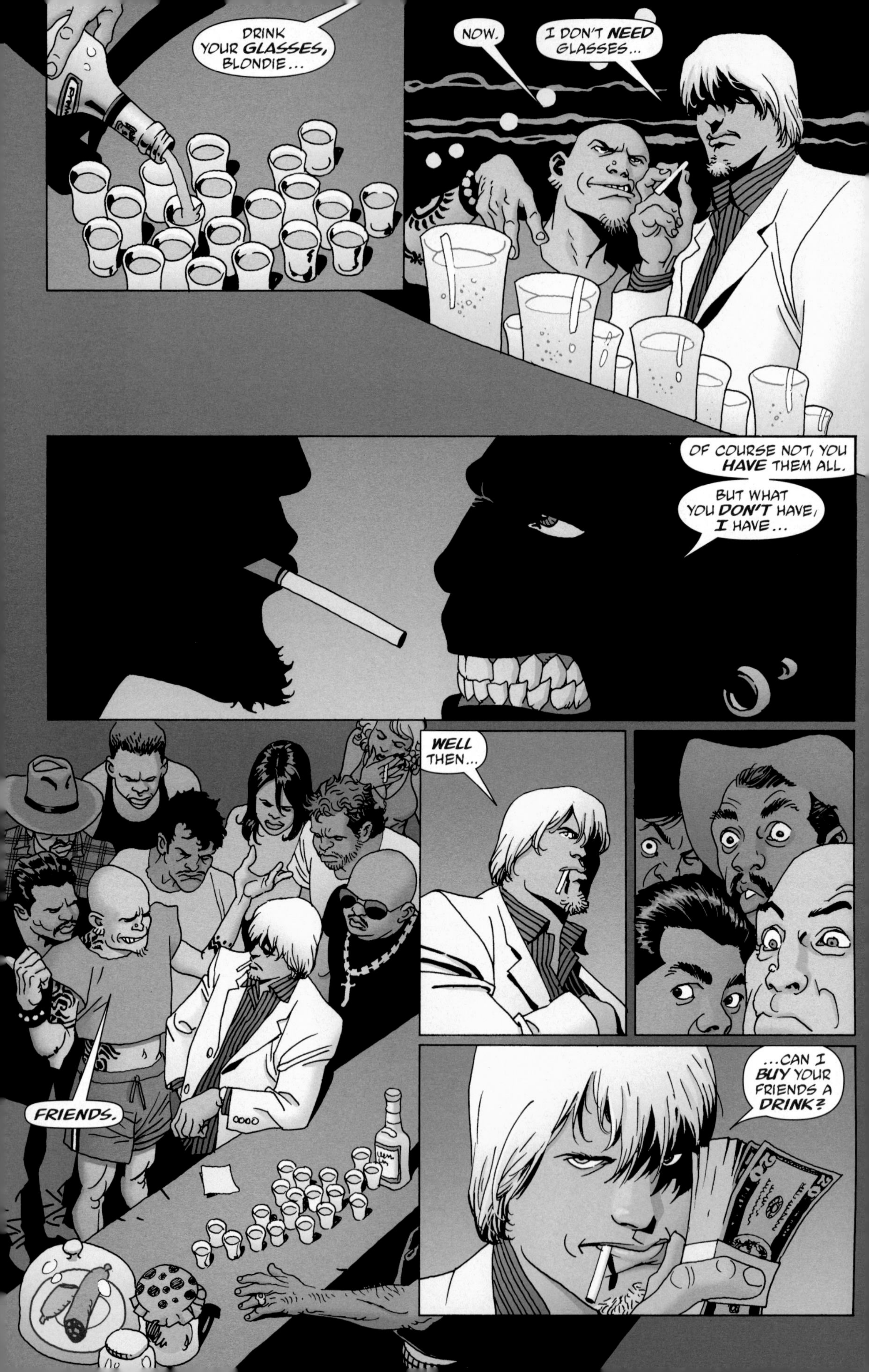

DRINK YOUR GLASSES, BLONDIE...
NOW.
I DON'T NEED GLASSES...
OF COURSE NOT, YOU HAVE THEM ALL.
BUT WHAT YOU DON'T HAVE, I HAVE...
FRIENDS.
WELL THEN...
...CAN I BUY YOUR FRIENDS A DRINK?

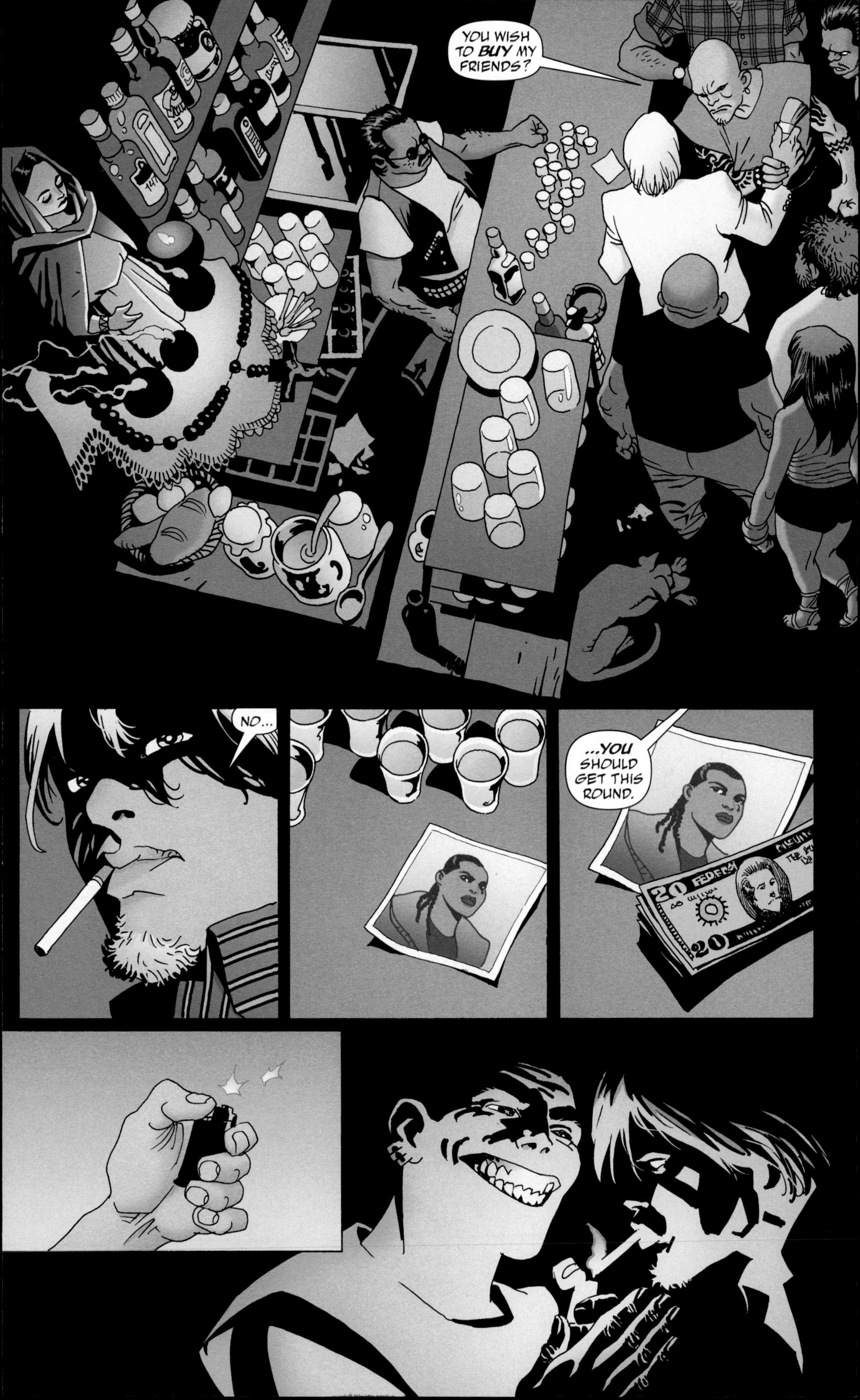
YOU WISH TO BUY MY FRIENDS?
NO...
...YOU SHOULD GET THIS ROUND.

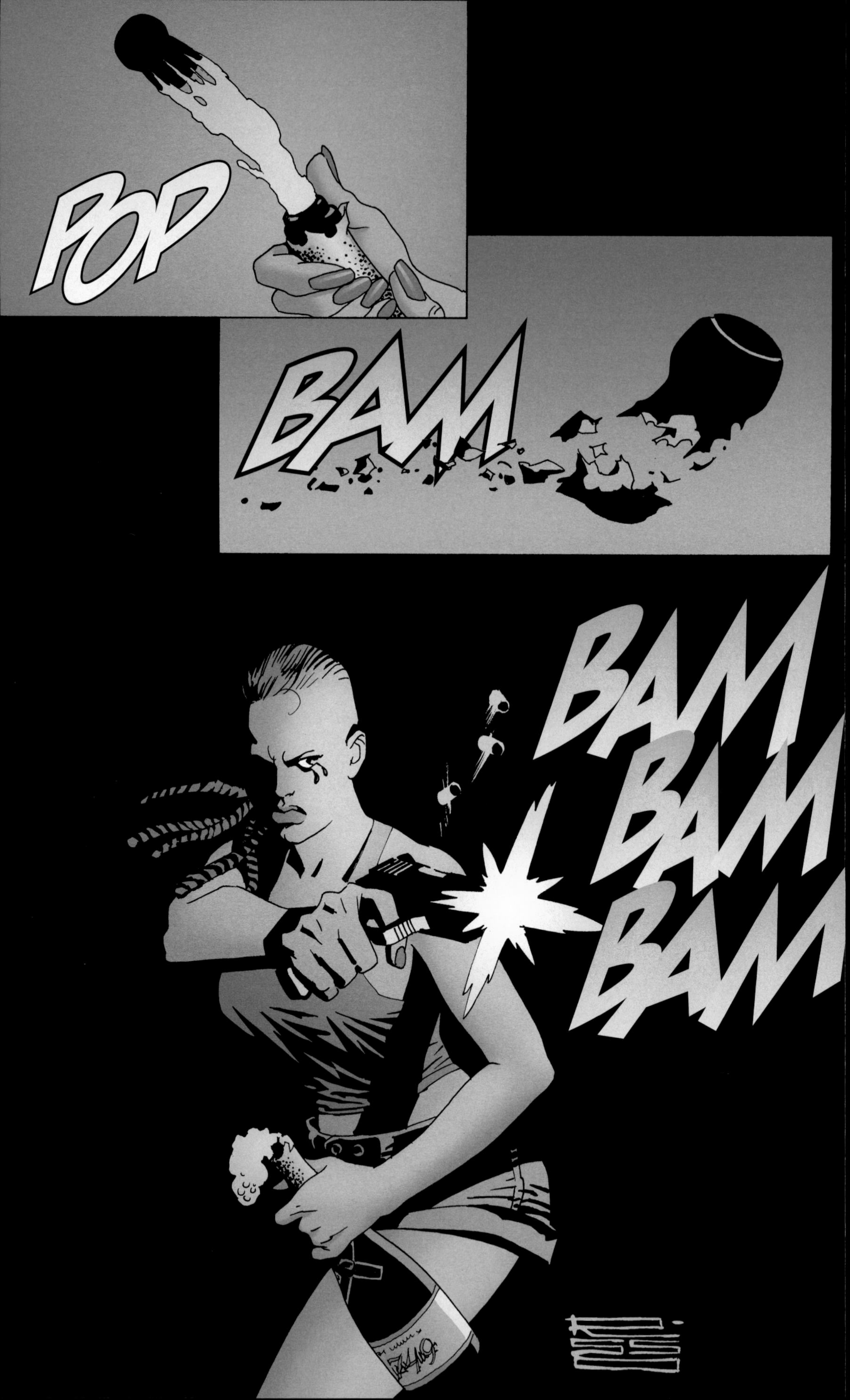
POP
BAM
BAM
BAM
BAM

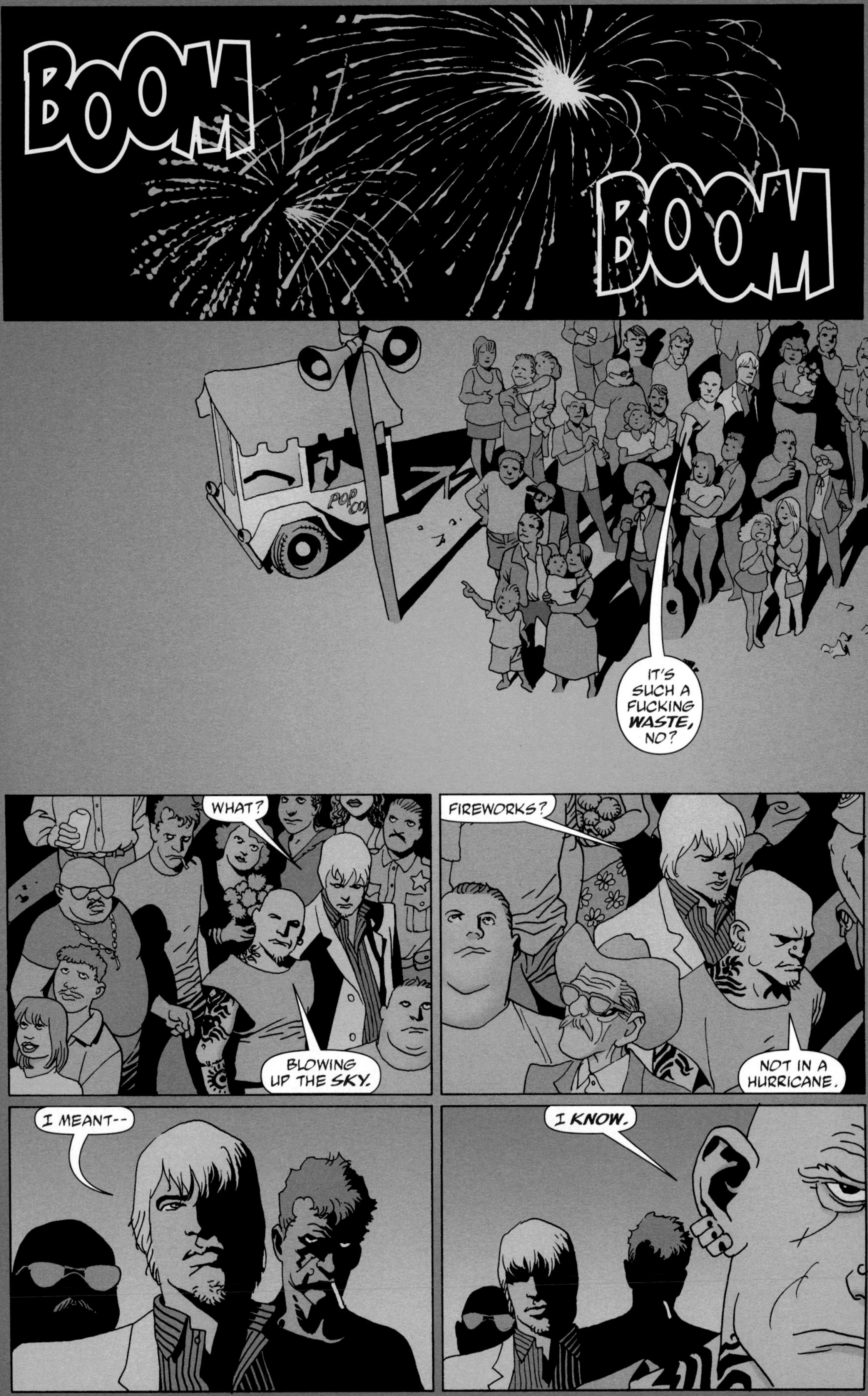
BOOM
BOOM
POP CO
IT'S SUCH A FUCKING WASTE, NO?
WHAT?
BLOWING UP THE SKY.
FIREWORKS?
NOT IN A HURRICANE.
I MEANT--
I KNOW.

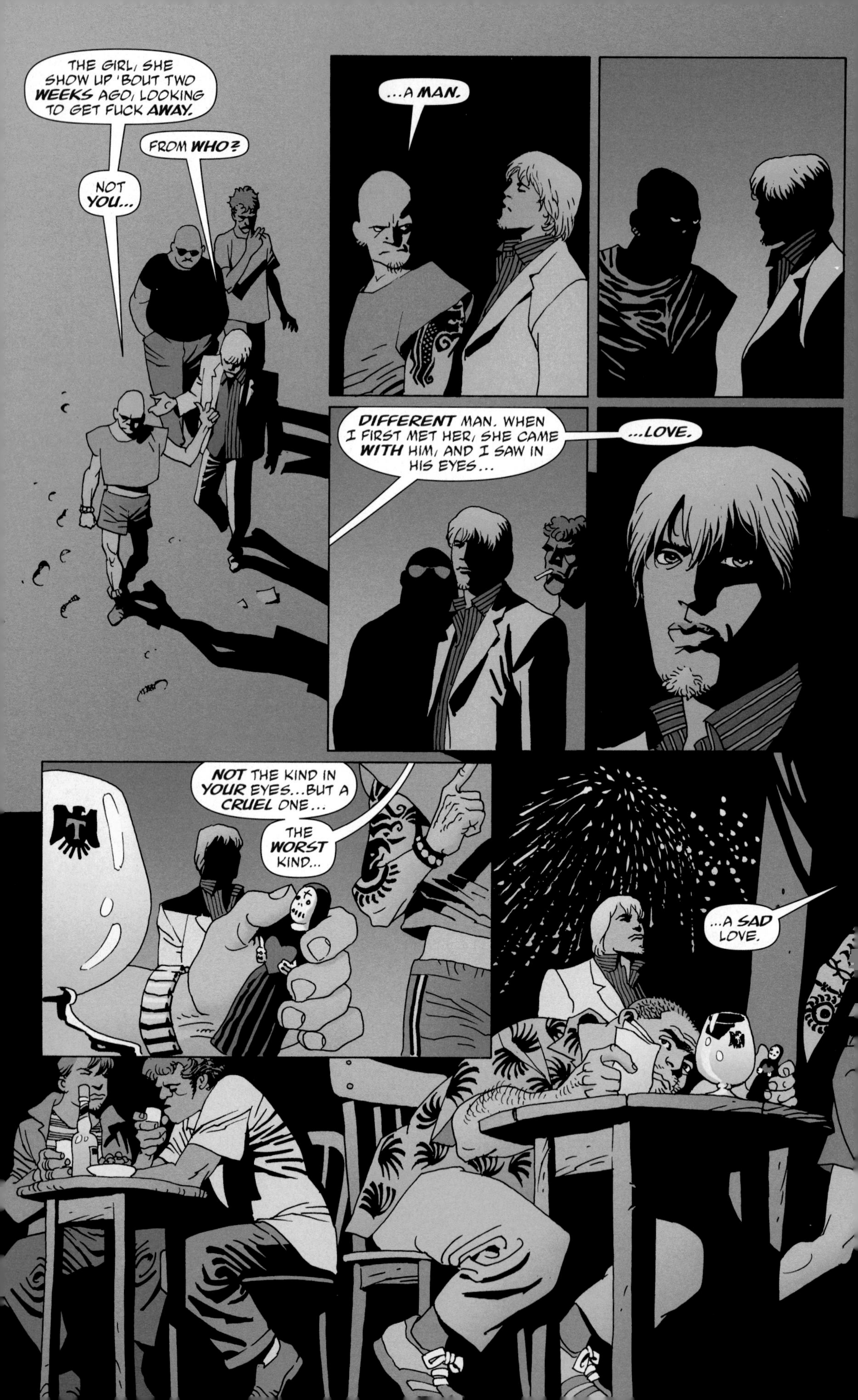
THE GIRL, SHE SHOW UP 'BOUT TWO WEEKS AGO, LOOKING TO GET FUCK AWAY.
FROM WHO?
NOT YOU...
...A MAN.
DIFFERENT MAN. WHEN I FIRST MET HER, SHE CAME WITH HIM, AND I SAW IN HIS EYES...
...LOVE.
NOT THE KIND IN YOUR EYES...BUT A CRUEL ONE...
THE WORST KIND...
...A SAD LOVE.

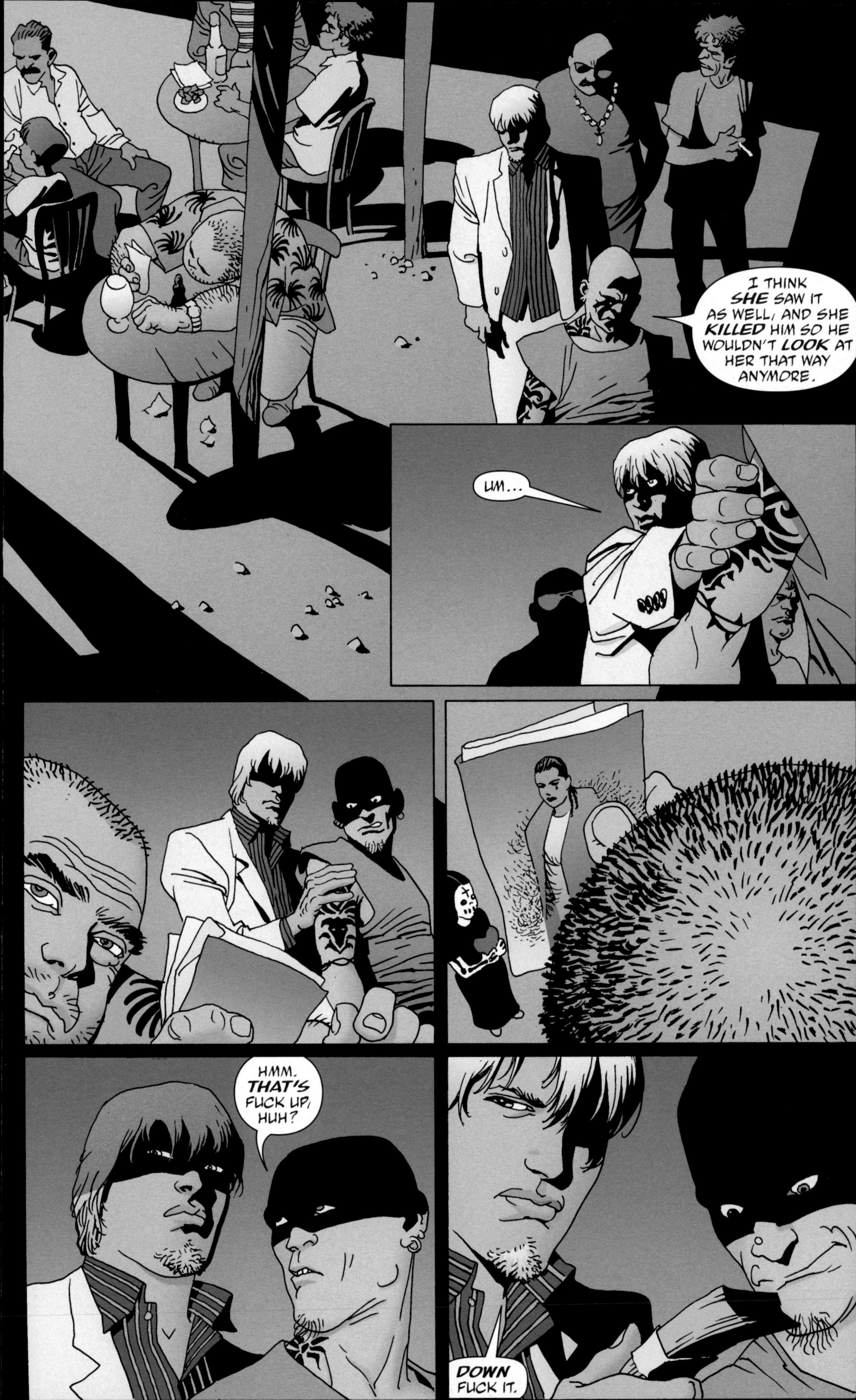
I THINK SHE SAW IT AS WELL, AND SHE KILLED HIM SO HE WOULDN'T LOOK AT HER THAT WAY ANYMORE.
UM...
HMM. THAT'S FUCK UP, HUH?
DOWN FUCK IT.

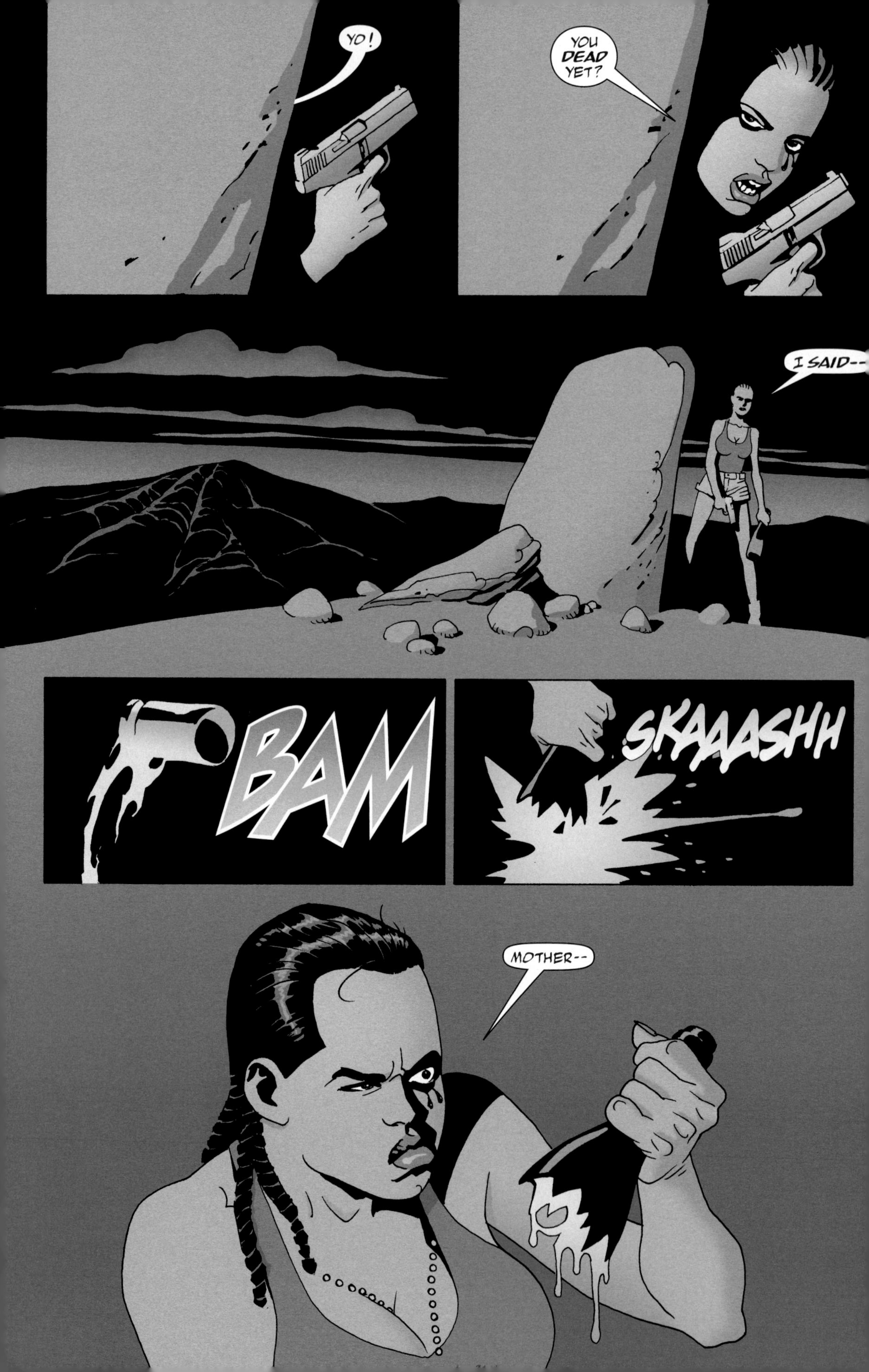
YO!
YOU DEAD YET?
I SAID--
BAM
SKAAASHH
MOTHER--

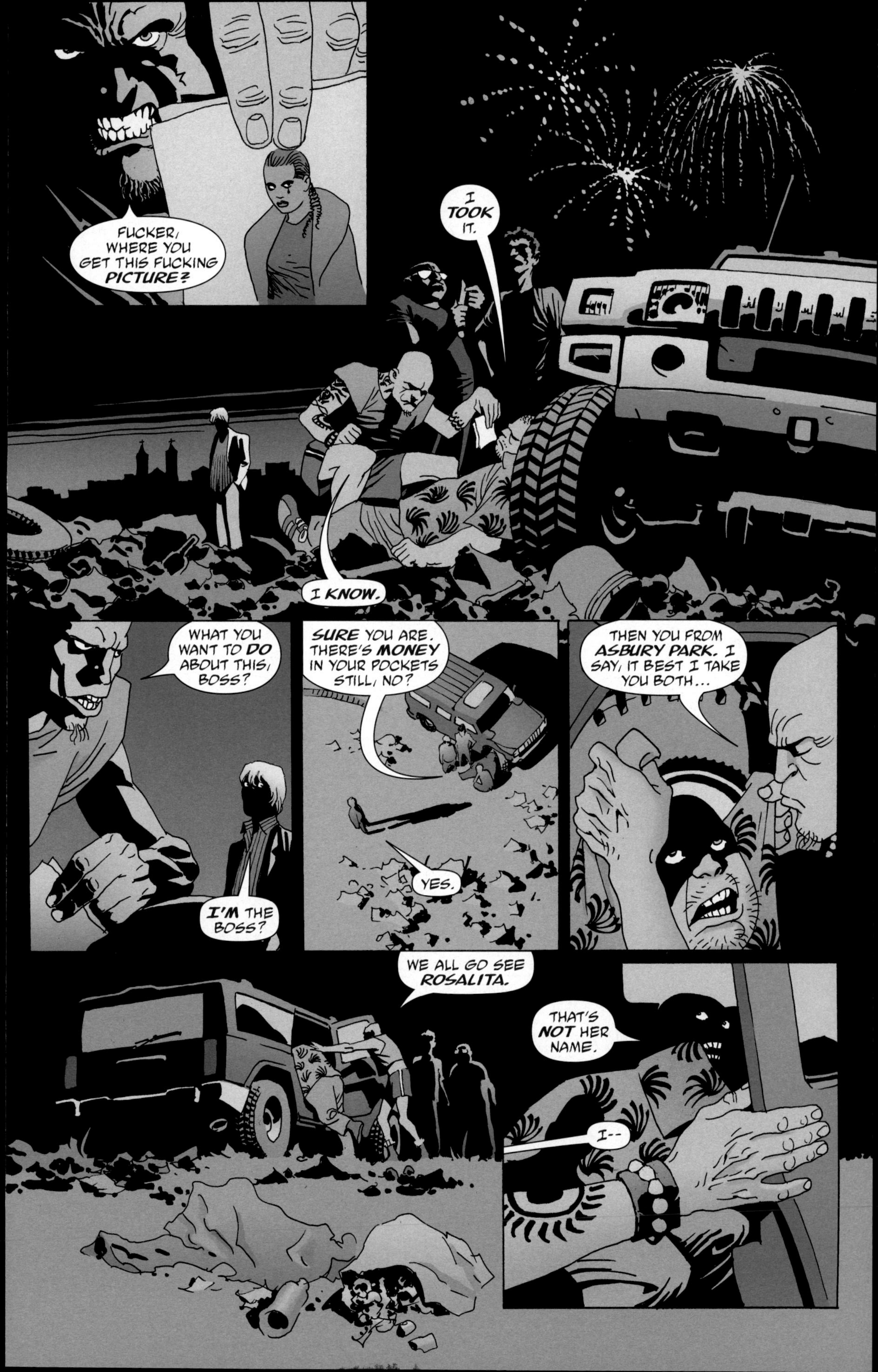
FUCKER, WHERE YOU GET THIS FUCKING PICTURE?
I TOOK IT.
I KNOW.
WHAT YOU WANT TO DO ABOUT THIS, BOSS?
I'M THE BOSS?
SURE YOU ARE. THERE'S MONEY IN YOUR POCKETS STILL, NO?
YES.
THEN YOU FROM ASBURY PARK. I SAY, IT BEST I TAKE YOU BOTH...
WE ALL GO SEE ROSALITA.
THAT'S NOT HER NAME.
I--

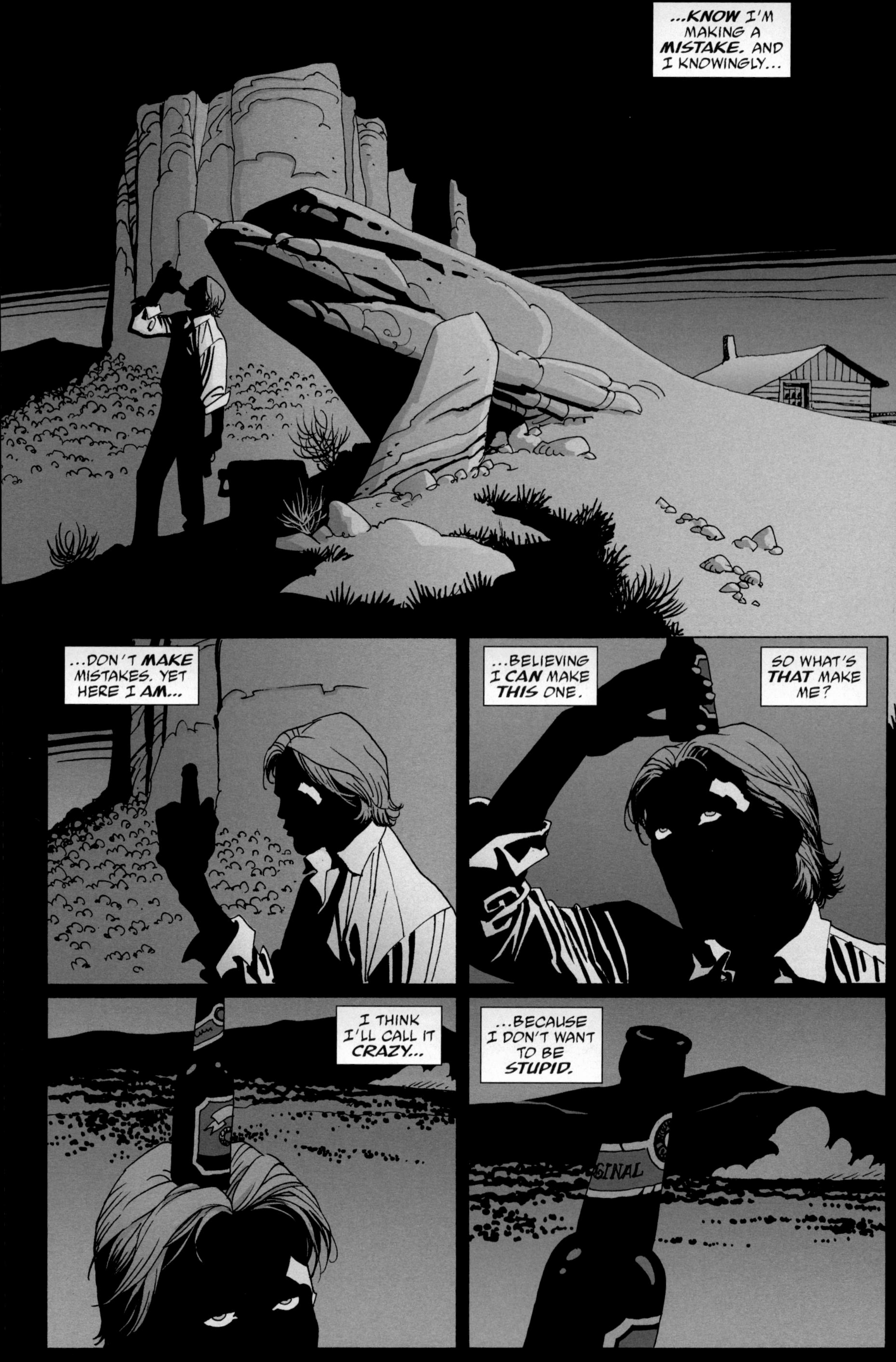
...KNOW I'M MAKING A MISTAKE. AND I KNOWINGLY...
...DON'T MAKE MISTAKES. YET HERE I AM...
...BELIEVING I CAN MAKE THIS ONE.
SO WHAT'S THAT MAKE ME?
I THINK I'LL CALL IT CRAZY...
...BECAUSE I DON'T WANT TO BE STUPID.

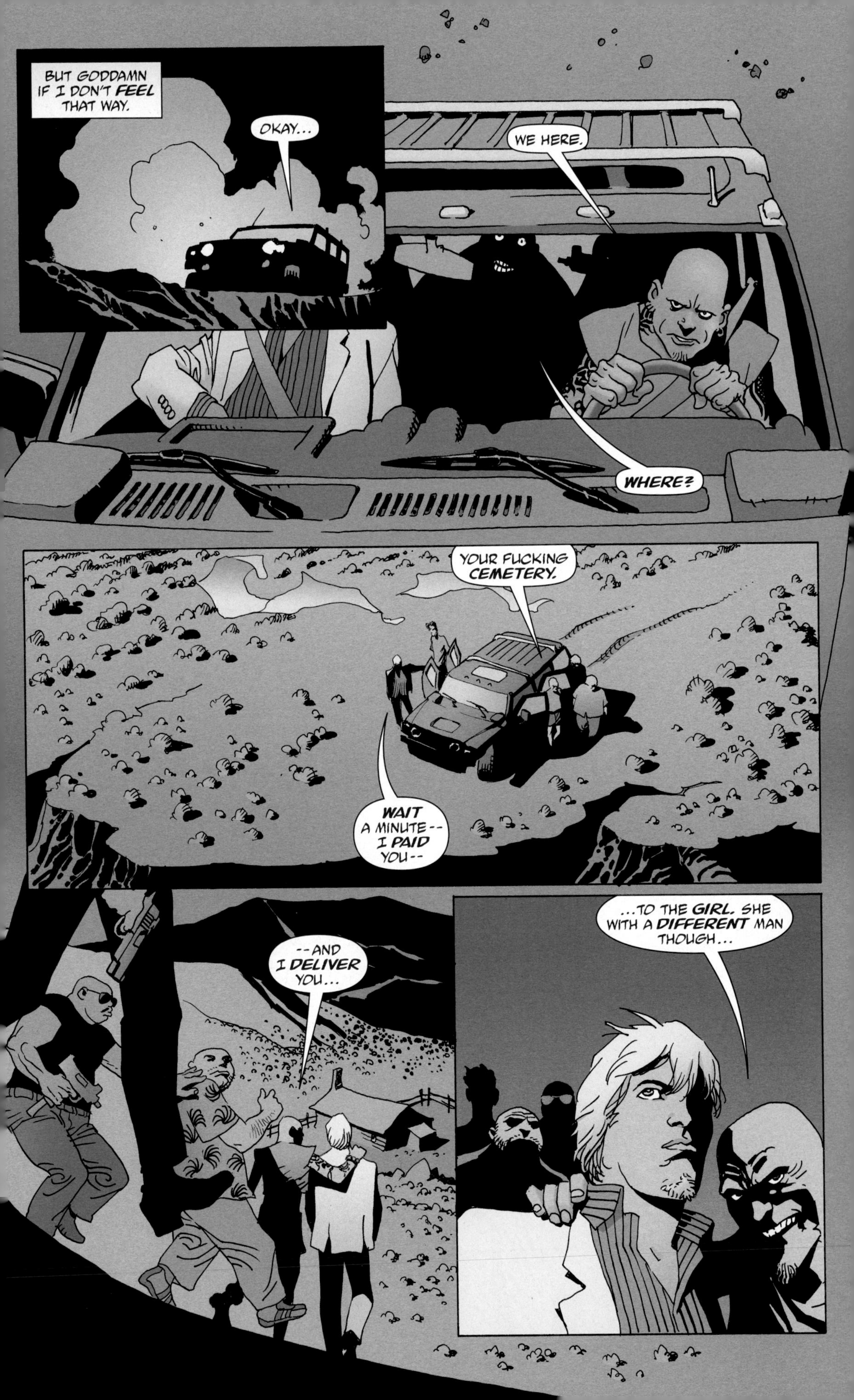
BUT GODDAMN IF I DON'T FEEL THAT WAY.
OKAY...
WE HERE.
WHERE?
YOUR FUCKING CEMETERY.
WAIT A MINUTE-- I PAID YOU--
--AND I DELIVER YOU...
...TO THE GIRL. SHE WITH A DIFFERENT MAN THOUGH...

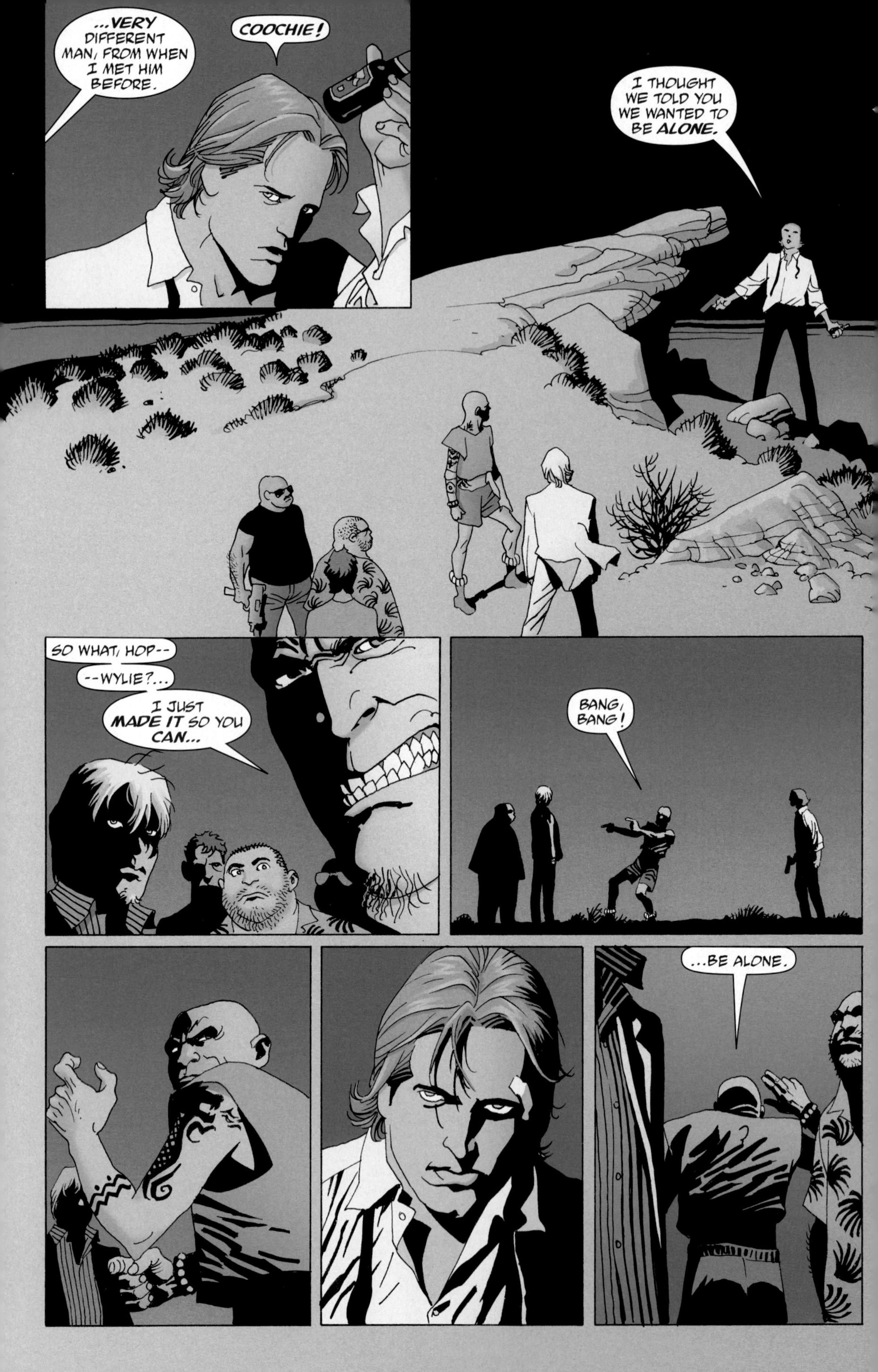
...VERY DIFFERENT MAN, FROM WHEN I MET HIM BEFORE.
COOCHIE!
I THOUGHT WE TOLD YOU WE WANTED TO BE ALONE.
SO WHAT, HOP--
--WYLIE?...
I JUST MADE IT SO YOU CAN...
BANG, BANG!
...BE ALONE.

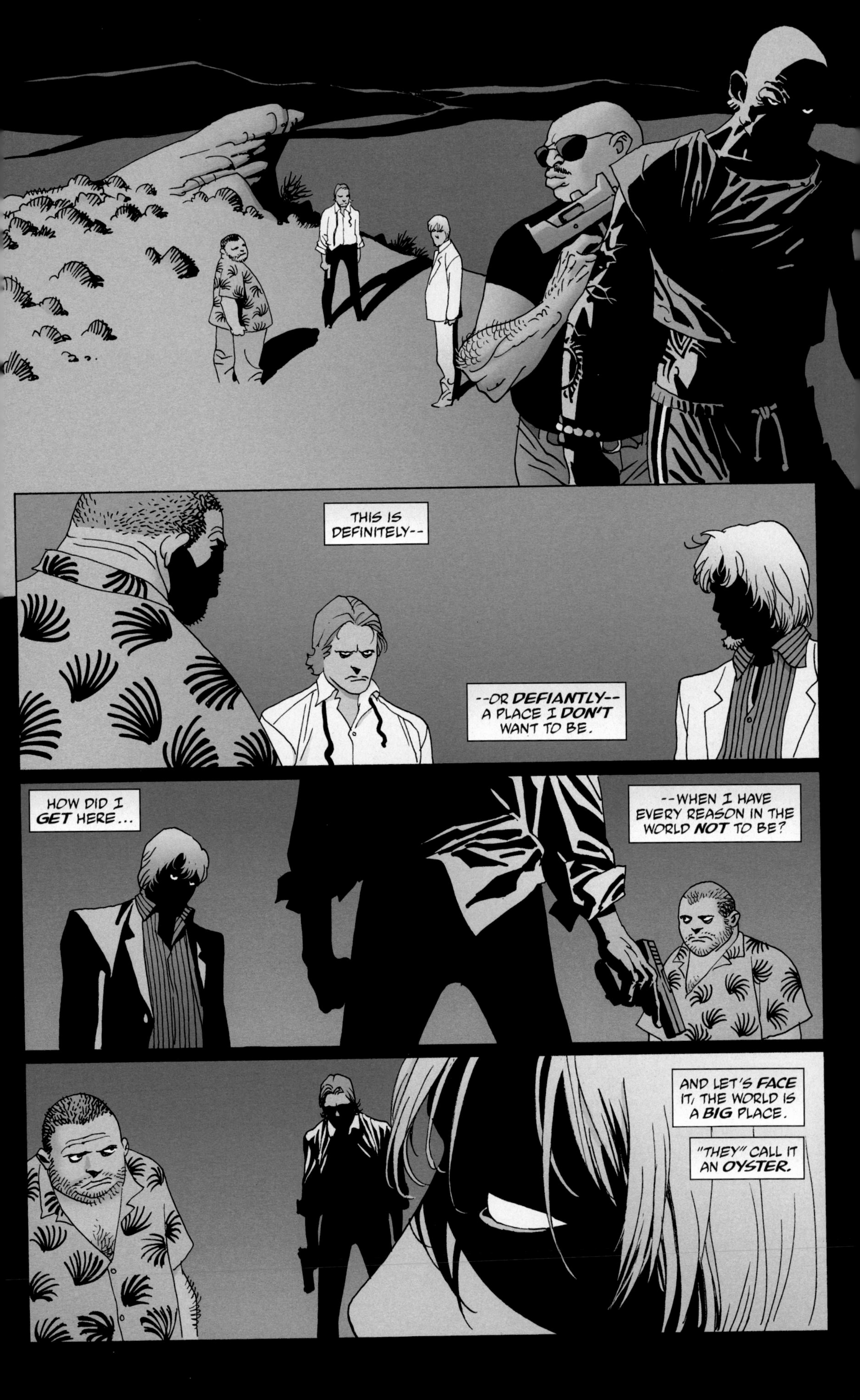
THIS IS DEFINITELY--
--OR DEFIANTLY-- A PLACE I DON'T WANT TO BE.
HOW DID I GET HERE...
--WHEN I HAVE EVERY REASON IN THE WORLD NOT TO BE?
AND LET'S FACE IT, THE WORLD IS A BIG PLACE.
"THEY" CALL IT AN OYSTER.

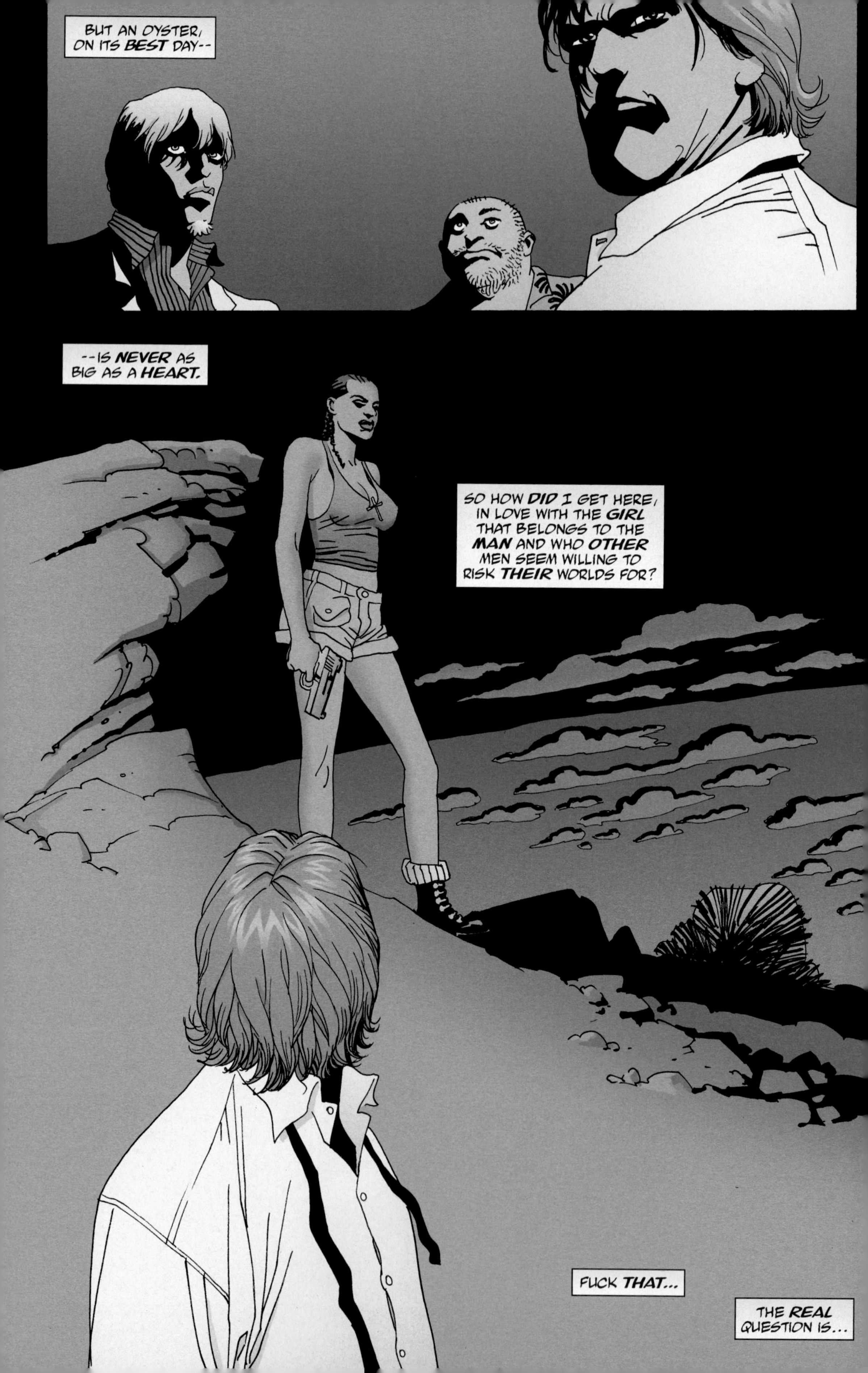
BUT AN OYSTER, ON ITS BEST DAY--
--IS NEVER AS BIG AS A HEART.
SO HOW DID I GET HERE, IN LOVE WITH THE GIRL THAT BELONGS TO THE MAN AND WHO OTHER MEN SEEM WILLING TO RISK THEIR WORLDS FOR?
FUCK THAT...
THE REAL QUESTION IS...

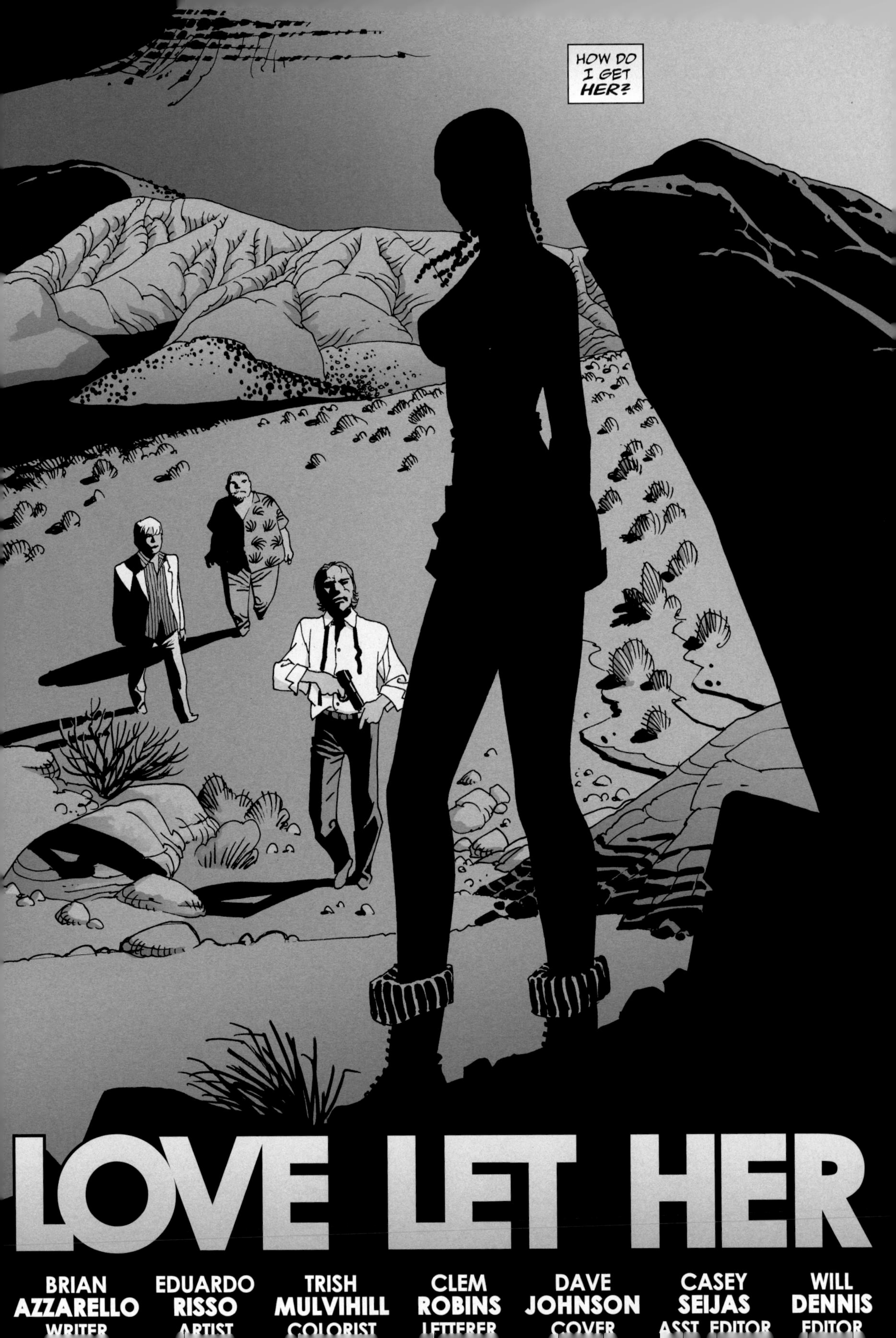
HOW DO I GET HER?
LOVE LET HER
BRIAN AZZARELLO WRITER
EDUARDO RISSO ARTIST
TRISH MULVIHILL COLORIST
CLEM ROBINS LETTERER
DAVE JOHNSON COVER
CASEY SEIJAS ASST. EDITOR
WILL DENNIS EDITOR

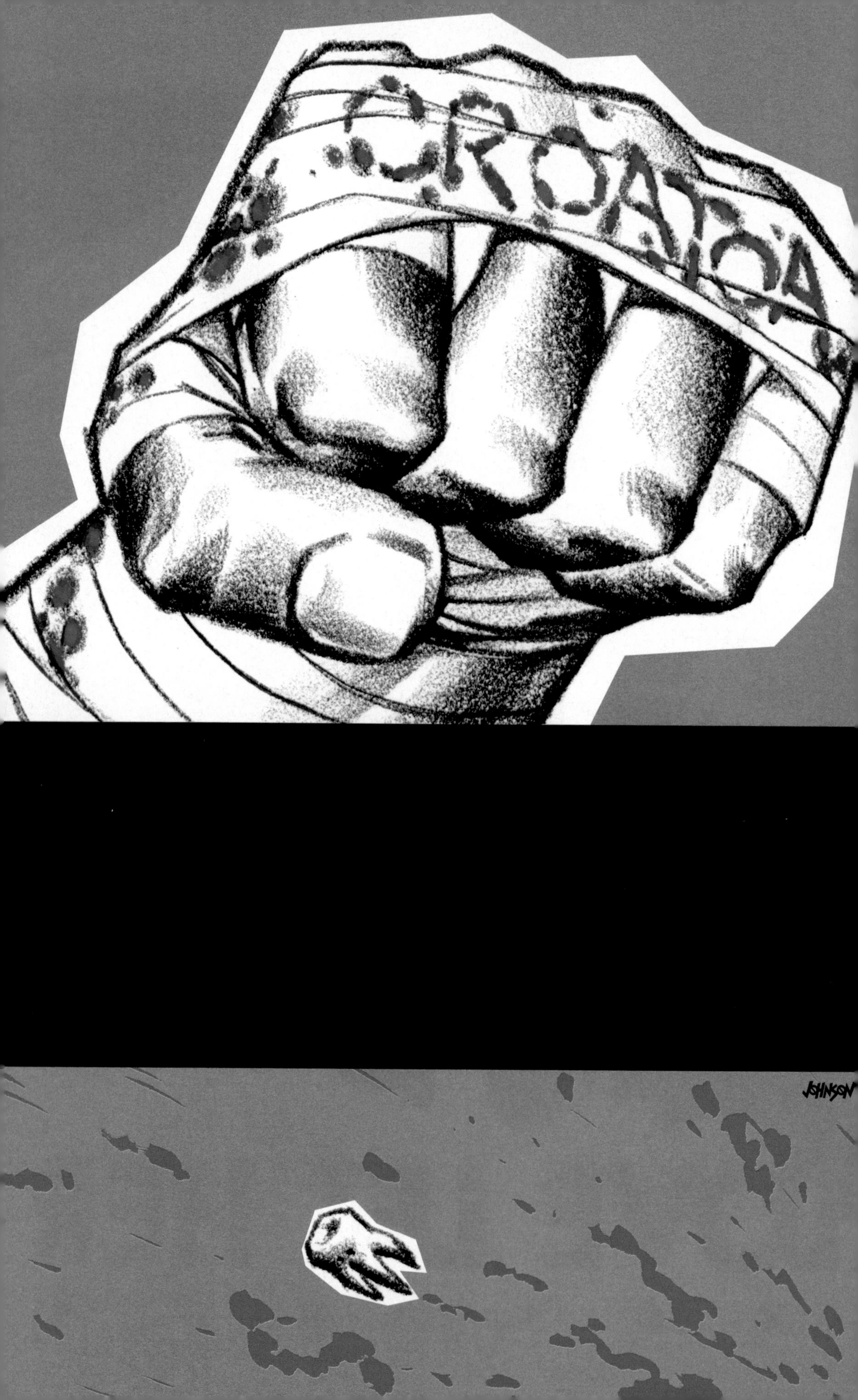
CROATOA
JOHNSON

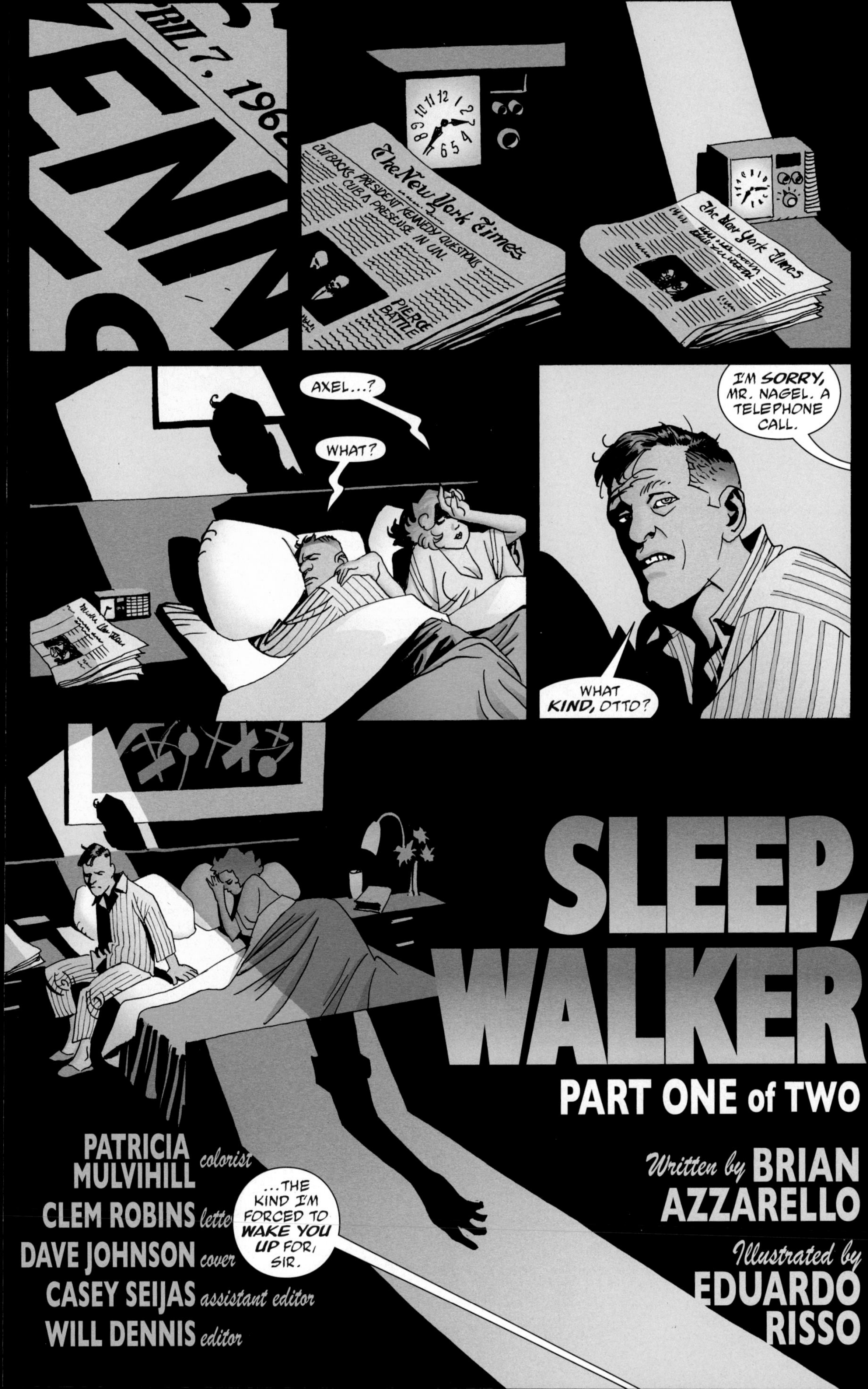

The New York Times
CUTBACKS PRESIDENT KENNEDY QUESTIONS CUBA PRESENSE IN U.N.
The New York Times
AXEL...?
WHAT?
I'M SORRY, MR. NAGEL. A TELEPHONE CALL.
WHAT KIND, OTTO?
...THE KIND I'M FORCED TO WAKE YOU UP FOR, SIR.
SLEEP, WALKER
PART ONE of TWO
Written by BRIAN AZZARELLO
Illustrated by EDUARDO RISSO
PATRICIA MULVIHILL colorist
CLEM ROBINS letterer
DAVE JOHNSON cover
CASEY SEIJAS assistant editor
WILL DENNIS editor

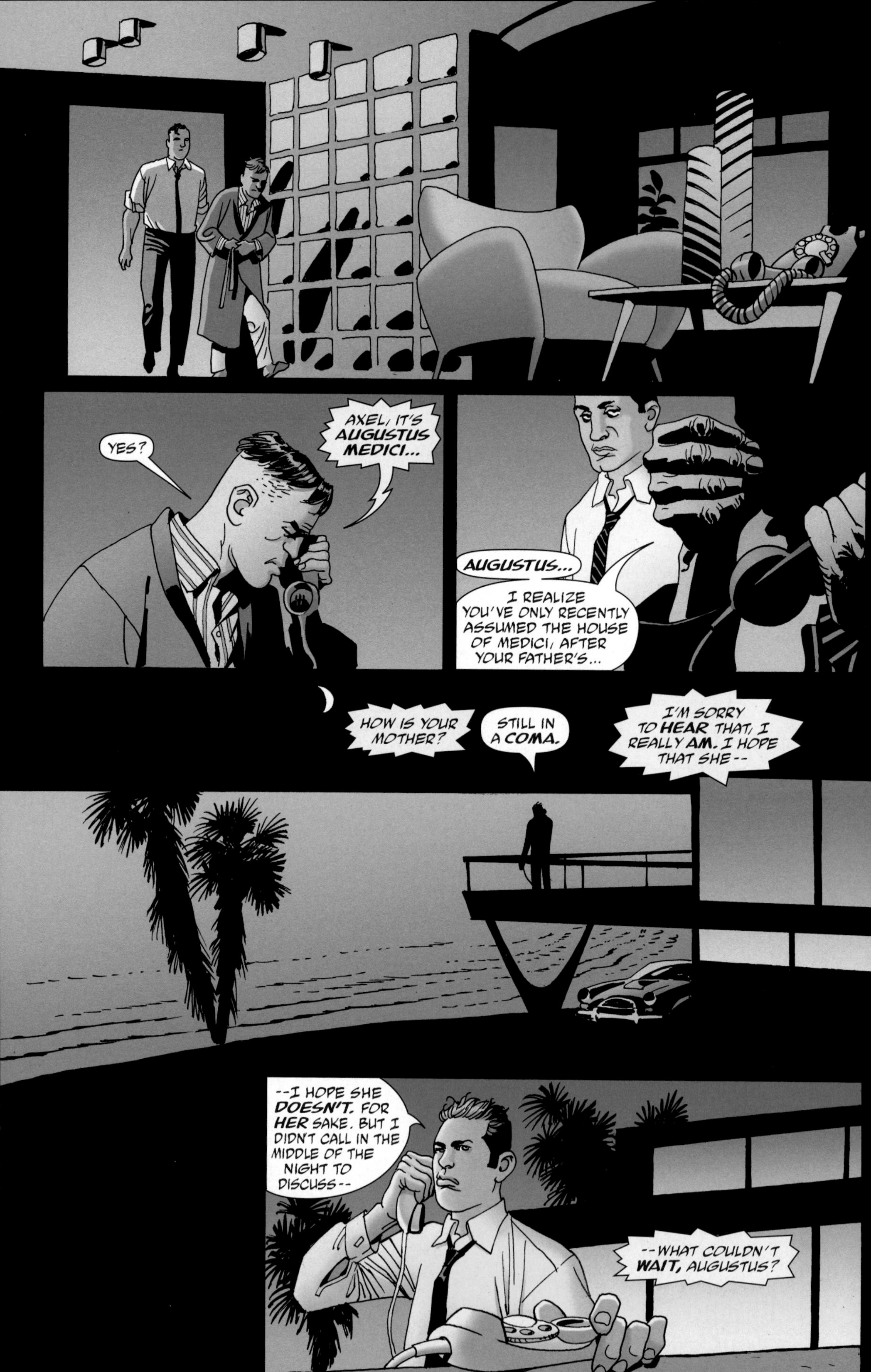
YES?
AXEL, IT'S AUGUSTUS MEDICI...
AUGUSTUS...
I REALIZE YOU'VE ONLY RECENTLY ASSUMED THE HOUSE OF MEDICI, AFTER YOUR FATHER'S...
HOW IS YOUR MOTHER?
STILL IN A COMA.
I'M SORRY TO HEAR THAT, I REALLY AM. I HOPE THAT SHE--
--I HOPE SHE DOESN'T. FOR HER SAKE. BUT I DIDN'T CALL IN THE MIDDLE OF THE NIGHT TO DISCUSS--
--WHAT COULDN'T WAIT, AUGUSTUS?

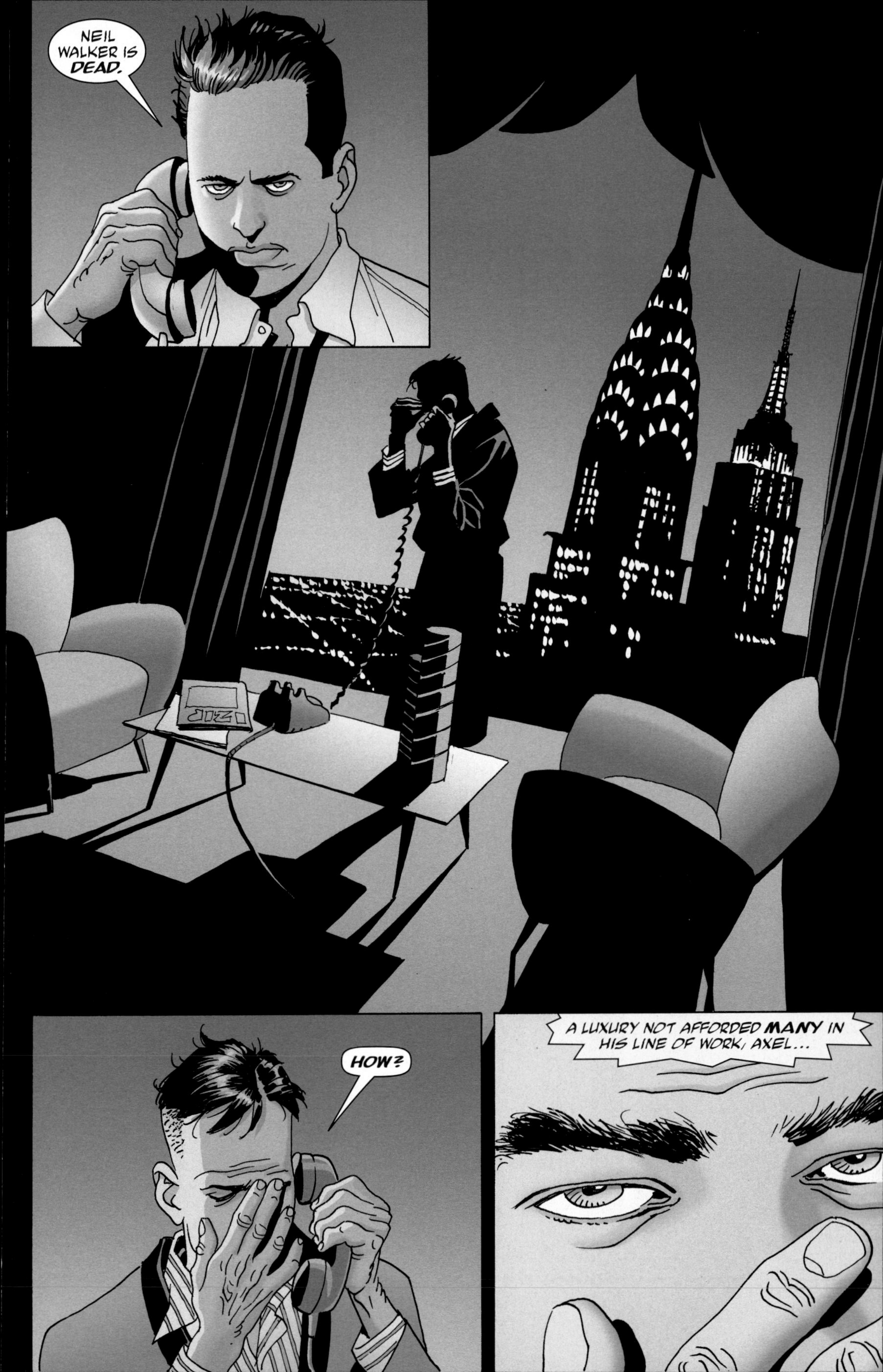
NEIL WALKER IS DEAD.
HOW?
A LUXURY NOT AFFORDED MANY IN HIS LINE OF WORK, AXEL...

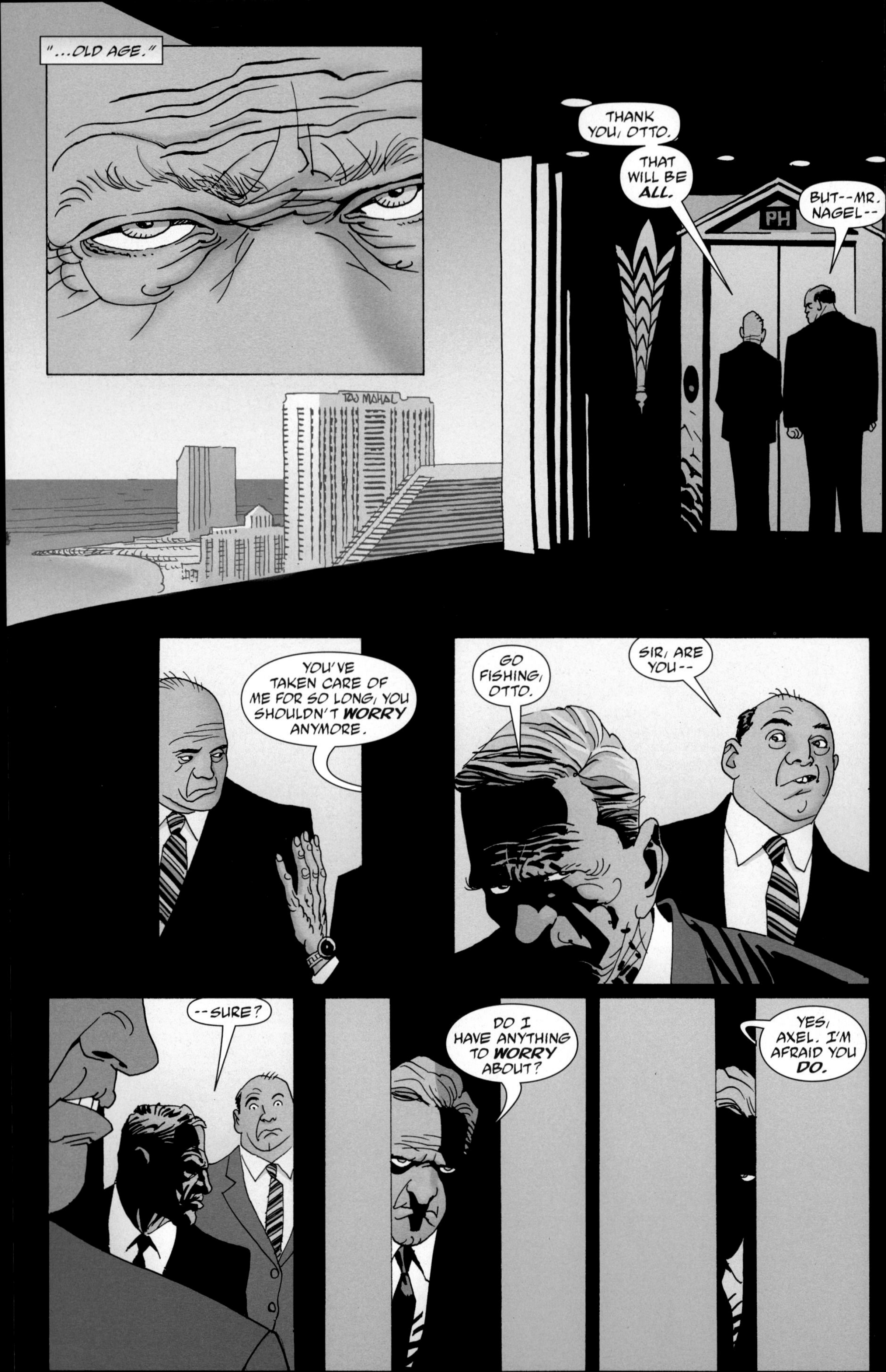
"...OLD AGE."
TAJ MAHAL
THANK YOU, OTTO.
THAT WILL BE ALL.
PH
BUT--MR. NAGEL--
YOU'VE TAKEN CARE OF ME FOR SO LONG, YOU SHOULDN'T WORRY ANYMORE.
GO FISHING, OTTO.
SIR, ARE YOU--
--SURE?
DO I HAVE ANYTHING TO WORRY ABOUT?
YES, AXEL. I'M AFRAID YOU DO.

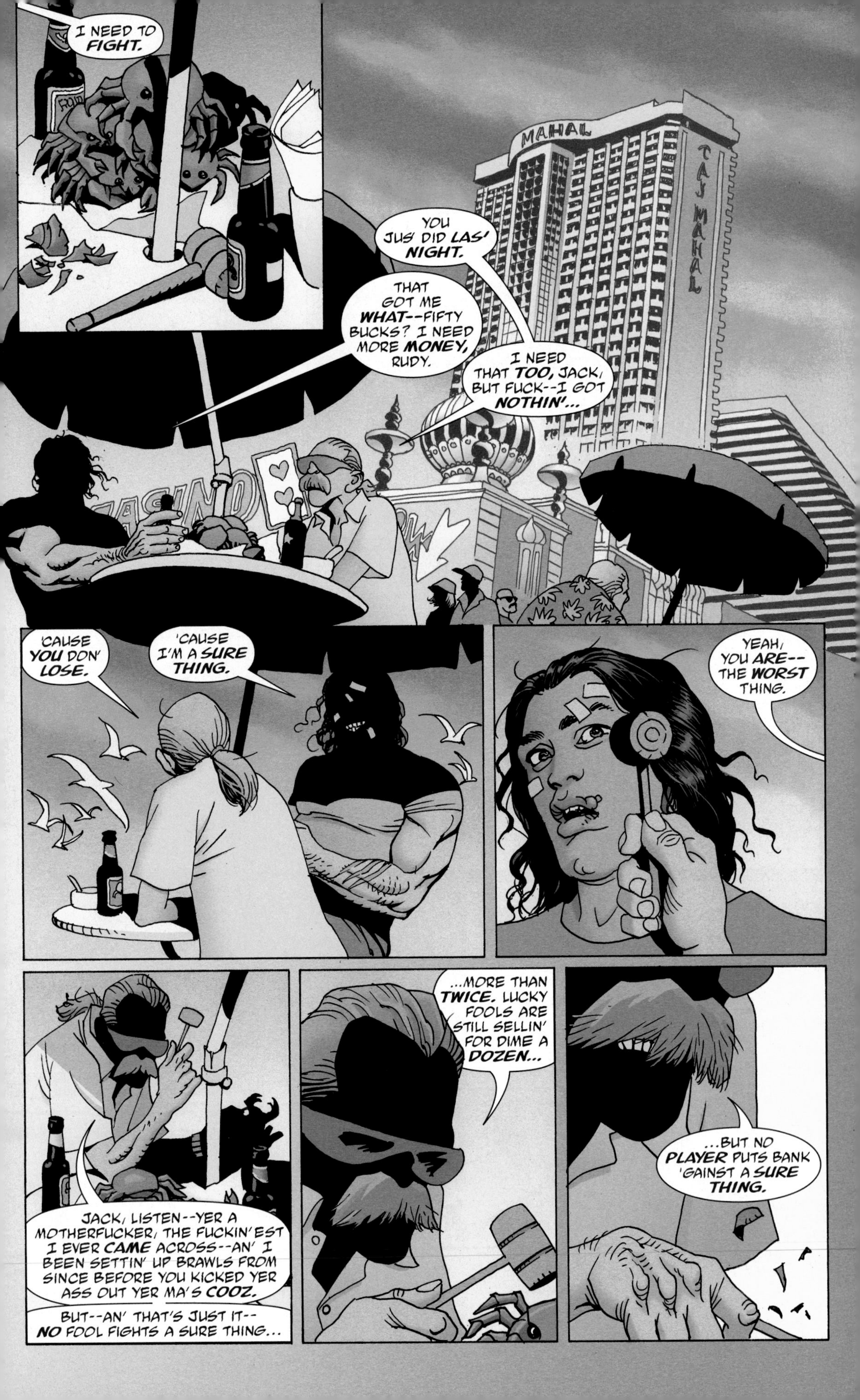
I NEED TO FIGHT.
YOU JUS' DID LAS' NIGHT.
THAT GOT ME WHAT--FIFTY BUCKS? I NEED MORE MONEY, RUDY.
I NEED THAT TOO, JACK, BUT FUCK--I GOT NOTHIN'...
MAHAL
TAJ MAHAL
'CAUSE YOU DON' LOSE.
'CAUSE I'M A SURE THING.
YEAH, YOU ARE--THE WORST THING.
JACK, LISTEN--YER A MOTHERFUCKER, THE FUCKIN'EST I EVER CAME ACROSS--AN' I BEEN SETTIN' UP BRAWLS FROM SINCE BEFORE YOU KICKED YER ASS OUT YER MA'S COOZ.
BUT--AN' THAT'S JUST IT--NO FOOL FIGHTS A SURE THING...
...MORE THAN TWICE. LUCKY FOOLS ARE STILL SELLIN' FOR DIME A DOZEN...
...BUT NO PLAYER PUTS BANK 'GAINST A SURE THING.

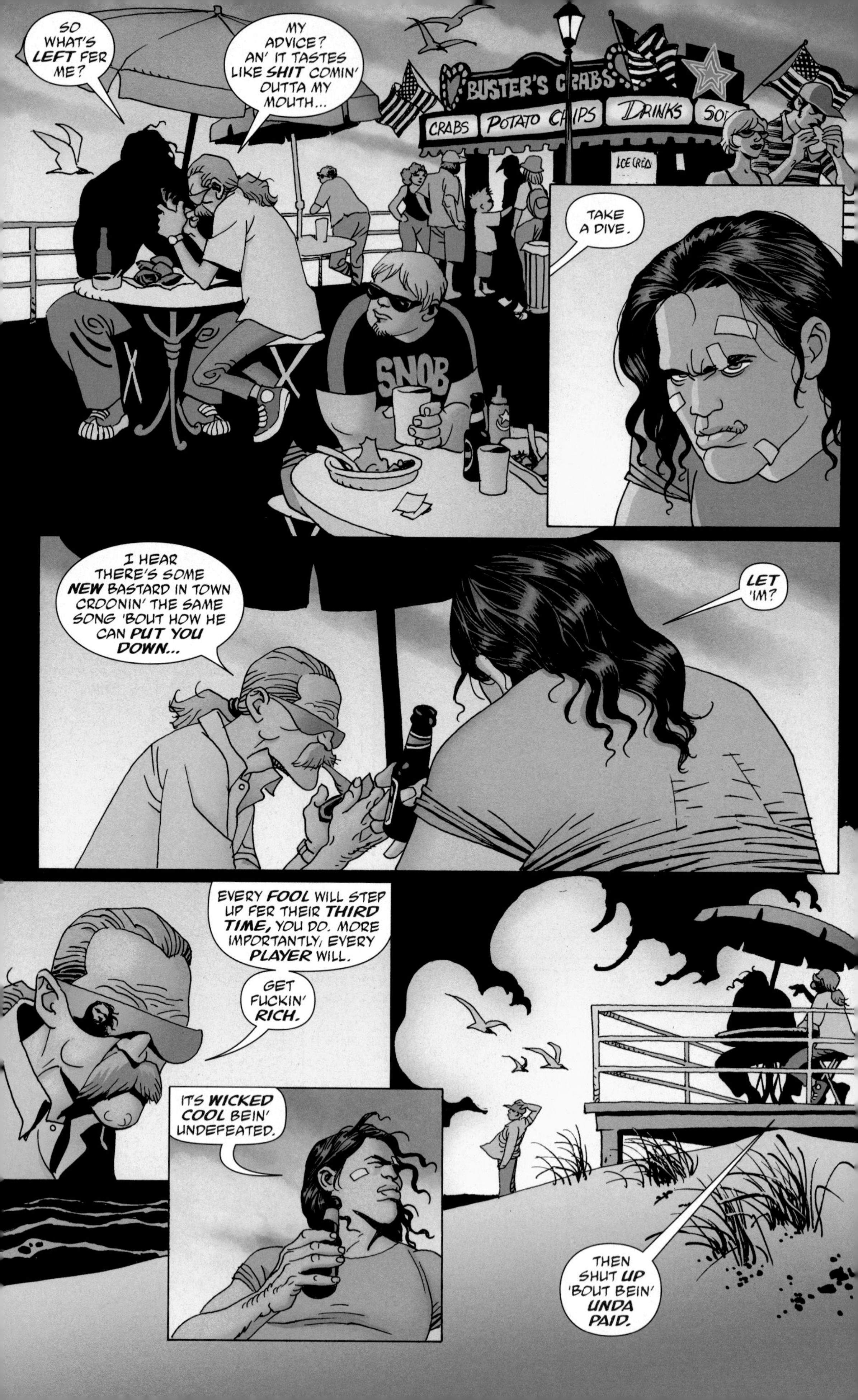
SO WHAT'S LEFT FER ME?
MY ADVICE? AN' IT TASTES LIKE SHIT COMIN' OUTTA MY MOUTH...
BUSTER'S CRABS
CRABS
POTATO CHIPS
DRINKS
ICE CREAM
SNOB
TAKE A DIVE.
I HEAR THERE'S SOME NEW BASTARD IN TOWN CROONIN' THE SAME SONG 'BOUT HOW HE CAN PUT YOU DOWN...
LET 'IM?
EVERY FOOL WILL STEP UP FER THEIR THIRD TIME, YOU DO. MORE IMPORTANTLY, EVERY PLAYER WILL.
GET FUCKIN' RICH.
IT'S WICKED COOL BEIN' UNDEFEATED.
THEN SHUT UP 'BOUT BEIN' UNDA PAID.

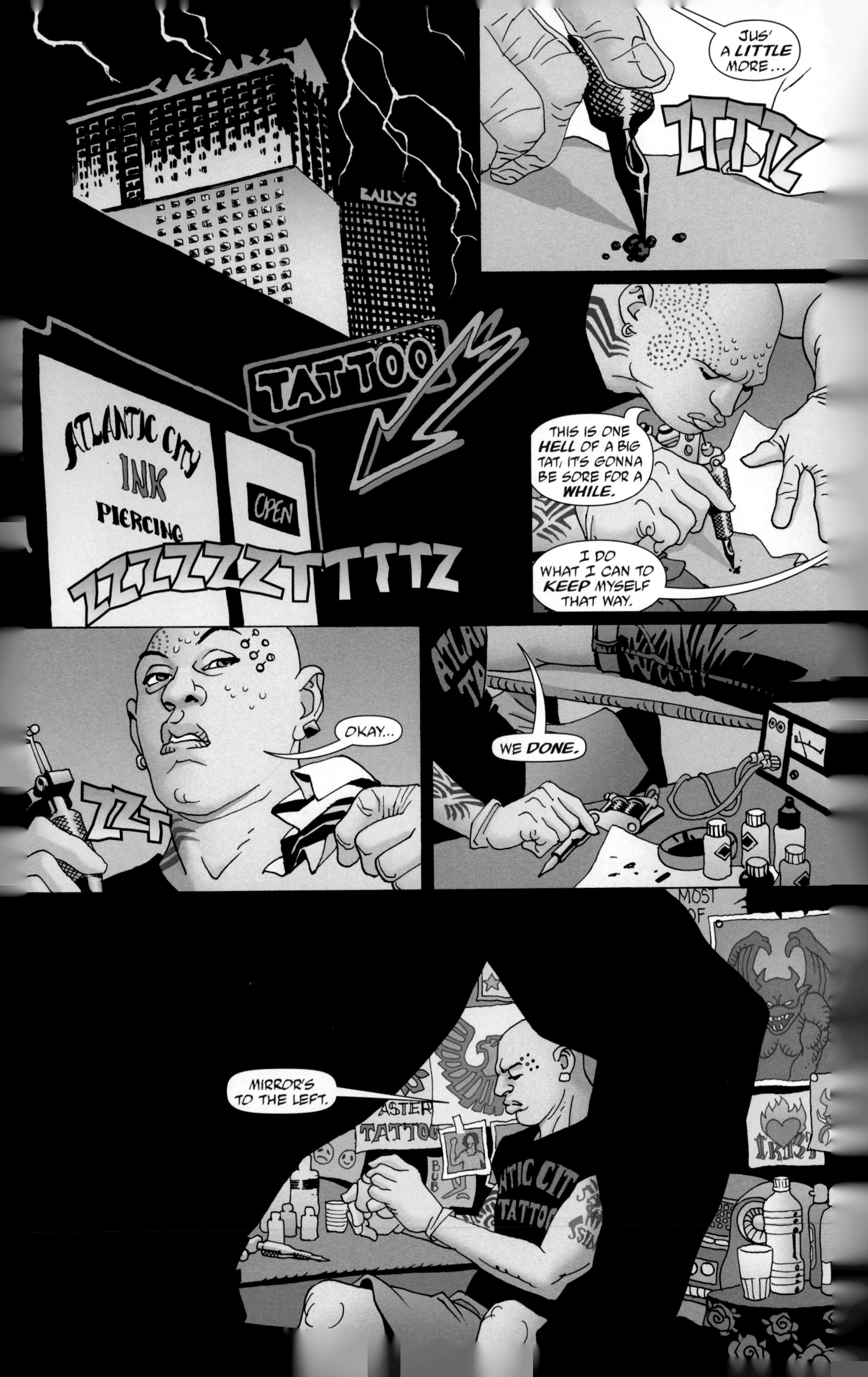

CAESARS
BALLY'S
JUS' A LITTLE MORE...
ZTTTZ
TATTOO
ATLANTIC CITY INK PIERCING
OPEN
ZZZZZZTTTTZ
THIS IS ONE HELL OF A BIG TAT, IT'S GONNA BE SORE FOR A WHILE.
I DO WHAT I CAN TO KEEP MYSELF THAT WAY.
ZZT
OKAY...
WE DONE.
MIRROR'S TO THE LEFT.

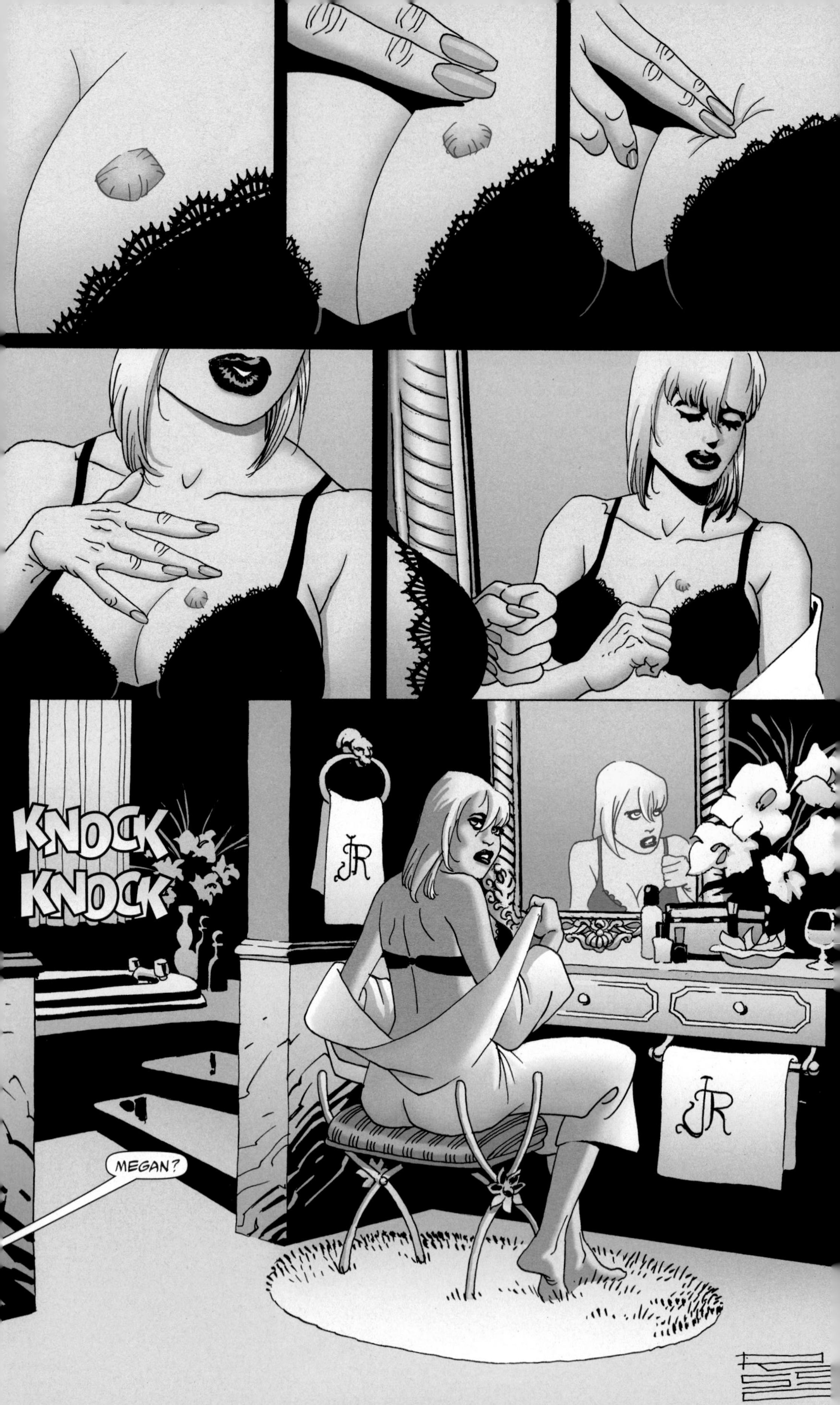
KNOCK
KNOCK
MEGAN?

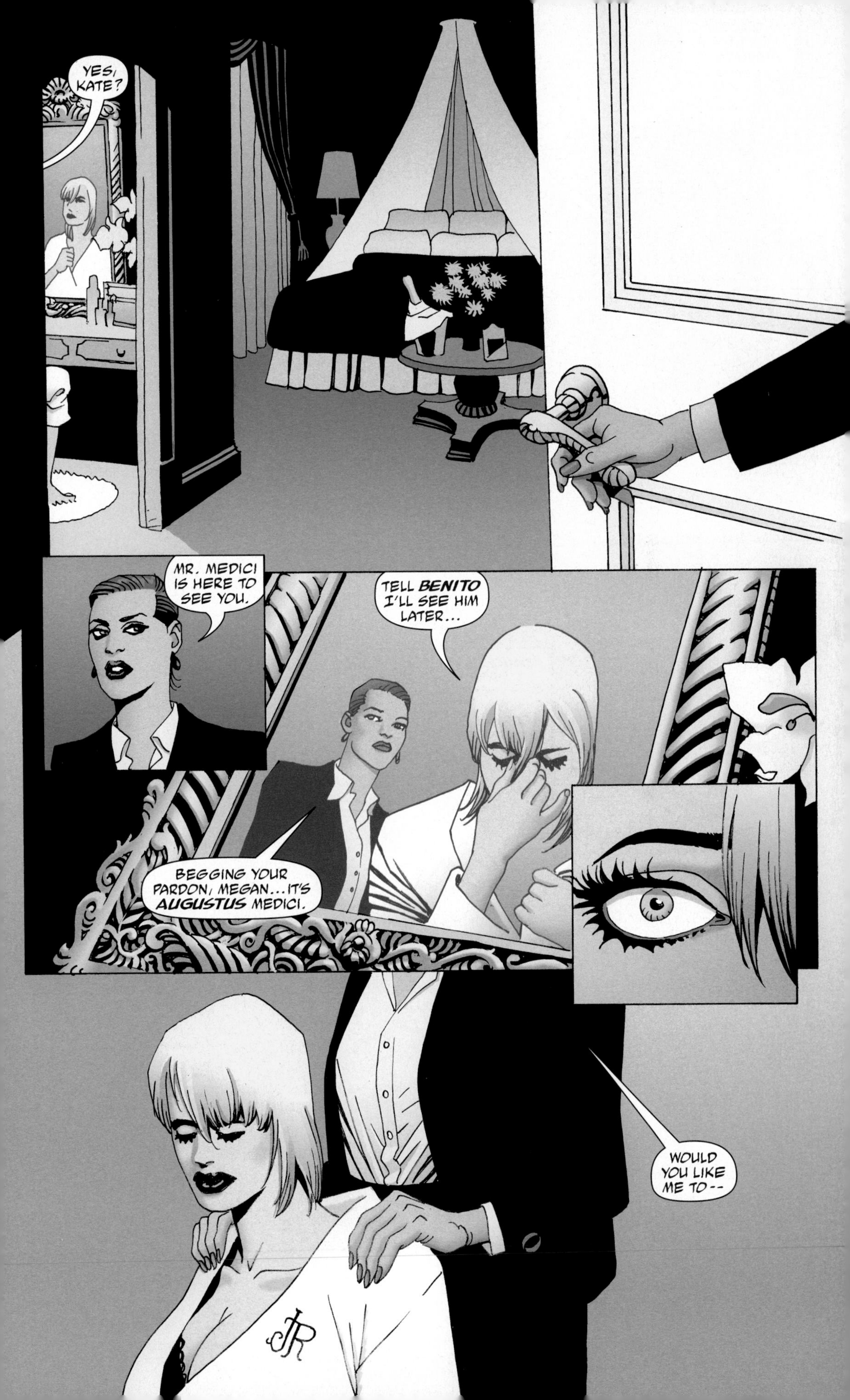
YES, KATE?
MR. MEDICI IS HERE TO SEE YOU.
TELL BENITO I'LL SEE HIM LATER...
BEGGING YOUR PARDON, MEGAN... IT'S AUGUSTUS MEDICI.
WOULD YOU LIKE ME TO--

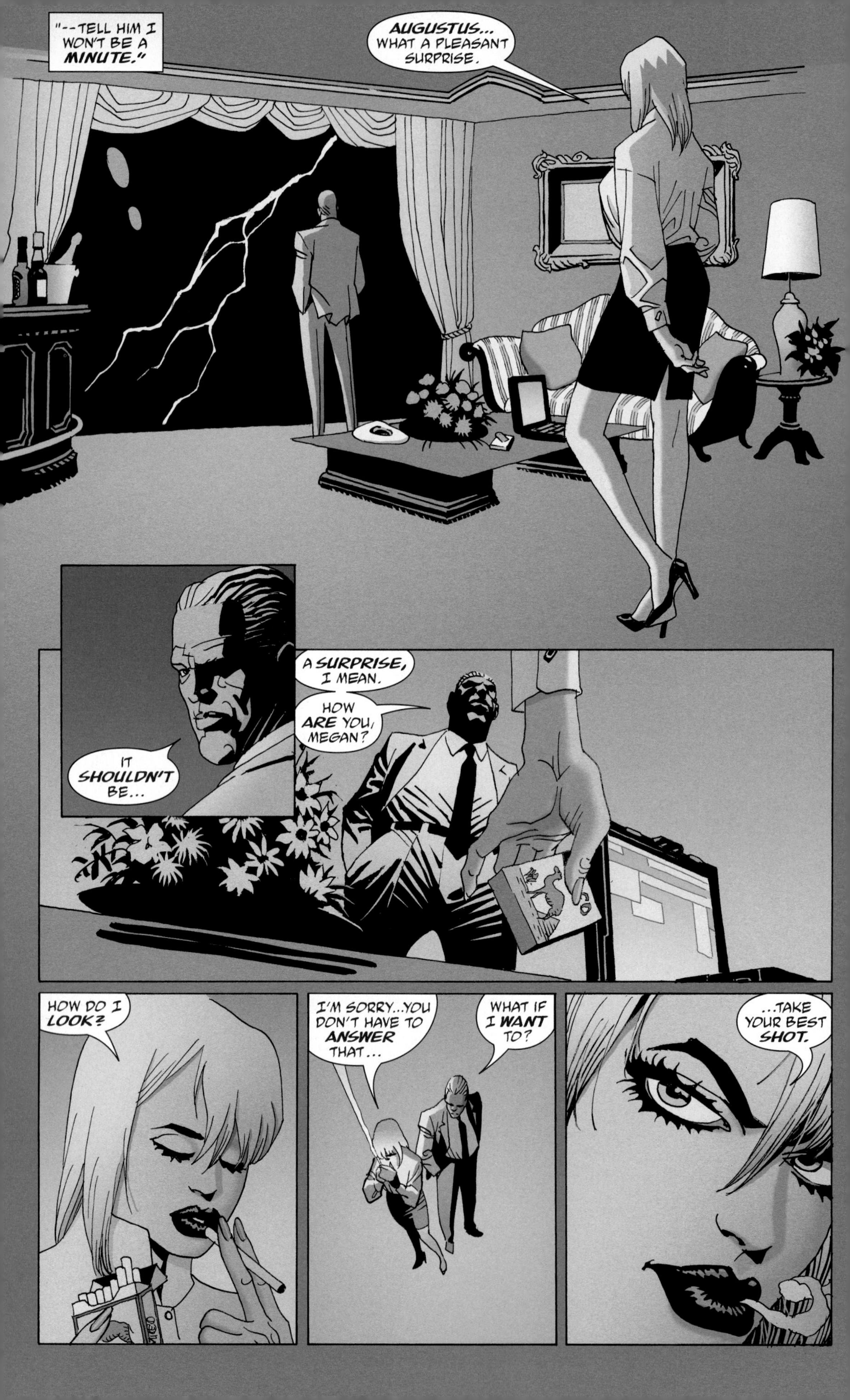
"--TELL HIM I WON'T BE A MINUTE."
AUGUSTUS... WHAT A PLEASANT SURPRISE.
IT SHOULDN'T BE...
A SURPRISE, I MEAN.
HOW ARE YOU, MEGAN?
HOW DO I LOOK?
I'M SORRY...YOU DON'T HAVE TO ANSWER THAT...
WHAT IF I WANT TO?
...TAKE YOUR BEST SHOT.

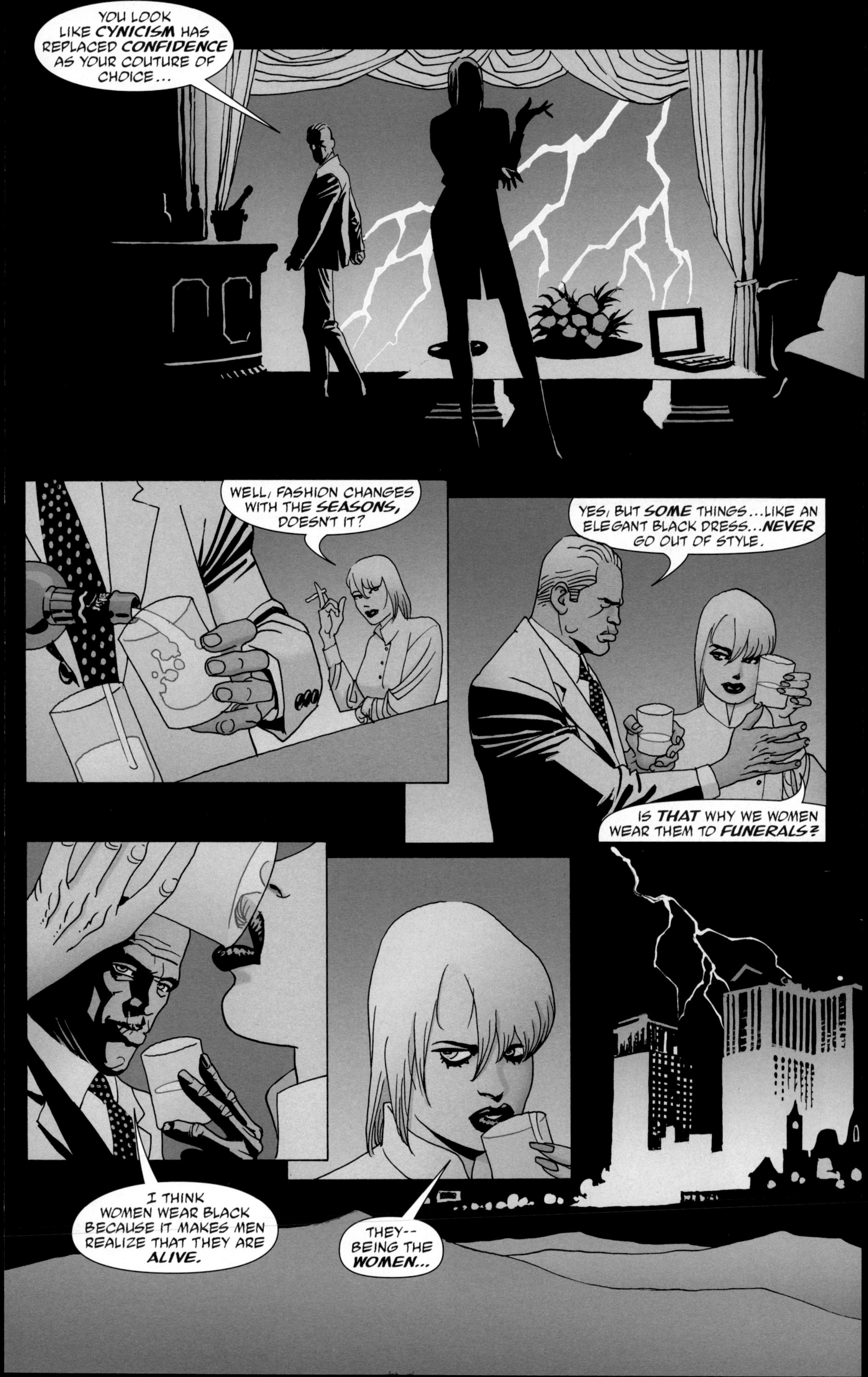

YOU LOOK LIKE CYNICISM HAS REPLACED CONFIDENCE AS YOUR COUTURE OF CHOICE...
WELL, FASHION CHANGES WITH THE SEASONS, DOESN'T IT?
YES, BUT SOME THINGS...LIKE AN ELEGANT BLACK DRESS...NEVER GO OUT OF STYLE.
IS THAT WHY WE WOMEN WEAR THEM TO FUNERALS?
I THINK WOMEN WEAR BLACK BECAUSE IT MAKES MEN REALIZE THAT THEY ARE ALIVE.
THEY-- BEING THE WOMEN...

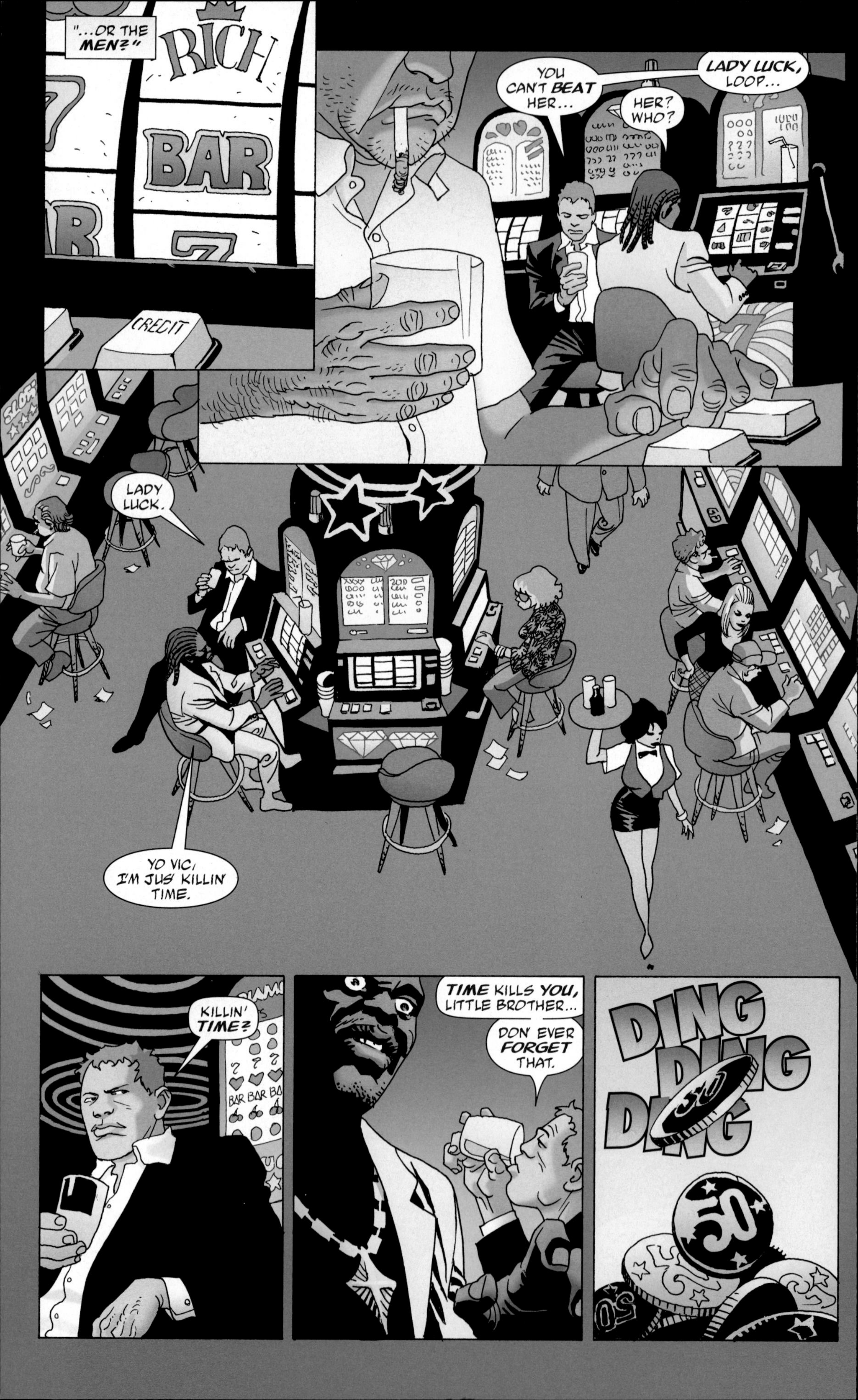
"...OR THE MEN?"
YOU CAN'T BEAT HER...
HER? WHO?
LADY LUCK, LOOP...
LADY LUCK.
YO VIC, I'M JUS' KILLIN' TIME.
KILLIN' TIME?
TIME KILLS YOU, LITTLE BROTHER...
DON' EVER FORGET THAT.
DING DING DING

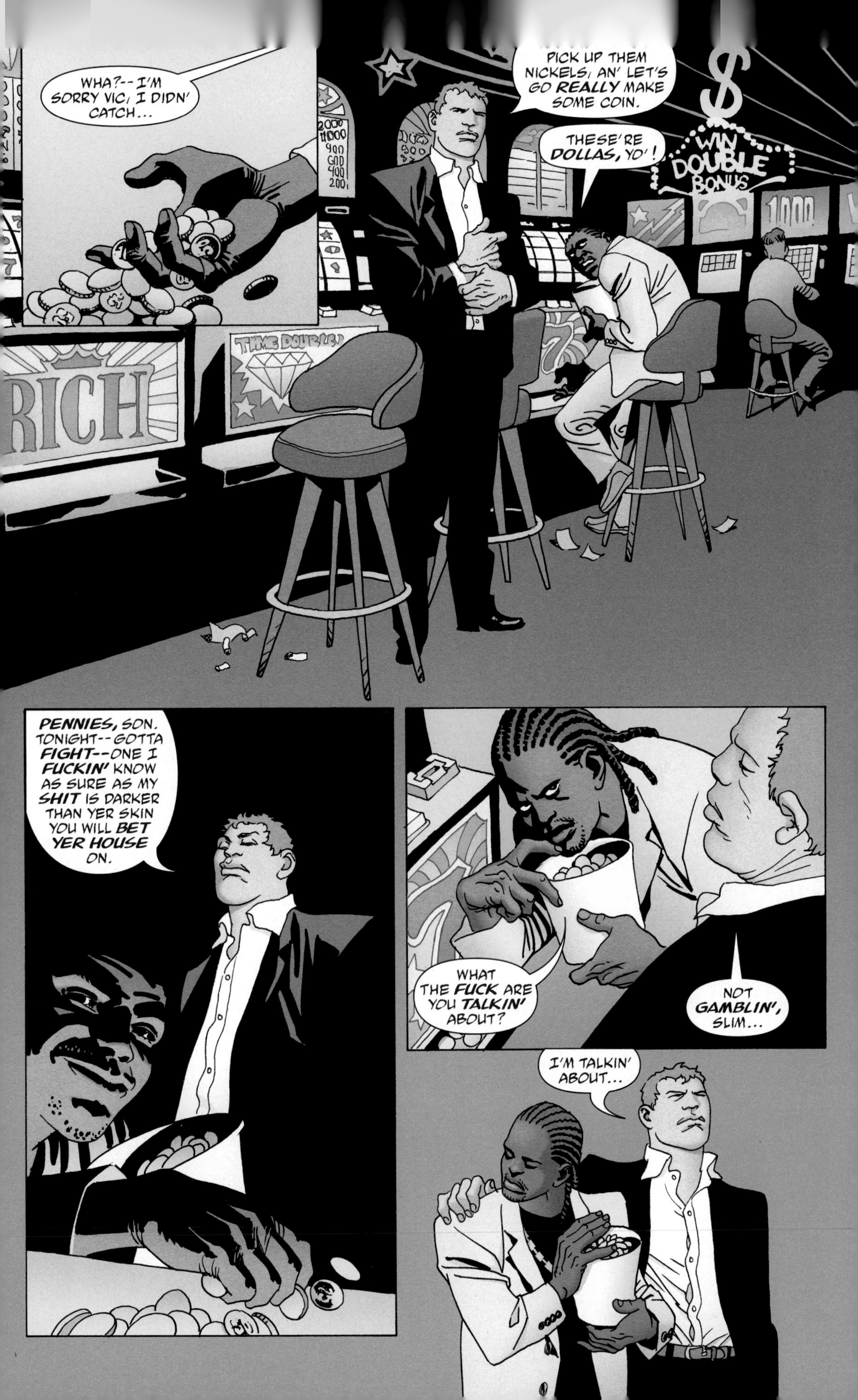
WHA?-- I'M SORRY VIC, I DIDN' CATCH...
PICK UP THEM NICKELS, AN' LET'S GO REALLY MAKE SOME COIN.
THESE'RE DOLLAS, YO'!
WIN DOUBLE BONUS
RICH
PENNIES, SON. TONIGHT-- GOTTA FIGHT--ONE I FUCKIN' KNOW AS SURE AS MY SHIT IS DARKER THAN YER SKIN YOU WILL BET YER HOUSE ON.
WHAT THE FUCK ARE YOU TALKIN' ABOUT?
NOT GAMBLIN', SLIM...
I'M TALKIN' ABOUT...

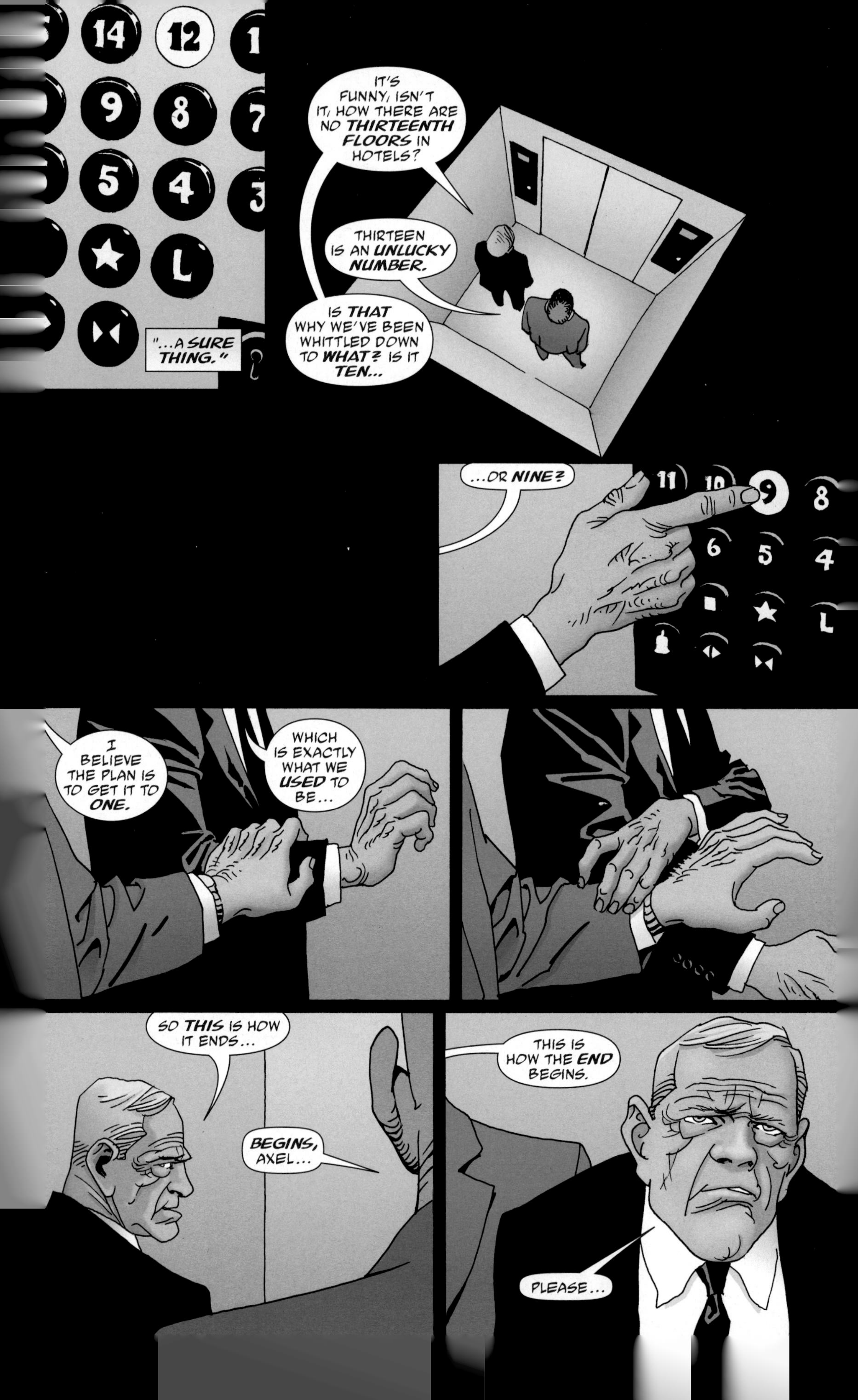
14
12
9
8
5
4
L
"...A SURE THING."
IT'S FUNNY, ISN'T IT, HOW THERE ARE NO THIRTEENTH FLOORS IN HOTELS?
THIRTEEN IS AN UNLUCKY NUMBER.
IS THAT WHY WE'VE BEEN WHITTLED DOWN TO WHAT? IS IT TEN...
...OR NINE?
11
10
9
8
6
5
4
L
I BELIEVE THE PLAN IS TO GET IT TO ONE.
WHICH IS EXACTLY WHAT WE USED TO BE...
SO THIS IS HOW IT ENDS...
BEGINS, AXEL...
THIS IS HOW THE END BEGINS.
PLEASE...

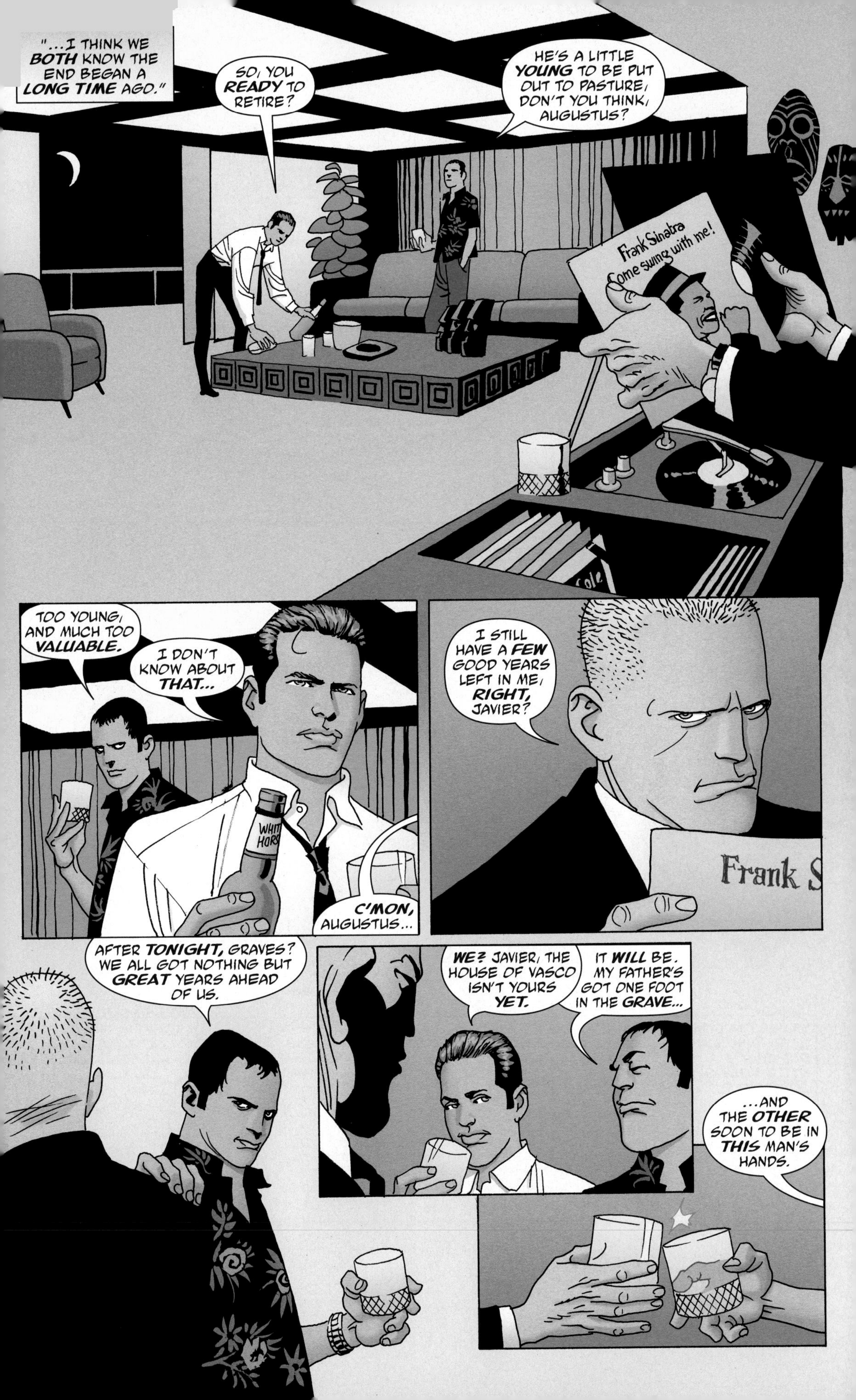
"...I THINK WE BOTH KNOW THE END BEGAN A LONG TIME AGO."
SO, YOU READY TO RETIRE?
HE'S A LITTLE YOUNG TO BE PUT OUT TO PASTURE, DON'T YOU THINK, AUGUSTUS?
Frank Sinatra
Come swing with me!
TOO YOUNG, AND MUCH TOO VALUABLE.
I DON'T KNOW ABOUT THAT...
C'MON, AUGUSTUS...
I STILL HAVE A FEW GOOD YEARS LEFT IN ME, RIGHT, JAVIER?
Frank S
AFTER TONIGHT, GRAVES? WE ALL GOT NOTHING BUT GREAT YEARS AHEAD OF US.
WE? JAVIER, THE HOUSE OF VASCO ISN'T YOURS YET.
IT WILL BE. MY FATHER'S GOT ONE FOOT IN THE GRAVE...
...AND THE OTHER SOON TO BE IN THIS MAN'S HANDS.

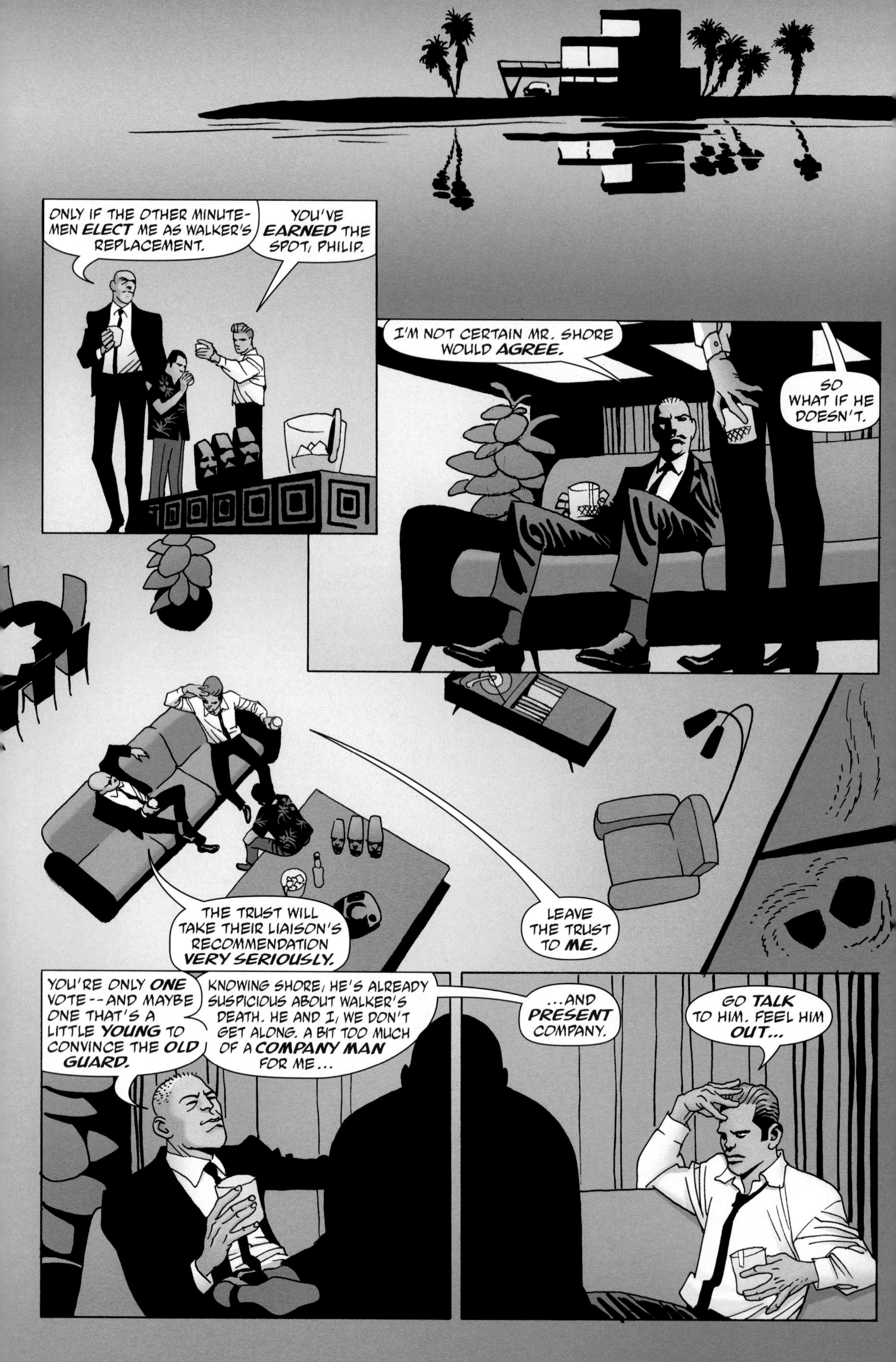
ONLY IF THE OTHER MINUTE-MEN ELECT ME AS WALKER'S REPLACEMENT.
YOU'VE EARNED THE SPOT, PHILIP.
I'M NOT CERTAIN MR. SHORE WOULD AGREE.
SO WHAT IF HE DOESN'T.
THE TRUST WILL TAKE THEIR LIAISON'S RECOMMENDATION VERY SERIOUSLY.
LEAVE THE TRUST TO ME.
YOU'RE ONLY ONE VOTE--AND MAYBE ONE THAT'S A LITTLE YOUNG TO CONVINCE THE OLD GUARD.
KNOWING SHORE, HE'S ALREADY SUSPICIOUS ABOUT WALKER'S DEATH. HE AND I, WE DON'T GET ALONG. A BIT TOO MUCH OF A COMPANY MAN FOR ME...
...AND PRESENT COMPANY.
GO TALK TO HIM. FEEL HIM OUT...

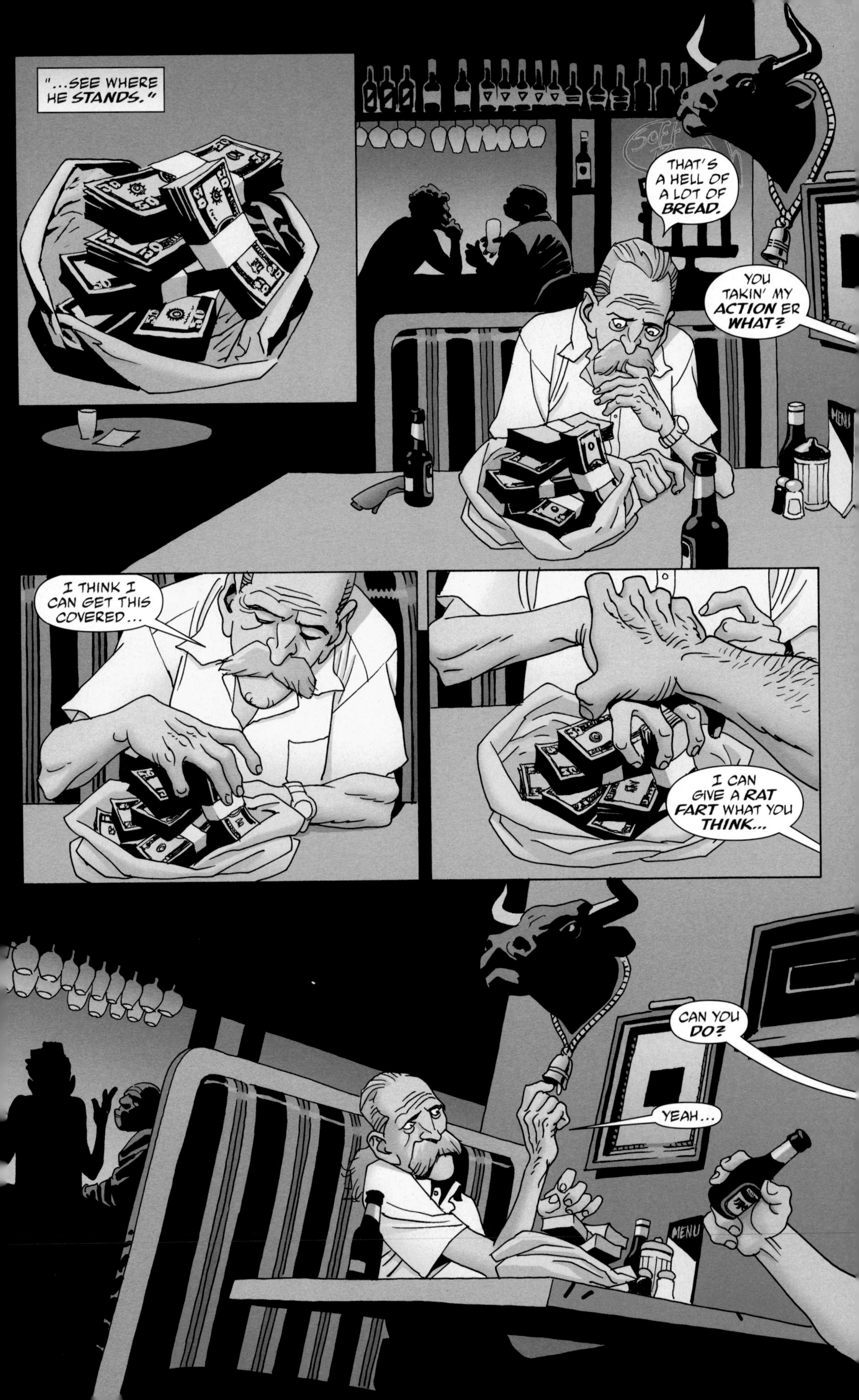
"...SEE WHERE HE STANDS."
THAT'S A HELL OF A LOT OF BREAD.
YOU TAKIN' MY ACTION ER WHAT?
I THINK I CAN GET THIS COVERED...
I CAN GIVE A RAT FART WHAT YOU THINK...
CAN YOU DO?
YEAH...

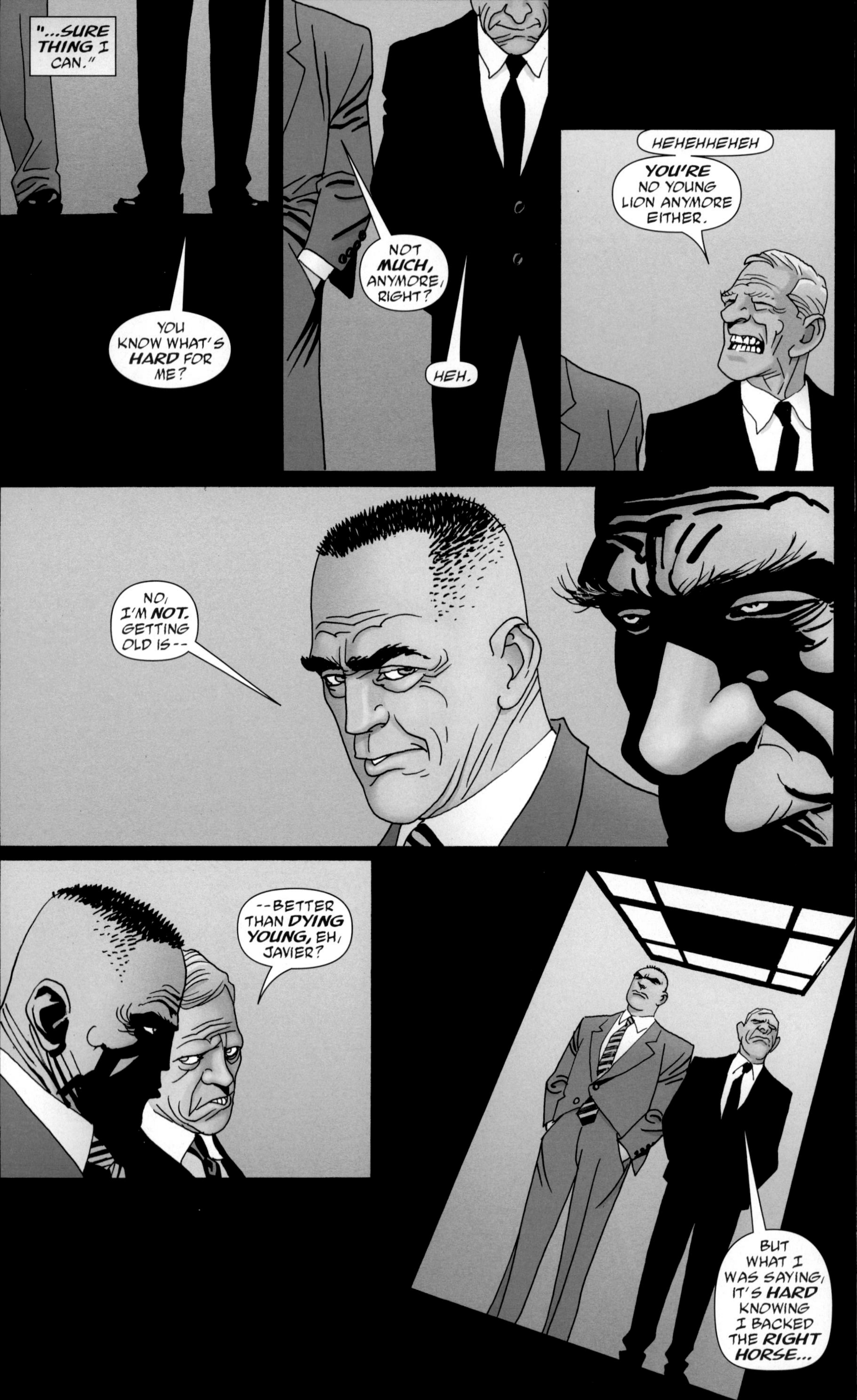
"...SURE THING I CAN."
YOU KNOW WHAT'S HARD FOR ME?
NOT MUCH, ANYMORE, RIGHT?
HEH.
HEHEHHEHEH
YOU'RE NO YOUNG LION ANYMORE EITHER.
NO, I'M NOT. GETTING OLD IS--
--BETTER THAN DYING YOUNG, EH, JAVIER?
BUT WHAT I WAS SAYING, IT'S HARD KNOWING I BACKED THE RIGHT HORSE...

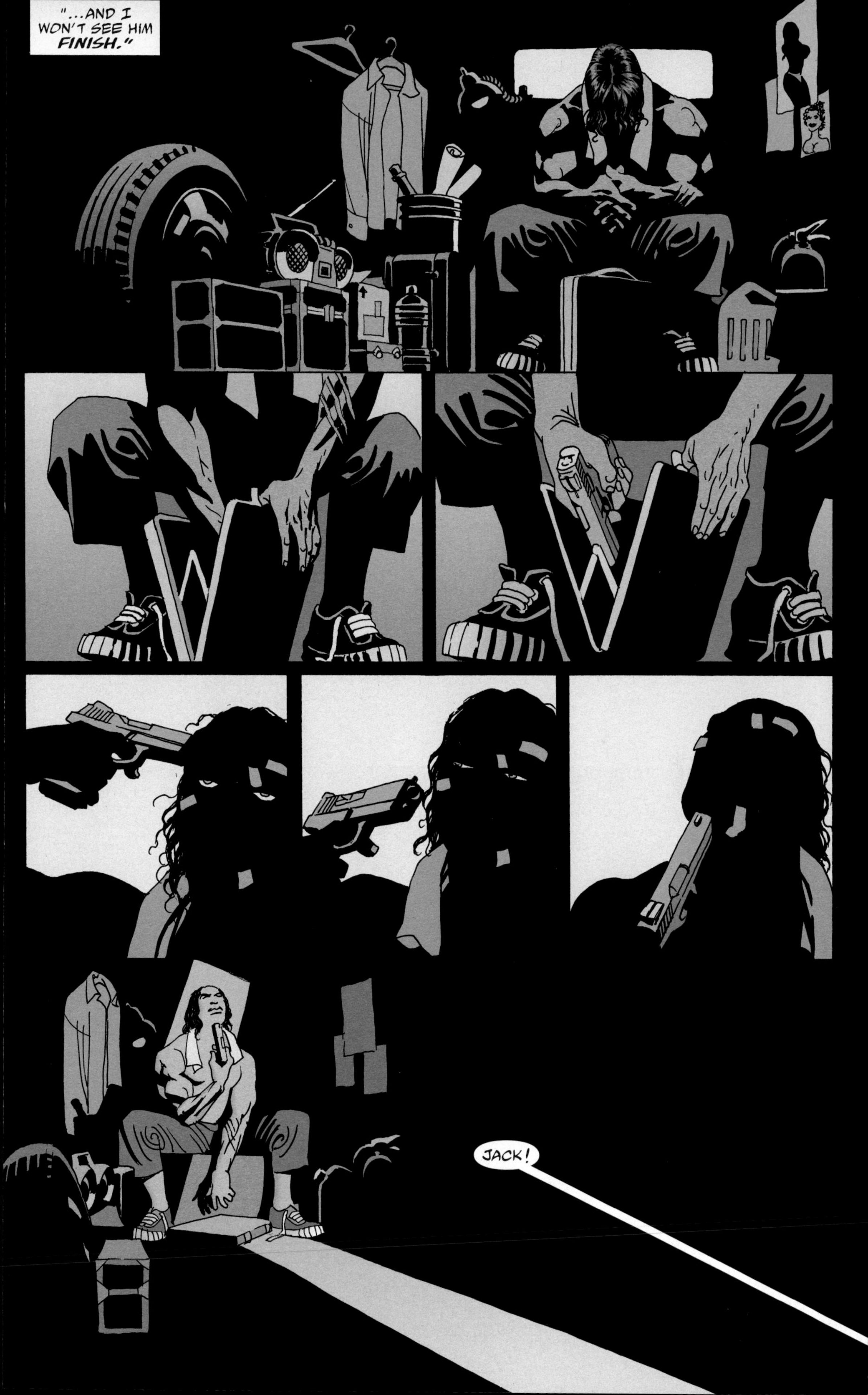
"...AND I WON'T SEE HIM FINISH."
JACK!

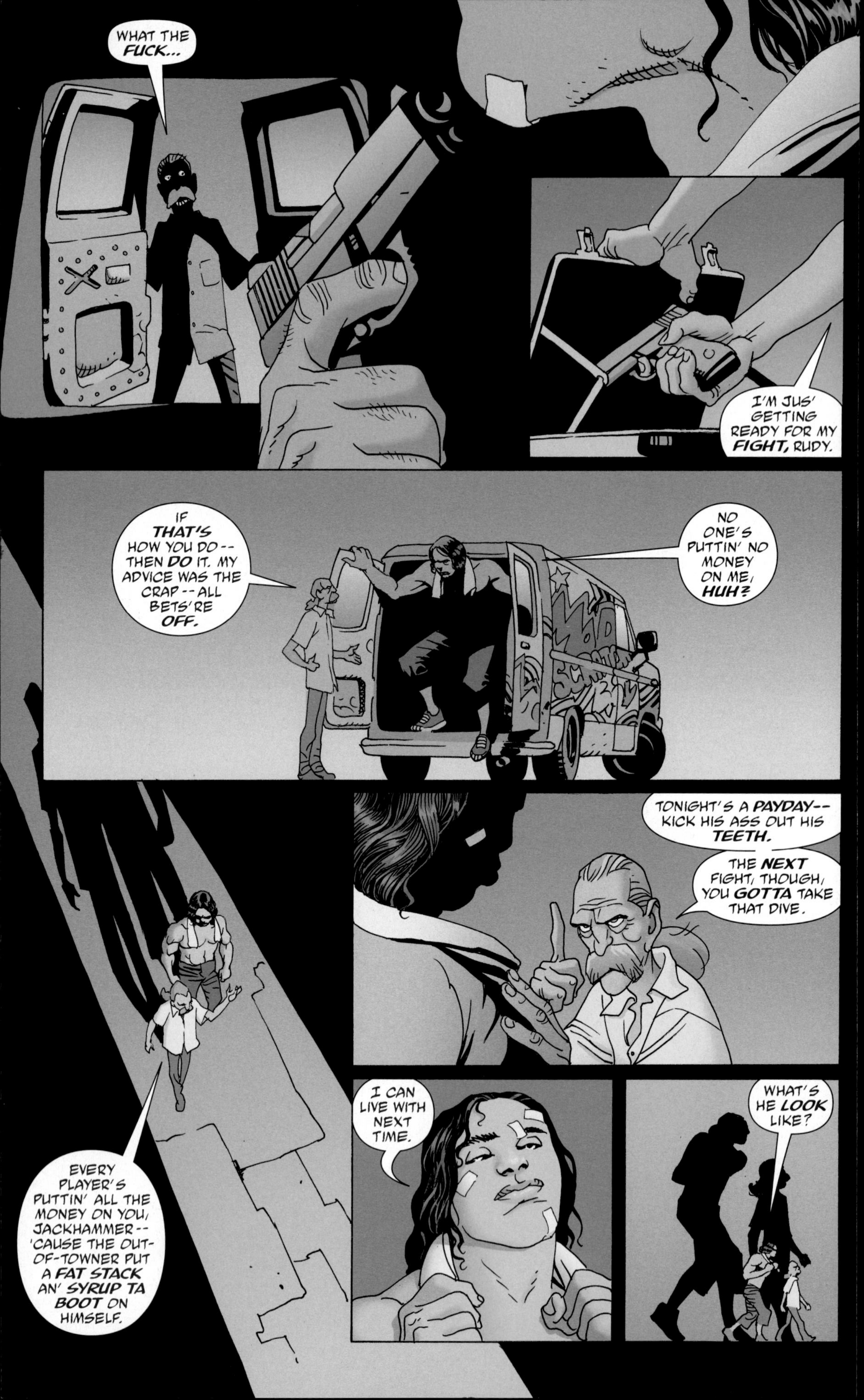
WHAT THE FUCK...
I'M JUS' GETTING READY FOR MY FIGHT, RUDY.
IF THAT'S HOW YOU DO-- THEN DO IT. MY ADVICE WAS THE CRAP--ALL BETS'RE OFF.
NO ONE'S PUTTIN' NO MONEY ON ME, HUH?
EVERY PLAYER'S PUTTIN' ALL THE MONEY ON YOU, JACKHAMMER-- 'CAUSE THE OUT-OF-TOWNER PUT A FAT STACK AN' SYRUP TA BOOT ON HIMSELF.
TONIGHT'S A PAYDAY-- KICK HIS ASS OUT HIS TEETH.
THE NEXT FIGHT, THOUGH, YOU GOTTA TAKE THAT DIVE.
I CAN LIVE WITH NEXT TIME.
WHAT'S HE LOOK LIKE?

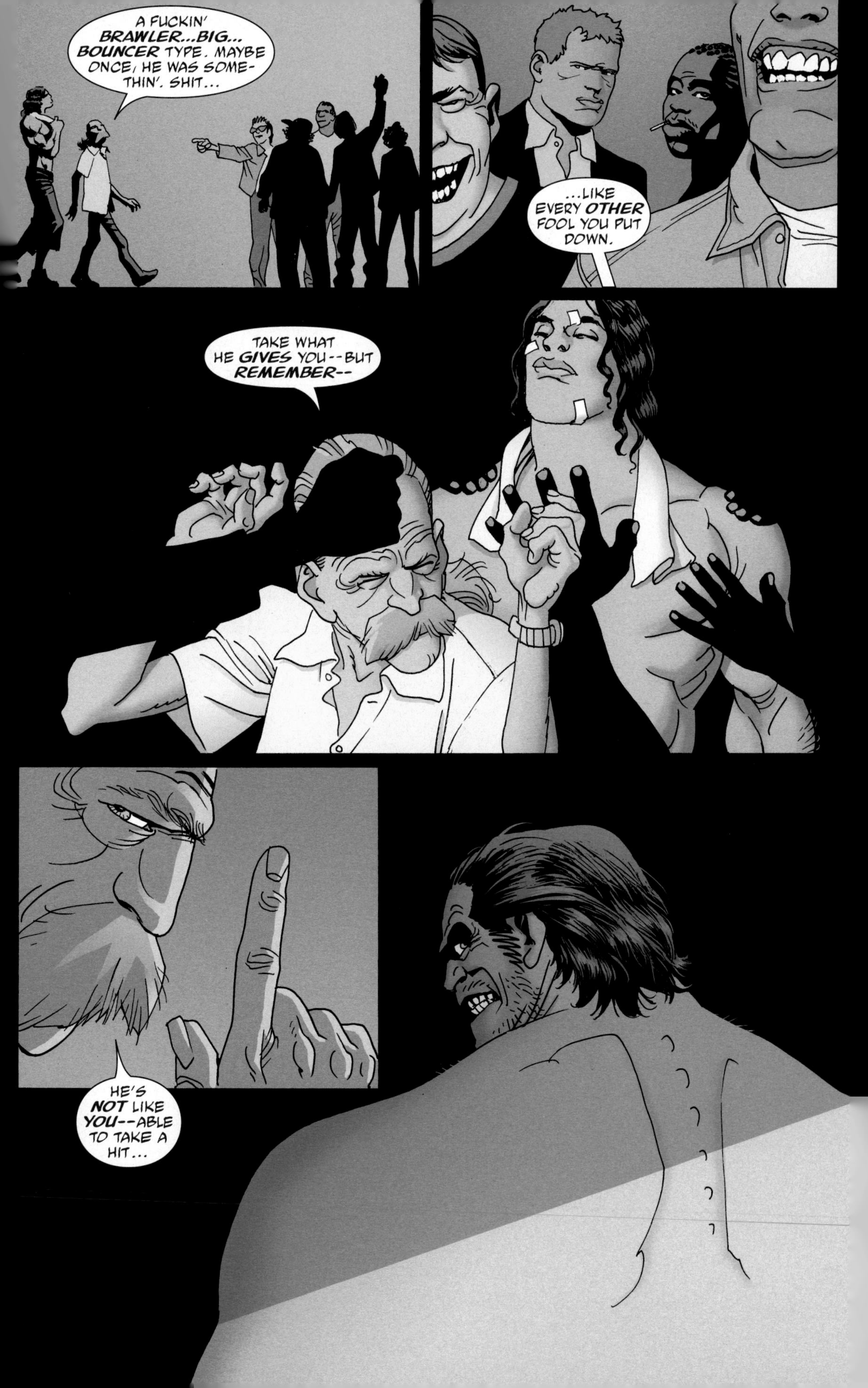
A FUCKIN' **BRAWLER...BIG... BOUNCER** TYPE. MAYBE ONCE, HE WAS SOME-THIN'. SHIT...
...LIKE EVERY **OTHER** FOOL YOU PUT DOWN.
TAKE WHAT HE **GIVES** YOU--BUT **REMEMBER--**
HE'S **NOT** LIKE **YOU**--ABLE TO TAKE A HIT...

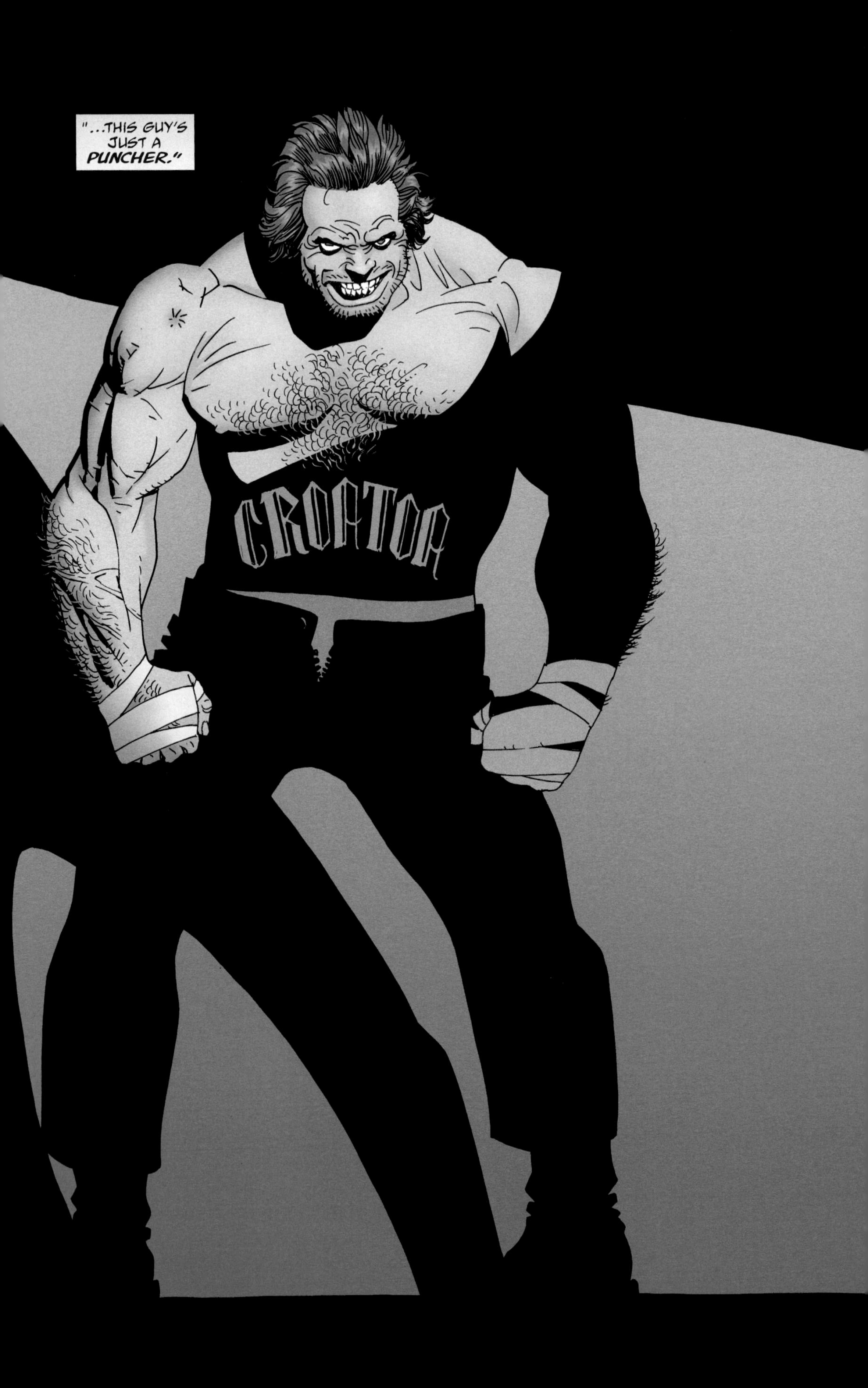
"...THIS GUY'S JUST A PUNCHER."
CROATOR

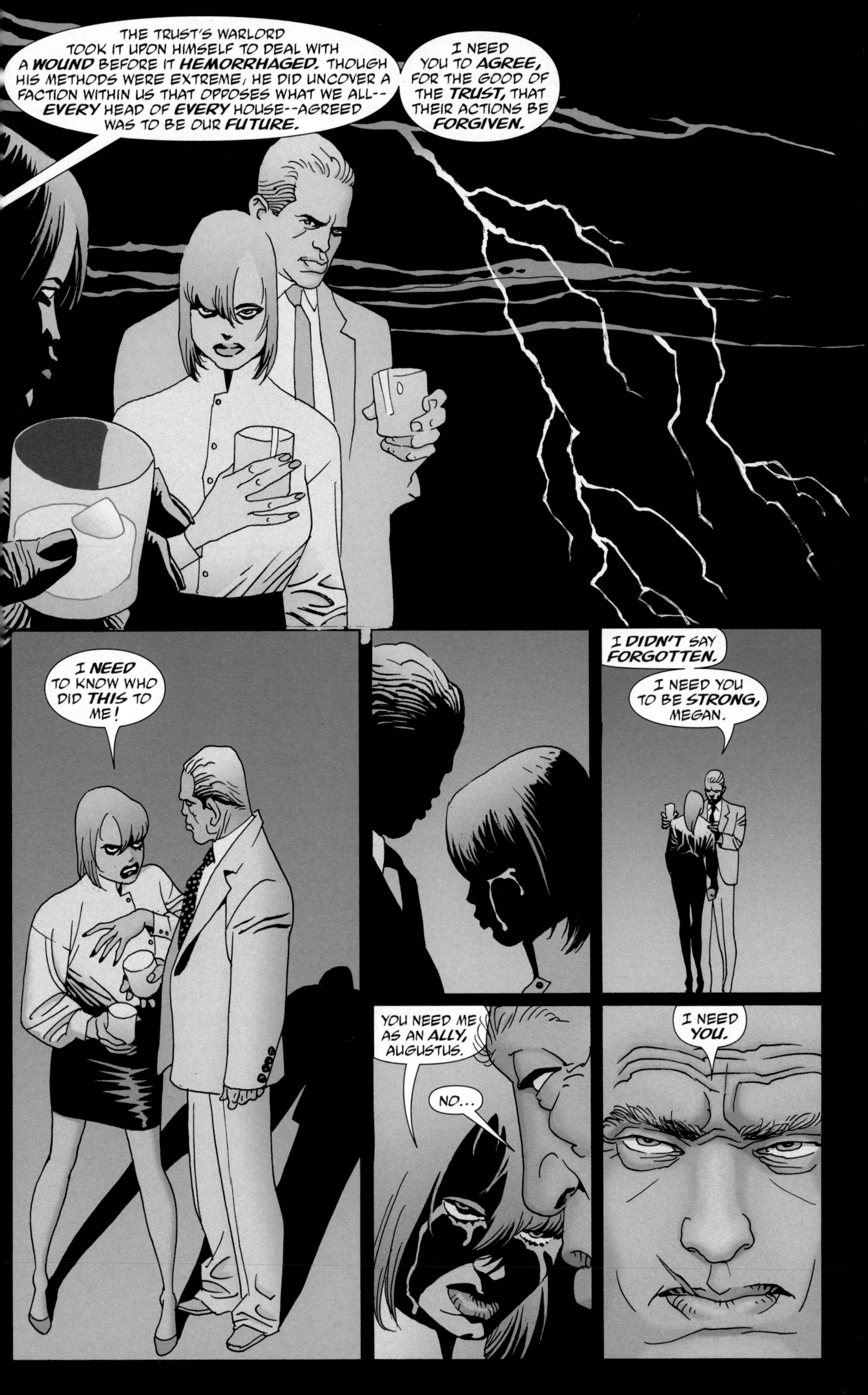
THE TRUST'S WARLORD TOOK IT UPON HIMSELF TO DEAL WITH A **WOUND** BEFORE IT **HEMORRHAGED.** THOUGH HIS METHODS WERE EXTREME, HE DID UNCOVER A FACTION WITHIN US THAT OPPOSES WHAT WE ALL-- **EVERY** HEAD OF **EVERY** HOUSE--AGREED WAS TO BE OUR **FUTURE.**
I NEED YOU TO **AGREE,** FOR THE GOOD OF THE **TRUST,** THAT THEIR ACTIONS BE **FORGIVEN.**
I **NEED** TO KNOW WHO DID **THIS** TO ME!
I **DIDN'T** SAY **FORGOTTEN.**
I NEED YOU TO BE **STRONG,** MEGAN.
YOU NEED ME AS AN **ALLY,** AUGUSTUS.
NO...
I NEED **YOU.**

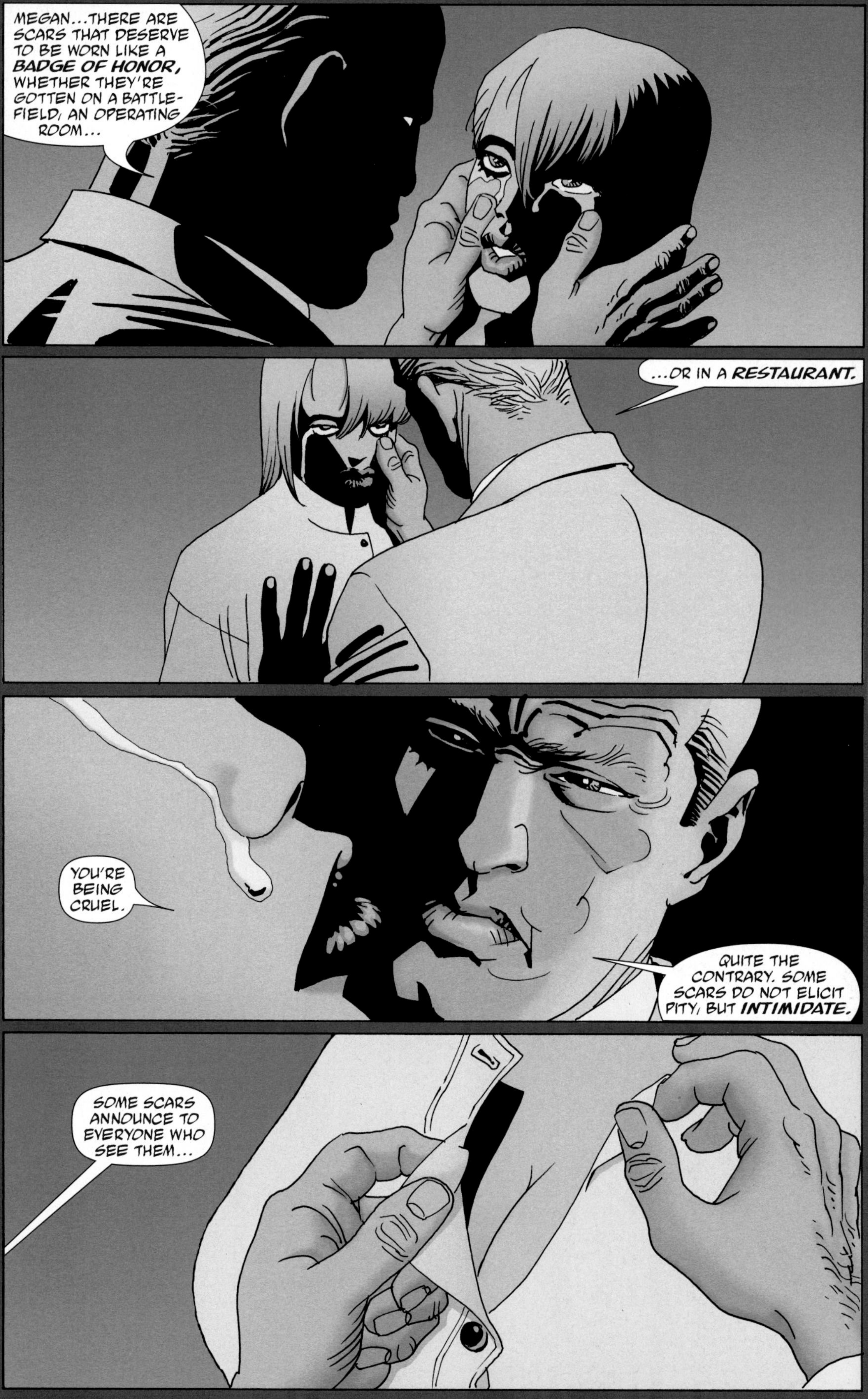
MEGAN...THERE ARE SCARS THAT DESERVE TO BE WORN LIKE A BADGE OF HONOR, WHETHER THEY'RE GOTTEN ON A BATTLEFIELD, AN OPERATING ROOM...
...OR IN A RESTAURANT.
YOU'RE BEING CRUEL.
QUITE THE CONTRARY. SOME SCARS DO NOT ELICIT PITY, BUT INTIMIDATE.
SOME SCARS ANNOUNCE TO EVERYONE WHO SEE THEM...

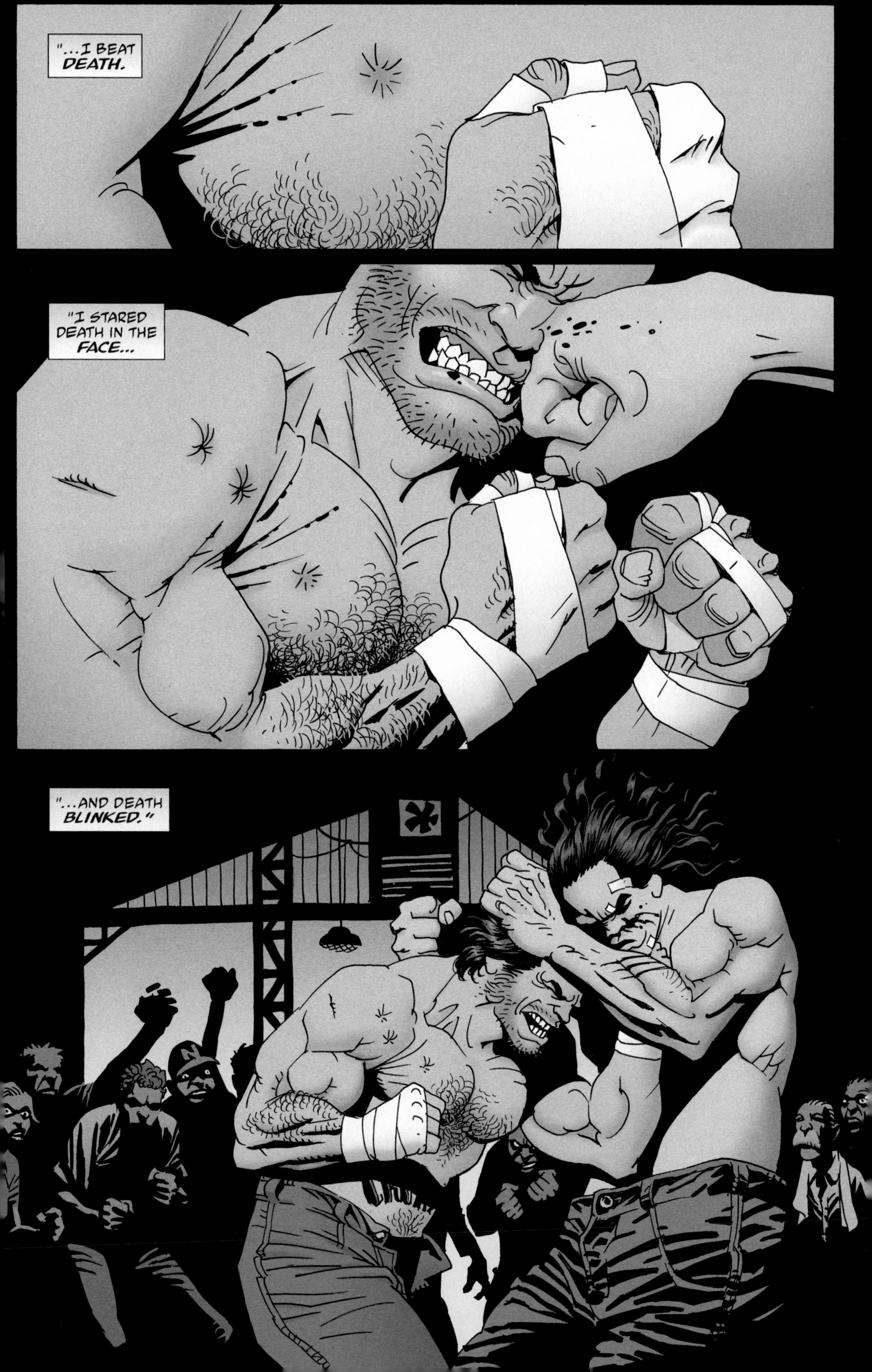
"...I BEAT DEATH.
"I STARED DEATH IN THE FACE...
"...AND DEATH BLINKED."

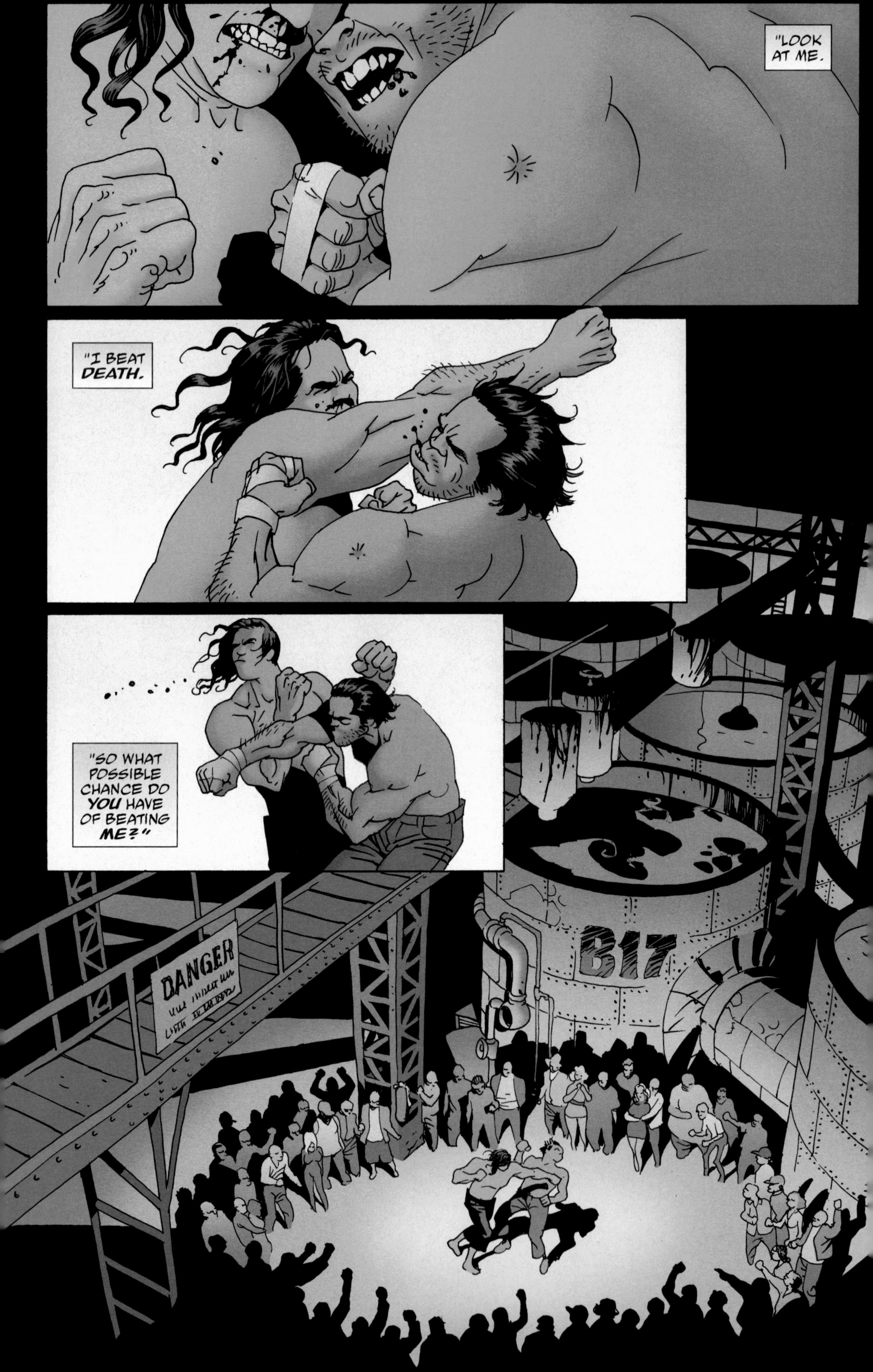
"LOOK AT ME.
"I BEAT DEATH.
"SO WHAT POSSIBLE CHANCE DO YOU HAVE OF BEATING ME?"
DANGER
B17

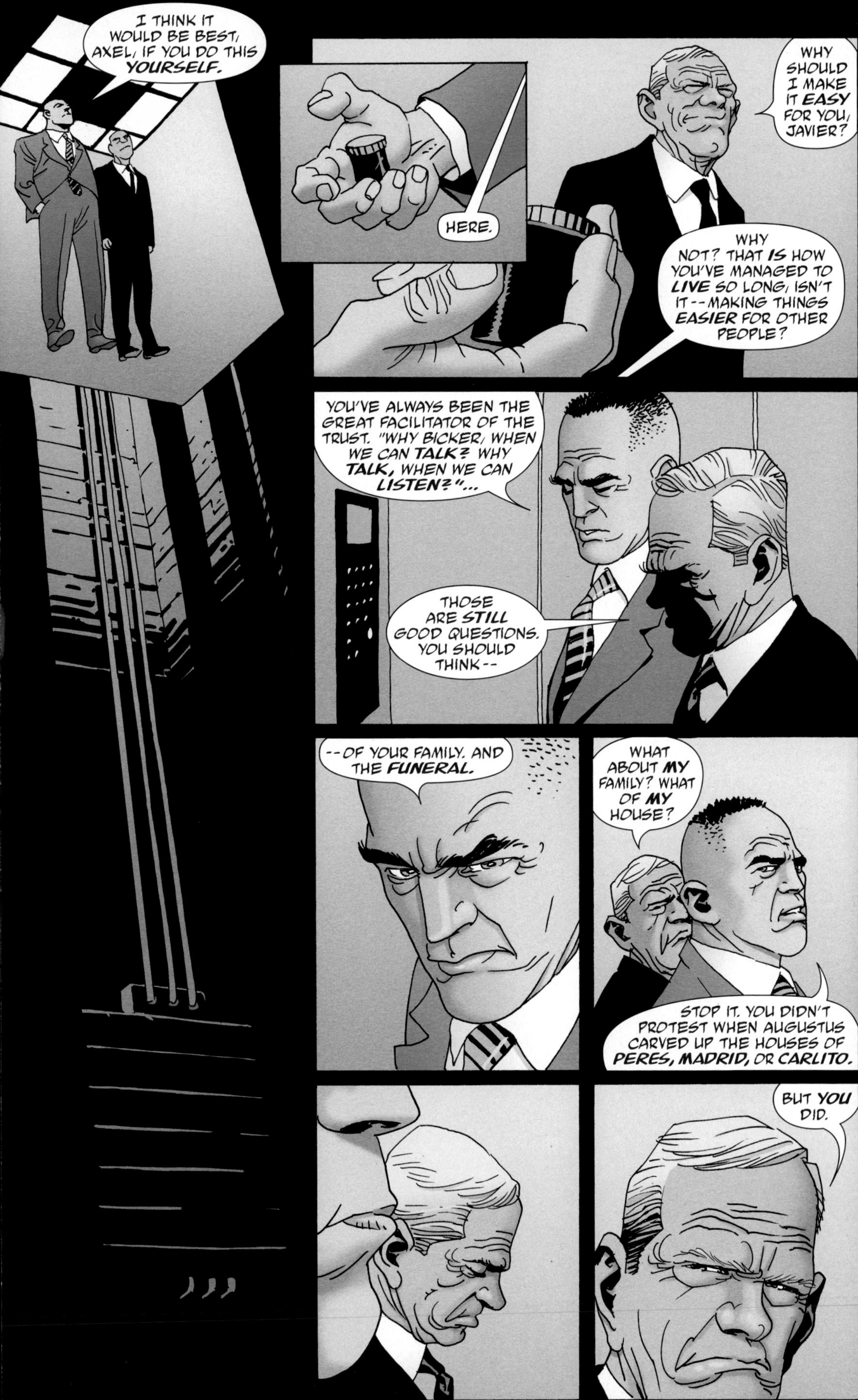
I THINK IT WOULD BE BEST, AXEL, IF YOU DO THIS YOURSELF.
HERE.
WHY SHOULD I MAKE IT EASY FOR YOU, JAVIER?
WHY NOT? THAT IS HOW YOU'VE MANAGED TO LIVE SO LONG, ISN'T IT--MAKING THINGS EASIER FOR OTHER PEOPLE?
YOU'VE ALWAYS BEEN THE GREAT FACILITATOR OF THE TRUST. "WHY BICKER, WHEN WE CAN TALK? WHY TALK, WHEN WE CAN LISTEN?"...
THOSE ARE STILL GOOD QUESTIONS. YOU SHOULD THINK--
--OF YOUR FAMILY. AND THE FUNERAL.
WHAT ABOUT MY FAMILY? WHAT OF MY HOUSE?
STOP IT. YOU DIDN'T PROTEST WHEN AUGUSTUS CARVED UP THE HOUSES OF PERES, MADRID, OR CARLITO.
BUT YOU DID.

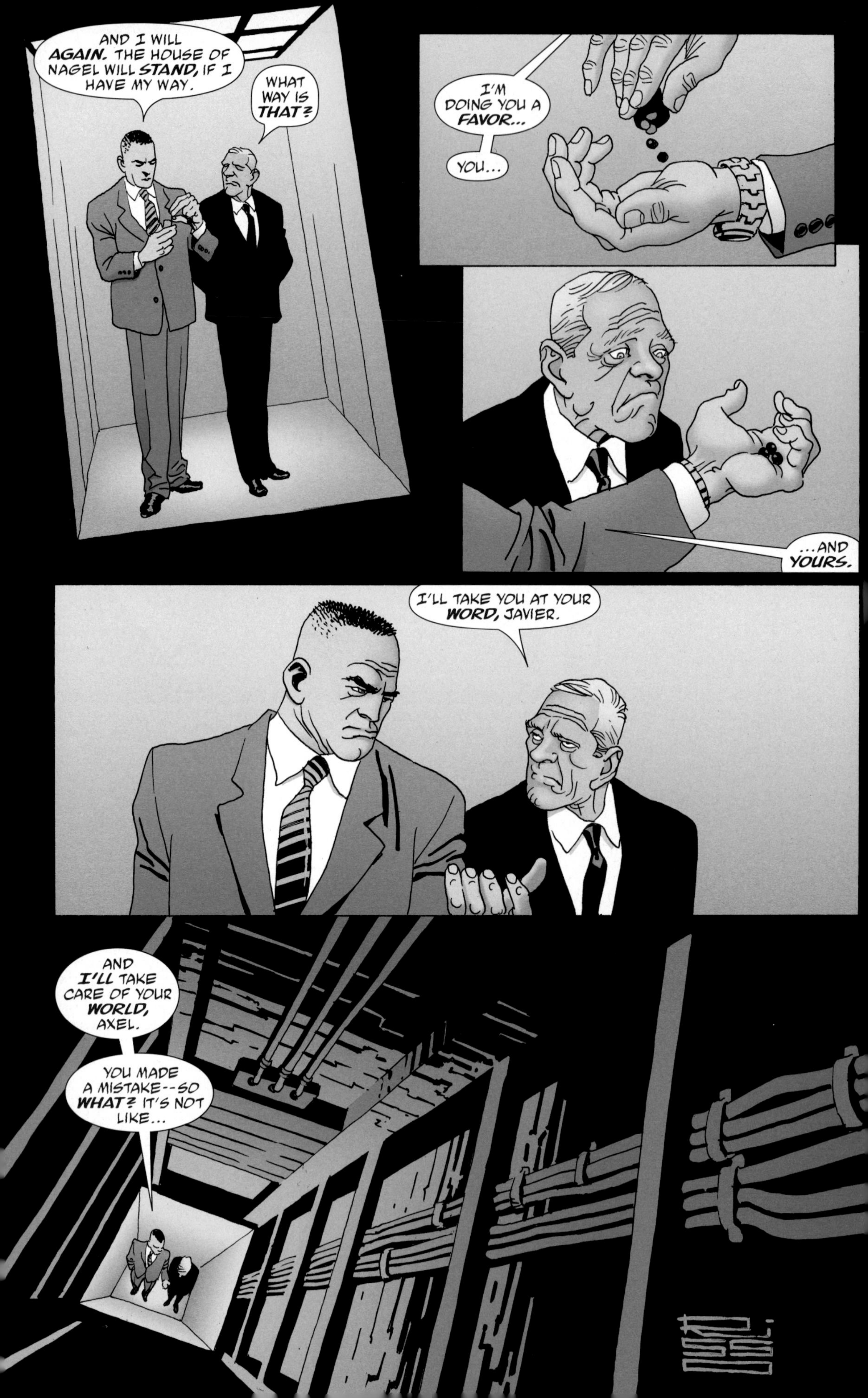
AND I WILL **AGAIN.** THE HOUSE OF NAGEL WILL **STAND,** IF I HAVE MY WAY.
WHAT WAY IS **THAT?**
I'M DOING YOU A **FAVOR...**
YOU...
...AND **YOURS.**
I'LL TAKE YOU AT YOUR **WORD,** JAVIER.
AND **I'LL** TAKE CARE OF YOUR **WORLD,** AXEL.
YOU MADE A MISTAKE--SO **WHAT?** IT'S NOT LIKE...

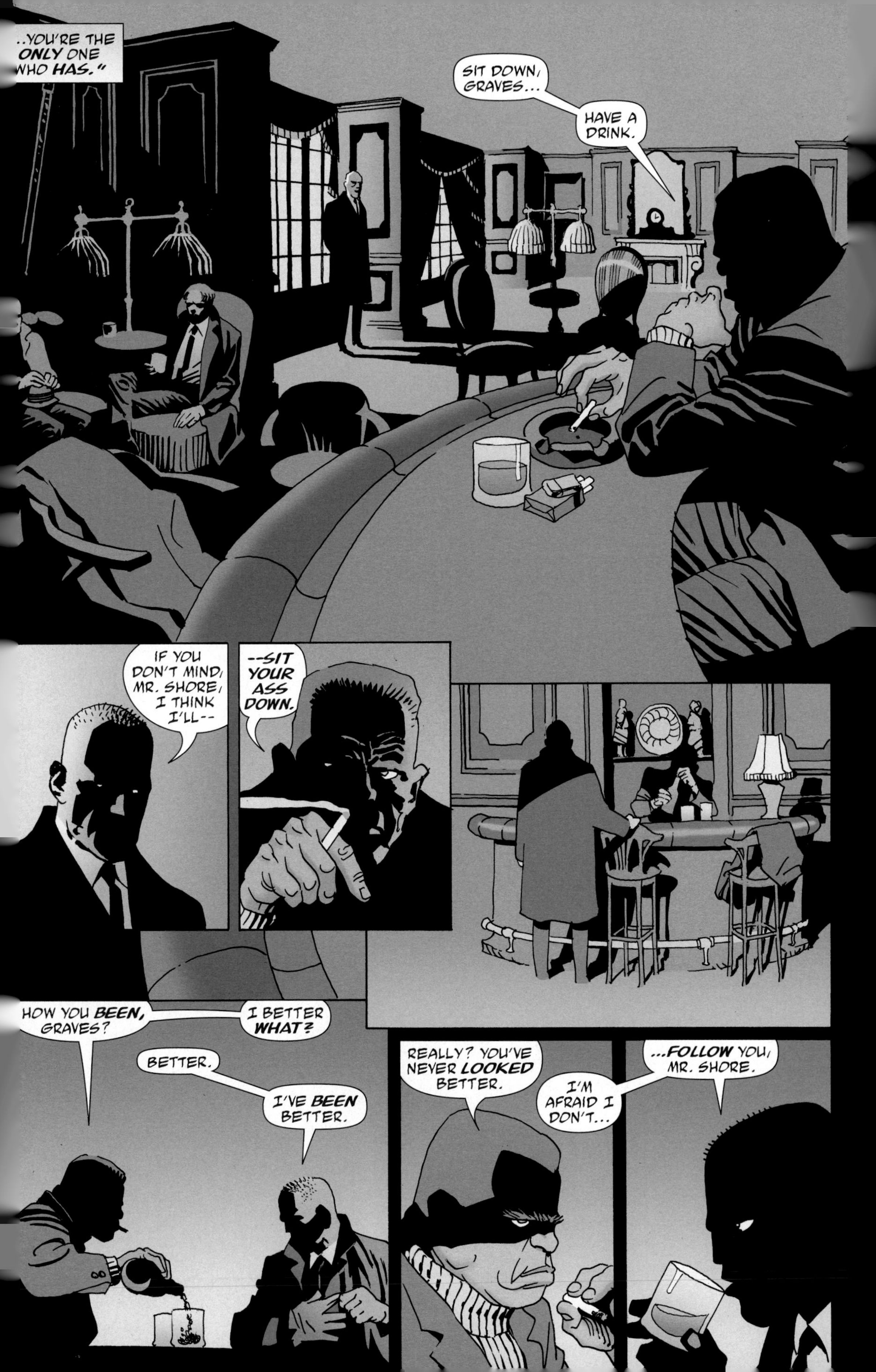
..YOU'RE THE ONLY ONE WHO HAS."
SIT DOWN, GRAVES...
HAVE A DRINK.
IF YOU DON'T MIND, MR. SHORE, I THINK I'LL--
--SIT YOUR ASS DOWN.
HOW YOU BEEN, GRAVES?
BETTER.
I'VE BEEN BETTER.
I BETTER WHAT?
REALLY? YOU'VE NEVER LOOKED BETTER.
I'M AFRAID I DON'T...
...FOLLOW YOU, MR. SHORE.

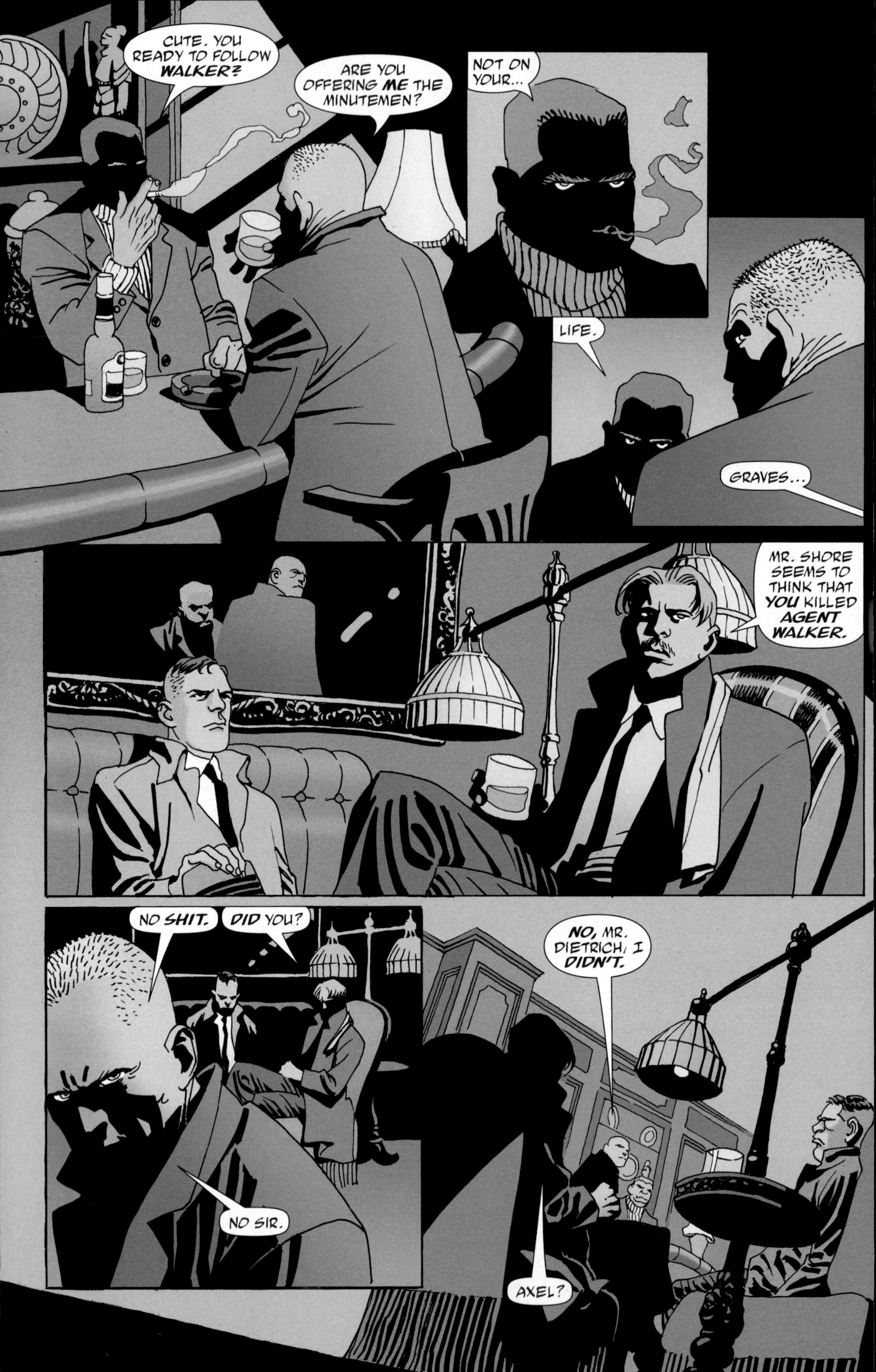
CUTE. YOU READY TO FOLLOW WALKER?
ARE YOU OFFERING ME THE MINUTEMEN?
NOT ON YOUR...
LIFE.
GRAVES...
MR. SHORE SEEMS TO THINK THAT YOU KILLED AGENT WALKER.
NO SHIT.
DID YOU?
NO SIR.
NO, MR. DIETRICH, I DIDN'T.
AXEL?

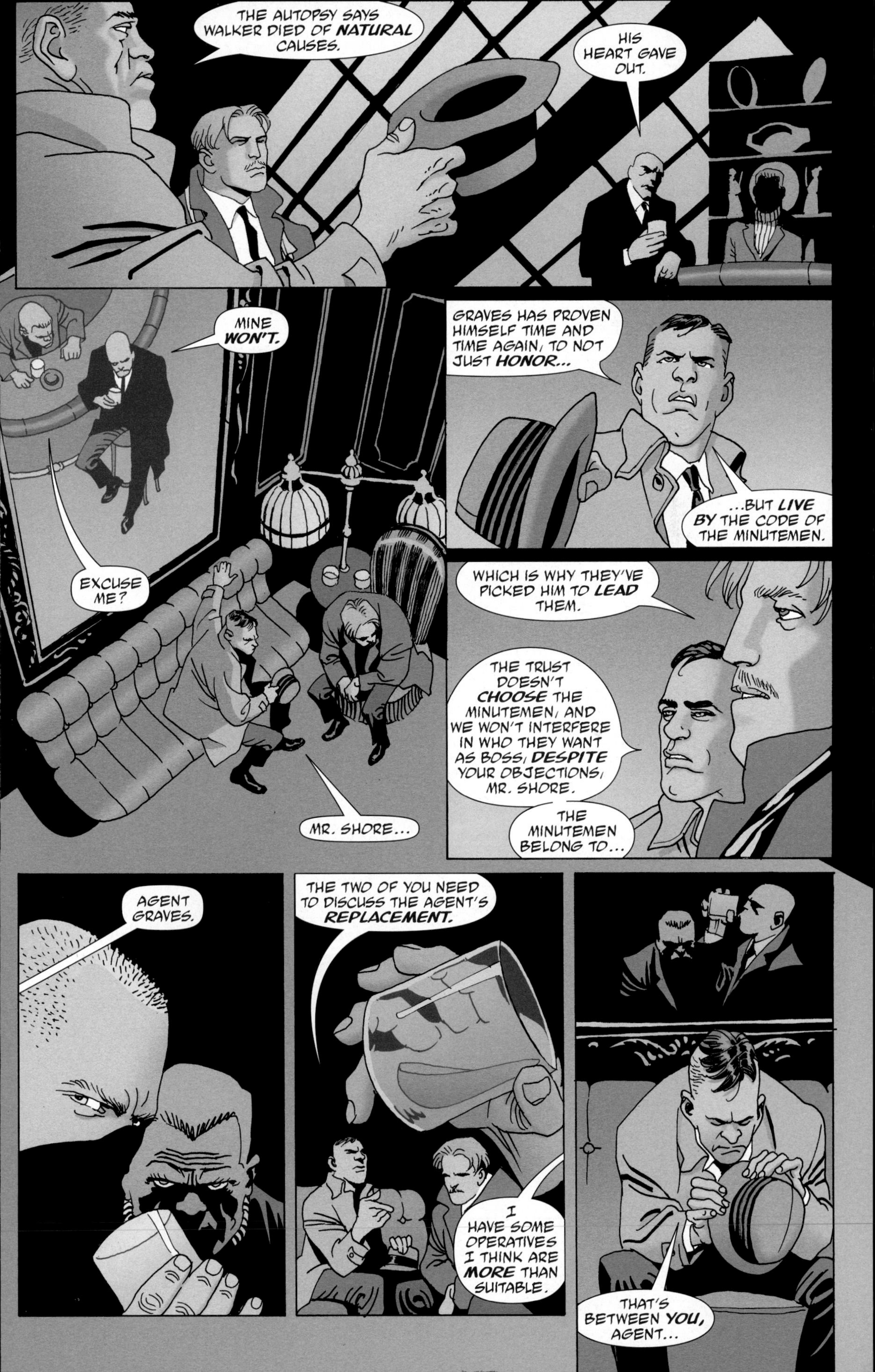
THE AUTOPSY SAYS WALKER DIED OF NATURAL CAUSES.
HIS HEART GAVE OUT.
MINE WON'T.
EXCUSE ME?
GRAVES HAS PROVEN HIMSELF TIME AND TIME AGAIN, TO NOT JUST HONOR...
...BUT LIVE BY THE CODE OF THE MINUTEMEN.
WHICH IS WHY THEY'VE PICKED HIM TO LEAD THEM.
THE TRUST DOESN'T CHOOSE THE MINUTEMEN, AND WE WON'T INTERFERE IN WHO THEY WANT AS BOSS, DESPITE YOUR OBJECTIONS, MR. SHORE.
MR. SHORE...
THE MINUTEMEN BELONG TO...
AGENT GRAVES.
THE TWO OF YOU NEED TO DISCUSS THE AGENT'S REPLACEMENT.
I HAVE SOME OPERATIVES I THINK ARE MORE THAN SUITABLE.
THAT'S BETWEEN YOU, AGENT...

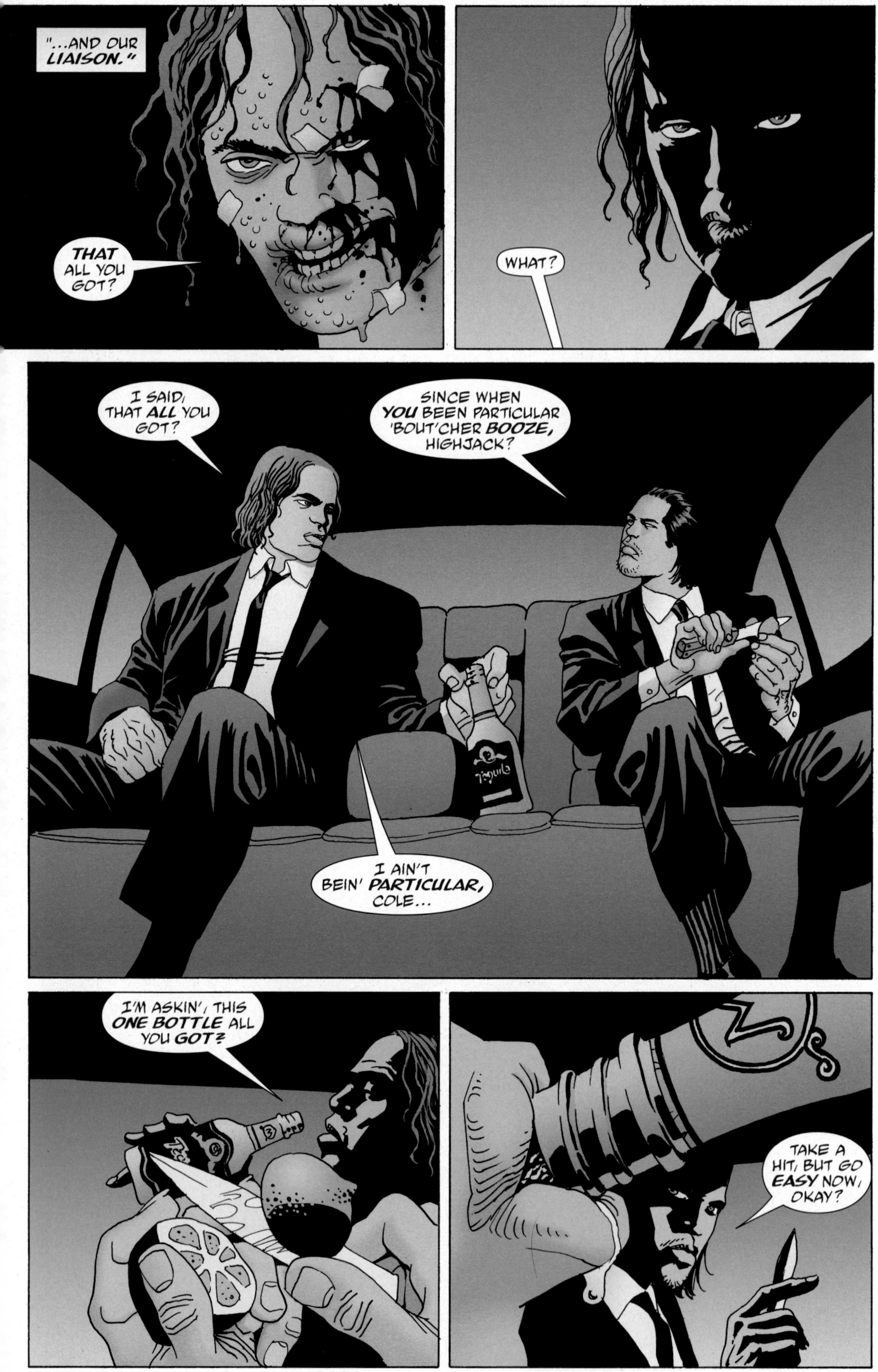
"...AND OUR LIAISON."
THAT ALL YOU GOT?
WHAT?
I SAID, THAT ALL YOU GOT?
SINCE WHEN YOU BEEN PARTICULAR 'BOUT'CHER BOOZE, HIGHJACK?
I AIN'T BEIN' PARTICULAR, COLE...
I'M ASKIN', THIS ONE BOTTLE ALL YOU GOT?
TAKE A HIT, BUT GO EASY NOW, OKAY?

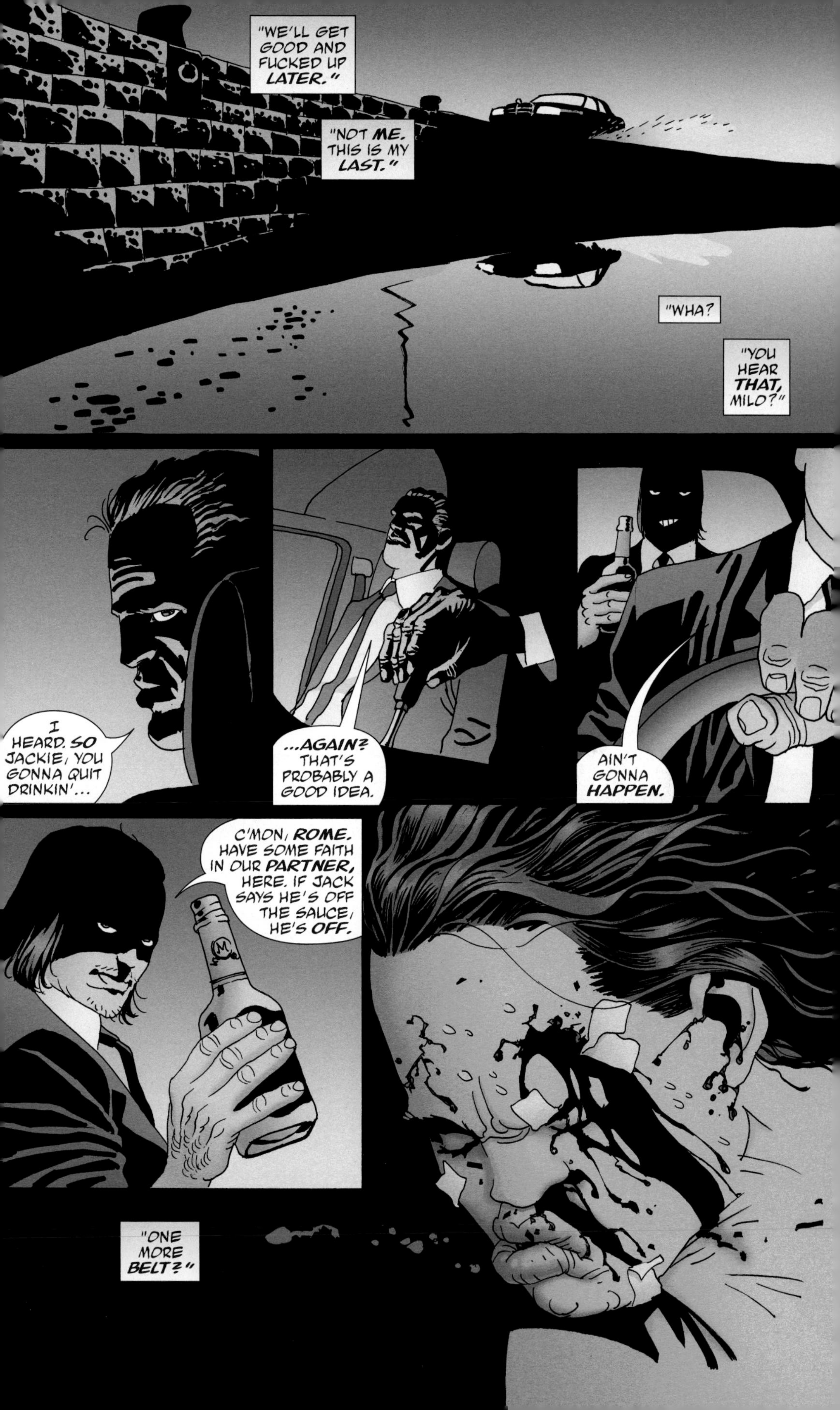
"WE'LL GET GOOD AND FUCKED UP LATER."
"NOT ME. THIS IS MY LAST."
"WHA?
"YOU HEAR THAT, MILO?"
I HEARD. SO JACKIE, YOU GONNA QUIT DRINKIN'...
...AGAIN? THAT'S PROBABLY A GOOD IDEA.
AIN'T GONNA HAPPEN.
C'MON, ROME. HAVE SOME FAITH IN OUR PARTNER, HERE. IF JACK SAYS HE'S OFF THE SAUCE, HE'S OFF.
"ONE MORE BELT?"

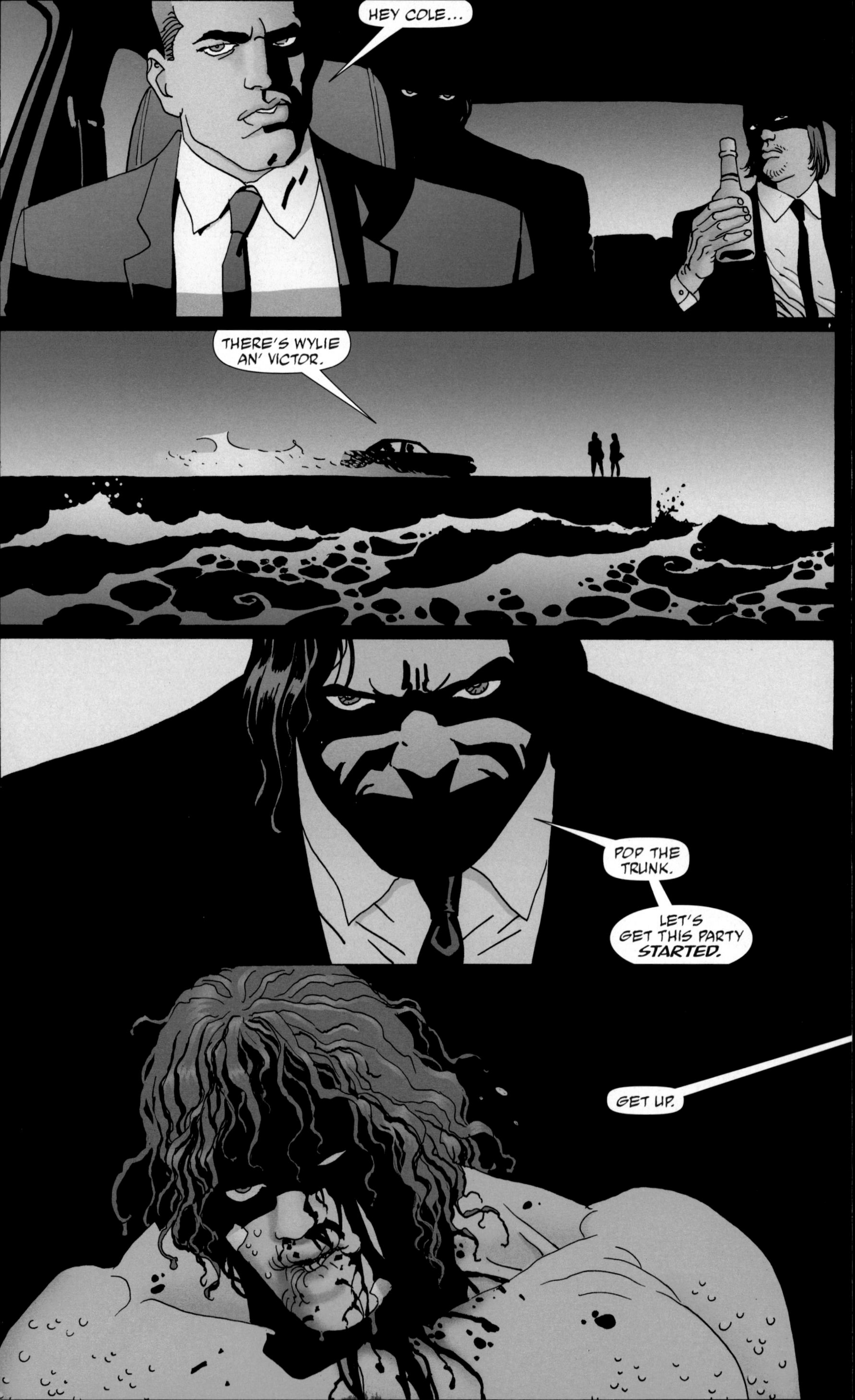
HEY COLE...
THERE'S WYLIE AN' VICTOR.
POP THE TRUNK.
LET'S GET THIS PARTY STARTED.
GET UP.

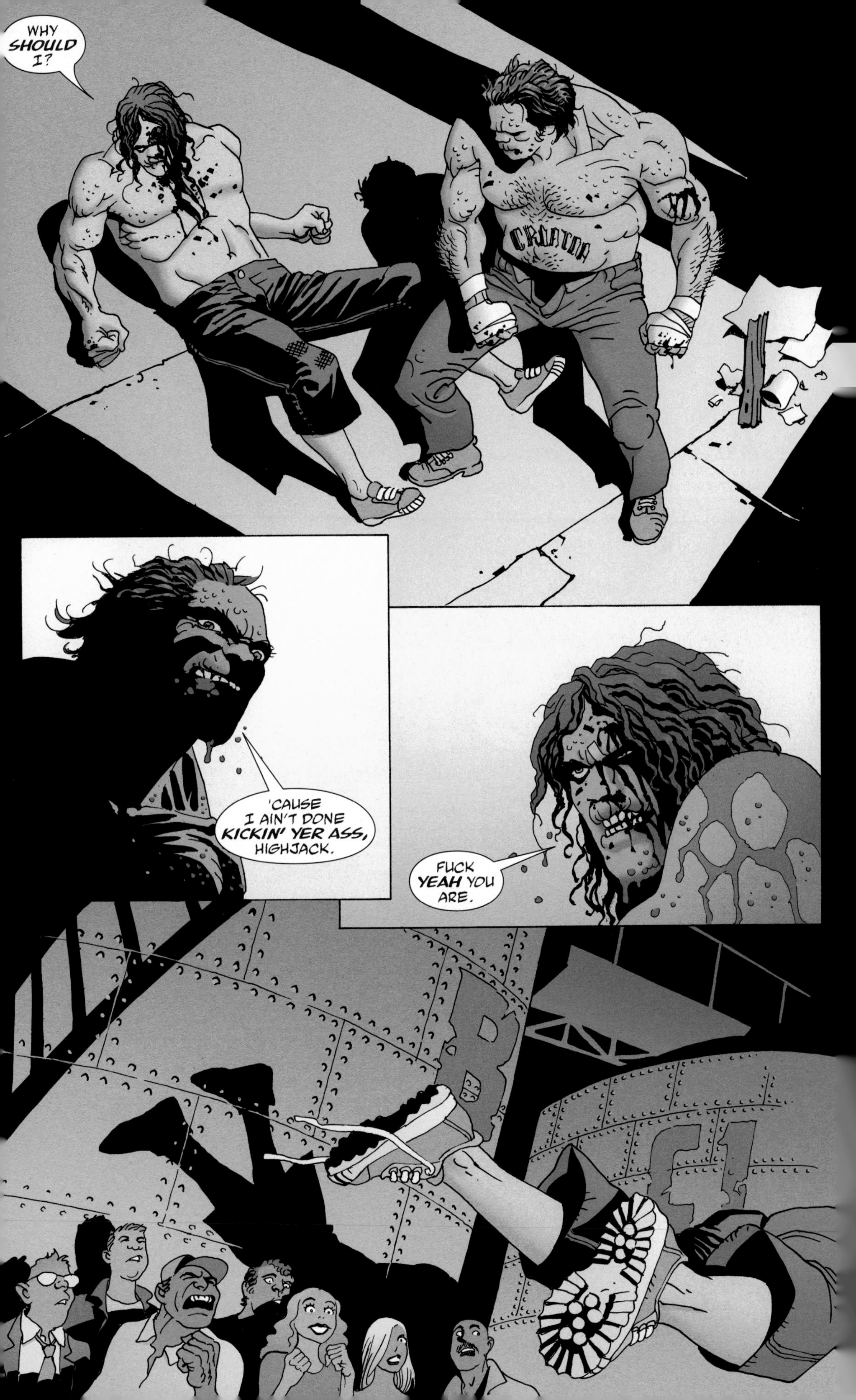
WHY SHOULD I?
'CAUSE I AIN'T DONE KICKIN' YER ASS, HIGHJACK.
FUCK YEAH YOU ARE.

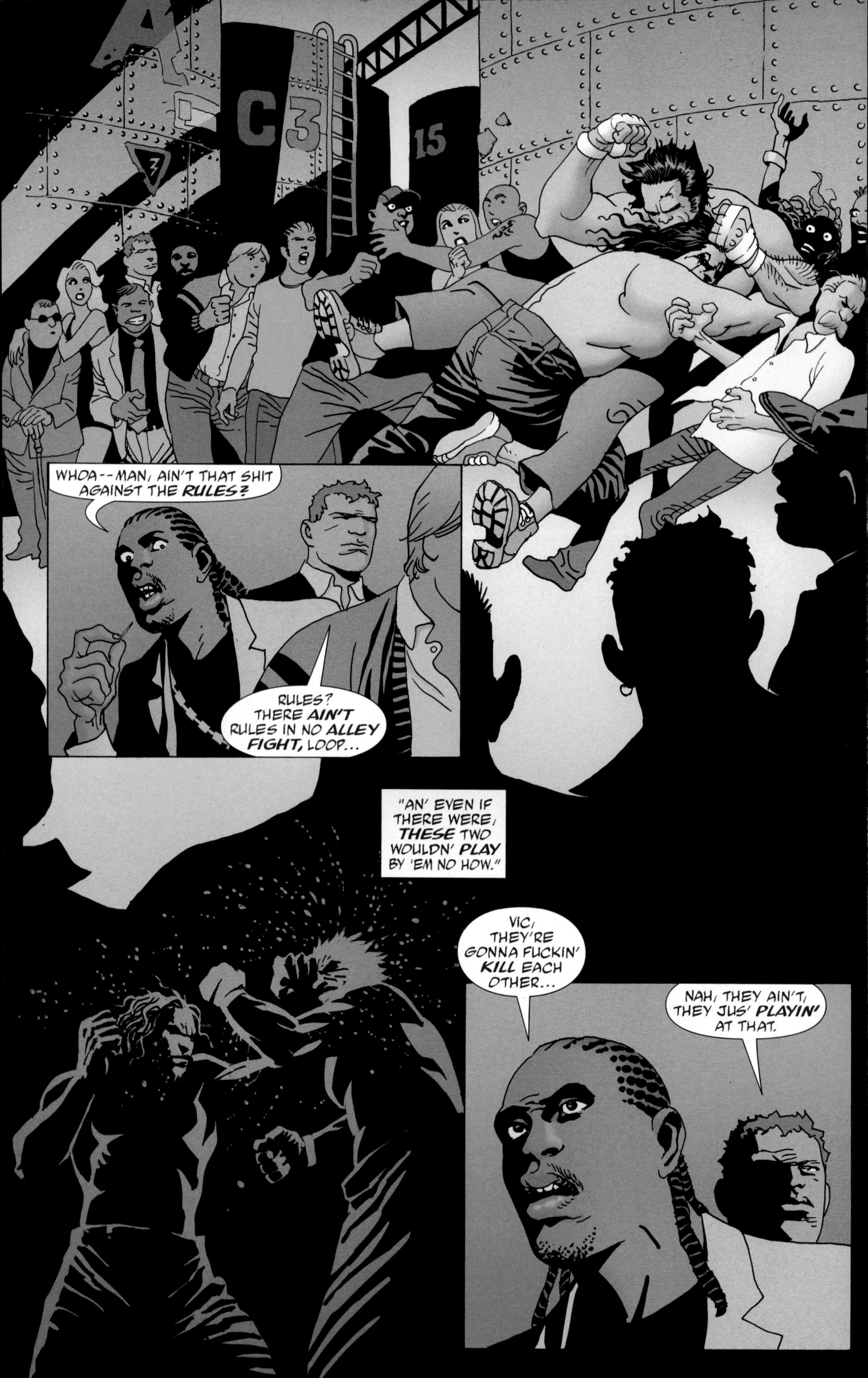

WHOA--MAN, AIN'T THAT SHIT AGAINST THE RULES?
RULES? THERE AIN'T RULES IN NO ALLEY FIGHT, LOOP...
"AN' EVEN IF THERE WERE, THESE TWO WOULDN' PLAY BY 'EM NO HOW."
VIC, THEY'RE GONNA FUCKIN' KILL EACH OTHER...
NAH, THEY AIN'T, THEY JUS' PLAYIN' AT THAT.

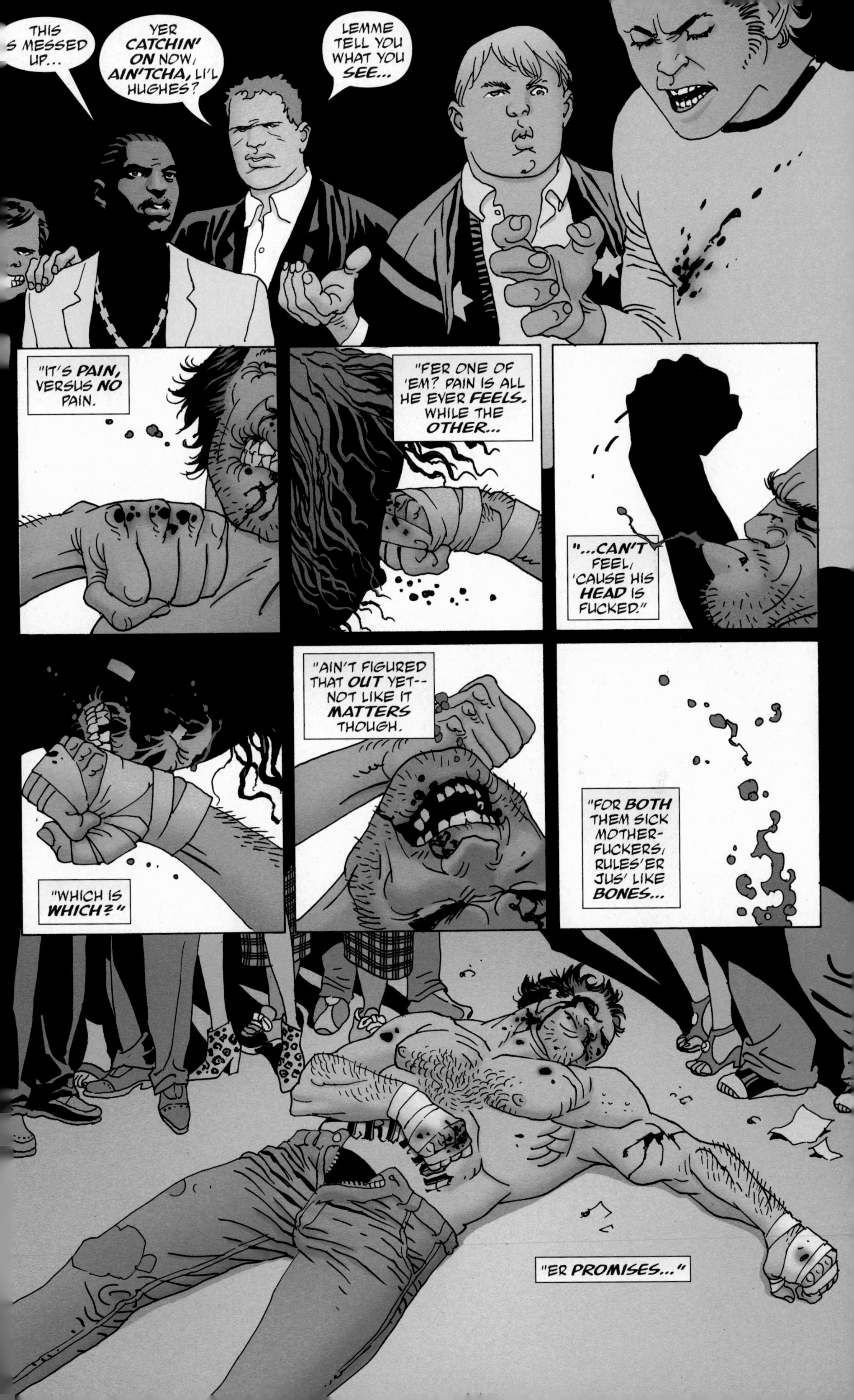

THIS 'S MESSED UP...
YER CATCHIN' ON NOW, AIN'TCHA, LI'L HUGHES?
LEMME TELL YOU WHAT YOU SEE...
"IT'S PAIN, VERSUS NO PAIN.
"FER ONE OF 'EM? PAIN IS ALL HE EVER FEELS. WHILE THE OTHER...
"...CAN'T FEEL, 'CAUSE HIS HEAD IS FUCKED."
"WHICH IS WHICH?"
"AIN'T FIGURED THAT OUT YET-- NOT LIKE IT MATTERS THOUGH.
"FOR BOTH THEM SICK MOTHER-FUCKERS, RULES'ER JUS' LIKE BONES...
"ER PROMISES..."

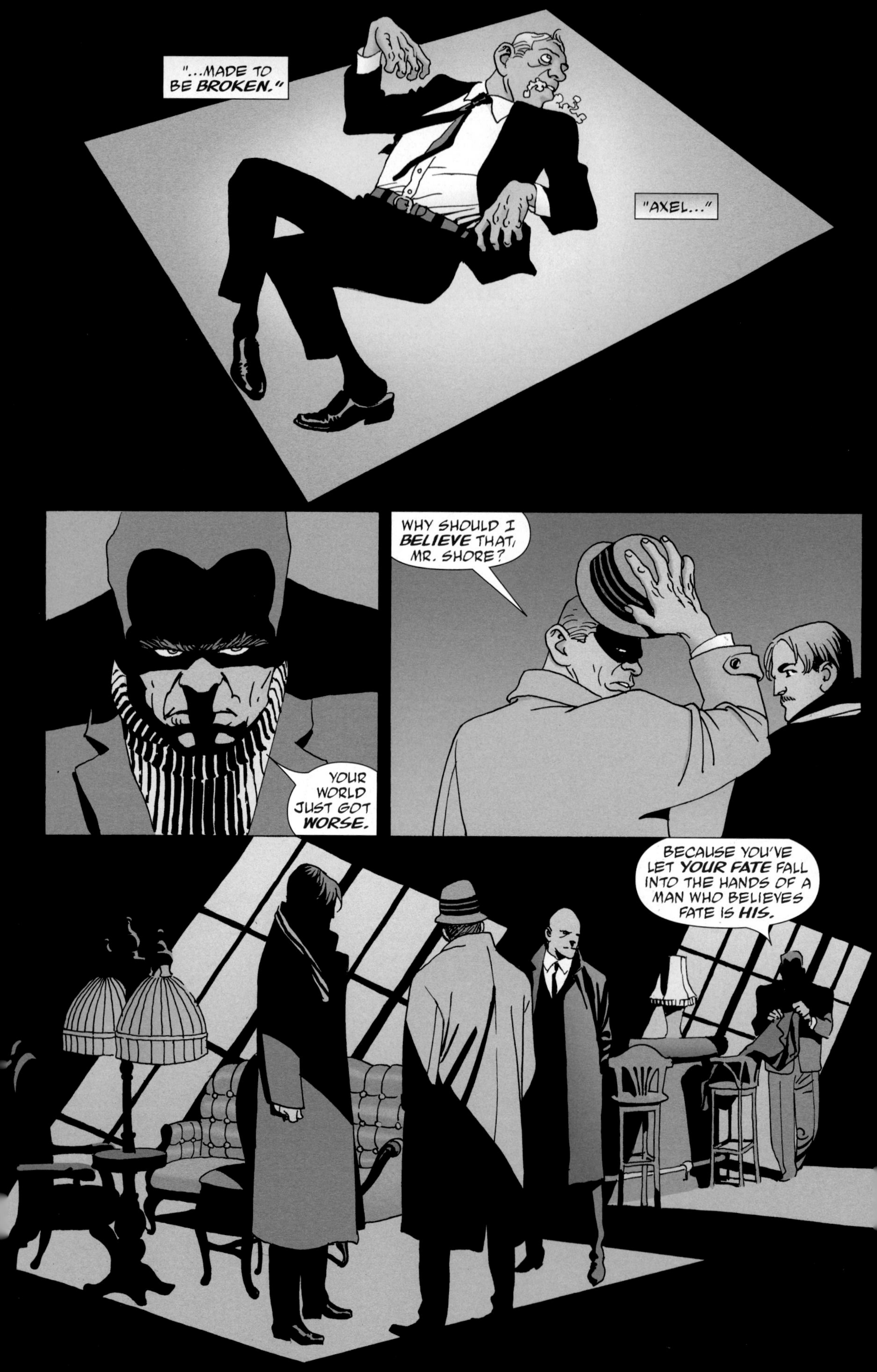
"...MADE TO BE BROKEN."
"AXEL..."
YOUR WORLD JUST GOT WORSE.
WHY SHOULD I BELIEVE THAT, MR. SHORE?
BECAUSE YOU'VE LET YOUR FATE FALL INTO THE HANDS OF A MAN WHO BELIEVES FATE IS HIS.

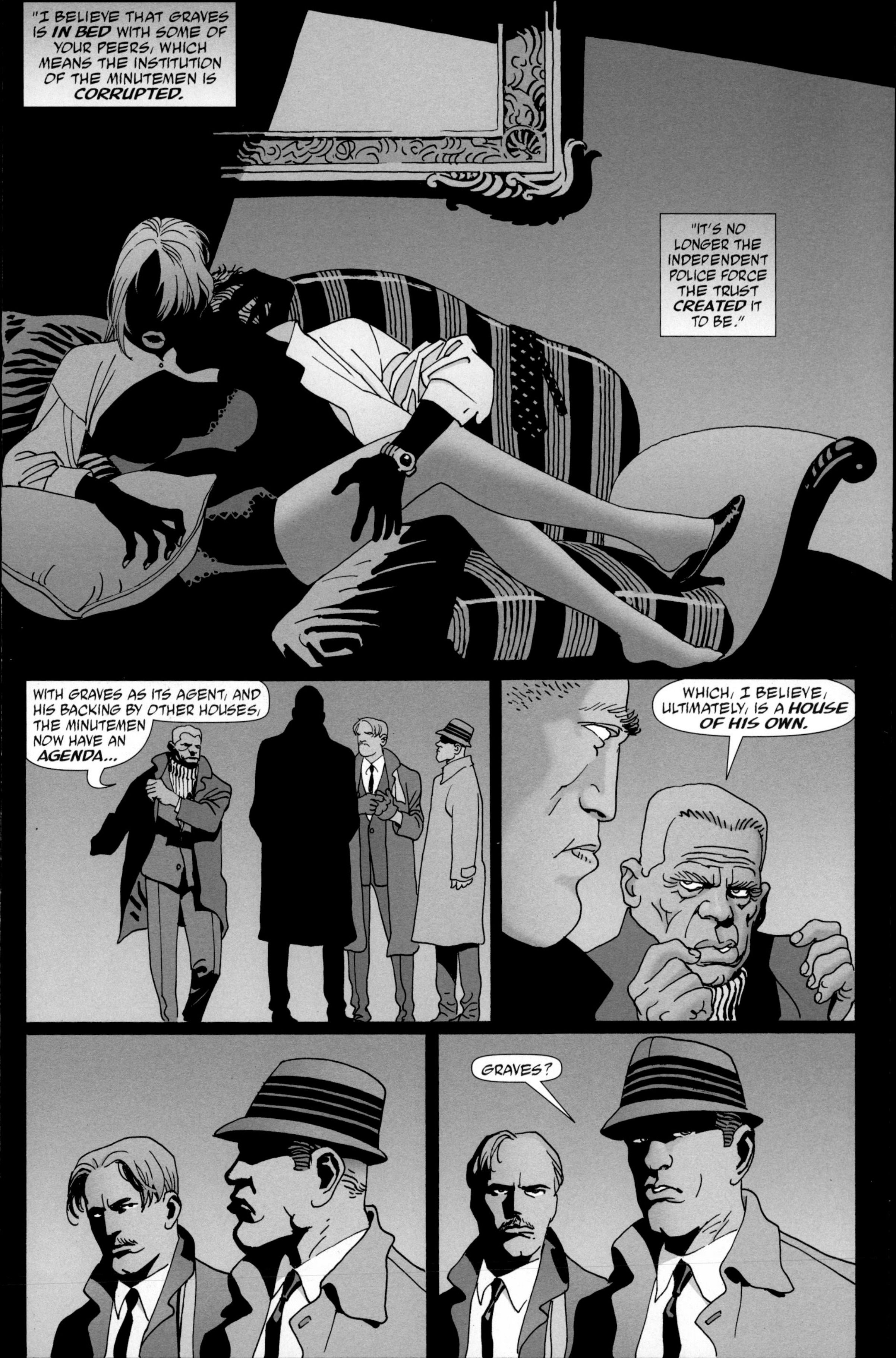
"I BELIEVE THAT GRAVES IS IN BED WITH SOME OF YOUR PEERS, WHICH MEANS THE INSTITUTION OF THE MINUTEMEN IS CORRUPTED.
"IT'S NO LONGER THE INDEPENDENT POLICE FORCE THE TRUST CREATED IT TO BE."
WITH GRAVES AS ITS AGENT, AND HIS BACKING BY OTHER HOUSES, THE MINUTEMEN NOW HAVE AN AGENDA...
WHICH, I BELIEVE, ULTIMATELY, IS A HOUSE OF HIS OWN.
GRAVES?

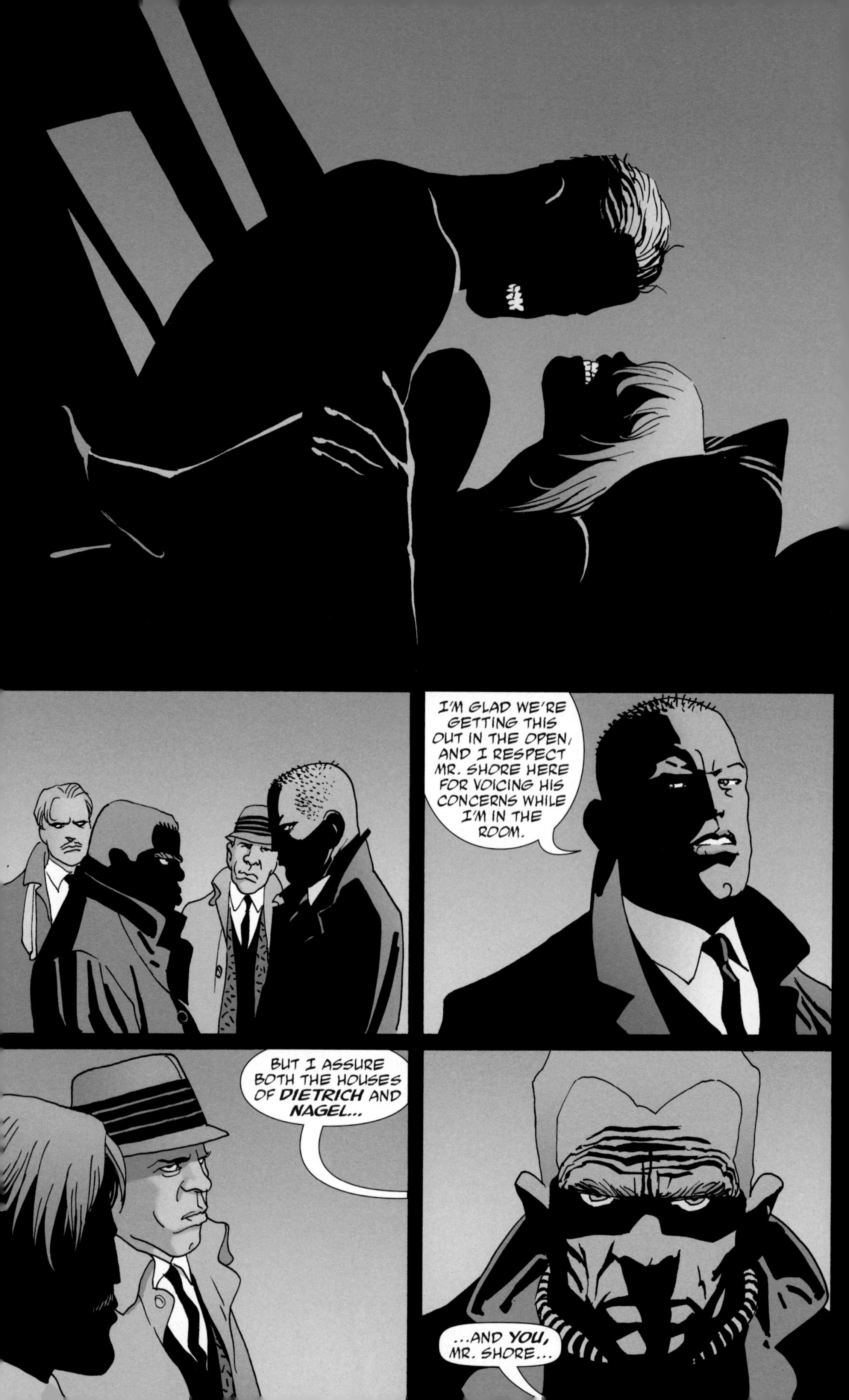
I'M GLAD WE'RE GETTING THIS OUT IN THE OPEN, AND I RESPECT MR. SHORE HERE FOR VOICING HIS CONCERNS WHILE I'M IN THE ROOM.
BUT I ASSURE BOTH THE HOUSES OF **DIETRICH** AND **NAGEL...**
...AND **YOU,** MR. SHORE...

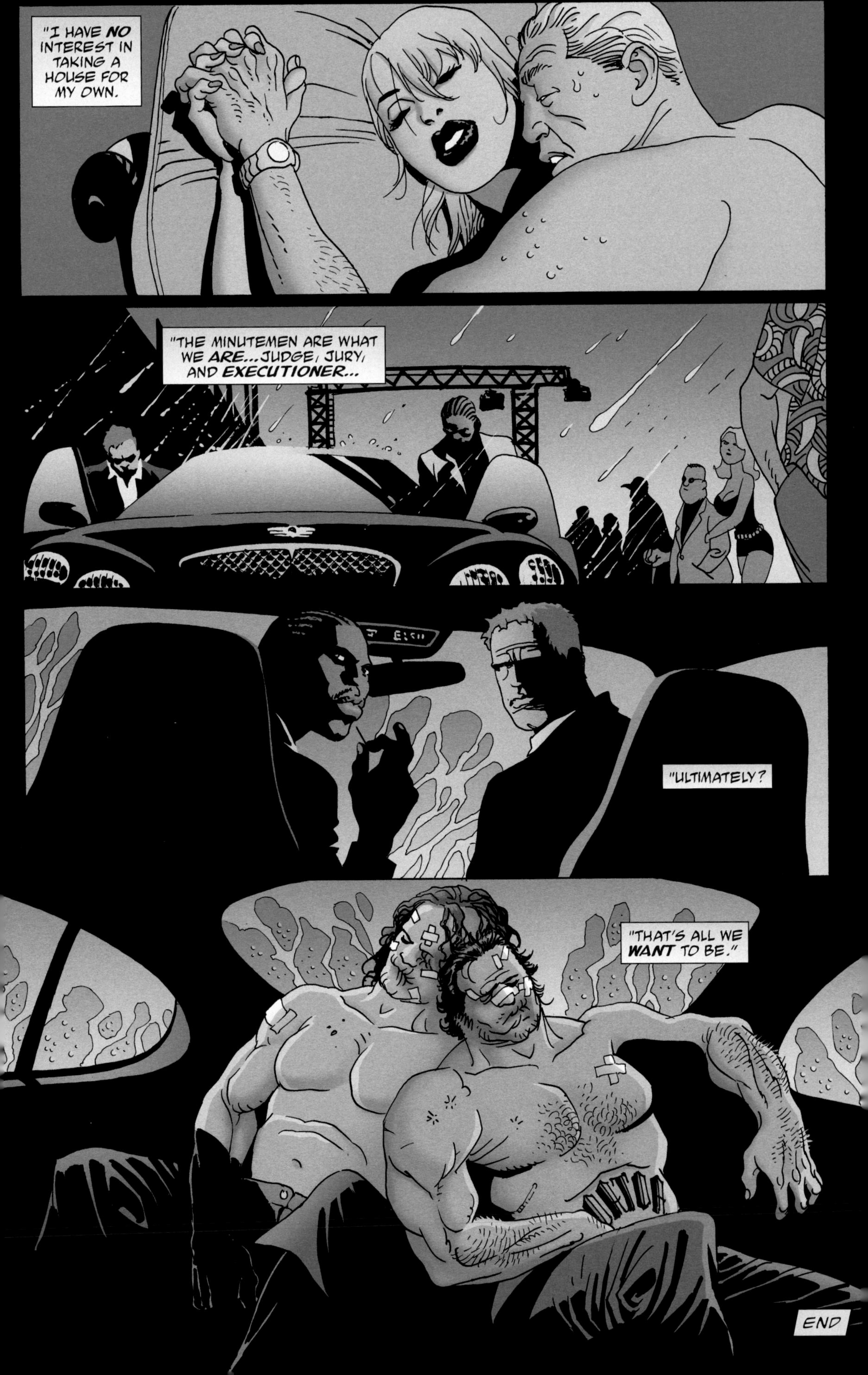
"I HAVE NO INTEREST IN TAKING A HOUSE FOR MY OWN.
"THE MINUTEMEN ARE WHAT WE ARE...JUDGE, JURY, AND EXECUTIONER...
"ULTIMATELY?
"THAT'S ALL WE WANT TO BE."
END

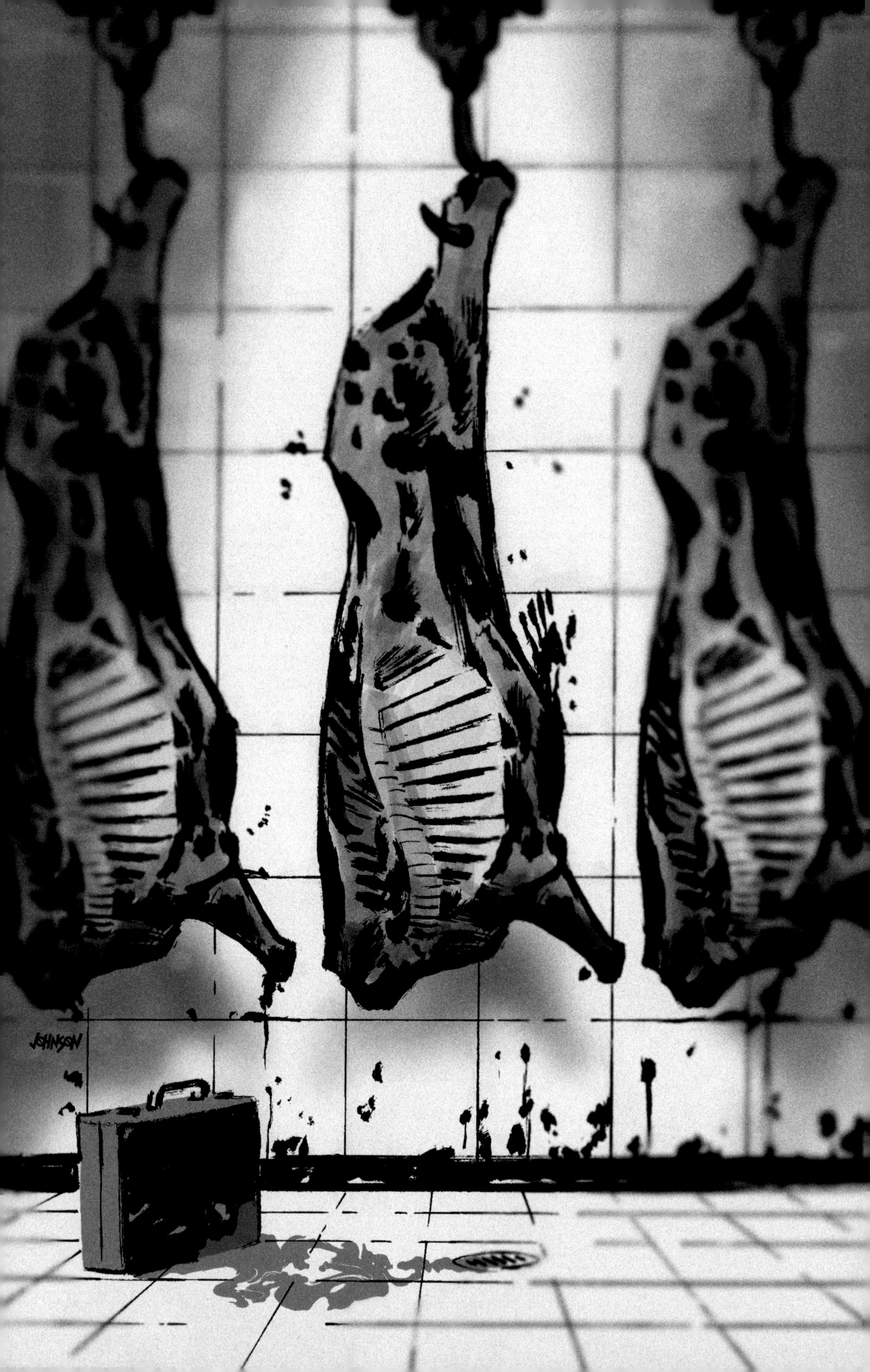
JOHNSON

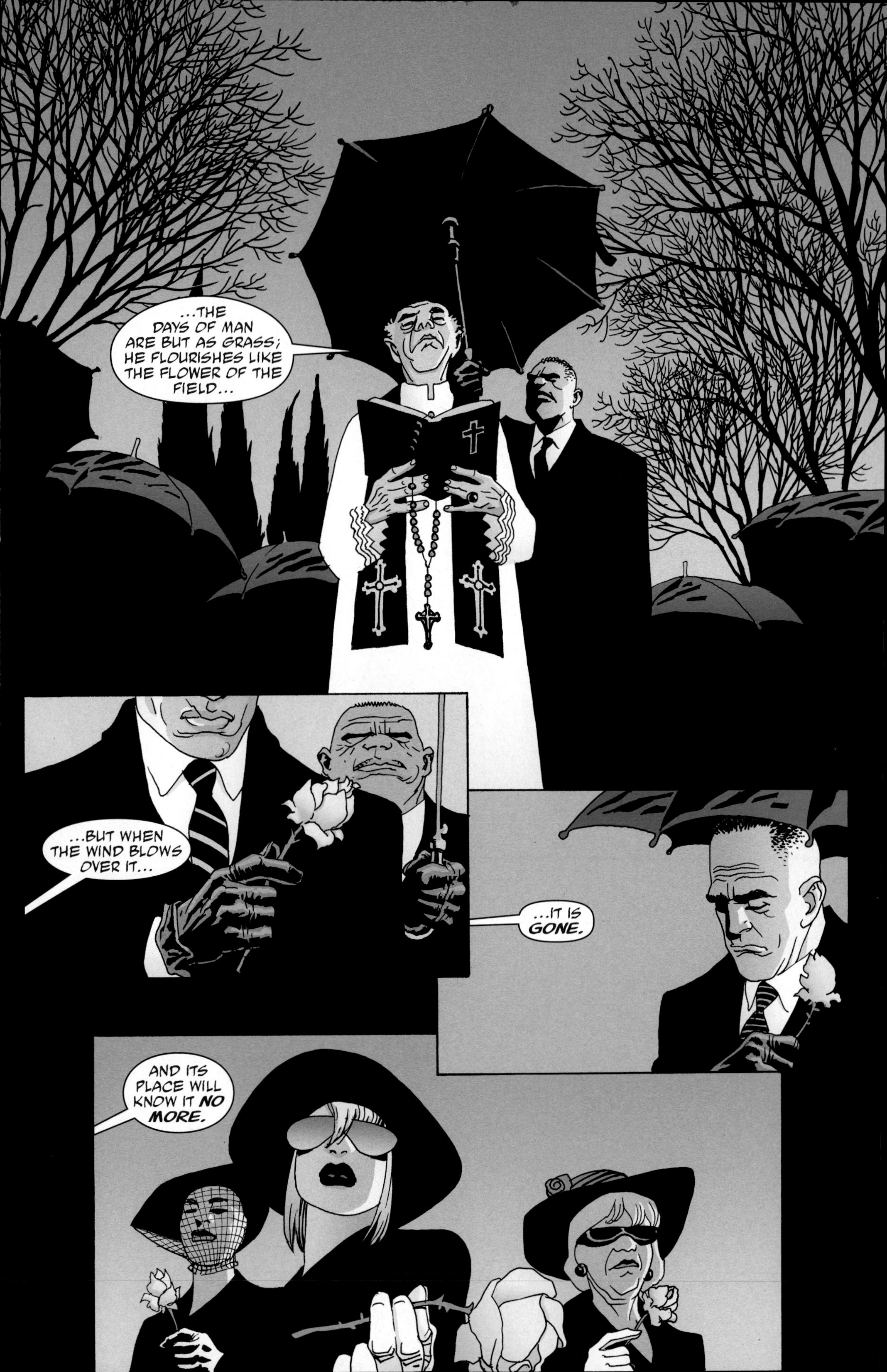
...THE DAYS OF MAN ARE BUT AS GRASS; HE FLOURISHES LIKE THE FLOWER OF THE FIELD...
...BUT WHEN THE WIND BLOWS OVER IT...
...IT IS *GONE.*
AND ITS PLACE WILL KNOW IT *NO MORE.*

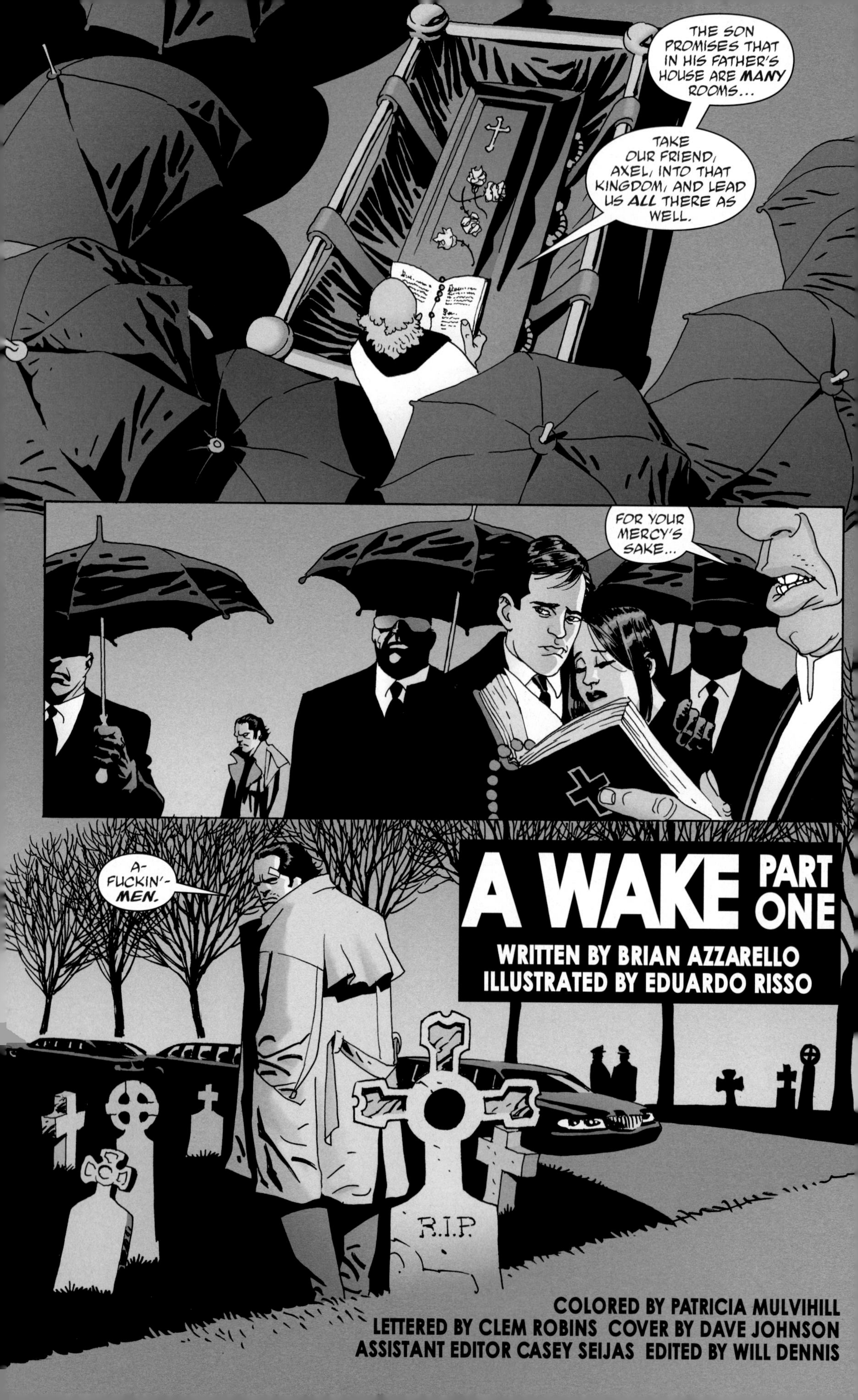
THE SON PROMISES THAT IN HIS FATHER'S HOUSE ARE MANY ROOMS...
TAKE OUR FRIEND, AXEL, INTO THAT KINGDOM, AND LEAD US ALL THERE AS WELL.
FOR YOUR MERCY'S SAKE...
A-FUCKIN'-MEN.
A WAKE PART ONE
WRITTEN BY BRIAN AZZARELLO
ILLUSTRATED BY EDUARDO RISSO
R.I.P.
COLORED BY PATRICIA MULVIHILL
LETTERED BY CLEM ROBINS COVER BY DAVE JOHNSON
ASSISTANT EDITOR CASEY SEIJAS EDITED BY WILL DENNIS

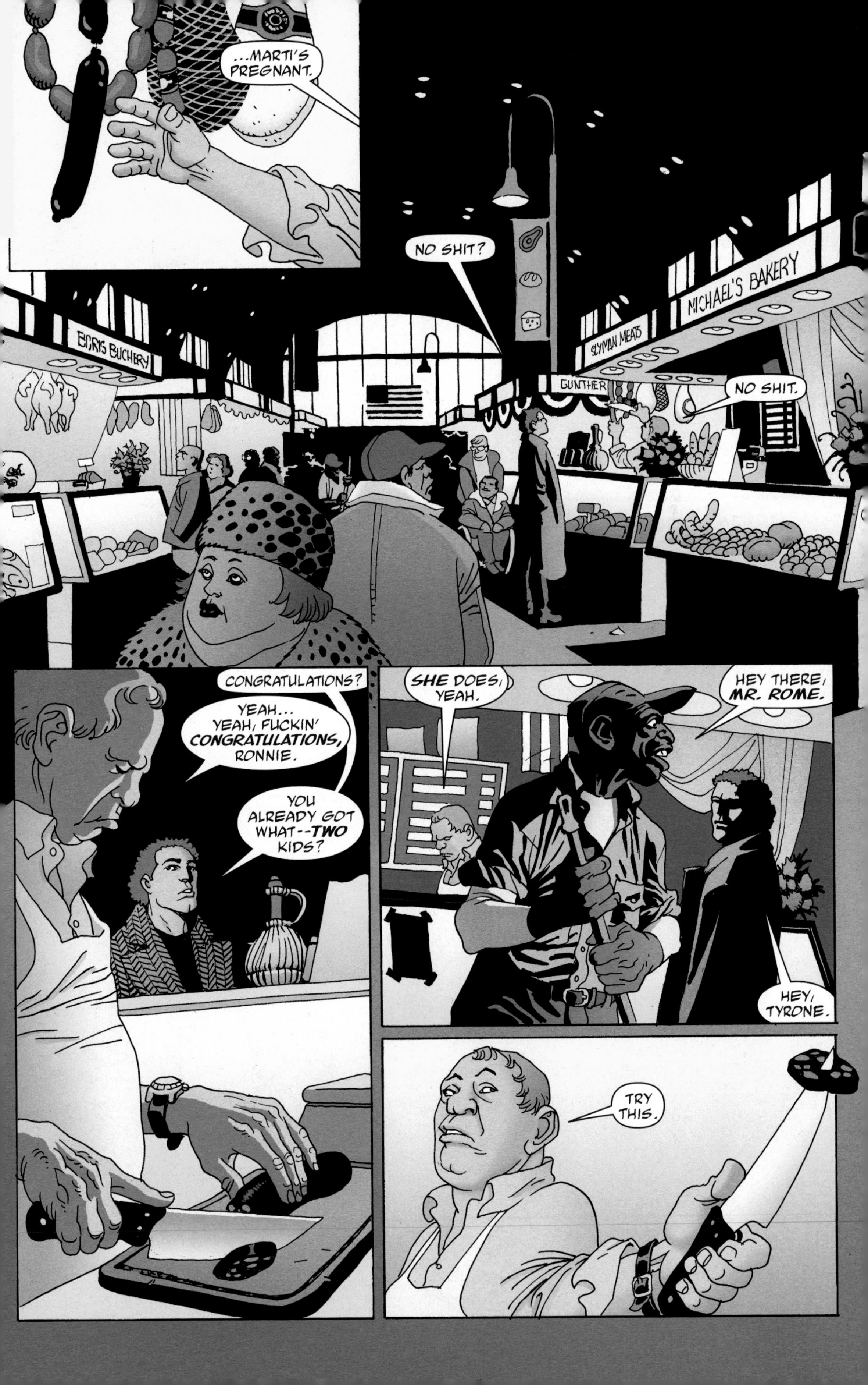
...MARTI'S PREGNANT.
NO SHIT?
BORIS BUCHERY
MICHAEL'S BAKERY
SLYMAN MEATS
GUNTHER
NO SHIT.
CONGRATULATIONS?
YEAH... YEAH, FUCKIN' **CONGRATULATIONS,** RONNIE.
YOU ALREADY GOT WHAT--**TWO** KIDS?
SHE DOES, YEAH.
HEY THERE, **MR. ROME.**
HEY, TYRONE.
TRY THIS.

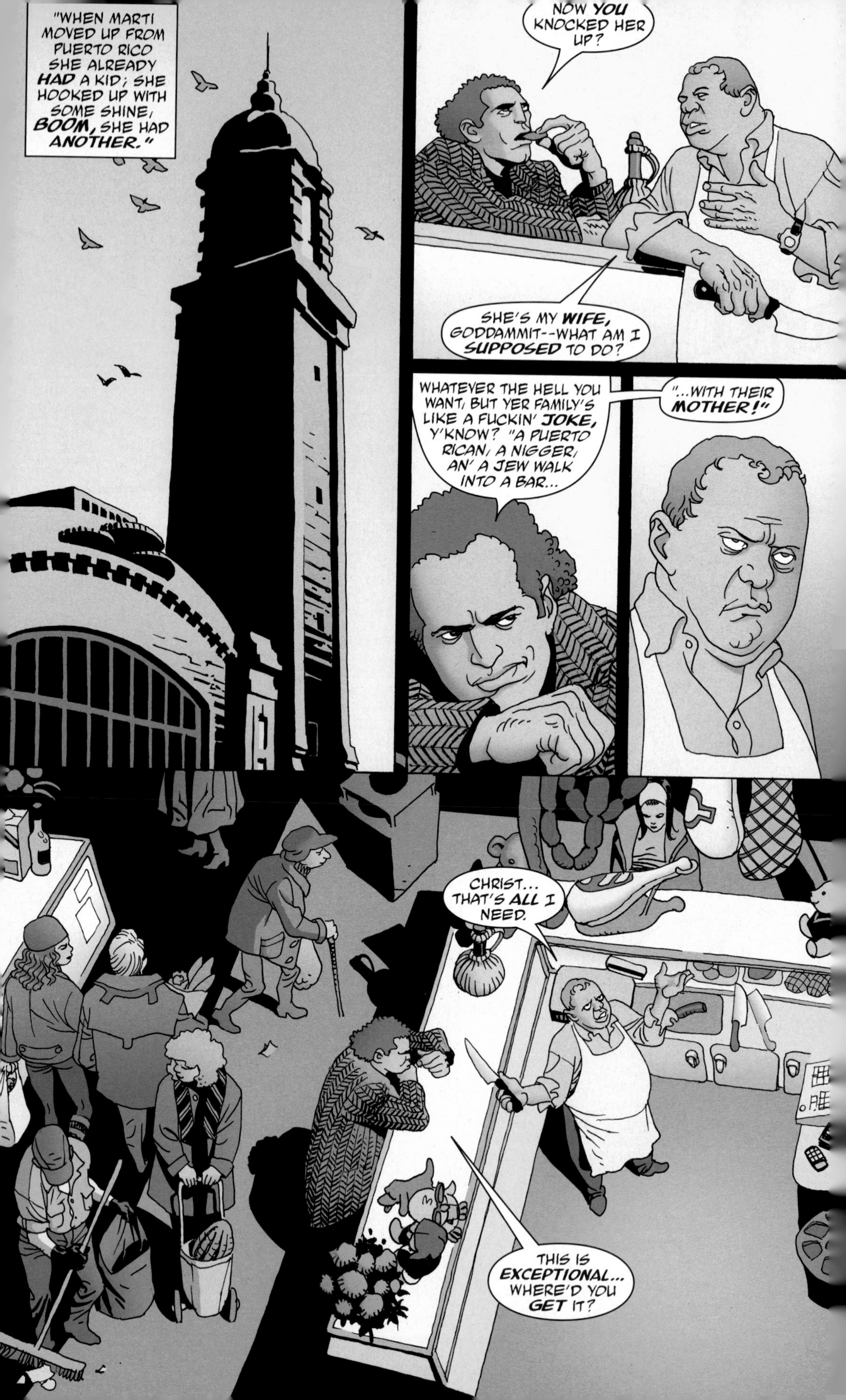
"WHEN MARTI MOVED UP FROM PUERTO RICO SHE ALREADY HAD A KID; SHE HOOKED UP WITH SOME SHINE, BOOM, SHE HAD ANOTHER."
NOW YOU KNOCKED HER UP?
SHE'S MY WIFE, GODDAMMIT--WHAT AM I SUPPOSED TO DO?
WHATEVER THE HELL YOU WANT, BUT YER FAMILY'S LIKE A FUCKIN' JOKE, Y'KNOW? "A PUERTO RICAN, A NIGGER, AN' A JEW WALK INTO A BAR...
"...WITH THEIR MOTHER!"
CHRIST... THAT'S ALL I NEED.
THIS IS EXCEPTIONAL... WHERE'D YOU GET IT?

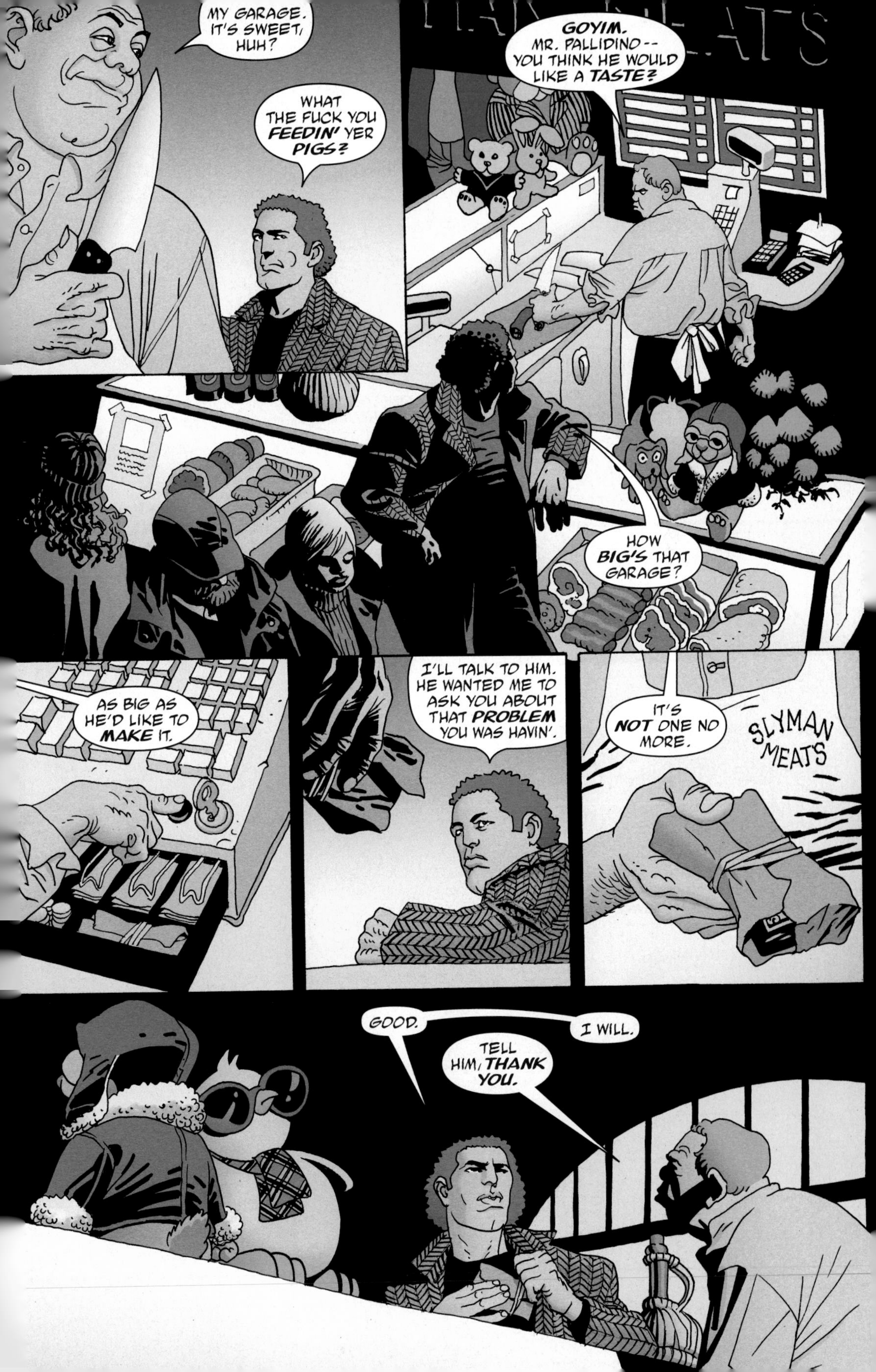
MY GARAGE. IT'S SWEET, HUH?
WHAT THE FUCK YOU FEEDIN' YER PIGS?
GOYIM. MR. PALLIDINO -- YOU THINK HE WOULD LIKE A TASTE?
HOW BIG'S THAT GARAGE?
AS BIG AS HE'D LIKE TO MAKE IT.
I'LL TALK TO HIM. HE WANTED ME TO ASK YOU ABOUT THAT PROBLEM YOU WAS HAVIN'.
IT'S NOT ONE NO MORE.
SLYMAN MEATS
GOOD.
I WILL.
TELL HIM, THANK YOU.

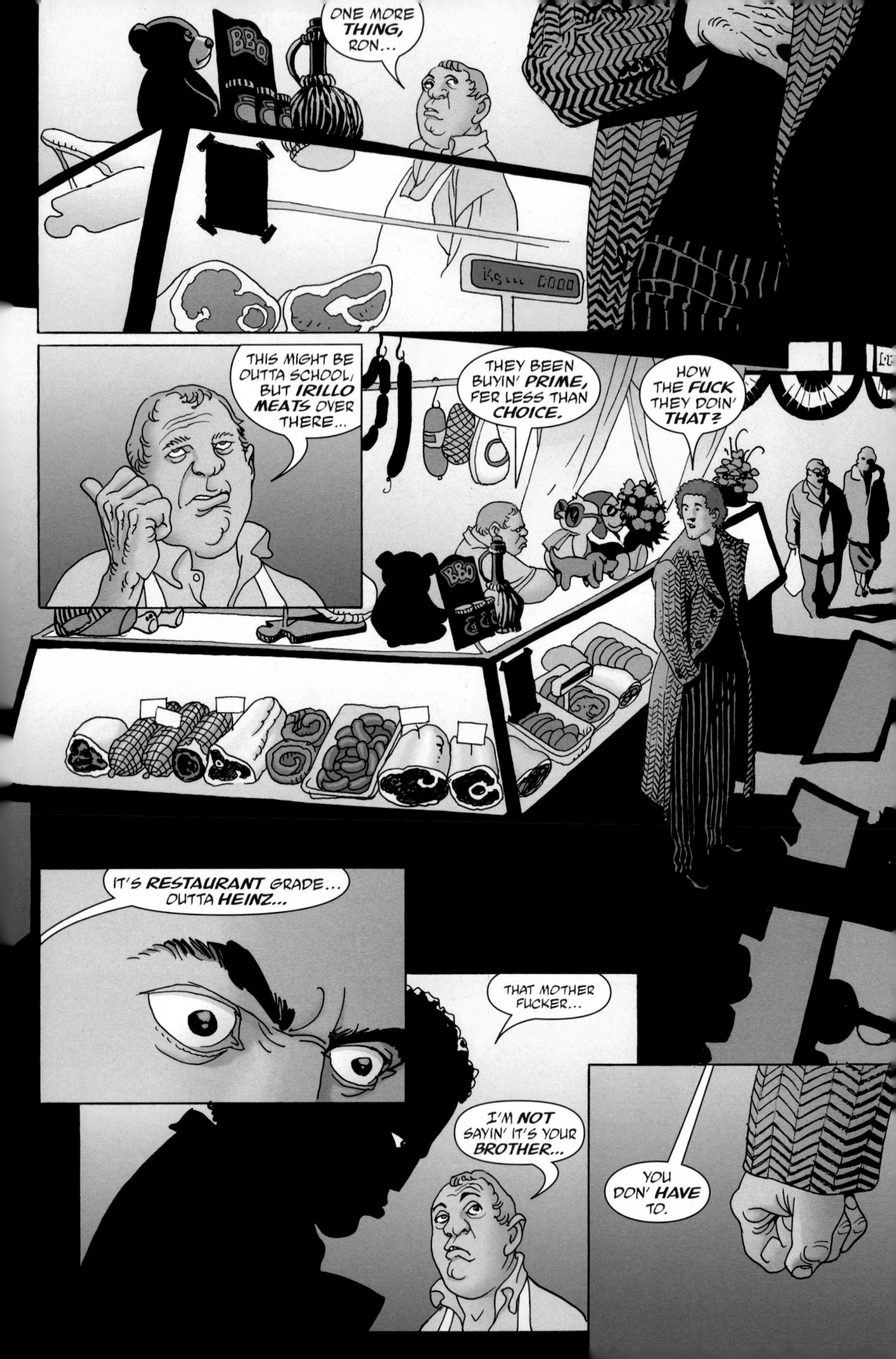
ONE MORE THING, RON...
THIS MIGHT BE OUTTA SCHOOL, BUT IRILLO MEATS OVER THERE...
THEY BEEN BUYIN' PRIME, FER LESS THAN CHOICE.
HOW THE FUCK THEY DOIN' THAT?
IT'S RESTAURANT GRADE... OUTTA HEINZ...
THAT MOTHER FUCKER...
I'M NOT SAYIN' IT'S YOUR BROTHER...
YOU DON' HAVE TO.

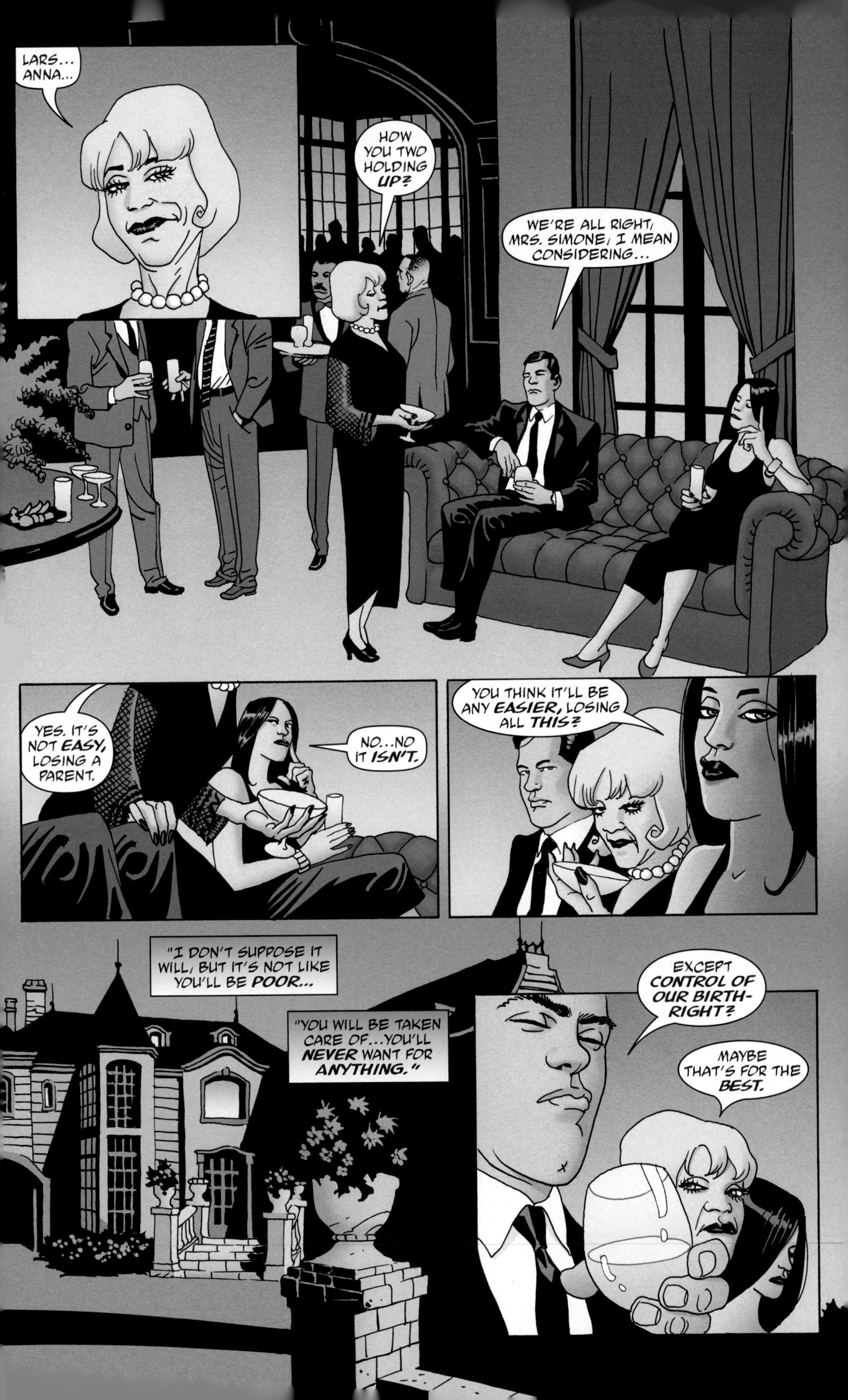

LARS... ANNA...
HOW YOU TWO HOLDING UP?
WE'RE ALL RIGHT, MRS. SIMONE, I MEAN CONSIDERING...
YES. IT'S NOT EASY, LOSING A PARENT.
NO...NO IT ISN'T.
YOU THINK IT'LL BE ANY EASIER, LOSING ALL THIS?
"I DON'T SUPPOSE IT WILL, BUT IT'S NOT LIKE YOU'LL BE POOR...
"YOU WILL BE TAKEN CARE OF...YOU'LL NEVER WANT FOR ANYTHING."
EXCEPT CONTROL OF OUR BIRTH-RIGHT?
MAYBE THAT'S FOR THE BEST.

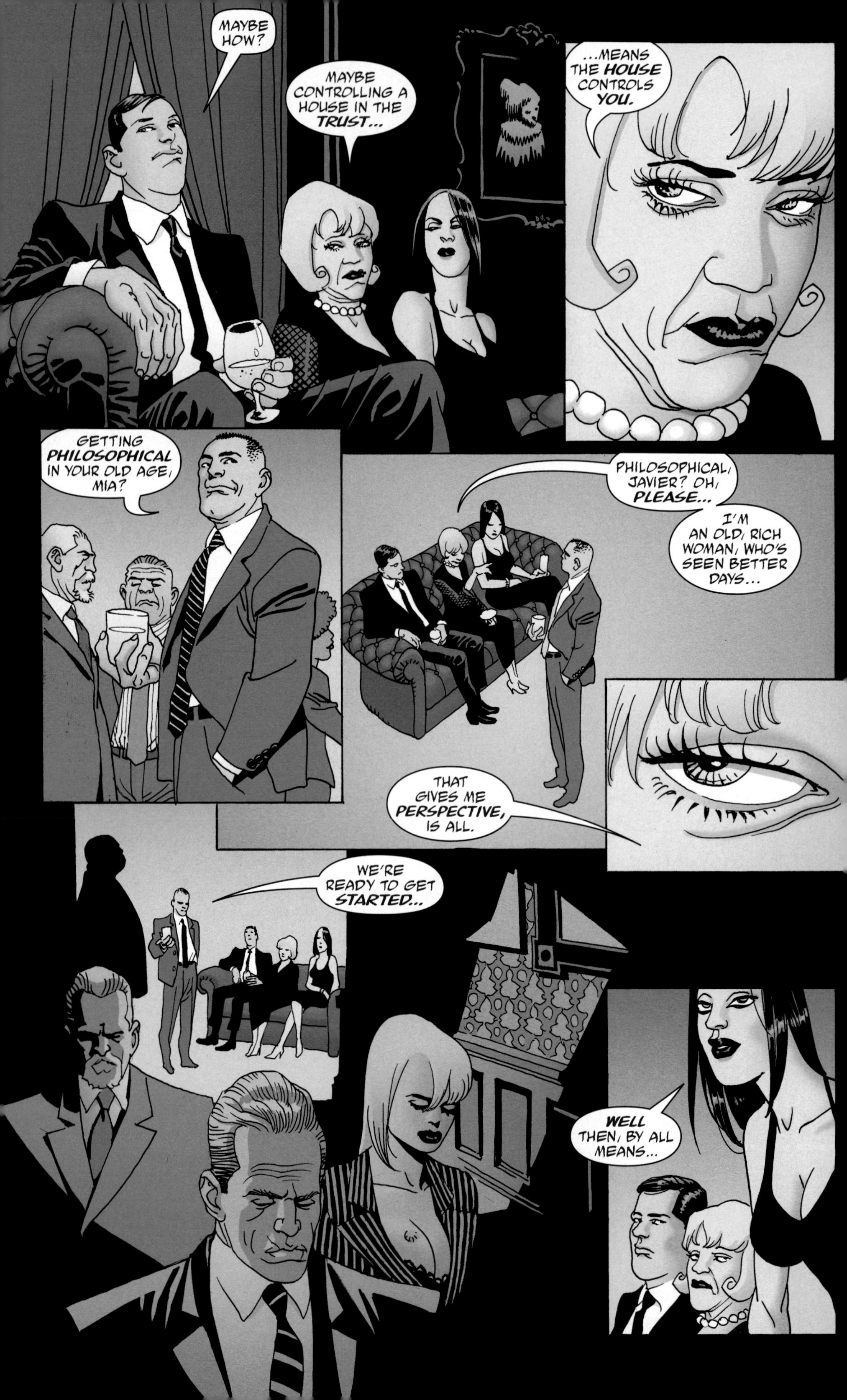
MAYBE HOW?
MAYBE CONTROLLING A HOUSE IN THE TRUST...
...MEANS THE HOUSE CONTROLS YOU.
GETTING PHILOSOPHICAL IN YOUR OLD AGE, MIA?
PHILOSOPHICAL, JAVIER? OH, PLEASE...
I'M AN OLD, RICH WOMAN, WHO'S SEEN BETTER DAYS...
THAT GIVES ME PERSPECTIVE, IS ALL.
WE'RE READY TO GET STARTED...
WELL THEN, BY ALL MEANS...

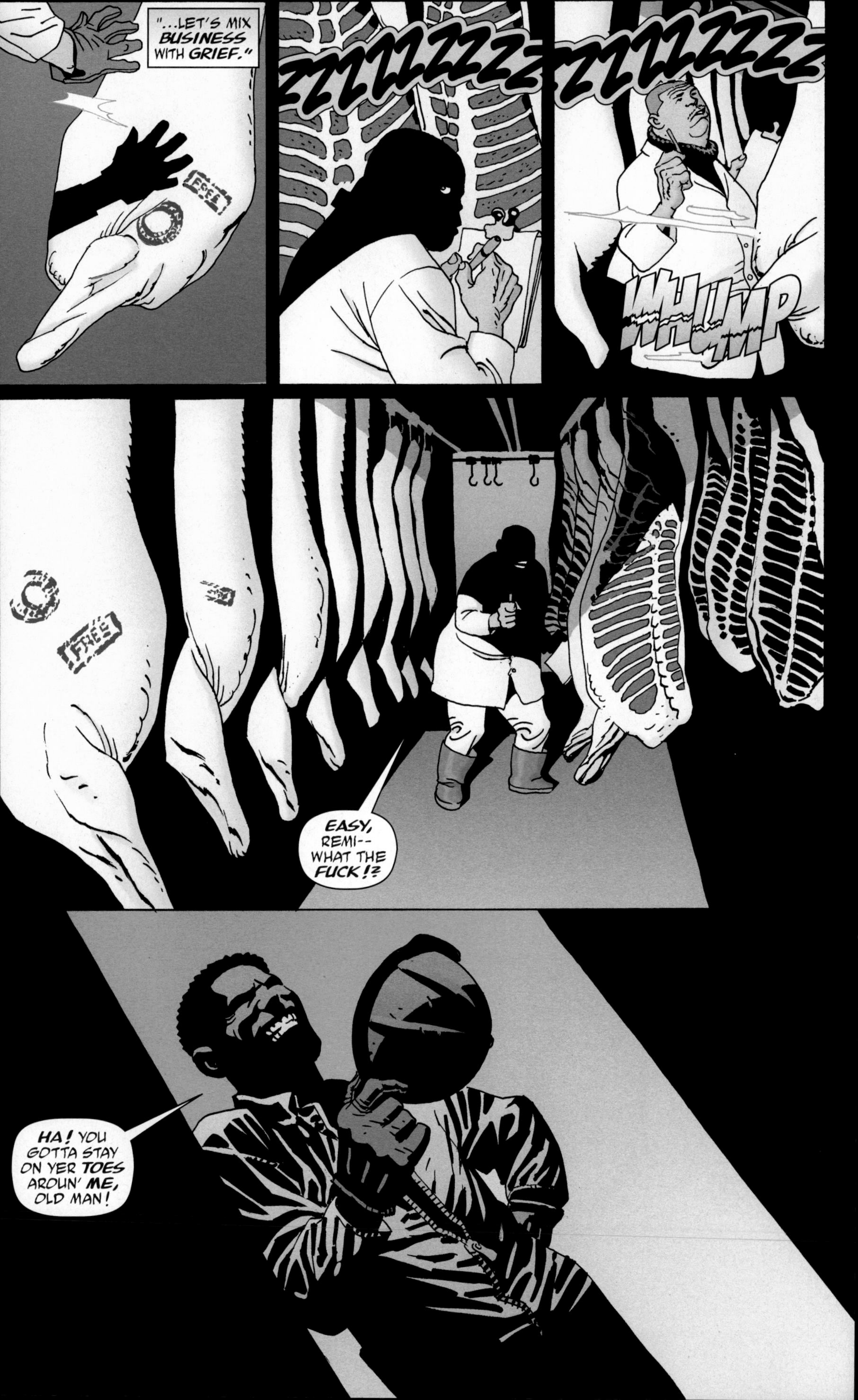
"...LET'S MIX BUSINESS WITH GRIEF."
ZZZZZZZZZZZZZZZZ
WHUMP
FREE
FREE
EASY, REMI-- WHAT THE FUCK!?
HA! YOU GOTTA STAY ON YER TOES AROUN' ME, OLD MAN!

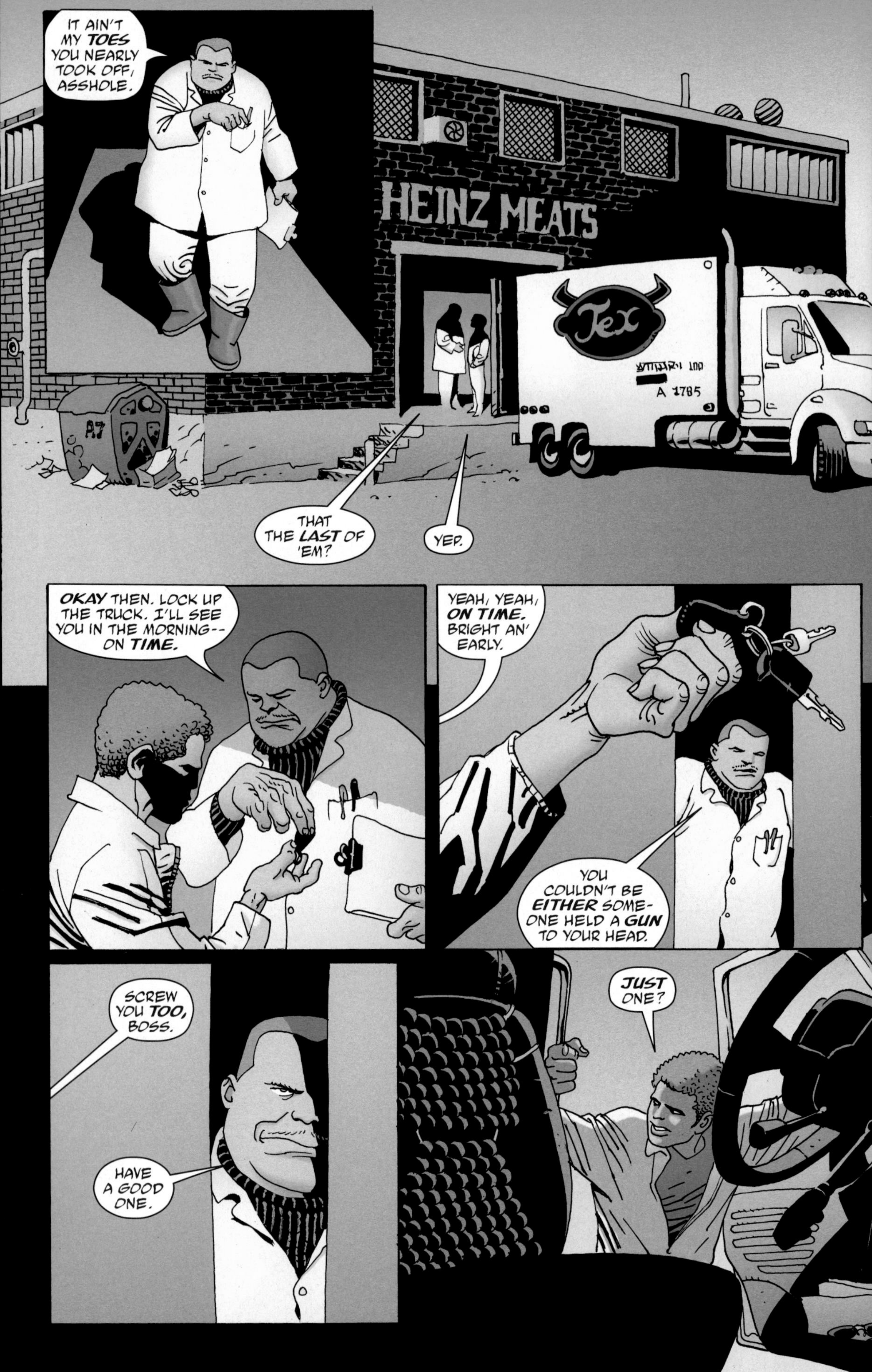
HEINZ MEATS
Tex
A 1785
A7
IT AIN'T MY TOES YOU NEARLY TOOK OFF, ASSHOLE.
THAT THE LAST OF 'EM?
YEP.
OKAY THEN. LOCK UP THE TRUCK. I'LL SEE YOU IN THE MORNING-- ON TIME.
YEAH, YEAH, ON TIME. BRIGHT AN' EARLY.
YOU COULDN'T BE EITHER SOME-ONE HELD A GUN TO YOUR HEAD.
SCREW YOU TOO, BOSS.
HAVE A GOOD ONE.
JUST ONE?

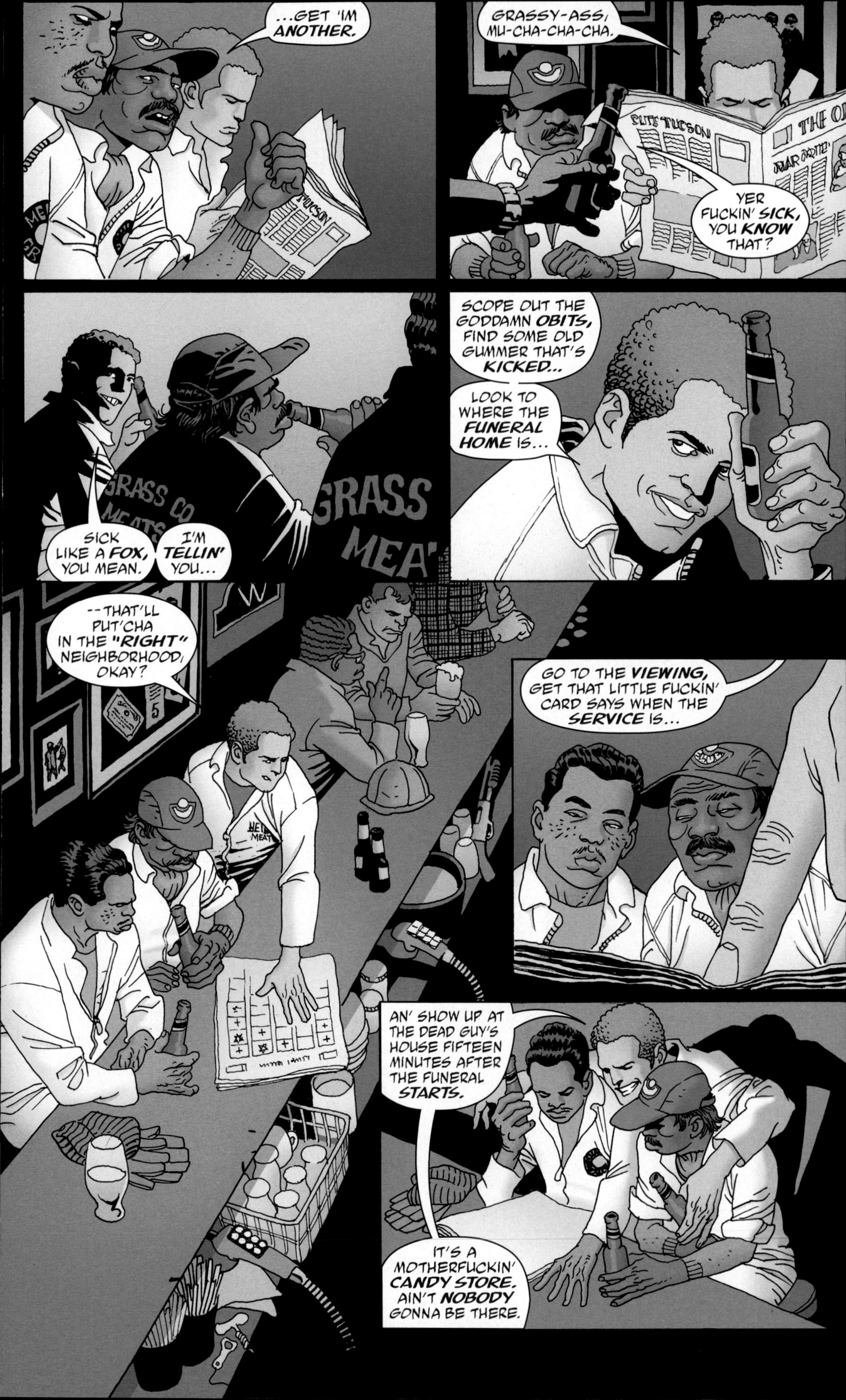
...GET 'IM ANOTHER.
GRASSY-ASS, MU-CHA-CHA-CHA.
YER FUCKIN' SICK, YOU KNOW THAT?
SICK LIKE A FOX, YOU MEAN.
I'M TELLIN' YOU...
SCOPE OUT THE GODDAMN OBITS, FIND SOME OLD GUMMER THAT'S KICKED...
LOOK TO WHERE THE FUNERAL HOME IS...
--THAT'LL PUT'CHA IN THE "RIGHT" NEIGHBORHOOD, OKAY?
GO TO THE VIEWING, GET THAT LITTLE FUCKIN' CARD SAYS WHEN THE SERVICE IS...
AN' SHOW UP AT THE DEAD GUY'S HOUSE FIFTEEN MINUTES AFTER THE FUNERAL STARTS.
IT'S A MOTHERFUCKIN' CANDY STORE. AIN'T NOBODY GONNA BE THERE.

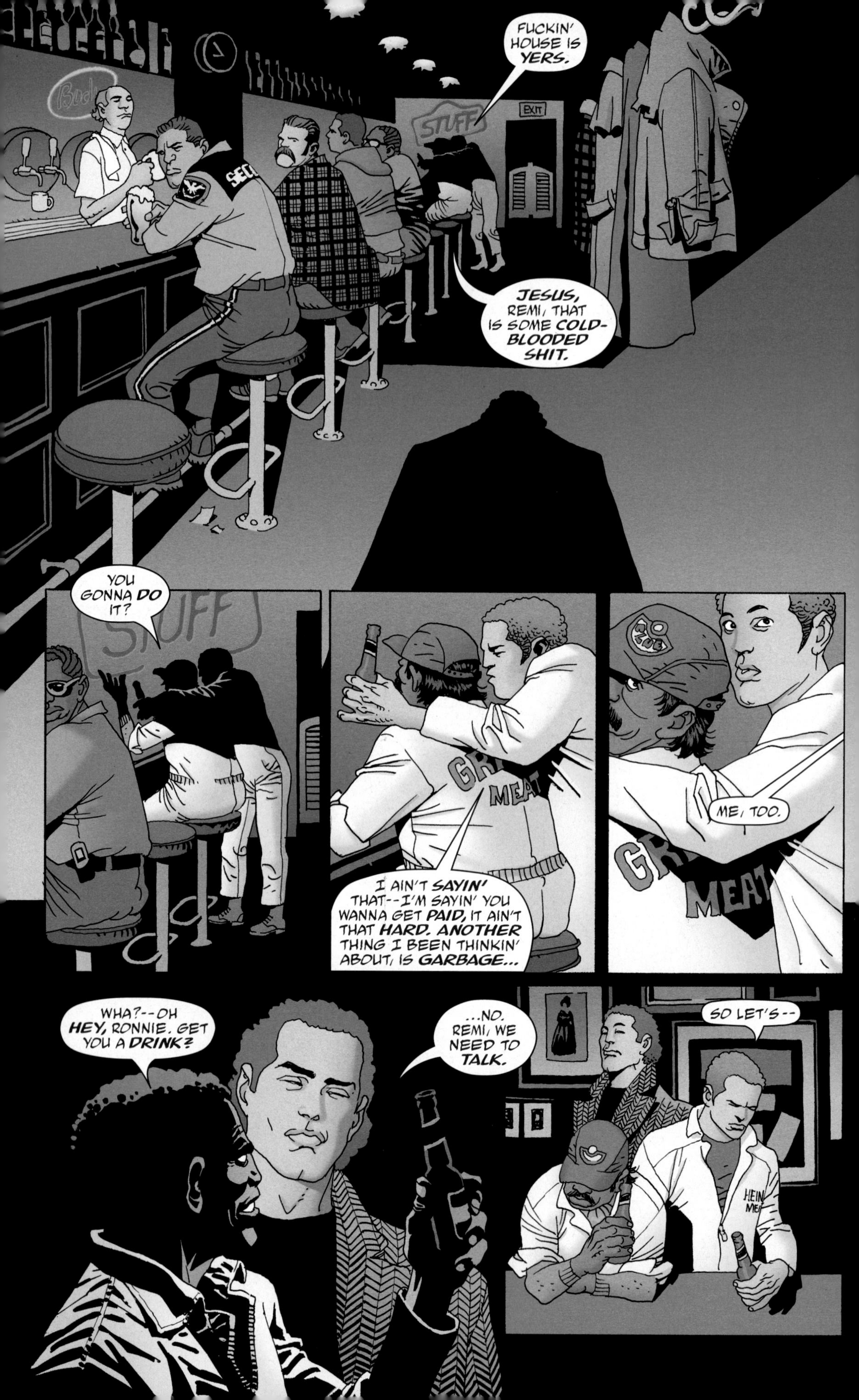
FUCKIN' HOUSE IS YERS.
JESUS, REMI, THAT IS SOME COLD-BLOODED SHIT.
YOU GONNA DO IT?
I AIN'T SAYIN' THAT--I'M SAYIN' YOU WANNA GET PAID, IT AIN'T THAT HARD. ANOTHER THING I BEEN THINKIN' ABOUT, IS GARBAGE...
ME, TOO.
WHA?--OH HEY, RONNIE. GET YOU A DRINK?
...NO. REMI, WE NEED TO TALK.
SO LET'S--

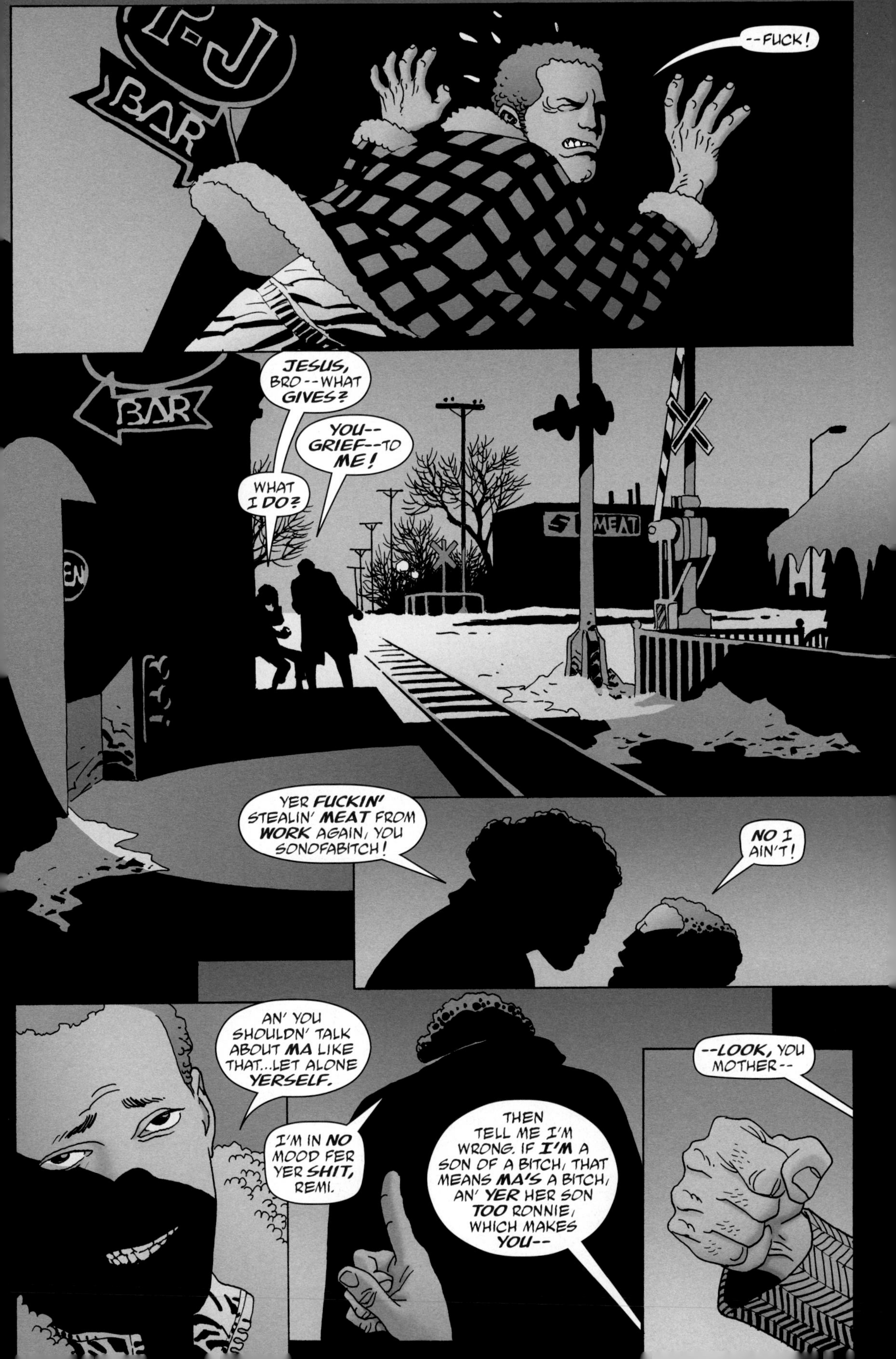
P-J
BAR
--FUCK!
BAR
JESUS, BRO--WHAT GIVES?
YOU--GRIEF--TO ME!
WHAT I DO?
MEAT
YER FUCKIN' STEALIN' MEAT FROM WORK AGAIN, YOU SONOFABITCH!
NO I AIN'T!
AN' YOU SHOULDN' TALK ABOUT MA LIKE THAT...LET ALONE YERSELF.
I'M IN NO MOOD FER YER SHIT, REMI.
THEN TELL ME I'M WRONG. IF I'M A SON OF A BITCH, THAT MEANS MA'S A BITCH, AN' YER HER SON TOO RONNIE, WHICH MAKES YOU--
--LOOK, YOU MOTHER--

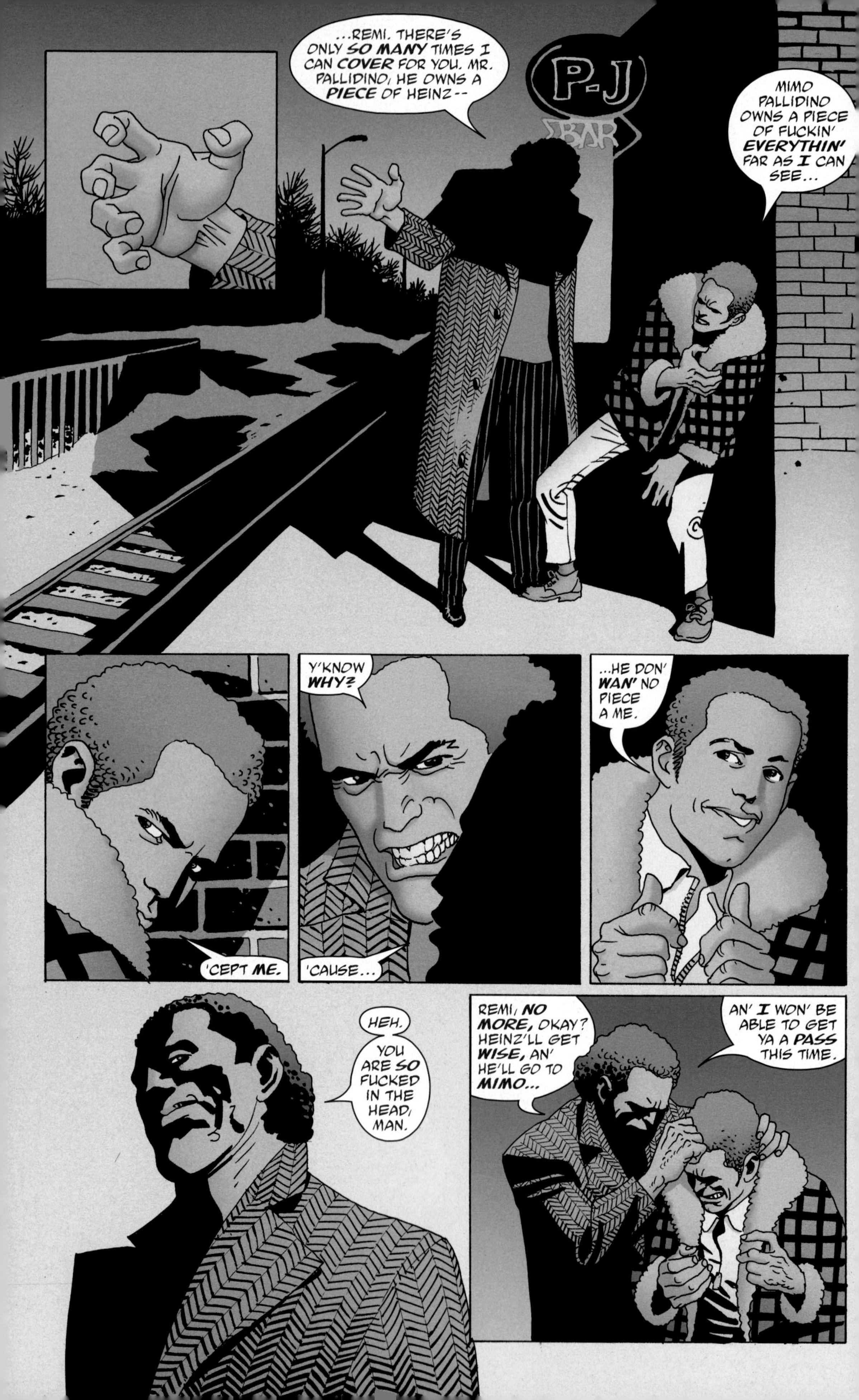
...REMI. THERE'S ONLY SO MANY TIMES I CAN COVER FOR YOU. MR. PALLIDINO, HE OWNS A PIECE OF HEINZ--
P-J
BAR
MIMO PALLIDINO OWNS A PIECE OF FUCKIN' EVERYTHIN' FAR AS I CAN SEE...
'CEPT ME.
Y'KNOW WHY?
'CAUSE...
...HE DON' WAN' NO PIECE A ME.
HEH.
YOU ARE SO FUCKED IN THE HEAD, MAN.
REMI, NO MORE, OKAY? HEINZ'LL GET WISE, AN' HE'LL GO TO MIMO...
AN' I WON' BE ABLE TO GET YA A PASS THIS TIME.

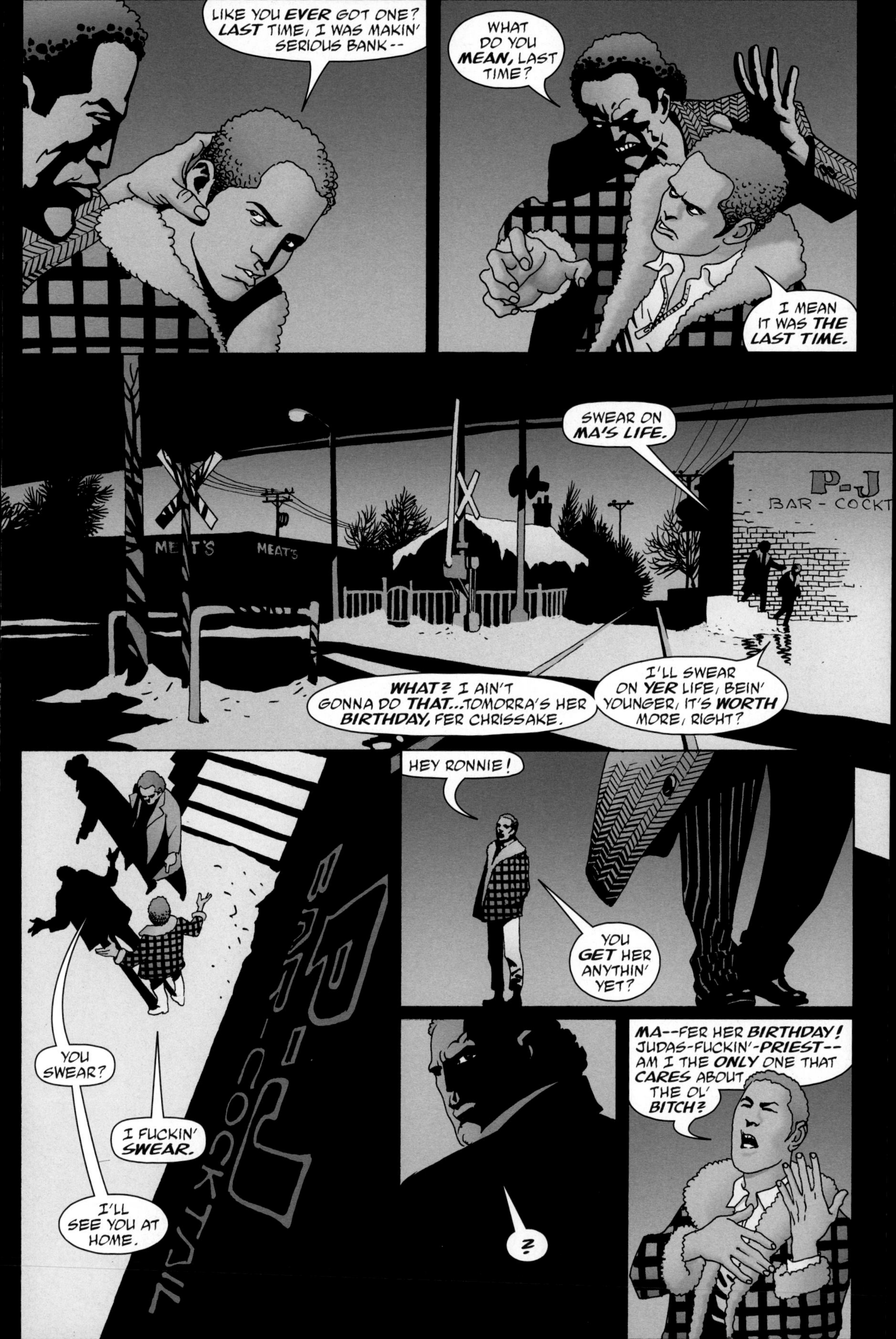
LIKE YOU EVER GOT ONE? LAST TIME, I WAS MAKIN' SERIOUS BANK --
WHAT DO YOU MEAN, LAST TIME?
I MEAN IT WAS THE LAST TIME.
SWEAR ON MA'S LIFE.
P-J
BAR-COCKT
MEAT'S
MEAT'S
WHAT? I AIN'T GONNA DO THAT...TOMORRA'S HER BIRTHDAY, FER CHRISSAKE.
I'LL SWEAR ON YER LIFE, BEIN' YOUNGER, IT'S WORTH MORE, RIGHT?
YOU SWEAR?
I FUCKIN' SWEAR.
I'LL SEE YOU AT HOME.
HEY RONNIE!
YOU GET HER ANYTHIN' YET?
?
MA--FER HER BIRTHDAY! JUDAS-FUCKIN'-PRIEST-- AM I THE ONLY ONE THAT CARES ABOUT THE OL' BITCH?

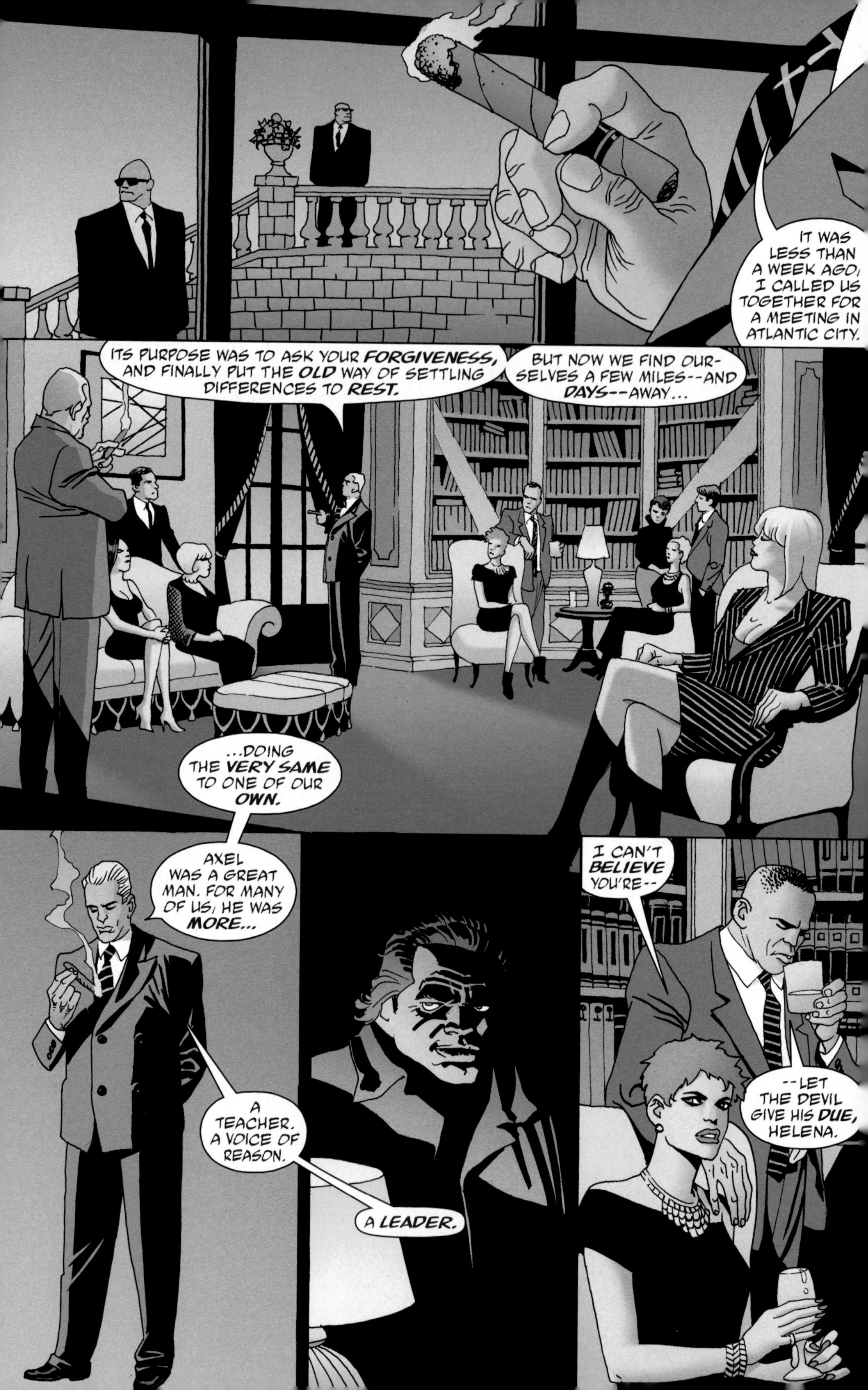

IT WAS LESS THAN A WEEK AGO, I CALLED US TOGETHER FOR A MEETING IN ATLANTIC CITY.
ITS PURPOSE WAS TO ASK YOUR FORGIVENESS, AND FINALLY PUT THE OLD WAY OF SETTLING DIFFERENCES TO REST.
BUT NOW WE FIND OURSELVES A FEW MILES--AND DAYS--AWAY...
...DOING THE VERY SAME TO ONE OF OUR OWN.
AXEL WAS A GREAT MAN. FOR MANY OF US, HE WAS MORE...
A TEACHER. A VOICE OF REASON.
A LEADER.
I CAN'T BELIEVE YOU'RE--
--LET THE DEVIL GIVE HIS DUE, HELENA.

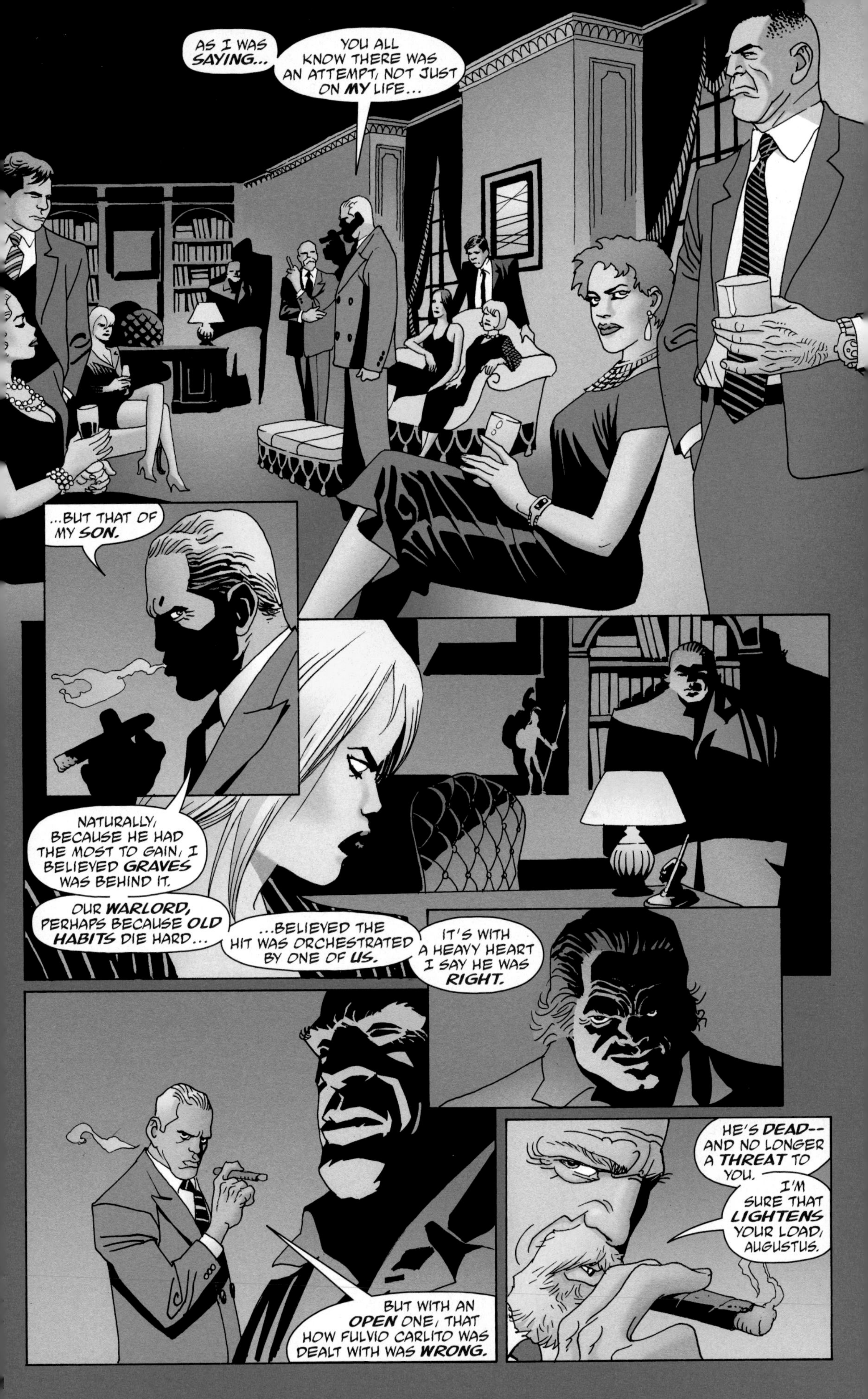
AS I WAS SAYING...
YOU ALL KNOW THERE WAS AN ATTEMPT, NOT JUST ON MY LIFE...
...BUT THAT OF MY SON.
NATURALLY, BECAUSE HE HAD THE MOST TO GAIN, I BELIEVED GRAVES WAS BEHIND IT.
OUR WARLORD, PERHAPS BECAUSE OLD HABITS DIE HARD...
...BELIEVED THE HIT WAS ORCHESTRATED BY ONE OF US.
IT'S WITH A HEAVY HEART I SAY HE WAS RIGHT.
BUT WITH AN OPEN ONE, THAT HOW FULVIO CARLITO WAS DEALT WITH WAS WRONG.
HE'S DEAD-- AND NO LONGER A THREAT TO YOU.
I'M SURE THAT LIGHTENS YOUR LOAD, AUGUSTUS.

IT DOESN'T, SIGMAR. BECAUSE FULVIO CONFESSED THAT HE DIDN'T ACT *ALONE.*

ARE YOU SAYING--

--NO, I'M *NOT.* THAT'S MY *POINT...*

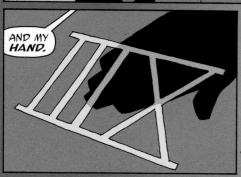

AND MY *HAND.*

GRAVES WANTS US ALL *DEAD.*

WELL, WE *CAN'T* DIE ANYMORE. I AM *NOT* THE ENEMY...

AND NEITHER ARE *YOU.*

WHAT'S PAST IS PAST. THERE'S NOTHING THAT CAN *CHANGE* THAT. BUT FOR THE TRUST TO SURVIVE, *EVERY* HOUSE MUST STAND TOGETHER.

INCLUDING THE HOUSE OF NAGEL.

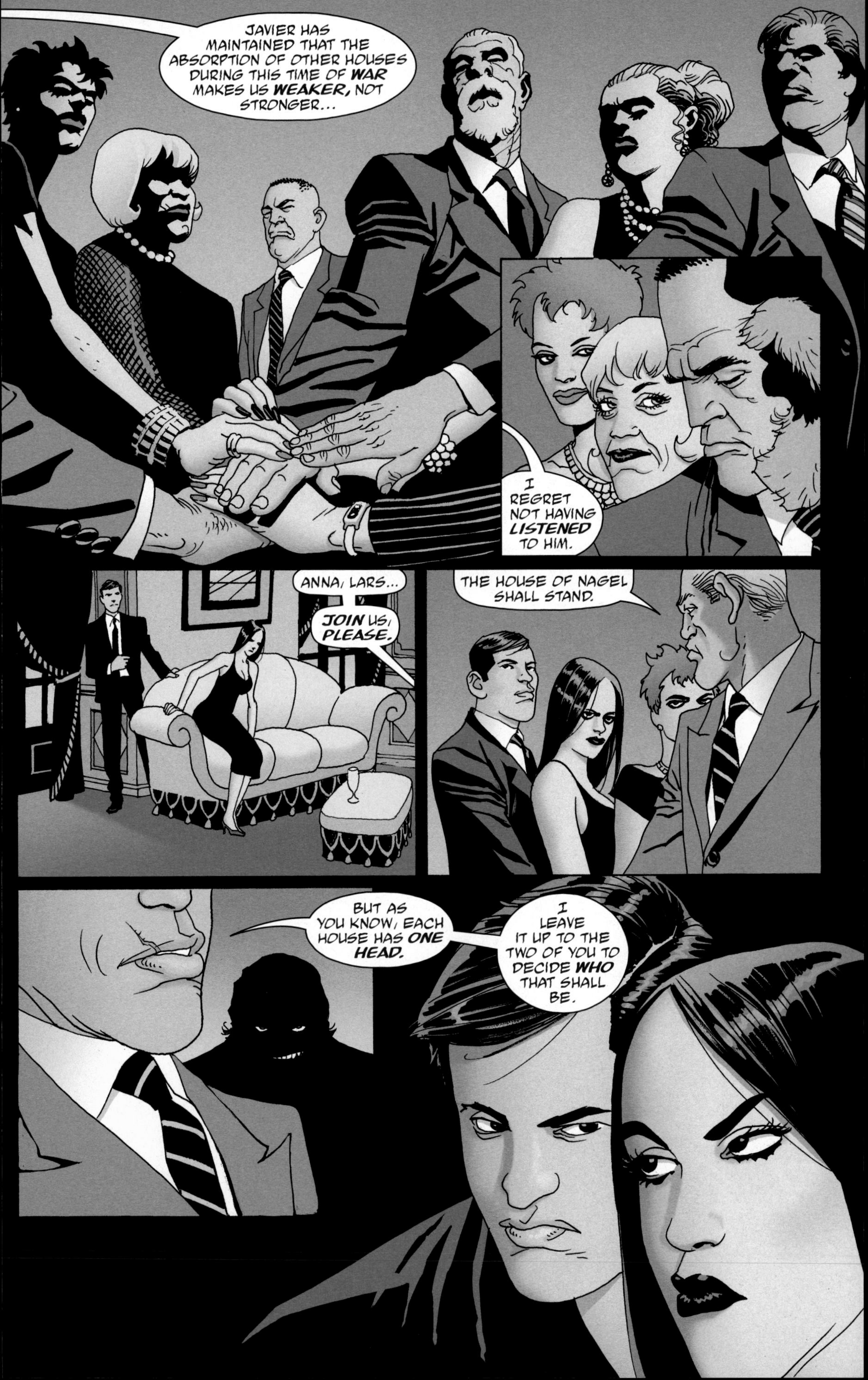
JAVIER HAS MAINTAINED THAT THE ABSORPTION OF OTHER HOUSES DURING THIS TIME OF WAR MAKES US WEAKER, NOT STRONGER...
I REGRET NOT HAVING LISTENED TO HIM.
ANNA, LARS...
JOIN US, PLEASE.
THE HOUSE OF NAGEL SHALL STAND.
BUT AS YOU KNOW, EACH HOUSE HAS ONE HEAD.
I LEAVE IT UP TO THE TWO OF YOU TO DECIDE WHO THAT SHALL BE.

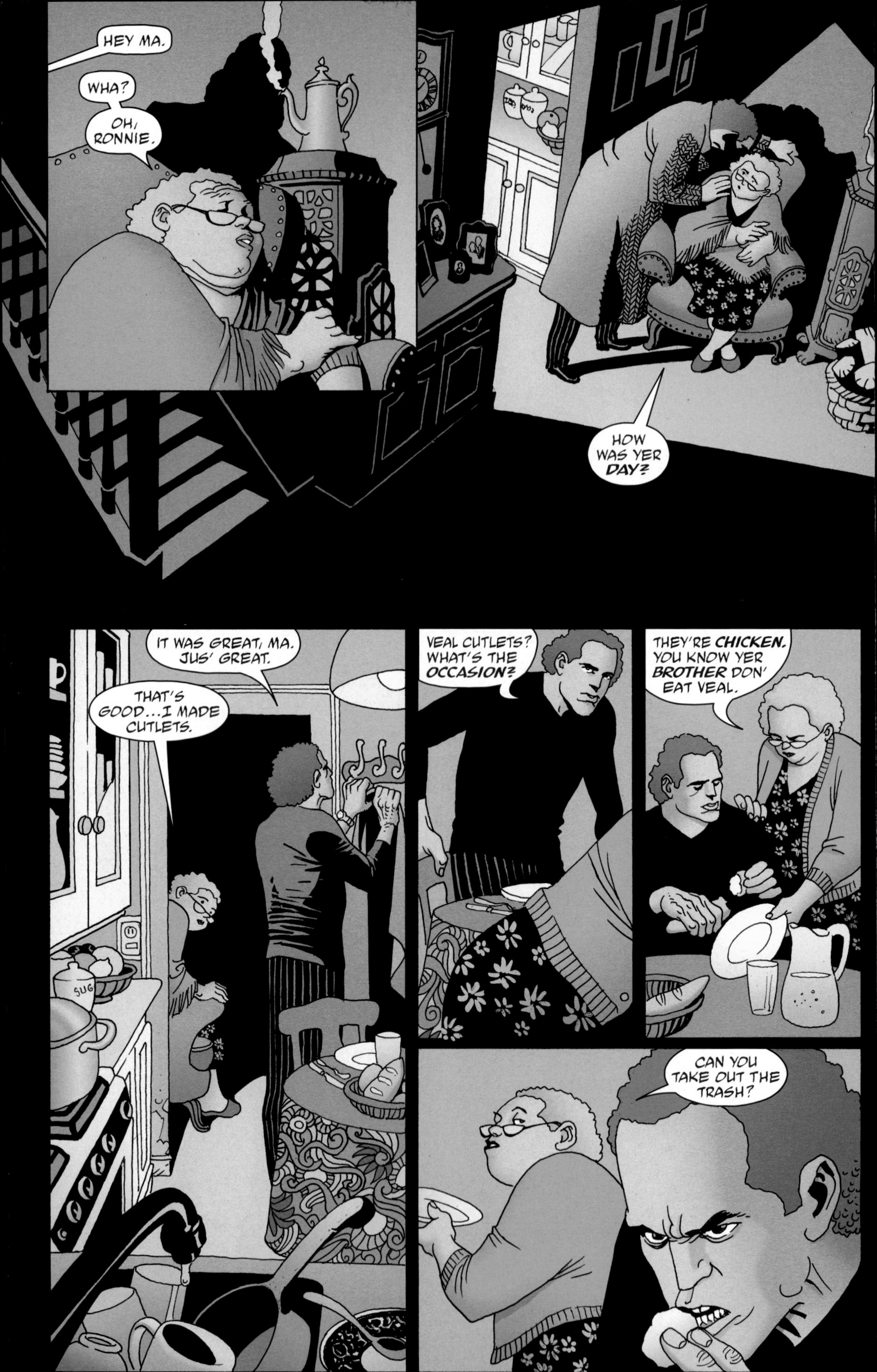
HEY MA.
WHA?
OH, RONNIE.
HOW WAS YER DAY?
IT WAS GREAT, MA. JUS' GREAT.
THAT'S GOOD...I MADE CUTLETS.
VEAL CUTLETS? WHAT'S THE OCCASION?
THEY'RE CHICKEN. YOU KNOW YER BROTHER DON' EAT VEAL.
CAN YOU TAKE OUT THE TRASH?

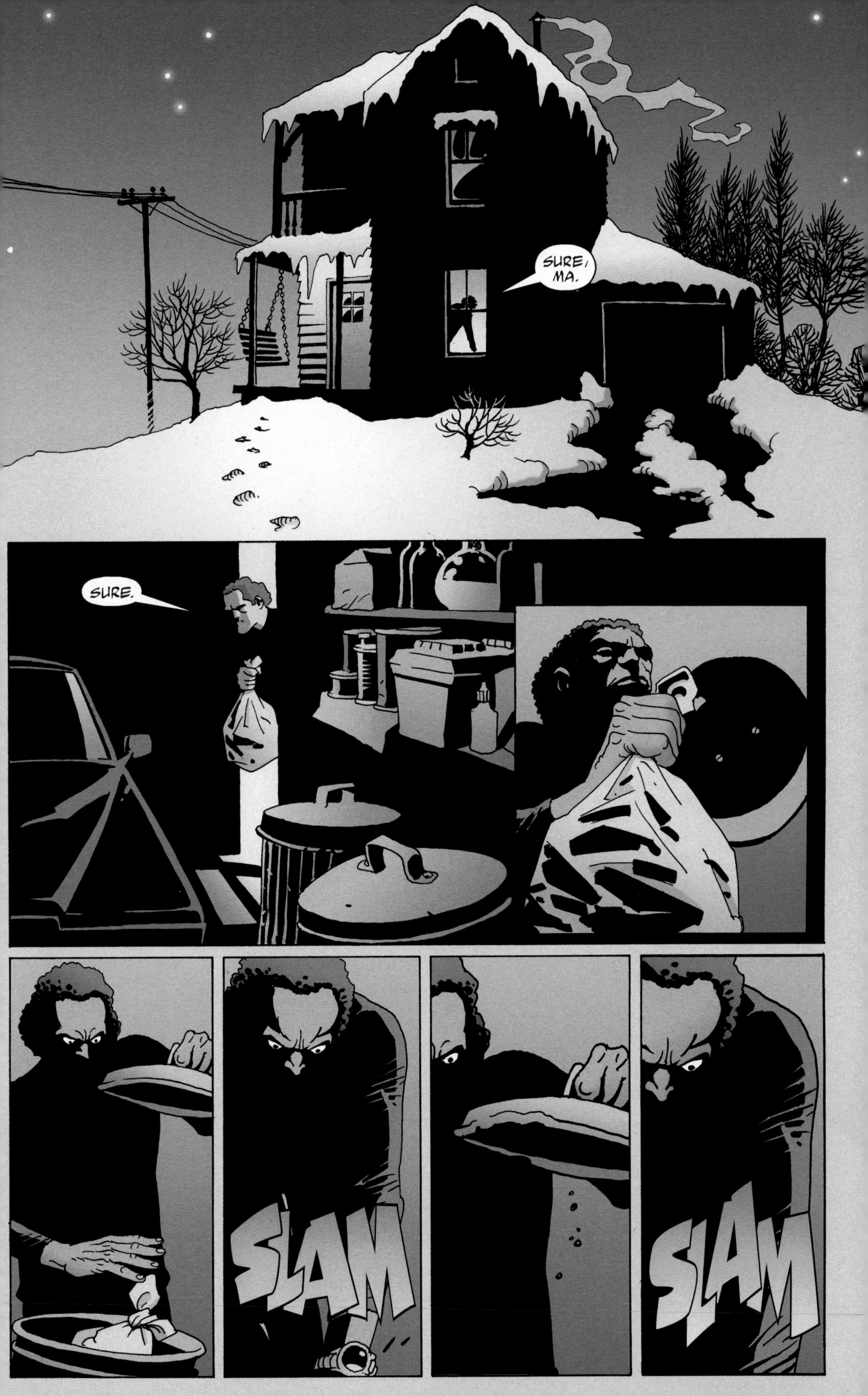
SURE, MA.
SURE.
SLAM
SLAM

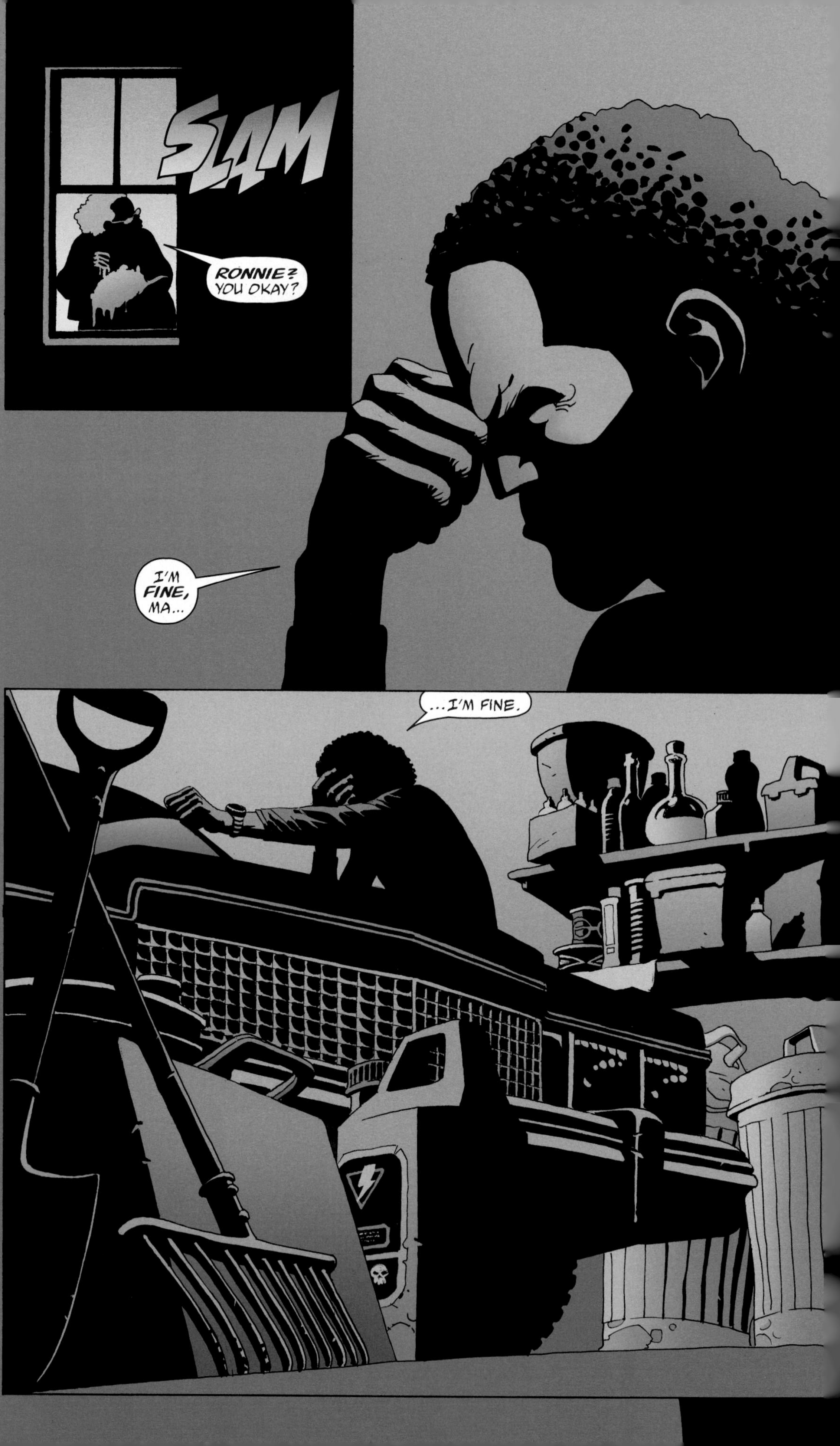
SLAM
RONNIE? YOU OKAY?
I'M FINE, MA...
...I'M FINE.

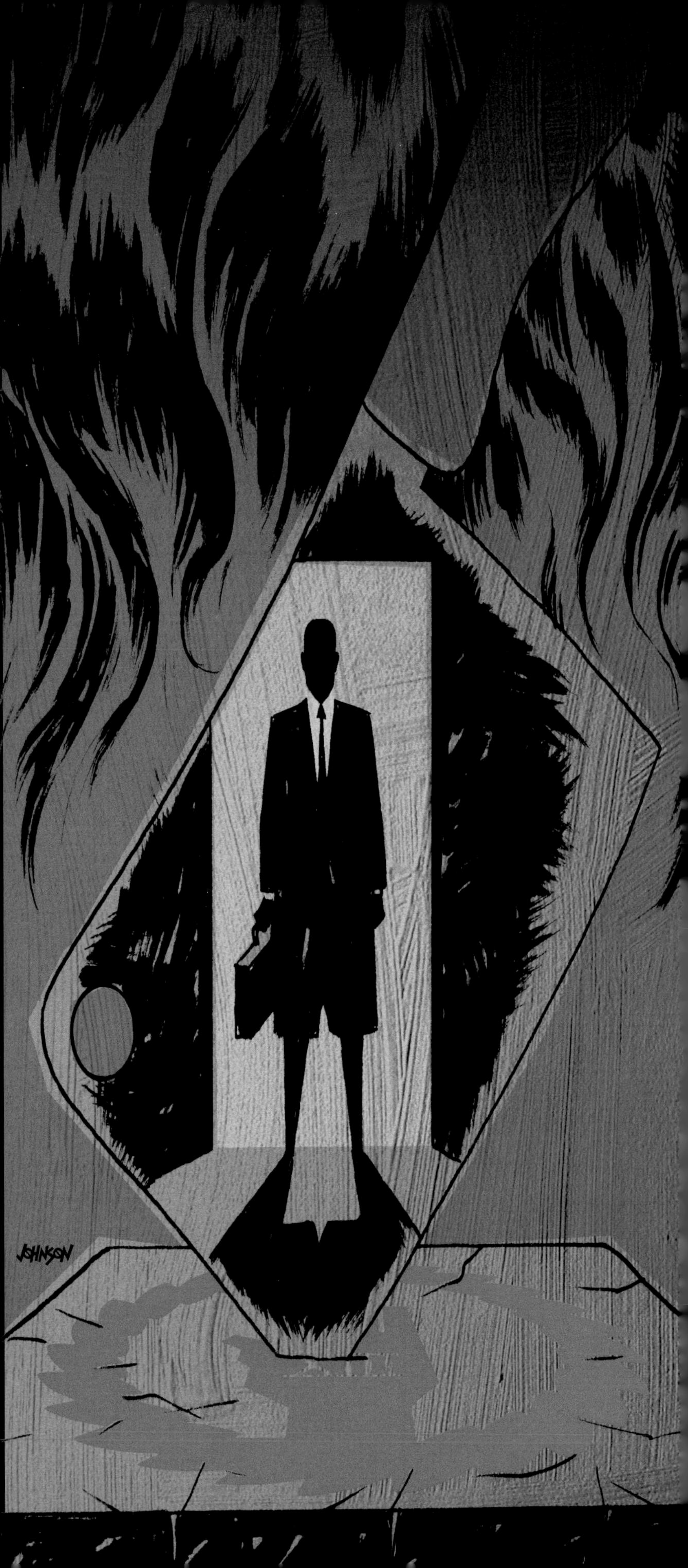
JOHNSON

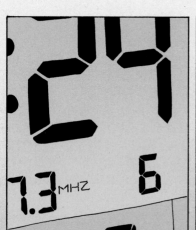

--WE GOT A THANG, THAT'S CALL' RADAH LUH-HU

HEY...

--NO RADIA'AT ALL!--

PAMMY--

HUH? WHAT *TIME* IS IT...

TIME FER *YOU* TO GO.

I'M STILL SLEEPIN'...

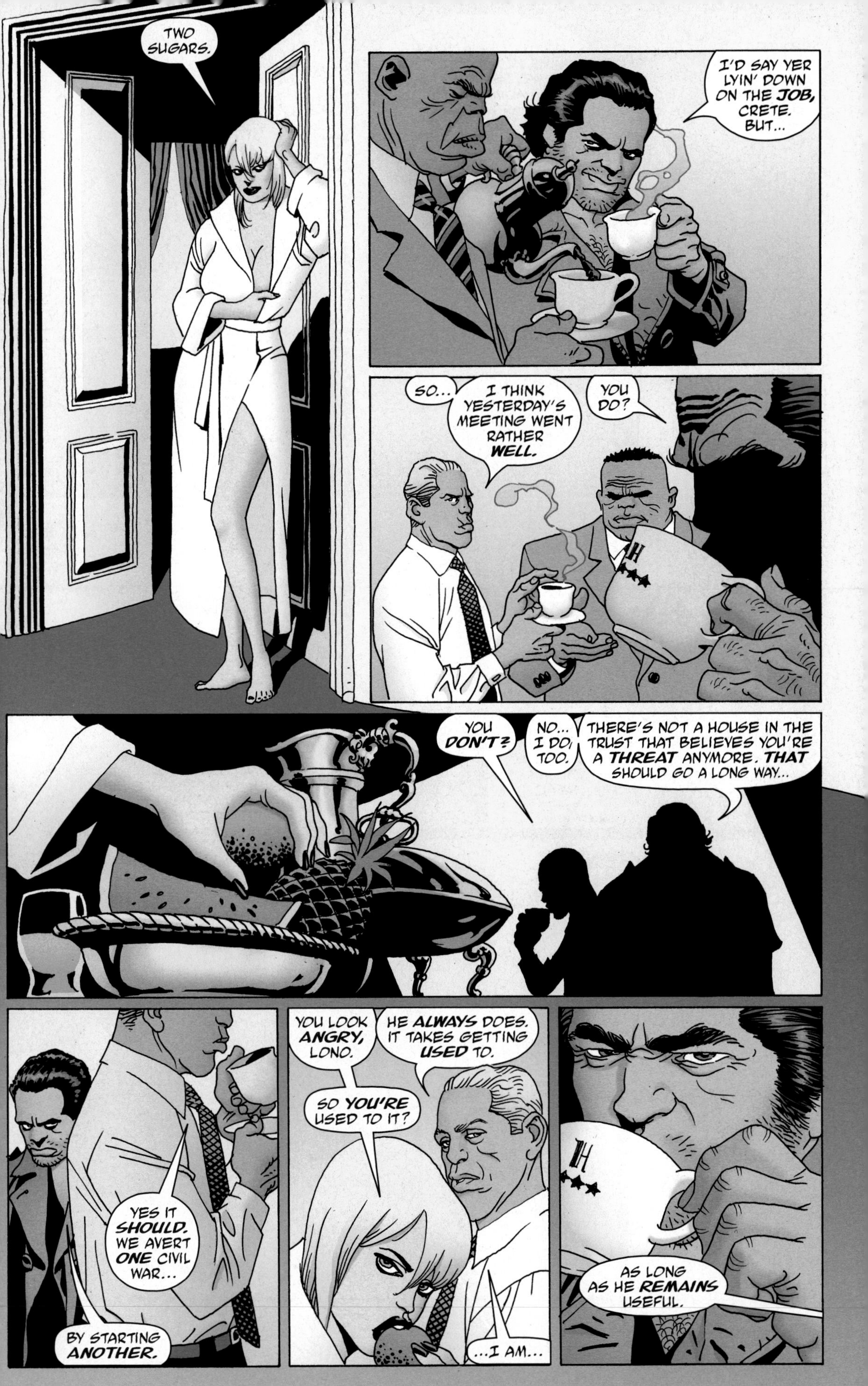
TWO SUGARS.
I'D SAY YER LYIN' DOWN ON THE JOB, CRETE. BUT...
SO...
I THINK YESTERDAY'S MEETING WENT RATHER WELL.
YOU DO?
YOU DON'T?
NO... I DO, TOO.
THERE'S NOT A HOUSE IN THE TRUST THAT BELIEVES YOU'RE A THREAT ANYMORE. THAT SHOULD GO A LONG WAY...
YES IT SHOULD. WE AVERT ONE CIVIL WAR...
BY STARTING ANOTHER.
YOU LOOK ANGRY, LONO.
HE ALWAYS DOES. IT TAKES GETTING USED TO.
SO YOU'RE USED TO IT?
...I AM...
AS LONG AS HE REMAINS USEFUL.

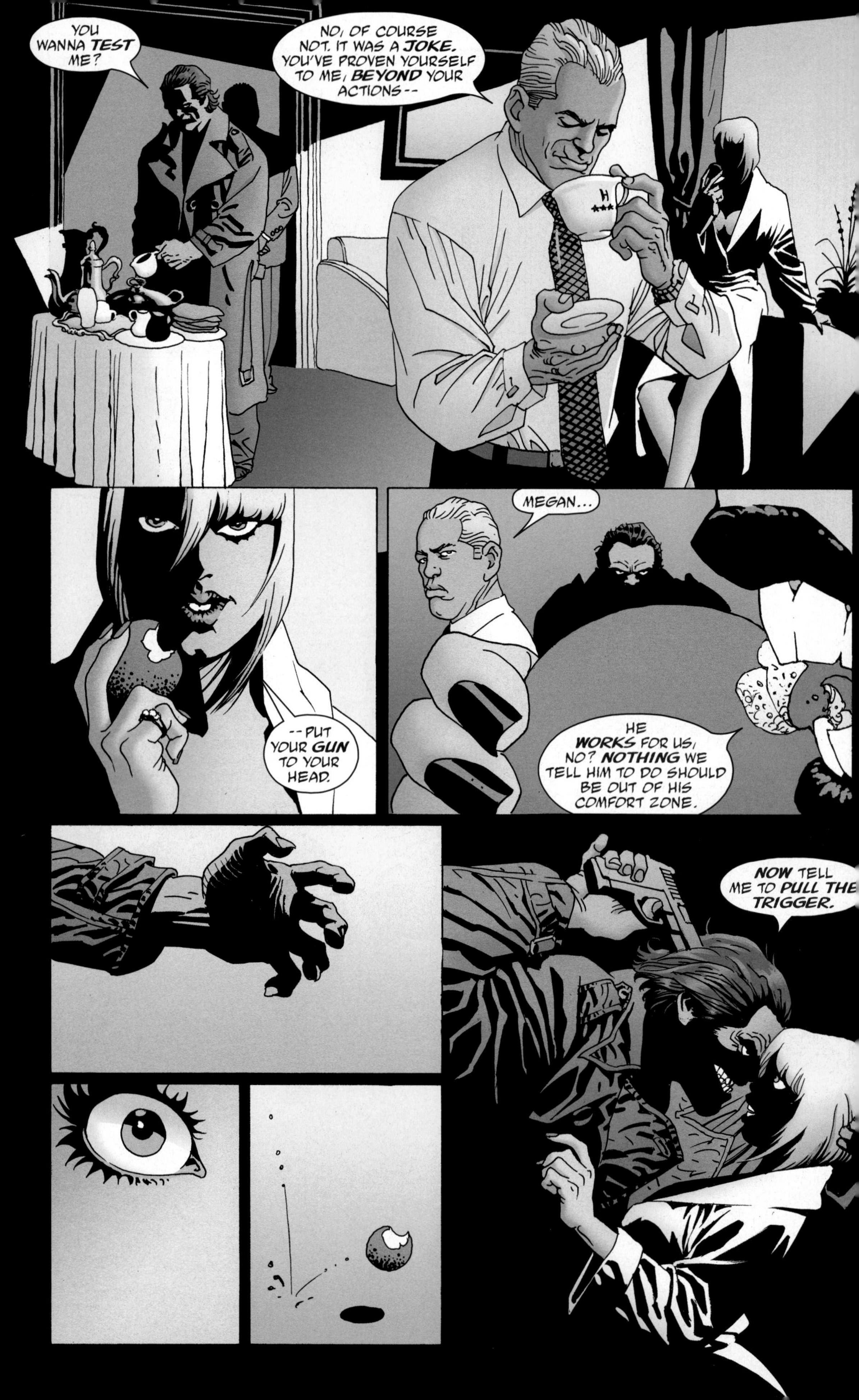
YOU WANNA **TEST** ME?
NO, OF COURSE NOT. IT WAS A **JOKE.** YOU'VE PROVEN YOURSELF TO ME, **BEYOND** YOUR ACTIONS--
--PUT YOUR **GUN** TO YOUR HEAD.
MEGAN...
HE **WORKS** FOR US, NO? **NOTHING** WE TELL HIM TO DO SHOULD BE OUT OF HIS COMFORT ZONE.
NOW TELL ME TO **PULL THE TRIGGER.**

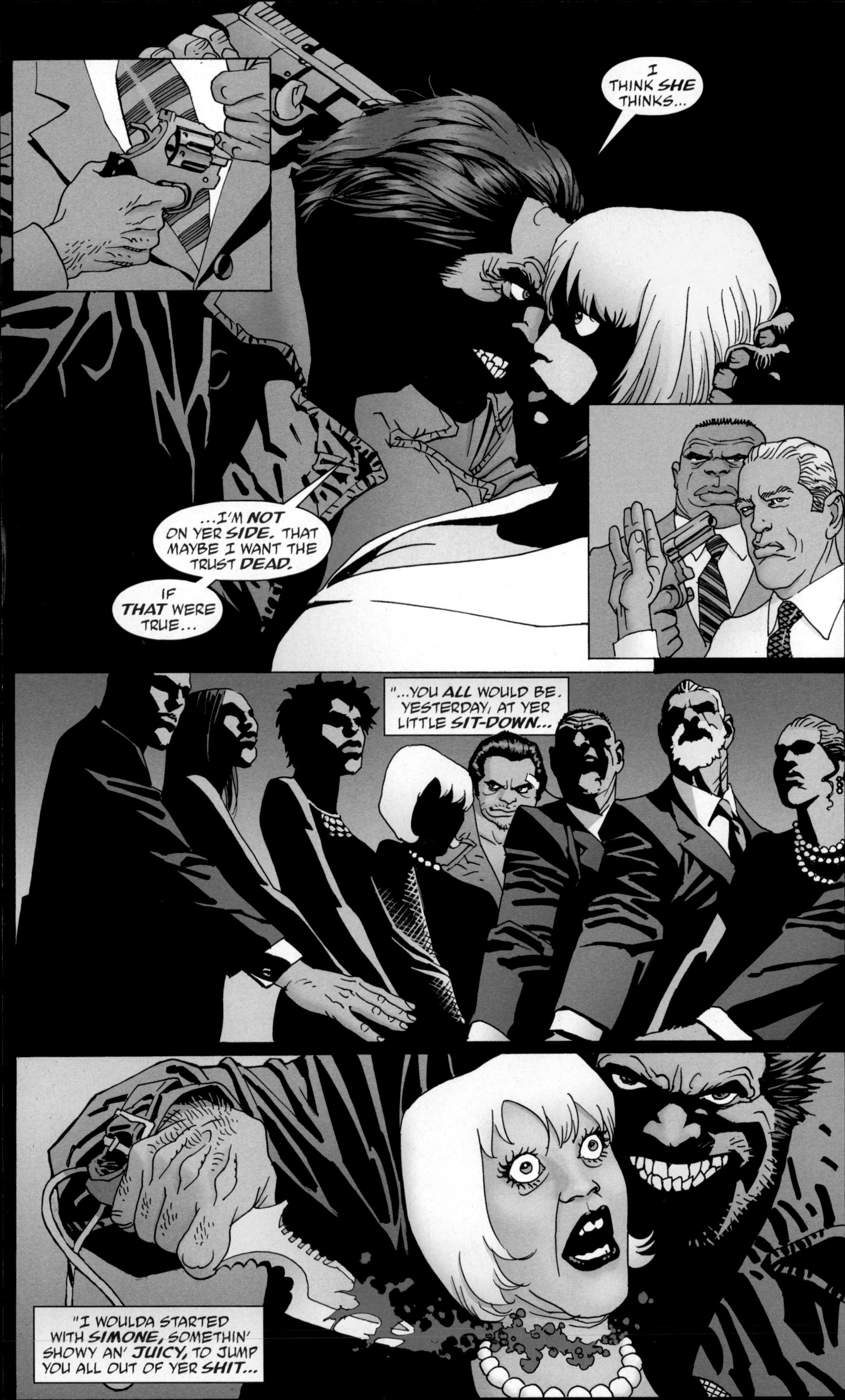
I THINK SHE THINKS...
...I'M NOT ON YER SIDE. THAT MAYBE I WANT THE TRUST DEAD.
IF THAT WERE TRUE...
"...YOU ALL WOULD BE. YESTERDAY, AT YER LITTLE SIT-DOWN...
"I WOULDA STARTED WITH SIMONE, SOMETHIN' SHOWY AN' JUICY, TO JUMP YOU ALL OUT OF YER SHIT...

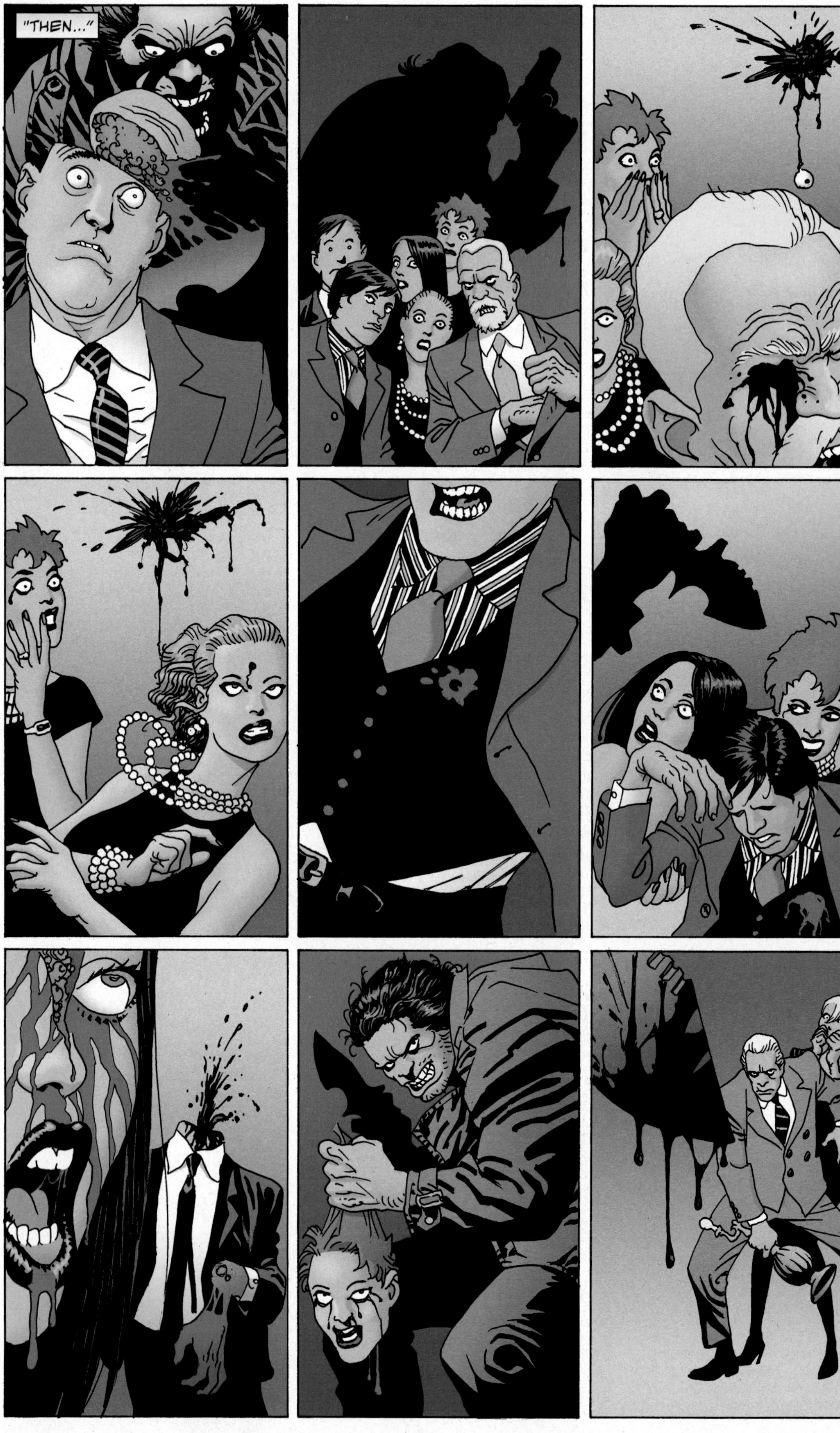
"THEN..."

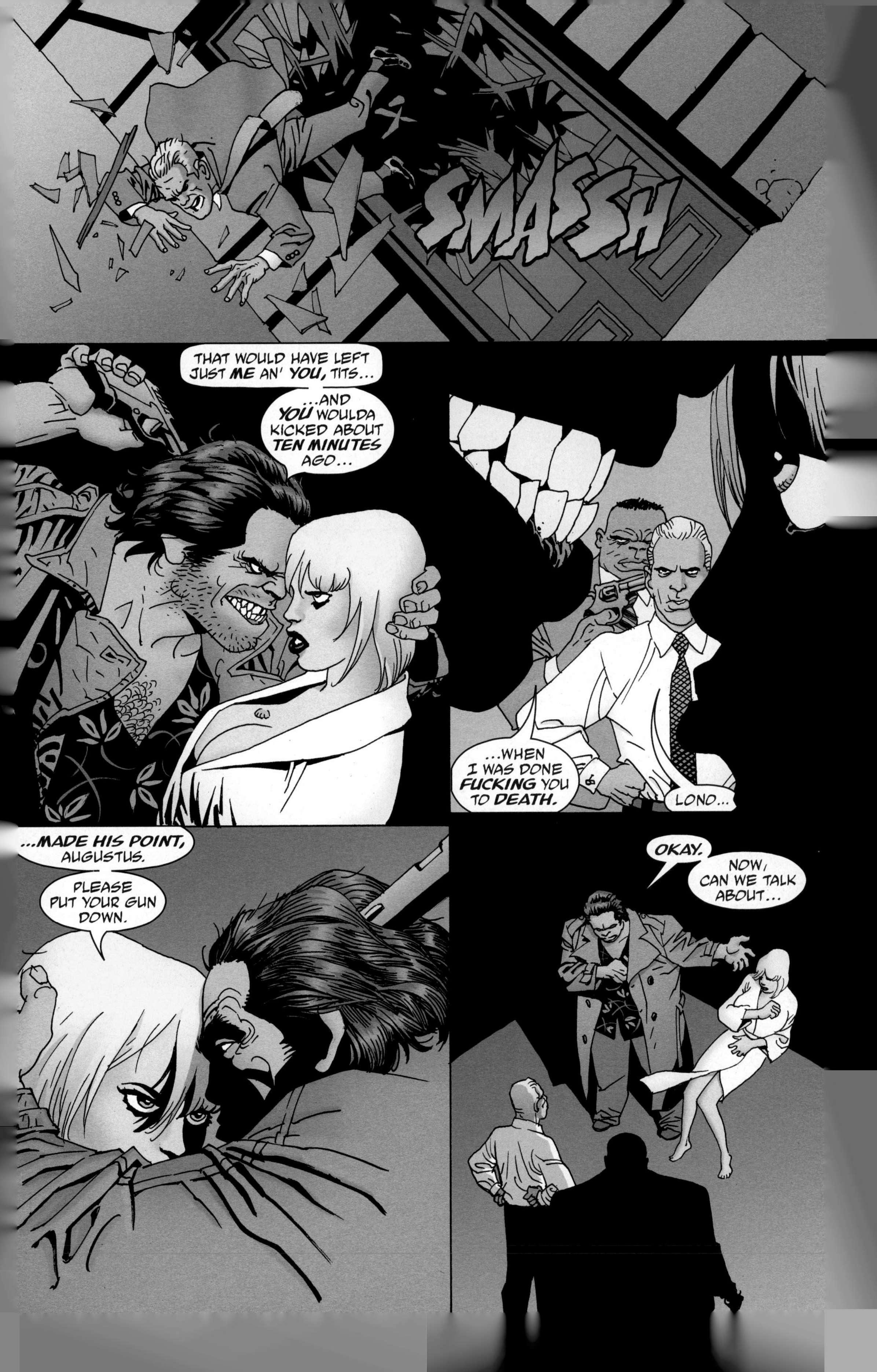
SMASH
THAT WOULD HAVE LEFT JUST ME AN' YOU, TITS...
...AND YOU WOULDA KICKED ABOUT TEN MINUTES AGO...
...WHEN I WAS DONE FUCKING YOU TO DEATH.
LONO...
...MADE HIS POINT, AUGUSTUS.
PLEASE PUT YOUR GUN DOWN.
OKAY.
NOW, CAN WE TALK ABOUT...

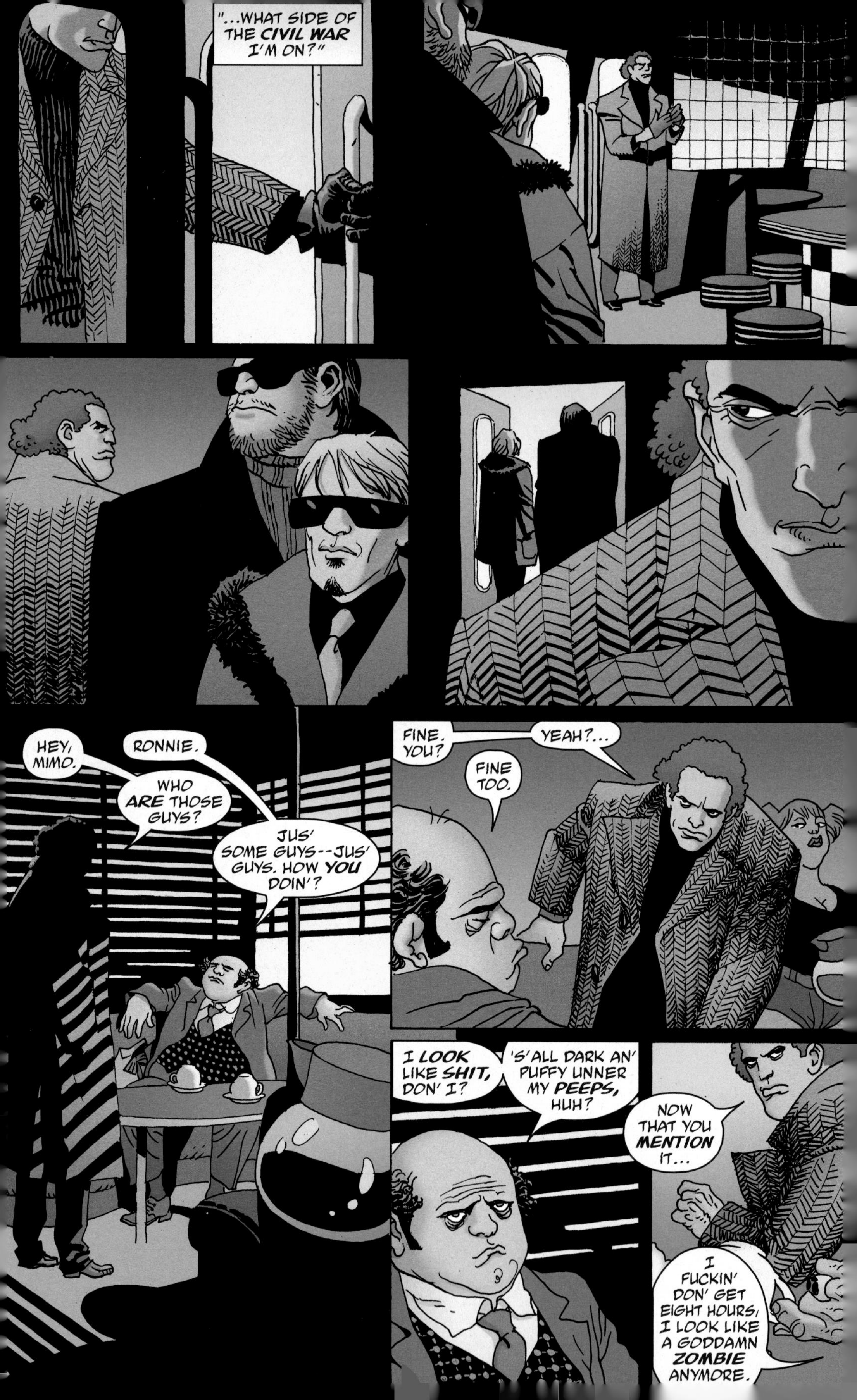
"...WHAT SIDE OF THE CIVIL WAR I'M ON?"
HEY, MIMO.
RONNIE.
WHO ARE THOSE GUYS?
JUS' SOME GUYS--JUS' GUYS. HOW YOU DOIN'?
FINE. YOU?
YEAH?...
FINE TOO.
I LOOK LIKE SHIT, DON' I?
'S'ALL DARK AN' PUFFY UNNER MY PEEPS, HUH?
NOW THAT YOU MENTION IT...
I FUCKIN' DON' GET EIGHT HOURS, I LOOK LIKE A GODDAMN ZOMBIE ANYMORE.

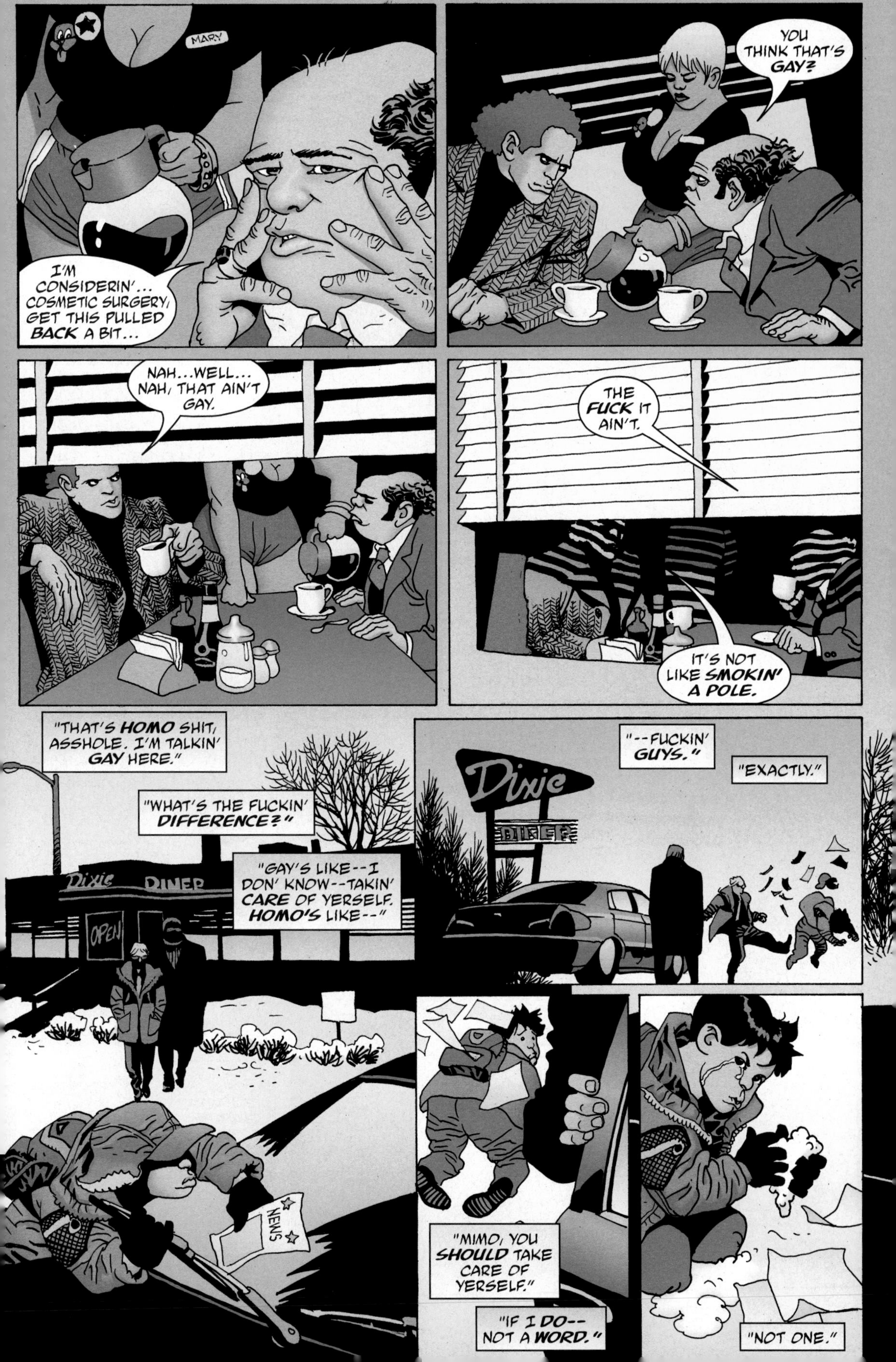
MARY
I'M CONSIDERIN'... COSMETIC SURGERY, GET THIS PULLED BACK A BIT...
YOU THINK THAT'S GAY?
NAH...WELL... NAH, THAT AIN'T GAY.
THE FUCK IT AIN'T.
IT'S NOT LIKE SMOKIN' A POLE.
"THAT'S HOMO SHIT, ASSHOLE. I'M TALKIN' GAY HERE."
"WHAT'S THE FUCKIN' DIFFERENCE?"
DIXIE DINER
OPEN
"GAY'S LIKE--I DON' KNOW--TAKIN' CARE OF YERSELF. HOMO'S LIKE--"
"--FUCKIN' GUYS."
"EXACTLY."
Dixie
NEWS
"MIMO, YOU SHOULD TAKE CARE OF YERSELF."
"IF I DO-- NOT A WORD."
"NOT ONE."

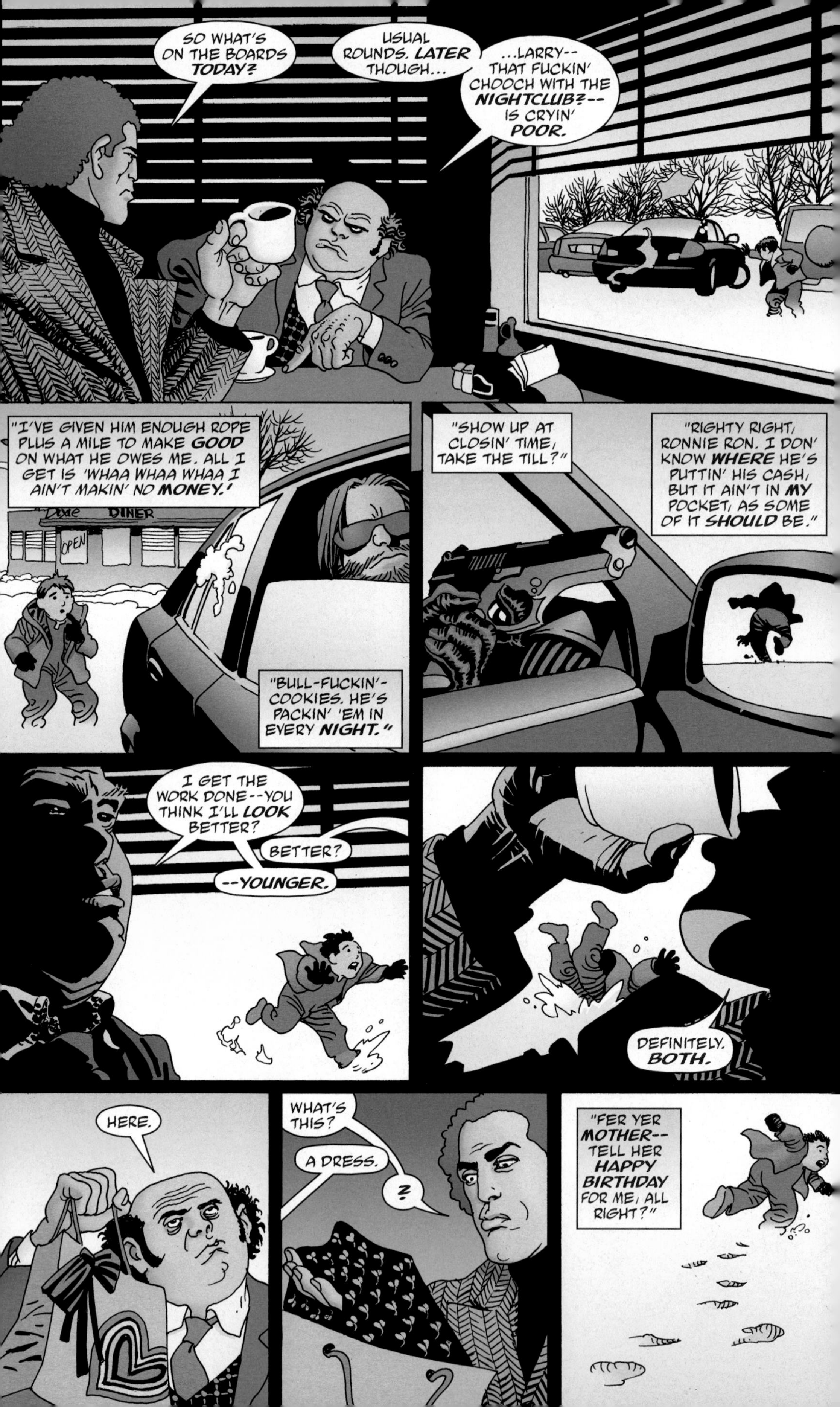

SO WHAT'S ON THE BOARDS TODAY?
USUAL ROUNDS. LATER THOUGH...
...LARRY-- THAT FUCKIN' CHOOCH WITH THE NIGHTCLUB?-- IS CRYIN' POOR.
"I'VE GIVEN HIM ENOUGH ROPE PLUS A MILE TO MAKE GOOD ON WHAT HE OWES ME. ALL I GET IS 'WHAA WHAA WHAA I AIN'T MAKIN' NO MONEY.'
DIXIE DINER
OPEN
"BULL-FUCKIN'-COOKIES. HE'S PACKIN' 'EM IN EVERY NIGHT."
"SHOW UP AT CLOSIN' TIME, TAKE THE TILL?"
"RIGHTY RIGHT, RONNIE RON. I DON' KNOW WHERE HE'S PUTTIN' HIS CASH, BUT IT AIN'T IN MY POCKET, AS SOME OF IT SHOULD BE."
I GET THE WORK DONE--YOU THINK I'LL LOOK BETTER?
BETTER?
--YOUNGER.
DEFINITELY. BOTH.
HERE.
WHAT'S THIS?
A DRESS.
?
"FER YER MOTHER-- TELL HER HAPPY BIRTHDAY FOR ME, ALL RIGHT?"

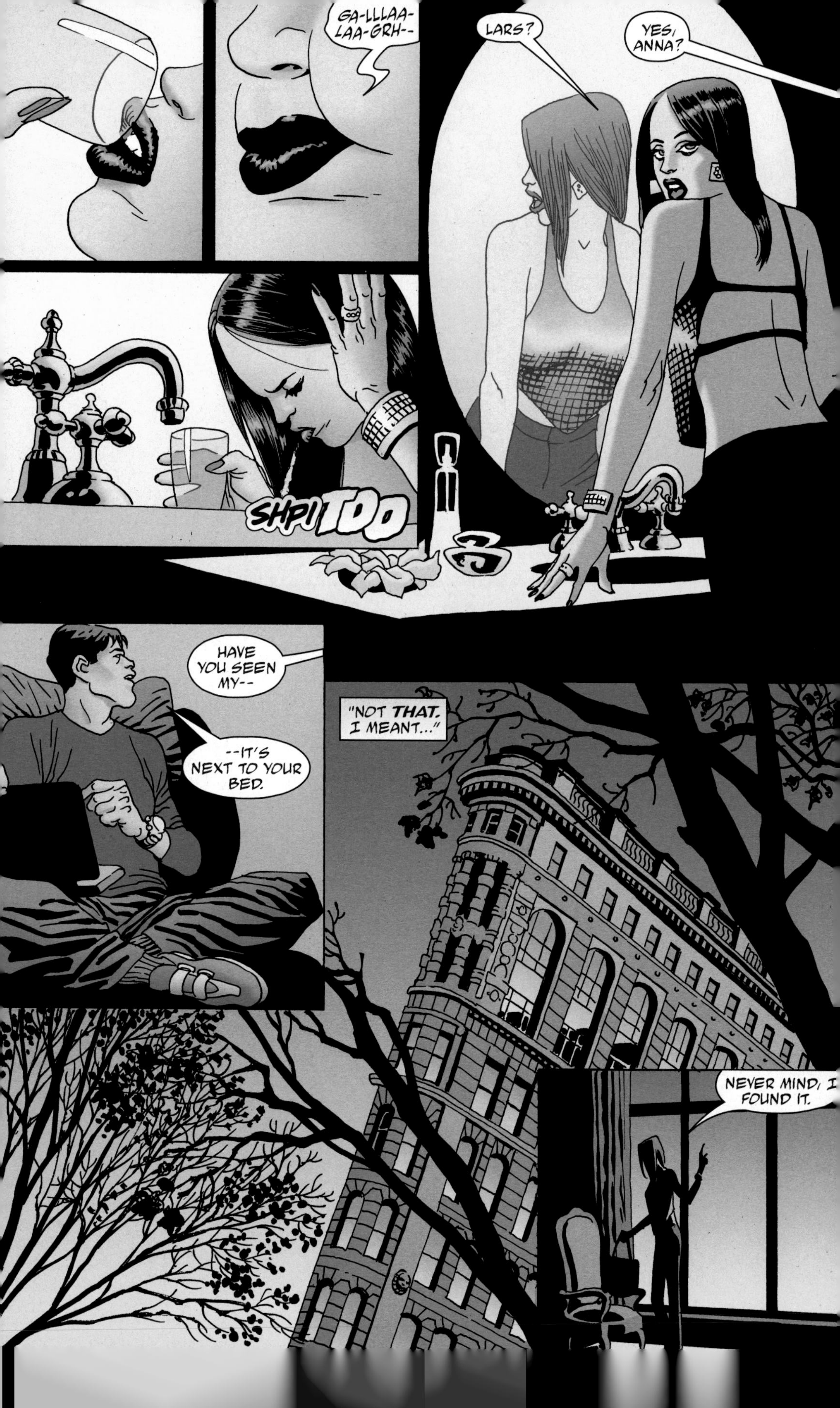
GA-LLLAA-LAA-GRH--
SHPITOO
LARS?
YES, ANNA?
HAVE YOU SEEN MY--
--IT'S NEXT TO YOUR BED.
"NOT THAT. I MEANT..."
NEVER MIND, I FOUND IT.

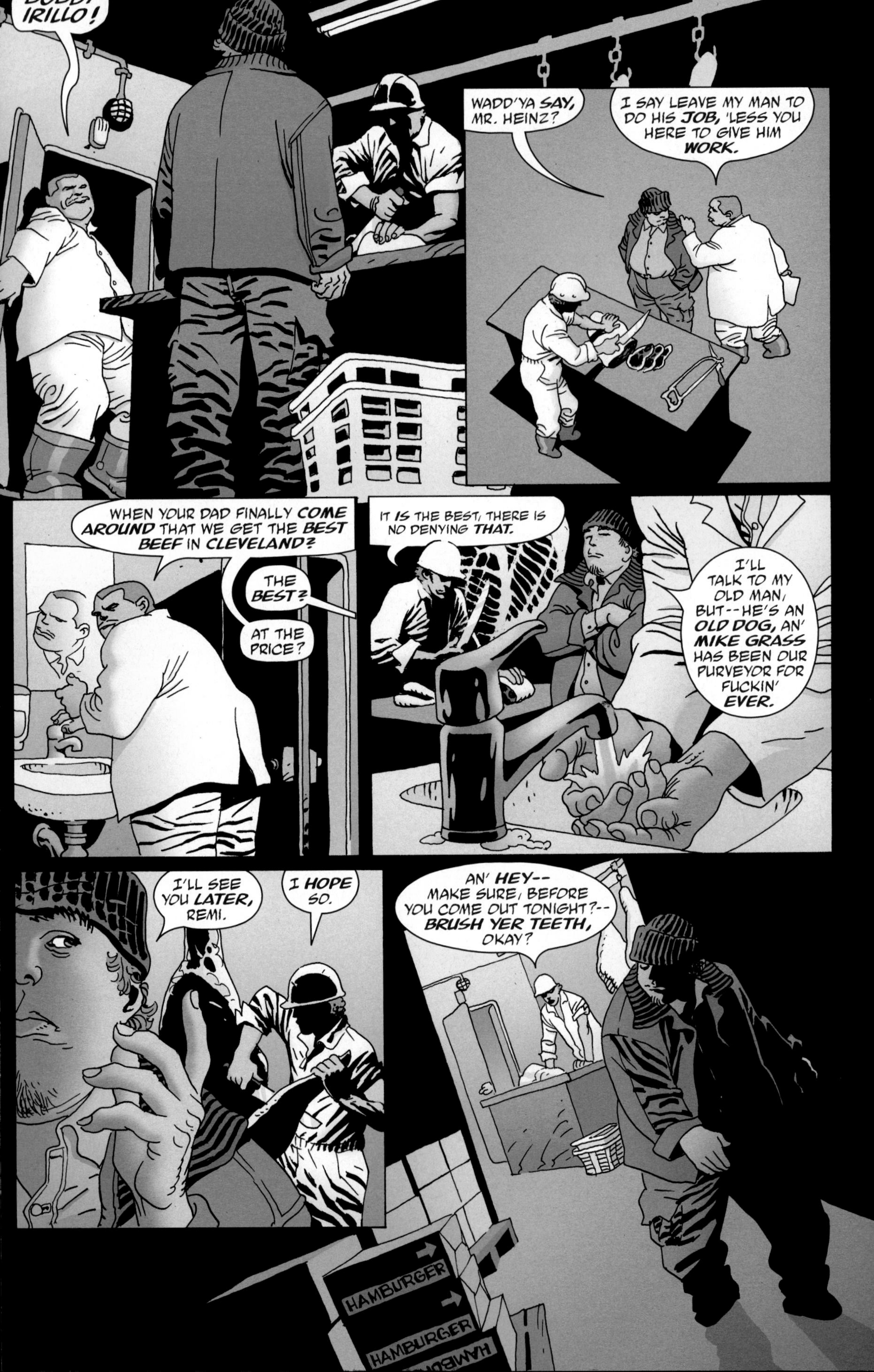
BOBBY IRILLO!
WADD'YA SAY, MR. HEINZ?
I SAY LEAVE MY MAN TO DO HIS JOB, 'LESS YOU HERE TO GIVE HIM WORK.
WHEN YOUR DAD FINALLY COME AROUND THAT WE GET THE BEST BEEF IN CLEVELAND?
THE BEST?
AT THE PRICE?
IT IS THE BEST, THERE IS NO DENYING THAT.
I'LL TALK TO MY OLD MAN, BUT--HE'S AN OLD DOG, AN' MIKE GRASS HAS BEEN OUR PURVEYOR FOR FUCKIN' EVER.
I'LL SEE YOU LATER, REMI.
I HOPE SO.
AN' HEY-- MAKE SURE, BEFORE YOU COME OUT TONIGHT?-- BRUSH YER TEETH, OKAY?
HAMBURGER
HAMBURGER
HAMBURGER
HAMBURGER

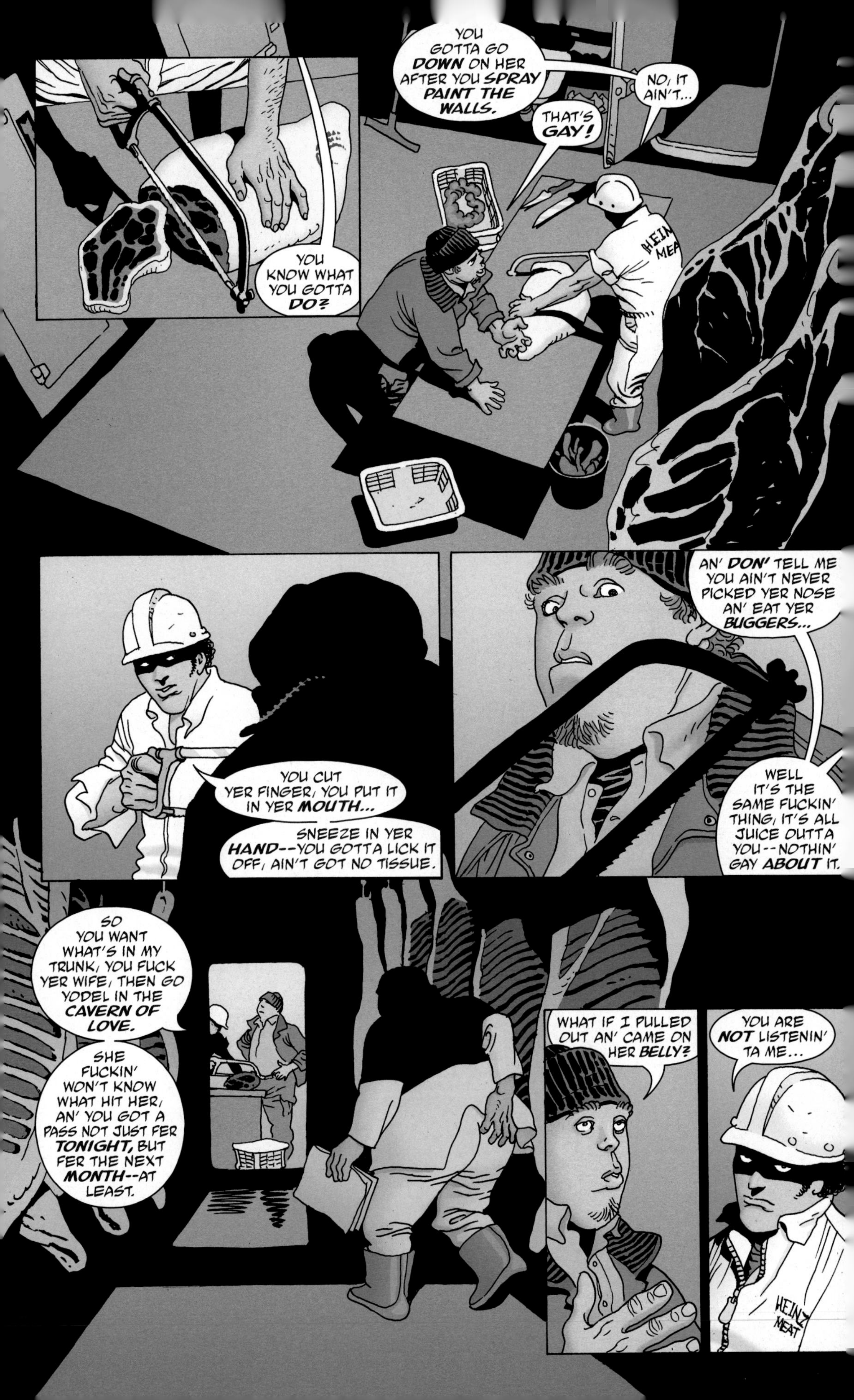
YOU KNOW WHAT YOU GOTTA DO?
YOU GOTTA GO DOWN ON HER AFTER YOU SPRAY PAINT THE WALLS.
THAT'S GAY!
NO, IT AIN'T...
YOU CUT YER FINGER, YOU PUT IT IN YER MOUTH...
SNEEZE IN YER HAND--YOU GOTTA LICK IT OFF, AIN'T GOT NO TISSUE.
AN' DON' TELL ME YOU AIN'T NEVER PICKED YER NOSE AN' EAT YER BUGGERS...
WELL IT'S THE SAME FUCKIN' THING, IT'S ALL JUICE OUTTA YOU--NOTHIN' GAY ABOUT IT.
SO YOU WANT WHAT'S IN MY TRUNK, YOU FUCK YER WIFE, THEN GO YODEL IN THE CAVERN OF LOVE.
SHE FUCKIN' WON'T KNOW WHAT HIT HER, AN' YOU GOT A PASS NOT JUST FER TONIGHT, BUT FER THE NEXT MONTH--AT LEAST.
WHAT IF I PULLED OUT AN' CAME ON HER BELLY?
YOU ARE NOT LISTENIN' TA ME...
HEINZ MEAT

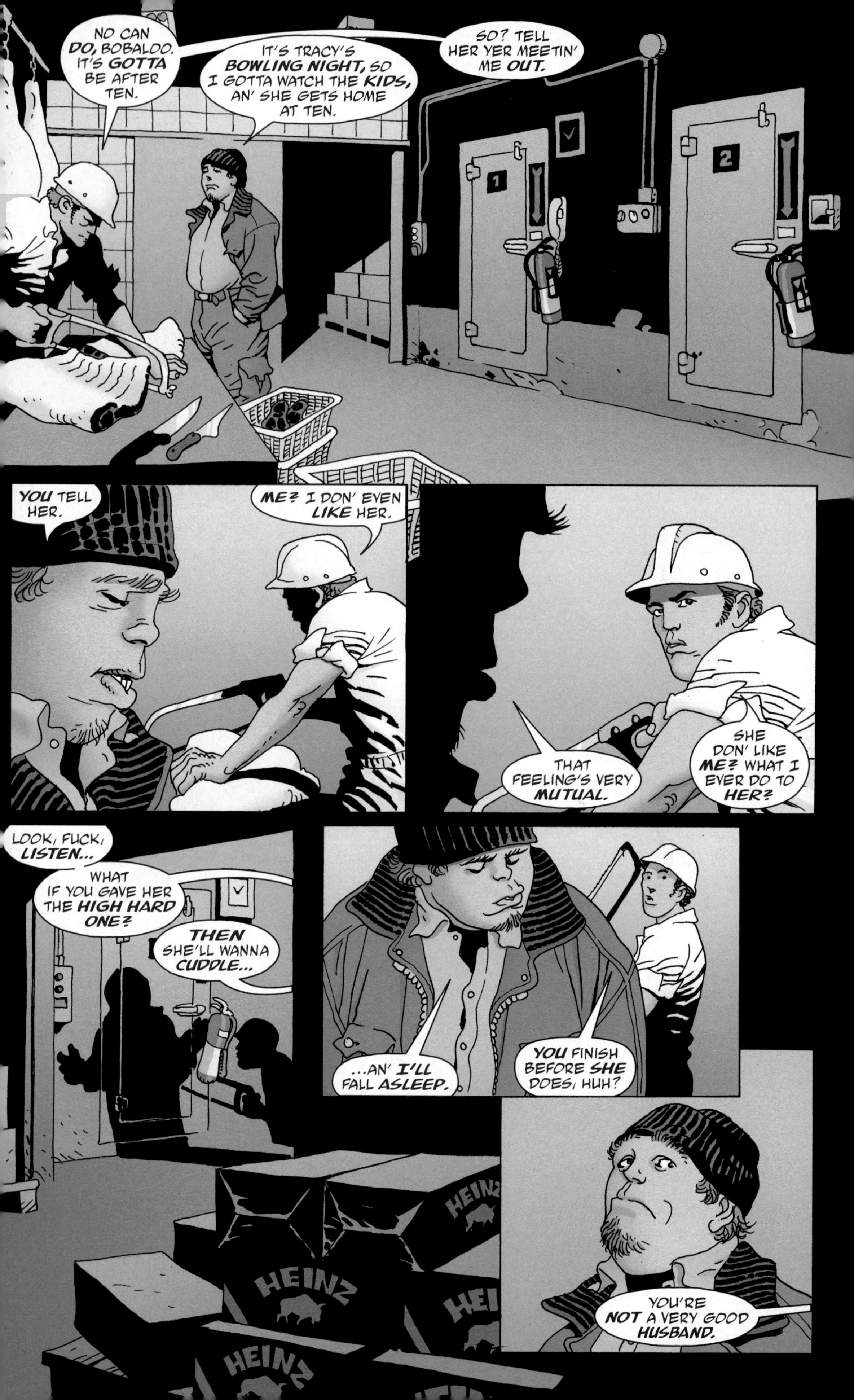
NO CAN DO, BOBALOO. IT'S GOTTA BE AFTER TEN.
IT'S TRACY'S BOWLING NIGHT, SO I GOTTA WATCH THE KIDS, AN' SHE GETS HOME AT TEN.
SO? TELL HER YER MEETIN' ME OUT.
YOU TELL HER.
ME? I DON' EVEN LIKE HER.
THAT FEELING'S VERY MUTUAL.
SHE DON' LIKE ME? WHAT I EVER DO TO HER?
LOOK, FUCK, LISTEN...
WHAT IF YOU GAVE HER THE HIGH HARD ONE?
THEN SHE'LL WANNA CUDDLE...
...AN' I'LL FALL ASLEEP.
YOU FINISH BEFORE SHE DOES, HUH?
YOU'RE NOT A VERY GOOD HUSBAND.
HEINZ
HEINZ
HEINZ

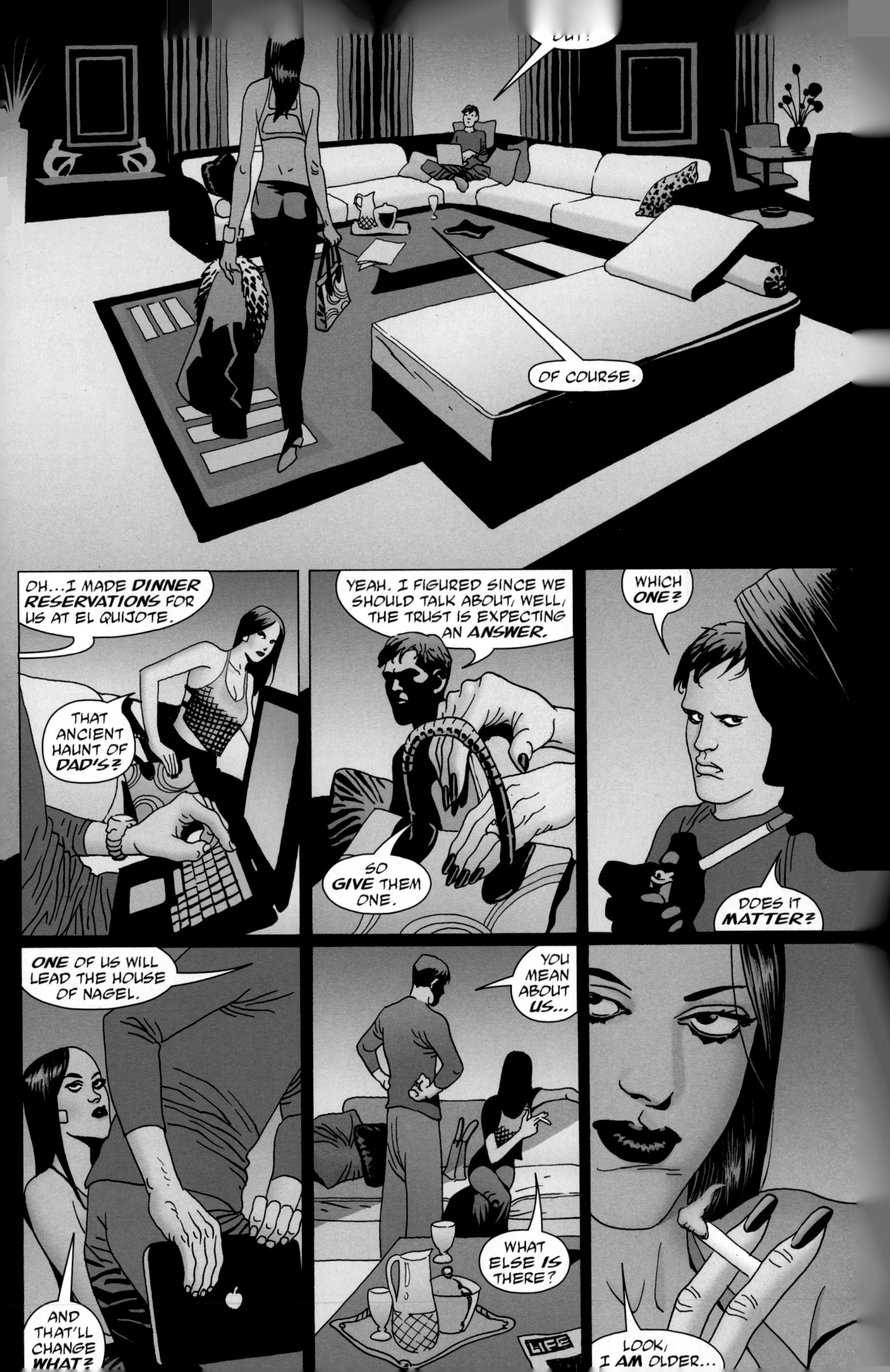
OUT?
OF COURSE.
OH...I MADE DINNER RESERVATIONS FOR US AT EL QUIJOTE.
THAT ANCIENT HAUNT OF DAD'S?
YEAH. I FIGURED SINCE WE SHOULD TALK ABOUT, WELL, THE TRUST IS EXPECTING AN ANSWER.
SO GIVE THEM ONE.
WHICH ONE?
DOES IT MATTER?
ONE OF US WILL LEAD THE HOUSE OF NAGEL.
AND THAT'LL CHANGE WHAT?
YOU MEAN ABOUT US...
WHAT ELSE IS THERE?
LIFE
LOOK, I AM OLDER...

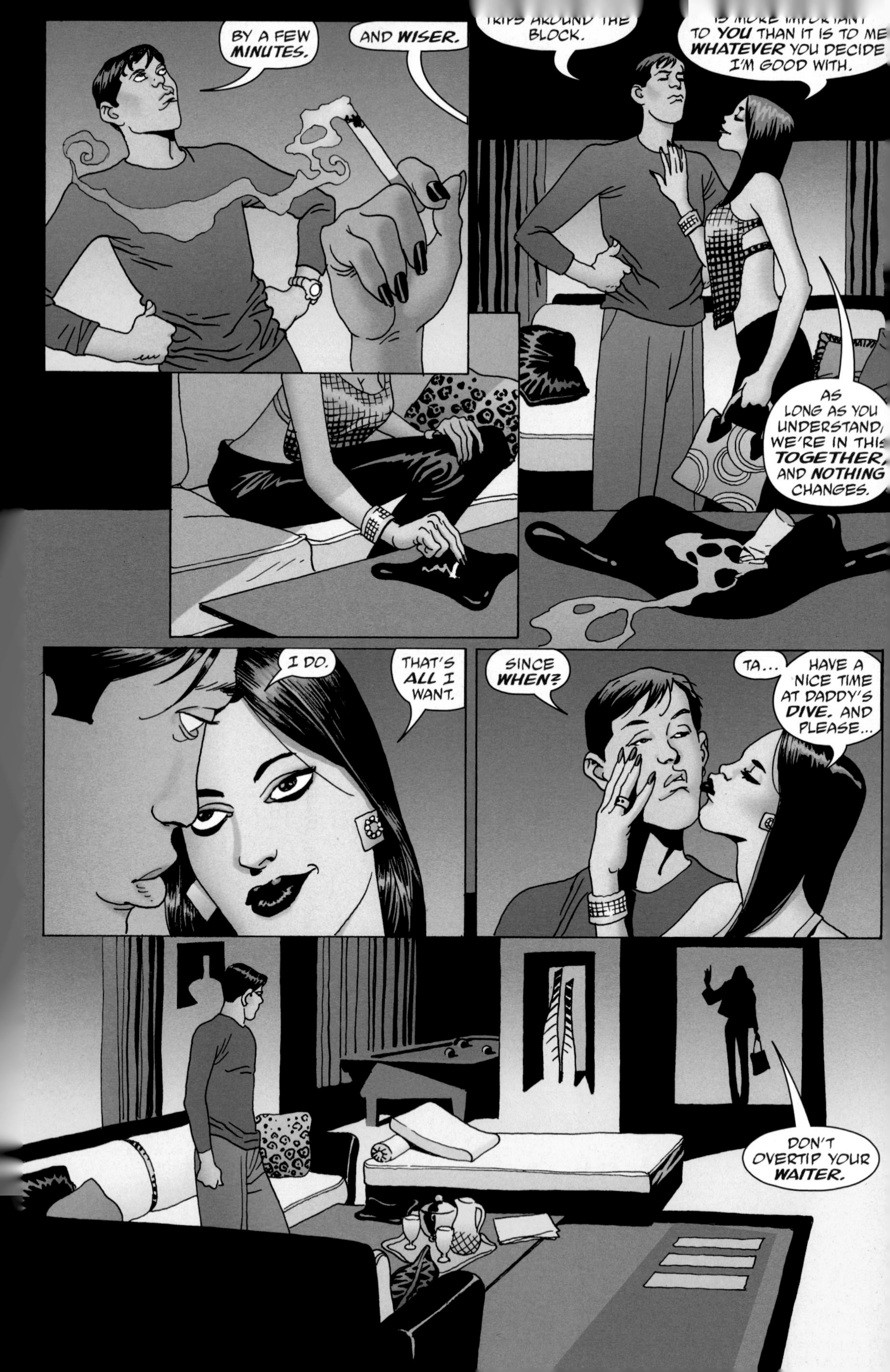
BY A FEW MINUTES.
AND WISER.
TRIPS AROUND THE BLOCK.
TO YOU THAN IT IS TO ME. WHATEVER YOU DECIDE I'M GOOD WITH.
AS LONG AS YOU UNDERSTAND, WE'RE IN THIS TOGETHER, AND NOTHING CHANGES.
I DO.
THAT'S ALL I WANT.
SINCE WHEN?
TA...
HAVE A NICE TIME AT DADDY'S DIVE. AND PLEASE...
DON'T OVERTIP YOUR WAITER.

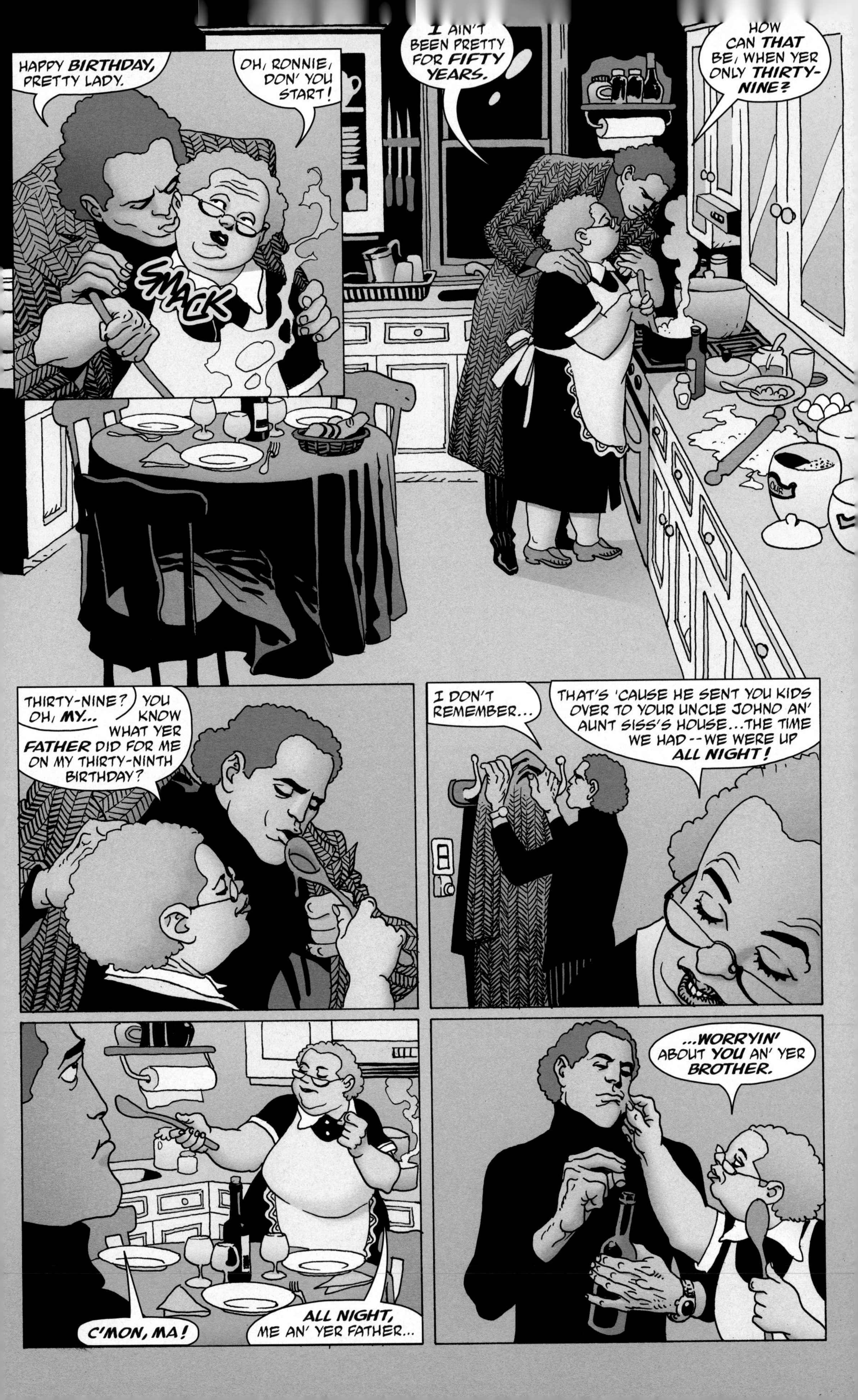
HAPPY BIRTHDAY, PRETTY LADY.
OH, RONNIE, DON' YOU START!
SMACK
I AIN'T BEEN PRETTY FOR FIFTY YEARS.
HOW CAN THAT BE, WHEN YER ONLY THIRTY-NINE?
THIRTY-NINE? OH, MY...
YOU KNOW WHAT YER FATHER DID FOR ME ON MY THIRTY-NINTH BIRTHDAY?
I DON'T REMEMBER...
THAT'S 'CAUSE HE SENT YOU KIDS OVER TO YOUR UNCLE JOHNO AN' AUNT SISS'S HOUSE...THE TIME WE HAD--WE WERE UP ALL NIGHT!
C'MON, MA!
ALL NIGHT, ME AN' YER FATHER...
...WORRYIN' ABOUT YOU AN' YER BROTHER.

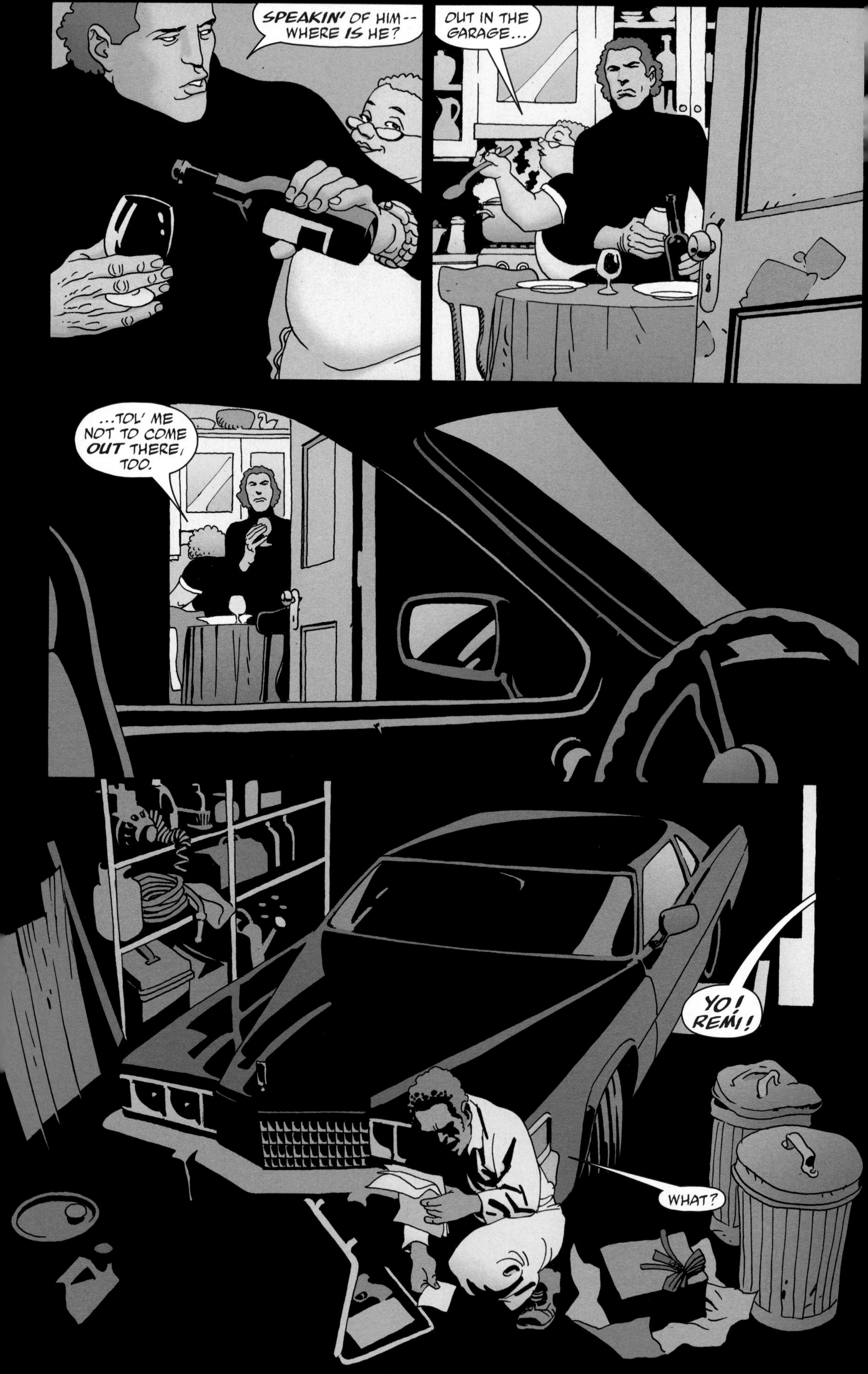
SPEAKIN' OF HIM-- WHERE IS HE?
OUT IN THE GARAGE...
...TOL' ME NOT TO COME OUT THERE, TOO.
YO! REMI!
WHAT?

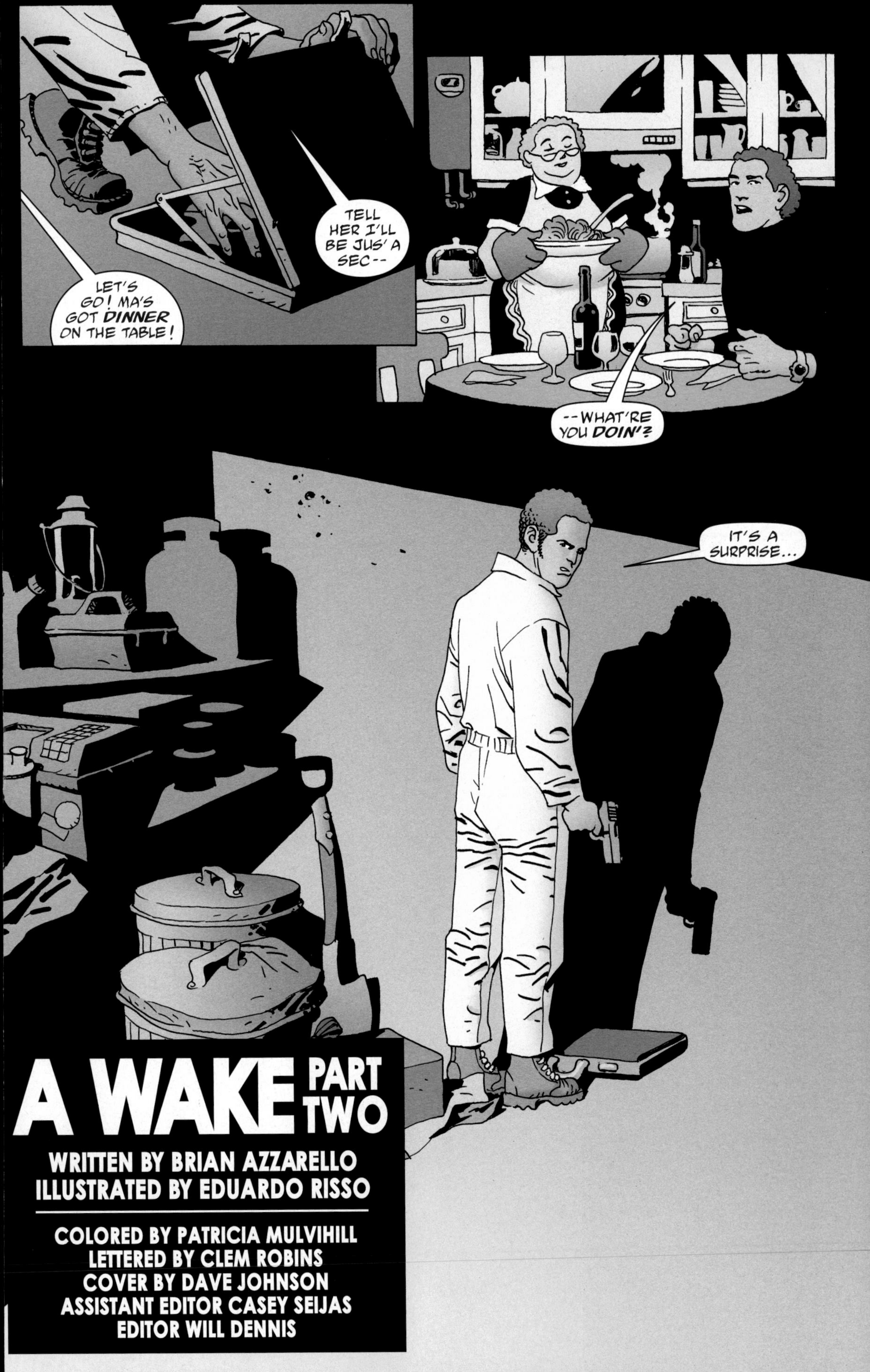
LET'S GO! MA'S GOT DINNER ON THE TABLE!
TELL HER I'LL BE JUS' A SEC--
--WHAT'RE YOU DOIN'?
IT'S A SURPRISE...

A WAKE PART TWO

WRITTEN BY BRIAN AZZARELLO
ILLUSTRATED BY EDUARDO RISSO

COLORED BY PATRICIA MULVIHILL
LETTERED BY CLEM ROBINS
COVER BY DAVE JOHNSON
ASSISTANT EDITOR CASEY SEIJAS
EDITOR WILL DENNIS

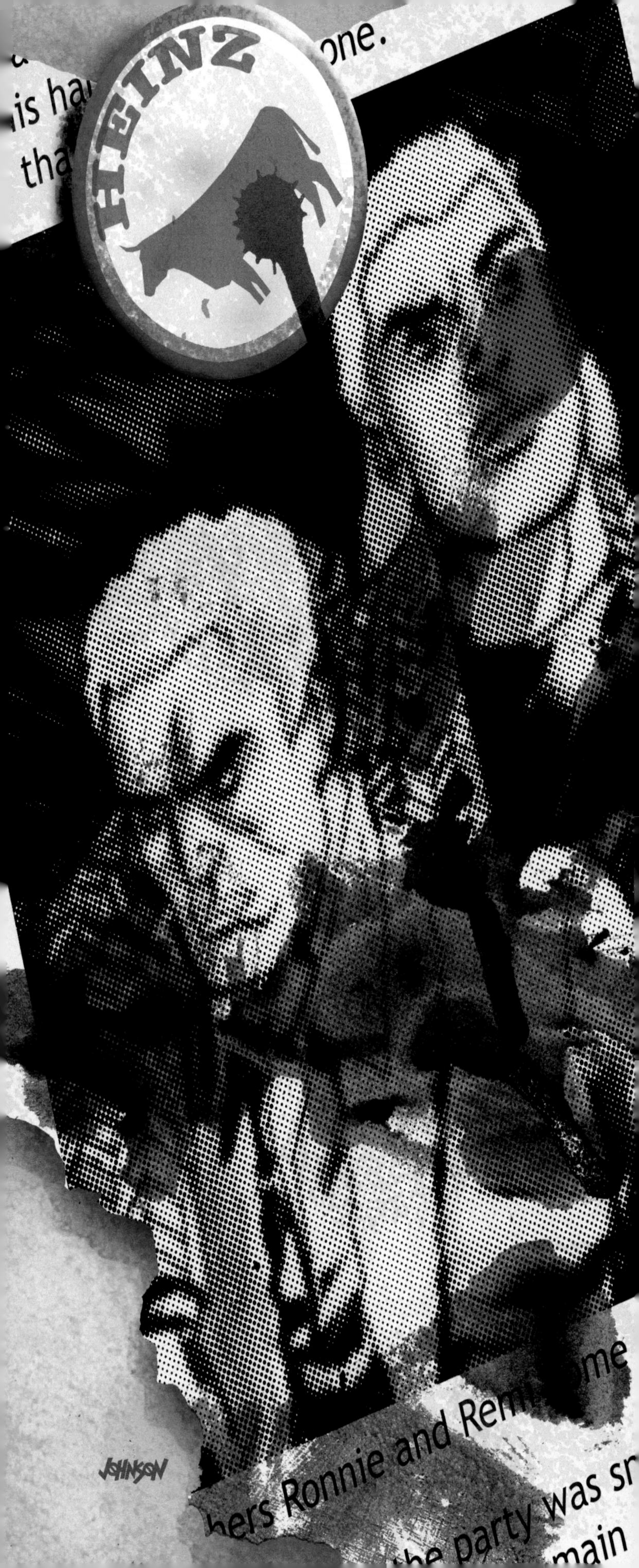
HEINZ
one.
is ha
tha
hers Ronnie and Rem
me
party was s
main
JOHNSON

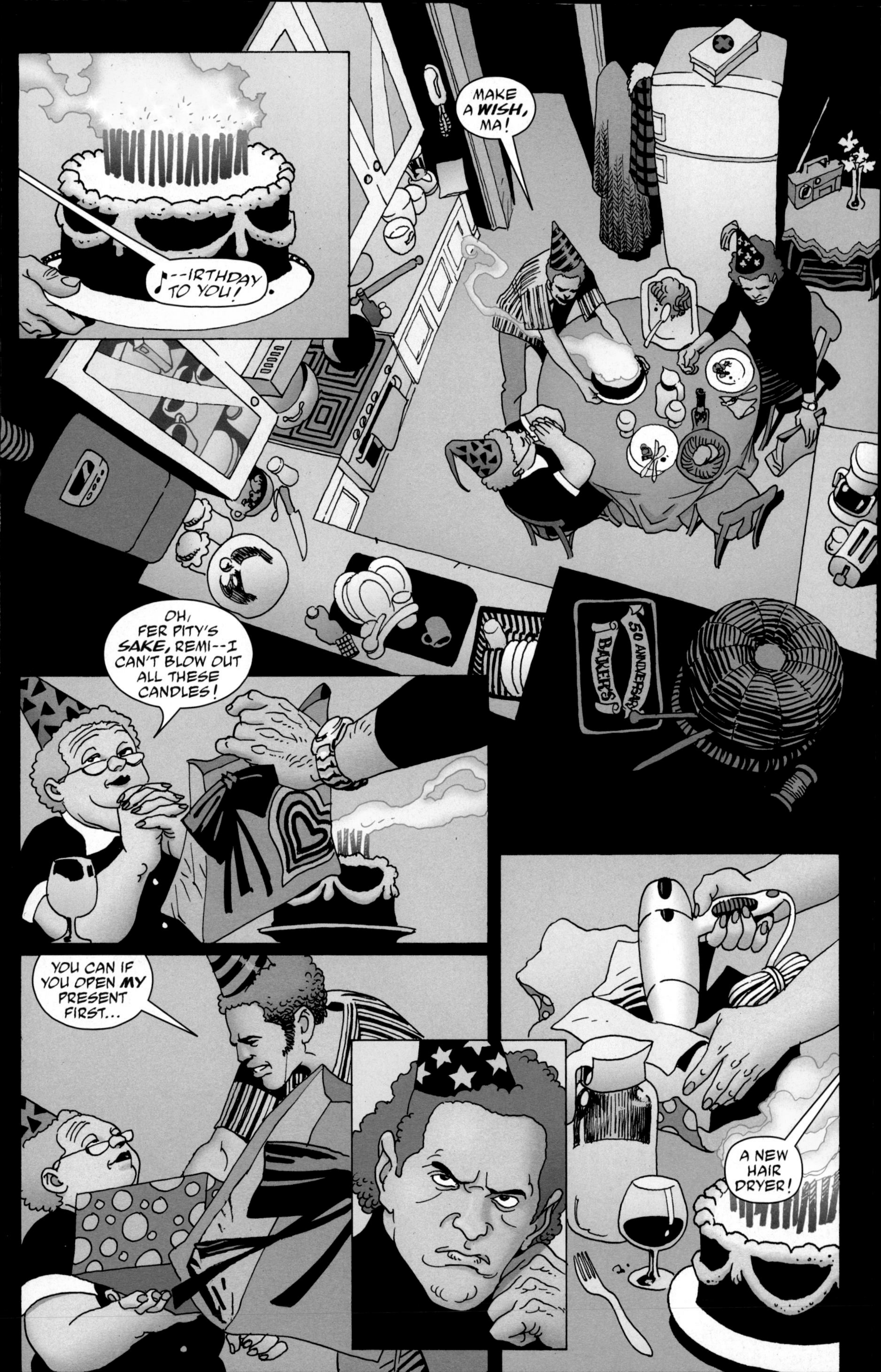
♪--IRTHDAY TO YOU!
MAKE A WISH, MA!
50 ANNIVERSARY
BAKER'S
OH, FER PITY'S SAKE, REMI--I CAN'T BLOW OUT ALL THESE CANDLES!
YOU CAN IF YOU OPEN MY PRESENT FIRST...
A NEW HAIR DRYER!

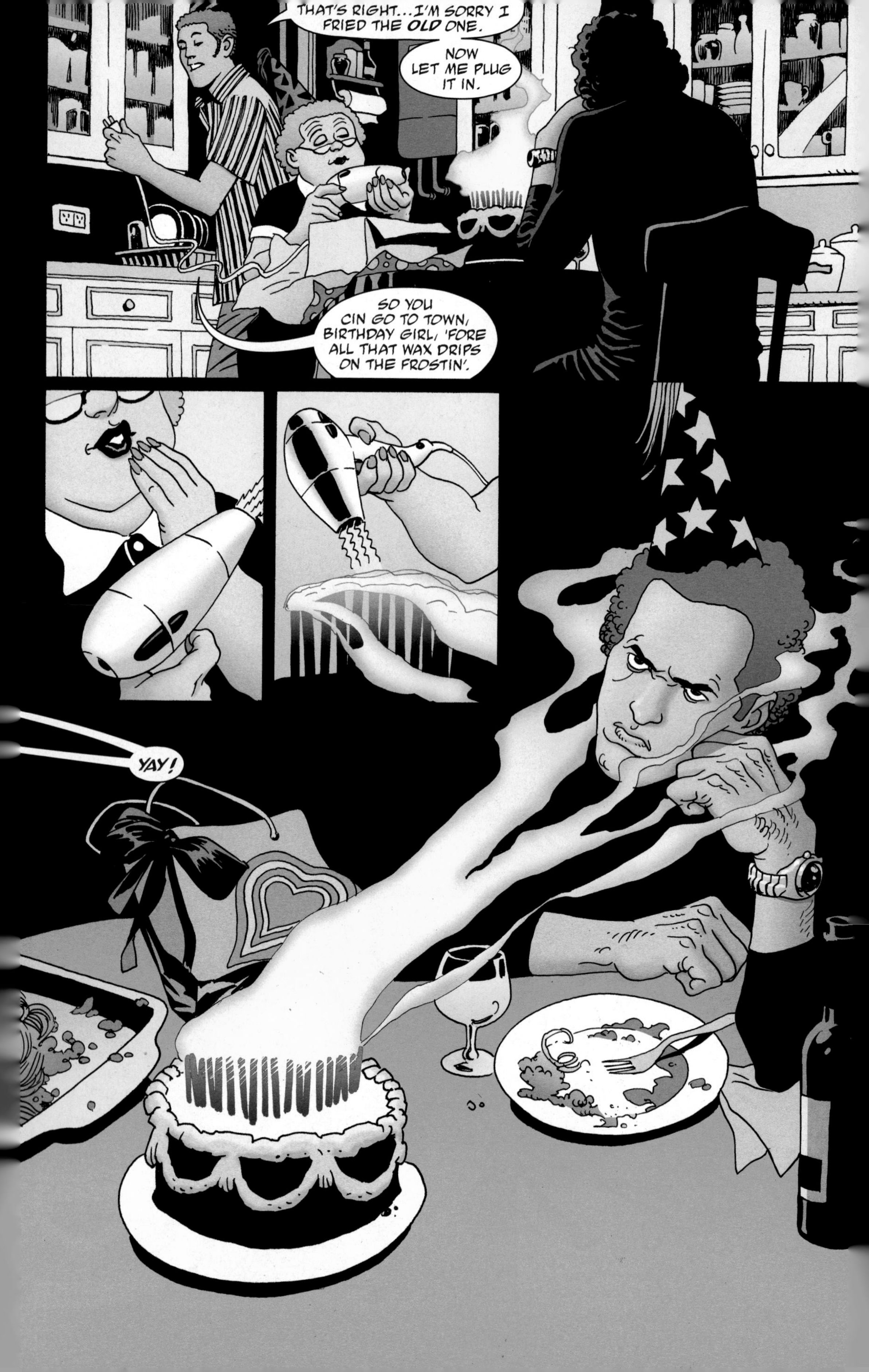
THAT'S RIGHT... I'M SORRY I FRIED THE OLD ONE.
NOW LET ME PLUG IT IN.
SO YOU CIN GO TO TOWN, BIRTHDAY GIRL, 'FORE ALL THAT WAX DRIPS ON THE FROSTIN'.
YAY!

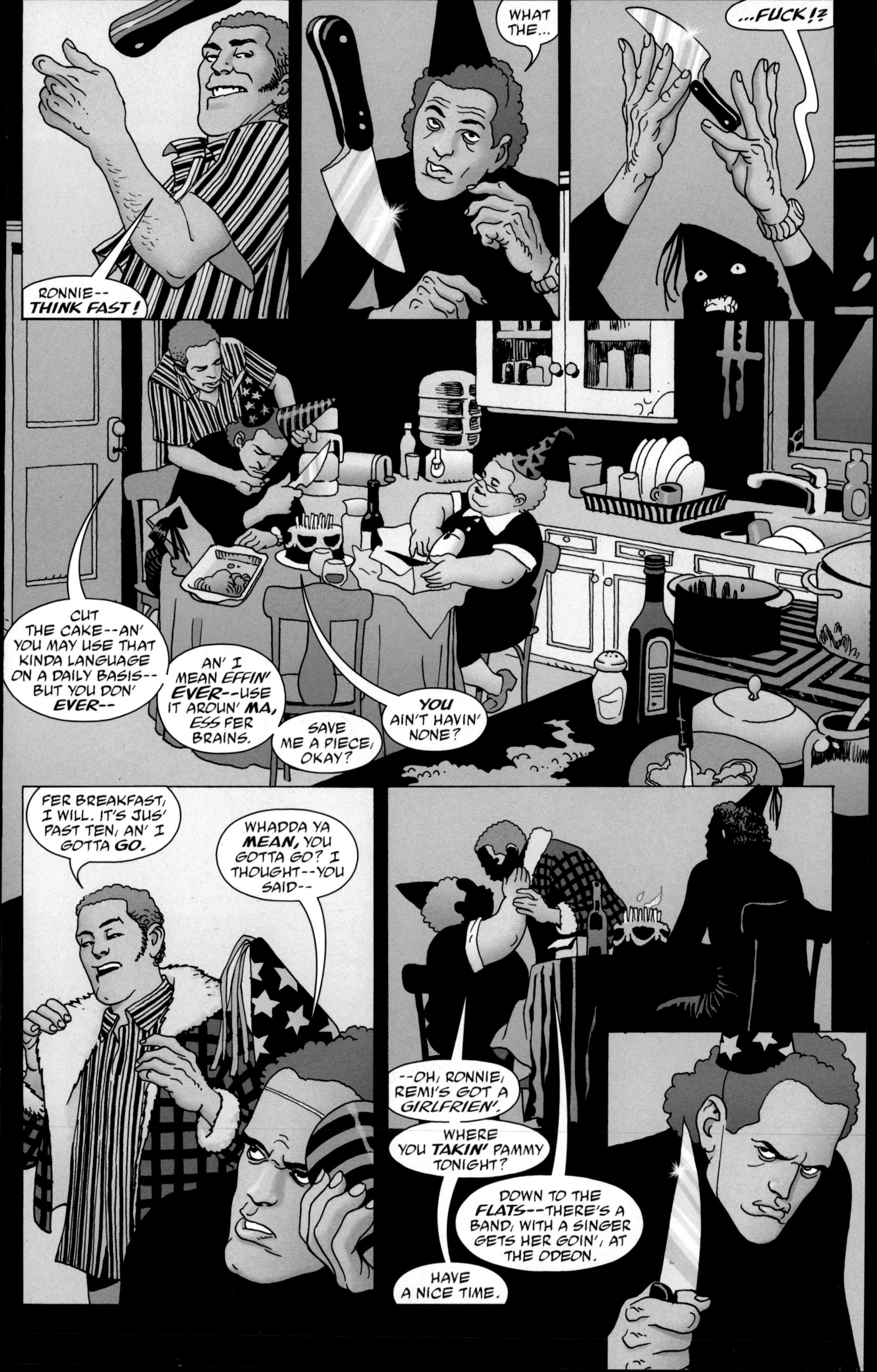

RONNIE-- THINK FAST!
WHAT THE...
...FUCK!?
CUT THE CAKE--AN' YOU MAY USE THAT KINDA LANGUAGE ON A DAILY BASIS--BUT YOU DON' EVER--
AN' I MEAN EFFIN' EVER--USE IT AROUN' MA, ESS FER BRAINS.
SAVE ME A PIECE, OKAY?
YOU AIN'T HAVIN' NONE?
FER BREAKFAST, I WILL. IT'S JUS' PAST TEN, AN' I GOTTA GO.
WHADDA YA MEAN, YOU GOTTA GO? I THOUGHT--YOU SAID--
--OH, RONNIE, REMI'S GOT A GIRLFRIEN'.
WHERE YOU TAKIN' PAMMY TONIGHT?
DOWN TO THE FLATS--THERE'S A BAND, WITH A SINGER GETS HER GOIN', AT THE ODEON.
HAVE A NICE TIME.

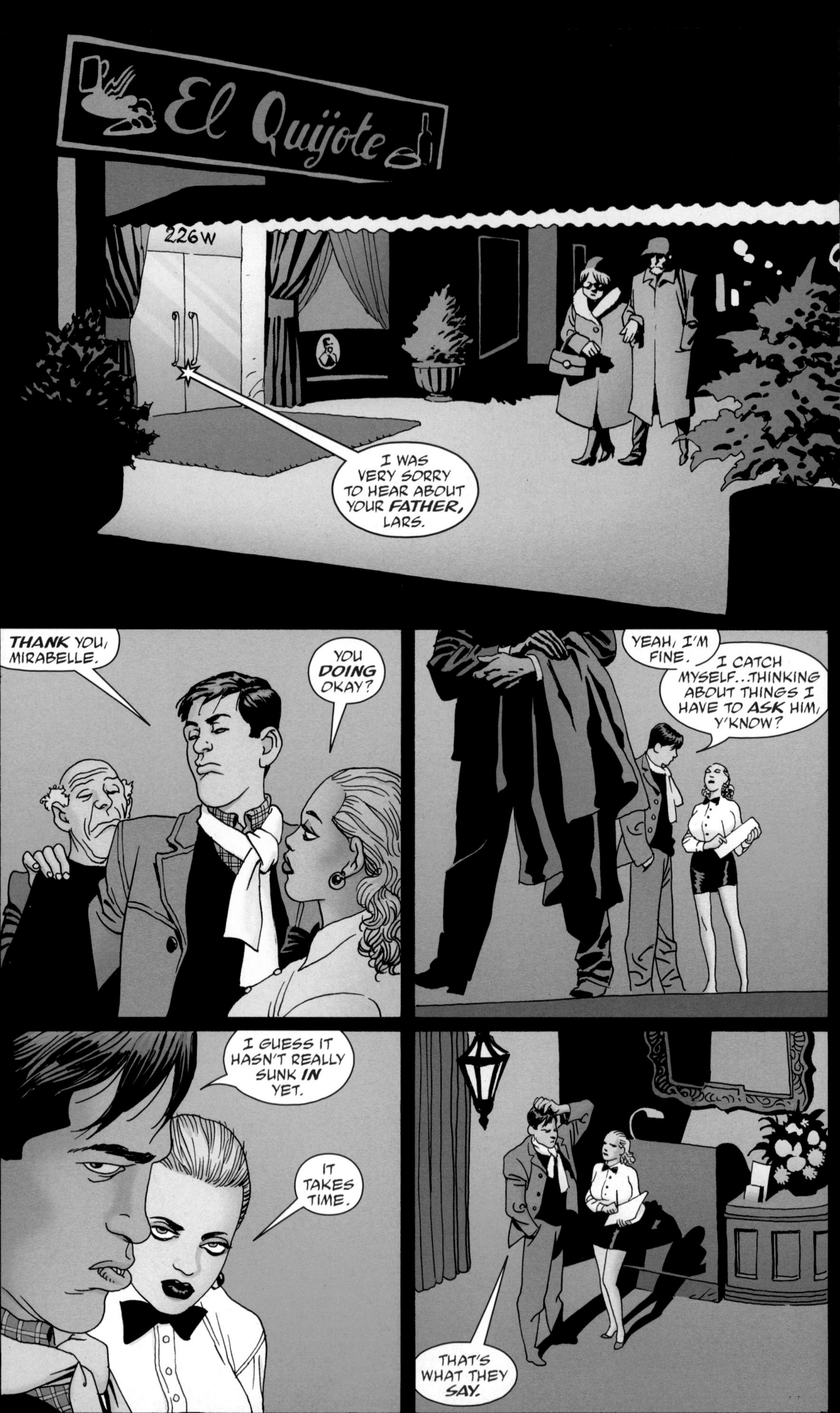
El Quijote
226 W
I WAS VERY SORRY TO HEAR ABOUT YOUR FATHER, LARS.
THANK YOU, MIRABELLE.
YOU DOING OKAY?
YEAH, I'M FINE.
I CATCH MYSELF... THINKING ABOUT THINGS I HAVE TO ASK HIM, Y'KNOW?
I GUESS IT HASN'T REALLY SUNK IN YET.
IT TAKES TIME.
THAT'S WHAT THEY SAY.

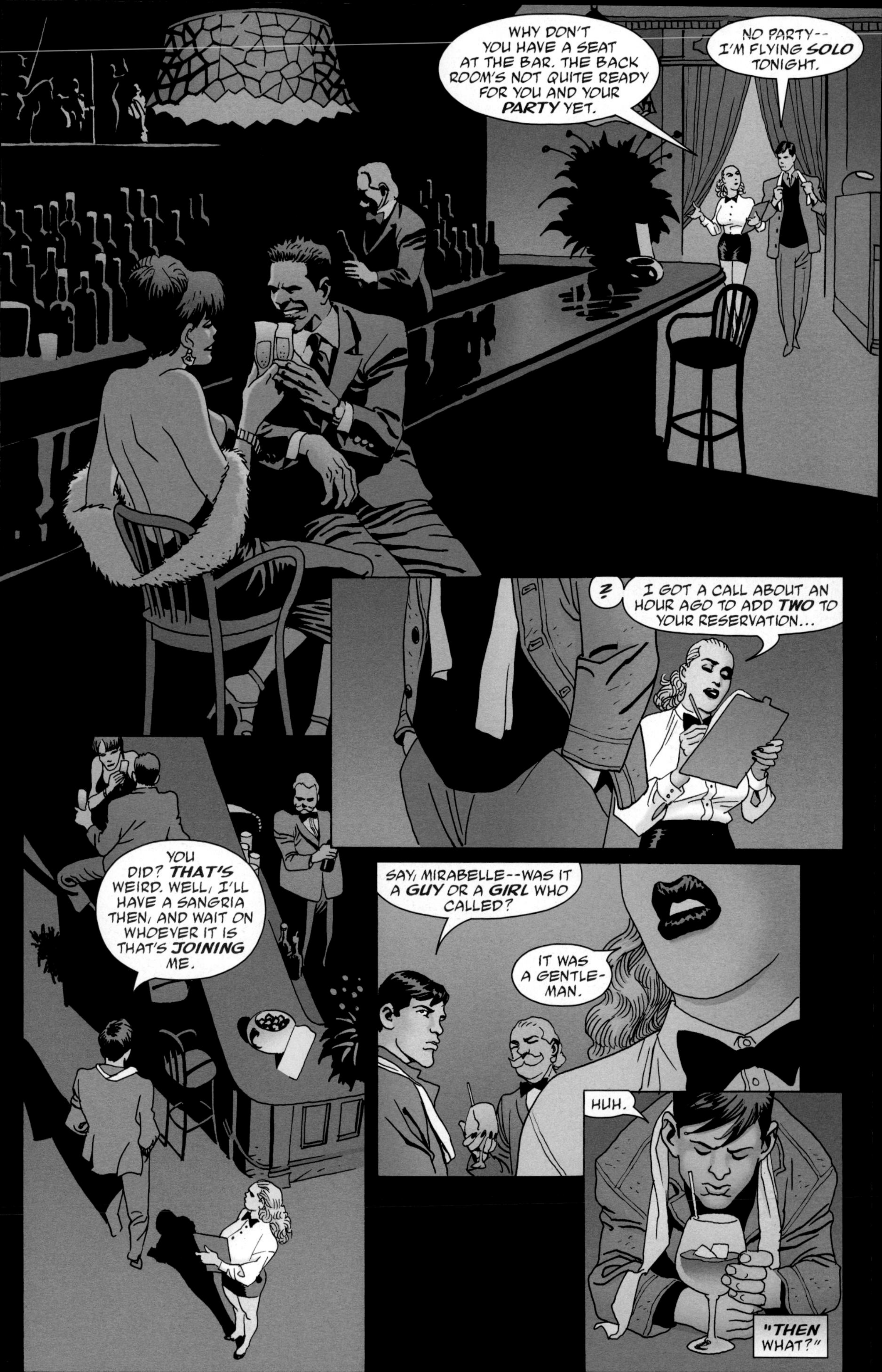
WHY DON'T YOU HAVE A SEAT AT THE BAR. THE BACK ROOM'S NOT QUITE READY FOR YOU AND YOUR PARTY YET.
NO PARTY-- I'M FLYING SOLO TONIGHT.
?
I GOT A CALL ABOUT AN HOUR AGO TO ADD TWO TO YOUR RESERVATION...
YOU DID? THAT'S WEIRD. WELL, I'LL HAVE A SANGRIA THEN, AND WAIT ON WHOEVER IT IS THAT'S JOINING ME.
SAY, MIRABELLE--WAS IT A GUY OR A GIRL WHO CALLED?
IT WAS A GENTLE-MAN.
HUH.
"THEN WHAT?"

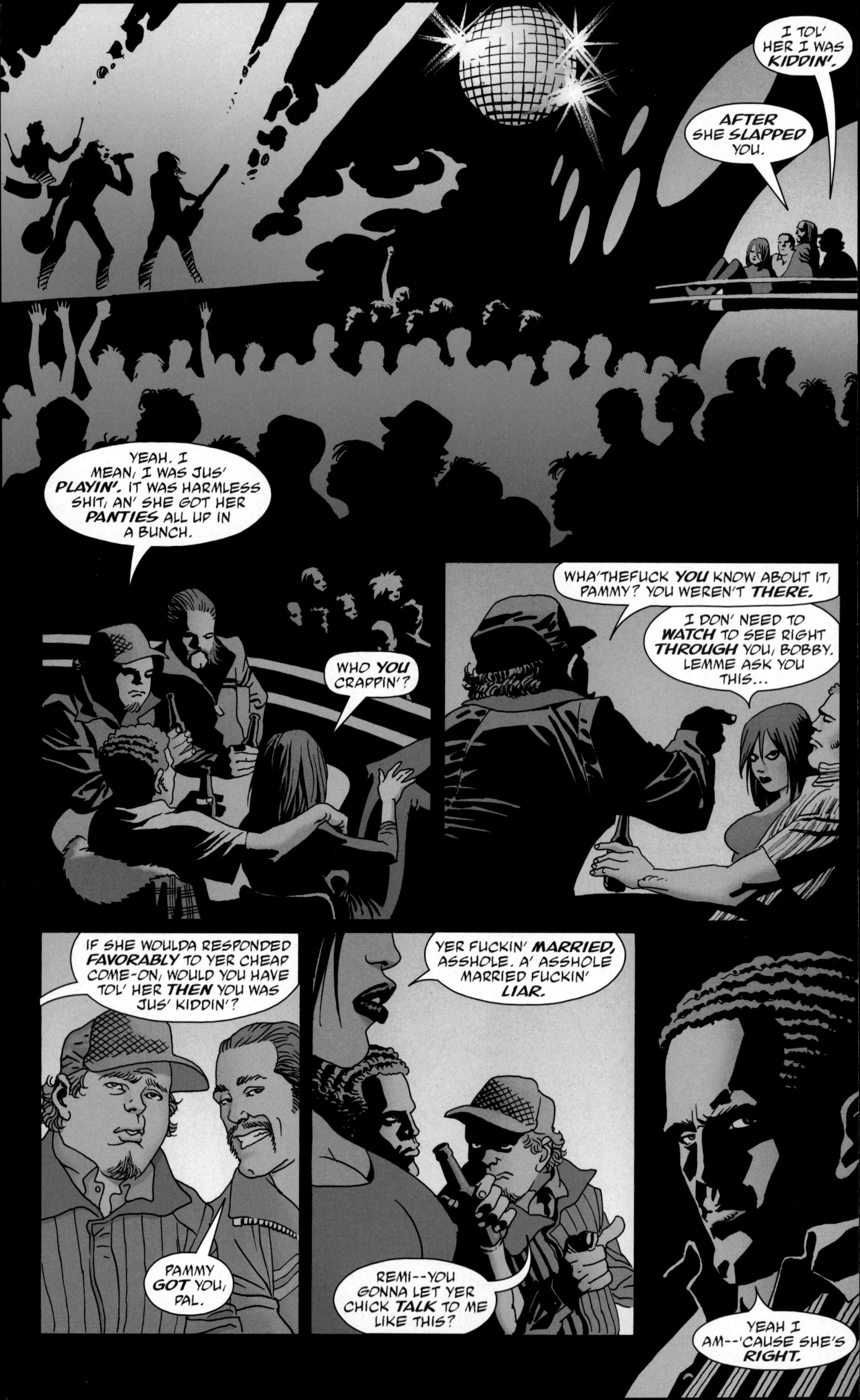
I TOL' HER I WAS KIDDIN'.
AFTER SHE SLAPPED YOU.
YEAH. I MEAN, I WAS JUS' PLAYIN'. IT WAS HARMLESS SHIT, AN' SHE GOT HER PANTIES ALL UP IN A BUNCH.
WHO YOU CRAPPIN'?
WHA'THEFUCK YOU KNOW ABOUT IT, PAMMY? YOU WEREN'T THERE.
I DON' NEED TO WATCH TO SEE RIGHT THROUGH YOU, BOBBY. LEMME ASK YOU THIS...
IF SHE WOULDA RESPONDED FAVORABLY TO YER CHEAP COME-ON, WOULD YOU HAVE TOL' HER THEN YOU WAS JUS' KIDDIN'?
PAMMY GOT YOU, PAL.
YER FUCKIN' MARRIED, ASSHOLE. A' ASSHOLE MARRIED FUCKIN' LIAR.
REMI--YOU GONNA LET YER CHICK TALK TO ME LIKE THIS?
YEAH I AM--'CAUSE SHE'S RIGHT.

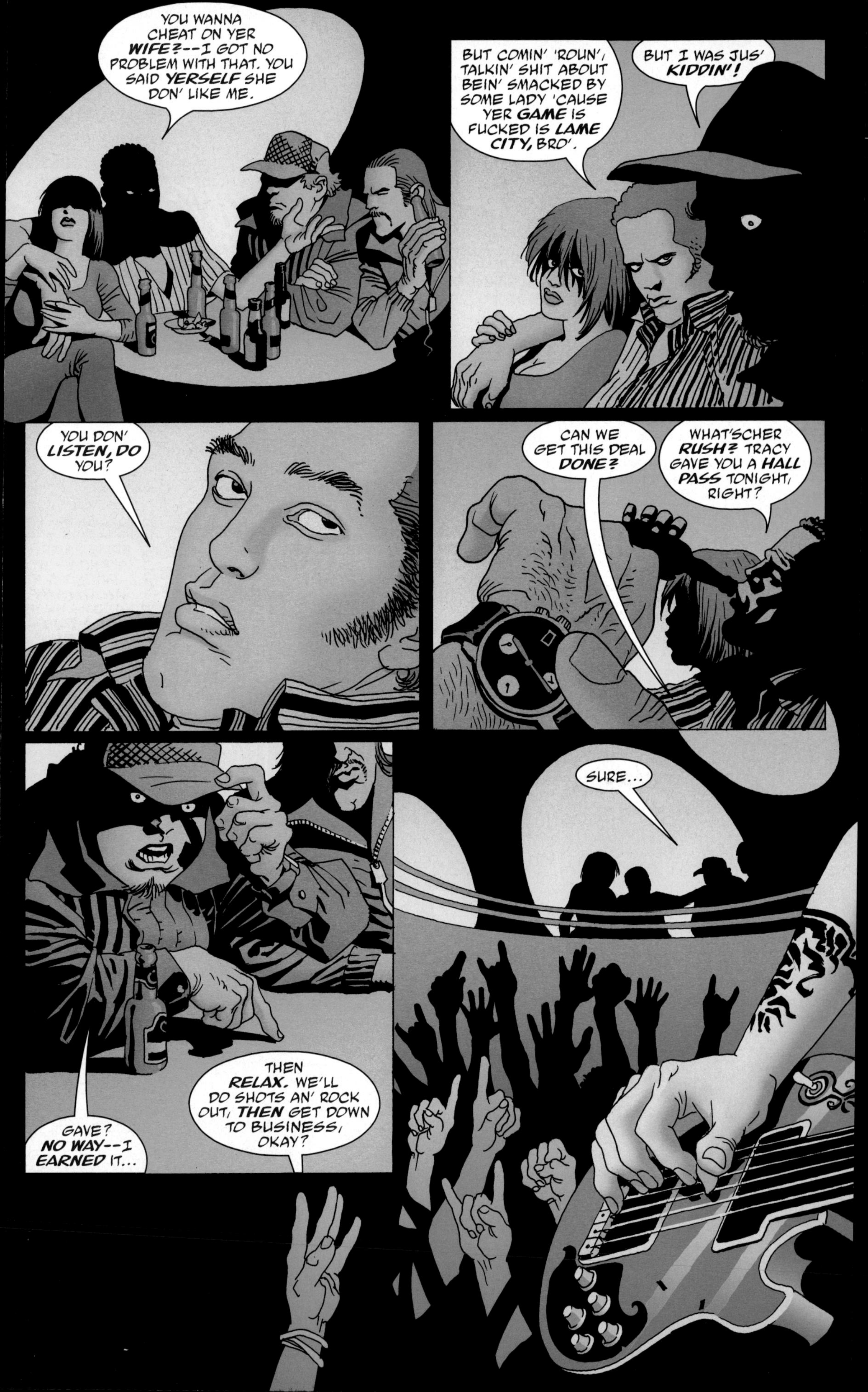
YOU WANNA CHEAT ON YER WIFE?--I GOT NO PROBLEM WITH THAT. YOU SAID YERSELF SHE DON' LIKE ME.
BUT I WAS JUS' KIDDIN'!
BUT COMIN' 'ROUN', TALKIN' SHIT ABOUT BEIN' SMACKED BY SOME LADY 'CAUSE YER GAME IS FUCKED IS LAME CITY, BRO'.
YOU DON' LISTEN, DO YOU?
CAN WE GET THIS DEAL DONE?
WHAT'SCHER RUSH? TRACY GAVE YOU A HALL PASS TONIGHT, RIGHT?
GAVE? NO WAY--I EARNED IT...
THEN RELAX. WE'LL DO SHOTS AN' ROCK OUT, THEN GET DOWN TO BUSINESS, OKAY?
SURE...

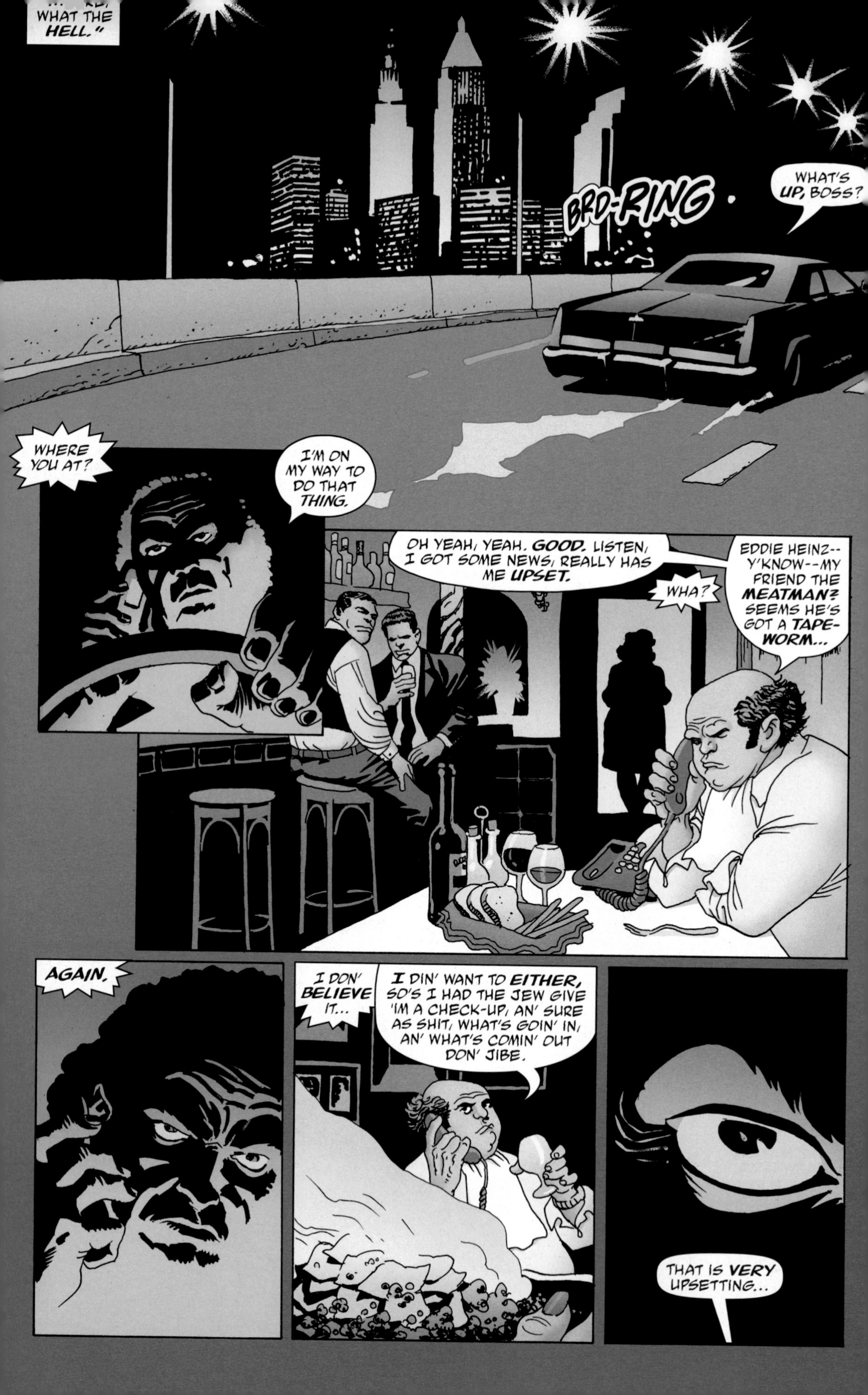
WHAT THE HELL."
BRD-RING
WHAT'S UP, BOSS?
WHERE YOU AT?
I'M ON MY WAY TO DO THAT THING.
OH YEAH, YEAH. GOOD. LISTEN, I GOT SOME NEWS, REALLY HAS ME UPSET.
WHA?
EDDIE HEINZ-- Y'KNOW--MY FRIEND THE MEATMAN? SEEMS HE'S GOT A TAPE-WORM...
AGAIN.
I DON' BELIEVE IT...
I DIN' WANT TO EITHER, SO'S I HAD THE JEW GIVE 'IM A CHECK-UP, AN' SURE AS SHIT, WHAT'S GOIN' IN, AN' WHAT'S COMIN' OUT DON' JIBE.
THAT IS VERY UPSETTING...

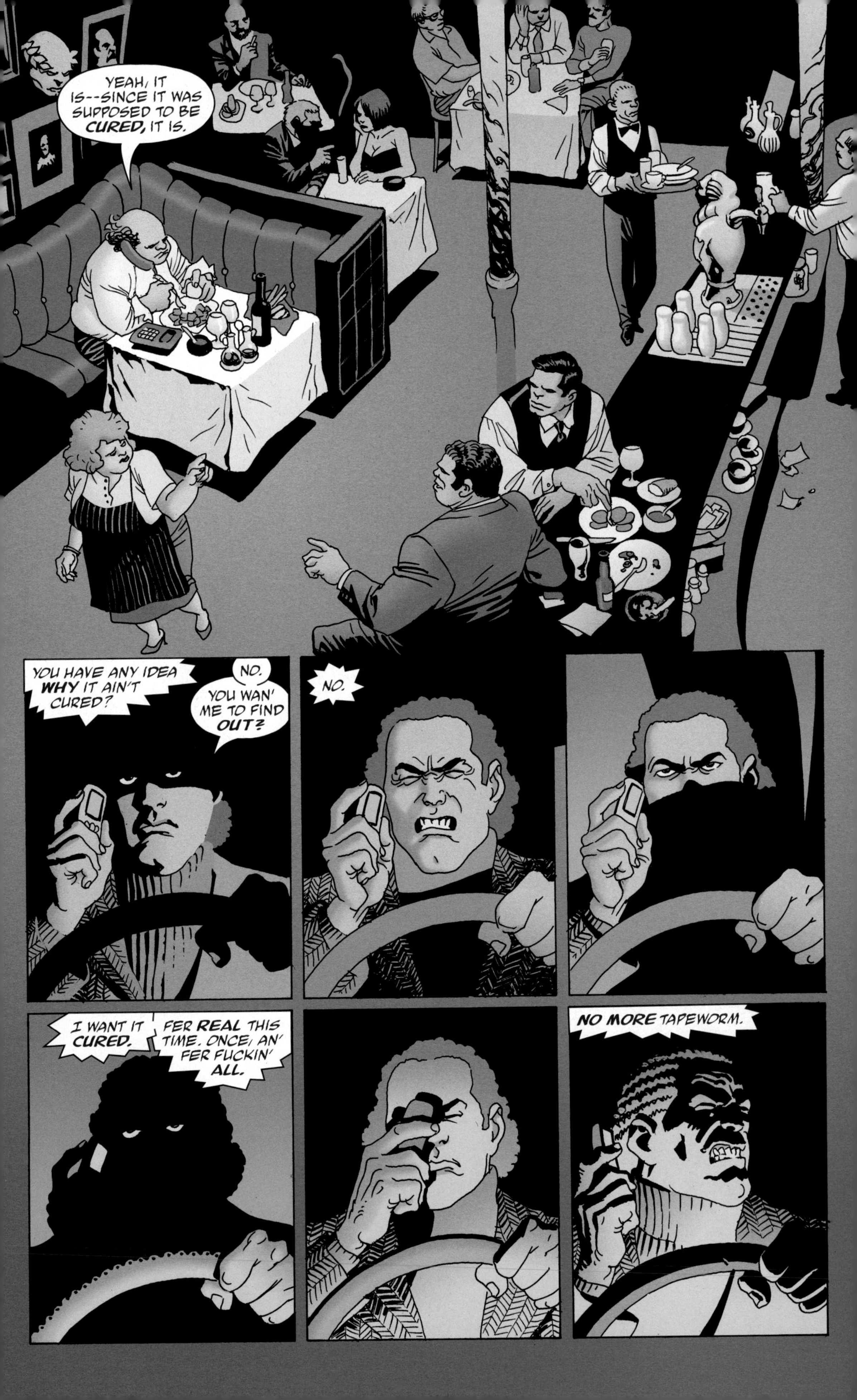
YEAH, IT IS--SINCE IT WAS SUPPOSED TO BE CURED, IT IS.
YOU HAVE ANY IDEA WHY IT AIN'T CURED?
NO.
YOU WAN' ME TO FIND OUT?
NO.
I WANT IT CURED.
FER REAL THIS TIME. ONCE, AN' FER FUCKIN' ALL.
NO MORE TAPEWORM.

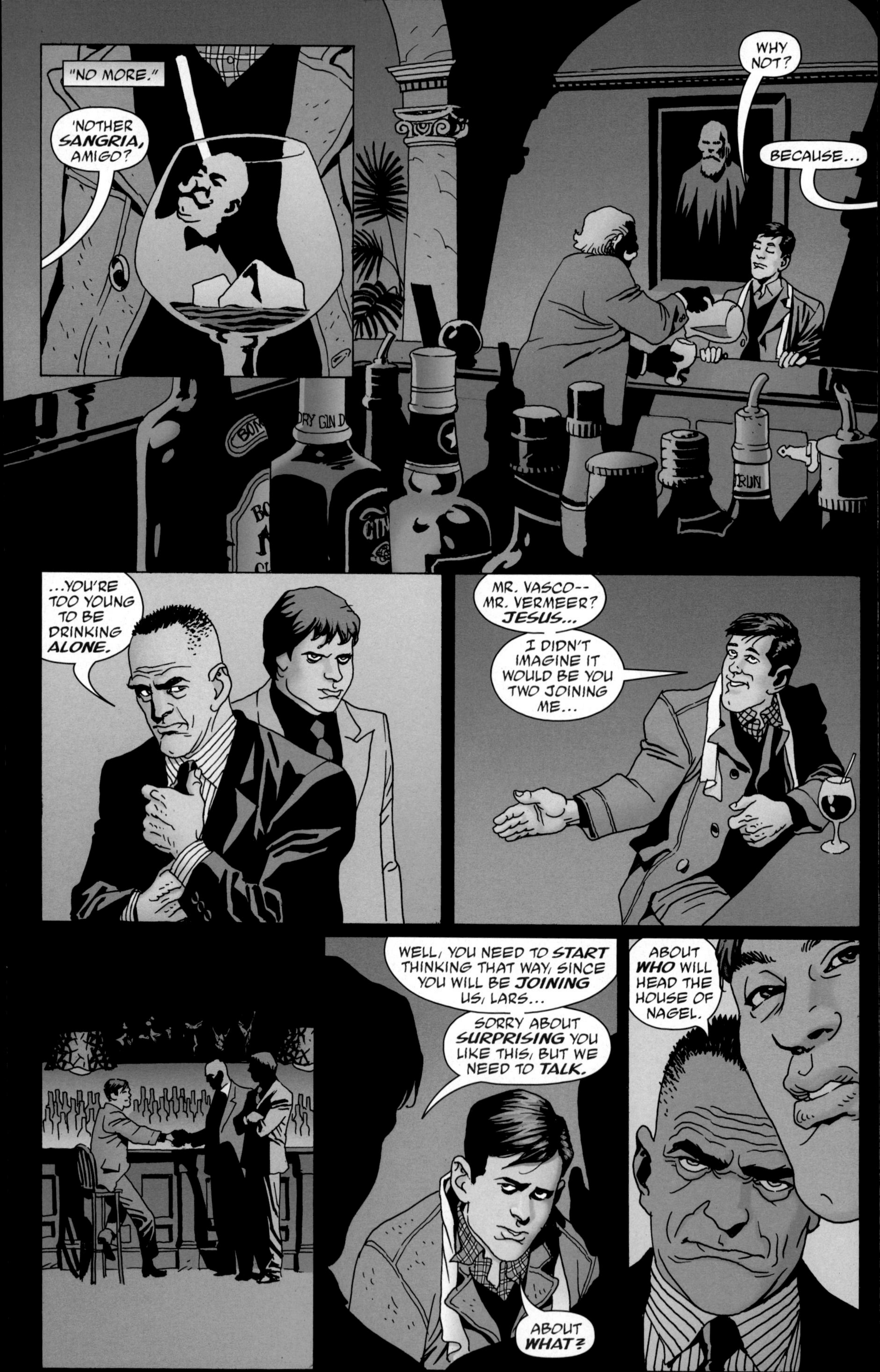

"NO MORE."
'NOTHER SANGRIA, AMIGO?
WHY NOT?
BECAUSE...
...YOU'RE TOO YOUNG TO BE DRINKING ALONE.
MR. VASCO-- MR. VERMEER? JESUS...
I DIDN'T IMAGINE IT WOULD BE YOU TWO JOINING ME...
WELL, YOU NEED TO START THINKING THAT WAY, SINCE YOU WILL BE JOINING US, LARS...
SORRY ABOUT SURPRISING YOU LIKE THIS, BUT WE NEED TO TALK.
ABOUT WHAT?
ABOUT WHO WILL HEAD THE HOUSE OF NAGEL.

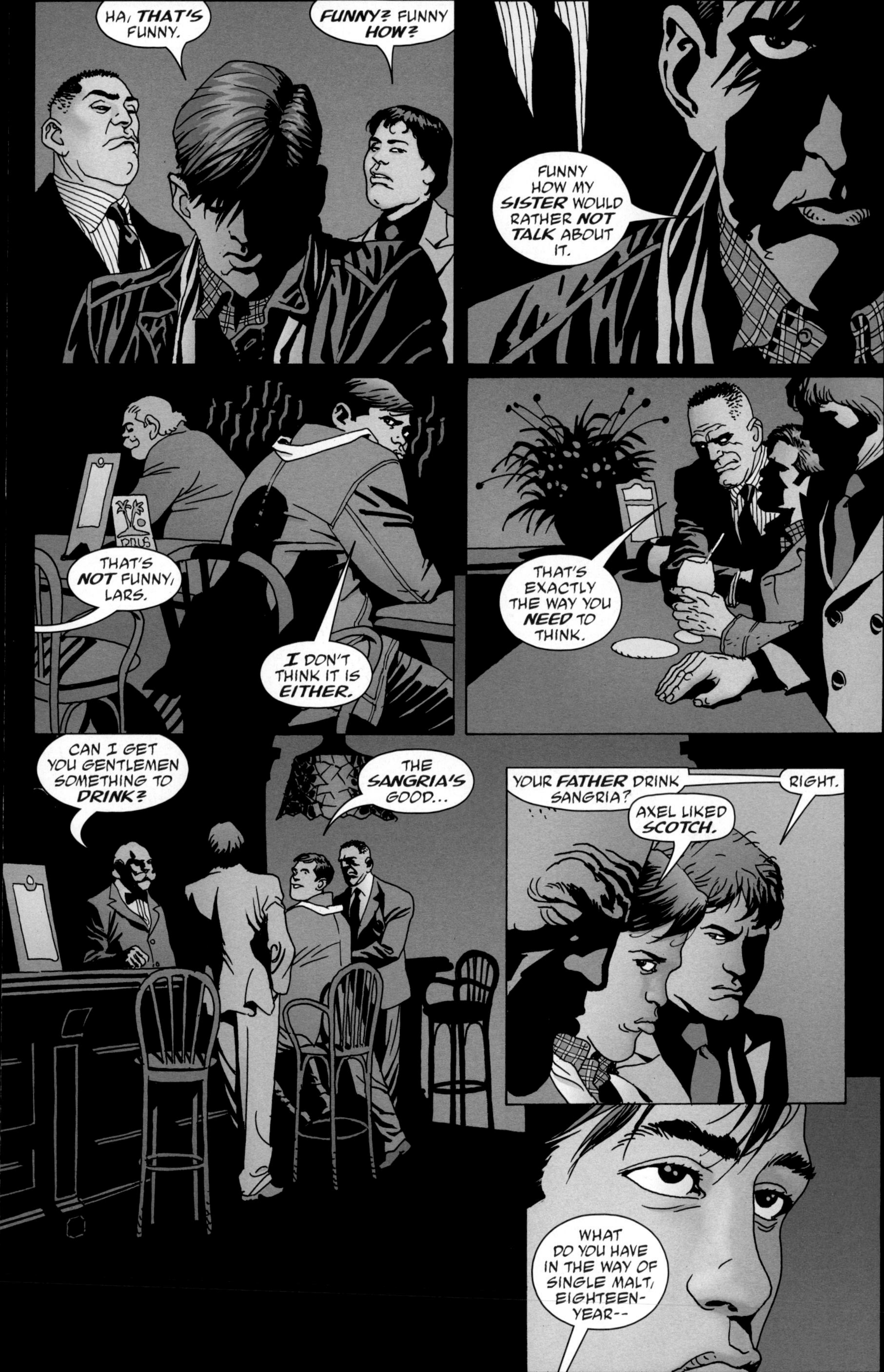
HA, **THAT'S** FUNNY.
FUNNY? FUNNY **HOW?**
FUNNY HOW MY **SISTER** WOULD RATHER **NOT TALK** ABOUT IT.
THAT'S **NOT** FUNNY, LARS.
I DON'T THINK IT IS **EITHER.**
THAT'S EXACTLY THE WAY YOU **NEED** TO THINK.
CAN I GET YOU GENTLEMEN SOMETHING TO **DRINK?**
THE **SANGRIA'S** GOOD...
YOUR **FATHER** DRINK SANGRIA?
RIGHT.
AXEL LIKED **SCOTCH.**
WHAT DO YOU HAVE IN THE WAY OF SINGLE MALT, EIGHTEEN-YEAR--

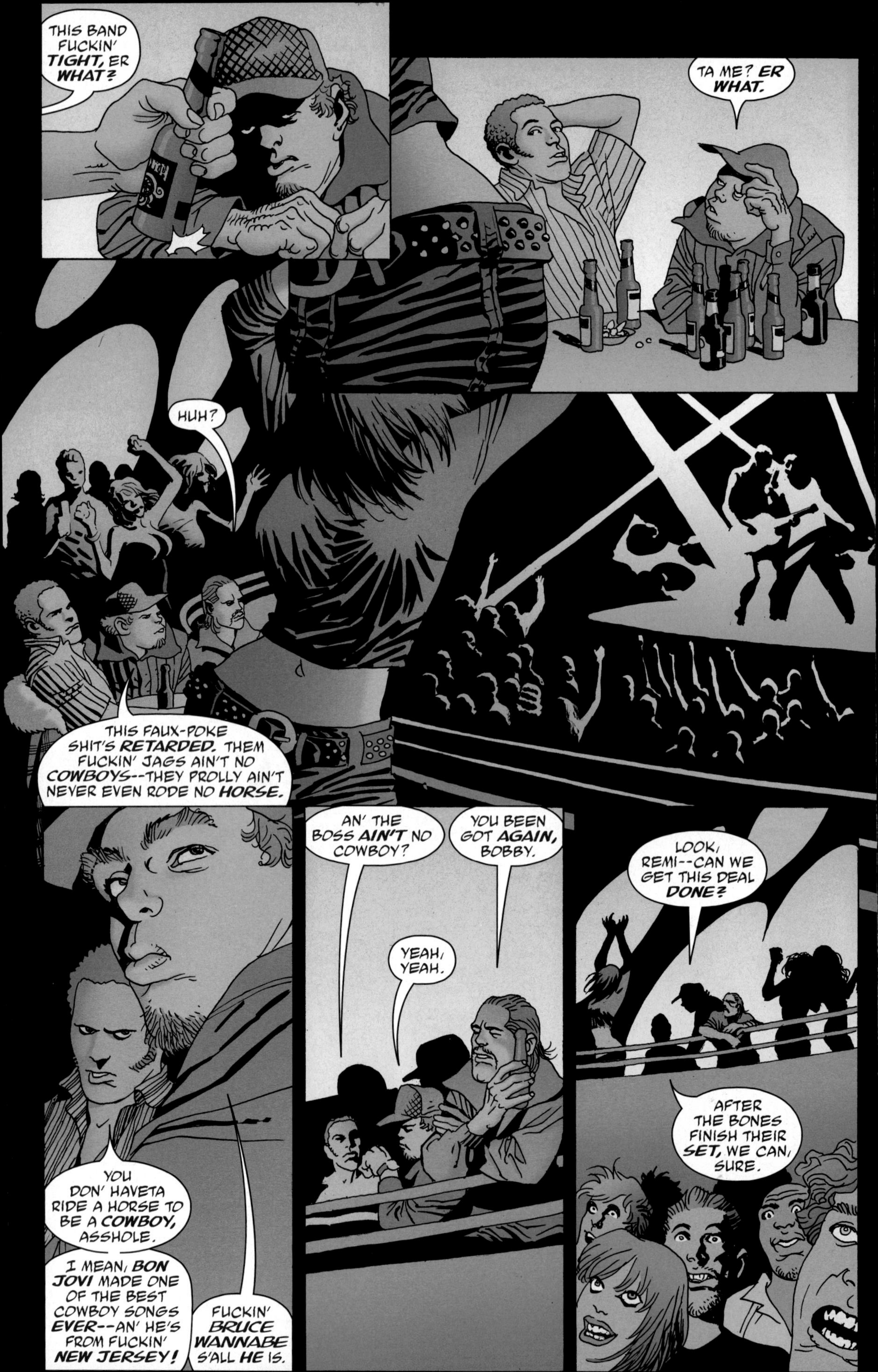
THIS BAND FUCKIN' TIGHT, ER WHAT?
TA ME? ER WHAT.
HUH?
THIS FAUX-POKE SHIT'S RETARDED. THEM FUCKIN' JAGS AIN'T NO COWBOYS--THEY PROLLY AIN'T NEVER EVEN RODE NO HORSE.
YOU DON' HAVETA RIDE A HORSE TO BE A COWBOY, ASSHOLE.
I MEAN, BON JOVI MADE ONE OF THE BEST COWBOY SONGS EVER--AN' HE'S FROM FUCKIN' NEW JERSEY!
FUCKIN' BRUCE WANNABE S'ALL HE IS.
AN' THE BOSS AIN'T NO COWBOY?
YOU BEEN GOT AGAIN, BOBBY.
YEAH, YEAH.
LOOK, REMI--CAN WE GET THIS DEAL DONE?
AFTER THE BONES FINISH THEIR SET, WE CAN, SURE.

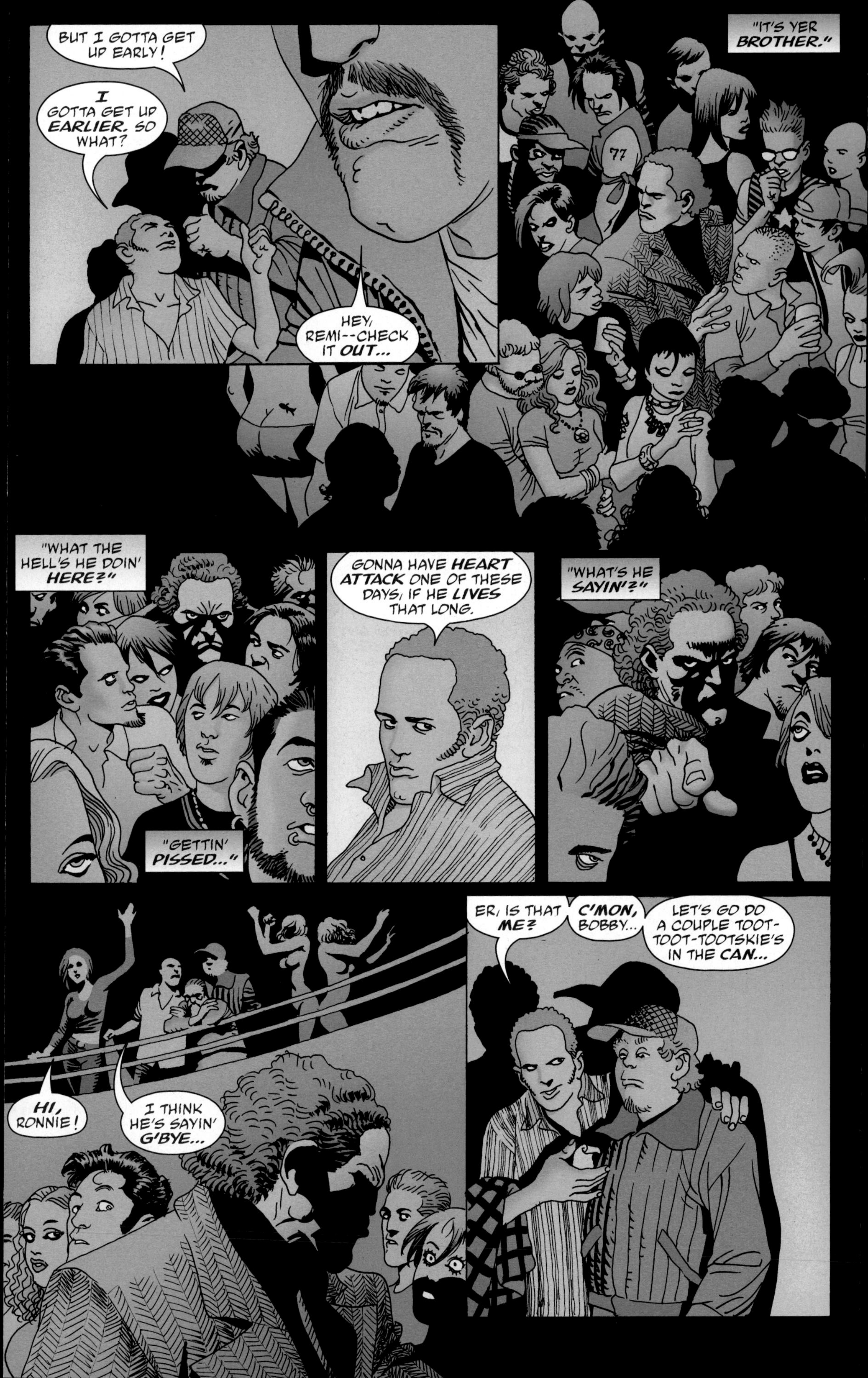
BUT I GOTTA GET UP EARLY!
I GOTTA GET UP EARLIER. SO WHAT?
HEY, REMI--CHECK IT OUT...
"IT'S YER BROTHER."
"WHAT THE HELL'S HE DOIN' HERE?"
"GETTIN' PISSED..."
GONNA HAVE HEART ATTACK ONE OF THESE DAYS, IF HE LIVES THAT LONG.
"WHAT'S HE SAYIN'?"
HI, RONNIE!
I THINK HE'S SAYIN' G'BYE...
ER, IS THAT ME?
C'MON, BOBBY...
LET'S GO DO A COUPLE TOOT-TOOT-TOOTSKIE'S IN THE CAN...

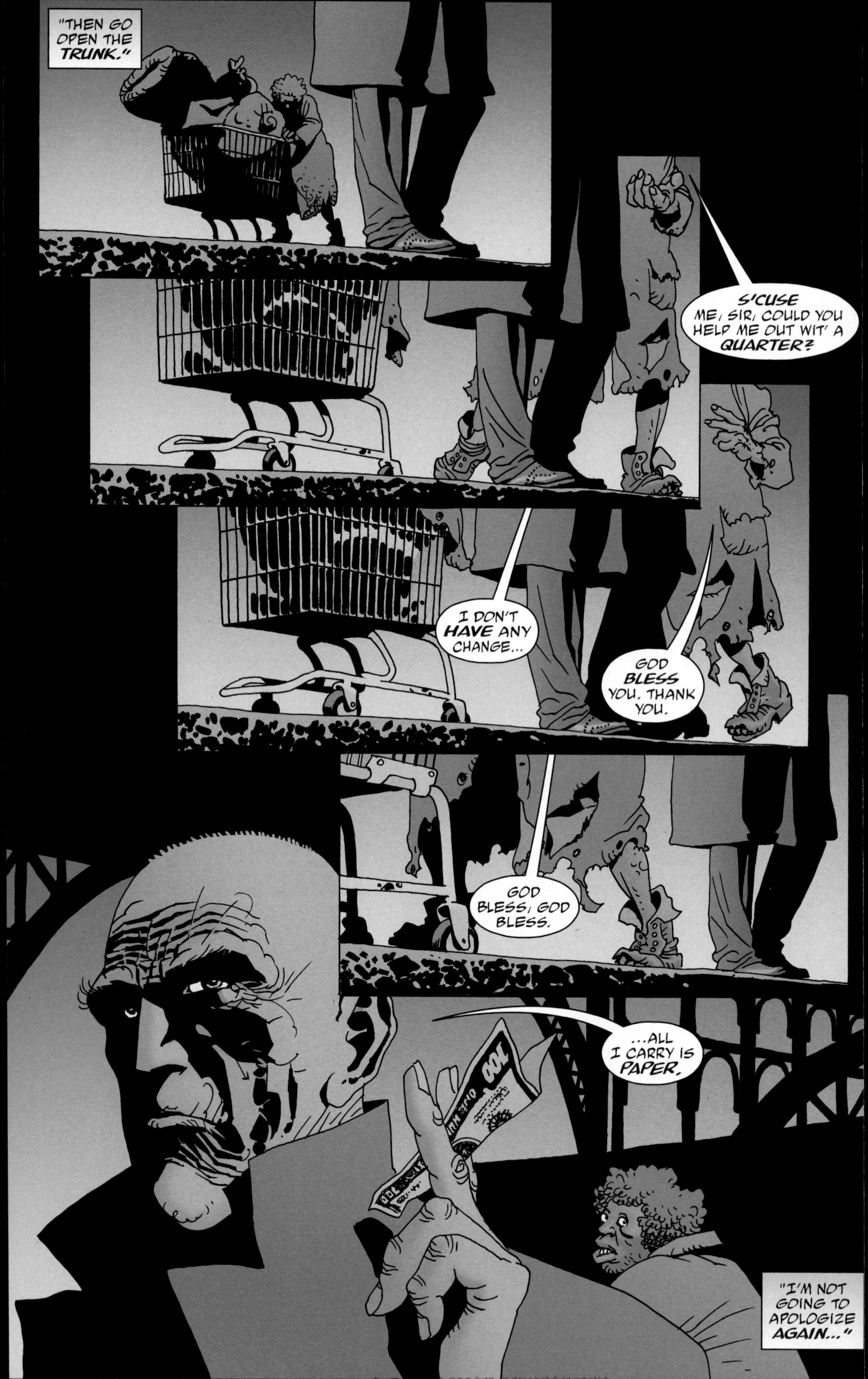
"THEN GO OPEN THE TRUNK."
S'CUSE ME, SIR, COULD YOU HELP ME OUT WIT' A QUARTER?
I DON'T HAVE ANY CHANGE...
GOD BLESS YOU. THANK YOU.
GOD BLESS, GOD BLESS.
...ALL I CARRY IS PAPER.
"I'M NOT GOING TO APOLOGIZE AGAIN..."

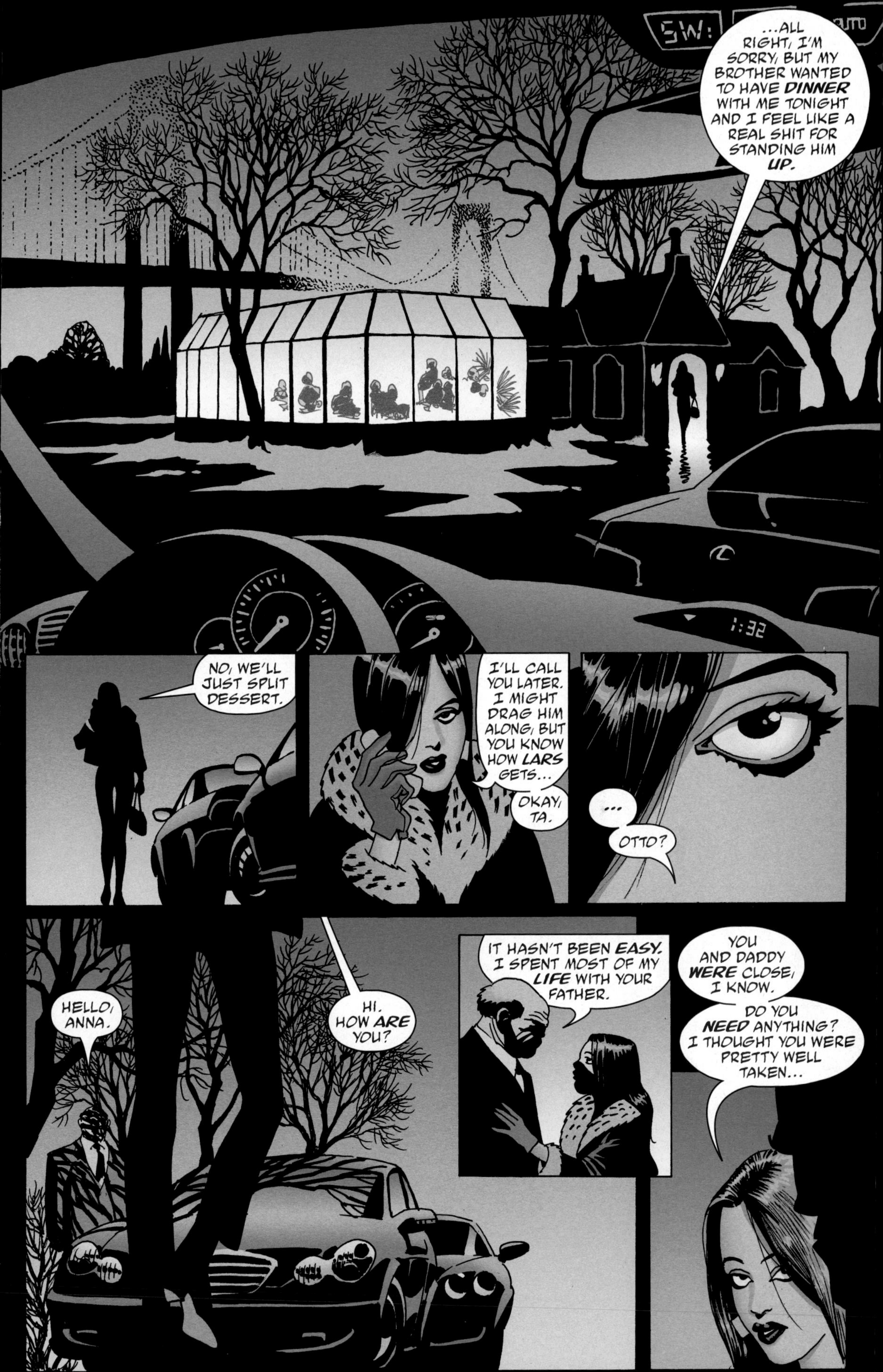
SW:
...ALL RIGHT, I'M SORRY, BUT MY BROTHER WANTED TO HAVE DINNER WITH ME TONIGHT AND I FEEL LIKE A REAL SHIT FOR STANDING HIM UP.
1:32
NO, WE'LL JUST SPLIT DESSERT.
I'LL CALL YOU LATER. I MIGHT DRAG HIM ALONG, BUT YOU KNOW HOW LARS GETS...
OKAY, TA.
...
OTTO?
HELLO, ANNA.
HI. HOW ARE YOU?
IT HASN'T BEEN EASY. I SPENT MOST OF MY LIFE WITH YOUR FATHER.
YOU AND DADDY WERE CLOSE, I KNOW.
DO YOU NEED ANYTHING? I THOUGHT YOU WERE PRETTY WELL TAKEN...

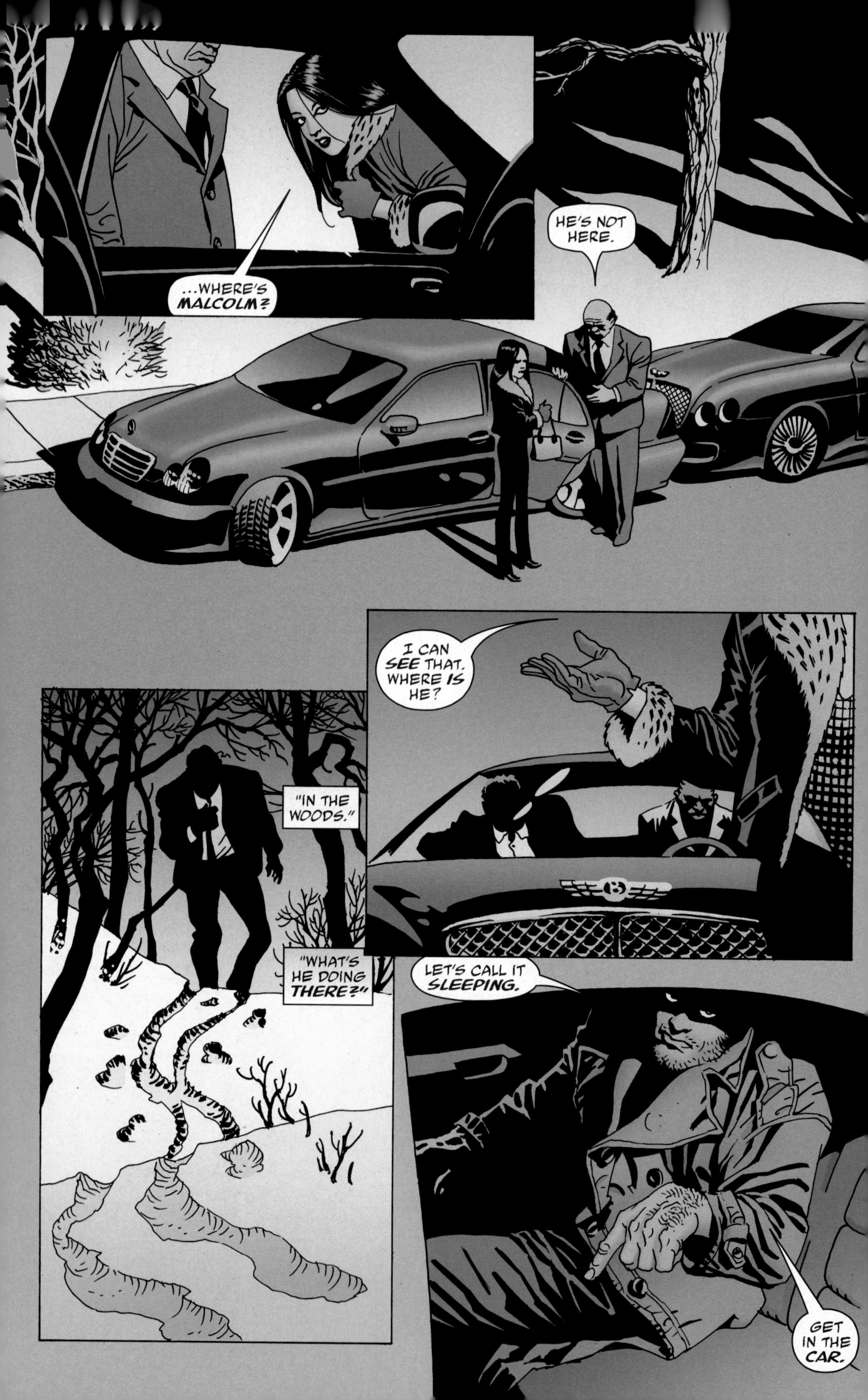
...WHERE'S MALCOLM?
HE'S NOT HERE.
I CAN SEE THAT. WHERE IS HE?
LET'S CALL IT SLEEPING.
"IN THE WOODS."
"WHAT'S HE DOING THERE?"
GET IN THE CAR.

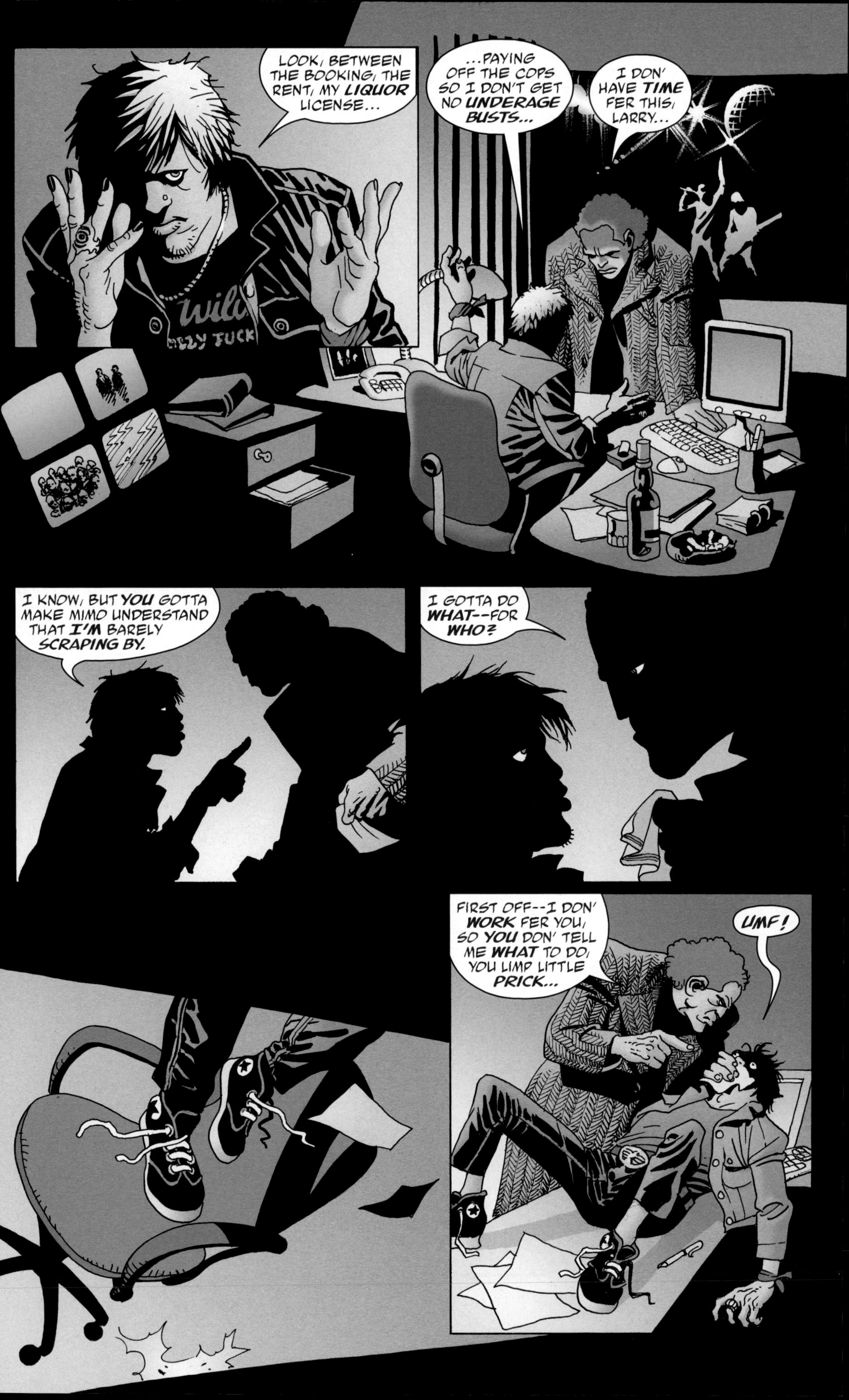
LOOK, BETWEEN THE BOOKING, THE RENT, MY LIQUOR LICENSE...
...PAYING OFF THE COPS SO I DON'T GET NO UNDERAGE BUSTS...
I DON' HAVE TIME FER THIS, LARRY...
I KNOW, BUT YOU GOTTA MAKE MIMO UNDERSTAND THAT I'M BARELY SCRAPING BY.
I GOTTA DO WHAT--FOR WHO?
FIRST OFF--I DON' WORK FER YOU, SO YOU DON' TELL ME WHAT TO DO, YOU LIMP LITTLE PRICK...
UMF!

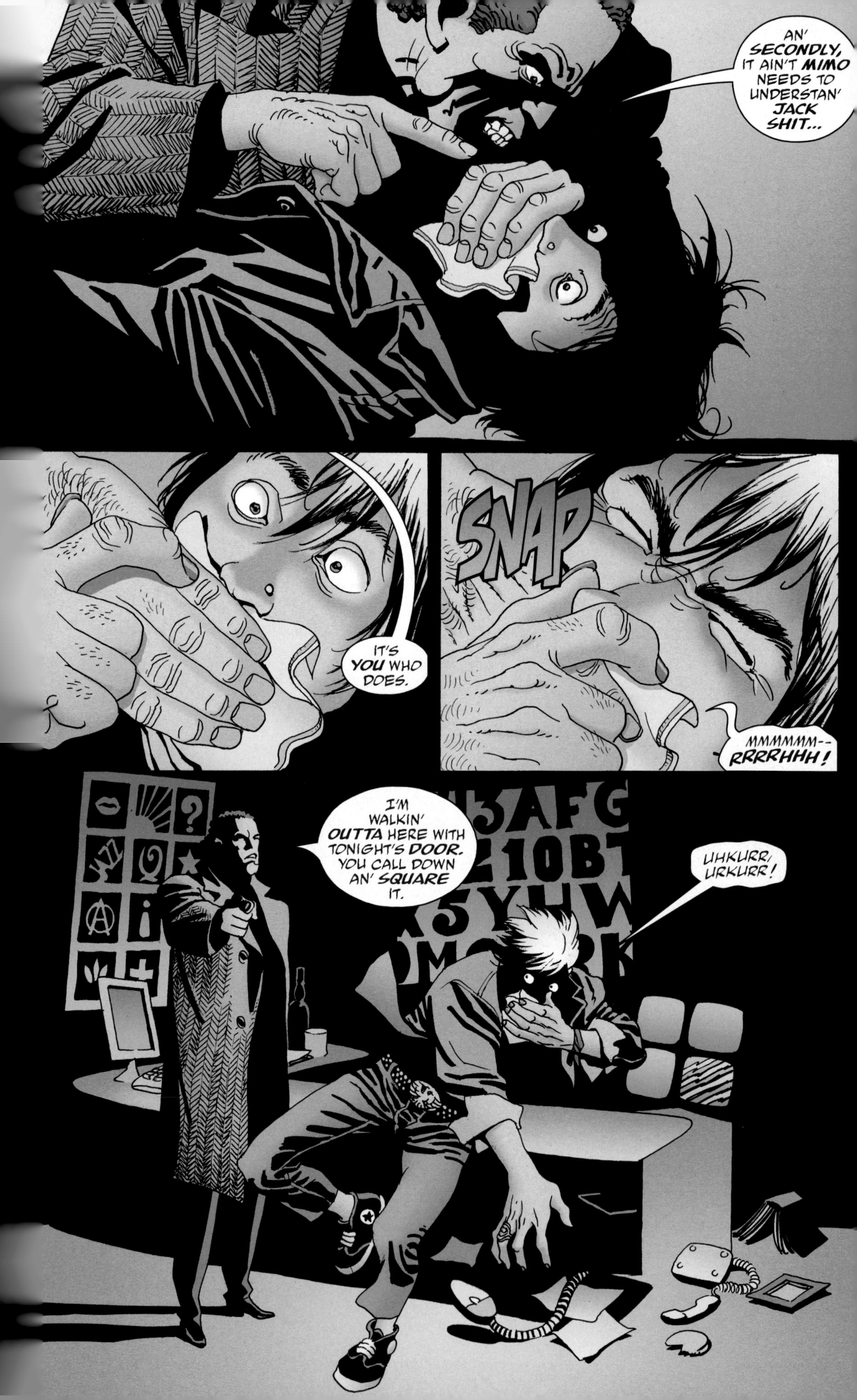
AN' SECONDLY, IT AIN'T MIMO NEEDS TO UNDERSTAN' JACK SHIT...
IT'S YOU WHO DOES.
SNAP
MMMMMM-- RRRRHHH!
I'M WALKIN' OUTTA HERE WITH TONIGHT'S DOOR. YOU CALL DOWN AN' SQUARE IT.
UHKURR, URKURR!

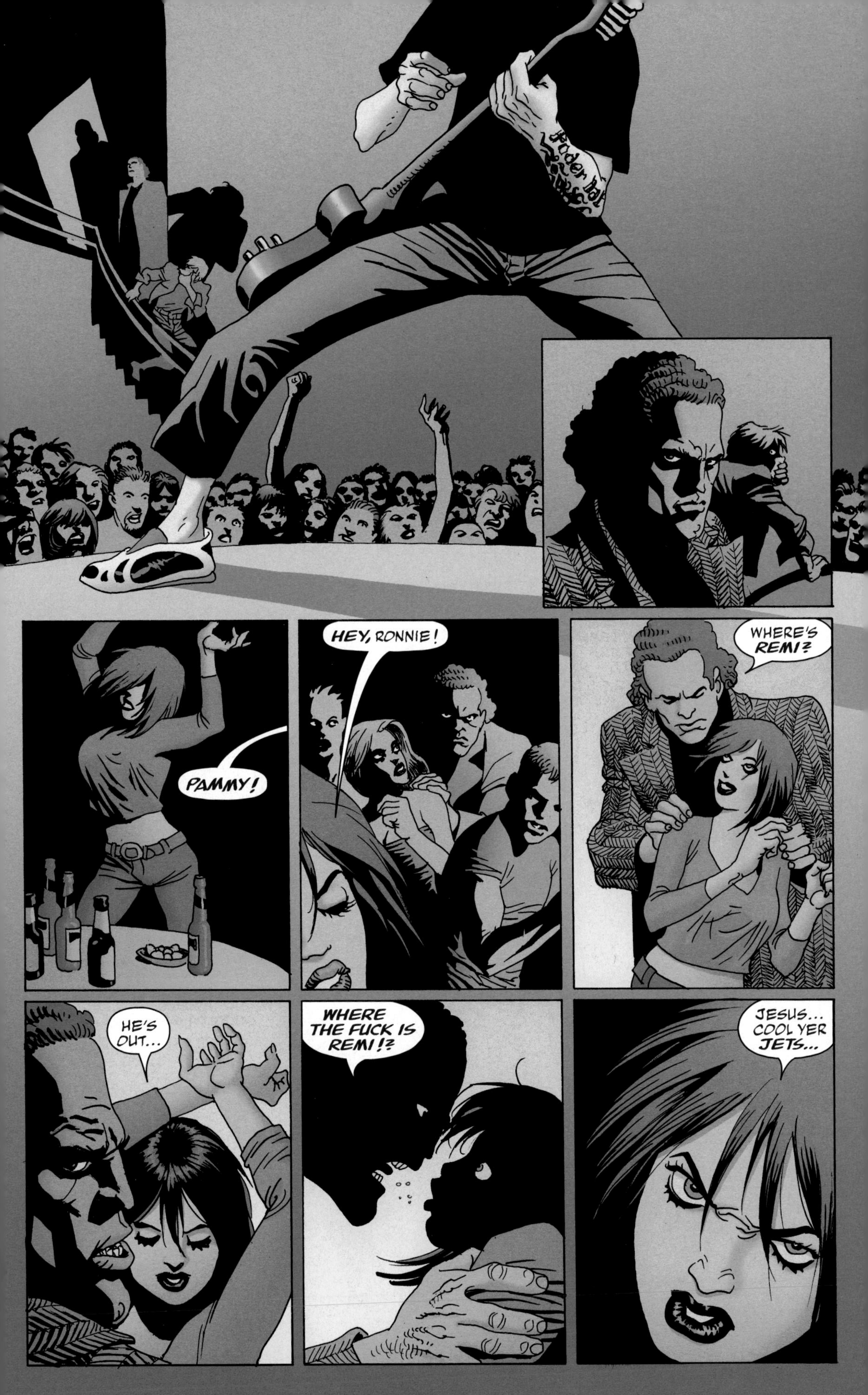
PAMMY!
HEY, RONNIE!
WHERE'S REMI?
HE'S OUT...
WHERE THE FUCK IS REMI!?
JESUS... COOL YER JETS...

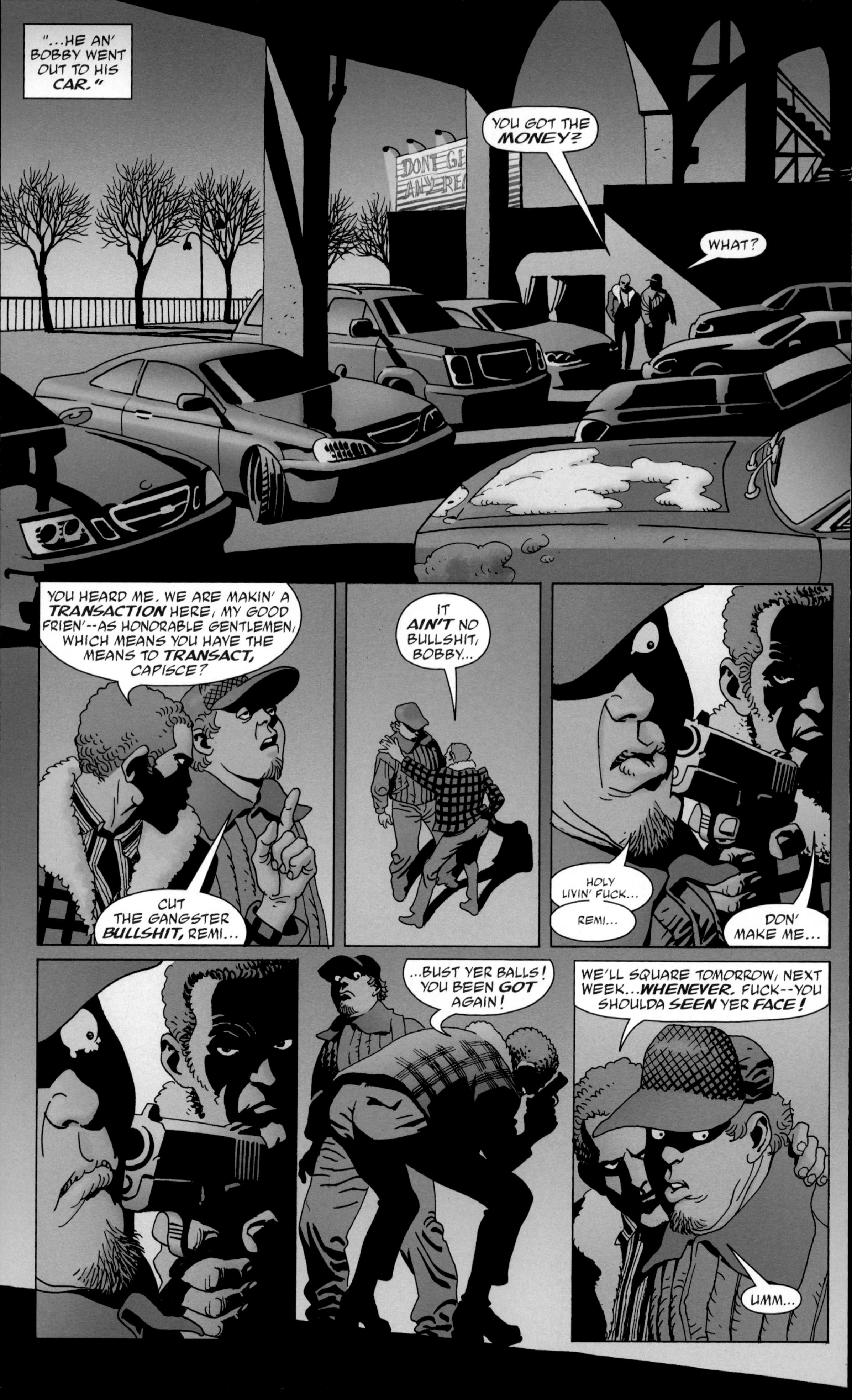
"...HE AN' BOBBY WENT OUT TO HIS CAR."
DON'T GE ANY REA
YOU GOT THE MONEY?
WHAT?
YOU HEARD ME. WE ARE MAKIN' A TRANSACTION HERE, MY GOOD FRIEN'--AS HONORABLE GENTLEMEN, WHICH MEANS YOU HAVE THE MEANS TO TRANSACT, CAPISCE?
CUT THE GANGSTER BULLSHIT, REMI...
IT AIN'T NO BULLSHIT, BOBBY...
HOLY LIVIN' FUCK...
REMI...
DON' MAKE ME...
...BUST YER BALLS! YOU BEEN GOT AGAIN!
WE'LL SQUARE TOMORROW, NEXT WEEK...WHENEVER. FUCK--YOU SHOULDA SEEN YER FACE!
UMM...

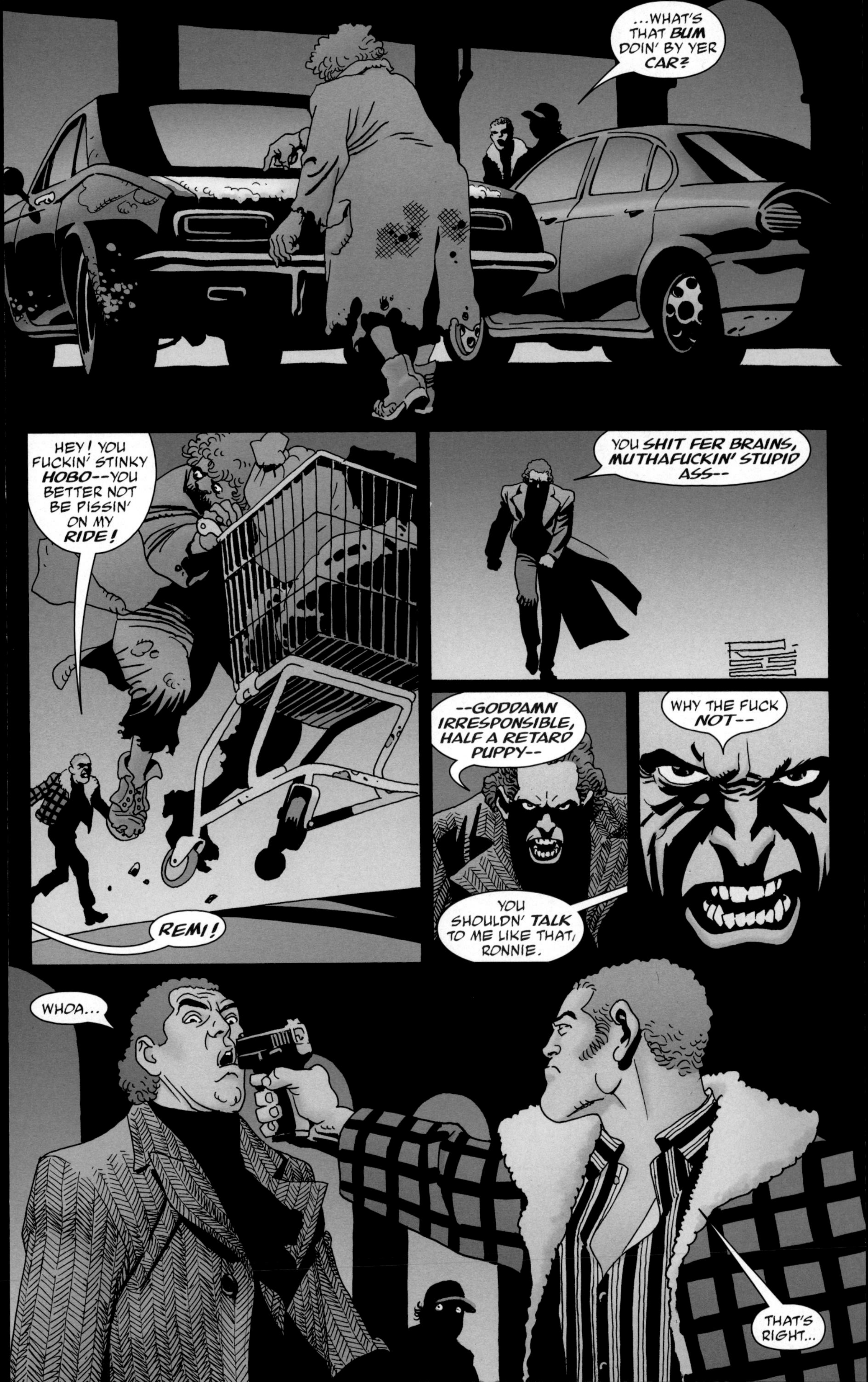
...WHAT'S THAT BUM DOIN' BY YER CAR?
HEY! YOU FUCKIN' STINKY HOBO--YOU BETTER NOT BE PISSIN' ON MY RIDE!
REMI!
YOU SHIT FER BRAINS, MUTHAFUCKIN' STUPID ASS--
--GODDAMN IRRESPONSIBLE, HALF A RETARD PUPPY--
WHY THE FUCK NOT--
YOU SHOULDN' TALK TO ME LIKE THAT, RONNIE.
WHOA...
THAT'S RIGHT...

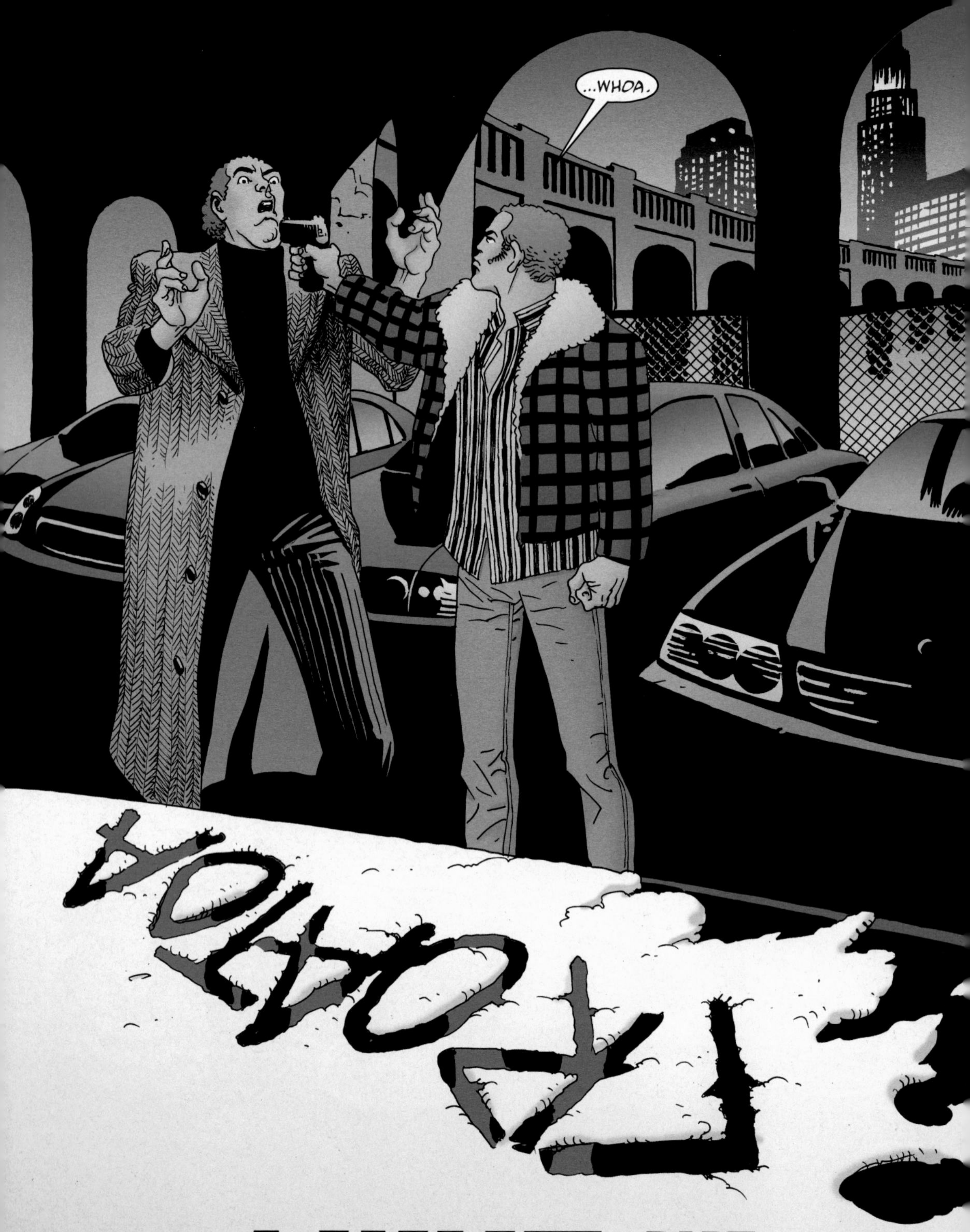
...WHOA.

A WAKE PART THREE

WRITTEN BY BRIAN AZZARELLO
ILLUSTRATED BY EDUARDO RISSO

COLORED BY PATRICIA MULVIHILL
LETTERED BY CLEM ROBINS COVER BY DAVE JOHNSON
ASSISTANT EDITOR CASEY SEIJAS EDITED BY WILL DENNIS

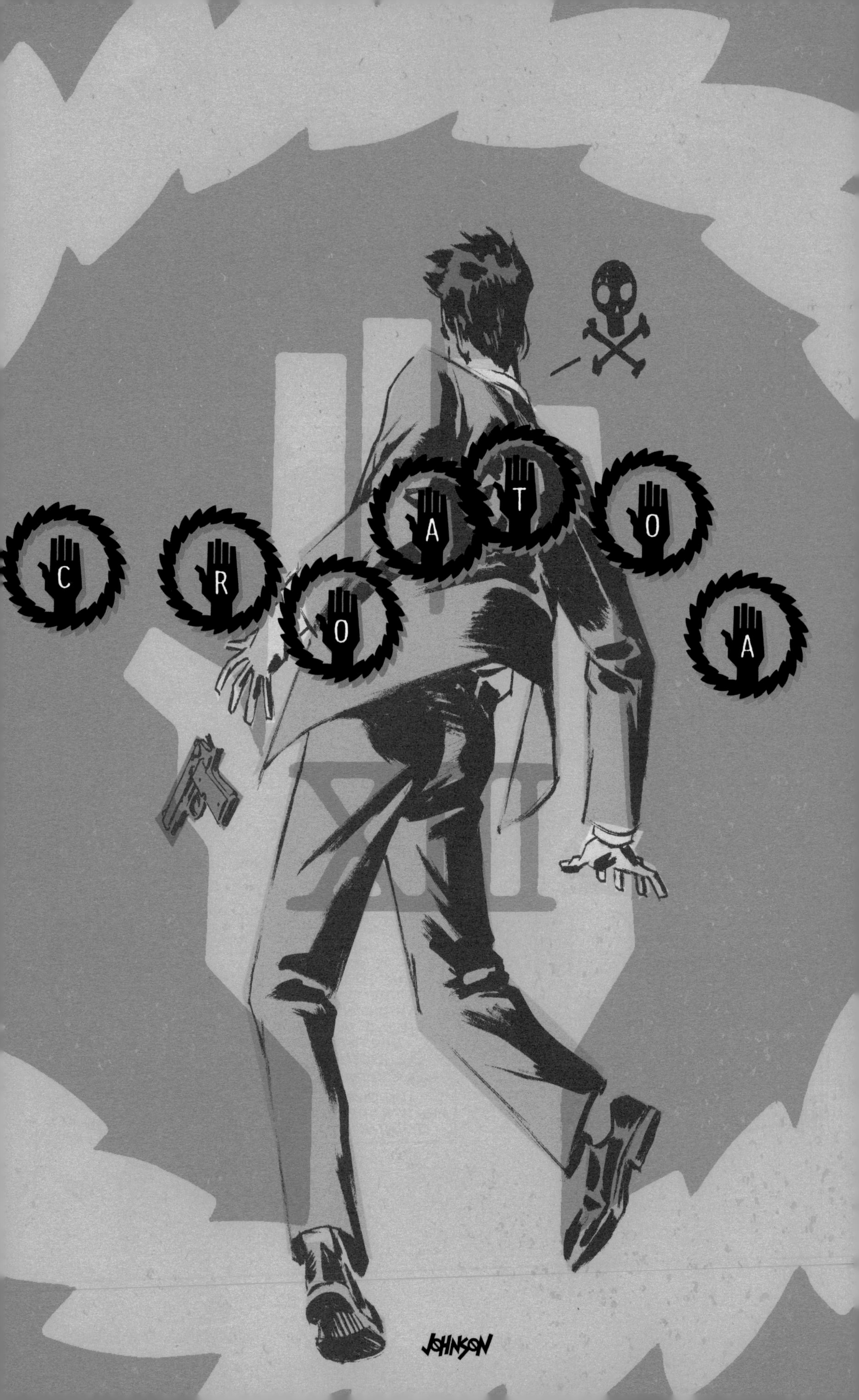
C
R
O
A
T
O
A
JOHNSON

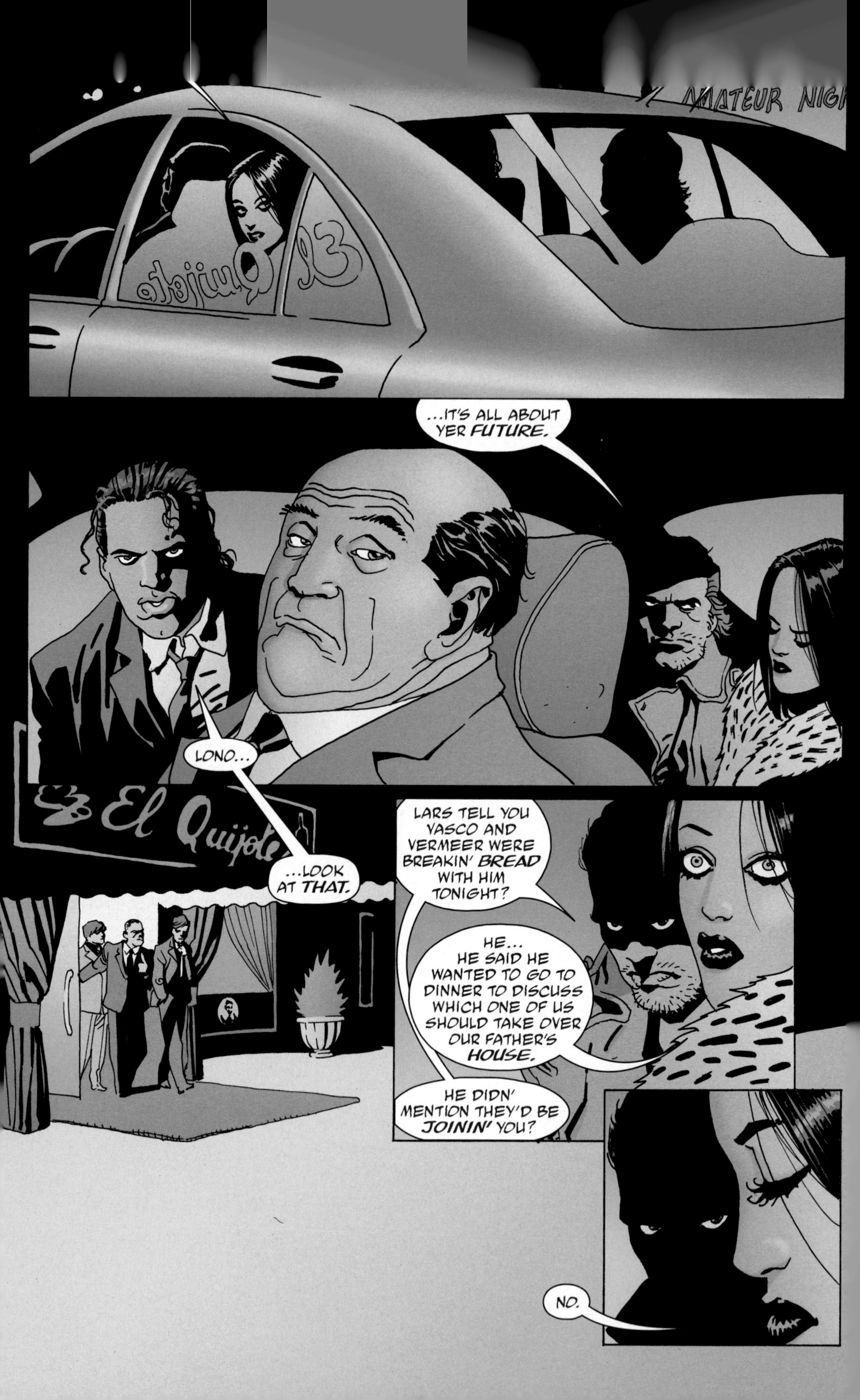

AMATEUR NIGH
El Quijote
...IT'S ALL ABOUT YER FUTURE.
LONO...
El Quijote
...LOOK AT THAT.
LARS TELL YOU VASCO AND VERMEER WERE BREAKIN' BREAD WITH HIM TONIGHT?
HE... HE SAID HE WANTED TO GO TO DINNER TO DISCUSS WHICH ONE OF US SHOULD TAKE OVER OUR FATHER'S HOUSE.
HE DIDN' MENTION THEY'D BE JOININ' YOU?
NO.

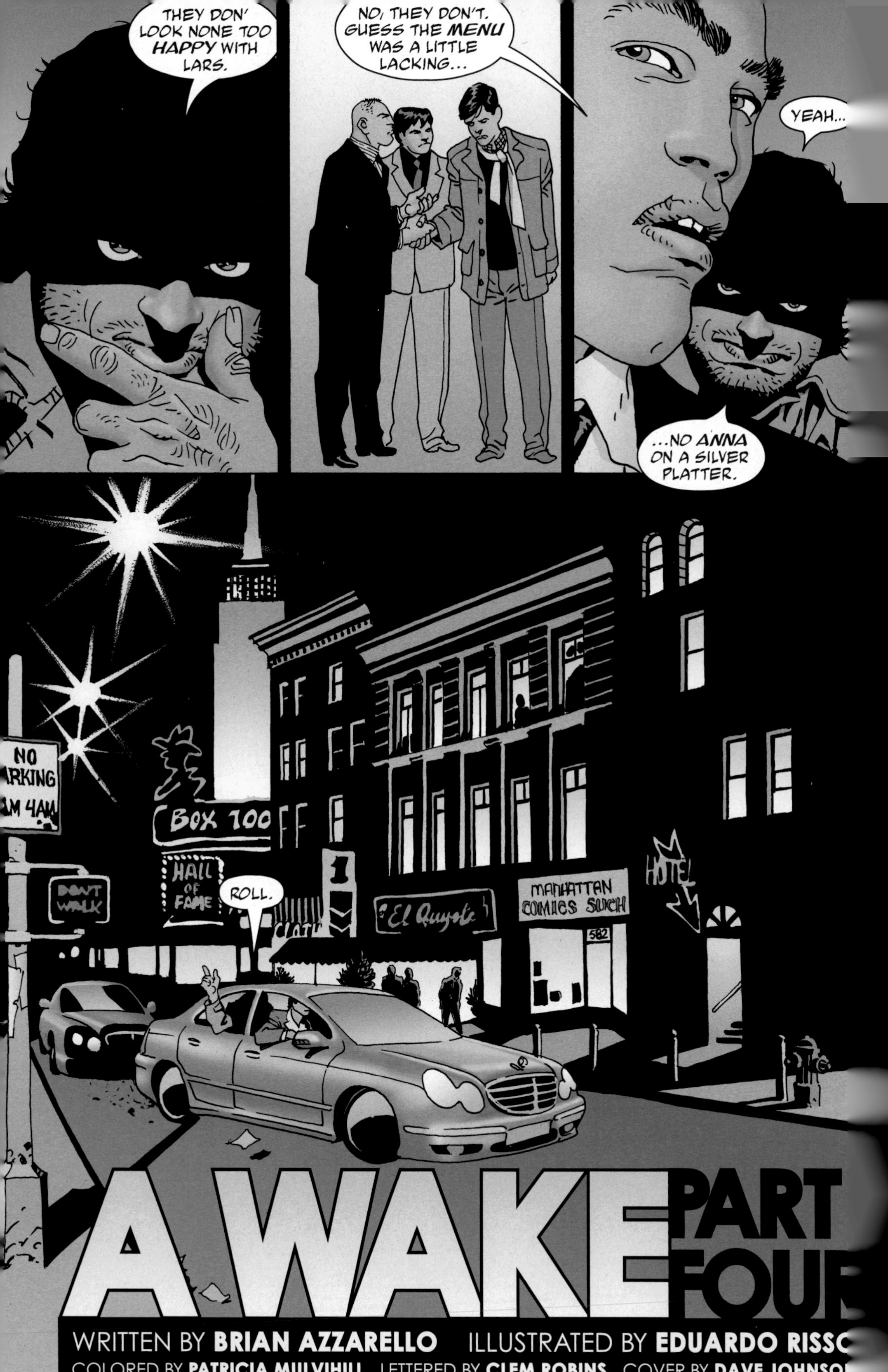
THEY DON' LOOK NONE TOO HAPPY WITH LARS.
NO, THEY DON'T. GUESS THE MENU WAS A LITTLE LACKING...
YEAH...
...NO ANNA ON A SILVER PLATTER.
NO
HALL OF FAME
DON'T WALK
ROLL.
MANHATTAN COMICS
582
HOTEL
A WAKE PART FOUR

WRITTEN BY **BRIAN AZZARELLO** ILLUSTRATED BY **EDUARDO RISSO**
COLORED BY **PATRICIA MULVIHILL** LETTERED BY **CLEM ROBINS** COVER BY **DAVE JOHNSON**
ASSISTANT EDITOR **CASEY SEIJAS** EDITED BY **WILL DENNIS**

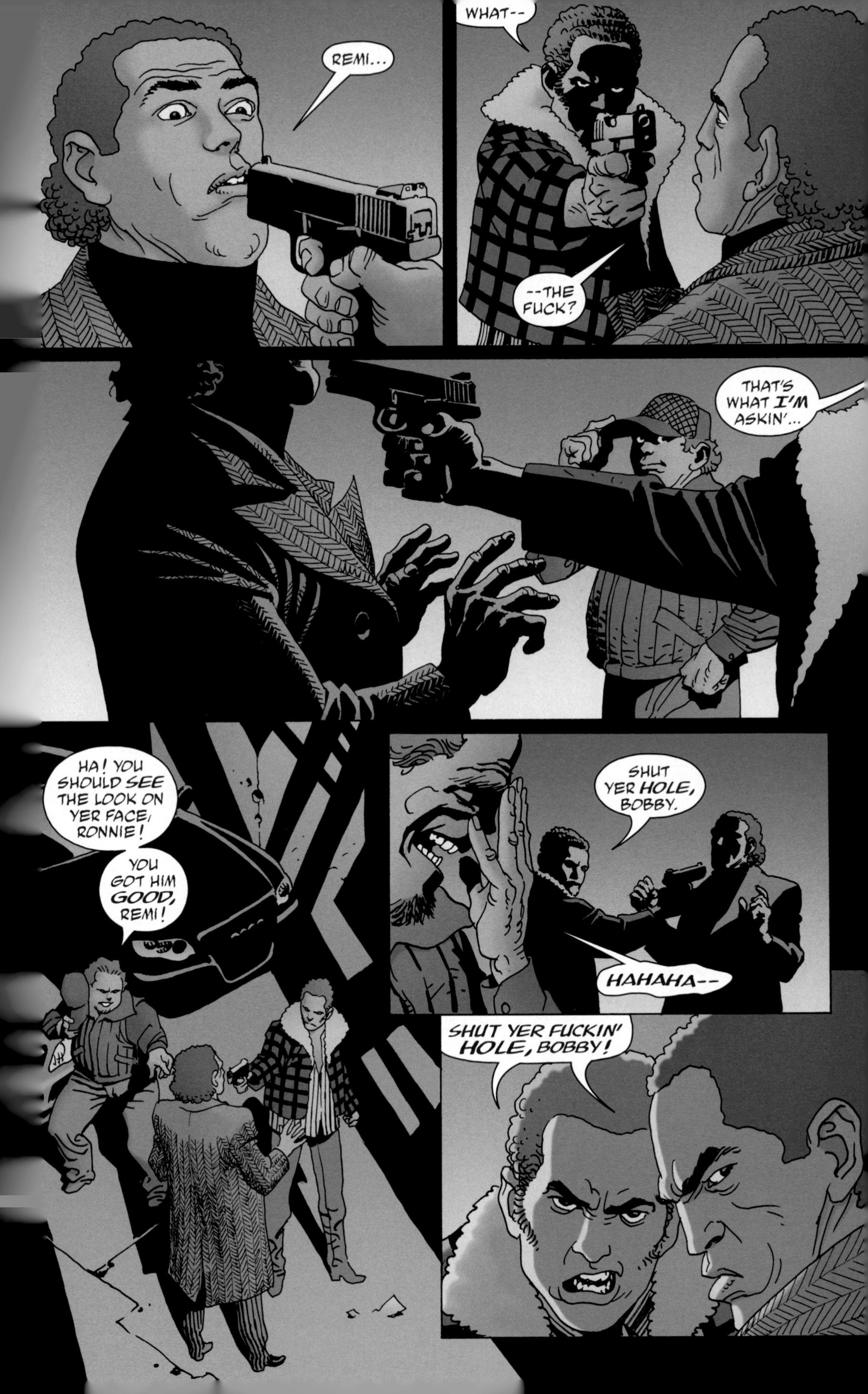
REMI...
WHAT--
--THE FUCK?
THAT'S WHAT I'M ASKIN'...
HA! YOU SHOULD SEE THE LOOK ON YER FACE, RONNIE!
YOU GOT HIM GOOD, REMI!
SHUT YER HOLE, BOBBY.
HAHAHA--
SHUT YER FUCKIN' HOLE, BOBBY!

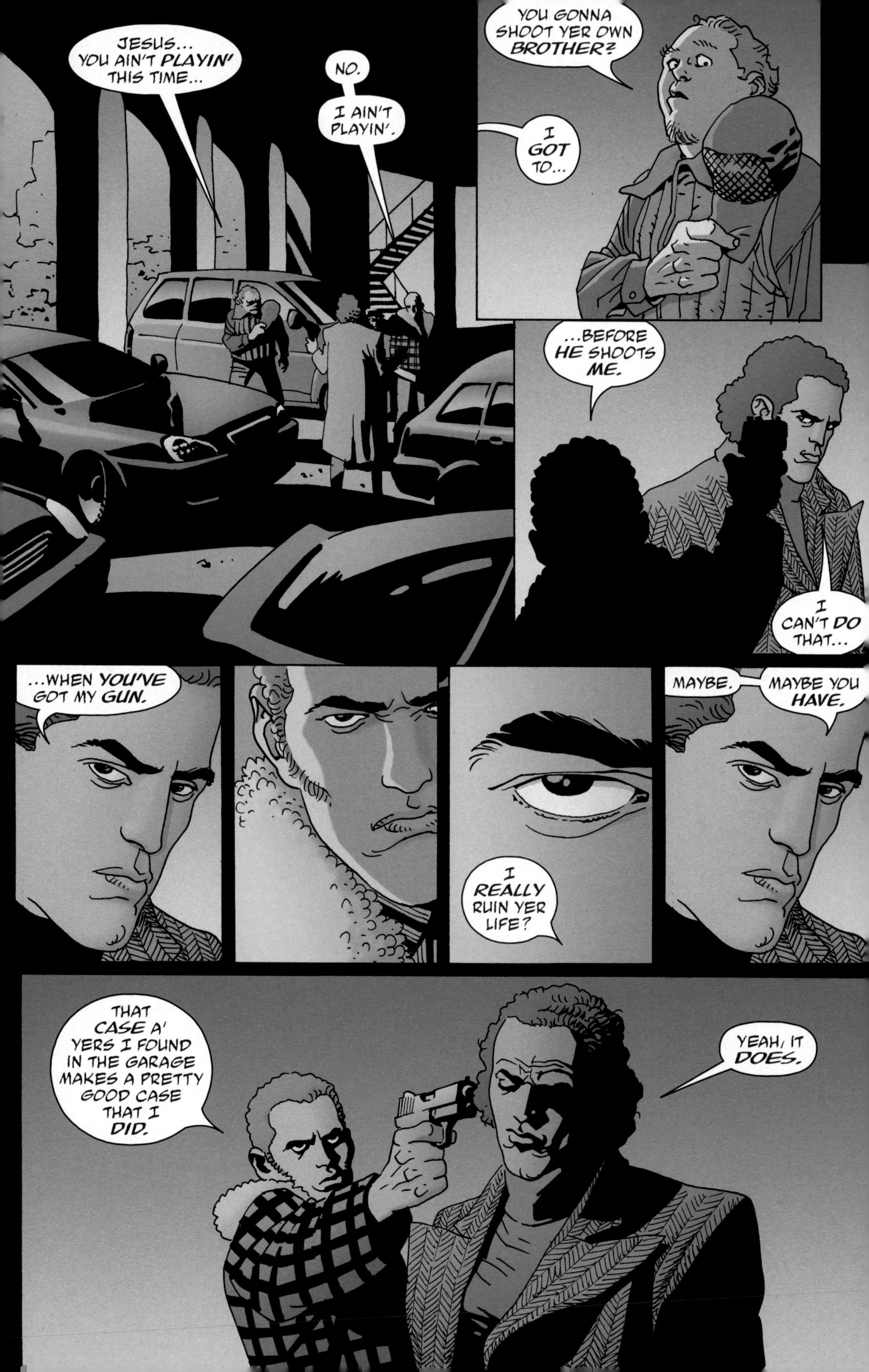
JESUS... YOU AIN'T PLAYIN' THIS TIME...
NO.
I AIN'T PLAYIN'.
YOU GONNA SHOOT YER OWN BROTHER?
I GOT TO...
...BEFORE HE SHOOTS ME.
I CAN'T DO THAT...
...WHEN YOU'VE GOT MY GUN.
I REALLY RUIN YER LIFE?
MAYBE.
MAYBE YOU HAVE.
THAT CASE A' YERS I FOUND IN THE GARAGE MAKES A PRETTY GOOD CASE THAT I DID.
YEAH, IT DOES.

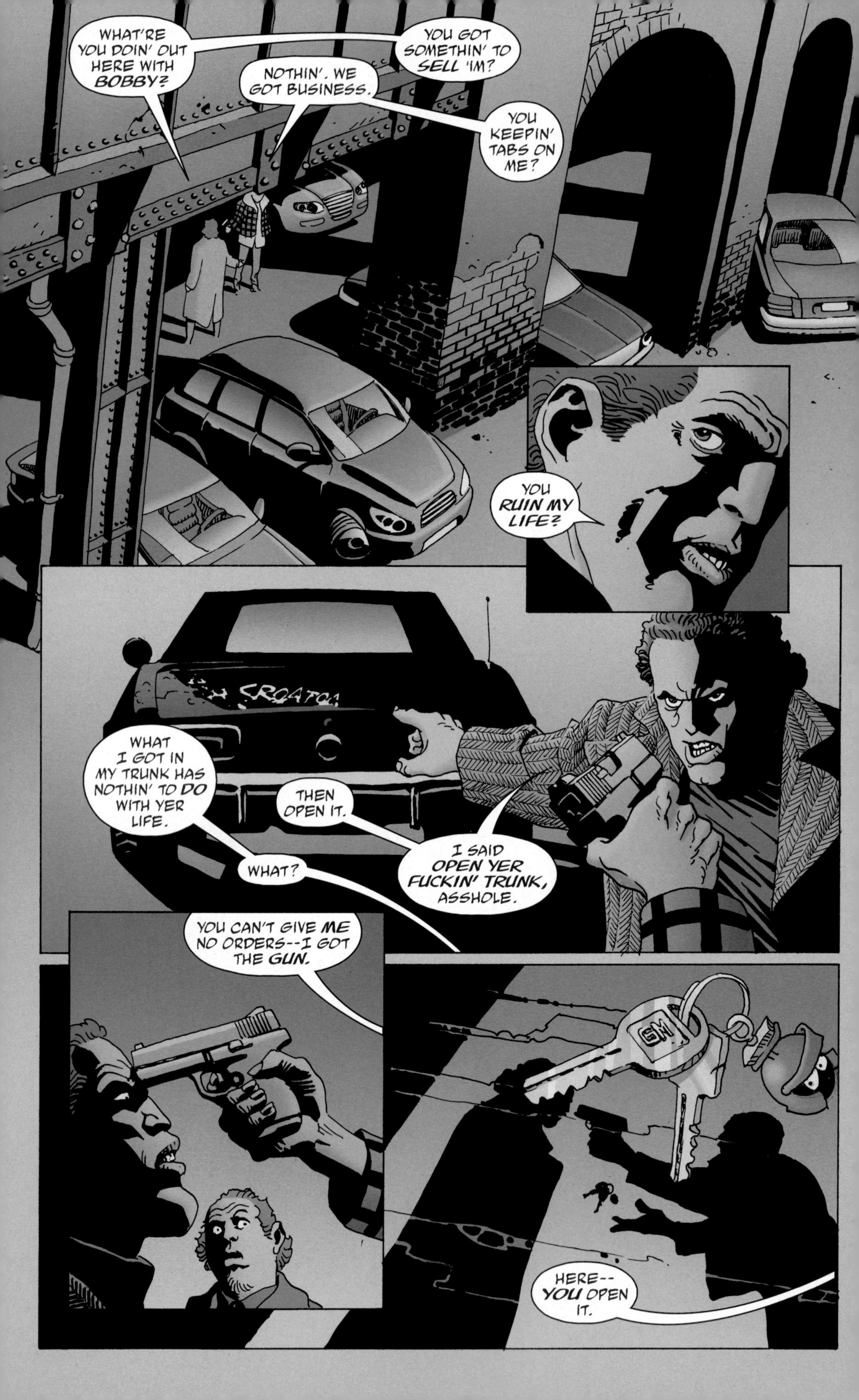
WHAT'RE YOU DOIN' OUT HERE WITH BOBBY?
YOU GOT SOMETHIN' TO SELL 'IM?
NOTHIN'. WE GOT BUSINESS.
YOU KEEPIN' TABS ON ME?
YOU RUIN MY LIFE?
WHAT I GOT IN MY TRUNK HAS NOTHIN' TO DO WITH YER LIFE.
THEN OPEN IT.
WHAT?
I SAID OPEN YER FUCKIN' TRUNK, ASSHOLE.
YOU CAN'T GIVE ME NO ORDERS--I GOT THE GUN.
HERE--YOU OPEN IT.

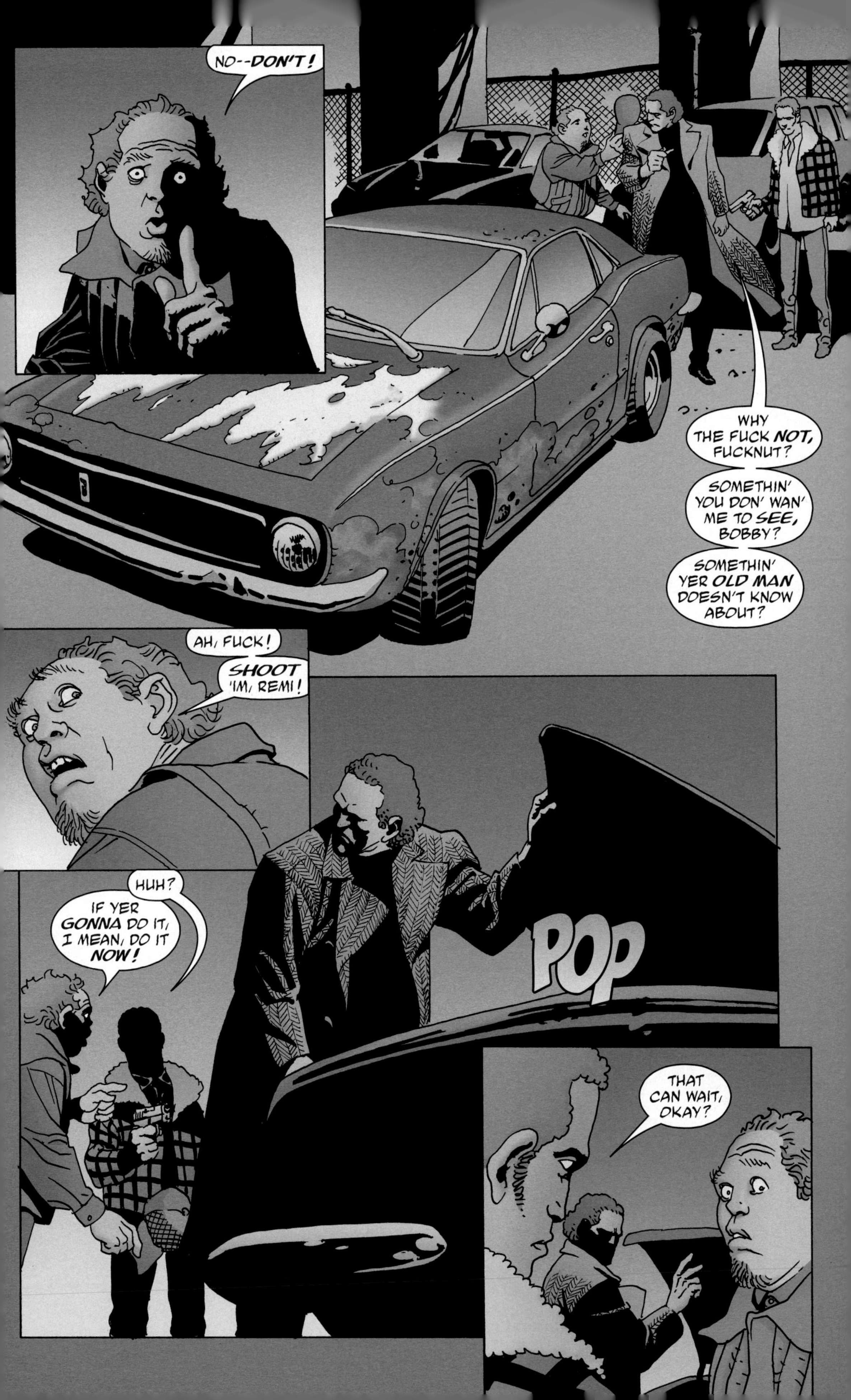
NO--DON'T!
WHY THE FUCK NOT, FUCKNUT?
SOMETHIN' YOU DON' WAN' ME TO SEE, BOBBY?
SOMETHIN' YER OLD MAN DOESN'T KNOW ABOUT?
AH, FUCK!
SHOOT 'IM, REMI!
POP
HUH?
IF YER GONNA DO IT, I MEAN, DO IT NOW!
THAT CAN WAIT, OKAY?

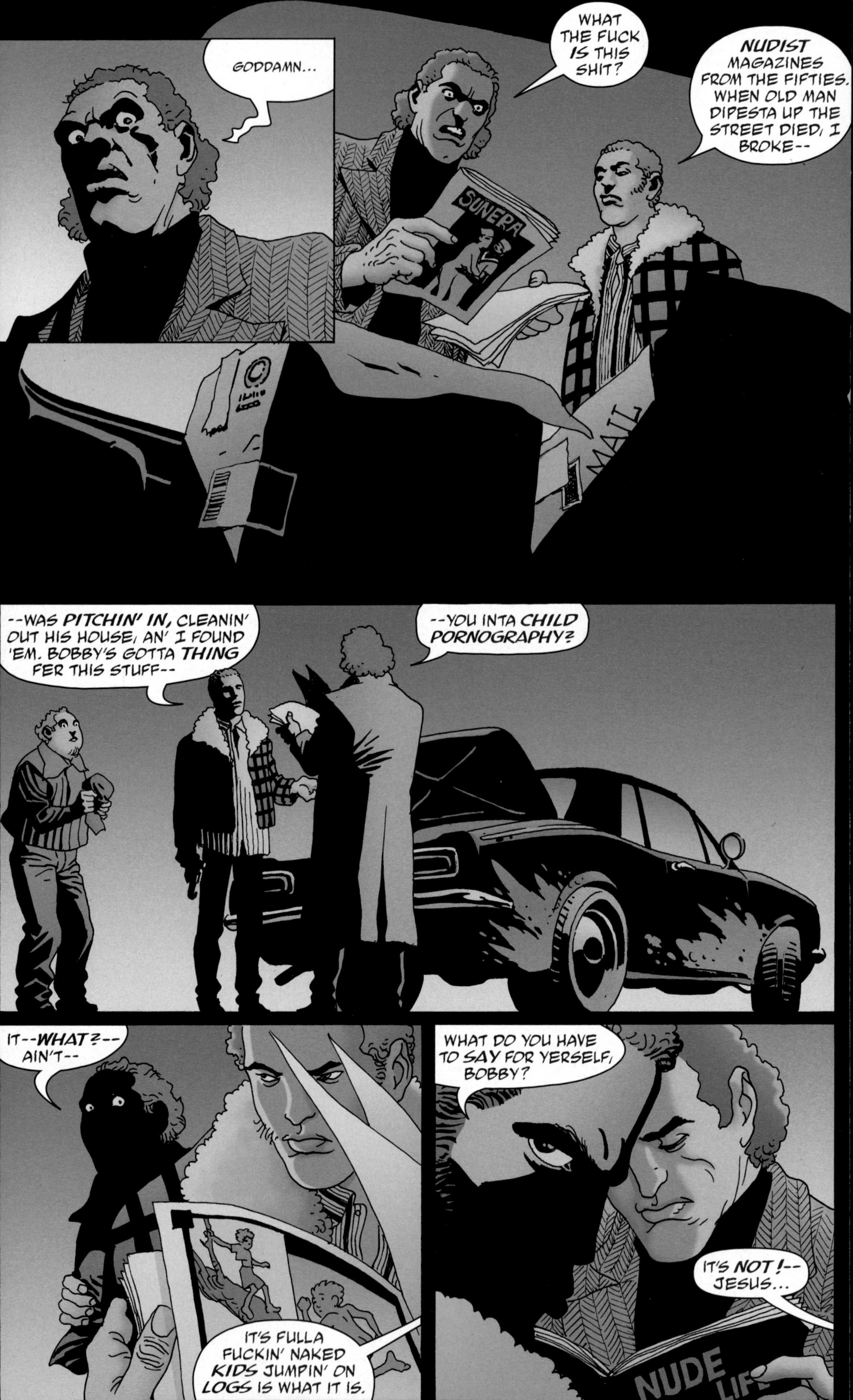
GODDAMN...
WHAT THE FUCK IS THIS SHIT?
NUDIST MAGAZINES FROM THE FIFTIES. WHEN OLD MAN DIPESTA UP THE STREET DIED, I BROKE--
SUNERA
MAIL
--WAS PITCHIN' IN, CLEANIN' OUT HIS HOUSE, AN' I FOUND 'EM. BOBBY'S GOTTA THING FER THIS STUFF--
--YOU INTA CHILD PORNOGRAPHY?
IT--WHAT?-- AIN'T--
IT'S FULLA FUCKIN' NAKED KIDS JUMPIN' ON LOGS IS WHAT IT IS.
WHAT DO YOU HAVE TO SAY FOR YERSELF, BOBBY?
IT'S NOT!-- JESUS...
NUDE

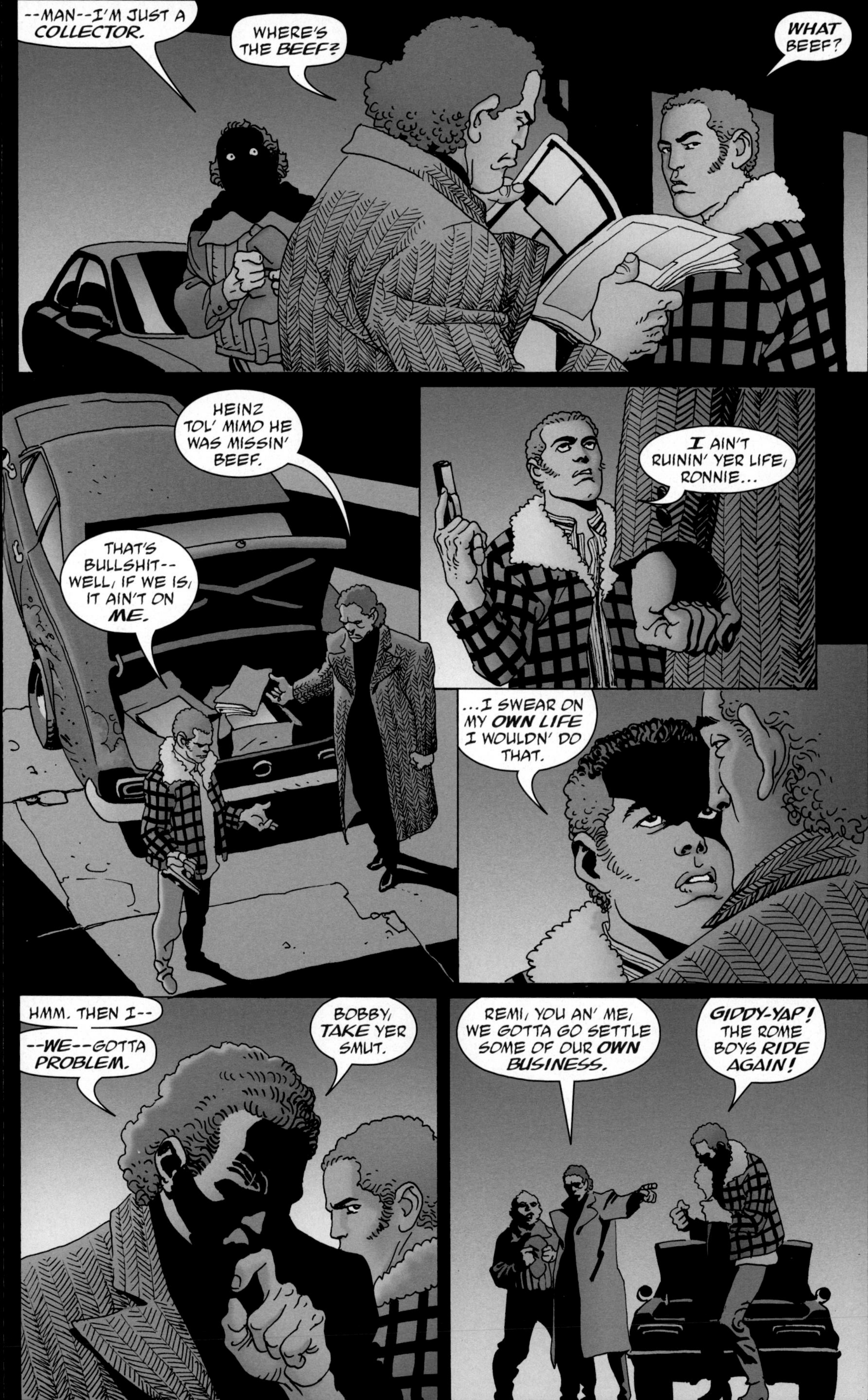
--MAN--I'M JUST A COLLECTOR.
WHERE'S THE BEEF?
WHAT BEEF?
HEINZ TOL' MIMO HE WAS MISSIN' BEEF.
THAT'S BULLSHIT--WELL, IF WE IS, IT AIN'T ON ME.
I AIN'T RUININ' YER LIFE, RONNIE...
...I SWEAR ON MY OWN LIFE I WOULDN' DO THAT.
HMM. THEN I--
--WE--GOTTA PROBLEM.
BOBBY, TAKE YER SMUT.
REMI, YOU AN' ME, WE GOTTA GO SETTLE SOME OF OUR OWN BUSINESS.
GIDDY-YAP! THE ROME BOYS RIDE AGAIN!

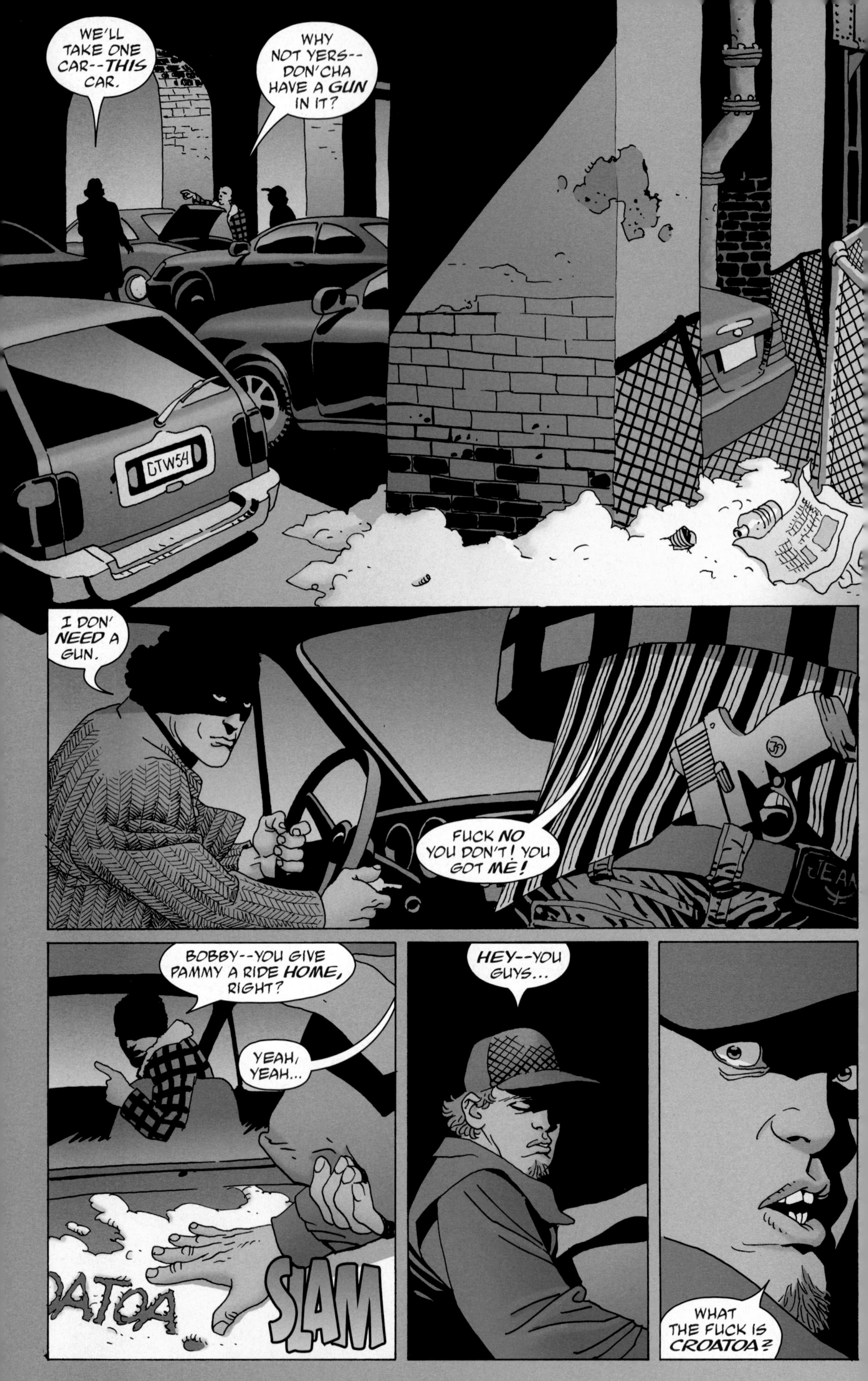
WE'LL TAKE ONE CAR--THIS CAR.
WHY NOT YERS--DON'CHA HAVE A GUN IN IT?
GTW54
I DON' NEED A GUN.
FUCK NO YOU DON'T! YOU GOT ME!
BOBBY--YOU GIVE PAMMY A RIDE HOME, RIGHT?
YEAH, YEAH...
OATOA
SLAM
HEY--YOU GUYS...
WHAT THE FUCK IS CROATOA?

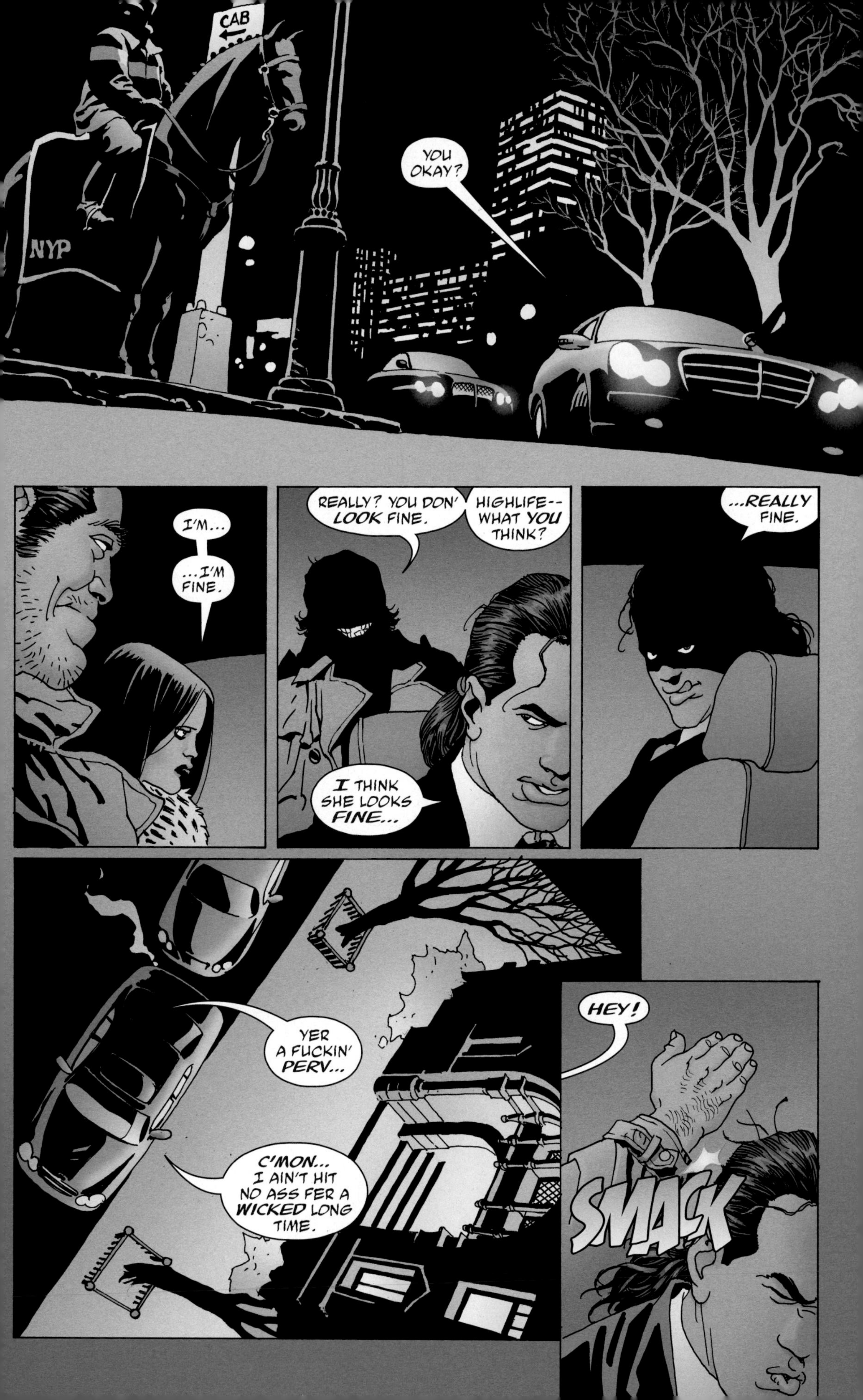
CAB
NYP
YOU OKAY?
I'M...
...I'M FINE.
REALLY? YOU DON' LOOK FINE.
HIGHLIFE-- WHAT YOU THINK?
I THINK SHE LOOKS FINE...
...REALLY FINE.
YER A FUCKIN' PERV...
C'MON... I AIN'T HIT NO ASS FER A WICKED LONG TIME.
HEY!
SMACK

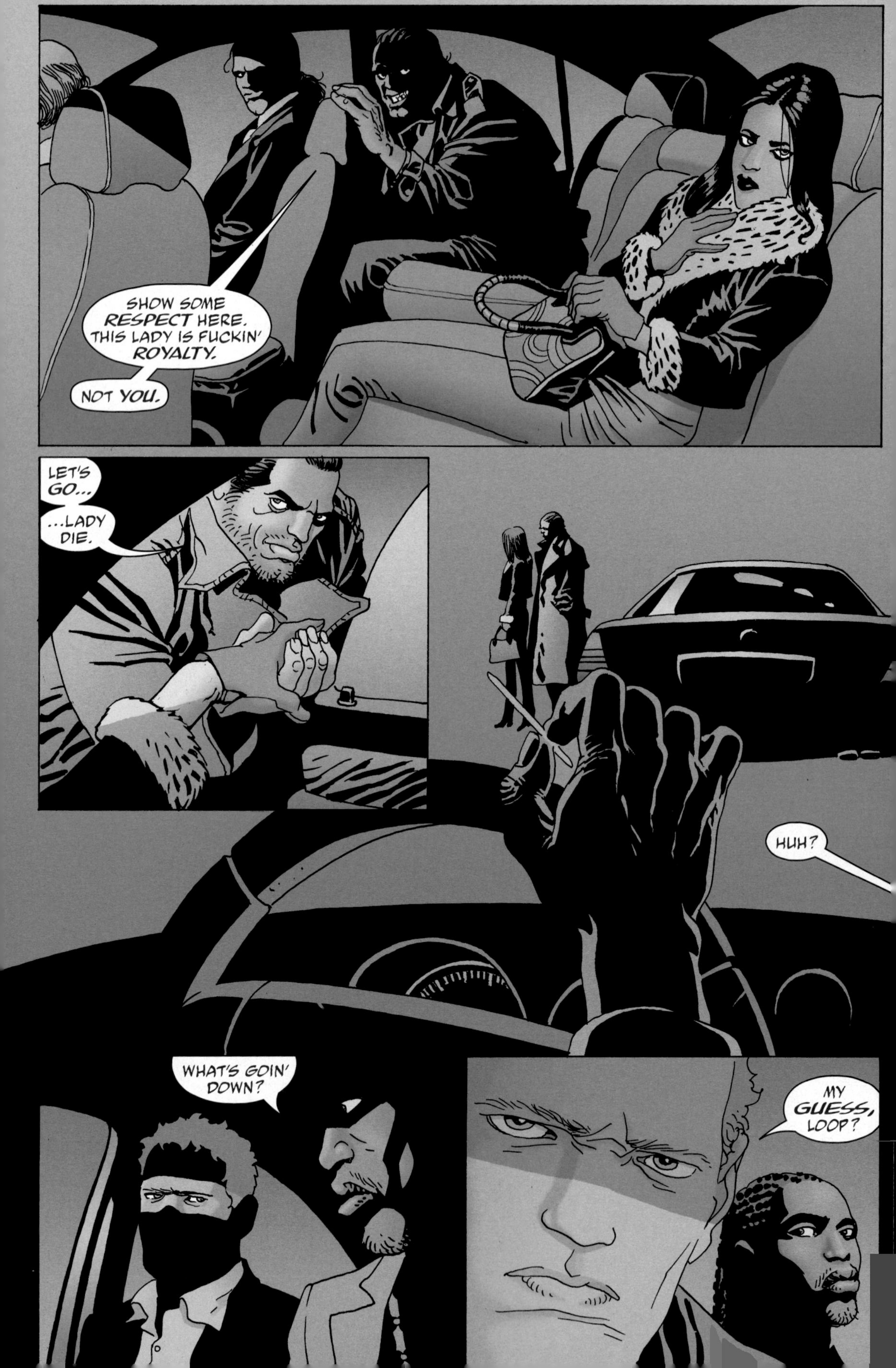
SHOW SOME RESPECT HERE. THIS LADY IS FUCKIN' ROYALTY.
NOT YOU.
LET'S GO...
...LADY DIE.
HUH?
WHAT'S GOIN' DOWN?
MY GUESS, LOOP?

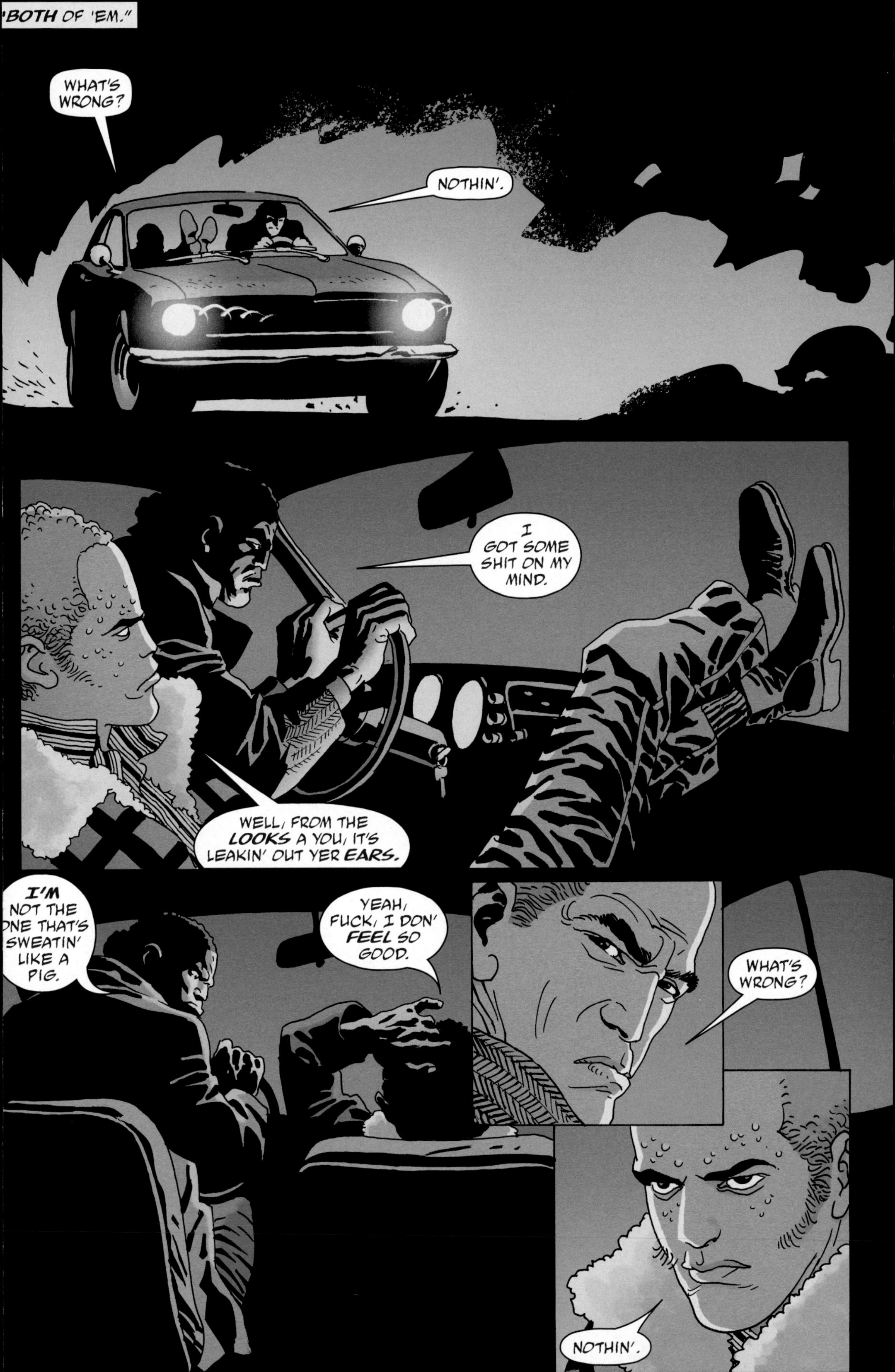
"BOTH OF 'EM."
WHAT'S WRONG?
NOTHIN'.
I GOT SOME SHIT ON MY MIND.
WELL, FROM THE LOOKS A YOU, IT'S LEAKIN' OUT YER EARS.
I'M NOT THE ONE THAT'S SWEATIN' LIKE A PIG.
YEAH, FUCK, I DON' FEEL SO GOOD.
WHAT'S WRONG?
NOTHIN'.

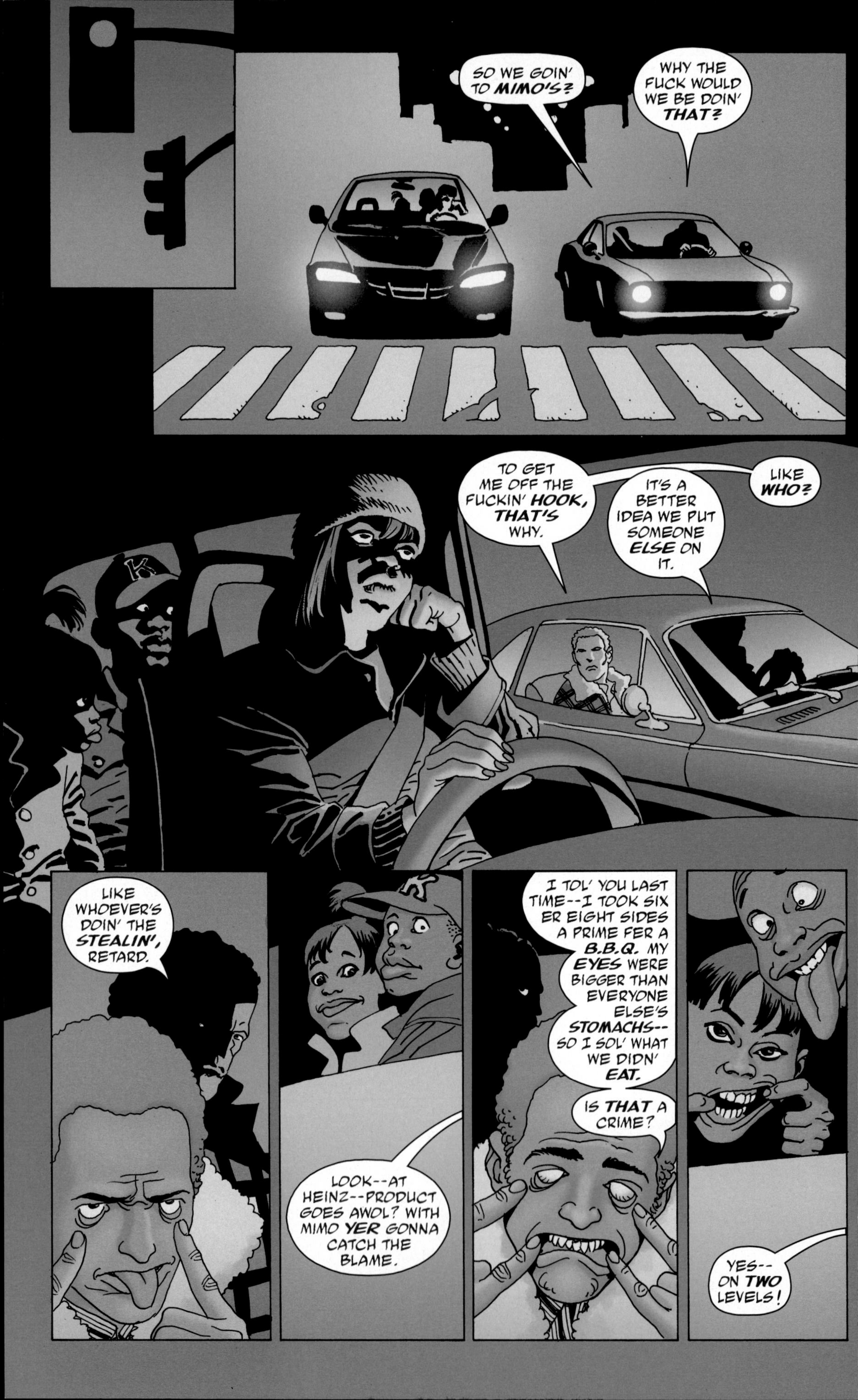
SO WE GOIN' TO MIMO'S?
WHY THE FUCK WOULD WE BE DOIN' THAT?
TO GET ME OFF THE FUCKIN' HOOK, THAT'S WHY.
IT'S A BETTER IDEA WE PUT SOMEONE ELSE ON IT.
LIKE WHO?
LIKE WHOEVER'S DOIN' THE STEALIN', RETARD.
LOOK--AT HEINZ--PRODUCT GOES AWOL? WITH MIMO YER GONNA CATCH THE BLAME.
I TOL' YOU LAST TIME--I TOOK SIX ER EIGHT SIDES A PRIME FER A B.B.Q. MY EYES WERE BIGGER THAN EVERYONE ELSE'S STOMACHS--SO I SOL' WHAT WE DIDN' EAT.
IS THAT A CRIME?
YES--ON TWO LEVELS!

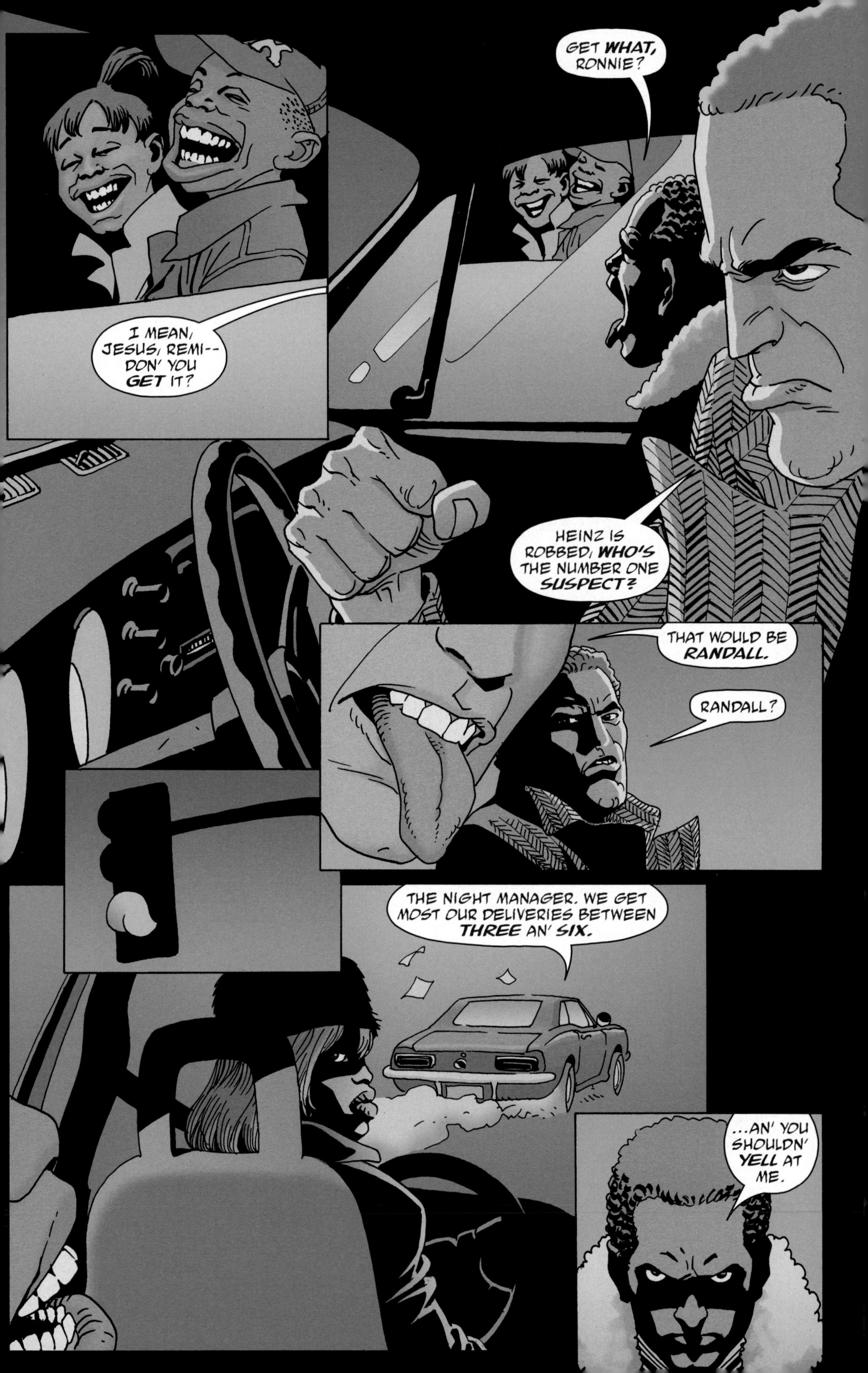
I MEAN, JESUS, REMI-- DON' YOU GET IT?
GET WHAT, RONNIE?
HEINZ IS ROBBED, WHO'S THE NUMBER ONE SUSPECT?
THAT WOULD BE RANDALL.
RANDALL?
THE NIGHT MANAGER. WE GET MOST OUR DELIVERIES BETWEEN THREE AN' SIX.
...AN' YOU SHOULDN' YELL AT ME.

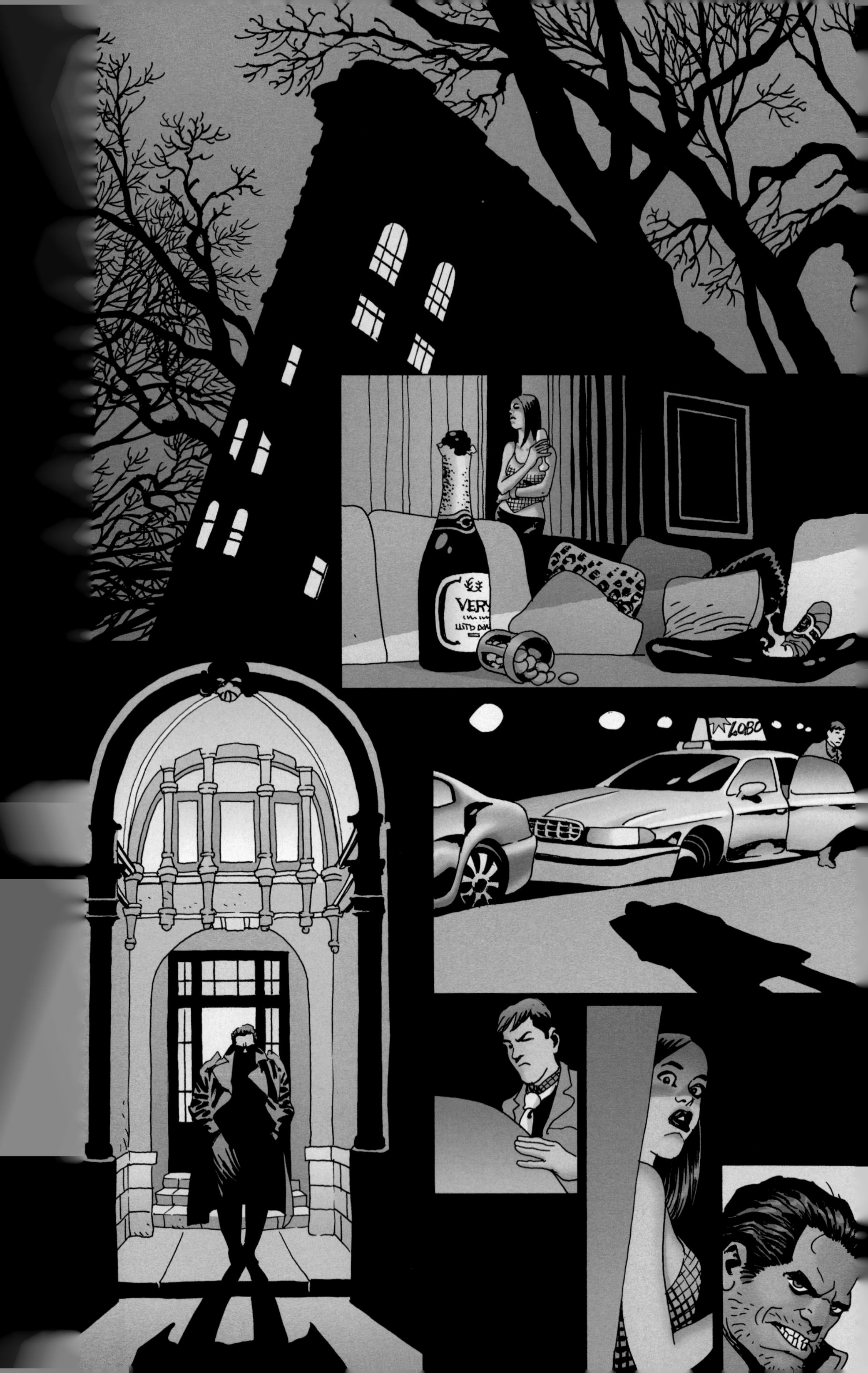
VERY
LOBO

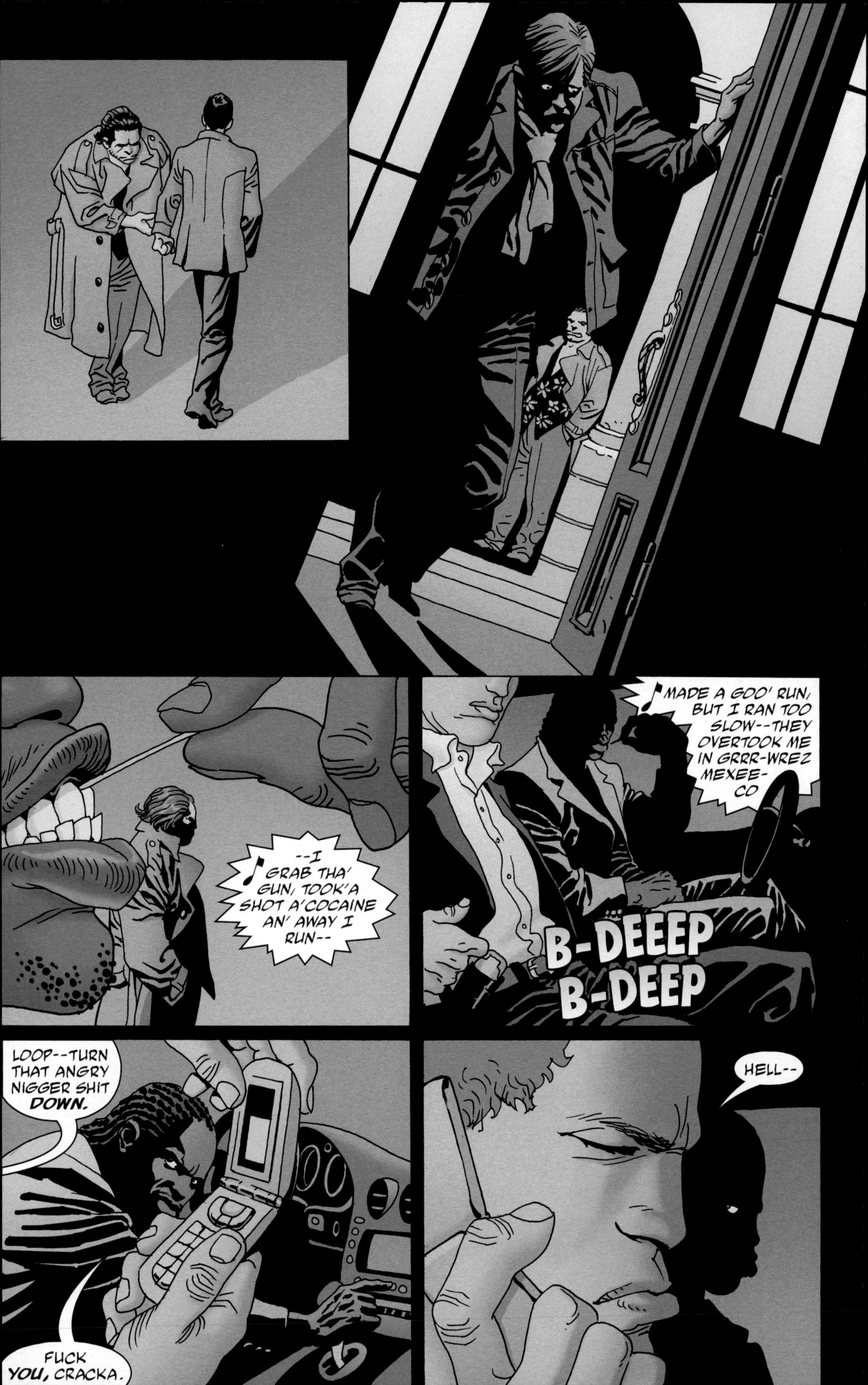
--I GRAB THA' GUN, TOOK'A SHOT A'COCAINE AN' AWAY I RUN--
MADE A GOO' RUN, BUT I RAN TOO SLOW--THEY OVERTOOK ME IN GRRR-WREZ MEXEE-CO
B-DEEEP B-DEEP
LOOP--TURN THAT ANGRY NIGGER SHIT DOWN.
FUCK YOU, CRACKA.
HELL--

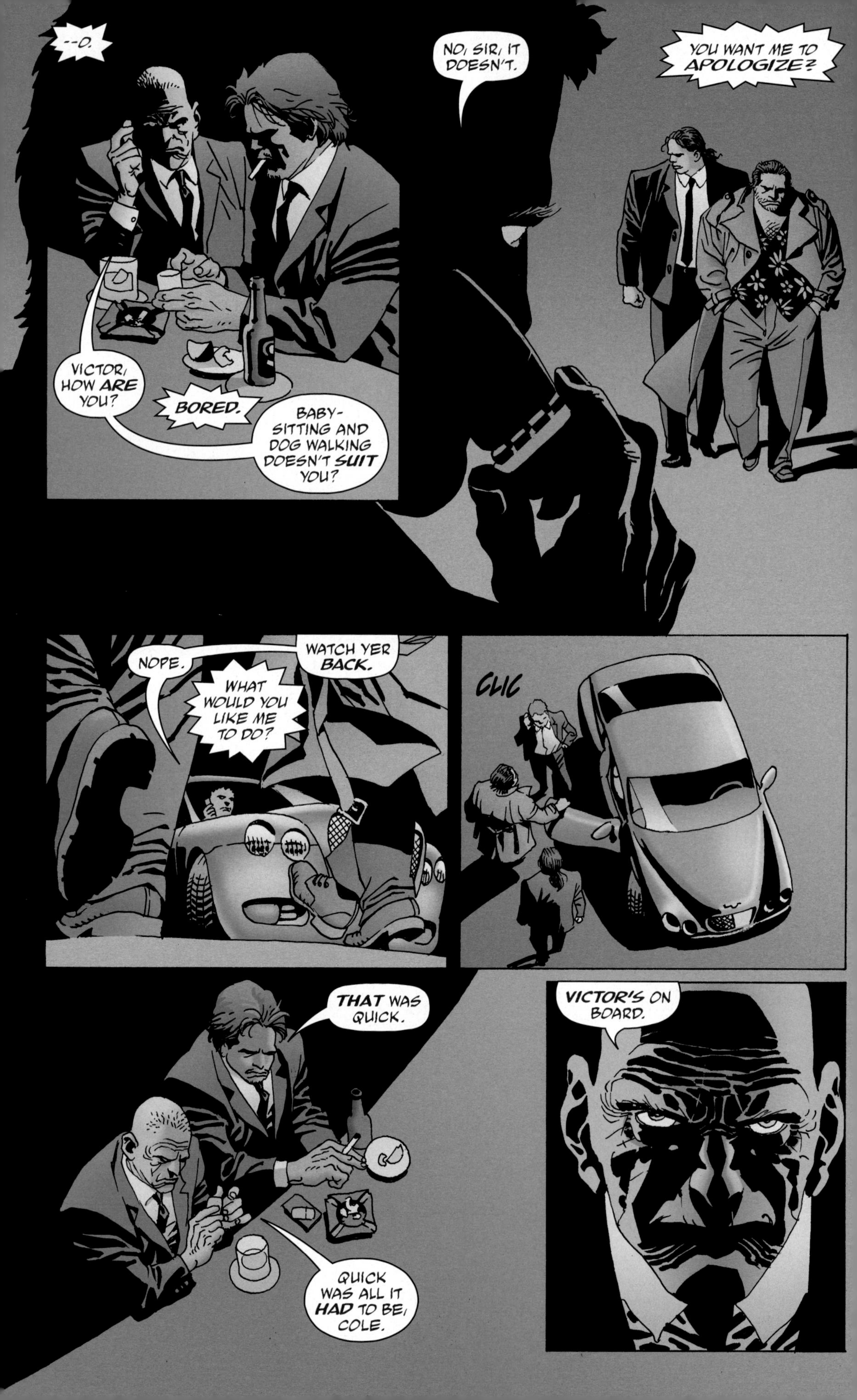
--O.
VICTOR, HOW ARE YOU?
BORED.
BABY-SITTING AND DOG WALKING DOESN'T SUIT YOU?
NO, SIR, IT DOESN'T.
YOU WANT ME TO APOLOGIZE?
NOPE.
WHAT WOULD YOU LIKE ME TO DO?
WATCH YER BACK.
CLIC
THAT WAS QUICK.
QUICK WAS ALL IT HAD TO BE, COLE.
VICTOR'S ON BOARD.

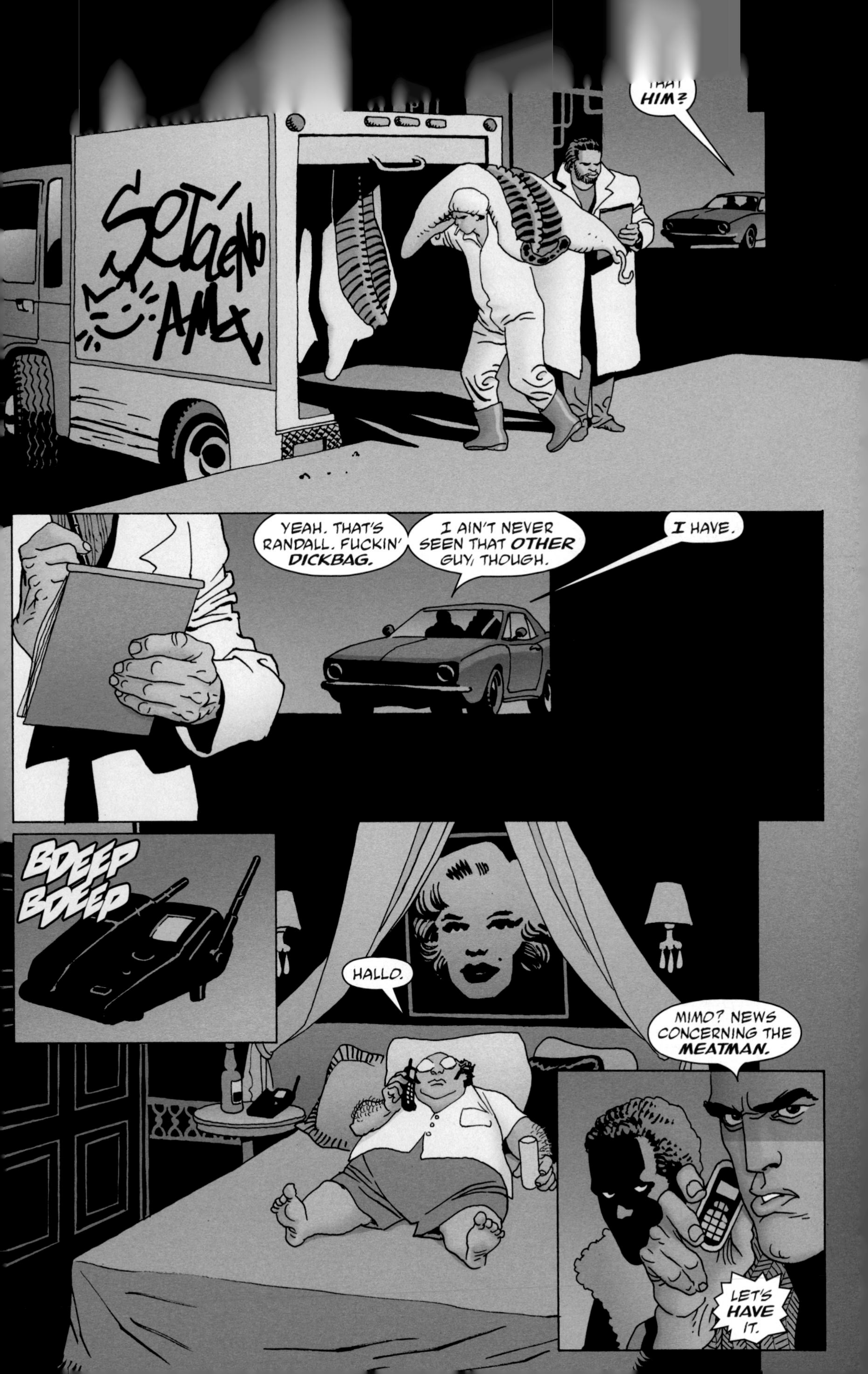

HIM?
YEAH. THAT'S RANDALL. FUCKIN' DICKBAG.
I AIN'T NEVER SEEN THAT OTHER GUY, THOUGH.
I HAVE.
BDEEP BDEEP
HALLO.
MIMO? NEWS CONCERNING THE MEATMAN.
LET'S HAVE IT.

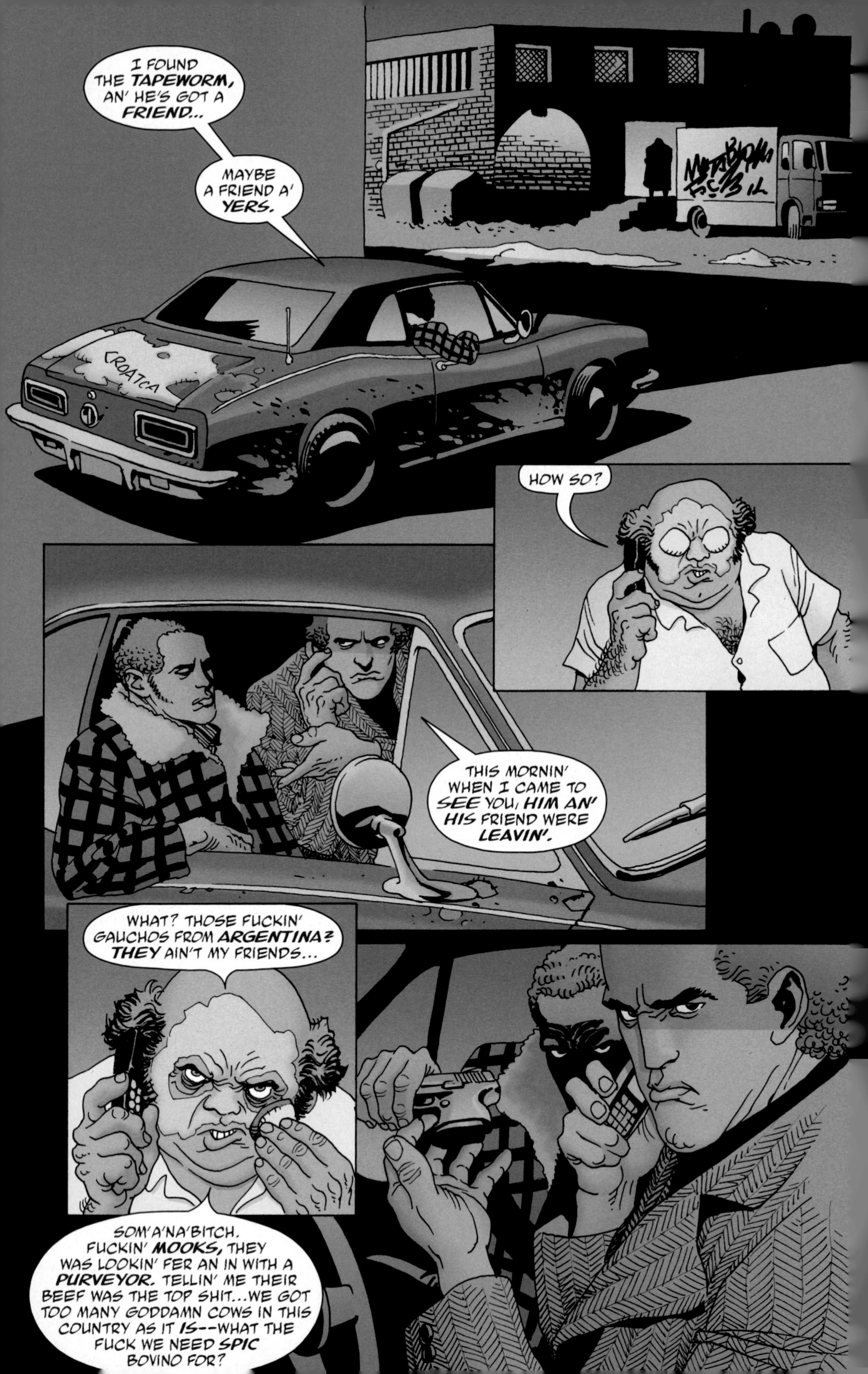
I FOUND THE TAPEWORM, AN' HE'S GOT A FRIEND...
MAYBE A FRIEND A' YERS.
CROATCA
HOW SO?
THIS MORNIN' WHEN I CAME TO SEE YOU, HIM AN' HIS FRIEND WERE LEAVIN'.
WHAT? THOSE FUCKIN' GAUCHOS FROM ARGENTINA? THEY AIN'T MY FRIENDS...
SOM'A'NA'BITCH. FUCKIN' MOOKS, THEY WAS LOOKIN' FER AN IN WITH A PURVEYOR. TELLIN' ME THEIR BEEF WAS THE TOP SHIT...WE GOT TOO MANY GODDAMN COWS IN THIS COUNTRY AS IT IS--WHAT THE FUCK WE NEED SPIC BOVINO FOR?

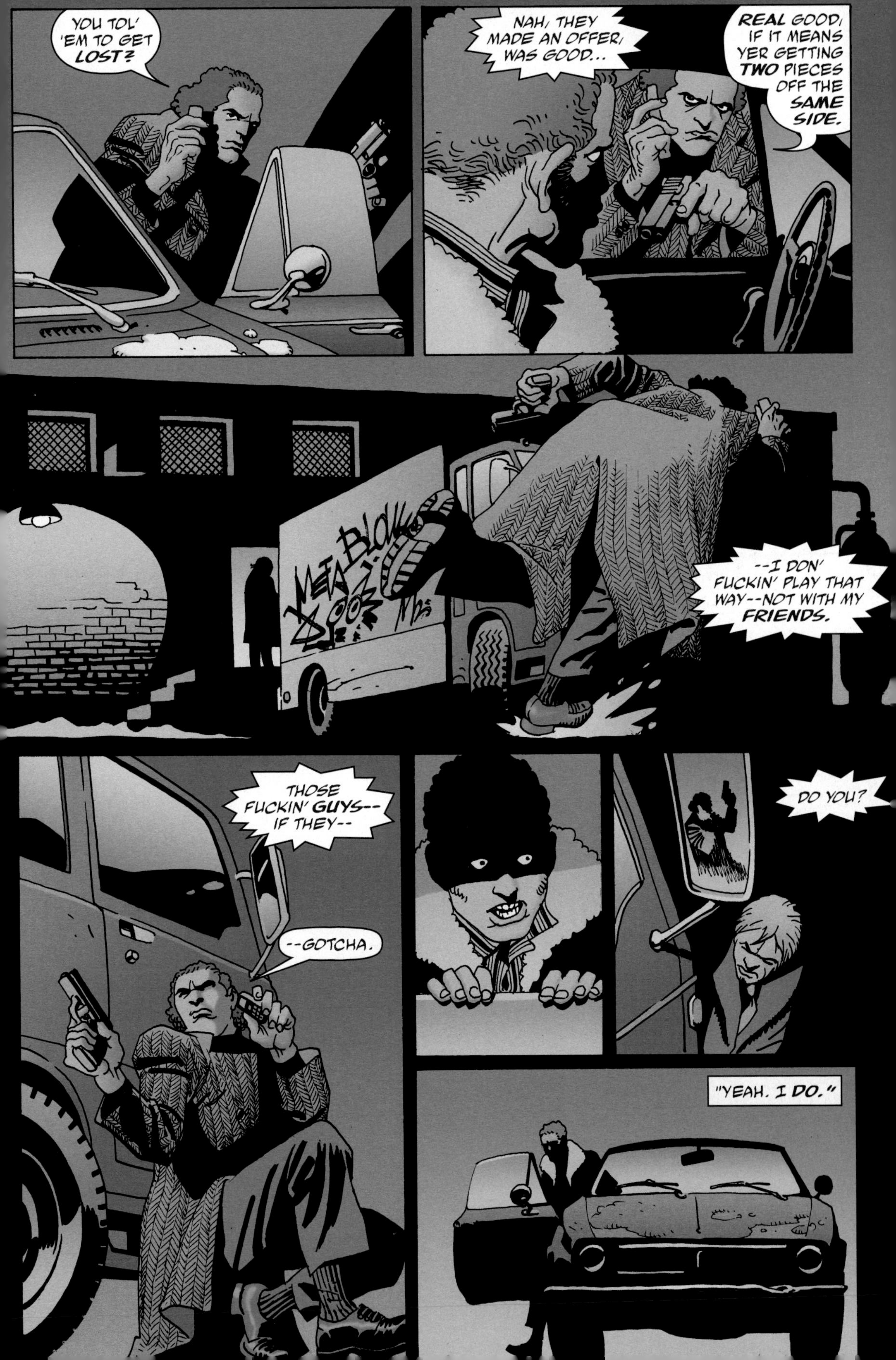
YOU TOL' 'EM TO GET LOST?
NAH, THEY MADE AN OFFER, WAS GOOD...
REAL GOOD, IF IT MEANS YER GETTING TWO PIECES OFF THE SAME SIDE.
--I DON' FUCKIN' PLAY THAT WAY--NOT WITH MY FRIENDS.
THOSE FUCKIN' GUYS-- IF THEY--
--GOTCHA.
DO YOU?
"YEAH. I DO."

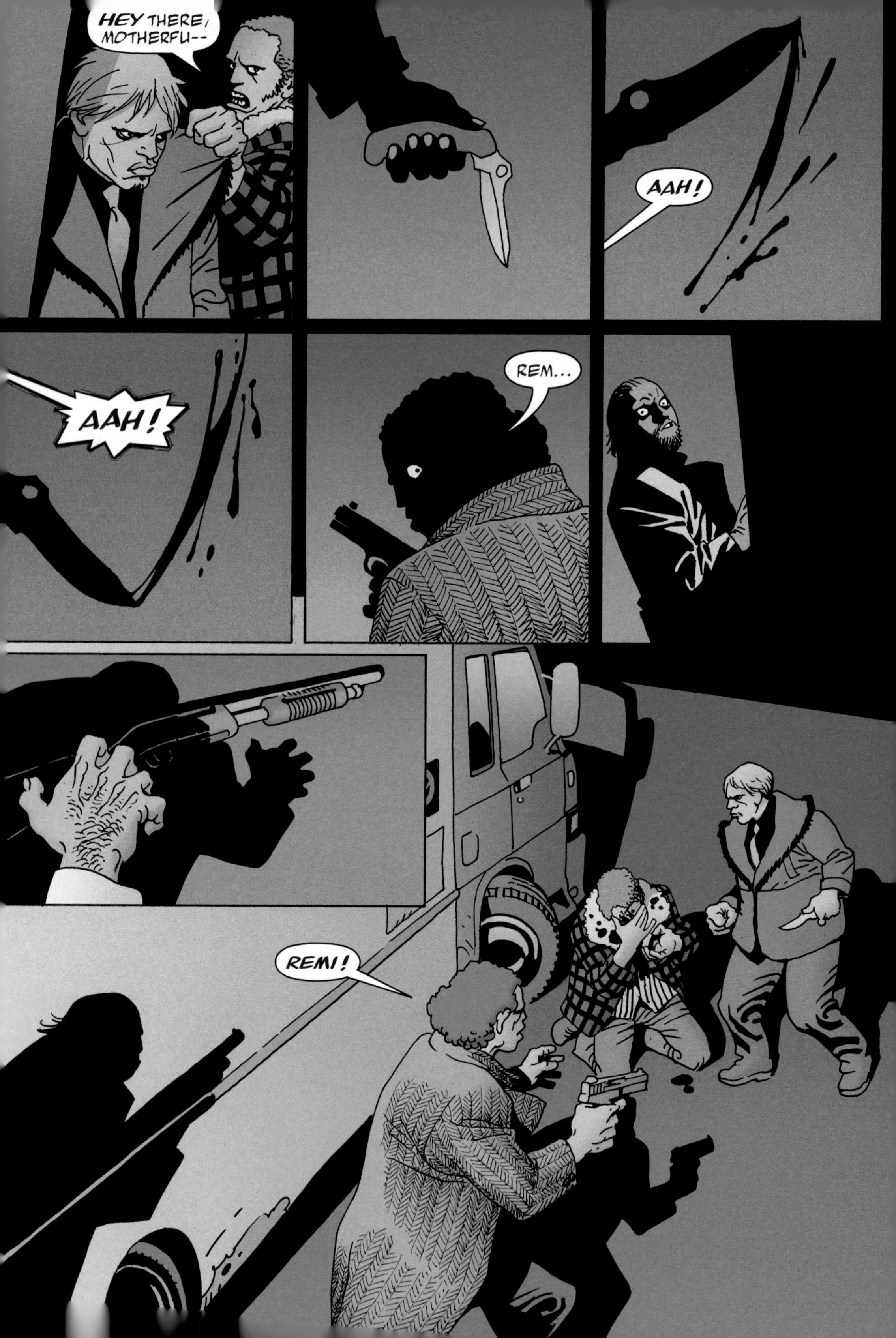
HEY THERE, MOTHERFU--
AAH!
AAH!
REM...
REMI!

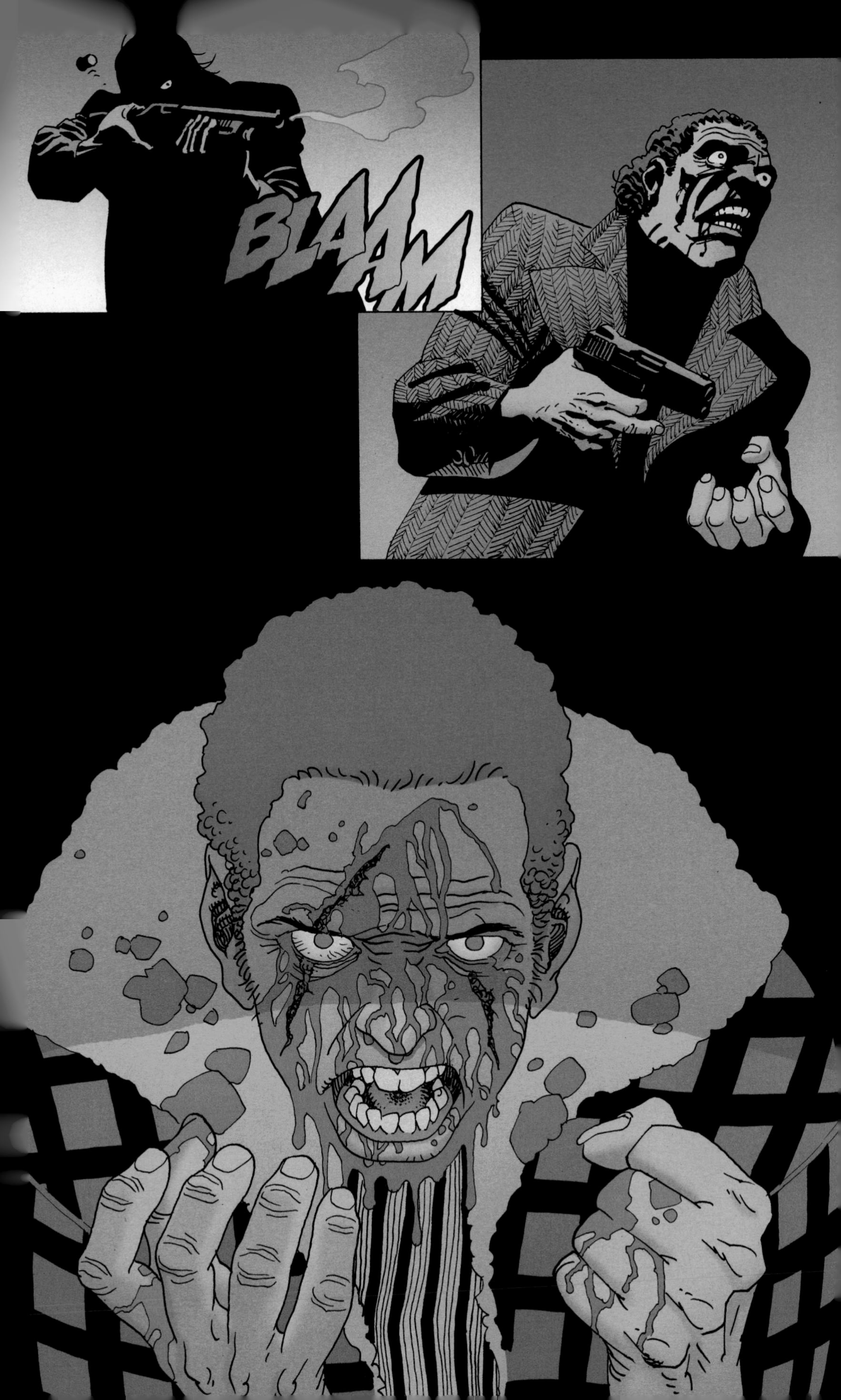
BLAAM

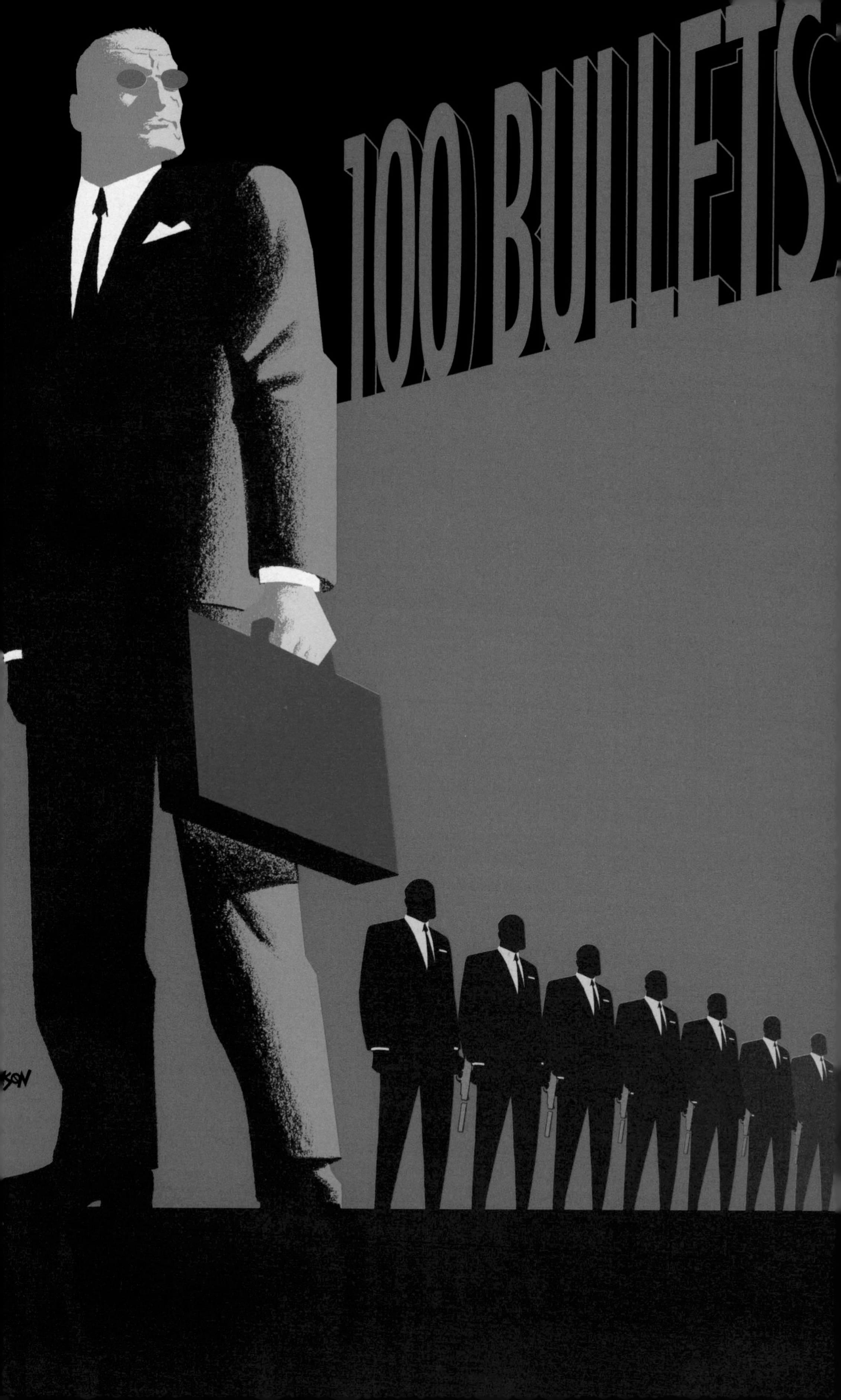
100 BULLETS

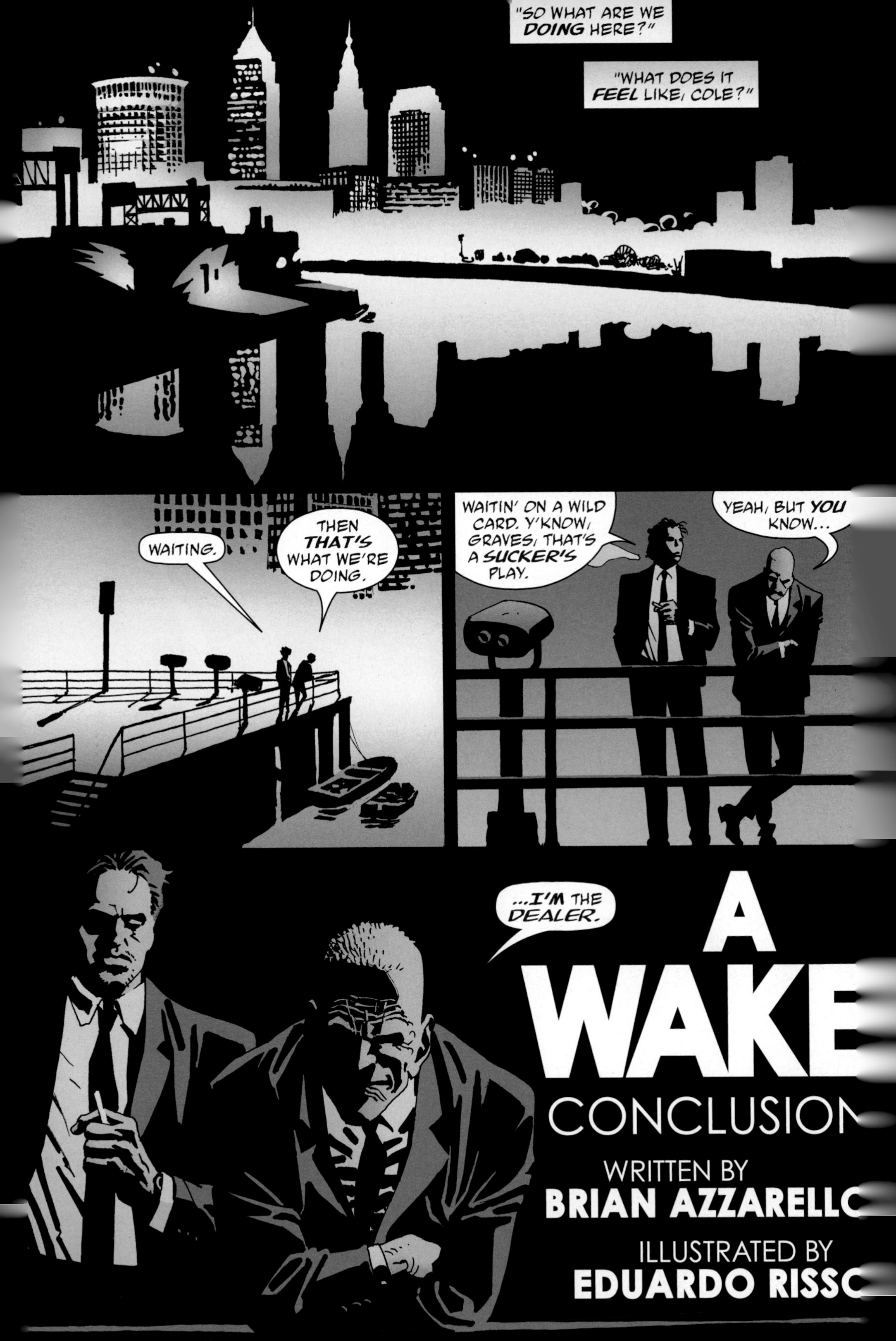
"SO WHAT ARE WE DOING HERE?"
"WHAT DOES IT FEEL LIKE, COLE?"
WAITING.
THEN THAT'S WHAT WE'RE DOING.
WAITIN' ON A WILD CARD. Y'KNOW, GRAVES, THAT'S A SUCKER'S PLAY.
YEAH, BUT YOU KNOW...
...I'M THE DEALER.
A WAKE
CONCLUSIO
WRITTEN BY
BRIAN AZZARELL
ILLUSTRATED BY
EDUARDO RISS

OLORED BY PATRICIA MULVIHILL LETTERED BY CLEM ROBINS COVER BY DAVE JOHNSO
ASSISTANT EDITOR CASEY SEIJAS EDITOR WILL DENNIS

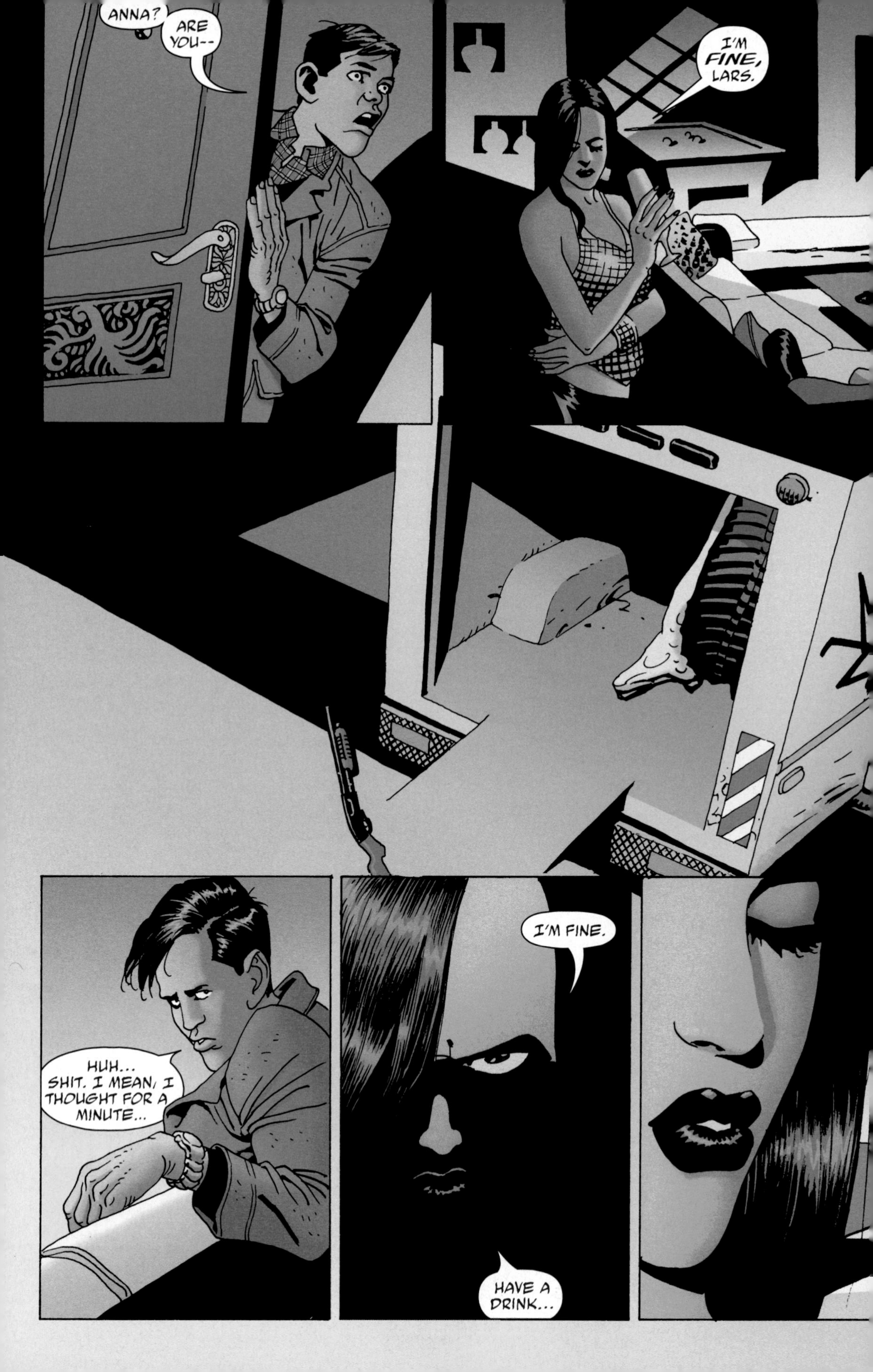
ANNA?
ARE YOU--
I'M FINE, LARS.
HUH... SHIT. I MEAN, I THOUGHT FOR A MINUTE...
I'M FINE.
HAVE A DRINK...

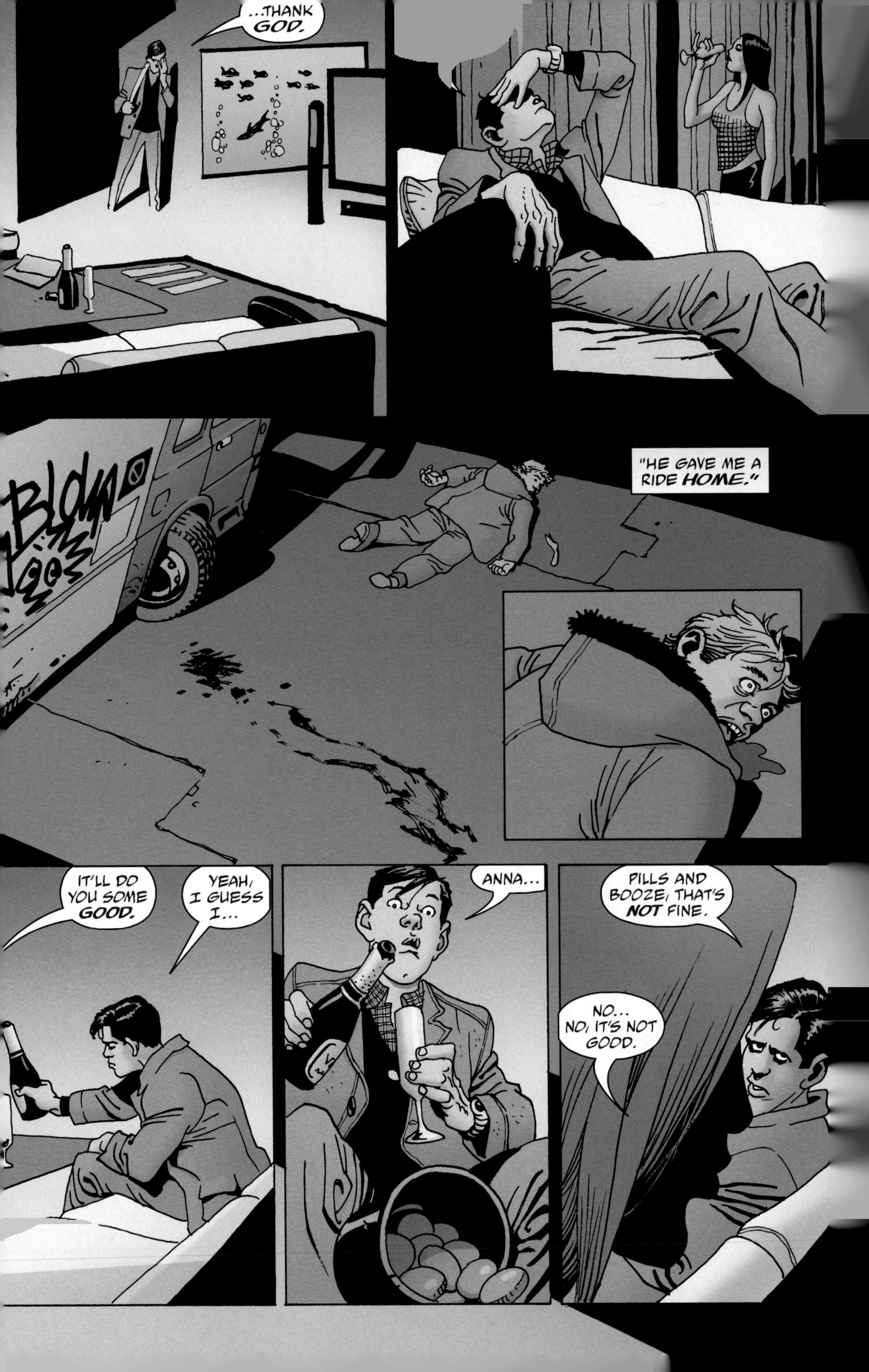
...THANK GOD.
"HE GAVE ME A RIDE HOME."
IT'LL DO YOU SOME GOOD.
YEAH, I GUESS I...
ANNA...
PILLS AND BOOZE, THAT'S NOT FINE.
NO... NO, IT'S NOT GOOD.

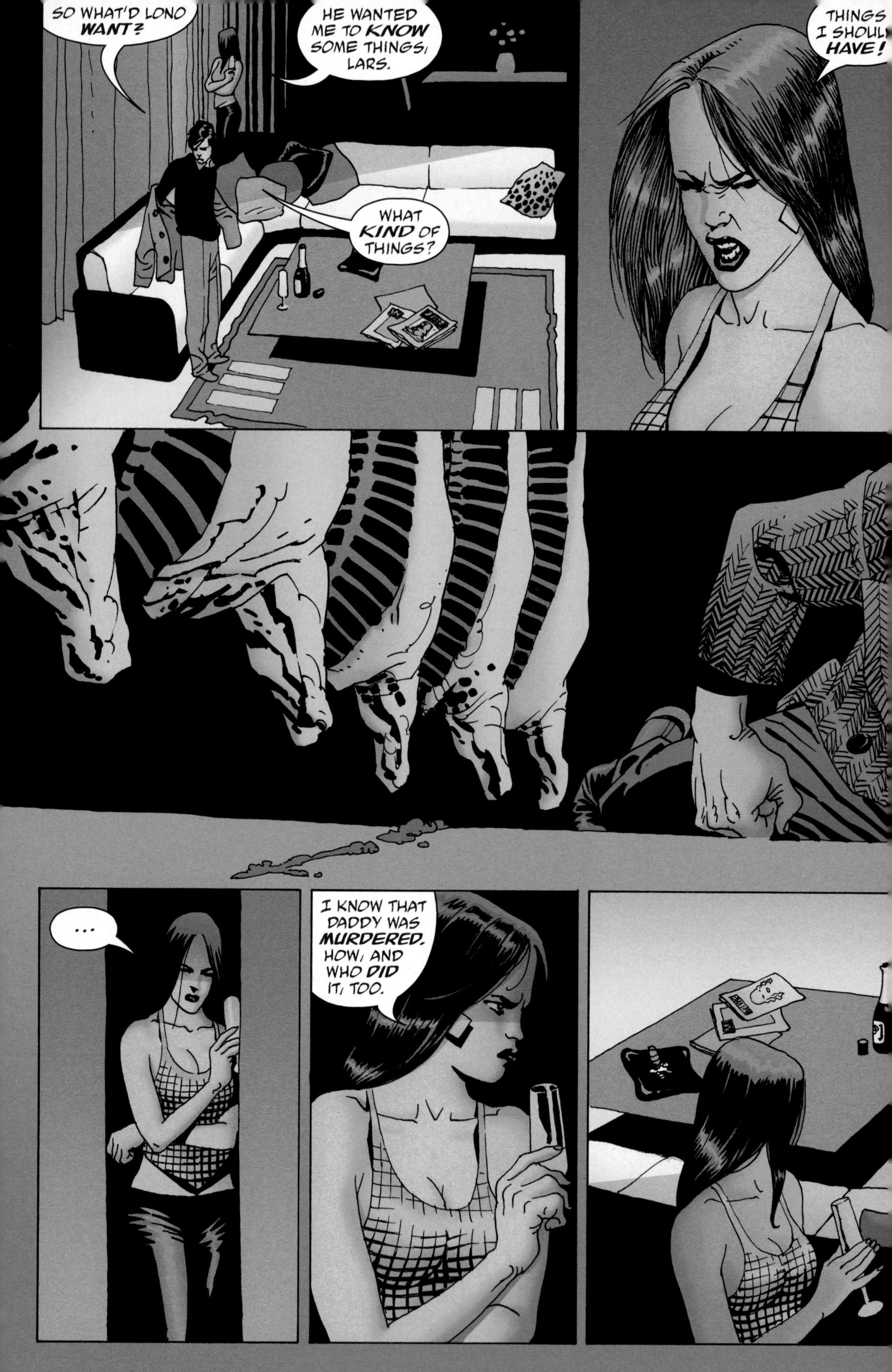
SO WHAT'D LONO **WANT?**
HE WANTED ME TO **KNOW** SOME THINGS, LARS.
WHAT **KIND** OF THINGS?
THINGS I SHOUL **HAVE!**
...
I KNOW THAT DADDY WAS **MURDERED.** HOW, AND WHO **DID** IT, TOO.

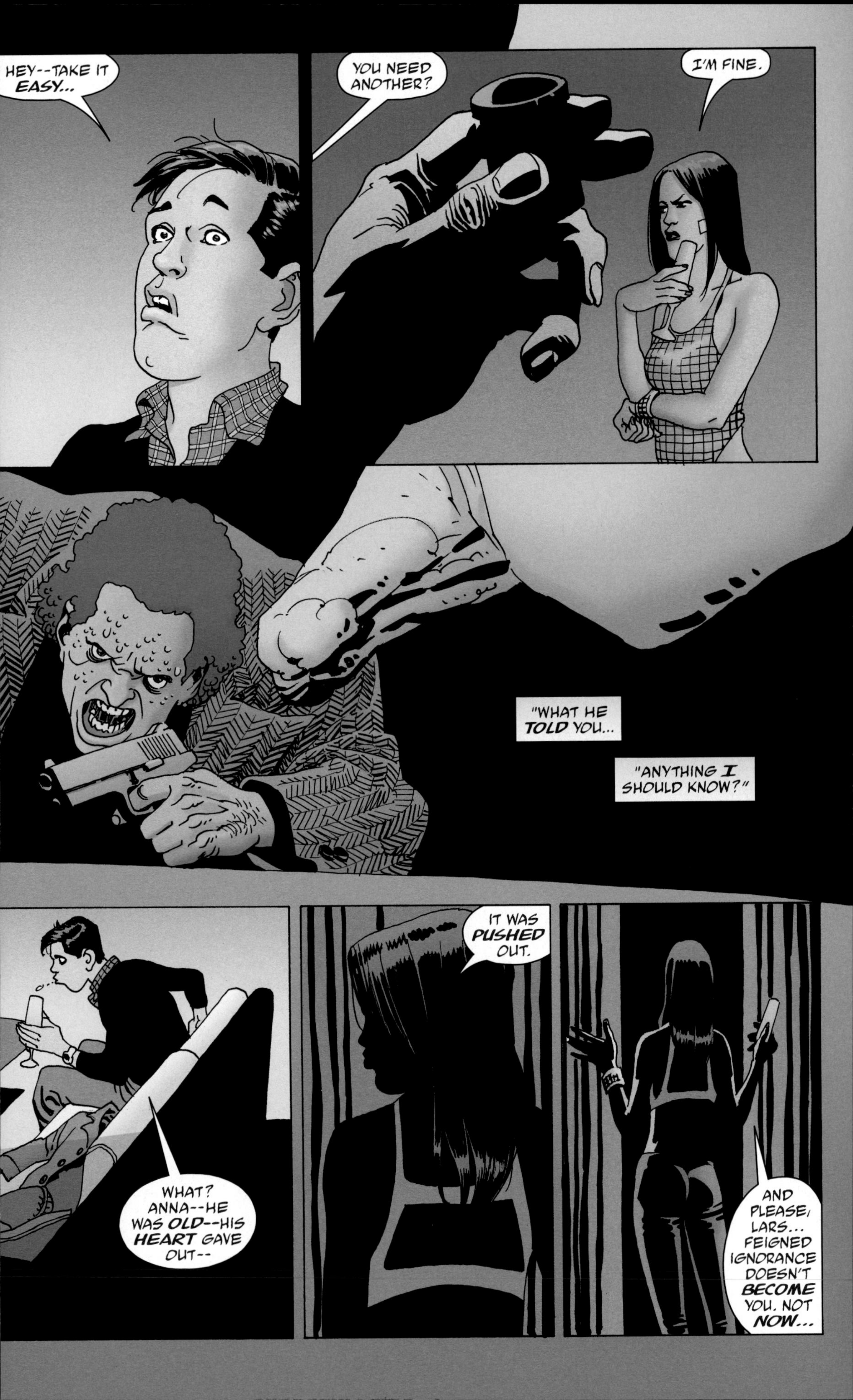
HEY--TAKE IT EASY...
YOU NEED ANOTHER?
I'M FINE.
"WHAT HE TOLD YOU...
"ANYTHING I SHOULD KNOW?"
WHAT? ANNA--HE WAS OLD--HIS HEART GAVE OUT--
IT WAS PUSHED OUT.
AND PLEASE, LARS... FEIGNED IGNORANCE DOESN'T BECOME YOU. NOT NOW...

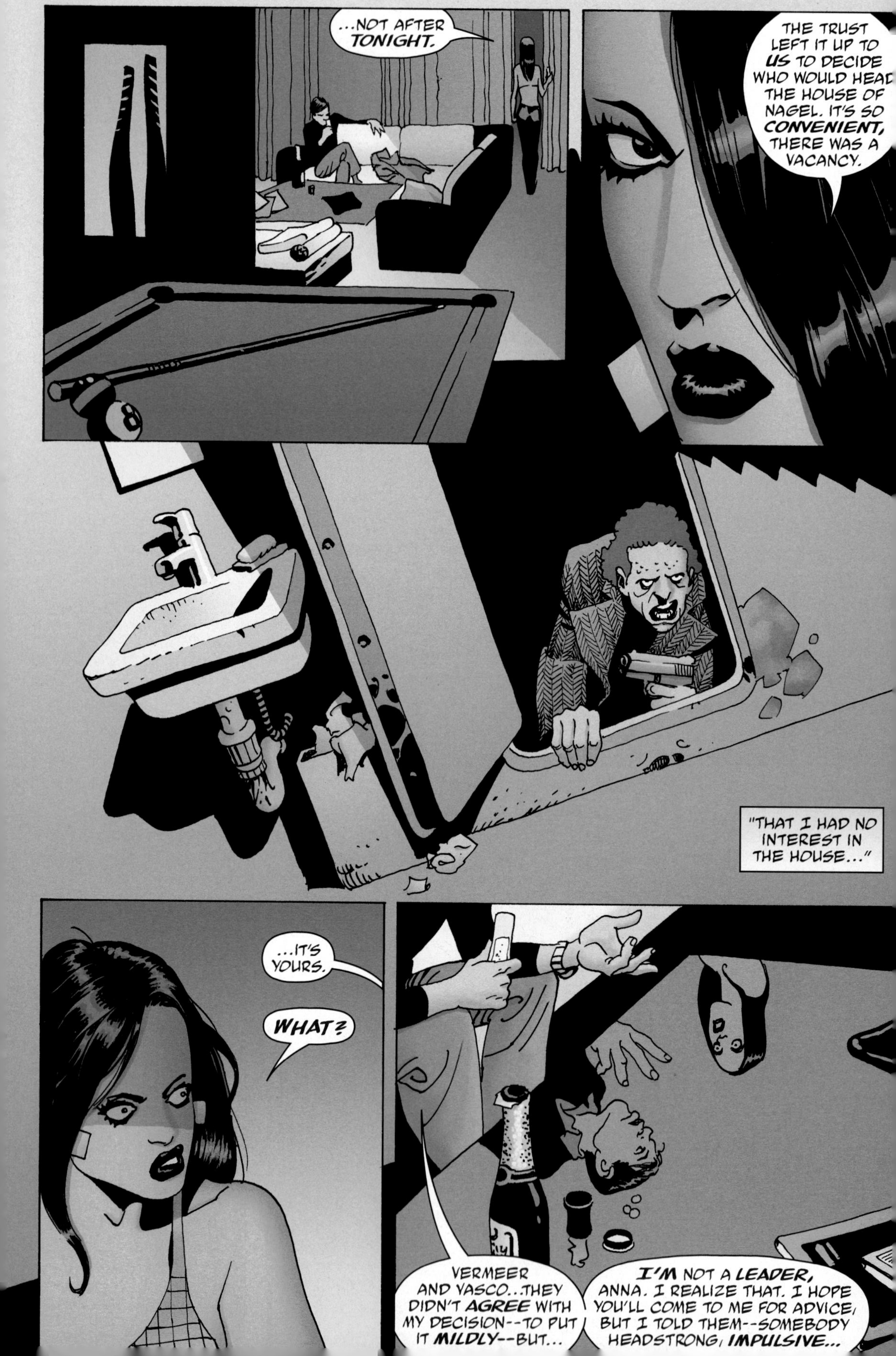
...NOT AFTER TONIGHT.
THE TRUST LEFT IT UP TO US TO DECIDE WHO WOULD HEAD THE HOUSE OF NAGEL. IT'S SO CONVENIENT, THERE WAS A VACANCY.
"THAT I HAD NO INTEREST IN THE HOUSE..."
...IT'S YOURS.
WHAT?
VERMEER AND VASCO...THEY DIDN'T AGREE WITH MY DECISION--TO PUT IT MILDLY--BUT...
I'M NOT A LEADER, ANNA. I REALIZE THAT. I HOPE YOU'LL COME TO ME FOR ADVICE, BUT I TOLD THEM--SOMEBODY HEADSTRONG, IMPULSIVE...

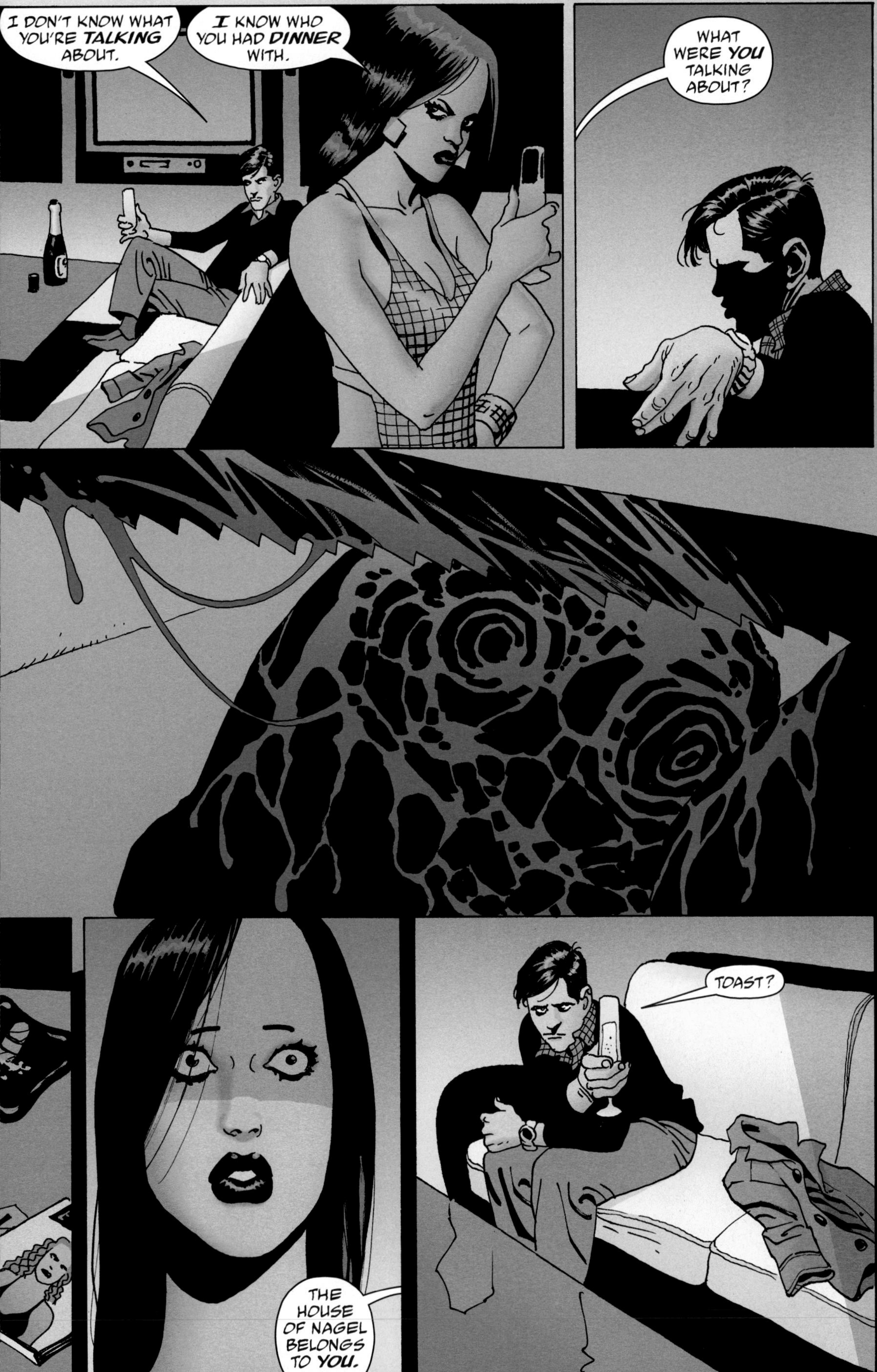
I DON'T KNOW WHAT YOU'RE TALKING ABOUT.
I KNOW WHO YOU HAD DINNER WITH.
WHAT WERE YOU TALKING ABOUT?
THE HOUSE OF NAGEL BELONGS TO YOU.
TOAST?

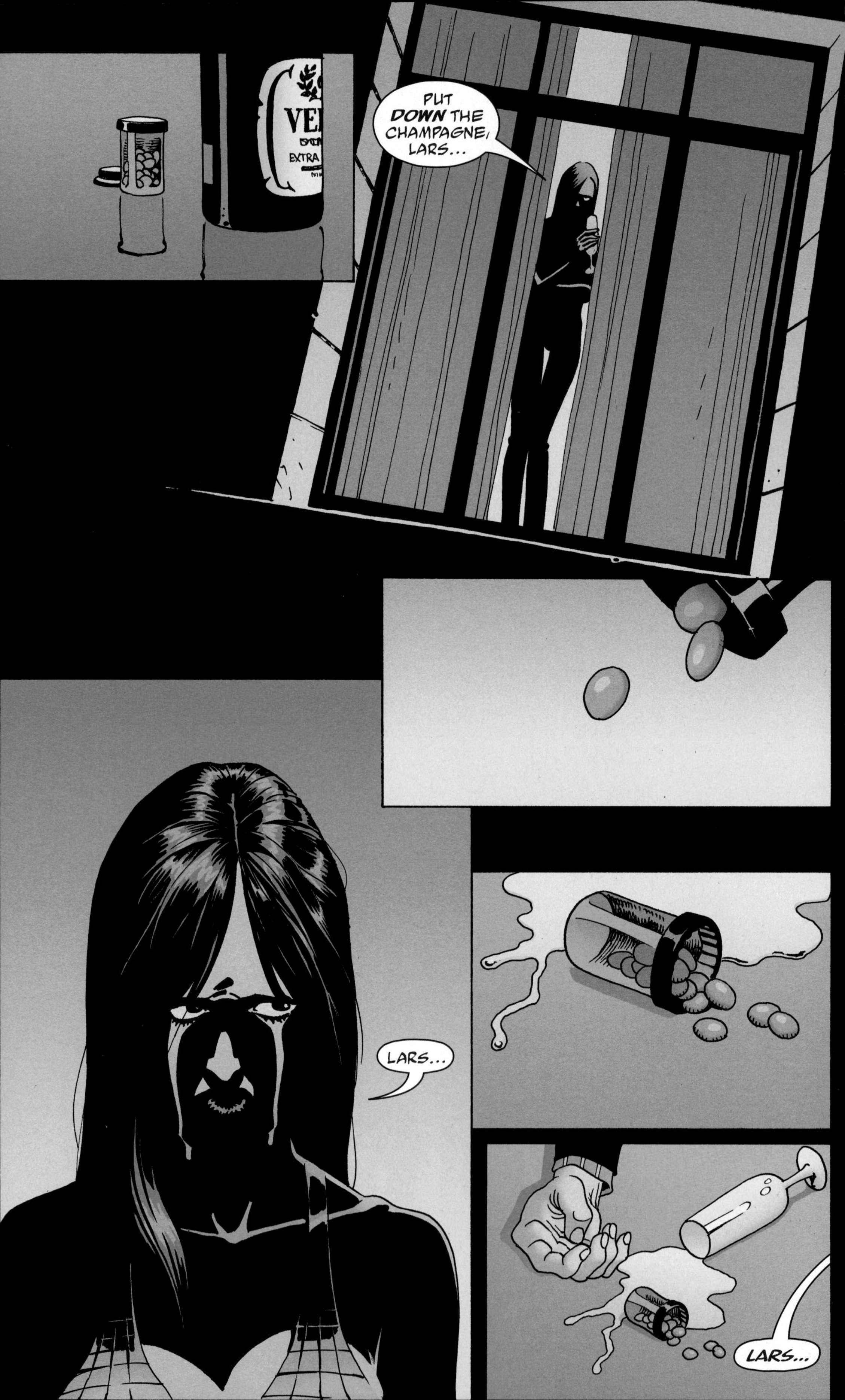

PUT **DOWN** THE CHAMPAGNE, LARS...
LARS...
LARS...

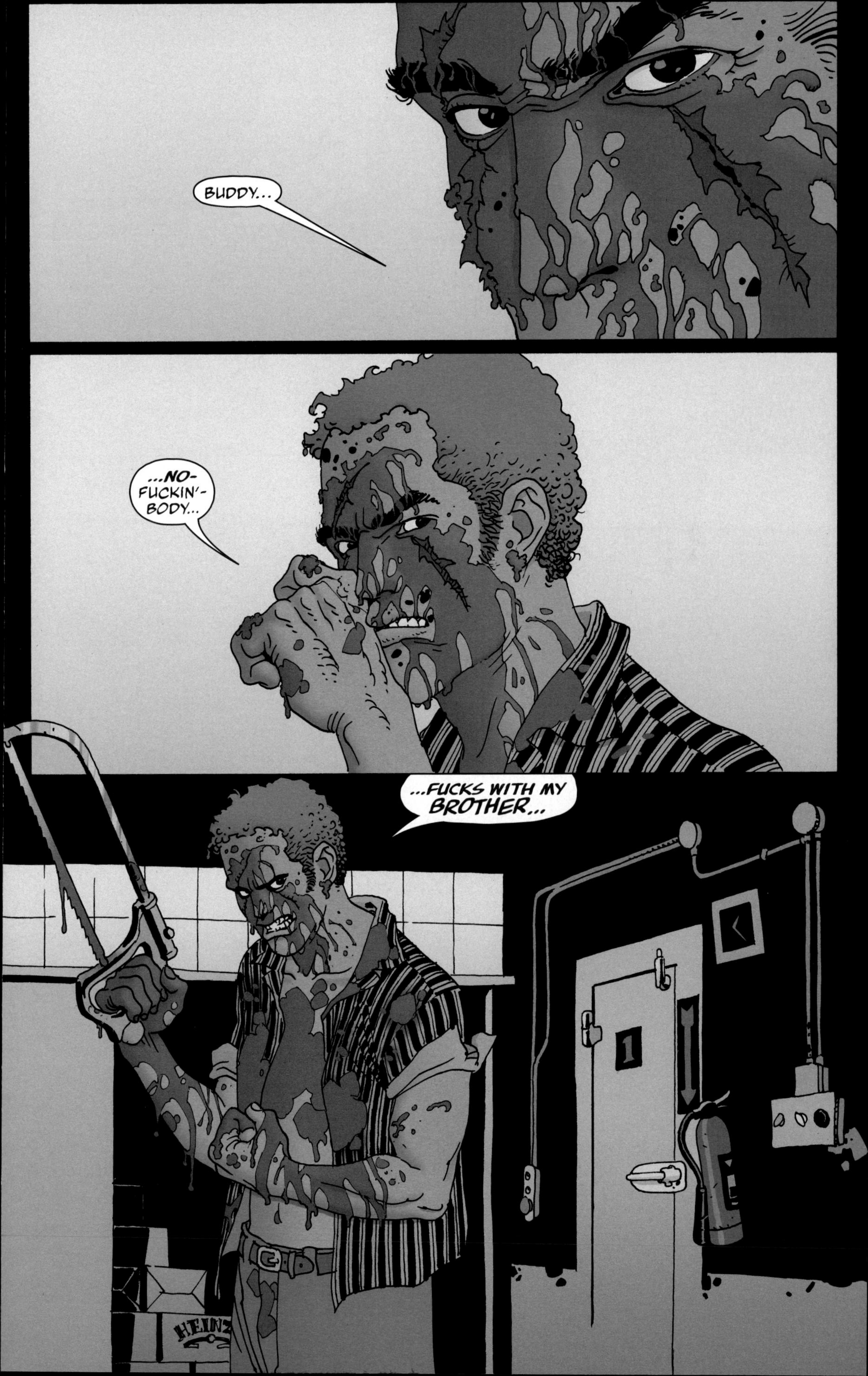
BUDDY...
...NO-FUCKIN'-BODY...
...FUCKS WITH MY BROTHER...
HEINZ

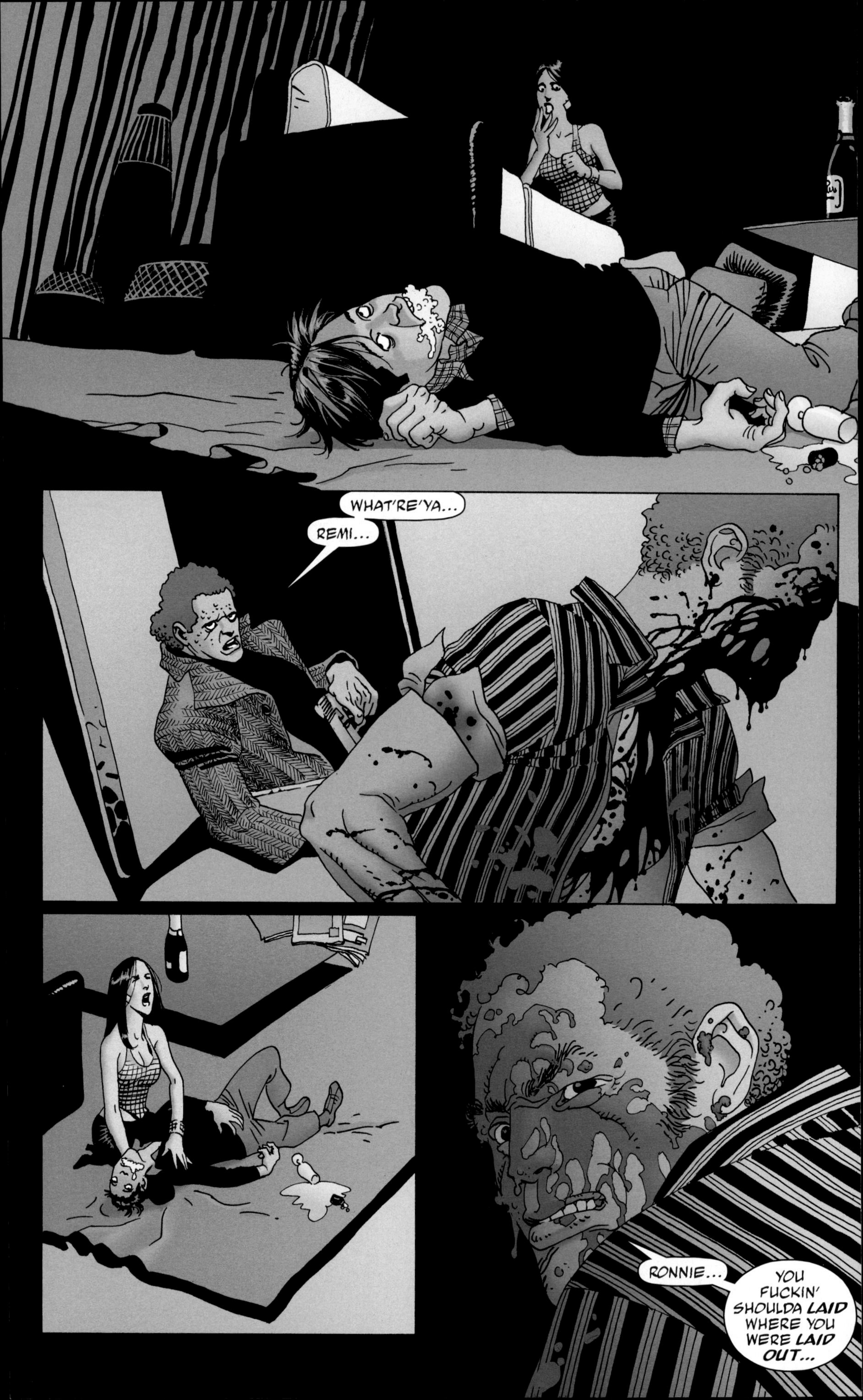
WHAT'RE'YA...
REMI...
RONNIE...
YOU FUCKIN' SHOULDA **LAID** WHERE YOU WERE **LAID OUT...**

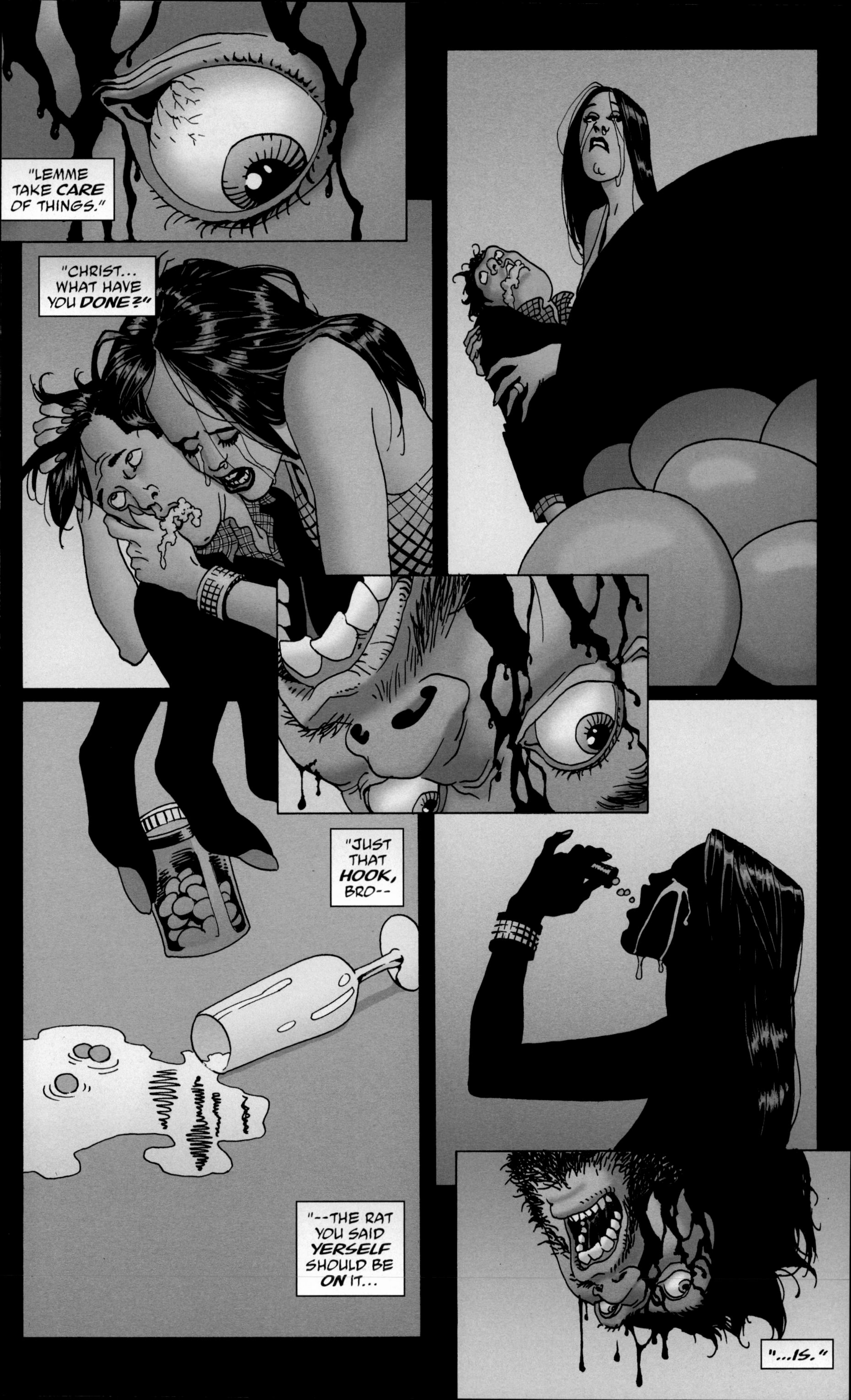
"LEMME TAKE CARE OF THINGS."
"CHRIST... WHAT HAVE YOU DONE?"
"JUST THAT HOOK, BRO--
"--THE RAT YOU SAID YERSELF SHOULD BE ON IT...
"...IS."

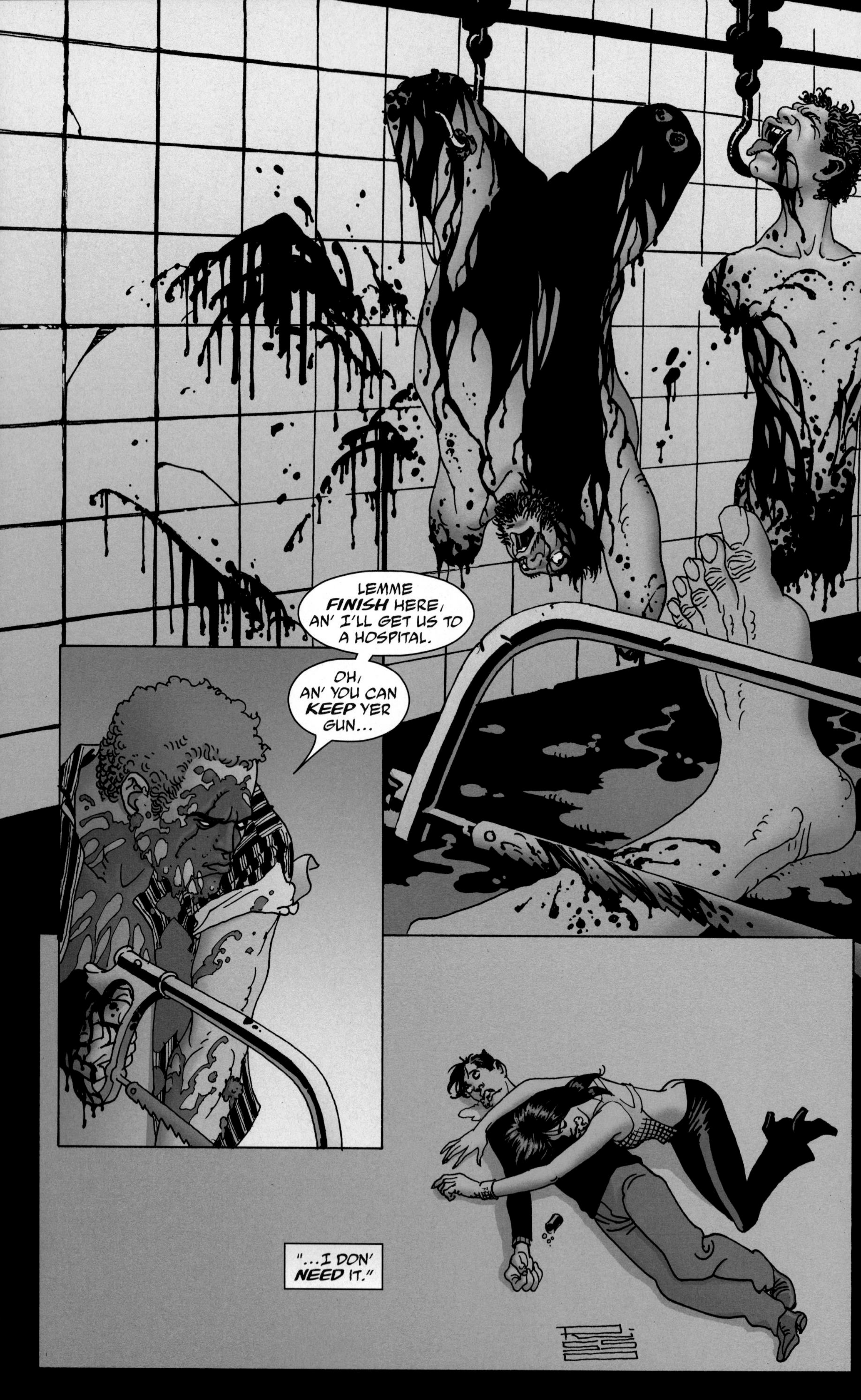
LEMME FINISH HERE, AN' I'LL GET US TO A HOSPITAL.
OH, AN' YOU CAN KEEP YER GUN...
"...I DON' NEED IT."

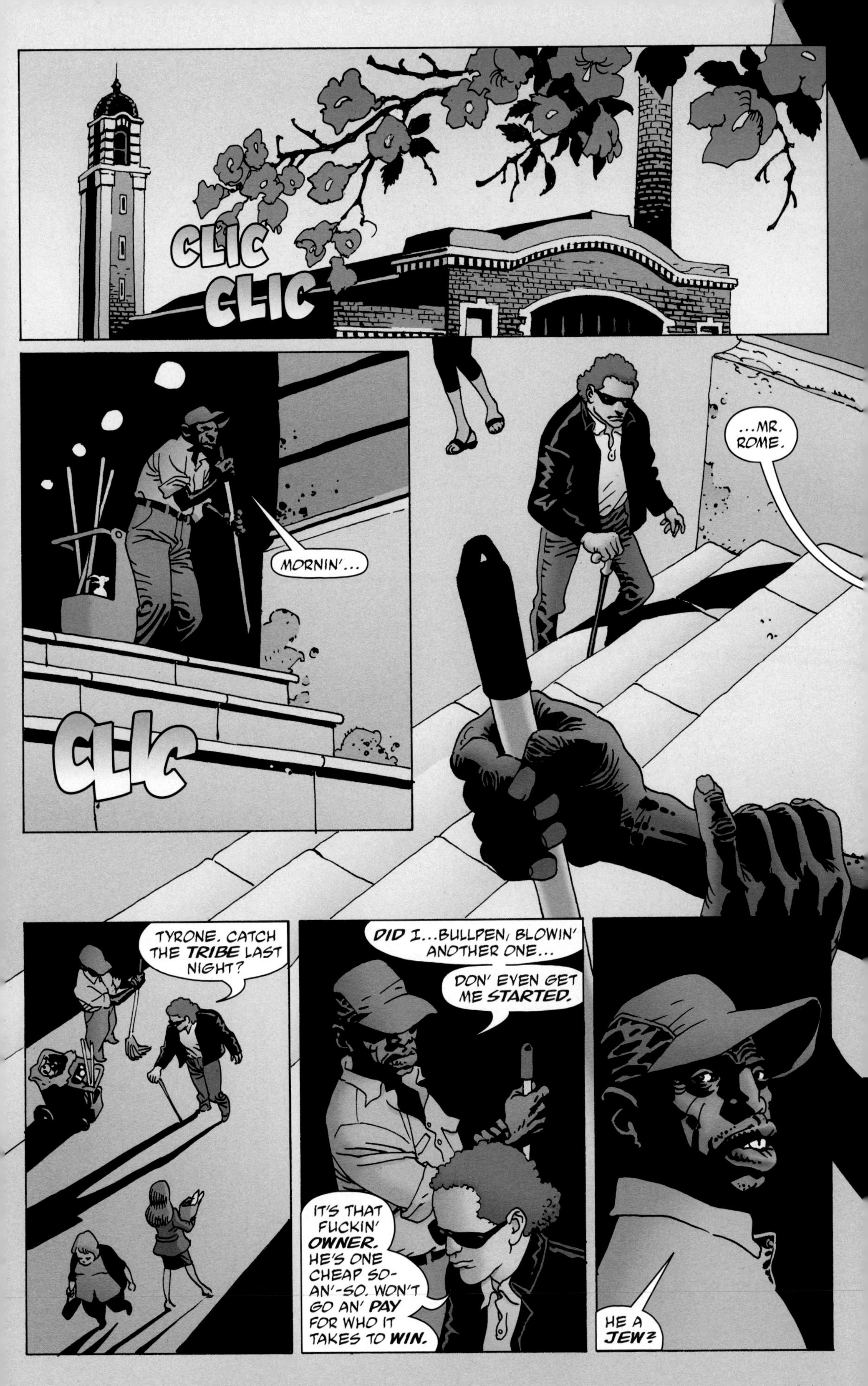
CLIC
CLIC
MORNIN'...
CLIC
...MR. ROME.
TYRONE. CATCH THE TRIBE LAST NIGHT?
DID I...BULLPEN, BLOWIN' ANOTHER ONE...
DON' EVEN GET ME STARTED.
IT'S THAT FUCKIN' OWNER. HE'S ONE CHEAP SO-AN'-SO. WON'T GO AN' PAY FOR WHO IT TAKES TO WIN.
HE A JEW?

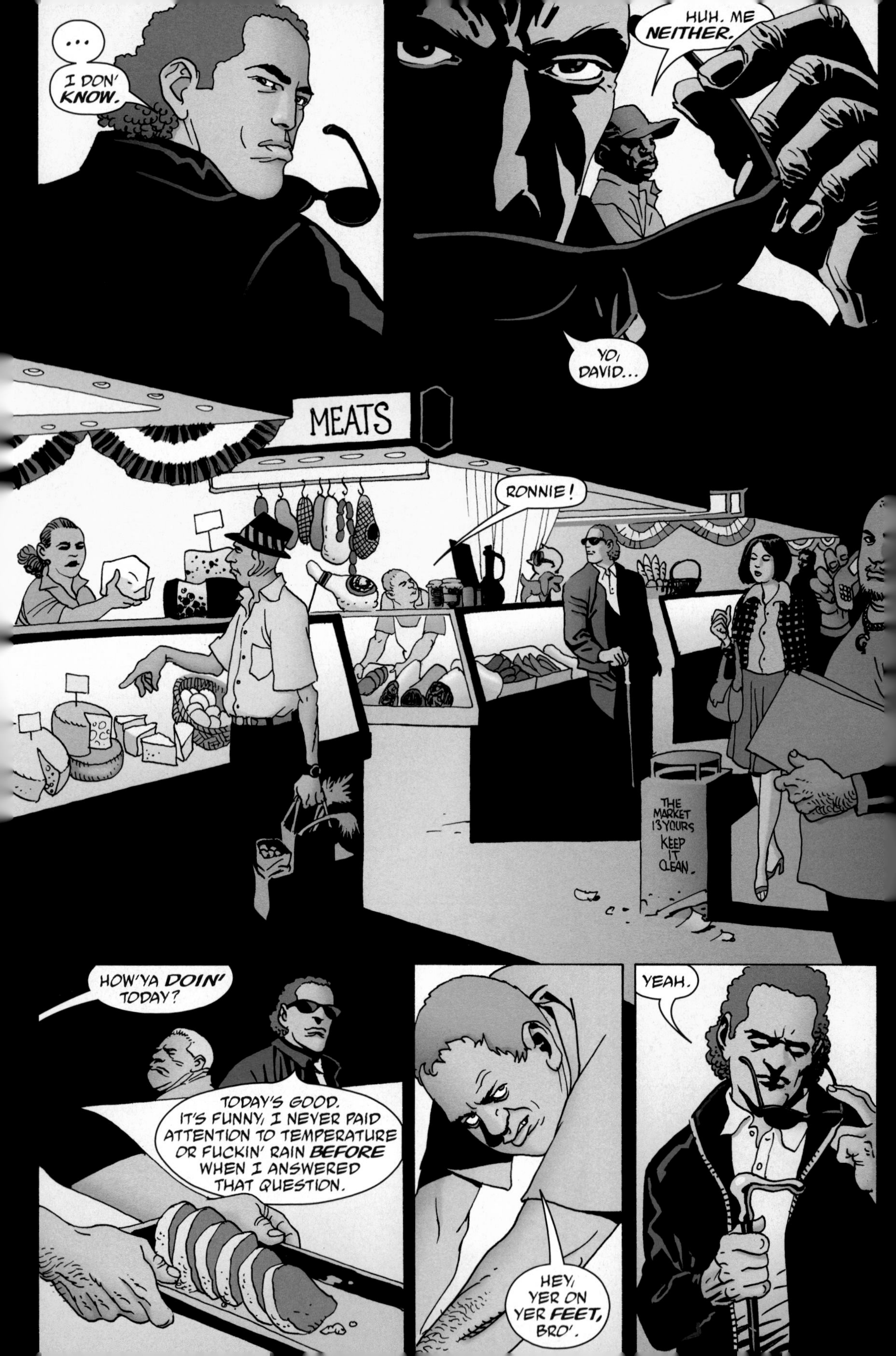
...
I DON' KNOW.
HUH. ME NEITHER.
YO, DAVID...
MEATS
RONNIE!
THE MARKET IS YOURS KEEP IT CLEAN.
HOW'YA DOIN' TODAY?
TODAY'S GOOD. IT'S FUNNY, I NEVER PAID ATTENTION TO TEMPERATURE OR FUCKIN' RAIN BEFORE WHEN I ANSWERED THAT QUESTION.
HEY, YER ON YER FEET, BRO'.
YEAH.

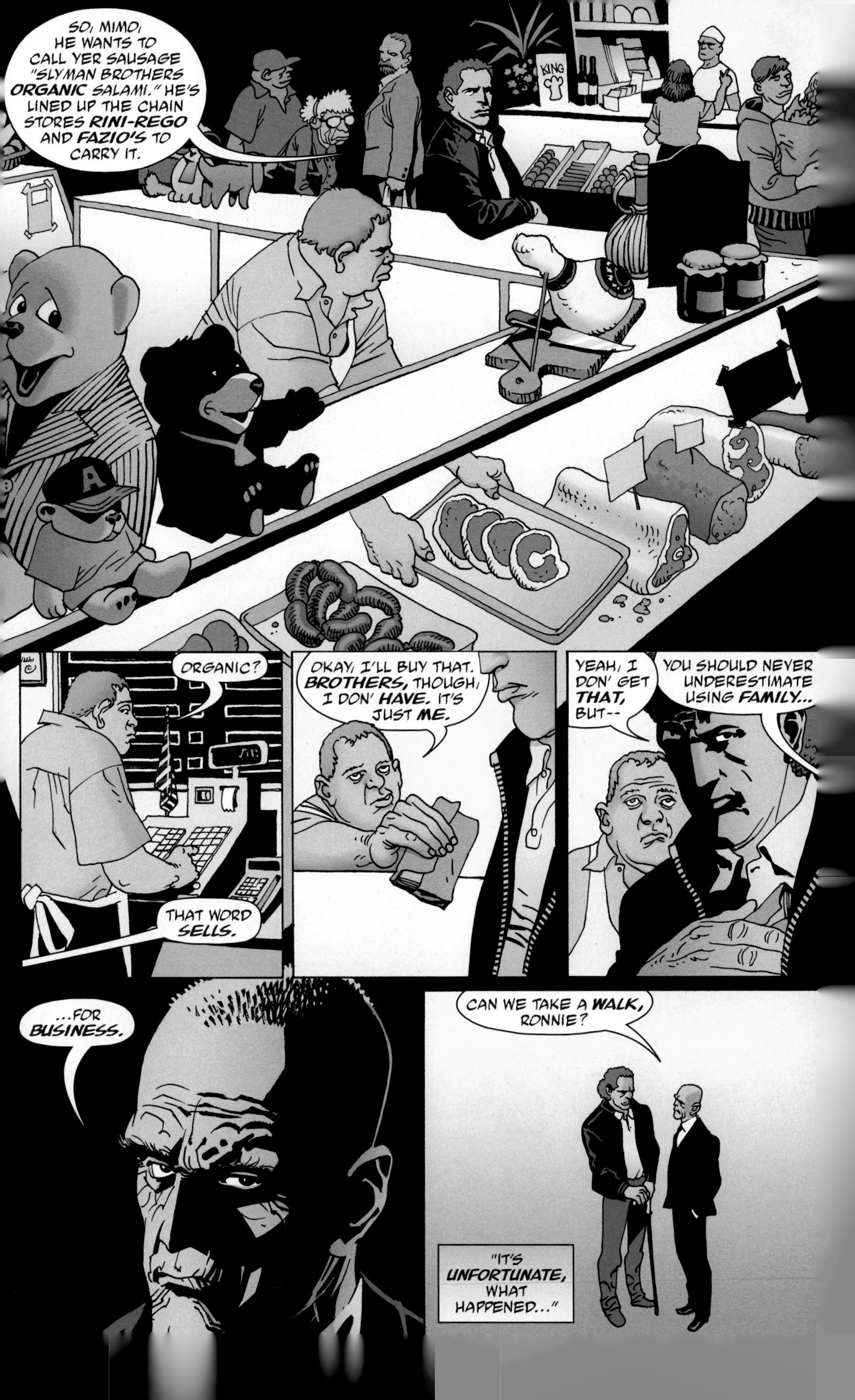
SO, MIMO, HE WANTS TO CALL YER SAUSAGE "SLYMAN BROTHERS ORGANIC SALAMI." HE'S LINED UP THE CHAIN STORES RINI-REGO AND FAZIO'S TO CARRY IT.
KING
ORGANIC?
THAT WORD SELLS.
OKAY, I'LL BUY THAT. BROTHERS, THOUGH, I DON' HAVE. IT'S JUST ME.
YEAH, I DON' GET THAT, BUT--
YOU SHOULD NEVER UNDERESTIMATE USING FAMILY...
...FOR BUSINESS.
CAN WE TAKE A WALK, RONNIE?
"IT'S UNFORTUNATE, WHAT HAPPENED..."

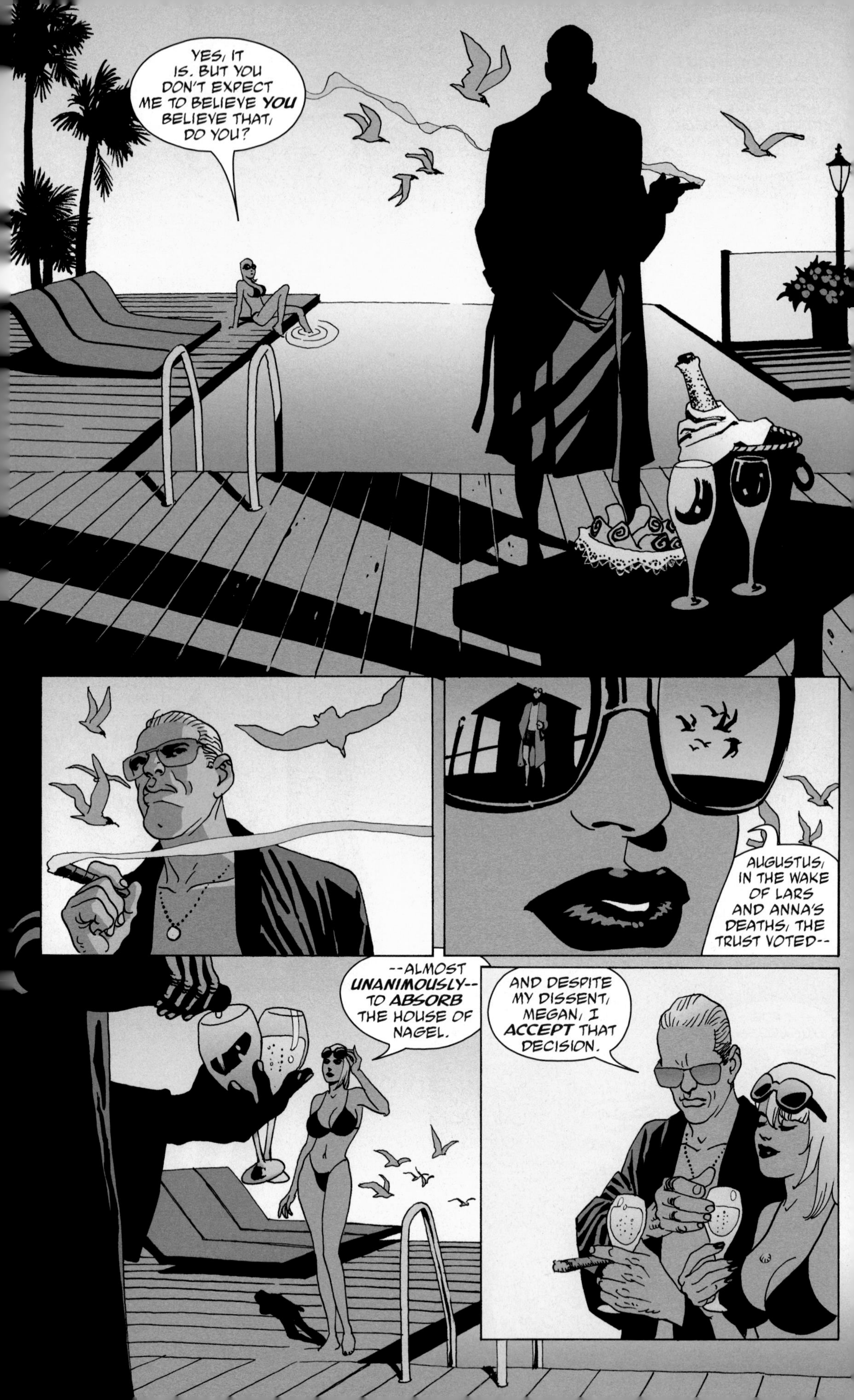
YES, IT IS. BUT YOU DON'T EXPECT ME TO BELIEVE YOU BELIEVE THAT, DO YOU?
AUGUSTUS, IN THE WAKE OF LARS AND ANNA'S DEATHS, THE TRUST VOTED--
--ALMOST UNANIMOUSLY-- TO ABSORB THE HOUSE OF NAGEL.
AND DESPITE MY DISSENT, MEGAN, I ACCEPT THAT DECISION.

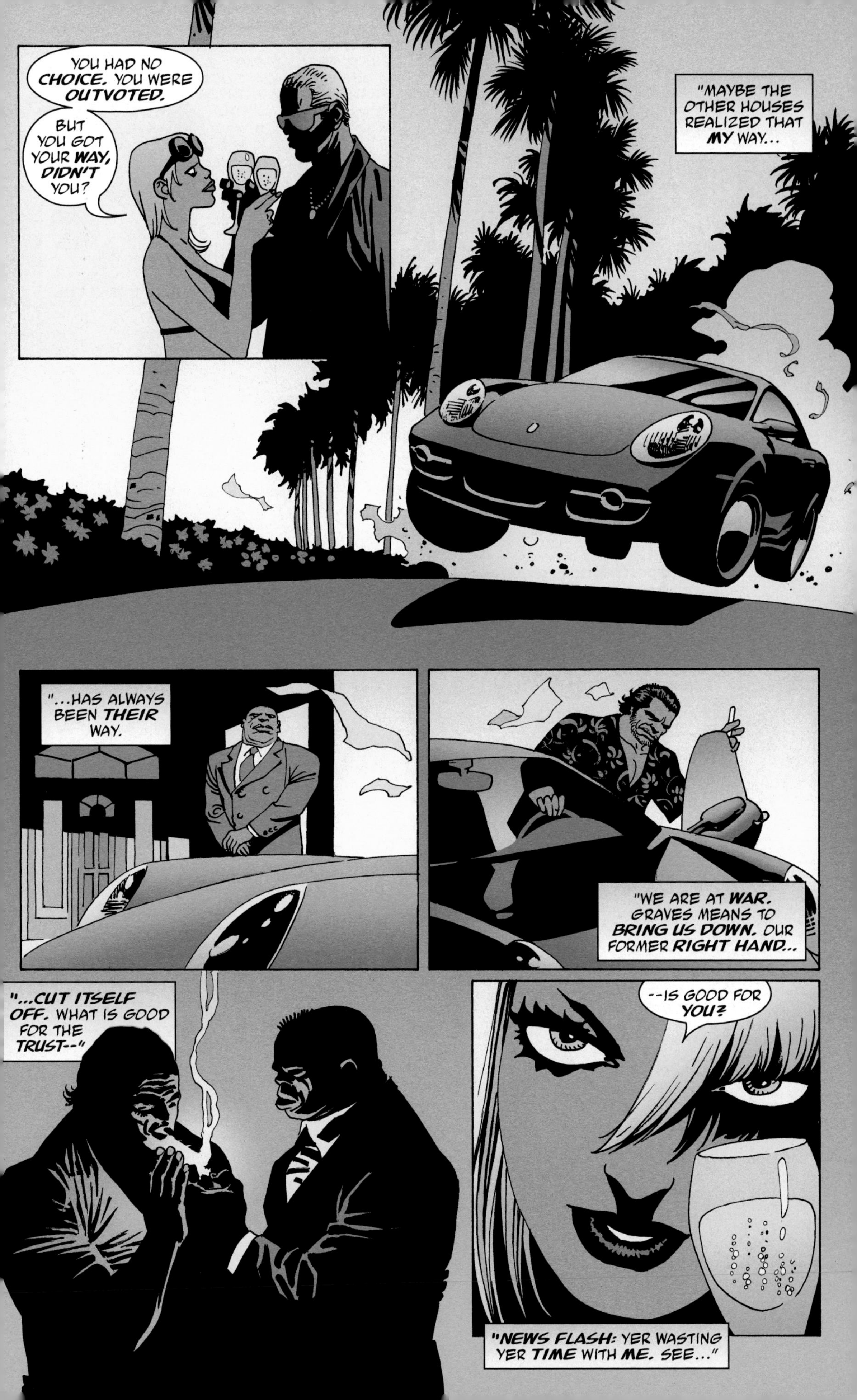

YOU HAD NO CHOICE. YOU WERE OUTVOTED.
BUT YOU GOT YOUR WAY, DIDN'T YOU?
"MAYBE THE OTHER HOUSES REALIZED THAT MY WAY...
"...HAS ALWAYS BEEN THEIR WAY.
"WE ARE AT WAR. GRAVES MEANS TO BRING US DOWN. OUR FORMER RIGHT HAND...
"...CUT ITSELF OFF. WHAT IS GOOD FOR THE TRUST--"
--IS GOOD FOR YOU?
"NEWS FLASH: YER WASTING YER TIME WITH ME. SEE..."

I CAN'T DO WHAT YOU ASKED ME TO, AGENT GRAVES.

REMI'S GONE. I HAVEN'T SEEN 'IM IN THREE MONTHS.

I MERELY POINTED OUT THAT SOMEONE HAD RUINED YOUR LIFE, AND PROVIDED YOU WITH THE MEANS TO DEAL WITH IT. I DIDN'T ASK YOU TO DO ANYTHING, RONNIE.

YEAH. WELL, EVEN IF I SAY YOU DID, THE ANSWER IS NO.

KALIL ORANGE

CUCUMBER FROM ARGEL

WHIZ

ZIHM

REMI DIN' FUCK UP MY LIFE. REMI'S REMI, LIKE ALWAYS.

HE'S MY FUCKIN' BROTHER, SO FUCK YOU.

THERE'S NO DENYING THE FACT THAT SIDING WITH HIM HAS PREVENTED YOU FROM MOVING UP THE LADDER IN THE PALLIDINO FAMILY. THAT'S DANGEROUS. IT'S MADE YOU EXPENDABLE.

SCREW MIMO TOO--HE KNOWS I'M LOYAL. REMI...

...IS FAMILY. AN' YOU KNOW WHAT? IF FAMILY RUINS YER LIFE, WELL, THAT'S WHAT FAMILY IS...

...YER LIFE.

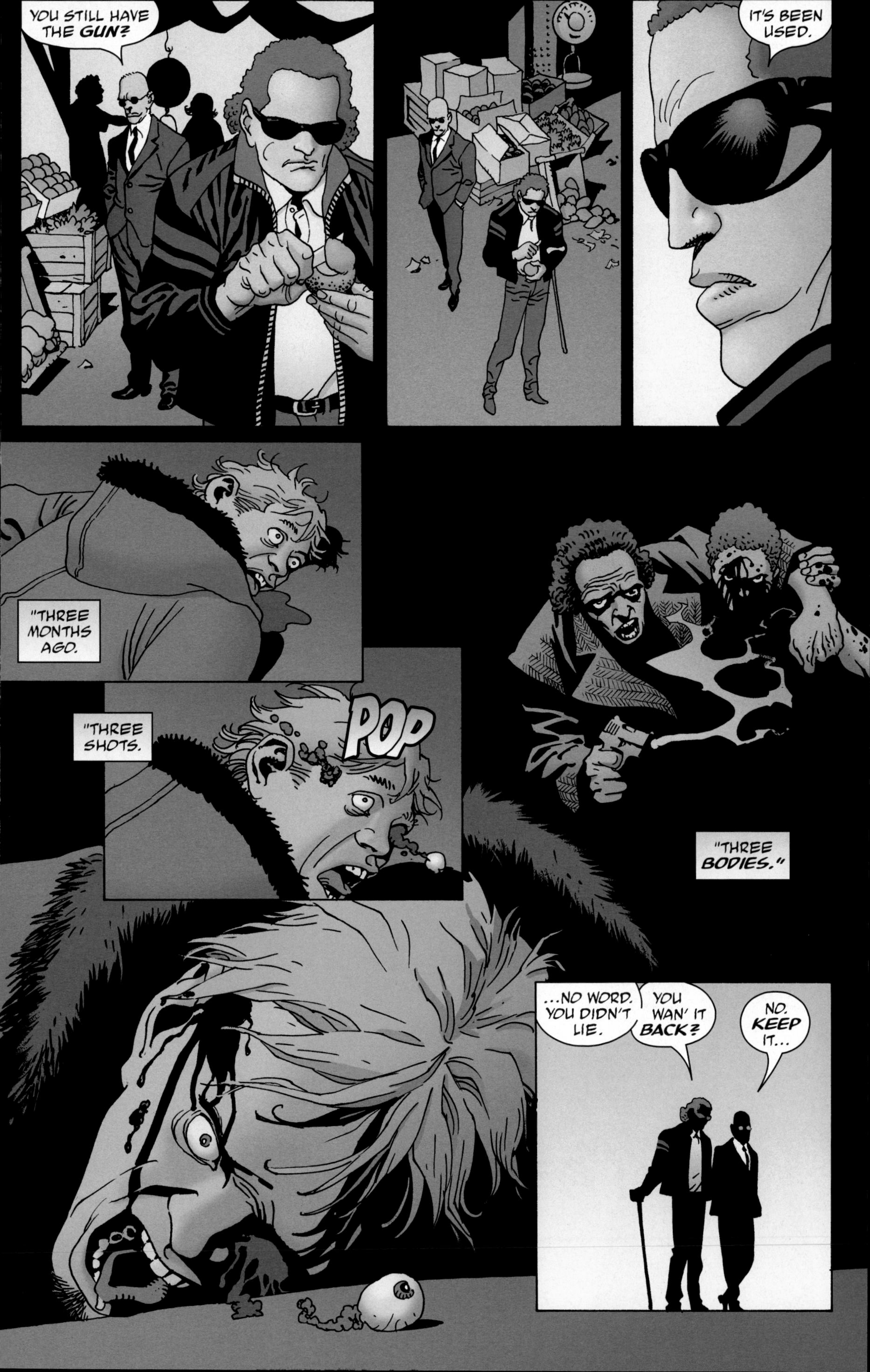
YOU STILL HAVE THE GUN?
IT'S BEEN USED.
"THREE MONTHS AGO.
"THREE SHOTS.
POP
"THREE BODIES."
...NO WORD. YOU DIDN'T LIE.
YOU WAN' IT BACK?
NO. KEEP IT...

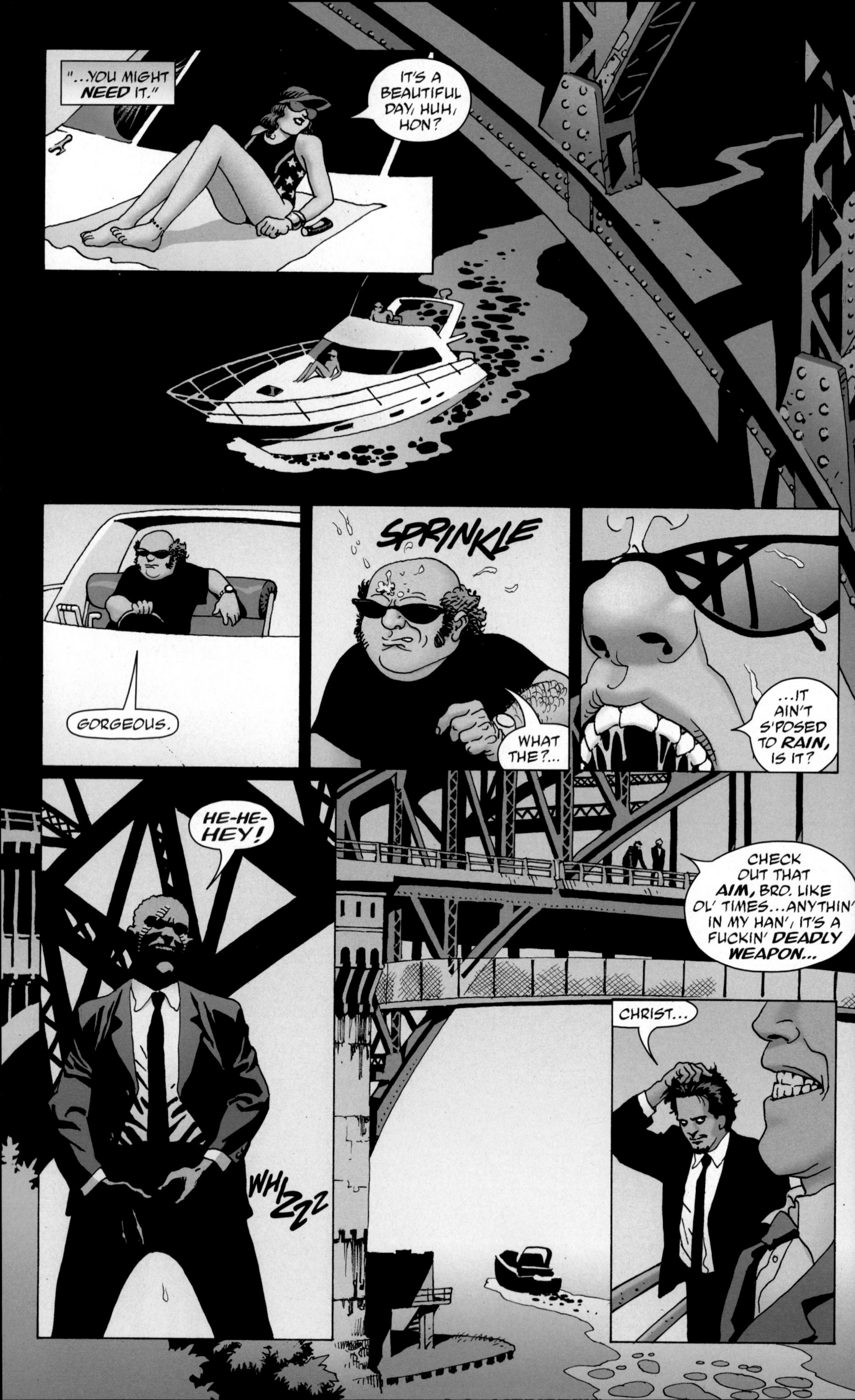
"...YOU MIGHT NEED IT."
IT'S A BEAUTIFUL DAY, HUH, HON?
GORGEOUS.
SPRINKLE
WHAT THE?...
...IT AIN'T S'POSED TO RAIN, IS IT?
HE-HE-HEY!
CHECK OUT THAT AIM, BRO. LIKE OL' TIMES...ANYTHIN' IN MY HAN', IT'S A FUCKIN' DEADLY WEAPON...
WHIZZZ
CHRIST...

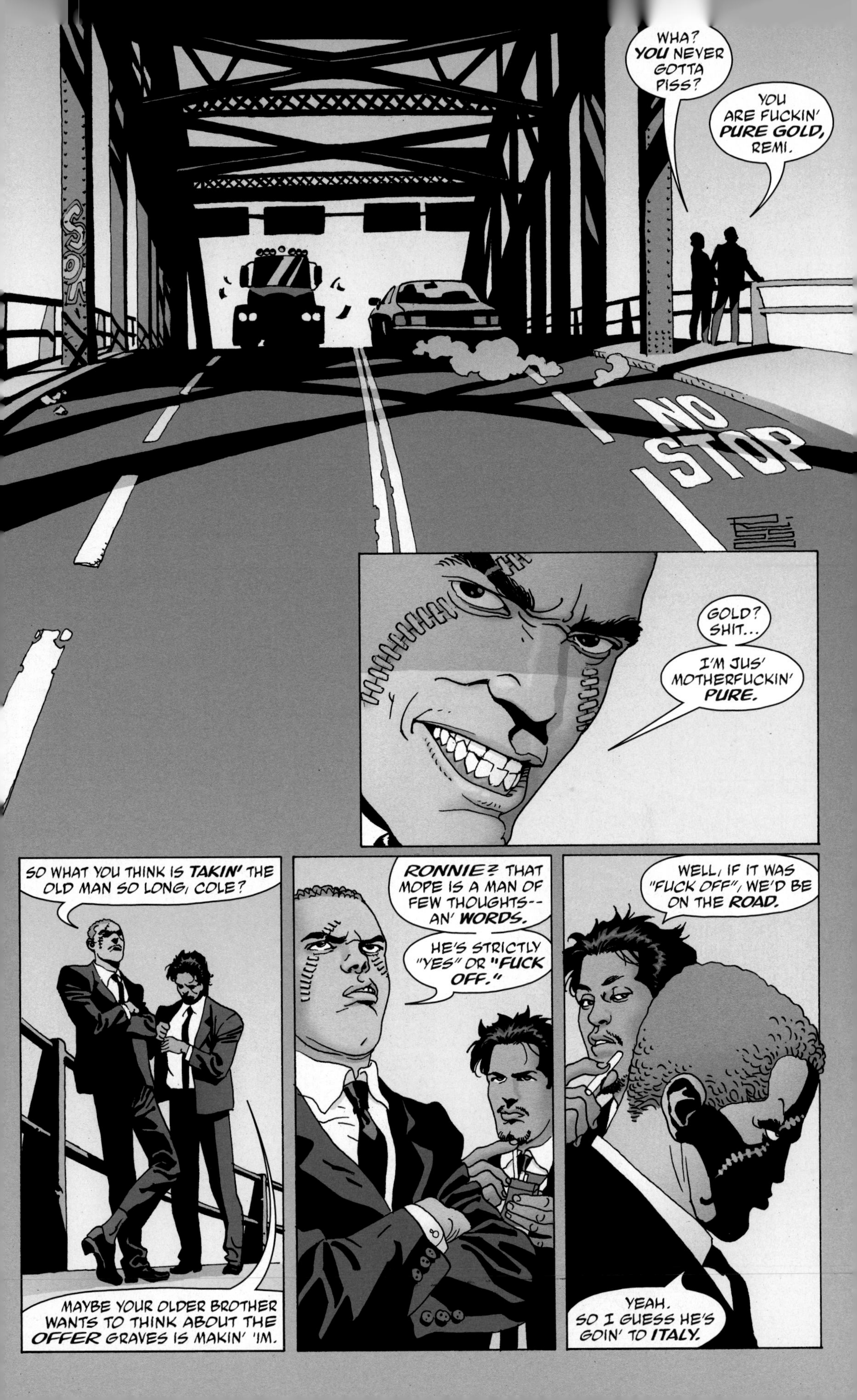
WHA? YOU NEVER GOTTA PISS?
YOU ARE FUCKIN' PURE GOLD, REMI.
NO STOP
GOLD? SHIT...
I'M JUS' MOTHERFUCKIN' PURE.
SO WHAT YOU THINK IS TAKIN' THE OLD MAN SO LONG, COLE?
MAYBE YOUR OLDER BROTHER WANTS TO THINK ABOUT THE OFFER GRAVES IS MAKIN' 'IM.
RONNIE? THAT MOPE IS A MAN OF FEW THOUGHTS-- AN' WORDS.
HE'S STRICTLY "YES" OR "FUCK OFF."
WELL, IF IT WAS "FUCK OFF", WE'D BE ON THE ROAD.
YEAH. SO I GUESS HE'S GOIN' TO ITALY.

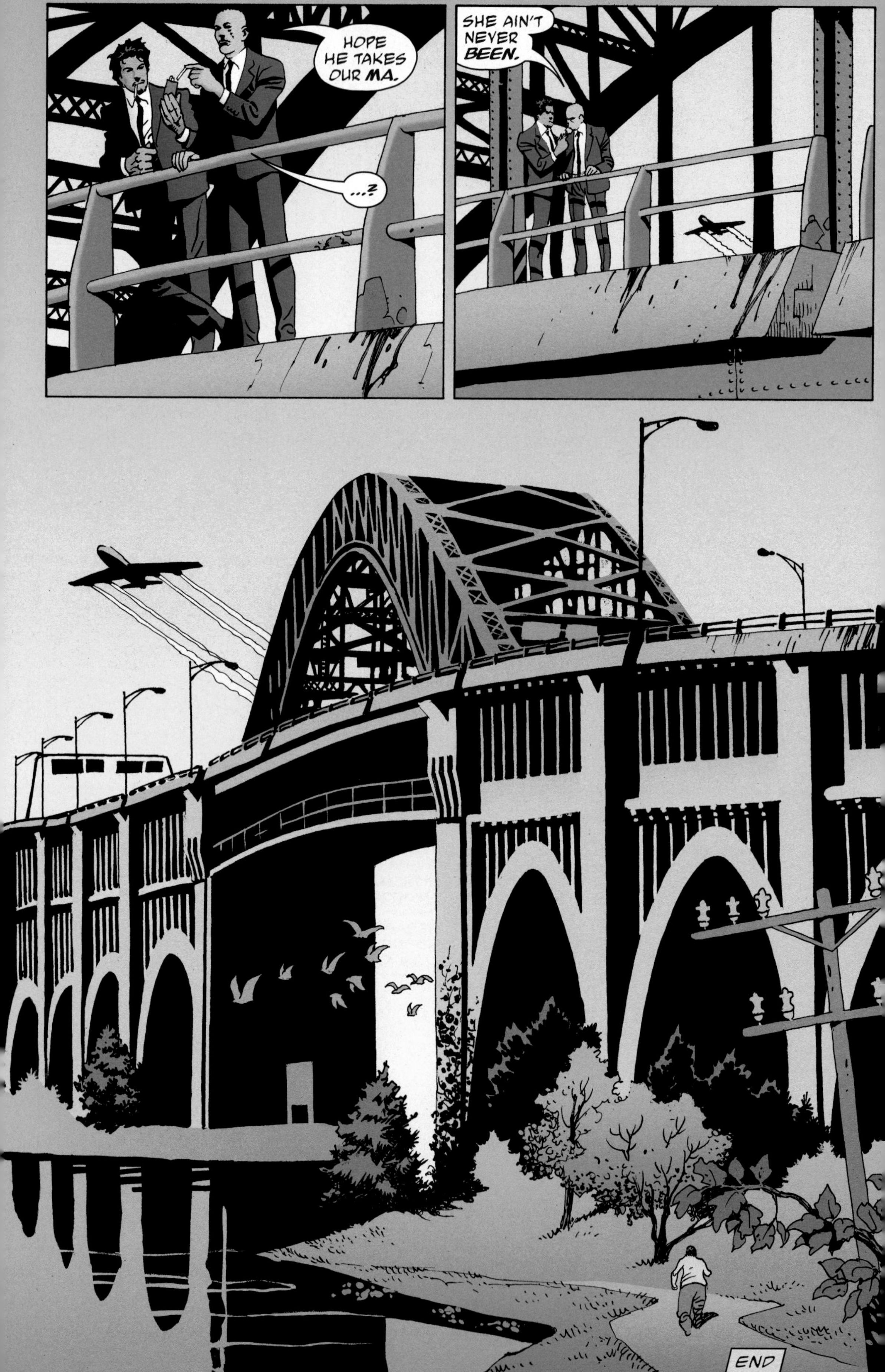
HOPE HE TAKES OUR MA.
...?
SHE AIN'T NEVER BEEN.
END

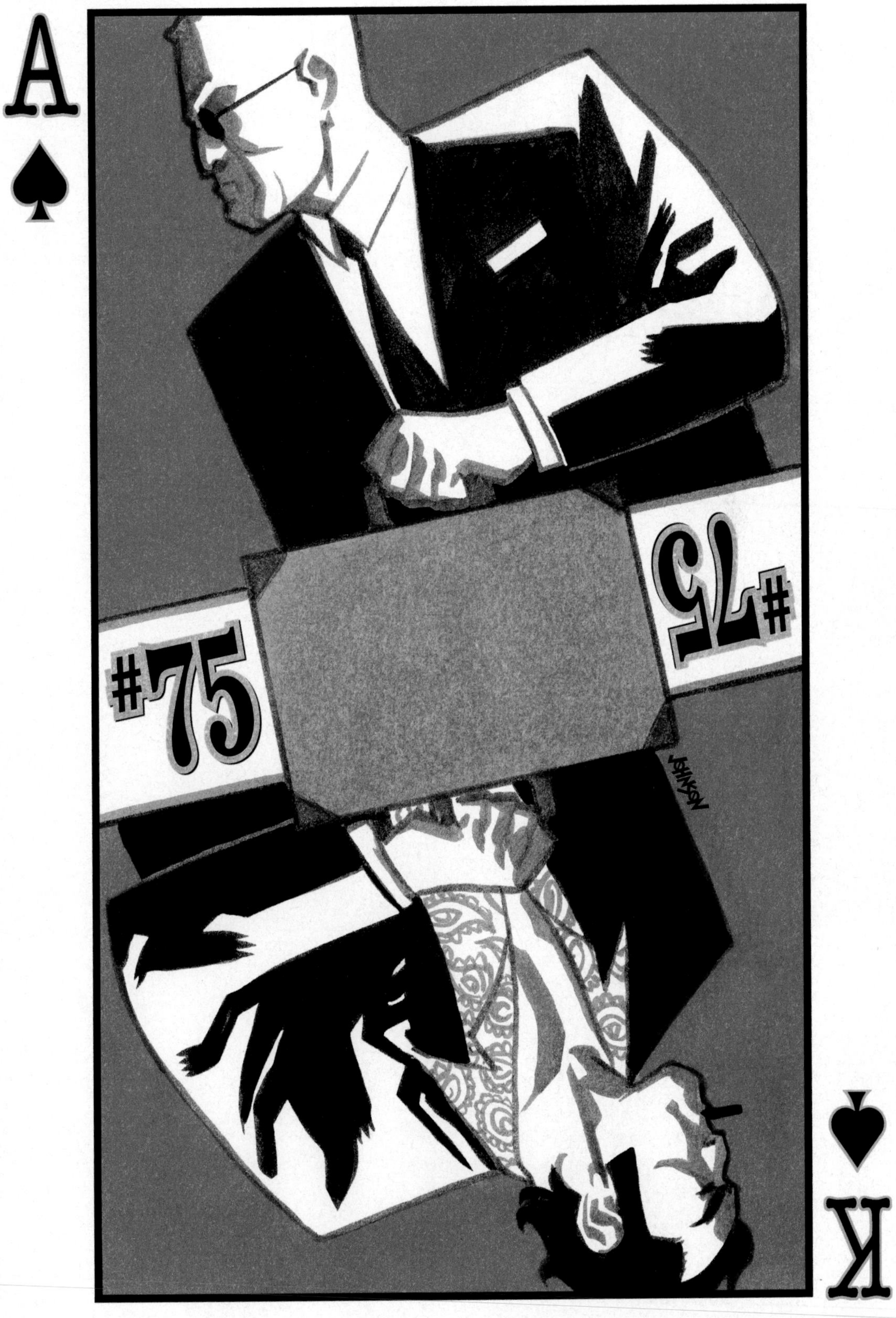
A
#75
#75
K

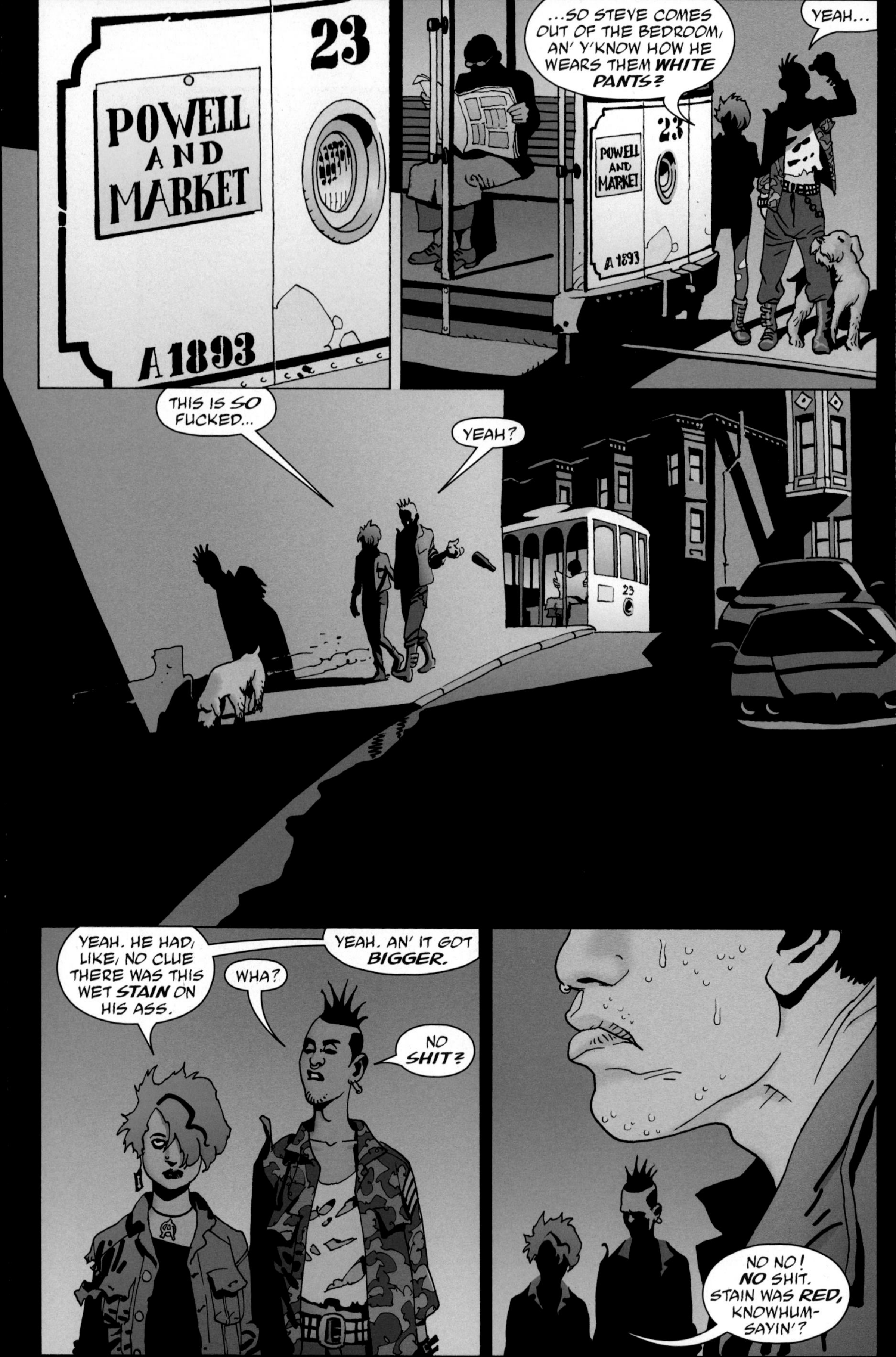
POWELL AND MARKET
23
A 1893
...SO STEVE COMES OUT OF THE BEDROOM, AN' Y'KNOW HOW HE WEARS THEM WHITE PANTS?
YEAH...
THIS IS SO FUCKED...
YEAH?
YEAH. HE HAD, LIKE, NO CLUE THERE WAS THIS WET STAIN ON HIS ASS.
WHA?
YEAH. AN' IT GOT BIGGER.
NO SHIT?
NO NO! NO SHIT. STAIN WAS RED, KNOWHUM-SAYIN'?

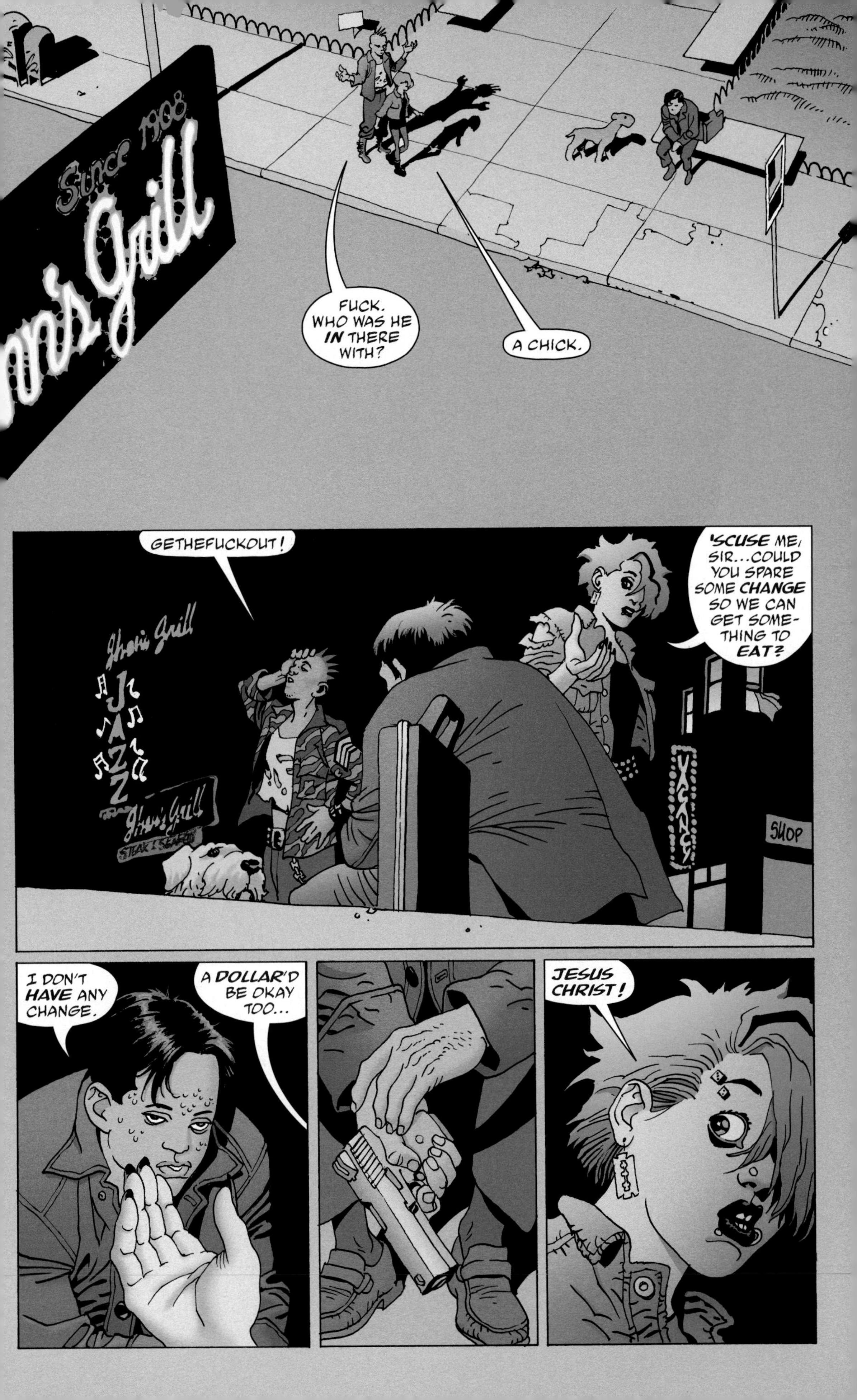

Since 1908
FUCK. WHO WAS HE *IN* THERE WITH?
A CHICK.
GETHEFUCKOUT!
'*SCUSE* ME, SIR...COULD YOU SPARE SOME *CHANGE* SO WE CAN GET SOMETHING TO *EAT?*
JAZZ
SHOP
I DON'T *HAVE* ANY CHANGE.
A *DOLLAR'D* BE OKAY TOO...
JESUS CHRIST!

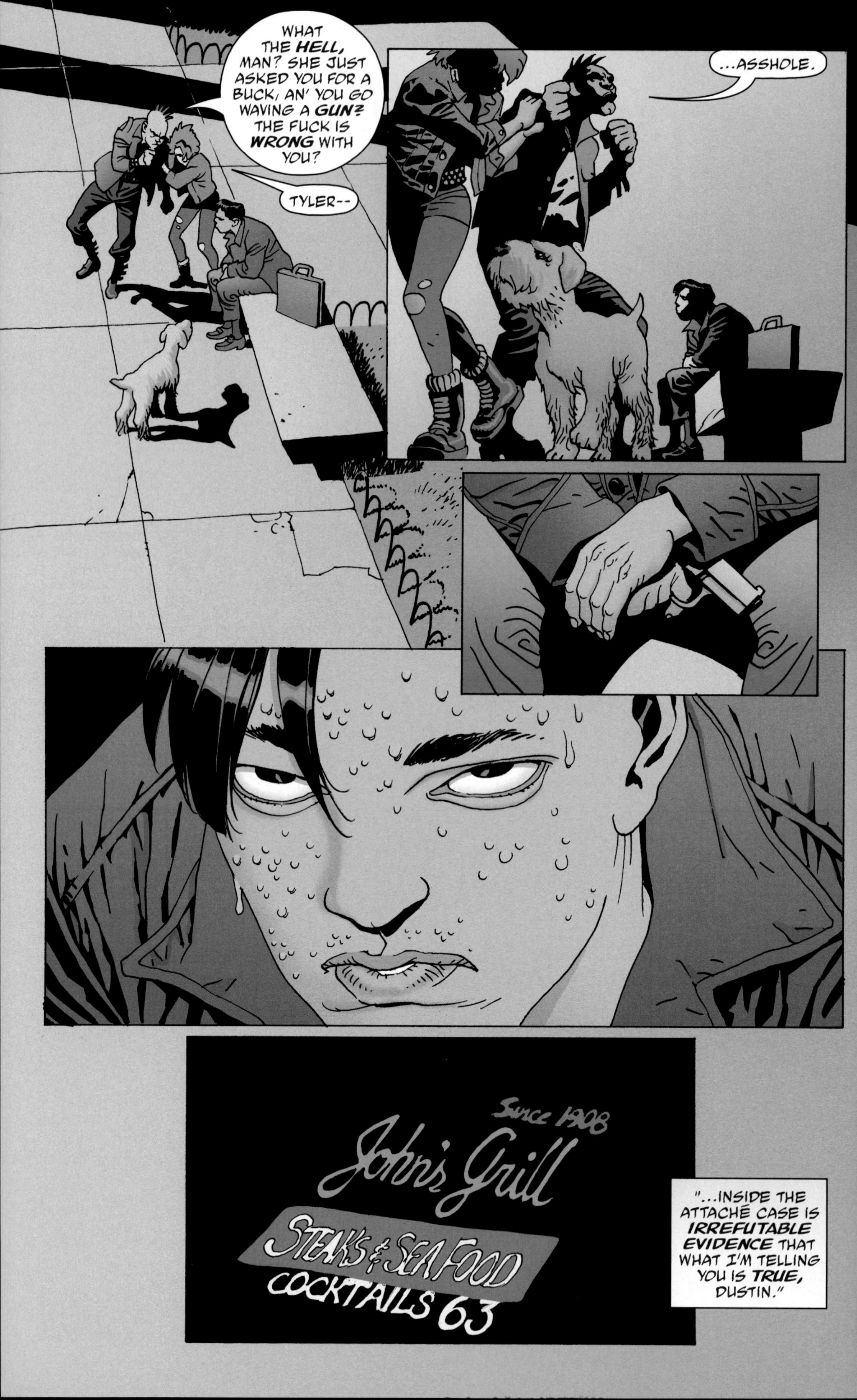
WHAT THE **HELL,** MAN? SHE JUST ASKED YOU FOR A BUCK, AN' YOU GO WAVING A **GUN?** THE FUCK IS **WRONG** WITH YOU?
TYLER--
...ASSHOLE.
Since 1908
John's Grill
STEAKS & SEA FOOD
COCKTAILS 63
"...INSIDE THE ATTACHÉ CASE IS **IRREFUTABLE EVIDENCE** THAT WHAT I'M TELLING YOU IS **TRUE,** DUSTIN."

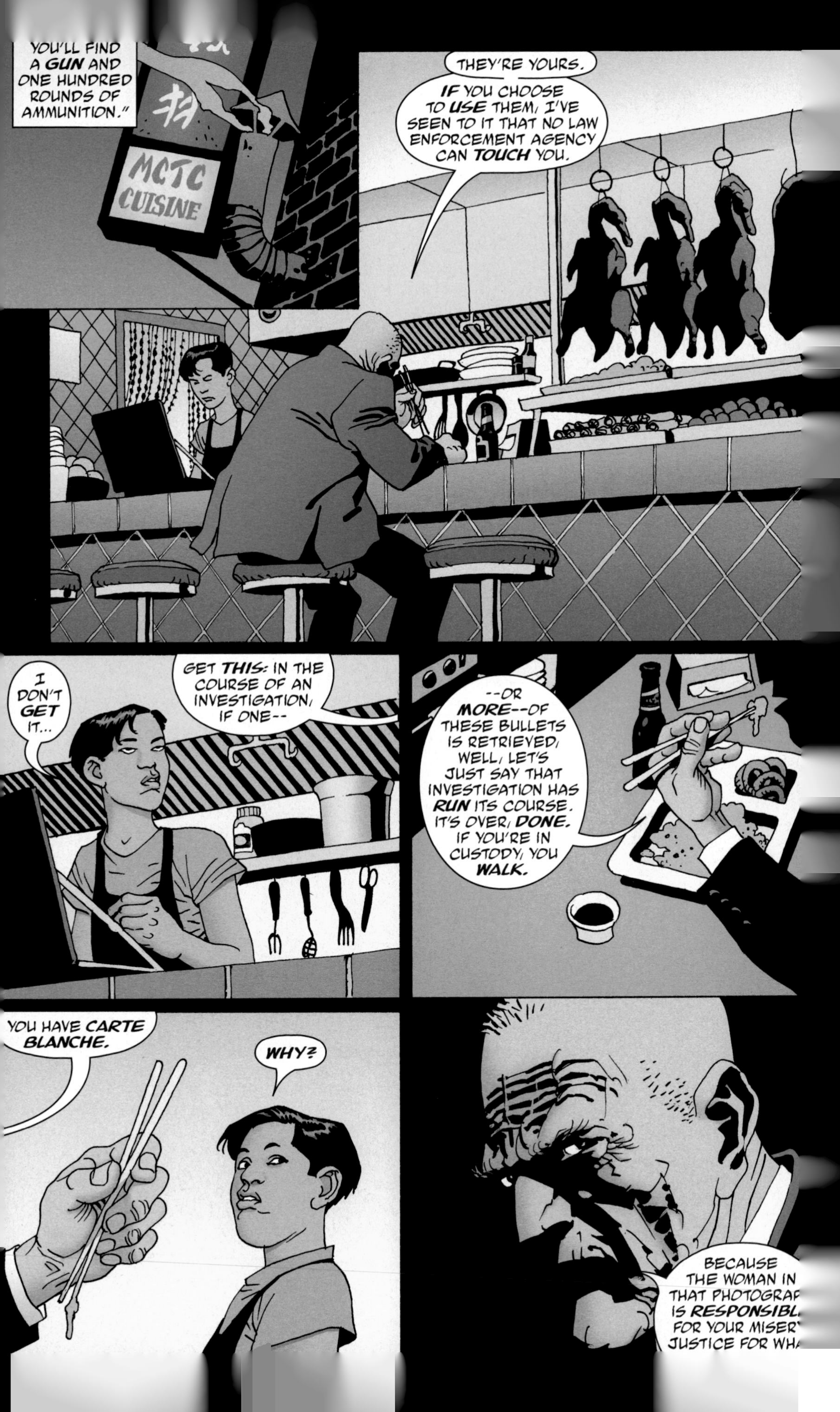

YOU'LL FIND A **GUN** AND ONE HUNDRED ROUNDS OF AMMUNITION."
MCTC CUISINE
THEY'RE YOURS.
IF YOU CHOOSE TO **USE** THEM, I'VE SEEN TO IT THAT NO LAW ENFORCEMENT AGENCY CAN **TOUCH** YOU.
I DON'T **GET** IT...
GET **THIS**: IN THE COURSE OF AN INVESTIGATION, IF ONE--
--OR **MORE**--OF THESE BULLETS IS RETRIEVED, WELL, LET'S JUST SAY THAT INVESTIGATION HAS **RUN** ITS COURSE. IT'S OVER, **DONE.** IF YOU'RE IN CUSTODY, YOU **WALK.**
YOU HAVE **CARTE BLANCHE.**
WHY?
BECAUSE THE WOMAN IN THAT PHOTOGRAP IS **RESPONSIBL** FOR YOUR MISER JUSTICE FOR WHA

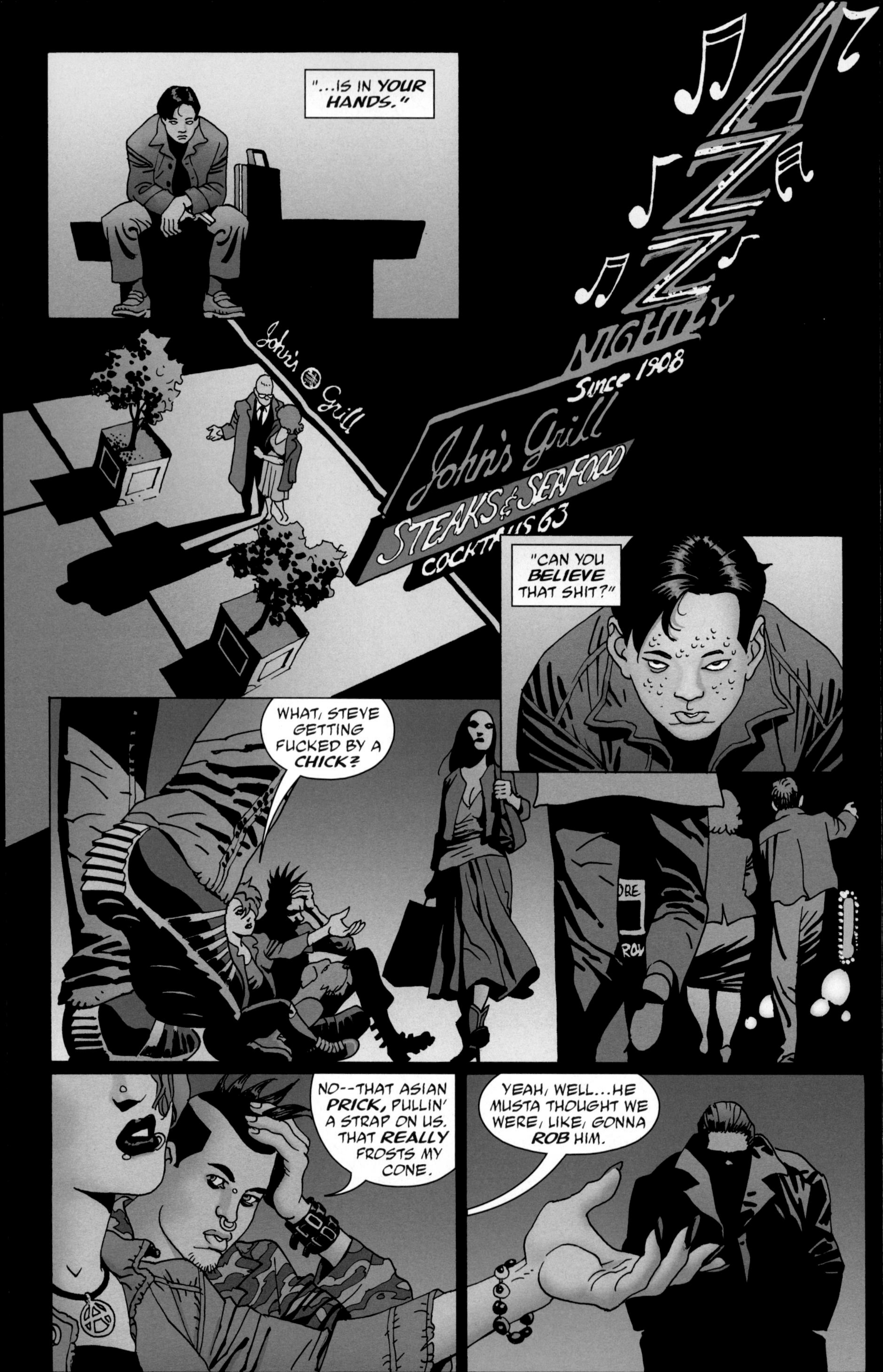
"...IS IN YOUR HANDS."
JAZZ NIGHTLY
John's Grill
Since 1908
John's Grill
STEAKS & SEAFOOD
COCKTAILS 63
"CAN YOU BELIEVE THAT SHIT?"
WHAT, STEVE GETTING FUCKED BY A CHICK?
NO--THAT ASIAN PRICK, PULLIN' A STRAP ON US. THAT REALLY FROSTS MY CONE.
YEAH, WELL...HE MUSTA THOUGHT WE WERE, LIKE, GONNA ROB HIM.

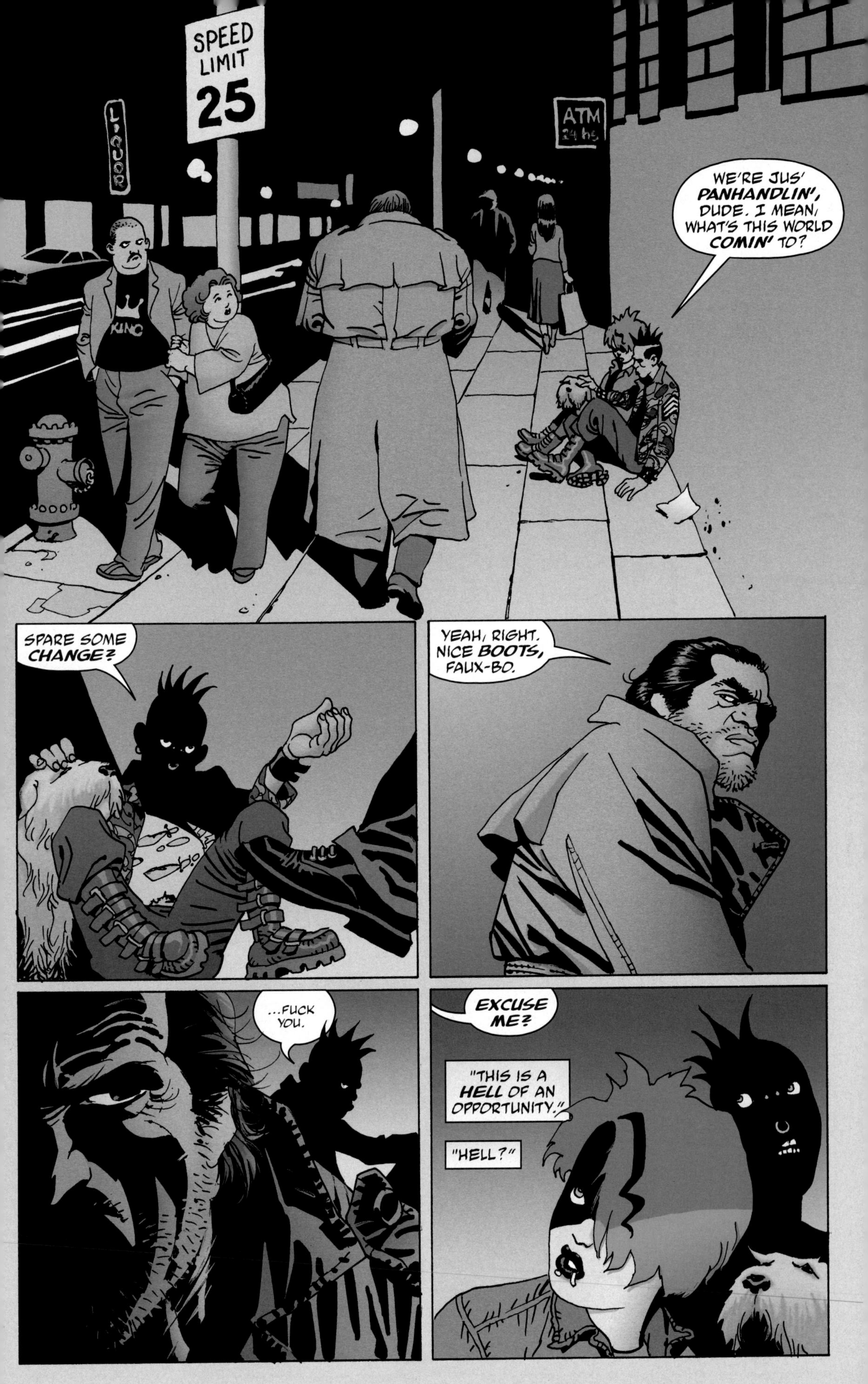
SPEED LIMIT 25
LIQUOR
ATM 24 hs
KING
WE'RE JUS' PANHANDLIN', DUDE. I MEAN, WHAT'S THIS WORLD COMIN' TO?
SPARE SOME CHANGE?
YEAH, RIGHT. NICE BOOTS, FAUX-BO.
...FUCK YOU.
EXCUSE ME?
"THIS IS A HELL OF AN OPPORTUNITY."
"HELL?"

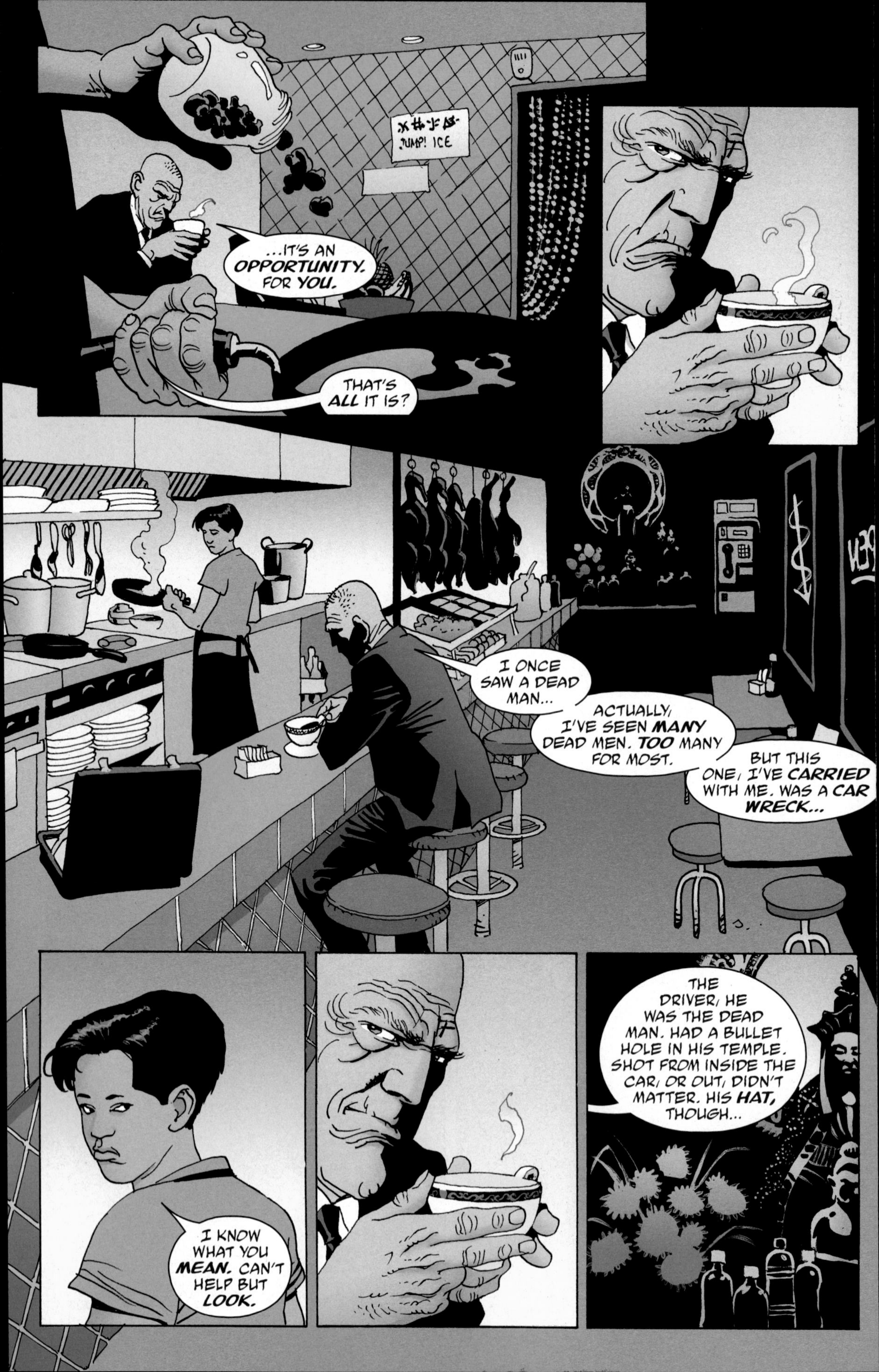
JUMP! ICE
...IT'S AN OPPORTUNITY. FOR YOU.
THAT'S ALL IT IS?
I ONCE SAW A DEAD MAN...
ACTUALLY, I'VE SEEN MANY DEAD MEN. TOO MANY FOR MOST.
BUT THIS ONE, I'VE CARRIED WITH ME. WAS A CAR WRECK...
I KNOW WHAT YOU MEAN. CAN'T HELP BUT LOOK.
THE DRIVER, HE WAS THE DEAD MAN. HAD A BULLET HOLE IN HIS TEMPLE. SHOT FROM INSIDE THE CAR, OR OUT, DIDN'T MATTER. HIS HAT, THOUGH...

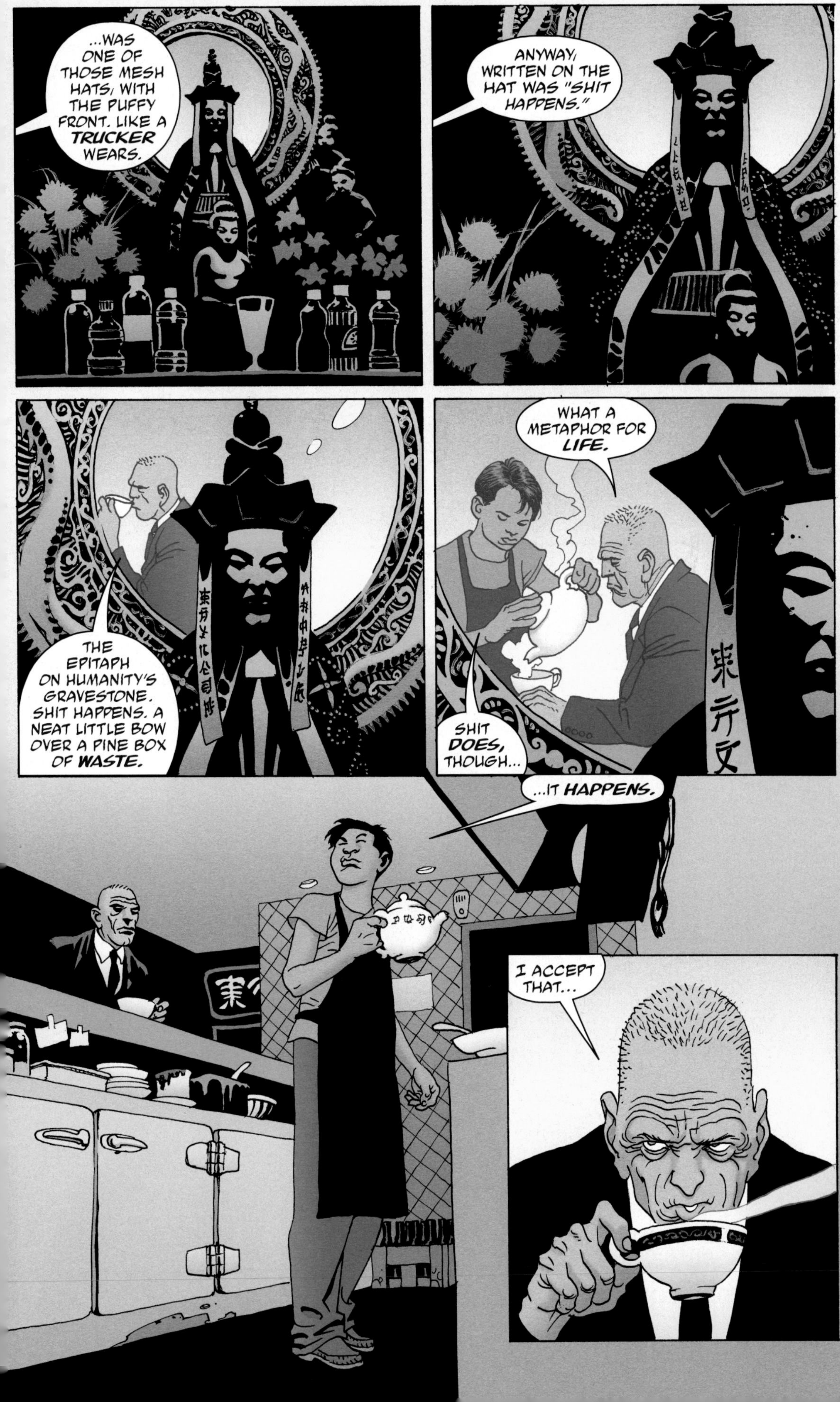
...WAS ONE OF THOSE MESH HATS, WITH THE PUFFY FRONT. LIKE A TRUCKER WEARS.
ANYWAY, WRITTEN ON THE HAT WAS "SHIT HAPPENS."
THE EPITAPH ON HUMANITY'S GRAVESTONE. SHIT HAPPENS. A NEAT LITTLE BOW OVER A PINE BOX OF WASTE.
WHAT A METAPHOR FOR LIFE.
SHIT DOES, THOUGH...
...IT HAPPENS.
I ACCEPT THAT...

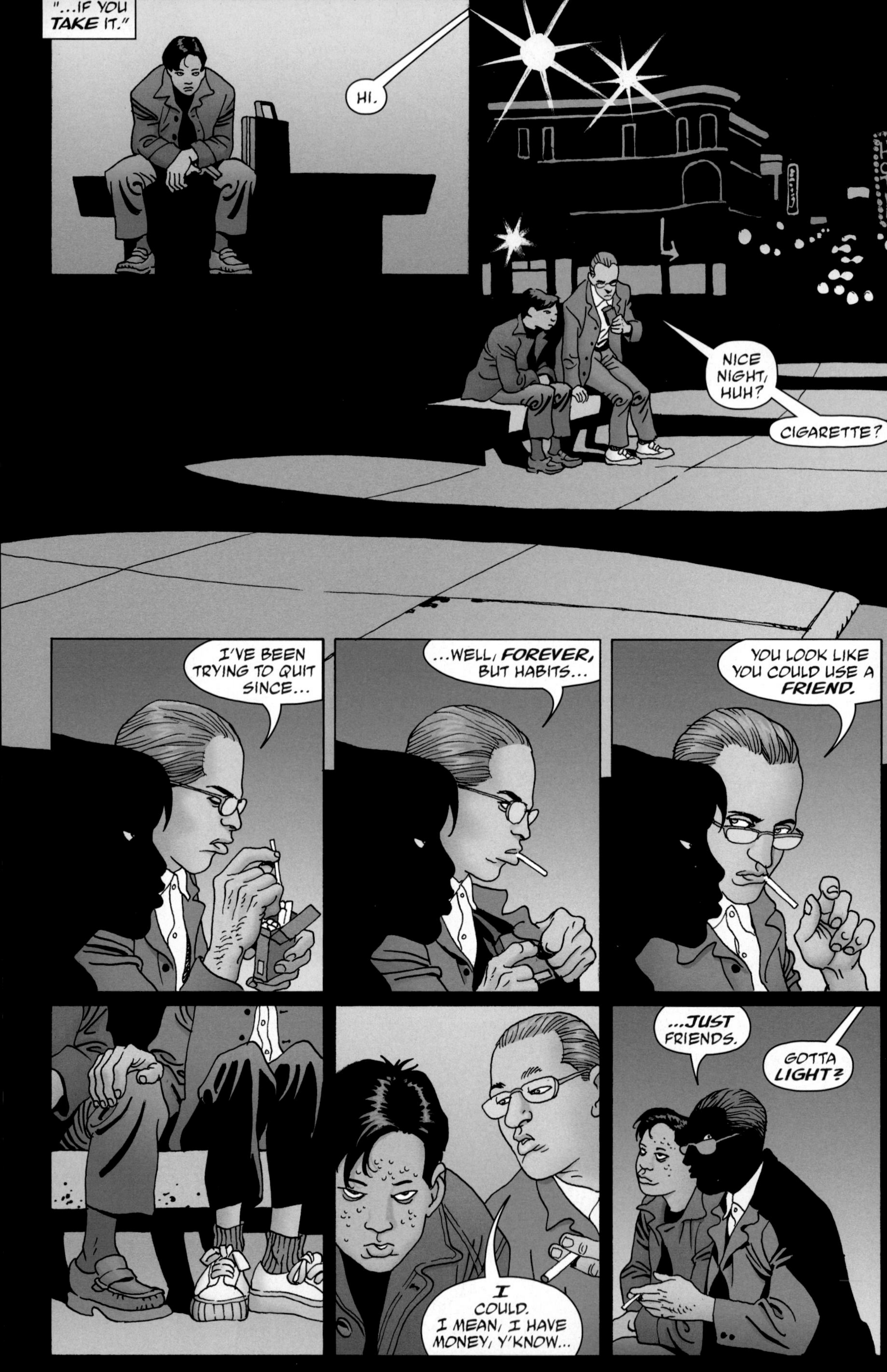
"...IF YOU TAKE IT."
HI.
NICE NIGHT, HUH?
CIGARETTE?
I'VE BEEN TRYING TO QUIT SINCE...
...WELL, FOREVER, BUT HABITS...
YOU LOOK LIKE YOU COULD USE A FRIEND.
I COULD. I MEAN, I HAVE MONEY, Y'KNOW...
...JUST FRIENDS.
GOTTA LIGHT?

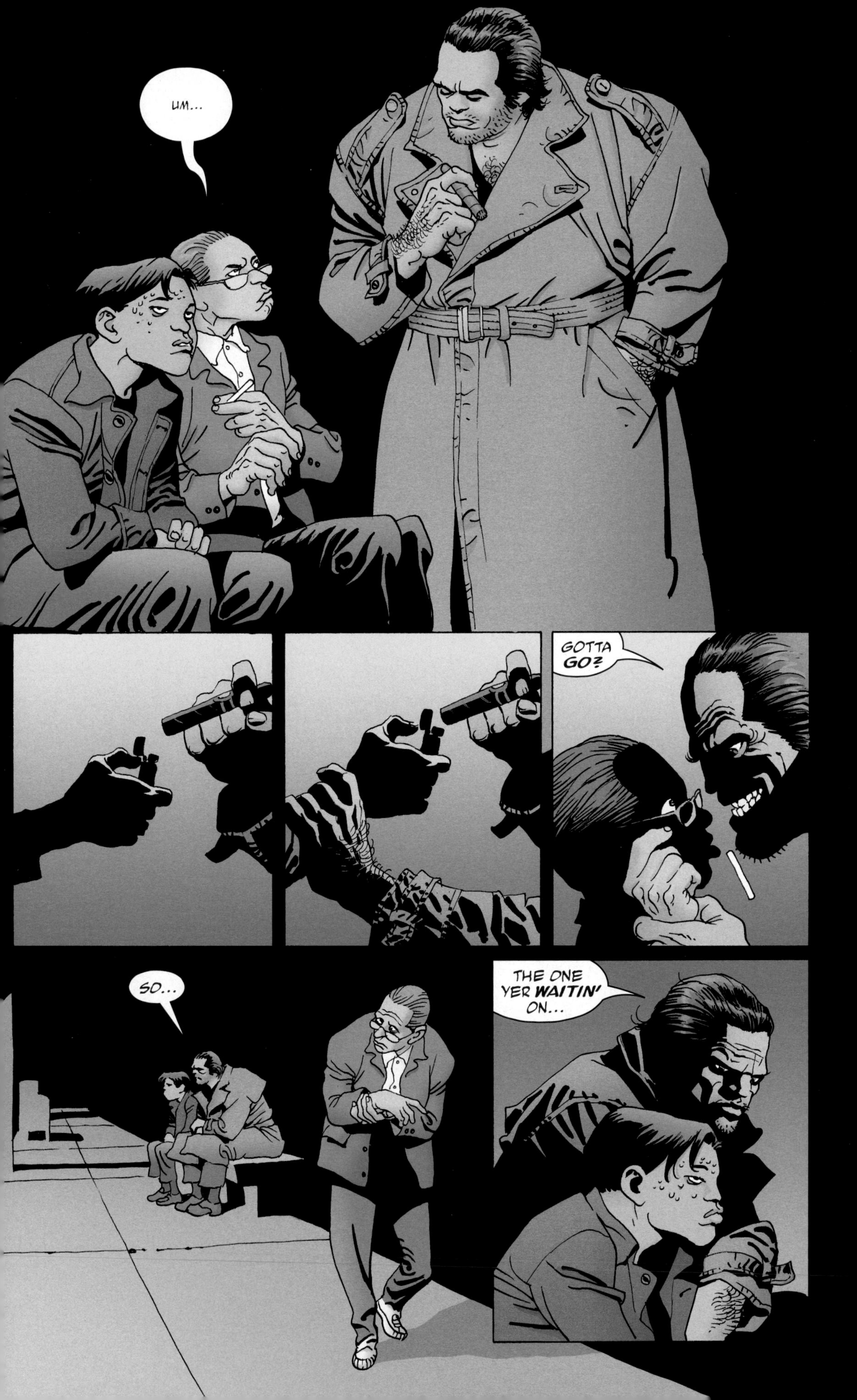
UM...
GOTTA GO?
SO...
THE ONE YER WAITIN' ON...

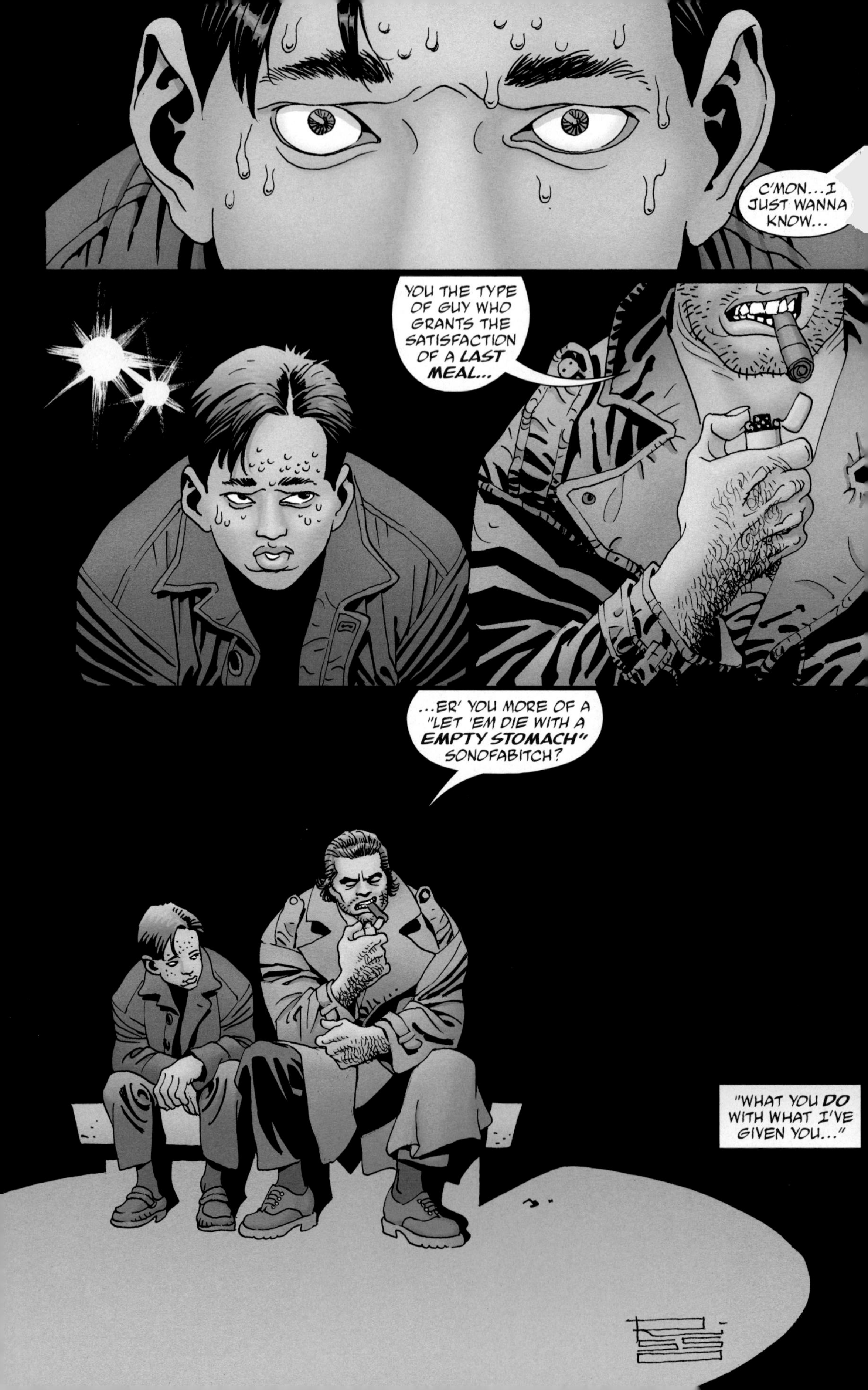
C'MON...I JUST WANNA KNOW...
YOU THE TYPE OF GUY WHO GRANTS THE SATISFACTION OF A LAST MEAL...
...ER' YOU MORE OF A "LET 'EM DIE WITH A EMPTY STOMACH" SONOFABITCH?
"WHAT YOU DO WITH WHAT I'VE GIVEN YOU..."

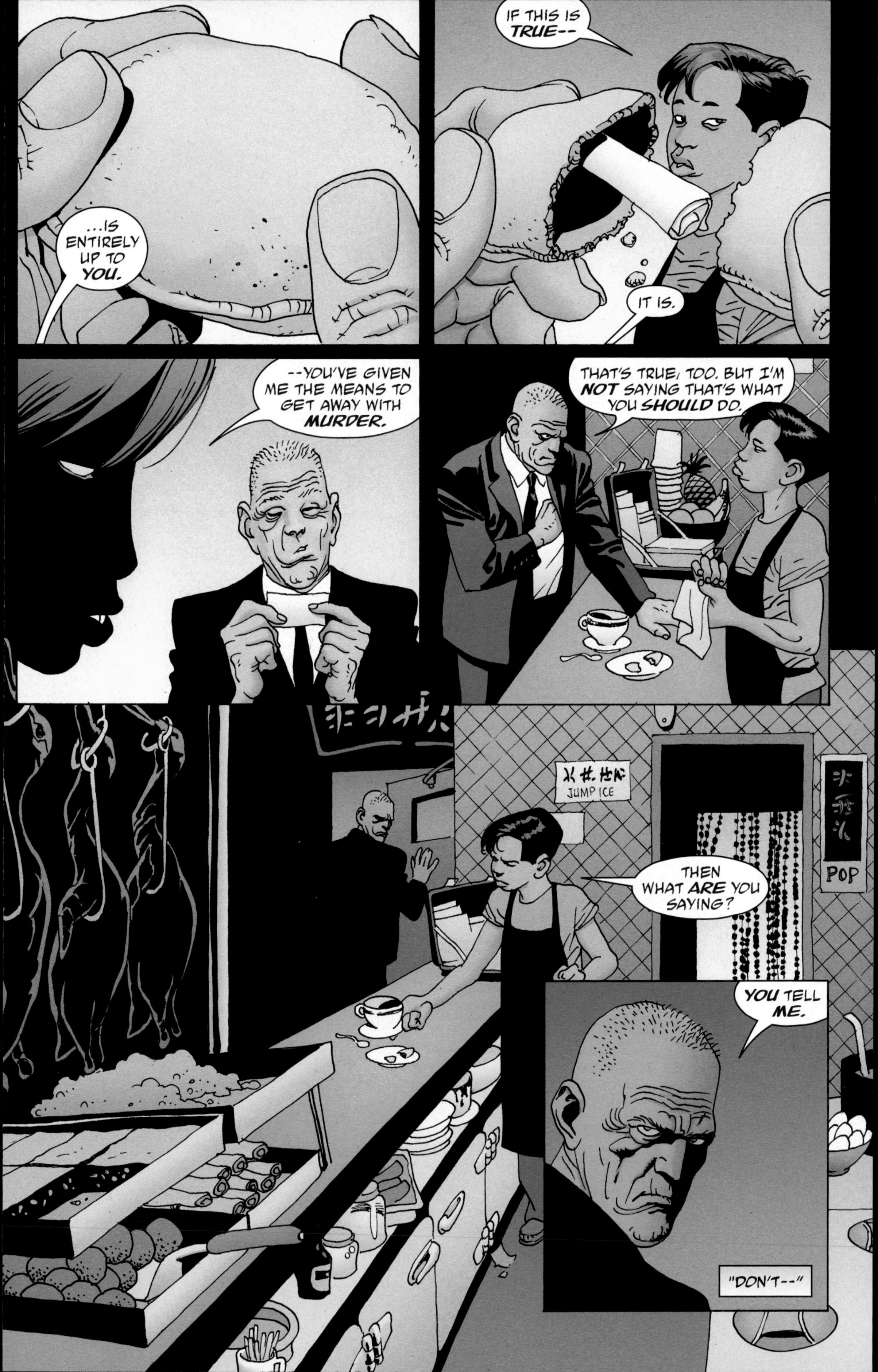

IF THIS IS TRUE--
...IS ENTIRELY UP TO YOU.
IT IS.
--YOU'VE GIVEN ME THE MEANS TO GET AWAY WITH MURDER.
THAT'S TRUE, TOO. BUT I'M NOT SAYING THAT'S WHAT YOU SHOULD DO.
JUMP ICE
POP
THEN WHAT ARE YOU SAYING?
YOU TELL ME.
"DON'T--"

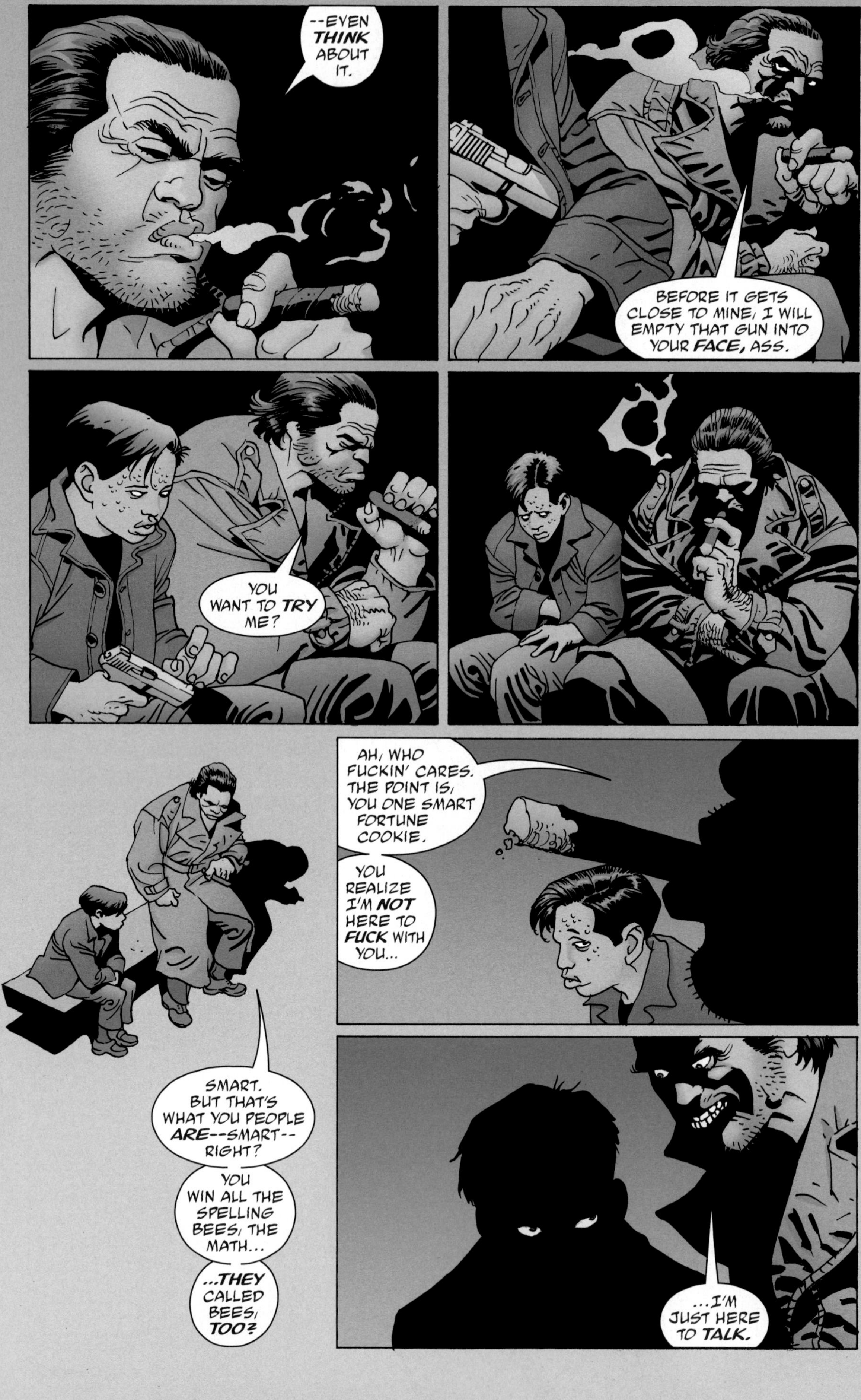
--EVEN THINK ABOUT IT.
BEFORE IT GETS CLOSE TO MINE, I WILL EMPTY THAT GUN INTO YOUR FACE, ASS.
YOU WANT TO TRY ME?
SMART. BUT THAT'S WHAT YOU PEOPLE ARE--SMART--RIGHT?
YOU WIN ALL THE SPELLING BEES, THE MATH...
...THEY CALLED BEES, TOO?
AH, WHO FUCKIN' CARES. THE POINT IS, YOU ONE SMART FORTUNE COOKIE.
YOU REALIZE I'M NOT HERE TO FUCK WITH YOU...
...I'M JUST HERE TO TALK.

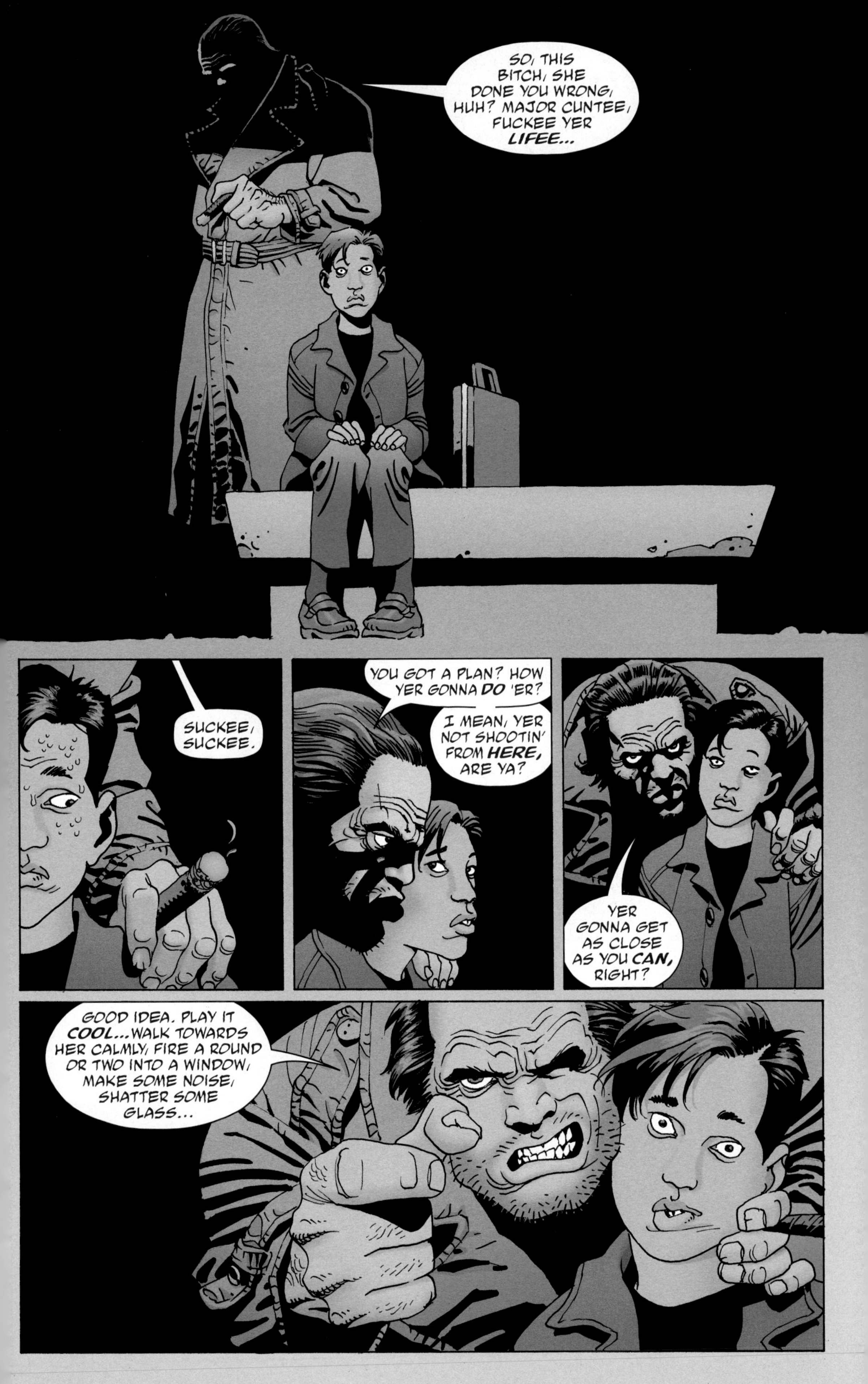
SO, THIS BITCH, SHE DONE YOU WRONG, HUH? MAJOR CUNTEE, FUCKEE YER LIFEE...
SUCKEE, SUCKEE.
YOU GOT A PLAN? HOW YER GONNA DO 'ER?
I MEAN, YER NOT SHOOTIN' FROM HERE, ARE YA?
YER GONNA GET AS CLOSE AS YOU CAN, RIGHT?
GOOD IDEA. PLAY IT COOL... WALK TOWARDS HER CALMLY, FIRE A ROUND OR TWO INTO A WINDOW, MAKE SOME NOISE, SHATTER SOME GLASS...

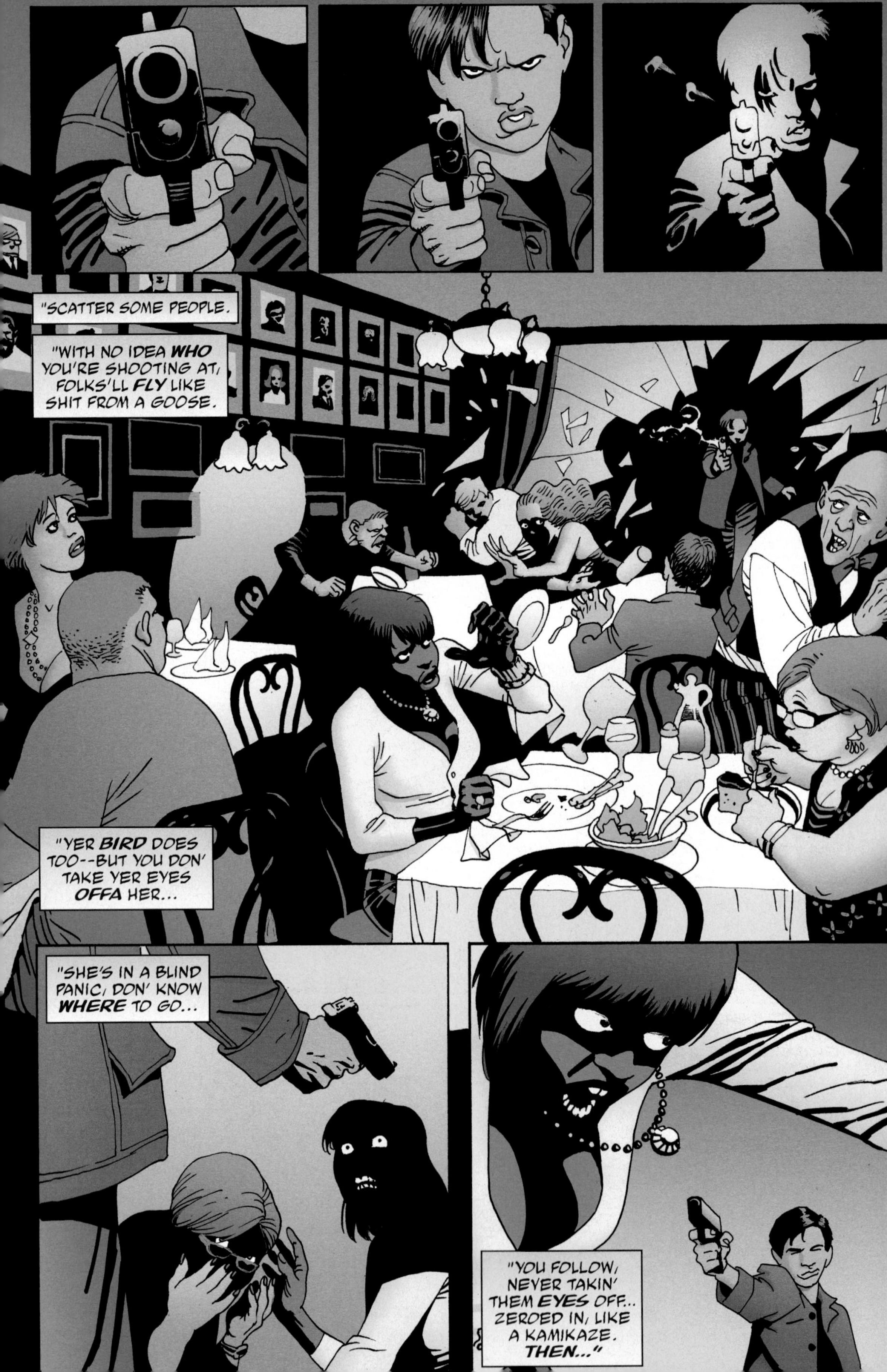
"SCATTER SOME PEOPLE.
"WITH NO IDEA WHO YOU'RE SHOOTING AT, FOLKS'LL FLY LIKE SHIT FROM A GOOSE.
"YER BIRD DOES TOO--BUT YOU DON' TAKE YER EYES OFFA HER...
"SHE'S IN A BLIND PANIC, DON' KNOW WHERE TO GO...
"YOU FOLLOW, NEVER TAKIN' THEM EYES OFF... ZEROED IN, LIKE A KAMIKAZE. THEN..."

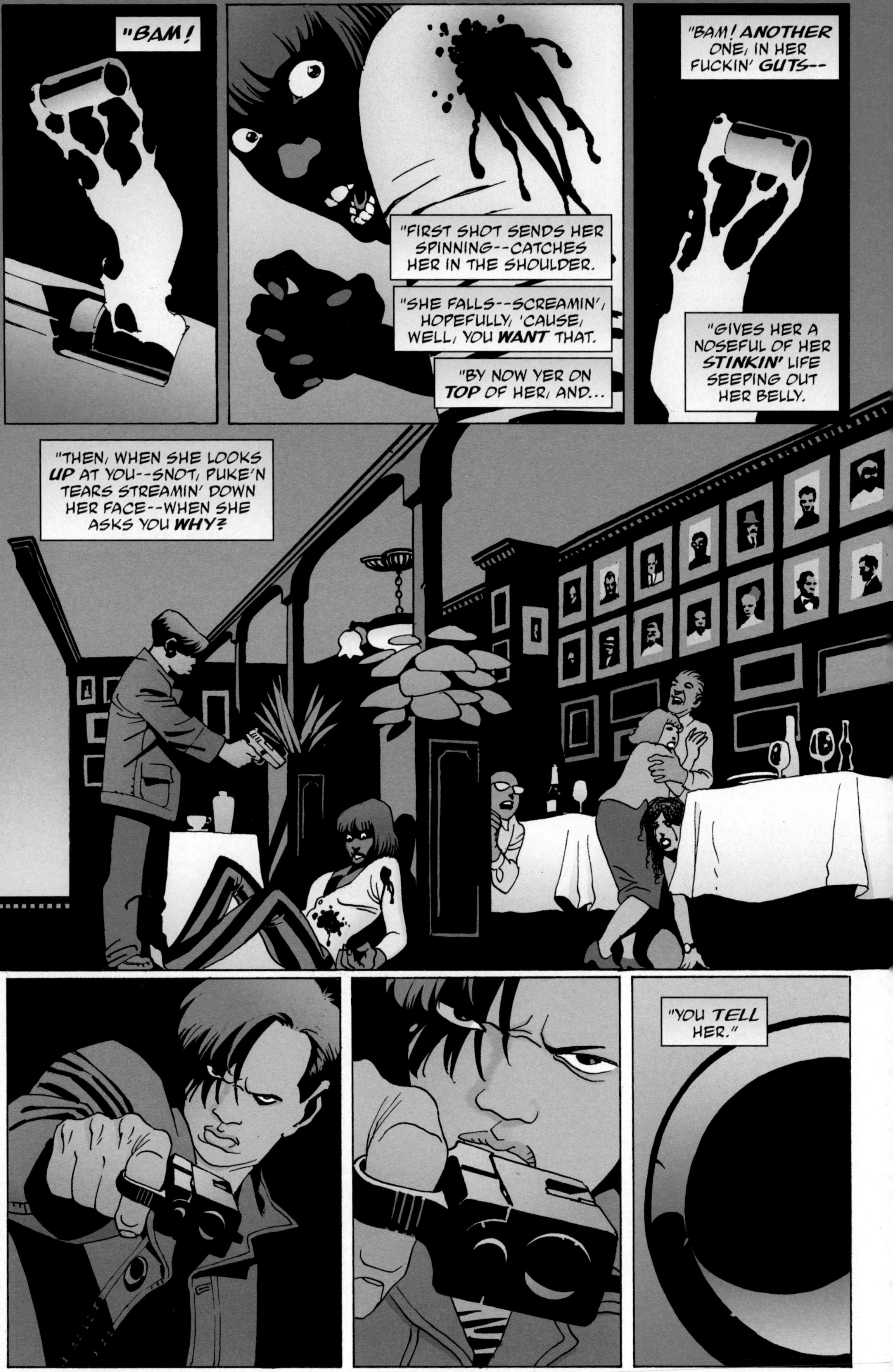
"BAM!
"FIRST SHOT SENDS HER SPINNING--CATCHES HER IN THE SHOULDER.
"SHE FALLS--SCREAMIN', HOPEFULLY, 'CAUSE, WELL, YOU WANT THAT.
"BY NOW YER ON TOP OF HER, AND...
"BAM! ANOTHER ONE, IN HER FUCKIN' GUTS--
"GIVES HER A NOSEFUL OF HER STINKIN' LIFE SEEPING OUT HER BELLY.
"THEN, WHEN SHE LOOKS UP AT YOU--SNOT, PUKE'N TEARS STREAMIN' DOWN HER FACE--WHEN SHE ASKS YOU WHY?
"YOU TELL HER."

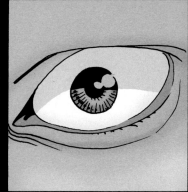

"BOOM."

HEAD SHOT. NECK SNAPS, THUD ON THE CONCRETE. **GAME OVER.**

GOOD **PLAN,** DUDE. NO WORRIES.

I MEAN, **FUCK** ALL THEM OTHERS. WHAT THE HELL DO **THEY** MATTER, HUH?

OTHER **WHAT?**

FUCK 'EM. LIKE I SAID, **YOU** CAN'T BE BOTHERED.

BY **WHAT?**

LIVES, BOSS...

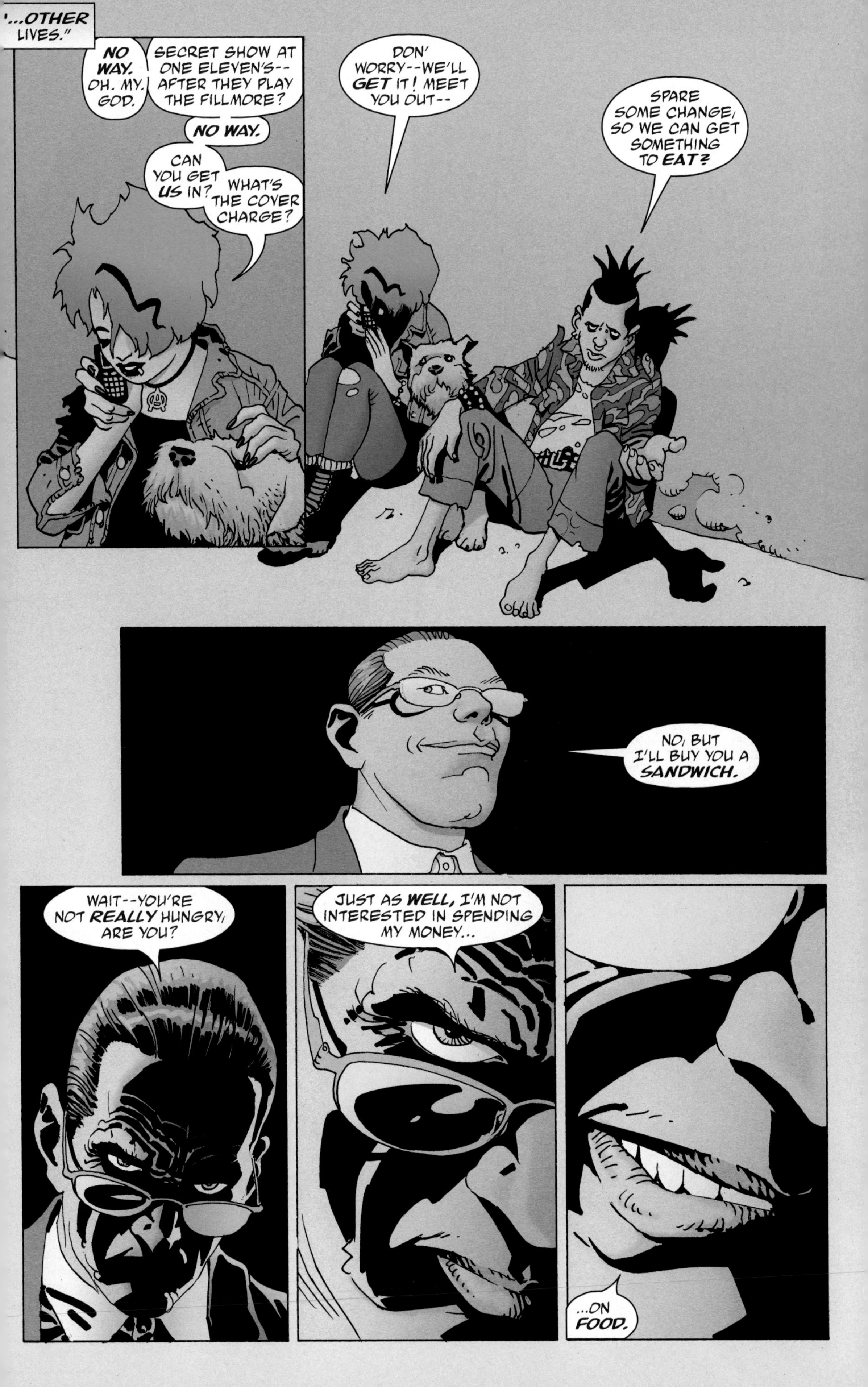
"...OTHER LIVES."
NO WAY. OH. MY. GOD.
SECRET SHOW AT ONE ELEVEN'S-- AFTER THEY PLAY THE FILLMORE?
NO WAY.
CAN YOU GET US IN?
WHAT'S THE COVER CHARGE?
DON' WORRY--WE'LL GET IT! MEET YOU OUT--
SPARE SOME CHANGE, SO WE CAN GET SOMETHING TO EAT?
NO, BUT I'LL BUY YOU A SANDWICH.
WAIT--YOU'RE NOT REALLY HUNGRY, ARE YOU?
JUST AS WELL, I'M NOT INTERESTED IN SPENDING MY MONEY...
...ON FOOD.

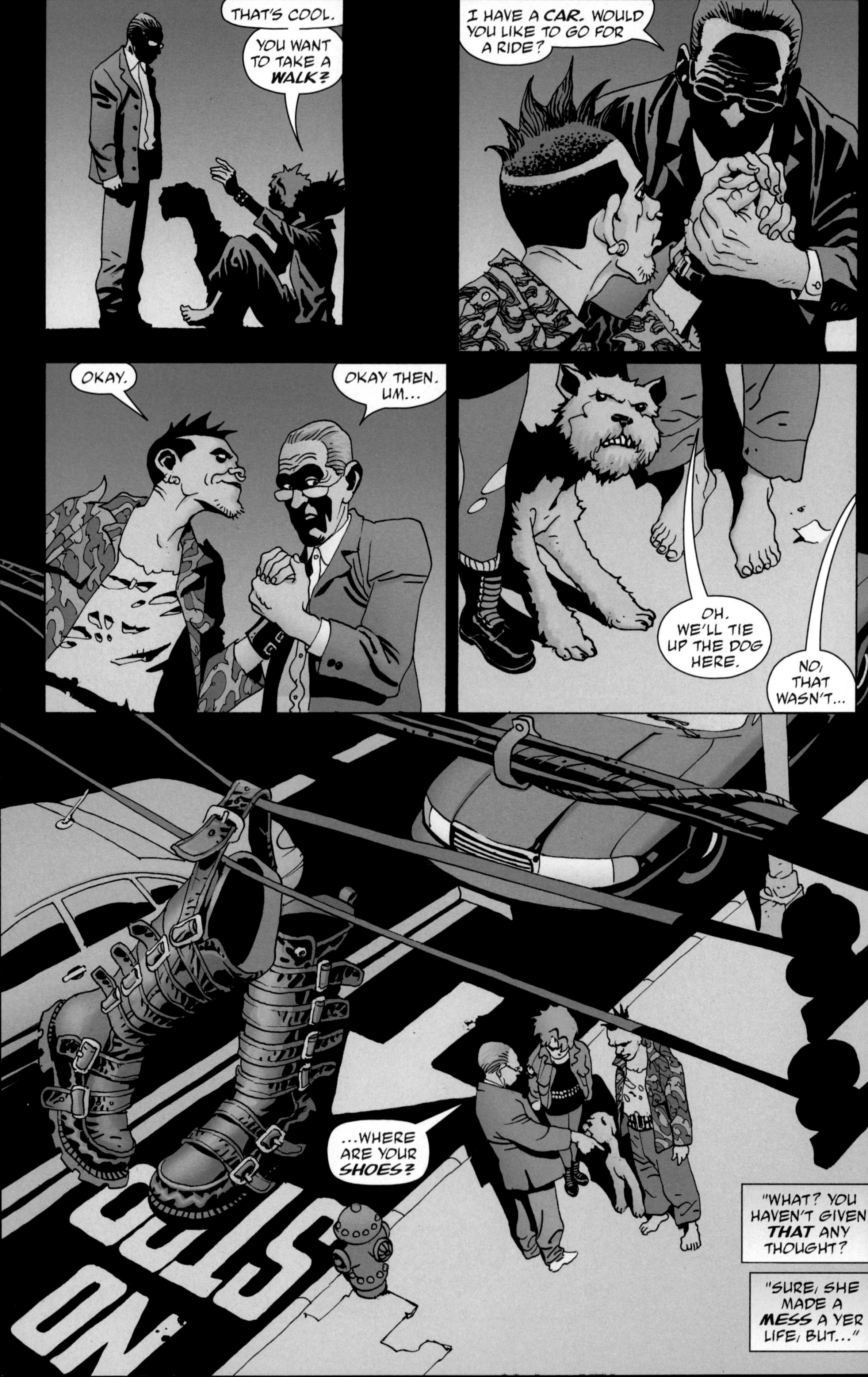
THAT'S COOL.
YOU WANT TO TAKE A WALK?
I HAVE A CAR. WOULD YOU LIKE TO GO FOR A RIDE?
OKAY.
OKAY THEN. UM...
OH. WE'LL TIE UP THE DOG HERE.
NO, THAT WASN'T...
...WHERE ARE YOUR SHOES?
"WHAT? YOU HAVEN'T GIVEN THAT ANY THOUGHT?
"SURE, SHE MADE A MESS A YER LIFE, BUT..."
NO STOP

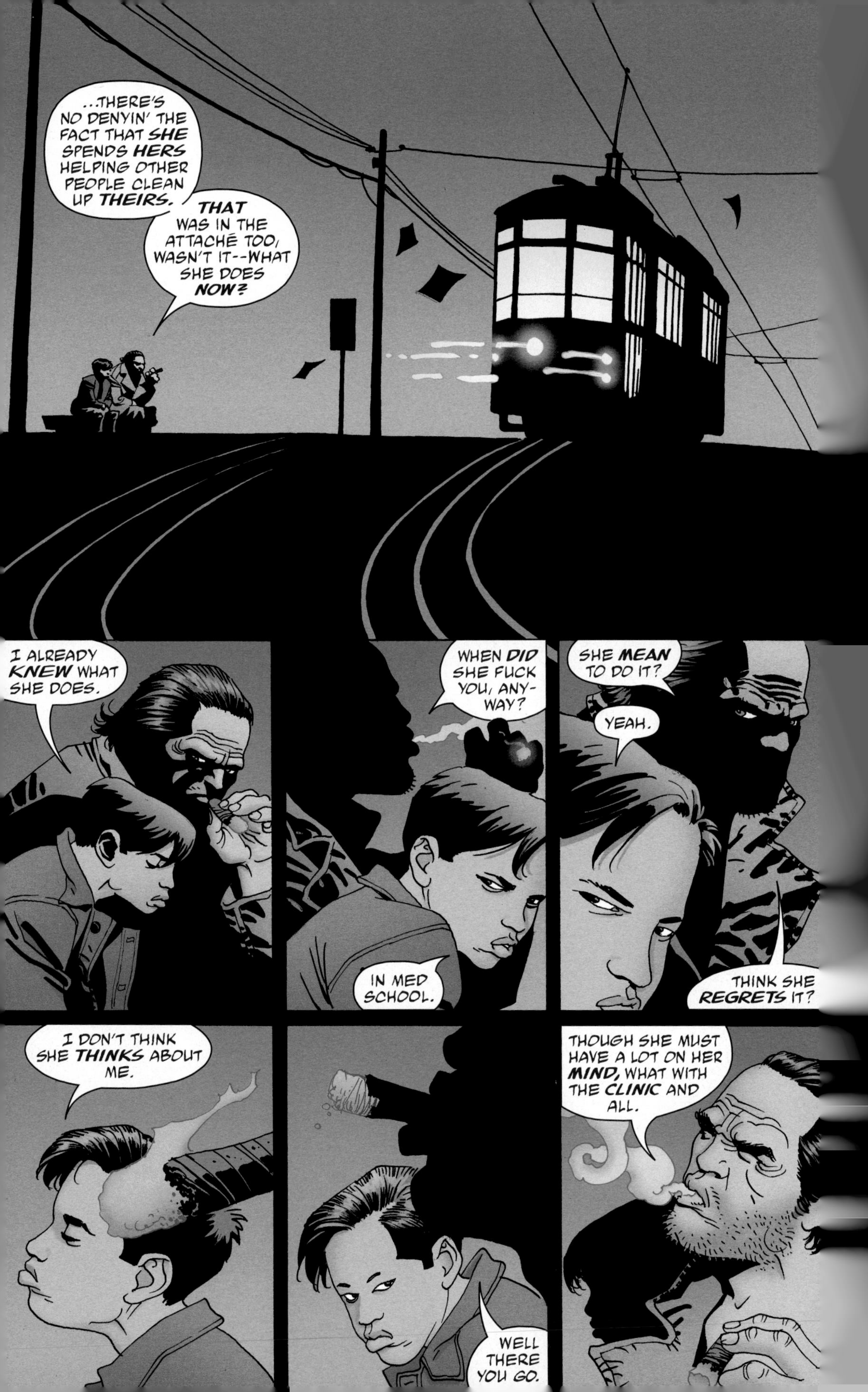
...THERE'S NO DENYIN' THE FACT THAT SHE SPENDS HERS HELPING OTHER PEOPLE CLEAN UP THEIRS.
THAT WAS IN THE ATTACHÉ TOO, WASN'T IT--WHAT SHE DOES NOW?
I ALREADY KNEW WHAT SHE DOES.
WHEN DID SHE FUCK YOU, ANYWAY?
IN MED SCHOOL.
SHE MEAN TO DO IT?
YEAH.
THINK SHE REGRETS IT?
I DON'T THINK SHE THINKS ABOUT ME.
WELL THERE YOU GO.
THOUGH SHE MUST HAVE A LOT ON HER MIND, WHAT WITH THE CLINIC AND ALL.

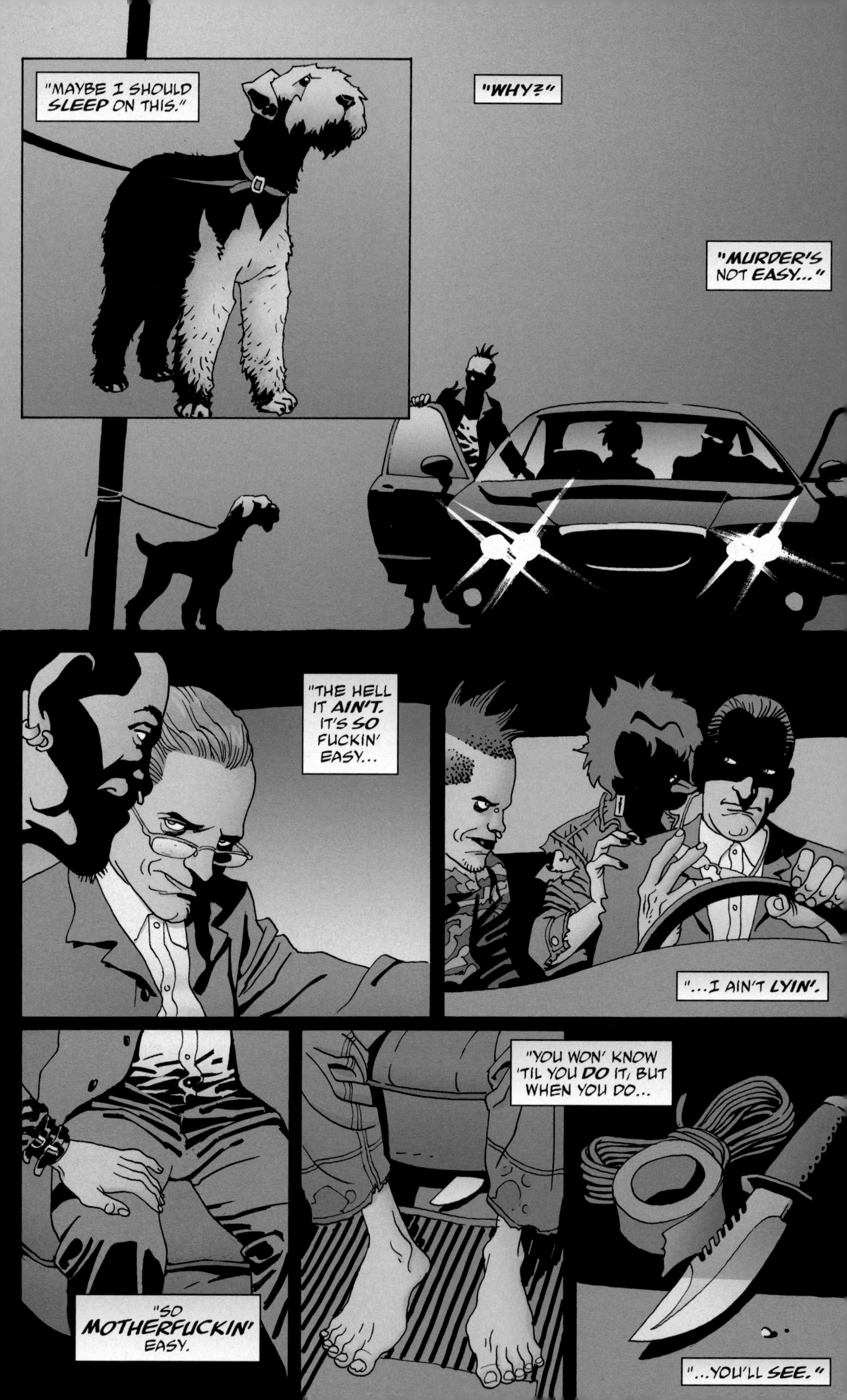
"MAYBE I SHOULD SLEEP ON THIS."
"WHY?"
"MURDER'S NOT EASY..."
"THE HELL IT AIN'T. IT'S SO FUCKIN' EASY...
"...I AIN'T LYIN'.
"SO MOTHERFUCKIN' EASY.
"YOU WON' KNOW 'TIL YOU DO IT, BUT WHEN YOU DO...
"...YOU'LL SEE."

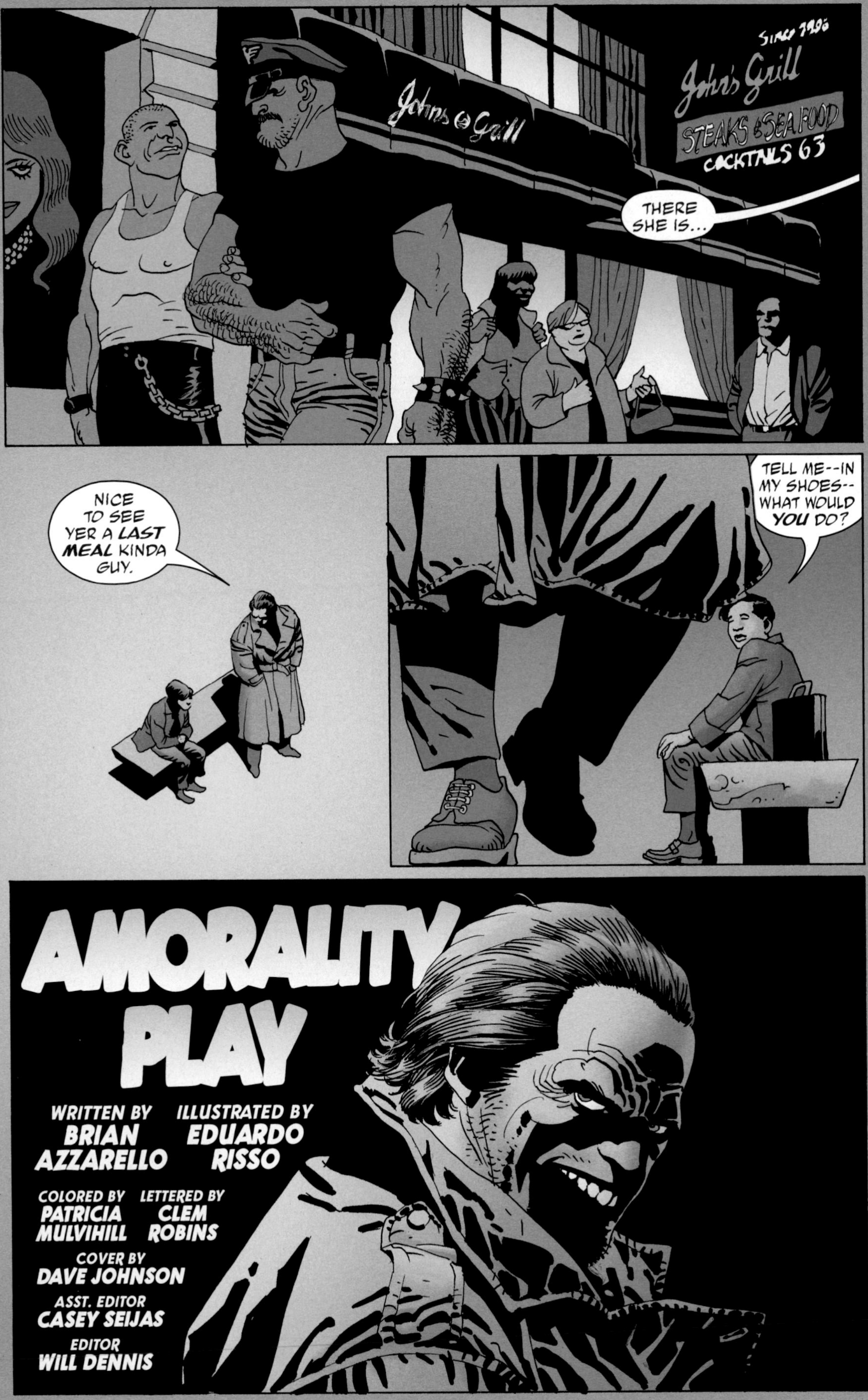
SINCE 1906
John's Grill
STEAKS & SEA FOOD
COCKTAILS 63
John's Grill
THERE SHE IS...
NICE TO SEE YER A LAST MEAL KINDA GUY.
TELL ME--IN MY SHOES--WHAT WOULD YOU DO?
AMORALITY PLAY
WRITTEN BY BRIAN AZZARELLO
ILLUSTRATED BY EDUARDO RISSO
COLORED BY PATRICIA MULVIHILL
LETTERED BY CLEM ROBINS
COVER BY DAVE JOHNSON
ASST. EDITOR CASEY SEIJAS
EDITOR WILL DENNIS

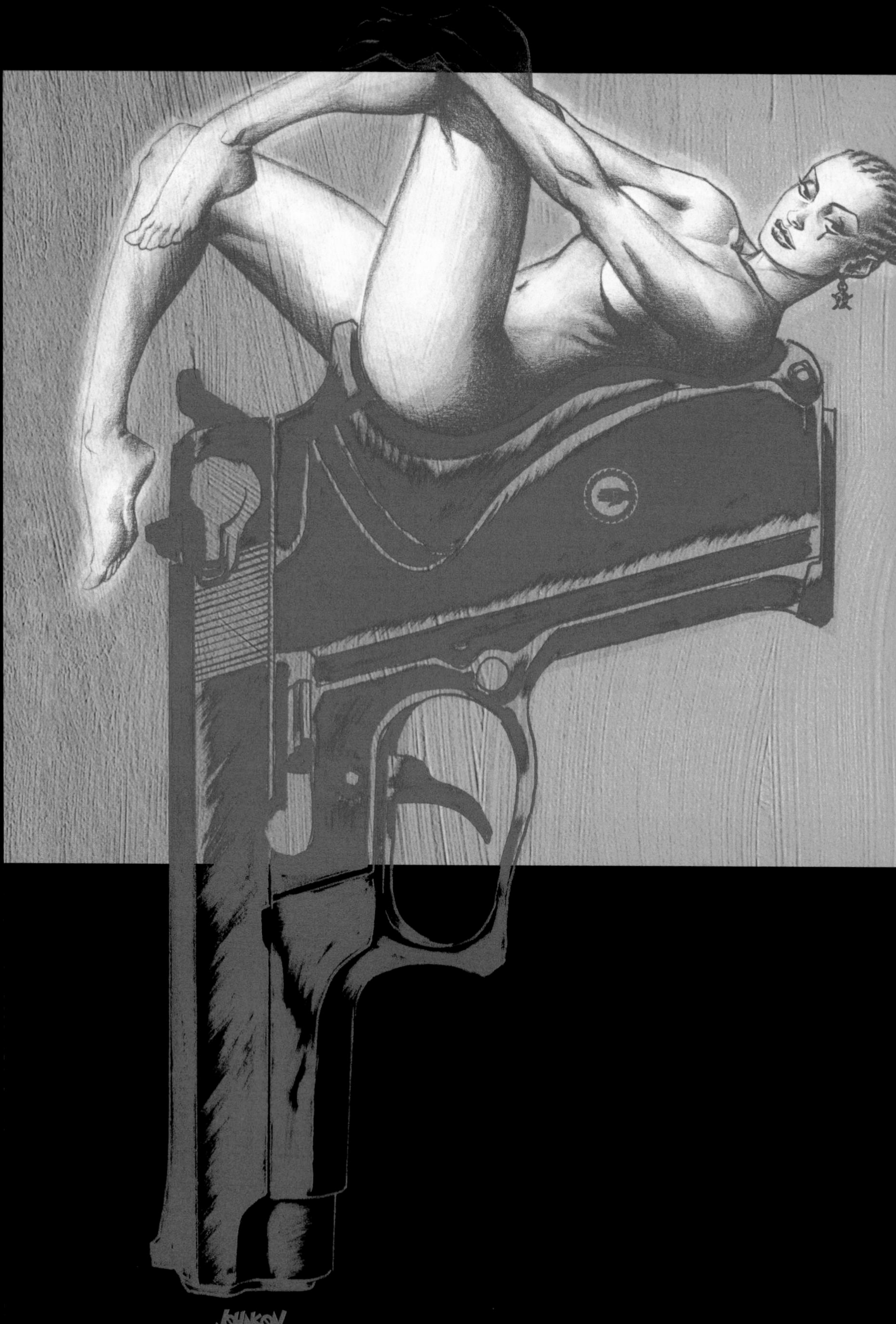
JOHNSON

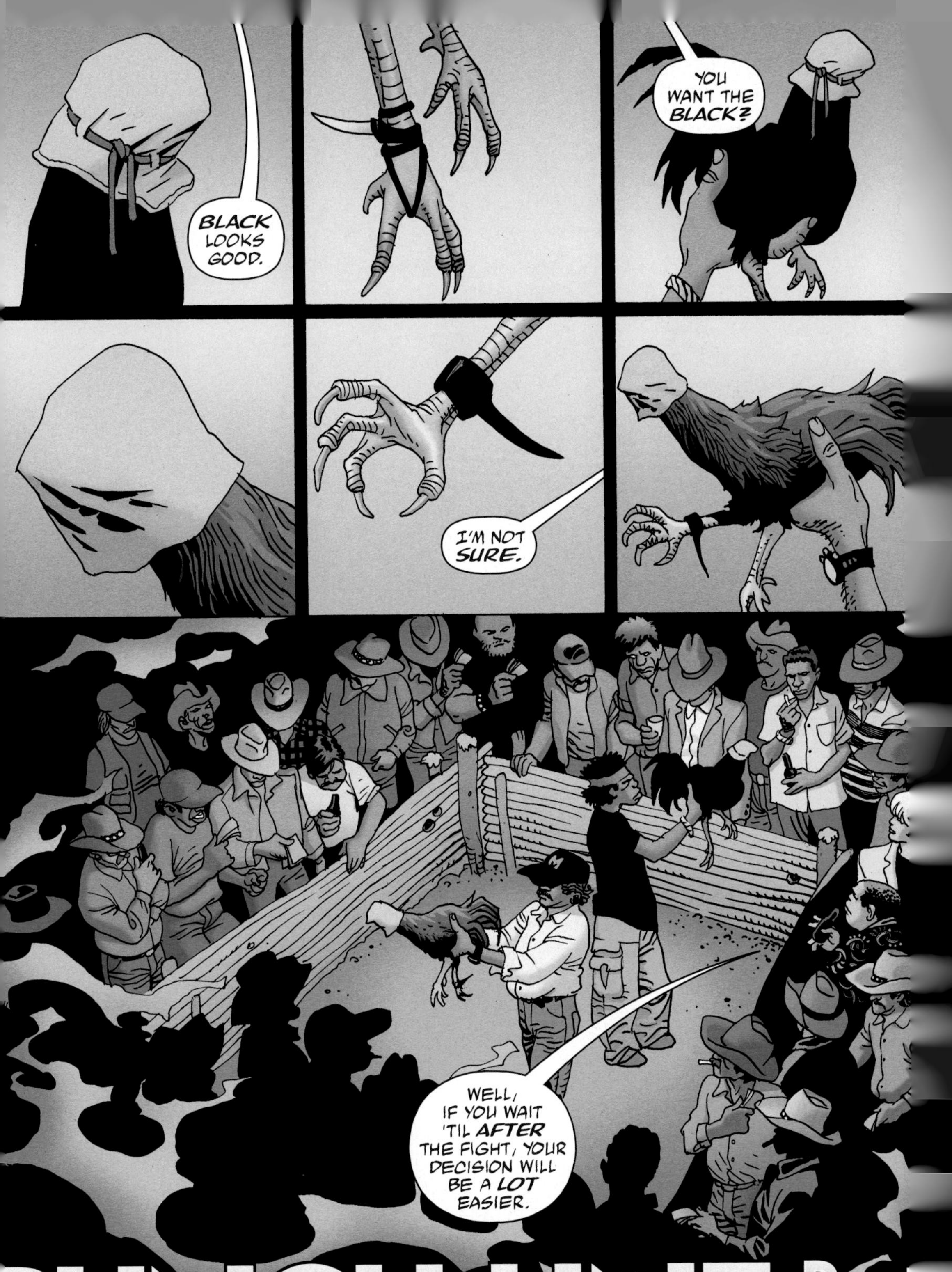
BLACK LOOKS GOOD.
YOU WANT THE BLACK?
I'M NOT SURE.
WELL, IF YOU WAIT 'TIL AFTER THE FIGHT, YOUR DECISION WILL BE A LOT EASIER.

PUNCH LINE Part One

Written by Brian Azzarello Illustrated by Eduardo Riss

Colored by Patricia Mulvihill Lettered by Clem Robins Cover by Dave Johnson

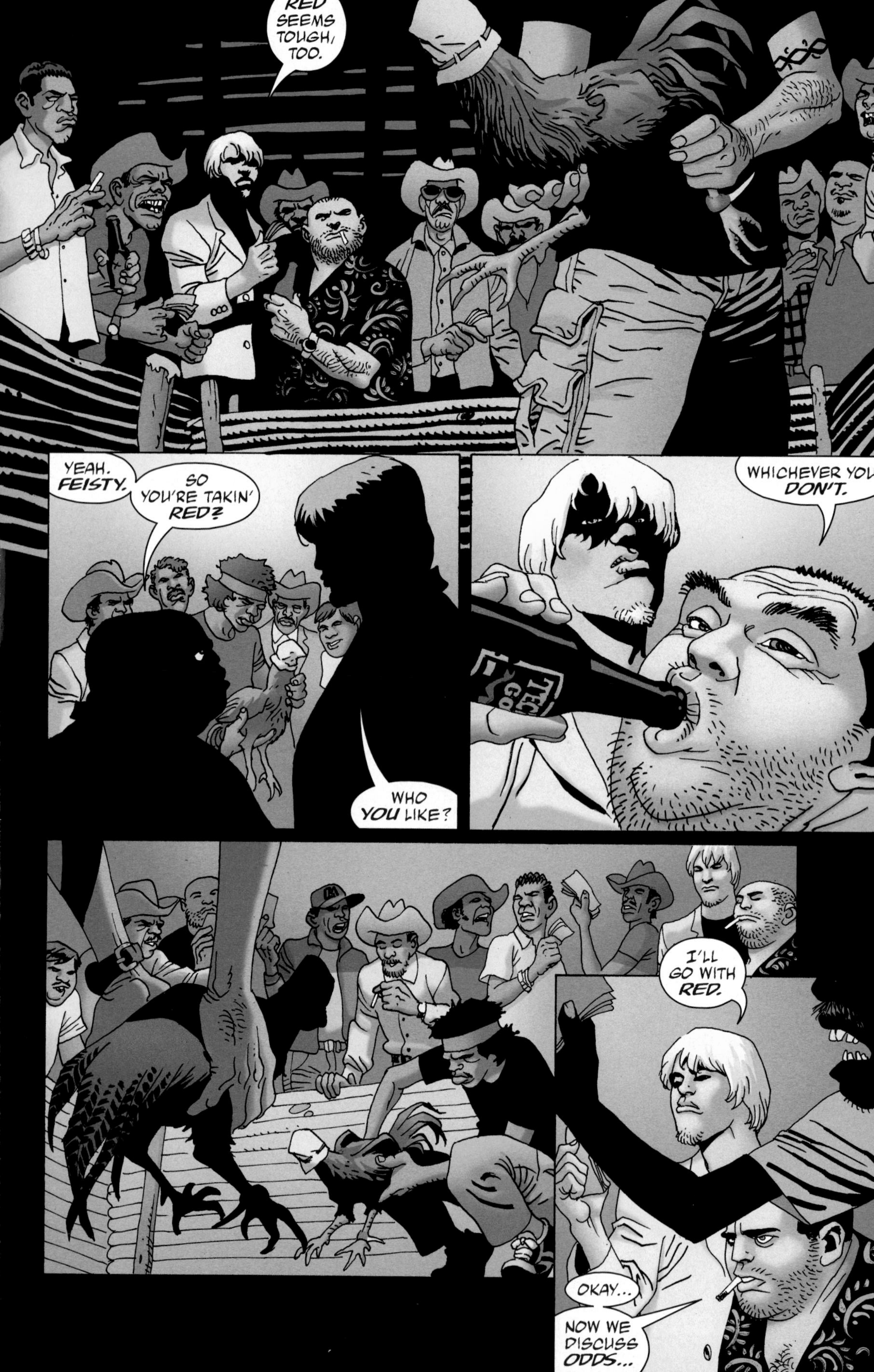
RED SEEMS TOUGH, TOO.
YEAH. FEISTY.
SO YOU'RE TAKIN' RED?
WHO YOU LIKE?
WHICHEVER YOU DON'T.
I'LL GO WITH RED.
OKAY...
NOW WE DISCUSS ODDS...

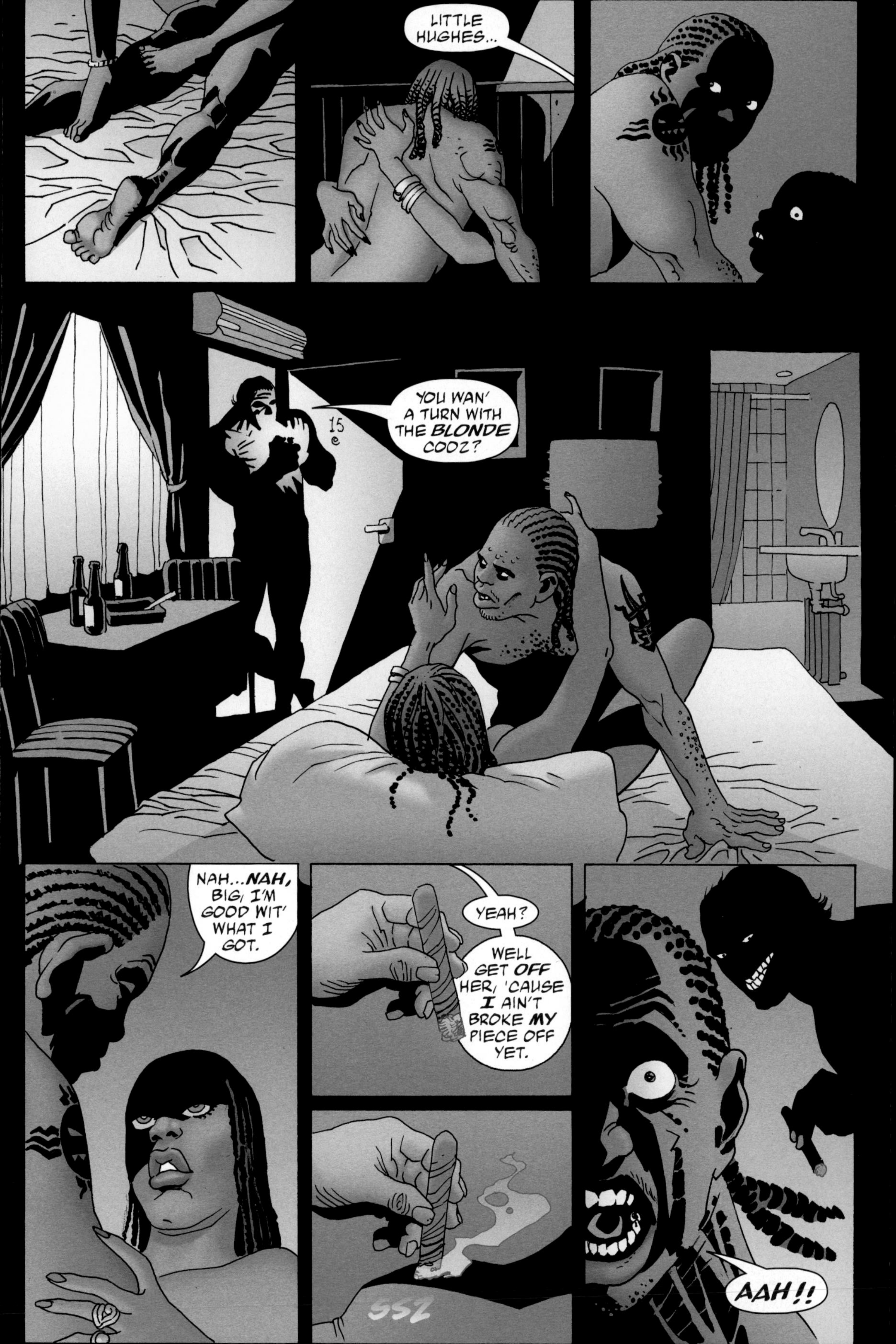

LITTLE HUGHES...
YOU WAN' A TURN WITH THE BLONDE COOZ?
NAH...NAH, BIG, I'M GOOD WIT' WHAT I GOT.
YEAH?
WELL GET OFF HER, 'CAUSE I AIN'T BROKE MY PIECE OFF YET.
AAH!!

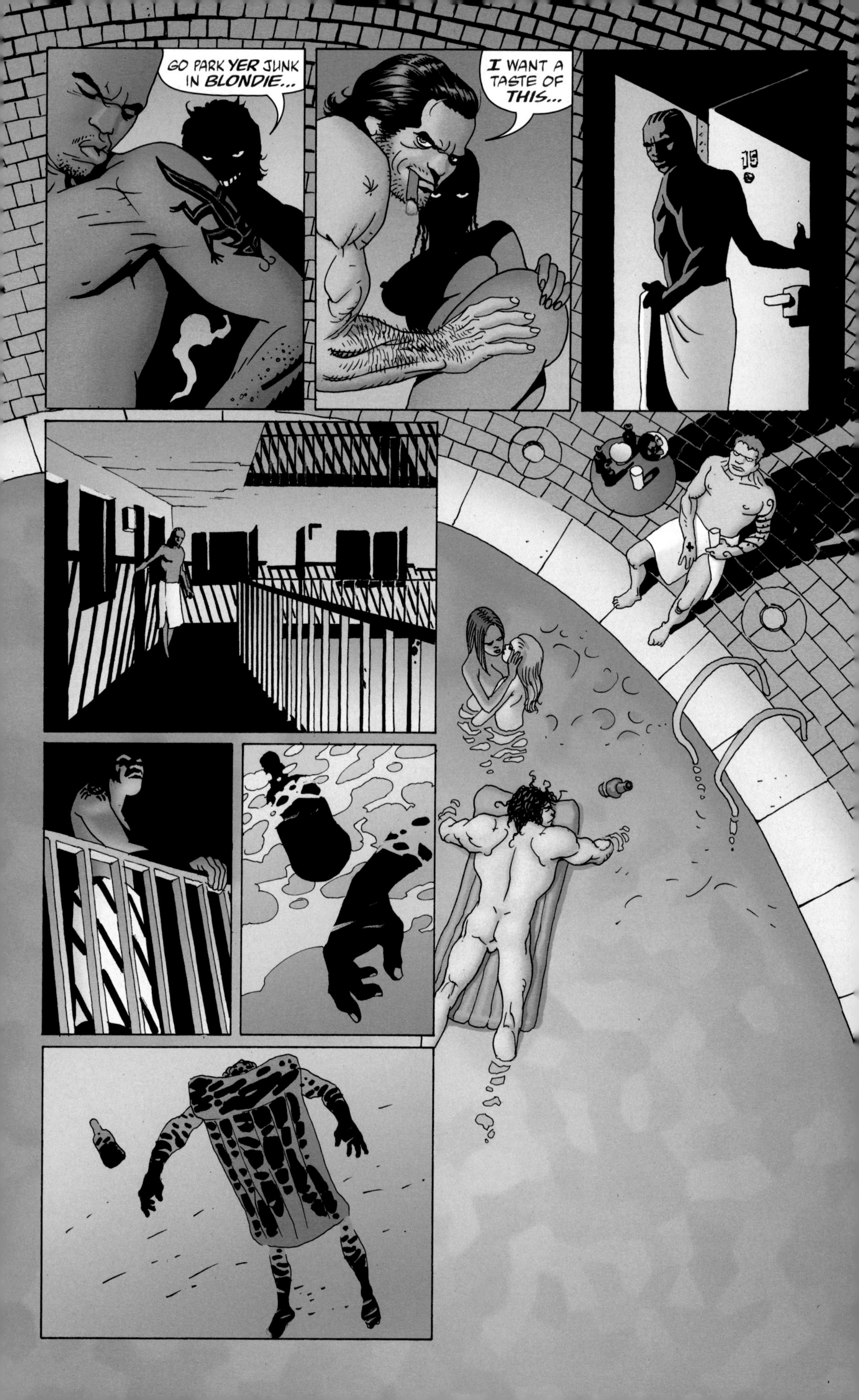
GO PARK YER JUNK
IN BLONDIE...
I WANT A
TASTE OF
THIS...
15

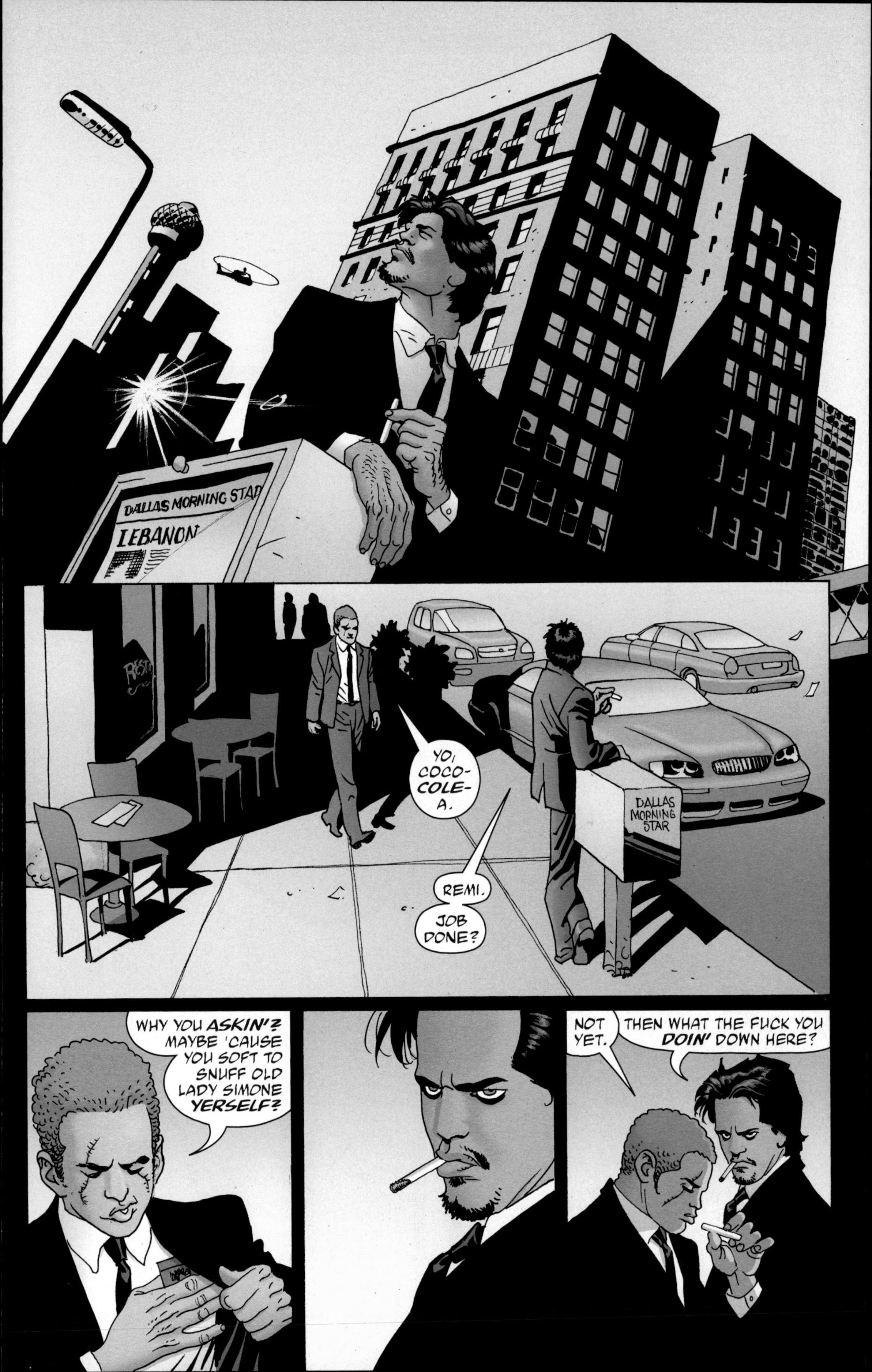

DALLAS MORNING STAR
LEBANON
YO, COCO-COLE-A.
REMI.
JOB DONE?
DALLAS MORNING STAR
WHY YOU ASKIN'? MAYBE 'CAUSE YOU SOFT TO SNUFF OLD LADY SIMONE YERSELF?
NOT YET.
THEN WHAT THE FUCK YOU DOIN' DOWN HERE?

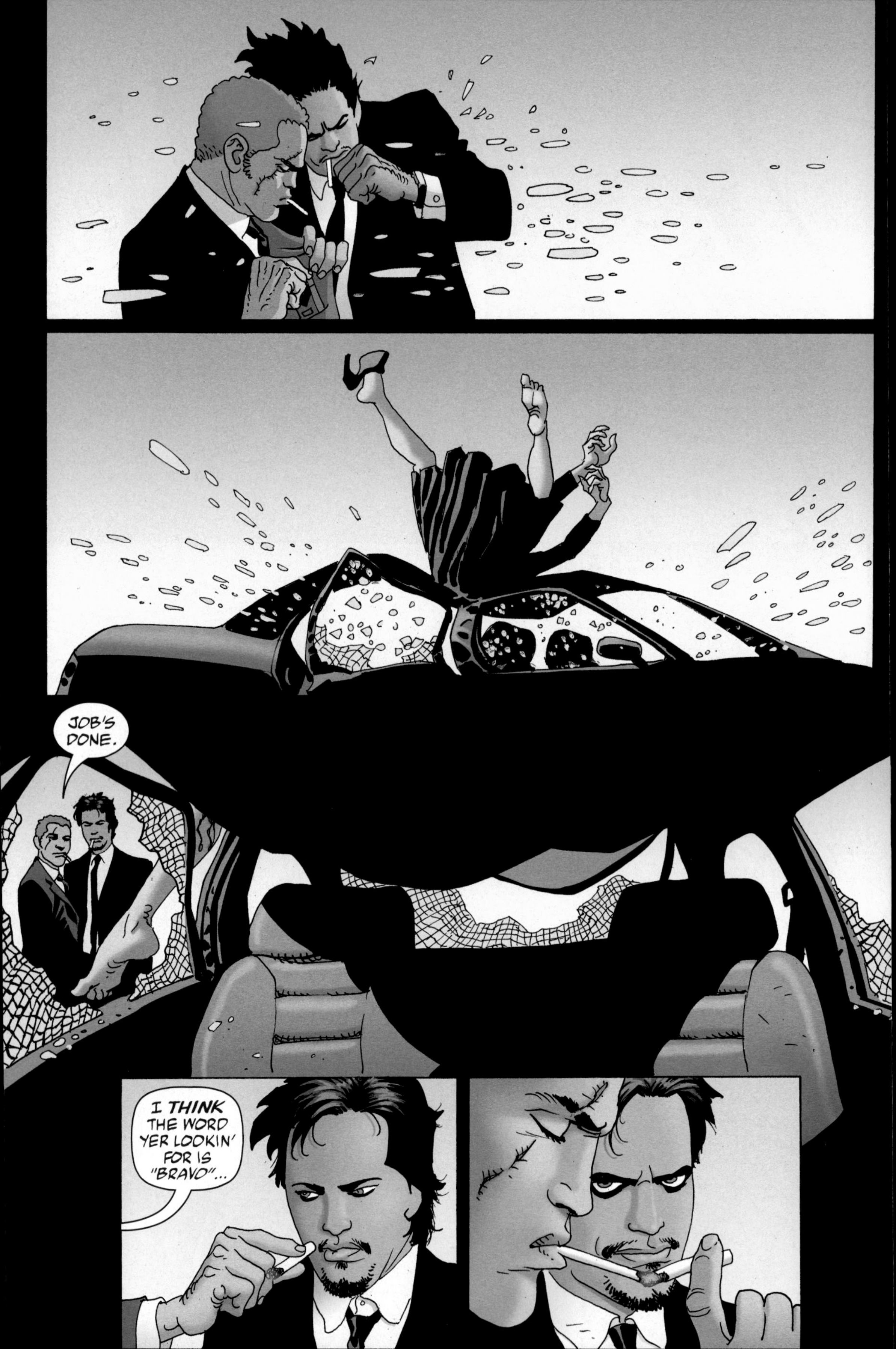
JOB'S DONE.
I THINK THE WORD YER LOOKIN' FOR IS "BRAVO"...

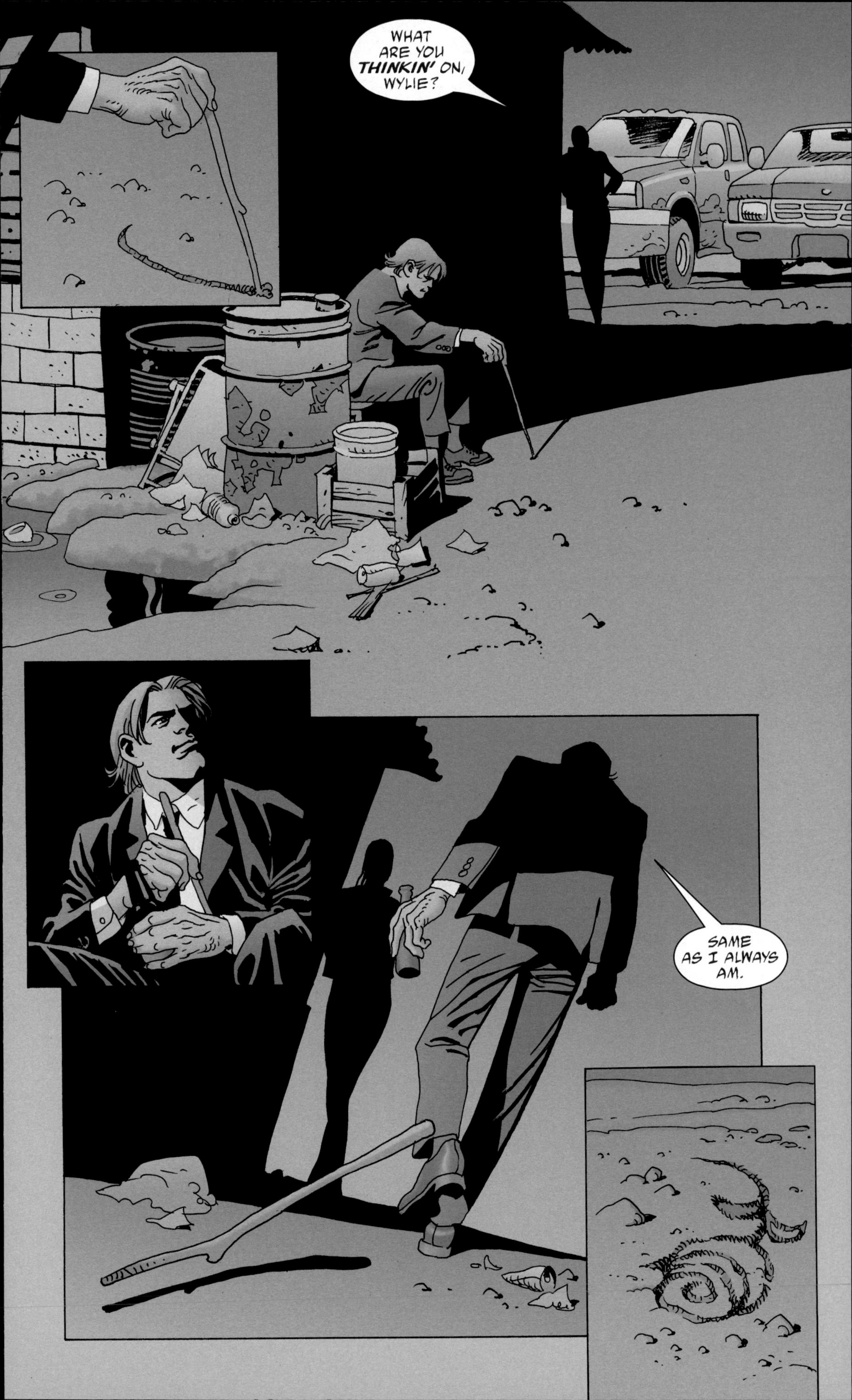
WHAT ARE YOU *THINKIN'* ON, WYLIE?
SAME AS I ALWAYS AM.

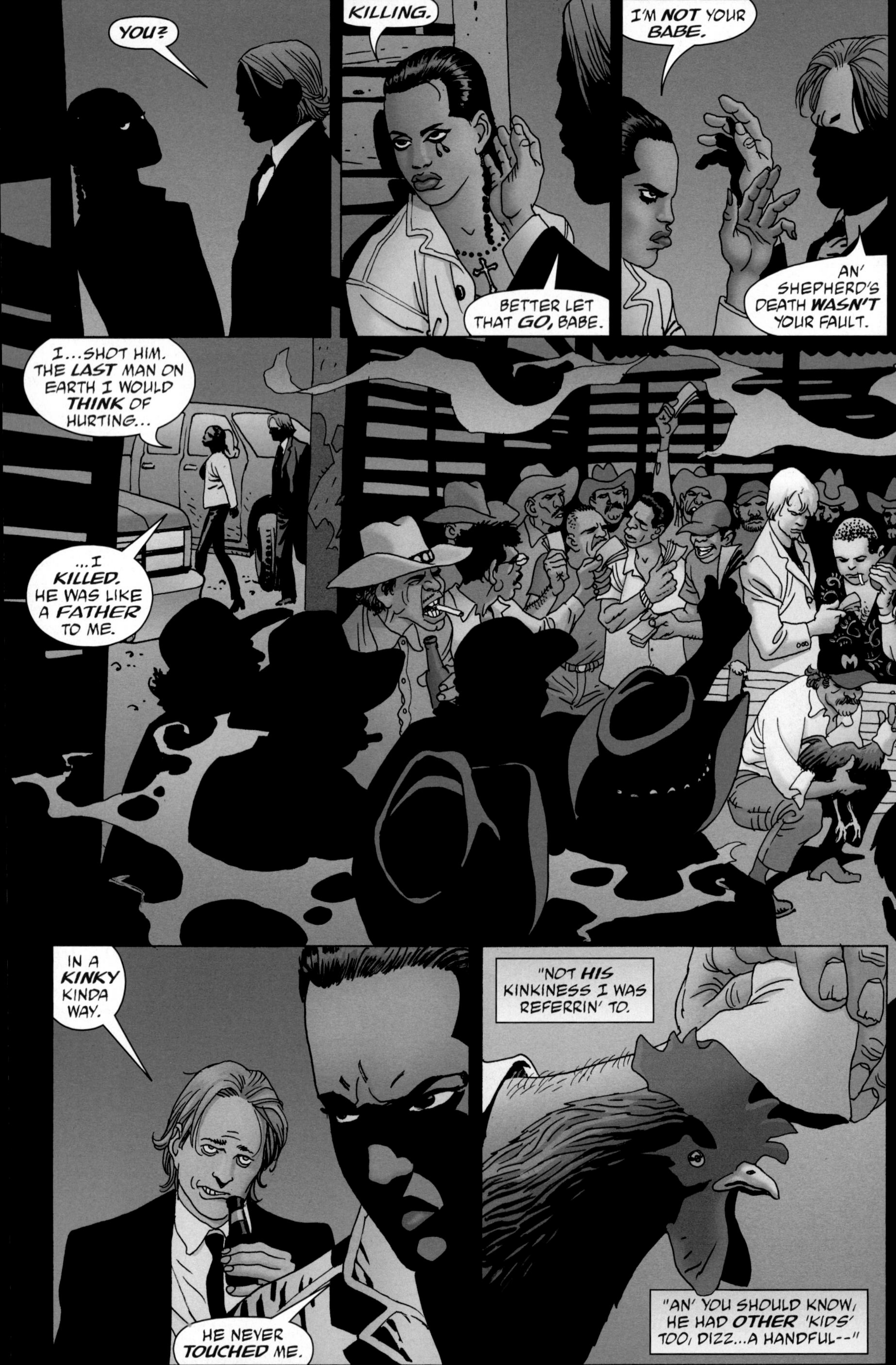
YOU?
KILLING.
BETTER LET THAT GO, BABE.
I'M NOT YOUR BABE.
AN' SHEPHERD'S DEATH WASN'T YOUR FAULT.
I...SHOT HIM. THE LAST MAN ON EARTH I WOULD THINK OF HURTING...
...I KILLED. HE WAS LIKE A FATHER TO ME.
IN A KINKY KINDA WAY.
HE NEVER TOUCHED ME.
"NOT HIS KINKINESS I WAS REFERRIN' TO.
"AN' YOU SHOULD KNOW, HE HAD OTHER 'KIDS' TOO, DIZZ...A HANDFUL--"

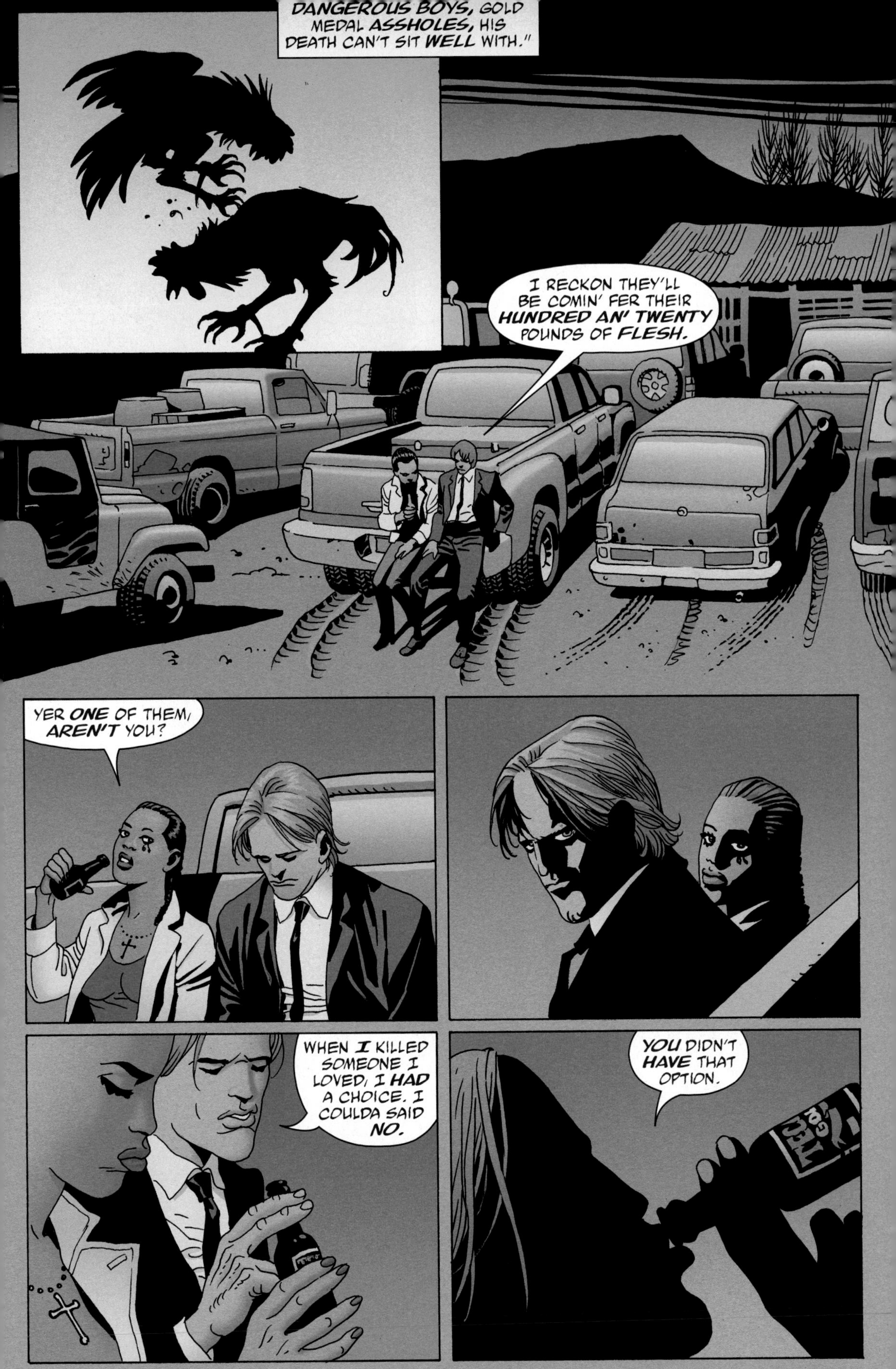
DANGEROUS BOYS, GOLD MEDAL ASSHOLES, HIS DEATH CAN'T SIT WELL WITH."
I RECKON THEY'LL BE COMIN' FER THEIR HUNDRED AN' TWENTY POUNDS OF FLESH.
YER ONE OF THEM, AREN'T YOU?
WHEN I KILLED SOMEONE I LOVED, I HAD A CHOICE. I COULDA SAID NO.
YOU DIDN'T HAVE THAT OPTION.

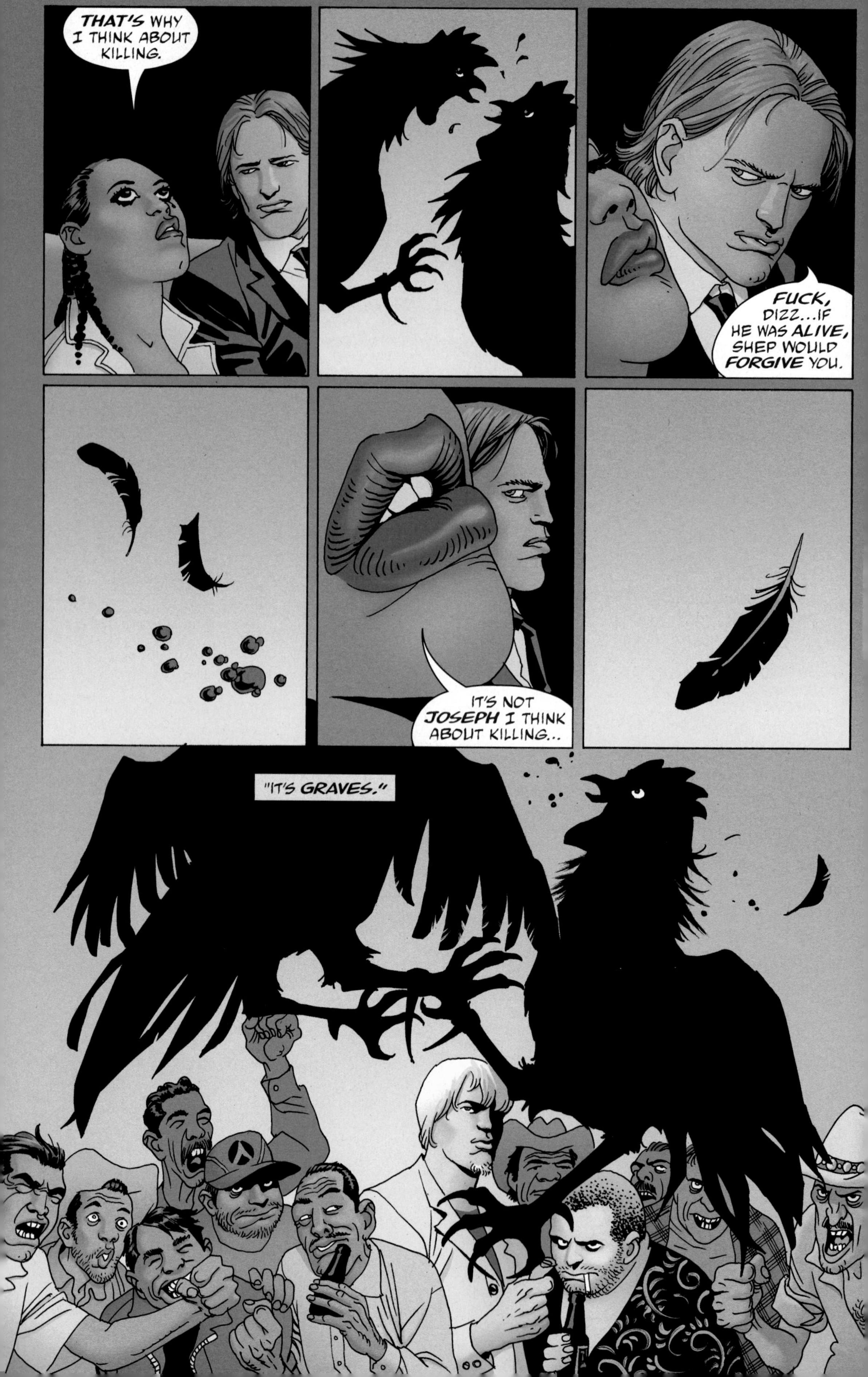
THAT'S WHY I THINK ABOUT KILLING.
FUCK, DIZZ...IF HE WAS ALIVE, SHEP WOULD FORGIVE YOU.
IT'S NOT JOSEPH I THINK ABOUT KILLING...
"IT'S GRAVES."

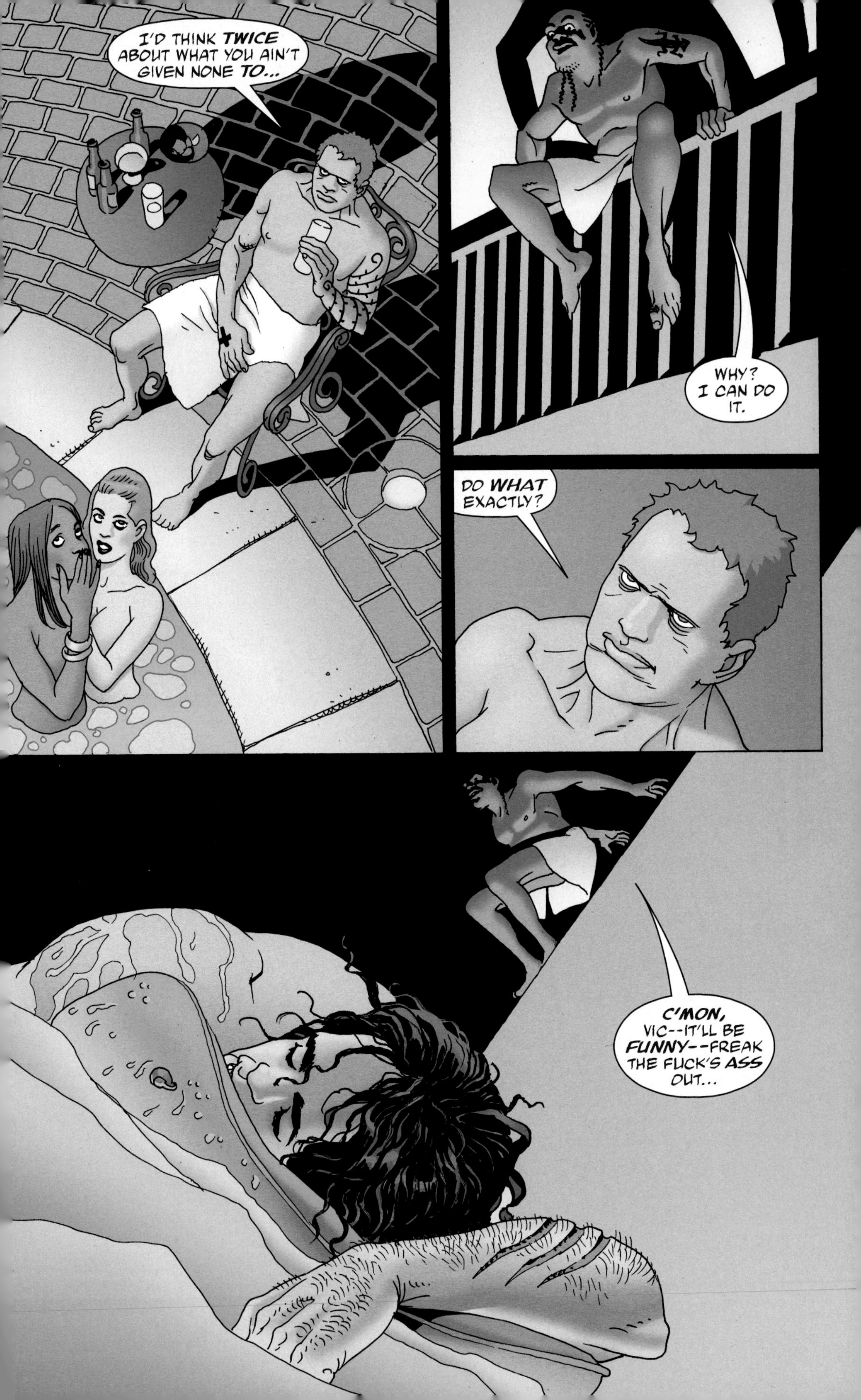
I'D THINK TWICE ABOUT WHAT YOU AIN'T GIVEN NONE TO...
WHY? I CAN DO IT.
DO WHAT EXACTLY?
C'MON, VIC--IT'LL BE FUNNY--FREAK THE FUCK'S ASS OUT...

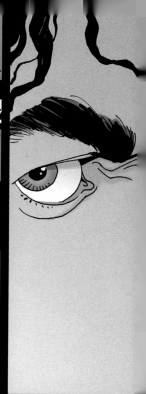

AIN'T THE FREAK IN THE FUCK'S ASS YOU SHOULD BE **CONCERNED** WITH...

SPLASH

"SO HOW'D IT **GO?**"

"NOT ACCORDING TO **PLAN**, BUT--"

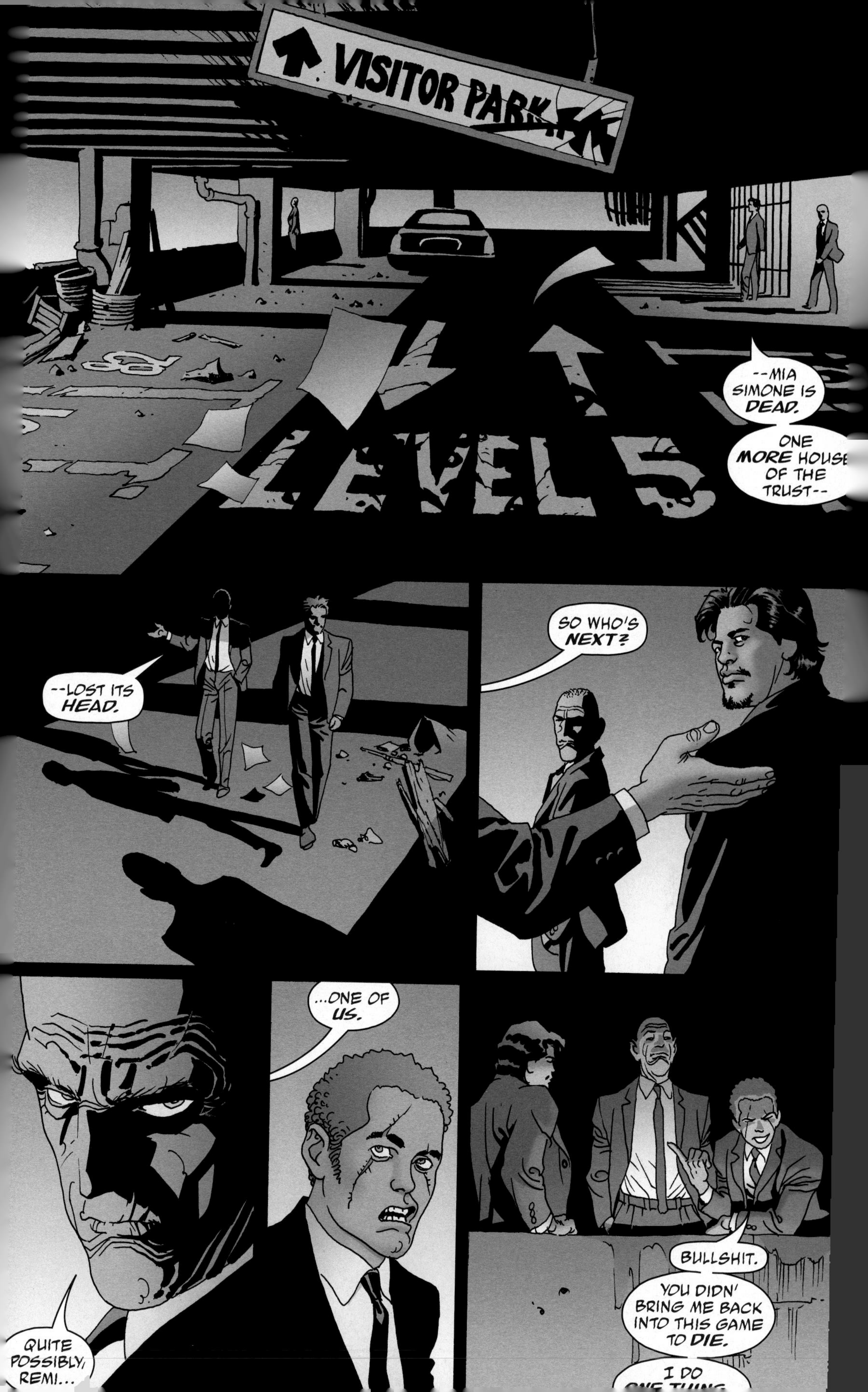

VISITOR PARK
LEVEL 5
--MIA SIMONE IS DEAD.
ONE MORE HOUSE OF THE TRUST--
--LOST ITS HEAD.
SO WHO'S NEXT?
QUITE POSSIBLY, REMI...
...ONE OF US.
BULLSHIT.
YOU DIDN' BRING ME BACK INTO THIS GAME TO DIE.
I DO

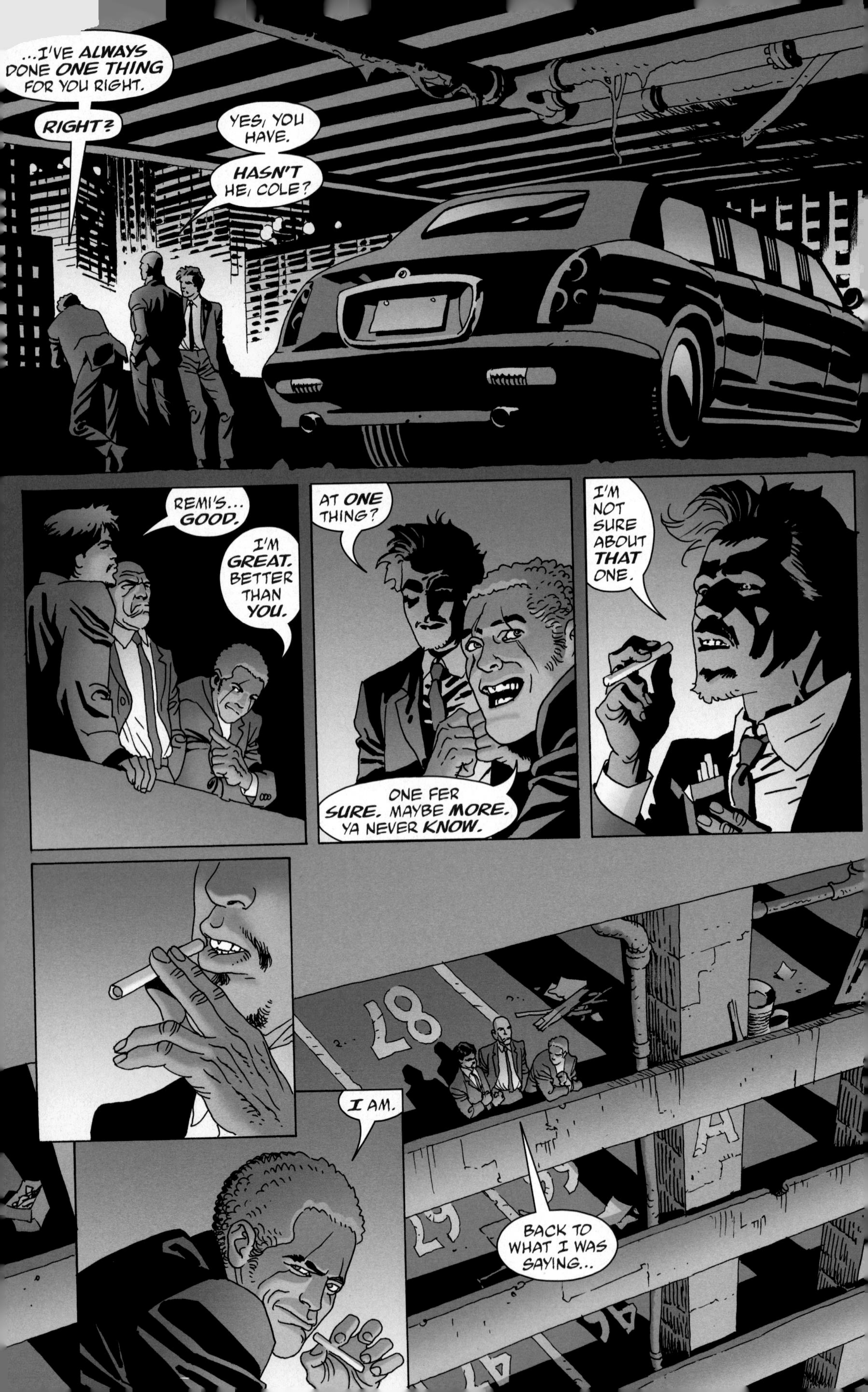

...I'VE ALWAYS DONE ONE THING FOR YOU RIGHT.
RIGHT?
YES, YOU HAVE.
HASN'T HE, COLE?
REMI'S... GOOD.
I'M GREAT. BETTER THAN YOU.
AT ONE THING?
ONE FER SURE. MAYBE MORE. YA NEVER KNOW.
I'M NOT SURE ABOUT THAT ONE.
I AM.
BACK TO WHAT I WAS SAYING...

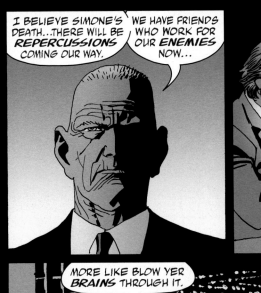

I BELIEVE SIMONE'S DEATH...THERE WILL BE *REPERCUSSIONS* COMING OUR WAY.

WE HAVE FRIENDS WHO WORK FOR OUR *ENEMIES* NOW...

THAT BIG DICK HAWAIIAN CUNT CAN *SUCK MY ASS.*

MORE LIKE BLOW YER *BRAINS* THROUGH IT.

MORE IMPORTANT, WE HAVE FRIENDS WHO-- RIGHT NOW...

"...DON'T WORK FOR *ANYONE*..."

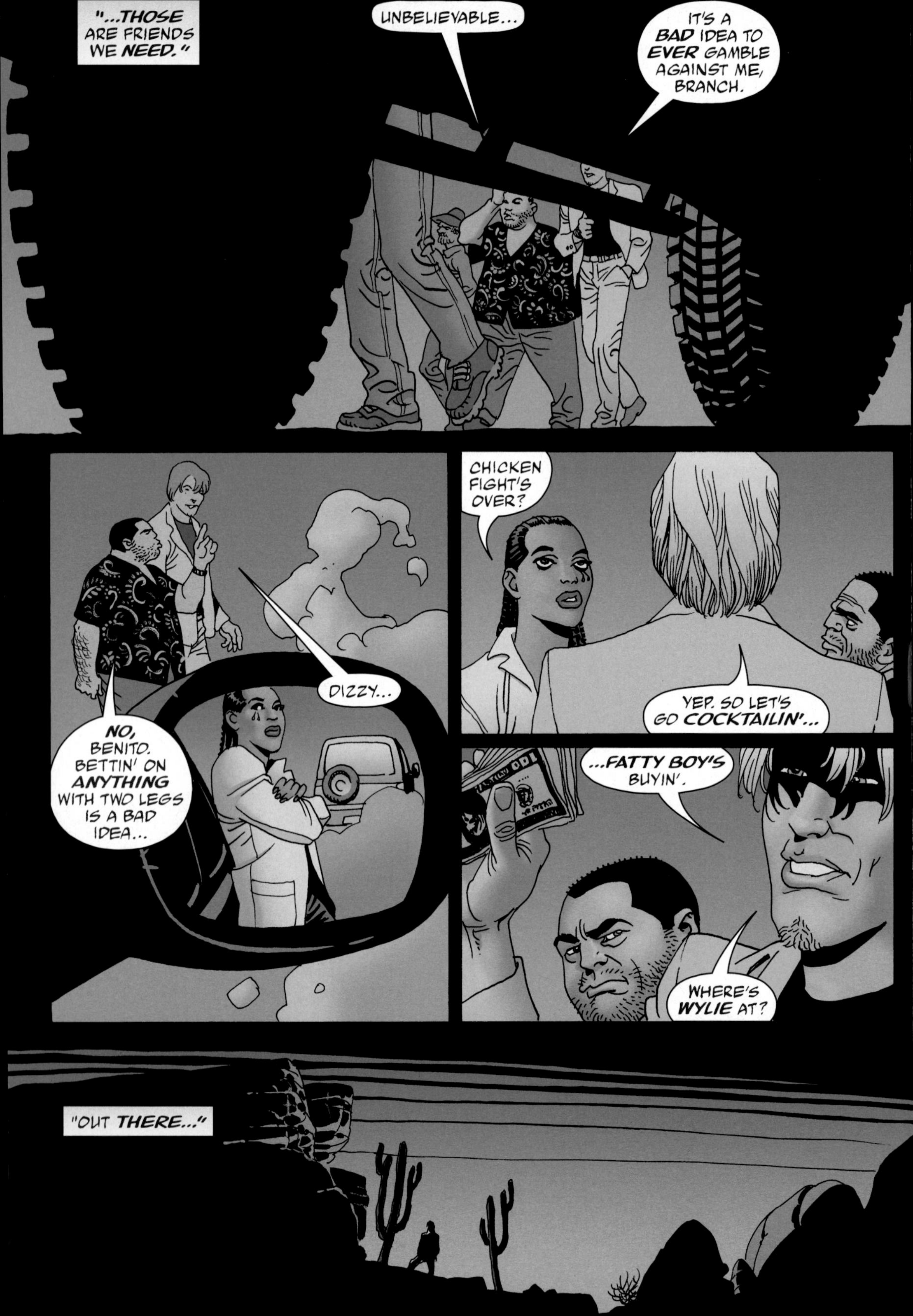
"...THOSE ARE FRIENDS WE NEED."
UNBELIEVABLE...
IT'S A BAD IDEA TO EVER GAMBLE AGAINST ME, BRANCH.
DIZZY...
NO, BENITO. BETTIN' ON ANYTHING WITH TWO LEGS IS A BAD IDEA...
CHICKEN FIGHT'S OVER?
YEP. SO LET'S GO COCKTAILIN'...
...FATTY BOY'S BUYIN'.
WHERE'S WYLIE AT?
"OUT THERE..."

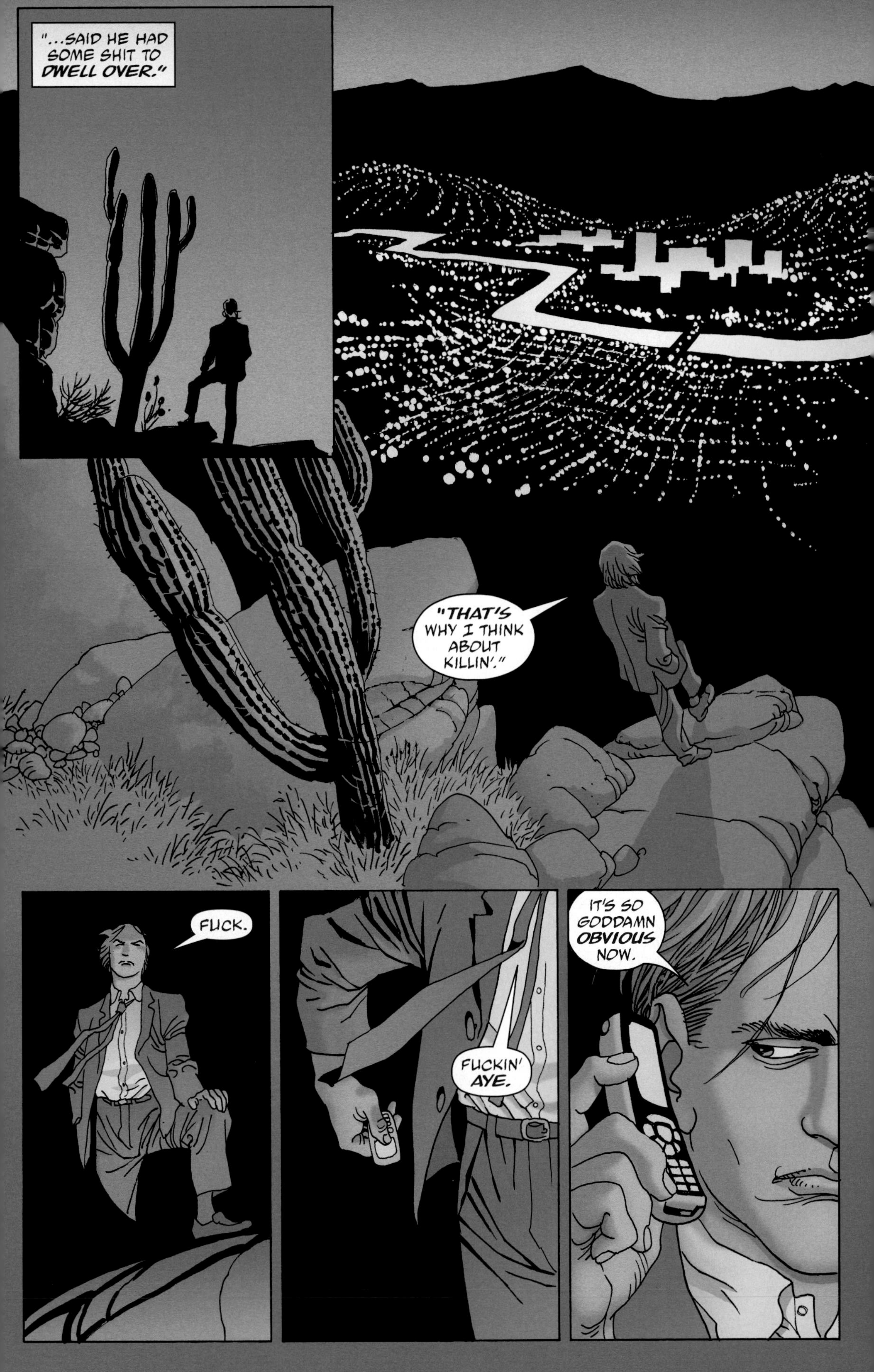
"...SAID HE HAD SOME SHIT TO DWELL OVER."
"THAT'S WHY I THINK ABOUT KILLIN'."
FUCK.
FUCKIN' AYE.
IT'S SO GODDAMN OBVIOUS NOW.

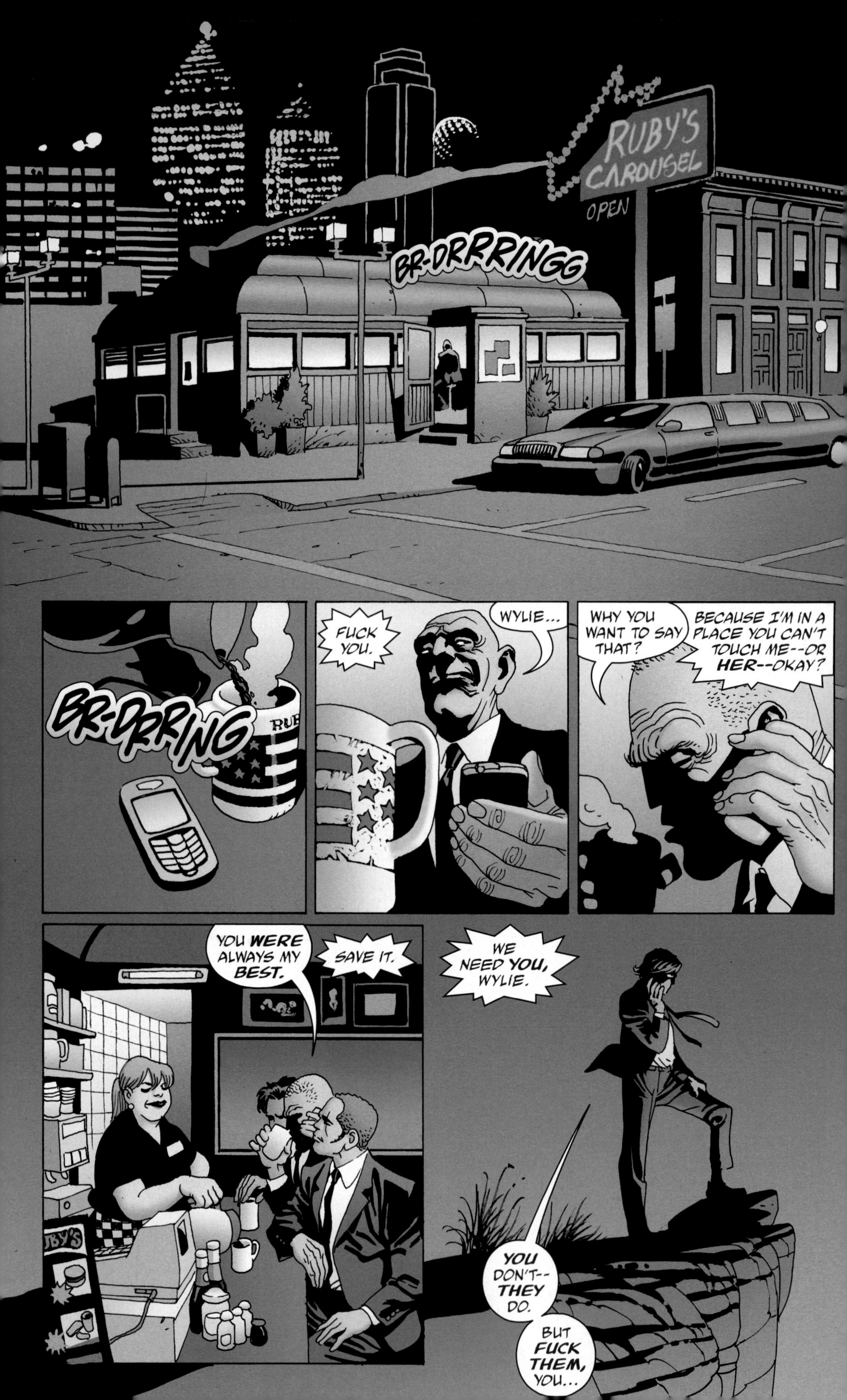
RUBY'S CAROUSEL
OPEN
BR-DRRRINGG
BR-DRRRING
RUB
FUCK YOU.
WYLIE...
WHY YOU WANT TO SAY THAT?
BECAUSE I'M IN A PLACE YOU CAN'T TOUCH ME--OR HER--OKAY?
YOU WERE ALWAYS MY BEST.
SAVE IT.
WE NEED YOU, WYLIE.
YOU DON'T--THEY DO.
BUT FUCK THEM, YOU...
UBY'S

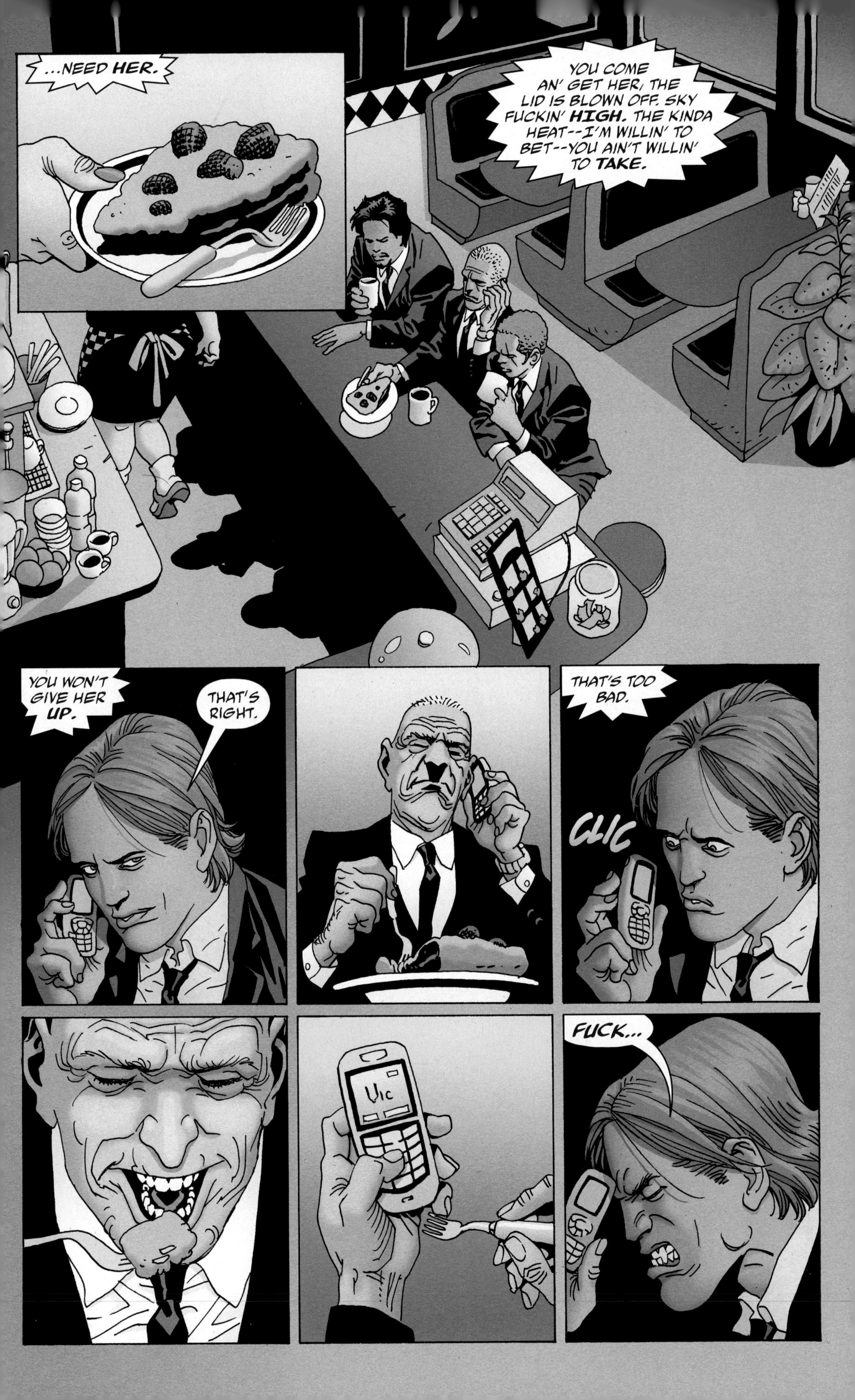
...NEED HER.
YOU COME AN' GET HER, THE LID IS BLOWN OFF. SKY FUCKIN' HIGH. THE KINDA HEAT--I'M WILLIN' TO BET--YOU AIN'T WILLIN' TO TAKE.
YOU WON'T GIVE HER UP.
THAT'S RIGHT.
THAT'S TOO BAD.
CLIC
VIC
FUCK...

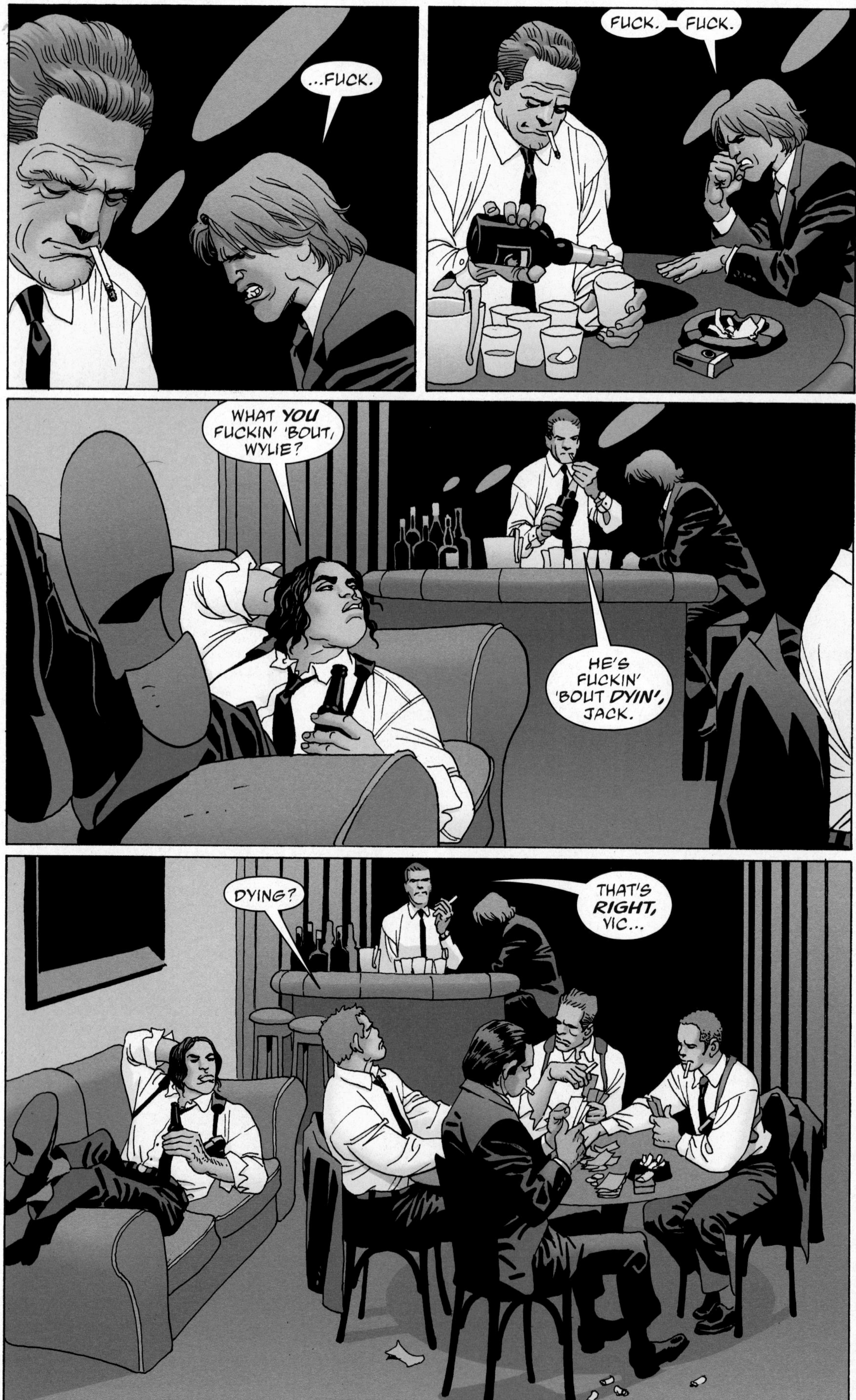
...FUCK.
FUCK.
FUCK.
WHAT YOU FUCKIN' 'BOUT, WYLIE?
HE'S FUCKIN' 'BOUT DYIN', JACK.
DYING?
THAT'S RIGHT, VIC...

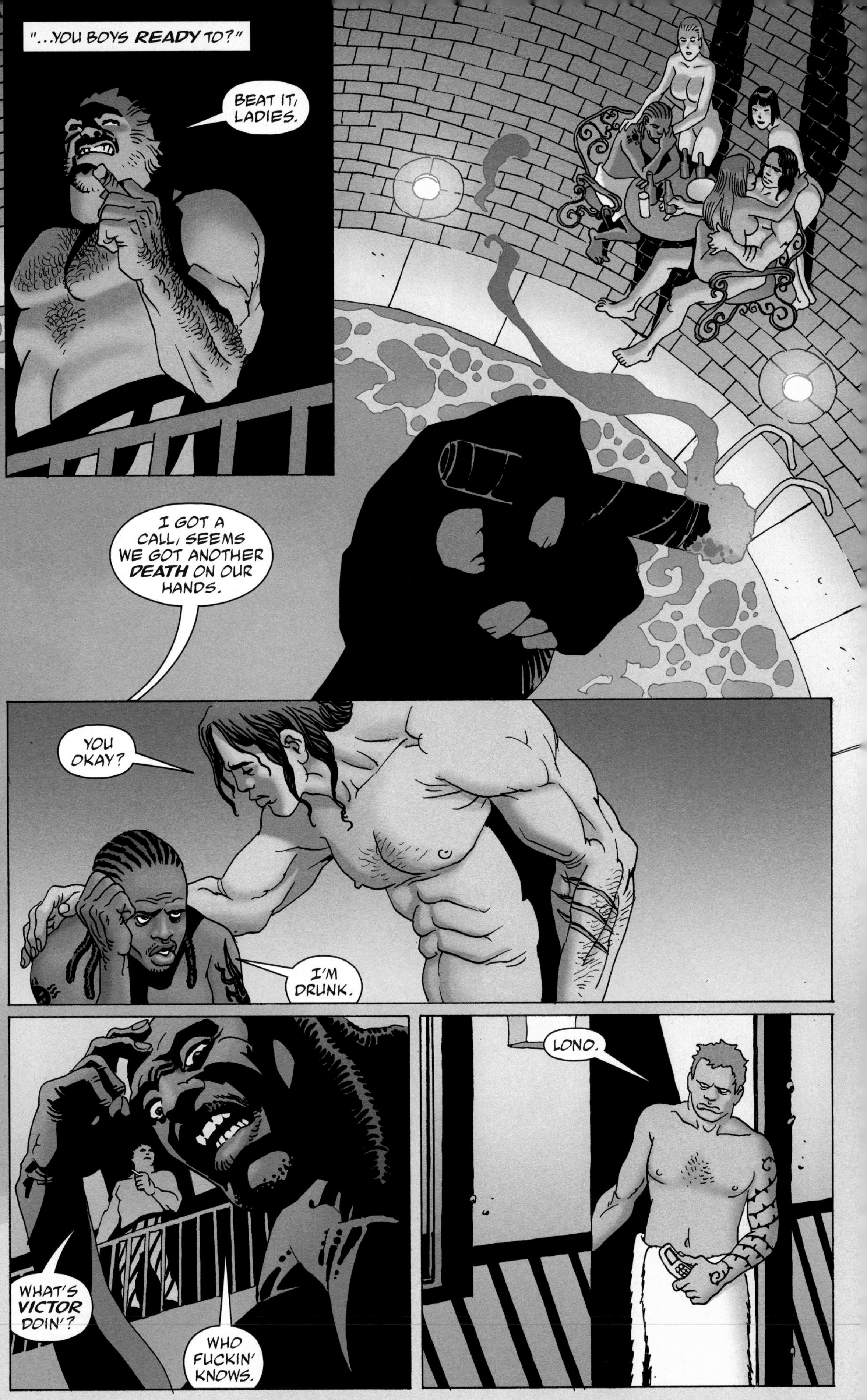
"...YOU BOYS READY TO?"
BEAT IT, LADIES.
I GOT A CALL, SEEMS WE GOT ANOTHER DEATH ON OUR HANDS.
YOU OKAY?
I'M DRUNK.
WHAT'S VICTOR DOIN'?
WHO FUCKIN' KNOWS.
LONO.

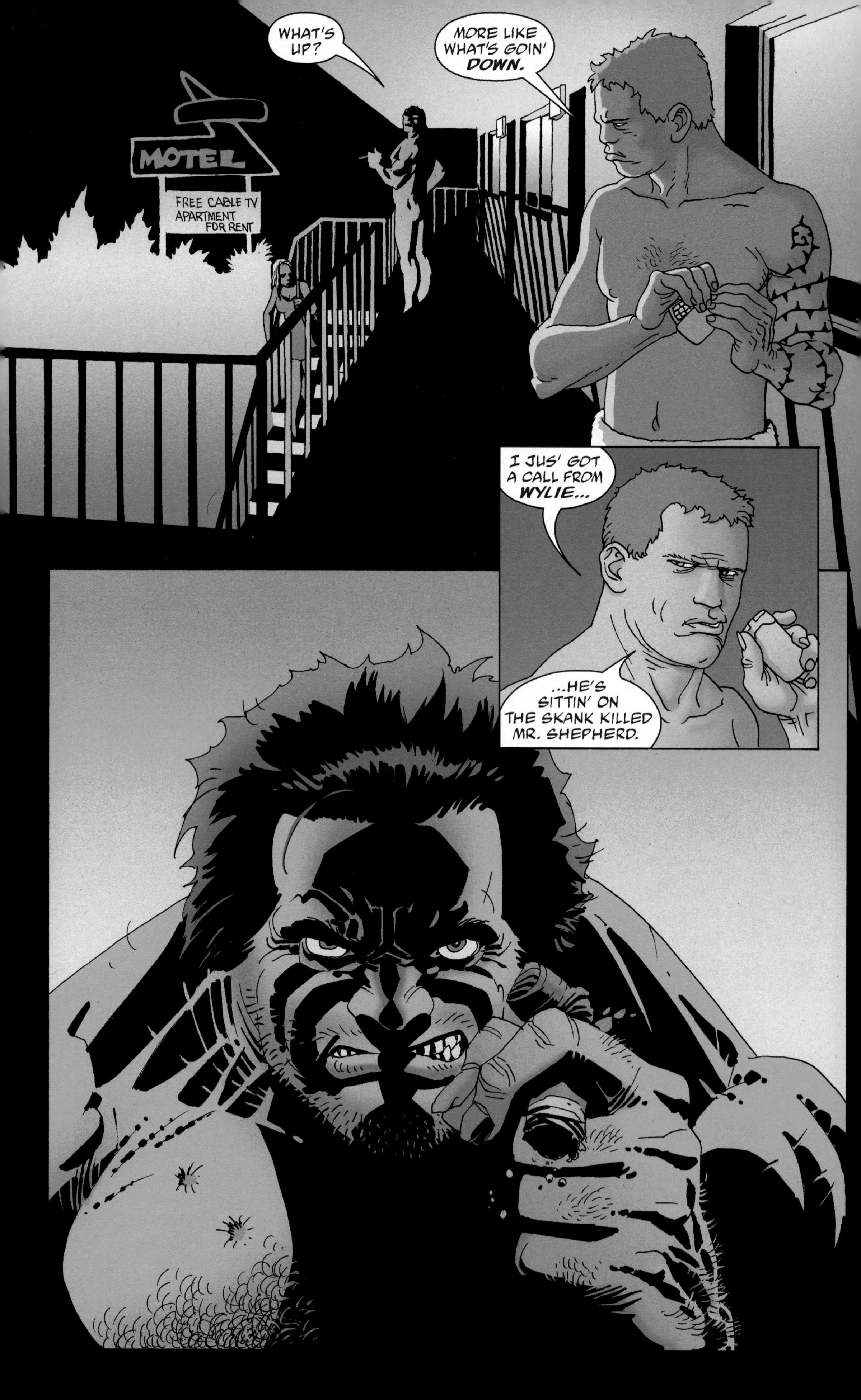
WHAT'S UP?
MORE LIKE WHAT'S GOIN' DOWN.
MOTEL
FREE CABLE TV
APARTMENT FOR RENT
I JUS' GOT A CALL FROM WYLIE...
...HE'S SITTIN' ON THE SKANK KILLED MR. SHEPHERD.

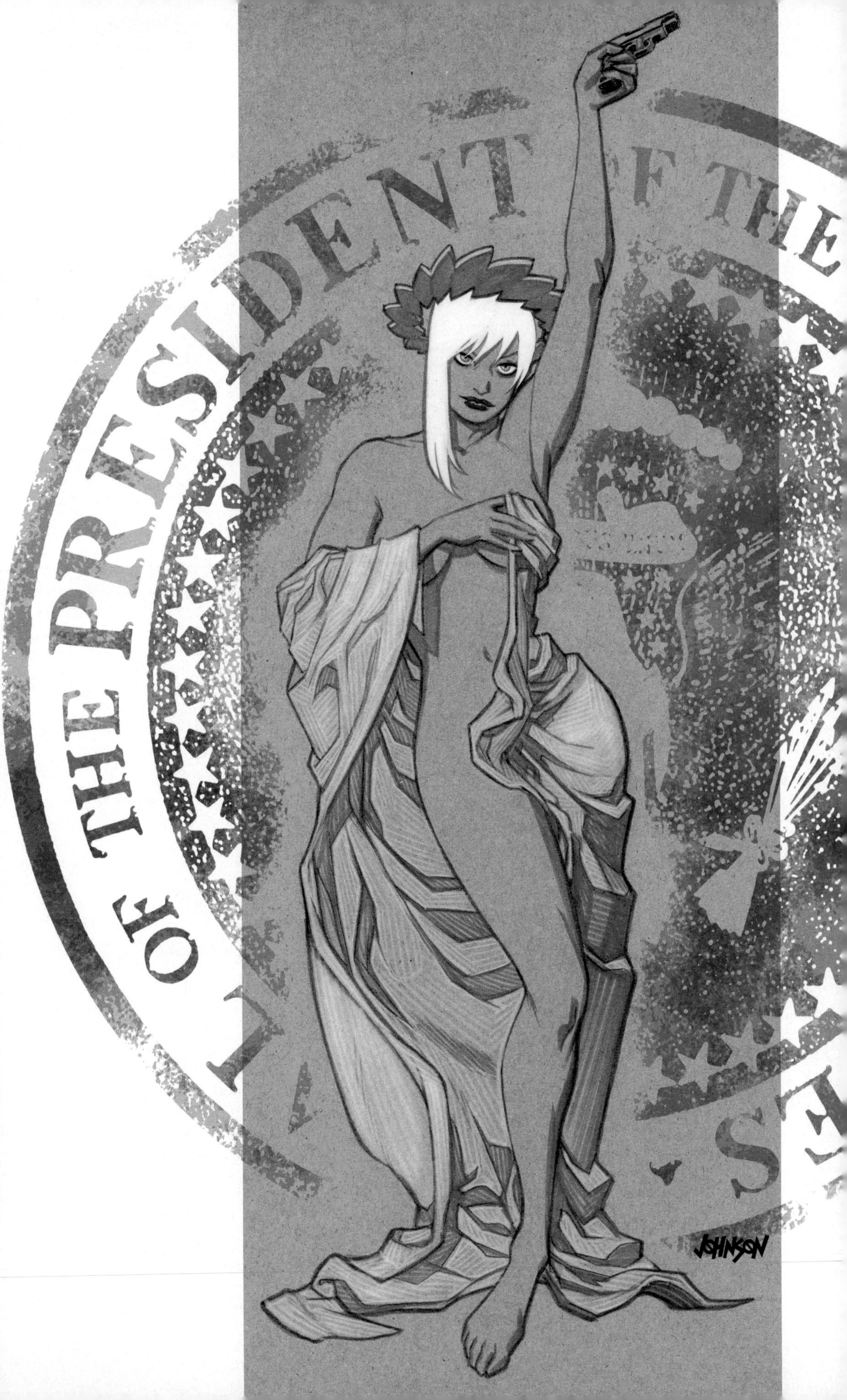
OF THE PRESIDENT OF THE
JOHNSON

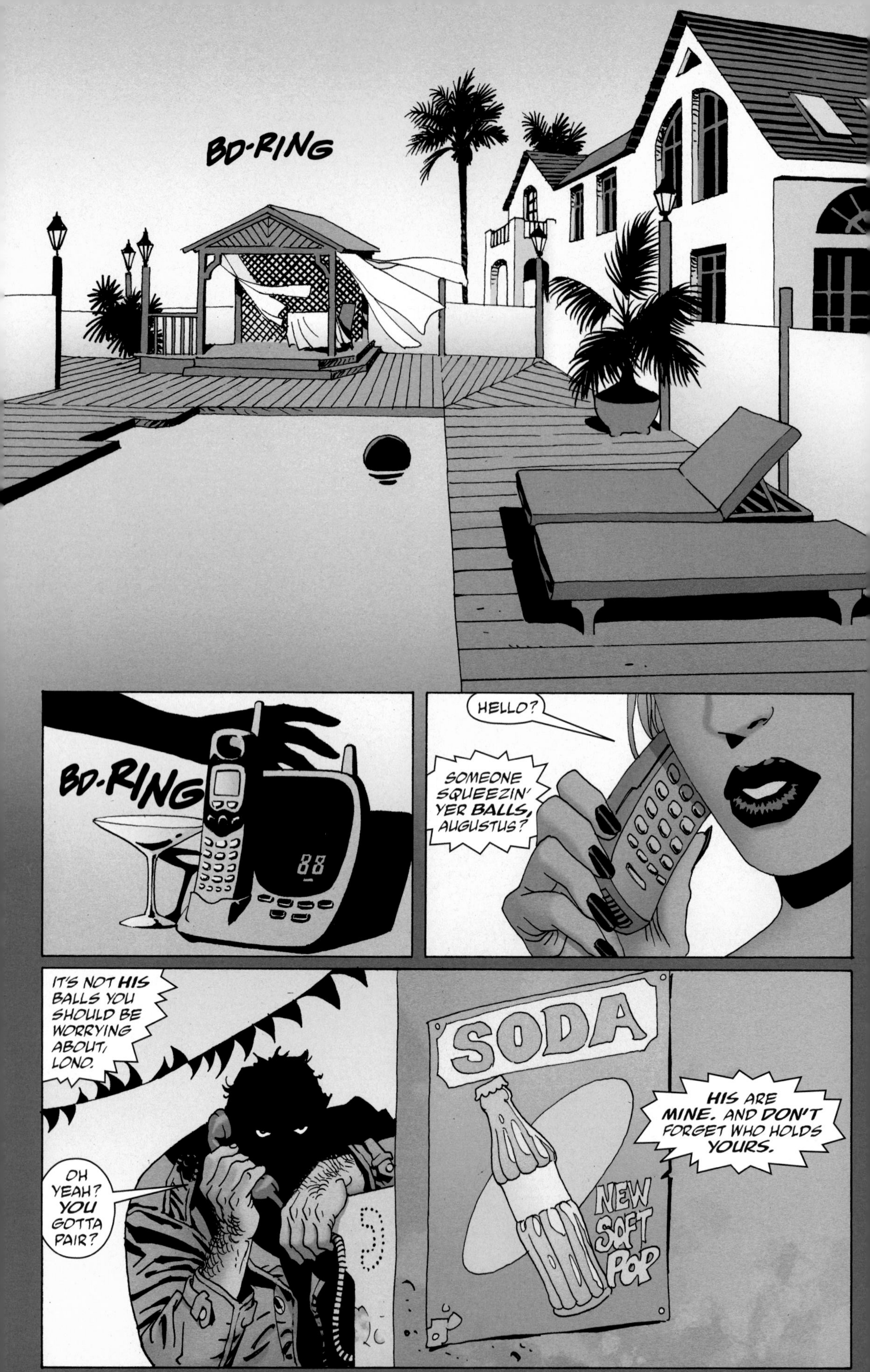
BD-RING
BD-RING
HELLO?
SOMEONE SQUEEZIN' YER BALLS, AUGUSTUS?
IT'S NOT HIS BALLS YOU SHOULD BE WORRYING ABOUT, LONO.
OH YEAH? YOU GOTTA PAIR?
SODA
NEW SOFT POP
HIS ARE MINE. AND DON'T FORGET WHO HOLDS YOURS.

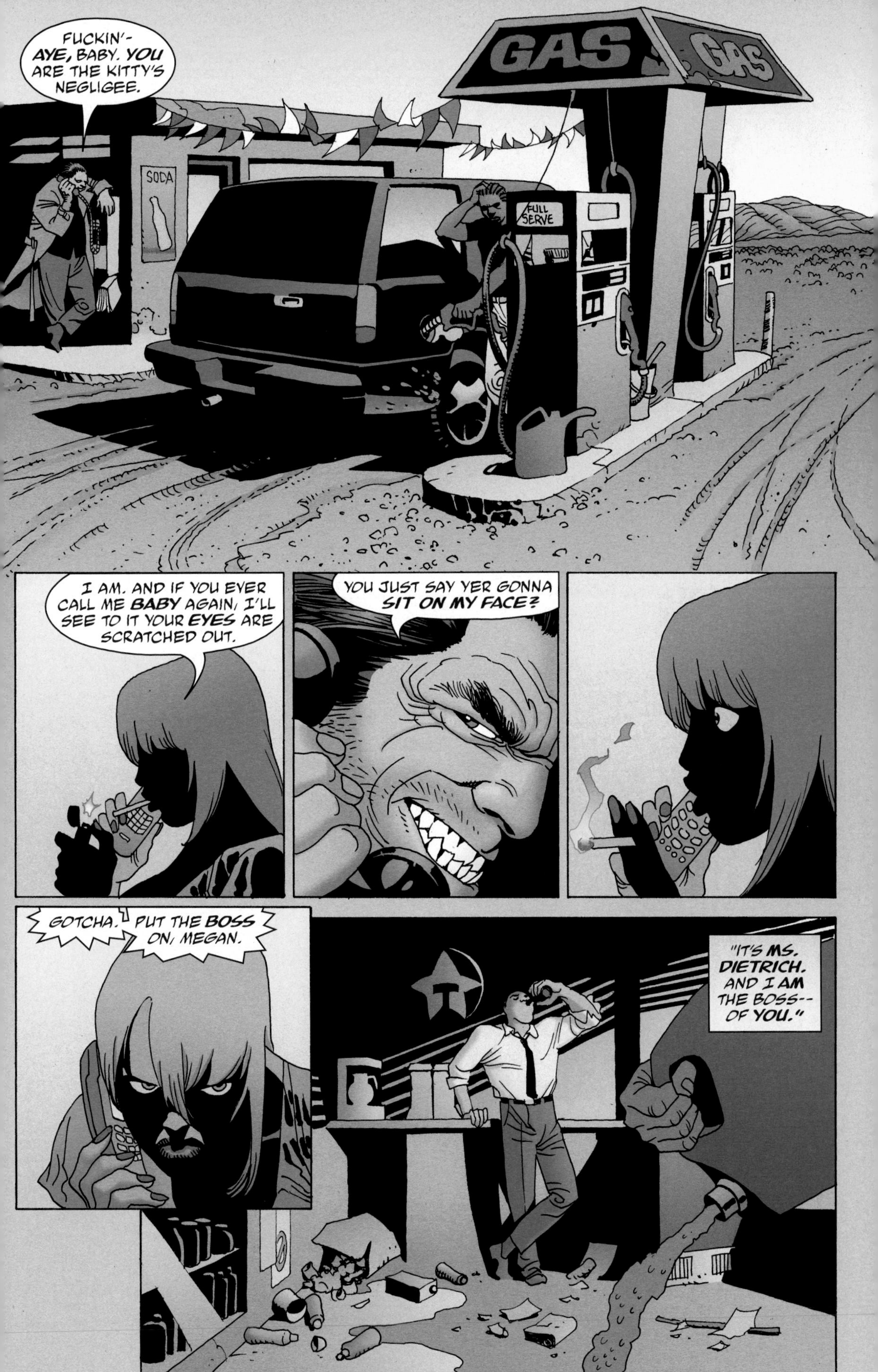
FUCKIN'-
AYE, BABY. YOU ARE THE KITTY'S NEGLIGEE.
GAS
GAS
SODA
FULL SERVE
I AM. AND IF YOU EVER CALL ME BABY AGAIN, I'LL SEE TO IT YOUR EYES ARE SCRATCHED OUT.
YOU JUST SAY YER GONNA SIT ON MY FACE?
GOTCHA.
PUT THE BOSS ON, MEGAN.
"IT'S MS. DIETRICH. AND I AM THE BOSS-- OF YOU."

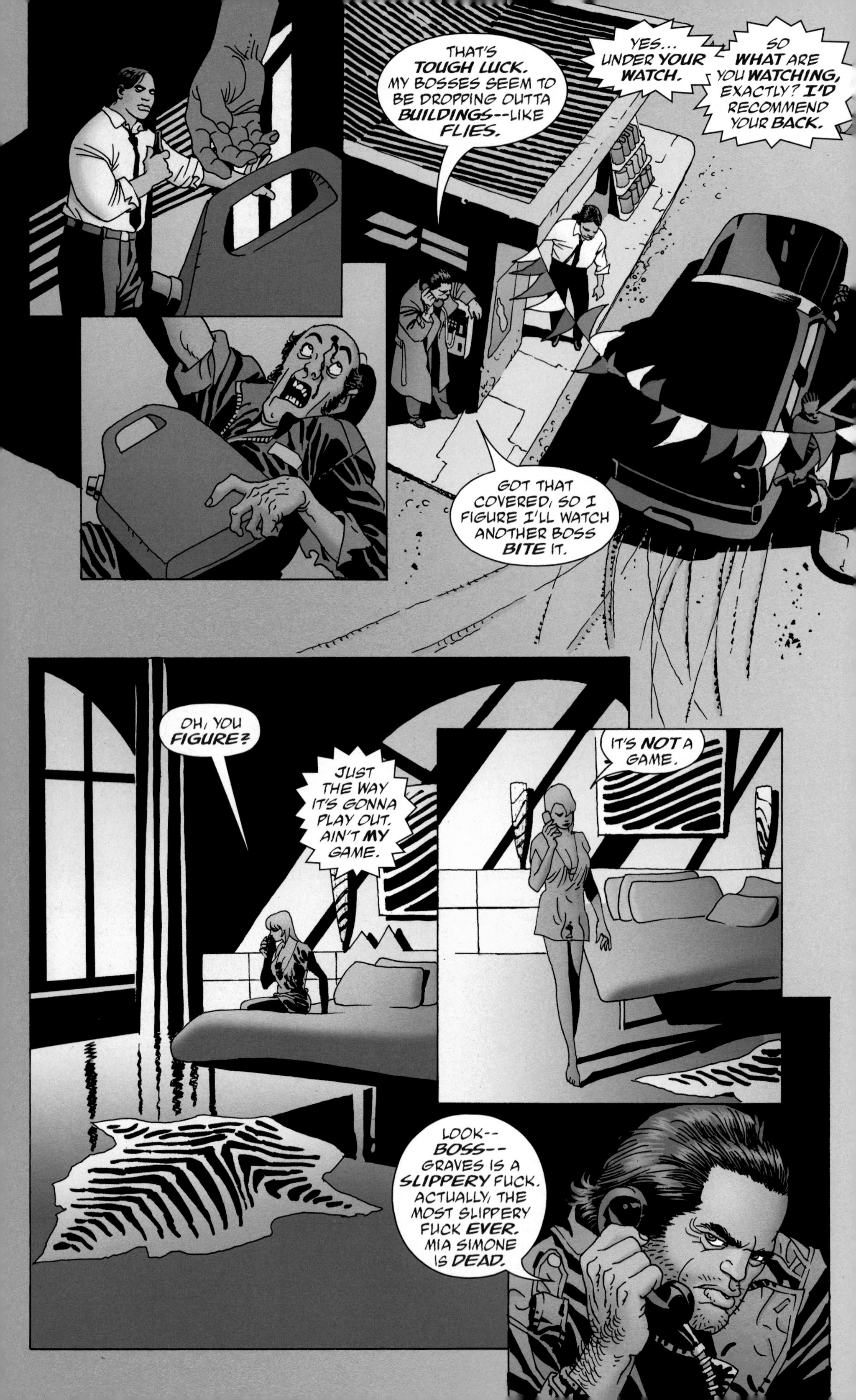
THAT'S TOUGH LUCK. MY BOSSES SEEM TO BE DROPPING OUTTA BUILDINGS--LIKE FLIES.
YES... UNDER YOUR WATCH.
SO WHAT ARE YOU WATCHING, EXACTLY? I'D RECOMMEND YOUR BACK.
GOT THAT COVERED, SO I FIGURE I'LL WATCH ANOTHER BOSS BITE IT.
OH, YOU FIGURE?
JUST THE WAY IT'S GONNA PLAY OUT. AIN'T MY GAME.
IT'S NOT A GAME.
LOOK-- BOSS-- GRAVES IS A SLIPPERY FUCK. ACTUALLY, THE MOST SLIPPERY FUCK EVER. MIA SIMONE IS DEAD.

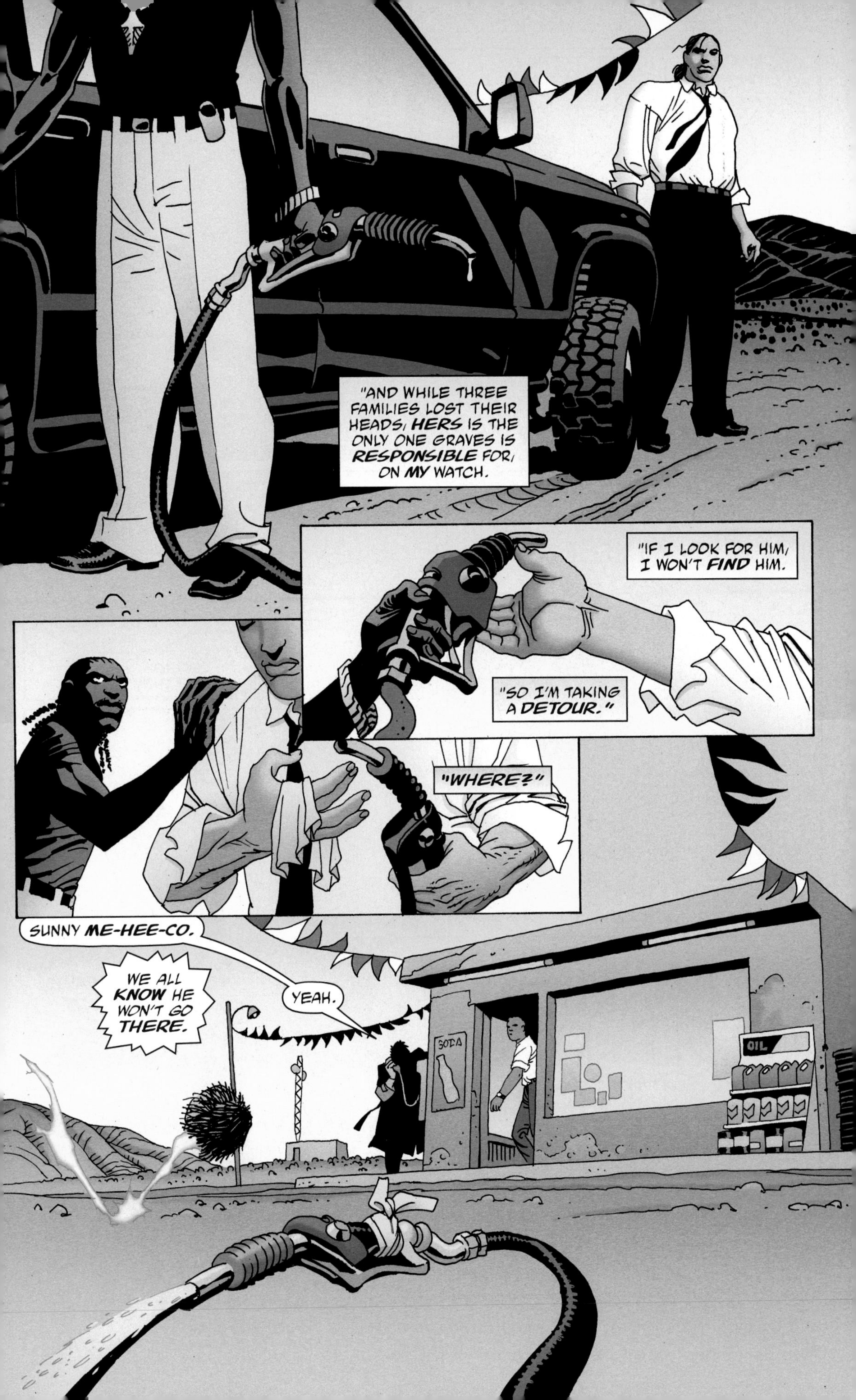
"AND WHILE THREE FAMILIES LOST THEIR HEADS, HERS IS THE ONLY ONE GRAVES IS RESPONSIBLE FOR, ON MY WATCH.
"IF I LOOK FOR HIM, I WON'T FIND HIM.
"SO I'M TAKING A DETOUR."
"WHERE?"
SUNNY ME-HEE-CO.
WE ALL KNOW HE WON'T GO THERE.
YEAH.
SODA
OIL

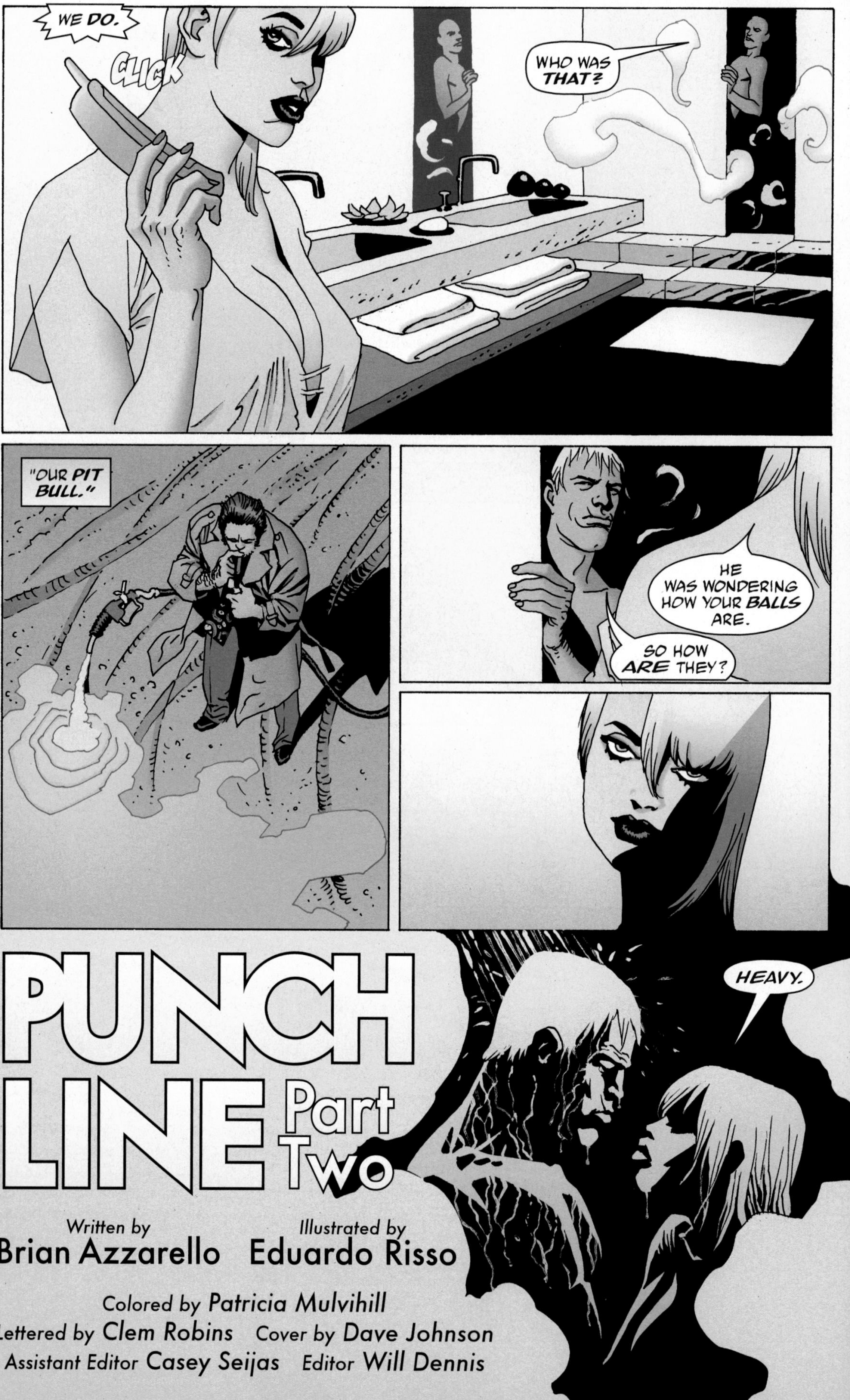
WE DO.
CLICK
WHO WAS THAT?
"OUR PIT BULL."
HE WAS WONDERING HOW YOUR BALLS ARE.
SO HOW ARE THEY?
HEAVY.

PUNCH LINE Part Two

Written by
Brian Azzarello

Illustrated by
Eduardo Risso

Colored by Patricia Mulvihill
Lettered by Clem Robins Cover by Dave Johnson
Assistant Editor Casey Seijas Editor Will Dennis

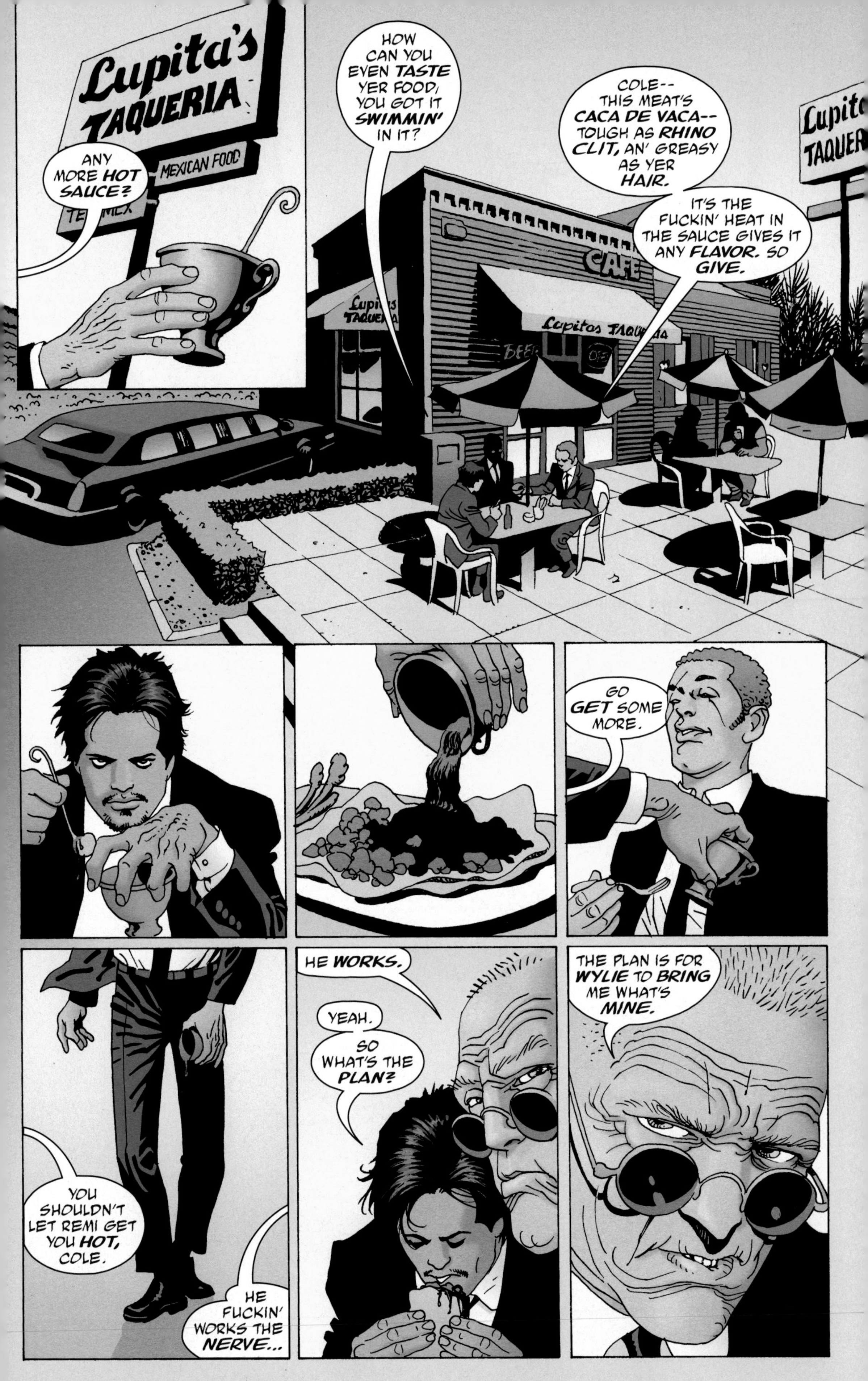

Lupita's TAQUERIA
MEXICAN FOOD
ANY MORE HOT SAUCE?
HOW CAN YOU EVEN TASTE YER FOOD, YOU GOT IT SWIMMIN' IN IT?
COLE-- THIS MEAT'S CACA DE VACA-- TOUGH AS RHINO CLIT, AN' GREASY AS YER HAIR.
IT'S THE FUCKIN' HEAT IN THE SAUCE GIVES IT ANY FLAVOR. SO GIVE.
CAFE
Lupitas TAQUERIA
GO GET SOME MORE.
YOU SHOULDN'T LET REMI GET YOU HOT, COLE.
HE FUCKIN' WORKS THE NERVE...
HE WORKS.
YEAH.
SO WHAT'S THE PLAN?
THE PLAN IS FOR WYLIE TO BRING ME WHAT'S MINE.

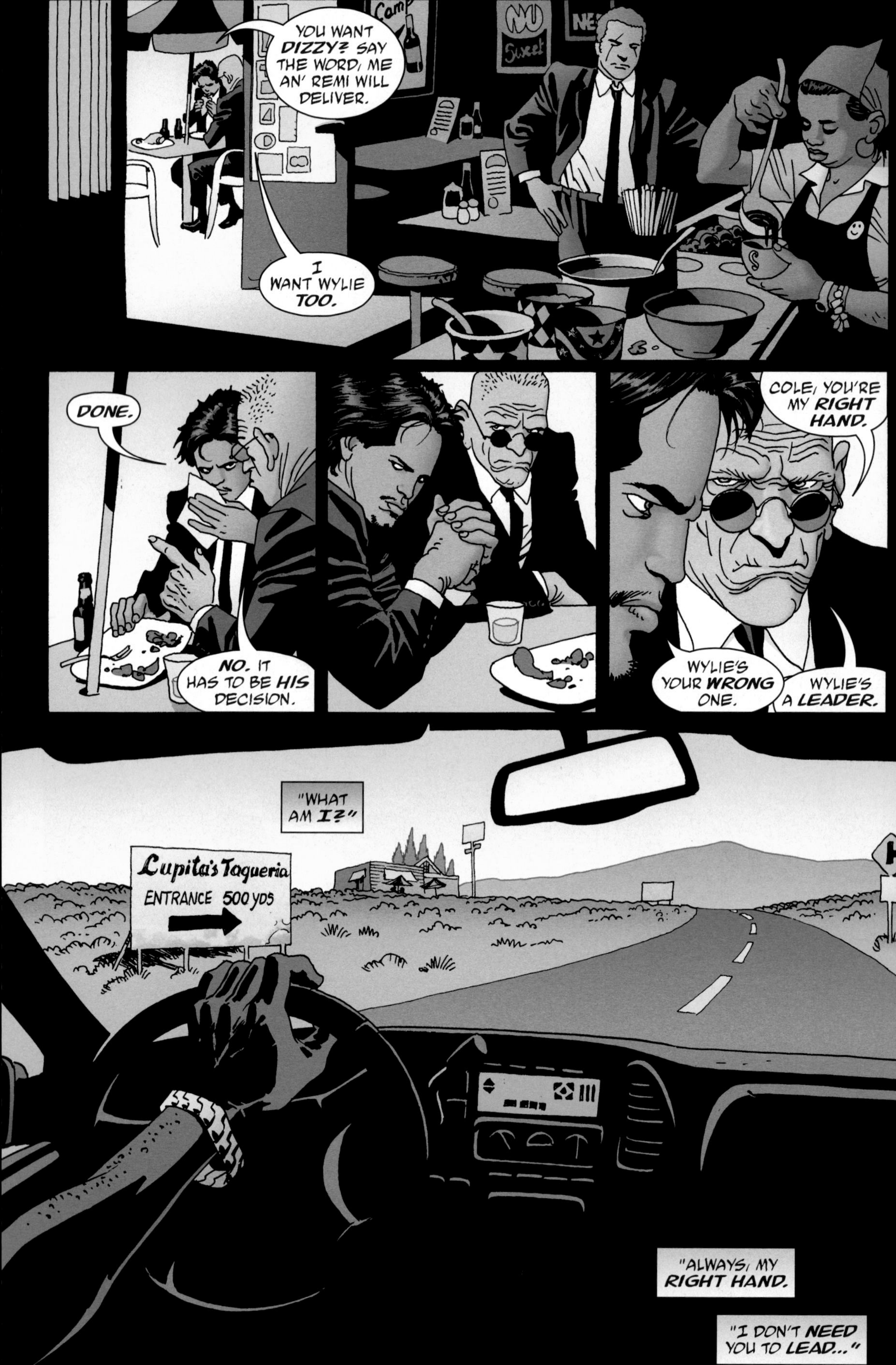
YOU WANT DIZZY? SAY THE WORD, ME AN' REMI WILL DELIVER.
I WANT WYLIE TOO.
DONE.
NO. IT HAS TO BE HIS DECISION.
COLE, YOU'RE MY RIGHT HAND.
WYLIE'S A LEADER.
WYLIE'S YOUR WRONG ONE.
"WHAT AM I?"
Lupita's Taqueria
ENTRANCE 500 YDS
"ALWAYS, MY RIGHT HAND.
"I DON'T NEED YOU TO LEAD..."

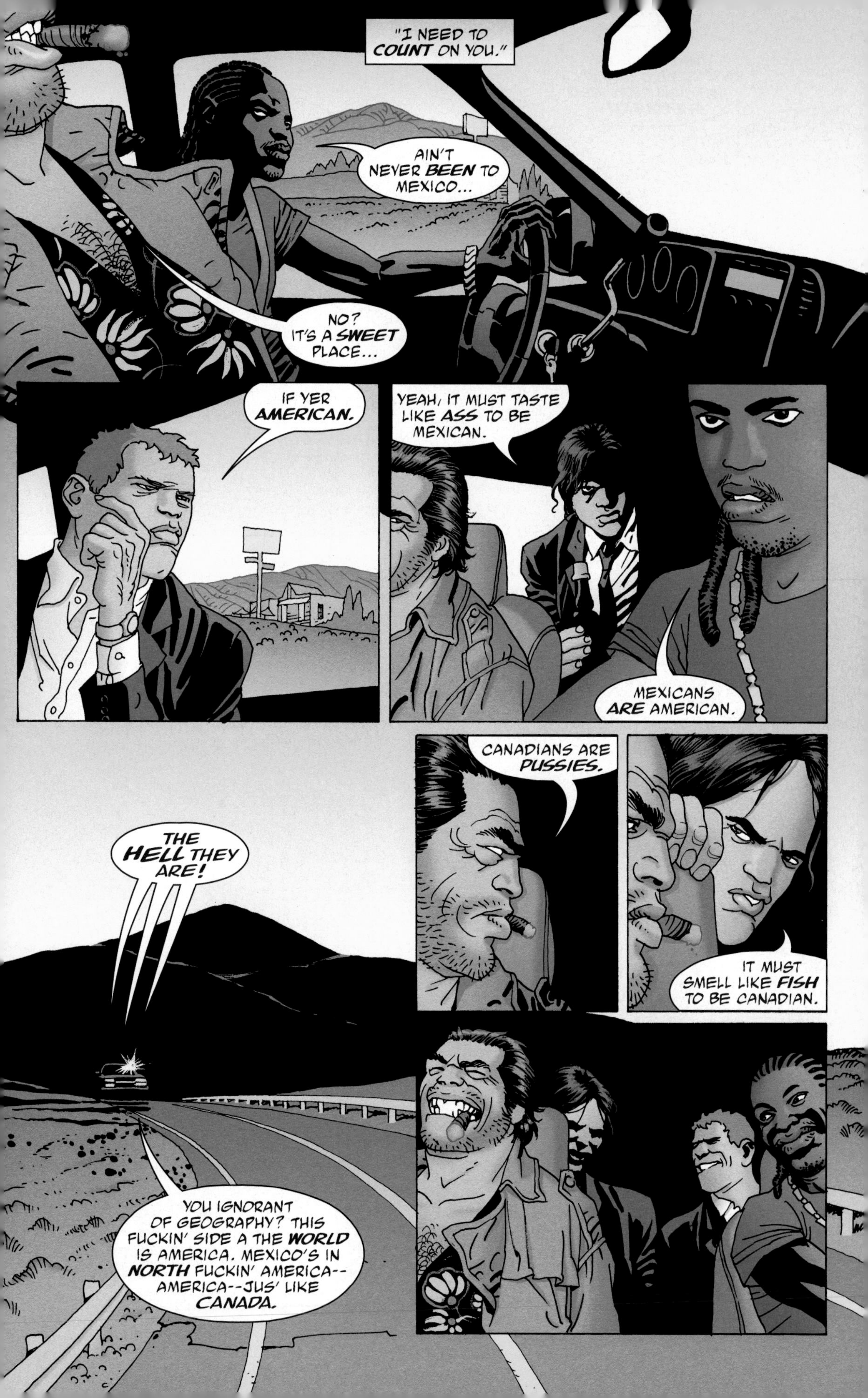
"I NEED TO COUNT ON YOU."
AIN'T NEVER BEEN TO MEXICO...
NO? IT'S A SWEET PLACE...
IF YER AMERICAN.
YEAH, IT MUST TASTE LIKE ASS TO BE MEXICAN.
MEXICANS ARE AMERICAN.
CANADIANS ARE PUSSIES.
IT MUST SMELL LIKE FISH TO BE CANADIAN.
THE HELL THEY ARE!
YOU IGNORANT OF GEOGRAPHY? THIS FUCKIN' SIDE A THE WORLD IS AMERICA. MEXICO'S IN NORTH FUCKIN' AMERICA--AMERICA--JUS' LIKE CANADA.

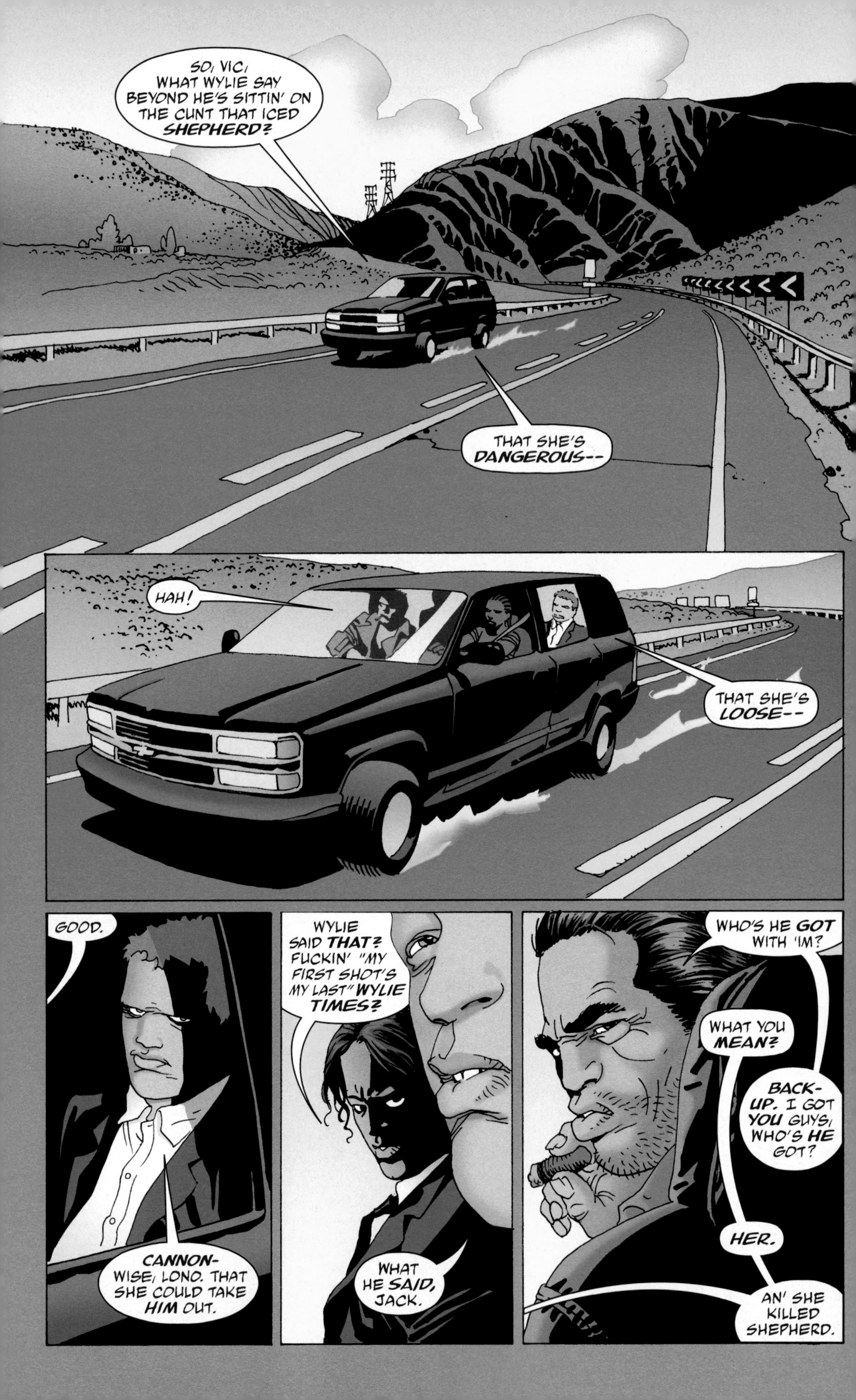
SO, VIC, WHAT WYLIE SAY BEYOND HE'S SITTIN' ON THE CUNT THAT ICED SHEPHERD?
THAT SHE'S DANGEROUS--
HAH!
THAT SHE'S LOOSE--
GOOD.
CANNON-WISE, LONO. THAT SHE COULD TAKE HIM OUT.
WYLIE SAID THAT? FUCKIN' "MY FIRST SHOT'S MY LAST" WYLIE TIMES?
WHAT HE SAID, JACK.
WHO'S HE GOT WITH 'IM?
WHAT YOU MEAN?
BACK-UP. I GOT YOU GUYS, WHO'S HE GOT?
HER.
AN' SHE KILLED SHEPHERD.

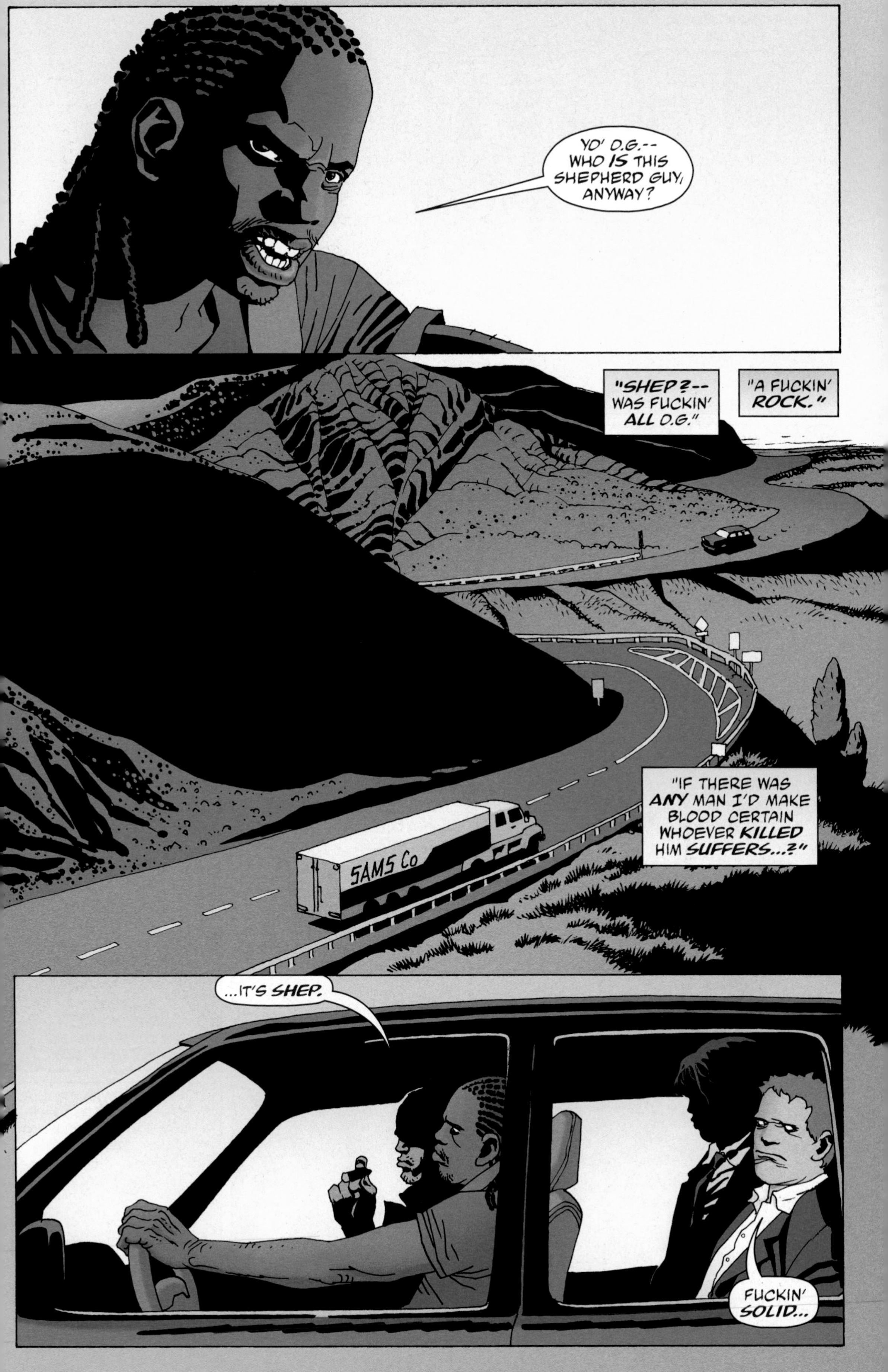

YO' O.G.-- WHO IS THIS SHEPHERD GUY, ANYWAY?
"SHEP?-- WAS FUCKIN' ALL O.G."
"A FUCKIN' ROCK."
SAMS Co
"IF THERE WAS ANY MAN I'D MAKE BLOOD CERTAIN WHOEVER KILLED HIM SUFFERS...?"
...IT'S SHEP.
FUCKIN' SOLID...

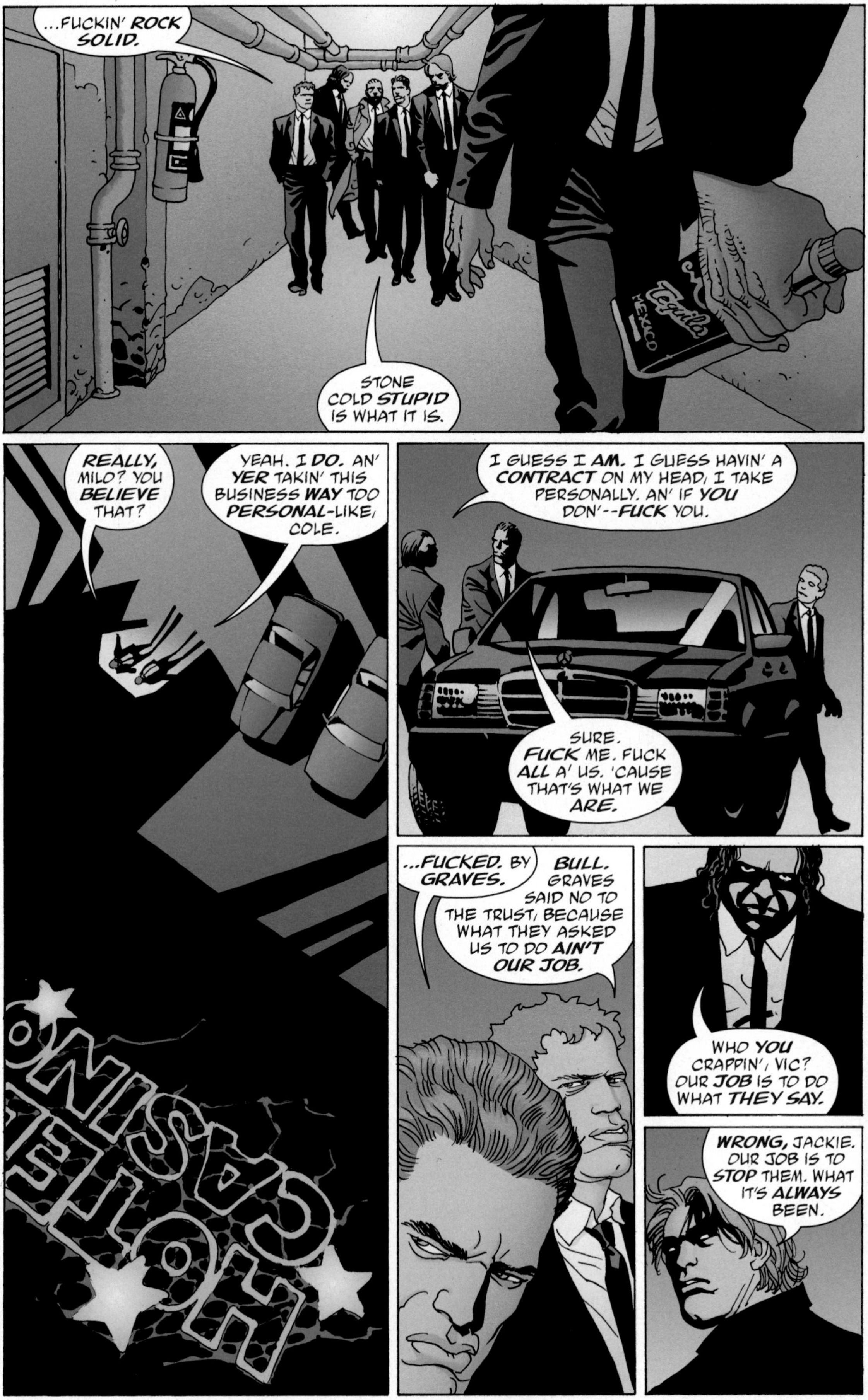

...FUCKIN' ROCK SOLID.
Tequila
MEXICO
STONE COLD STUPID IS WHAT IT IS.
REALLY, MILO? YOU BELIEVE THAT?
YEAH. I DO. AN' YER TAKIN' THIS BUSINESS WAY TOO PERSONAL-LIKE, COLE.
I GUESS I AM. I GUESS HAVIN' A CONTRACT ON MY HEAD, I TAKE PERSONALLY. AN' IF YOU DON'--FUCK YOU.
SURE. FUCK ME. FUCK ALL A' US. 'CAUSE THAT'S WHAT WE ARE.
...FUCKED. BY GRAVES.
BULL. GRAVES SAID NO TO THE TRUST, BECAUSE WHAT THEY ASKED US TO DO AIN'T OUR JOB.
WHO YOU CRAPPIN', VIC? OUR JOB IS TO DO WHAT THEY SAY.
WRONG, JACKIE. OUR JOB IS TO STOP THEM. WHAT IT'S ALWAYS BEEN.

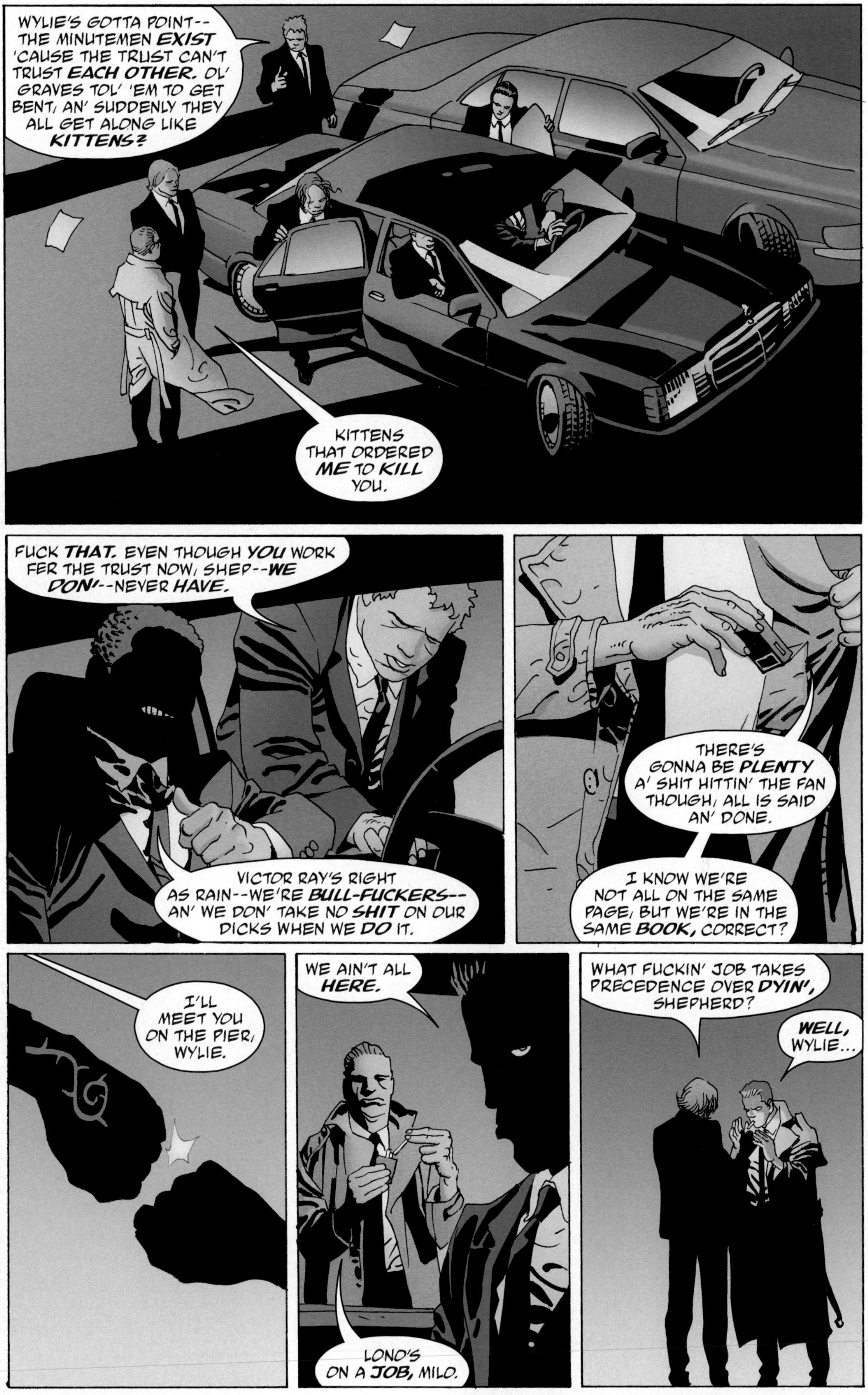
WYLIE'S GOTTA POINT-- THE MINUTEMEN EXIST 'CAUSE THE TRUST CAN'T TRUST EACH OTHER. OL' GRAVES TOL' 'EM TO GET BENT, AN' SUDDENLY THEY ALL GET ALONG LIKE KITTENS?
KITTENS THAT ORDERED ME TO KILL YOU.
FUCK THAT. EVEN THOUGH YOU WORK FER THE TRUST NOW, SHEP--WE DON'--NEVER HAVE.
VICTOR RAY'S RIGHT AS RAIN--WE'RE BULL-FUCKERS--AN' WE DON' TAKE NO SHIT ON OUR DICKS WHEN WE DO IT.
THERE'S GONNA BE PLENTY A' SHIT HITTIN' THE FAN THOUGH, ALL IS SAID AN' DONE.
I KNOW WE'RE NOT ALL ON THE SAME PAGE, BUT WE'RE IN THE SAME BOOK, CORRECT?
I'LL MEET YOU ON THE PIER, WYLIE.
WE AIN'T ALL HERE.
LONO'S ON A JOB, MILO.
WHAT FUCKIN' JOB TAKES PRECEDENCE OVER DYIN', SHEPHERD?
WELL, WYLIE...

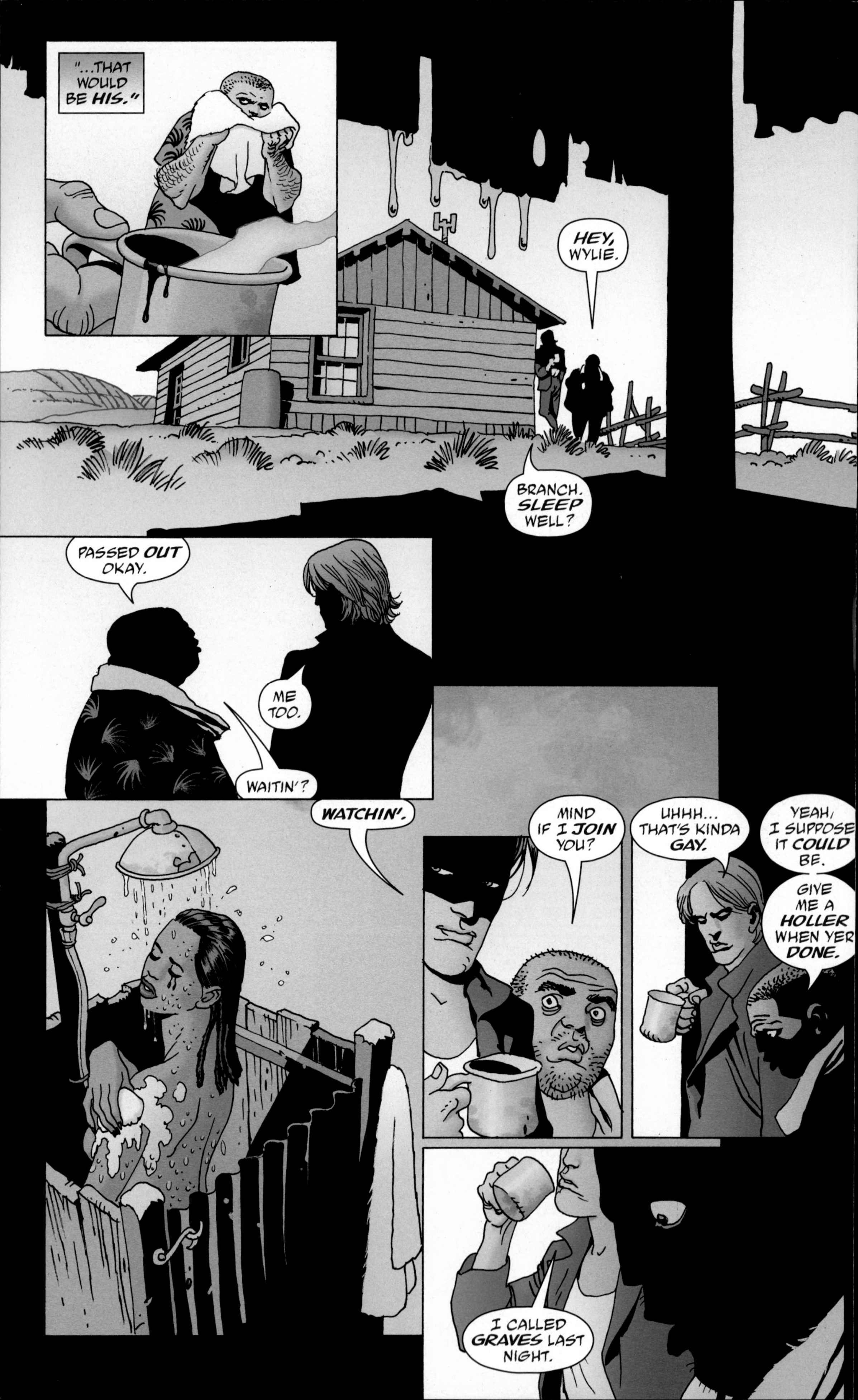
"...THAT WOULD BE HIS."
HEY, WYLIE.
BRANCH. SLEEP WELL?
PASSED OUT OKAY.
ME TOO.
WAITIN'?
WATCHIN'.
MIND IF I JOIN YOU?
UHHH... THAT'S KINDA GAY.
YEAH, I SUPPOSE IT COULD BE.
GIVE ME A HOLLER WHEN YER DONE.
I CALLED GRAVES LAST NIGHT.

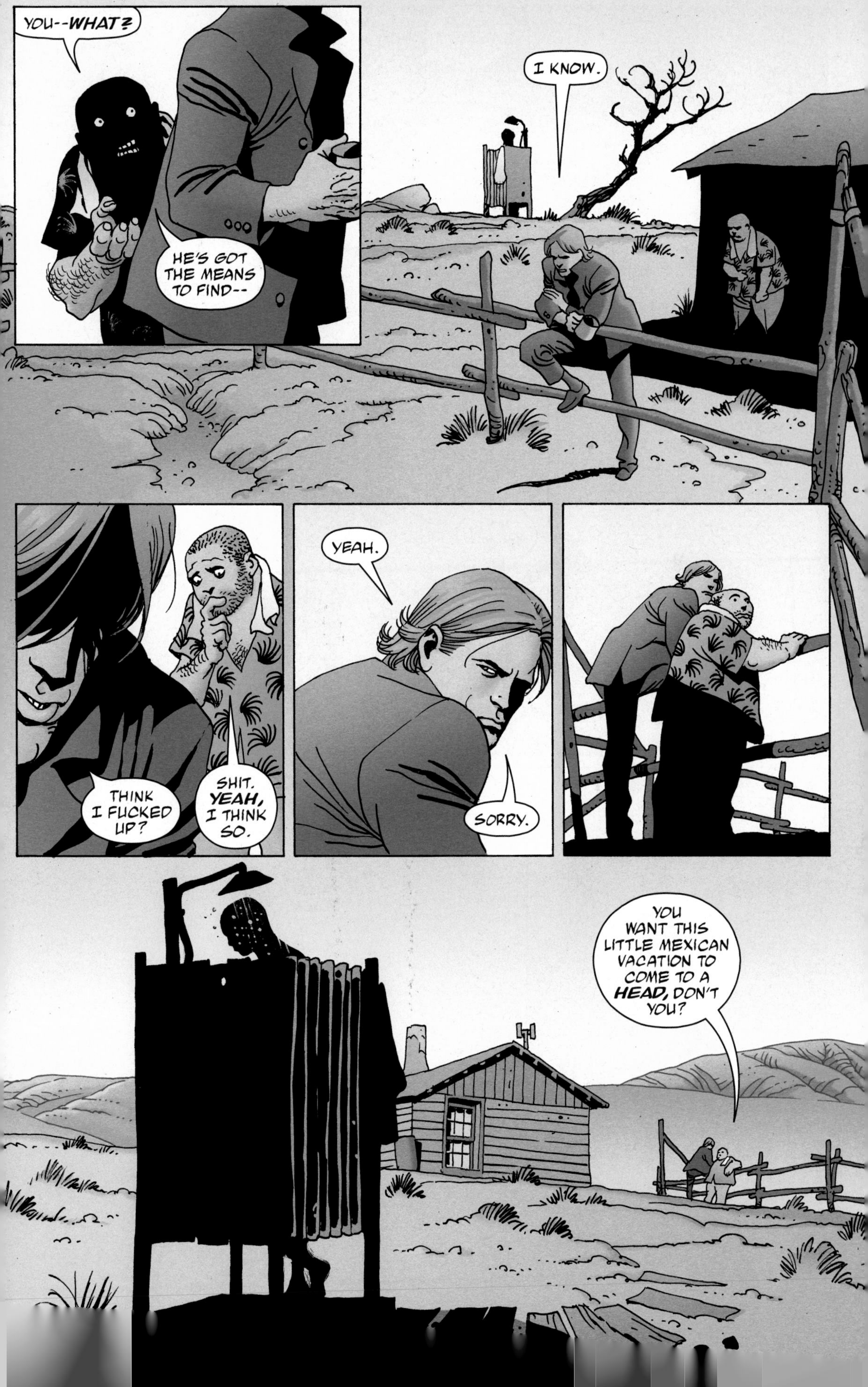
YOU--WHAT?
HE'S GOT THE MEANS TO FIND--
I KNOW.
THINK I FUCKED UP?
SHIT. YEAH, I THINK SO.
YEAH.
SORRY.
YOU WANT THIS LITTLE MEXICAN VACATION TO COME TO A HEAD, DON'T YOU?

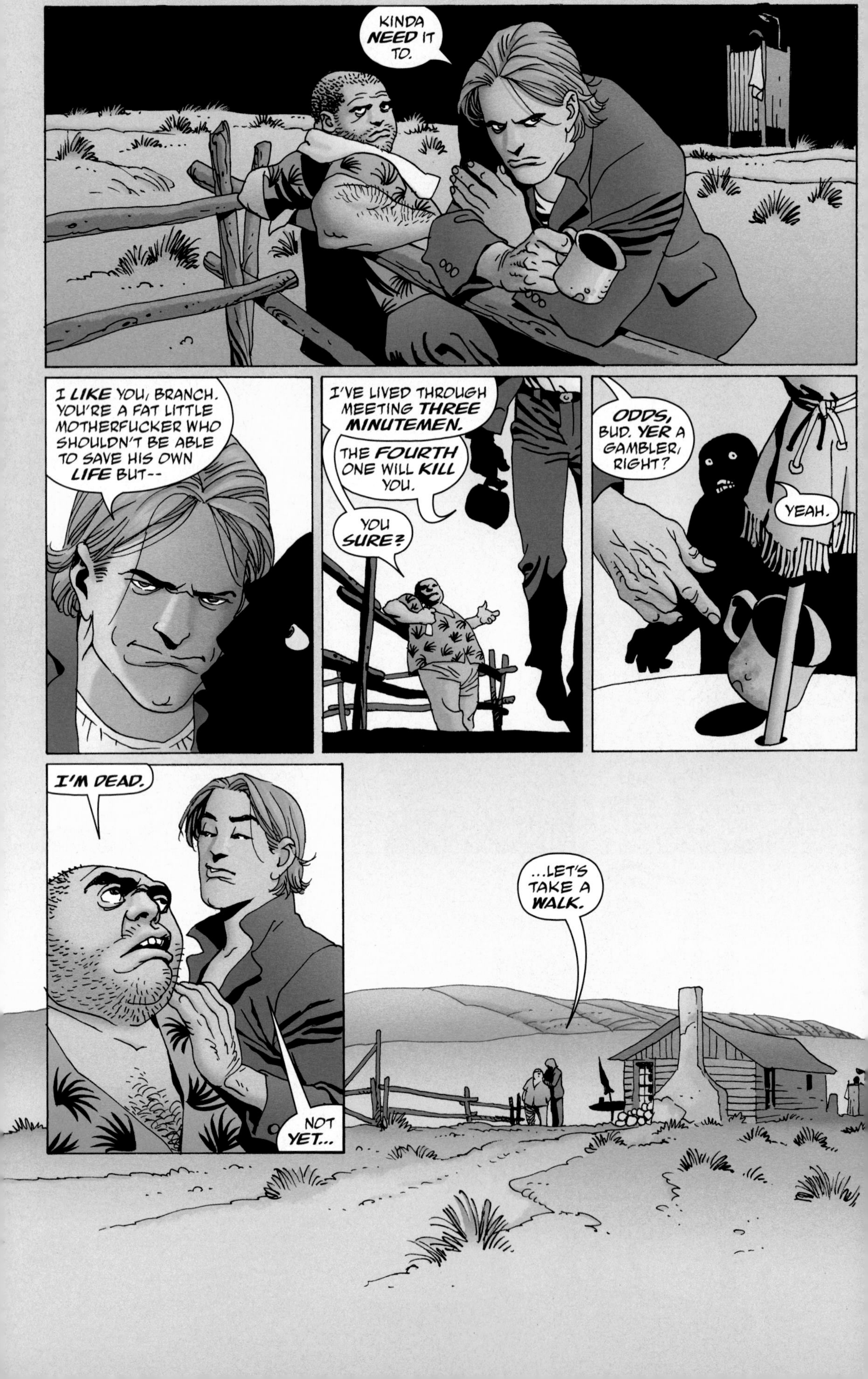
KINDA NEED IT TO.
I LIKE YOU, BRANCH. YOU'RE A FAT LITTLE MOTHERFUCKER WHO SHOULDN'T BE ABLE TO SAVE HIS OWN LIFE BUT--
I'VE LIVED THROUGH MEETING THREE MINUTEMEN.
THE FOURTH ONE WILL KILL YOU.
YOU SURE?
ODDS, BUD. YER A GAMBLER, RIGHT?
YEAH.
I'M DEAD.
NOT YET...
...LET'S TAKE A WALK.

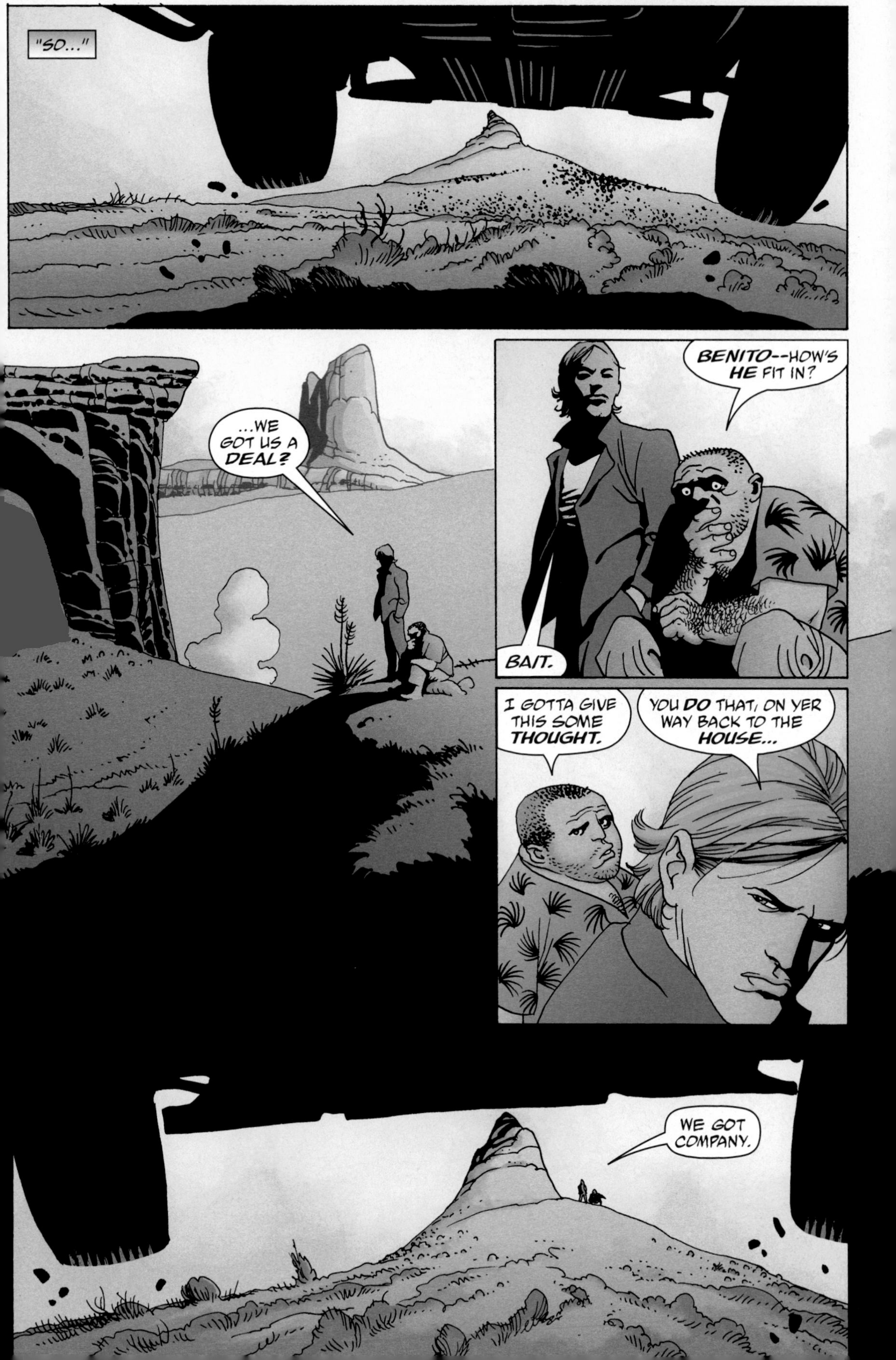
"SO..."
...WE GOT US A DEAL?
BENITO--HOW'S HE FIT IN?
BAIT.
I GOTTA GIVE THIS SOME THOUGHT.
YOU DO THAT, ON YER WAY BACK TO THE HOUSE...
WE GOT COMPANY.

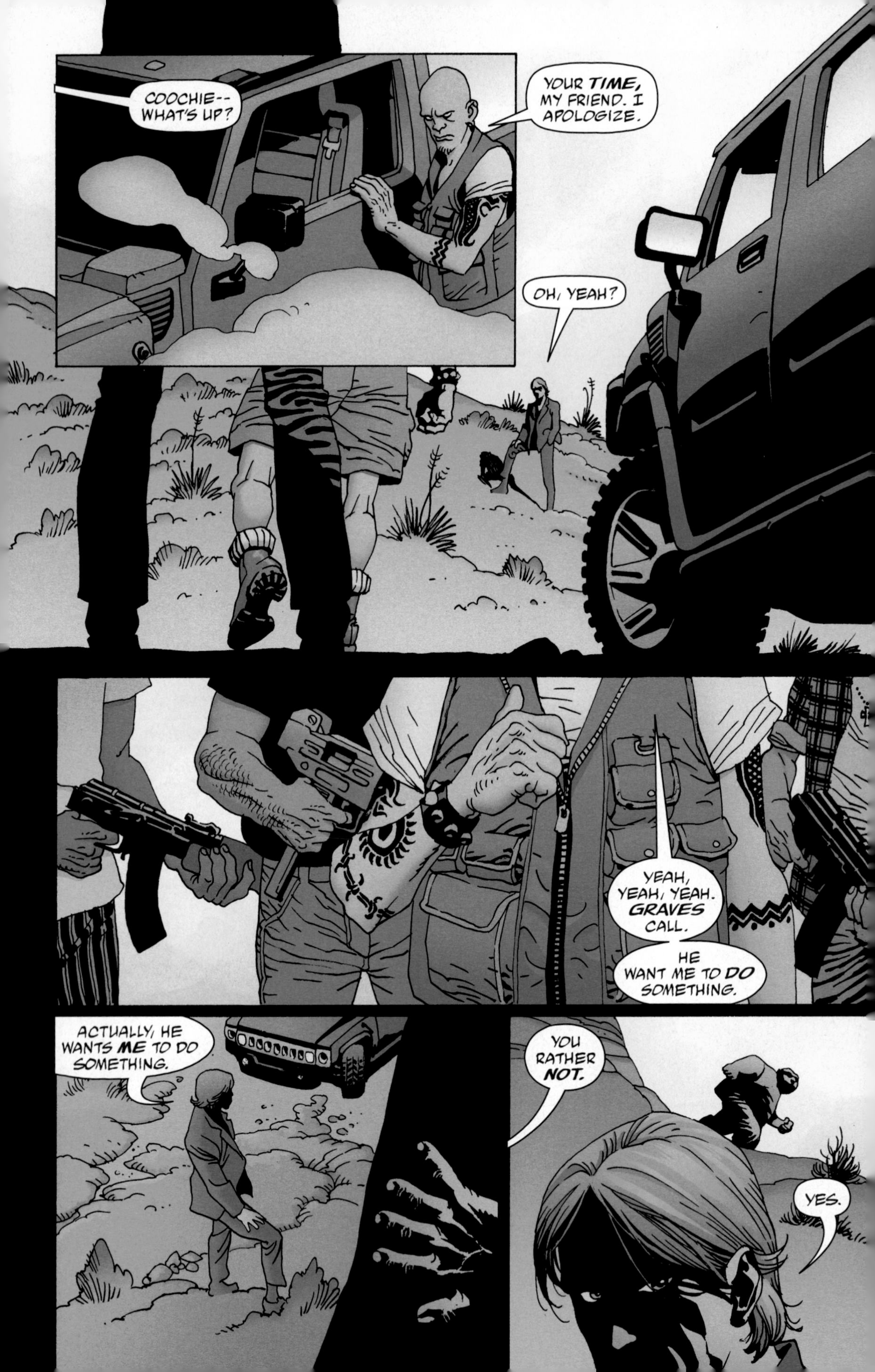
COOCHIE--
WHAT'S UP?
YOUR TIME, MY FRIEND. I APOLOGIZE.
OH, YEAH?
YEAH, YEAH, YEAH. GRAVES CALL.
HE WANT ME TO DO SOMETHING.
ACTUALLY, HE WANTS ME TO DO SOMETHING.
YOU RATHER NOT.
YES.

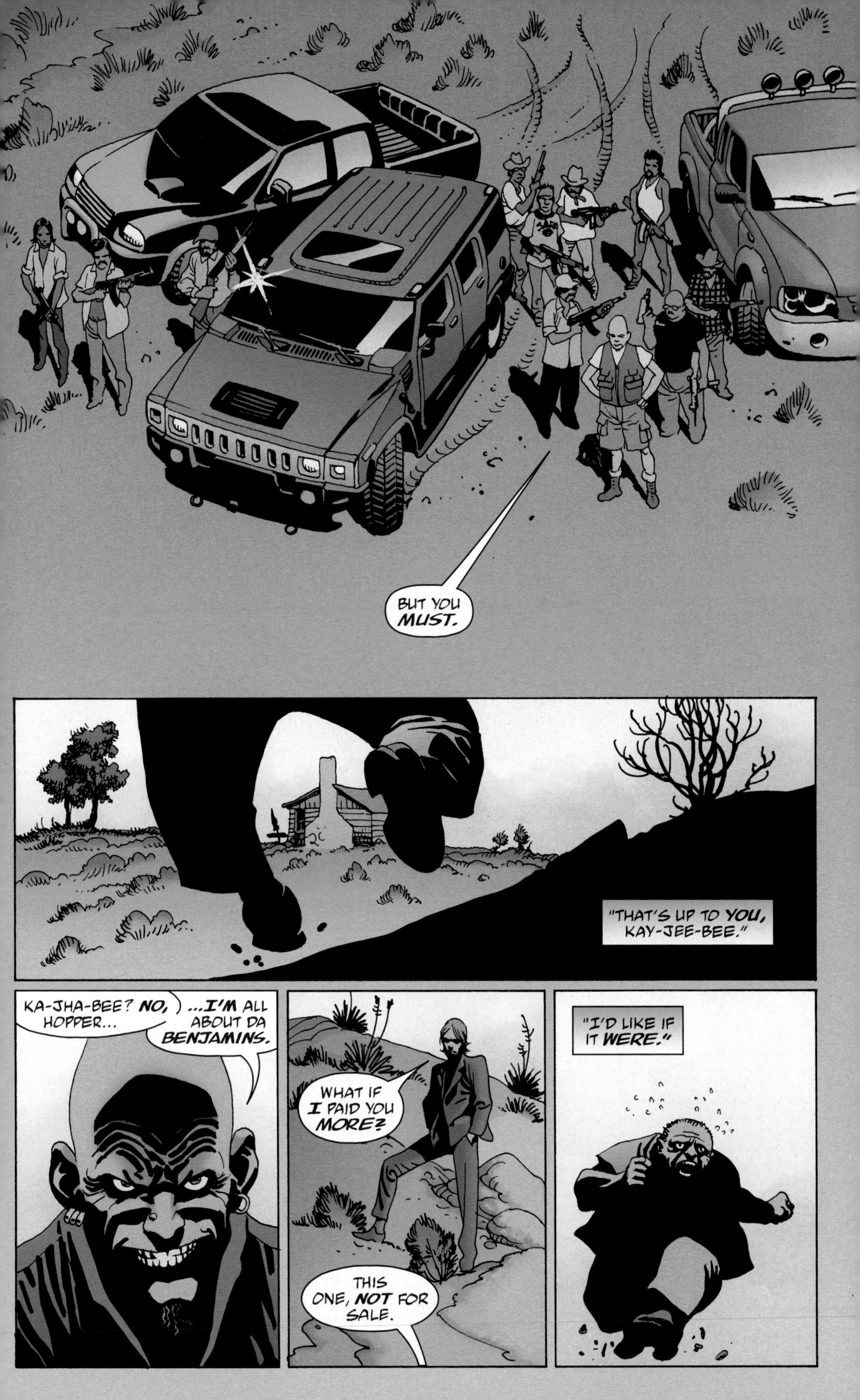
BUT YOU MUST.
"THAT'S UP TO YOU, KAY-JEE-BEE."
KA-JHA-BEE? NO, HOPPER...
...I'M ALL ABOUT DA BENJAMINS.
WHAT IF I PAID YOU MORE?
THIS ONE, NOT FOR SALE.
"I'D LIKE IF IT WERE."

THAT'S OKAY... I'M NOT SURE IF I COULD MEET YER *PRICE*.

THAT? NEGOTIATION. DIFFERENT *TIME*...

...*MR.* TIMES. SHEPHERD... HE KNEW *FINESSE.* WOULD NOT HAVE LET THIS *HAPPEN.*

I...YER RIGHT.

SHEPHERD WAS *GOOD MAN*.

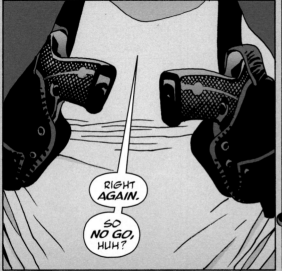

RIGHT *AGAIN*.

SO *NO GO,* HUH?

NO.

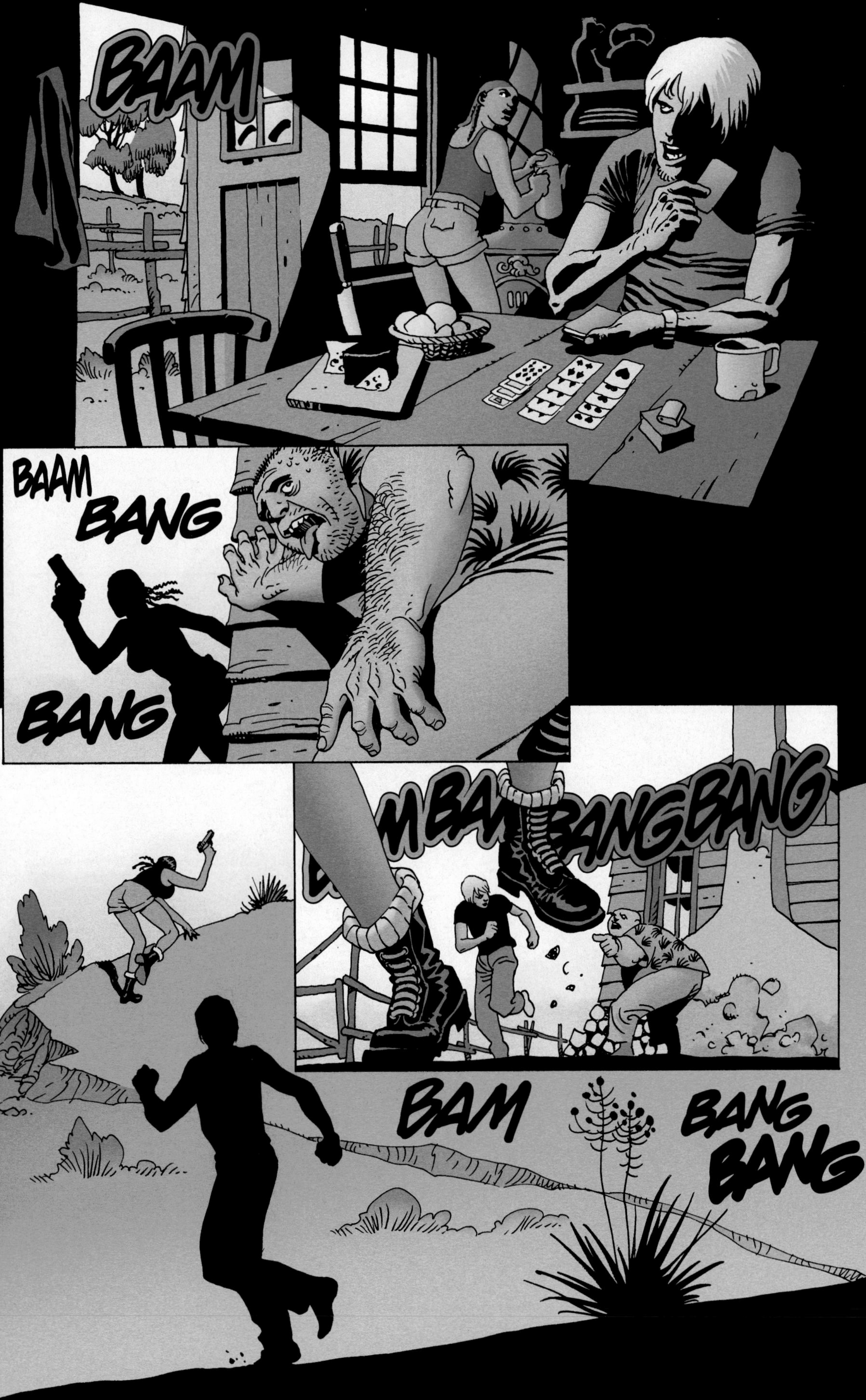
BAAM
BAAM
BANG
BANG
BANG BANG
BAM
BANG
BANG

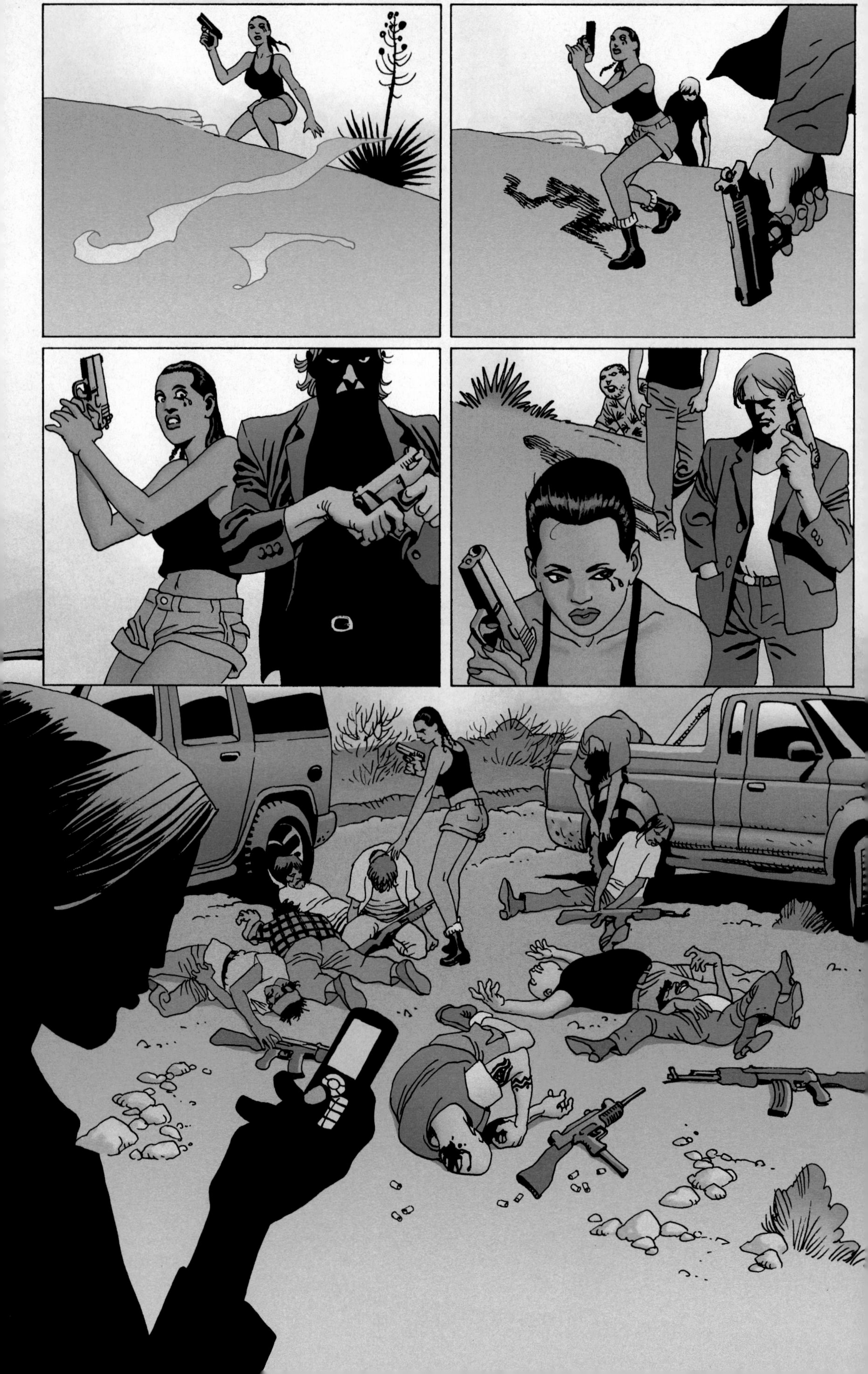

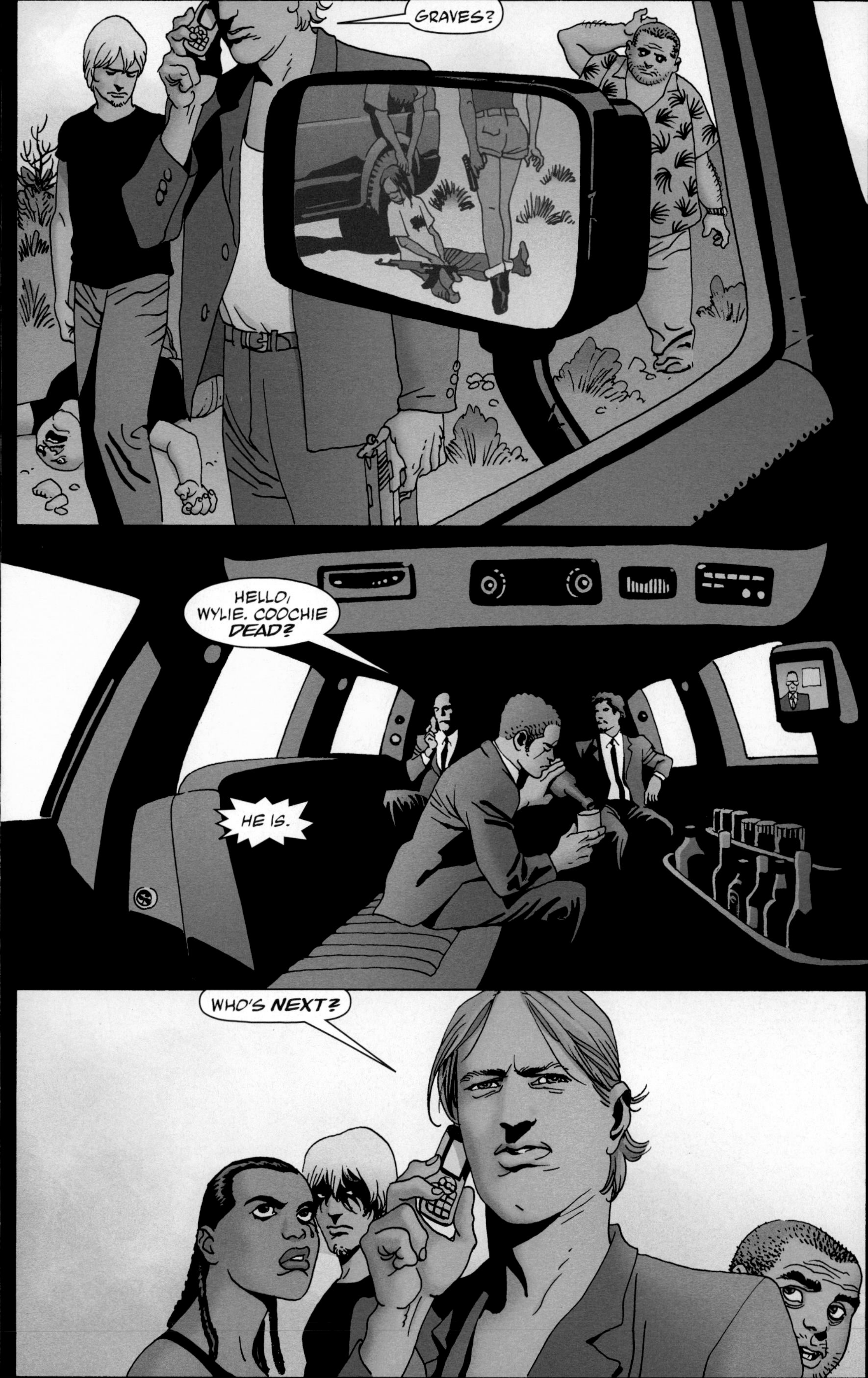
GRAVES?
HELLO, WYLIE. COOCHIE DEAD?
HE IS.
WHO'S NEXT?

"Cuatro Jinetes" Parque de Carreras d
allos
¡APUESTOS AQU
Cerveza Fria y Tac
Las Puertas
abren a las
11:00 am
JOHNSON

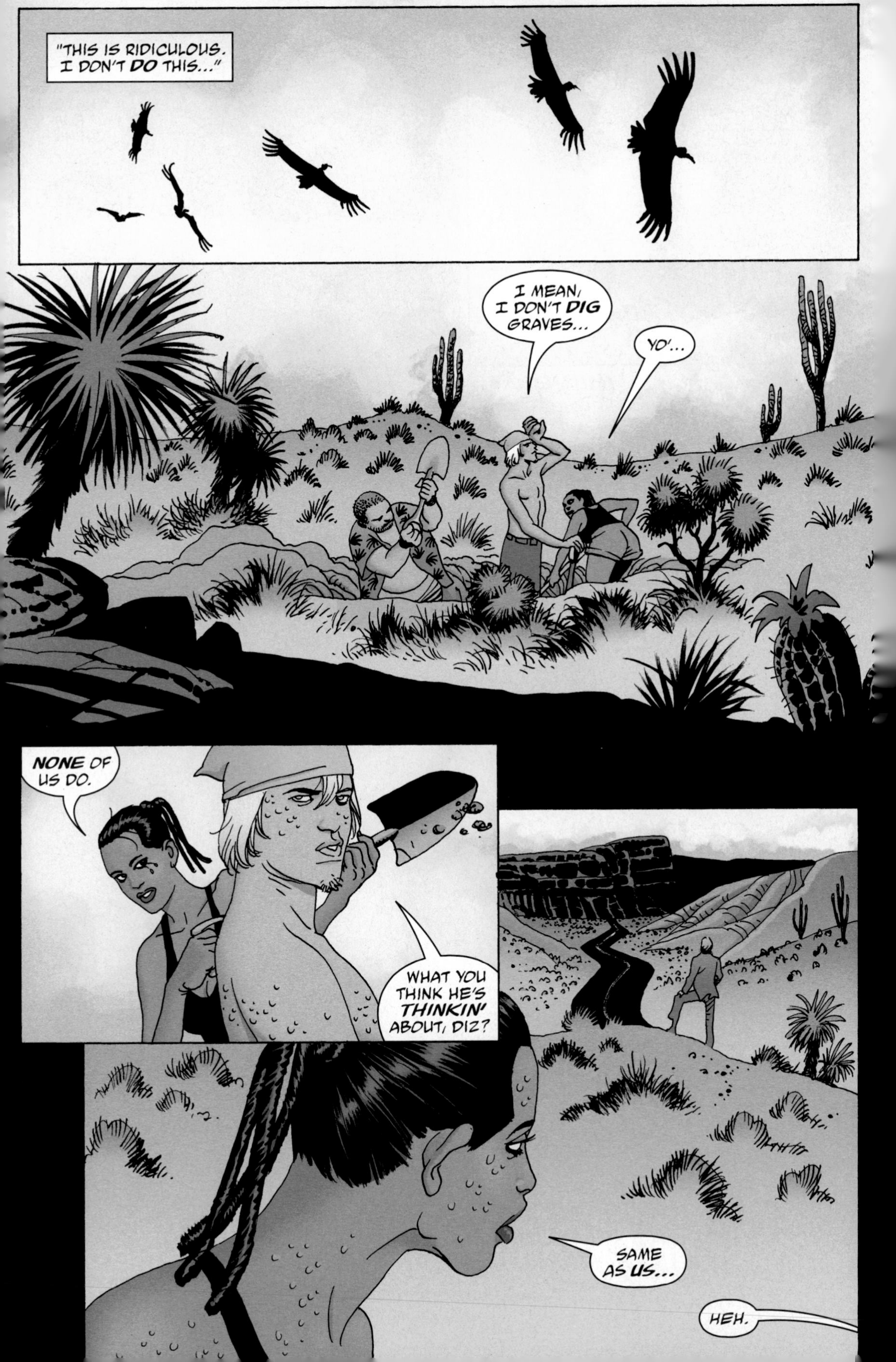
"THIS IS RIDICULOUS. I DON'T DO THIS..."
I MEAN, I DON'T DIG GRAVES...
YO'...
NONE OF US DO.
WHAT YOU THINK HE'S THINKIN' ABOUT, DIZ?
SAME AS US...
HEH.

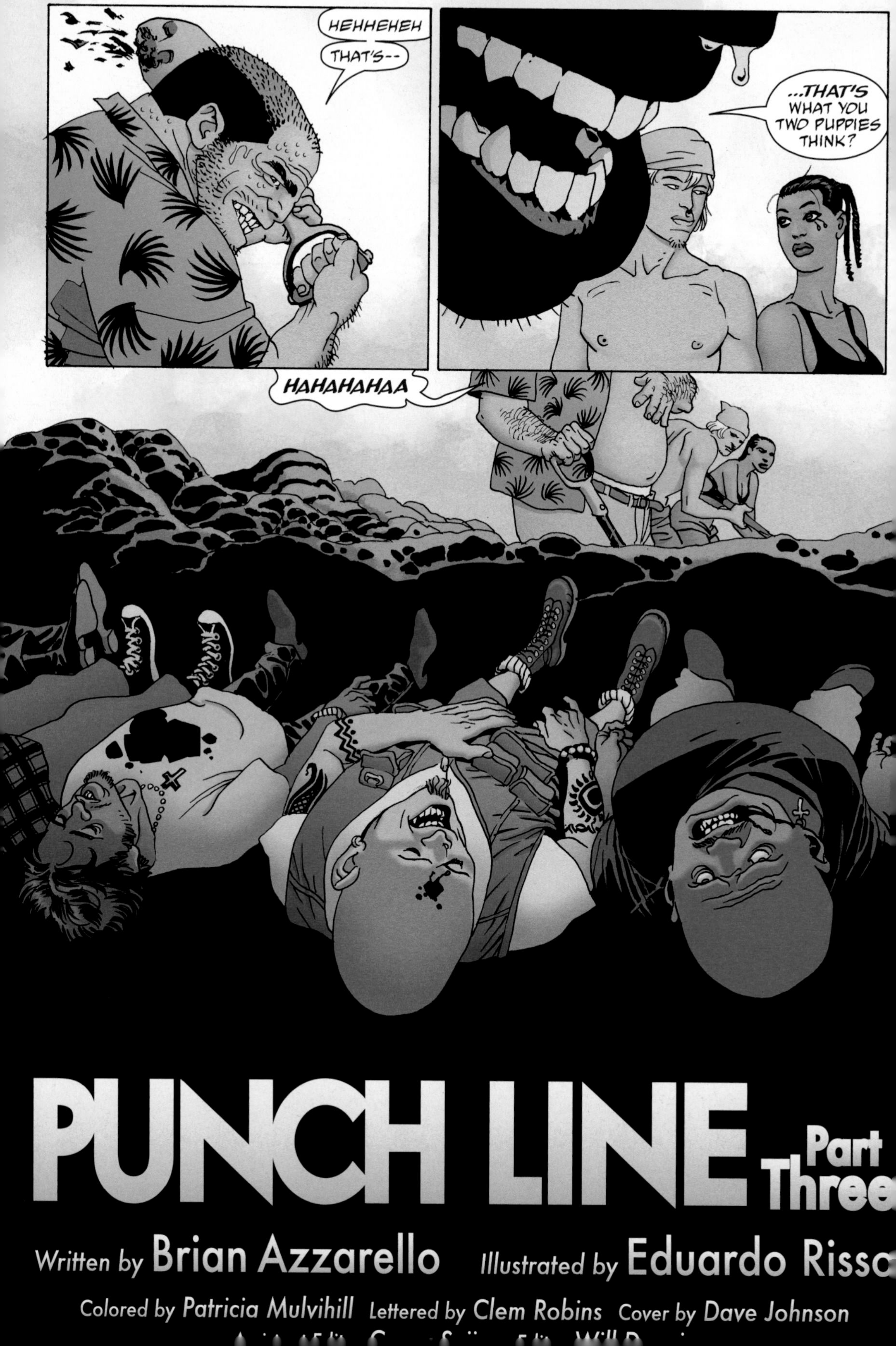
HEHHEHEH
THAT'S--
...THAT'S WHAT YOU TWO PUPPIES THINK?
HAHAHAHAA

PUNCH LINE Part Three

Written by Brian Azzarello Illustrated by Eduardo Risso

Colored by Patricia Mulvihill Lettered by Clem Robins Cover by Dave Johnson

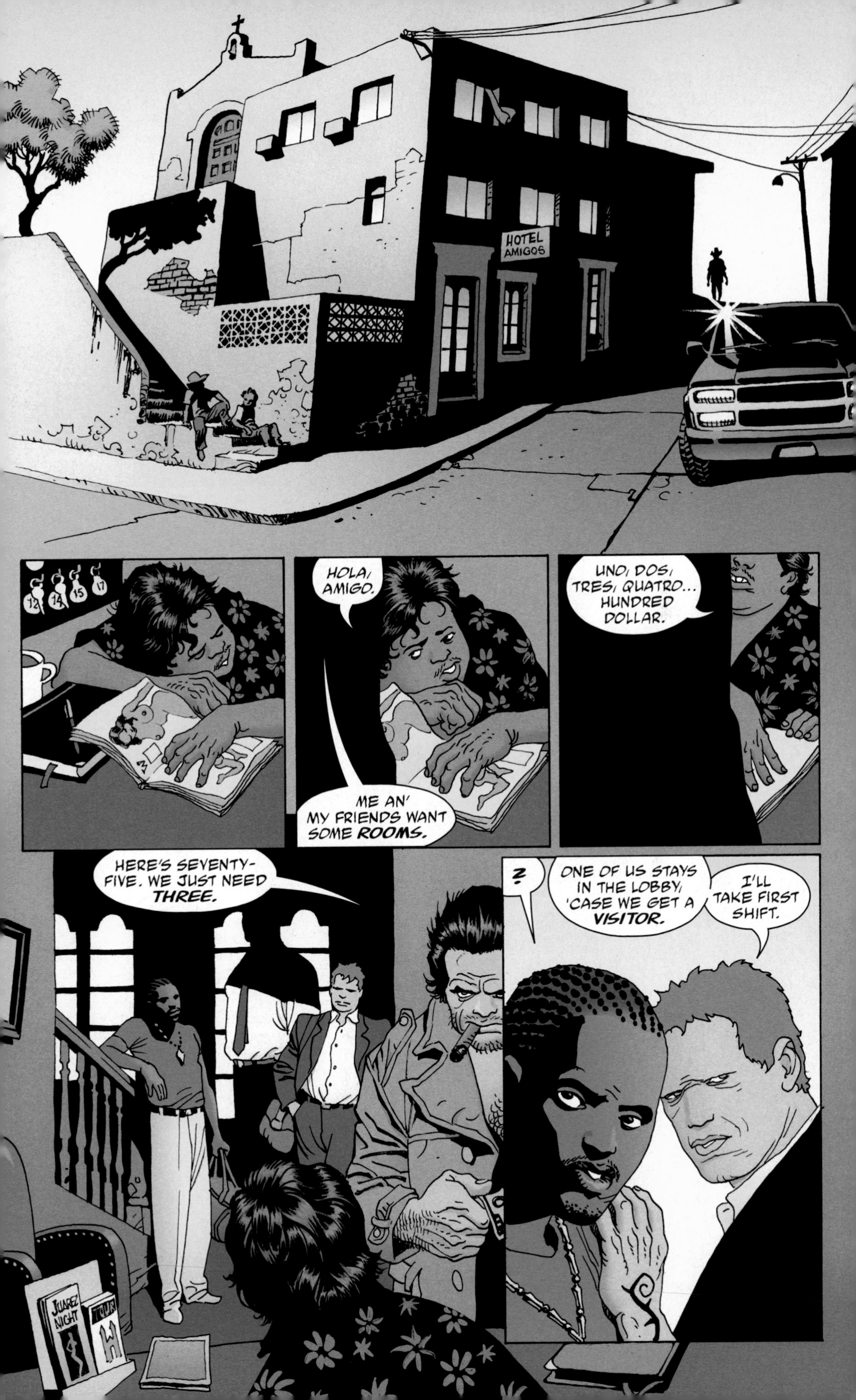
HOTEL AMIGOS
12
14
15
17
HOLA, AMIGO.
ME AN' MY FRIENDS WANT SOME **ROOMS.**
UNO, DOS, TRES, QUATRO... HUNDRED DOLLAR.
HERE'S SEVENTY-FIVE. WE JUST NEED **THREE.**
?
ONE OF US STAYS IN THE LOBBY, 'CASE WE GET A **VISITOR.**
I'LL TAKE FIRST SHIFT.
JUAREZ NIGHT
TOUR

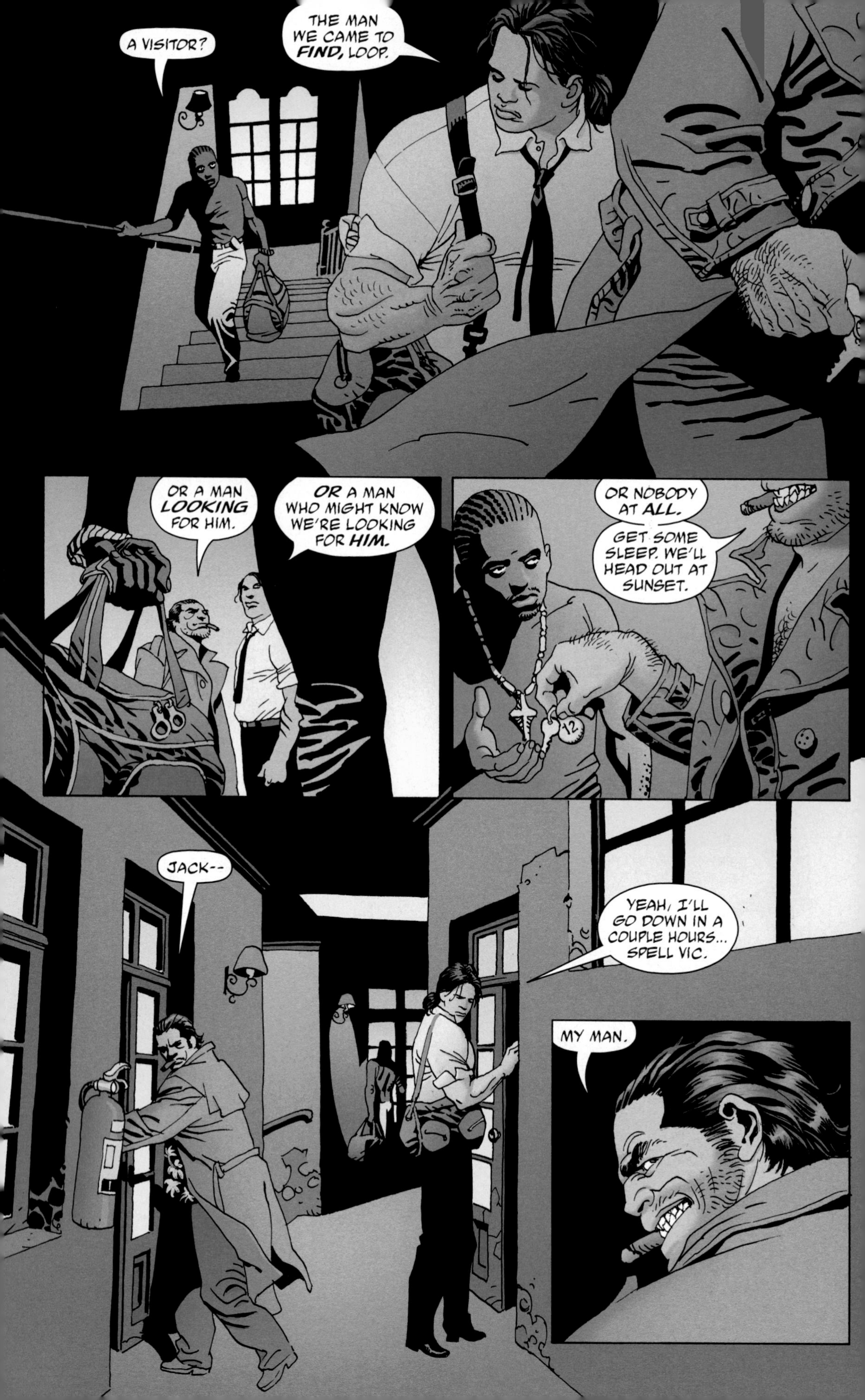
A VISITOR?
THE MAN WE CAME TO FIND, LOOP.
OR A MAN LOOKING FOR HIM.
OR A MAN WHO MIGHT KNOW WE'RE LOOKING FOR HIM.
OR NOBODY AT ALL.
GET SOME SLEEP. WE'LL HEAD OUT AT SUNSET.
12
JACK--
YEAH, I'LL GO DOWN IN A COUPLE HOURS... SPELL VIC.
MY MAN.

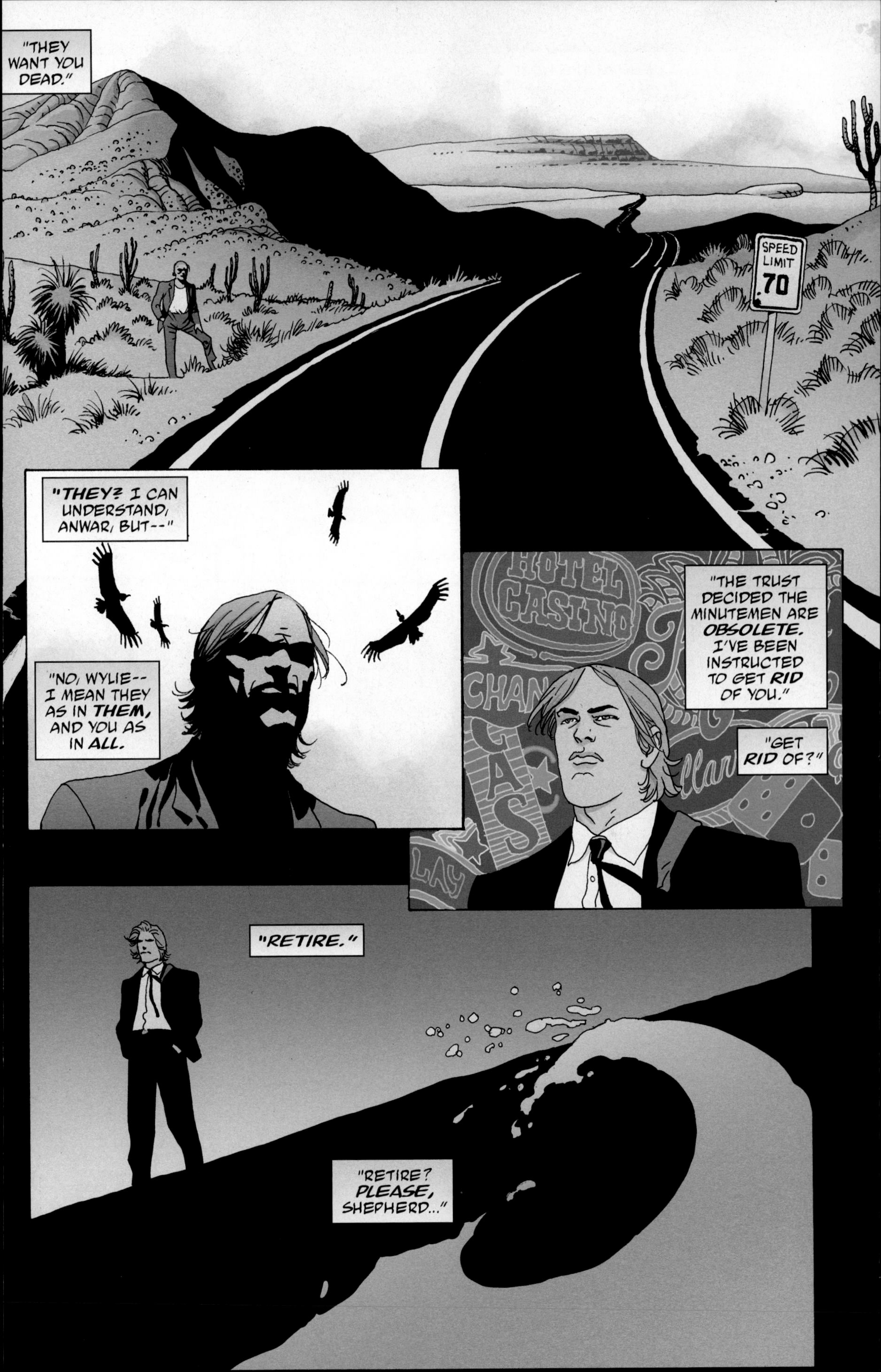
"THEY WANT YOU DEAD."
SPEED LIMIT 70
"THEY? I CAN UNDERSTAND, ANWAR, BUT--"
"NO, WYLIE-- I MEAN THEY AS IN THEM, AND YOU AS IN ALL.
HOTEL CASINO
"THE TRUST DECIDED THE MINUTEMEN ARE OBSOLETE. I'VE BEEN INSTRUCTED TO GET RID OF YOU."
"GET RID OF?"
"RETIRE."
"RETIRE? PLEASE, SHEPHERD..."

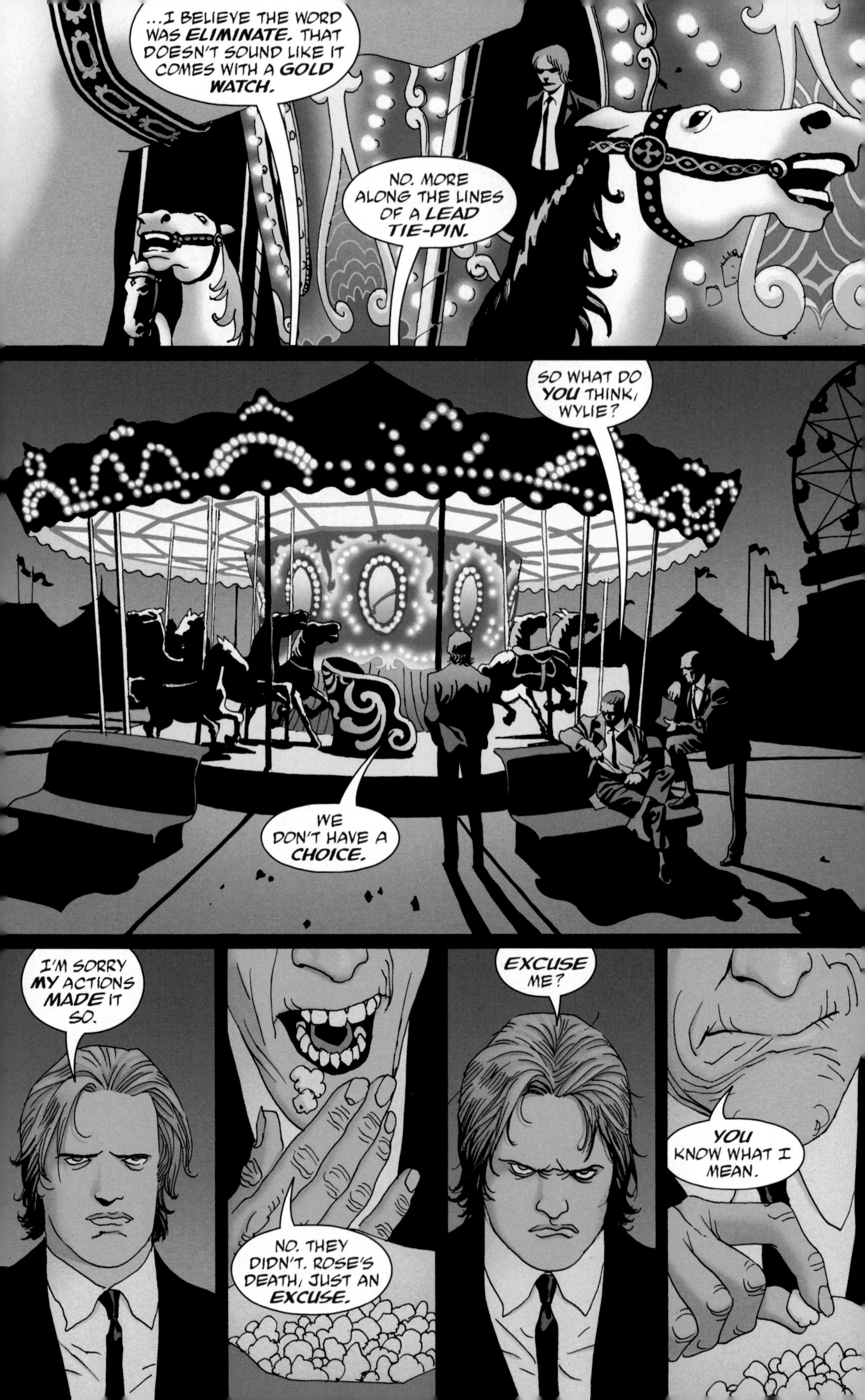
...I BELIEVE THE WORD WAS ELIMINATE. THAT DOESN'T SOUND LIKE IT COMES WITH A GOLD WATCH.
NO. MORE ALONG THE LINES OF A LEAD TIE-PIN.
SO WHAT DO YOU THINK, WYLIE?
WE DON'T HAVE A CHOICE.
I'M SORRY MY ACTIONS MADE IT SO.
NO. THEY DIDN'T. ROSE'S DEATH, JUST AN EXCUSE.
EXCUSE ME?
YOU KNOW WHAT I MEAN.

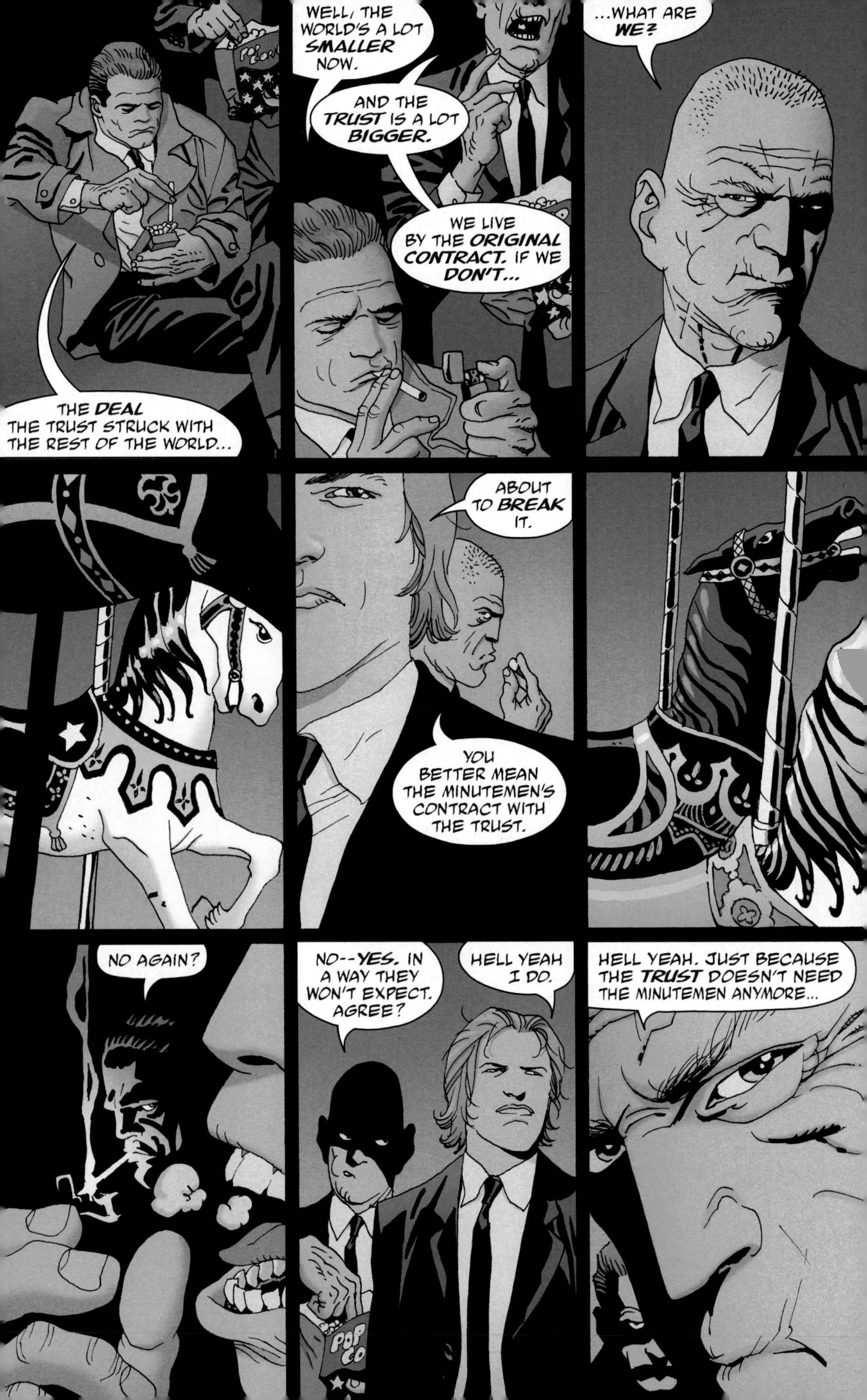
THE DEAL THE TRUST STRUCK WITH THE REST OF THE WORLD...
WELL, THE WORLD'S A LOT SMALLER NOW.
AND THE TRUST IS A LOT BIGGER.
WE LIVE BY THE ORIGINAL CONTRACT. IF WE DON'T...
...WHAT ARE WE?
ABOUT TO BREAK IT.
YOU BETTER MEAN THE MINUTEMEN'S CONTRACT WITH THE TRUST.
NO AGAIN?
NO--YES. IN A WAY THEY WON'T EXPECT. AGREE?
HELL YEAH I DO.
HELL YEAH. JUST BECAUSE THE TRUST DOESN'T NEED THE MINUTEMEN ANYMORE...

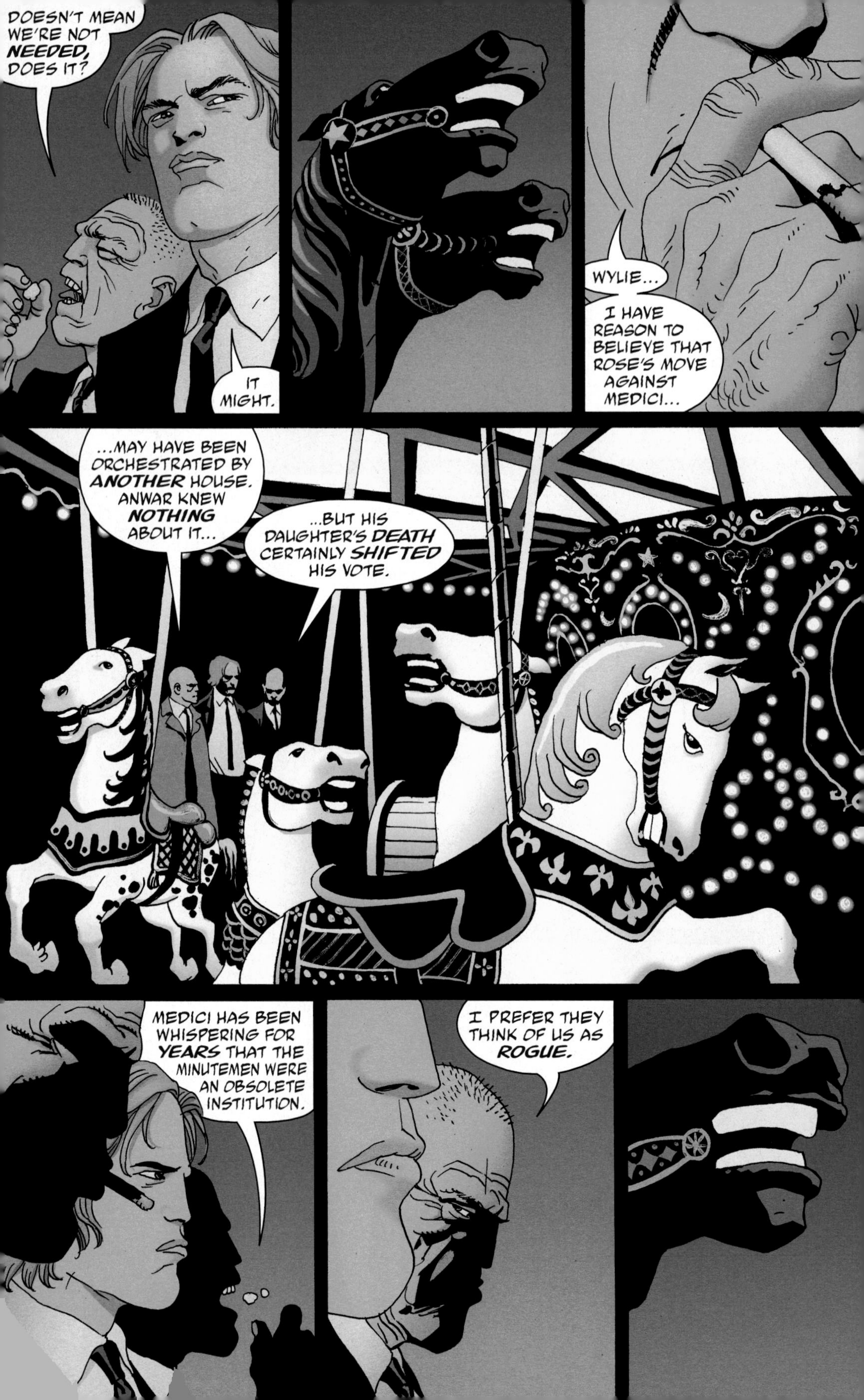
DOESN'T MEAN WE'RE NOT **NEEDED,** DOES IT?
IT MIGHT.
WYLIE...
I HAVE REASON TO BELIEVE THAT ROSE'S MOVE AGAINST MEDICI...
...MAY HAVE BEEN ORCHESTRATED BY **ANOTHER** HOUSE. ANWAR KNEW **NOTHING** ABOUT IT...
...BUT HIS DAUGHTER'S **DEATH** CERTAINLY **SHIFTED** HIS VOTE.
MEDICI HAS BEEN WHISPERING FOR **YEARS** THAT THE MINUTEMEN WERE AN OBSOLETE INSTITUTION.
I PREFER THEY THINK OF US AS **ROGUE.**

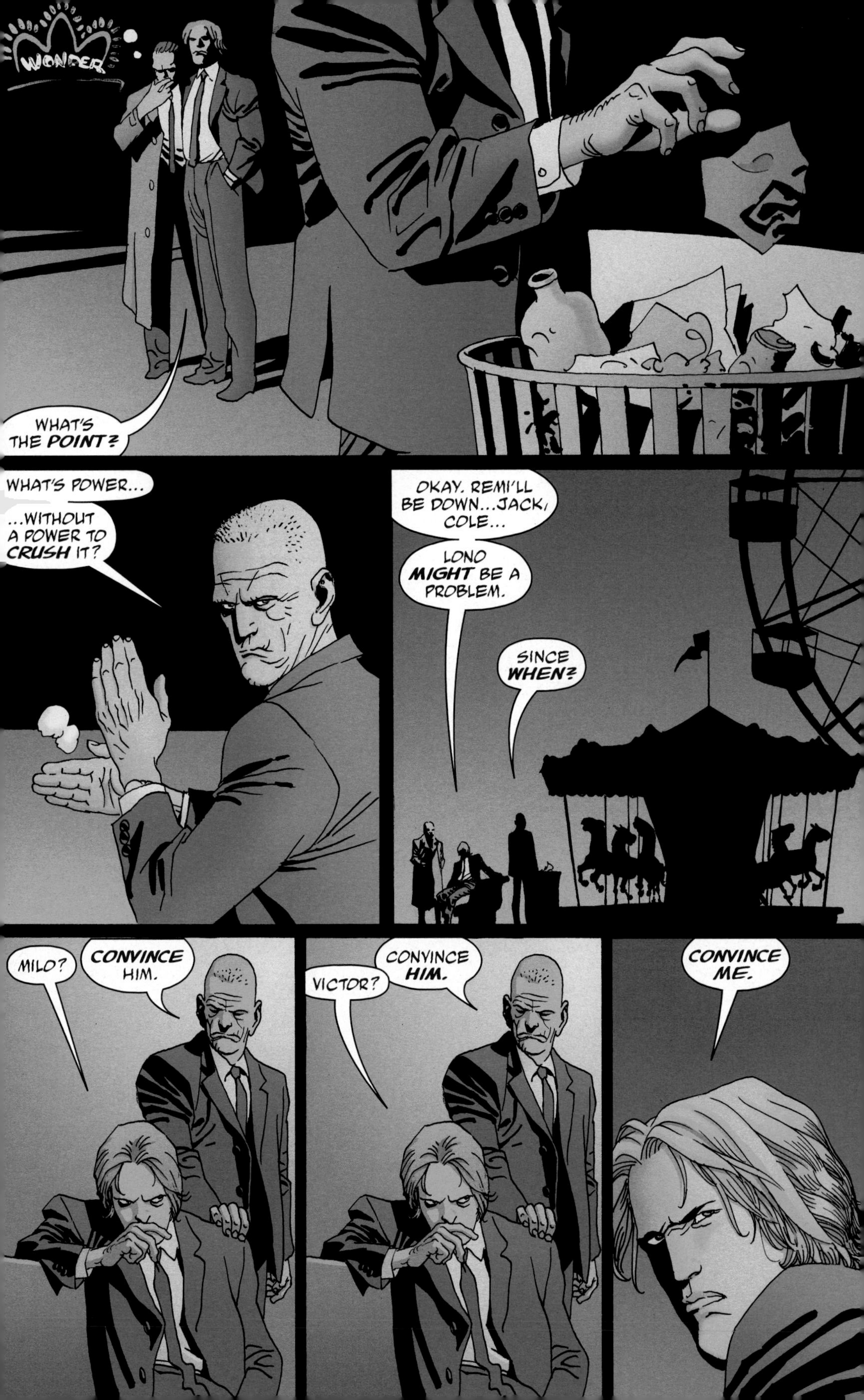
WONDER
WHAT'S THE POINT?
WHAT'S POWER...
...WITHOUT A POWER TO CRUSH IT?
OKAY. REMI'LL BE DOWN...JACK, COLE...
LONO MIGHT BE A PROBLEM.
SINCE WHEN?
MILO?
CONVINCE HIM.
VICTOR?
CONVINCE HIM.
CONVINCE ME.

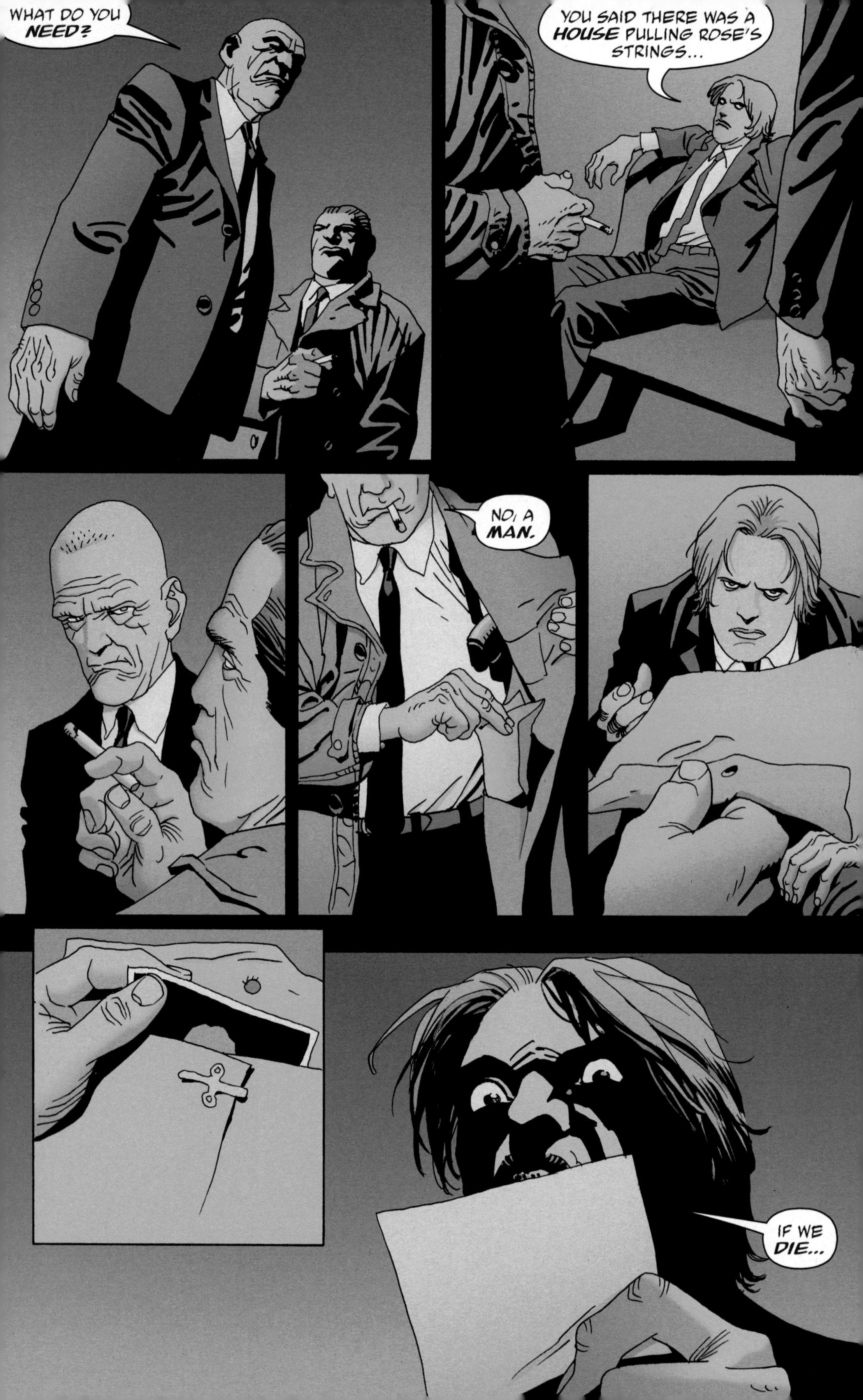
WHAT DO YOU NEED?
YOU SAID THERE WAS A HOUSE PULLING ROSE'S STRINGS...
NO, A MAN.
IF WE DIE...

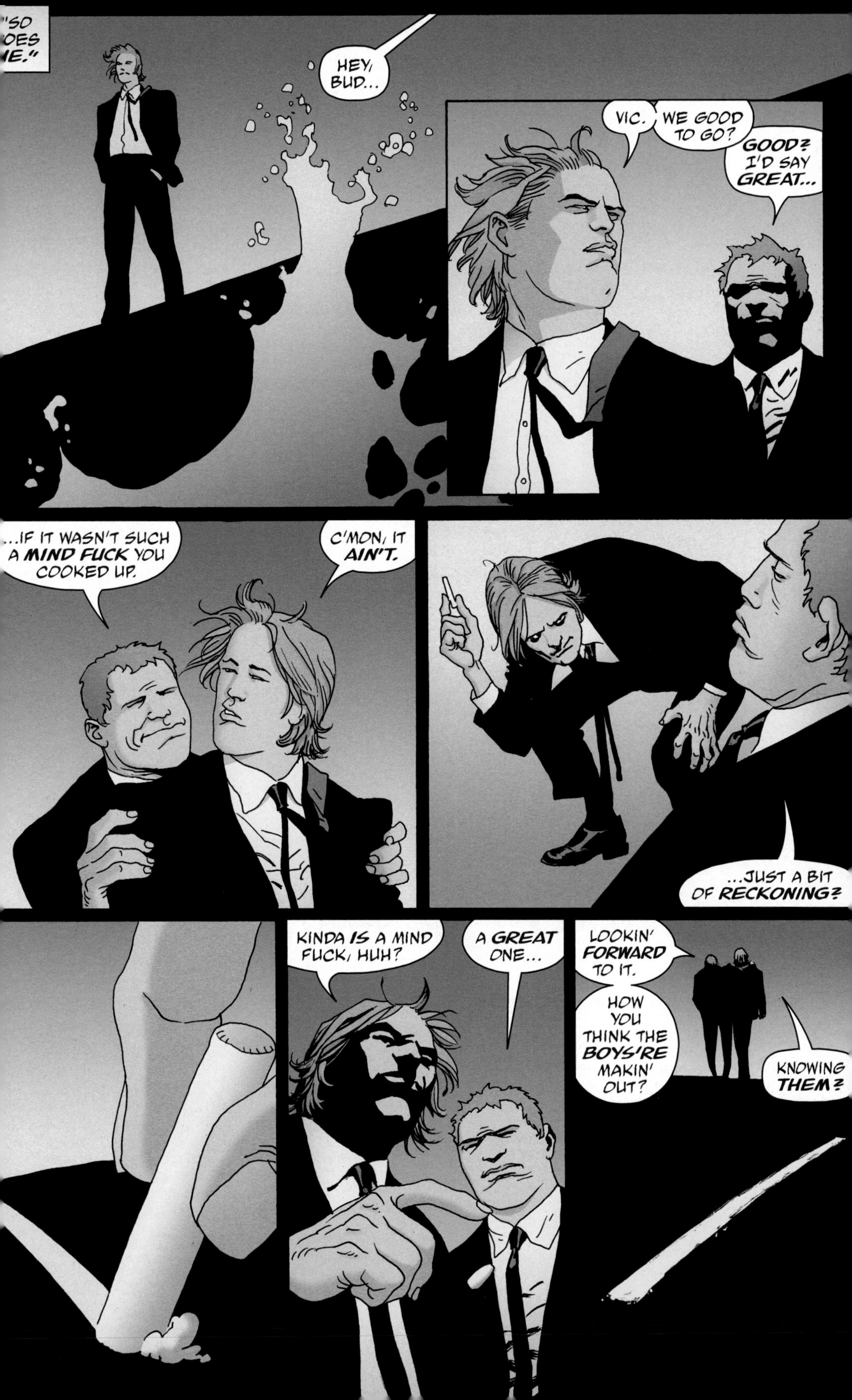
"SO
OES
IE."
HEY, BUD...
VIC.
WE GOOD TO GO?
GOOD? I'D SAY GREAT...
...IF IT WASN'T SUCH A MIND FUCK YOU COOKED UP.
C'MON, IT AIN'T.
...JUST A BIT OF RECKONING?
KINDA IS A MIND FUCK, HUH?
A GREAT ONE...
LOOKIN' FORWARD TO IT.
HOW YOU THINK THE BOYS'RE MAKIN' OUT?
KNOWING THEM?

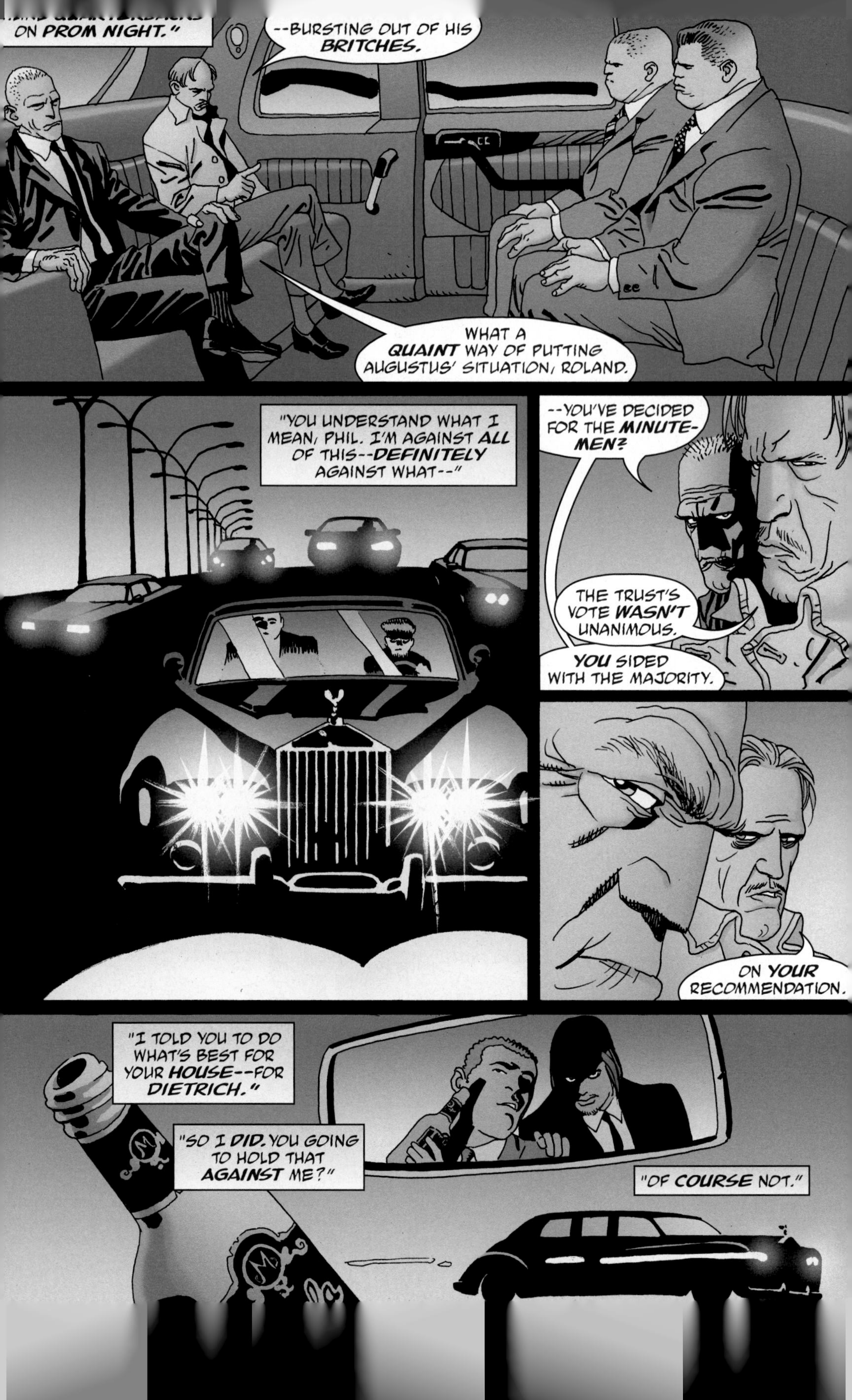

"...AND QUARTERBACKS ON PROM NIGHT."
--BURSTING OUT OF HIS BRITCHES.
WHAT A QUAINT WAY OF PUTTING AUGUSTUS' SITUATION, ROLAND.
"YOU UNDERSTAND WHAT I MEAN, PHIL. I'M AGAINST ALL OF THIS--DEFINITELY AGAINST WHAT--"
--YOU'VE DECIDED FOR THE MINUTE-MEN?
THE TRUST'S VOTE WASN'T UNANIMOUS.
YOU SIDED WITH THE MAJORITY.
ON YOUR RECOMMENDATION.
"I TOLD YOU TO DO WHAT'S BEST FOR YOUR HOUSE--FOR DIETRICH."
"SO I DID. YOU GOING TO HOLD THAT AGAINST ME?"
"OF COURSE NOT."

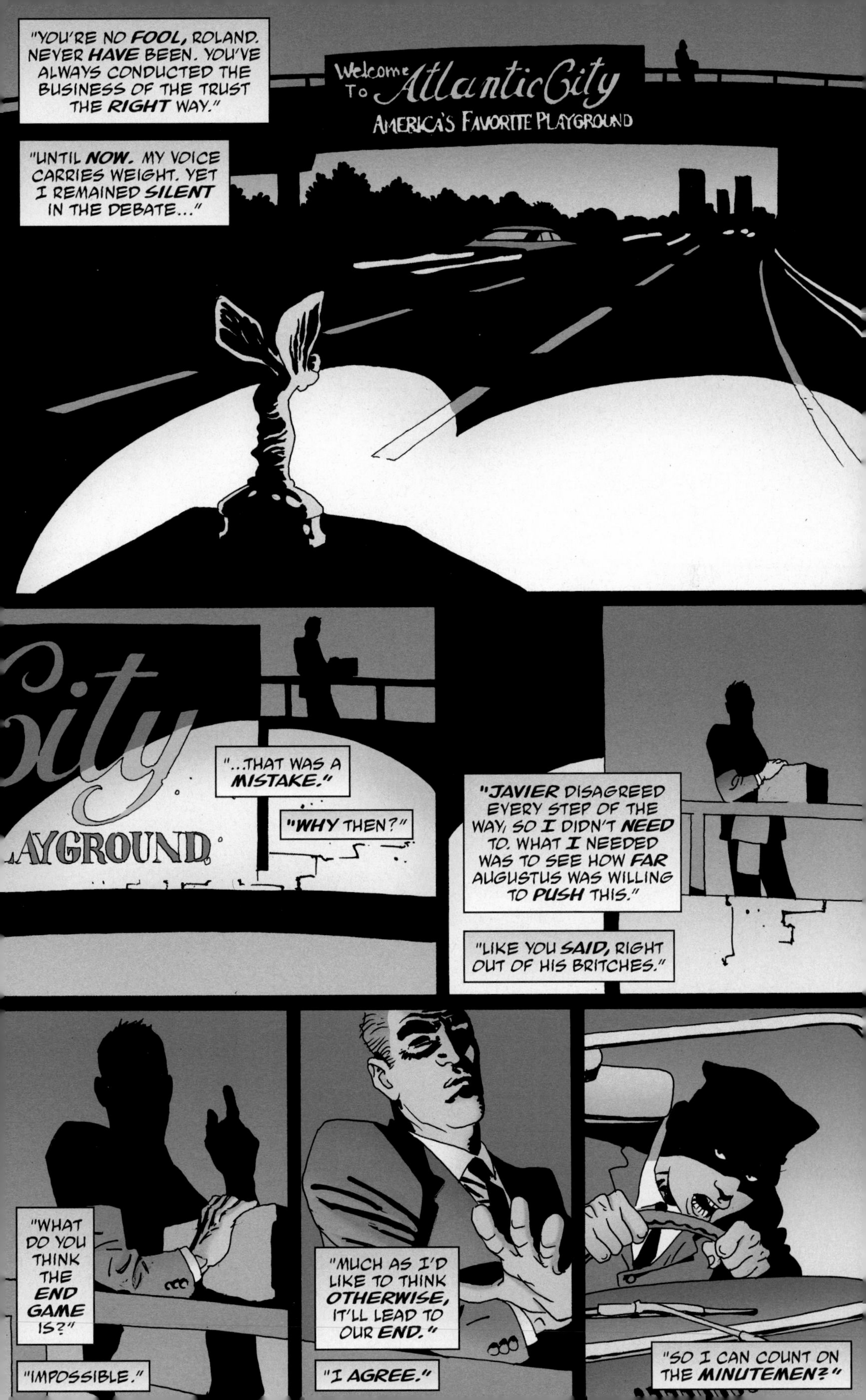
"YOU'RE NO FOOL, ROLAND. NEVER HAVE BEEN. YOU'VE ALWAYS CONDUCTED THE BUSINESS OF THE TRUST THE RIGHT WAY."
Welcome To Atlantic City
AMERICA'S FAVORITE PLAYGROUND
"UNTIL NOW. MY VOICE CARRIES WEIGHT. YET I REMAINED SILENT IN THE DEBATE..."
"...THAT WAS A MISTAKE."
"WHY THEN?"
"JAVIER DISAGREED EVERY STEP OF THE WAY, SO I DIDN'T NEED TO. WHAT I NEEDED WAS TO SEE HOW FAR AUGUSTUS WAS WILLING TO PUSH THIS."
"LIKE YOU SAID, RIGHT OUT OF HIS BRITCHES."
"WHAT DO YOU THINK THE END GAME IS?"
"IMPOSSIBLE."
"MUCH AS I'D LIKE TO THINK OTHERWISE, IT'LL LEAD TO OUR END."
"I AGREE."
"SO I CAN COUNT ON THE MINUTEMEN?"

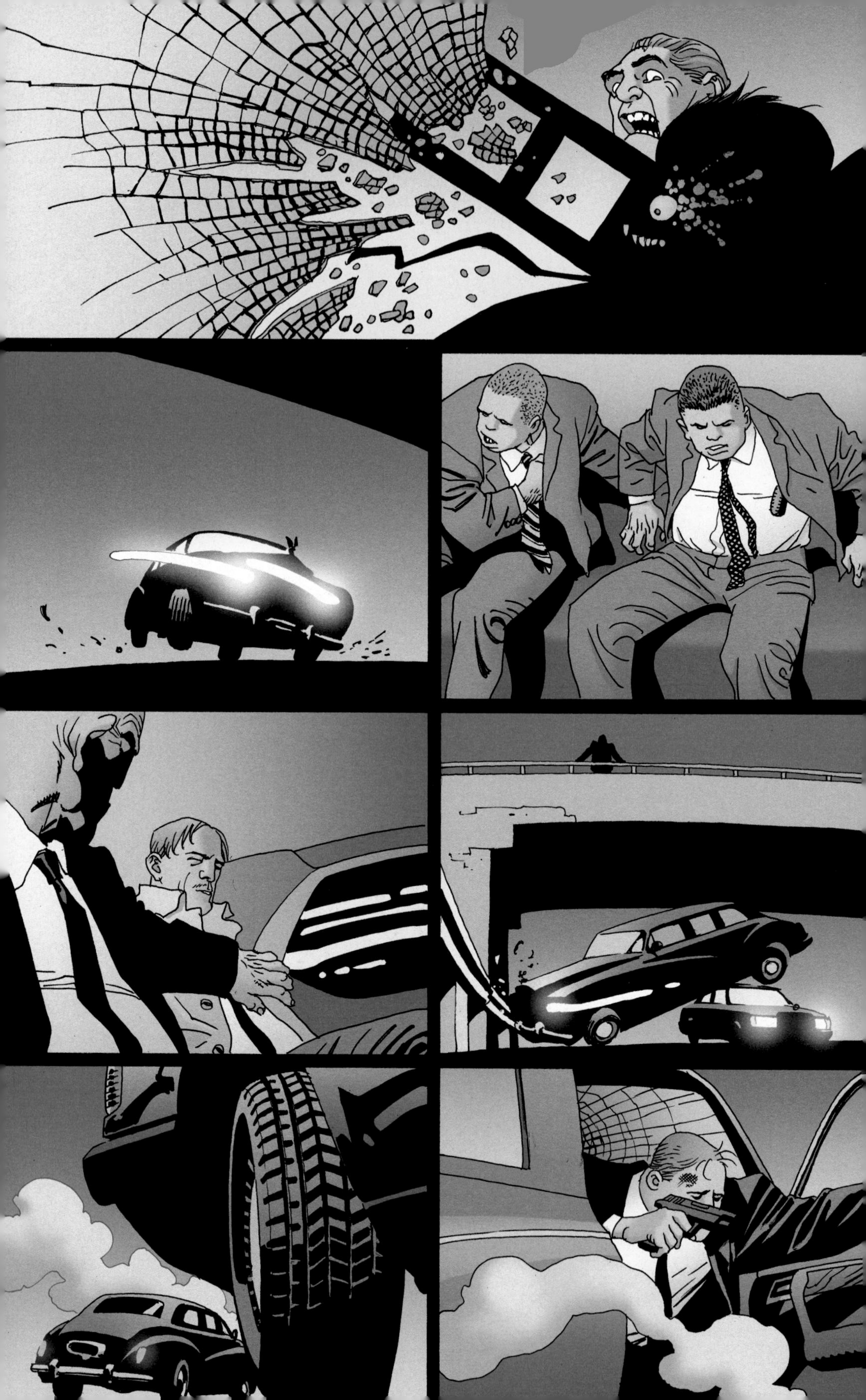

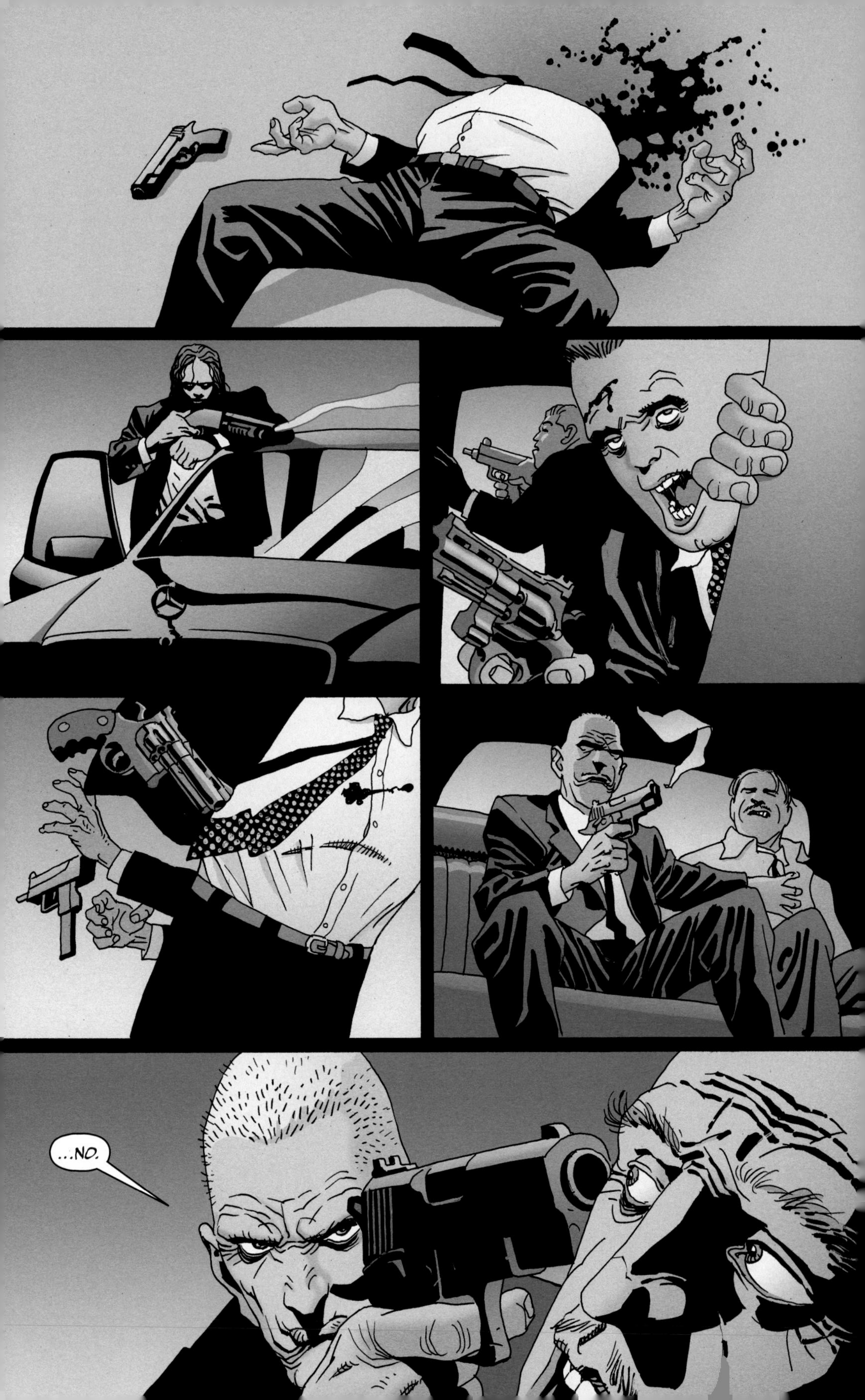
...NO.

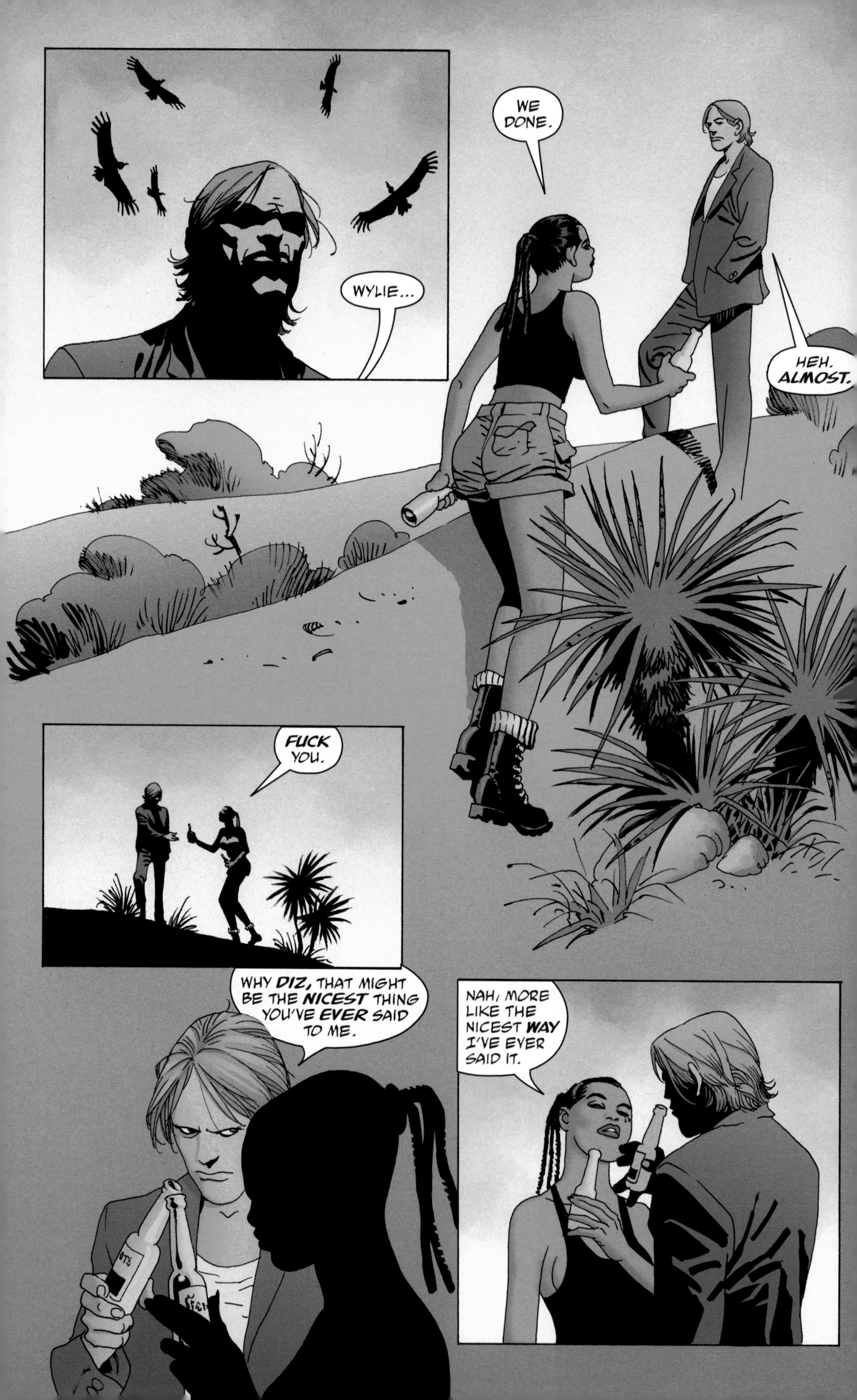
WYLIE...
WE DONE.
HEH. ALMOST.
FUCK YOU.
WHY DIZ, THAT MIGHT BE THE NICEST THING YOU'VE EVER SAID TO ME.
NAH, MORE LIKE THE NICEST WAY I'VE EVER SAID IT.

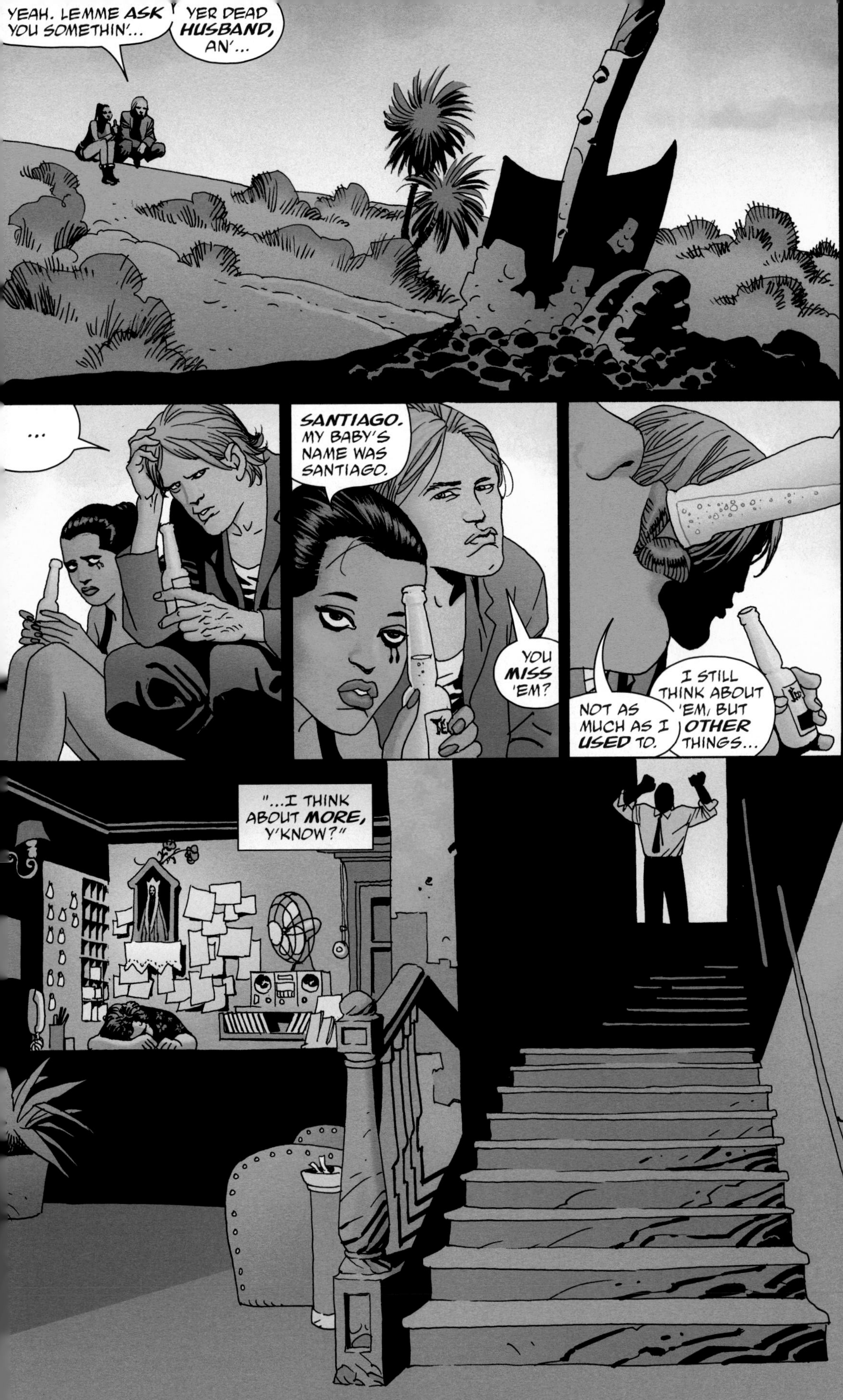
YEAH. LEMME ASK YOU SOMETHIN'...
YER DEAD HUSBAND, AN'...
...
SANTIAGO. MY BABY'S NAME WAS SANTIAGO.
YOU MISS 'EM?
NOT AS MUCH AS I USED TO.
I STILL THINK ABOUT 'EM, BUT OTHER THINGS...
"...I THINK ABOUT MORE, Y'KNOW?"

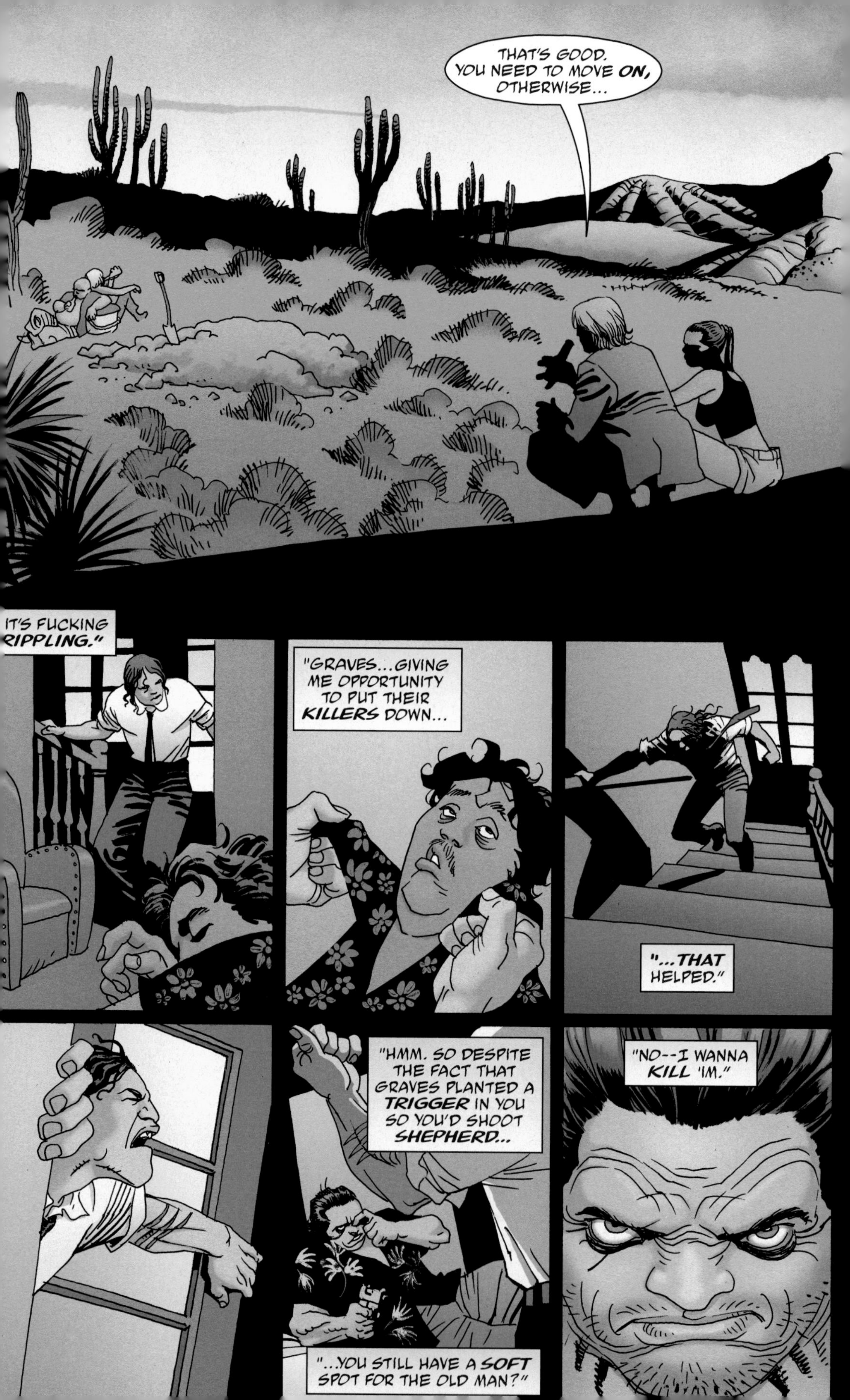
THAT'S GOOD. YOU NEED TO MOVE ON, OTHERWISE...
IT'S FUCKING CRIPPLING."
"GRAVES... GIVING ME OPPORTUNITY TO PUT THEIR KILLERS DOWN...
"...THAT HELPED."
"HMM. SO DESPITE THE FACT THAT GRAVES PLANTED A TRIGGER IN YOU SO YOU'D SHOOT SHEPHERD...
"...YOU STILL HAVE A SOFT SPOT FOR THE OLD MAN?"
"NO--I WANNA KILL 'IM."

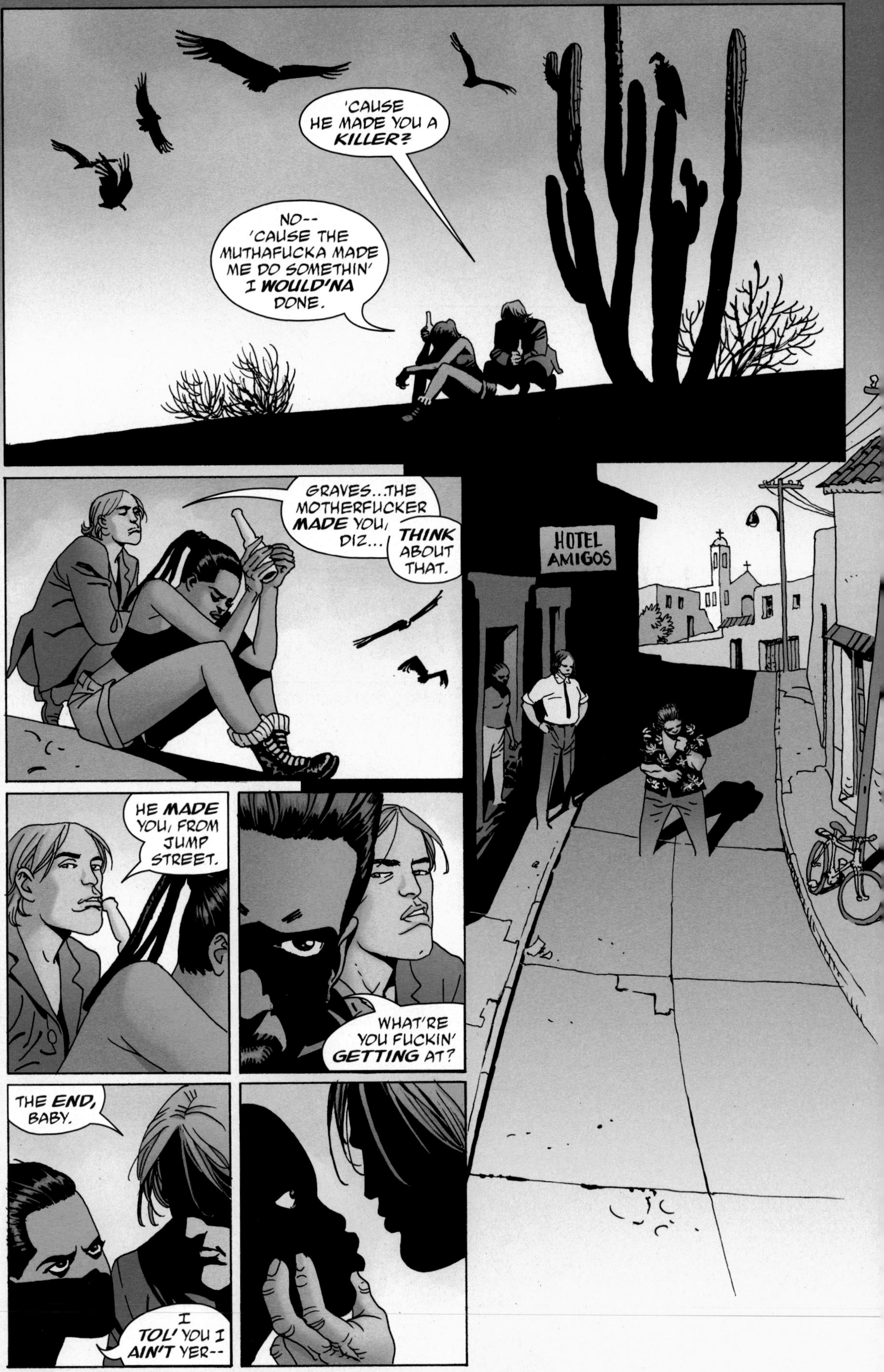
'CAUSE HE MADE YOU A KILLER?
NO-- 'CAUSE THE MUTHAFUCKA MADE ME DO SOMETHIN' I WOULD'NA DONE.
GRAVES...THE MOTHERFUCKER MADE YOU, DIZ...
THINK ABOUT THAT.
HOTEL AMIGOS
HE MADE YOU, FROM JUMP STREET.
WHAT'RE YOU FUCKIN' GETTING AT?
THE END, BABY.
I TOL' YOU I AIN'T YER--

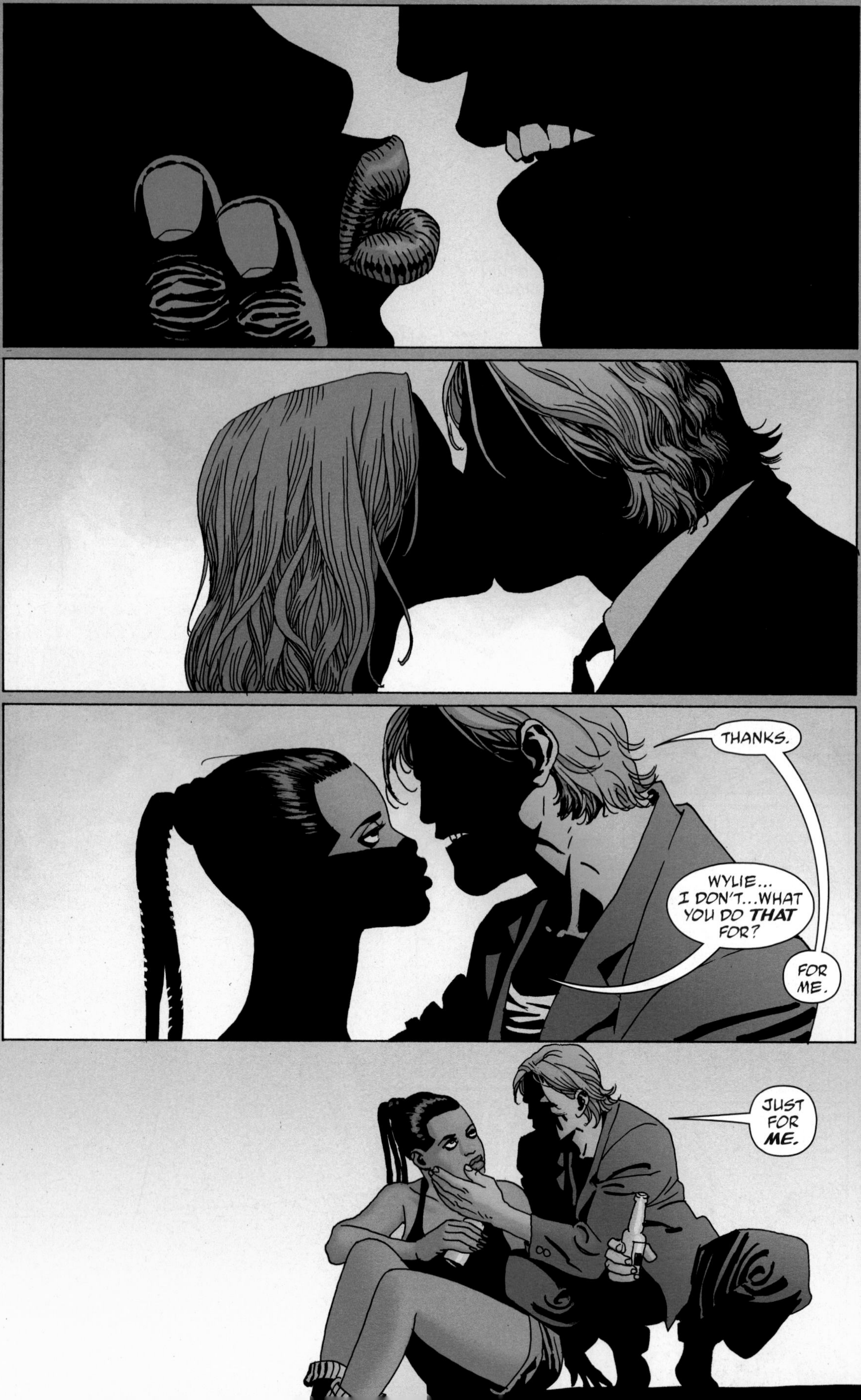
THANKS.
WYLIE... I DON'T...WHAT YOU DO THAT FOR?
FOR ME.
JUST FOR ME.

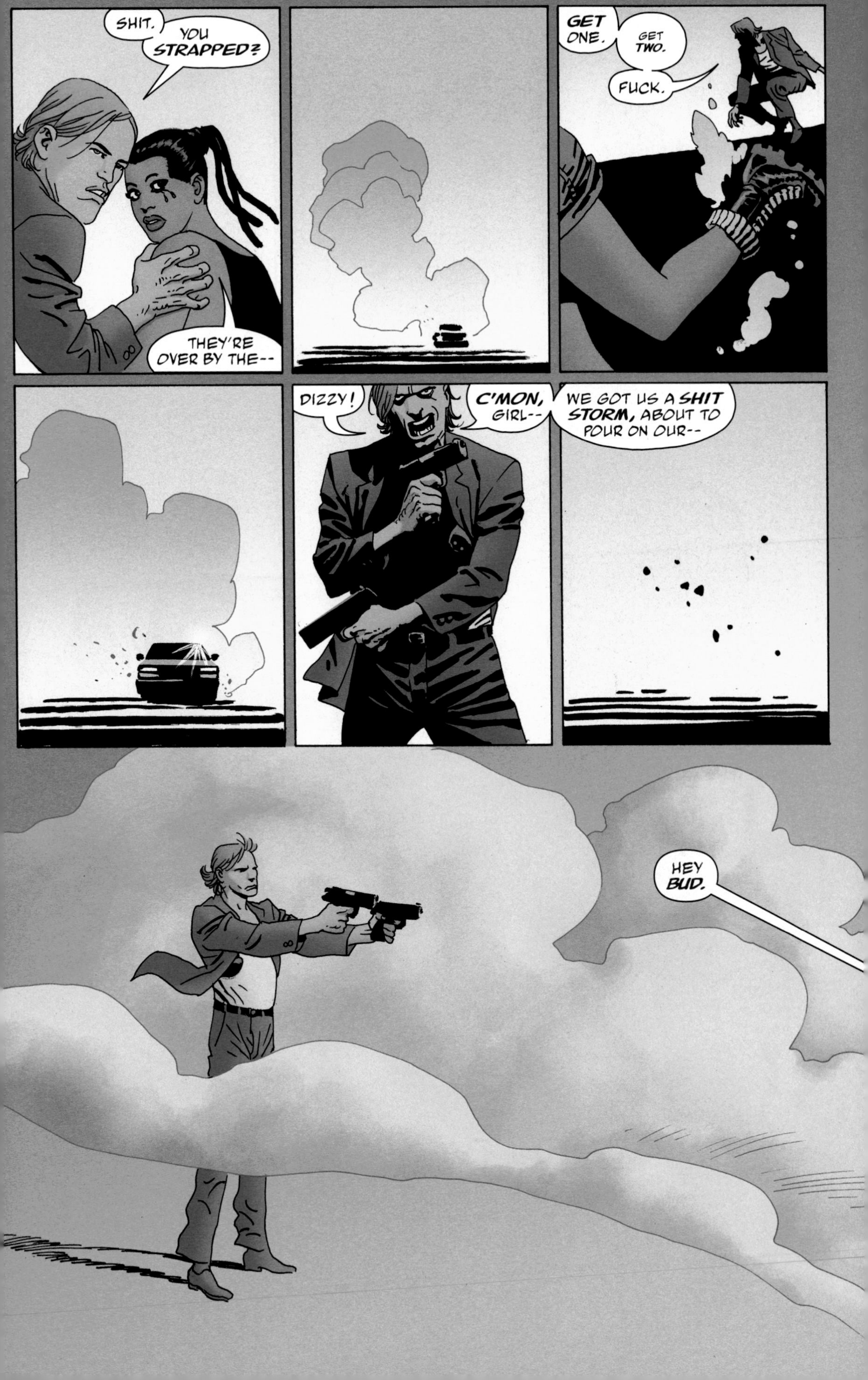
SHIT.
YOU STRAPPED?
THEY'RE OVER BY THE--
GET ONE.
GET TWO.
FUCK.
DIZZY!
C'MON, GIRL--
WE GOT US A SHIT STORM, ABOUT TO POUR ON OUR--
HEY BUD.

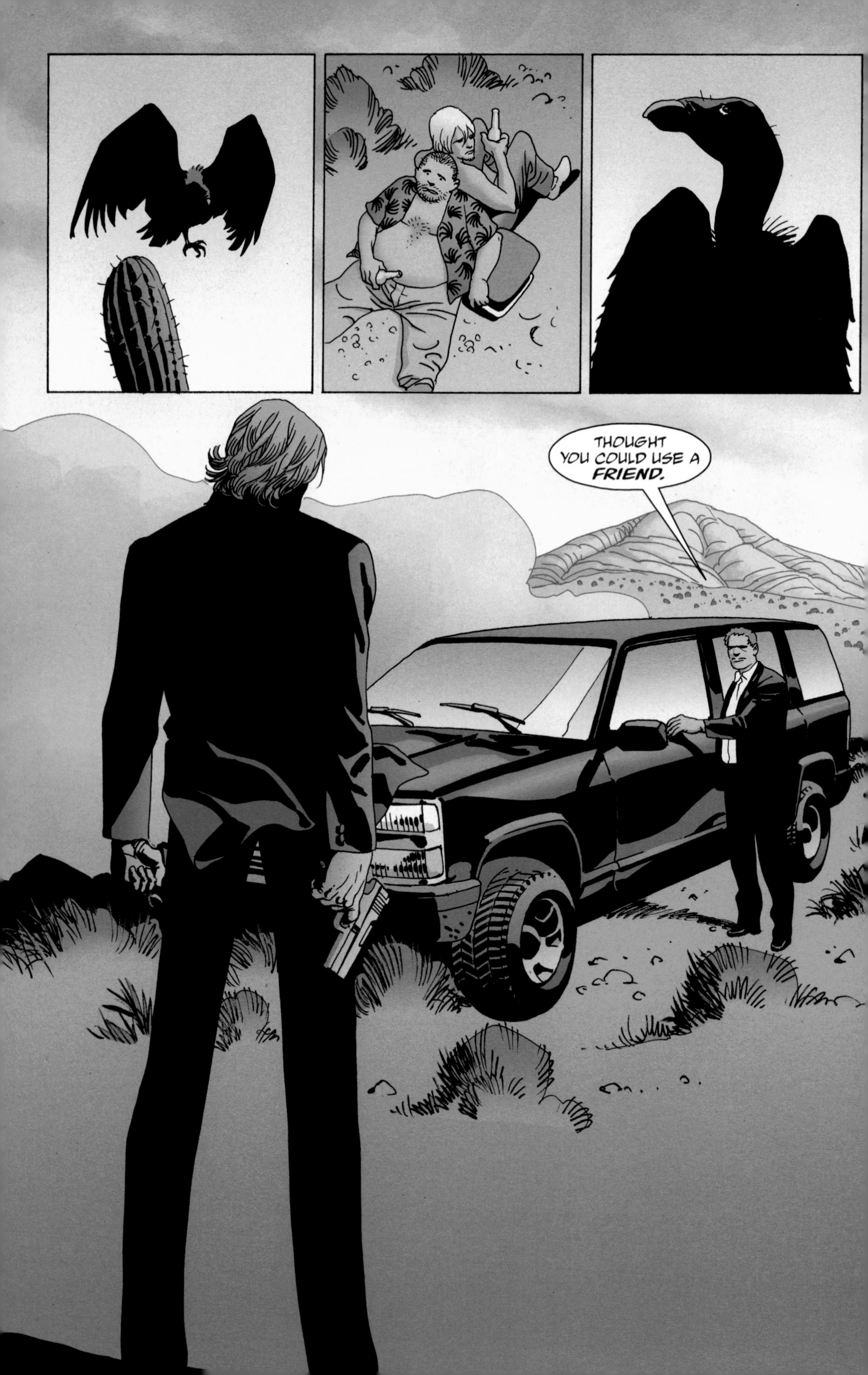
THOUGHT YOU COULD USE A *FRIEND.*

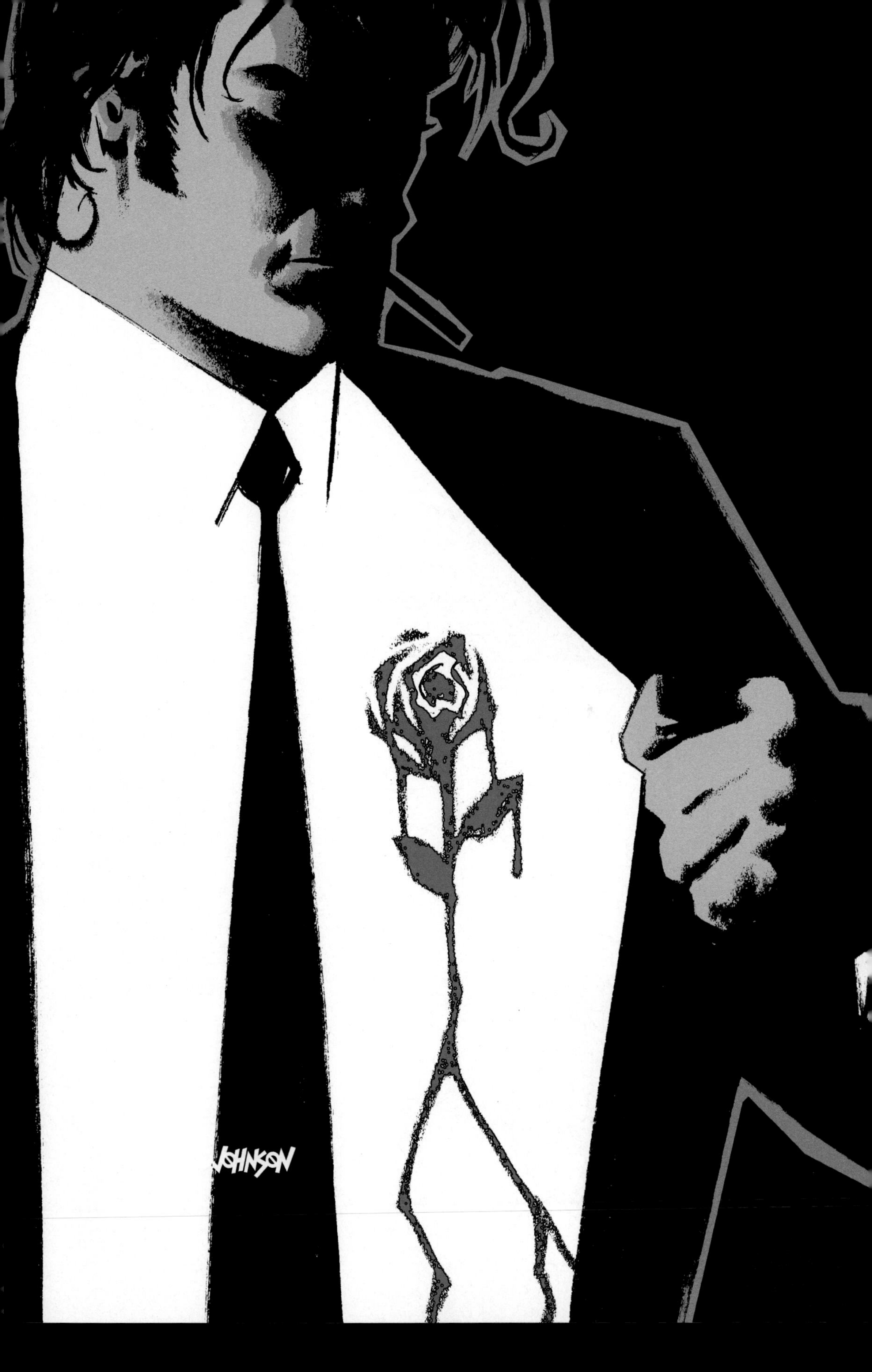
JOHNSON

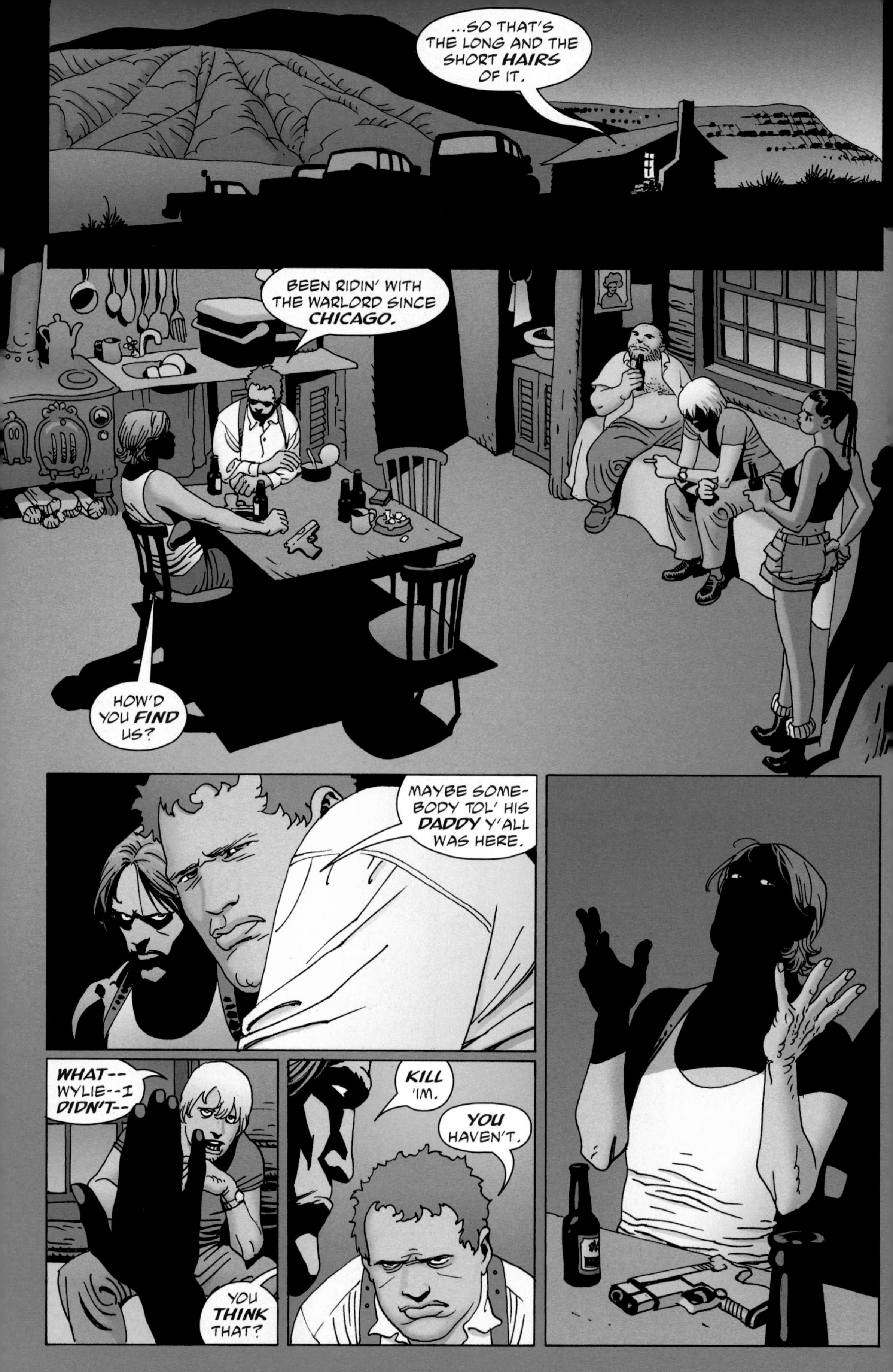
...SO THAT'S THE LONG AND THE SHORT HAIRS OF IT.
BEEN RIDIN' WITH THE WARLORD SINCE CHICAGO.
HOW'D YOU FIND US?
MAYBE SOME-BODY TOL' HIS DADDY Y'ALL WAS HERE.
WHAT-- WYLIE--I DIDN'T--
YOU THINK THAT?
KILL 'IM.
YOU HAVEN'T.

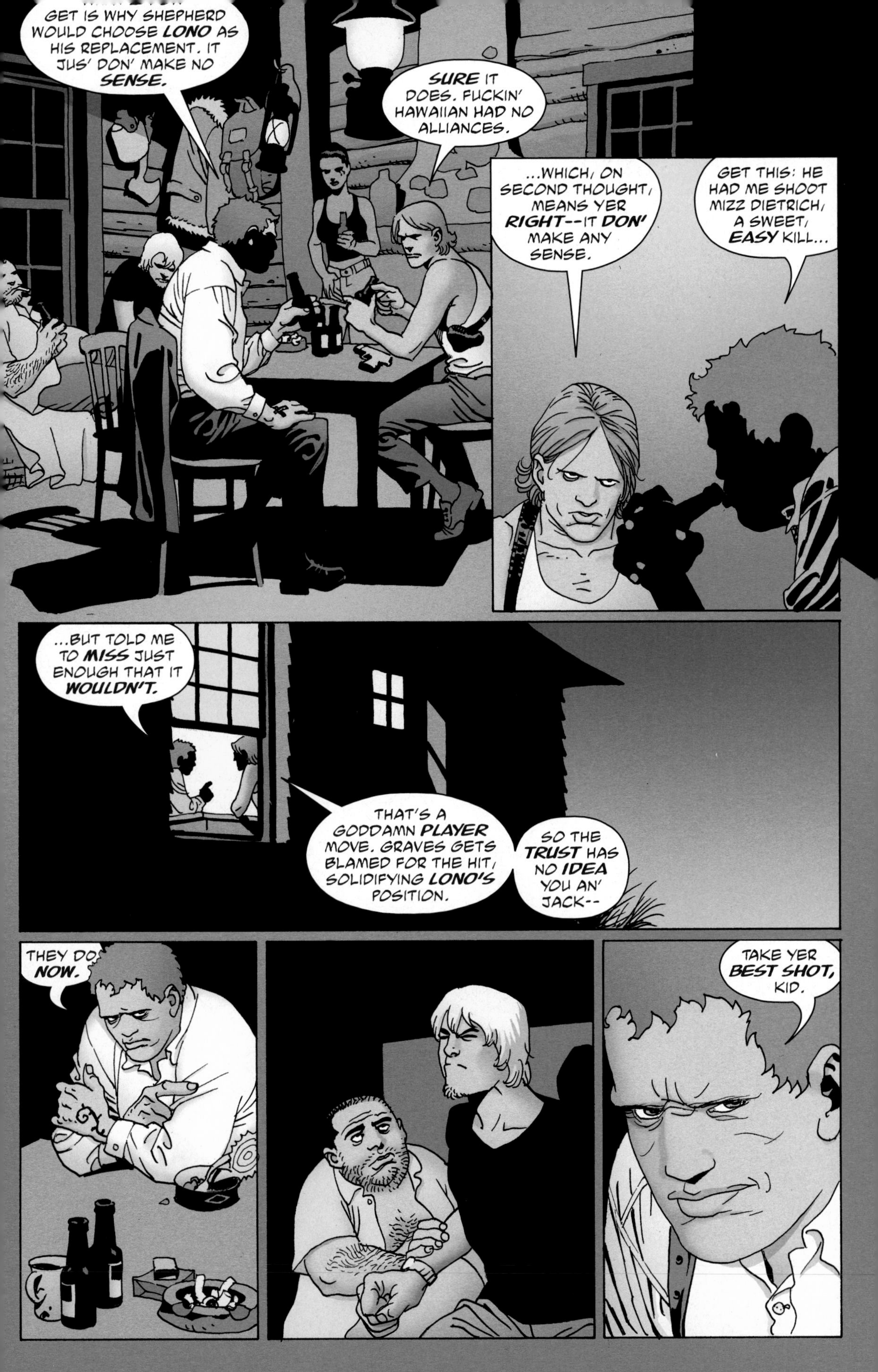
GET IS WHY SHEPHERD WOULD CHOOSE LONO AS HIS REPLACEMENT. IT JUS' DON' MAKE NO SENSE.
SURE IT DOES. FUCKIN' HAWAIIAN HAD NO ALLIANCES.
...WHICH, ON SECOND THOUGHT, MEANS YER RIGHT--IT DON' MAKE ANY SENSE.
GET THIS: HE HAD ME SHOOT MIZZ DIETRICH, A SWEET, EASY KILL...
...BUT TOLD ME TO MISS JUST ENOUGH THAT IT WOULDN'T.
THAT'S A GODDAMN PLAYER MOVE. GRAVES GETS BLAMED FOR THE HIT, SOLIDIFYING LONO'S POSITION.
SO THE TRUST HAS NO IDEA YOU AN' JACK--
THEY DO NOW.
TAKE YER BEST SHOT, KID.

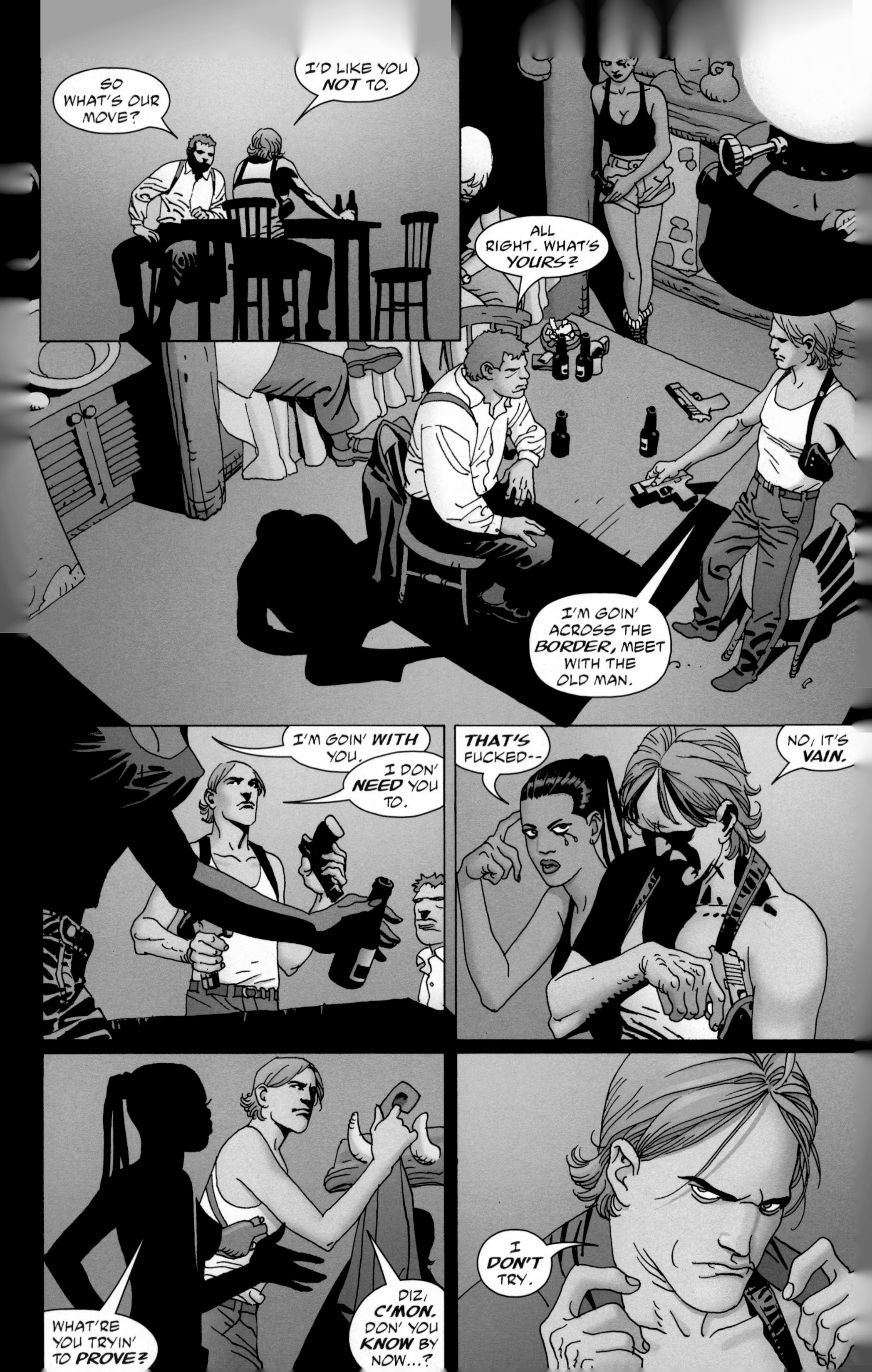

SO WHAT'S OUR MOVE?
I'D LIKE YOU NOT TO.
ALL RIGHT. WHAT'S YOURS?
I'M GOIN' ACROSS THE BORDER, MEET WITH THE OLD MAN.
I'M GOIN' WITH YOU.
I DON' NEED YOU TO.
THAT'S FUCKED--
NO, IT'S VAIN.
WHAT'RE YOU TRYIN' TO PROVE?
DIZ, C'MON. DON' YOU KNOW BY NOW...?
I DON'T TRY.

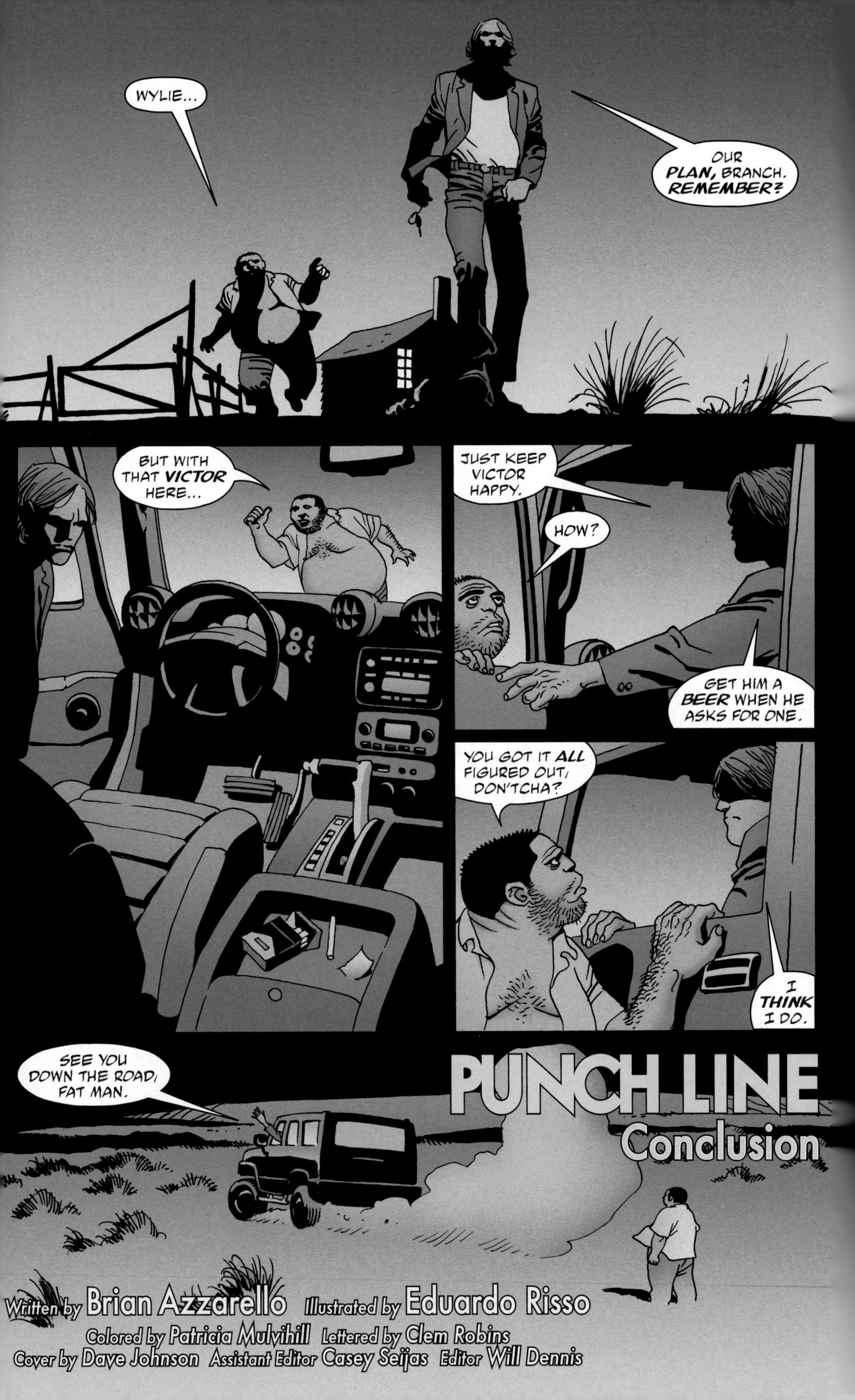
WYLIE...
OUR **PLAN,** BRANCH. **REMEMBER?**
BUT WITH THAT **VICTOR** HERE...
JUST KEEP VICTOR HAPPY.
HOW?
GET HIM A **BEER** WHEN HE ASKS FOR ONE.
YOU GOT IT **ALL** FIGURED OUT, DON'TCHA?
I **THINK** I DO.
SEE YOU DOWN THE ROAD, FAT MAN.
PUNCH LINE
Conclusion
Written by Brian Azzarello Illustrated by Eduardo Risso
Colored by Patricia Mulvihill Lettered by Clem Robins
Cover by Dave Johnson Assistant Editor Casey Seijas Editor Will Dennis

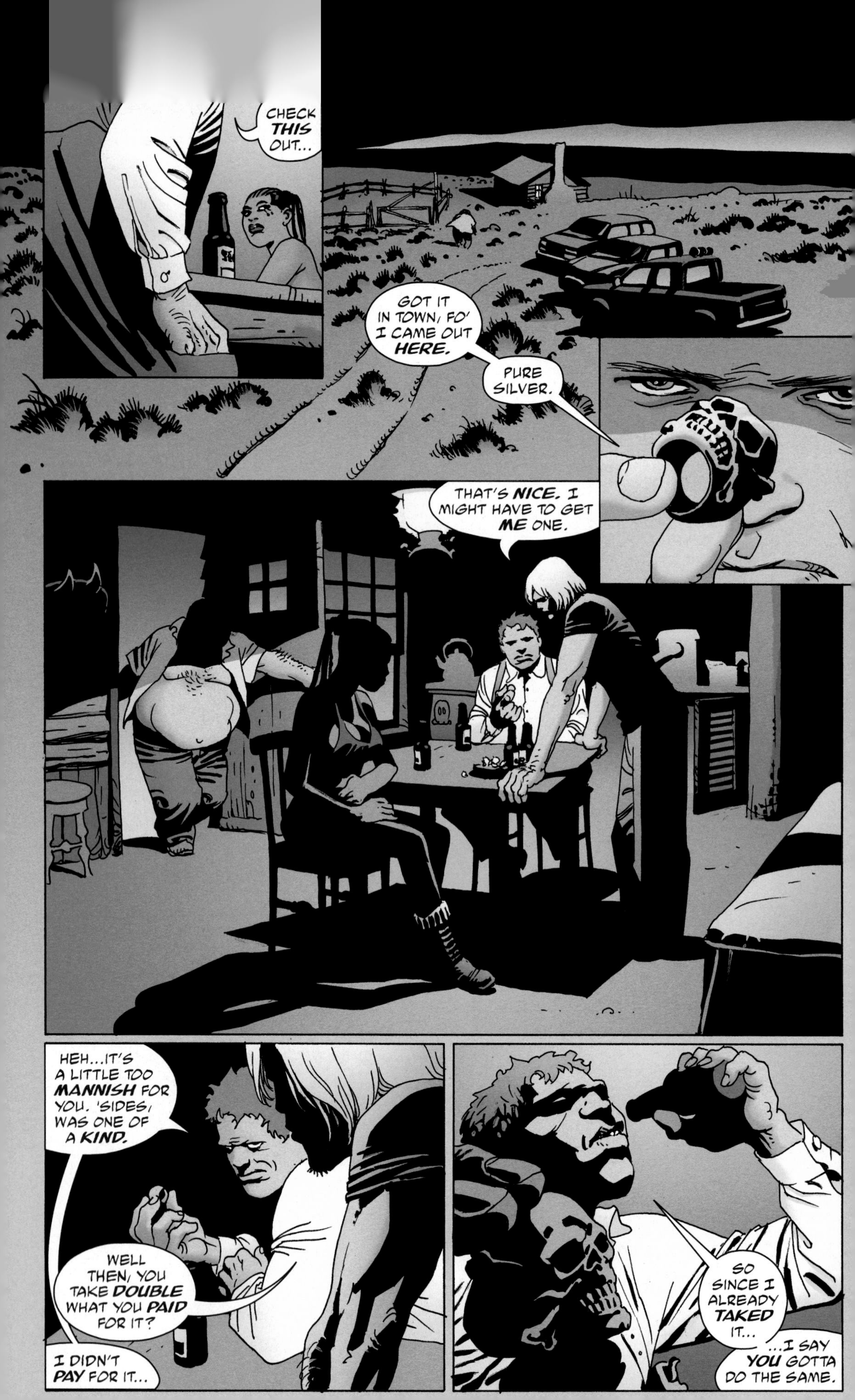
CHECK THIS OUT...
GOT IT IN TOWN, FO' I CAME OUT HERE.
PURE SILVER.
THAT'S NICE. I MIGHT HAVE TO GET ME ONE.
HEH...IT'S A LITTLE TOO MANNISH FOR YOU. 'SIDES, WAS ONE OF A KIND.
WELL THEN, YOU TAKE DOUBLE WHAT YOU PAID FOR IT?
I DIDN'T PAY FOR IT...
SO SINCE I ALREADY TAKED IT...
...I SAY YOU GOTTA DO THE SAME.

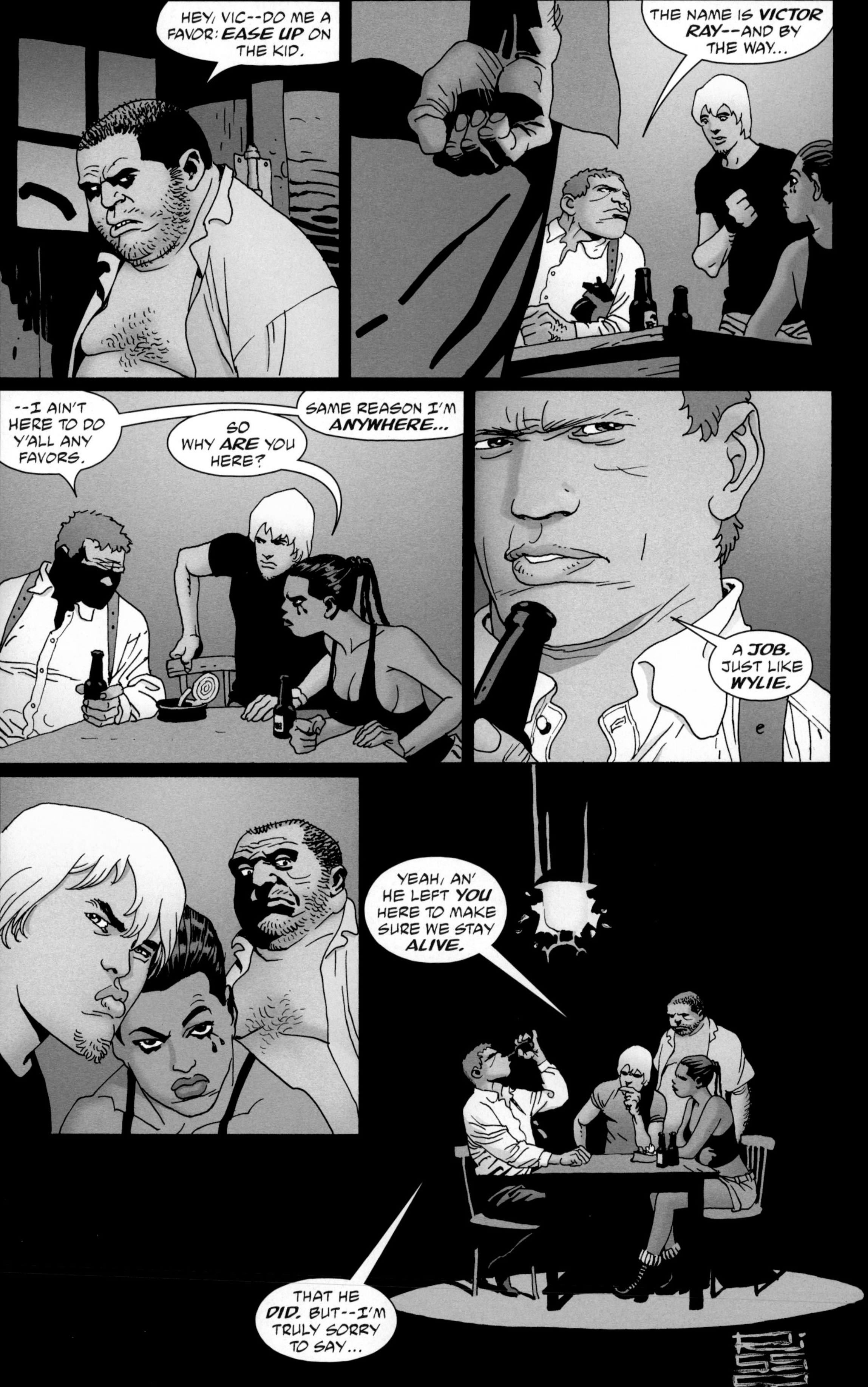
HEY, VIC--DO ME A FAVOR: EASE UP ON THE KID.
THE NAME IS VICTOR RAY--AND BY THE WAY...
--I AIN'T HERE TO DO Y'ALL ANY FAVORS.
SO WHY ARE YOU HERE?
SAME REASON I'M ANYWHERE...
A JOB. JUST LIKE WYLIE.
YEAH, AN' HE LEFT YOU HERE TO MAKE SURE WE STAY ALIVE.
THAT HE DID. BUT--I'M TRULY SORRY TO SAY...

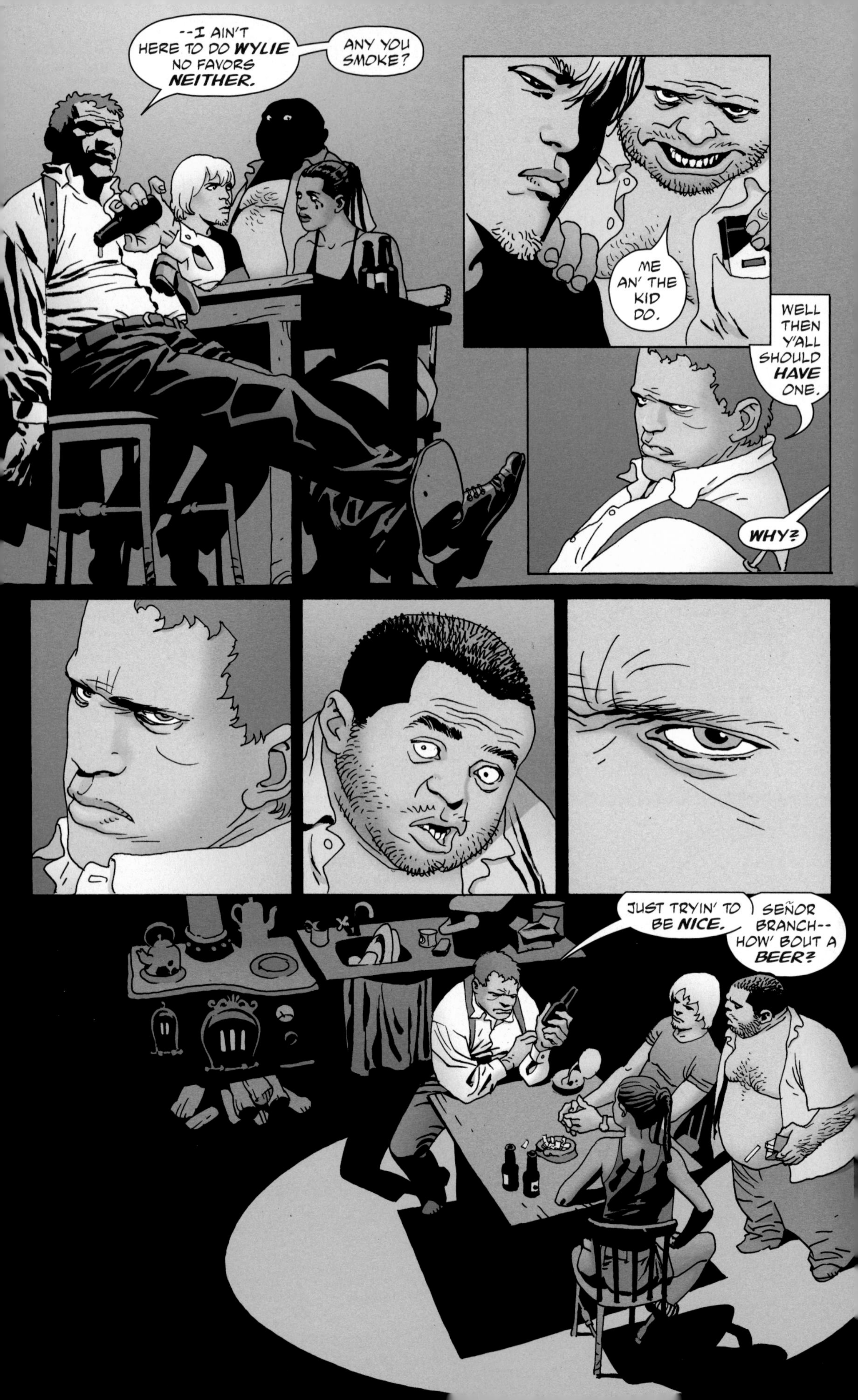
--I AIN'T HERE TO DO WYLIE NO FAVORS NEITHER.
ANY YOU SMOKE?
ME AN' THE KID DO.
WELL THEN Y'ALL SHOULD HAVE ONE.
WHY?
JUST TRYIN' TO BE NICE.
SEÑOR BRANCH-- HOW' BOUT A BEER?

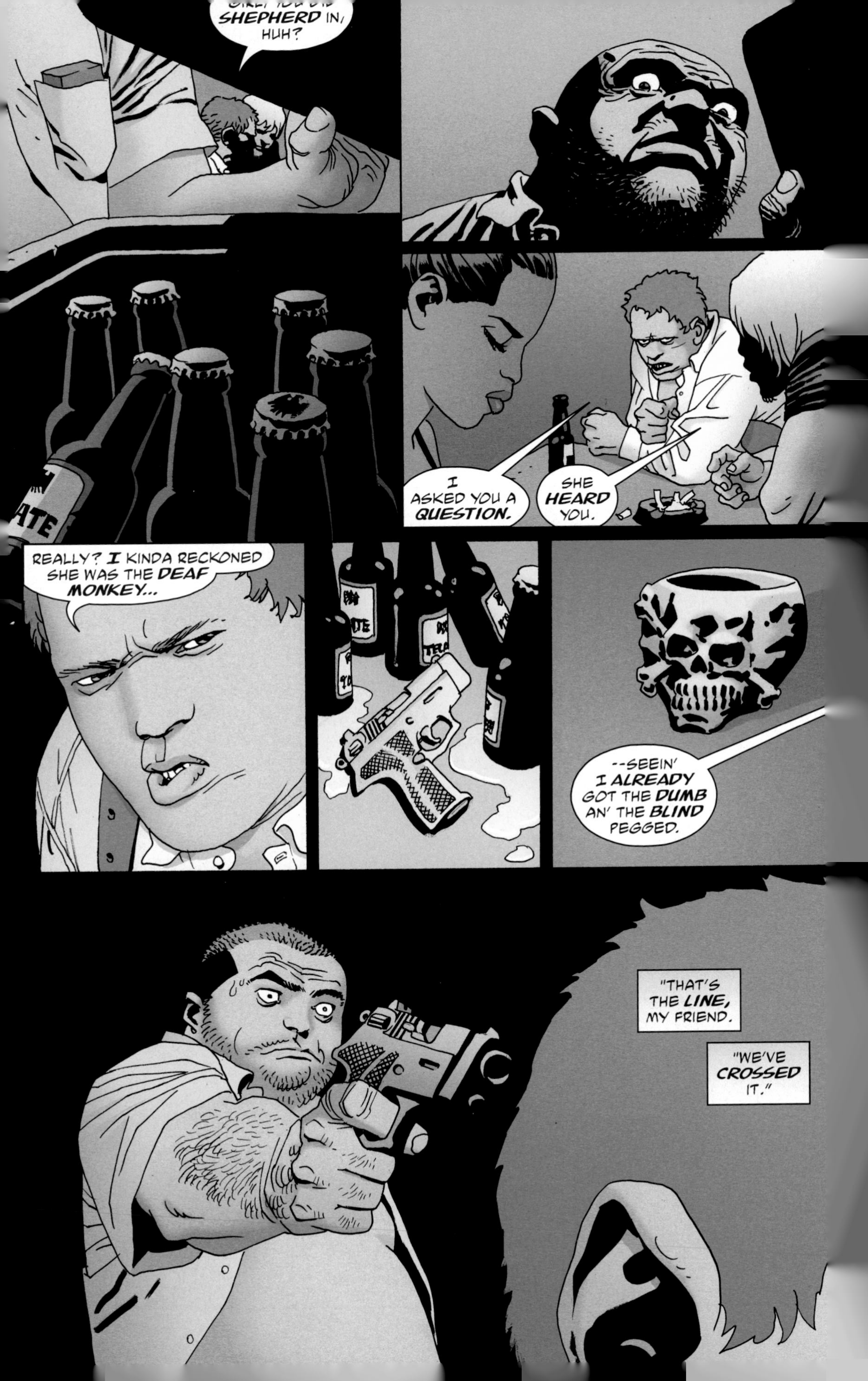
SHEPHERD IN, HUH?
I ASKED YOU A QUESTION.
SHE HEARD YOU.
REALLY? I KINDA RECKONED SHE WAS THE DEAF MONKEY...
--SEEIN' I ALREADY GOT THE DUMB AN' THE BLIND PEGGED.
"THAT'S THE LINE, MY FRIEND.
"WE'VE CROSSED IT."

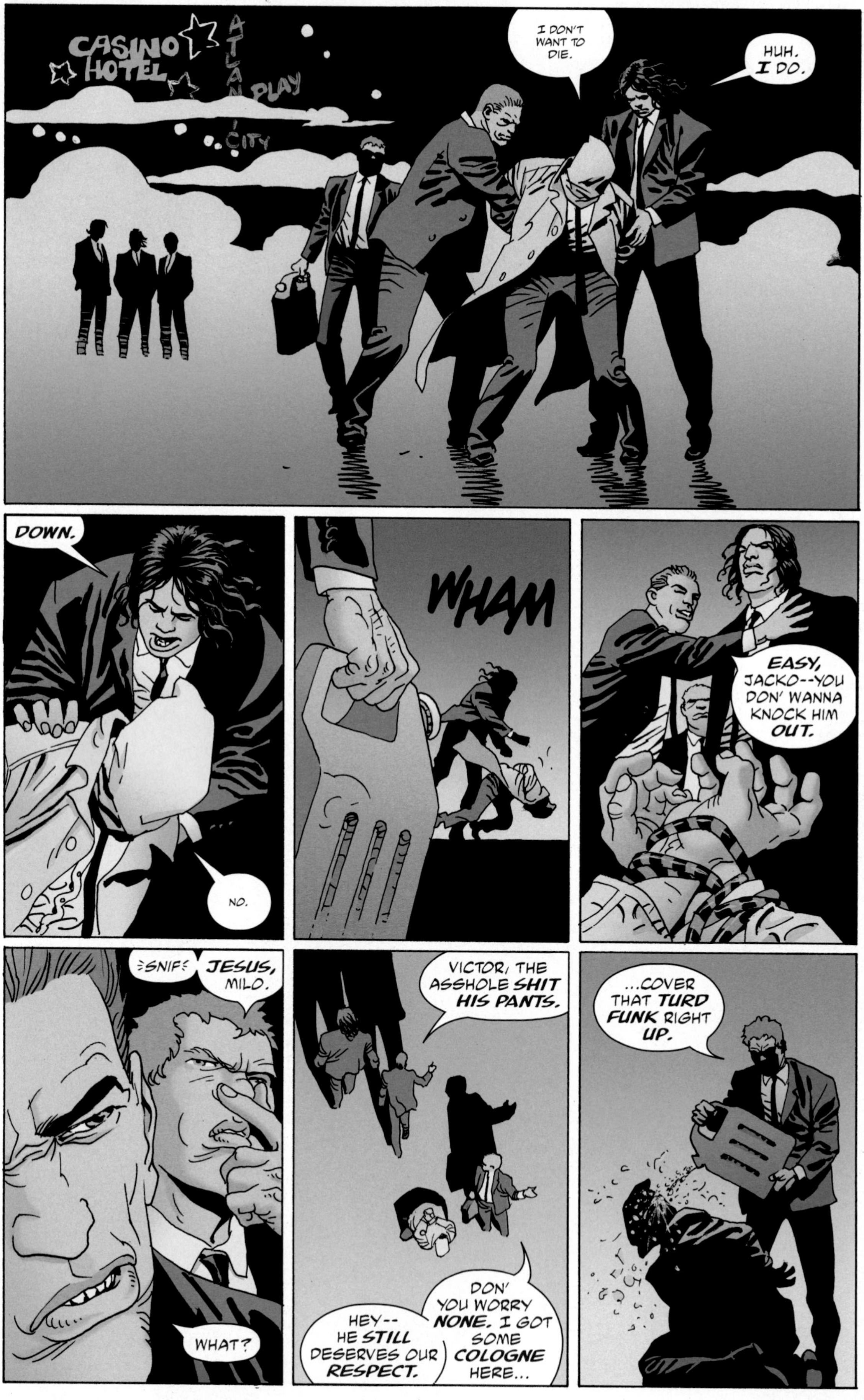
CASINO HOTEL
ATLANTIC CITY
PLAY
I DON'T WANT TO DIE.
HUH. I DO.
DOWN.
NO.
WHAM
EASY, JACKO--YOU DON' WANNA KNOCK HIM OUT.
SNIF
JESUS, MILO.
WHAT?
VICTOR, THE ASSHOLE SHIT HIS PANTS.
HEY-- HE STILL DESERVES OUR RESPECT.
DON' YOU WORRY NONE. I GOT SOME COLOGNE HERE...
...COVER THAT TURD FUNK RIGHT UP.

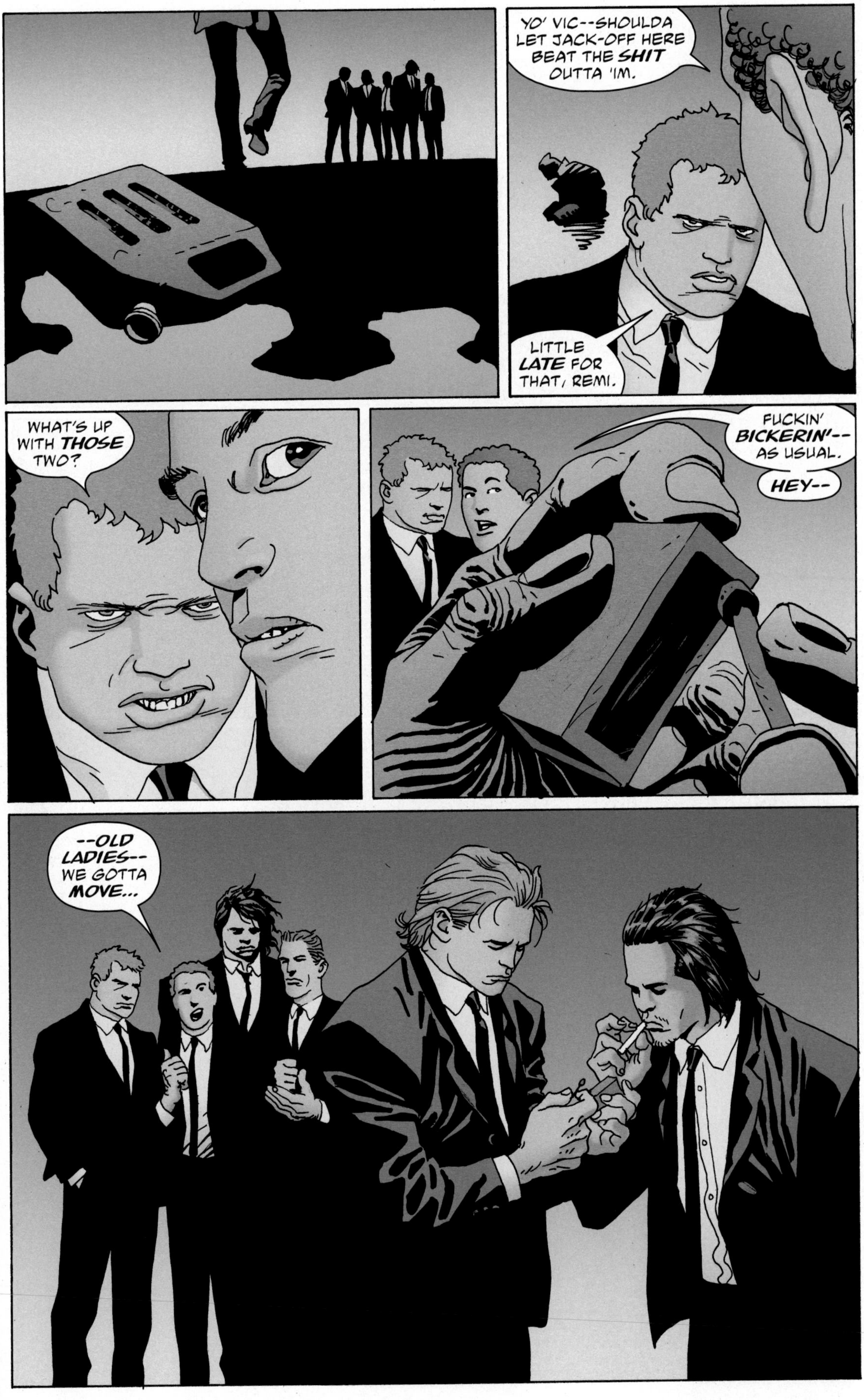
YO' VIC--SHOULDA LET JACK-OFF HERE BEAT THE SHIT OUTTA 'IM.
LITTLE LATE FOR THAT, REMI.
WHAT'S UP WITH THOSE TWO?
FUCKIN' BICKERIN'-- AS USUAL.
HEY--
--OLD LADIES-- WE GOTTA MOVE...

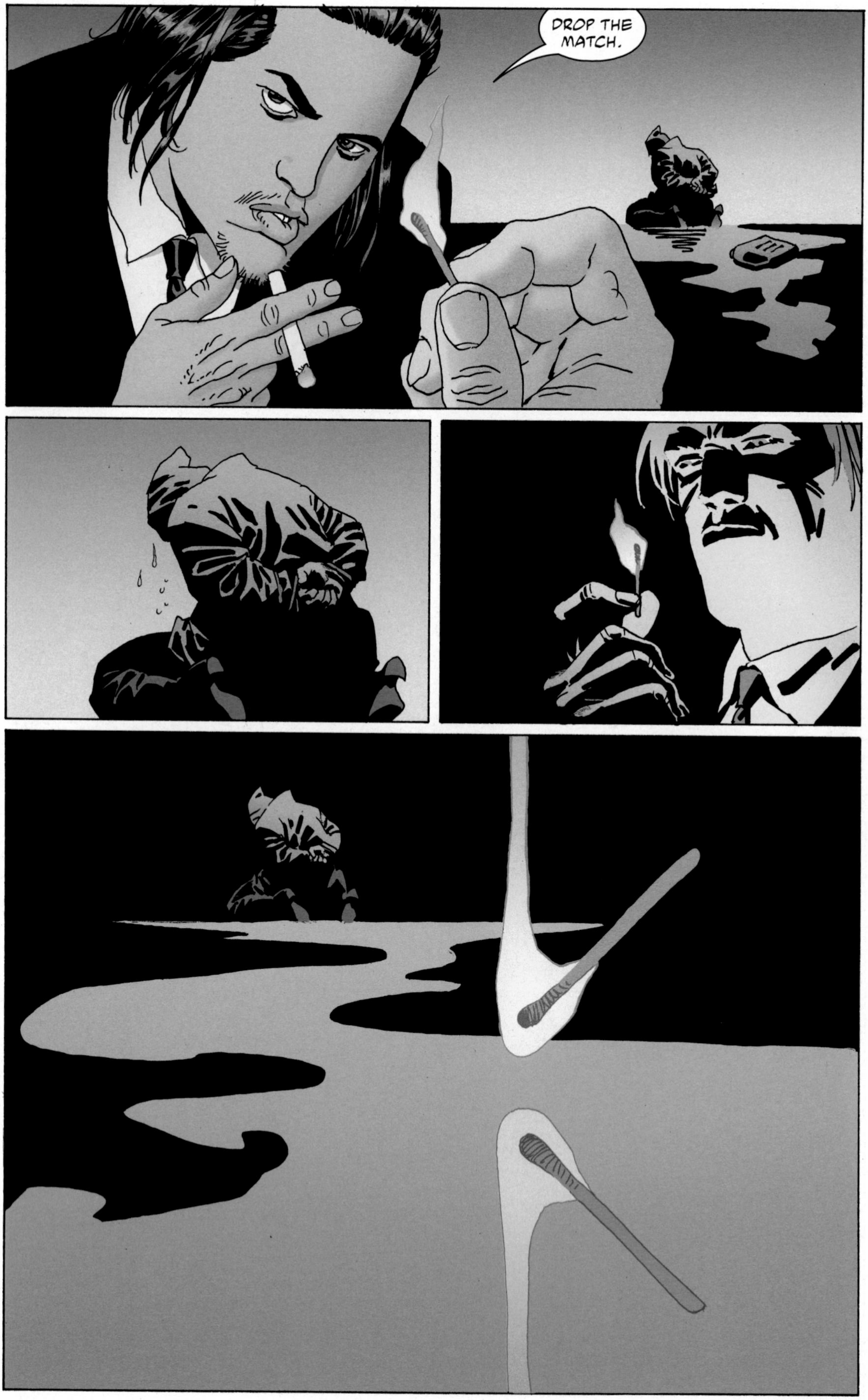
DROP THE MATCH.

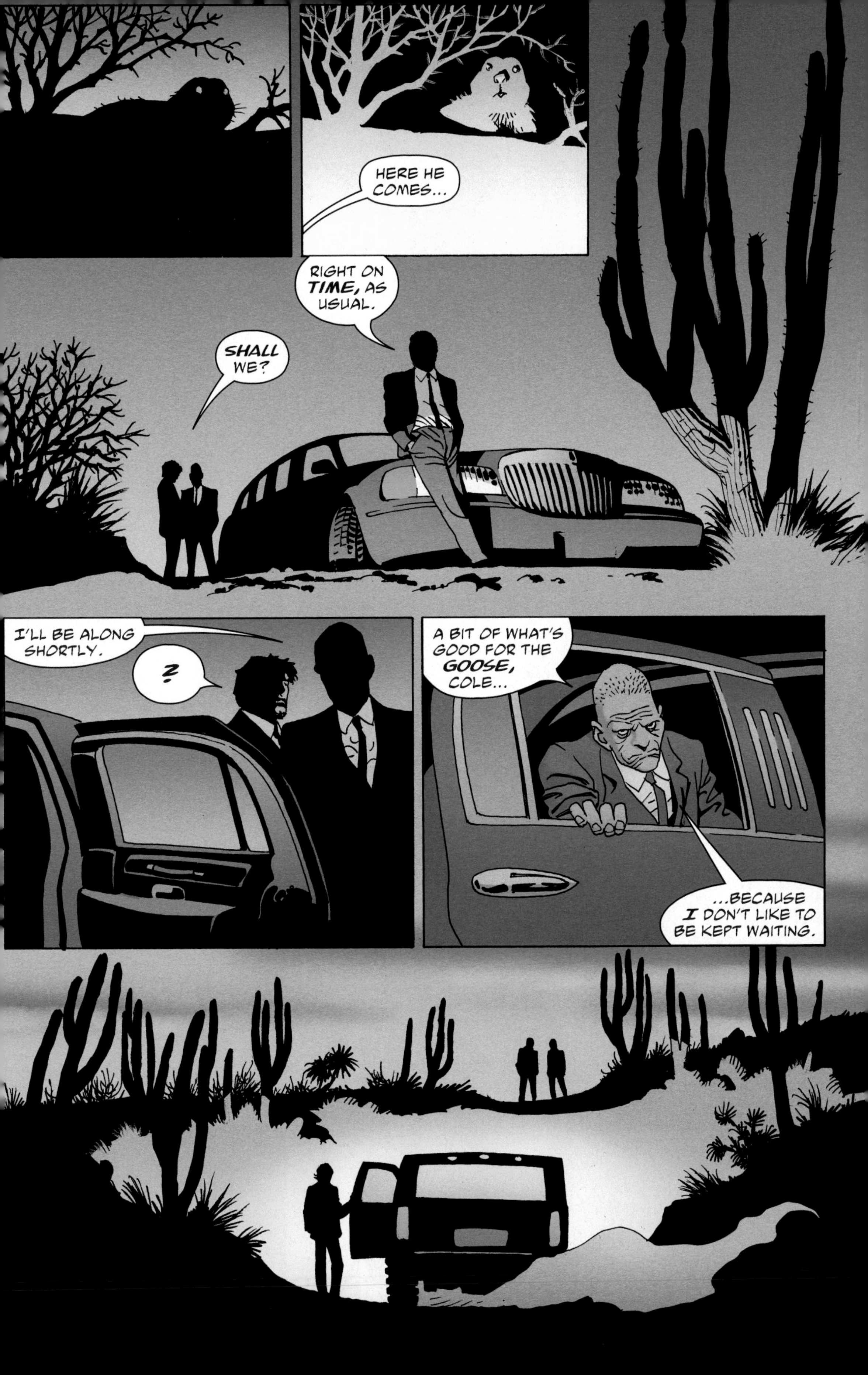
HERE HE COMES...
RIGHT ON TIME, AS USUAL.
SHALL WE?
I'LL BE ALONG SHORTLY.
?
A BIT OF WHAT'S GOOD FOR THE GOOSE, COLE...
...BECAUSE I DON'T LIKE TO BE KEPT WAITING.

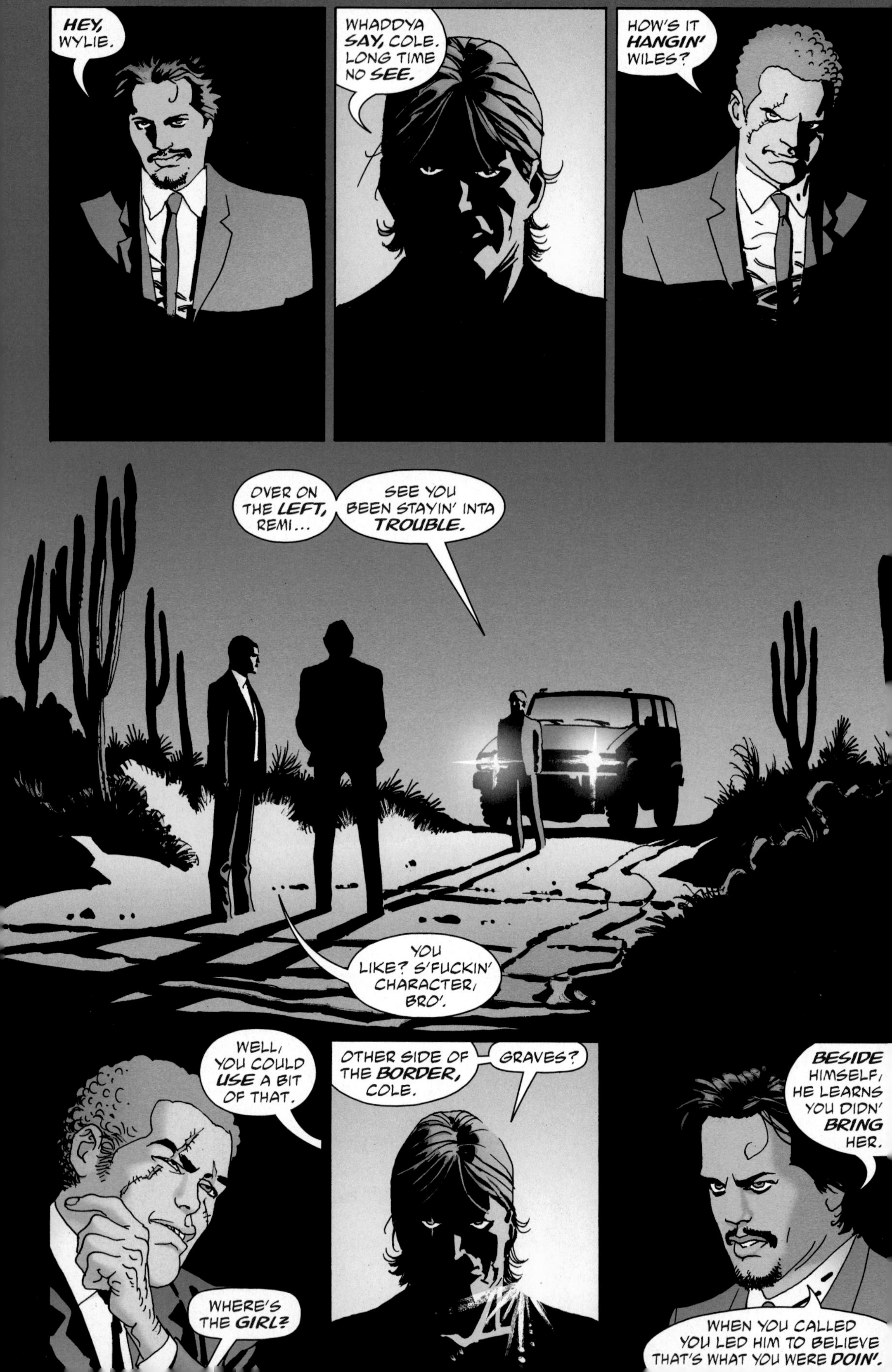
HEY, WYLIE.
WHADDYA SAY, COLE. LONG TIME NO SEE.
HOW'S IT HANGIN' WILES?
OVER ON THE LEFT, REMI...
SEE YOU BEEN STAYIN' INTA TROUBLE.
YOU LIKE? S'FUCKIN' CHARACTER, BRO'.
WELL, YOU COULD USE A BIT OF THAT.
WHERE'S THE GIRL?
OTHER SIDE OF THE BORDER, COLE.
GRAVES?
BESIDE HIMSELF, HE LEARNS YOU DIDN' BRING HER.
WHEN YOU CALLED YOU LED HIM TO BELIEVE THAT'S WHAT YOU WERE DOIN'.

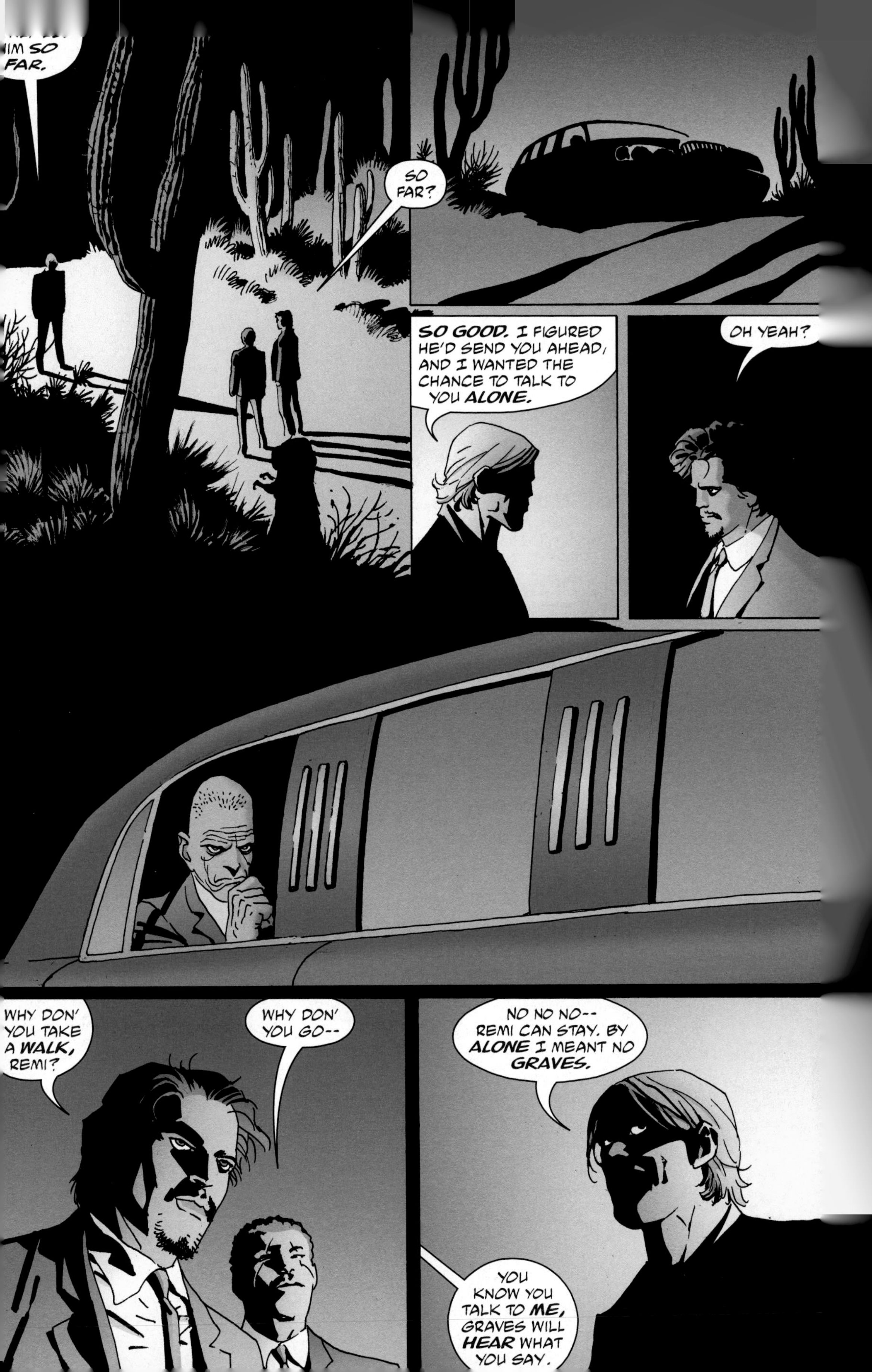

...IM SO FAR.
SO FAR?
SO GOOD. I FIGURED HE'D SEND YOU AHEAD, AND I WANTED THE CHANCE TO TALK TO YOU ALONE.
OH YEAH?
WHY DON' YOU TAKE A WALK, REMI?
WHY DON' YOU GO--
NO NO NO-- REMI CAN STAY. BY ALONE I MEANT NO GRAVES.
YOU KNOW YOU TALK TO ME, GRAVES WILL HEAR WHAT YOU SAY.

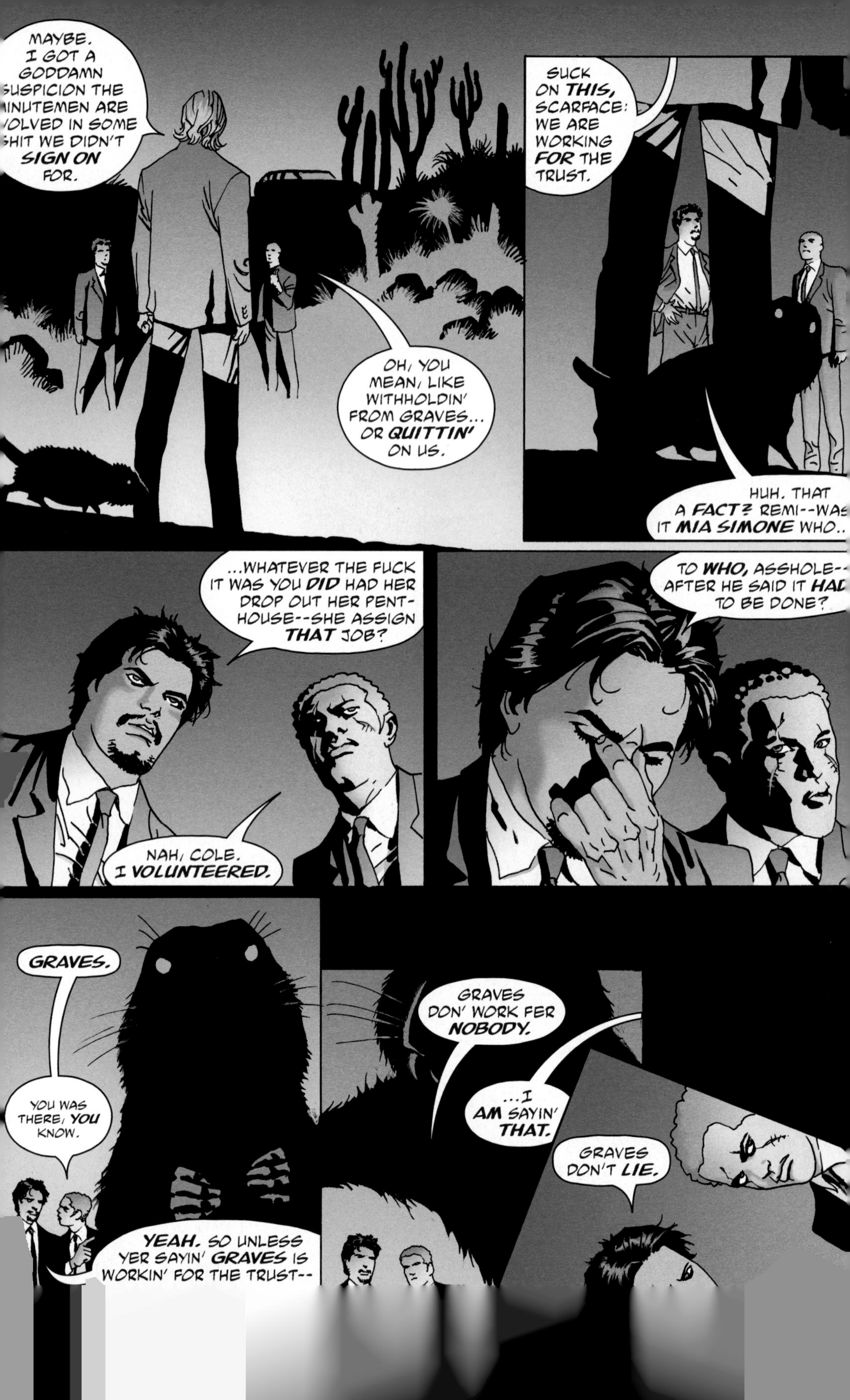

MAYBE. I GOT A GODDAMN SUSPICION THE MINUTEMEN ARE INVOLVED IN SOME SHIT WE DIDN'T SIGN ON FOR.
OH, YOU MEAN, LIKE WITHHOLDIN' FROM GRAVES... OR QUITTIN' ON US.
SUCK ON THIS, SCARFACE: WE ARE WORKING FOR THE TRUST.
HUH. THAT A FACT? REMI--WAS IT MIA SIMONE WHO...
...WHATEVER THE FUCK IT WAS YOU DID HAD HER DROP OUT HER PENT-HOUSE--SHE ASSIGN THAT JOB?
NAH, COLE. I VOLUNTEERED.
TO WHO, ASSHOLE--AFTER HE SAID IT HAD TO BE DONE?
GRAVES.
YOU WAS THERE, YOU KNOW.
YEAH. SO UNLESS YER SAYIN' GRAVES IS WORKIN' FOR THE TRUST--
GRAVES DON' WORK FER NOBODY.
...I AM SAYIN' THAT.
GRAVES DON'T LIE.

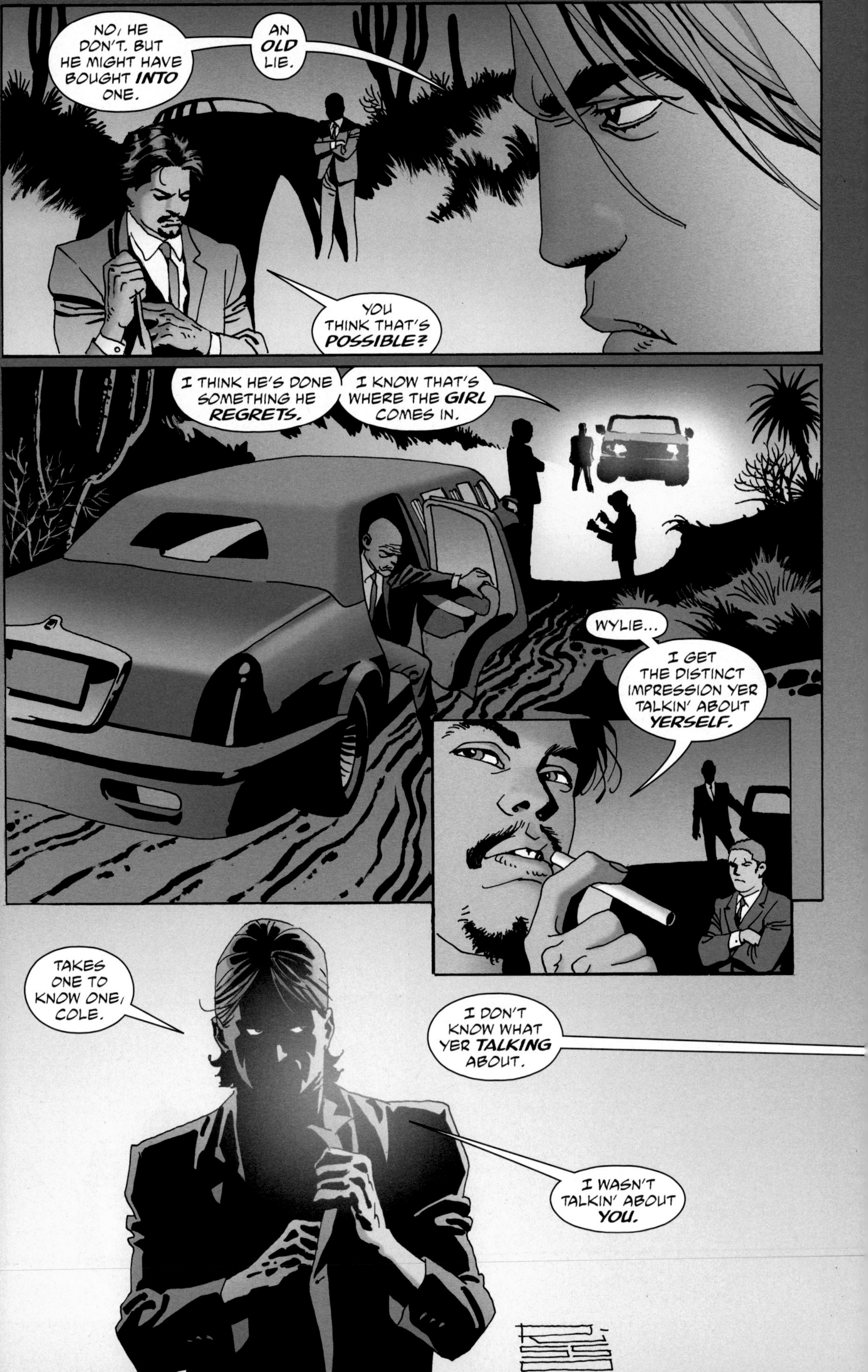
NO, HE DON'T. BUT HE MIGHT HAVE BOUGHT INTO ONE.
AN OLD LIE.
YOU THINK THAT'S POSSIBLE?
I THINK HE'S DONE SOMETHING HE REGRETS.
I KNOW THAT'S WHERE THE GIRL COMES IN.
WYLIE...
I GET THE DISTINCT IMPRESSION YER TALKIN' ABOUT YERSELF.
TAKES ONE TO KNOW ONE, COLE.
I DON'T KNOW WHAT YER TALKING ABOUT.
I WASN'T TALKIN' ABOUT YOU.

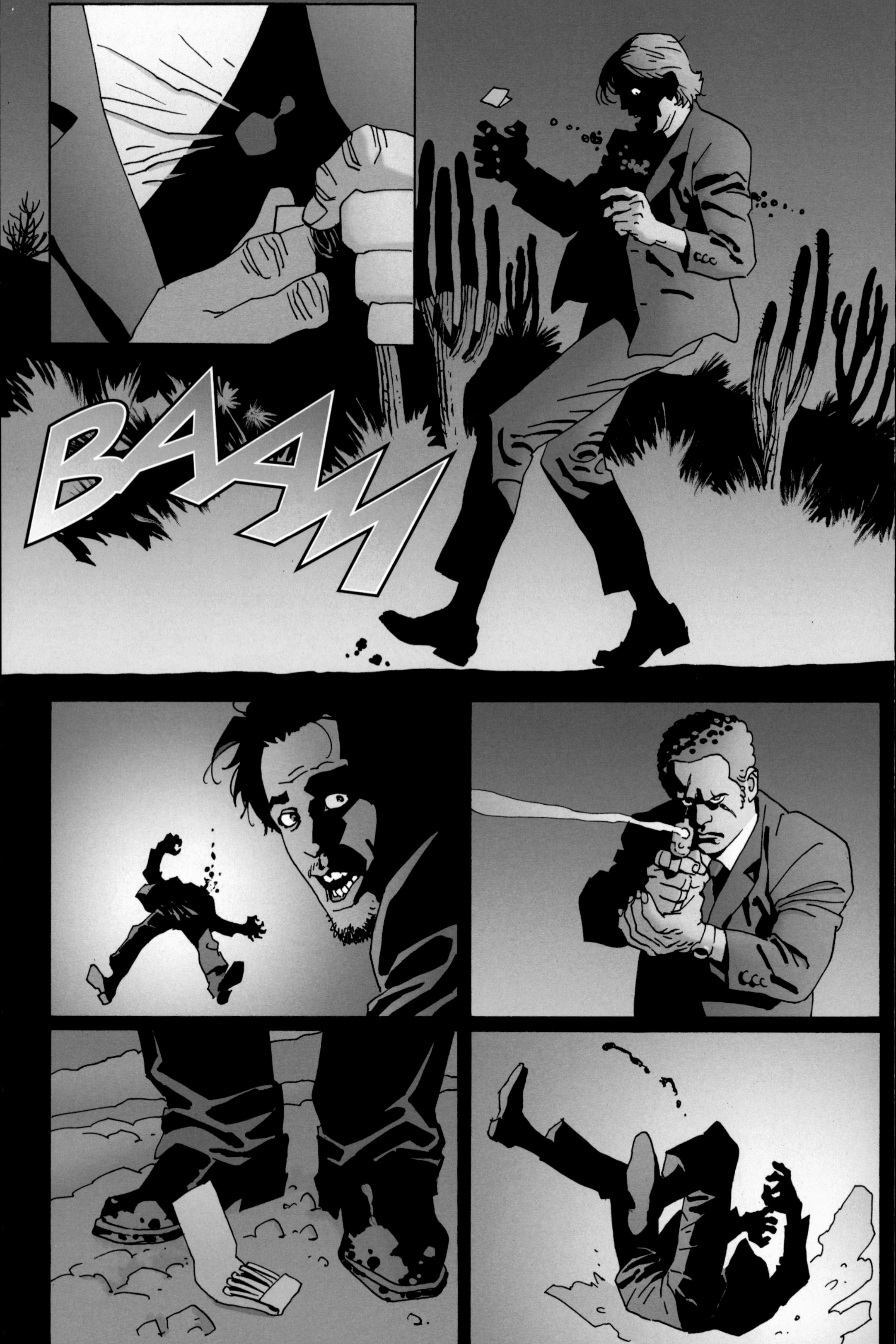
BAAM

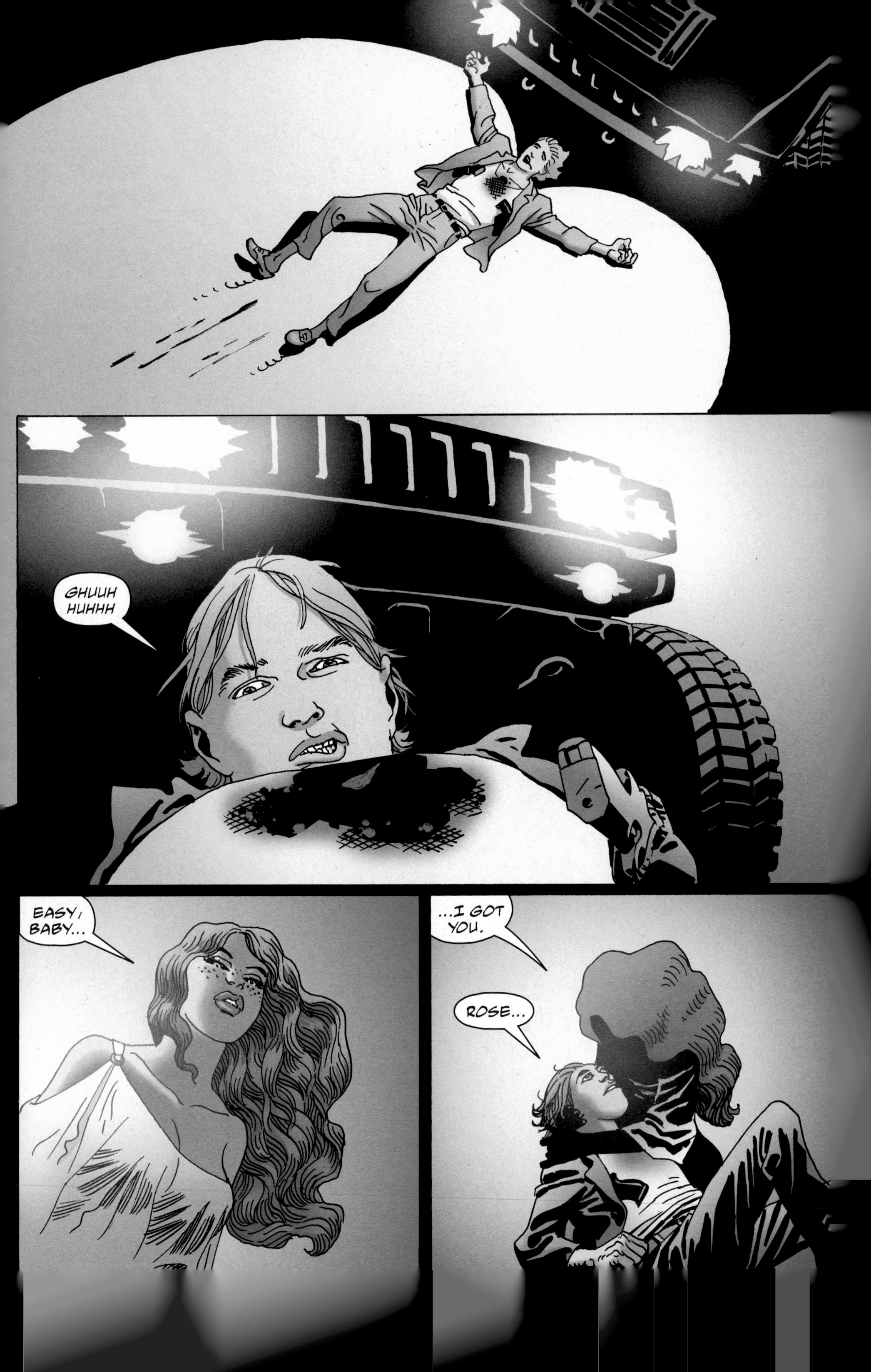
GHUUH HUHHH
EASY, BABY...
...I GOT YOU.
ROSE...

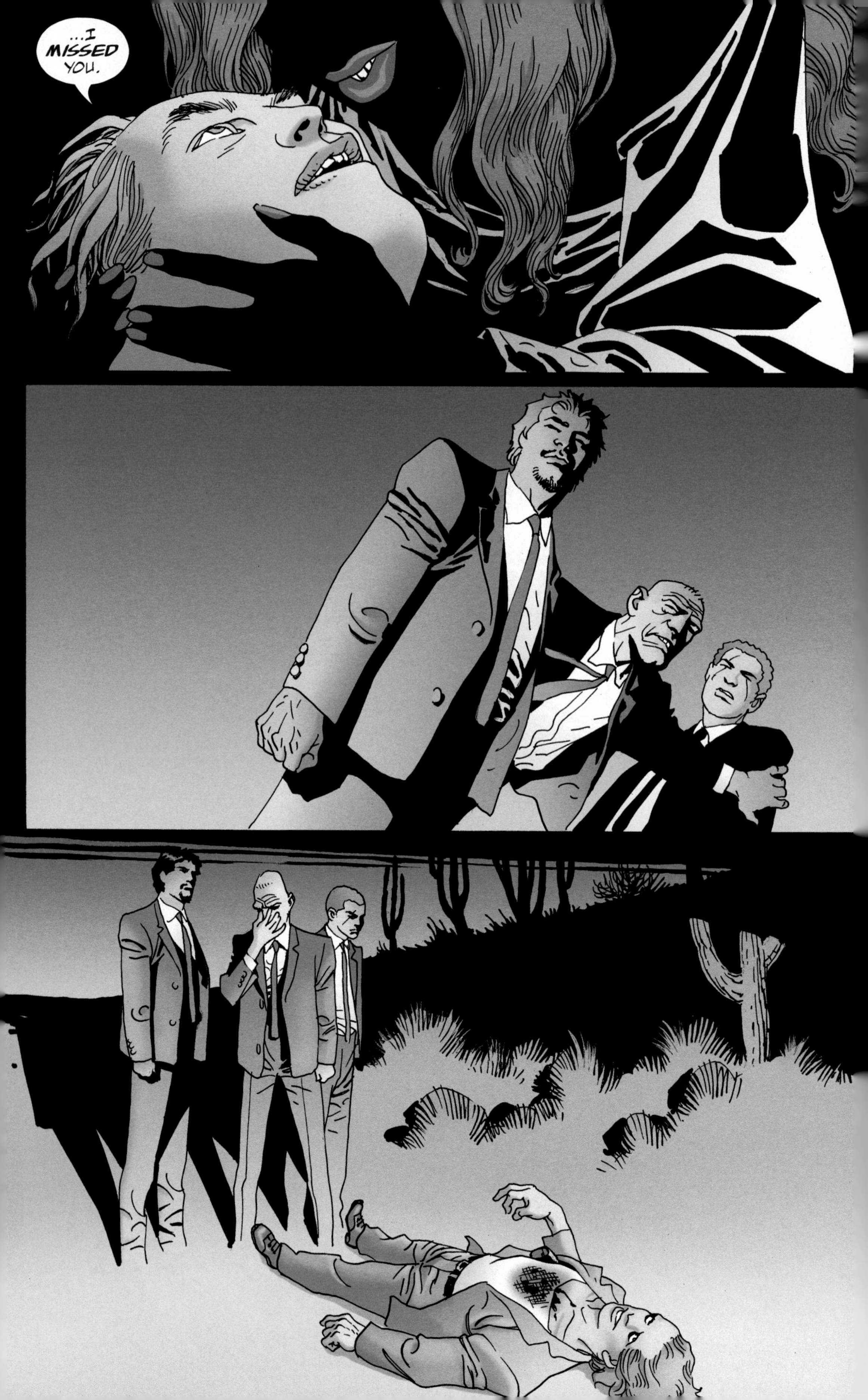
...I MISSED YOU.

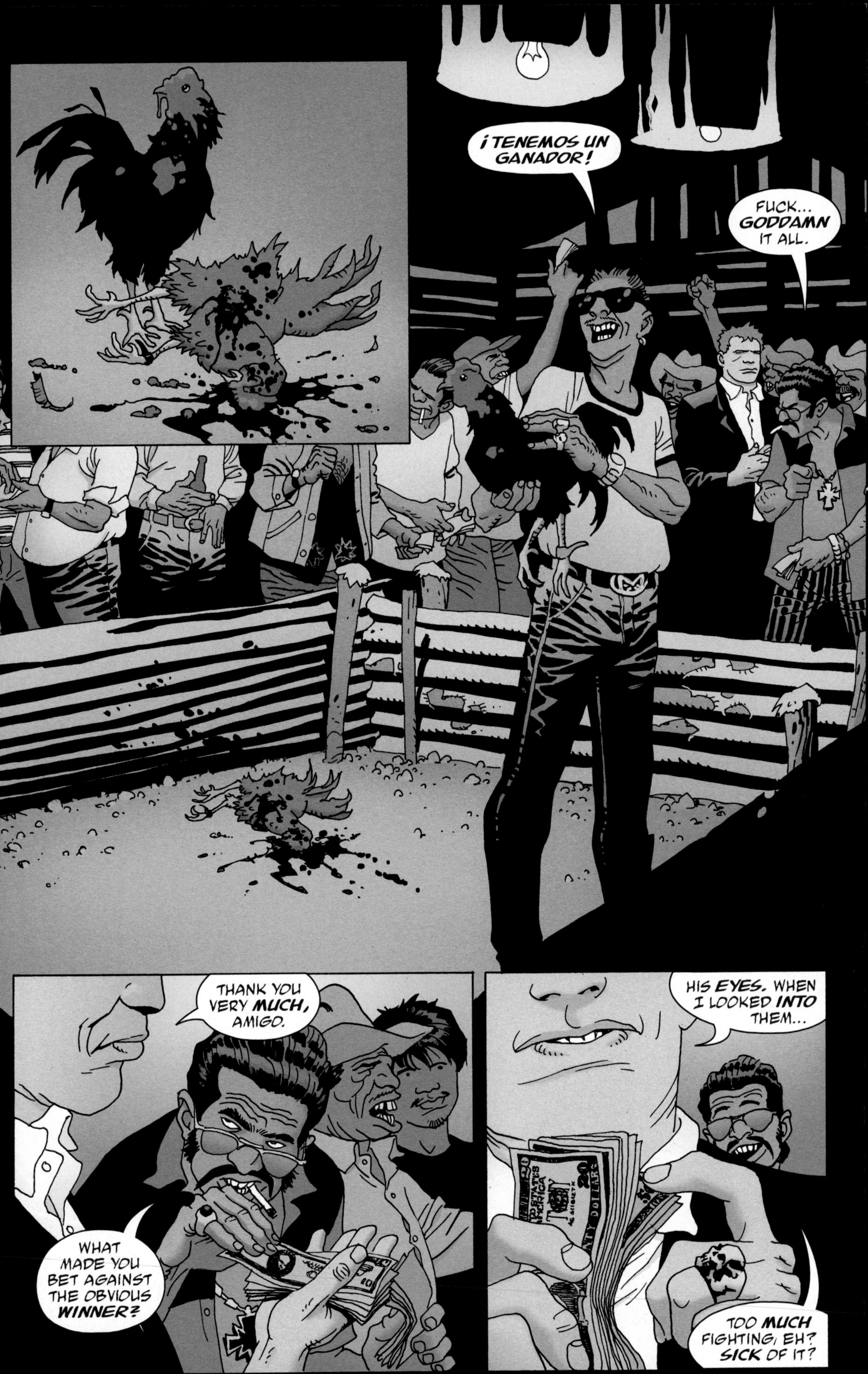
¡TENEMOS UN GANADOR!
FUCK... GODDAMN IT ALL.
THANK YOU VERY MUCH, AMIGO.
WHAT MADE YOU BET AGAINST THE OBVIOUS WINNER?
HIS EYES. WHEN I LOOKED INTO THEM...
TOO MUCH FIGHTING, EH? SICK OF IT?

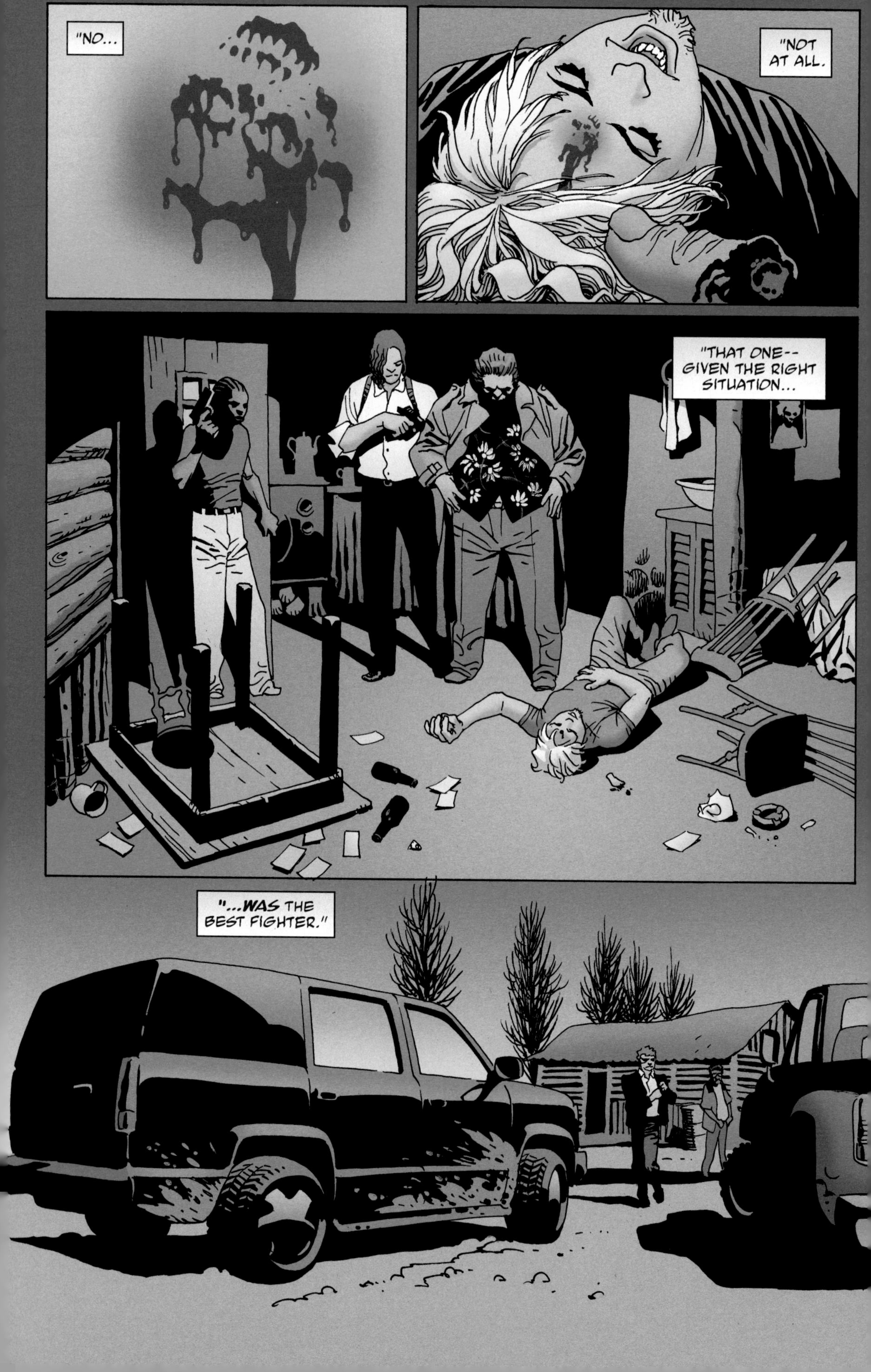
"NO...
"NOT AT ALL.
"THAT ONE-- GIVEN THE RIGHT SITUATION...
"...WAS THE BEST FIGHTER."

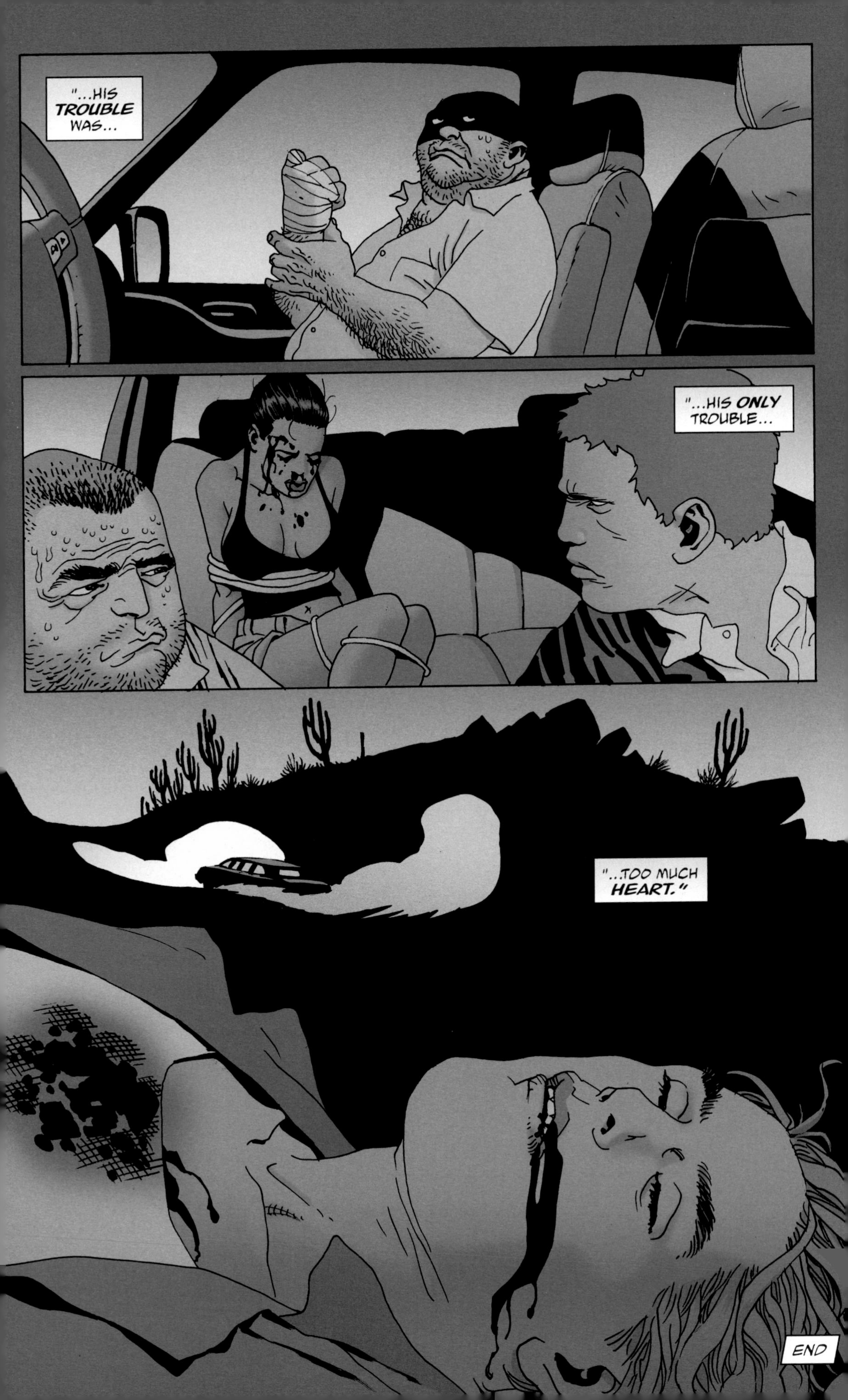
"...HIS TROUBLE WAS...
"...HIS ONLY TROUBLE...
"...TOO MUCH HEART."
END

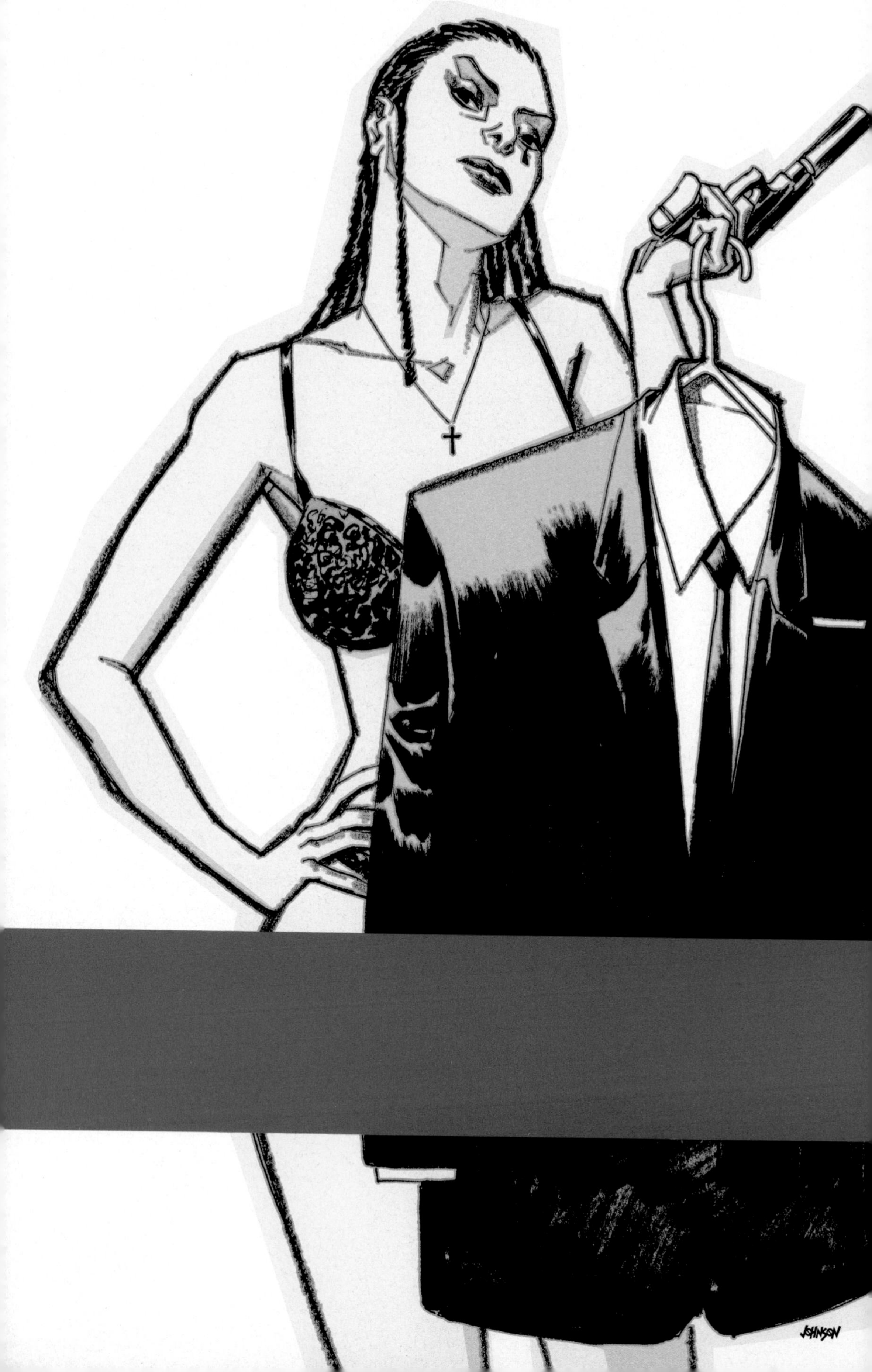
JOHNSON

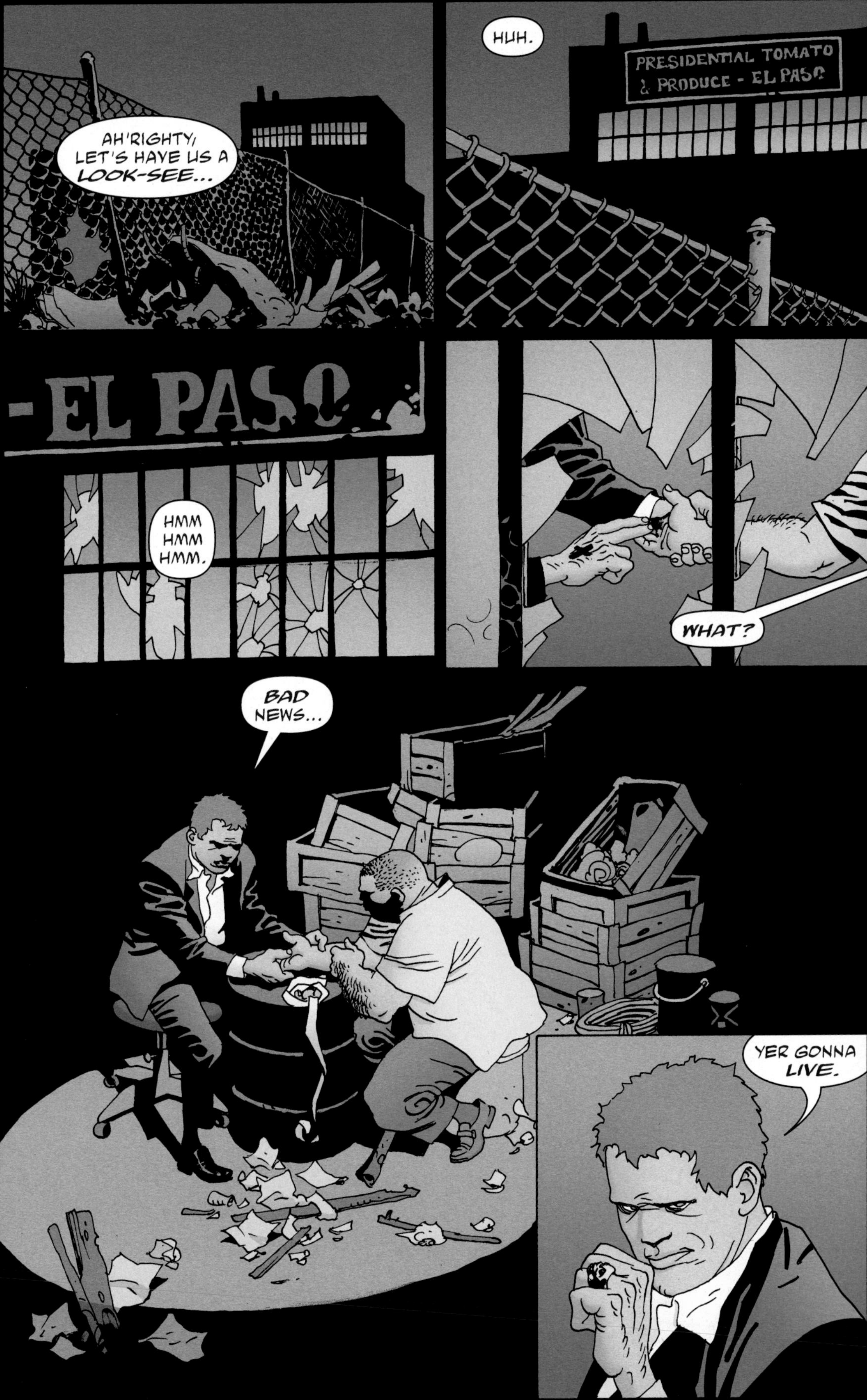
AH'RIGHTY, LET'S HAVE US A LOOK-SEE...
HUH.
PRESIDENTIAL TOMATO & PRODUCE - EL PASO
- EL PASO
HMM HMM HMM.
WHAT?
BAD NEWS...
YER GONNA LIVE.

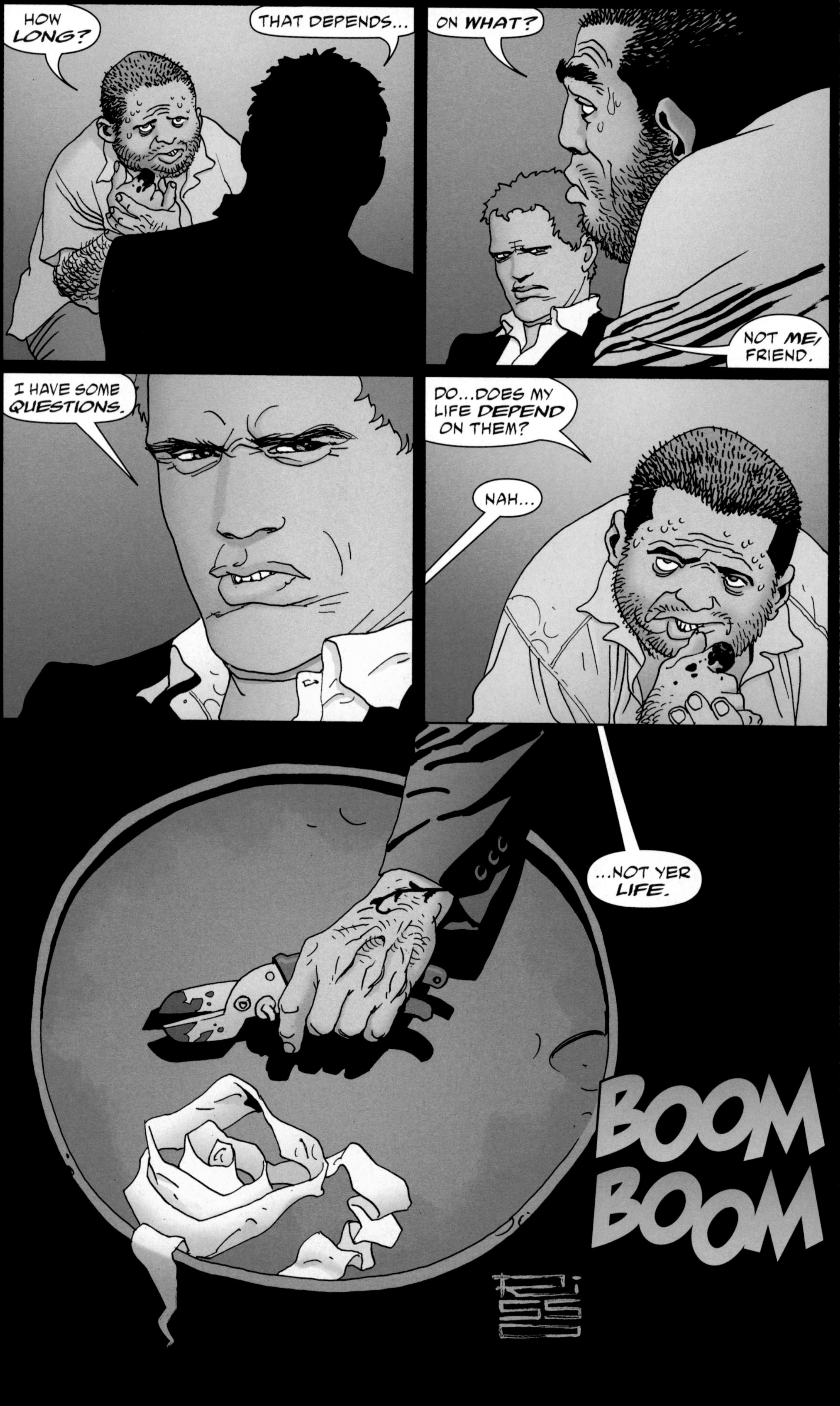
HOW LONG?
THAT DEPENDS...
ON WHAT?
NOT ME, FRIEND.
I HAVE SOME QUESTIONS.
DO...DOES MY LIFE DEPEND ON THEM?
NAH...
...NOT YER LIFE.
BOOM BOOM

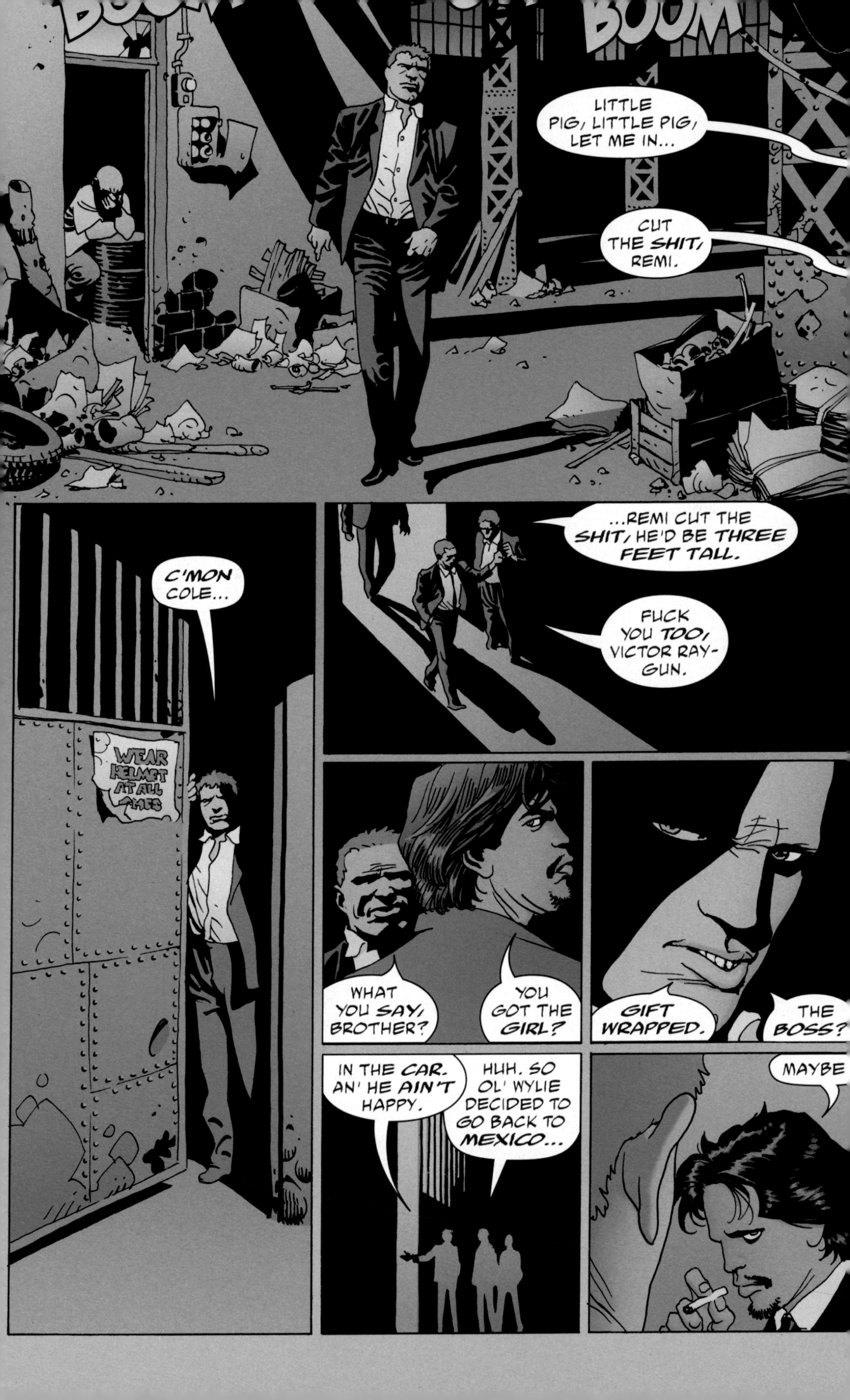
BOOM
BOOM
LITTLE PIG, LITTLE PIG, LET ME IN...
CUT THE SHIT, REMI.
C'MON COLE...
WEAR HELMET AT ALL TIMES
...REMI CUT THE SHIT, HE'D BE THREE FEET TALL.
FUCK YOU TOO, VICTOR RAY-GUN.
WHAT YOU SAY, BROTHER?
YOU GOT THE GIRL?
GIFT WRAPPED.
THE BOSS?
IN THE CAR. AN' HE AIN'T HAPPY.
HUH. SO OL' WYLIE DECIDED TO GO BACK TO MEXICO...
MAYBE

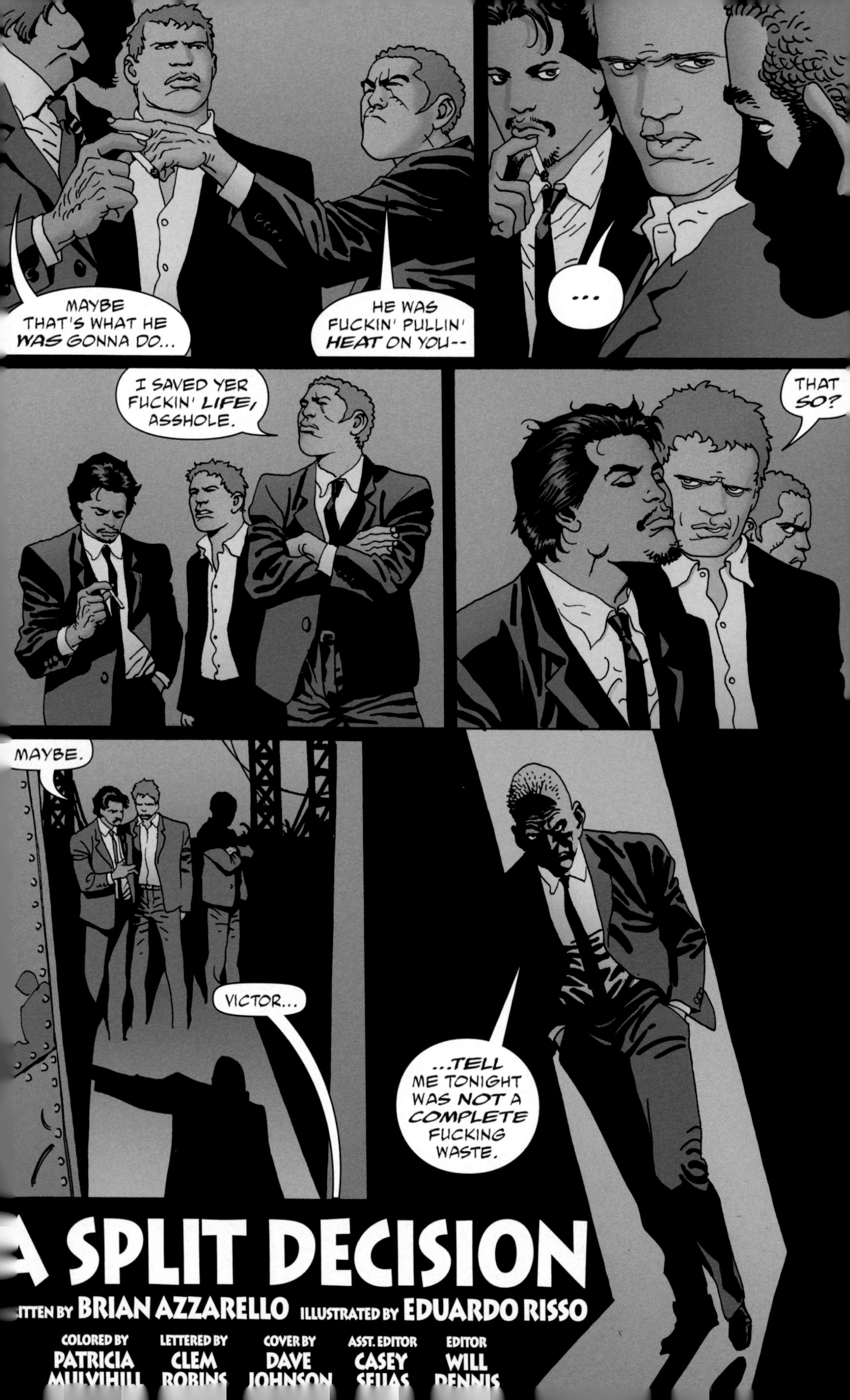
MAYBE THAT'S WHAT HE *WAS* GONNA DO...
HE WAS FUCKIN' PULLIN' *HEAT* ON YOU--
...
I SAVED YER FUCKIN' *LIFE,* ASSHOLE.
THAT *SO?*
MAYBE.
VICTOR...
...*TELL* ME TONIGHT WAS *NOT* A *COMPLETE* FUCKING WASTE.
A SPLIT DECISION
ITTEN BY BRIAN AZZARELLO ILLUSTRATED BY EDUARDO RISSO
COLORED BY PATRICIA MULVIHILL
LETTERED BY CLEM ROBINS
COVER BY DAVE JOHNSON
ASST. EDITOR CASEY SEIJAS
EDITOR WILL DENNIS

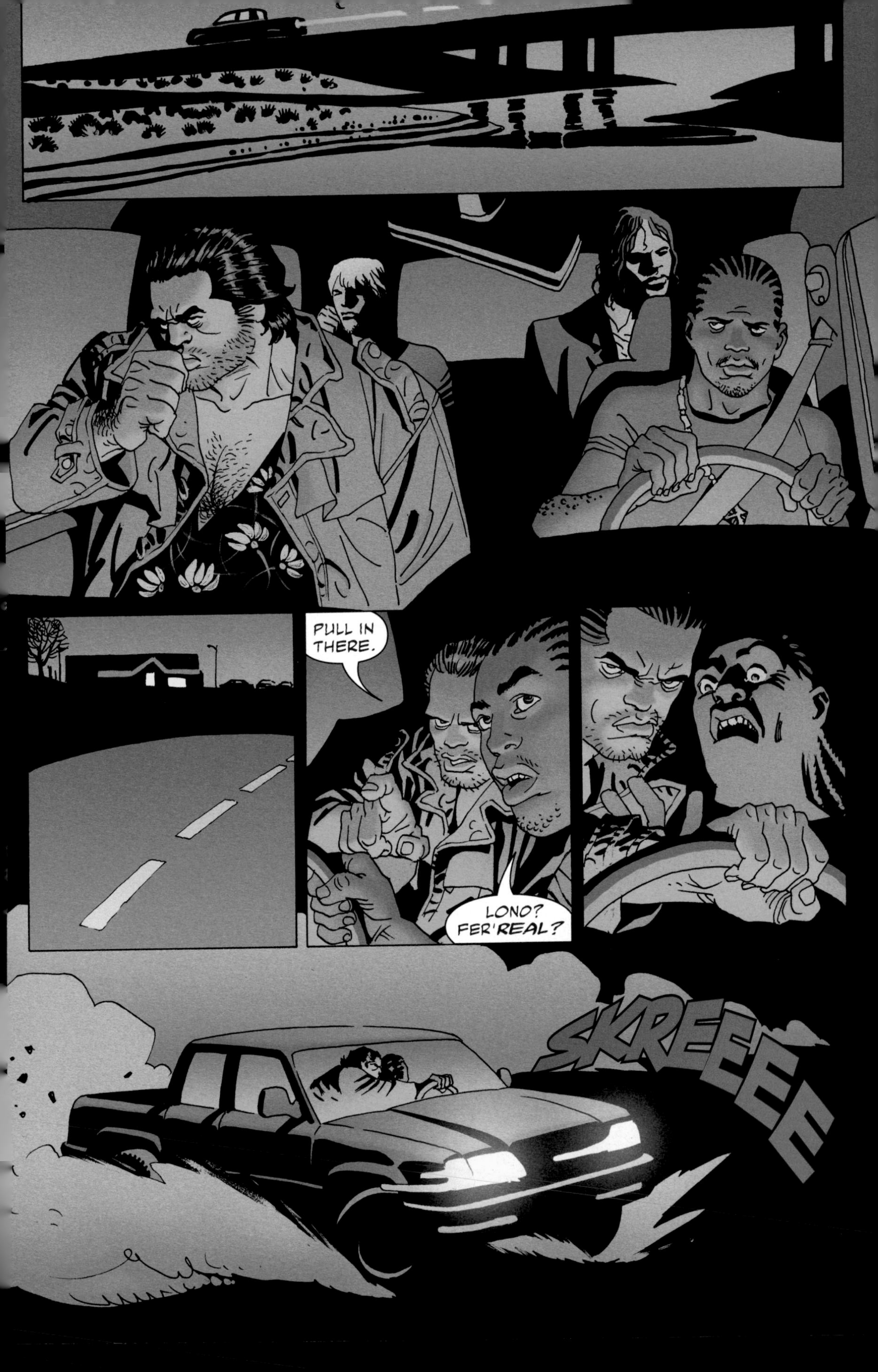
PULL IN THERE.
LONO? FER'REAL?
SKREEEEE

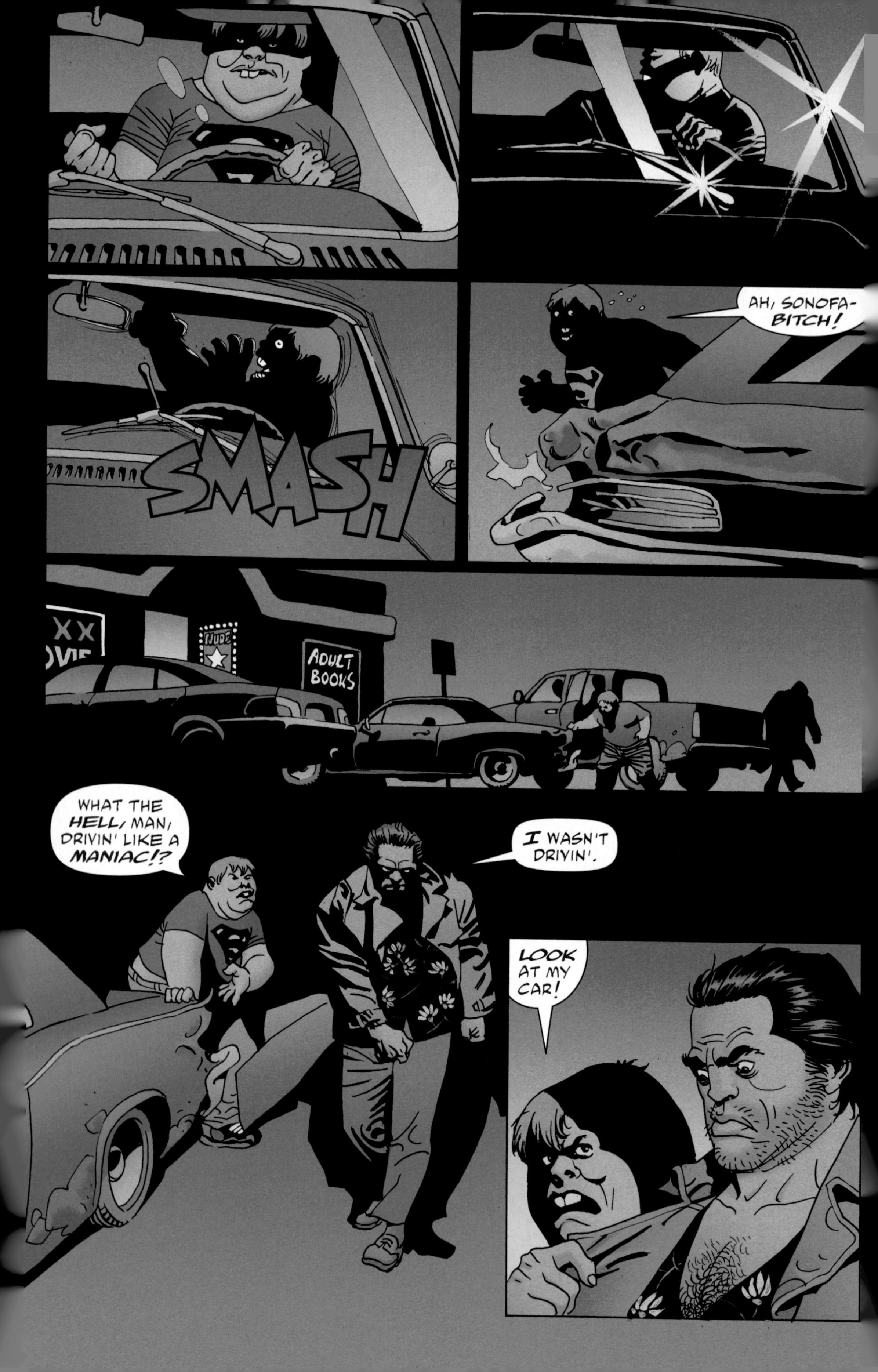

AH, SONOFA-BITCH!
SMASH
XX
OVIE
NUDE
ADULT BOOKS
WHAT THE HELL, MAN, DRIVIN' LIKE A MANIAC!?
I WASN'T DRIVIN'.
LOOK AT MY CAR!

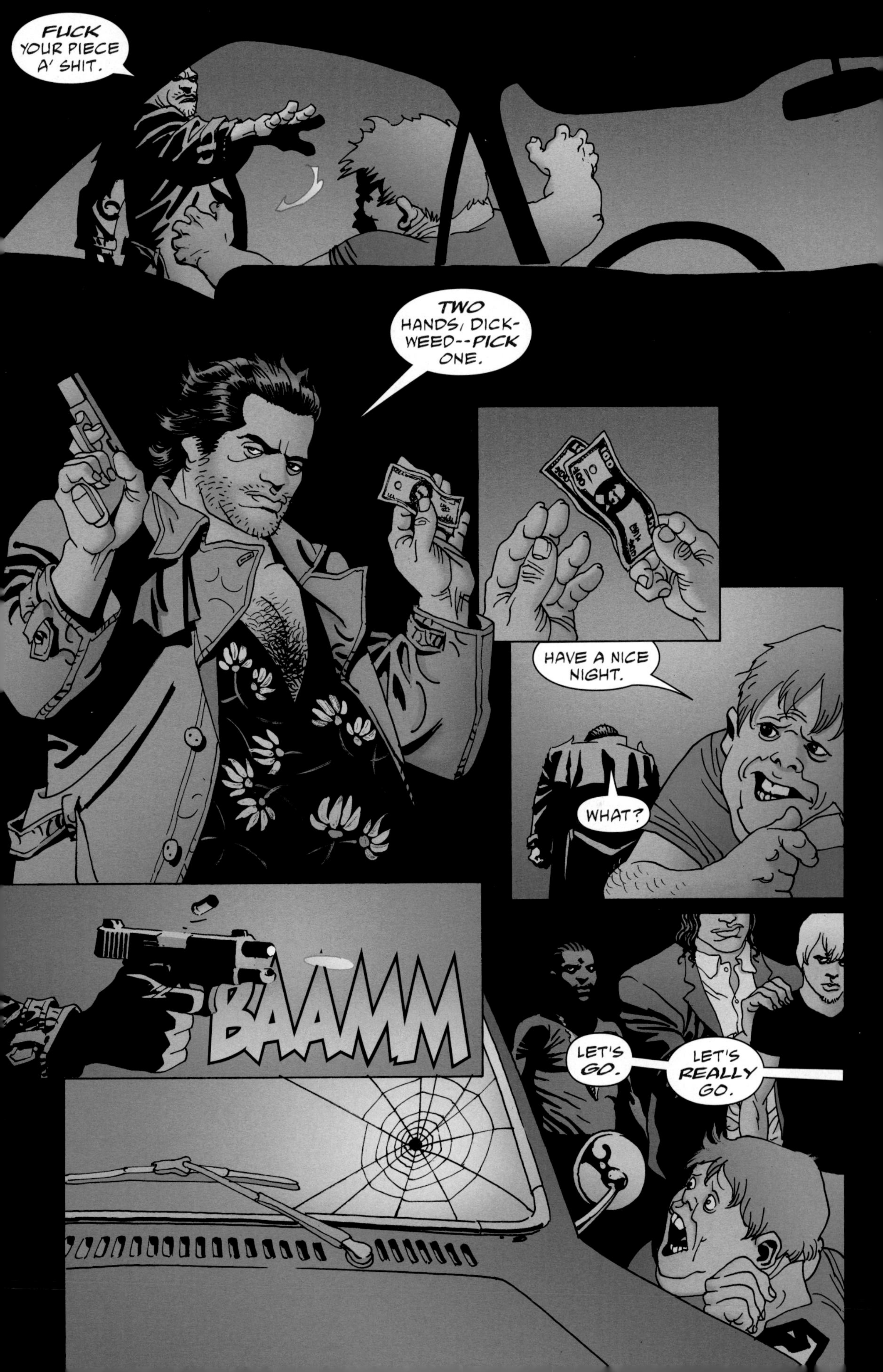
FUCK YOUR PIECE A' SHIT.
TWO HANDS, DICK-WEED--PICK ONE.
HAVE A NICE NIGHT.
WHAT?
BAAMM
LET'S GO.
LET'S REALLY GO.

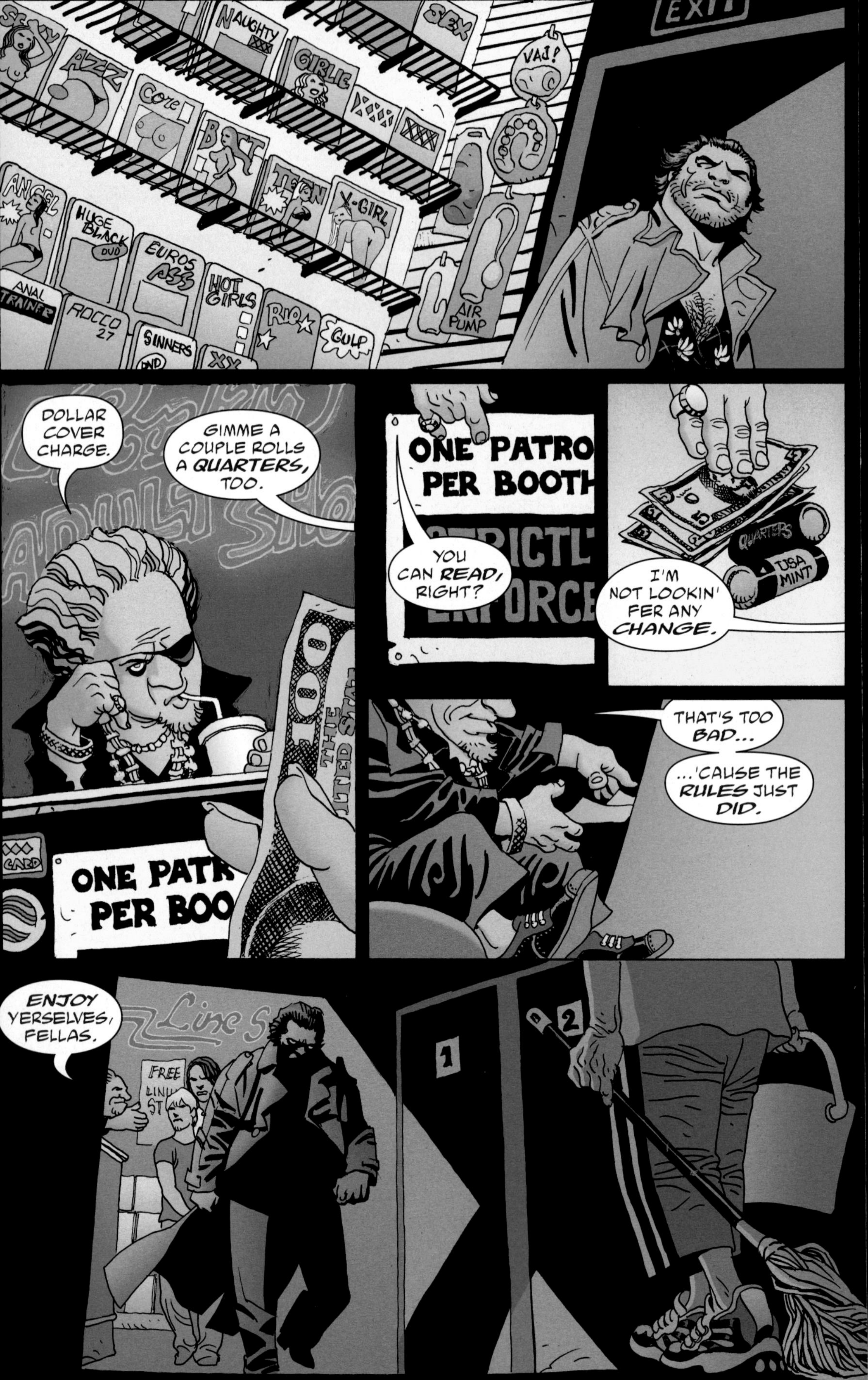
DOLLAR COVER CHARGE.
GIMME A COUPLE ROLLS A QUARTERS, TOO.
YOU CAN READ, RIGHT?
I'M NOT LOOKIN' FER ANY CHANGE.
THAT'S TOO BAD...
...'CAUSE THE RULES JUST DID.
ENJOY YERSELVES, FELLAS.

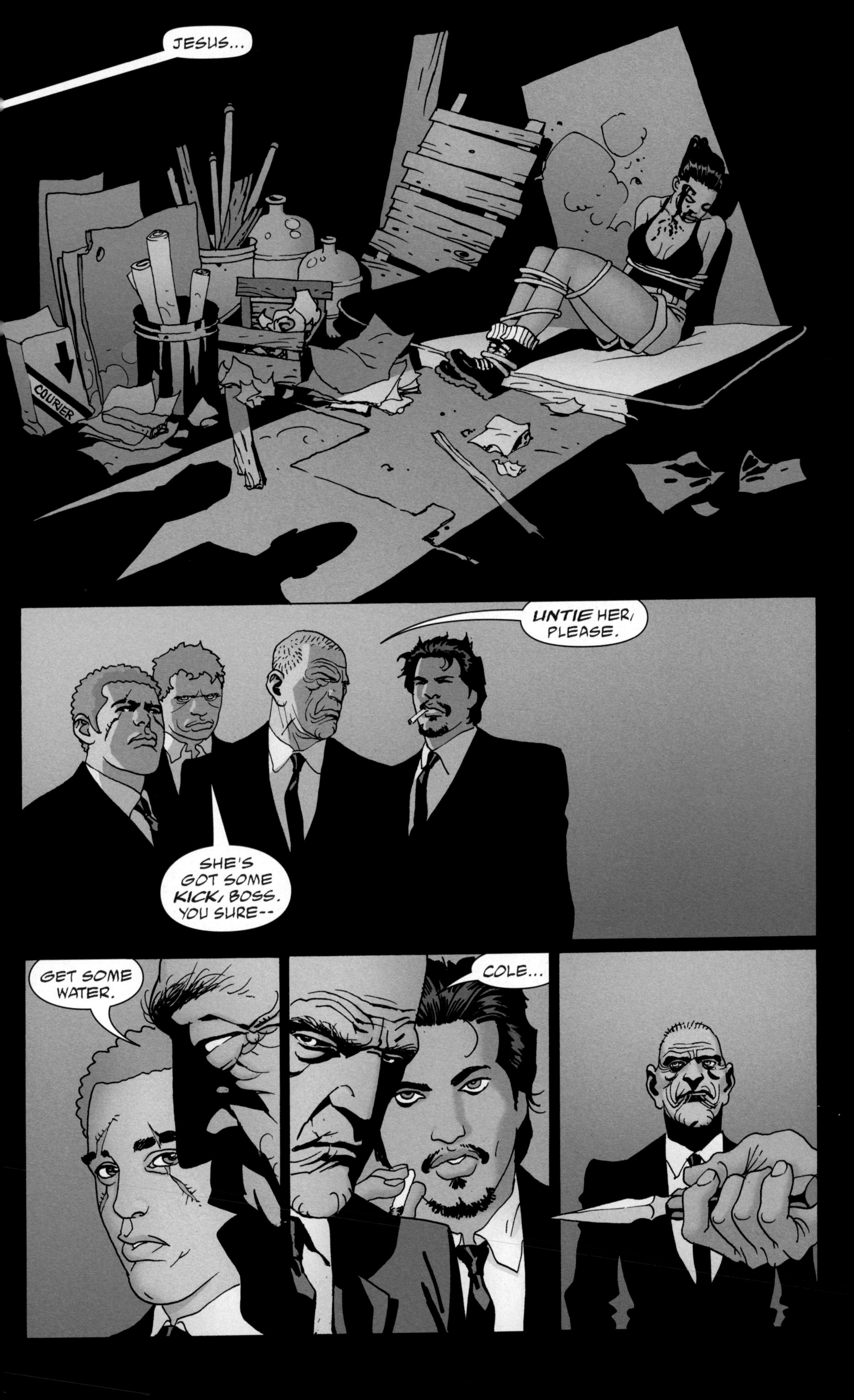
JESUS...
UNTIE HER, PLEASE.
SHE'S GOT SOME KICK, BOSS. YOU SURE--
GET SOME WATER.
COLE...
COURIER

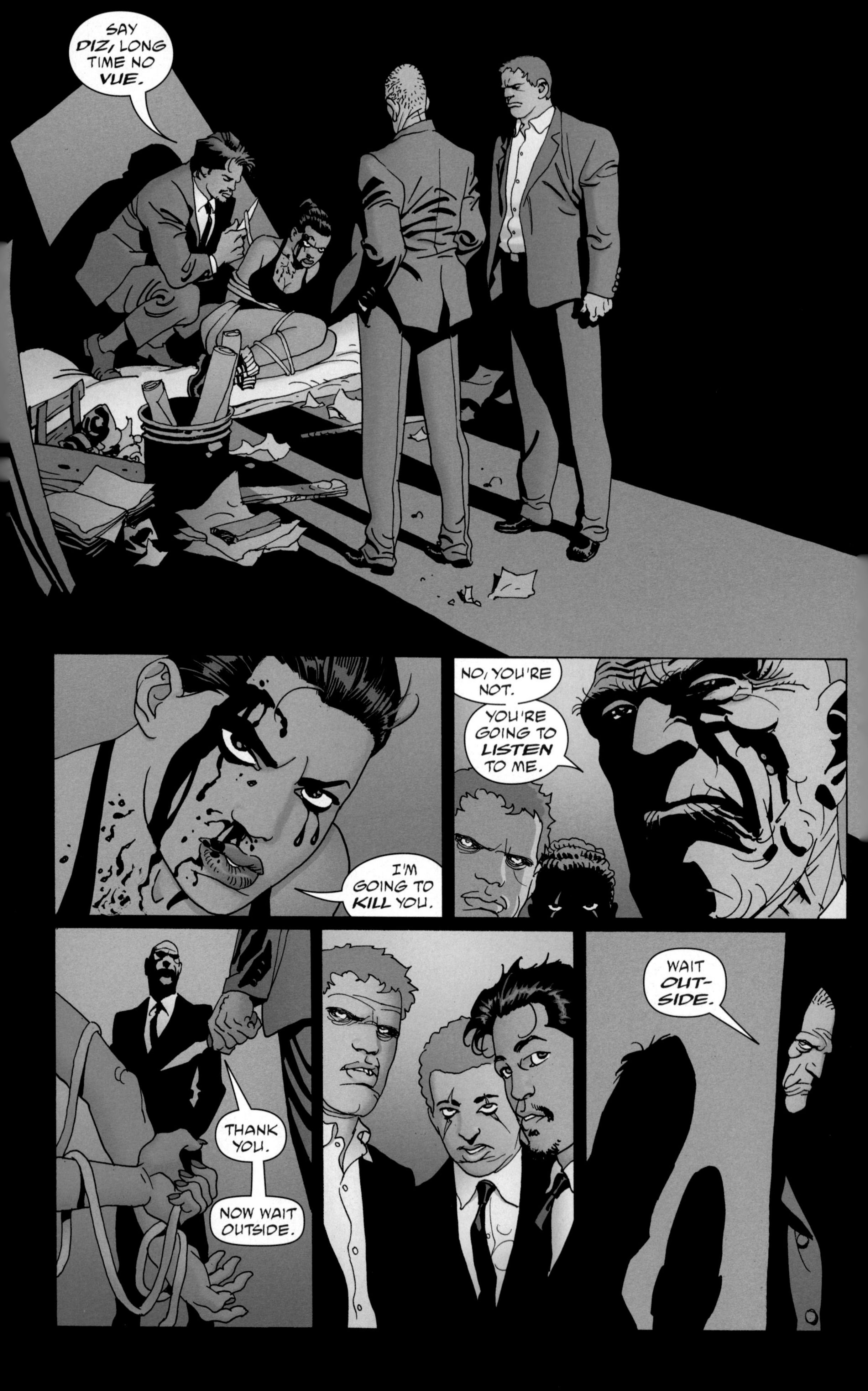
SAY DIZ, LONG TIME NO VUE.
I'M GOING TO KILL YOU.
NO, YOU'RE NOT.
YOU'RE GOING TO LISTEN TO ME.
THANK YOU.
NOW WAIT OUTSIDE.
WAIT OUT-SIDE.

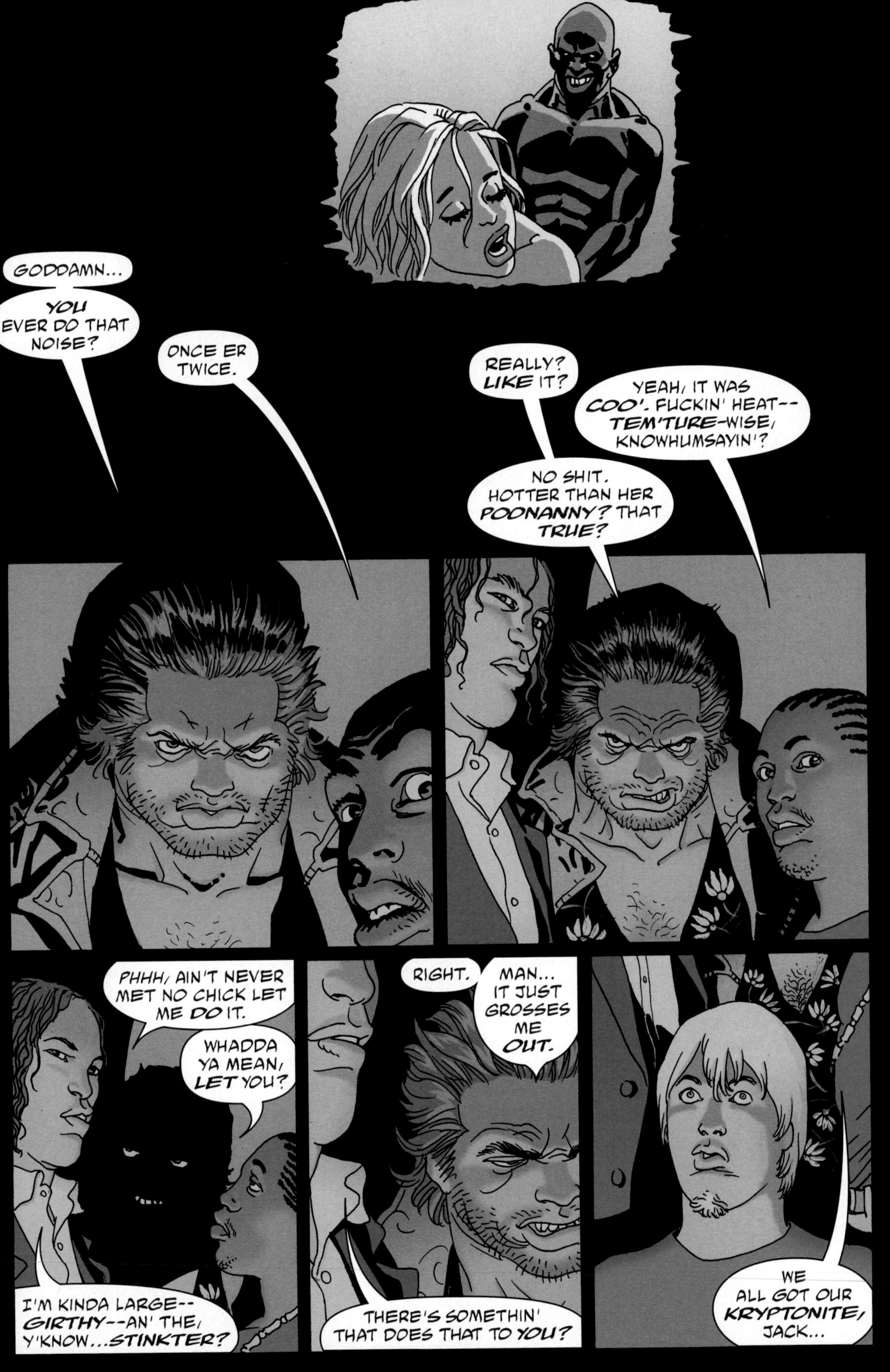
GODDAMN...
YOU EVER DO THAT NOISE?
ONCE ER TWICE.
REALLY? LIKE IT?
YEAH, IT WAS COO'. FUCKIN' HEAT-- TEM'TURE-WISE, KNOWHUMSAYIN'?
NO SHIT. HOTTER THAN HER POONANNY? THAT TRUE?
PHHH, AIN'T NEVER MET NO CHICK LET ME DO IT.
WHADDA YA MEAN, LET YOU?
I'M KINDA LARGE-- GIRTHY--AN' THE, Y'KNOW...STINKTER?
RIGHT.
MAN... IT JUST GROSSES ME OUT.
THERE'S SOMETHIN' THAT DOES THAT TO YOU?
WE ALL GOT OUR KRYPTONITE, JACK...

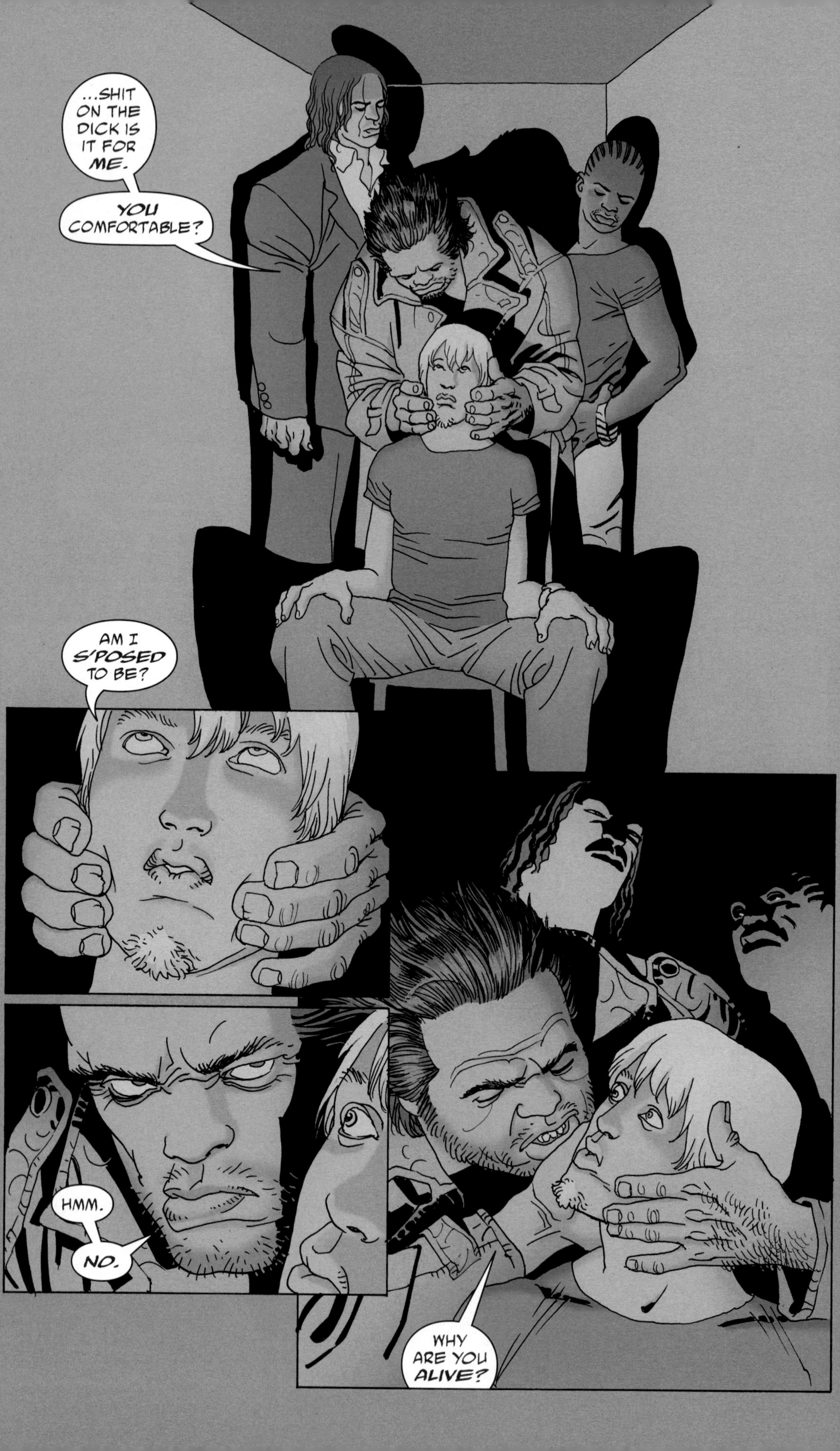
...SHIT ON THE DICK IS IT FOR ME.
YOU COMFORTABLE?
AM I S'POSED TO BE?
HMM.
NO.
WHY ARE YOU ALIVE?

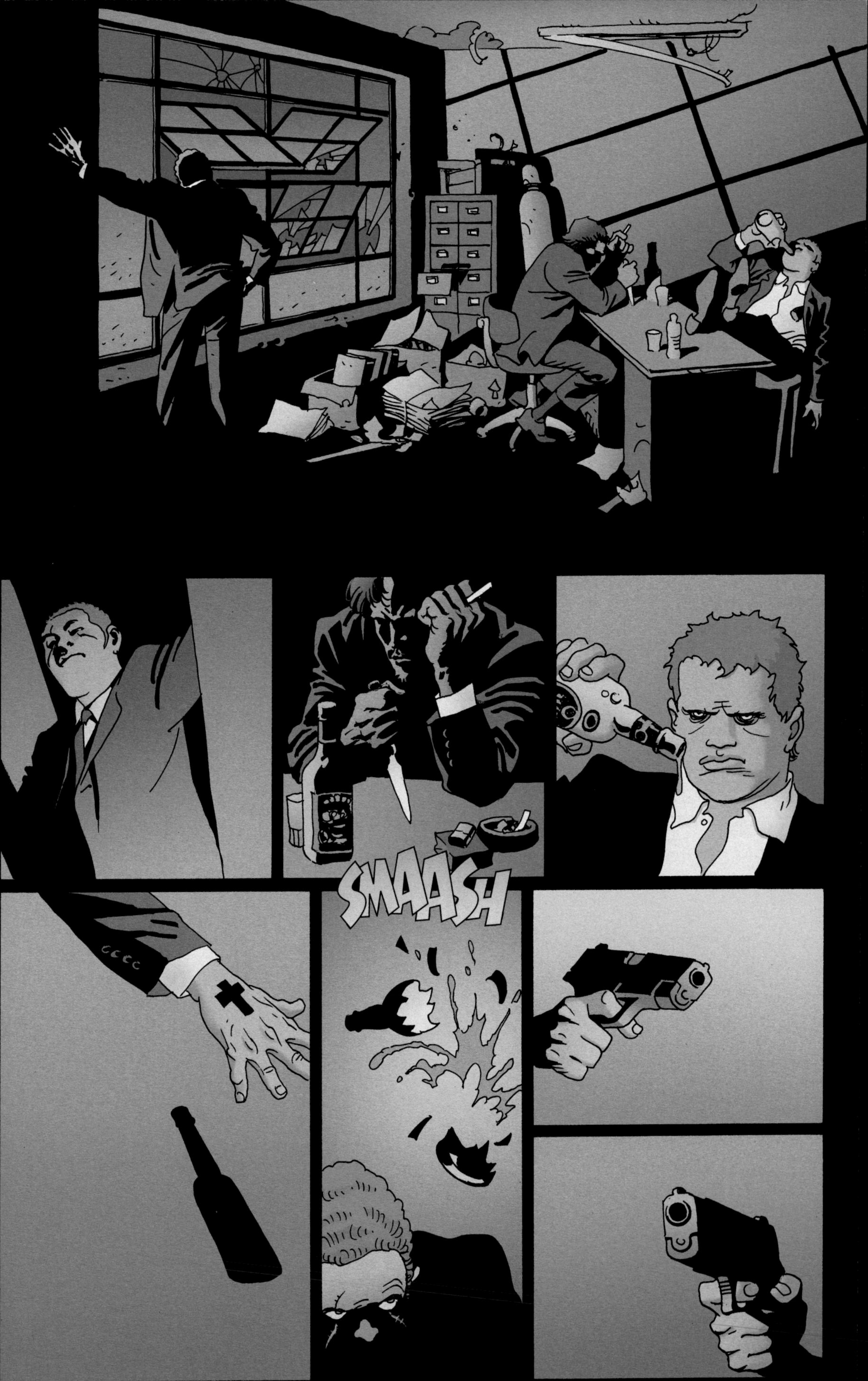
SMAASH

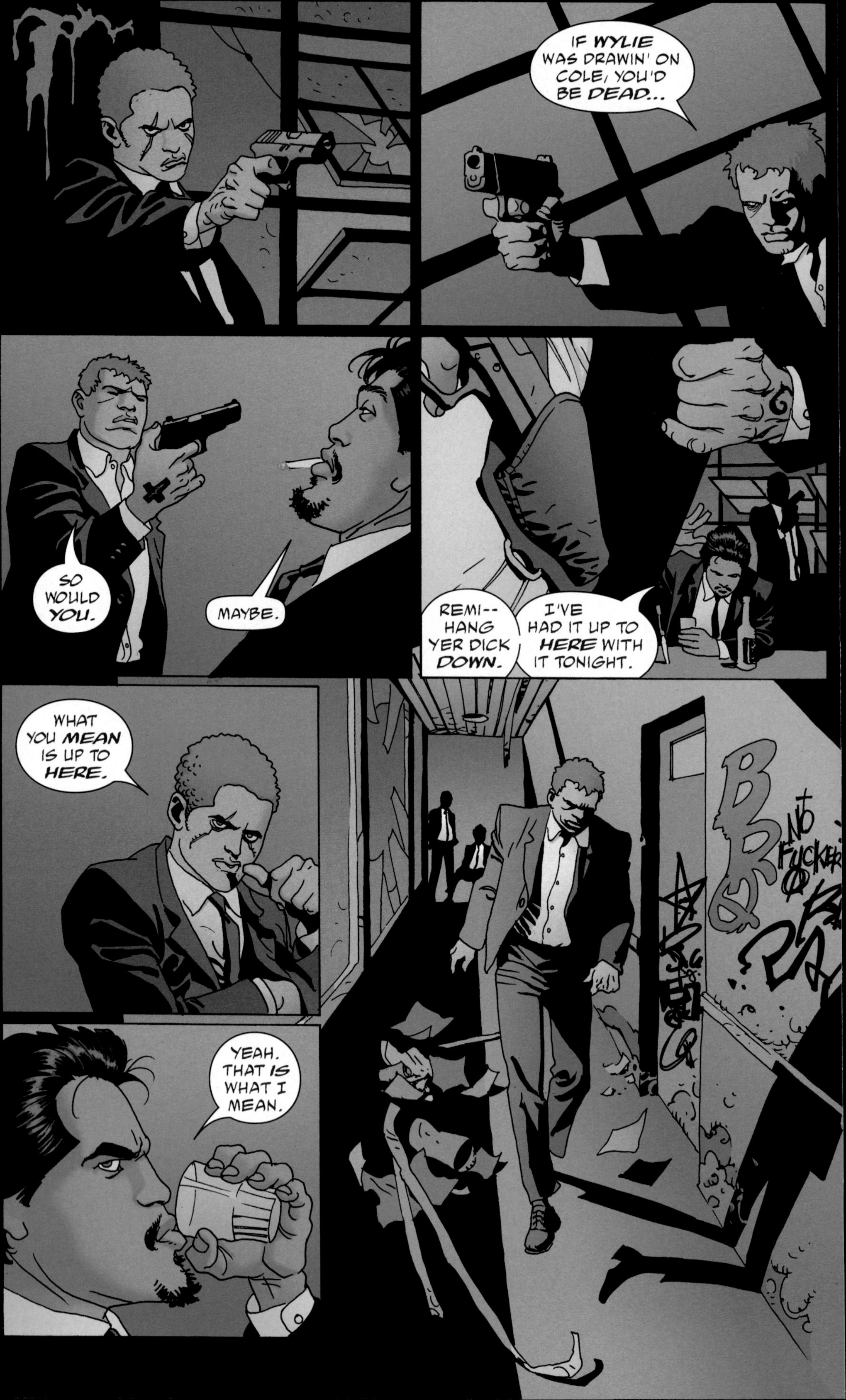
IF WYLIE WAS DRAWIN' ON COLE, YOU'D BE DEAD...
SO WOULD YOU.
MAYBE.
REMI-- HANG YER DICK DOWN.
I'VE HAD IT UP TO HERE WITH IT TONIGHT.
WHAT YOU MEAN IS UP TO HERE.
YEAH. THAT IS WHAT I MEAN.
NO FUCKER

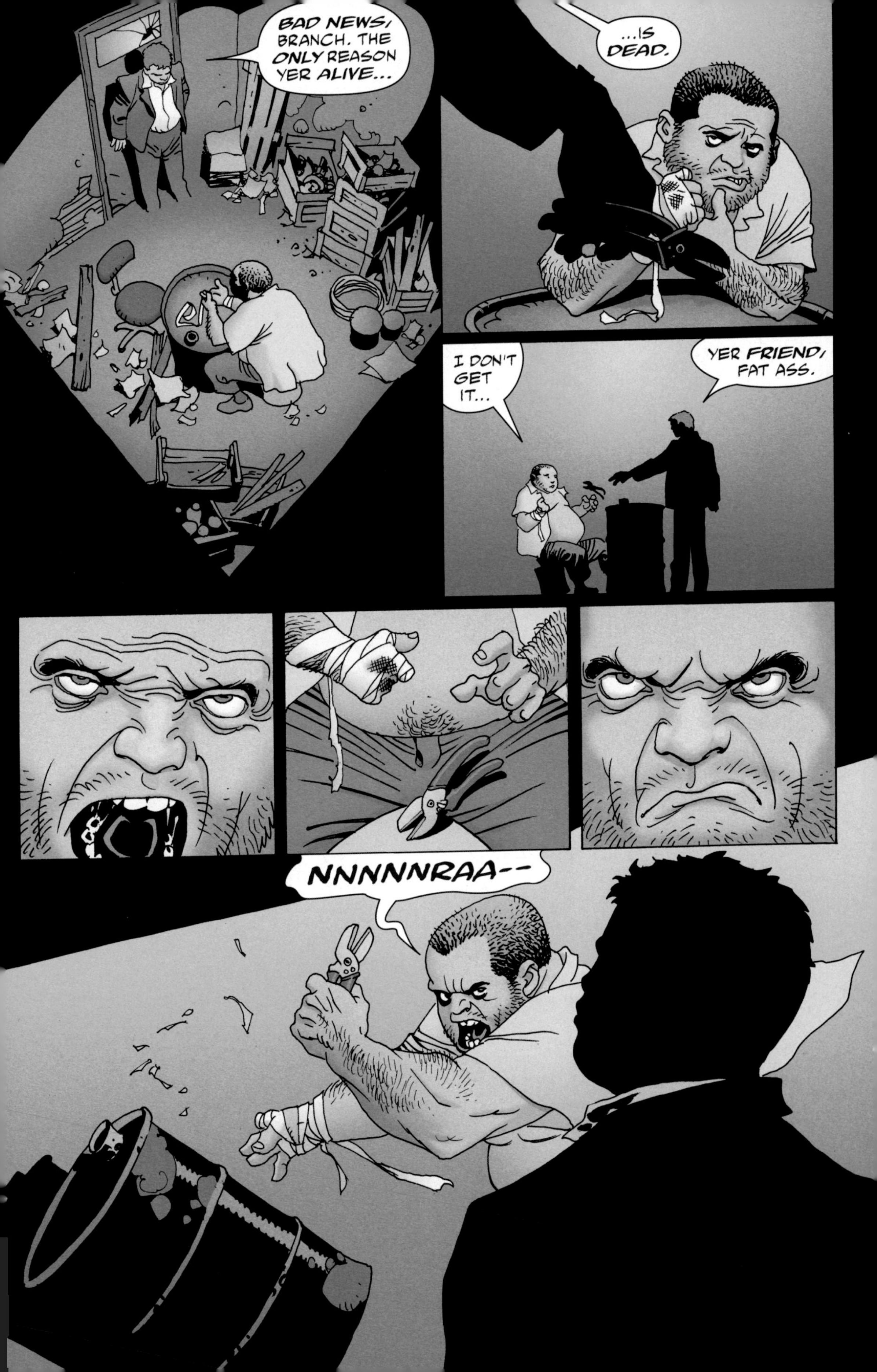
BAD NEWS, BRANCH. THE ONLY REASON YER ALIVE...
...IS DEAD.
I DON'T GET IT...
YER FRIEND, FAT ASS.
NNNNNRAA--

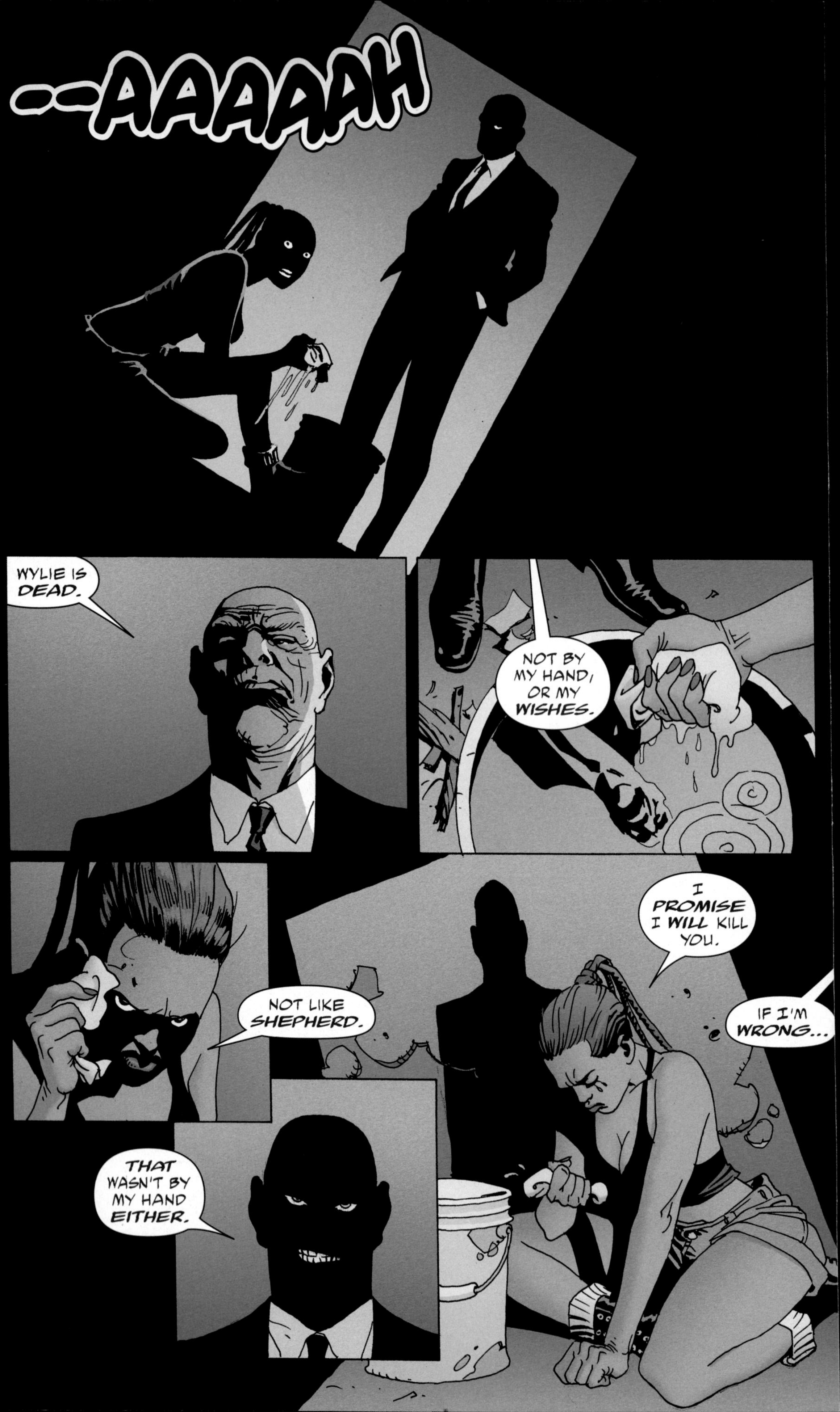
--AAAAAH
WYLIE IS DEAD.
NOT BY MY HAND, OR MY WISHES.
NOT LIKE SHEPHERD.
THAT WASN'T BY MY HAND EITHER.
I PROMISE I WILL KILL YOU.
IF I'M WRONG...

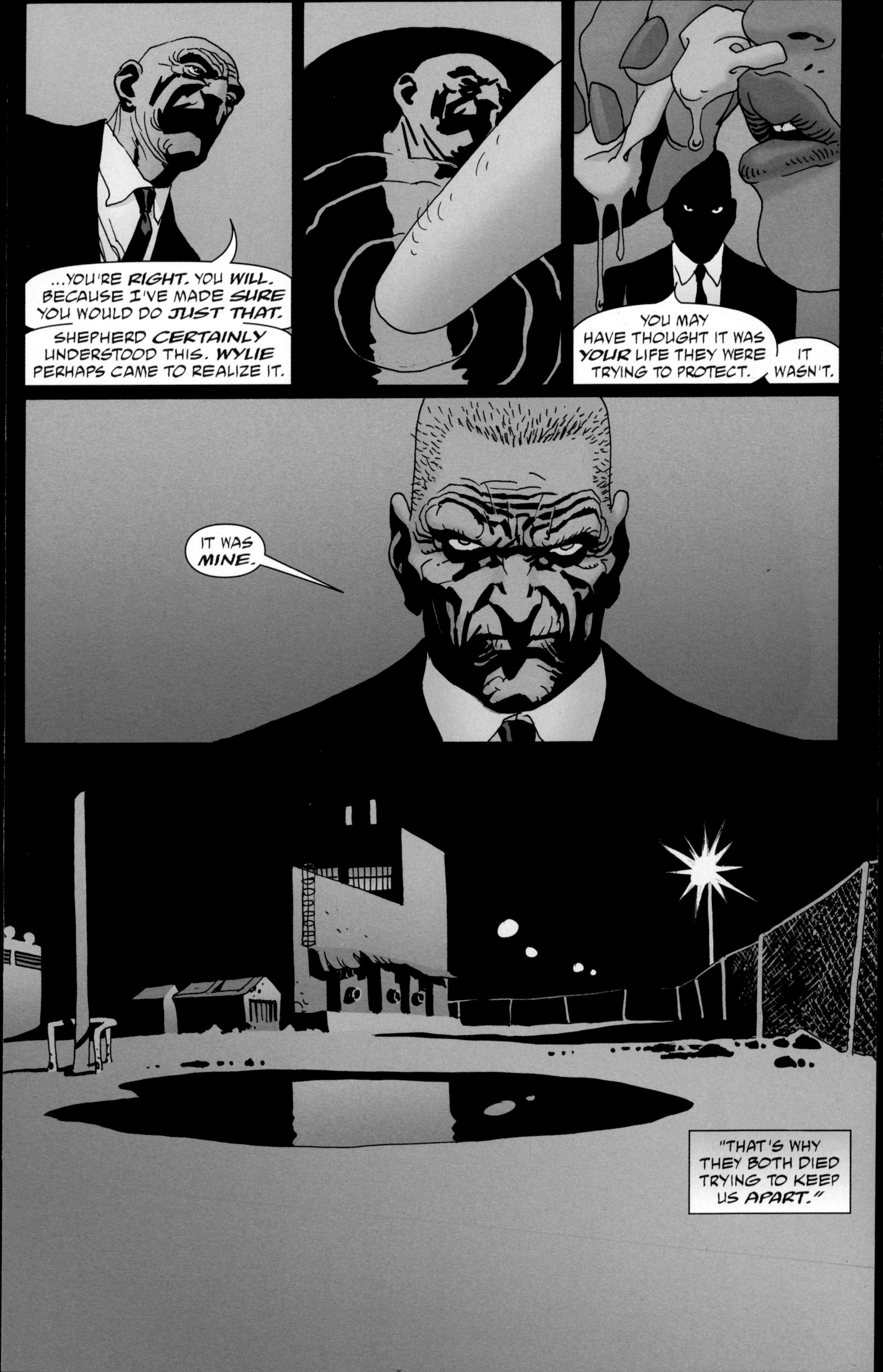
...YOU'RE RIGHT. YOU WILL. BECAUSE I'VE MADE SURE YOU WOULD DO JUST THAT.
SHEPHERD CERTAINLY UNDERSTOOD THIS. WYLIE PERHAPS CAME TO REALIZE IT.
YOU MAY HAVE THOUGHT IT WAS YOUR LIFE THEY WERE TRYING TO PROTECT.
IT WASN'T.
IT WAS MINE.
"THAT'S WHY THEY BOTH DIED TRYING TO KEEP US APART."

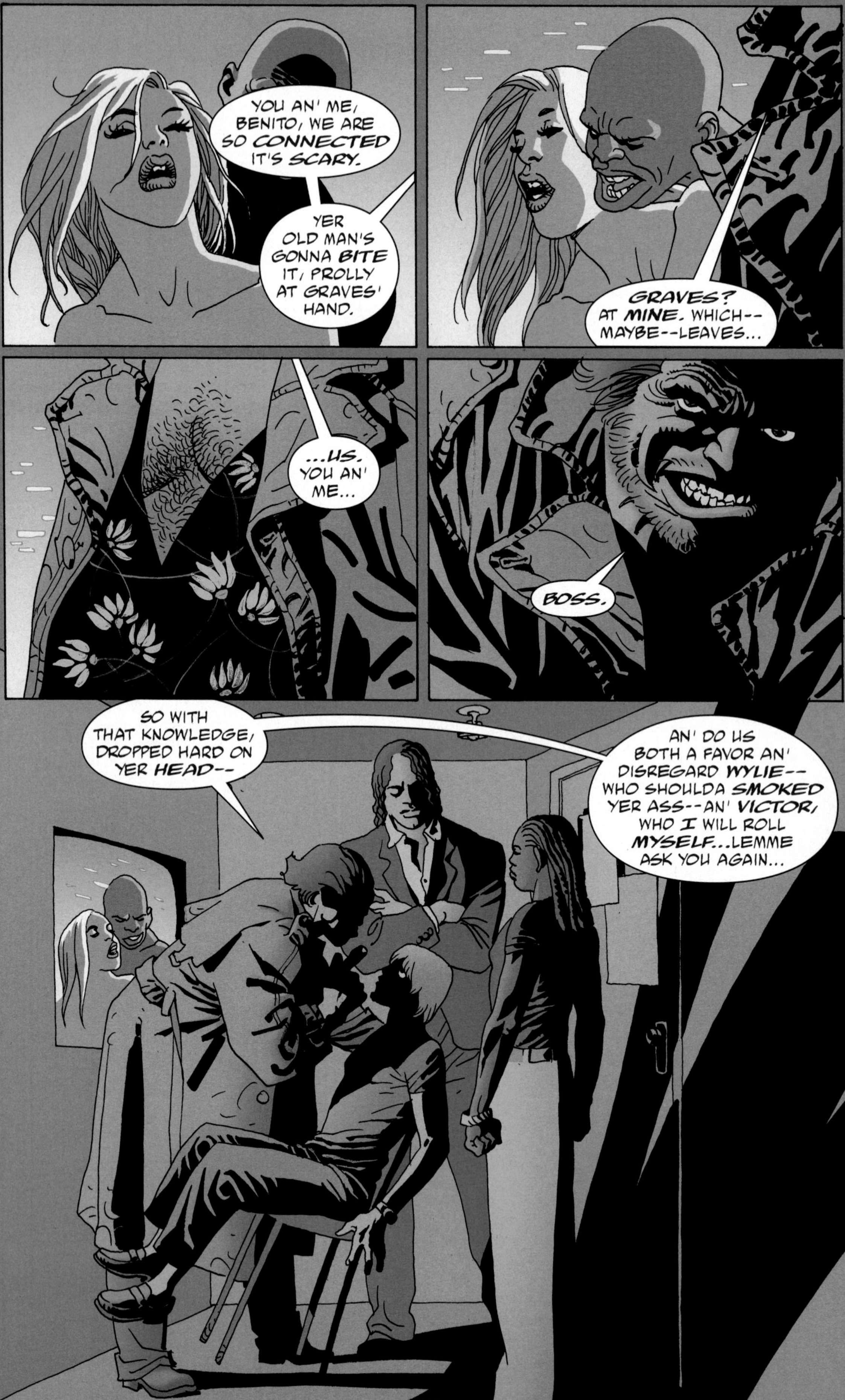
YOU AN' ME, BENITO, WE ARE SO CONNECTED IT'S SCARY.
YER OLD MAN'S GONNA BITE IT, PROLLY AT GRAVES' HAND.
GRAVES? AT MINE. WHICH-- MAYBE--LEAVES...
...US. YOU AN' ME...
BOSS.
SO WITH THAT KNOWLEDGE, DROPPED HARD ON YER HEAD--
AN' DO US BOTH A FAVOR AN' DISREGARD WYLIE-- WHO SHOULDA SMOKED YER ASS--AN' VICTOR, WHO I WILL ROLL MYSELF...LEMME ASK YOU AGAIN...

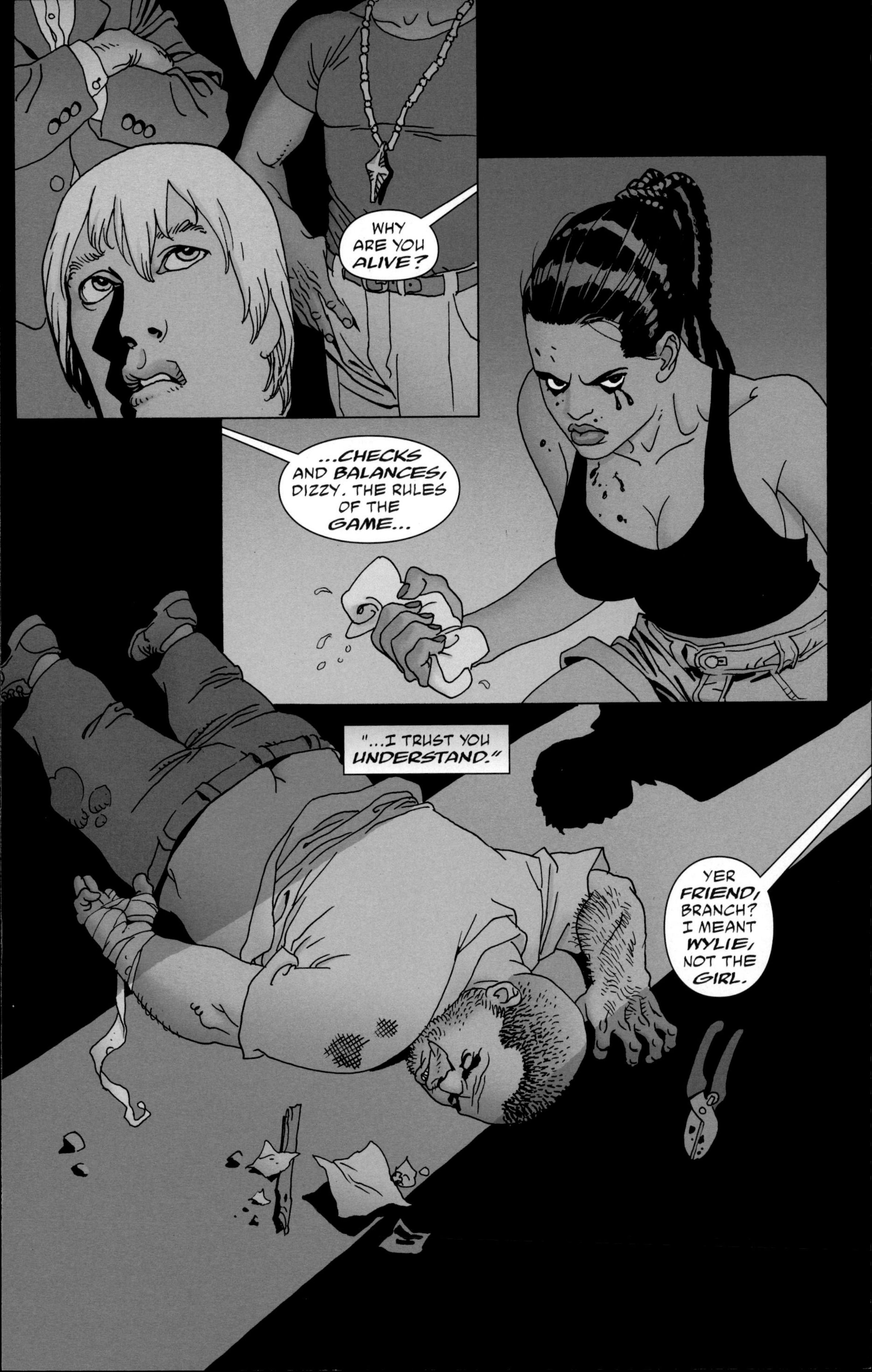
WHY ARE YOU ALIVE?
...CHECKS AND BALANCES, DIZZY. THE RULES OF THE GAME...
"...I TRUST YOU UNDERSTAND."
YER FRIEND, BRANCH? I MEANT WYLIE, NOT THE GIRL.

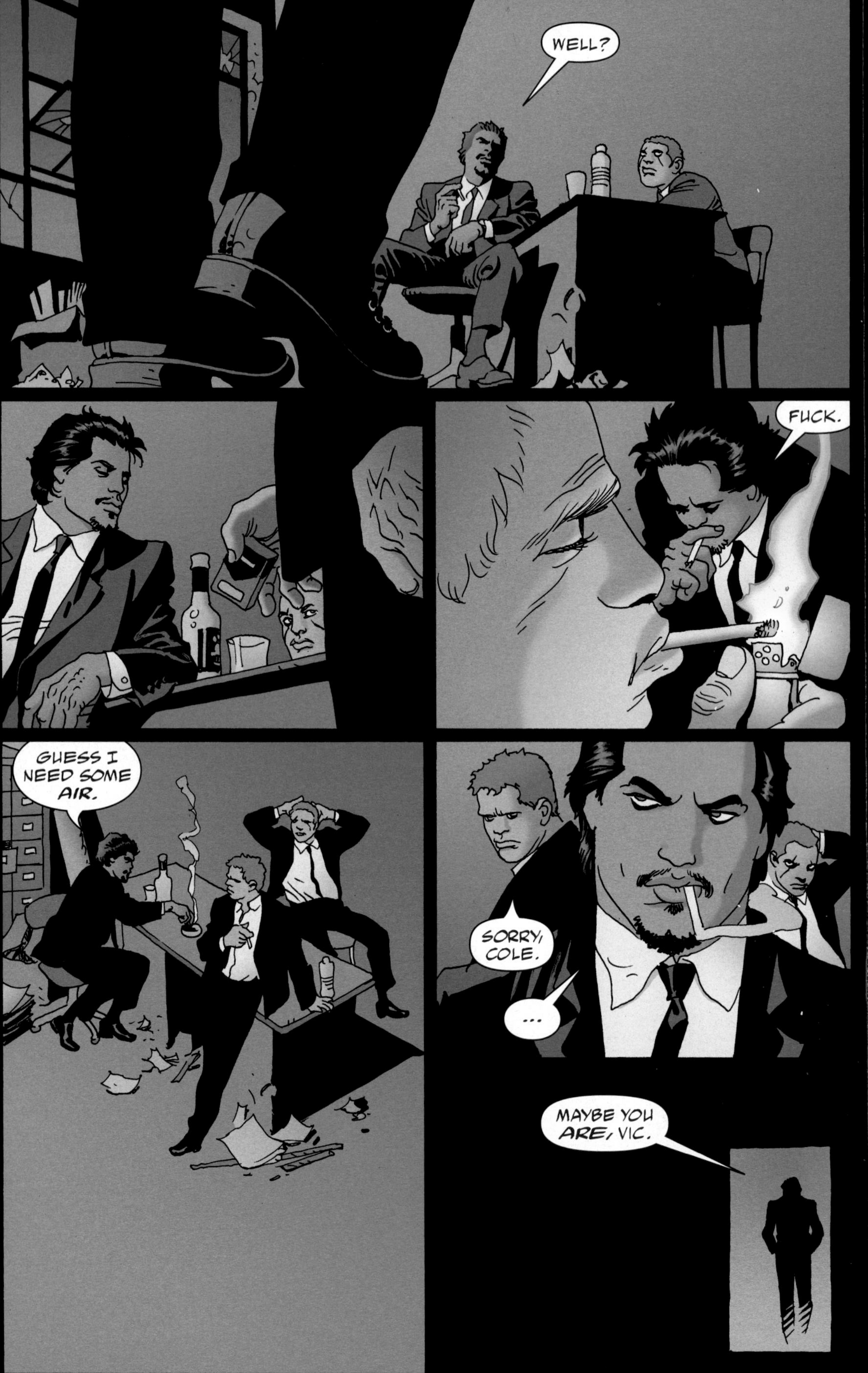
WELL?
FUCK.
GUESS I NEED SOME AIR.
SORRY, COLE.
...
MAYBE YOU ARE, VIC.

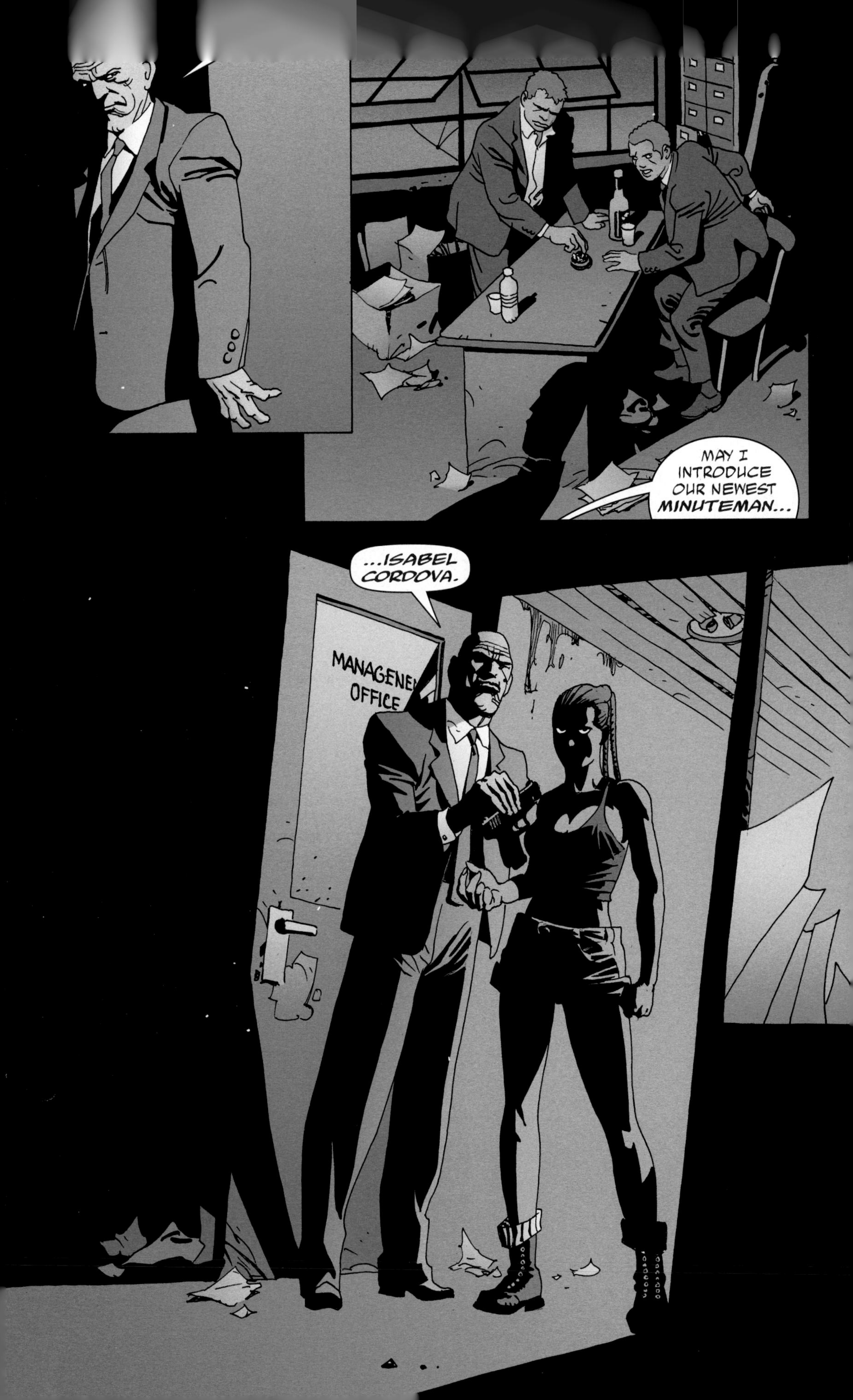
MAY I INTRODUCE OUR NEWEST MINUTEMAN...
...ISABEL CORDOVA.
MANAGEMENT OFFICE

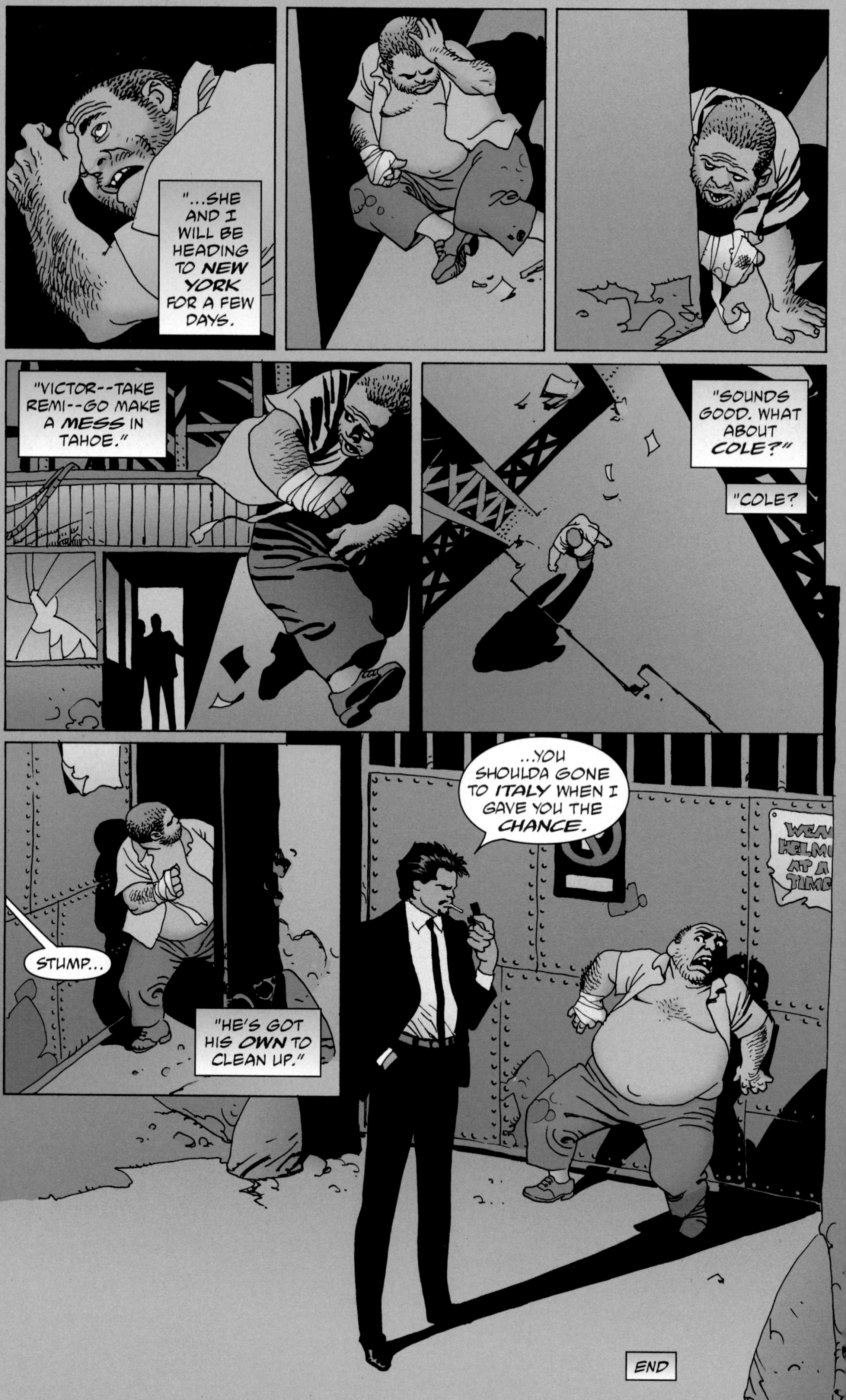
"...SHE AND I WILL BE HEADING TO NEW YORK FOR A FEW DAYS.
"VICTOR--TAKE REMI--GO MAKE A MESS IN TAHOE."
"SOUNDS GOOD. WHAT ABOUT COLE?"
"COLE?
STUMP...
"HE'S GOT HIS OWN TO CLEAN UP."
...YOU SHOULDA GONE TO ITALY WHEN I GAVE YOU THE CHANCE.
END